African American National Biography

SECOND EDITION

HENRY LOUIS GATES JR. EVELYN BROOKS
HIGGINBOTHAM

Editors in Chief

VOLUME 5: GAYLE, ADDISON, JR. – HITE, LES

OXFORD
UNIVERSITY PRESS

OXFORD

UNIVERSITY PRESS

Oxford University Press is a department of the University of Oxford.
It furthers the University's objective of excellence in research, scholarship,
and education by publishing worldwide.

Oxford   New York

Auckland   Cape Town   Dar es Salaam   Hong Kong   Karachi
Kuala Lumpur   Madrid   Melbourne   Mexico City   Nairobi
New Delhi   Shanghai   Taipei   Toronto

With offices in

Argentina   Austria   Brazil   Chile   Czech Republic   France   Greece
Guatemala   Hungary   Italy   Japan   Poland   Portugal   Singapore
South Korea   Switzerland   Thailand   Turkey   Ukraine   Vietnam

Oxford is a registered trademark of Oxford University Press in the UK and certain other countries.

Published in the United States of America by
Oxford University Press
198 Madison Avenue, New York, NY 10016

Library of Congress Cataloging-in-Publication Data
African American national biography / editors in chief Henry Louis Gates Jr., Evelyn Brooks Higginbotham. – 2nd ed.
p. cm.
Includes bibliographical references and index.
ISBN 978-0-19-999036-8 (volume 1; hdbk.); ISBN 978-0-19-999037-5 (volume 2; hdbk.); ISBN 978-0-19-999038-2 (volume 3; hdbk.);
ISBN 978-0-19-999039-9 (volume 4; hdbk.); ISBN 978-0-19-999040-5 (volume 5; hdbk.); ISBN 978-0-19-999041-2 (volume 6; hdbk.);
ISBN 978-0-19-999042-9 (volume 7; hdbk.); ISBN 978-0-19-999043-6 (volume 8; hdbk.); ISBN 978-0-19-999044-3 (volume 9; hdbk.);
ISBN 978-0-19-999045-0 (volume 10; hdbk.); ISBN 978-0-19-999046-7 (volume 11; hdbk.); ISBN 978-0-19-999047-4 (volume 12;
hdbk.); ISBN 978-0-19-992077-8 (12-volume set; hdbk.)
1. African Americans – Biography – Encyclopedias.   2. African Americans – History – Encyclopedias.   I. Gates, Henry
Louis.   II. Higginbotham, Evelyn Brooks, 1945-
E185.96.A4466 2012
920'.009296073 – dc23
[B]
2011043281

1 3 5 7 9 8 6 4 2
Printed in the United States of America
on acid-free paper

African American National Biography

G CONTINUED

Gayle, Addison, Jr. (2 June 1932–3 Oct. 1991), literary critic and Black Arts proponent, was born in Newport News, Virginia, the son of Addison Gayle Sr., a Communist Party spokesperson, and Carrie (Holloman) Gayle. Gayle was born during the Depression, and his parents divorced early in his life. Despite his mother's well-paying job at a nearby military base during World War II, Gayle and his immediate family remained well acquainted with poverty. He grew up in a black enclave and rarely saw whites. Still, he envied the apparent success that he believed all whites had.

In his autobiography *Wayward Child: A Personal Odyssey*, Gayle maintains that he was penalized by many of his high school teachers for being racially unmixed, poor, and seemingly arrogant. They despised him because he excelled on state exams and because he boasted about reading works by the Russian writer Fyodor Dostoyevsky and the African American writer RICHARD WRIGHT. Gayle had been introduced to these writers by his father, who encouraged him to rely on his intellect and not on his emotions. Fearing his teachers' wrath Gayle transferred to a high school in Hampton, Virginia, to complete his senior year. He graduated and finished writing a novel that represented both the anguish that he felt as a poor, ostracized African American and his aspirations for his life.

After high school Gayle joined the U.S. Air Force and befriended officers of different races, believing that within the confines of the corps, racial distinctions were blurred. His honorable discharge from the air force because of a heart condition (which

caused him to return to Virginia), the rejection of his writings by literary journals, his father's death, and an aunt's cajoling prompted Gayle to leave the South in search of better opportunities. Gayle moved nomadically throughout the North and Midwest before settling finally in New York City. Disgruntled with discriminatory treatment in the city and on his jobs (he worked as a hospital orderly and a porter) Gayle enrolled in the City College of New York in 1960.

College was a positive experience for Gayle, then twenty-eight. There his peers and teachers revered him; he excelled academically, and he envisioned greater achievements. Among those achievements was the completion of his second novel in 1961. This novel was influenced by writers like FREDERICK DOUGLASS and JAMES BALDWIN and was promoted by JACKIE ROBINSON, a civil rights advocate and the first African American to play baseball in the modern major leagues. Despite widespread promotion the novel received unfavorable criticism, and Gayle focused on finishing college.

Gayle's tunnel-vision approach to completing his schoolwork precluded him from fully participating in the political activities for which the 1960s have come to be known. Plagued by the guilt of his inactivity, Gayle still pondered events like the Birmingham, Alabama, church bombing of four little girls and the assassinations of John F. Kennedy and MALCOLM X in his personal journal even though he wished to make further educational strides. Completing a BA in Literature in the fall of 1965 and an MA in English Literature from the University of California at Los Angeles in 1967, and by that time having been married for a year to fellow undergraduate alumna Rosalie Norwood, Gayle was on his way to achieving the American dream.

After finishing graduate school Gayle accepted a lectureship in the English department at his undergraduate alma mater, during which time he explored black art and culture. As a result he changed the core curriculum of his classes to include authors of color, attended many Black Power and Black Arts meetings (political and cultural movements of the 1960s and 1970s that encouraged black pride), and befriended many of the movements' leaders and representative authors such as AMIRI BARAKA (formerly LeRoi Jones), HOYT FULLER, and GWENDOLYN BROOKS.

Gayle's publishing career was also at its height. He produced numerous books in succession, including *Black Expression: Essays by and about Black Americans in the Creative Arts* (1969), *The Black Situation* (1970), *The Black Aesthetic* (1971), *Bondage, Freedom, and Beyond: The Prose of Black Americans* (1971), *Oak and Ivy: A Biography of Paul Laurence Dunbar* (1971), and *Claude McKay: The Black Poet at War* (1972). Gayle perhaps gained his literary reputation for his fiery introduction to *The Black Aesthetic*, a collection of works by several Black Arts Movement writers that sought a solely black American literary canon based on the often enraging and separatist-inducing experiences of its authors. Gayle's introduction became a manifesto of sorts for the movement.

Gayle's appointment in 1970 as an assistant professor of English at Bernard Baruch College in New York and the dissolution of his marriage to Norwood in August 1971 increased his anxiety, which caused him to seek help from the psychologist Raphael Rosell. Gayle's breakthrough came outside of the confines of therapy, though, when he attended a weeklong literary conference at historically black Clark University in Atlanta, Georgia. There he was embraced by students, faculty, and upper-class politicians alike. Feeling a part of the African American community for the first time, Gayle reconciled his long-held tensions with the South. As a result he ended his sessions with Rosell and embarked on a lifelong journey of self-recovery.

Gayle continued to write prolifically throughout his career, publishing *The Way of the New World: The Black Novel in America* in 1975, his autobiography in 1977, and *Richard Wright: Ordeal of a Native Son* in 1980. He received a distinguished professorship in 1980 at Baruch College, teaching there for more than two decades. Later in his life Gayle remarried, wedding Lou Ethel Roliston. The manuscript of his final book, a biography of W.E.B. DuBois, was completed shortly before his death in 1991. It remains unpublished.

FURTHER READING

A copy of Addison Gayle's eulogy as given by John A. Williams on 9 October 1991 at Friendship Baptist Church in New York City may be found in the John A. Williams Papers in the Department of Rare Books, Special Collections and Preservation, at the University of Rochester, Rochester, New York. Correspondence in 1968 between Addison Gayle Jr. and the writer Julian Mayfield is in the Julian Mayfield Papers, 1949–1984, at the New York Public Library and through the library's online Digital Library Collection. Correspondence between Addison Gayle Jr. and the poet James A. Emanuel from 1966 to 1970 is in the Papers of James A. Emanuel housed in the Manuscript Reading Room at the Library of Congress, Washington, D.C. Annotated pages of Addison Gayle's books may be found in the Larry Neal Papers, 1961–1985, at the New York Public Library and through the library's online Digital Library Collection.

Gayle, Addison, Jr. *Wayward Child: A Personal Odyssey* (1977).

Major, Clarence. *The Dark and Feeling: Black American Writers and Their Work* (1974).

Obituary: *New York Times*, 5 Oct. 1991.

TOMEIKO ASHFORD CARTER

Gaynor, Gloria (7 Sept. 1949–), disco singer, was born Gloria Fowles in Newark, New Jersey, the daughter of Daniel Fowles, a professional singer, and Queenie May, a short order cook. Gaynor grew up with five brothers and one sister. Her father left before she was born, forcing her mother to care for the impoverished family alone. After graduating with honors from high school, she went to beauty school in New Jersey and started to play small engagements with different R&B acts, among them Johnny Nash (who gave Gaynor her stage name) and the Soul Satisfiers. The late 1960s and early 1970s saw Gaynor touring extensively with moderate success and without a recording contract. NAT KING COLE, ELLA FITZGERALD, Frank Sinatra, and MARVIN GAYE were among her early influences.

In 1972 Gaynor began playing with City Life, which would become her backing group for years to come. She signed with Columbia and recorded the sexually suggestive single "Honey Bee" in 1973, which became a major disco hit. At the time, disco was still an underground phenomenon with a largely urban, gay following. For her next record, Gaynor switched to MGM/Polydor in 1973. "Never Can Say Goodbye," which had been recorded by the Jackson 5 and ISAAC HAYES, was Gaynor's breakthrough into the pop market. At first, the record industry promoted the song only as a dance track to be played in discos, but ultimately it made it onto the playlists of AM radio and became the first #1 single on *Billboard*'s newly established dance chart in 1974. The song helped to promote disco as a widely recognized musical genre and was featured on the album of the same title from 1975. Gaynor's first three full-length albums, *Never Can Say Goodbye*, *Experience Gloria Gaynor*, and *I've Got You*, were slickly produced by Meco Monardo, Tony Bongiovi, and Jay Ellis, and signaled a break from previous recording traditions: side one of each album was a non-stop disco mix with one song segueing into the next, whereas side two of each album included more traditional R&B songs with breaks between them. In a publicity stunt, Gaynor was crowned Queen of Disco at the dance club Le Jardin by New York City mayor Abraham D. Beane on 3 March 1975. Gloria Gaynor's next three albums, *Glorious*, *Park Avenue Sound*, and *I Have a Right*, with different producers were less revolutionary and commercially less successful. In 1978 Gaynor fell from the stage while performing at Beacon Theater in New York City, injured her spine and had to undergo surgery. While staying at the hospital, the singer, who was grappling with alcohol, drug, and weight problems, began intensively studying the Bible. Like her colleague DONNA SUMMER, Gaynor would eventually become a born-again Christian, in 1982. In 1979 Gloria Gaynor recorded "I Will Survive," which was to become her signature song and biggest hit. Originally issued as a B side, the upbeat disco song about a failed relationship was put on heavy rotation by Richie Kacznor, DJ at Studio 54 in New York City. It eventually climbed to the #1 spot on the pop charts, sold more than seven million copies in 1979 alone and was awarded the Grammy for Best Disco Recording the same year (in the one-time only appearance of this category). Afterward, the song turned up in numerous movies and TV shows and was adopted by feminists, AIDS patients, and France's 1998 World Cup champion soccer team as a theme song. In 2000 the music TV network VH-1 proclaimed it the greatest dance song of all time. Not surprisingly, the accompanying album *Love*

Tracks, produced by Dino Fekaris, made it to #4 on the pop charts.

Also in 1979 Gloria Gaynor married the nightclub owner and music publisher Linwood Simon, who became her manager. Gaynor, however, was not able to continue the massive success of "I Will Survive." After she became a born-again Christian, she began to incorporate gospel into her repertoire and successfully toured in Europe and South America. Her 1984 disco version of "I Am What I Am" from the gay-themed musical *La Cage Aux Folles* was a hit in Europe, and Gaynor continued to appear at gay festivals and disco revival shows throughout the 1990s. In 1997 she published her autobiography.

Gaynor also starred in the Broadway musical *Smokey Joe's Cafe* and received the coveted Legend Award at the World Music Awards in 2002. The same year she released her first internationally distributed album in fifteen years, titled *I Wish You Love*. The single "I Never Know" reached #1 on the *Billboard* dance charts.

Gloria Gaynor's career represents the movement of disco from an underground phenomenon with a largely gay following in the early to mid-1970s to a mainstream phenomenon in the late 1970s. Her use of soulful vocals on top of a disco beat was extremely influential for house music in the 1990s, which used the same technique. More specifically, Gaynor's hit song "I Will Survive" created a memorable anthem for women and gay men. Gaynor's lyrical and vocal assertiveness on the track continued the tradition of self-assured female perspectives typified by artists such as ARETHA FRANKLIN in a highly danceable fashion.

Gloria Gaynor, performing at a concert at the Burj Al Arab Hotel in Dubai, United Arab Emirates, 31 December 2006. (AP Images.)

FURTHER READING

Gaynor, Gloria. *I Will Survive* (1997).

Holden, Stephen. "Gloria Gaynor's Gospel of Survival," *Rolling Stone* (17 May 1979).

Lawrence, Tim. *Love Saves the Day: A History of American Dance Music Culture, 1970–1979* (2003).

ULRICH ADELT

Gentry, Herbert (17 July 1919–8 Sept. 2003), expressionist painter, was born Herbert Alexander Gentry in Pittsburgh, Pennsylvania, the son of James Gentry, a commercial printer from Virginia, and Violet Howden, a dancer who immigrated to the United States from Kingston, Jamaica. Herbert's parents married in Pittsburgh and had two children. The elder, Elsa died at age four of pneumonia. In 1923 young Herbert and his mother moved to Harlem where she was hired as a Ziegfeld Follies showgirl and later took the stage name of Theresa Jentry. They lived on 126th Street and St. Nicholas Avenue, surrounded by the jazz music, theatrical productions, and art of the Harlem Renaissance. As the son of a dancer, Gentry was continuously exposed to the imaginative world of artists and entertainment. His mother took him to art museums and introduced him to performers, like DUKE ELLINGTON, PAUL ROBESON, COUNT BASIE, and Ethel Barrymore. This creative focus during his childhood fostered his interests in the visual arts.

Gentry's proclivity for drawing began in art classes at Cooper Junior High School in Harlem. At seventeen he enrolled in drawing courses at the 135th Street YMCA and, in the evenings, traveled to Roosevelt High School in the Bronx to attend a Works Progress Administration school arts program. Gentry graduated from George Washington High School and attended New York University from 1940 to 1942. He was drafted into the army in 1942 and served in the racially segregated 90th Coastal Artillery Regiment stationed in Casablanca, French Morocco. He was subsequently stationed in Corsica, Italy, Austria, Germany, and France, where his unit participated in the liberation of Paris. Gentry's experiences during World War II, as a black American with the segregated armed forces had a lasting impact on his perspectives of race and personal identity.

In 1945, at age twenty-six, Gentry was discharged from the military and returned home to America. Anticipating GI Bill funding, he continued his interrupted education in France, arriving in Paris in 1946 and settling in the Montparnasse quarter. He studied painting and drawing at L'École des Beaux-Arts but was not comfortable with their classical, representation-oriented training. He then enrolled at L'Académie de la Grande Chaumière, which provided an open studio program and a teaching philosophy that gave students more freedom in their work.

Gentry married American singer Evelyn Tadea Werfelman, whose stage name was Honey Johnson, in London, England, in 1949. The couple lived in Paris and had two children, Alain Herbert, born in 1949, and Therese Elsie, born in 1950. In 1949, the couple opened a club-gallery in Paris called Chez Honey on rue Jules-Chaplin in Montparnasse. The nightclub featured live jazz music and became a popular hangout for European intelligentsia and black and white expatriates. Performers included Kenny Clark, James Moody, Don Byars, and Zoot Simms. Johnson, who had sung with the REX STEWART Orchestra, performed nightly. Gentry displayed his paintings at Chez Honey along with canvasses by fellow American artists. In 1951 Chez Honey closed when the Gentrys left Paris for New York to follow Honey's career as a solo performer. The couple separated but would not divorce until 1970.

In 1953 Gentry returned alone to Paris. By 1955 he was producing entertainment shows for the Allied and American Armed Forces in France. His subsequent decision to return to painting marked his permanent exit from the entertainment field. In 1956, Gentry studied painting informally under painter Georges Braque, which, added to the influences of African Art, German Expressionism, Surrealism, and Abstract Expressionism, inspired him to explore introspective expression in his own work. In the 1960s, Gentry's style evolved from gestural abstraction to figurative expressionism. His rhythmic choreographies of figures, groups, couples, and faces emerged as a recurring motif. These compositions, he claimed, were painted from his subconscious.

Although aware of the New York School painters, and admiring the work of Jackson Pollock and Willem deKooning, Gentry's artistic associations were international and included the European CoBrA group and Cuban painter Wilfredo Lam. Spending considerable time in the Parisian cafés, particularly café Le Dôme, and café le Tournon, he enjoyed the camaraderie of fellow artists and expatriates BEAUFORD DELANEY, OLIVER W. HARRINGTON, and EDWARD CLARK, as well as American writers RICHARD WRIGHT, JAMES BALDWIN, and CHESTER HIMES. Gentry was invited to have a solo exhibition at the Hybler Gallery in 1958. Gentry was admired by critics and fellow artists across Europe, and collectors began acquiring his work. During the following years he traveled and exhibited in Malmö, Gothenburg, Stockholm, Copenhagen, Paris, Zurich, Geneva, Munich, and Amsterdam. Keeping a studio in Paris while basing himself in Copenhagen, life abroad provided Gentry with exhibition opportunities not afforded many black artists living in America.

In 1962 Gentry met his wife, Ingrid Katarina Stenvinkel, whom he married in 1970. The couple resided in Stockholm and had three children: Stephan James, born in 1963; Nickolas Torlum, born in 1966; and Elsa Katarina, born in 1968. The marriage ended in divorce in 1978.

Gentry returned to the New York art scene in 1972 and moved into the historic Chelsea Hotel in Manhattan. He would spend the rest of his professional career commuting between his studio-residence at the Chelsea, and his home in Sweden. In 1975, the Swedish Royal Academy of Art sponsored a retrospective of his work that spanned his twenty-year career. He had the distinct honor of being the first American painter invited to exhibit at the Royal Academy. While in New York in 1977, ROMARE BEARDEN introduced Gentry to printmaker ROBERT BLACKBURN, who ran the Printmaking Workshop in Chelsea, where Gentry intermittently worked creating monoprints and etchings. Gentry married his third wife, American painter Mary Anne Rose, in Copenhagen in 1984. Referring to himself as an expressionist, the next twenty years were prolific as he painted and exhibited extensively. In 1996, he was featured in a notable group exhibition at the Studio Museum in Harlem titled, Explorations in the City of Light: African-American Artists in Paris, 1945–1965.

After a long illness, Gentry died in Stockholm at the age of eighty-four. His art was an intimate reflection of his upbringing in Harlem, his life in Paris, Scandinavia, and New York City, as well as his love and compassion for family and friends. These themes are reflected in titles of his paintings such as *Mobility* (1978), *Yes I Like You* (1991), and *Among Others and with Friends* (2000). Gentry's work is represented in the collections of major museums and galleries internationally and in the United States.

FURTHER READING

African American Artists in the City of Light, a Studio Museum in Harlem exhibition catalogue of the 1990s.

Archives of American Art, Smithsonian Institution, *Oral History Interview with Herbert Gentry* (1991). Available at www.aaa.si.edu.

Bearden, Romare, and Harry Henderson. *A History of African-American Artists: From 1792 to the Present* (1993).

Hatch, James V., ed. *Artist and Influence* (2000).

The Studio Museum in Harlem. *Explorations in the City of Light: African-American Artists in Paris, 1945–1965* (1996).

Obituary: "Pioneering Artist Herb Gentry Passes at 84," *New York Amsterdam News*, 11–17 September 2003.

BRENDA K. DELANY

George, David (c. 1742–1810), lay preacher and émigré to Nova Scotia and Sierra Leone, was born on a Nottoway River plantation in Essex County, Virginia. His parents, slaves known as John and Judith, were of African origin and had nine children. While a youth David labored in the corn and tobacco fields and witnessed frequent whippings of other slaves, including his mother, who was the master's cook.

When he was about nineteen, George ran away to North Carolina, worked for a brief time, but was pursued and fled to South Carolina. He worked as a hired hand for about two years. After hearing that his first master was again pursuing him, George escaped to central Georgia where he hid among the Creek Indians. George became the personal servant of Chief Blue Salt, who later sold him to the Natchez chief, King Jack.

A trader with the white settlers, King Jack sold George to the Indian trader George Galphin of Silver Bluff, Georgia. Galphin sent George to work for John Miller, his agent. George mended deerskins and took care of Miller's horses until about 1766, when he went to live at Galphin's frontier trading post. Galphin, an Ulsterman who traded with the Creeks and Choctaws, treated George well.

About 1770 George married a woman known only as Phillis. Soon after his marriage he began attending slave prayer meetings led by a slave named Cyrus. George and his wife experienced conversion after hearing the preaching of GEORGE LIELE, the African American Baptist who conducted an itinerant ministry on plantations along the Savannah River. As a child, George had known Liele when the two were slaves in Virginia.

George and his wife were baptized about 1777 by Wait Palmer, a radical white Baptist who belonged to the Separate Baptist movement, which was zealously revivalistic, espousing the need for a "new birth." Liele encouraged George to preach with instruction from Palmer. Galphin employed a schoolmaster who, along with Galphin's children, taught George to read and write. Of learning these skills at the age of thirty, George later said, "The reading so ran in my mind, that I think I learned in my sleep …, and I can now read the Bible, so that what I have in my heart, I can see again in the Scriptures."

With assistance from Palmer, George organized a Baptist congregation on Galphin's Silver Bluff plantation that began with eight members; it expanded to about thirty members by 1778. During the Revolutionary War, John Murray, Lord Dunmore offered emancipation to any slaves who sought sanctuary behind British lines. George went to Charleston. When the British evacuated Charleston in 1782, he and his family were among the Charleston refugees who went to New York City and then to Halifax, Nova Scotia.

Finding no opportunity to preach among blacks in Halifax, George settled in Shelburne. Because white justices, fearing civil disorder, would not let him preach in town, George had to content himself with a hut in the woods, where his preaching attracted whites as well as blacks. He soon had fifty members in what was only the second Baptist church organized in Nova Scotia. In 1784 recently disbanded British soldiers, resenting competition from free black laborers, attacked and destroyed many of their houses. George and his family fled to Birchtown. After six months George returned to Shelburne and regained possession of his old meetinghouse. During the next years he conducted missionary trips in the Maritime Provinces. Though only a lay preacher, George was known for his rousing sermons and hymns and was responsible for the organization of seven Baptist churches in Nova Scotia before he left for Africa.

In 1791 Lieutenant John Clarkson of the British navy arrived in Nova Scotia to recruit Nova Scotia blacks for the British-sponsored "Free Settlement on the Coast of Africa" at Sierra Leone, West Africa. George was by now forty-eight years old, the father of six, the largest black landowner in Nova Scotia, and the pastor of two churches. He talked privately with Clarkson and became convinced of the merits of the Sierra Leone enterprise. On 15 January 1792 the George family departed Halifax for Cape Sierra Leone with about 1,200 other black Nova Scotians.

Soon after landing, George expressed his evangelical enthusiasm: "I preached the first Lord's Day (it was a blessed time) under a sail, and so I did for several weeks after. We then erected a hovel for a meeting-house, which is made of posts put into the ground, and poles over our heads, which are covered with grass." George led the formation of the first Baptist church in West Africa at Freetown, Sierra Leone. He and his members supported Clarkson when other settler factions challenged the authority of the British governor. In 1796, however, George opposed Governor Zachary Macaulay because Macaulay issued a decree that restricted the authority to perform marriages to the ordained clergy of the Anglican church and the governor. George was more moderate in his protest of British authority than some Nova Scotians, as those who had come with Clarkson were known. More strident settlers called George "Macaulay's tool."

While in Sierra Leone, George did limited missionary work among the indigenous Temne. Conflict among the various ethnic groups prevented him from carrying out plans for establishing Baptist churches in areas outside those occupied by the colonists. George and THOMAS PETERS, another Nova Scotian, were the first unofficial members of the Sierra Leone Legislative Council. George traveled to Britain in December 1792, remaining six months visiting English Baptists and telling his story. After returning to Sierra Leone, George devoted himself to church work, especially as an advocate for the Baptists when opposition arose from Methodists in the colony. He died in Sierra Leone.

FURTHER READING

Bill, Ingraham E. *Fifty Years with the Baptist Ministers and Churches of the Maritime Provinces of Canada* (1880).

George, David. *Baptist Annual Register for … 1793*, 473–84.

Kirk-Greene, Anthony. "David George: The Nova Scotia Experience," *Sierra Leone Studies* 14 (1960): 93–120.

Walker, James W. St. G. *The Black Loyalists: The Search for a Promised Land in Nova Scotia and Sierra Leone, 1783–1870* (1976).

Wilson, Ellen Gibson. *The Loyal Blacks* (1976).

This entry is taken from the *American National Biography* and is published here with the permission of the American Council of Learned Societies.

MILTON C. SERNETT

George, Nelson (1 Sept. 1957–), journalist, music critic, author, filmmaker, and television producer, was born and raised in Brooklyn, New York. He attended St. John's University, and while there began his writing career at the black newspaper the *Amsterdam News*, where he was a college intern. During this time he also contributed to the music trade journal *Billboard*. After graduating from St. John's in 1979, George worked as a freelance writer and lived with his mother and sister in a poverty-stricken neighborhood in Brooklyn. It did not take him long, though, to begin what would prove to be a flourishing career. George found employment as a black music editor, first for *Real World* magazine from 1981 to 1982, and then at *Billboard* from 1982 to 1989. He moved on to write a successful column titled "Native Son" for the *Village Voice*, from 1989 to 1992, and contributed to dozens of major publications, including *Essence, Esquire, Playboy, Rolling Stone, Spin*, and the *New York Times Magazine*.

George authored many works of both fiction and nonfiction, but he was best known for the latter, which received widespread critical acclaim. He wrote extensively about topics related to African American popular culture, including music, basketball, and hip hop. George wrote his first published work, *The Michael Jackson Story* (1984), in four months during the summer of 1983. The book was a huge success; it reached number three on the *New York Times* bestseller list and sold over one million copies. George

Nelson George, arriving for the screening of his film *Life Support* at the Sundance Film Festival in Park City, Utah, 26 January 2007. (AP Images.)

also wrote other critically acclaimed works. *Where Did Our Love Go: The Rise and Fall of the Motown Sound* (1985), a history of BERRY GORDY JR., his recording company, and the many well-known artists associated with the label, won the ASCAP Deems Taylor Award for music writing and was identified by the British publication *Q* as one of the best books about rock history. His next nonfiction work, *The Death of Rhythm & Blues* (1988), about the evolution of black music in the mid-twentieth century and the pitfalls of the drive for assimilation and crossover success, also won the ASCAP Deems Taylor Award and was nominated for a National Book Critics Circle award. *Elevating the Game: Black Men and Basketball* (1992) examined the role of blacks in basketball, from the first black intercollegiate conference in 1916 to the early 1990s. It won an American Book Award and an Amateur Athletic Association award. *Hip Hop America* (1999), a personal account about the creation, development, and influence of hip-hop culture, based on Nelson's memories, interviews, and clippings was a finalist for the National Book Critics Circle Award in Criticism and won an American Book Award. *Blackface: Reflections on African-Americans and the Movies* (2002) examined African American cinema and some of the black film industry's most notable contributors. *Post-Soul Nation: The Explosive, Contradictory, Triumphant, and Tragic 1980s as Experienced by African Americans (Previously Known as Blacks and Before that Negroes)* (2004) was a chronological exploration of the contributions of African Americans during the 1980s and the successes and failures of the decade. Although *Post-Soul Nation* was told with a third-person narrator, both it and *Hip Hop America*, which was written in the first person, might be considered to be partially autobiographical because the books' themes relate to many of the themes of George's life and offer reflections on his own experiences. George's fiction contained autobiographical elements as well. Most of his novels are set in New York City and take place in the post–civil rights era when African Americans had greater opportunities yet continued to encounter racial barriers. His first novel was *Urban Romance* (1993); it was followed by *Seduced: The Life and Times of a One Hit Wonder* (1996), *One Woman Short* (2000), *Show & Tell* (2001), *Night Work* (2003), and *The Accidental Hunter* (2004). The six novels are related by theme and by characters who travel between the books, sometimes as protagonists, other times as minor characters.

In addition to his successful writing career, George worked in television and film. The royalties from *The Michael Jackson Story* enabled him to invest in the SPIKE LEE film *She's Gotta Have It* (1986). He was hired first as a co-supervising producer and then became a consulting producer of the award-winning *Chris Rock Show*, which aired for five years on HBO. In 2004 he served as a consulting producer for VH1's *Hip Hop Honors*, a tribute and awards show dedicated to celebrating the history of hip hop. He continued to work on the show as consulting producer and coexecutive producer after it became an annual event in 2005.

George also produced, directed, and wrote a number of films. He cowrote *Strictly Business* (1991), a comedy that starred HALLE BERRY, and cowrote and produced *CB4* (1993), which starred Chris Rock in the story of the rise of the fictitious rap group CB4. He wrote and directed the independent documentary *To Be a Black Man* (1996), a short film based on a well-known essay by the same title that George wrote for the *Village Voice*. Narrated by SAMUEL L. JACKSON, the film explored the lives of both well-known and unknown black men. He was also the executive producer of the HBO film *Everyday People* (2004), which revolved around contemporary racial issues and was filmed in Brooklyn. The film debuted at the Sundance Film Festival. He made his directorial debut in 2007 with the HBO film *Life Support*, starring QUEEN LATIFAH.

George became one of the preeminent analysts and producers of contemporary black culture in the 1990s and 2000s, reaching a sizable audience and at the same time achieving enormous critical success. With his contemporary Greg Tate, he paved the way for the development of a new cadre of black popular music critics during the rise of hip hop. He continued to live and write in Brooklyn into the 2000s.

FURTHER READING

George, Nelson. *Post-Soul Nation: The Explosive, Contradictory, Triumphant, and Tragic 1980s as Experienced by African Americans (Previously Known as Blacks and Before that Negroes)* (2004).

DIANE TODD BUCCI

George, Zelma Watson (8 Dec. 1903–3 July 1994), musicologist, opera singer, and diplomat, was born Zelma Watson in Hearne, Texas, the daughter of Samuel Watson, a Baptist minister, and Lena Thomas, a domestic worker. Zelma's parents attached a great deal of importance to education. As the former principal of a boarding school, Samuel Watson instilled into each of his six children an understanding of the value of education; until sixth grade their mother taught all the Watson children at home. The Watsons were also keen musicians, and family music-making sessions were a staple of Zelma's early life. As the eldest of the children, Zelma clearly took note of both of her parents' pet projects and made scholarship and song central to her own life.

Due to her father's job as a preacher, Zelma's early life was rather peripatetic. At age five she moved to Palestine, Texas, and then to Dallas, Texas, at the age of ten. Her father was a proud man and patently refused to accept the second-class citizenship that the American South served up—a trait his daughter unquestionably imbibed. Such attitudes however, meant that the Watson family was driven from Texas in 1917 by a group of white vigilantes. The family eventually settled in Topeka, Kansas, where Zelma attended public high school, graduating in 1920. Following high school, Zelma enrolled at the University of Chicago to study sociology. Although accepted in the course, her time at university provided an insight into the vagaries of racial discrimination such that she was denied dormitory accommodation by the university. Upon graduating in 1924 with a degree in sociology, Zelma set about cultivating her musical talents. She took pipe organ classes at Northwestern University while spending her evenings at the American Conservatory of Music with a voice coach. Following her father's death in 1925, the family's pecuniary need forced Zelma to find employment. She served as a social worker in Evanston, Illinois, and a probation officer for the juvenile court in Chicago. In 1932 Watson took a post as a personnel administrator at Tennessee State University in Nashville. Soon she was promoted to dean of women. Although she only remained at the institution for five years, it was during this time that she met her first husband, Baxter Duke. They married at Zelma's father's former Baptist church in Chicago.

The newlyweds soon left the Midwest, moving in 1937 to Los Angeles, where they joined the Avalon Christian Church. During her five years in Los Angeles, Zelma oversaw the church's community center. As had been the case throughout her childhood, it was because of this involvement with the church that she met many nationally important figures, including Jester Hairston, the celebrated African American musician, whose choir performed at the center. In her spare time Zelma also began research at the University of Southern California for what she believed would become her doctoral dissertation. Following the dissolution of her marriage to Reverend Duke in 1942, she received a grant from the Rockefeller Foundation that made possible a trip to Cleveland to study the collections of the bibliophile John White.

While engrossed in this research project, Zelma also completed a master's degree in personnel administration at New York University. During this period she met her second husband, the well-known Cleveland attorney and civil-service commissioner Clayborne George. They married in September 1944. Neither study nor matrimony could sap Zelma George's creative energies. By 1949 she had written her first play, *Chariot's a Comin'*. Later that year she also performed in the opera *The Medium*, at Cleveland's recently opened Karamu Theatre. With the encouragement of the theater's director Rowena Jelliffe, George played what had previously been deemed a "white" role, the part of Madam Flora. Playing the part from the position of a wheelchair because she was considerably larger than actors traditionally used for the role, George starred in the show sixty-seven times before Gian Carlo Menotti asked her to take the production to Broadway. To rapturous applause, George made her New York debut at the Edison Hotel's Arena Theatre in July 1950. Following that show, George returned to Cleveland in the fall of 1950 and ultimately assumed leading roles in Menotti's *The Consul* as well as Kurt Weill's *The Threepenny Opera*. Amateur dramatics always figured in George's life, as seen by her part in the musical *Enshrined Forever* just three years before her death in 1991. It was with other enterprises that she devoted her attention to in the postwar years.

Drawing on her research from the mid-1940s, George enrolled at New York University in 1950 and began work on her doctorate. By 1953 she had completed the work, turning out a comprehensive listing of African American songs and scores. Titled *A Guide to Negro Music*, George's PhD dissertation cataloged over twelve thousand titles of compositions written, influenced, or inspired by African Americans. George's personal friend RAOUL ABDUL, the celebrated black journalist and musicologist, later insisted that the study was "indispensable [for] anyone involved in research on Black music" (104). It was not until 1973, however, that the work finally became a published book, although previously a copy had been kept in Howard University's library. Throughout her life George continued to find fascination in all manner of topics about African American music and theater, and she wrote widely, regularly contributing articles to popular journals

and to works like John Preston Davis's *The American Negro Reference Book* (1966).

Through her published work, others took note of George's talents as an intellectual and a discrete political commentator. Her first federal appointment came in 1954, when she was placed on a committee to assess the role of women in the U.S. Army, a position that took her across the United States. Two years later, because of her training in sociology, the Dwight D. Eisenhower administration chose George to serve on a presidential commission to plan a conference on youth and children. If such appointments were intended as a sop to silence her, then they failed. Instead, George frequently used such positions as a platform for her challenges to the administration's record on civil rights, and she frequently lamented President Eisenhower's failure to speak out on racial violence and discrimination in the South. Even though she was one of the administration's most vocal critics, the State Department provided a grant that made possible a six-month lecture tour across three continents and thirteen countries in 1959. The tour concluded at the Pan Pacific Women's Assembly in Singapore, where George was the principal American delegate. Upon her return to the United States in 1960, Congress awarded George with an even more prestigious post, naming her to the fifteenth U.S. delegation to the United Nations General Assembly. In this capacity, as an alternate delegate for economics and finance, she attained the height of her recognition and influence.

Drawing from the knowledge and experience of these appointments, George easily pieced together a career once she left the government's pay. In 1963 the Danforth Foundation recognized her talents as a public speaker and funded her travel and lectures at colleges across the Midwest. Her enjoyment of travel, politics, and art also found expression in the projects she undertook. In 1963 she visited Ghana to attend the "Ban the Bomb" Conference. Three years later she accompanied the musical legends MARIAN ANDERSON and DUKE ELLINGTON to Senegal for the inaugural World Festival of Negro Art. Back in Cleveland, she busied herself with work for the Alpha Kappa Alpha sorority and became involved with the Cleveland Jobs Corps. George would end up devoting increasing amounts of her time to the latter project and ultimately served as its director from 1966 until her retirement in 1974. Widely known for her keen engagement with politics and respected for her social work, she was also selected by the organizers of the Miss America Contest to become its first African American judge in 1969.

Despite the strains of age and the heartache of her husband's death in 1970, George continued to exude energy and determination in her later life. And such efforts did not go without recognition. In late 1971 President Richard Nixon appointed George to the Corporation for Public Broadcasting, where she devoted her one-year term to improving the educational content of programs. Educational institutions around Ohio rewarded George's lifelong intellectual contributions, and Cleveland State University presented her with an honorary doctorate in 1974. In recognition of her work at the United Nations, she received the prestigious Dag Hammarskjöld Award for helping the cause of world peace, and the U.S. State Department presented her with a Distinguished Citizen Award. For her contributions to Cleveland's African American community, she received a Mary Bethune Gold Medallion in 1973.

George's final years were spent mostly in Cleveland, where she engaged in the educational, welfare, musical, and political projects that had always occupied her. She died in the Shaker Heights area of that city. When the playwright LANGSTON HUGHES claimed, shortly before his own death, that "it would take a volume to catalogue [Zelma George's] achievements," he was clearly not exaggerating (Abdul, 104). Throughout her life—regardless of the activity or the country she happened to be in—George embraced her work with an extraordinary combination of vigor and erudition.

FURTHER READING

George's papers are at the Western Reserve Historical Society, Cleveland, Ohio.

Abdul, Raoul. *Blacks in Classical Music: A Personal History* (1977).

Jelliffe, Rowena Woodham. *Here's Zelma* (1971).

Smith, Jessie Carney, ed. *Epic Lives: One Hundred Black Women Who Made a Difference* (1993).

Obituary: *Cleveland Plain Dealer* and *Call and Post*, 5 July 1994.

ANDREW M. FEARNLEY

Gervin, George (27 Apr. 1952–), basketball player, was born in Detroit, Michigan, one of six children. When Gervin was two his father abandoned the family, leaving his mother to support the children alone. Growing up in the 1950s and 1960s Gervin experienced first-hand the desperation caused by urban poverty and racial discrimination, tensions that culminated in the 1967 Detroit riots.

As a 5'8" sophomore Gervin failed to make the Martin Luther King High School basketball team in

1967. However, assistant coach Willie Meriweather saw his potential and offered him a place on the junior varsity squad. Gervin made the most of the opportunity. After befriending the high school janitor, he gained after-hours access to the gymnasium for late-night shooting practice in exchange for sweeping up afterward.

By his senior year Gervin had grown to just below his full height of 6'7", and had developed a silky shooting touch. Averaging thirty-one points and twenty rebounds a game, the All-Conference, All-State, All-American forward led his team to the 1969 state quarterfinals and earned a scholarship to Long Beach State in California. Experiencing intense homesickness, however, he left Long Beach before the end of his first semester. He enrolled at Eastern Michigan, where he averaged 29.5 points a game as a sophomore during the 1971–1972 season and established school records for most points (886), rebounds (458), and field goals made (339) in a season.

Gervin's college career came to a sudden end after a violent incident during a 1972 Division II tournament game in Evansville, Indiana. In an uncharacteristic display of temper, Gervin struck an opponent, Roanoke College player Jay Piccola, twice before being ejected from the game. Gervin was not immediately kicked off the team, but in August school administrators informed him that he could not return, ostensibly for missing an NCAA eligibility exam. Try-out offers for the Pan-Am Games and the 1972 Olympic basketball teams were also revoked. Rather than quit the game, however, Gervin joined the minor league Eastern Basketball Association where he earned $500 a month while averaging forty points for the Pontiac (Michigan) Chaparrals. Playing in the league gave him a chance to showcase and develop his talents, including his signature "finger roll," the shot he popularized in which, with his hand under the ball, he would extend his arm toward the hoop and lay it in with a quick flick of the wrist.

In 1973 the Virginia Squires of the upstart American Basketball Association (ABA) made Gervin their first-round draft choice, signing him to a lucrative contract. The Squires also featured JULIUS ERVING, then a second-year player out of the University of Massachusetts. After appearing in only thirty games that season, Gervin was named to the All-Rookie team. He averaged a modest (by his standards) 14.1 points a game while Erving scored a league-leading 31.9.

It was also during his first year in Virginia that Gervin gained his famous moniker, "Iceman."

Teammate Fatty Taylor began to call Gervin "Iceberg Slim" because of his physical resemblance to the Chicago hustler, ROBERT BECK, who had published the 1969 book *Pimp*, detailing his life on the streets. The nickname was shortened simply to "Iceman" in recognition of Gervin's smooth moves and cool demeanor on the court. The Iceman image would become iconic in early 1980s with a Nike poster that featured Gervin in a silver sweat suit, palming two silver basketballs, and seated on an ice-throne.

In 1974 the Squires, facing financial troubles, traded Gervin to the ABA's San Antonio Spurs. Two years later the league folded, and the Spurs, along with the Denver Nuggets, Indiana Pacers, and New Jersey Nets, joined the better-established National Basketball Association (NBA). Gervin quickly emerged as a star in the NBA, winning four scoring titles, earning five All-NBA First Team awards, and making nine All-Star games in his thirteen-year NBA career.

In 1976 Gervin married Joyce King whom he had met when they attended rival high schools in Detroit. They would be divorced in 1984 only to remarry the year after. Their children include George Gervin Jr. (known as "Gee"), a standout hoopster at the University of Houston and professionally in the newly-revived ABA, the Swedish League, and the NBA Developmental League.

During the 1977–1978 season Gervin, along with DAVID THOMPSON, engaged in one of the most dramatic scoring-title races in league history. Throughout the year they had jockeyed for first. Then on the final night of the season Thompson scored a remarkable seventy-three points. Gervin would have to score at least fifty-three to take the title. He opened the final game, against the New Orleans Jazz, with six straight misses, but quickly recovered to score an NBA-record thirty-three points in the second quarter and sixty-three for the game, claiming the title.

In addition to Gervin's phenomenal success, he also experienced a number of near-misses. He was runner-up for the NBA Most Valuable Player to Bill Walton of the Portland Trailblazers in the 1977–1978 season and to MOSES MALONE of the Houston Rockets the following year. When the Spurs joined the Western Conference, Gervin led the team to the conference finals, but lost in both 1982 and 1983 to the Los Angeles Lakers. He never won an NBA championship.

In 1985 Gervin was traded to the Chicago Bulls, where he stepped in for an injured MICHAEL JORDAN by averaging 16.2 points and appearing in every game. After retiring from the NBA, Gervin played for Banco Roma in the Italian League and for the Quad City Thunder of the Continental Basketball Association in his short-lived 1989–1990 comeback effort.

Away from the court, Gervin battled substance abuse in the late 1980s, finally getting clean at a rehabilitation facility run by his former Spurs teammate (and recovered drug abuser) John Lucas. Lucas would later hire Gervin as a San Antonio assistant coach after being named head coach in 1992. Gervin coached for two years before returning to a position in the Spurs' community relations division in 1994.

Gervin's life after basketball has centered on addressing the very problems he experienced as a child growing up in Detroit. In 1989 he founded the George Gervin Youth Center (now the George Gervin Academy), whose mission was to create training and educational opportunities for disadvantaged young people and their families. In 1996 Gervin was named to the NBA's 50th anniversary All-Time Team and inducted into the Naismith Memorial Basketball Hall of Fame. The Spurs retired his number 44 jersey in 1999.

In 2007 Gervin was named Head of Basketball Operations for the Rio Grande Valley Vipers of the NBA Developmental League, a position he holds while continuing his work with the Spurs and his Academy.

FURTHER READING

Kirkpatrick, Curry. "The Iceman Cometh and Scoreth," *Sports Illustrated* 48 (6 Mar. 1978).

O'Connor, Richard. "The Lonest Star in Texas," *Sports Illustrated* 72 (3 Mar. 1981).

Pluto, Terry. *Loose Balls: The Short, Wild Life of the American Basketball Association as Told by the Players, Coaches, and Movers and Shakers Who Made It Happen* (1991).

ADAM BRADLEY

Gibbs, James Lowell (13 June 1931–), anthropologist, was born in Syracuse, New York, to Huldah Hortense Dabney, a schoolteacher, and James Lowell Gibbs Sr., executive director of a community center. He attended public primary and secondary schools in Ithaca, New York. He continued his education in Ithaca, receiving a BA in Sociology and Anthropology from Cornell University in 1952. During the 1953–1954 school term he attended the University of Cambridge in Cambridge, England, where he was enrolled under the faculty of archaeology and anthropology. In addition Gibbs received a number of other graduate fellowships and honors, including a National Woodrow Wilson Fellowship. From 1956 to 1958 he was a Ford Foundation Foreign Area Training Fellow, and in 1958–1959 he was a National Science Foundation Predoctoral Fellow. Gibbs received his PhD in Social Anthropology from Harvard University in 1961. His dissertation, "Some Judicial Implications of Marital Instability among the Kpelle," examined a West African ethnic group.

In 1956 Gibbs married Jewelle Althea Taylor, who became a professor of social welfare. Gibbs taught at the University of Minnesota (1959–1966) as an instructor and then assistant professor of anthropology. From July 1965 to July 1966 he continued his study of Kpelle law. In 1966 he joined the Stanford University anthropology department, which became his academic home for the next three decades. In 1967 he received tenure, the first African American to do so at that institution. He was Stanford's first dean of undergraduate studies (1970–1976) and served as acting director, until the appointment of St. Clair Drake as director, of the Stanford faculty committee that shaped the undergraduate program in African and Afro-American Studies.

In the summer of 1981 Gibbs studied law in Botswana and traveled throughout East Africa. He has also been a notable classroom teacher, developing innovative courses on ethnographic film as well as African American film. From 1985 to 1987 Gibbs served as co-director of the Stanford-Berkeley Center for African studies. In 1986 he received Stanford's highest undergraduate teaching award, the Dinkelspiel Award. From 1987 to 1990 he was chair of the anthropology department. In 1984–1985 Gibbs was a senior fellow at the W. E. B. DuBois Institute for Afro-American Research at Harvard University. He was named Martin Luther King Jr. Centennial Professor in 1988.

Gibbs edited *Peoples of Africa* (1965), which became a standard in African studies, and his article "The Kpelle Moot: A Therapeutic Model for the Informal Settlement of Disputes" was also considered seminal. In addition, Gibbs co-wrote *Law in Radically Different Cultures* (1983), another major work in the field. He co-produced and co-directed several anthropological films, including *The Cows of Dolo Ken Paye* (1970) and *Dolo Ken Paye's People Go to the Movies* (2000), which were effective teaching tools in both general anthropology and Africanist courses. Gibbs also wrote *Television and Diversity: The Quantum Leap Model*, a textbook published in 2000.

Among his other academic honors, Gibbs was a fellow of the Center for Advanced Study in the Behavioral Sciences, Stanford, California (1969–1970); a fellow of the Woodrow Wilson International Center for Scholars, Smithsonian Institution (1976–1977); and a senior fellow at the Research Institute of the Center for Comparative Studies in Race and Ethnicity, Stanford University (2001–2004). A member of the National Research Council's Committee on the Status of Black Americans, he helped produce its 1989 work *A Common Destiny: Blacks and American Society*. Additionally Gibbs served on the Committee on Policy for Racial Justice, Joint Center for Political and Economic Studies; on the Board of Trustees of the Carnegie Corporation of New York; as a trustee (later trustee emeritus) of Cornell University; and as an adviser to the NAACP Legal Defense Fund of Northern California.

In 1996 Gibbs was inducted into Stanford University's Hall of Fame. Through it all he remained an open, gracious colleague of good cheer and pleasant demeanor. His accomplishments were great and worn with grace. In 1997 he became Martin Luther King Jr. Centennial Professor of Anthropology Emeritus.

FURTHER READING
Harrison, Ira E., and Faye V. Harrison, eds. *African-American Pioneers in Anthropology* (1999).

FRANK A. SALAMONE

Gibbs, Jonathan C. (c. 1827–14 Aug. 1874), clergyman, educator, and politician, was born free in Philadelphia, Pennsylvania, the son of Maria Jackson and Jonathan C. Gibbs, a Methodist minister. He learned carpentry as a youth and followed that trade until the Presbyterian Assembly helped him enroll at Dartmouth College in 1848. Gibbs, who was one of only two black students at Dartmouth, claimed that he had been rejected by eighteen colleges before being accepted. After graduating from Dartmouth in 1852 he attended the Princeton Theological Seminary. He was ordained as a Presbyterian minister and went on to pastor churches in Troy, New York, and in Philadelphia. While in New York Gibbs campaigned for the extension of black suffrage in the state. When he moved to Philadelphia in 1859 he became prominent in the local Underground Railroad. During the Civil War he joined the freed people's relief efforts, campaigned against segregated city streetcars, encouraged black enlistments in the army, served as vice president of the Pennsylvania State Equal Rights League, and continued his participation in the black convention movement. He represented Philadelphia at the black national convention in Syracuse in 1864, which severely criticized the Republican Party for its failure to endorse black suffrage and which gave birth to the National Equal Rights League.

In April 1865 Gibbs went to Wilmington, North Carolina, to establish churches and schools for freed people. He cooperated with white missionaries in the area but was deeply troubled by their paternalism and racism. Nevertheless, he saw the last few months of 1865 as a period of remarkable gains for blacks. In 1866 Gibbs exclaimed, "We have progressed a century in a year." In 1867 Gibbs was transferred to Florida to organize churches and schools among former slaves. When the congressional Reconstruction Act of 1867 mandated black suffrage, he concluded that talented black men were as badly needed in politics as in religion and education. Voters elected him as a delegate to the Florida Constitutional Convention, which met in Tallahassee in January 1868. When Republican delegates divided into conservative and radical factions, he joined the latter but did not blindly support them, and his speeches were generally temperate. He sought a constitution that would protect the rights of both blacks and property owners. Gibbs proved to be an exemplary delegate. Press accounts described him as being of medium build with "a good intelligent yellow African face," an orator, "not a roarer but a convincing, argumentative, pleasant speaker: in this respect the most talented man in the Convention." Many members agreed with the *New York Tribune* reporter who wrote that there was "no fitter man" at the convention, "white or black."

In 1868 Gibbs was appointed secretary of state; working closely with the Florida governor Harrison Reed, he became a well-respected public official. In the governor's absence Gibbs served as chairman pro tem of the Board of Commissioners of Public Institutions with the support and confidence of other cabinet members. Even the Democrats occasionally praised Gibbs for the equitable manner in which he administered government contracts. His impartiality did not shield him from Ku Klux Klan hatred, however. His brother, during a visit to Tallahassee while Gibbs was secretary of state, found him well-armed and sleeping in the attic, ready to defend himself against the Klan, which had threatened his life. Gibbs fought for civil rights and equal economic opportunity. Emphasizing black history at a time when it received little attention, in 1871 he wrote a series of sketches of distinguished blacks for Florida newspapers in an effort to "incite" black youth to "fit themselves for the higher walks of usefulness." The future, he added, is "to the young man

of color who is in earnest. Everything is before us; everything to win!"

When Ossian B. Hart succeeded Reed as governor in 1873, he appointed Gibbs as superintendent of public instruction. Florida had no viable system of public education before Republican Reconstruction, and Gibbs played a large role in placing it on a firm foundation. The manuscript records of superintendent Gibbs reveal him to have been an intelligent, able administrator who was devoted to public education. County superintendents were charged with keeping complete, accurate records, and Gibbs closely supervised their work. He succeeded in securing the adoption of uniform texts for the state. Although the system of public education experienced rapid growth under Gibbs's brief leadership, he was not satisfied, claiming that white fear of integrated schools inhibited the system at the county level. The mental, moral, and physical possibilities of the black man, Gibbs said, "strikes terror to the hearts of men who have so long trampled him underfoot." He was not always so pessimistic, however. In an address to the National Educational Association at Elmira, New York, in August 1873, he acknowledged Florida's educational shortcomings but offered impressive statistics to illustrate the great improvements that had taken place since the Civil War. His speech received flattering notice in New York journals, which seemed to relate with pride that an African American from the South "had delivered with the dignity of an educated gentleman" a speech that in "breadth of thought and liberality of sentiment" marked him as a "worthy son" of Dartmouth.

Gibbs's sudden death was a serious loss to the state. S. B. McLin, his successor as superintendent of public instruction, wrote that blacks "have lost one of their noblest representatives, our State one of its most valued citizens, and our public school system one of its most intelligent advocates and one of its best friends." Gibbs, in apparent good health, had given a rousing speech at a Republican meeting in Tallahassee but died later the same night. Although he probably suffered a heart attack, it was whispered and widely believed that he had been poisoned by white enemies. Gibbs was an outstanding African American leader during the Reconstruction era.

FURTHER READING
Gibbs, Mifflin Wistar. *Shadow and Light: An Autobiography* (1902).
Richardson, Joe M. *The Negro in the Reconstruction of Florida* (1965).

Sterling, Dorothy, ed. *The Trouble They Seen: Black People Tell the Story of Reconstruction* (1976).

Obituaries: Tallahassee *Weekly Floridian*, 25 Aug. 1874; Jacksonville *Tri-Weekly Union*, 18 Aug. 1874; and the Jacksonville *New South*, 19 Aug. 1874.

This entry is taken from the *American National Biography* and is published here with the permission of the American Council of Learned Societies.

JOE M. RICHARDSON

Gibbs, Mifflin Wistar (17 Apr. 1823–11 July 1915), businessman, politician, and race leader, was born in Philadelphia, Pennsylvania, the son of Jonathan C. Gibbs, a Methodist minister, and Maria Jackson. His parents were free blacks. His father died when Mifflin was seven years old, and his mother was an invalid. As a teenager Mifflin attended the Philomathean Institute, a black men's literary society, and, like his brother JONATHAN C. GIBBS (who would serve as secretary of state in Florida during Reconstruction), became a carpenter's apprentice, and subsequently a journeyman contractor. During the 1840s Mifflin Gibbs aided fugitive slaves by participating in local Underground Railroad efforts and worked with its famous conductor WILLIAM GRANT STILL. It was through this work that he became acquainted with the preeminent black abolitionist FREDERICK DOUGLASS, accompanying him on an 1849 tour of New York State.

During this tour Gibbs learned that gold had been discovered in California, and he set out to find his fortune. Reaching San Francisco in 1850, he decided that more money could be made in business than in panning for gold. Consequently, along with a black partner, Peter Lester, Gibbs established a clothing and dry goods store. His business prospered, and he quickly became a well-known and successful entrepreneur. He also kept up his interest in the abolitionist movement, attending three state black conventions (1854, 1855, 1857) and in 1855 purchasing and becoming the editor of a local black antislavery newspaper, the *Mirror of the Times*.

During an economic recession in the United States in 1857–1858, Gibbs followed a new gold rush to Victoria, British Columbia, Canada, where he opened another store. He briefly returned to the United States in 1859 to marry Maria A. Alexander, a former Oberlin student who became the mother of their five children. During the next decade Gibbs repeated his California business success in Canada by speculating in real estate, becoming the director of the Queen Charlotte Island Anthracite Coal Company,

and building a wharf and railroad spur to transport coal. His business ventures brought him influence, and in 1866 he was elected to the first of two terms as a member of Victoria's Common Council. After the second term, however, disgruntled by the direction of local politics, he returned to the United States to complete a formal course in law at a business school in Oberlin, Ohio. Touring the southern states to find a suitable location to establish a law practice, Gibbs settled in the rapidly growing town of Little Rock, Arkansas, in 1871. Beginning as a lawyer, he was later appointed county attorney, and in 1873 he won election as municipal judge of Little Rock, reportedly the first black man in the nation to be so honored. In 1875 when the Democrats returned to power, Gibbs lost the judgeship, but he quickly rose to prominence in the Republican Party, attending national Republican conventions and serving as a presidential elector for Arkansas in 1876 and as secretary of the Republican state central committee from 1887 to 1897. In 1877 he was appointed by President Rutherford B. Hayes as register of the U.S. Land Office for the Little Rock

Mifflin Wistar Gibbs, politician, diplomat, businessman, and lawyer. (Schomburg Center for Research in Black Culture, New York Public Library.)

District of Arkansas. He served in the land office for twelve years, the last four as receiver of public monies. In 1897 he was appointed U.S. consul to Tamatave, Madagascar (1898–1901).

In 1901 Gibbs returned to Arkansas and the next year published *Shadow and Light, an Autobiography with Reminiscences of the Last and Present Century* (repr. 1968), a lively account of his life and times, with an introduction by the famous black leader BOOKER T. WASHINGTON. That Washington would introduce the book was no accident; Gibbs epitomized Washington's self-help philosophy. In Little Rock, Gibbs not only speculated in real estate but eventually owned a number of brick office buildings and rental properties. In 1903 Gibbs became president of the city's Capital City Savings Bank (it failed after five years) and later bought shares in several local companies while becoming a partner in the Little Rock Electric Light Company. He was also an active member of the National Negro Business League, founded by Washington to encourage entrepreneurship among blacks.

Although closely tied to the Republican machine in Arkansas, Gibbs fought for equal rights for blacks and supported emigration from the South as a cure for racial oppression (a radical stance in the late 1870s). After Theodore Roosevelt summarily dismissed black soldiers accused of inciting a race riot in Brownsville, Texas, in 1906, Gibbs abandoned the Republican Party and endorsed the Democrat William Jennings Bryan for the presidency. The common thread linking these diverse elements was Gibbs's commitment to what he termed "the progress of the race." Although he fought for equality and fair treatment, he believed that property acquisition and education were the keys to racial advancement and that African Americans should establish a skilled middle class in order to compete in the marketplace.

During the last decade of his life, using the income from his rental properties, Gibbs lived quietly and comfortably in Little Rock. After an illness of several months, he died at his home. He was survived by several notable children, among them HARRIET GIBBS MARSHALL, who founded the Washington Conservatory of Music, and IDA GIBBS HUNT, who married WILLIAM HENRY HUNT, Gibbs's successor as U.S. consul to Madagascar. A man of education, talent, energy, and property, Gibbs had a remarkably varied career.

FURTHER READING

Dillard, Tom W. "'Golden Prospects and Fraternal Amenities,' Mifflin W. Gibbs's Arkansas Years,"

Arkansas Historical Quarterly 35 (Winter, 1976): 307–333.

Obituaries: *Arkansas Gazette* and *Arkansas Democrat*, 12 July 1915; Washington *Bee*, 17 July 1915.

This entry is taken from the *American National Biography* and is published here with the permission of the American Council of Learned Societies.

LOREN SCHWENINGER

Gibson, Althea (25 Aug. 1927–28 Sept. 2003), tennis champion and professional golfer, was born in Silver, South Carolina, the first of five children of Daniel Gibson and Annie Gibson, who worked as sharecroppers. The family moved to New York City in 1930, and Gibson grew up in Harlem. As a youth Gibson rejected rules and authority; a frequent truant, she dropped out of high school after one year. She did, however, enjoy competition, playing basketball and paddleball, and shooting pool. After Gibson won a 1941 Police Athletic League paddleball championship, Buddy Walker, a tournament official, suggested that she try playing tennis. With Walker's assistance, she began tennis lessons at Harlem's Cosmopolitan Club.

The following summer, Gibson was ready for tournament play. She won the 1942 New York State Open in the girls' division, a victory that began her rise through the ranks of the American Tennis Association (ATA), the governing body of black tennis in the United States. In 1944 and 1945 she won consecutive ATA girls' national championships. As an eighteen-year-old, Gibson qualified to play in the women's division in 1946. Despite losing in the finals of the women's singles competition, her play impressed HUBERT A. EATON and Robert W. Johnson, two southern physicians who were active in the ATA. Eaton and Johnson believed Gibson had the potential to become a world-class player. They felt that with proper training and instruction, she could break the color line, which had prohibited earlier black tennis players like LUCY DIGGS SLOWE and ORA MAE WASHINGTON from competing in tournaments sponsored by the United States Lawn Tennis Association (USLTA). Following the advice of her friend the boxer SUGAR RAY ROBINSON (whom she had met in a bowling alley) and his wife, Gibson left Harlem in 1946 and boarded at Eaton's home in Wilmington, North Carolina. She enrolled in Wilmington's segregated public high school and began training year-round on Eaton's private tennis court. During the summers, Gibson practiced her tennis at Johnson's home in Lynchburg, Virginia.

She created a sensation on the ATA tournament circuit, capturing eight mixed-doubles championships, with Johnson as her partner, and winning nine women's singles titles, including the first of her ten consecutive ATA women's championships in 1947.

Gibson graduated from high school in 1949 and received an athletic scholarship to attend Florida A&M University (FAMU) in Tallahassee, where she played softball, volleyball, basketball, and tennis. Before she arrived at the FAMU campus, she competed against white players in tournament action for the first time, at two indoor events sponsored by USLTA. Although she made it to the quarterfinals in both tournaments, Gibson did not receive invitations to play at outdoor tournaments because most major USLTA events were held at segregated country clubs, such as the West Side Tennis Club in Forest Hills, New York.

After Gibson was shut out of USLTA tournament play in the summer of 1949, Alice Marble, the winner of four U.S. Open titles and a former Wimbledon champion, wrote in support of Gibson's struggle to break the color line in tennis, just as JACKIE ROBINSON had ended baseball's color bar in 1947. In an editorial published in the July 1950 issue of *American Lawn Tennis*, Marble criticized the USLTA for its pro-segregation stance. The piece made an immediate impact, and Gibson entered several USLTA outdoor tournaments in the summer of 1950, including the USLTA National Clay Court and the Eastern Grass Court Championships. She also qualified to play in the USLTA National Championship tournament (later the U.S. Open) at Forest Hills. On 28 August 1950 Gibson became the first African American to compete in this tournament, winning her first round match in straight sets, 6-2, 6-2. In the second round, she nearly pulled a stunning upset of the three-time Wimbledon champion, Louise Brough. With Gibson leading 1-6, 6-3, 7-6 and needing just one game to win, play was stopped because of severe weather. Brough rallied and won when play was resumed the next day. Gibson's performance in this and subsequent tournaments at Forest Hills established her as a fixture on the USLTA tour until her retirement from tennis.

Gibson continued to break racial barriers with each tournament appearance. In 1951 she became the first African American—male or female—to play on the grass courts of the All England Club at Wimbledon. She also captured her first international title that year, winning the Caribbean Open in Jamaica. By 1952 Gibson was ranked number nine among all American women tennis players.

However, because tennis was an amateur sport during this era, after graduating from Florida A&M in 1953 she took a teaching position in the athletic department at Lincoln University in Jefferson City, Missouri. She struggled in the years following her graduation, and her tennis career appeared to stall. Gibson contemplated leaving the tour, but was convinced to continue by the tennis coach Sydney Llewellyn, with whom she began training in 1954. Her career was revitalized when she returned from playing a series of goodwill exhibition matches in Southeast Asia sponsored by the U.S. Department of State during the winter of 1955–1956.

As she approached thirty, Gibson began a remarkable tournament run in which she took eight Grand Slam titles between 1956 and 1958. This streak began with her first, and only, appearance at the French Open. On her way to capturing that tournament's women's title, 6-0, 12-10 over the defending champion, Angela Mortimer, Gibson also won the French doubles title with her partner,

Althea Gibson, posing with a tennis ball and racket, 20 November 1958. (Library of Congress/Carl Van Vechten.)

Angela Buxton. Pairing again with Buxton, she won her first women's doubles title at Wimbledon in June 1956. Before the year was over, Gibson claimed singles titles in the Italian Open and the Asian Championship, in addition to other international events, including the New South Wales, Pan American, and South Australian tournaments. With each new title and tournament appearance, a piece of the color line broke away.

Gibson was at the top of her game in 1957, the year in which she won the women's singles championship and defended her doubles title at Wimbledon. She later recalled that receiving her trophy from Queen Elizabeth II and shaking hands with her "was a long way from being forced to sit down in the colored section of the bus going into downtown Wilmington, N.C." (*New York Times*, 29 Sept. 2003). When Gibson returned to New York City she was welcomed as a heroine, receiving the medallion of the city from Mayor Robert Wagner after a ticker tape parade. On 8 September 1957 she continued her pioneering career by becoming the first African American to win the U.S. Open, defeating Louise Brough in straight sets, 6-3, 6-2. This win was the first part of her clean sweep of the tournament, as she also captured the women's doubles with Darlene Hard and the mixed-doubles championships with Kurt Nielsen. By year's end, Gibson was ranked as the number one woman tennis player in the world and named Female Athlete of the Year by the Associated Press (AP), a first for an African American woman.

Gibson became a repeat winner of the AP Female Athlete of the Year award in 1958, successfully defending her Wimbledon singles title and taking a third straight doubles crown, this time with Maria Bueno. She also won her second straight U.S. National Championship at Forest Hills. Soon afterward Gibson retired from amateur tennis, leaving the tennis circuit with one hundred tournament victories.

Gibson kept her place in the public eye after her tennis career ended. She wrote her first autobiography, *I Always Wanted to Be Somebody* (1958), recorded an album titled *Althea Gibson Sings* (1958), and also appeared in the John Ford film *The Horse Soldiers* (1959) with John Wayne and William Holden. In 1960 she signed a hundred-thousand-dollar contract with the Harlem Globetrotters to stage tennis exhibitions in conjunction with Globetrotter appearances. However, this did not satisfy Gibson's competitive fire, and she began to explore the possibility of joining the newly constituted Ladies Professional Golf Association (LPGA). By earning her tour card in 1964, Gibson broke another part of the color line by becoming the first African American woman professional golfer. Although Gibson did not record any tournament victories while on the tour, she remained with the LPGA for seven years, playing in 171 tournaments. She briefly attempted a tennis comeback when Grand Slam tournaments were opened to both professionals and amateurs in 1968. She was inducted into the Tennis Hall of Fame in 1971.

Gibson, who married Will Darben in 1965, had settled in East Orange, New Jersey, upon her retirement from tennis. As well as coaching and teaching tennis, she also held a position in the East Orange Department of Recreation. In 1975 she was named New Jersey State athletic commissioner, becoming the first woman to serve in such a position anywhere in the United States. Gibson was honored for her groundbreaking accomplishments on and off the court with numerous awards, including induction to the International Women's Hall of Fame in 1980.

Althea Gibson died of respiratory failure in East Orange in September 2003. She was predeceased by Darben, and by her second husband, her former coach, Sydney Llewellyn. Gibson had no children. Her legacy continues to be carried out through the Althea Gibson Foundation, an organization founded to identify, encourage, and provide financial support for urban students seeking to develop their skills in tennis or golf. Her enduring significance lies in becoming the first African American to win Wimbledon, the world's premier tennis tournament. Gibson took great pride in that victory, which she viewed as the first-ever world championship won by a black woman. That victory inspired a young Billie Jean King, who greatly admired Gibson's courage, and set a precedent for ARTHUR ASHE, who won the men's Wimbledon title in 1975. Gibson showed a particular interest in encouraging the relatively small cohort of African American women on the tennis circuit. Despite her failing health, she traveled to London in 1990 to cheer on Zina Garrison, the first African American to reach the Wimbledon finals since Gibson's last appearance in 1958. She also took great pleasure in the Wimbledon triumphs of VENUS AND SERENA WILLIAMS, who like her had grown up in poverty. "The crowds will love you," Gibson told Venus on one occasion, reminding her, however, that it was important to "be who you are and let your racket do the talking" (Vecsey).

FURTHER READING

Gibson, Althea, edited by Ed Fitzgerald. *I Always Wanted to Be Somebody* (1958).

Gibson, Althea, with Richard Curtis. *So Much to Live For* (1968).

Vecsey, George. "Gibson Deserved a Better Old Age," *New York Times*, 29 Sept. 2003.

Wade, Virginia, with Jean Rafferty. *Ladies of the Court: A Century of Women at Wimbledon* (1984).

Obituary: *New York Times*, 29 Sept. 2003.

MICHAEL A. ANTONUCCI

Gibson, Bob (9 Nov. 1935–), baseball player, was born Pack Robert Gibson in Omaha, Nebraska, the last of the eight children of Pack Gibson, a carpenter, and Victoria Gibson, later Victoria Borden, a laundry worker. Upon reaching adulthood, Gibson legally changed his name to Robert Gibson. Pack Gibson died of tuberculosis five months before Bob's birth, leaving fifteen-year-old Leroy (known as "Josh") to run the family with his mother. The Gibsons lived in Omaha's North Side, where, surrounded almost exclusively by poor African Americans, Bob first recognized segregation.

Bob, who was born with severe asthma that would dissipate with age, had many health problems as a child, including rickets and a case of pneumonia that nearly killed him at age three. According to family lore, young Bob pulled through after Josh promised him a baseball glove if he survived. Josh taught his brother to play baseball and in 1947, after JACKIE ROBINSON's integration of Major League Baseball convinced him that African Americans would gain acceptance in professional sports, told his brother that he ought to choose between athletics and academics. Bob, who did not enjoy schoolwork, chose the former. Josh was a mentor to his brother and to many other North Side youngsters. While working at the local YMCA, he began a youth baseball team called the Monarchs that in 1951, with Bob as a star, became the first African American team to win Nebraska's state championship.

At Omaha Technical High School, Gibson played basketball, ran track, and during his senior year became one of the school's first two African American baseball players. After graduation in 1953, the lanky 6'1", 190-pound right-hander was offered a contract with the Negro League's Kansas City Monarchs, which he declined, on Josh's advice, in order to take a basketball scholarship at Omaha's Creighton University. Gibson was the first African American basketball player in the history of the university. As a pitcher and catcher on Creighton's baseball team, he led the

Nebraska College Conference in batting his senior year. In 1957 Gibson married Charline Johnson, the niece of Josh's wife, whom he had met at the YMCA during his senior year of high school. They had two children before they divorced in 1974.

After he graduated from Creighton, Gibson was offered a contract by the Harlem Globetrotters basketball team. He signed for the 1957–1958 winter but declined a more substantial commitment due to insufficient pay, disruptive travel schedules, and the unsatisfactory level of competition inherent in Globetrotter showmanship. As Gibson once stated, "I don't let my ten-year-old daughter beat me at tic-tac-toe" (Lipman and Wilks, 41). On 9 June 1957 the Omaha Cardinals, the American Association affiliate of the St. Louis Cardinals, signed Gibson for $4,000. Gibson pitched ten games for Omaha, going 2-1 before being demoted to Columbus, Georgia, in the South Atlantic or "Sally" League, where he went 4-3. While in Columbus, Gibson was repeatedly subjected to racist taunts from the stands.

Gibson split 1958 between Omaha and triple-A Rochester, where he was voted the fastest right-handed pitcher in the International League. On 10 April 1959 he signed with St. Louis, and later that week he made his major league debut. He went back and forth between the majors and minors before finding a permanent place with St. Louis in 1960. Gibson attributed his lackluster performance at the time to player-manager Solly Hemus, whom he regarded as racially insensitive. A turning point came in mid-1961, when his former Omaha manager, Johnny Keane, replaced Hemus. Gibson went 11-6 after Keane took over, posting a 3.24 earned run average (ERA) that ranked fifth in the National League and emerging as one of the most impressive and competitive players in the game. He was an all-around phenom who hit twenty-four home runs in his career, including a .303 batting average in 1970, and won nine straight Gold Gloves from 1965 to 1973. To his opponents, he was the most intimidating pitcher in baseball. At All-Star Games, Gibson refused to fraternize with National League teammates lest they feel comfortable facing him from the batter's box. "I wouldn't say Gibson was unfriendly when he pitched," commented the opponent and later teammate Joe Torre. "Hateful is more like it" (Gibson, *Stranger to the Game*, 6). In 1963 Gibson's ERA improved to 2.85, and he led the National League with five shutouts, earning his first of eight career all-star selections before suffering a broken leg at the end of the season. Gibson came back the next year to go 18-9, with a second-half

9-2 record, including eight consecutive complete games and a last-game pennant clincher. Gibson went on to set a World Series record by striking out thirty-one New York Yankees over the course of three games, winning the series finale on two days' rest and earning the 1964 Most Valuable Player (MVP) Award. Gibson went 7-2 over three career World Series appearances with a 1.89 ERA, including at one point seven straight wins and eight straight complete games. "I never have jitters," he once explained. "The only thing that makes me nervous is my wife" (Lipman and Wilks, 137).

To Gibson's dismay, Keane resigned as St. Louis's manager after the 1964 World Series to take over the Yankees. Gibson was pleased with his experience in St. Louis, despite its distinction as the southernmost city in baseball until the Houston Astros joined the National League in 1962. The Cardinals made a deliberate effort to minimize racial tensions by reporting inappropriate comments and demanding equal accommodations for white and black players. According to the center fielder CURT FLOOD, "The men on that team were as close to being free of racist poison as a diverse group of twentieth-century Americans could possibly be" (Gibson, *Stranger to the Game*, 82–83). Gibson, vocal but by his own admission not always active in addressing racial injustice, began a lifelong effort to promote African American entrepreneurship during the mid-1960s, when he spearheaded a project to purchase radio station KOWH in Omaha and later to operate a bank, stating, "The answer for ghettos now is not black power but green power" (Lipman and Wilks, 119).

Gibson won twenty games for the first time in 1965, followed by twenty-one the next year, despite a severely strained elbow and a second-division Cardinals performance. On 15 July 1967 Gibson's leg was broken by a line drive off the bat of the Pittsburgh Pirates great ROBERTO CLEMENTE. Gibson pitched to three more batters before collapsing to the ground in pain. He returned only two months later, on 6 September, and clinched the pennant with a win on 18 September. In the World Series, against the Boston Red Sox, he earned a second series MVP by throwing 3 complete game victories while posting a 1.00 ERA with twenty-six strikeouts and a home run in game seven. The Boston pitcher Jose

Bob Gibson, firing the ball in the ninth inning of the first game of the World Series at Busch stadium in St. Louis, Missouri, 2 October 1968. (AP Images.)

Santiago lamented, "You've got to pitch a shutout to beat Gibson" (Lipman and Wilks, 134).

In 1968, the Year of the Pitcher, Gibson had what many regard as the finest pitcher's season in baseball history, earning the National League Cy Young Award and the MVP with a 22-9 record, 268 strikeouts, thirteen shutouts, twenty-eight complete games, and a league record 1.12 ERA. At one point Gibson went 472/3 innings without an earned run and also won fifteen straight games. In game one of the World Series versus the Detroit Tigers, Gibson fanned a record seventeen batters and, despite St. Louis's seven-game loss, broke his own record with thirty-five strikeouts in the series. That year he published an autobiography, *From Ghetto to Glory.*

Gibson went on to win twenty games in both of the next two seasons, claiming the 1970 Cy Young Award and in 1971 throwing his only no-hitter against the Pirates. After that season Gibson was rewarded with a $150,000 contract, the most ever given to a St. Louis Cardinal or a major league pitcher at the time. In 1972 he recorded two hundred strikeouts for a record ninth time and passed the pitcher Jesse Haines for the most wins in Cardinals history. Gibson struggled through his last three seasons with persistent leg problems and finally retired in 1975 with 251 wins, 3,117 strikeouts, and a 2.91 career ERA. The Cardinals retired his uniform number 45 in 1975, and he was elected to the Baseball Hall of Fame in 1981.

After rejecting offers from the Cardinals and the San Francisco Giants, Gibson returned to Omaha to his two daughters and his new wife, Wendy Nelson, with whom he had a son. He attended to business interests in Omaha until he accepted the manager Torre's offer to be an "attitude coach" for the New York Mets in 1981. When Torre was fired at the end of the season and hired by the Atlanta Braves, Gibson followed him as pitching coach, where he served until 1984. In 1982 the Braves lost to the Cardinals in the National League Championship Series. From 1985 to 1989 Gibson hosted pre- and postgame shows for KMOX in St. Louis before joining ESPN for the 1990 season. He had previously broadcast college basketball for WPIX in New York and the 1970 and 1971 National League Championship Series for NBC Sports. In 1994 Gibson published his second autobiography, *Stranger to the Game,* with Lonnie Wheeler. He became a special instructor to the Cardinals in 1996, and in 1997 he began hosting an annual charity golf tournament in Omaha, featuring prominent athletes and celebrities.

Gibson will be regarded by baseball history as one of its most talented and fiercest competitors.

His ability to excel under pressure produced some of the game's most memorable performances, but to Gibson the challenges of the game were secondary to those of life. "Pressure?" he once scoffed during a pennant race. "I had more pressure on me when I was growing up as a kid in Omaha" (Lipman and Wilks, 51).

FURTHER READING
Gibson, Bob, with Lonnie Wheeler. *Stranger to the Game: The Autobiography of Bob Gibson* (1994).
Gibson, Bob, with Phil Pepe. *From Ghetto to Glory* (1968).
Lipman, David, and Ed Wilks. *Bob Gibson: Pitching Ace* (1975).
Owens, Tom. *Greatest Baseball Players of All Time* (1990).
Shatzkin, Mike, ed. *The Ballplayers* (1990).

CHRISTOPHER DEVINE

Gibson, John Trusty (4 Feb. 1878–17 June 1937), theater entrepreneur and prominent Philadelphia businessman, was born in Baltimore, Maryland, the son of George Henry and Elizabeth Gibson. In his biography in the 1929 edition of *Who's Who in Colored America* Gibson claimed to have attended public school in Baltimore but it is unclear whether he graduated from high school. The historian Henry T. Sampson in his book *Blacks in Blackface* reports that Gibson attended Morgan State Preparatory School (later Morgan State University) for two years. In 1928, however, he would receive an honorary doctorate from Morgan State. Sometime around 1899 Gibson moved to Philadelphia, Pennsylvania, where he worked in various jobs, including weaving, upholstering furniture, and peddling meat. In 1910 he became part owner with Samuel Reading of the North Pole Theater in Philadelphia. This small theater in the black Philadelphia community offered silent films and vaudeville acts. Around 1912 Gibson bought out his partner and became sole owner of the North Pole Theater, becoming the first African American to own a theater in Philadelphia. He later changed the name to the Auditorium, but the name change failed to increase business and it soon closed.

In April 1913 Gibson became part owner of the New Standard Theater in Philadelphia, a larger and more successful vaudeville house. He married Ella Lewis of Chester, Pennsylvania, in 1914, and the next year he became sole owner of the Standard, renaming it Gibson's New Standard Theater. That same year he financed Irvin C. Miller's new musical comedy show, *Broadway Rastus.* With a score composed by W. C. HANDY and a cast of popular performers such as Leigh Whipper and Lottie Grady, the show was a hit and established Gibson as a producer. Later in 1925 he produced the musical comedy *Chocolate Box Revue*. Gibson preferred, however, to have others like the vaudevillians Sandy Burns and Sam Russell produce his theater shows. Early vaudeville acts at the Standard included J. ROSAMOND JOHNSON, AIDA OVERTON WALKER, Tom Brown, Salem Tutt Whitney, JOSEPHINE BAKER, and BESSIE SMITH. The popular Whitmore Sisters credited Gibson with giving them their first show business break. African Americans compared the New Standard to black theaters like the Lafayette Theater in Harlem, the Pekin Theater in Chicago, and the Howard Theater in Washington, D.C. In 1919 the Dunbar Theater, owned by the African American banker Edward Cooper Brown, opened in Philadelphia and gave Gibson's Standard Theater stiff competition. But in 1921 Gibson bought the Dunbar from Brown for $120,000. Gibson then renamed the house Gibson's Dunbar Theater and once again became the only black theater owner in Philadelphia. Gibson's Dunbar Theater opened on 26 September 1921 as a Theater Owners' and Bookers Association (TOBA) vaudeville circuit house. The TOBA was a theatrical syndicate similar to the Keith and Albee vaudeville circuits but established tours for African American entertainers. Gibson wanted to be part of TOBA because by purchasing stock in the association, he won the right to stage appearances by TOBA artists. In 1921 Gibson was appointed by the TOBA chief, Milton Starr, to be vice president and eastern region representative of TOBA. With acquisition of the Dunbar, however, came unexpected labor and financial problems. In 1921 the National Association of Colored Stage Employees complained that Gibson, unlike Brown, was reluctant to hire black people. Around the same time the musicians in the house orchestra demanded a 50-percent wage increase and walked out on Gibson. These labor difficulties were compounded by the fact that black Philadelphians shunned the Dunbar, which offered the Lafayette Players in black versions of white Broadway shows. They seemed to prefer the older Standard Theater with its silent moving pictures and exciting TOBA vaudeville shows.

Vaudeville performers resented spending all of their salary on travel from town to town on trains. This and other complaints about unfair TOBA routing practices led E. L. Lummings to form a new vaudeville circuit, the Managers and Performers Association (M&P) in March 1922. M&P competed with TOBA for the business of touring black vaudeville performers. On 24 July 1922 the entertainment newspaper *Billboard* announced that John T. Gibson was now vice president of the Managers and Performers vaudeville circuit. It is not clear whether Gibson had given up his job as vice president of TOBA. By December 1922, however, the two organizations would merge to become one black vaudeville circuit: TOBA. Among the black vaudevillians Gibson brought to the Standard Theater in the late 1920s were LOUIS ARMSTRONG, PAUL ROBESON, Salem Tutt Whitney and J. Homer Tutt, ROSE MCCLENDON, DUKE ELLINGTON, ETHEL WATERS, Bessie Smith, FATS WALLER, and the Lafayette Players.

In addition to managing theaters, Gibson was active in the civic life of Philadelphia. He served on the board of Douglass Hospital, the Chamber of Commerce, and the Board of Trade. He belonged to the Citizens Republican Club, which was a black Republican organization, and he was a member of the Masons and the black fraternity Kappa Alpha Psi. Gibson's prosperity and prestige enabled him to purchase an estate in the Philadelphia suburb of Bethayes, Montgomery County, Pennsylvania. He also bought Philadelphia real estate, including an apartment building, row houses, and tenement buildings. For reasons that are unclear, Gibson's closed its doors in 1928. Gibson lost money in the stock market crash of 1929, and this disaster, along with the arrival of talking motion pictures and radio, as well as vaudeville's decline, hurt Gibson's business. He was forced to lease Gibson's Dunbar Theater in November 1929 to a group of Jewish businessmen. They eventually bought it and changed its name to the Lincoln in 1931. In 1932 the comedian and black theater owner SHERMAN H. DUDLEY became part owner of the Standard Theater. As the nation entered the Great Depression, Gibson lost control of his other real estate, plus the Standard Theatre, and he died in Philadelphia. His stunning career as an African American theater owner and promoter of black musicals put Philadelphia on the map during the Harlem Renaissance.

FURTHER READING

"John T. Gibson," in *The Harlem Renaissance: A Historical Dictionary for the Era*, ed. Bruce Kellner (1987).

Richardson, Clement. *The National Cyclopedia of the Colored Race*, vol. 1 (1919).

Sampson, Henry T. *Blacks in Blackface: A Source Book on Early Black Musical Shows* (1980).

Obituary: *Philadelphia Tribune*, 17 June 1937.

ERIC LEDELL SMITH

Gibson, Joseph Deighton (Jack) (13 May 1920–30 Jan. 2000), disc jockey, record executive, publisher, better known by his radio names—Jockey Jack and Jack the Rapper—was born in Chicago. His parents, Lillian Schwiech Gibson, a teacher, and Joseph Jack Gibson, a doctor, expected that he would attend college and perhaps follow in his father's footsteps, but the young Jack decided against a career in medicine. He found himself instead attracted to the performing arts, and after attending Lincoln University in Jefferson City, Missouri, in the early 1940s, he returned to Chicago to seek work on the radio. In the mid-1940s, radio dramas were still quite popular, and he became an actor in the first black soap opera, *Here Comes Tomorrow*, on station WJJD, beginning in 1947. Because he had studied drama in college, he had a polished on-air style that impressed a number of advertisers and led to more radio jobs. Then a lucky turn of events took him to Atlanta and a career as an announcer. One of his friends in Chicago was JESSE BEE BLAYTON JR. Gibson found out that Jesse's father, a successful Atlanta banker, had bought a failing radio station in 1949. Jesse Blayton Sr. was not a radio expert, but he understood business, and he knew the station, WERD, could be profitable if it programmed to Atlanta's black audience. Both Jesse Blayton Jr. and Gibson were invited to join the new venture, the first radio station ever owned by a black person. When the new WERD went on the air in early October 1949, the first voice the listeners heard was Gibson's.

Not only was "Jockey Jack" (the "jockey" was a shortened version of "disc jockey") a capable entertainer but he was also knowledgeable about music. In an era when announcers could still choose the songs they played, Gibson became known for playing everything from soul to jazz to classical. Partly this was a result of his eclectic tastes, but as he later admitted, it was also because the station was so new that everyone simply emulated whatever they heard other stations doing. Once Gibson and Blayton Jr. had fine-tuned the music mix and created a more consistent sound, WERD became a hit-oriented black music station with a huge audience of fans. "Jockey Jack" Gibson became one of the most popular DJs in Atlanta. The early years of black radio were dominated by the "personality DJ," a larger-than-life figure who the audience admired and trusted. As Gibson recalled "[T]he Disc Jockey was the leader in town. We didn't have a MARTIN LUTHER KING, WHITNEY YOUNG, JESSE JACKSON, or BEN HOOKS, to talk to the community yet … so therefore the

Disc Jockey was the leader … and if something went wrong or somebody couldn't pay their rent, the Disc Jockey would hold [an event] on the air and get money together, and tell the world across the air waves, 'we paid Ms. Jones' rent.' Whatever [the] city, our powerful voices became the boss for the community" (Washington-George, 1).

By 1951 Gibson had moved to WLOU in Louisville. It was there that he turned his radio nickname "Jockey Jack" into an on-air persona, complete with his signature jockey silks attire and show-opening Kentucky Derby-style bugle call. Like most personality DJs, he didn't stay in any one city for too long—as he became more famous, there was always a bigger and better opportunity. His career took him to Miami, Florida, where he not only was on the air but also was program director, first at WMBM and then at WFEC. By 1954 Gibson had been convinced to return to WERD in Atlanta, this time as program director. It was at that time when he became more involved in community activism, using his influence and popularity to exert a positive influence when there was a disturbance in one of the black neighborhoods. Gibson also met and worked with the Reverend Martin Luther King Jr. and praised King's work on the air.

Gibson became an advocate for black announcers as well. He founded the National Association of Rhythm and Blues, Gospel and Jazz Disc Jockeys of America in the early 1950s. Originally made up of the thirteen most influential black DJs, it was soon re-named the National Association of Radio Announcers, and, in the 1960s, the National Association of Television and Radio Announcers. Ostensibly an organization to help black DJs network and advance, it become known for its annual convention, which was, by all accounts, an extended party (George, 112).

Gibson also redesigned his studio so that the announcer would work standing up rather than seated: he believed that standing up would help a DJ to project the voice better, and it became a common practice in radio.

After a radio career that also included stops in Cincinnati and Cleveland, Gibson joined Motown Records in 1963 (some sources say 1962), doing public relations work for the label. He later worked as a record promoter for Decca Records and became vice president of special projects for Stax Records, where he worked from 1969 to 1972. Gibson was known for being outspoken and for having strong views about the future of the black radio format. In 1976 he started a weekly industry publication using the name "Jack the Rapper." The newsletter, known as the *Mello Yello*, gave tips about hot new records to play and provided a forum to discuss what Gibson saw as black radio's problems. Among these, he thought, was a tendency of some stations to call their format "urban" rather than "black." Gibson felt that these stations were wrong to try to appeal to the white audience by pretending they were not really black stations. He knew from his own experience on the air that white listeners did like black music, but he wanted black stations to appeal first and foremost to the black audience. He also opposed black stations that hired white consultants or added records from white top 40 lists to the play list. Gibson believed black stations should be proud of their identity and not run away from it. He also used the pages of his publication to speak out about racism in society, criticize black record companies and certain black artists for hiring so many white personnel, and encourage black announcers to be advocates for the black community.

In 1977 Gibson began to host an annual convention called the Family Affair. It started as "a handful of black radio and record people getting together and sharing war stories about the industry," but grew to be one of the biggest gatherings in the industry, a place where celebrities performed and new bands tried to make contacts with announcers who might play their songs. Unfortunately, by the early 1990s the convention had attracted controversy, becoming known more for fights and vandalism than for networking.

In the mid-1990s Gibson, who married Else and had two children, Jamilla (Jill) and Joseph III, moved to Las Vegas, where even though he was in semi-retirement he continued to be involved with the Family Affair, which he now copromoted with his daughter Jill. He also did a Sunday oldies show on station KCEP. Winner of many awards, including honors from the Nevada Broadcasters Hall of Fame (1997) and the Rock and Roll Hall of Fame in Cleveland in 1998, Gibson died of cancer at the age of seventy-nine.

FURTHER READING

Barlow, William. *Voice Over: The Making of Black Radio* (1998).

George, Nelson. *The Death of Rhythm and Blues* (1988)

Mills, David. "Tuned In to Jockey Jack: Tribute to a Black Radio Pioneer and Personality," *Washington Post*, 23 June 1990.

Washington-George, Marsha. "The Reign of Black DJs in Georgia: One Hell of an Era," *Atlanta Enquirer*, 21 June 1997.

Williams, Gilbert A. *Legendary Pioneers of Black Radio* (1998).

Obituaries: *Pittsburgh Courier*, 2 Feb. 2000; *Atlanta Journal and Constitution*, 7 Feb. 2000.

DONNA HALPER

Gibson, Josh (21 Dec. 1911–20 Jan. 1947), baseball player, was born Joshua Gibson in Buena Vista, Georgia, the son of Mark Gibson, a sharecropper and steel mill worker and the son of former slaves, and Nancy Woodlock. Josh's two younger siblings, Jerry and Annie, were also children of this union. Around 1921 Josh's father left the uncertain work environment of southwestern Georgia and migrated north to Pittsburgh, Pennsylvania. After securing employment as a laborer with Carnegie-Illinois Steel, he arranged for his family to rejoin him. Josh had completed five years of elementary education in Georgia and enrolled at Allegheny Pre-Vocational School with the intention of becoming an electrician. After completing the ninth grade he left school for an apprenticeship in a Westinghouse Airbrake factory and began playing with a sandlot baseball team, the Pleasant Valley Red Sox. He then joined the semipro Pittsburgh Crawford Giants in 1928. In the spring of 1930 he married Helen Mason, but three months later she died in childbirth, while fraternal twins Helen and Josh Jr. survived.

Gibson began his professional career when he was recruited by the Homestead Grays' player-manager JUDY JOHNSON in July 1930, after their catcher suffered a split finger. With Gibson as their regular catcher, the Grays capped a successful season by defeating the New York Lincoln Giants in a playoff for the Eastern Championship. In the series Gibson batted .368 and hit three home runs, including a 460-foot drive at Yankee Stadium. A right-handed batter, he had extraordinary power and established himself as a superstar in his first full season, 1931. The press credited him with seventy-five home runs that year, although most were against semipro opposition, and the Grays again reigned as the best team in the east. In 1932 the Pittsburgh Crawfords' owner Gus Greenlee raided the Grays, signing Gibson and other key players. With the flamboyant SATCHEL PAIGE pitching and Gibson catching, the Crawfords had one of baseball's stellar batteries, and for the next five years they were easily the finest team in the Negro Leagues.

In 1933 Gibson met Hattie Jones, and the couple soon established residence together. The first East-West All-Star game was played that year, and Gibson made the first of four straight All-Star appearances. In those seasons he batted .464, .383, .440, and .457 and was the premier slugger in the Negro Leagues. In 1934 he was credited with sixty-nine home runs against all levels of opposition, and in the 1935 playoff against the New York Cubans for the Negro National League pennant, he hit .407 and smashed a dramatic game-winning, two-run home run in the ninth inning of the final game. The 1935 Crawfords are considered to be the greatest team in the history of the Negro Leagues. In a postseason exhibition game that year, Gibson hit a home run off the white St. Louis Cardinals ace pitcher Dizzy Dean. Over his career Gibson would compile a .412 lifetime batting average against major leaguers. In 1936 the Crawfords won another pennant, and, during the season, Gibson and a select black All-Star team were entered in the Denver Post Tournament and won the championship with ease.

In March 1937 Gibson was returned to the Homestead Grays in the biggest transaction in Negro Leagues history. Soon after signing with the Grays he went to the Dominican Republic, where he led the league with a .453 batting average and powered the dictator Rafael Trujillo's All-Stars to the championship. Upon his return to the Grays, Gibson teamed with BUCK LEONARD to form a power tandem that the press dubbed the "Thunder Twins." Gibson was called the "black Babe Ruth," and the duo formed the nucleus of the Grays' "Murderers' Row" that in 1937 won the first of nine straight Negro National League pennants for the Grays.

In 1938 the media urged the major leagues to sign Gibson and other black stars, but to no avail. Around this time, Gibson and Leonard were called into the office of the Washington Senators' owner Clark Griffith and asked about their interest in playing in the major leagues, but despite their expressed confidence that they could make the team, Griffith told them, "Nobody wants to be the first." In 1938 the champion Grays made the first of two postseason tours of Cuba, with Gibson batting .347 in the series. Afterward he remained to play in the Cuban Winter League and powered Santa Clara to the championship, batting .356 and leading the league in home runs. One blast traveled an incredible 704 feet and is the longest home run in Cuban history.

In 1939 the Grays won their third straight pennant, Gibson recording a .440 batting average and a slugging percentage (the ratio of bases reached on hits to at bats) of 1.190. A postseason four-team tournament was held, with the Grays losing in the final round despite Gibson's pair of home runs.

Gibson opted to spend the 1939–1940 winter in Puerto Rico as Santurce's playing manager, and he batted .380 while leading the league in home runs. He jumped to Venezuela for the 1940 season, but, when the league folded, he signed with Veracruz in the Mexican League, where he batted .467. Gibson returned to Veracruz for the entire 1941 season and led the league with 33 home runs and batted .374, as Veracruz repeated as champions. He then returned to Santurce in the Puerto Rican Winter League, where he led the league with a .480 batting average, a .959 slugging percentage, and 13 home runs, to win the league's Most Valuable Player trophy. One of his home runs traveled more than 600 feet and was the longest in the history of Puerto Rican baseball.

When the Grays' owner CUM POSEY filed a ten-thousand-dollar lawsuit against Gibson for breach of contract and sought to take his house as compensation for alleged damages, a settlement was reached, and Gibson returned to the Grays for the 1942 season. With Gibson back in the fold, the Grays won another pennant, though the Kansas City Monarchs swept them in the first Negro World Series between the Negro National League and the Negro American League. But as the result of alcoholic excesses and, possibly, drug abuse, Gibson's physical and psychological condition deteriorated during the season. This decline was apparent to many by the end of the year. In January 1943 he was committed to a hospital after suffering a nervous breakdown. He lapsed into a coma and was diagnosed with a brain tumor. Upon recovery, he decided not to have the tumor removed for fear that he might have permanent brain damage, and he did not inform the Grays of his condition. Gibson developed a relationship with Grace Fournier, a rumored drug addict whose husband was stationed overseas in the army, and her influence contributed to his continued debilitation. As his substance abuse worsened, Gibson's behavior became more erratic, and he was frequently hospitalized or committed to sanatoriums throughout the remainder of his life.

World War II was at its peak, but Gibson was ineligible for the draft because of bad knees from many years of catching, both summer and winter. Despite the problems in his personal life, he still maintained his high standard of performance, and the Grays won back-to-back Negro World Series from the Birmingham Black Barons in 1943 and 1944. In the 1943 World Series, Gibson hit a grand-slam home run, and, in the 1944 series, he batted .500 and also hammered a home run. By 1945 Gibson had lost some of his power, but he still batted .398

for the season, as the Grays won their ninth straight pennant but were swept by the upstart Cleveland Buckeyes in the Negro World Series. Gibson began the winter season in Puerto Rico, but he did not play well and was involved in another dark episode when he ran naked through a San Juan plaza and had to be physically subdued, after which arrangements were made for his return to Pittsburgh for a long rest.

The 1946 season was Gibson's last. A distinct difference was noticeable, both in his health and his playing skills. His defensive skills had eroded, and he could not even squat down behind the plate in a catcher's position. Observers were saddened to see what had happened to the once seemingly indestructible player. He suffered excruciating headaches and dizziness and was plagued by occasional disorientation, incoherence, and conversations with imaginary people. Two All-Star games were played that season, and, despite his debilitation, Gibson was the starting catcher in both games. The consistency of his power had diminished, but the potential was still present, and though he was only a shadow of his former self, Gibson retained his smooth swing and bashed several long home runs, including a 550-foot shot in St. Louis against the Cleveland Buckeyes.

By the end of 1946 Gibson was unable to care for himself and, after a weekend of intense headaches, he suffered a stroke and died at his mother's home in Pittsburgh only three months before JACKIE ROBINSON broke the major league color line. In 1972 Josh Gibson became the second player from the Negro Leagues, after Satchel Paige (1971), to be inducted into the National Baseball Hall of Fame at Cooperstown, New York.

FURTHER READING

Brashler, William. *Josh Gibson: A Life in the Negro Leagues* (1978).

Peterson, Robert. *Only the Ball Was White* (1970).

Ribowsky, Mark. *The Power and the Darkness: The Life of Josh Gibson in the Shadows of the Game* (1996).

Obituary: *Pittsburgh Courier*, 25 Jan. 1947.

JAMES A. RILEY

Gibson, Truman Kella, Jr. (22 Jan. 1912–23 Dec. 2005), lawyer, presidential adviser, and boxing promoter, was born in Atlanta, Georgia, the eldest of the three children of the insurance executive Truman K. Gibson Sr. and Alberta Dickerson Gibson, a school teacher. The family first moved to Columbus, Ohio, to escape the menacing racial environment of the South, and then in 1929 they moved to Chicago so that Gibson Sr. could pursue his business interests. There Truman K. Gibson Jr. enrolled at the University of Chicago. While an undergraduate he worked as a researcher for Harold Gosnell, helping Gosnell gather information for his book *Negro Politicians: The Rise of Negro Politics in Chicago* (1935).

After graduating from the University of Chicago Law School in 1935 Gibson was recruited to join the legal team representing the real estate broker CARL HANSBERRY, who was challenging a restrictive racial real estate covenant that prohibited African Americans from living in the Washington Park subdivision in Chicago. Gibson spent months examining land deeds to develop the factual case for the lawsuit. The U.S. Supreme Court struck down the covenant on 12 November 1940. Hansberry's daughter, LORRAINE HANSBERRY, used the emotional upheaval of her family's being evicted from a Washington Park apartment as inspiration for her 1959 Pulitzer Prize–winning play *A Raisin in the Sun*.

Clearly a young man who had impressed Chicago's African American elite, Gibson was named in 1940 to be executive director of the American Negro Exposition—in effect a black world's fair in Chicago, organized to commemorate the seventy-fifth anniversary of Emancipation. Though largely forgotten today, the exposition opened with great fanfare on the Fourth of July, beginning a two-month celebration of African American contributions to U.S. history and a tribute to African American accomplishment in the arts and entertainment. PAUL ROBESON, DUKE ELLINGTON, LIONEL HAMPTON, COUNT BASIE, FATS WALLER, LANGSTON HUGHES, and HORACE CAYTON were just a few of the luminaries attracted to participate in the exposition.

With war raging in Europe, Gibson found himself drawn into the nation's military preparations. President Franklin D. Roosevelt had appointed blacks to New Deal agencies as advocates for African Americans, creating what would be remembered as the "black cabinet," and he had chosen WILLIAM HASTIE to be civilian aide to the secretary of war to represent the interests of Negro soldiers. Gibson became Hastie's assistant on 9 December 1940; after Hastie resigned on 6 January 1943, Gibson was promoted to civilian aide.

The War Department had imposed strict segregation on the army, and Gibson spent years seeking to reverse this policy. Working through the Advisory Committee on Negro Troop Policies, Gibson persuaded the army to insist that officers assume responsibility for race relations in units that they commanded, and he persuaded the department's civilian brass to ask—usually unsuccessfully—for the Justice Department to prosecute assaults and murders of black soldiers stationed at training bases in the South. Gibson never missed an opportunity to promote black troops. His lobbying of radio producers resulted in "America's Negro Soldiers," a nationwide radio broadcast on 12 August 1941. He consulted with the filmmaker Frank Capra on the filming of *The Negro Soldier*, a 1944 movie short credited with advancing the cause of desegregation. Gibson persuaded his friend and world heavyweight boxing champion JOE LOUIS to organize a troupe of boxing champions to put on exhibition matches at bases in the United States and abroad. A top priority for Gibson was getting black soldiers into the war. Though the army had created two all-black infantry divisions, it considered African American troops unreliable, and as late as 1944 neither division had been committed to combat. White northern politicians joined Negro leaders and newspapers in complaining about the army's relegating black soldiers to digging ditches, hauling supplies, and doing other support work for white combat soldiers. Gibson pressed the case with the Advisory Committee, and finally the decision was made to send the Ninety-second Infantry Division to Italy.

The black soldiers were pitted against the heavily fortified German Gothic Line in mountainous northern Italy in early February 1945. Their attack failed. The generals saw the failure as evidence backing their preconceived notions and damned the division's infantrymen for "melting away" from battle. Traveling to Italy, Gibson got the commanders to back off from their threat to pull the black soldiers out of combat. He interviewed hundreds of soldiers from the Ninety-second and defended their valor. He argued that the army's racial attitudes, segregated facilities, discriminatory promotion policies, and assignment of incompetent white officers to the division had wounded its fighting spirit. Newspaper articles tended to ignore Gibson's defense of the troops and his attack on segregation while reporting that he had acknowledged the army's account that some black GIs engaged in disorderly retreats. As a result Gibson was unfairly pilloried in black newspapers. Gibson said that his critics "want to say that segregation is wrong and yet that the end product, segregated divisions, is all right." His insistence that black soldiers be kept in the fight ensured that the men of the Ninety-second participated in the assault in April that finally broke the Gothic Line. Black troops thrown into battle elsewhere also proved to be courageous fighters.

Gibson resigned as civilian aide on 1 December 1945 after urging the department to develop a postwar policy based on the proven performance of black troops. The next year President Harry S. Truman appointed him as the only black member of the Advisory Commission on Universal Training, and Gibson seized it as a platform to campaign for integration. The commission's 1947 report denounced segregation as unfair and as an impediment to a sound and efficient military. On 26 July 1948 Truman signed Executive Order 9981 mandating integration of the armed forces. Truman also awarded Gibson the Presidential Medal of Merit, the highest honor accorded a civilian for service to the military, making him the first African American to receive the honor.

After the war Gibson helped Joe Louis deal with his considerable obligations on back taxes. One business venture with Louis in 1949 resulted in Gibson's becoming secretary and later president of the International Boxing Club. Gibson saw television as the financial salvation of boxing, and he labored to make the Wednesday and Friday night fights the winners of the TV ratings in the 1950s. So successful was the IBC that it came to dominate the sport, but on 12 January 1959 the U.S. Supreme Court declared it to be an illegal monopoly. Allegations of mob influence dogged boxing. Gibson acknowledged that the sport attracted shady characters but told a U.S. Senate hearing on 5–6 December 1960 that fixing a fight would have killed the TV cash cow. Still, in 1961 he was put on probation after being convicted, with several mob figures, of trying to take over the management of a fighter. Gibson maintained that prosecutors railroaded him.

His boxing career at an end, Gibson returned to private law practice in Chicago and attempted several business ventures; a couple of them were ill-advised and landed him in legal difficulties. In 2005, a few months before his death at age ninety-three, Gibson published his memoir *Knocking Down Barriers: My Fight for Black America*. The heart of the book was his battle against segregation in the military. Today no segment of American society has matched the armed forces in achieving the goals of integration. This is perhaps Gibson's most enduring legacy.

FURTHER READING

The papers of Truman K. Gibson are housed in the Manuscript Division of the Library of Congress, Washington, D.C.

Gibson, Truman K., Jr., with Steve Huntley. *Knocking Down Barriers: My Fight for Black America* (2005).

Lee, Ulysses Grant. *The Employment of Negro Troops* (1966).

MacGregor, Morris J., Jr. *Integration of the Armed Forces, 1940–1965* (1981).

STEVE HUNTLEY

Giddens, Rhiannon (21 Feb. 1977–), musician, was born in Greensboro, North Carolina, to an African American mother, Deborah A. Jamieson, and a white father, David Monroe Giddens, both of whom had some Native American heritage as well. Giddens became a central figure in the early-twenty-first-century movement to reclaim the banjo's roots in southern black communities, where it was once a musical mainstay, and its greater historical lineage in Africa.

As a youngster, Giddens was exposed to a variety of musical influences. Her parents listened to bluegrass, classic blues, and jazz, and her father sometimes sang folk music around town. Nonetheless, she came late to the realization that music would be her consuming passion.

Through much of her education at one of North Carolina's few surviving predominantly black high schools, and the prestigious North Carolina School of Science and Mathematics, Giddens focused on becoming a computer animator. The turning point was her 1994 attendance of the choral music program at Governor's School, an intensive summer program where North Carolina's most talented high-school students study a subject in which they excel.

After graduating from high school, Giddens enrolled in the Oberlin Conservatory of Music from 1995 to 2000; it was there she developed her soprano singing voice and pursued opera. During her stay in Ohio, Giddens made her professional debut with the Cleveland Opera and frequently sang the lead in *Madama Butterfly*. She appeared in five operas, including *Cosi fan Tutte* and *Romeo and Juliette*. After graduating in 2000, Giddens returned to Greensboro, where she eventually continued her classical education at the Music School of the University of North Carolina at Greensboro from 2001 to 2002. She continued to sing opera, appearing in several productions of the music school and participating as one of the artists in the Greensboro Opera's outreach program.

Even as Giddens honed her vocal abilities, she ventured into other genres. After launching a professional career in opera, she began to explore calling, the rhythmic and often humorous vocal style that instructs contra dancers (somewhat similar to square dancing) how to move. In the tradition of musicians with diverse interests, during the early 2000s she worked, often at the same time, with various performing groups, including Eleganza, a female duo devoted to classical music; Gaelwynd, a Celtic traditional band; and Sankofa Strings, a fiddle and banjo trio tinged with global influences. In 2004, she released a self-distributed solo album, *Many Voices*, that reflected the diversity of her musical interests, incorporating influences from blues, country, and Gaelic music.

It was not until 2000 that Giddens purchased her first fiddle with proceeds from months of restaurant waitressing, and then her first banjo a year later. She played on her own for some time, but eventually connected with a group of like-minded enthusiasts through an online discussion group called Black Banjo Then and Now, founded in 2004 by the Miami banjoist Tony Thomas. The group immediately began planning a gathering where they could play, swap stories and techniques, and celebrate the black banjo heritage.

That meeting, the Black Banjo Then and Now Gathering at Appalachian State University in 2005, turned out to be a life-changing experience for Giddens. As she commented in a newspaper interview, "I dreamt of being in an all-black string band, but I didn't feel like part of a community" before the gathering. "I felt like I was forcing my way into this all-white club" (Humes, 2005). The gathering allowed her to connect directly with a community of musicians and, in particular, with the Arizona banjoist Dom Flemons and the North Carolina fiddler Justin Robinson, who were equally interested in the banjo's plucky sound, its diminished visibility in black music, and its resurgence as a fixture in bluegrass and old-time music.

Giddens, Robinson, and Flemons discovered a common interest, and they also connected with the fiddler Joe Thompson, whose string band performed for black and white audiences throughout North Carolina at a time when many public institutions were still divided by segregation. Thompson, known for the Piedmont string style in which the banjo enjoyed equal billing with the often more "vocal" violin, adopted the trio.

Under Thompson's tutelage, Giddens and her colleagues formed the Carolina Chocolate Drops, an exclusively African American string band in which Giddens sang and played both the banjo and the fiddle. The group's name harked back to the Tennessee Chocolate Drops, one of the few African American acoustic string bands to achieve some degree of commercial success in the early twentieth century. Decades after the Tennessee Chocolate Drops recorded, the Carolina Chocolate Drops released its first album, *Dona Got a Ramblin Mind*, in 2006.

Giddens moved to Durham, North Carolina, in 2005, where she continued to research the musical connections between Africa and America. She also continued to teach, giving private lessons in banjo and voice, performing with the Carolina Chocolate Drops at various workshops and K–12 outreach events, and serving as an instructor at the Augusta Heritage Center in West Virginia. In July 2006 she traveled on a delegation to the West African nation of the Gambia. During a two-week stay there, she learned at the feet of master Gambian musicians, who played a stringed instrument called the akonting, possibly a close relative of the banjo. As a North Carolina native, Giddens sought to learn from and revitalize a black banjo tradition that stretched from the trans-Atlantic slave trade of the 1700s through the Piedmont frolic and string bands of the twentieth century.

Once again a resident of Greensboro, Giddens was married in September 2007 to Michael V. Laffan, from Limerick, Ireland. The couple had a daughter, Aoife, in 2009. Giddens's continuing interest in Celtic music was reflected by her appearance, along with her pianist husband, on *Indian Summer*, a 2007 album by the Scottish based American singer, Talitha MacKenzie. The Chocolate Drops toured extensively in North America and Europe, appeared on the soundtrack of the film *The Great Debaters* (2007), starring DENZEL WASHINGTON as MELVIN B. TOLSON, the charismatic coach of the famed Wiley College debate team in the 1930s, and in 2008 became the first black string band to play Nashville's Grand Ole Opry. The band then released three more albums: *Heritage* (2008); *The Carolina Chocolate Drops & Joe Thompson* (2009); and *Genuine Negro Jig* (2010). The latter album, on Nonesuch Records, the leading Roots label in America, reached Number One on Billboard's Bluegrass charts and got as high as 150 on the regular Billboard CD charts, a rare achievement for a bluegrass record. *Genuine Negro Jig* also appeared on many end of year lists as best album of 2010. The Drops' cover of R&B singer Blu Cantrell's "Hit 'Em Up Style," was a joyous slab of hillbilly hip hop. In 2011 *Genuine Negro Jig* won the Grammy award for Best Traditional Folk Album. That same year Giddens and other members of the Carolina Chocolate Drops worked with Chicago's Old Town School of Folk Music to curate *Keep a Song in Your Soul: The Black Roots of Vaudeville*.

FURTHER READING

Conway, Cecelia. *African Banjo Echoes in Appalachia: A Study of Folk Traditions* (1995).

Hume, Pete. "Musical Roots," *Richmond Times-Dispatch*, 9 May 2005.

Jefferson, Thomas. *Notes on the State of Virginia*, ed. William Paden (1954).

CYNTHIA GREENLEE-DONNELL

Giddings, Paula J. (16 Nov. 1947–), journalist, author, editor, and professor, grew up in Yonkers, New York. Her parents were Curtis G. Giddings and Virginia Stokes Giddings, and both were college educated. Her father was a teacher and guidance counselor, and her mother was employed as a guidance counselor as well. The family's neighborhood was integrated, and Giddings was the first African American to attend her private elementary school, where she was the victim of racial attacks. Even now, Giddings regrets that she allowed herself to be silenced by these attacks. This, no doubt, is what compelled her to develop her voice as a writer. Giddings graduated from Howard University with a BA in English in 1969, and she worked as an editor for several years. Her first job was as an editorial

Paula J. Giddings, scholar, writer, educator, and committed advocate on behalf of African American women. (Austin/Thompson Collection.)

assistant at Random House from 1969 to 1970, and then she became a copy editor at Random House from 1970 to 1972. She went on to work as an associate book editor at Howard University Press from 1972 to 1975, was Paris Bureau chief of *Encore American and Worldwide News*, 1975 to 1977, and was its associate editor from 1977 to 1979.

Giddings came of age in the 1960s, when she was influenced by the revolutionary movements and attitudes that helped make that decade so turbulent. She was especially inspired by the Freedom Riders, young adults who traveled from the North to assist African Americans throughout the South in their efforts to desegregate bus stations and interstate transportation. Not surprisingly, the Freedom Riders met much opposition and violence, but they refused to be defeated. Giddings was moved by their courage in the face of the racism and hatred that they encountered. The Freedom Rides and other events during the struggle for civil rights during the 1960s, as well as Giddings's experiences with discrimination while growing up in an integrated neighborhood, had an impact on her research and writing interests. She resolved to give voice to those who had been silenced throughout history, especially black women.

In her first work, *Black Women: When and Where I Enter: The Impact of Black Women on Race and Sex in America* (1984), Giddings uses primary sources such as letters, diaries, and speeches to explore how black women have impacted the racial and women's movements in the United States, from nineteenth-century antilynching campaigns to the civil rights movement of the 1960s. The work garnered much respect and began to be used in college classrooms throughout the country and was even translated into Dutch and Japanese. Giddings was named the United Negro College Fund Distinguished Scholar in 1986, and from 1986 to 1987 she taught at Spelman College.

In her second work, *In Search of Sisterhood: Delta Sigma Theta and the Challenge of the Black Sorority Movement* (1988), Giddings examines the birth of Delta Sigma Theta at Howard University and its development into the largest black women's sorority in the United States. The book contains interviews with numerous sorority members, as well as rare photographs of many of its noteworthy sisters. Giddings points out that the organization confronts political, racial, and class-related concerns and that its members have been outspoken in their pursuit of change, yet, at the same time, the sorority also encourages the successful development of the individual. The sorority's membership

includes a variety of prominent women, including Texas Congresswoman BARBARA JORDAN and performers LENA HORNE and ROBERTA FLACK; often, its members remained active long after they completed college.

Giddings's career in academia flourished from the 1990s into the twenty-first century. She received an Honorary Doctor of Humane Letters degree from Bennett College in 1990. And from 1989 to 1991 she was the New Jersey Laurie Chair in Women's Studies at Douglass College/Rutgers University. She returned to Spelman College to teach from 1991 to 1992. From 1992 to 1993 she was a visiting professor at Princeton University. She was a Fellow of the John Simon Guggenheim Foundation in 1993 and a Fellow of the National Humanities Center from 1993 to 1995. She received an honorary doctorate from Wesleyan University in 1995. She was Phi Beta Kappa Visiting Scholar from 1995 to 1996 and research professor of Women and African American Studies at Duke University from 1996 to 2001. Giddings coedited with CORNEL WEST the work *Regarding Malcolm X: A Reader* (1998), and she edited *Burning All Illusions: Writings from the Nation on Race 1866–2002* (2002), which is a compilation of articles covering a variety of perspectives on race and civil rights previously published by the *Nation*, founded in 1865 by abolitionists. The collection contained two sections: "Beholders" included first-person accounts, and "Reporters" included third-person accounts. The book contained the work of well-known authors such as CLAUDE MCKAY, LANGSTON HUGHES, RALPH ELLISON, and JAMES BALDWIN. The book also covered an expansive time period: from Reconstruction to the events surrounding the Supreme Court's 1954 *Brown v. Board of Education* decision (which ended racial segregation in schools) to contemporary racial concerns.

In 2001 Giddings joined the faculty at Smith College as professor of Afro-American Studies and was a founding member and senior editor of the peer-reviewed journal *Meridians: Feminism, Race, Transnationalism*. In 2005 Giddings published *Ida: A Sword Among Lions: Ida B. Wells and the Campaign Against Lynching*, and her work was also published in many newspapers, including the *Washington Post*, the *New York Times*, the *Philadelphia Inquirer*, the *Nation*, *Jeune Afrique* (a news magazine based in Paris), and prominent journals such as *Meridians: Feminism, Race, Transnationalism* and *Sage: A Scholarly Journal on Black Women*.

She received a Ford Foundation Grant in 1982 and awards from the National Coalition of 100

Black Women, 1985, the Howard University Alumni Club, 1985, the New York Urban League, 1986, and the Westchester Black Women's Political Caucus, 1986.

FURTHER READING

Llosa-Sandor, Tamara. "Paula Giddings, Afro-American Studies: Paula Giddings Makes Career Fighting for Equality," *Smith College Sophian*, 30 Sept. 2004.

Schiller, Naomi. "A Short History of Black Feminist Scholars," *Journal of Blacks in Higher Education* (2000).

DIANE TODD BUCCI

Gilbert, John Wesley (9 Jan. 1865–18 Nov. 1923), professor of ancient Greek, philologist, ordained Methodist minister in the Colored Methodist Episcopal (CME) Church, and missionary to the Congo, was born in Hephzibah, Georgia, not far from Augusta, to Gabriel and Sarah Gilbert. His parents were field hands, and scholars are not certain whether John was born free or enslaved. Some sources give his birth date as 6 July 1864. As a child he was eager to learn, but he had to mix long hours of farm work with brief periods of school. At last overwhelmed by poverty he was forced to withdraw from the Baptist Seminary in Augusta. After a three-year hiatus from schooling he resumed his work when Dr. George Williams Walker, a Methodist pastor who had come to Augusta to teach in 1884, and Warren A. Candler, pastor of Augusta's St. John Church, offered him assistance. With the help of these men Gilbert became the first student to enroll at the Paine Institute, named for Bishop Robert Paine and dedicated to the religious training and general education of African American students. The Institute, chartered as Paine College in 1903, had recently opened in a suite of rented rooms located on Broad Street in Augusta. It began under the aegis of the General Conference of the Methodist Church and took shape under the eye of an appointed task force of Bishop George F. Pierce, Pastor Chandler, and Bishop Lucius Holsey of the Colored Methodist Episcopal Church.

A gifted and motivated student with an uncommon facility in languages Gilbert made rapid progress. In 1884 he matriculated at Brown University and earned his BA four years later in ancient Greek. In 1888 he returned to Augusta to teach at Paine. He was the first black faculty member and his controversial appointment led to the resignation of Professor C. N. Carson Jr., who left in protest in 1888. From 1890 to 1891, with a scholarship from Brown University, Gilbert attended the American School of Classical Studies in Athens, Greece, which Brown University helped to found in 1881 to further the study of ancient Greek life and culture. He was the first African American to perform advanced work in classical archaeology. He worked on excavations at Eretria on the island of Euboea and designed a map of the site with John Pickard, a student from Dartmouth College. The map was published in the *American Journal of Archaeology* (7 Dec. 1891). This work was done in conjunction with a special course of study on Homer, the Homeric Question, Plato, and Demosthenes, as well as a thesis "The Demes of Attica," with which he earned his MA degree from Brown University in 1891. Sadly, Gilbert's thesis has disappeared from Brown University's archives and almost all of his personal papers have been lost, except for some portions of his diaries, which are housed in the archives at Paine College.

Gilbert returned to his scholarly work at Paine. In 1897 he joined the American Philological Association and was affiliated with the group until 1907. In the spring of 1889 he married Osceola K. Pleasant and began a family. He involved himself in various social and political issues of the day. On 23 September 1895 he wrote a letter congratulating BOOKER T. WASHINGTON on his Cotton Exposition speech. But he was not in full agreement with Washington's focus on manual training, and at the end of 1897 he suggested in an address delivered in Atlanta that African American education should not be limited to industrial programs. In 1902 he published an essay titled "How Can the Negroes Be Induced to Rally More to Negro Enterprises and to their Professional Men?" in D. W. Culp's *Twentieth Century Negro Literature*. In 1904 the text of a speech he presented on New Year's Day at a celebration of the Emancipation Proclamation at the Tabernacle Baptist Church in Augusta was published later that year as a twenty-four-page pamphlet. Titled *The Problems of the Races*, Gilbert's speech was a reply to lectures delivered by John Temple Graves in New York and Chicago concerning the supposed innate inferiority and criminality of people of African descent and the natural inequality between the white and black races. He corrected the many prejudices and misconceptions Graves held concerning the history and achievements of black people in the United States.

In 1911 Walter Russell Lambuth, a white bishop in the Methodist Episcopal Church South and secretary of the Board of Missions, planned a trip to

Africa. Lambuth and Gilbert had known each other for two decades, and when they found out that the man chosen to accompany Lambuth had died in North Carolina, Gilbert agreed to go in his place. On 14 September 1911 Gilbert sailed from New York to meet Lambuth in London. They arrived in Dakar on 24 October 1911 and began a long, arduous trek by boat and on foot through the Congo region into the country of the Atetela tribes. That trip took them to places such as Lusambo, Dema, Pangu, Luebo, Kinshasa, Ba Wakina, Ndumba, and Malamala. Gilbert's talents at languages were immediately employed. On 1 February 1912 the pair officially established a mission at the village of Ewangu in central Africa with the permission of the village's chief, Wembo-Nyama. While in Luebo the the two travelers had gained African names. Gilbert was known as Mutombo Kutchi and Lambuth as Kabengele. The mission began to grow, and in March 1912, Lambuth and Gilbert returned to the United States to find more recruits. It is not known why Gilbert failed to come back in 1913 with a second wave of missionaries. Some suspect without firm evidence that the other white missionaries were not comfortable with Gilbert. Others conjecture that a man of Gilbert's achievements was perceived as a stimulus to revolt among the Congolese and a challenge to the Belgian Government. For Gilbert and Lambuth, however, the mission was a success and showed how they themselves and other like-minded men within the Methodist church could transcend race prejudice. Their spirit of cooperation was later celebrated by the erection of the Gilbert-Lambuth Memorial Chapel on Paine's campus in 1968. Inside the vestibule is an oil painting by Ann Barnes of the two men in a jungle setting.

In Chicago in 1918 the General Conference of the Colored Methodist Episcopal Church established a Sunday School Department and selected Gilbert to be its first Sunday school editor. But his health broke down and he spent the last four years of his life as an invalid, eventually dying from a curious illness thought to have been contracted in Africa. JOHN HOPE, a contemporary of Gilbert's and an African American educational leader, suggested that Gilbert was infected by a tse-tse fly. Gilbert's body was buried in Cedar Grove Cemetery in Augusta, Georgia.

FURTHER READING

Calhoun, E. Clayton. *Of Men Who Ventured Much and Far: The Congo Quest of Dr. Gilbert and Bishop Lambuth* (1961).
Colclough, J. C. *The Spirit of John Wesley Gilbert* (1925).
Kasongo, M. O. "A Spirit of Cooperation in Mission: Professor John Wesley Gilbert and Bishop Walter Russell Lambuth," *Methodist History* 36 (1998).
Ronnick, Michele Valerie. "John Wesley Gilbert," *Classical Outlook* 78 (2001).

MICHELE VALERIE RONNICK

Gilbert, Mercedes (1889–1 Mar. 1952), actress and writer, was born in Jacksonville, Florida, the daughter of Daniel Marshall Gilbert, the owner of a furniture business, and Edna Earl Knott, the owner of a dressmaking business. In an unfinished autobiographical manuscript Gilbert wrote that because of her parents' jobs, she was cared for and educated by a nurse. She enrolled in the Boylan Home, a seminary for girls in Jacksonville, when she was in the fourth grade. After her family moved to Tampa, Florida, Gilbert attended a Catholic school and the Orange Park Normal and Industrial School. She went to Edward Waters College in Jacksonville and after graduation taught school in southern Florida before deciding that she wanted a different profession. She then entered the Brewster Hospital Nurses Training School and graduated three years later, staying on the staff for two more years as the assistant superintendent.

After moving to New York City in 1916, first possibly having spent some time in Chicago, Gilbert searched for a nursing job. She found, however, that her hospital in Florida did not have the appropriate qualifications to make it a Grade One training school, so she would have had to spend three more years in postgraduate training at Lincoln Hospital. Since she had been writing poems and plays with some success for most of her life, in the early 1920s Gilbert began to take seriously the advice of friends who told her to find a songwriter to collaborate with her in setting some of her poetry to music. Though she may have worked as a private nurse for some periods of time in New York City, in 1922 Gilbert began to achieve status as a songwriter. She notes in her autobiographical manuscript, "Strange to say, the first was a song about the 'sport of kings,' horse racing, titled 'The Also Ran Blues.' This song became quite a hit and was recorded by most of the record companies" (Roses and Randolph, 123). Gilbert managed an eight-piece jazz band and a blues singer who recorded the popular "The Decatur Street Blues" and "Got the World in a Jug," both of which she wrote in the early 1920s. In 1922 she married Arthur J. Stevenson.

Her marriage did not interfere with her blossoming career in the arts. Though she had been successfully composing songs and writing for the Associated Negro Press, she got her first significant part as an actress in *The Lace Petticoat*, a Broadway musical comedy in which all the members of the cast were white, "except the singers and myself" (Roses and Randolph, 123). She subsequently appeared in many Broadway shows, including *Lost*; *Bomboola*; *Play Genius*; *Play*; *Malinda*; *How Come Lawd?*; *The Searching Wind*; and *Carib Song*. Of special note is her performance as Zipporah, the wife of Moses, throughout the five-year run of *Green Pastures*, which played in New York City and on tour during the early 1930s. Her obituary in the *New York Times* notes that her portrayal of Zipporah and her performance as Cora Lewis in *Mulatto* were her most notable. The role of Cora Lewis, the wife of Colonel Norwood in LANGSTON HUGHES's *Mulatto*, is especially significant not only because it contains excellent monologues that would highlight any actress's skills but also because she unexpectedly had to take over the role previously played by Rose McClendon, being handed the script on a Saturday evening and set to appear onstage on Tuesday. A reviewer in the *New York World Telegram* notes on 8 May 1936 that "Mercedes Gilbert pinch-hits successfully.... Hers is a perilous part and she makes hay with it" (quoted in Roses and Randolph, 122). She played the role on Broadway for a year, the rest of the 1935–1936 season, and on tour for seven months. Another contemporary reviewer notes, "Miss Gilbert, as Cora Lewis ... is performing so remarkably and being so well received by different audiences that both author Langston Hughes and producer Martin Jones predict a long run at the Ambassador Theatre ... where 'Mulatto' has now been running more than eleven months" (Stewart, 7).

Gilbert also appeared on radio, television, and in such silent pictures as *The Call of His People*, *Secret Sorrow*, and *Body and Soul*. In *Body and Soul*, which was directed by one of the most famous black filmmakers of the 1920s, OSCAR MICHEAUX, Gilbert worked with the popular black actor PAUL ROBESON. Also of note are her performances in the all-black productions of *Lysistrata* and *Tobacco Road*. In the 1940s she began to tour the United States and Canada in a one-woman show consisting of recitals of her work. During this time she also toured colleges performing and lecturing on black history. A collection of her work, *Selected Gems of Poetry, Comedy, and Drama* (1931), contains comments on the dust jacket stating that Gilbert's monologues were performed on national radio. The publishers note that "the work is mainly in Southern dialect, because the direct appeal of this soft speech is intriguing and amusing to readers both North and South" (Roses and Randolph, p. 123). She was also a member of the Olympic Committee for the 11th Olympiad (1936). Her only novel, *Aunt Sara's Wooden God*, was published in 1938 with a foreword by Langston Hughes. The novel, like much of Gilbert's other work, has fallen into undeserved obscurity. She also wrote three plays, *Environment*, *In Greener Pastures*, and *Ma Johnson's Harlem Rooming House*; this latter was first produced by the Harlem YMCA in 1938.

The last record of Mercedes Gilbert in the Schomburg Collection is an invitation to her and her husband's twenty-fifth wedding anniversary on 19 July 1947. There is no information available that indicates children or further public activity after 1947. Her obituary in the *New York Times* states that she was living in Jamaica, New York, when she died in the Queens General Hospital.

FURTHER READING

An autobiographical manuscript and other information available through the Schomburg Center for Research in Black Culture of the New York Public Library and through Gilbert's publisher, Christopher House.

Gloster, Hugh Morris. *Negro Voices in American Fiction* (1948).

Roses, Lorraine E., and Ruth E. Randolph. *Harlem Renaissance and Beyond: Literary Biographies of 100 Black Women Writers, 1900–1945* (1990).

Obituary: *New York Times*, 6 Mar. 1952.

This entry is taken from the *American National Biography* and is published here with the permission of the American Council of Learned Societies.

SHARON L. BARNES

Gilbert, Robert Alexander (1869–7 Jan. 1942), photographer and naturalist, was born in Natural Bridge, Virginia. His parents' names and occupations are unknown. In 1881, after attending primary schools in Lexington, Virginia, Gilbert was taken by his family to Lynchburg, Virginia, to complete his education. In 1886 he followed his brother William north to Boston, where he found employment as a porter on the *Portland Boston* steamship line. He would work various odd jobs until 1896, when psychologist James Chadbourne hired him to help with laboratory rats. Gilbert, as he was generally known in the Boston white community, also took a temporary job setting up a bird museum in Cambridge, Massachusetts, with the renowned nineteenth-century ornithologist William Brewster. Brewster subsequently hired Gilbert as a full-time manservant, field assistant, factotum, and, as some of the early private journal records state, "friend," to the well-respected Brewster.

Under Brewster's tutelage Gilbert learned how to develop and print photographs and then took up the art himself. His images, mixed in with photographs taken by his employer, were discovered in 1974 in the attic of an old estate in Lincoln, Massachusetts. Gilbert's photographic work favored landscapes, especially images of water and woodland roads. His work is representative of the contemporary popular photographic style known as pictorialism—misty, soft-focused, romantic images that evoked a certain sense of mystery.

Gilbert was something of an entrepreneur and a self-made man. He was a skilled pianist and is listed in two different federal census records as "piano teacher." But at some point in the 1920s he developed a shoe polish formula, which, according to anecdotal accounts, he took to Stockholm, where he made a fortune in the business. Piecing together unofficial evidence, it appears that by the late twenties he lost his money and fled to Paris, where, in 1926 or 1927, he seems to have linked up with a group of American expatriates.

By 1931 he was back in the United States living at 66 Inman Street in Cambridge, Massachusetts, and working at the Harvard Museum of Comparative Zoology as assistant to the curator. Gilbert remained at the museum for the rest of his life and gained renown as a skilled craftsman who mounted and maintained the exhibits. During this period he was also recognized as an imaginative cook, who entertained visiting Harvard dignitaries.

A quiet, unassuming man, Gilbert married Anna Scott, with whom he had three daughters. In the 1920s, before he went to Paris, either through his shoe polish formula, or possibly using an inheritance from William Brewster, he managed to send one daughter to Radcliffe College, one to Boston University, and one to a teacher's college in New York. He was fondly remembered in the African American Cambridge community long after his death.

Early on in his career, white ornithologists recognized Robert A. Gilbert as a skilled observer of birds—one of the few naturalists with the ability to spot and identify birds in the field without resorting to killing the animals, which was commonly done by ornithologists then. Many of his sightings are entered in the Brewster field journals and in Brewster's posthumously published books, *The Birds of the Cambridge Region of Massachusetts, October Farm, from the Concord Journals and Diaries of William Brewster* and *Concord River; Selections from the Journals of William Brewster*. Gilbert is even listed in one record as co-author of Brewster's book *The Birds of the Lake Umbagog Region*, although his name does not appear on the final edition. Gilbert's photographs (also uncredited) appear in Brewster's book *October Farm*.

All this places Gilbert as one of the early African American naturalists and, along with William Henry Trotter, one of the few African American photographers who specialized in landscapes. Up until the 1960s very few, if any, African Americans were working in the field of natural history, and although there were many black photographers in Gilbert's time, most were working in studios rather than outdoors in natural light. Gilbert's life would have gone unrecognized save for the work of John Hanson Mitchell, who discovered a trove of glass plate negatives originally attributed to William Brewster.

FURTHER READING
Mitchell, John Hanson. *Looking for Mr. Gilbert* (2005).
JOHN HANSON MITCHELL

Gilchrist, Carlton Chester "Cookie" (25 May 1935– 10 Jan. 2011), professional football player, was born in Brackenridge, Pennsylvania, to Pittsburgh steelworkers Otto and Rose Gilchrist. Gilchrist loved sweets as a child, and was thus given the nickname "Cookie." He attended Har-Brack High School in nearby Natrona Heights, where he was a star player, leading his team to an area championship in 1953. Though in his youth he had visions of becoming a doctor, Gilchrist's increasingly apparent physical gifts steered him toward sports. A gifted athlete, a bruising runner and blocker—"Cookie" was Jim Brown before there was a Jim Brown. With over one hundred college scholarship offers by his junior year, Gilchrist signed a professional contract with owner Paul Brown of the Cleveland Browns of the National Football League (NFL). Because he was nineteen years old, the contract violated NFL rules, so Gilchrist left the Browns' training camp for Canada, where he played in the Ontario Rugby Football Union for two years. In 1956 he joined the Hamilton Tiger-Cats of the Canadian Football League (CFL), leading them to a Gray Cup championship in 1957. Gilchrist played six seasons in the

CFL, with Hamilton (1956–57), Saskatchewan (1958), and Toronto (1959–1962). Although he was named a CFL All-Star five years in a row (1956–1960) as a fullback and defensive linebacker, controversy followed Gilchrist, and in 1962 he was suspended by Toronto Argonauts coach Lou Agase for violating the team curfew. Having signed a five-year contract with Toronto in 1961, with other teams reluctant to absorb his salary, Gilchrist was waived out of the league in July 1962.

In August, Gilchrist signed a one-year contract with the Buffalo Bills of the American Football League (AFL) in August. An AFL rookie at twenty-seven, he set or tied several league records in his first season: the AFL's first 1,000-yard rusher, the most 100-yard rushing games in a season (6), the most consecutive games scoring a touchdown (7), and the single-season rushing touchdown record (tied at 13). For his efforts, he was named AFL Player of the Year and All-AFL—he was also an AFL All-Star. Kicking placements for Buffalo in 1962, Cookie converted on eight of twenty field goal attempts and fourteen of seventeen points after touchdown. When the Bills drafted Syracuse All-American and Heisman Trophy winner Ernie Davis, Gilchrist was signed by Buffalo as insurance. Ironically Davis signed with the Cleveland Browns of the NFL instead. Gilchrist, like Davis, was an outspoken advocate for African American rights who would take the lead in protests against perceived racism. In all, Cookie played three memorable seasons in Buffalo and is still the team's fifth leading all-time rusher. In 1963 against the New York Jets he rushed for a then professional record 243 yards and five touchdowns.

Two events following the 1964 season changed Gilchrist and football. Selected to the AFL post-season all star game scheduled in New Orleans, Gilchrist led a player revolt when black players were denied cab rides and admission to New Orleans restaurants and clubs. Twenty-two black players refused to play, and the game was quickly moved to Houston. After the boycott, New Orleans ended public desegregation and was awarded an NFL franchise in 1967. His racial views then led Cookie into a salary dispute with Buffalo owner Ralph Wilson and he was traded to Denver, where he had an All-Star—the AFL equivalent of All-Pro—year.

At age thirty, time and injuries caught up with the powerful back. Gilchrist played only eight games with Miami in 1966 and one game back in Denver before he retired (1967). In four full AFL seasons Gilchrist rushed for over 4,000 yards and scored thirty-seven touchdowns. Former teammate and broadcaster Paul Maguire remembers him as the meanest and most fearless player he ever saw—not an uncommon assessment by those who played against Gilchrist.

Ever outspoken, Cookie Gilchrist refused induction into the Canadian Football Hall of Fame and enshrinement on the Bills' Wall of Fame. He squabbled with owners, coaches, and players. Crying racism and exploitation, and saying he played only to get paid, Gilchrist worked for civil rights causes, protested the Vietnam War, and knew pivotal leaders such as Dr. MARTIN LUTHER KING JR. and MUHAMMAD ALI. After football came several failed business ventures, but Gilchrist remained a fan favorite who never apologized for his stance on racial issues.

At the end of his life he was working on an unfinished biography and screenplay about the pivotal New Orleans boycott. In 2007 he told a sportswriter he had throat cancer and that his weight had fallen to 180. Gilchrist finally reconciled with Bills owner Wilson before his death and changed his mind on accepting a place on the Bills' Ring of Honor, although he was not enshrined before his death. Survived by sons Jeffrey and Scott and daughter Christina, Gilchrist died in an assisted living facility in Pittsburgh in January 2011. Gilchrist's legacy is certainly tied to football and the records he set, but his unrelenting beliefs in equality and the influence he had on others to make that same stand are his most enduring traits.

FURTHER READING
Marshall, Brian. "Pro Football Career of Cookie Gilchrist." *Coffin Corner* 24, no. 2 (2000). Available at http://www.profootballresearchers.org/Coffin_Corner/24-02-933.pdf.
Miller, Jeffrey, and Billy Shaw. *Rockin' the Rockpile: The Buffalo Bills of the American Football League* (2007).
Warren, MattRich. "Memorial Celebrated Cookie Gilchrist's Legacy On, Off Field." *Buffalo Rumblings*, 20 Apr. 2011. Available at http://www.buffalorumblings.com/2011/4/20/2121373/Cookie-Gilchrist-Legacy-Memorial-Buffalo-Bills.

BOYD CHILDRESS

Gilchrist, Samuel (1839– ?), Civil War soldier and Butler Medal recipient, was born in Surry County, Virginia. Likely a former slave, Gilchrist enlisted for service in the 2nd North Carolina Colored Volunteers Regiment at Hampton, Virginia, on 3 October 1863 for three years. Military records list his age as twenty-four, his height 5'10½", his skin color as brown, and his occupation as carpenter. One of the regiment's enlistees at its inception, composed largely of blacks from North Carolina and Virginia, Gilchrist surely showed leadership qualities from the start as he soon rose from the rank of private to sergeant in Company K. He was likely promoted because of his aptitude, age, and size; nearly all of the other men in his company were farmers or laborers with an average age of approximately twenty-two years and averaged around 5'6" in height. Indeed, Gilchrist's intelligence, demonstrated by his skilled profession, and relative maturity and imposing physical presence were all desirable qualities in a non-commissioned officer.

Gilchrist's official military service in the Union army, as well as that of the approximately 178,000 other black soldiers during the later half of the Civil War, was made possible by the War Department's General Order Number 143 on 22 May 1863, which established the Bureau of Colored Troops. Among the first black regiments were those established in Louisiana, South Carolina, and Massachusetts, and later in thirty-two other states, both North and South. Though black soldiers were discriminated against in the pay they received, and their use was controversial at times for political reasons, their excellent combat performance could not be denied. Indeed, it was the 54th Massachusetts Regiment's heroic actions during the assault on Fort Wagner in South Carolina in July 1863, personified by the valor of the standard bearer Sergeant WILLIAM CARNEY, that helped establish the fighting reputation of black soldiers in the public eye.

Samuel Gilchrist's 2nd North Carolina Colored Volunteer Regiment was first established at the state level in October 1863, and thereafter was reorganized and accepted into the Union army as the 36th U.S. Colored Troop (USCT) Regiment in February 1864. Interestingly, among the soldiers in Gilchrist's Company K was one John Brown, 5'2" barber from New Castle, Maine, and one of over 100 black soldiers to serve in the Civil War from that state. The 36th USCT was first assigned to Wild's African Brigade in the Department of Virginia and North Carolina and subsequently at Point Lookout, Maryland, to guard Confederate prisoners and serving in several expeditions in the area through the end of June 1864. Gilchrist and the men of the 36th USCT went to the front lines at Richmond in July 1864 as part of Major Benjamin Butler's Army of the James during its siege of the Confederate capital. It was here that Gilchrist would earn his stripes as a company sergeant in fierce combat that

would gain the Union's black regiments even further renown.

Late September 1864 found the 36th USCT stationed near New Market Heights, south of Richmond. In an attempt to breach the enemy's ring of defenses, Ulysses S. Grant ordered Benjamin Butler's Army of the James, composed of many USCT regiments, to attack Confederate fortifications and capture four key forts. The two-day battle on 29–30 September 1864 resulted in some of the fiercest fighting of the Richmond campaign and over 5,000 Union casualties. Though Butler's army captured only one of the Confederate positions, Fort Harrison, and its success was short-lived, the Battle of New Market Heights proved yet again that black troops in combat were as determined, skilled, and brave as any white soldier in the Union army. In the early morning fighting on 29 September at New Market Heights, many white officers were killed in action, their places of leadership immediately taken over by black non-commissioned officers, first sergeants, like Samuel Gilchrist, JAMES BRONSON, MILTON HOLLAND, POWHATTAN BEATY, ROBERT PINN, EDWARD RATCLIFF, and others. Perhaps with the massacre of their fellow black troops at Fort Pillow in western Tennessee just five months earlier fresh in their minds, and with the rallying cry of "No quarter, No quarter" rising above the din of battle, Gilchrist of the 35th USCT and sergeants in other black regiments gallantly led their men in the assault on Confederate positions.

Major General Benjamin Butler, always a friend to his black troops and rightfully proud of their conduct in battle, stated eleven days after the battle that at New Market Heights "The colored soldiers by coolness, steadiness, and determined courage and dash have silenced every cavil of the doubters of their soldierly capacity … this war is ended when a musket is in the hands of every able bodied negro who wishes to use one" (Official Records, 163). In commenting on the individual acts of heroism of several black sergeants that led their companies in battle, Butler would later "cause a special medal to be struck in honor of these gallant colored soldiers" (Official Records, 168). First called the Colored Troop Medal, and later more commonly referred to as the Butler Medal, this silver medal, engraved with the words "With distinguished courage—Campaign before Richmond 1864" and depicting black soldiers advancing toward enemy fortifications, was awarded to several hundred black soldiers during the campaign and would be the only army decoration ever approved solely for black troops. As for Samuel Gilchrist, he, too, was recognized for his heroism in leading the men of Company K; Butler's order of 11 October 1864 to the Army of the James succinctly states that Gilchrist "has a medal for gallantry" (Official Records, 169). Interestingly, while most of the sergeants so honored at New Market also received the Medal of Honor, Gilchrist is the only such man listed in Butler's order who did not. The explanation for this lack of a higher award for Gilchrist is unknown, but likely a simple error in the confused aftermath of battle.

Following the battle of New Market Heights, during which he was severely wounded, Sergeant Samuel Gilchrist was hospitalized at the U.S. General Hospital at Fort Monroe, Virginia. He was subsequently mustered out of the army due to his disabilities on 17 June 1865. Though the details of Samuel Gilchrist's later life are uncertain, he nonetheless deserves recognition for his gallantry and courage in the Civil War, which served to exemplify the contribution of thousands of black soldiers to the Union cause and the higher ideals of freedom and equality.

FURTHER READING

North Carolina. "Regimental Service Records for the 2nd North Carolina Colored Volunteers/36th United States Colored Infantry." Available at http://www.rootsweb.com/~ncust/36regt.htm.

United States, Government Printing Office. *The War of the Rebellion: A Compilation of the Official Records of the Union and Confederate Armies*, volume 42, series I, part III (1893): 163–169.

GLENN ALLEN KNOBLOCK

Gillam, Cora T. (c. 1851– ?), sharecropper and clubwoman, was born Cora Alice McCarroll in Greenville, Mississippi, the youngest of three children of a slave woman whose surname was Warren and an Ohioborn white overseer named McCarroll. In the early nineteenth century Gillam's mother and her siblings, who were part Cherokee, were taken from their mother's home in North Carolina and sold into slavery in Mississippi. Interviewed by the Federal Writers' Project in the 1930s, Gillam recalled that her maternal grandmother left North Carolina and tracked her children to Greenville, where she remained. Gillam never met her father, who died shortly before she was born. His early death also denied her the opportunity of the northern education her siblings had enjoyed, her brother Tom in Cincinnati and her sister at Oberlin College. McCarroll had set aside funds for Cora's education, but her mother's second husband, a slave named Lee, "took my school money and put me

in the cotton patch," Gillam noted with some bitterness more than eighty years later (Rawick, 8). Despite widespread opposition to educating slaves in most of the South, Gillam nevertheless learned to read and write with the assistance of her brother, whom she remembered as "the best reader, white or black, for miles" (Rawick, 28).

The outbreak of the Civil War in 1861 disrupted family life for Gillam and other southern slaves. Her mother left Greenville to work as a cook for Confederate troops stationed in Little Rock, Arkansas, leaving her ten-year-old daughter in the care of her mistress, who made her knit gloves and socks for Confederate soldiers. Gillam also lost contact with her brother for several years after he was arrested, jailed, and nearly lynched for reading newspaper accounts of war developments to his fellow slaves. Released from jail by advancing Union troops, Tom later joined the Fifty-fourth Regiment, U.S. Colored Infantry, in Arkansas.

The end of the war and the abolition of slavery reunited Gillam with her mother and stepfather, who had moved to Helena, Arkansas. "When slaves got free," Gillam recalled in the 1930s, "they didn't have nothing but their two hands to start out with. I never heard of any master giving a slave money or land." Like many of the freed people in the cotton-rich lands of central east Arkansas, Gillam and her parents entered into a new working relationship with their former owners, who "put up the cotton and seed and corn and food for us" and "told us we could work on shares, half and half." It soon became apparent, however, that sharecropping was far from fair and equal. "Some white folks was so mean," Gillam remembered, noting that her family barely broke even once their landowners deducted the cost of seed, rent, and food from their account at the end of the year. Realizing that "we was just about where we was in slave days," Gillam and her mother abandoned sharecropping in favor of wage labor, receiving $1.50 for every hundred pounds of cotton they picked (Rawick, 30). That pay rate was fairly high for the late 1860s though not so unusual in Arkansas, which was suffering from a severe labor shortage at that time. Within a few years Gillam had saved enough money to escape the backbreaking labor of the Delta cotton fields, and she moved to Little Rock to be with her husband, ISAAC T. GILLAM, whom she had married in 1867. She may have met him through her brother Tom, who had served with him in the Arkansas Colored Infantry.

Her husband's thriving business as a blacksmith and a horse breeder as well as his prominent role in Arkansas politics ensured Gillam a level of social and financial security that was rare among postwar southern black women. Relieved of the need to labor for wages, she devoted herself to looking after her nine children, seven of whom reached adulthood, and five of whom became teachers. Three of her daughters taught in the Little Rock schools, while a fourth taught in Cincinnati after studying at Howard University, the University of Paris, and the University of Cincinnati. A son, Isaac Gillam Jr., served as principal of Little Rock's black high school for fifty years and also taught at Shorter College in North Little Rock, which Cora and Isaac Gillam had helped found as Bethel University in 1886. Like other southern black middle-class women, Cora Gillam was active in the club movement at the beginning of the twentieth century. She won awards for her quilts, which she continued to make into her eighties without the benefit of eyeglasses.

Gillam had strong political views, though it is possible that she tempered them somewhat for Beulah Sherwood Hagg, the white Federal Writers' Project employee who interviewed her in the 1930s. Gillam told Hagg that "if the rough element from the north had stayed out of the south the trouble of reconstruction would not [have] happened" (Rawick, 31). She also contradicted comments she had made earlier in her interview about the unfairness of sharecropping by stating that "the white folks was still kind to them what had been their slaves. They would have helped to get them started." Gillam was more forceful, however, in her defense of black voting rights, telling Hagg, "I guess you don't find any colored folks what think they get a fair deal" (Rawick, 32). Gillam particularly resented the denial of the vote to African Americans who paid their poll taxes and criticized the Little Rock school board for threatening to fire black teachers who registered to vote. It is not known precisely when Gillam died, but in 1937, in her eighty-sixth year, she remained active and full of energy. Perhaps because she had "not had it hard like lots of ex-slaves," Gillam told her interviewer, "I still feel young inside. I feel that I have had a good life" (Rawick, 33).

FURTHER READING

Gillam, Cora. "Interview of Mrs. Cora Gillam," in *The American Slave: A Composite Autobiography*, ed. George P. Rawick, supp. 9, pt. 3 (1972).

STEVEN J. NIVEN

Gillam, Isaac T. (c. 1839–18 Apr. 1904), blacksmith and politician, was born a slave in Hardin County, Tennessee. It is unknown whether he was still living there in April 1862, during the battle of Shiloh, one of the bloodiest of the Civil War. By 15 September 1863 he was living in Little Rock, Arkansas, more than 250 miles west of his birthplace. On that day, five days after Little Rock fell to the Union army, Gillam enlisted in Company I, Second Regiment, Arkansas Infantry, which was later renamed Company I, Fifty-fourth Regiment, U.S. Colored Infantry. Since he immediately assumed the rank of sergeant, he probably knew how to read and write (noncommissioned officers in the Union army were expected to be able to read orders and file reports). After serving for three years, primarily in Arkansas and Kansas, he left the army in 1866, having reached the rank of first sergeant.

Gillam settled in Little Rock, where he began working as a blacksmith. In 1867 he married Cora Alice McCarrell, a fifteen-year-old Mississippi native who had moved to Little Rock after the Civil War and who had a brother who was also a veteran of the Fifty-fourth Regiment. The couple had nine children, seven of whom survived to adulthood, and five of whom became teachers. In the 1930s CORA GILLAM recalled that her husband enjoyed a good business as a blacksmith and that he once nursed to health a badly injured cavalry horse that later competed in and won several races in Kentucky. Gillam was also a successful horse breeder, supplying foals to customers as far away as Texas.

That he named one of his favorite stallion Pinchback, after the Louisiana senator P. B. S. PINCHBACK, is also suggestive of Gillam's other main interest in Reconstruction-era Arkansas: politics. An active member of the Republican Party, he was appointed to the post of city jailer in 1872 and was also prominent two years later in the so-called Brooks-Baxter War, in which more than two hundred Arkansans died as a result of internecine fighting within the state Republican Party. Gillam served as a captain in the predominantly African American militia loyal to the Ohio-born Joseph Brooks, which suffered most of the casualties. Perhaps as a result of Gillam's efforts as one of the few black officers in the Brooks militia, voters of Little Rock's predominantly African American Sixth Ward elected him to the city council in April 1877. Along with another black Republican councilman, he served on the important Ways and Means Committee, which was responsible for city finances and public spending.

Partisan divisions on the city council were intense, but Gillam increasingly allied with members of the new Greenback Party, which had emerged in response to the 1873 depression. The Greenbackers' proposal to increase the paper money supply appealed to farmers and laborers of both races suffering from tight credit policies. In the 1878 congressional elections, the Greenback Party won more than a million votes, elected fourteen members of Congress, and won hundreds of local races nationwide. Among the victorious was Gillam, still a Republican alderman in Little Rock, who fought for and won a seat in the Arkansas House of Representatives on the Greenback ticket. He also ran as a Greenback candidate for the Little Rock city council in 1879 but was defeated when another Greenback candidate split the black vote and enabled a white Democrat to win.

Gillam returned to political office in 1882, this time as the successful Democratic Party candidate for coroner of Pulaski County, a post he held until 1886. Four years later he again sought the office of coroner, this time as the nominee of the Populist Party, whose economic reform policies owed much to the Greenbackers. This time, however, Gillam lost; any further political ambitions he may have had were rendered moot in 1894, when Democrats in the Arkansas legislature followed the lead of other southern states and disenfranchised African American voters. Gillam remained active in civic and religious affairs in Little Rock, serving on the board of trustees of the city's Bethel AME Church, and was a prominent Mason. Gillam died suddenly in Little Rock in April 1904 on the day he was to serve on a grand jury in that city. He is buried in the National Cemetery in Little Rock.

Gillam's political career mirrored that of black southerners generally in the late nineteenth century. He began as a Republican, the party of Abraham Lincoln and Reconstruction, but later joined the Greenbackers and Populists when the economic policies of those parties offered hope to struggling black farmers and laborers. His brief flirtation with the Democrats in the early 1880s r eflected a pragmatic willingness to work with the party of white supremacy as long as that party was willing to work with African Americans. After disenfranchisement in 1894, Gillam returned to the Republican Party fold.

FURTHER READING

Dillard, Tom W. "Isaac T. Gillam: Black Pulaski Countian," *Pulaski County Historical Review* 24 (Spring 1976).

Gillam, Cora. "Interview of Mrs. Cora Gillam," in *The American Slave: A Composite Autobiography*, ed. George P. Rawick, supp. 9, pt. 3 (1972).

STEVEN J. NIVEN

Gillespie, Dizzy (21 Oct. 1917–6 Jan. 1993), jazz trumpeter, composer, and bandleader, was born John Birks Gillespie at Cheraw, South Carolina, the ninth and youngest child of James Gillespie, a brick mason, builder, and amateur musician, and Lottie Powe, a laundress. The earliest musical influences on Gillespie were the sounds of the town band, in which his father played and whose instruments were stored in the family home, together with the singing and hand clapping of the parishioners of the Sanctified Church a few doors away from his house. James Gillespie was cruel and sadistic, regularly beating his sons, but he died from an asthma attack when Gillespie was ten. Not long afterward, he was formally introduced to playing music by Alice Wilson, a schoolteacher at the Robert Smalls School in Cheraw. Growing up as the youngest child of a large single-parent family, Gillespie developed an early penchant for mischief, but music was a stabilizing influence in his life. After first playing trombone and then settling on trumpet, Gillespie joined a local amateur band of young musicians, playing for social events in and around Cheraw. He eventually won

Dizzy Gillespie performs at the Famous Door in New York City, c. June 1946. Gillespie's most memorable and widely performed composition is "A Night in Tunisia." (© William P. Gottlieb; www.jazzphotos.com.)

a music scholarship to the Laurinburg Institute in Laurinburg, North Carolina.

Although the music tutor there, Philmore "Shorty" Hall, was a proficient trumpeter from Tuskegee College, Alabama, he had little time to pass on his knowledge to Gillespie, who consequently was largely self-taught, sharing his diligent trumpet practice routines with a cousin, Norman Powe, who later became a professional trombonist. In due course Gillespie also became a competent pianist, using the piano to help him understand harmony and developing the trick of playing the trumpet with his right hand while accompanying himself on the piano with his left. Gillespie left the institute before graduating in 1935 and moved with his family to Philadelphia, Pennsylvania, where he joined the big band of Frankie Fairfax. This gave him a thorough musical apprenticeship, including touring throughout Pennsylvania and travels on the territory band circuit of the South and Southwest under the temporary leadership of the drummer TINY BRADSHAW. During his time in Fairfax's band, Gillespie acquired the nickname "Dizzy" for his occasionally outlandish behavior and frequent practical jokes, and he soon became popularly known by this name alone.

His contemporaries described Gillespie's early solos as redolent of LOUIS ARMSTRONG, but his trumpet-section colleagues CHARLIE SHAVERS and Carl Warwick introduced him to the stylistic innovations of ROY ELDRIDGE. These became the dominant influences on Gillespie's playing, which he refined by studying Eldridge's work from records, broadcasts, and occasional live appearances in Philadelphia. In 1937 Shavers and Warwick persuaded Gillespie to move to New York City to join LUCKY MILLINDER's orchestra, but when this plan fell through, Gillespie joined Teddy Hill's band and almost immediately set sail for a European tour that took him to France and Britain. Before leaving, Gillespie, at age nineteen, made his first records; his solo on Hill's "King Porter Stomp" reveals a remarkably mature player, already developing a style distinct from that of Eldridge.

During the Atlantic crossing, the trumpeter Bill Dillard coached Gillespie in the art of section playing. After appearances at the Moulin Rouge in Paris and the London Palladium, he returned to New York a seasoned big-band musician, continuing to work with Hill and with Edgar Hayes, Al Cooper, and the Cuban flutist Alberto Socarras. In 1939 he joined CAB CALLOWAY's orchestra, one of the most high-profile bands in jazz. This move brought Gillespie's playing to the attention of a large public.

He not only recorded many solos with Calloway but also contributed arrangements to the band, including the innovative "Picking the Cabbage," which prefigured some of the rhythmic and structural devices he was to use in such later compositions as "A Night in Tunisia."

However, Gillespie found the endless routine of backing up Calloway's singing and dancing, and the relatively limited musical vocabulary of the majority of the music, to be highly restrictive. He fooled around onstage and played ever more daring solos that ventured into new harmonic directions, delivered at dazzling speed. Calloway disliked this "Chinese music," and matters came to a head in September 1941, when Calloway accused Gillespie of throwing a spitball on stage. Gillespie—innocent for once—responded by drawing a knife and stabbing his bandleader in the rear end. He was immediately fired.

Gillespie was one of a small number of African American musicians actively seeking to expand the vocabulary of jazz. In June 1940, in Kansas City, Gillespie had met CHARLIE PARKER, thus beginning their highly productive collaboration. In New York, Gillespie, Parker, and other young innovative players, including the drummer KENNY CLARKE, who had worked with Gillespie in Hayes's orchestra, and the pianist THELONIOUS MONK, would jam after hours at such Harlem clubs as Minton's Playhouse and Monroe's Uptown House. These informal and experimental jam sessions allowed the musicians to play in small groups where they could develop their own personal styles and where they began to move jazz itself in a new direction. Unfortunately, because of a strike by the American Federation of Musicians in the early 1940s, these earliest forays into what came to be known as bebop are largely unrecorded.

The relationship of Parker and Gillespie developed further when both men played in the big band led by EARL HINES, during the first nine months of 1943. Together, Parker and Gillespie became figureheads of the new bebop movement, which drew together several revolutionary elements. Among their innovations they employed unusual, often dissonant harmonies, such as ninths, elevenths, and thirteenths, as well as habitually flattening some regularly used intervals, such as fifths and sevenths. They also used brief thematic formulas to construct long, flowing melodic lines, often delivered at high speed, which ran over the conventional four- and eight-measure phrase lengths of popular songs, and they introduced cross-rhythms and uneven accents to the playing of rhythm accompaniments.

If Parker was the mercurial, short-lived genius whose inspirational playing was the heart of the new style, Gillespie became its head, documenting their repertoire of new tunes, arranging and voicing them for small and large ensembles, and tirelessly teaching his contemporaries the necessary harmonic and rhythmic structures. As improvisers the two were evenly matched, and Gillespie described Parker as "the other half of my heartbeat."

Gillespie first brought bebop to Fifty-second Street in New York, leading a band at the Onyx Club from late 1943 until early the following year. With Parker temporarily home in Kansas City, Gillespie worked with the saxophonists LESTER YOUNG, DON BYAS, and BUDD JOHNSON to develop the style. Later in 1944 he joined BILLY ECKSTINE's orchestra, which marked an early attempt to transfer the new ideas to a large ensemble. However, it was the quintet that Parker and Gillespie led at the Three Deuces in New York, from the spring until the late summer of 1945, that cemented the principles of bebop, and the recordings they made together at that time capture the inspirational brilliance of their playing. Their repertoire included "Dizzy Atmosphere," "Groovin' High," and "Salt Peanuts."

After a short-lived attempt to launch his own big band in mid-1945, Gillespie went with Parker to California, a visit marred by Parker's growing drug dependence and unreliability. Gillespie returned to New York, subsequently launching a successful big band, which he led until the end of the decade, making numerous recordings and traveling to Europe in 1948. This group demonstrated how to transfer bebop to large groups successfully and introduced several new concepts, including the use of modal structures and Afro-Cuban rhythms, notably on "Cubano Be, Cubano Bop," a composition by Gillespie, the theorist GEORGE RUSSELL, and the band's Cuban percussionist, CHANO POZO.

Gillespie's repertoire of songs became big-band standards, including "Things to Come" and "Algo Bueno," as well as lighthearted vehicles for the scat singing of Dizzy and the vocalists Joe Carroll or Kenny Hagood, such as "Oop-Pop-a-Dah." Most significantly, Gillespie's ebullient personality, ready wit, and show-business experience made this difficult new music palatable to large audiences, helped by the eccentric visual image he adopted, sporting a beret, horn-rimmed spectacles, and a goatee. Lampooned in the press, his fashions were adopted by many of the band's fans.

In the early 1950s Gillespie's big band ceased to be economically viable, and his wife, Lorraine Willis, whom he had married in 1940, encouraged him to abandon it. He temporarily experimented in rhythm and blues and with his own record label, Dee Gee. This was an unsuccessful period for him musically. Then, as the 1950s developed, his regular quintet with the pianist WYNTON KELLY and the baritone saxophonist Bill Graham became a regular feature of the touring circuit, visiting Scandinavia, Germany, and France as well as traveling widely in the United States. In 1953 Gillespie took part in a celebrated reunion with Parker at Massey Hall in Toronto.

Gillespie continued to develop as a soloist, appearing from 1954 in Jazz at the Philharmonic concerts and on record for the entrepreneur Norman Granz, who was instrumental in helping Gillespie re-form his big band. This was when Gillespie adopted his trademark upswept trumpet, its bell angled upward at a forty-five-degree angle. Combined with his unusually puffed-out cheeks, he became one of the most visually distinctive figures in music.

Following tours on behalf of the U.S. State Department to the Middle East and South America, Gillespie kept his new big band going through 1956 and 1957, thereafter only returning to larger ensembles sporadically and preferring to tour regularly with his quintet. During the early 1960s Gillespie formed a productive partnership with the Argentinean composer Lalo Schifrin, performing *Gillespiana*, a five-movement suite for trumpet and big band, at Carnegie Hall in March 1961. Schifrin worked as pianist in Gillespie's quintet and composed for the small group and larger forces, including "New Continent" in 1962.

By this time Gillespie was beginning to be regarded as a father figure of the jazz trumpet, gradually assuming the role that Louis Armstrong had previously enjoyed. Gillespie's solo touring for Granz and his group's appearances on the burgeoning festival circuit ensured his worldwide popularity. This became the pattern of his life for the next two decades: consistent touring with his quintet, solo appearances on disc and in all-star bands, and extension of his ambassadorial activities. The latter included, on one hand, being among the first American jazz players to visit Castro's Cuba and, on the other, appearing on *The Muppet Show*.

In his final years Gillespie adopted the tenets of the Baha'i faith. His last major musical venture in 1988 was to found his United Nation Orchestra, a big band that brought together musicians from North and South America and the Caribbean. After final quintet appearances at the Blue Note in New York during the summer of 1992, he became unable to play following the onset of pancreatic cancer. He died in Englewood, New Jersey, where he had lived for many years. He was survived by Lorraine and by his daughter, Jeanie Bryson, born in March 1958 to the songwriter Connie Bryson.

Gillespie's role as one of the principal architects of modern jazz has tended to be overlooked in favor of the achievements of Parker, who died in 1955. Gillespie's technical innovations in the speed and range of the trumpet, his codification of the harmonic structures and repertoire of bebop, and his role as mentor to generations of younger players made him an equally significant figure. In particular, he encouraged the careers of the trumpeters LEE MORGAN, Jon Faddis, Claudio Roditi, and Arturo Sandoval and brought jazz to a vast international audience.

FURTHER READING
An oral history interview with Gillespie is in the Institute for Jazz Studies at Rutgers University, Newark, New Jersey. Some of his earliest autograph arrangements survive in the Cab Calloway Collection at the Mugar Memorial Library, Boston University.
Gillespie, Dizzy, with Al Fraser. *To Be or Not to Bop* (1980).
Gentry, Tony. *Dizzy Gillespie* (1991).
McRae, Barry. *Dizzy Gillespie: His Life and Times* (1988).
Shipton, Alyn. *Groovin' High* (1999, rev. ed. with recordings list 2001).
Obituary: *New York Times*, 7 Jan. 1993.

DISCOGRAPHY
The French company Média 7 is issuing a comprehensive edition of Gillespie's output, including private recordings and broadcasts. Volumes 1–5 are MJCD 31, 41, 45, 86, and 110.
Dizzy Gillespie: The Complete RCA Bluebird Recordings (Bluebird 66528-2).
Dizzy's Diamonds (Verve 513875).

ALYN SHIPTON

Gilliam, Earl B. (17 Aug. 1931–28 Jan. 2001), federal judge and educator, was born Earl Ben Gilliam in Clovis, New Mexico, the son of James Earl Gilliam, a small-business owner, and Lula Mae Gooden. Gilliam spent most of his boyhood in Oklahoma City before his family moved to San Diego, California, in 1941. At the end of World War II his father opened the Louisiana Fish Market on Imperial Avenue in the heart of the city's African American community, and while attending San Diego High School—where he was an outstanding tackle on the football team—Gilliam spent many after-school hours assisting the family business. While attending San Diego State College he enjoyed acting in plays and was one of the earliest pledges of the school's first black fraternity, Kappa Alpha Psi. Upon earning his bachelor's degree in Accounting in 1953 Gilliam entered the University of California's Hastings College of Law in San Francisco and was a classmate of the future San Francisco mayor WILLIE BROWN. Gilliam's marriage in 1956 to Barbara Jean Crawford, a county Probation Department employee, produced two sons. Completing his J.D. and passing the bar exam in 1957, Gilliam returned to San Diego and started work as a criminal investigator for the district attorney's office and later was a deputy district attorney for three and a half years. He resigned in 1961 and went into private practice as a general practitioner.

Gilliam's high standing in Southeast San Diego, the city's predominantly black community, and his connections in the Democratic Party undoubtedly helped him to become the first African American judge in San Diego County when Governor Edmund G. Brown named him to fill a vacancy on the San Diego Municipal Court in 1963. Subsequently Gilliam was elected by the voters to serve a six-year term on the court and eventually became its presiding judge. During the late 1950s and early 1960s Gilliam, an active liberal Democrat, distinguished himself in the community and professional service as a member of the city's Interracial Council, as a county juvenile justice commissioner, as a member of the Southeast Chamber of Commerce, as a member of the advisory committee to the San Diego Board of Education, and as a member of the federal, municipal, and reconciliation committees of the San Diego County Bar Association. In 1969 Gilliam served as professor and head of the trial practice department at the Western State University Law School in San Diego and also taught classes at the city's newly established Thomas Jefferson School of Law in 1996. He also taught in the urban and rural studies department at the University of California at San Diego and was a lecturer at United States International University. In 1975 Gilliam became the first African American to serve as a judge of the Superior Court for the state of California. President Jimmy Carter appointed Gilliam to the United States District Court for the Southern District of California in 1980. He reached senior status on this court in 1993.

Gilliam presided over some of the most sensational and far-reaching cases in San Diego in the postwar era, among them the 1985 trial of the attorney Phillip A. DeMassa on charges relating to his connection with the notorious Coronado Company, which since the late 1970s had smuggled unprecedented amounts of marijuana and hashish into the United States; the prolonged 1986 criminal trial *United States v. Telink* in which government employees allegedly took kickbacks and bribes from a telecommunications company; the 1988 case concerning the fraudulent multimillion-dollar Ponzi scheme of the investment pitchman J. David Dominelli and his mistress, business partner, and former mayor of Del Mar, California, Nancy Hoover; the 1989 case of *Daubert v. Merrell Dow Pharmaceuticals*, which resulted in a national standard for trial courts authenticating scientific evidence; and the 1992 overbilling fraud case involving National Health Laboratories, in which government prosecutors won a record-setting $110 million judgment.

Blessed with the keen intellect necessary to untangle and explain legal complexities, Gilliam also possessed a warm and gregarious personality and was widely revered. He was particularly outspoken on matters concerning racial equality, women's rights, and youth education and guidance. Gilliam chafed at federal sentencing guidelines, which he contended discounted what he called "the human factor" in determining punishment. Members of the Association of Black Attorneys of San Diego County were so impressed with his accomplishments and his performance as a mentor and role model that in 1982 they renamed their group the Earl B. Gilliam Bar Association—a rare honor for someone still living—and later initiated a scholarship fund in appreciation of his contributions to his profession and his promotion of a civil society.

Gilliam was quite active in community development, and he founded, inspired, and served on the boards of many San Diego organizations, including the Burn Institute, the Villaview Hospital Foundation, the YMCA, the Salvation Army, and the Urban League. Gilliam suffered a personal setback and public embarrassment in 1990 when his eldest son, Earl Kenneth Gilliam, a cocaine addict, was convicted of robbing two cab drivers. The son died in 1999. In 1995 Gilliam and Crawford divorced, and Gilliam married his second wife, the locally prominent feminist attorney Rebecca Prater.

In his last years on the bench Gilliam received a host of honors and recognitions, including being named San Diego County Bar Association Legal Professional of the Year and garnering the National Bar Association Wiley A. Branton Award and the NAACP Civil Rights Pioneer Award. A portrait of Gilliam was displayed at his high school, and the moot courtroom at the Thomas Jefferson School of Law was named in his honor. Following Gilliam's death from heart disease the Earl B. Gilliam Memorial Golf Tournament was launched, a memorial plaque and bust of Gilliam was enshrined in the San Diego Hall of Justice, and a new U.S. postal facility near his former home was christened the Earl B. Gilliam Post Office Building.

FURTHER READING
Judges of the United States, 2d ed. (1983).
Moran, Greg. "Memorial Honors Late Judge Gilliam," *San Diego Union-Tribune*, 20 June 2003.
Obituary: *San Diego Union-Tribune*, 29 Jan. 2001.

ROBERT FIKES JR.

Gilliam, Sam (30 Nov. 1933–), artist, was born in Tupelo, Mississippi, the seventh of eight children of Sam Gilliam, a carpenter and truck driver, and Estery C. Cousin, a schoolteacher. Around 1942 the Gilliams moved to Louisville, Kentucky, where Sam's artistic promise was encouraged by his parents and his teachers at Virginia Avenue Elementary School, Madison Junior High School, and Central High School, all segregated public facilities. Following high school graduation in 1951, he enrolled at the newly desegregated University of Louisville, earning a BA in Fine Arts in 1955. After serving two years in the U.S. Army, he returned to the University of Louisville and completed an MA in Painting in 1961. The following year Gilliam moved to Washington, D.C., and married the journalist Dorothy Butler. Over the next several years they had three daughters. For the next twenty-five years Gilliam worked as a teacher, first at McKinley High School (1962–1967) and later at the Maryland Art Institute (1967–1982), the University of Maryland (1982–1985), and Carnegie Mellon University (1985–1989).

In 1963 in his first show after moving to Washington, Gilliam showed a series of moody figurative works, mostly watercolors, influenced by Paul Klee, the German Expressionists, particularly Emil Nolde, and the California artist Nathan Olivera, whose paintings Gilliam had seen in Louisville. By the following year, however, Gilliam had fully embraced abstraction, encouraged by the radical color experiments of Mark Rothko, Barnett Newman, and Helen Frankenthaler and the work of a number of local painters who came to be known as the Washington Color School. From the Color School painters, with whom he had become friendly, Gilliam adopted a passionate devotion to color and color relationships and the technique of pouring paint onto unstretched canvas. Like ALMA THOMAS, another artist associated with the Washington Color School, Gilliam shared the Washington painters' focus on vivid color, optical effects, and the processes of preparing and treating canvases and paints. But, also like Thomas, he eventually eschewed the precision of hard-edged effects that sought to flatten the picture plane and do away with visible brush stokes in favor of a more gestural, tactile approach more consistent with earlier abstract expressionist action painters like Jackson Pollock and Willem de Kooning.

Beginning with small watercolors on rice paper, Gilliam experimented with and learned to control broad applications of paint. By 1966 he had switched from oil to the acrylic paints popular with the Washington Color School painters. With works like *Paleo* (1966) and *Red Petals* (1967) he threw himself into color, staining canvases with broad flows of paint, producing interpenetrating areas of color evocative of mood and atmosphere. He soon introduced a new technique that diverged from the work of other Washington Color School painters. Folding or rolling huge, wet, painted canvases, Gilliam created vertical striations and patches of symmetrical, Rorschach-like elements in works such as *Restore* (1968) and *Elephanta* (1970) that in their abstract patterning variously recall natural phenomena like rock formations and textile techniques like tie-dye.

Gilliam had already exhibited in a number of Washington galleries when in 1966 he received a grant from the National Council on the Arts, an NEA Individual Artist Grant in 1967, and his first solo museum show at the prestigious Phillips Collection. In 1968 he was included in a touring exhibition of African American artists organized by the Minneapolis Institute of Art. That same year his work was added to a Museum of Modern Art exhibition honoring the recently assassinated MARTIN LUTHER KING JR. following protests from black artists, including FAITH RINGGOLD, who forced the museum to include black artists in the exhibition. In 1968 the Washington Gallery of Modern Art awarded Gilliam a five-year grant and a rent-free studio, thus providing the support he needed to pioneer his next breakthrough.

In 1968 Gilliam innovated the unsupported canvas or "drape painting." Blurring the line between painting and sculpture—painted on a two-dimensional surface yet operating in three-dimensional space— Gilliam's huge paintings (as large as thirty by forty and ten by seventy-five feet) were suspended from walls and ceilings or draped across poles and beams. With each new presentation, works like *Relative* (1969), *Horizontal Extension* (1969), and *Lithe* (1970) were altered in their form, composition, and color relationships, changing the interplay of background and foreground within each work as well as the work's relationship to its special environment. "The gravity-formed or suspended paintings," Gilliam wrote in 1991 in the *Art Journal*, "consisted of paint poured directly onto raw canvas and exhibited in a way consistent with the manner in which they were made ... now the canvas was not only the means to, but a primary part of, the object. The suspended paintings began by celebrating the working process and ended with the involvement of the wall, the floor, and the ceiling." Mobile and responsive to site conditions, the drape painting firmly launched the themes that inform all of Gilliam's work: process, materials, and the serendipitous and performative elements of painting.

That Gilliam had altered the trajectory of painting is clear from his reception by artists, critics, and curators, who immediately featured his suspended works. In 1969 Gilliam's drape paintings were shown in exhibitions at the Corcoran Gallery of Art, the Whitney Museum of Art, and the newly established Studio Museum in Harlem. Other museum and gallery shows quickly followed, and in 1971 he received a Guggenheim Memorial Foundation Grant and a solo exhibition at the Museum of Modern Art. The following year he represented the United States at the Venice Biennale. "Sam Gilliam is free-wheeling and adventurous in his work," the curator Jacqueline Days Serwer wrote in 1974. "He ignores conventional limits, not only on the size and shape of his paintings, but also what a painting is ... they have come out of the frame, off the wall and into the available space." When the three suspended panels of *Mr. Robeson* were exhibited at the Corcoran in 1975, the *Washington Star* exclaimed that Gilliam was creating cathedrals out of canvas.

With *Seahorses*, commissioned by the Philadelphia Museum of Art in 1975, Gilliam moved his drape paintings outdoors, furthering the impact of factors such as rain, wind, and temperature on the creation and exhibition of his works. The massive piece, six canvases comprising 16,800 square feet of material and 250 gallons of paint, was later reinstalled at the Brooklyn Museum. For an installation at Artpark in Lewiston, New York, in 1977, Gilliam installed fourteen "sculptural fabric placements" along a cliff overlooking the Niagara River. After wind and rain had dragged the pieces down the gorge, he sculpted and exhibited the canvases on wooden supports. Gilliam continued to make outdoor works in a variety of media and completed more than twenty public art projects for both indoor and outdoor sites, including works for airports in Atlanta, New York, and Washington, D.C., subway stations in Buffalo, Manhattan, Queens, and Somerville, Massachusetts, and federal buildings in Atlanta, Detroit, Trenton, New Jersey, Fort Lauderdale, and Philadelphia.

While producing his giant drapes, Gilliam also experimented with painting, cutting, hanging, and suspending smaller indoor pieces, including the *Quadrille* and *Cowl* series. By the early 1970s he had returned to large stretched canvases, turning his attention to the alchemy and application of paint. Working with a variety of acrylic, translucent, and metallic paints, lacquer thinners and aniline dyes, and rakes, combs, and brooms, Gilliam poured, spattered, built up, and scratched canvases, producing large, lyrical paintings like *On a Landless Sea* (1973) and *Orpheus* (1973). Soon he was adding bits of paper, stitched fabric, household items, ephemeral and found objects, photographs, toys, and what Gilliam called "relics." The resulting works, including *Dark As I Am* (1971), an assemblage of artist's tools and paint-encrusted clothes and shoes, led to the *Jail Jungle* series (1973), mixed-media constructions hung on clothes hangers and encased in wood and glass. In the mid-1970s Gilliam introduced a series of quiltlike collages, created by cutting and reassembling pieces from previously painted canvases. Over time the circular format and pie-shaped pieces of works like *For Day One* (1974–1975) and *Over* (1974–1975) evolved into irregular, crazy-quilt-like canvases typified by *Arc Maker I and II* (1981) and *Crazy Indiana* (1982). In the latter half of the 1970s Gilliam used the monochromatic palettes, especially in his *White Paintings* (1976) and *Black Paintings* (1977), to experiment with surface treatment and texture, and impasto and overglazing techniques. Having built up his canvas with an almost architectural attention to paint, Gilliam began building out, incorporating metal appendages and other three-dimensional elements to his paintings.

By the late 1980s and 1990s Gilliam was producing mixed-media installations of various combinations of paints, dyes, natural and man-made fabrics, computer-generated images, glass, wood, and metals. As the twentieth century drew to a close he turned to wood construction, crafting abstract still lifes and pieces with movable parts and piano hinges inspired in part by the Dutch modernists Piet Mondrian and Gerrit Rietveld. About these works the *Washington Post* critic Ferdinand Potzman wrote:

> They are like cubist African kimono sculptures. They have the flow and formal presence of the Japanese garment, the fractured planes of a Braque painting, the vivid colors of West African art and structural and compositional elements drawn from European, American and West African sculpture.... He's a master synthesizer, following his own path but constantly absorbing influences and turning them into something fresh, unique and compelling. (4 Nov. 1999)

After his early experiments painting, folding, cutting, and shaping paper in preparation for his canvas innovations, Gilliam periodically returned to printmaking and works on paper. In the 1990s and 2000s Gilliam used handmade paper, paint, dyes, wood veneer, and such techniques as silkscreening, stitching, appliqué, collage, and paper cutouts to create mixed-media monotypes ranging in size from small, intimate pieces to *Fireflies and Ferriswheels* (1997), a 1,500-yard print.

The recipient of numerous awards, including a second NEA Individual Artist Grant in 1989 and nine honorary doctorates, Gilliam has exhibited his work in more than 120 solo exhibitions and in 129 group shows. His works are held in the collections of more than fifty museums, including the National Gallery of Art and National Museum of American Art in Washington, D.C.; the Metropolitan Museum of Art, Museum of Modern Art, and Whitney Museum of American Art in New York City; and the Tate Gallery in London.

The critic Paul Richard has described Gilliam's work as "a struggle between opposites, between chaos and control, between the intuitively improvised and the predetermined" (*Washington Post*, 24 Mar. 1983). Throughout his career, in his supported and unsupported canvas paintings, assemblages, installations, collages, and works on paper, Gilliam has investigated the visceral, cerebral, and emotional properties of color, geometry, texture, and form. His works reveal a deep respect for craft and medium, a rich knowledge of history and art, and a passion for experimentation and evolution.

FURTHER READING

Gilliam, Sam. "Solids and Veils," *Art Journal* (Spring 1991).

Davies, Hugh. *Sam Gilliam: Indoor and Outdoor Paintings 1967–1978* (1978).

Serwer, Jacqueline. *Gilliam/ Edwards/ Williams: Extensions* (1974).

Studio Museum in Harlem. *Red & Black to "D": Paintings by Sam Gilliam* (1983).

LISA E. RIVO

Gilliard, James E. M. (c. 1835–6 June 1876), activist and educator, was born in Baltimore, Maryland. Nothing is known of his parentage or youth. He was probably the James Gilliard listed in the 1860 Federal Census of Stockton, California; if this is the case, he was a barber, his wife was named Charlotte (c. 1835– ?), and had a step-daughter, Mary E. Jones (c. 1848– ?). In the late 1860s Gilliard worked as a teacher and sometime-minister in the African Methodist Episcopal (AME) Church and spent time in both Los Angeles and San Francisco. He wrote several short pieces for the San Francisco *Elevator*—sometimes under his full name and sometimes using simply "J. E. M."—and was noted by the editor Philip Bell as one of the weekly's best contributors (along with Thomas Detter and Jennie Carter). Gilliard was even occasionally noted as the paper's "associate editor."

Gilliard lectured throughout California in 1870 and 1871—generally on race and education. In letters of recommendation later published in the 13 February 1873 and 27 November 1873 *Christian Recorder*, Bishop Thomas M. D. Ward said that "as an orator, he has no superior and few equals on this side of the American Continent," and Governor Newton Booth praised him as "a co-worker in the elevation of the colored people in our country." The endorsement from Booth, who was not always a friend to California blacks, suggests that Gilliard was willing to cross partisan lines to aid in civil rights efforts. His willingness to work with Democrats could be seen in what was perhaps his most famous speech, given at Los Angeles's 1870 celebration of the Fifteenth Amendment, where he shared the podium with the seemingly repentant Southern sympathizer Democrat Edward Kewen. He forgave Kewen and crossed the stage to shake hands with him. Gilliard's peace-making abilities were also called upon when he accepted the chair a meeting of the Executive Committee—a planning group of several of the state's Colored Conventions in the 1860s and 1870s—when the quarreling factions of Bell and rival editor Peter Anderson clashed.

Still, finding opportunities in California more limited than he had hoped and drawn by a call from the African Methodist Episcopal Church, Gilliard moved to Texas in 1872, where he was given the dual charge of Austin's AME Church and the AME Conference high school, which had ties to Paul Quinn College. Gilliard, who had traveled the nation and was both sophisticated and multilingual (he spoke several romance languages and Chinese), likely chafed in Austin, where, in the words of former student Hightower T. Kealing, the church was "a rough, unplanned, barn-like structure" (67) Gilliard, "a man who would go into a white church and take a seat forward," was reportedly attacked several times by whites angered at his sense of equality and justice (67).

Gilliard received a new charge in 1873: to travel North to raise funds for the struggling high school. He lectured in Philadelphia on 13 February 1873 on "The Colored American," as well as in Baltimore and Washington, and published work in the *Christian Recorder*. When he returned to Texas, he was named the Presiding Elder of the Palestine District—though he continued work with the Conference high school His work was not without controversy; a summary of the March 1875 San Antonio District meeting published in the *Recorder* notes that charges of an unknown nature were brought against Gilliard and then dismissed after "a very spirited discussion." In late 1875 he again returned North to raise funds. According to the 28 October 1875 *Recorder*, audiences spoke "in glowing terms" of his "scholarly discourse and gentlemanly bearing"; late 1875 and early 1876 saw him criss-cross Texas, offering lectures on blacks and education.

His outspoken advocacy for black rights, though, continued to threaten many Texas whites. On 6 June 1876, while in Van Zandt County, Gilliard was again attacked by local whites and then arrested on a trumped-up charge of assault and battery. While in custody, he was shot twice by two men who authorities described only as "unknown" and who were never apprehended. This brutal murder occasioned mass meetings and resolutions not only in Texas but also in Gilliard's old home, California. In asserting that Gilliard was a martyr, some AME ministers claimed that the murderers were members of the Texas White League, an anti-black organization similar to the Ku Klux Klan. An important early figure in the battles for civil rights in both California and Texas, Gilliard deserves further study.

FURTHER READING

Kealing, Hightower T. *History of African Methodism in Texas* (1885).

Shaffer, Ralph E. *California and the Coming of the Fifteenth Amendment* (2005).

Obituary: *Christian Recorder*, 10 Aug. 1876.

ERIC GARDNER

Gilpin, Charles Sidney (20 Nov. 1878–7 May 1930), actor, was born in Richmond, Virginia, the youngest of fourteen children of Peter Gilpin, a steel mill laborer, and Caroline (White) Gilpin, a trained nurse who worked at Richmond City Hospital. Gilpin attended St. Francis Catholic School for Colored Children, where, through the encouragement of his teachers, he performed in school theatricals. He left school at age twelve to apprentice himself in the print shop of the *Richmond Planet* newspaper, but left Richmond in 1896 to pursue a career on stage. While earning a living in a series of odd jobs, Gilpin appeared in minstrel shows, reviews, and vaudeville. He joined the Big Spectacular Log Cabin Company and, after this troupe went bust, he was picked up by the Perkus & Davis Great Southern Minstrel Barnstorming Aggregation. This company, too, went bankrupt and so Gilpin supported himself with jobs as a barber and trainer of prizefighters.

In 1903 Gilpin joined the Carey and Carter Canadian Jubilee Singers and in 1906 he performed with the BERT WILLIAMS and GEORGE WALKER Abyssinia Company, billed as a "baritone soloist." From 1908 to 1911 he appeared with Robert T. Motts' Pekin Theater, one of the first legitimate black theatre companies in Chicago, where in 1907 he was hailed for his performance in the Irvin C. Miller and Aubrey Lyles play *The Mayor of Dixie* (1907). He toured the United States with the Pan-American Octettes from 1911 to 1913 before joining Rogers and Creamer's Old Man's Boy Company. He made his way from Chicago to New York and in 1915 joined one of the earliest black theatrical stock companies in New York, the Anita Bush Players.

When the troupe moved from the Lincoln Theater in Harlem to the Lafayette Theater they became known as the Lafayette Players. The players mounted a new production each week with Gilpin as the featured performer. In 1916 he appeared in whiteface as the character Jacob McCloskey in the Dion Boucicault play *The Octoroon*. Gilpin left the company in a dispute over salary. In 1919 John Drinkwater's play *Abraham Lincoln* premiered at the Cort Theatre in New York to positive reviews from the local press. Gilpin performed as the character William Custis, a former slave turned minister who travels to Washington, D.C., for a conference with President Lincoln.

It was during this period that the thirty-two-year-old Eugene O'Neill enjoyed some success as a playwright with the production of his work by the Provincetown Players of New York. The company had established a precedent by using black actors to play black parts, for example, in the mounting of O'Neill's one-act play about the Harlem underworld, *The Dreamy Kid* (1918). The Provincetown Players knew that Gilpin would be ideal for the part of the leading-man in O'Neill's latest drama on black life.

The Emperor Jones, featuring Gilpin, debuted in November 1920 at the Provincetown Theatre in Greenwich Village. The play dramatizes the story of Brutus Jones, a Pullman car train porter who, through bluff and brutality, installs himself as the titular head, the emperor, of an island inhabited by black citizens. Jones's rise to power, and his slow, painful descent and death are vividly portrayed on stage. In several scenes, Jones remains alone, delivering lengthy passages of haunting and compelling soliloquy. Gilpin's deep resonant voice, flawless diction, commanding presence, and histrionic acting skills mesmerized audiences. Noted the author Edith J. R. Isaacs, "when the play and the player met they became one." Indeed, as the doomed Emperor Jones, Gilpin took the theatre community of New York by storm.

Critics from the black and mainstream press were effusive in their praise of Gilpin. Alexander Woollcott, drama critic for the *New York Times*, called Gilpin's performance "amazing and unforgettable ... superb acting." By December, the production had been moved to the Princess Theatre to accommodate the crowds and ran for more than 200 performances before commencing a two-year, national and international road tour. When the play arrived in the District of Columbia, the *Washington Post* called *The Emperor Jones*, "one of the season's greatest successes," and recognized Gilpin as, "one of the greatest of contemporary actors."

In early 1921 the New York Center of the Drama League of America nominated Gilpin as one of the ten individuals who had done the most for American theater during the year 1920. He was the first black actor to receive the honor and storm clouds quickly arose over whether Gilpin should be allowed to attend the annual dinner at a hotel that barred black guests. Some, including local writers and league members, called for the invitation to be withdrawn.

But the Drama League stood firm in its resolve. The controversy put Gilpin in a difficult position. He did not wish to offend the black community, nor did he want to alienate himself from the white men upon whom he depended for his living. He chose to attend the dinner, arriving promptly at 7 p.m. He ate the meal while sitting at a table with his theatre colleagues, and accepted his award with grace.

Gilpin later commented on the affair, with his words appearing in the *New Times*: "'Against those who do not care to sit in the same dining room with me I have no complaint.' ... He then quoted poet Alexander Pope: 'Real people everywhere, without regard to color or estate, realize that Honor and shame from no condition rise. Act well your part: there all the honor lies.'"

In June 1921 the National Association for the Advancement of Colored People (NAACP) awarded Gilpin the Spingarn Medal, an annual prize established in 1914, given to black citizens of high achievement. In September that same year he was invited by President Warren G. Harding to visit the White House, where the two men talked of ways to uplift the black race.

Gilpin's post-*Emperor Jones* years were full of ups and downs. In March 1924 he appeared as the character Cicero Brown in the black-cast production of the Nan Bagby Stephensen play *Roseanne*. A review appearing in the *New York Times* described his performance as, "a disappointing one." That same year, when the Provincetown Players revived *The Emperor Jones*, the *New York Times* announced that the part of Brutus Jones, the role made famous by Gilpin, would be played by another actor, PAUL ROBESON. Some have contended that O'Neill chose Robeson because he tired of Gilpin's appearances on stage in an inebriated state, or of his tendency to exchange O'Neill's dialogue for his own, or because Gilpin refused to speak the racial epithets written into the play. The truth about Gilpin's interpretation of the play and his relationship with O'Neill is still debated by theatre scholars.

In September 1924 Gilpin appeared in a review with FLORENCE MILLS called *Dixie to Broadway*. In 1925, in the Joe Byron-Totten play *So That's That*, Gilpin was "handicapped by an inadequate role" in an "inept play," noted the *New York Times*. Over the next few years he worked odd jobs, made recordings of dramatic readings, performed monologues on the new medium of radio, appeared in a silent all-black independent film called *Ten Nights in a Barroom* (1926), made public appearances, performed at benefits for needy black actors, and

supported his family which included a common-law wife, a sister, and college-aged son. For Gilpin, his unheralded success as Brutus Jones became a curse. He was hopelessly typecast, with his every appearance compared to *The Emperor Jones*, so much so that he eventually gave in and initiated his own 1926–1927 revival of *The Emperor Jones*, serving as director as well as lead actor.

In 1927 Gilpin announced his return to vaudeville, but by this time he had begun to succumb to the effects of his drinking. Suffering from fragile health, he lost his most important asset: his voice, forcing him to return to odd jobs, including his old post as an elevator operator at a local department store. In 1929 he was scheduled to appear as lead in the play *The Bottom of the Cup*, but the actor DANIEL HAYNES opened the show for Gilpin, who was afflicted with pneumonia.

Charles S. Gilpin died at the age of fifty-one in Eldridge Park, New Jersey. According to the *New York Times*, he left the sum of $25 to his sister, Lelia Brown, and the bulk of his estate to Alma Bynum, his common-law wife and their son Paul. In August of that year, a woman calling herself Lillian Wood Gilpin claimed to be Gilpin's wife and she sued for a portion of his $2,500 estate.

Though his career as a performer spanned some forty years, Charles Gilpin is most often cited solely for his performance in *The Emperor Jones*. Indeed, noted JAMES WELDON JOHNSON, when Gilpin took on the role of Brutus Jones, "another important page in the history of the Negro in the theatre was written." Gilpin, too, must be recognized as one of the best actors of his times.

FURTHER READING

Gill, Glenda. *No Surrender! No Retreat!: African American Pioneer Performers of the 20th Century American Theater* (2003).

Hill, Errol, and James Hatch. *A History of African American Theatre* (2003).

Isaacs, Edith J. R. *The Negro in the American Theatre* (1968).

Johnson, James Weldon. *Black Manhattan* (1968).

Krasner, David. *A Beautiful Pageant: African American Theatre Drama and Performance in the Harlem Renaissance, 1910–1927* (2002)

PAMALA S. DEANE

Gines, Bernadine Alberta Coles (8 Apr. 1926–), certified public accountant (CPA), was born Bernadine Alberta Coles in Charlottesville, Virginia, to Bernard Albert Coles, a dentist, and the former Ruth Wyatt, a teacher. Bernadine and her younger sister enjoyed playing "office" so much that she once asked Santa Claus to bring her paper clips for Christmas. Later her grandfather gave the girls a portable typewriter, further encouraging their interest. Bernadine was the oldest of three daughters (the second of whom, RUTH COLES HARRIS, became the first African American female CPA in Virginia in 1963), and her father encouraged her to follow in his footsteps and become a dentist. But she was not interested, partly because she did not know any female dentists. She also considered becoming a teacher like her mother, but believed she lacked the patience required for that field. As valedictorian of her class at Jefferson High School in Charlottesville, she was awarded a scholarship to attend Virginia State College for Negroes (later Virginia State University), where she chose to major in business.

In the mid-1940s few black colleges had well-developed business programs. Both because there were few opportunities for their graduates and because there were few African Americans trained to teach business disciplines, class offerings were sparse and included typing and shorthand rather than more advanced courses in accounting and finance. Gines's favorite professor, the chair of the business department, George G. Singleton, taught the two accounting courses that Virginia State offered. The advanced-level course was in such low demand that it was only offered every other year. In contrast, during the same period the whites-only University of Virginia offered four courses in accounting, including audit, accounting information systems, and advanced financial reporting courses. Nevertheless Gines excelled at accounting, and Singleton recommended that she pursue graduate education in the field.

By the 1940s most southern states had developed plans to prevent integration in their universities and graduate schools. In 1938 the U.S. Supreme Court had ruled against allowing segregation in the University of Missouri Law School, because no "separate but equal" law school was available to African Americans. Several southern states responded by providing out-of-state scholarships to black students who wanted to attend graduate programs that were not available to nonwhites in the state. When Gines graduated as valedictorian from Virginia State in 1946, Singleton recommended that she avail herself of the tuition program developed by the state of Virginia and attend his alma mater, New York University, for graduate work in

accounting. He also recommended that she pursue the pinnacle of the profession and become a certified public accountant.

Gines followed Singleton's advice, but she was unaware of the obstacles that she would face in trying to enter the accounting profession. She headed to New York city in September 1946, where she thought that career opportunities would be much more open than they were in Virginia. This was particularly important to her because she knew that in order to become a CPA she would have to pass the certified public accountancy examination as well as meet a three-year experience requirement working for a CPA. Upon graduation from her MBA program at NYU in 1947, she sought a position with a CPA firm in New York. But Gines did not receive any interviews with the public accounting firms whose sponsorship she required in order to earn her CPA. She found a position with an African American accountant, but he was not a CPA and she knew that she could not become a CPA while working for him. She then accepted a position as a bookkeeper for the famed black newspaper the *New York Age*, where she was employed from October 1948 to November 1949. There she learned that there was one small black-owned CPA firm in New York, but that it would not hire women. This was not uncommon for accounting firms in the early 1950s; most would not hire women until the 1970s. But it seemed doubly harsh to Gines that she could not find a position because of her race and because of her gender.

At the outset of her job search, Gines lived at the YWCA in Harlem. When she sent out applications for positions in CPA firms, she did not get any responses. She did not fully understand the reason until later. On 18 June 1949 she married Richard Edward Gines, a reporter with the *New York Age* whom she had met while she was in college and he was stationed at a nearby army base. The couple moved to Queens, where Gines continued to submit job applications, and where she suddenly received several offers for interviews. She realized that this was because—as was not the case when she lived in Harlem—her address no longer revealed her race. She visited several firms, but no offers were made. At the first firm at which she interviewed, the prospective employer told her that he could not possibly hire her, but that his wife needed a maid. He asked if Gines could help him find one.

Gines's job search lasted for over two years. Finally, in 1949, she had an interview with two young

Jewish men who owned a small CPA firm, Goodman and Ehrlich. They were surprised to find that their applicant was African American but, after several interviews, offered her a position. Once she started working there she looked at the application files from the others who had applied for her job and found that her educational credentials and passage of the relevant parts of the CPA examination had far surpassed those of her competitors for the position. At the time New York had only recently required that new CPAs be college graduates, and Gines had a master's degree. She did not realize that she was part of a trend among the handful of African Americans who became CPAs in the 1950s. With the exception of those who earned their CPAs by working for one of the three or four black-owned firms in the United States, virtually every one of them worked for a Jewish employer. At the time the major firms rarely hired Jews.

In the early 1950s it was common for white CPAs to claim that, while they themselves were not prejudiced, their client base would never allow an African American to oversee their financial records. But Gines enjoyed working for the firm and found the predominantly Jewish clientele of the small firm to be welcoming of her presence. In this way she earned her CPA, working at the firm five and a half days a week at $45 dollars per week. She was the first black woman in New York to earn her CPA in September 1954, and she soon found that her new qualifications made her more marketable. When her son, Richard, was born in April 1953 she decided that it would be a good time to find a position that required fewer hours, and she soon found an accounting job at a printing company that paid $75 for a five-day week.

Gines's father had long encouraged her to join the civil service, stressing the dependability of such a position. African American professionals in the 1950s found more opportunities in federal and northern state and city government than in the private sector. Additionally, the Gines family's landlady worked for the city, and Gines noticed that she left work at 4:00 p.m. in the summers. Gines applied for, and got, a job as an accountant for the City of New York. She joined the Field Audit unit of the Bureau of Excise Taxes. The department's manager got his first choice of new recruits and always selected from among the new hires who had earned CPAs. Impressed by the talent and hard work Gines had evidenced in the city's six-week training program, he chose her for the group and set her to work auditing sales tax receipts. Over the course of her career in the city, Gines helped computerize its accounting systems and helped the firm to weather the financial crisis of the 1970s.

Gines retired in 1991 and engaged in extensive volunteer work, including as a volunteer tax preparer for the American Association of Retired Persons. She was honored by New York University Stern School's Association of Hispanic and Black Business Students as an outstanding alumnus in 2003. In 2004 she was honored by the New York State Society of Certified Public Accountants on the fiftieth anniversary of her having become the state's first female African-American CPA

FURTHER READING

Some of the information for this article was gathered during interviews with Gines on 11 March 1992.

Hammond, Theresa. *A White-Collar Profession: African American Certified Public Accountants since 1921* (2002).

Tushnet, Mark. *The NAACP's Legal Strategy Against Segregated Education, 1925–1950* (1987).

THERESA A. HAMMOND

Giovanni, Nikki (7 June 1943–), poet, lecturer, and educator, was born Yolande Cornelia Giovanni Jr. in Knoxville, Tennessee, the second of two daughters of Jones "Gus" Giovanni, a teacher and probation officer born in a small town in Alabama, and Yolande Cornelia Watson, a teacher and social worker from Knoxville. Shortly after Giovanni's birth, her family moved to Cincinnati, Ohio, to seek employment better than that available in the segregated South. Giovanni was a quiet and somewhat introverted child, though unafraid to fight anyone who tried to bully her or her older sister, Gary. While Giovanni was still a toddler, her sister began calling her "Nikki," a name she was known by from then on. Although they were poor, her parents instilled in their children pride in who they were and a belief in their ability to become whatever they wanted. As Giovanni later wrote in "Nikki Rosa," "black love is black wealth." From her mother she learned the importance of dreaming, from her father the necessity of taking action to fulfill dreams. A bright, obedient child, Giovanni would frequently forget what she had been sent to the store to buy because her mind was caught up in daydreams. She loved to read and, early on, to write.

Giovanni's early education was at Oak Avenue School, a public school, and St. Simon's, an Episcopal school, both in suburbs of Cincinnati. After completing her first year of high school at Lockland High School, she moved to Knoxville to live with her grandparents, John Brown Watson and Emma Louvenia Watson. Giovanni developed

Nikki Giovanni (left), with Kay Mazzo, a dancer with the New York City Ballet, and fashion designer Betsey Johnson, receiving the first Sun Shower Award in New York City, January 1971. (AP Images.)

a close relationship with her grandmother, the most important influence on her life, who taught her to be generous and to fight against racial injustice and inequality. These values inform her poetry as well as her life.

In 1960, after two years at Austin High School in Knoxville, Giovanni enrolled as an early entrant to Fisk University, her grandfather's alma mater. However, instead of the intellectual excitement she had anticipated, Giovanni found a conservative environment governed by inflexible rules. She immediately clashed with the dean of students and by the end of her first semester had been expelled. For the next few years, she lived with her parents in Cincinnati. Recognizing the importance of finishing her undergraduate degree, and determined to do so at Fisk, she sought and gained readmittance. Both Giovanni and the college had changed by 1964, and her experience this time was fruitful.

She majored in history, revived the campus chapter of SNCC (Student Nonviolent Coordinating Committee), edited the school's literary magazine, enrolled in the writing workshops offered by writer-in-residence JOHN OLIVER KILLENS, and immersed herself in the rhetoric and ideas of the Black Power movement and the emergent Black Arts Movement. When she graduated from Fisk in January 1967, she had already started to publish small pieces, both prose and verse, in *Negro Digest*.

The death of her grandmother in March 1967 was a tremendous blow, but Giovanni channeled her grief into her writing, producing a substantial body of poems. After a short and unsuccessful stint at the University of Pennsylvania's School of Social Work, she moved to New York City in the summer of 1968. She borrowed money to privately print her first volume of poems, *Black Feeling Black Talk*. By the end of 1968, with money generated by the book's sales, she was able to self-publish her second volume, *Black Judgement*, which was distributed by Broadside Press. When the master of fine arts program at Columbia University, in which she had enrolled, refused to accept these volumes as fulfillment of its writing requirements, she abandoned the program.

Giovanni's overnight success resulted from many factors. Her poems touched responsive chords in the thousands of people she read them to, whether chords of anger from "The Great Pax Whitie," chords of joy from "Beautiful Black Men," or chords of pride from "Ego Tripping." The oral quality of Giovanni's poetry, one of its distinctive features, gave it an appeal to people who did not typically like poetry, and many rap artists recognize her as the mother of rap music. In addition to the quality of her poetry, Giovanni's charisma and charm, together with her quick wit and waiflike appearance, drew people to her. For the next several years she appeared regularly on the black entertainment and talk show *Soul!* on WNET television, giving her a national audience rarely available to poets. When she became a single mother with the birth of her son, Thomas, in 1969, she seemed to embody women's liberation. People were shocked but also enamored.

Giovanni published her third volume of poetry, *Re: Creation*, with Broadside Press in 1970. That same year, she signed a contract with William Morrow, which published *Black Feeling Black Talk/Black Judgement* as one volume. Recognizing the publishing obstacles women face, she edited an anthology of poems by black women, *Night Comes Softly*. The following year, Bobbs-Merrill published her autobiography, *Gemini: An Extended Autobiographical Statement on My First Twenty-five Years of Being a Black Poet*, which was nominated for a National Book Award. She also published a volume of poems for children, *Spin a Soft Black Song* (1971).

In 1971 Giovanni extended her appeal by releasing a recording of her poetry read with gospel music performed by the New York Community Choir. *Truth Is on Its Way* was introduced at a concert she performed with the choir at Canaan Baptist Church in Harlem before a crowd of 1,500. Despite the audience's enthusiastic reception, no one could have predicted the success of this album; within six months, *Truth* sold more than one hundred thousand copies and was played by radio stations across the country. More than any other single factor, *Truth* made Giovanni's poems almost as familiar to people as the hit songs they heard on the radio. Decades after the album's release, many

people know the words to her poems, even though they may never have seen them in print.

In December 1971 Giovanni traveled to London to videotape a conversation with the writer JAMES BALDWIN for *Soul!* The Baldwin sessions aired on the program in December 1971 and were subsequently transcribed and made into the book *A Dialogue: James Baldwin and Nikki Giovanni* (1973). She began accumulating awards and honors, including an honorary doctorate from Wilberforce University. Giovanni maintained a busy lecture schedule, both to promote her poetry and to support herself and her son. Despite the sometimes frantic pace of her life, she continued to write, and in 1972 published *My House*, named one of the best books of 1973 by the American Library Association. *My House* turns away from the militant rhetoric characteristic of some of her early poems and explores themes related to language and female identity.

During the period 1972–1978, Giovanni engaged in a variety of activities. She became a consultant and regular contributor to the black news magazine *Encore*, and she gave public readings to large audiences throughout the country, including a sold-out performance at New York City's Philharmonic Hall. In addition, she published three volumes of poetry and a dialogue with the poet MARGARET WALKER, and released several more spoken-word albums. She continued to travel extensively, taking on an African lecture tour for the U.S. Information Agency.

Her father's stroke and subsequent diagnosis of cancer in 1978 brought Giovanni and her son back to Cincinnati, where she became the financial and emotional mainstay of the family. Her family responsibilities essentially ended what can be regarded as the first stage of her writing career. She had little time to write, and between 1978 and 1988 she published only three books, although one them was the remarkable *Those Who Ride the Night Winds* (1983), in which she began to develop the poetic form characteristic of her later volumes.

In 1987 Giovanni accepted a faculty position at Virginia Tech in Blacksburg. Although she had held brief teaching appointments earlier in her career, the tenured position at Virginia Tech, which eventually evolved into a University Distinguished Professorship, was her first experience of stable employment. Once she settled into the position, Giovanni came to enjoy teaching, especially the time it gave her to think and to write. She published several new books, including *Racism 101* (1994), a book popular with college students.

Just as she had started to establish new directions for her career, however, Giovanni was diagnosed with lung cancer, and in January 1995 doctors told her she had about six months to live. Always a fighter, she traveled to Cincinnati for a second opinion, and remained to have successful surgery. Miraculously, the cancer did not spread.

Giovanni's encounter with cancer reenergized and refocused her imagination, and she entered another period of high productivity, publishing seven books between 1996 and 2002. Of these, three—*Love Poems* (1997), *Blues: For All the Changes* (1999), and *Quilting the Black-eyed Pea* (2002)—won NAACP Image awards, the awards of which she was proudest. Giovanni continued her productive streak with the publication of *The Collected Poetry* (2003), *Acolytes* (2007), and a children's book about the life of ROSA PARKS, *Rosa* (2005). Her work was collected together for the first time in the volume, *The Prosaic Soul of Nikki Giovanni* (2003).

Giovanni's powerful poetical and oratorical skills were called on after the tragic massacre at Virginia Tech on 16 April 2007, where thirty-two students were murdered by Cho Sueng-Hui, who subsequently committed suicide. She had taught Cho in a creative writing class and alerted senior college officials to his disturbing compositions. During the official memorial service Giovanni addressed the crowd with a "chant poem," which asserted: "We are the Hokies. We will prevail. We will prevail. We will prevail. We are Virginia Tech."

Today, as much as when she started her career, Giovanni is a "poet of the people," drawing record audiences to her lectures and readings. These are matched by dozens of honors and awards, including twenty-two honorary doctorates. She continues to speak the truth as she sees it and to celebrate black people and black culture.

FURTHER READING

Nikki Giovanni's papers are housed in the Special Collections division of the Mugar Memorial Library at Boston University.

Giovanni, Nikki. *The Collected Poetry of Nikki Giovanni: 1968-1998* (2003).

Giovanni, Nikki. *Gemini: An Extended Autobiographical Statement on My First Twenty-five Years of Being a Black Poet* (1971).

Giovanni, Nikki. "In Sympathy with Another Motherless Child (One View of the Profession of Writing)," in *Sacred Cows ... and Other Edibles* (1988).

Fowler, Virginia C. *Nikki Giovanni* (1992).

Giddings, Paula. "Taking a Chance on Feeling," in *Black Women Writers (1950–1980)*, ed. Mari Evans (1983).

VIRGINIA C. FOWLER

Girandy, Alphonse (21 Jan. 1868–3 Apr. 1941), seaman in the U.S. Navy and Medal of Honor recipient, was born on the island of Guadeloupe, a French possession in the Caribbean located in the Leeward Island chain. Like many born in Guadeloupe, Girandy had direct ties to Africa; his father Alfred was from the French colony of Algeria in North Africa, whose native language was Arabic, while his mother was a native of Reunion, a French possession in the Indian Ocean. Prior to coming to the United States in 1896, Girandy is thought to have spent some of his early adult years in Spain, and though details are lacking, he seems to have been well traveled prior to arriving in America, possibly plying the trade of a sailor. On 13 June 1896 Girandy arrived in New York from Santiago, Cuba, aboard the steamship *Niagara*. He was married to a woman named Maggie, and their son Frank Girandy was born later in 1896.

Alphonse Girandy joined the U.S. Navy in 1898, likely as a result of the Spanish-American War, but nothing specific is known of his early naval career and individual achievements. By 1901 he was serving in the Philippine Islands aboard the gunboat U.S.S. *Petrel*, which arrived there in April 1898 as part of Admiral George Dewey's fleet during the campaign against the Spanish. The men of the *Petrel* subsequently took part in the Battle of Manila Bay, afterward heading to the navy yard at Cavite to force the surrender of the Spanish and to destroy any remaining enemy ships. The *Petrel* and its crew, with Alphonse Girandy aboard, continued to serve for the next two years during military operations in the Philippines. On the early morning of 31 March 1901 the ship was off Cavite when an accidental fire broke out below decks in the sail room, located next to the ship's ammunition magazine. Led by their captain, LCDR Jesse Roper, the crew quickly sprang into action to save their ship. While one group of men was sent below to remove the ammunition to prevent its detonation, Roper led a team below to fight the fire in the sail room. While the flames of the fire were slight, the compartment was filled with thick black smoke and toxic fumes, making conditions difficult. These conditions were compounded by the fact that the fire had to be fought in the dark, as the ship's electric generator had been turned off earlier that morning. As the fumes worsened, men below had great difficulty breathing and were soon overcome. Captain Roper quickly ordered everyone out of the sail room, but one man, Seaman Patrick Toner was in distress and unable to make it out. Led by Roper, three men, Cadet Lewis, Gunner's Mate Flaherty, and Storekeeper Kessler, went below to rescue Toner, but were themselves overcome and in need of rescue. Knowing his shipmates were in distress, Seaman Alphonse Girandy went into action and made his way below with a line tied around his waist. "the moment he got his feet below deck, and by the time he was waist deep below, he was yelling fiendishly and clawing the air desperately like a demon. Yet he went on to his duty, and had the grit, even in his condition, to pass up Kessler and Flaherty, who had consciousness enough left to grab him and hold on while he helped them up the ladder. Finally, in his searching around the ladder's foot, he found Toner ... and although losing consciousness himself, the black hero bravely held on to his shipmate's body until the men above, pulling hard on the bow-line, had hauled them within reach and out on deck" (Waters, p. 126). The other men still left below, Cadet Lewis and Captain Roper, were subsequently brought from below by Marine Private Louis Thiess and Seaman Thomas Cahey; while Roper was dead, having succumbed to the fumes, Lewis survived. Within hours, the fire aboard *Petrel* was fully extinguished and the ship saved. For their heroic actions in rescuing their fellow crewmen, Girandy, Thiess, and Cahey were subsequently awarded the Medal of Honor.

Medal of Honor recipient Alphonse Girandy is an important figure for several reasons; not only is he the last African American sailor to have received this most important of U.S. military decorations, but he is also representative of a largely forgotten group, men like JOSEPH NOIL and ROBERT SWEENEY, who earned the medal for heroic deeds that did not occur in combat circumstances. The Medal of Honor continued to be awarded in noncombat situations until 1916, when the requirements changed and were narrowed to include only feats of heroism during wartime. While Alphonse Girandy and others like him earned their award in noncombat situations, it is important to remember that they acted without hesitation and regard for their own safety to help a shipmate in extremis, thus going above and beyond in upholding the finest traditions of service in the U.S. armed forces.

Following his service in the navy, Alphonse Girandy lived the rest of his life in Philadelphia, becoming a naturalized citizen on 4 February 1905. He was working in and around the city as a laborer by 1910 and in 1917, when he registered for the draft in World War I, was working for the Concrete Steel Company in nearby Camden, New Jersey. While Girandy registered for the draft, it is unknown if he actually served during the war; this seems unlikely due to his age. By 1920 he worked at the Philadelphia Navy Yard, and his occupation was later listed as that of a janitor. Early on, Girandy seems to have divorced his first wife, Maggie, but by 1930 had a new wife, Rose. Alphonse Girandy died on 3 April 1941 and was buried in the Philadelphia National Cemetery in grave number N-66.

FURTHER READING

Hanna, Charles W. *African American Recipients of the Medal of Honor: A Biographical Dictionary, Civil War through Vietnam War* (2010).

Waters, Theodore. "American Heroes: Lieutenant-Commander Roper," *The New England Magazine*, Sept. 1901.

GLENN ALLEN KNOBLOCK

Gladwell, Malcolm (3 Sept. 1963–), *New Yorker* columnist and author of popular nonfiction, was born in Fareham, England, the youngest of three sons born to Graham M. L. Gladwell, a British mathematician, and Joyce (Nation) Gladwell, a Jamaican-born family therapist. His parents met while attending university in England in the 1950s; during that time interracial couples were not common, and Joyce Gladwell later wrote of the couple's struggle for acceptance, as well as of her own experiences growing up a "brown face" in Jamaica, in her book *Brown Face, Big Master*, which was published in 1969. That same year the Gladwell family relocated to Elmira, Canada, which is just outside Toronto, after Graham Gladwell—who has authored numerous mathematical texts—accepted a teaching position at the University of Waterloo.

In "Black Like Them," a 1996 article written for the *New Yorker*, Gladwell described Elmira as a close-knit, sleepy town in which he was rarely confronted with racial intolerance; he has attributed the generally progressive atmosphere to the influence of the town's large Mennonite population. Raised in a Presbyterian family that did not own a television, he began reading the Bible at the age of six. He was fond of cars, and at the age of twelve, after purchasing his first typewriter, he began writing letters to automotive companies, requesting photographs of the expensive models that he liked. The letters were so well written that on one occasion, much to his mother's surprise, a car salesman knocked on their front door asking to speak with "Mr. Gladwell," apparently unaware that his potential customer was a twelve-year-old boy. In high school Gladwell published his own zine, *Ad Hominen: A Journal of Slander and Critical Opinion*, and won a short-story contest for a piece in which he imagined himself conducting an interview with God.

After receiving his BA in History in 1984 from the University of Toronto's Trinity College, Gladwell applied for jobs at the *Toronto Star* and the *Globe and Mail* and in the advertising industry but was roundly rejected. He then moved to Bloomington, Indiana, where he interned briefly at the *American Spectator* before being fired—which he has speculated was because of his tendency to oversleep. In 1987 he began working for the *Washington Post* as a business reporter, and in 1990 he switched to the health beat, writing many articles on the burgeoning HIV/AIDS crisis. Three years later he was promoted to chief of the newspaper's New York bureau.

While working for the *Washington Post* Gladwell met the reporter David Remnick, who in 1998 was named the editor in chief of the *New Yorker*. Shortly after joining the *New Yorker* as a staff writer in 1992, Remnick recommended his former coworker to then editor in chief Tina Brown, and Gladwell soon began writing freelance articles for the "Comment" and "Talk of the Town" columns. In 1996 he was hired as staff writer. Early on he made a positive impression on the editors by taking unconventional approaches to his articles. For example, in "Conquering the Coma" he intertwined the sensational story of a woman who was attacked by a deranged assailant in New York City's Central Park with an examination of how changing medical protocol had helped a neurosurgeon save her life.

The typical Gladwell piece begins with the micro—a story about a particular person or event—and then once the reader is involved the writer addresses the macro—some organizing principle or theory that not only addresses the story that he has already introduced but also addresses larger patterns in society. For example, in "Troublemakers" he used the story of a pit bull that attacked a Canadian child—causing the Ontario legislature to ban ownership of the breed altogether—as an entrée into a critique of racial profiling. Gladwell, who in his youth would accompany his father to university libraries, sees himself as an intermediary between academia and the popular media; he has spent countless hours wandering the stacks of New York University's library, browsing academic journals in search of brilliant ideas that might not otherwise reach general audiences.

Gladwell's work not only earned the respect of his editors but also garnered him a large fan base among *New Yorker* readers and caught the attention of media executives. Shortly after Gladwell published "The Coolhunt," a 1997 article about a fashion scout for the sneaker manufacturer Reebok, Danny DeVito's production company, Jersey Films, a division of Universal Studios, optioned it and set a screenwriter to work on developing it for the big screen. "The Dead Zone," Gladwell's 1999 article about the great flu pandemic of 1918 and the possibility of another such outbreak, was turned into a television movie, the thriller *Runaway Virus* (2002) for ABC.

Gladwell was also offered an unusually large advance—$1.5 million—to write a book based on his 1996 article "The Tipping Point," in which he applied the principles of epidemiology (the study of disease) to explain the falling crime rate in New York City. When epidemiologists refer to a "tipping point," they are describing the moment an outbreak of a disease reaches critical mass and becomes a full-blown epidemic; in his magazine article Gladwell discussed the increasingly popular notion among social scientists that "social problems behave like infectious agents," pointing out that the addition of a few more officers to a Brooklyn precinct had resulted in a disproportionate drop in crime.

"Epidemics are a function of the people who transmit the infectious agents, the infectious agent itself, and the environment in which the infectious agent is operating," Gladwell wrote in the introduction to his book *The Tipping Point: How Little Things Can Make a Big Difference*, which was published in 2002. "And when an epidemic tips, when it is jolted out of equilibrium, it tips because something has happened, some change occurred in one (or two or three) of those areas." The three areas, or determinants, that Gladwell argued are necessary for the successful spread of social epidemics are "The Law of the Few," which dictates that the spread of the epidemic is dependent on the involvement of people with a rare set of social gifts; "The Stickiness Factor," which is the ability of the audience to absorb the message; and "The Power of Context," which refers to the environment that fosters an epidemic's effects.

In the book Gladwell also posited that even in this age of electronic communication, word of mouth was still the most important factor in the spread of social epidemics. Indeed, word of mouth about Gladwell's book spread like wildfire, and the hardback edition was on the *New York Times* best-seller list for twenty-eight weeks. For a time the term "tipping point" became ubiquitous in the media, and the business community eagerly embraced Gladwell's book, viewing the author as a new business guru of sorts. The high-profile companies Ketchum (a public relations agency) and Simmons Market Research began developing databases that attempted to identify the sort of people described in Gladwell's "The Law of the Few."

Gladwell was inspired to write his second book after changing his hairstyle. A light-skinned man who wore his hair closely cropped for most of his life, Gladwell had found—occasionally to the chagrin of acquaintances who in unguarded moments made bigoted remarks about the Jamaican community—that most people were unaware of his Afro-Caribbean roots. In his thirties, when he began growing his hair out, Afro style, he was surprised at how people's attitudes toward him changed. Most notably, one day when he was walking along Fourteenth Street in New York City, three police officers confronted him, thinking that he was the suspect in a rape case. After twenty minutes of questioning, and after Gladwell pointed out that he looked nothing like the man in the police sketch, the officers left him alone. But it was at that moment that Gladwell realized how important appearances can be; he soon set to work on *Blink: The Power of Thinking without Thinking* (2004), which examined rapid cognition—the snap judgments that people make within the first few seconds of their introduction to a new person or situation. The book was on the *New York Times* best-seller list for more than a year.

After the phenomenal success of his two books, Gladwell began to receive offers in the neighborhood of forty thousand dollars for lecture appearances. In February 2006 he launched a blog on his Web site, http://www.gladwell.com, which also offers an archive of all of his *New Yorker* articles. The singular approach that he has taken in these articles has ensconced him in the long tradition of such great prose stylists as E. B. White and A. J. Liebling, who also established their names at what is considered by many to be America's premier literary magazine. In 2008 Gladwell published *Outliers: The Story of Success*, which immediately went to the top of the *New York Times* best-selling list and remained there for three months. His next book, *What the Dog Saw: And Other Adventures* (2009), was a collection of his essays from the *New Yorker*.

FURTHER READING

Gladwell, Malcolm. "Black like Them," *New Yorker* (29 Apr. 1996).

Gladwell, Malcolm. "Lost in the Middle," *Washington Post*, 17 May 1998.

Kahn, Joseph P. "Malcolm in the Milieu: New Yorker Scribe Draws Accolades for His Quirky Thinking," *Boston Globe*, 4 May 2000.

Stoffman, Judy. "Journalist a Treat to Read," *Toronto Star*, 14 June 1999.

JENNIFER CURRY

Glass, Charlie (187?–1937), cowboy, was apparently born in the Indian Territory (later Oklahoma). Little is known of his parents or early life. According to "The Ballad of Charlie Glass," by William Leslie Clark, Glass was "one quarter Cherokee" (Wyman and Hart). Legend has it that he moved to western Colorado after shooting the man who had killed his father. What is known to be factual is that by 1909 Glass was working as a cowboy for the S-Cross Ranch in western Colorado.

Glass was, by reputation, a colorful character. He was known for going to town in fancy silk shirts and enjoying the saloons, card games, and brothels of the "Barbary Coast," the red-light district of Grand Junction, Colorado. By 1917 he had found employment with Oscar L. Turner, a cattleman with large ranch holdings in the counties of Mesa, Garfield, and Rio Blanca in western Colorado and Grand and Uintah counties across the state line in Utah. He was reputedly well respected by neighboring ranchers and cattlemen, cowboy and owner alike. African American cowboys were not uncommon on the Colorado range, but Glass was exceptional in being advanced to foreman on Turner's ranch.

Except for one fateful incident, Glass might have faded, like most cowboys, into obscurity. The Colorado-Utah border was still largely open range in the early 1900s, although agreements were reached by ranchers concerning who would graze where. Ranchers usually "homesteaded" the water resources on the arid pasturage and enjoined their cowboys to do the same; the cowboys then assigned their rights to the ranch owner. Glass was no exception; he established a homestead under the Homestead Act and later surrendered his property rights to Turner.

Range wars between cattle and sheep ranchers were very much a part of this period in Colorado history, and it was a conflict over grazing rights that gave Glass his claim to fame. According to later court testimony, sheepmen routinely "trespassed" their stock onto traditional cattle ranges near the Colorado-Utah border. This led to confrontation, and during one such incident Glass shot and killed a trespassing Basque sheepherder named Felix Jesui.

The trial of Glass for this killing provides the little historical evidence of his existence. The Moab, Utah, courthouse's records of the trial were mysteriously lost, but the *Moab Times-Independent* carried a close account. Glass never denied shooting Jesui, but he claimed it was only in self-defense. Local antisheep sentiments made Glass a folk hero for taking a "might-makes-right" stand against what the ranchers saw as a violation of grazing rights.

Testimony transcribed into the newspaper account of the court proceedings revealed several facts about the case. Felix Jesui was with sheep near the Turner ranch on the morning of 23 February 1921. He was in possession of a rifle and a .25-caliber automatic pistol. Witnesses heard four shots. Shortly after the gunfire Glass rode into the Turner ranch headquarters and asked Oscar Turner and Alvee Field, a sheepman, to come out to the scene of the shooting and witness the body and the guns.

What happened during the shooting will never be known for sure. Field testified that he saw a rifle in Jesui's possession but no other gun. The county coroner testified that three .32-caliber shells, from Glass's automatic pistol, were found "some twenty-five feet from the body." The sheriff, J. B. Skewes, testified that he found the rifle and the .25-caliber automatic on Jesui's body and that "he also found one .25-caliber shell about fifteen feet from the body" (*Times-Independent*, 24 Nov. 1921), which, with the three shots fired by Glass, would account for the four shots heard by Field and Turner.

Testifying on his own behalf, Glass said that he had confronted Jesui about trespassing on the Turner range and that the Basque sheepherder was "armed with two guns, a rifle and a pistol, and was very defiant" (*Times-Independent*, 1 Dec. 1921). He said he decided that, rather than argue with Jesui, he would take up the matter with the herder's boss, and he turned toward his horse to leave. According to Glass, as he reached his horse, Jesui fired his rifle, and by the time Glass was able to draw his pistol Jesui had fired his own pistol twice more. Glass then shot the herder in self-defense, returned to the Turner ranch, and surrendered to the sheriff upon his arrival.

The trial lasted more than a week, but the jury's deliberation took less than two hours. A verdict of acquittal seemed reasonable to the entire community, who saw the killing as an appropriate solution for trespassing sheepmen. Glass returned to his job as Turner's foreman and might have faded again into the sunset except for his mysterious death.

Sixteen years after the killing of Felix Jesui, Glass was involved in a poker game in the Denver and Rio Grande Western Railroad town of Thompson, Utah. Some of the players suggested that the group travel to nearby Cisco and join in a high-stakes poker game there. Within a couple of hours two Basque sheepherders, Andre Sartan and Joe Savorna, were involved in a suspicious car accident in which Glass was killed.

The two sheepherders insisted that they had been drunk and rolled a pickup truck, killing Glass. Many local cattlemen were sure that Sartan and Savorna, cousins of Jesui, staged the accident in order to kill the man who had shot their cousin sixteen years earlier. Even in the 1960s area residents who had known Glass were reluctant to speak to the historians Walker Wyman and John Hart, who were writing a short history of Glass.

Whether Glass killed Jesui in self-defense or murdered him to scare sheepmen off the open range will never be known. Nor will it ever be discovered whether Jesui's cousins killed Glass in retribution. What is known is that Glass was a rarity: an African American foreman on a cattle ranch, responsible for giving orders to Anglo as well as African American and Hispanic cowboys. Although much of his life remains the subject of speculation and legend, it is significant that he is recalled at all—very few of the legendary cowboys are remembered by name, and even fewer of those were of African American heritage. According to a newspaper tribute at Glass's death, "cattlemen, former employees and acquaintances of Glass all agree that fiction could produce no more colorful nor picturesque character than Glass" (*Grand Junction Sentinel*, 24 Feb. 1937).

FURTHER READING

Durham, Philip, and Everett L. Jones. *The Adventures of the Negro Cowboys* (1966).

Durham, Philip, and Everett L. Jones. *The Negro Cowboys* (1965).

Wyman, Walker D., and John D. Hart. *The Legend of Charlie Glass, Negro Cowboy on the Colorado-Utah Range* (1970).

Obituary: *Grand Junction Sentinel*, 24 Feb. 1937.

This entry is taken from the *American National Biography* and is published here with the permission of the American Council of Learned Societies.

J. C. MUTCHLER

Glass, Dick (fl. 1878–June 1885), black Creek partisan and whiskey runner, came to prominence amid the interracial and intertribal conflicts in the Indian Territory after the Civil War. As the accused killer of the seventeen-year-old Cherokee Billy Cobb, he spent his last five years with bounties on his head, making a living stealing horses and selling liquor. During his lifetime, the *Muskogee Indian Journal* compared him to Jesse James; the historian Kenneth Porter likened him to Robin Hood. Little is known of Glass's personal history. One source describes him as "much more Indian than Negro." Another contemporary account refers to him as "a full-blooded Negro" (*Arkansas City Traveler*), which seems to have been how he understood himself. After his death, he was described physically as having "a bad scar across the side of his neck, running from his ear down to his chest, caused by a burn of some kind, over which the skin had grown red instead of black … [and] a scar on one hand, made by a bullet which had passed through it when he was in one of his shooting scrapes" (Burton, 26).

By 1878 hostility between black Creeks and mixed-blood Cherokee aristocrats, who had supported slavery and the Confederacy, erupted into undeclared warfare along the Creek-Cherokee border. Cherokee warriors attacked black Creek lighthorsemen, or mounted police, and fired into black homes. Black Creeks, in turn, took Cherokee livestock. Black Creek spokesmen wrote to Chief Samuel Checote for assistance on 23 February 1880, stating that Cherokees had recently killed four and wounded six of their people. The locus of black resistance was Marshalltown, in the "Point" between the Arkansas and the Verdigris rivers, said to be a haven for horse and cattle thieves led by Dick Glass.

On the night of 26 July 1880, Cherokees posing as U.S. deputy marshals seized two alleged horse thieves, Monday Roberts and Robert Jones, took them out of Marshalltown, and lynched them. The next day, Glass led a search party, as he later wrote, "to bury the dead and investigate the cause" (Burton, 20). While seeking Monday Roberts's body, the party encountered two young men from prominent Cherokee families, Billy Cobb and Alex Cowan. In the gunfight that followed, Alex Cowan and Billy Cobb were both shot; Cobb died. Glass had his horse killed under him. Knocked unconscious by a bullet through the cheekbone, he was reported dead.

The mixed-blood Cherokees were enraged, and more than a hundred decamped from Fort Gibson, vowing to destroy Marshalltown. Dennis W. Bushyhead, the chief of the Cherokees, managed to restrain them by placing large bounties on Glass and his men. Bounty hunters tracked down four of the fugitives. Two of them, Jim Samson and Ben Roberts, were killed "while resisting arrest." Two others, Daniel Luckey and Douglass Murrell, were kidnapped and turned over for trial by the Cherokees. The trials resulted in death sentences for both men. On the personal intervention of Samuel Checote, the Creek chief, and since the trials had been irregular, Bushyhead pardoned Luckey and gave Murrell an "indefinite respite." The two principal suspects in the lynchings of Monday Roberts and Robert Jones, for their part, were tried and acquitted in Cherokee court.

Glass evaded capture. Avoiding Marshalltown and the Cherokee country, he took up a lucrative trade route, exchanging stolen horses for whiskey in Denison, Texas, liquor that commanded a high price in the dry Indian Territory. In June 1882 Creek lighthorsemen attacked Glass, Ben Doaker, and Douglass Murrell, who were driving a herd of stolen horses near Okmulgee. Doaker was killed, and Glass was hurt so badly that he was reported killed for the second time. In September of the same year, a sheriff put Glass in jail in Winfield, Kansas, then started with his prisoner on the way to claim the $600 Cherokee reward. Glass escaped en route; his friends may have paid more than the Cherokees' price. The story that appeared in the *Winfield Courier* had Glass filing down his shackles with the tongue of a jaw harp, then running off "amid a shower of bullets."

At the end of 1882, Glass led a column of black Creeks in the "Green Peach War," a struggle between full-blood and mixed-blood Creeks. The black Creeks sided with Isparecher, the conservative full-blood leader, against Samuel Checote. The conflict subsided by the summer of 1883.

Glass disappeared from view for over a year. The *Muskogee Indian Journal* reported on 9 April 1885 that the rewards on Glass had come to total upward of $1,000. The fugitive, however, had written the newspaper to the effect that "he wished to become a law-abiding citizen if the officers would not molest him." After the publication of Glass's letter, the *Indian Journal* continued, two Texas sheriffs had found him in the Arbuckle Mountains, near the Texas border, where they shot him off his horse. For the third and last time, Glass was taken for dead. Yet he had worn a bulletproof breastplate; as the officers approached his prone body, he shot them both. They survived long enough to detail his pioneering body armor before dying.

On 24 April 1885 Glass wrote another letter, this time to J. C. Atkins, the commissioner of Indian affairs, in Washington. In his final text, preserved in the National Archives, he recounted the shootout with Billy Cobb. Cobb "swore he would kill every black … of us," and fired the first shot, killing Glass's horse (Burton, 20). Alex Cowan had testified that Glass's men fired the first shot. The horse, furthermore, had died a half mile into Creek territory, and Glass argued that the Creeks should have jurisdiction over the case. (The Cherokees had claimed that the horse had run across the border into the Creek Nation after being shot.) Recounting the circumstances of his men's deaths at the hands of bounty hunters, Glass declared himself "ready to be tried [by any court] except in the Cherokee Nation, there it would be death, I know" (Burton, 21).

To Atkins, he concluded, "I ask you as a man who has borne and suffered much, in the cause of humanity and for the sake of my family to make some effort in my behalf, that I may not be for the sake of a reward, put up by private parties in the Cherokee authorities hands, killed as were my companions" (Burton, 21). Less than two months later, on 15 June 1885, the *Cheyenne Transporter* (of Darlington, Indian Territory) ran the front page story that Glass had been shot and killed by Sam Sixkiller, a member of the Indian Police, and his posse. Among the effects of the outlaw Glass were a pearl-handled revolver and two ivory-handled pistols.

FURTHER READING

Arkansas City Traveler, 5 Dec. 1883, available online at http://www.ausbcomp.com/~bbott/cowley/Oldnews/Papers/Trav61.htm.

Burton, Arthur T. *Black, Red, and Deadly: Black and Indian Gunfighters of the Indian Territory, 1870–1907* (1991).

Debo, Angie. *The Road to Disappearance: A History of the Creek Indians* (1987).

Katz, William Loren. *Black Indians: A Hidden Heritage* (1986).

Porter, Kenneth Wiggins. "Glass, Dick," in *Dictionary of American Negro Biography*, eds. Rayford W. Logan and Michael R. Winston (1982).

Teall, Kaye M., ed. *Black History in Oklahoma: A Resource Book* (1971).

BENJAMIN LETZLER

Glave, Thomas (1964–), writer, gay activist, and educator, developed a fascination with language early in life. Born in the Bronx, New York, Glave grew up both there and in Kingston, Jamaica, in neighborhoods populated with storytellers. These people, Glave recalled in a 2000 article in the *Village Voice*, could "go from irony to outrage to feigned surprise to deep drama with all of these gesticulations, intonations, and coded references in the span of just one sentence."

From an early age Glave worked to capture this vibrant language in his own writing. He attended private schools in New York and began sending his stories to magazines while still in high school. He graduated from Bowdoin College with honors in 1993, and his writing first gained attention when he was in the MFA program at Brown University. In 1997 his story "The Final Inning" won an O. Henry Prize, making Glave only the second black gay writer to receive the honor (JAMES BALDWIN was the first). Upon graduating from Brown the following year, Glave spent a year in Jamaica as a Fulbright scholar, studying Caribbean literature and culture and Jamaican historiography. While there he also helped found the Jamaica Forum of Lesbians, All-Sexuals, and Gays (J-FLAG).

Glave's writing explores the connections—and clashes—among race, sexuality, and identity. In 2000 shortly before the publication of his debut story collection, *Whose Song? and Other Stories*, the *Village Voice Literary Supplement* deemed him one of their "Writers on the Verge." Kera Bolonik argues that Glave "fearlessly delves into the interior worlds of African American and Caribbean men whose secret desires and personal histories threaten the connection to both their families and communities." The collection garnered critical acclaim for its jarring mix of deeply lyrical prose and shockingly graphic violence, a pairing that earned Glave comparisons to TONI MORRISON in her early work.

"The Final Inning," Glave's prizewinning story that appears in *Whose Song?*, captures the cacophony among mourners at the funeral of a proud, openly gay black man named Duane. While his family tries to deny his identity, his gay friends linger in the back rows of the service, disgusted. The story demonstrates Glave's willingness to bend style and structure to fit the emotional demands of his work. At its climax the story splits into two columns, one representing Duane's family and the other the voice of the friend who cared for Duane before he died. "And no you won't make me SHUT UP," rages Duane's friend James, "cause I'm PROUD to be here today as a GAY friend of DUANE'S and a *(shouting over the rage)* HUMAN BEING GODDAMNIT just like DUANE WAS TOO and now why won't you SAY IT he died of AIDS of AIDS." Across the page Duane's family responds, "Jesus Jesus Jesus! No my son ain't no homosexual no my cousin ain't no faggot no my nephew didn't have no damn AIDS the devil's disease don't you say that in this church and O you you filthy:—"

In a review of *Whose Song?* in *Gay & Lesbian Review Worldwide* Amy Sickels explains that "Glave interrupts sentences with parentheses, colons, semicolons, and ellipses, merging past with present and mapping the ripples of desire and oppression." Later she asserts, "Unlike many current experimental writers, Glave's work is not inaccessible or aloof, but creates an intimate bridge with the reader." Glave's quiet, poetic voice and sharp use of images keeps readers from turning away from even the most troubling scenes—the young man who must spurn his male lover in order to marry the woman his father wants him to, the white woman who believes her desire for a black man keeps her from being racist, and the rape of a lesbian teenager by three neighborhood boys.

Glave became assistant professor of English at Binghamton University, State University of New York, where he taught creative writing, literature, and Africana studies. He previously taught at Brown University, Cleveland State University, Naropa University, and the University of Virginia, as well as at various creative writing conferences. His awards include a James Michener Scholarship from the Caribbean Writers' Institute at the University of Miami, a travel grant from the National Endowment for the Arts, a fiction fellowship from the Fine Arts Center in Provincetown, Massachusetts, and a fiction fellowship from the New York Foundation for the Arts. He was a frequent contributor of both fiction and nonfiction to *Callaloo*, and his work has also appeared in the *Kenyon Review*, the *Massachusetts Review*, *Children of the Night: The Best Short Stories by Black Writers, 1967 to the Present*, edited by Gloria Naylor (1995), *Best American Gay Fiction*, and other publications. Glave's first collection of nonfiction, *Words to Our Now: Imagination and Dissent*, was published by the University of Minnesota Press in fall of 2005.

FURTHER READING

Glave, Thomas. *Whose Song? and Other Stories* (2000).

Bolonik, Kera. "Writers on the Verge," *Village Voice Literary Supplement* (June 2000).

Jarrett, Gene. "'Couldn't Find Them Anywhere': Thomas Glave's *Whose Song?*, (Post)Modernist Literary Queerings, and the Trauma of Witnessing, Memory, and Testimony," *Callaloo* 23 (2000).

Sickels, Amy. "No Shield for the Endangered," *Gay & Lesbian Review Worldwide* 8 (2001).

Tettenborn, Eva. "'Will the Big Boys Finally Love You?' The Impossibility of Black Male Homoerotic Desire and the Taboo of Black Homosexual Solidarity in Thomas Glave's *Whose Song?*" *Callaloo* 26 (2003).

MAGGIE GERRITY

Gleason, Eliza Veleria Atkins (15 Dec. 1909– 15 Dec. 2009), librarian and educator, was born in Winston-Salem, North Carolina. Gleason earned an AB degree from Fisk University in 1926 and a bachelor of science in 1931 from the University of Chicago Library School. Gleason began her library employment that same year as an assistant librarian at the Louisville Municipal College for Negroes in Kentucky. In 1932 Gleason became head librarian and taught library classes in the new library department she had created. The department, in conjunction with the Louisville Western Colored Branch Library, offered the only available library classes for African Americans in Kentucky between 1932 and 1951. In 1936 Gleason left Kentucky, earned a master's of arts degree in Library Science from the University of California, Berkeley, and taught at Fisk University in Tennessee as an assistant professor through 1937.

Gleason's impressive academic career reached a zenith in 1940, when she became the first African American woman to earn a PhD in Library Science, which she earned from the Graduate Library School of the University of Chicago. Her dissertation, "Government and Administration of Public Library Service to Negroes in the South," was published in 1941 as the landmark text *The Southern Negro and the Public Library* and traced the history of library service to African Americans up to that time, laying the foundation for all other histories of that aspect of library service. Considered an exceptional resource by both peers and, later, academics, Gleason's text represents a specific critical analysis of library services available to African Americans in thirteen southern states during the early twentieth century and includes vital statistics and facts, such as the Covington Public Library's special status as the only desegregated library in Kentucky.

Although the exact date of marriage is not known, records indicate that Eliza Atkins married Maurice F. Gleason, a physician, around 1939. From 1940 until 1941, Gleason was the director of libraries at Talladega College and a professor at Atlanta

University in Atlanta, Georgia, from 1941 to 1946. Gleason's efforts to structure and organize the library school at Atlanta University Library School for Negroes earned her a position as the first African American library school dean in 1942. From 1942 to 1946 Gleason served on the council of the American Library Association (ALA).

From 1954 to 1965, Gleason served as associate professor at the Chicago Teachers College and was later appointed professor at the Illinois Institute of Technology, from 1967 to 1970. She was employed as assistant from 1967 to 1970 at the John Crerar Library, University of Chicago, and from 1970 to 1973 was the assistant chief librarian at the Chicago Public Library, most notably teaching accredited college library courses in her last year there. From 1974 to 1975 Gleason taught at Northern Illinois University as one of only two professors of library science and in 1976 became chief librarian with a professorship at the Illinois Institute of Technology. In 1979 Gleason was appointed to the board of directors of the Chicago Public Library and continued to work throughout her career as a professional consultant to public and academic libraries.

In 2004 the Library History Round Table of the ALA instituted the Eliza Atkins Gleason Book Award, given every three years in recognition of the best book written in English in the field of library history, including the history of libraries, librarianship, and book culture.

Gleason died in Louisville Kentucky on her 100th birthday.

FURTHER READING

Jones, Reinette F. *Library Service to African Americans in Kentucky, from the Reconstruction to the 1960s* (2002).

Josey, E. J. *The Black Librarian in America Revisited* (1994).

SYLVIA M. DESANTIS

Gloster, Hugh Morris (11 May 1911–16 Feb. 2002), president of Morehouse College, was born in the small West Tennessee community of Brownsville, the eldest of four children born to John R. and Dora Gloster. Both parents were teachers by profession, and his father attended Roger Williams University, one of four Nashville colleges established for the education of freedmen after the Civil War. However, the family found life in Brownsville plagued by intolerable lynching and relocated to Memphis in 1915. While the age difference between Gloster and his siblings made his childhood experiences akin to that of an only child, his parents stressed the value of education for all their children. After studying at the Howe Institute, Gloster received a junior diploma from LeMoyne College (later LeMoyne-Owen College), also in Memphis. As had his older brothers, Gloster attended Morehouse College, where he received a BA in 1931 in English. Two years later he was awarded an MA in English from Atlanta University, another black Atlanta college that had just begun its formal affiliation with Morehouse and Spelman Colleges as the Atlanta University System.

Gloster returned to Memphis and to LeMoyne in 1933 to begin his professional career as a teacher. Recognizing the need to exchange scholarly research about their professional interests and the collegiate communities they served, Gloster, along with nine other scholars from black colleges and universities, founded the College Language Association on the LeMoyne campus in 1937. As the association's first (1937–1938) and fifth president (1948–1950) as well as an executive board member until 2002, Gloster helped to guide the CLA for sixty-five years.

Gloster left Memphis to study for the PhD at New York University in 1941. Living among African American intellectuals, writers, and artists in New York just two decades removed from the Harlem Renaissance, Gloster expanded his interest in black literature, and he was awarded with a doctorate in English in 1943. His return to teaching, however, was postponed when he was drafted for military service that same year. Sent to Fort Huachuca, Arizona, where the Tenth Cavalry, Buffalo Soldiers, had been stationed for twenty years, he worked as the facility's organization program director then as associate regional director in Atlanta, Georgia, before ending his military career in 1946 to return to the educational sector at Hampton Institute in Hampton, Virginia.

Once at Hampton, Gloster distinguished himself as a scholar and administrator. Hailed as the definitive study of black literature, Gloster's 1948 publication *Negro Voices in American Fiction* earned him the respect of his peers as a leading black literary critic. That same year, he coedited the best-selling college textbook *My Life–My Country–My World*. Meanwhile, Gloster also traveled extensively throughout Europe, Africa, the Middle East, and Japan, where he was a Fulbright Professor of English at Hiroshima University from 1953 to 1955. In addition to urging the creation of Hampton's precollege program in 1952, Gloster served for ten years as director of the university's summer sessions

(1952–1962). His fund-raising successes as dean of faculty to the tune of $21 million undoubtedly helped to secure his appointment as president of Morehouse College in 1967.

Gloster guided the university's rejuvenation and expansion. In addition to constructing twelve buildings valued at $30 million, the college also acquired thirty acres of adjacent urban land, a classroom building, an apartment complex, and the president's residence during Gloster's presidency. On the academic front, the college established a major in international studies, eight new majors in the department of business, and embarked on a dual-degree engineering program with the Georgia Institute of Technology and Boston University. Under Gloster's leadership, Morehouse successfully completed capital campaigns for $20 million in the mid-1970s and mid-1980s. Since the university operated without a deficit during the 1970s and 1980s, Gloster led efforts to double the size and salaries of Morehouse faculty. Still, Gloster's most lasting contribution to the college is likely the founding and development of the Morehouse School of Medicine in 1981 and his success in quadrupling the college's endowment to $29 million by the time he retired in 1987.

While he declined several subsequent offers of college and interim presidencies, Gloster dedicated the remainder of his life to working with educational organizations such as the United Negro College Fund and LeMonye-Owen College. A member of Alpha Phi Alpha Fraternity, Sigma Pi Phi Boule, and Phi Beta Kappa National Honor Society, Gloster was the recipient of a host of awards and honorary degrees before his death in 2002 at age ninety. He was survived by his third wife Yvonne King, a lawyer (and his executive assistant while at Morehouse, two daughters, Alice and Evelyn (by his first wife Louise), son Hugh Jr. (by his second wife Beulah), four stepchildren and a host of grand- and great-grandchildren.

FURTHER READING

Many of Hugh M. Gloster's papers are housed at the Archives and Special Collections of Atlanta University Center Woodruff Library in Atlanta, Georgia.

Banks, William M. *Black Intellectuals: Race and Responsibility in American Life* (1996).

Bobia, Rosa. "Hugh Gloster," in *Notable Black American Men, Book II*, ed. Jessie Carney Smith (2007).

Gloster, Hugh Morris. *Negro Voices in American Fiction* (1965).

Obituary: *Atlanta Inquirer*, 2 Mar. 2002.

CRYSTAL A. DEGREGORY

Gloucester, John (1776?–2 May 1822), founder of African American Presbyterianism and abolitionist, born a slave in Kentucky, was a "body servant" called "Jack" and purchased as a young man by the Tennessee Presbyterian minister Gideon Blackburn. Gloucester's parentage is unclear because of his early enslavement; although in 1806, while a member of the New Providence Presbyterian Church of Maryville, Tennessee, he was bought by Blackburn from an undisclosed owner. His intelligence and comprehension of theological principles motivated Blackburn, an evangelical preacher and abolitionist, to unsuccessfully seek Tennessee legislative help to free Gloucester. Blackburn had been born an orphan and moved into the Presbyterian ministry in the early 1790s before establishing missions to "educate" the Cherokee in Tennessee. He visited Philadelphia with Gloucester and freed him under the guidance of the Reverend Archibald Alexander, pastor of the Third Presbyterian Church. By that time, in Tennessee, Gloucester had converted many whites and blacks to Christianity, even under the burden of his wife, Rhoda, and his children still being held as slaves. Although their exact marriage date is not known, with Rhoda's maiden name unclear probably because of her slavery status that often meant having no designated surname, they were joined in matrimony and had children before 31 May 1811, when the cornerstone of Gloucester's Philadelphia church, the First African Presbyterian Church, was dedicated (Smith, 463).

With the help of the famed colonial physician Benjamin Rush and the black businessman JAMES FORTEN, Gloucester eventually raised funds to free his family by speaking against slavery in the United States and Europe. He also led several of his Princeton-educated sons into the Presbyterian ministry. They included his first-born son Jeremiah Gloucester, who in 1824 founded the Second African Presbyterian Church; Stephen Gloucester, who in 1844 founded the Central Presbyterian Church; James M. Gloucester, who migrated to Brooklyn, New York, and supported the white abolitionist John Brown; and John Gloucester Jr., who was vehemently opposed to the colonization of black Americans back to Africa. The couple also had a daughter, Mary Gloucester, whose political and religious activities are not known.

John Gloucester Jr.'s views on colonization mirrored those of his father, who became part of the elite Committee of Twelve, which consisted of Philadelphia's most prominent African American ministers and others associated with the Free African Society (FAS), the first black rights organization in the United States. Founded in 1787 the FAS, an umbrella to the first independent black churches in the United States, gave birth to the Committee of Twelve, which included Forten; RICHARD ALLEN of Mother Bethel African Methodist Episcopal (AME) Church, where FAS met in 1817 to debate colonization, attracting an estimated 3,000 participants, the largest documented mass black rights meeting in the United States at that time; and ABSALOM JONES, a close associate of Allen and the minister of St. Thomas African Episcopal Church.

In the early 1800s, while his family was still enslaved, Gloucester preached with a booming voice on street corners and in the homes of Philadelphia. He advocated the development of a black Presbyterian church, an idea supported more by white Presbyterian power brokers than by the white hierarchy behind Allen and Jones. The Reverend William T. Catto, father of the well-known Philadelphia black activist OCTAVIUS CATTO, who was assassinated in 1871 while advocating for black voting rights, noted that Gloucester did face some opposition. "Let it suffice the reader for me to say, there was no cause of ill-treatment upon the part of existing organizations or Churches, to drive the colored membership to seek a separation," wrote Catto about the history of the church in *A Semi-Centenary Discourse, Delivered in the First African Presbyterian Church, Philadelphia, on the Fourth Sabbath of May, 1857* (19).

However, before officially taking the helm of the church, Gloucester had to deal with the Philadelphia Presbytery. Although by 1807 the First African Presbyterian Church was organized with an initial membership of about twenty-five, that same year the Philadelphia Presbytery rejected Gloucester's ordination, indicating it was the responsibility of the Tennessee jurisdiction. In Tennessee further examination required that Gloucester study such subjects as philosophy and astronomy before he was eventually ordained on 30 April 1810. All the while he commuted between the two states and kept his Philadelphia congregation growing. Gloucester, the first African American to study at Tennessee's Greeneville College, where Blackburn was a trustee, became a member of the Philadelphia Presbytery in April 1811.

Gloucester was a powerful and absorbing preacher, with a strong evangelistic style similar to Blackburn's. "He abounded in anecdotes, for he was a close observer of everything that was transpiring around him," Catto wrote. "His manner was bold, his voice clear and loud" (32).

The congregation was meeting on street corners, in schools, and even in members' homes, so the next order of business was to establish a church. Furthermore, according to Catto, the black Presbyterians found it "inconvenient and unpleasant, for reasons which need not now be stated, to attend the houses of worship frequented by white people" (52). Gloucester did receive some opposition from white elements owing to "bigotry," Catto said, despite the support of Alexander, who had become a leader of the presbytery. Still, Gloucester pressed forward, and with the help of the Evangelical Society, a lot was purchased at Shippen (later Lombard) and Seventh streets. "The cornerstone of the church was laid in 1810, and the structure was dedicated on 31 May 1811. It was a plain brick building capable of seating 650 people in comfort. At the time of its dedication the church had 123 members" (Smith, 463).

Gloucester had become involved with educating African Americans by 1818, when he founded the Pennsylvania Augustine Society for the Education of People of Color and other like organizations. During this period SAMUEL ELI CORNISH, who started New York City's first African American Presbyterian church and established, with JOHN RUSSWURM, the nation's first African American newspaper, *Freedom's Journal*, in 1827, was educated and trained for the ministry by Gloucester.

Yet Gloucester began to suffer from tuberculosis. By 27 June 1820, as his health deteriorated, he began to ask for substitute ministers, including Cornish, who filled in for several months. Gloucester's son Jeremiah Gloucester was ordained and briefly took over the pulpit. Jeremiah "led a greater part of the [First African] congregation into the Second African Presbyterian Church" after his father's death (Smith, 464). John Gloucester's legacy lives on in the First African Presbyterian Church, which celebrated its 195th anniversary in May 2002, nearly two centuries after Gloucester left, in the words of Catto, "his footprints on time, and his impressions on the world" (Catto, 31).

FURTHER READING

Apperson, George M. "African Americans on the Tennessee Frontier: John Gloucester and His Contemporaries," *Tennessee Historical Quarterly* 59 (Spring 2000): 2–19.

Catto, William T. *A Semi-Centenary Discourse, Delivered in the First African Presbyterian Church, Philadelphia, on the Fourth Sabbath of May, 1857: With a History of the Church from Its First Organization; Including a Brief Notice of Rev. John Gloucester, Its First Pastor* (1857).

Hopper, Matthew S. "From Refuge to Strength: The Rise of the African American Church in Philadelphia, 1787–1949" (1999).

Lane, Roger. *William Dorsey's Philadelphia and Ours: On the Past and Future of the Black City in America* (1991).

Preservation Alliance for Greater Philadelphia. Preservation News. "Origins of the African American Church in Philadelphia, 1787–1830" (2005). Available at http://www. preservationalliance.com/rise_index.php.

Smith, Jessie Carney, ed. *Notable Black American Men* (1999).

Winch, Julie. *A Gentleman of Color: The Life of James Forten* (2002).

Winch, Julie. *Philadelphia's Black Elite: Activism, Accommodation, and the Struggle for Autonomy, 1787–1848* (1988).

DONALD SCOTT SR.

Glover, Danny (22 July 1947–), actor, activist, producer, and director, was born in San Francisco, California, the eldest of five children born to James and Carrie Glover, lifelong postal workers and political activists in the NAACP and Postal Workers Union. As a child, Glover spent the school year with his parents, living in a government housing project in the Haight-Ashbury district. During summer vacations, however, he stayed with his grandparents on their farm in rural Louisville, Georgia, in the mid-1950s. The Glovers' ride from California across the South was always fearful, as the country was still in the grip of Jim Crow laws. Upon their arrival in Georgia they would have to use the back door for restroom use and sit at separate lunch counters apart from whites. These experiences stayed with Glover throughout his life and fueled his commitment to civil and human rights causes in the United States and abroad. Glover's early years were uncomfortable. He was very skinny and awkwardly tall; these features, coupled with his dark skin color, made him a target for relentless teasing. He performed poorly in school because of his undiagnosed dyslexia. Mathematics, therefore, was his best subject. At age eleven, he delivered newspapers before school, earning as much as $150 a month, plus tips. As a teenager he excelled at football, but epileptic seizures ended his dream of pursuing a sports career. Glover frequented pool halls, and once lost all his newspaper earnings rolling dice (he has never gambled since). He was also arrested several times for joyriding and shoplifting. Despite his reading disabilities he earned a high school diploma in 1965.

After high school Glover attended City College of San Francisco, but he dropped out after two semesters. With no direction and an uncertain future, he began washing dishes for $1.50 an hour at a women's college, Lone Mountain College. Everything changed for Glover, however, after a friend suggested that he volunteer at San Francisco State University (SFSU), tutoring inner city youths in a program sponsored by the Black Student Union. Danny Glover was about to find his calling.

It was 1966 and SFSU, like other college campuses, was in the midst of a social and political upheaval. Glover discovered that black was beautiful, and he demanded that the college offer courses on African American culture and heritage. He became a full-time student in 1967, and worked in the Black Panther Party's "breakfast program" as part of its community work. He began speaking at rallies in the Black Student Union as chairman of its Art and Cultural Committee. He helped organize a strike to block the college's decision to eliminate the Ethnic Studies Department, and he was arrested for his effort. And somehow Glover still had time to coordinate three reading centers for children. But most of all, Glover began to realize that he could make a difference in the world. From 1966 to 1975 Glover concentrated on classes in economics, and was a civil service employee, evaluating housing, education, and social programs for San Francisco and Berkeley.

Glover's first acting role came in 1967, with a role in AMIRI BARAKA's play *Pappa's Daughter*, staged at SFSU. His acting interests had begun simultaneously with his political involvement, and he played activist roles in many of Baraka's plays. After college, Glover pursued acting at the Black Box Theater Company. He also began to attend the Black Actor's Workshop at the American Conservatory Theater. In 1975 Glover married his college sweetheart, Asake Bomani; and in 1976 their only child, Mandisa, was born.

By 1977 Glover was twenty-nine years old and a family man. Yet he left his secure government job to drive a cab at night so he could pursue casting calls during the day. Soon, the Glovers moved to Los Angeles, and in 1979, Glover made his film debut in *Escape from Alcatraz* with Clint Eastwood.

Danny Glover, addressing a rally on Capitol Hill calling for congressional action to stop the global AIDS epidemic, 10 April 2002. (AP Images.)

The following year they moved to New York City, where Glover earned money scooping ice cream while developing his acting skills by studying the Stanislavski method with Uta Hagen.

In 1980 Glover's hard work paid off when he won the lead role in the Off-Broadway play *Blood Knot*, written by the white South African writer Athol Fugard. Glover credits Fugard as the reason he became an actor. After seeing Glover's performance in *Blood Knot*, Fugard was so impressed that he offered him the role of Willie in his upcoming Broadway production of *Master Harold ... and the Boys*, for which the actor eventually won the 1981–1982 Theatre World Award. Director Robert Benton saw the performance and offered Glover the lead role with Sally Field, in *Places in the Heart* (1984). This was the role that catapulted him into national stardom.

More film and television offers followed. In 1985 Glover starred in the film adaptation of ALICE WALKER's *The Color Purple*, Lawrence Kasdan's western-themed film *Silverado*, and *Witness*, a thriller. In 1987 he starred in the first of four *Lethal Weapon* films, and as Nelson Mandela in the made-for-television movie *Mandela*. *Dead Man Out* and *Lonesome Dove* followed in 1989, and in 1990 Glover starred in *To Sleep with Anger* by acclaimed director CHARLES BURNETT, a role for which he won an Independent Spirit Award for Best Actor. In 1991 he appeared in the film adaptation of CHESTER HIMES's *A Rage in Harlem*, and in 2001 he appeared in *The Royal Tenenbaums*. After the success of the first *Lethal Weapon*, he would reprise his role as Sergeant Roger Murtaugh in *Lethal Weapon 2* (1989), *Lethal Weapon 3* (1992), and *Lethal Weapon 4* (1998), each time playing the straight man opposite Mel Gibson's unconventional Martin Riggs character.

Starting in 1990, with *To Sleep with Anger*, Glover acted as producer on many of his films, including *Buffalo Soldiers* (1997, TV), *3 A.M.* (2001), and *Good Fences* (2003). Through his production company, L'Ouverture Films, he also produced a number of films focusing on important historical figures and events, including *Bamako* (2006), *Toussaint* (2007), and *Africa Unite* (2007).

Glover was the recipient of numerous awards, including NAACP Image Awards for his roles in *Freedom Song* (2000, TV), the film adaptation of Toni Morrison's *Beloved* (1998), *Queen* (1993, TV), *Lethal Weapon*, and *Mandela* (1987, TV). He was also nominated for other awards, including four Emmy Awards, Image Awards, MTV Movie Awards, and Black Reel Awards, among others.

In addition to his acting pursuits, Glover actively engaged in human rights issues. He fought against South African apartheid and challenged U.S. policy toward Caribbean and Haitian refugees. He was a spokesman for literacy, mathematics, and kidney disease campaigns (his father died of kidney disease in 2001), and crusaded against the death penalty. He was appointed the first Goodwill Ambassador for the United Nations Development Programme. He also filed a racial discrimination complaint with New York City's Taxi and Limousine Commission in November 1999. For his work both in the artistic and political spheres, Glover was the recipient of the Lifetime Achievement Award at the Los Angeles Pan African Film Festival in 2003; and in 2006, the Directors Guild of America honored Glover for his humanitarian work. He was a recipient of a Lifetime Achievement Award from Amnesty International. Glover has continued to appear in films, ranging from small budget independent dramas like *Moozlum* (2010), about an African American Muslim family after 9-11, to the big budget disaster movie, *2012*, in which Glover played the U.S. President. He also provided his voice for animated features such as *Alpha and Omega* (2009), a 3-D animated comedy, and documentaries, most notably *The People Speak* (2009), an adaptation of Howard Zinn's radical history, *The People's History of America*. Glover struggled to find Hollywood backing, however, for his planned directorial debut, a biopic about the Haitian revolutionary Toussaint L'Ouverture. In Glover's view this was because the mainstream motion picture industry was wary of financing a film that had no white heroes. Venezuelan leader Hugo Chavez—whom Glover had long championed—stepped into the breach by providing $18 million and offering his nation as a location to shoot the film, *Toussaint*, which had not been completed as of November 2011. Glover supported the political candidacy of BARACK OBAMA, once his preferred candidate, North Carolina Senator John Edwards, dropped out of the 2008 race, but has criticized Obama's presidency for continuing many of George W. Bush's domestic and foreign policies. In 2011 Glover was a prominent backer of the Occupy Wall Street and Occupy Oakland protests against corporate greed and growing economic inequality in America.

FURTHER READING

Barsamian, David. "Danny Glover," *Progressive* (Dec. 2002).

Blakely, Gloria. *Danny Glover* (2002).

Graham, Judith, ed. *Current Biography Yearbook 1992* (1992).

DAVID KOENIGSTEIN

Glover, Melvin. *See* Grandmaster Melle Mel (Melvin Glover).

Glover, Nathaniel, Jr. (9 Mar. 1943–), sheriff and college president, was born in Jacksonville, Florida. His father, Nathaniel Glover Sr., was a part-time Baptist pastor, and his mother, Arsie Singletary Glover, cleaned houses; together they raised five children in a two-room house in downtown Jacksonville. As a boy, Glover worked to provide funds for his family, first selling copies of the city's black newspaper, and later working at a local cafe. While walking home from work in 1960, Glover encountered a crowd of white segregationists protesting against the integration of the food counter at the cafe. The group noticed he was a dishwasher and clubbed him with an ax handle. When he appealed to a white officer for help, Glover was told to "Get out of town." The incident was a defining moment in Glover's life, and he became resolved that it might have been prevented had his tormentors been given proper educational opportunities.

Known to his fans as "Cannonball," Glover received a scholarship to Edward Waters College, a historically black college in Jacksonville, for football. He became a linebacker, made all conference, and was captain for two years. But he wanted to pursue his childhood dream of becoming a detective. After graduating with a bachelor of science in Social Science in 1965, he attended the Jacksonville police academy, where he was the sole African American to graduate in a class of about twenty.

In 1966 he joined the Jacksonville Sheriff's Office. He moved up the ranks quickly, being promoted to investigator in the detective division in 1969, and then to sergeant in 1974. He became a leading spokesman for the Brotherhood of Police Officers. In 1977, as head of the Police Hostage Negotiation Team and Chief of Services, he successfully negotiated with a hijacker of a Greyhound Bus carrying thirty-two passengers. Glover received a master's degree in Education in 1987 from the University of North Florida.

In 1995 Glover decided to seek the office of sheriff of Jacksonville, a position that would place in him in charge of the city's police force. He faced many challenges. Former sheriff Jim McMillan expressed a primary one: "Whether or not our community is progressed enough to be able to elect a black sheriff, I don't know." At that time no African American had been elected sheriff in Florida since the end of Reconstruction in the 1870s; however, this criticism did not deter Glover. He focused on three issues during the campaign: placing police officers back in neighborhoods, reducing the bureaucracy in the sheriff's office, and promoting community involvement. To prove how serious he was about serving the community, he promised that he would donate part of his pension to a scholarship fund after he retired. On 1 July 1995, Nathaniel Glover Jr. became the first elected African American sheriff in Jacksonville, Florida, in the one hundred years of the history of the office. Though Jacksonville was only 24 percent African American, Glover obtained 55 percent of all votes, defeating two white opponents.

As sheriff, Glover increased the education level of police officers, requiring all new hired officers to hold a bachelor's degree. He supervised one of the largest departments in the state, with more than 2,200 police and correctional officers covering the largest patrol territory outside of Juneau, Alaska. He accomplished the reorganization of the office of sheriff, resulting in $200,000 savings per year. On 1 May 1996, 109 more officers were assigned to patrol the division. He was instrumental in founding COPS AHEAD, a three-year federally funded program that increased the number of community officers in local departments across the nation. Additionally, he often personally walked each of the ninety-two beats in Jacksonville, stating that "We're going to be just like the postman."

After serving thirty-seven years with the sheriff's department, Glover ran for mayor in 2003 on a platform of education, economic development, and management of city growth. Despite losing the election to the Republican candidate John Peyton by roughly 16 percent, Glover persisted in active service to the community. He donated $250,000 to the Jacksonville Commitment scholarship and became a special assistant to the University of North Florida president John Delaney, where he played a role in the prevention of student drop-outs.

Over the course of his career Glover received the following honors: Law Enforcement Officer of the Year (1977); Sallye B. Mathis Award for outstanding community service (1991); Outstanding Alumni award from the University of North Florida (1995); FBI Director's Community Leadership award (1999); and the Martin Luther King Humanitarian award.

Glover married Doris J. Bailey, his high school sweetheart, on 22 November 1964. They had two children, Clementine and Michael, two grandsons, and a granddaughter. In May 2010 he was named the twenty-ninth president of Edward Waters College.

FURTHER READING
A collection of Nathaniel Glover Jr.'s papers is held at the Thomas G. Carpenter Library at the University of Northern Florida.
McGoff, Amanda. "The Beat Goes On: A Day in the Life of Jacksonville Sheriff Nat Glover." *UNF Journal* (winter 1995).

KELSEY SCHURER AND
MARINA REASONER

Glover, Ruth (23 Aug. 1916–), basketball player and teacher, was born in Bennett, North Carolina, the eighth of ten children of William Green Glover, a farmer and lumberjack, and Carrie Marsh. As a youngster Ruth acquired and honed her basketball skills, playing with her brothers on a makeshift court in the family's yard. These experiences helped prepare her for the competitive basketball she played in high school and college. Glover graduated from Chatham County High School in Siler City, North Carolina, in 1933 and then earned a BA in Elementary Education from Bennett College in Greensboro, North Carolina, in 1937.

The year Glover entered Chatham County High School, a girls' basketball team was established, providing female students at the all-black school the same opportunities their peers already had at the all-white Siler City High School. Glover, eager to test the skills learned playing informally with her brothers, signed up immediately for the team. Glover's basketball talents, including her ability to score points, quickly became evident to Zenobia Bost, the coach of the fledgling team. Bost, a recent graduate of Bennett College and a former member of its basketball squad, soon became Glover's mentor, providing support both on and off the court. Intent upon seeing Glover succeed, Bost strove to help make the path less turbulent by offering assistance across a range of settings and situations. Bost's efforts included gifts of clothing when Glover needed an outfit for a special occasion and securing on-campus employment, thus enabling Glover to enroll at Bennett College in the fall of 1933.

Far from unusual, Bost's wide-ranging support of Glover reflected and underscored a much broader legacy of commitment to education among many African Americans during this period. Family, friends, church leaders, and other community members made up a complex network of support that sought to clear a path toward higher education for young African American men and women. On the surface, educational achievement may have appeared as a marker of individual success. It was, however, more often conceptualized as a collective accomplishment, benefiting the entire community while simultaneously serving to eradicate racism.

By the time Glover entered Bennett College, the school's basketball program was firmly in place. Initially established by the Methodist Episcopal Church as a coeducational institution in 1873, Bennett reorganized as a women's college in 1926 and initiated a basketball team shortly thereafter. Despite the team's newcomer status, Glover joined a respected program. Her athletic talents rapidly helped transform the team from a worthy opponent to an unbeatable one, competing against schools in North Carolina and beyond. With a relatively high number of black colleges and universities in North Carolina, it was not difficult to find competition, enabling the Bennett team to routinely play ten to twenty games per season. Women's basketball enjoyed a solid level of notoriety and respectability at Bennett and the dozens of other black colleges and universities throughout the South that offered the sport. With few requirements in terms of equipment and playing facilities, basketball's feasibility helped propel it to the favored game status it enjoyed among financially strapped black colleges and universities in the first half of the twentieth century. Furthermore at single-sex Bennett College the basketball program did not have to compete for campus resources with a men's team, as was the case for virtually all other women's teams during this period.

Glover's impact on Bennett's basketball success was immediate. In her first week of collegiate competition as a freshman, Glover led her team to victory, scoring 32 of Bennett's 59 points over a two-game span. Bennett ended the 1934 season with an undefeated record against college opponents, losing only to the Philadelphia Tribune team, a semiprofessional squad captained by ORA WASHINGTON. Annie Bowers of Shaw University clearly remembered Glover: "She never dribbled the regular way. She would throw it over you and run around you and get it. It was pretty difficult to keep up with

her" (Bowers, quoted in Liberti, 88.) Teammates and opponents knew well of her athletic ability, and Glover became familiar to a wider audience as the black press reported her feats with frequency. Glover's athleticism and her reddish hair gave the press a unique identifier for the Bennett star, dubbing her the "titian-haired flash," "Red Glover," or the "auburn-haired luminary," among other monikers. The press had much to report about Glover and the Bennett squad as over the next three years the team lost only one game of dozens played. Glover's career at Bennett ended as it began, with individual as well as team honors. During Bennett's championship 1937 season, the team amassed 377 points over eleven games, with Glover's 168 points leading all scorers.

The prominent place afforded competitive basketball on the Bennett College campus can be attributed at least in part to the fact that the game and the values it was believed to instill blended well with the overall mission of the school. Bennett president David D. Jones and other school officials were committed to preparing graduates to face the challenges of sexism and racism. It was believed that competitive basketball provided one of many opportunities on Bennett's campus for young women to demand for themselves and those around them a greater standard of performance and strength of character. Basketball's place within this strategy was derived in part from an expansive conceptualization of womanhood, one that did not construct femininity and athleticism as mutually exclusive categories. Rather, the qualities necessary to play basketball, including physicality, were seen to strengthen notions of what it meant to be a woman. Such was not the case for women enrolled at predominantly white colleges in this period. Finite notions of femininity, grounded in frailty and weakness, precluded involvement in basketball and other physical activities deemed injurious to a woman's health and well-being.

Through basketball Glover learned important lessons about team effort, tenacity, commitment, and the relationship between herself and the community that helped send her to Bennett College. Like so many other female athletes from this period, Glover's graduation from Bennett marked the beginning of a long tenure of giving back to the community from which she had come, working to provide a path to success for others like the one Zenobia Bost helped establish for her. Glover's career as a teacher spanned nearly four decades, including a position from 1937 to 1955 at Currituck County Union School in Moyock, North Carolina, where she also coached a championship girls' basketball team. In 1937 Glover married John Thomas Mullen, her husband of sixty-four years, who died in 2001. The couple had one child. Glover continued her career at the Chester Upland School District in Pennsylvania from 1963 until her retirement in 1982, while spending the summer months working in the Chester City Recreation Department as a playground supervisor. After her retirement she remained active in numerous church, community, and Bennett College fund-raising programs. In 1985 she was recognized by officials in Delaware County, Pennsylvania, for her participation in various service projects in the area. For her volunteer efforts as Sunday school and Bible school teacher and her membership in the aide guild and on the scholarship committee, the United Methodist Women of St. Daniels presented her with an award in appreciation for many years of dedicated service.

Since its inception in 1891, basketball has been a part of African American communities across the United States and especially in the rural South. Glover's experiences on the court and her contributions off of it provide an important lens through which to better understand the richness of women's basketball history and the profound connections between individual achievement and collective will within the African American community during the first half of the twentieth century.

FURTHER READING

Grundy, Pamela, and Susan Shackelford. *Shattering the Glass: The Remarkable History of Women's Basketball* (2005).

Liberti, Rita. "'We Were Ladies, We Just Played Like Boys': African American Womanhood and Competitive Basketball at Bennett College, 1928–1942," *Journal of Sport History* 26.3 (Fall 1999): 567–584.

RITA LIBERTI

Glover, Savion (19 Nov. 1973–), dancer, choreographer, and musical performer, was born in Newark, New Jersey, to the singer and actress Yvette Glover, who chose her son's name as a variation on "saviour." Glover and his two elder brothers, Carlton and Abron, were raised by their mother and their grandmother, Anna Lundy Lewis, who was a minister of music at the New Point Baptist Church in Newark.

Glover began drumming on pots and pans at age two. At four, he enrolled in drum lessons; however, he was asked to leave the class for being "too

Savion Glover, performing at the Jacob's Pillow Dance Festival in Becket, Massachusetts, 15 June 2002. (AP Images.)

advanced." The teacher instead arranged an interview at the Newark Community School of the Arts, where at five he became their youngest student ever to receive a full scholarship. Glover attended the José Feliciano School for the Performing Arts in Manhattan, and graduated in 1992 from the Arts High School in Newark.

Drumming led Glover to tap dancing at age seven. While taking classes at the Broadway Dance Center in New York City, he first saw the tap superstars Lon Chaney and Chuck Green dance. They performed rhythm tap, a style that involves making sound with the whole foot, not just the heel and toe. "This is what I want to do," he told his mother afterward, and he began making rhythms constantly. "Once he hit the floor to get up in the morning, what you'd hear was tapping … when he walked to school, he tapped," Yvette Glover told John Lahr for the *New Yorker* (Lahr, 90).

Glover's first big role came at age twelve, when he began a two-year spell playing the lead in the Broadway production of *The Tap Dance Kid.*

Glover played Willie, a ten-year-old boy who wants to follow in his grandfather's footsteps and be a tap dancer—against the wishes of his father, a lawyer who wants his son to pursue the law.

Next, he tapped for a production of *Black and Blue* on Broadway in 1989. The show, a tribute to black dancers and blues performers from the pre–World War II era, allowed Glover to perform with some of his heroes: Lon Chaney, JIMMY SLYDE, BUNNY BRIGGS, and Ralph Brown. Glover was nominated for a Tony Award for his performance, becoming one of the youngest men to be nominated. The tap dancer GREGORY HINES saw *Black and Blue* and came backstage to suggest to Glover that they work together. Shortly afterward, Glover was cast alongside Hines and SAMMY DAVIS JR. in the movie *Tap* (1989), the story of a young dancer struggling to decide between a life in dance and a life of crime. The next year, Glover debuted his first choreographed piece at the Apollo Theater, and began appearing on the children's television program *Sesame Street*.

Glover and Hines reunited in 1991 for a Broadway production of *Jelly's Last Jam*. This musical biography of JELLY ROLL MORTON, directed by GEORGE C. WOLFE, was a huge hit and earned Hines a Tony Award. Critics praised Glover's performance in the show, and in 1991 he received a MARTIN LUTHER KING JR. Outstanding Youth Award. The eighteen-year-old Glover soon embarked on a national tour with "Jelly's Last Jam."

The National Endowment for the Arts awarded Glover a grant for choreography in 1992, making him the youngest-ever recipient of the prestigious NEA grant. Thus began the next phase of his career, as a choreographer as well as a dancer. Glover became a major star with the debut of his 1995 show *Bring in 'Da Noise, Bring in 'Da Funk: A Tap/Rap Discourse on the Staying Power of the Beat*. A collaboration between Glover and Wolfe, *Bring in 'Da Noise* uses tap to tell stories about African American history. "In every dance, Glover has managed to make the tapping communicate not just as music but as narrative," wrote Joan Acocella in the *New York Review of Books* (Acocella, 4). "In the 'Slave Ships' section, we see only one figure (Glover), sitting on the floor and leaning back, as though in the galleys of those fateful ships. Haltingly, he rises and executes a series of very slow *ronds de jambe* (semicircles on the floor), trying to find his legs again. Meanwhile, in the scraping of his metal taps on the floor, we are made to feel the chains." Other numbers in the show included a machine dance, after the Russian Constructivist avant-garde artistic movement of the early twentieth century; a cakewalk; a Charleston; and a buck and wing. "Sometimes the four lead dancers look like boys in a schoolyard, passing a phrase like a basketball.... In a section about Harlem during the 1977 blackout, the four of them simply move forward, from the back of the stage to the front, in what seem like fixed slots, their feet drumming a relentless phrase—the four tappers of the apocalypse," wrote critic Rick Simas in a 1997 *Theater Journal* review (Simas, 220).

The show opened at the Public Theater to great critical acclaim, and swiftly moved to Broadway. *Bring in 'Da Noise* won Glover a Tony Award for Best Choreography as well as a 1996 Dance Magazine award; Wolfe won the Tony for Best Direction of a Musical. Several national and international tours followed.

After the success of *Bring in 'Da Noise*, Glover was in demand both as a choreographer and a performer. He starred in the SPIKE LEE film *Bamboozled*, a satire about network television and modern-day minstrelsy. Solo tours followed, and he choreographed some award-winning commercials for Nike.

On the road again in 2000, Glover toured nationally with *Footnotes: The Concert*, in which he reunited with the tap stars Jimmy Slyde, James "Buster" Brown, and Dianne Walker. In 2004 he debuted a show called *Improvography* at the Joyce Theater in New York City. In it, Glover soloed with a five-piece jazz band playing jazz standards. After singing briefly, Glover broke into a breathtaking tap passage. "To me, Glover has never been anything but classical—floor-bound, not aerial; aural, not visual; a drummer, almost, more than a dancer—and his shows have always been full of tap pietas, invocations of the elders," Joan Acocella wrote in the *New Yorker* (Acocella, 77).

Glover married in 2003 and his son Sea Glover was born in 2004. In 2005 Glover began a thirteen-city solo tour called *Classical Savion*, with a similar format. This time, however, music by Bach and Vivaldi backed up his signature urban tap moves. The same year, he starred in *Vision of a Bible* at the Joyce Theater, in which he starred and wrote the title song. The year 2006 saw him starring in the fourth national tour of *Classical Savion*. Glover performed in a motion-capture suit to create the slick moves for Mumble, the dancing penguin hero of the Academy Award-winning animated film *Happy Feet*. "Savion is possibly the best tap dancer that ever lived," Gregory Hines has said of the young dancer. "Every now and then someone comes along who is just better than everyone else. That's how I feel about Savion" (Lahr, 90).

FURTHER READING

Acocella, Joan. "On Tap," *The New York Review of Books* (6 June 1996).

Acocella, Joan. "Taking Steps," *The New Yorker* (12 Jan. 2004).

Lahr, John. "King Tap," *The New Yorker* (30 Oct. 1995).

Simas, Rick. "Performance Review," *Theatre Journal* (May 1997).

MEREDITH BROUSSARD

Goines, Donald Joseph (15 Dec. 1937–21 Oct. 1974), writer, was born in Detroit, Michigan, to Joseph Leonard and Myrtle Baugh Goines, business owners. He attended parochial schools, and his parents expected him to work in the family dry cleaning and laundry business. Donnie, as he was known, first had difficulties in his studies at school in the third grade and was held back that year. He lost interest in classes, dropped out after finishing the ninth grade, and, beginning in 1952, served three years in the U.S. Air Force, having used a fake ID to enlist because he was too young to serve. It was during his overseas assignments in Japan and Korea that he became addicted to heroin.

Goines's street legend finds him returning to the United States, becoming a street hustler, running numbers and bootleg liquor, and pimping prostitutes. All of this he purportedly documented in his later autobiographical works. In reality, however, Goines was addicted to drugs and lived on the streets. He was arrested for armed robbery and, all told, spent six and one-half years in jail throughout his lifetime for his illegal activities.

His first two novels were written in prison. As an inmate, Goines read the unpublished work of other prisoners, as well as various forms of pulp fiction. He enjoyed writing westerns, but publishers turned down the western novels he wrote and submitted from prison. Goines then discovered the street literature of ROBERT BECK, better known as Iceberg Slim. Goines's first novel, *Dopefiend: The Story of a Black Junkie*, was inspired by Beck's novel *Pimp: The Story of My Life*. Goines was released from prison in 1970, moved his family to Los Angeles and began writing. His second novel *Whoreson*, about a Detroit pimp, was published by Holloway House in 1971. Goines typically took just over a month to complete a novel, even though he had a serious addiction to heroin. His younger sister Joan worked as his proofreader and editor.

Goines wrote five novels under the pen name Al C. Clark. The main character in this series, Kenyatta, takes his name from Jomo Kenyatta, the adopted name of the first president of Kenya. Goines attributed superhero-like actions to his protagonists, who work to rid the ghettos of drugs, prostitution, and white police officers—all classified by Goines as exploiters of black inner-city residents. *Crime Partners*, published in 1974, is the first in the Kenyatta series. *Black Girl Lost* claims to trace the ghetto experience of a black girl on the streets and was later adopted as a song title by female hip-hop and rap performers. *Street Players*, the fourth Goines novel, comes closest to Goines's mentor Iceberg Slim in relating the semi-autobiographical story of a street youth who talks tough and fights to the top of his profession as a hustler. *White Man's Justice, Black Man's Grief* focuses on prison life and the systematic discrimination of black men. Holloway published these three novels in 1973.

Goines published eight more novels the following year. *Daddy Cool* tells the story of an avenging hit man on a personal mission when his daughter is forced to work as a prostitute for a local pimp. The novel *Crime Partners* continued the Kenyatta series. *Eldorado Red* borrows from Goines's own experience robbing a local gambling house to fund his heroin addiction. *Never Die Alone* chronicles a cocaine dealer's life on the streets. *Swamp Man* is purportedly the only novel Goines wrote that did not relate to his own life experiences. The main character of the novel was born and lived in Mississippi, rather than the streets of a northern town. *Cry Revenge* deals with a Los Angeles gang war between blacks and Chicano gangs, and *Death List* and *Kenyatta's Escape* continue building the persona of Kenyatta. *Inner City Hoodlum* is the story of a teen living in Los Angeles who steals from the local freight yard to support his family. The final novel of the Kenyatta series, *Kenyatta's Last Hit*, ends with the main character dying in a dramatic gunfight. Goines's last two novels were published posthumously in 1975.

The story of the deaths of Goines and his common-law wife Shirley reads like one of his novels. Goines disliked Los Angeles and was disappointed that he could not make a career in the film industry. Having lived in California after his release from prison in 1970, the family returned to Detroit after only two years. The couple was brutally murdered in their home in Highland Park, a suburb of Detroit, in what law enforcement officials believe was a dispute over drugs. Some fans believe that Goines was killed to silence him as a writer from writing about the life of a black man living in poverty. The couple's two young daughters were locked in a basement for hours and were discovered after the crime was reported to police the following morning. The murders received only a few sentences in local papers and were one of several murders that night in the neighborhood; the case remains unsolved.

Daddy Cool: The Story of a Hit Man's Fearful Vengeance in Defense of His Teenage Daughter's Honor was re-written and released as a graphic novel by Los Angeles publisher Melrose Square in 1984. The rappers and hip-hop artists TUPAC SHAKUR, Noreaga, JAY-Z, DMX, and Busta Rhymes all credited Goines as among their inspirations. Popular rapper Kool Genius Rap called himself the "Donald Goines of Rap," while rapper DMX bought the rights for the film adaptation of Goines's *Never Die Alone* and worked to bring the novel to the big screen in 2004. *Crime Partners 2000*, directed by J. Jesses Smith, was released in 2001. Both films received mixed critical and fan reviews.

Many fans consider *Black Gangster* to be Goines's seminal work. *Gangster* details the rise of a young man who becomes the head of organized crime in Detroit. The themes of ghetto or street life ring true with many youth living in the inner city. Goines's work also found a large audience with middle-class white youth living in the suburbs. The works of Iceberg Slim and Donald Goines continued to be popular reading for both whites and blacks in prison. Goines's novels were popular in Europe and sold in excess of five million copies worldwide.

FURTHER READING
Donald Goines's sister Joan holds many of his unpublished manuscripts.
Allen, Eddie B., Jr. *Low Road: The Life and Legacy of Donald Goines* (2004).
Stone, Eddie. *Donald Writes No More: A Biography of Donald Goines* (2001).

PAMELA LEE GRAY

Goldberg, Whoopi (13 Nov. 1955–), actress and comedian, was born Caryn Elaine Johnson in New York City, the second of two children of Emma Harris, a sometime teacher and nurse, and Robert Johnson, who left the family when Goldberg was a toddler. Goldberg attended St. Columbia School, a parochial school located several blocks from the family's working-class neighborhood. New York provided a stimulating, multicultural environment that encouraged Goldberg to reject the strictures of her Catholic education. By age eight, with the support of her mother, she began acting at the Hudson Guild in the Helena Rubinstein Children's Theater, and she also showed a precocious interest in ballet and music.

Goldberg appeared in as many Hudson Guild productions as possible, but was less focused on her schoolwork. Her academic difficulties were exacerbated by dyslexia, though this was not diagnosed until later, and she dropped out of Washington Irving High School at age fourteen. Although Goldberg's teenage insecurities were hardly atypical, she was particularly discouraged by the racism endemic in the career path that she hoped to follow: the movie industry. In Hollywood, a white standard of beauty predominated, and glamorous roles for black actresses had traditionally been reserved for light-skinned and lithe performers like DOROTHY DANDRIDGE and LENA HORNE. Caryn Johnson, however, was a brown-skinned beauty with full features of a type not yet acceptable to the entertainment industry's limited and racially determined ideas of beauty. But such racism did not deter her thespian ambitions, and she appeared in the chorus of the Broadway musicals *Jesus Christ Superstar* and *Hair*.

After leaving school, Goldberg had an unexpected pregnancy and abortion, and she became, as she later explained, "chemically dependent on many things for many years." Later, the escapades, pain, and difficulties of this period became fodder for her stand-up comedy routines, finding their way into her one-woman show. Eventually she entered treatment for substance abuse, and in 1973 she married her drug counselor, Alvin Martin. Their daughter, Alexandra, was born a year later, but the couple separated in the mid-1970s and Goldberg moved with her young daughter to San Diego, California. There she worked as a beautician, funeral home hairstylist, and bank teller while performing in local theater groups. She was also, for a few years, on welfare before finding success at the San Diego Repertory Company, appearing in Bertolt Brecht's *Mother Courage*, and with Spontaneous Combustion, an improvisational comedy group. Making her professional aspirations a reality required one more thing: to change her name, which she found boring, to a memorable moniker. She first chose "Whoopi Cushion" and then dropped Cushion for Goldberg, after her Jewish relatives. In the late 1970s Goldberg moved to Berkeley, California, where she lived with her daughter and the playwright-performer David Schein. Performing at the Blake Street Hawkeyes Theater in 1982, she developed a one-woman play, *The Spook Show*, which she based on characters derived from life. The show included monologues spoken by

Whoopi Goldberg, joking around as she reads to children inside the Scholastic tent at the Tribeca Family Festival in New York City, 8 May 2004. (AP Images.)

a thirteen-year-old valley girl–surfer chick who uses a hanger to give herself an abortion, a seven-year-old black girl who pines for blue eyes, and Fontaine, a junkie with a PhD in Literature. Her performance and some of her characters were controversial; but more importantly, they were fresh, anarchic, and hilarious. Goldberg toured the United States and Europe with *The Spook Show* and in 1983 performed at the Dance Theater Workshop in New York, where the director Mike Nichols approached her about bringing the production to Broadway. Instead, Goldberg returned to San Francisco and mounted *Moms*, a one-woman show that she cowrote as a tribute to the vaudevillian MOMS MABLEY. A year later Goldberg returned to New York and to Nichols. Her debut on Broadway, in the newly renamed show, *Whoopi Goldberg*, won her Theatre World and Drama Desk awards, and in 1985 she received a Grammy Award for Best Comedy Recording.

In 1985 Goldberg made her film debut in Steven Spielberg's adaptation of ALICE WALKER's *The Color Purple*. Grossing more than $80 million at the box office and earning an additional $50 million in home video rentals, the film was an unexpected commercial success. Its reception among African Americans was more controversial, however, as some black viewers believed that an African American filmmaker should have directed the movie; others took issue with what they deemed to be the material's unsympathetic depiction of black men. There was no such disagreement about Goldberg's strong, subtle performance, for which she received an Oscar nomination and a Golden Globe Award.

In addition to performing stand-up and touring with her one-woman show *Living on the Edge of Chaos*, Goldberg worked steadily in film and on television during the last half of the 1980s, although, with the exception of *Jumpin' Jack Flash* (1986), her films—*Burglar* (1987), *Fatal Beauty* (1987), *Clara's Heart* (1988), and *The Telephone* (1988)—were only marginal hits. Goldberg became a household name with *Ghost* (1990). The film grossed more than $517 million worldwide and earned Goldberg an Academy Award for Best Supporting Actress, the second Oscar awarded to a black woman. (HATTIE MCDANIEL had won in 1939.) In 1992's *Sister Act*, Goldberg again struck box-office gold and won a second Golden Globe, although this time, Hollywood acknowledged, she carried the film.

Having proved her financial value, Goldberg began balancing her Hollywood film appearances in comedies such as *Made in America* (1993), *Eddie* (1996), and *The Associate* (1996) with roles in smaller, independent films, including *The Long Walk Home* (1990), a film about the 1955 Montgomery bus boycott; a hilarious role as a cop in Robert Altman's Hollywood satire *The Player* (1992); *Sarafina!* (1992), a musical drama set in apartheid South Africa; *Corrina, Corrina* (1994), a 1950s period film in which she unexpectedly ends up as the romantic interest opposite the white actor Ray Liotta. She also appeared in *Boys on the Side* (1995), *How Stella Got Her Groove Back* (1998), and *Girl, Interrupted* (1999). In 1996 Goldberg portrayed MYRLIE EVERS-WILLIAMS, the wife of the slain civil rights leader MEDGAR EVERS, in the film *Ghosts of Mississippi*.

Goldberg's television career has been even more prodigious. In 1986, along with comedians Billy Crystal and Robin Williams, she began hosting the semiannual live broadcast *Comic Relief*, a comedy showcase fund-raiser for the homeless, and in 1992 she launched a short-lived, self-titled, late-night talk show. As she became one of America's most recognizable cultural figures, Goldberg was increasingly tapped to host television tributes and to appear in cameos as "herself." She also appeared in her own HBO stand-up specials and had a recurring role (1988–1993) as Guinan on *Star Trek: The Next Generation*. Her pivotal role in the 1994 and 2002 *Star Trek* films further proved her popularity and crossover appeal. In 1994 Goldberg hosted the 66th Annual Academy Awards, becoming the first black woman to preside over the Oscars since DIANA ROSS had cohosted in 1974. She returned to emcee the awards in 1996, 1999, and 2002. From 1998 until 2002 she was also executive producer and appeared as the center square of the Emmy Award–winning television game show *Hollywood Squares*.

Following her successful return to Broadway in 1997 as the lead in *A Funny Thing Happened on the Way to the Forum*, Goldberg expanded her theatrical activities, coproducing the Broadway revival of *Thoroughly Modern Millie* (2002) and *Harlem Song* (2002), a new musical by GEORGE C. WOLFE, and starring in and producing the Broadway revival of AUGUST WILSON's *Ma Rainey's Black Bottom* (2002), though the reviews for her performance were mixed.

Offscreen, Goldberg married David Claessen, a Dutch-born director of photography, in 1986, after her relationship with Schein ended in 1985.

Goldberg's subsequent private relationship with the actor Ted Danson sparked public controversy after Danson performed in blackface at the Friars Club roast of the actress in 1993. The following year she entered into a one-year marriage with the union organizer Lyle Trachtenberg, whom she met when he was unionizing the crew of *Corrina, Corrina*. From 1995 through 2000 she was involved with the actor Frank Langella.

The author of the best-selling *Book* (1997), Goldberg is the recipient of more than forty awards, including six People's Choice awards, five Kids' Choice awards, and nine NAACP Image awards; she has garnered fourteen Emmy nominations and the 2001 Kennedy Center's Mark Twain Prize for American Humor. Goldberg has been recognized as well for her humanitarian efforts on behalf of children, the homeless, human rights, substance abuse, and the battle against AIDS. (Her father died in 1993 from stomach cancer and complications from HIV infection.) In 1995 her hands, feet, and signature braids were pressed in cement outside Mann's Chinese Theatre in Los Angeles, and in 2001, on her forty-sixth birthday, she received a star on Hollywood's Walk of Fame.

Despite being an African American woman in a white-dominated industry, Goldberg has become a mainstay in American entertainment. An iconoclastic comedian and commentator, she uses humor both to critique and to amuse her audiences. Over the years there has been a mixed response to her celebrity. Some film critics and historians argue that her asexual characters perpetuate the iconic stereotype of the black mammy in the white household, while others interpret her screen persona differently, viewing Goldberg as an iconoclastic figure and countercultural force. However, even Whoopi—whose name signifies both flatulence and lovemaking—has expressed frustration with the selective editing of sex scenes that have landed on the cutting room floor. Goldberg returned to television in 2003 with the sitcom *Whoopi*, in which she played Mavis Rae, a one-hit wonder who now runs a small New York hotel. "Why not be active doing stuff that's still interesting to me? This was handed to me on a silver platter with no restrictions and no hassles. I have the ability to do the show I wanted to do" (*Jet* 104, no. 18 [2003]). Critics generally praised the show and compared the prickly, politically incorrect Mavis Rae to the Archie Bunker character in the 1970s sitcom *All in the Family*. In 2006, Goldberg appeared on an episode of *African*

American Lives, in which host HENRY LOUIS GATES, JR. traced her ancestry back to Florida of the Reconstruction Era.

Often described as too fat, too funny, too noisy, and too rebellious, Whoopi Goldberg, who is willing to offend and to be offensive, has become what the critic Kathleen Rowe has termed an "unruly woman." In Broadway performances, movies, and television appearances, she has played defiant characters who overturn social hierarchies, cross racial boundaries, and subvert conventional authority. Since 2007 Goldberg has been a regular contributor to the television talk show, *The View*, and in 2009 shared an Emmy Award for Outstanding Talk Show Host with her colleagues. In 2010 Goldberg appeared in *For Colored Girls*, Tyler Perry's adaptation of Ntozake Shange's play *For Colored Girls Who Have Considered Suicide When the Rainbow Is Enuf*. In 2011 she appeared as God in the romantic comedy, *A Little Bit of Heaven*, in a cameo in *The Muppets*, and was the narrator of *Being Elmo: A Puppeteer's Journey*, a documentary film on the career of KEVIN CLASH, the puppeteer and voice of *Sesame Street*'s Elmo.

FURTHER READING

Adams, Mary. *Whoopi Goldberg: From Street to Stardom* (1993).

Parish, James Robert. *Whoopi Goldberg: Her Journey from Poverty to Megastardom* (1997).

MIA L. MASK

Golden, Charles Franklin (24 Aug. 1912–17 Nov. 1984), Methodist bishop, was born in Holly Springs, Mississippi, to Dr. J. W. Golden and Mary Tyson. Both his father and a grandfather were Methodist ministers. Charles attended the precollegiate program at Rust College in Holly Springs, received his AB degree from Clark College in Atlanta, Georgia, and received a master of sacred theology degree from Boston University in 1938. He was ordained a deacon in the Methodist Episcopal Church in 1936 and was ordained an elder in 1938. He married Ida Elizabeth Smith on 24 May 1937, and their marriage lasted until his death.

While serving as pastor of Wesley Methodist Church in Little Rock, Arkansas, between 1938 and 1942, Golden was also professor of religion at Philander Smith College, one of twelve black colleges supported by the Methodist Church. He joined the U.S. Army chaplain's corps in 1942 and served in North Africa and Europe while rising to the rank of captain. In 1946 he returned to civilian life and joined the Methodist Church Board of Missions in the Department of Negro Work. In this capacity he traveled throughout the Central Jurisdiction, the all-black jurisdictional conference created by the Methodist Church (formed by the union of three Methodist denominations in 1939). Golden promoted the development of new churches and growth within existing congregations.

Golden was also an outspoken opponent of racial segregation, and in 1951 he authored a petition in the Lexington Annual Conference of the Central Jurisdiction that called for a racially inclusive policy within the Methodist Church. He was elected to the Methodist General Conference in 1956 and 1960, and he served on the Commission on Inter-jurisdictional Relations during the 1956–1960 quadrennium. On this seventy-member body he was an advocate of a target date for the end of the Central Jurisdiction, a position that was more militant than that taken by some of his fellow commission members from the Central Jurisdiction. DR. JAMES P. BRAWLEY, president of Clark College and also a member of the commission from the Central Jurisdiction, felt that a target date was unrealistic given the opposition of southern states to the *Brown v. Board of Education* desegregation decision. Golden wanted the church to establish a clear moral example, while Brawley feared that pious proclamations might energize segregationists more than advocates of integration.

At the 1960 meeting of the Central Jurisdiction, Golden was elected bishop and assigned to supervise annual conferences in Alabama, Mississippi, and Tennessee. He served on the Commission of Thirty-Six to speed desegregation in the Methodist Church, but he led the fight within the Central Jurisdiction against the commission's proposals that he felt were inadequate and piecemeal. Most dramatically, he joined Methodist clergy who were protesting racial segregation by white Methodist congregations in Jackson, Mississippi. On Easter Sunday 1964 Golden and Bishop James K. Mathews, a liberal white bishop from Boston, attempted to integrate the congregation of Galloway Methodist church. They were turned away, despite a statement made earlier by the Council of Bishops of the Methodist Church condemning segregationist policies. This Easter incident led the 1964 General Conference of the Methodist Church to legislate that all Methodist congregations be open for worship and membership without regard to race. Ironically, the church acted only a couple of months before the United States Congress passed the Civil Rights Act, signed by President Lyndon Johnson on 2 July 1964.

After the end of the Central Jurisdiction and the creation of the United Methodist Church in 1968, Golden transferred to the Western Jurisdiction and served as bishop over San Francisco and later Los Angeles. He served as president of the United Methodist Church Council of Bishops in 1973–1974. He supported the formation of Black Methodists for Church Renewal as an independent caucus for change, and he embraced the Black Power movement through his participation in the National Conference of Black Churchmen (NCBC). Formed in 1966 as the National Committee of Negro Churchmen, the organization met annually and interpreted the "Black Manifesto" of James Forman and attacked racism in American churches and Christian theology. The NCBC first issued statements in advance of JAMES H. CONE's *Theology and Black Power*, a seminal work published in 1969, and Golden continued to skewer racism in American churches.

The anti–Vietnam War movement also garnered Golden's time and energy, especially demonstrations at the Oakland, California, armory. In 1978 Golden defended the United Methodist Church on the CBS program *60 Minutes* in a segment on the Pacific Homes, a chain of twelve retirement communities affiliated with his annual conference that went bankrupt because of high inflation and inadequate financial reserves. The case had enormous implications for Methodists and other denominations because plaintiffs held the entire denomination responsible for the actions of an affiliated institution.

Bishop Golden retired in 1980, but for a generation of African American Methodist ministers such as Rev. JAMES M. LAWSON JR. and JOSEPH E. LOWERY he was a towering figure. When many Methodist leaders lamented the United Methodist Church's steep decline in membership that began in the 1960s, Bishop Golden attributed the loss to a lack of commitment to social justice. To him the greatest tool available to the church was through proclaiming a gospel that transformed believers. His courage to preach the gospel fearlessly and his willingness to take part in social action were unsurpassed among his generation of black Methodist leaders.

FURTHER READING
Murray, Peter C. *Methodists and the Crucible of Race, 1930–1975* (2004).

Wilmore, Gayraud S., and James H. Cone, eds. *Black Theology: A Documentary History, 1966–1979*, 2d ed. (1993).

PETER C. MURRAY

Golden, Lily (18 July 1934–), academic and writer, was born in Tashkent, Uzbekistan, to OLIVER JOHN GOLDEN, an African American agronomist, and Bertha Bialek, an English teacher of Polish-Jewish descent. Communist sympathizers who found life in America as an interracial couple extremely difficult, Oliver and Bertha led an expedition of sixteen African American agricultural experts to the Soviet Union in 1931 in an attempt to assist the USSR's agricultural development, specifically the cotton industry in Uzbekistan. Shortly after Golden's birth, her parents were offered work at universities in Tashkent, capital of the then-named Uzbek Soviet Socialist Republic. In 1937, the family was given an ultimatum by the Soviet government: to leave the country or renounce their American citizenship. As Golden later wrote, "Neither my father nor my mother was inclined to take their newly born child back to the racism and intolerance that they had experienced in the United States" (p. 15).

Golden's father died of heart failure and an old kidney injury in 1940; to compensate during the war, her mother took on two more jobs using her translating skills, and rented out two of their apartment rooms. Golden showed a high proficiency for music and tennis at an early age; while attending high school in Tashkent, she played in national youth tennis tournaments before her graduation in 1952. Urged by the actor and fellow African American emigré Wayland Rudd, Golden left home to attend Moscow State University that fall, but was initially turned away, ironically, because of her Jewish roots. Through the connections of Robert Ross, a leader of the black community of Moscow, Golden was accepted into the university, becoming the first student of African descent at Moscow State.

Golden sought special dispensation from the administration to study black history at the school, though—like her parents, who had occasionally been harassed by the KGB—she was subjected to state suppression. Her thesis, "The Struggle of Radical Republicans in the American Congress against Slavery," was initially rejected because it did not include any quotations from the late dictator Joseph Stalin, who had died four years earlier. Lacking employment opportunities following her graduation in 1957, she was ordered by the university administration to teach German in a small village school near the city of Saratov. Golden escaped the assignment by landing a job with the nascent African Department at Moscow's Oriental Institute of the Academy of Science.

Golden had been married briefly in 1956—her husband was killed shortly after their wedding in an automobile crash—but received a new proposal in 1960 from Abdulla Kassim Hanga, a Zanzibari revolutionary who had harbored a crush since hearing friends' reports of her work at a Moscow International Youth Festival in 1957. When Golden demurred, Hanga transferred from Oxford to Moscow's New Peoples' Friendship University to complete his degree and continue his courtship. The two wed in 1961, causing ripples in international relations: just as Britain's House of Commons debated the continental effects of an African revolutionary marrying a Soviet academic, Russia's KGB began investigating her for marrying a foreigner.

In May 1962, Golden gave birth to a daughter, YELENA KHANGA; disappointed that the child wasn't a son, Hanga abruptly left the country for Zanzibar. Following his release from political prison in 1963, Hanga was named to a high cabinet post in the post-revolutionary government of Tanzania, the country merged from Taganyika and Zanzibar. When Hanga visited Moscow as part of a state delegation, his more conservative religious views drove him and Golden further apart. In 1965, he disappeared; only in the 1970s did Golden discover he had been the victim of a political assassination.

After finishing her dissertation on African music for the Soviet Academy of Science, Golden settled in for life as an academic, but also acted in Russian films that required people of African descent. Originally blocked from giving speeches by the Communist Party Committee of her scientific institute, Golden began lecturing throughout the USSR, and was elected secretary of the Scientific Council on Culture and Literature of the Society of Knowledge.

She came under further scrutiny by the Soviet government when her old friend Svetlana Alliluyeva, Stalin's daughter, escaped the country and began publishing books about life within the USSR, mentioning Golden in glowing terms. Despite being the subject of travel restrictions and constant investigations, Golden continued to publish articles on African history and culture. In 1978, she married her third husband, a well-known novelist and journalist, Boris Yakovlev.

As the Russian state moved toward glasnost in the 1980s, Golden was invited to the United States as part of a "Peace Committee," a delegation of non-Party-affiliated Russians. She visited America three times between 1987 and 1989, giving lectures at universities and traveling to various cities. After the television program 20/20 ran a show on the Afro-Russian family of Golden and her daughter, Yelena, a journalist for the Moscow News, an American cousin organized a homecoming for her in Chicago. In 1992, another family reunion brought together 130 of Golden's cousins from both her black Alabaman and white, Jewish New York roots.

After the dissolution of the Soviet Union, Golden continued her role as a cultural ambassador, escorting black artists from Russia to America, and serving on the Board of Directors of the Center of Citizen Initiatives, the Council of Elders of the International Cross-cultural Black Women's Studies Institute, and the United Nations' Committee on Racism. She was invited to be Chicago State University's "Distinguished Scholar in Residence" in 1993. In the following years Golden split her time between Chicago, where she also held a professorship from 1993 to 2003, and Moscow, where her daughter Yelena and grandchild lived.

FURTHER READING
Golden, Lily. My Long Journey Home (2002).
Khanga, Yelena, with Susan Jacoby. Soul to Soul (1994).
                                        ADAM W. GREEN

Golden, Marita (28 Apr. 1950–), novelist, essayist, educator, and activist, was born and raised in Washington, D.C. She was an only child. Golden's mother, a native of Greensboro, North Carolina, was a cleaning woman who played the lottery and became wealthy enough to afford many properties; her father was a taxicab driver. Neither parent had any formal education, but Golden was inspired to write by her father's bedtime stories, which involved African American history and culture. Her mother encouraged her writing talents, too. At age ten Golden had a letter published in the editorial section of the Washington Post. Around age fourteen Golden's mother told her that she was going to write books. This was surprising to Golden because she never even saw her mother reading.

In 1968 Golden graduated from high school and attended American University in Washington, D.C., on a FREDERICK DOUGLASS Scholarship that was developed as a result of the riots that occurred a year earlier upon the assassination of DR. MARTIN LUTHER KING JR. While at American University she was very active in the revolutionary fervor of the Black Power philosophy. Along with friends who were charter members of the Student Nonviolent Coordinating Committee, her activist spirit grew. As a student at American University she sat on a panel to help develop a program in African American studies and upon graduation gained experience as a journalist by interning with the *Baltimore Sun*; she later became a general assignment reporter. She then attended Columbia University and graduated with an MFA in Journalism. Upon graduation she became an editorial assistant and wrote freelance articles in the evenings. Her articles were published in the *New York Times*, the *Washington Post*, and *Essence* magazine. In 1975 she married a native Nigerian and later moved to Africa with him. While in Nigeria she taught at the University of Lagos and began writing *Migrations of the Heart: An Autobiography*.

After living in Nigeria for many years Golden returned to the United States, residing in Boston and then Washington, D.C. Upon her return Golden founded the African American Writers Guild with her friend Clyde McElevene so that African American writers could meet, write, and focus their efforts in order to establish a strong literary tradition in the Washington, D.C., area. Determined to encourage literature among African Americans, Golden founded the ZORA NEALE HURSTON/RICHARD WRIGHT Foundation in 1990 in order to reward talented college writers and to stimulate the documentation of the African American experience through literature. The foundation was the first organization of its kind committed to recognizing African and African American literature throughout the African diaspora. The foundation now rewards writers of African descent with a number of awards, including the Hurston/Wright Award for College Writers and the Hurston/Wright Legacy Award.

Golden's spirit of activism was not limited to literature. While in Washington, D.C., she confronted the harsh reality of alarming mortality rates among African American males within the District and surrounding areas. In 1996 she wrote *Saving Our Sons*, reflecting her emotional distress as the mother of a young African American male and her perceptions about the mortality rates of young black men in the District of Columbia. *Skin Deep*, coauthored with Susan Shreve, addressed the issues within the context of gender, raising children, friendship, and self-identity.

By 2006 Golden was the author of eleven books and was still writing. She resided in the Washington, D.C., metropolitan area and was an activist for literacy and the accurate portrayal of the African American existence in literature. Golden received numerous awards, including an honorary doctorate from the University of Richmond and the Distinguished Alumni Award from American University. She was honored with the 2002 Authors Guild Award for Distinguished Service to the Literary Community, an award that recognized her as a "literary cultural worker." She also received the Barnes and Noble 2001 Writers for Writers Award presented by Poets and Writers. She was inducted into the International Hall of Fame for Writers of African Descent at the Gwendolyn Brooks Center at Chicago State University, and she received the Woman of the Year award from Zeta Phi Beta. In addition to her awards and prizes Golden is on the advisory committee for the Mobil Pegasus Prize for Literature. She also was a member of the board of the Girl Scouts of America and the Authors Guild and served as a member of the PEN/Faulkner board.

FURTHER READINGS
Golden, Marita. *Don't Play in the Sun: One Woman's Journey through the Color Complex* (2004).
Golden, Marita. *Migrations of the Heart: An Autobiography* (1984).

DAMARIS B. HILL

Golden, Oliver John (18 Nov. 1887–1940), a trained agronomist who organized a team to help the Soviet Union develop its economy, and remained in the Uzbek Soviet Socialist Republic until his death, was born on a cotton farm in Yazoo County, Mississippi, the son of Hilliard and Catherine Golden.

Golden's father was born in Mississippi in 1844, to parents born in North Carolina, while his mother was born in Texas, to a father born in North Carolina and a mother born in Virginia. He had older sisters born between the years 1862 and 1886 (Mary, Martha, Elizabeth, Rebecca, Biddie, Miriam, Virginia Mamie), and younger brothers and sisters born between 1891 to 1900 (Willie, Lily, and Viola). Golden's parents and grandparents had all been enslaved from birth until 1863. After emancipation, Hilliard Golden saved money to acquire a substantial cotton farm, but when his hired workforce came to include people classified by law as "white," in addition to people classified as "black," a mob burned down the family home in the 1890s, and again in 1909. The second time the family was forced to abandon the property and move to Memphis, Tennessee. Later, Hilliard and Catherine Golden resettled in Moorhead, Mississippi (Census, 1920).

Golden enrolled at Alcorn State College in Mississippi, then spent two years at Tuskegee

Institute, where he worked closely with Dr. GEORGE WASHINGTON CARVER, but had to be spirited away in 1913 after getting into a fight with a local resident considered "white." Drafted into the army in Clarksdale, Mississippi, during World War I he served in noncombat support assignments with the 92nd Division. Honorably discharged 14 July 1919—Bastille Day in France—he worked in post office jobs and as a railroad chef out of Chicago. He married for the first time in 1925 to a woman named Jane.

Lovett Fort-Whiteman, an African American communist recently returned from the Soviet Union, encouraged his old friend Golden to go to school in Moscow. In 1925 Golden traveled with Jane to the Soviet Union, along with a contingency that included the prominent communists Otto Hall and HARRY HAYWOOD, to attend the University for Oriental Workers, known by its Russian acronym, KUTV. Golden later remarked, "I would have done anything to get off those dining cars" (Carew, p. 10). Haywood joked that Golden was "the only person in the world who speaks Russian with a Mississippi dialect" (Golden, p. 4).

Despite the respectful turnout of the entire university for Jane's funeral, her death that year of an infectious illness drove Golden into depression. He was nursed back to health by a Soviet-Asian woman named Anya, and had a son by her named Ollava. He had no further contact with either after his return to the United States in November 1927, but his daughter later reestablished contact with her half-brother in the 1950s, learning that Anya had been a highly decorated partisan during World War II.

Plunging back into political activity in New York, Golden opened a cooperative restaurant, served as a member of the executive committee of the Negro Workers Relief Committee (initially the Negro Committee for Miners Relief) chaired by Grace P. Campbell, and according to family legend, met his future wife Bertha Bialek in a New York jail after being arrested at a demonstration. The daughter of Polish-Jewish immigrants, Bialek married Golden against the wishes of her family, including the communist brother who had inspired her work with the International Ladies Garment Workers Union. One of her oldest friends later told Bertha's granddaughter, "Bertha and your grandfather had a shared belief in equal justice for all, regardless of race, color, or creed. She didn't fall in love with Golden *because* he was a black man. It's just that Bertha wouldn't have let his color stop her from seeing the person inside." (Carew, p. 100).

Golden conceived the idea of aiding the economic development of the non-European peoples of the USSR, who in American terms were considered "colored," while in the USSR the term "national minorities" was being introduced. While "Fifty of America's largest industrial concerns [including giants like Ford Motor Company] have sent 2,000 of their representatives to Soviet Russia to help develop the Russian industry," Golden wrote, "so far we have not on record any Negro specialists in Russia" (Carew, p. 92). In this effort Golden wanted African Americans in leading roles.

In December 1930, he initiated correspondence with Dr. Carver about assembling a team of skilled African American agronomists trained in the production of cotton. Carver responded positively, and recommended some of his best students, including John Sutton and George Tynes, but declined Golden's solicitation to visit the Soviet Union himself. "Russia is the only country in the world today," Golden wrote, "that gives equal chances to black and white alike" (Carew, p. 90).

A team of fourteen, including graduates of Tuskegee, Hampton Institute, and Wilberforce and Howard Universities, departed by ship for Hamburg, Germany, in 1931. They arrived in Leningrad the same year, and on the anniversary of the Bolshevik revolution, proceeding to Tashkent, Uzbekistan, and finally to the remote rural village of Yangiyul. Their primary assignment was to develop productive cotton farming in the Syr Darya river valley, which they did so well that cotton remains a major commodity there today, albeit with unanticipated environmental problems.

The Goldens had one daughter, LILY GOLDEN, born in Tashkent, 19 July 1934. Lily's daughter YELENA KHANGA would later write that her grandparents would have returned to the United States in 1937, but did not want to raise a racially mixed child in America (Carew, p. 160). The Goldens were offered teaching positions in Tashkent; Oliver a professorship in agronomy and Lily a professorship in English at the Institute of Foreign Languages. They received visits from Americans touring the USSR, including LANGSTON HUGHES and the family of PAUL ROBESON. The Soviet authorities' open invitation for foreign help—though speeding up economic production in the 1930s—gave way to a growing paranoia about any ties to foreign countries, and in 1936 the Goldens applied for Soviet citizenship.

Golden died in 1940 in Tashkent, the result of heart failure and a long-standing kidney ailment inflicted by a police night stick in New York in the 1920s. He was survived by his wife and daughter, who remained in the Soviet Union. In 1958, when W. E. B. DuBois suggested to Nikita Krushchev the creation of an African Institute within the Soviet Academy of Sciences, Lily Golden became its first scholar. She eventually reclaimed her American citizenship (since she was born before her parents renounced theirs), but her daughter Yelena, born to a brief marriage in Russia with Zanzibari independence leader Abdulla Kassim Khanga, continued to identify herself as "Russian to the core."

FURTHER READING

Carew, Joy Gleason. *Blacks, Reds, and Russians: Sojourners in Search of the Soviet Promise* (2008).

Golden, Lily. *My Long Journey Home* (2002).

Gilmore, Glenda Elizabeth. *Defying Dixie: The Radical Roots of Civil Rights, 1919–1950* (2008).

Haybes, Karima A. "Soul to Soul: How a Black/Jewish/Polish/Russian/African Woman Found Her Roots," *Ebony*, Dec. 1992.

Khanga, Yelena. *Soul to Soul: A Black Russian American Family, 1865–1992* (1992).

CHARLES ROSENBERG

Goldsby, Crawford (Cherokee Bill) (8 Feb. 1876–19 Mar. 1896), western outlaw, was born at Fort Concho, Texas, the second of four children of George and Ellen (Beck) Goldsby. Born a slave near Selma, Alabama, Crawford's father George Goldsby was serving a Confederate officer when he ran off to Union lines during the Battle of Gettysburg. When the Civil War ended, he enlisted in the Tenth U.S. Cavalry, eventually becoming that regiment's sergeant major. A Cherokee freedwoman, Ellen Beck was of African, white, and Cherokee ancestry; she also served as a laundress for the cavalrymen. Her marriage to George was not a success, and the couple would soon separate.

Although Crawford Goldsby, according to some sources, was barely literate, from the age of seven, he spent three years at the "Indian School" in Cherokee, Kansas; and from the age of ten, he spent two years at the Carlisle Indian Industrial School, in Carlisle, Pennsylvania. When Crawford returned home, he found that his mother had remarried. However, Crawford did not get along with his stepfather, Private William Lynch, Company K, Ninth U.S. Cavalry, and his discipline soon became a problem. At the age of fifteen, he was sent to live with his sister Georgia and her husband Mose Brown in the town of Nowata, in what was then Indian Territory (and would eventually become Oklahoma).

Very soon after his arrival, Crawford began to quarrel with his brother-in-law, then packed his bags and left. Until he reached the age of eighteen, Crawford—who grew into a burly six-foot-tall man—worked on farms and ranches in the area. Although he had a good reputation among his peers and his employers, he got into serious trouble. Back in Fort Gibson, while attending a dance, his younger brother Clarence got into an altercation with an older black man named Jake Lewis. Crawford went to his brother's defense, but both he and Clarence were severely beaten. Crawford decided to settle matters. He picked up a pistol and shot Lewis off his horse.

Thinking that he had killed Lewis, Crawford mounted Lewis's horse and rode away. Lewis survived his wounds, but by the time Crawford learned this, he had met Jim and Bill Cook, two part-Cherokee brothers who, with several other African American and Indian outlaws, would form the Cook Gang. They robbed banks, trains, grocery stores, stagecoaches, railroad stations, and express offices in the Indian Territory.

In June 1894 a posse of lawmen rode to the town of Tahlequah in an attempt to serve a warrant on Jim Cook, only to be met by gunfire from Goldsby and the Cook brothers. Posse member Sequoyah Houston was shot and killed by Goldsby, while Jim Cook, seriously wounded, was left behind and captured. It was after this fight that Goldsby got the nickname "Cherokee Bill." When a witness was asked if Goldsby had been present, the witness replied, "No, it was Cherokee Bill," and the name stuck (Burton).

After separating from Bill Cook, Cherokee Bill rode to his sister's home, attempting to find a hideout. There are several different stories behind what brought about the next event, but all accounts agree that Bill was on the move once again, as he had shot and killed his brother-in-law Mose Brown. While making his escape, Goldsby hopped a Missouri-Pacific train. The train's conductor, Sam Collins, demanded that Bill pay for a ticket. So Goldsby shot him dead.

The Cook Gang continued its rampage throughout Indian Territory for several more months. On 31 July 1894, the Cook Gang robbed the Lincoln County Bank in Chandler, Indian Territory, and Cherokee Bill shot and killed the town barber, J. M. Mitchell. On 8 November 1894, the Cook Gang attempted to rob a general store in Lenapah,

Indian Territory; in the middle of the robbery, a housepainter named Ernest Melton peered through the store's window and soon fell dead with a bullet in his brain, courtesy of Goldsby. Now with a $1,500 reward on his head, Cherokee Bill broke away from the gang and, with two others, robbed the railway station at Nowata, killing the station agent, R. L. "Dick" Richards.

On 29 January 1895 Cherokee Bill was captured by U.S. deputy marshals at the home of Ike Rogers near Nowata, where Goldsby had been meeting one of his girlfriends, Maggie Glass. He was brought to Fort Smith, Arkansas, to stand trial in the court of U.S. District Judge Isaac C. Parker, also known as the "Hanging Judge." Cherokee Bill was found guilty and sentenced to hang the following June. While awaiting the execution of the sentence, he was confined in Fort Smith, and as the days passed, he grew somewhat uneasy. News that his counsel had obtained a stay of execution was not a comfort to him, nor to his jailers who heard rumors that Goldsby was planning an escape.

These rumors proved true, and on 26 July 1895 Cherokee Bill attempted a jailbreak using a pistol that had been smuggled in to him. He shot and killed one of the turnkeys, Lawrence Keating, and held off twenty lawmen for several hours until fellow inmate, an Indian named Henry Starr, volunteered to try and persuade Goldsby to give up. After ten minutes, Starr reappeared holding Goldsby's pistol, and the siege was over.

On 8 August 1895, Goldsby was brought to trial for Lawrence Keating's murder; although he pleaded not guilty, on 10 September 1895 he was convicted of murder. The verdict was appealed to the U.S. Supreme Court, and a stay of execution was granted; however, on 2 December 1895 the Supreme Court affirmed Goldsby's conviction, and he was scheduled to hang on 17 March 1896. When asked if he had any last words, Cherokee Bill scowled and said, "I came here to die, not to make a speech" (Burton). He was only twenty years old. His mother and sister claimed his body and buried him in the family plot at the Cherokee National Cemetery in Fort Gibson, Oklahoma.

FURTHER READING

Burton, Arthur T. *Black, Red, and Deadly: Black and Indian Gunfighters of the Territory, 1870–1907* (1991).

Shirley, Glenn. *Law West of Fort Smith* (1968).

Shirley, Glenn. *Marauders of the Indian Nation: The Bill Cook Gang and Cherokee Bill* (1994).

REGINALD H. PITTS

Gomes, Peter John (22 May 1942– 28 Feb. 2011), Plummer Professor of Christian Morals and Pusey Minister in the Memorial Church at Harvard University, was born in Boston, Massachusetts. He was the only child of Peter Lobo Gomes, a cranberry bog laborer who had immigrated from the Cape Verde Islands, and Orissa Josephine Gomes (née White), a member of a prominent family in the black aristocracy of Boston, a graduate of the New England Conservatory of Music, and the first black woman to work in the Massachusetts State House, where she was a principal Clerk. Peter J. Gomes was raised in the predominantly white town of Plymouth, Massachusetts, where he was the only black student in his class. An exceptional student and the president of his class, Gomes devoted himself to the First Baptist Church of Plymouth, where his mother played the organ and directed the choir and where Gomes preached his first sermon at the age of twelve. On Sunday evenings Gomes and his mother attended the Bethel African Methodist Episcopal (AME) Church to worship among the handful of other black Christians of Plymouth.

Gomes received an AB in History from Bates College in 1965, planning a career as a museum curator, but at the suggestion of a Bates religion professor instead enrolled at Harvard Divinity School. In 1968, after receiving the STB and the prestigious Billings Prize in preaching at Harvard Divinity School, where he was a Rockefeller Fellow, and being ordained as an American Baptist minister by the First Baptist Church of Plymouth, Gomes accepted the position of instructor of history and director of the freshman experimental program at the Tuskegee Institute in Alabama. His two years at Tuskegee represented the first time that Gomes had been to the South and the first time that he had been part of a predominantly black community.

In 1970 Gomes accepted an offer from the Reverend Charles P. Price, preacher to the University and Plummer Professor of Christian Morals, to return to Harvard as the assistant minister in the Memorial Church. After Price retired in 1972 Gomes served as acting minister, and then in 1974 was appointed by President Derek C. Bok to the position of Plummer Professor of Christian Morals and Minister in the Memorial Church. Gomes also served as an administrator and trustee and on numerous advisory boards throughout his career. From 1978 until 1982 he was national chaplain for the American Guild of Organists. An accomplished organist in his own right, Gomes often spent his summers serving as an organist at the church in which he was ordained: the First Baptist Church of Plymouth, Massachusetts.

From his opening prayer at Freshman Sunday to his benediction at commencement, Gomes's voice was the first and last official voice heard by every Harvard student. An avowed conservative and Republican, Gomes delivered the benediction at President Ronald W. Reagan's second inauguration and the sermon at President George H. W. Bush's inauguration. Widely regarded as one of America's most distinguished preachers Gomes also regularly preached and lectured in the British Isles.

At Harvard in 1990 he was acting director of the W. E. B. DuBois Institute for Afro-American Research. He was director of the English-Speaking Union, on the board of *The Living Pulpit* and the advisory board of the Winterthur Museum in Delaware, and was a trustee of the Museum of Fine Arts in Boston, the Public Broadcasting Service, Donation to Liberia, Bates College, Wellesley College, the Charity of Edward Hopkins, Boston Freedom Trail, Plymouth Plantation, Roxbury Latin School, the Boston Foundation, Plymouth Public Library, Handel and Haydn Society, Pilgrim Society of Plymouth, Massachusetts, and the International Fund for Defense and Aid in South Africa. He served as president of the Signet Society, Harvard's oldest literary society, and of the Pilgrim Society of Plymouth and the International Fund for Defense and Aid in South Africa. He was a member of the Massachusetts Historical Society, the Colonial Society of Massachusetts, the Council of Sarum College in Salisbury, England, the Farmington Institute of Christian Studies, the Royal Society of Church Music, the American Baptist Historical Society, the Unitarian Historical Society, and was a Fellow of the Royal Society of Arts in London, England, and an honorary member of the Country Day School Headmasters Association.

In November 1991 Gomes spoke at a student gathering on the steps of Memorial Church following the publication of a conservative undergraduate magazine that had characterized homosexuality as immoral and pitiable. Before a few hundred students Gomes affirmed the rightful place of homosexual men and women in the church, and concluded with the proclamation that he was "a Christian who happens as well to be gay." Word of Gomes's "coming out" spread quickly on campus, and soon thereafter the national media picked up his story, resulting in articles in the *Washington Post* and *Time* and appearances on *Nightline*. Gomes did not wish to be an activist and he did not want the attention, but the exposure nonetheless vaulted him into a more national role as a prominent clergyman.

The publication of *The Good Book: Reading the Bible with Mind and Heart* (1996), a work that appeared on the *New York Times* best-seller list, spread Gomes's perspectives on the Bible internationally, both among clergy and laity. *The Good Book* was Gomes's towering literary achievement, both in its scope and in its influence. No longer merely an academic fixture, Gomes became far better known in the greater ecclesiastical and secular world. In 1997 Gomes's position at the church became endowed as the Pusey Minister, named in honor of Dr. Nathan March Pusey, Harvard's twenty-fourth president. Under Gomes's leadership and preaching, the Memorial Church underwent a revivification in attendance and influence on campus. Gomes became an iconic figure for his excellent humor and sharp wit, his unparalleled knowledge of the history of Harvard University, his popular classes in Harvard College and the Divinity School, and for his memorable sermons, which combined the oratory and verbal play of African American preaching with a rigorously intellectual rhetoric. He opened Sparks House, the Harvard parsonage, to the university and Cambridge communities for tea on Wednesday afternoons in term time, a valued tradition which he reclaimed from his days as a seminarian.

In 1998 he wrote *Sermons: Biblical Wisdom for Daily Living*. That same year he was named Clergy of the Year by Religion in American Life; he also presented the Lyman Beecher Lectures on Preaching at Yale Divinity School in 1998. He had special pride in being included in the summer 1999 premiere issue of *Talk* magazine as part of its feature article, "The Best Talkers in America: Fifty Big Mouths We Hope Will Never Shut Up." He delivered the University Sermon before the University of Cambridge and the Millennial Sermon in Canterbury Cathedral in 2000, served as Missioner to Oxford University, preached in the University Church of St. Mary the Virgin in 2001 and in the same year garnered the Phi Beta Kappa Teaching Award at Harvard University. In 2002 he traveled as the Hein Fry Lecturer for the Evangelical Lutheran Seminaries in the United States.

Gomes continued to write books, publishing *The Good Life: Truths That Last in Times of Need* (2002), *Strength for the Journey: Biblical Wisdom for Daily Living* (2003), and *The Backward Glance and the Forward Look* (2005). Gomes received over thirty honorary doctorates from colleges and universities throughout the United States, and was an Honorary Fellow of Emmanuel College at the University of Cambridge, where John Harvard, the founder of Harvard University, had studied, and where the Gomes Lectureship was established in his name. He delivered the Lyttleton Addresses at Eton College in 2003, offered the Convocation Address at Harvard Divinity School in 2004, and presented a series of sermons in England's St. Edmundsbury Cathedral in the presence of the Prince of Wales and the Duchess of Cornwall in 2005. Gomes was profiled by Robert Boynton in the *New Yorker*, interviewed by Morley Safer on *60 Minutes*, and named in a Baylor University study as one of the "12 Most Effective Preachers in the English-Speaking Language." Gomes died in Boston at the age of 68 from stroke-related complications.

FURTHER READING

Gomes, Peter J. *The Backward Glance and the Forward Look* (2005).

Gomes, Peter J. *The Good Book: Reading the Bible with Heart and Mind* (1996).

Gomes, Peter J. *The Good Life: Truths That Last in Times of Need* (2002).

Gomes, Peter J. *Sermons: Biblical Wisdom for Daily Living* (1998).

Gomes, Peter J. *Strength for the Journey: Biblical Wisdom for Daily Living* (2003).

STEPHEN BUTLER MURRAY

Gomez, Joseph (26 Nov. 1890–28 Apr. 1979), bishop of the African Methodist Episcopal Church, was born Joseph Antonio Guminston Gomes in the village of Willikies on the island of Antigua. His father, Manoel Gomes, was the son of Catholic immigrants who had settled on the island from Portugal and after some initial hardships became part of the Portuguese merchant class that established themselves below the British elite and above the black majority in the island's social and economic hierarchy. Sexual liaisons between European men and local women were common; Manoel Gomes had fathered at least one child through such an illicit relationship before meeting Joseph's mother, Rebecca Richardson, a woman of African descent. However, he violated all social norms when he took Rebecca as his common-law wife sometime in the 1880s and then secretly married her in an Episcopal service in 1896. Their union, which may have been unprecedented, ultimately produced nine children; Joseph was the third child, but he was the most favored because he was the first male.

At birth Joseph was named after his paternal grandfather, Antonio, but when he was baptized a year later in the Catholic Church he was given the name Joseph because that grandfather had refused to recognize him. Though disinherited, for a time Joseph's family lived fairly prosperous lives as the proprietors of a successful bakery. They had servants, and a private British tutor was hired to give Joseph his early classical education. Joseph resented the way that his mother and her children were ostracized from white social circles, and they thus preferred to worship at the Zion Hill Methodist Church, which later changed its name to Gilbert Memorial in honor of its founder. Gomez occasionally felt hostility from blacks who thought that families such as his were attempting to claim a higher status by virtue of their mixed-race ancestry, but since he was taught not to regard his lighter complexion as a privilege, he learned to ignore such sentiments. He was bright and studious, his father was affectionate and indulgent, and when he got into trouble it was his mother who assumed the role of the firm disciplinarian.

When the family fell on hard economic times, they lost their home and the bakery. In an effort to make a new start they moved to the island of Trinidad and established a bakery in the capital of Port of Spain. There Joseph enrolled in a private Methodist school and then, because of dwindling finances, enrolled in a local public school and finished his education. In 1908 at the age of seventeen he immigrated to the United States in search of better career opportunities.

In New York City he settled in the Tenderloin District of lower Manhattan. Gomez, as he began to spell his name, dreamed of becoming a lawyer, but he soon discovered that his high school diploma was not sufficient to gain him entrance to a college in the city. He resolved to attend school at night while he worked as an elevator operator and as a busboy in a Jewish restaurant during the day. On Sundays he attended the Bethel African Methodist Episcopal (AME) Church on West Twenty-fifth Street. What he experienced there altered the course of his life. Reverend Cassius Ransom was the dynamic pastor of this church, and his sermons were laced with references to the burning political issues of the day. For the first time Gomez heard the writings of W. E. B. DuBois discussed from the pulpit, and black politicians such as P. B. S. Pinchback and the assertive AME bishop Henry McNeil Turner were frequent speakers.

Reverend Ransom had been one of the founders of the Niagara Movement with DuBois. He urged blacks to reconsider their political loyalty to the Republican Party because it had become indifferent to the suffering of black people; within the city, Ransom and his wife were patrons of the arts—particularly the emerging black theater—and they took an immediate interest in Gomez's welfare, inviting him to their home where he met such luminaries as JAMES WELDON JOHNSON and BERT WILLIAMS. In 1910 Gomez saw the black community of New York come to the defense of BOOKER T. WASHINGTON, who had been assaulted and maligned in the city. In addition he was moved by other ministers such as the Reverend ADAM CLAYTON POWELL Sr., who, like Ransom, preached a social gospel that addressed the problems of poverty, crime, and inferior schools. All these influences combined to cause Gomez to join the AME church of his mentor and to seek a career in the ministry.

With Ransom's assistance Gomez obtained a scholarship to Payne Theological Seminary at Wilberforce University, an institution run by the AME Church. He began his studies in the fall of 1911 and met his future wife, Hazel Eliza Jane, a fellow undergraduate and a native of Ohio. On 18 June 1914 he received his degree and married Hazel on the same day. Shortly thereafter he was ordained an AME elder and began the process of becoming a U.S. citizen. Over the next sixty-five years Gomez would build one of the longest and most distinguished careers in the history of his denomination.

His first appointment was to Bethel AME Church in Bermuda. There Gomez began to establish his reputation as a church builder. In just under four years he expanded the congregation from sixty members to one hundred and sixty. As a community activist he protested the segregation of black soldiers in the Bermuda Volunteer Rifle Corps during World War I. And as a progressive thinker he promoted the full participation of women in church governance—including ordination (though his position on women never became dominant within the AME).

In 1917 Gomez was transferred to the Saint Paul AME Church in Hamilton, Ontario. Like black Methodists in the West Indies and the antebellum South, black Methodists in Canada were attracted to the AME because of its racial autonomy, its support for an educated ministry and laity, and its commitment to social justice. Gomez had represented the best of this tradition at Saint Paul's for almost two years when he was rewarded with his first American appointment, at the two-thousand-member Bethel Church in Detroit. By 1926 he had

nearly doubled the size of the congregation with sermons that appealed to the mind and moved the heart. Under his leadership Bethel provided a platform for leaders of the race such as the union organizer A. PHILIP RANDOLPH and the editor of the *Messenger* Chandler Owens—even though many critics labeled these men as Communists.

The AME General Conference in 1923 was held in Louisville, Kentucky. Hazel Gomez always attended these meetings with her husband, but on this occasion she and several other women interrupted one session with banners that read, "We Want Women Suffrage and Want It Now" (Gomez-Jefferson, *Through Love to Light*, 90). Reverend Gomez and several other delegates loudly applauded their efforts to gain a greater voice in the affairs of the church.

Back in Detroit, Reverend Gomez faced fierce opposition from white residents who opposed his plan to acquire land in a white section of the city to build a larger church for his growing congregation, Greater Bethel, and a sixty-acre cemetery for its members. He became a leading critic of the local Council of Churches, which had refused to condemn the Ku Klux Klan for its blatant acts of terrorism. After a cross was burned in front of Bethel, members were agitated and ready to defend their building; even Hazel volunteered, claiming that she could "aim high and shoot straight" (Gomez-Jefferson, *Through Love to Light*, 90), but Gomez urged calm and avoided even the threat of violence.

After ten years of marriage Hazel and Joseph had their first child, Hazel, in 1926; they had Annetta the following year. Bishops Ransom and Charles S. Smith would be Gomez's staunchest allies and greatly champion his career, but appointments were made by the presiding bishop in each district and elevations to the bishopric in the AME were made democratically at hotly brokered conventions. As a result of internal politics, in 1927 Gomez was transferred to Kansas City, Missouri, over the strenuous objection of the members of Bethel. Gomez was so disappointed that he briefly contemplated leaving the church and studying law instead.

In 1928 Gomez took up his duties at Allen Chapel and continued to pursue his vision. He attended a dinner in 1929 at which Harry S. Truman spoke, and he then challenged the future president for referring to African Americans as "niggers." Truman sheepishly insisted, "I didn't say 'niggers.' I said 'negras.'" Later Gomez joked that Truman learned to say "Negro" clearly (Gomez-Jefferson, *Through Love to Light*, 112). In contrast to Detroit, the Council of

Churches in Kansas voted to admit black congregations, and in 1930 Gomez made his first European trip as a delegate to the World Christian Endeavor Convention in Germany. At the height of the Depression in 1932, Gomez was again transferred, this time to Saint Paul in Saint Louis. There he continued his studies and in 1934 became one of the first two black candidates to receive a master's degree in sacred theology from Eden Seminary. At the pastor's invitation, Carter G. Woodson spoke at Saint Paul about the history and importance of the black church. In 1936 Gomez made his first unsuccessful attempt to become a bishop and was then assigned to Saint James AME Church in Cleveland, Ohio.

During World War II Gomez spoke out against segregation in the American armed forces just as he had in Bermuda. He planned to participate in A. Philip Randolph's proposed March on Washington in 1941 until President Roosevelt acceded to their demands and issued Executive Order 8802 prohibiting racial discrimination in war industries. Gomez excoriated the Red Cross's policy of first not accepting blood from black donors and then segregating it by race. Gomez was one of the few leaders of any race to condemn the illegal incarceration of Japanese Americans and the use of atomic weapons on Hiroshima and Nagasaki, even though it was dangerous and unpopular to do so.

After four previous attempts, Gomez was elected the sixty-seventh bishop of the AME Church in May 1948. This time Gomez was to be assigned to South Africa. The death of a fellow bishop caused him to be sent to Texas, however, where he played an instrumental role in rebuilding Paul Quinn College, which named a new administrative building in his honor. He served there for eight years, after which he presided over Tennessee and Kentucky and then over much of the Midwest. Throughout his career he worked to expand the church and supported several attempts to facilitate a merger with the rival African Methodist Episcopal Zion Church, but his most outstanding achievements during his thirty-one years as a bishop occurred during the civil rights movement.

When MARTIN LUTHER KING JR. addressed the AME Conference in 1964 he thanked the body for its support but encouraged them to join him in taking bolder steps. Though Gomez disapproved of the rhetoric of the Black Power movement, he had enthusiastically supported the nonviolent tactics employed by Dr. King. Gomez described the struggle as a "fight to save America from herself. We must win for the sake of the Negro, to be sure …

but also for the sake of America, whose image remains blurred and distorted by the injustices perpetrated in America" (Gomez-Jefferson, *Through Love to Light*, 311). Gomez worked most closely with Dr. King during his northern campaign against poverty and racism in Chicago during the spring of 1965. After many of the riots, marches, and protests of 1965 and a few weeks after the assassination of MALCOLM X, Gomez and several other AME ministers met with President Johnson at the White House. Gomez had been critical of the Vietnam War, but he fervently believed in Johnson's Great Society programs and appreciated Johnson's courage in backing the Voting Rights Act of 1964 and the Civil Rights Act of 1965.

When Dr. King was assassinated in April 1968, Gomez ordered the ministers in his district to go into the streets in an attempt to quell the violence. At the AME Conference in May, Gomez, who was seventy-eight years old and had already suffered a heart attack, called for the creation of a "freedom budget" and more politically relevant youth programs. Both resolutions were passed, and rather than giving Gomez a new district he was assigned to write the policy of the church, which was published in 1971. Yet after the death of a fellow bishop Gomez was called back into active service to preside over the seventeenth district in southern and central Africa. Though he was well past his prime, he and Hazel welcomed the opportunity to visit the continent. In 1972 Gomez officially retired, and in 1979 he died of a heart attack at the age of eighty-nine. His life and career epitomize the best of the African American ministerial tradition in the twentieth century.

FURTHER READING

The main body of papers covering Bishop Gomez's life and career were in the possession of his daughter, Annetta Gomez-Jefferson, who used them as the basis for two books: *Through Love to Light: Excerpts from the Sermons, Addresses, and Prayers of Joseph Gomez, a Bishop in the A.M.E. Church* (1997) and a scholarly biography on his life titled *In Darkness with God: The Life of Joseph Gomez, a Bishop in the African Methodist Episcopal Church* (1998). Other useful collections include those at the Schomburg Center for Research in Black Culture of the New York Public Library; the Saint Louis Historical Society; the Archives of Wilberforce University and Payne Theological Seminary, Wilberforce, Ohio; the Archives of Paul Quinn College, Waco, Texas; and the Library of Congress, Washington, D.C.

Lincoln, C. Eric, and Lawrence H. Mamiya. *The Black
Church in the African American Experience* (1990).

Richardson, Harry V. *Dark Salvation: The Story
of Methodism as It Developed among Blacks in
America* (1976).

Smith, Charles S. *A History of the African Methodist
Episcopal Church 1856–1922* (1922).

Wright, Richard R. *The Bishops of the African
Methodist Episcopal Church* (1963).

SHOLOMO B. LEVY

Gomillion, Charles Goode (1 Apr. 1900–4 Oct.
1995), civil rights activist, clinical sociologist, and
educator, was born in Johnston, a small town in
rural Edgefield County, South Carolina. His father,
Charles, a laborer, was illiterate, and his mother,
Flora, a cook who took in washing, could barely
read and write. Both of his parents encouraged him
and the three younger children to work hard, be
frugal, ask questions, and read. Gomillion remembered going alone and with his mother to ask "white
folks to give us magazines," and remembered that
his mother regularly brought home copies of the
Chicago Defender and the NAACP's *Crisis*.

When he was sixteen years old Gomillion left
home to pursue his high school education at Paine
College in Augusta, Georgia. He was admitted on
probation because he had completed only twenty-six months of formal education. Although he
worked the whole time he was at Paine to pay for
his schooling, he was in debt to the school at the
start of each new academic year. Of the thirty-five
students in his entering class, Gomillion said that
he was one of only six to graduate in 1920.

After moving up to the college level at Paine,
Gomillion left school in December 1922 and married a classmate, Hermyne Hones, on 2 January
1923. During the next three years Gomillion was
a junior high school principal in Milledgeville,
Georgia, and he and his wife became the parents
of two daughters. Gomillion returned to Paine in
1926 and graduated cum laude in 1928 as a social
science major.

After finishing at Paine, Gomillion accepted
a one-year post in Alabama teaching history in
Tuskegee Institute's high school program. That
limited-term position developed into a relationship that lasted more than forty years. Gomillion
taught in Tuskegee's high school for five years and
then was promoted to the college program. He
became a professor of sociology and also served as
dean of the School of Education, dean of students,
chair of the Division of Social Sciences, and dean

of the College of Arts and Sciences. Gomillion said
that "he never wanted to be anything other than
a teacher" and reluctantly accepted a number of
administrative posts only because he was allowed
to teach one or two courses per academic session.

Gomillion arranged a leave from Tuskegee for
one year in 1933–1934 to take graduate courses at
Fisk University in Nashville, Tennessee. He was
able to do that because Fisk waived his tuition,
the Bethlehem Center in Nashville gave him room
and board, and Tuskegee gave him his full salary.
Gomillion needed that money to support his family. He had divorced his wife in 1932, and his sister
in Washington, D.C., cared for his daughters while
he attended Fisk. While there he studied under
Bertram Doyle, who had been at Paine College, E.
FRANKLIN FRAZIER, who had come to Fisk from
the Atlanta School of Social Work, and CHARLES
S. JOHNSON, who had been with the Urban League.
Seven years later in 1941 Gomillion was awarded a
scholarship that allowed him to spend one quarter
in the Ohio State University graduate program in
education. While there he was advised to enroll in
the graduate program in sociology. Eighteen years
later, after periodically dropping out for financial
reasons, he finally received his PhD in sociology at
the age of fifty-nine.

While working at Tuskegee and finishing the doctoral program at Ohio State University, Gomillion
became increasingly involved in the advancement
of civil rights through activity in political and advocacy. He also was a cofounder of the Tuskegee Civic
Association (TCA) in 1941 and was the soft-spoken,
determined, patient president of the TCA for more
than twenty years (1941–1945, 1951–1968, and 1970).
TCA members encouraged African Americans to
vote and taught them how to register.

In his capacity as TCA president, Gomillion
began to challenge the treatment of black citizens in
Macon County. The struggle was long and difficult.
Numerous legal actions were initiated, and a boycott
of the white-owned businesses in Tuskegee began
in the early 1950s. The boycott—known in Tuskegee
as the "trade-with-your-friends campaign"—was
officially endorsed in 1957 by the TCA and continued for two more years. It had a great effect. Half of
the white-owned businesses closed by the spring of
1958, and sales were down 45–60 percent for those
that survived. At the same time white resistance
began to diminish, voter registration began to take
place, and the courts started to be responsive.

Gomillion's most significant legal victory came in
1960 in the U.S. Supreme Court. As president of the

Tuskegee Civic Association, he was the lead plaintiff in *Gomillion v. Lightfoot*, in which the high court outlawed the racial gerrymandering that kept all but about ten African American residents from voting in the Tuskegee elections. Fred Gray, the attorney for the Tuskegee Civic Association, thought that the *Gomillion* case led to one of the landmark decisions of the century because it resulted in the redistricting and reapportioning of various legislative bodies from city hall to the U.S. capitol. He also thought that it laid the foundation for the idea of "one person, one vote," which the U.S. Supreme Court later affirmed in *Baker v. Carr* in 1962.

Even after retiring from his university position in 1971, Gomillion continued to be active in numerous organizations and gave donations to a large number of academic and community groups (more than sixty, for instance, in 1988). Dr. Gomillion lived most of his last years in Washington, D.C., with his second wife, Blondelia. He remained passionately interested in civil rights and deeply concerned about civic democracy. At one point, when he was in his late eighties, he went to court with other tenants from his apartment building to protest conditions in the facility. He also continued his work on behalf of Paine College, in part because he felt that he could never do enough to repay Paine for giving him an education.

It was only when he reached his nineties that Gomillion began to slow down. On 1 July 1995 he announced that he would no longer hold any office in any organization, which was for the first time since September 1916, when he had nominated himself for treasurer of the first-year class at Paine College. He said he was now going to "act his age— eat, sleep, eat, sleep."

On 1 August 1995 Gomillion returned to Tuskegee, Alabama, to reside in the house where he had lived from 1940 to 1975. He said that it would probably be his home for the rest of his life. Gomillion, who had heart problems and had undergone surgery for internal bleeding, died in a hospital in Montgomery, Alabama, at the age of ninety-five. Always a practical man, he had prepared the complete notification list (including addresses) and requested that there be no funeral or flowers. He bequeathed his body to the University of Alabama School of Medicine for use in its teaching program.

FURTHER READING
Fritz, Jan Marie. "Charles Gomillion, Educator-Community Activist," *Clinical Sociology Review* (1988).

Guzman, Jessie Parkhurst. *Crusade for Civic Democracy: The Story of the Tuskegee Civic Association* (1984).

Norrell, Robert J. *Reaping the Whirlwind: The Civil Rights Movement in Tuskegee* (1985).

Taper, Bernard. *Gomillion versus Lightfoot: Apartheid in Alabama* (1962).

Obituary: *New York Times*, 12 Oct. 1995.

JAN MARIE FRITZ

Gonzales, Babs (27 Oct. 1916?–23 Jan. 1980), jazz singer and conversationalist, was born Lee Brown in Newark, New Jersey. His parents' names are unknown. Accounts of his activities may be unreliable, owing to his fondness for hyperbole and disinformation. His birth year has always appeared as 1919 in reference works, but his *New York Times* obituary gave his age as sixty-three, hence the 1916 birth year. In his first book Gonzales claimed to be four years younger than the saxophonist IKE QUEBEC (who was born in 1918; hence c. 1922) and elsewhere in that book he made himself out to be still younger (for example, age eighteen in 1943; hence c. 1925), presumably none of which should be believed.

Regarding his nickname, he reported that his brothers played basketball at a time when there was a star player called Big Babbiad, so they became Big Babs and Middle-sized Babs, and he, Little Babs. He also reported that his mother ran a whorehouse. Later she opened a restaurant where he met many well-known jazz musicians, and one summer, probably in the late 1930s, he toured as the band boy for JIMMIE LUNCEFORD's orchestra. At a fine arts school in Newark he studied piano and then played drums and sang. Around 1940 he toured regionally as a pianist in a Newark-based band.

In 1941 he toured with Charlie Barnet's big band for a few weeks, serving as a backup singer to LENA HORNE. According to one of his accounts, he picked the surname Gonzales to pretend to be Hispanic and thereby avoid Jim Crow laws while on tour with Barnet, but elsewhere he claimed to have assumed the surname while working as a chauffeur for the actor Errol Flynn in Los Angeles in 1943. During this year he sang with Benny Carter's band. In 1945 he joined LIONEL HAMPTON's big band for about five months.

As Babs Brown he drummed while singing with his group Three Bips and a Bop, which included TAD DAMERON; he said that he grew tired of lugging around the drum set and focused on singing. The group formed at Minton's Playhouse in Harlem in 1946, transferred to Buffalo after a dispute over pay, and then returned to Minton's in 1947. In February of that year he recorded his compositions "Oop-Pop-a-Da" and "Low Pow," the latter arranged by Dameron. Later that year the trumpeter DIZZY GILLESPIE made a version of "Oop-Pop-a-Da" that became a hit recording, and Gonzales subsequently toured with Gillespie's big band for about three months, until the vocalist Joe Carroll took his place. Around 1947 or 1948 Gonzales published a now-obscure book, *The Be-bop Dictionary and History of Its- Famous Stars*, which gives delightful definitions ("gestapo": an out-of-town musicians union delegate) and brief colorful biographies.

In 1949 Gonzales made a few recordings, including "Capitolizing" and "Professor Bop," in New York City and Los Angeles with a crew of distinguished young jazz musicians among his sidemen. In 1951 he joined the Manhattan Singers to tour Scandinavia for four months with comedian the Reverend Carl Davis. Gonzales remained in Scandinavia and then traveled to Paris, where he met the saxophonist JAMES MOODY. Having returned to the United States by December 1951, he recorded Moody's albums *Cool Whalin'* and *The James Moody Story* (both 1952–1953) and stayed with Moody as manager and singer until 1953, when they had a falling out and EDDIE JEFFERSON took Gonzales's place. Later that year he toured Sweden leading a band that included the trumpeter BUCK CLAYTON and the drummer Kansas Fields.

Gonzales worked as a disc jockey in Newark, and around 1955 he sang with the tenor saxophonist JOHNNY GRIFFIN's band at the Blue Note Club in Chicago. At some point he wrote lyrics to instrumental jazz themes: HORACE SILVER's "The Preacher," Gillespie's "A Night in Tunisia," and THELONIOUS MONK's "Round Midnight." He returned to Paris several times during the mid-1950s, and he also performed in Holland, Spain, Switzerland, and Egypt. Back in the United States, he worked as a singer and comedian in several major cities and on a southern tour. In 1958 he recorded the album *Voilà*, including "Lullaby of the Doomed," which he wrote for BILLIE HOLIDAY, and the following year he made another album, *Cool Philosophy*.

Gonzales performed in nightclubs in Southern California in 1962 or 1963, and in the latter year he recorded the album *Sundays at Small's Paradise* in New York. In July 1963 he held a two-week engagement at Ronnie Scott's nightclub in London, and he also worked in Amsterdam and Paris. He continued to make regular summer visits to Europe into the 1970s.

Sometime in the late 1960s Gonzales produced the album *Tales of the Famous: Guess Who?*, on which he tells outrageous stories about well-known musicians whose identities are only thinly disguised. In his final decade he was often seen at jazz concerts, selling his books. He died in Newark, New Jersey.

The writer Jack Cooke best captured Gonzales's art: "He has two methods of expression in his songs: one of them is a harsh, gravelly approach in which he spits out the words of things like *Night in Tunisia* and *The Preacher* before going into his scat singing, hand-clapping, shouting and foot-stamping routine; the other is a gentler approach he reserves for his ballad material." Though his voice had limited range, his ear for harmony and sense of timing were excellent. But, as Cooke wrote, "More important than all his singing … was his talking…. He assumed the role of spokesman for the whole hipster world."

FURTHER READING

Gonzales, Babs. *I Paid My Dues: Good Times … No Bread* (1967).

Gonzales, Babs. *Moving on Down the Line* (c. 1975).

Cooke, Jack. "Babs Gonzales," *Jazz Monthly* 9 (Sept. 1963).

Wilmer, Valerie. *Jazz People* (1970).

Obituaries: *New York Times*, 24 Jan. 1980; *Down Beat* 47 (Apr. 1980); *Jazz Journal International* 33 (1980).

This entry is taken from the *American National Biography* and is published here with the permission of the American Council of Learned Societies.

BARRY KERNFELD

Goode, Malvin Russell (13 Feb. 1908–12 Sept. 1995), civil rights activist and pioneering journalist, was born in White Plains, Virginia, the third eldest of six children of William and Mary Goode. William Goode's father, Thomas, was born a slave and died after the Civil War, a free man. William and Mary moved their family to Homestead, Pennsylvania, a borough located seven miles from downtown Pittsburgh that was home to one of the world's most productive steel mills. Goode's parents relocated from Virginia to Pennsylvania so their children could attend school year-round and receive a better education than that offered in the South. The colored schools in Virginia closed at harvest time so black children, particularly boys, could work in the fields. The lure of better wages in the steel mills also prompted the family to migrate to the North.

Goode's father worked as a second helper on an open hearth furnace at Homestead Works, where he was later injured on the job and retired on a disability pension. Additionally, Goode's parents owned and operated a poultry store in the area for several years to support the family. Goode was educated in Homestead's public school system where he graduated from Homestead High School. He went on to graduate from the University of Pittsburgh in 1931 with a degree in political science. He worked as a laborer in the steel mills while in high school and college and for five years after he graduated.

In 1936, Goode married Mary Lavelle, and together they had seven children. One died from "crib death" when he was only five weeks old. The surviving children were Malvin Jr., Robert, Richard, Roberta, Rosalia, and Ronald.

Goode was eventually appointed to a position with the juvenile court system in Allegheny County. He was later hired as the boy's work secretary at the Centre Avenue YMCA in the Hill District, the famed black neighborhood in Pittsburgh. In this position, Goode led the fight against racial discrimination in the Pittsburgh branches of the YMCA. Following his tenure at the YMCA, he worked for the Pittsburgh Housing Authority for six years, and in 1948, he joined the celebrated *Pittsburgh Courier* newspaper staff in its circulation department. The *Pittsburgh Courier* courted Goode to join its operations because of his reputation at the YMCA, specifically working with young adults. That skill would come in handy at the *Courier* where Goode was put in charge of coordinating more than two hundred newsboys who worked for the paper, as well as the paper's sixteen national and international editions. He worked for the *Courier*, then the largest-circulated black weekly newspaper, for fourteen years. In addition to being in circulation, Goode worked as the paper's public relations representative.

A year after starting at the *Courier*, Goode further diversified his professional experiences by beginning a new "career" in radio broadcasting while he was still employed at the newspaper. He hosted a fifteen-minute news show called *Courier Speaks* two nights a week on public affairs station KQV. Soon after, Goode and the *Courier* were approached by another station to do a news segment. Along with his sister, Mary Dee, one of the first African American women in radio, and the first in the United States to break the color barrier with her own radio show, Goode co-hosted a morning show for six years on the station WHOD (later WAMO).

Goode was on a path that would lead to establishing his place in American history. Like his sister did in radio, Goode broke the color barrier in television. He became the first black network news correspondent when he was hired by ABC News in 1962. Goode was fifty-four years old at the time of his hire and was named a United Nations reporter for the network. Goode received the call from ABC executives about working for the network on the impetus of baseball player JACKIE ROBINSON, who was the first black player in the major leagues. Robinson, who met Goode through his association with the *Pittsburgh Courier*, complained to ABC News President James Hagerty about the lack of black reporters on television. ABC News invited nearly thirty possible candidates, all black men with either radio or local television news experience, to submit tapes for network consideration.

Goode traveled to New York for an interview with the network and calmly read a script he had prepared for the interview. He was offered the job about a month later, and consequently became the first black TV news reporter for a major network. Goode was hired as the back-up U.N. reporter behind John McVane. One of the first key stories Goode covered was the Cuban Missile Crisis, a thirteen-day confrontation during the Cold War between the Soviet Union and the United States regarding the Soviet deployment of nuclear missiles in Cuba. McVane was on a hunting trip with his son on the fateful Saturday afternoon in October when the crisis began to unfold. Goode, who had only been on the job for a month, was working at the U.N. on what started out as an uneventful day. "I went on at 25 minutes after 10 when they broke into the (regularly scheduled) program," Goode once said in an interview. "This was the first time my family saw me on TV, and they started calling from across the country" (*Communicator*). ABC News interrupted its regular programming nearly thirty times throughout the day to bring Goode's updates from the U.N. on the impending situation.

Goode worked for ABC for nearly twenty years and remained as a consultant for several years after he retired. In addition to the Cuban Missile Crisis, he covered the Poor People's March in Washington, D.C., and the assassination of MARTIN LUTHER KING JR. His position allowed him to bring the struggles of the civil rights movement into the homes of hundreds of thousands of Americans, while furthering his personal cause for racial justice and equality. As a television journalist, he interviewed a number of prominent people including the civil rights leaders

King and MALCOLM X, the boxer MUHAMMAD ALI and the musician NAT KING COLE. However, Goode never again held the national spotlight as he did during the missile crisis.

Goode also worked as an educator. For two months in 1963, he joined several colleagues to teach journalism courses to African students in seminars in Lagos, Nigeria; Addis Ababa, Ethiopia; and Dar es Salaam, Tanzania. In 1971, Goode became the first black member of the Radio and Television News Directors Association. He was later elected the organization's president.

A recipient of numerous honors, Goode was awarded his fraternity's highest distinction—Alpha Phi Alpha's Award of Merit. In 1990, he was inducted into the National Association of Black Journalists' hall of fame as a charter member.

Goode died from a stroke at St. Margaret's Memorial Hospital in Pittsburgh in 1995.

FURTHER READING

Mitchell, Patricia Pugh. *Beyond Adversity: African-Americans' Struggle for Equality in Western Pennsylvania, 1750–1990* (1993).

Papper, Bob, and Michael Gerhard. "Women & Minorities: Nine Who Changed the Face of News," *Communicator* (July 2000).

Obituary: *Jet Magazine*, 2 Oct. 1995.

MICHELLE K. MASSIE

Goode, Sarah E. (c. 1850s–early 1900s), inventor and entrepreneur, blazed a path for black female inventors, yet little is known of her early life. Neither her parents' names nor her exact date or place of birth are known one biographer indicates that she was born in the 1850s and grew up in slavery. After the Civil War ended and former slaves in the South were emancipated, Goode, like thousands of African Americans, made her way north, taking up residence in Chicago by the early 1880s. In Chicago, she owned and operated a furniture store, and her entrepreneurial endeavors led to her become the first African American woman to receive a patent from the United States Patent Office. On 14 July 1885 Goode received her patent for a "Folding Cabinet Bed," comparable to modern sofa or hideaway beds. The first of five black women to patent new inventions in the nineteenth century, she was a pioneer, and her efforts inspired other women and African Americans to pursue patents and take control over their creative contributions to American culture.

As did so many blacks of the time, Goode left the South in an effort to escape discrimination and violence and to build a better future for themselves and their families. Arriving in Chicago, she recognized the growing market for furniture as new arrivals found employment, rented apartments, and began to purchase items for making empty rooms into homes. Responding to this market, Goode set up her own furniture store, purchasing furniture wholesale from local manufacturers and selling it to customers moving into Chicago's ethnic neighborhoods.

At this time, Chicago, like most American urban centers, was a segregated city. Each ethnic group, whether Irish, Italian, or African American, was confined to a particular area of the city, and individuals within those ethnic groups tended not to live outside designated areas, even when they worked in other parts of the city. This form of segregated housing was particularly stringent for African Americans. City officials, real estate agents and agencies, and the white community worked cooperatively to prevent blacks from renting apartments or buying homes outside of the black section of the city. As more and more blacks arrived in Chicago and found themselves limited to living within a restricted segment of the city, conditions became more crowded and monthly rents continued to rise.

Goode's Folding Cabinet Bed was an invention designed specifically for the needs of people moving into apartments and homes with limited space and increasingly crowded conditions. Her customers needed high-quality furniture that was also flexible in application. Goode designed a piece of furniture that could function as a cabinet or desk during the day and be converted into a bed at night. The cabinet Goode designed looked like "an antique rolltop desk" (Sullivan, 13–16), with pockets and shelves for organizing correspondence and storing important papers. The desk could also be used as a table and, at night, as an extra bed. "It was the perfect solution for anyone who had limited living space. It was functional and inexpensive" (Sullivan, 13–14).

Goode filed her patent application on 12 November 1883. The patent application included a model of her Folding Cabinet Bed, drawings indicating the design and how to construct the item, and a description of her new invention. According to Goode's patent application, the purpose of her invention was:

first, to provide a folding bed of novel construction, adapted, when folded together, to form a desk suitable for office or general use; second, to provide for counterbalancing the weight of the folding sections of the bed, so that they may be easily raised or lowered in folding or unfolding the bed; third, to provide for holding the hinged or folding sections securely in place when the bed is unfolded, and fourth, to provide an automatic auxiliary support for the bedding at the middle when the bed is unfolded. (U.S. Patent #322,177)

Through her entrepreneurial founding of a furniture store and her invention and patenting of a folding cabinet bed, Sarah Goode made a memorable contribution to American society and culture. Overcoming barriers presented by racism and sexism, she proved that legal and economic restrictions faced by entrepreneurial blacks and women could be breached. As the first black woman to receive a patent, she paved the way for other creative and innovative black women who would seek patents for their inventions in the coming years. Her success was followed by Miriam E. Benjamin, who patented her so-called Gong and Signal Chair for Hotels (a call button on the chair allowed guests to summon waiters) in 1888, and Anna M. Mangin, who received a patent for a pastry fork just a few months before SARAH BOONE received her patent for an improved ironing board in 1892. By 1900, five African American women had patented their new inventions, and by the mid-twentieth century, black female inventors had contributed inventions ranging from a fruit press to heat regulators for furnaces to new hair-beauty techniques to torpedo discharge devices. Women, Goode among them, found creative ways to respond to the needs of their businesses, their communities, and the shifting consumer markets of the nineteenth century when they invented new technologies or improved on existing ones.

FURTHER READING

Goode, Sarah. Letter of Application and Letter Patent No. 322,177. Washington, D.C.: United States Patent Office, 13 Nov. 1883.

Sluby, Patricia Carter. "Black Women and Invention," *Sage: A Scholarly Journal on Black Women* 6.2 (Fall, 1989).

Sullivan, Otha Richard. *Black Stars: African American Women Scientists and Inventors* (2002).

PAMELA C. EDWARDS

Goode, W. Wilson (19 Aug. 1938–), mayor of Philadelphia, was born Woodrow Wilson Goode near Seaboard, Northampton County, North Carolina, the second youngest of seven children of Albert Goode and Rozelar, sharecroppers. His family moved every year to work for different landlords, which made for a lonely childhood for Goode, who was not able to establish long-term friendships. The whole family worked in the cotton and peanut fields from the early hours in the morning until the late hours of the evening. Goode dreamed of living in the city, residing in a big house, and working for himself, where he would be in control of his own destiny. He dreamed of becoming famous and having the power to change things for the better. Goode learned from his parents, especially his mother, that with faith in God, everything in life is possible. He saw education as his only way out of poverty and also as a weapon against bigotry.

Goode moved to Philadelphia with his family and graduated from John Bartram High School in January 1957. When he arrived on the campus of Morgan State University, he was the first member of his family to attend college; he graduated in 1961 with a BA in political science. During his college years, he met Velma Helen Williams, whom he married in 1960 at the First Baptist Church of Darby, Pennsylvania. The couple would have three children.

Goode was commissioned as a second lieutenant in the U.S. Army and was assigned to the Military Police Division at Fort Carson, Colorado. Following the failure of the U.S.-supported invasion at the Bay of Pigs in Cuba, Goode was assigned as a defense counsel for the men who were court-martialed. After finishing his duty in Fort Carson in 1963, Goode took the civil service exam and became a probation officer in the West Division of the Juvenile Section of the Probation Department in Philadelphia. During the early 1960s he held several other jobs, including insurance claims adjuster and building maintenance firm supervisor.

Goode spent his next twelve years as president and executive officer of the Philadelphia Council for Community Advancement (PCCA). PCCA was a nonprofit organization whose mission was to provide affordable housing for the poorer citizens. Goode embraced this opportunity and organized programs in education, employment, and economic development. He raised more than $60 million in housing investments. The PCCA built more housing units than any other agency at that time.

Goode received his master's degree in governmental administration from the University of Pennsylvania's Wharton School of Business in 1968. He also received fourteen honorary degrees, along with a thousand honors and awards. In 1979 Milton J. Shapp, then governor of Pennsylvania, appointed Goode head of the Pennsylvania Public Utilities Commission. Within a year Goode became the first African American managing director of Philadelphia. He had a particular interest in solving the city's problems of sanitation and urban decay. His interest, devotion, and hands-on approach to these problems made him popular. On 30 November 1982 Goode resigned from his position as managing director to think about the future of his career in government. He officially announced his candidacy for mayor of Philadelphia on 6 December 1982. On 8 November 1983 Goode was elected, and on 2 January 1984 he was sworn in as Philadelphia's 126th mayor. He was the first African American to hold that office in Philadelphia.

Goode entered an office suffering from many problems, including unemployment, poor trash disposal, and unfinished city building projects. He had spent only sixteen months in office when a major controversy hit his administration. The Philadelphia police dropped a bomb in a residential area in an effort to arrest members of MOVE, a militant organization made up of mostly black members who preached against technology and who were in favor of returning to Africa. The resulting fire burned down sixty-one houses and left 250 people homeless. The fire killed eleven people, including five children. During the blaze Police Commissioner Gregore Sambor and Fire Commissioner William Richmond delayed sending in firefighters to extinguish the blaze. A jury found that they violated the law and ordered the city of Philadelphia and the two officials to pay the survivors $1.5 million. The judge found the mayor exempt from charges.

This tragedy tarnished Goode's reputation, but he was reelected mayor of Philadelphia in the following election. Goode left office at the end of his second term on 6 January 1992, when Edward G. Rendell took over as mayor.

Goode published his autobiography, *In Goode Faith*, in 1992. He began attending Eastern Baptist Theological Seminary in 1996, and in 2000 he received his doctorate of ministry. In 1997 he was appointed deputy assistant secretary for regional and community services for the federal Office of Intergovernmental and Interagency Affairs. He continued to serve as chairman of four boards, the Free Library of Philadelphia, the Cornerstone Christian Academy, Self, Inc., and the Philadelphia Leadership Foundation.

FURTHER READING

Goode, W. Wilson, with Joann Stevens. *In Goode Faith* (1992).

Bowser, Charles W. *Let the Bunker Burn: The Final Battle with MOVE* (1989)

ARTHUR MATTHEW HOLST

Gooden, Dwight Eugene (16 Nov. 1964–), baseball player, was born in Tampa, Florida, the son of Dan Gooden, a chemical plant worker, and Ella Mae (maiden known unknown), a nurse's aide. The youngest of six children, Gooden grew up in a comfortable middle-class household where he was expected to do little more than play baseball well. The Goodens' Belmont Heights neighborhood was the kind of place that Gooden and his boyhood friend and fellow future major leaguer Floyd Youmans remembered as the kind of place where every adult was a surrogate parent and every child was eager to play sports. Dwight Gooden did concentrate on sports. Dan Gooden had played semipro baseball, and his overriding ambition was for his son to play in the major leagues. Dwight's Little League team made it to the 1975 Little League World Series, where they lost to Taiwan. Gooden earned his enduring nickname "Doctor K" ("K" is the symbol for a strikeout in baseball scoring), or the shortened "Doc," on the ball fields of Tampa.

After graduating from Tampa's Hillsborough High School, Gooden accepted a baseball scholarship to the University of Miami. But the Mets made Gooden their first-round pick in the 1982 amateur draft, and he signed a professional contract with the team. He spent only parts of two seasons with the team's low–minor league affiliates and then, at the age of nineteen, exploded onto the New York sports scene in the 1984 season with one of the greatest performances by a rookie pitcher ever recorded. With a 17-3 won-loss record, 276 strikeouts (the most in the league that year and a record for rookies), and an earned run average (ERA) of 2.60, Gooden easily won the National League's Rookie of the Year Award. He was second in the balloting for the league's Cy Young Award for most outstanding pitcher. Gooden followed that performance with a dominating 1985 season. He became the youngest Cy Young Award winner in history after posting a 24-1 record with a 1.53 ERA and 268 strikeouts. Gooden won the so-called triple crown of pitching in 1985, with more wins, more strikeouts, and a lower ERA than any other pitcher in the league.

Gooden's 1986 season was something of a disappointment but only by comparison with his previous performances. His 17-5 record, 2.84 ERA, and 200 strikeouts were good enough to garner a seventh-place finish in the votes for the Cy Young Award, and

Gooden's season capped arguably the most dominating three-year stretch of power pitching in the history of the game. After defeating the Houston Astros in the 1986 National Championship Series, the Mets won a truly epic seven-game clash with the Boston Red Sox in the World Series. Gooden's performance in both series was disappointing—he lost three of the four games he started—but by this time he may well have been the most popular athlete in New York.

Gooden's private life was a mess. Tellingly he missed the team's World Series victory parade through Manhattan; he said he had overslept after a night of heavy drinking. In December of that year Gooden brawled with Tampa police after a traffic stop. By Gooden's count more than a dozen officers beat him to the point that he feared for his life. Details of why the police stopped Gooden were sketchy, but the department hinted toward suspicions of drug involvement.

The Mets were concerned by rumors of Gooden's drug use that had persisted throughout the 1986 season. Davey Johnson, the Mets manager, worried that after Gooden signed his first million-dollar contract following the 1985 season, ne'er-do-well friends from Tampa had begun reentering his personal circle. Johnson believed that Gooden's greatest sin was an inability to say no to others. Major League Baseball marketed Gooden as the starting pitcher for the National League in the 1986 All-Star Game even while investigating the pitcher for using cocaine.

During spring training in 1987 Gooden and the team agreed to add a clause to his contract requiring him to undergo periodic random drug tests. Just days after Gooden signed it, he failed his first test. He tested positive for cocaine and immediately entered a month-long program at the Smithers Alcoholism and Treatment Center in Manhattan. Gooden emerged from treatment confident that he could control his cocaine addiction. He did win fifteen games that season, but he continued to drink heavily. According to Gooden, he began drinking heavily during the 1985 season. He married Monica Harris in 1987; they had four children. Gooden also fathered a child with Debra Hamilton, a former high school classmate, in 1986.

Gooden was suspended again for sixty days of the 1994 season for breaking the rules of his aftercare program and entered the Betty Ford Clinic for additional treatment. The Mets announced that Gooden would not return to the team. Gooden was again banned, this time for the entire 1995 season, after testing positive for cocaine use multiple times while under his second suspension. For many fans, Gooden came to personify the modern, spoiled professional athlete.

Gooden received one last chance to prove himself in 1996, when the New York Yankees offered Gooden an incentive-laden contract. He was a pedestrian pitcher for the Yankees through the first two months of the season. Then on 14 May, with Dan Gooden lying on his deathbed in a Tampa hospital, Dwight Gooden threw a complete-game no-hitter against the powerful Seattle Mariners. Gooden settled back into mediocrity and left Major League Baseball at the end of the 2000 season, but it was the emotional triumph of the no-hitter that many baseball fans remember. The memory will surely be tempered by Gooden's three drug suspensions and a suspicion that he wasted the raw, electric talent that comes along no more than once in a generation.

FURTHER READING
Gooden, Dwight, with Bob Klapisch. *Heat* (1999).
Klapisch, Bob. *High and Tight* (1996).
Pearlman, Jeff. *The Bad Guys Won* (2004).

J. TODD MOYE

Gooding, James Henry (1837–1864), sailor, poet, Civil War soldier, and newspaper correspondent, first appears in the historical record in 1856 as a nineteen-year-old sailor on a whaling vessel out of New Bedford, Massachusetts. His birthplace is uncertain. His marriage certificate and seaman's papers say he was born in Troy, New York, yet no Gooding family appears in the census records for Troy. In Seneca, New York, a state census in 1850 records the presence of a James Goodin (with no final *g*), who might have been Gooding's father and who probably worked as a rail or canal laborer in upstate New York. Whatever Gooding's early background, his education, whether self-directed or formal, was exceptional. The letters he published during the Civil War reveal his grounding in history and the classics. If he did grow up in Troy, Gooding received the benefits of membership in a black community vigorously committed to the abolition of slavery. The community had several schools for black children.

In the summer of 1856 Gooding, called by his middle name, Henry, signed up in New Bedford for a whaling voyage. He was issued a seaman's protection paper. The paper records that Gooding had brown skin, curly hair, and black eyes and was of medium height. His name was entered into a crew list of the whaler *Sunbeam*. The ship's record describes him as a "mulatto" and an inexperienced "green hand." Gooding's decision reflects the fact that in the nineteenth century the sea provided jobs for black men. In the whaling industry African Americans accounted for as many as one in six men. Gooding was assigned to the galley on his first trip to sea. While at sea Gooding wrote six poems, which were later published. One of the poems was a memorial to an African American sailor, "In Memory of Eli Dodge, Who Was Killed by a Whale, Sept. 4, 1868, off the coast of new Holland." His poetry was shaped by personal experience and the literary conventions of the time. It is unclear when the poems were printed, but the location can be inferred since their typography resembles that of the Mercury Job Printing Office in New Bedford.

The *Sunbeam* returned to the United States in 1860, and Gooding stayed on land for only a month before signing up as a steward for a whaling voyage to the east Arctic. His job as a steward would have entitled him to a larger "lay," or share of the profits. The profits for this voyage proved disappointing when he returned to New Bedford in 1861. He then left the whaling business and signed up for a merchant ship bound for Montevideo, Uruguay. When he returned he married Ellen Louisa Allen on 28 September 1862.

The U.S. War Department early in 1863 authorized Massachusetts Governor John A. Andrew to raise an infantry regiment composed of African Americans. On 14 February 1863 Gooding joined the Massachusetts Fifty-fourth Regiment. On 18 February a meeting of African American citizens was held in New Bedford's Liberty Hall to encourage enlistment. Gooding was listed as one of the vice presidents of the meeting. Gooding was enrolled in Company C of the Massachusetts Fifty-fourth (each regiment comprised several companies). Less than half the company came from New Bedford. Because Massachusetts had a relatively small black population, recruitment of the regiment took place nationwide, which was unusual for a Civil War regiment. Recruitment was led by the Massachusetts industrialist and abolitionist George Stearns, who had helped finance the 1859 raid on Harpers Ferry, Virginia, by John Brown. Recruiters included leading black abolitionists such as FREDERICK DOUGLASS, HENRY HIGHLAND GARNET, and MARTIN R. DELANY. Soldiers in the Fifty-fourth Massachusetts came from fifteen northern states, all four border states, and five Confederate states. The largest delegations came from Pennsylvania and New York. One-fourth of the men were born in one of the slave states.

During his time in the army Gooding rose to the rank of corporal and was viewed by his peers as an exceptional man. He served as a correspondent for the *New Bedford Mercury*, describing the activities of the regiment in great detail, usually on a weekly basis. His articles agitated for equal pay for black soldiers, and Gooding supported his fellow soldiers in refusing to accept pay until inequities in pay between whites and blacks were remedied. He also wrote an eloquent letter on the pay issue to Abraham Lincoln, which is preserved in the National Archives. His optimistic vision of the future was captured in one article in which he linked the military effort to recognizing "the right of every man in the Commonwealth to be a MAN and a citizen."

Gooding participated in raids near Darien, Georgia, and took part in the famous (and disastrous) charge of the Fifty-fourth at Fort Wagner outside of Charleston, South Carolina, on 18 July 1863. In that assault 1,515 Union soldiers died, and the Fifty-fourth suffered especially. As Gooding described it, "Fort Wagner is the Sebastopol of the rebels; but we went at it, over the ditch and on to the parapet through a deadly fire; but we could not get into the fort." Gooding participated in a siege of Charleston and then fought in Florida. He was captured by the Confederates in the Battle of Olustee in February 1864.

He was taken to the notoriously brutal Andersonville prisoner of war camp, where he died. The cause of death is uncertain and could have been due to wounds, exposure, malnutrition, or disease.

FURTHER READING

Gooding, James Henry. *On the Altar of Freedom: A Black Soldier's Civil War Letters from the Front*, ed. Virginia Matzke Adams (1991).

Blatt, Martin H., Thomas J. Brown, and Donald Yacovone, eds. *Hope and Glory: Essays on the Legacy of the Fifty-fourth Massachusetts Regiment* (2001).

Emilio, Luis F. *A Brave Black Regiment: History of the Fifty-fourth Regiment of Massachusetts Volunteer Infantry, 1863–65* (1894; rpt. 1995).

WALLACE HETTLE

Goodlett, Carlton Benjamin (23 July 1914–1 Feb. 1997), physician and newspaper publisher, was born in Chipley, southern Florida, but his family moved to Omaha, Nebraska, where he was educated in the local public schools.

Goodlet graduated from Howard University in 1935, having served as president of the student body and editor of *Hilltop*, the campus newspaper. He began graduate studies at the University of

California, receiving a doctorate in Child Psychology in 1938. For the next year, he was a member of the faculty at West Virginia State College in Institute, West Virginia. In 1939 he authored a report on "The Mental Abilities of Twenty-nine Deaf and Partially Deaf Negro Children," published in the *West Virginia Bureau of Negro Welfare Statistics*. Entering Meharry Medical College in Nashville, he was awarded an M.D. in 1944. Goodlett married Willette Hill on 27 November 1943; they divorced in 1968, after an eleven-year separation.

After completing medical school. Goodlett moved to San Francisco in 1945, encouraged by his friend Thomas Fleming, founding editor a year earlier of the *Reporter*, a newspaper launched by the businessman Frank Logan. Fleming recalled years later that Logan was a professional gambler who wanted to do something legitimate. The paper served the growing number of African Americans moving to San Francisco and the Bay Area to work in wartime production industries and military bases. Goodlett established a medical practice near the *Reporter* office, sharing space on Fillmore Street with Dr. Daniel Collins, a black dentist.

About one and a half years after arriving in San Francisco, Goodlett was invited to join the faculty of the California Labor School, established by the International Longshoremen's and Warehousemen's Union. This association inspired innuendo that Goodlett was a "red," which in the mid-twentieth century meant a Communist. (It was only in the early twenty-first century that "red states" came to be associated with the Republican Party.) At least, Goodlett was thought to be a "fellow traveler," someone vaguely sympathetic to communism, but not a party member. He didn't let this bother him; he persuaded the pastor of Third Baptist Church to host an appearance by the world-renowned actor, singer, and civil rights activist PAUL ROBESON, when most venues were refusing him because he was blacklisted for his refusal to cooperate with the cold war anticommunist hysteria. Goodlett served in the presidium of the World Peace Council, and in the 1960s was among the earliest voices urging DR. MARTIN LUTHER KING JR. to take a stand against American military intervention in Vietnam. In 1966 he was a sponsor of the Herbert Aptheker Testimonial Dinner in New York, honoring the scholarly work and publishing career of a historian who was a known Communist Party member.

A flourishing medical practice allowed Goodlett to invest in the *Reporter*; generally, this took the form of lending the paper money to pay the bills,

which Logan could not pay him back. Together with Collins, he acquired the paper in 1946. He combined the *Reporter* with another local paper, the *Sun*, after winning the latter from its owner, "white" businessman Frank Laurent, in a poker game. Owing Goodlett $4500, Laurent said for $1500 Goodlett could have the *Sun*. Goodlett became sole owner and publisher of the *Sun-Reporter* in 1951. Goodlett and Fleming took turns writing editorials for the next four decades.

Goodlett was elected president of the San Francisco NAACP, 1947–1949. Fleming recounted in 1999 to the reporter Max Millard that Goodlett had once been pulled over for running a red light, and after producing his license was addressed by the police officer "Well, Carlton." His response was "Listen here, I'm Dr. Goodlett to you, and you're officer to me." Handcuffed and arrested for "resisting arrest, or some silly thing," he was walked out of the Hall of Justice by Fleming, and charges were dropped next morning.

Goodlett was also arrested in 1959 after resisting a police officer's insistence on inspecting several packages he was carrying. It was common during the 1950s and early 1960s that police officers targeted anyone with a dark, complexion who dressed well, and appeared to be a professional, to be pulled over and humiliated. In an article in the *Sun-Reporter*, he wrote that not a few Bay Area policemen "believe that the best way to deal with any Negro…is to first crack him across the head so as to get his attention, second to knock him to his knees, and finally to place the Negro under arrest. This is the usual treatment given a stubborn mule in the Southland" (Crowe, p. 85).

Goodlett also wrote of other examples of police harassment of people of color, including business owners in their own stores, and elderly women who were subjected to brutal and capricious treatment. There had even been a case of tenants meeting inside a private apartment brutalized by police after a call from their landlord.

In 1963 Goodlett combined his medical practice and the *Sun-Reporter* in a single building on Turk Street near the corner of Fillmore. In 1966 he challenged the incumbent governor Edmund G. "Pat" Brown in the Democratic primary, challenging him to "go into the ghettos of Watts and Oakland." He came in third in a field of six candidates. Brown won the primary, but lost the general election to an actor with political aspirations named Ronald Reagan. Goodlett purchased the *California Voice* in 1971, and began publishing seven *Metro-Reporter* weeklies in as many California cities. Combined circulation of nine weeklies rose to 160,000.

Goodlett retired from the *Sun-Reporter* in 1994. He died in Cedar Rapids, Iowa, at the home of his surviving son, Dr. Garry M. Goodlett, after battling Parkinson's disease for several years. He was also survived by five grandchildren. In 1999 one block of Polk Street, San Francisco, where it runs between the city hall and Civic Center Plaza, was named in honor of Dr. Goodlet. City hall is now 1 Carleton Goodlett Place.

FURTHER READING
Crowe, Daniel Edward. *Prophets of Rage: The Black Freedom Struggle in San Francisco, 1945–1969* (2000).
Obituaries: *New York Times*, 2 Feb. 1997; *Jet*, 14 Apr. 1997.

CHARLES ROSENBERG

Goodridge, Glenalvin J. (1829–14 Nov. 1867), Wallace L. Goodridge (4 Sept. 1840–3 Mar. 1922), and William O. Goodridge (28 May 1846–17 Aug. 1890), photographers, were born in York, Pennsylvania, three of seven children of William C. Goodridge and Evalina Wallace. Among the first African Americans to work as professional photographers, Glenalvin J. Goodridge in 1847 established a studio in York that Wallace L. Goodridge and William O. Goodridge continued to operate after 1863 in Saginaw, Michigan, until Wallace's death in 1922. During three-quarters of a century the Goodridge brothers experimented with all forms of photography, from daguerreotypes and ambrotypes in the 1840s and 1850s, to X-ray images and motion pictures in the early twentieth century. Their portrait, landscape, and stereoscopic images gained the studio both national and international recognition.

The sons' success was due in part to the energy and enterprise of their father, a slave descendant of the Carrolls of Carrollton, born in Baltimore, Maryland, in 1806, and their mother, a free woman of the same city. Following an apprenticeship to a York tanner, William C. Goodridge gained his freedom in 1822, established a barbershop, and married Evalina in 1827. Before her death in 1852, the Goodridges made the barbershop the foundation for economic holdings in York that included Centre Hall, the largest business block west of the Susquehannal River; Goodridge's Reliance Line, a railroad package service between York and Philadelphia; a bathhouse; a jewelry and confectionary; an employment agency;

and residential holdings that brought their wealth to more than $250,000. William C. Goodridge also was an active participant in the Underground Railroad—often using the Reliance Line—and was reported to have assisted in the successful escape of OSBORNE PERRY ANDERSON following John Brown's raid on Harpers Ferry. The parents' success also presented the children with opportunities available to few young people at that time. The Goodridge daughters Emily and Mary attended St. Francis Academy in Baltimore, a finishing school for young African American women run by the Oblate Sisters of Providence. The Goodridge sons were educated at the York school for black children, where in 1847 Glenalvin became the first black high school teacher in the city. That year Glenalvin also opened Goodridge's Daguerrian Rooms and began making daguerreotypes (unique positive images on silver-sensitized copper plates) less than a decade after their introduction in France in 1839.

Glenalvin was not the first photographer to open a studio in York, but he soon became the most successful. He trained with the celebrated Montgomery P. Simons in Philadelphia during spring 1847 and by July, back in York, took over the studio of Joseph Reinhart, an itinerant daguerreotypist who had rented space in China Hall, one of the senior Goodridges' commercial ventures. By the end of 1848, when "M.R.D." visited York, he reported to the *Rochester North Star* (15 Dec. 1848) that Goodridge "keeps a fine gallery at his father's dwellings, where he has his private study, and operates at leisure hours." Until 1851 Glenalvin continued his dual career as photographer and high school teacher. That year, in the face of increasing competition from other York photographers, Glenalvin decided to devote his energy and talent to photography and with positive results. He moved the studio to a new location on the fifth floor of the family business block, Centre Hall, at the commercial crossroads of York. *Humphrey's Journal* (1 Jan. and 1 Oct. 1853), the prestigious photographer's magazine, described the new studio as "pleasant rooms, with every convenience for producing the finest Daguerreotypes and … with all that is desirable for the ladies of York." Increased business also prompted Glenalvin to train his brothers Wallace and William as studio assistants. In 1855 Goodridge's American Photographic Gallery, as the studio was then styled, became the first west of Philadelphia to offer its clients the latest form of photography, ambrotypes (unique positive images on glass). Enthusiastic responses to these developments appeared in the *York Gazette* (30 Oct. 1855), which characterized Glenalvin's ambrotypes as "decidedly superior to the Daguerreotype" and the young photographer as "constantly vigilant in the wonderful photographic art ... [and] never content to remain a single step in the rear of its progress." And between 1853 and 1856 the judges at the York County Agricultural Society Fair annually awarded Glenalvin both first and second premiums for the quality of his work.

Success enabled Glenalvin to marry Rhoda Cornelia Grey in 1851. They had four children, only one of whom survived his parents. A growing business and expanding family also prompted Glenalvin and Rhoda to invest in real estate. By 1857 the couple owned their own two-story town house and six rental properties. Because Glenalvin's business ventures had always been closely tied to those of his father, when the elder Goodridge declared bankruptcy following an economic downturn in 1859, both father and son were forced to sell their holdings to cover their debt. For a time in 1860 Glenalvin returned to teaching. The following year, however, photography had regained its hold on him, and Glenalvin, this time with Wallace as his partner, reopened his studio in York. The almost immediate return of success led the brothers to establish a branch of the studio in nearby Columbia, Pennsylvania. Then disaster struck. On 28 August 1862 Glenalvin was indicted for rape by the York County Grand Jury. His accuser, a white woman named Mary E. Smith, lived at the camp of the Union troops then stationed in York. On at least one occasion she had visited the Goodridge studio, where, testimony later revealed, young Wallace had paid for her services. When Smith realized she was pregnant, Wallace had disappeared to the West, where he had joined his sister Mary Goodridge Nichols in Saginaw, Michigan. Smith, attempting to make the best of a poor situation by extorting money from the family, named Glenalvin as the father in the place of the absent Wallace. In the highly charged political atmosphere of 1863 southeastern Pennsylvania, Glenalvin, although clearly innocent, was found guilty and sentenced to five years solitary confinement at Eastern State Penitentiary in Philadelphia before Wallace could be returned to testify on his brother's behalf. Because of his father's efforts, Glenalvin was pardoned and released from prison in December 1864 but only on the condition that he leave Pennsylvania. Glenalvin's two-year imprisonment ultimately became a life sentence as he contracted tuberculosis there. He and quite likely three of his four children would die from the disease within three years of his release.

In accordance with the terms of his pardon, Glenalvin and his family left York and by spring 1865 joined his sister Mary Nichols, who had settled in Saginaw with her barber husband, John Nichols. William C. Goodridge continued west to Minneapolis to live with his daughter Emily and her barber husband, Ralph Toyer Grey. He died there in 1873. In anticipation of Glenalvin's freedom, Wallace and young William O. Goodridge had also settled in Saginaw and had reopened the family studio there by July 1863. Because of his illness, Glenalvin did not again work actively as a photographer with his brothers. On 14 November 1867 he died of tuberculosis while visiting his sister Emily and her family in Minneapolis.

Unlike the York studio, which Glenalvin had devoted almost exclusively to portrait photography, the Saginaw studio from the outset offered a variety of photographic services. Portraiture, Wallace's specialty, continued to pay the bills, and that enabled William, the youngest and most artistic of the brothers, to direct his talent to landscape or "view" photography. The result was a clear and complementary division of labor between the two surviving Goodridge brothers that defined the studio's operations through the end of the century. At the time Saginaw was the focal point of Michigan's post–Civil War pine lumber boom. The wealth it generated and the simultaneous population growth in the area fueled the studio's commercial success. As a result in 1872 the brothers built their own studio complex, parts of which remain in the early twenty-first century. During the 1870s and 1880s Wallace and William were active and enthusiastic Republicans, and the studio often served as a political gathering place for Saginaw's African American community. In 1884 Wallace served as a delegate to the state assembly of the Knights of Labor. The following year he was a member of the committee of Michigan African Americans charged with designing the state's exhibit for the World's Industrial and Cotton Centennial Exposition in New Orleans. In 1888 William organized the Colored National Monument Association in Michigan that proposed creating a sculpture honoring the nation's black veterans. In 1879 William married Gertrude Watson. The couple had two sons, William O. Goodridge Jr. and John F. Goodridge, and a daughter, Altena Goodridge. Wallace did not marry until 1889. He and Margaret Jacques of Baltimore had no children, although before his death Wallace did acknowledge the existence of a son born in Philadelphia in 1862. The identity of the mother is not known.

In 1874 Wallace, having inherited his father's business acumen, negotiated a contract with the Flint and Pere Marquette Railroad, whose route traversed the best pinelands in the state. As the railroad's official photographer, William had unlimited access to the lumber camps it served. Through the 1870s he created several series of commercially successful stereo views variously titled *In the Pineries of Michigan* and *Lumbering in Michigan*. When stereo views lost their popularity by the mid-1880s, William shifted to larger format views of the lumber camps and river drives. The Forestry Division of the U.S. Department of Agriculture commissioned a series of twelve such views by William that served as a focal point for the department's extensive and celebrated exhibit at the 1889 Universal Exposition in Paris. Unfortunately William's success was cut short at its peak. On 17 August 1890 he died of blood poisoning contracted as a result of a darkroom accident.

For a time following their father's death, both William O. Goodridge Jr. and John F. Goodridge assisted their uncle Wallace in the studio, but neither chose to make photography his career. Through the rest of the century and until the final weeks before his death on 3 March 1922, the last of the Goodridge brothers continued to offer Saginaw Valley residents the newest techniques and most up-to-date technology of the profession. Wallace provided his customers with X-ray, magnesium flash, Cirkut panoramic, and thirty-five millimeter and sixteen millimeter motion picture photography. In 1892 he doubled the size of the existing studio to include photography supplies and lessons for amateur photographers captivated by the Kodak revolution in photography. After 1900 he also made the studio, often using William's views stored in the negative vault, a source of photographs for the penny postcard industry. When he died, the *Saginaw News Courier* (4 Mar. 1922) published a three-column obituary that reviewed the family's history in York and Saginaw and eulogized Wallace as the "First Saginaw Photographer" and "reputedly the oldest photographer of colored blood in America." The obituary also printed a photograph of Wallace taken shortly before his death, ironically the only time an image of the photographer appeared in the local news sheets.

FURTHER READING
Jezierski, John Vincent. "'Dangerous Opportunity': Glenalvin J. Goodridge and Early Photography in York, Pennsylvania," *Pennsylvania History* (Spring 1997).

Jezierski, John Vincent. *Enterprising Images* (2000).
Obituary: *Saginaw News Courier*, 4 Mar. 1922.
JOHN V. JEZIERSKI

Goodwin, Ruby Berkley (17 Oct. 1903–31 May 1961), actress and author, was born in Du Quoin, Illinois, the daughter of Braxton Berkley, a coalminer and union organizer, and Sophia Jane Holmes, who had nine other children. She graduated from high school there and in 1920 moved with her parents to Imperial Valley in California. She attended San Diego State Teachers' College for one year and later taught in El Centro, where in 1924 she married Lee Goodwin, an auto mechanic. They had five children and adopted another. In 1931 the Goodwin family moved to Fullerton, where she attended Fullerton Junior College, held various jobs, and was extensively involved in civic organizations. From 1936 to 1952 she worked as personal secretary to the actress HATTIE MCDANIEL and more briefly as secretary to the actress ETHEL WATERS.

During the 1920s Goodwin had won a $100 prize in a short-story contest and was encouraged to pursue a writing career. However, she remained unpublished until 1937, when she wrote a series of "literary treatments" (sketches) of black life to accompany *Twelve Negro Spirituals* (1937) by the noted composer WILLIAM GRANT STILL. Goodwin later wrote poems and articles for newspapers and magazines. The first collection of her poetry, *From My Kitchen Window*, appeared in 1942. "An Ode to Lincoln" is the best-known item in the collection, which also includes lyrics on a variety of social and religious themes. Another collection, *A Gold Star Mother Speaks*, followed two years later. Although Goodwin did not lose a son in World War II she was inspired to write the war-related poems by the highly publicized deaths of the five Sullivan brothers (who perished together on USS *Juneau* in 1942).

Goodwin began her stage career in the 1940s, when she appeared in a Los Angeles production of *The Little Foxes*. She later appeared in *Nine Pine Street*, *Anna Lucasta*, *The Member of the Wedding*, and *The Male Animal*. During that decade she also wrote a musical, *American Rhapsody* (1942), a syndicated newspaper column called "Hollywood in Bronze," and a series of radio plays based on the lives of black leaders. She also continued her education, eventually receiving her AB degree from San Gabriel State College in 1949. And she began lecturing to organizations and at colleges and universities. Her topics were race relations, black music, and literature. In her most popular lecture, "Democracy

Challenges America," Goodwin called for an end to racial segregation, and in the process she referred to her own mixed background of African American, Native American, and Scotch-Irish ethnic groups. She also wrote a novel about interracial marriage, "Pure White," which was accepted for publication but never appeared.

Goodwin's stage acting and her associations with Hattie McDaniel and Ethel Waters eventually led to a screen career. She appeared in *The View from Pompey's Head* (1955), *Strange Interlude* (1956), *The Alligator People* (1959), and *Wild in the Country* (1961), among other films. She also appeared in the television production of *The Life of Booker T. Washington* and in two noted TV dramatic programs, *The Loretta Young Show* and *Ford Theater*.

Goodwin also continued to write. Her best-known book was her last, *It's Good to Be Black* (1953), a series of heartwarming autobiographical sketches that portray her early life in Du Quoin and stress the positive impact of family relationships. Much of the author's racial and family pride was derived from her father, a man of little education but much wisdom and energy, who had earned the respect of blacks and whites alike: "He was the eldest son of an ex-slave, but because mining was a hard and dangerous job, no one was too concerned about a miner's background. If he knew his business he was accepted as a fellow worker, and that was his admittance card into the great fraternity of free men." Although racism is not absent from the book, *It's Good to Be Black* explicitly rejects the notion that it was the central fact of black life in Du Quoin. As the author says, "We were colored, but what of it?" Widely praised, the book won the Commonwealth Award for the best nonfiction work by a California writer.

In 1955 the American Mothers Committee selected Goodwin as the California State Mother of the Year. By that time she had moved to Los Angeles, where she died several years later.

FURTHER READING
Goodwin, Ruby Berkley. *It's Good to Be Black* (1953; repr. 1976).
Rush, Theressa Gunnels, et al., eds. *Black American Writers, Past and Present* (1975).
Obituary: *Los Angeles Examiner*, 2 June 1961.
This entry is taken from the *American National Biography* and is published here with the permission of the American Council of Learned Societies.

JOHN E. HALLWAS

Gordon (dates unknown), escaped slave and Union soldier, was likely born on the plantation of John Lyon near Washington, Louisiana, an important steamboat port before the Civil War. Lyon was a cotton planter whose property was located on the Atchafalya River. The names of Gordon's parents and details about his youth are not known.

Gordon received a severe whipping for undisclosed reasons from the plantation's overseer in the fall of 1862. This beating left him with horrible welts on much of the surface of his back, and for the next two months Gordon recuperated in bed. Although Lyon discharged the overseer who carried out this vicious attack, Gordon decided to escape.

In March 1863 Gordon fled his home, heading east toward the Mississippi River and Union lines. Upon learning of his flight, his master recruited several neighbors, and together they chased after him with a pack of bloodhounds. Gordon had anticipated that he would be pursued and carried with him onions from the plantation, which he rubbed on his body to throw the dogs off the scent. Such resourcefulness worked, and Gordon—his clothes torn and his body covered with mud and dirt—reached the safety of Union soldiers stationed at Baton Rouge after ten days and having traveled approximately eighty miles. While at this encampment Gordon decided to enlist in the Union army. As President Lincoln's Emancipation Proclamation in January called upon African Americans to serve in the army (they had served in the navy since the beginning of the war), Gordon was at the front of a movement that ultimately would involve nearly 179,000 African Americans. It was during his medical examination prior to being mustered into the army that military doctors discovered the extensive scars on his back. A local photographer, William D. McPherson, and his partner, a Mr. Oliver, were then in the camp, and Gordon was asked to pose for a picture that would reveal the harsh treatment he had recently received. At least two photographs of Gordon with his scarred back to the camera were taken. McPherson and Oliver sold copies of Gordon's portrait in the popular photographic format known as the carte de visite, a small albumen print often used as a visiting card. The image provoked an immediate response, and soon copies were circulating widely. Samuel K. Towle, a surgeon with the Thirtieth Regiment of the Massachusetts Volunteers, was then working at Baton Rouge and sent a copy of the photograph to the surgeon general of the State of Massachusetts. In his letter he wrote, "Few sensation writers ever depicted worse

RAID OF SECOND SOUTH CAROLINA VOLUNTEERS (COL. MONTGOMERY) AMONG THE RICE PLANTATIONS ON THE COMBAHEE, S. C.—[See Page 427.]

[A TYPICAL NEGRO.]

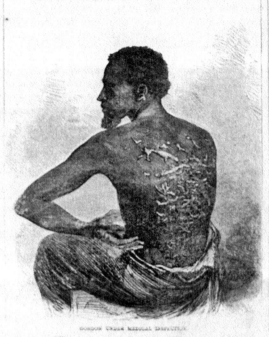

The journey of Gordon, a slave who escaped his master in Mississippi and found safety behind Union lines in Baton Rouge, Louisiana, during the Civil War, is depicted in this illustrated article published in *Harper's Weekly* on 4 July 1863. The pictures show: (left) Gordon as a runaway dressed in tattered rags, (center) the scars of repeated whippings on his back, and (right) Gordon in his uniform after enrolling in the Union army. (Library of Congress.)

punishments than this man must have received, though nothing in his appearance indicates any unusual viciousness—but on the contrary, he seems INTELLIGENT AND WELL-BEHAVED." Within months commercial photographers in Philadelphia, New York, Boston, and London had issued this image on their own studio mounts. McAllister & Brothers of Philadelphia printed an excerpt of Towle's letter on the verso of their mount and gave the picture the title "The Scourged Back." Recognized as a searing indictment of slavery, Gordon's portrait was presented as the latest evidence in the abolitionist campaign. An unidentified writer for the *New York Independent* wrote: "This Card Photograph should be multiplied by 100,000, and scattered over the States. It tells the story in a way that even Mrs. [Harriet Beecher] Stowe can not approach, because it tells the story to the eye." Abolitionist leaders such as William Lloyd Garrison referred to it repeatedly in their work. On 4 July 1863 *Harper's Weekly* reproduced the image as a wood engraving with the article "A Typical Negro." Two other portraits of Gordon—one "as he

entered our lines," and the other "in his uniform as a U.S. soldier"—were also included. Together these three images and the accompanying article about his harrowing journey and the brutality of southern slaveholders transformed Gordon into a symbol of African American courage and patriotism. His example also stimulated free African Americans in the North to enlist.

Records of Gordon's military service during the Civil War are incomplete. *Harper's Weekly* reported that he served as a Union guide in Louisiana, and that during one expedition he was taken captive by Confederate forces, beaten, and left for dead. Yet, he supposedly survived and returned to Union lines. The *Liberator* reported that he served as a sergeant in an African American regiment that fought bravely at the siege of Port Hudson, an important Confederate stronghold on the Mississippi River twenty miles north of Baton Rouge. This battle on 27 May 1863 marked the first time that African American soldiers played a leading role in an assault on a major Confederate position. Their heroism was widely noted and helped to convince many skeptics to accept the enlistment of African Americans into the U.S. Army. There are no further records indicating what became of Gordon. In 1999, in tribute to the African Americans who fought in the Civil War, the founders of the African American Civil War Memorial in the historic Shaw district of Washington, D.C., dedicated the memorial to the memory of Gordon.

FURTHER READING

Collins, Kathleen. "The Scourged Back," *History of Photography* (Mar. 1985).

Garrison, William L. "The Dumb Witness," *Liberator*, 12 June 1863.

"A Picture for the Times," *Liberator*, 3 July 1863.

"A Typical Negro," *Harper's Weekly* (4 July 1863).

FRANK H. GOODYEAR III

Gordon, Bruce S. (15 Feb. 1946–), president and CEO of the NAACP and telecommunications executive, was born in Camden, New Jersey, one of five children of Walter Gordon, a school administrator, and Violet, a teacher. His father cofounded and served as secretary-treasurer of the Camden chapter of the NAACP, and starting at the age of eight, Gordon accompanied his father to meetings. Because both of his parents were educators, he aspired to enter the field as well. Gordon attended Gettysburg College in Pennsylvania, where he majored in anthropology and sociology (liberal arts and sociology according to some sources), earning his bachelor's degree in 1968.

After meeting with an on-campus recruiter, Gordon accepted a management-trainee post with the local phone company, Bell of Pennsylvania. Completing the training program in 1970, he signed on as a business office manager and stayed with the company until his retirement. On 20 February 1970 Gordon married Genie Alston; they had one son before they divorced. Gordon married Tawana Tibbs.

Two years after he accepted the office manager position, a rumor began circulating through the office that Gordon was going to be dismissed. Carl Nurick, a general manager in sales who was Jewish and had been discriminated against himself, sympathized with Gordon and asked that he be transferred to the sales division. Gordon worked under Nurick until 1974, when he was promoted to personnel supervisor. Over the next few years, he rose steadily in the company.

American Telephone and Telegraph (AT&T) had enjoyed monopoly control over the government-supervised telephone industry for decades. But in the 1980s, after nearly ten years of litigation,

AT&T settled an antitrust suit filled by the U.S. Department of Justice and agreed to break the Bell System into "Baby Bells," seven regional companies that would be forced to compete under normal market conditions. In 1985 Gordon's employer, Bell of Philadelphia, became the Bell Atlantic Corporation. Gordon was appointed general manager of marketing and sales shortly after the reorganization. Seeing that the company would need to be more aggressive in attracting and retaining subscribers now that it faced competition, he tried several innovative approaches to marketing, including the installation of kiosks in shopping malls and sales outlets in Sears retail stores. Gordon earned a master's degree from the Massachusetts Institute of Technology's Sloan School of Management in 1988. That same year he was named the vice president of Bell Atlantic's marketing department, and in 1993 he was promoted to group president of the business unit.

Bell Atlantic became the second-largest telecommunications company in the United States in 1997, when it merged with Nynex, the New York and New England phone system. Gordon was responsible for establishing brand recognition for Bell Atlantic among the millions of new customers the company acquired under the $26 billion deal. He moved from Philadelphia to New York to lead the integration team, and in only three weeks consumer awareness of Bell Atlantic in the newly acquired markets rose from 4 percent to 79 percent, leading *Black Enterprise* magazine to name Gordon the executive of the year in 1998.

Bell Atlantic merged with the telecommunications company GTE in 2002, forming the largest telecommunications company in the country and changing its name to Verizon Communications, Inc. After the merger Gordon was promoted to president of the retail markets group. In 2003 *Fortune* ranked Gordon sixth on its list of the most powerful black executives.

By the time he retired from Verizon in 2003, Gordon had been placed in charge of the largest business unit, which employed 34,000 people, served thirty-three million telephone and Internet customers, and recorded more than $25 billion in sales annually. Throughout his career Gordon was instrumental in promoting racial diversity within the company, starting the Developmental Roundtable for Upward Mobility (DRUM), a self-help, self-mentoring group for African American men. He was also involved in the Accelerated Leadership Diversity program through the Consortium of

Information Technology Executives, a group of African Americans committed to helping their colleagues succeed professionally, and One Hundred Plus, a group of African American businessmen at the director level and above.

In December 2004 KWEISI MFUME resigned as president of the NAACP to run for a seat in the U.S. Senate. The NAACP's board of directors selected Gordon to replace Mfume at a meeting in Atlanta, Georgia, on 25 June 2005, but some members worried that Gordon's corporate background might be detrimental to the organization, that he might deviate from the organization's tradition of political activism through such techniques as boycotts, marches, leafleting, and picketing. For the previous thirty years every NAACP president had worked as either a politician or a clergyman; a businessman had not served in the role for nearly one hundred years. Gordon made it clear in press interviews that he did not intend to eschew traditional methods, but he explained that he intended to make slight adjustments in the purpose and focus of the organization in order to attract younger members by addressing such issues as de facto segregation as well as disparities in income, housing, and education. He also said he would place particular emphasis on economic equality, arguing that it is key to achieving social equality.

In July 2005, at the association's ninety-sixth annual convention in Milwaukee, Wisconsin, Gordon was officially confirmed as the fifteenth president and CEO of the NAACP. In his acceptance speech he vowed to help the organization extend its influence and to push for the establishment of more African American leaders in academia, politics, and the business world. Early in his tenure he set an ambitious fund-raising goal for the NAACP's endowment, which he argued was woefully small for an organization of its size. He also pledged to increase the NAACP's membership, which had been stagnant for about a decade, holding at around 500,000. Gordon resigned as president and CEO of the NAACP on 4 March 2007, after nineteen months of service.

Though Gordon's career did not follow that of a traditional activist, his legacy helps further the cause of racial equality. Through personal example he demonstrated that African Americans are as capable as their white counterparts, and he provided an entrée for other African Americans into positions of high prestige and influence.

FURTHER READING

Dao, James. "At N.A.A.C.P. Helm, an Economic Approach to Rights," *New York Times*, 5 July 2005.

Graves, Earl G., Sr. "A New Brand of Civil Rights Leadership," *Black Enterprise*, Sept. 2005.

Smith, Vern E. "Getting Down to Business," *Crisis*, July–Aug. 2005.

JENNIFER CURRY

Gordon, Dexter Keith (27 Feb. 1923–25 Apr. 1990), jazz tenor saxophonist, was born in Los Angeles, California, the son of Frank Alexander Gordon and Gwendolyn Baker. His father was a physician and surgeon who numbered among his patients the musicians DUKE ELLINGTON and LIONEL HAMPTON. His father's personal interest in jazz encouraged Dexter at an early age, and he first studied clarinet and elementary music theory at age seven with the New Orleans-born clarinetist John Sturdevant, a disciple of BARNEY BIGARD. Dexter's father died when Dexter was twelve, but he continued studying music, adding the alto saxophone when he was fifteen and playing in the school dance band. Other contemporaries at Jefferson High School, where Sam Brown directed the bands, were Chico Hamilton, drums; Ernie Royal, trumpet; and Vi Redd, alto saxophone. Dexter studied saxophone with Lloyd Reese, lead trumpet in the LES HITE Orchestra, and Reese formed a rehearsal band of his students that included both Dexter and Buddy Collette on saxophone and CHARLES MINGUS on bass. At seventeen Gordon took up the tenor saxophone, played in local clubs, and quit school to play in a local professional band, the Harlem Collegians. In December 1940 he joined the Lionel Hampton Orchestra, recorded with Hampton in 1941, and remained with Hampton for three years. His tenor partner in the band was ILLINOIS JACQUET.

Dexter Keith Gordon, performing at the Charlie Parker tribute at Carnegie Hall in New York City, 28 June 1980. (AP Images.)

Returning from New York to Los Angeles in 1943, he worked briefly with the Lee Young Sextet, the Jesse Price Band, and the FLETCHER HENDERSON Orchestra. That same year, Gordon made his first recordings as leader of a quintet with NAT KING COLE on piano and Harry Edison on trumpet.

Gordon played briefly and recorded with LOUIS ARMSTRONG in 1944 and with the BILLY ECKSTINE Orchestra during 1944 and 1945, the first big band to feature the new bebop style. Fellow musicians in the band included SARAH VAUGHAN, vocalist; DIZZY GILLESPIE, trumpet; SONNY STITT, alto saxophone; GENE AMMONS, tenor saxophone; John Malachi, piano; Tommy Potter, bass; and ART BLAKEY, drums. He left the band in St. Louis and returned to New York in 1945, had freelance associations with CHARLIE PARKER at the Spotlite, led his own group at the Three Deuces, and began a regular series of recordings under his own name. These activities placed Gordon among the leaders of bebop.

Between 1946 and 1949 Gordon traveled as a freelance artist to Los Angeles, Honolulu, and then back and forth between the East and West coasts. Between 1947 and 1952 he gained increased musical celebrity for his "saxophone duels"—live and recorded performances in which two soloists competed to outplay each other—with the tenor saxophonist WARDELL GRAY. Their 1947 recording for Dial Records, *The Chase*, became the model for many battles of the saxophones. Speaking of his association with Gray, Gordon said:

> I came back to LA in '47. And the jam session thing was going on very heavily at that time, at several different clubs … various tenors, altos, trumpets and an occasional trombone. But it seemed that in the wee small hours of the morning—always—there would be only Wardell and myself. It became kind of a traditional thing. (Quoted in Britt, 18)

Gordon, like many jazz musicians of the 1940s and 1950s, suffered from heroin addiction and was incarcerated from 1952 to 1954 at Chino Penitentiary in California. Although his return from prison was followed by recordings and a successful comeback, his musical activities during the 1950s were seriously curtailed when he was jailed a second time for drug use from 1956 to 1960. After his second return, he made several recordings that were well received. In September 1960 he joined the West Coast company of Jack Gelber's play about drug addicts, *The Connection*, as composer, musician, and actor. The play received mixed reviews, and in 1962 Gordon returned briefly to New York, but his parole conditions and lack of a cabaret card prevented him from performing in New York City.

In September 1962 Gordon played engagements in Europe and Great Britain and settled in Valby, Denmark, a suburb of Copenhagen, for fourteen years, making brief returns to the United States in 1965, 1969, 1970, and 1972. While in Europe, he married a second time (details of his first marriage are not known), appeared at jazz festivals, toured Japan, recorded frequently with European musicians, and taught and played regularly in Denmark. His drug addiction persisted, and he was arrested and jailed once again in Paris in 1966. Overall, however, his years abroad were successful and artistically satisfying. Of his years abroad, Gordon commented:

> Ira Gitler referred to me as an expatriate. That's true, you know, but at the time I hadn't really made up my mind to live there so I came back here in 1965 for about six months, mostly out on the coast. But with all the political and social strife during that time and the Beatles thing, I didn't really dig it. So I went back…. The fact that you're an artist in Europe means something. They treat you with a lot of respect. In America, you know, they say, "Do you make any money?" (Interview with Chuck Berg, *Down Beat*, Sept. 1989, 82)

A warm reception for his visit to the United States in 1976 led him to return permanently in 1977. He was selected Musician of the Year by *Down Beat* magazine in 1978 and 1980 and was elected to the Jazz Hall of Fame in 1980. He performed less frequently thereafter, but in 1986 he was acclaimed for his acting in the motion picture *Round Midnight*, for which he received an Academy Award nomination. The film, directed by Bertrand Tavernier, portrayed the trials of an expatriate jazz musician in France, and although the movie was based on the final years of BUD POWELL's life, it was, in fact, hauntingly autobiographical for Gordon. Partially as a result of the publicity received from the film's success, he began playing again. He died on tour in Philadelphia, Pennsylvania. He was survived by his second wife, Maxine (maiden name unknown), and five children.

During his career, Gordon recorded prolifically, but a few of his more important and representative recordings are *Long Tall Dexter* (1946), *The Chase* (1947), *Doin' All Right* (1961), *Our Man in Paris* (1963), and *Homecoming* (1976). He did his most innovative work during the late 1940s and 1950s.

When new styles developed in the late 1950s, he remained true to his ideals of bebop execution. Summarizing Gordon's career, Brian Priestley (*Jazz: The Essential Companion* [1987], 196) wrote:

> His combination of bop-inspired lines with an essentially pre-bop time feeling produced an inherent tension which was excruciatingly enjoyable. His tone quality, always vibrantly hot even when playing ballads, remained virtually unchanged for 40 years, despite adopting a few mannerisms from Coltrane in the 1960s and occasionally taking up the soprano. His authoritative delivery, however, only increased with the passing years.

Dexter Gordon was the first significant bebop tenor saxophonist, and he provided the key link between the music of LESTER YOUNG and JOHN COLTRANE. He combined a huge, hard tone with spare melodic lines and laid-back, behind-the-beat phrasing. An imposing figure, always elegantly attired and standing six feet five inches, he became, through his presence, manner, and expatriation, a representative African American figure fighting racial and social injustice. In his portrayal of Dale Turner in *Round Midnight*, and in his music, Gordon achieved his own apotheosis as a black artist struggling against the terrors of drugs, alcohol, and racism.

FURTHER READING

Oral history material and recordings are preserved at the Institute of Jazz Studies at Rutgers University in Newark, New Jersey.

Britt, Stan. *Dexter Gordon: A Musical Biography* (1989).

Gitler, Ira. *Jazz Masters of the Forties* (1966; repr., 1983).

Nieus, Robert. *A Discography of Dexter Gordon* (1986).

Sjøgren, Thorsten. *Long Tall Dexter: A Discography of Dexter Gordon* (1986).

Obituary: *New York Times*, 26 Apr. 1990.

This entry is taken from the *American National Biography* and is published here with the permission of the American Council of Learned Societies.

FRANK TIRRO

Gordon, Edmund Wyatt (13 June 1921–), Presbyterian minister, clinical and counseling psychologist, and educator, was born in Goldsboro, North Carolina, to Edmund Taylor Gordon, a physician, and Mabel Ellison Gordon, a schoolteacher. At the time of his birth and during Gordon's early life there, Goldsboro, a small city in eastern North Carolina, was typical of southern locales, with a pattern of racial segregation and racial prejudice. Despite the segregation that he experienced, Gordon grew up in privileged circumstances. His parents, both educated professionals, were firmly ensconced members of the black upper middle class.

After completing high school in Goldsboro, Gordon attended Howard University in Washington, D.C. During his early college years Howard University suspended Gordon for a semester for not making proper academic progress. When he returned, he was lucky enough to find a mentor in the person of Professor ALAIN LOCKE, the noted black philosopher and scholar who was at Howard University at that time. Professor Locke became the first in a series of mentors who came to the aid of Gordon at various stages in his educational and professional career. Gordon earned a degree in Zoology from Howard in 1942. Three years later, in 1945, he received a Bachelor of Divinity in Social Ethics from the Graduate School at Howard University. The year following his graduation from Divinity School, Gordon, an ordained minister of the Presbyterian Church, was a field missionary. From 1946 to 1950 he was the assistant dean of men at Howard. During that period he married Susan Elizabeth Git, a pediatrician, in November of 1948. They had four children: Edmund T., Christopher W., Jessica G., and Johanna S.

In 1950 Edmund Gordon completed the work for a Master of Arts in Social Psychology from American University in Washington, D.C. Following a move to New York City, Gordon attended the Jefferson School of Social Sciences. During these early years in New York City, he felt he was not as well read as some of his classmates. When he told this to another of his mentors, research psychologist Dr. Herbert G. Birch, Dr. Birch advised him to go to the library and remedy his deficiencies. Gordon became confident enough to meet weekly for discussions with W. E. B. DuBois, who had befriended him. He credits DuBois for the idea of paying attention to the "talented tenth" of blacks, which influenced Gordon's own work with the factors involved in the success or failure of a relatively elite group of minority students.

During these years in New York City, Professor Gordon and his wife founded in 1952 the Harriet Tubman Clinic for Children and served as co-directors from 1953 to 1959. Also at this time Professor Gordon was the assistant director and counseling psychologist for the Morningside Community Center and Mental Health Services. He additionally held clinical posts in psychology and psychiatry at the New York University Medical College, the Jewish Hospital of Brooklyn, and the Morris J. Solomon Clinic for the Rehabilitation of Retarded Children. The Teachers College of Columbia

University awarded him a Doctor of Education in Child Development and Guidance in 1957, following what must have been an exhausting period of work and study.

In the ensuing years he held a number of academic and counseling positions in prestigious colleges and universities in the northeastern United States. He was in great demand as a consultant on educational matters affecting minorities. He served as a consultant to the United States Office of Education from 1964 to 1966. During President Lyndon Johnson's administration, Gordon was the founding director of Research Evaluation for Project Head Start, a national program designed to give disadvantaged children a better start in school and life, which was a prime interest of Gordon. Project Head Start, inaugurated during the Johnson administration as a part of the war on poverty, was one of the most successful programs of the federal government, continuing nationwide into the twenty-first century. The National Academy of Education elected Gordon to membership in 1968.

In the years following his work in Project Head Start, Professor Gordon held positions at Columbia Teachers College. He was a professor of education and the chair of the Department of Guidance, the director of the National Center for Research and Information on Equal Educational Opportunity, and the head of the Institute of Urban and Minority Education (which he co-founded). From 1973 to 1979 Gordon consulted on projects for the Educational Testing Service, which administers the well-known Scholastic Assessment Test (SAT) and other undergraduate and graduate testing programs. He is the author of several books and numerous articles in professional publications.

Professor Gordon received honorary degrees from a number of prestigious colleges and universities, among them Yale University, Brown University, the Bank Street College, and Mount Holyoke College. In recognition of his many accomplishments, Gordon was elected a fellow of several professional organizations, including the American Psychological Society. He was a fellow and life member of the American Association for the Advancement of Science. In 1993 Columbia University Teachers College awarded him the Cleveland E. Dodge Teachers College Medal for Distinguished Service to Education. In recognition of his contributions to the Educational Testing Service, this organization established a chair to memorialize his career as an educator. In April of 2000, at their annual meeting, the American Educational Association honored Gordon for "Distinguished Contributions to Education."

Professor Edmund W. Gordon devoted more than half a century of his life to improving the opportunities for education, in particular those for children of ethnic and cultural minorities. His work informed the conceptual framework of many of the advances in educating disadvantaged children and youth.

FURTHER READING
Gross, Jane. "Studying Race, Privilege, and Intellectual Levels," *New York Times*, 8 Jan. 2003.
Yale Bulletin & Calendar 28.33 (26 May 2000).

BENJAMIN A. JACKSON

Gordon, Emmanuel Taylor (29 Apr. 1893–5 May 1971), singer, actor, and writer, was born in White Sulphur Springs, Montana, the youngest child of John Francis Gordon and Mary Anna Goodall, who were married in 1879. John Gordon claimed Zulu ancestry, while Mary Anna Goodall was born into slavery in Bourbon County, Kentucky, in 1853. Moving to Montana in 1881, John Gordon traveled by steamboat up the Missouri River to work as cook for a Fort Benton mining company. Mary joined him a year later with their son Robert, the first of their five children. An expert chef, John Gordon worked as a cook in several Montana mining camps. In 1893 John left to work as a cook for a Canadian railroad, but reportedly died in a train wreck. Mary Gordon, left to raise five children alone, supported her family with wages earned as a cook, laundress, and nurse—working for the cowboys, miners, and prostitutes that dominated the fledgling mining town of White Sulphur Springs.

The Gordon home was filled with music; all members of the family sang and played various instruments. Mary Gordon was renowned for the haunting beauty and power of the spirituals she sang. Taylor, or "Mannie" Gordon, as he was called, attended the local school and worked at whatever employment he could find—carrying messages for the local bawdy houses, serving drinks, setting bowling pins, selling "hop" and cleaning pipes in opium dens, and working as an automobile mechanic. Taking a cue from his mother, Gordon would sing as he worked. Although his was the only black family in White Sulphur Springs, Gordon later claimed to have thought little of race, even as his socially ambiguous position allowed him to move between classes, delivering messages between local prostitutes and their well-heeled clients and selling opium out of a Chinese laundry. Abandoning formal education, Gordon learned to ride and rope, working cattle for a wealthy rancher. He also became an able mechanic, a skill that would later serve him well as a driver for a Montana-based land-development company owned by the circus impresario John Ringling.

In 1910 the St. Paul, Minnesota, opera house manager Louis N. Scott, who had visited Montana as John Ringling's guest, hired Gordon as his personal chauffeur. Here, Gordon was forced to adapt to unfamiliar circumstances, encountering racial segregation for the first time and finding that he could no longer rely on Blue Steel Betty, the trusty revolver his mother had insisted he leave behind, to settle arguments. He was nevertheless enthralled by the prospects of urban life. Also working as a Pullman porter, doorman, and cook, he eventually made his way to New York, where he became Ringling's valet, traveling throughout the country on Ringling's private rail car. In 1915 in St. Louis, Missouri, a passerby overheard Gordon singing along to an Enrique Caruso record and suggested that he pursue a musical career. With Ringling's support, he moved to New York to study with the composer WILL MARION COOK and, after stints as a dockworker, bricklayer, elevator operator, and immigration agent, began performing with B. F. Keith's vaudeville revue in 1919. Beginning in 1925 he began touring major venues as a concert tenor, accompanied by JOHN ROSAMOND JOHNSON on piano, singing from *The Book of American Negro Spirituals*. He also sang with Johnson's vaudeville act known as the Inimitable Five. Gordon's career peaked in 1927 when he toured France and England, performing for a number of dignitaries, including England's King George V and Queen Mary.

By 1925 Gordon had come to the attention of Carl Van Vechten, the white arts patron, and with Van Vechten's help, published his autobiography, *Born to Be*, in 1929. With a foreword by Van Vechten, an introduction by Muriel Draper, and illustrations by Miguel Covarrubias, *Born to Be* was a remarkable achievement, as Gordon details his rugged upbringing in Montana, recounts many amorous adventures on both sides of the color line, offers blunt commentaries on racial politics, and drops names in copious quantities, paying tribute to "the world's greatest celebrities, artists, musicians, writers, bulldikers, hoboes, faggots, bankers, sweetbacks, hotpots, and royalty, who have framed my mind so that life goes on for me, one thrill after another" (235). Throughout the book he displayed a marked ambivalence toward African American identity, straightforwardly depicting the demeaning and sometimes violent facts of segregation while insisting that "the Race Question has never been the big ghost in my life" (234). His enthusiasm for further adventures seemed misguided, however, as the publication of *Born to Be* heralded a period of professional and personal decline. In addition to *Born to Be*, Gordon published "Malicious Lies Magnifying the Truth," an essay examining racial prejudice, in Nancy Cunard's *Negro* anthology in 1934. In the essay he identified prejudice as a universal trait among all races, but he detailed how prejudice became exacerbated in contemporary America, using analyses of the ideology of white supremacy, class distinctions among immigrants, and passing by black actresses in Hollywood.

Gordon continued entertaining privately and eventually pursued an acting career, appearing as a cast member on Broadway in *Shoot the Works* (1931), *Ol' Man Satan* (1932), *The Gay Divorce* (1932), and *After Such Pleasures* (1934), and in the film *The Emperor Jones* (1933); yet he never reclaimed his previous level of success. He completed the novel "Daonda" in 1935, but it was never published. In 1947 Gordon suffered a nervous breakdown and was institutionalized several times over the next decade.

In February 1959 Gordon was released to the care of his sister, ROSE BEATRIS GORDON, who still resided in White Sulphur Springs and who by this time had gained her own renown. Taylor Gordon supported himself through rental incomes, an antique business, occasional concerts and talks, and through his writing. His later books include *Born to Be Sequel* (1970) and *The Man Who Built the Stone Castle* (1967), which was about White Sulphur Springs' historic landmark. He died in White Sulphur Springs in 1971.

FURTHER READING

Gordon, Taylor. *Born to Be* (1929, repr. 1995).

Johnson, Michael K. "Migration, Masculinity, and Racial Identity in Taylor Gordon's *Born to Be*," in *Moving Stories: Migration and the American West, 1850–2000* (2001).

HUGH DAVIS JODIE FOLEY

Gordon, Eugene F. (23 Nov. 1891–18 Mar. 1974), author and journalist, was born in Oviedo, Florida, to Elijah and Lillian. Some early biographical sketches give his birth year as 1890. He was raised on his grandfather's farm in Hawkinsville, Georgia, and went to the only school in that town for black students. He attended Howard University Academy, a preparatory school run by Howard, but by 1917, when he was in his junior year, he left to join the military. He later explained that he was an idealist who believed his military service would gain him more respect in the still-segregated United States. In 1916 he married Edythe Mae Chapman of Washington, D.C. They would have one son together.

After his military service was completed, Gordon and his wife moved to Boston. He was hired by the *Boston Post* in 1919, becoming one of the few black reporters at a white-owned newspaper. He also edited copy and worked on feature stories. After taking some extra journalism courses at Boston University in the early 1920s, he was promoted to an editorial position at the *Post* in 1923. He not only supervised short fiction for the newspaper (newspapers regularly serialized popular books and offered works of fiction by well-known authors) but wrote editorials and commentary in the Sunday edition of the *Post* and sometimes in the daily edition. In the majority of American cities, even the most talented black journalists were hired only by the local black newspapers, so Gordon's position at the *Post* was unusual for its time.

During the mid-1920s, in addition to his work at the *Post*, Gordon began to freelance for a number of publications, including the National Urban League's *Opportunity* magazine and such mainstream publications as *Scribner's* and *American Mercury*. He also contributed a 1928 essay to the *Annals of the American Academy of Political and Social Science*, in which he evaluated the current state of black journalism. In that essay he praised the *Pittsburgh Courier* as the paper that took the most courageous editorial stands on issues. His magazine articles were usually social commentary about African American life in the United States. He also edited a short-lived literary journal called the *Saturday Evening Quill* from 1928 to 1930. The *Quill* evolved from a black literary club in Boston, whose members wanted to publish their own work independently, mainly for the enjoyment of friends and colleagues. They raised the money and put out three annual issues of the journal, which featured original poetry, short stories, and critical essays. W. E. B. DuBois, then editor of *The Crisis*, praised the *Quill*, as did CHARLES JOHNSON of *Opportunity*. In addition to contributions from such writers as Helene Johnson, Waring Cuning, and DOROTHY WEST, Gordon's wife Edythe, who was working on a master's degree at Boston University, contributed short fiction and poetry, and the *Quill* was the first place her work was published.

While definitive information about Gordon is not available, he seems to have become increasingly more frustrated by the limitations placed on him in the racist and segregated world of the 1920s and 1930s. In a 1934 essay he observed that even becoming an officer in the military had not earned him more respect from white society, and although the Harlem Renaissance had provided greater opportunities for black artists and intellectuals, he believed that society at large was still as racist as ever. He gave examples in his essays, describing how despite being both an educator and a journalist, he was still mistaken for a porter or an elevator operator by white people who did not know him.

At some point in the early 1930s Gordon and Edythe separated, though they were not formally divorced until 1942. But the most dramatic change in Gordon's life was his involvement with the Communist Party. In the 1930 edition of *Who's Who in Colored America*, he listed himself as a member, and he became increasingly more active as the decade progressed. That he joined was not in itself unique. A number of intellectuals, both black and white, identified with socialist or communist ideologies during the Great Depression. But for Gordon as a journalist, the episodes of racial injustice he observed made him more determined to speak out against racism, and he increasingly saw the Communist Party's journals as a good fit for his views. By 1934, when an unarmed black janitor named George Borden was shot and killed when he resisted being arrested for several outstanding (and relatively minor) traffic violations, Gordon published a commentary on the case for a communist publication, titled "The Borden Case: The Struggle for Negro Rights in Boston" (1935). It was far more outspoken than what he could have printed in the *Boston Post*. He also participated in demonstrations with the League of Struggle for Negro Rights. These activities began to attract the attention of some of the more mainstream media newspapers, which were critical of him and other "Reds" for demanding justice in a way that seemed too forceful.

By 1935 Gordon wrote exclusively for publications identified with the Communist Party. He began praising the Soviet Union as an example of egalitarianism, and in April 1935 he announced that he would go to Russia to study and work. He was hired by the *Moscow Daily News* as a reporter, and when he returned to the United States after three years in Moscow, he told the *New York Age* that "there is no color prejudice whatsoever in the USSR." He also praised the Moscow newspaper for giving him more opportunities to cover major stories than his U.S. paper did ("Eugene Gordon Back from Three Year Stay in Russia," 3). He moved to New York, where he wrote for many years for such publications as the *Daily Worker* and the *National*

Guardian. He became known for his investigative reporting. His focus was stories of injustice that had gone unpunished—innocent black men who had been subjected to police brutality or black women who were raped by white men. He felt that while the mainstream white press was quick to report on crimes allegedly committed by blacks, that same white press was usually silent when blacks were the victims of crime. Some of Gordon's columns in the communist press were quoted by black newspapers like the *Chicago Defender,* but more often than not the mainstream press ignored Gordon's reporting.

In the mid-1940s Gordon married June, who had once been the wife of Carl Reeve, a Communist Party leader and the son of the party matriarch Ella "Mother Bloor" Reeve. June Gordon ultimately faced deportation to Russia in 1960 because the U.S. government said she had entered the country illegally in 1928. Her supporters believed she was targeted for being a communist and for demonstrating on behalf of workers' rights. Eugene Gordon died in New York, seldom mentioned by the mainstream media, mourned only by his colleagues and friends in the Communist Party. Scholars have begun to pay more attention to Gordon's tireless efforts to gain respect for journalists of color.

Had Gordon not become an active member of the Communist Party, he might have been remembered as a pioneering journalist, one of the first African Americans to attain the position of editor at a white newspaper, a respected media critic, and editor of a critically acclaimed literary journal. But in a country where communists were reviled by people like Representative Martin Dies, cofounder of the House Committee on Un-American Activities, and Senator Joseph McCarthy, Gordon's career was marginalized by the mainstream press.

FURTHER READING

Daniel, Walter C. *Black Journals of the United States* (1982).

"Eugene Gordon Back from 3 Year Stay in Russia." *New York Age,* 5 Feb. 1938.

Miller, Eben Simmons. "A New Day Is Here: The Shooting of George Borden and 1930s Civil Rights Activism in Boston," *New England Quarterly* 73.1 (Mar. 2000): 3–31.

"To Study in Soviet Russia." *Chicago Defender,* 27 Apr. 1935.

"U.S. Orders Deportation of Known Red." *Gettysburg Pennsylvania Times,* 6 Aug. 1960.

DONNA HALPER

Gordon, Nora Antonia (25 Aug. 1866–Jan. 1901), missionary and printing supervisor, was born to former slaves (names unknown) in Columbus, Georgia. There is no additional information about Gordon's parents, childhood, or life before she entered Spelman Seminary (later to become Spelman College) in 1882 and graduated in 1888. Spelman, originally known as Atlanta Baptist Female Seminary, was founded in 1881 in the basement of Friendship Baptist Church (Atlanta's oldest black church) by Harriet E. Giles and Sophia B. Packard, two white teachers who were graduates of Oread Institute.

With $100 from the First Baptist Church of Medford, Massachusetts, and support from the Woman's American Baptist Home Mission Society, Atlanta Baptist Female Seminary opened, with eleven black female students enrolled.

Overcrowding forced the school to relocate in 1883 to a nine-acre site in Atlanta, close to the church where it had been originally founded. After a visit to the school in April 1884, John D. Rockefeller settled the debt on the property. The school's name was changed to Spelman Seminary, in honor of his wife, Laura Spelman Rockefeller, and her parents, Harvey Buel Spelman and Lucy Henry Spelman, longtime activists in the antislavery movement.

Nora Gordon was the first Spelman student to travel to Africa as a missionary. Her letters described her experiences in Africa and convinced several other Spelman graduates to volunteer for missionary work on that continent.

Gordon was sent out by the Woman's American Baptist Foreign Missionary Society of the West, an auxiliary of the American Baptist Missionary Union (ABMU), to the Livingstone Inland Mission of Great Britain, which founded the first mission station in the Congo at Palabala in 1878. However, the Livingstone Inland Mission was unable to continue financing the work in the Congo, and turned that responsibility over to the American Baptist Missionary Union in 1884.

Before going to her assignment, Gordon attended a missionary training institute in London, conducted by two former Congo missionaries. At the mission station in Palabala on the Congo River she worked with Louise Cecilia Fleming and taught fifty-seven pupils at the mission school, and an additional twenty-five students in her Sunday school class. In a report home in 1894, Gordon emphasized the need for a separate girls' schoolhouse where they could be educated and trained to become Christian wives and mothers.

Missionaries, regardless of their denominational affiliation, their location in Africa, or the colonial ruler of the colony, used similar tactics for conversion: the single traveling missionary, mission stations, or the founding of schools on mission posts. It was the last strategy that proved to be the most successful for increasing membership in mission churches, and especially effective was the organization of boarding schools for children. Missionaries constructed buildings where children would live year-round. They were encouraged to accept Western and Christian ideas and to reject their traditional cultures. Children proved easy converts, and in fact, a direct correlation existed between the establishment of boarding mission schools and the number of converts.

As disclosed in their letters and reports home, female missionaries faced some frustrations concerning the pace and progress of their work. They were disappointed that there never seemed to be enough resources for all mission programs, particularly those geared toward women and girls; they also lamented the scant resources available to mission stations and the paltry salaries of missionaries. Despite some improvements on the Palabala station, Gordon continued to complain that work among girls and women was progressing too slowly. A separate building for girls was never built probably because of the limited funds of mission societies in general.

In 1891, in adherence to the normal course of mission station transfers, Gordon was relocated to a mission station in the Lukunga region of the western Congo, a center for twenty-four schools. At the station she was put in charge of the afternoon school and was appointed supervisor of the printing office where she set up type for printing the first arithmetic textbook in the local language, Lingala.

Soon after her arrival at Lukunga, Gordon expressed a concern of most women missionaries in Africa. She rejoiced that some African women were converting, but she continued to be disappointed at not being able to reach more women. Despite the high conversion rates among children at the mission schools, missionaries did not have the same success in winning female converts in surrounding areas.

Gordon's letters did refer to fulfillment in other areas. She admitted that she had formed deep and lasting relationships with both women and men in the Congo. Rapport and bonds often developed between the black missionaries and the indigenous women and children, perhaps strengthened by the fact that African American female missionaries, particularly unmarried ones such as Gordon, had little companionship in Africa other than African women and children.

In 1893 Gordon took a furlough in the United States. Two years later, she married the Reverend S. C. Gardner of Jamaica, and they sailed to the Congo under appointment by a British Baptist mission society. Two daughters were born to the couple but neither child lived longer than a year. Nora Gordon Gardner returned to America in 1900 with failing health and died in Atlanta a year later at a mere thirty-four years of age.

FURTHER READING
Baptist Missionary Magazine (1890–1891). cannot do "Black Baptists in Mission," Pamphlet. International Ministries, American Baptist Churches in the U.S.A.
Hartshord, W. N., ed. *An Era of Progress and Promise, 1863–1910* (1910).
Read, Florence Matilda. *The Story of Spelman College* (1961).
Spelman Messenger, 1889–1893.
Woman's Baptist Foreign Missionary Society of the West (1890–1891).

SYLVIA M. JACOBS

Gordon, Rose Beatris (2 June 1885–19 Nov. 1968), physiotherapist, masseuse, businesswoman, and community organizer, was born in Barker, Montana, the second child and only daughter of Mary Ann Goodlow and John Francis Gordon. Mary had been born a slave in Kentucky in 1853. John, who claimed Zulu heritage, trained to be a chef at Wilberforce University in Ohio. He traveled to Montana Territory from Illinois by steamboat in 1881 to cook on the mining frontier. Mary followed a year later. In the mid-1880s, employed as a chef for the town's primary hotel, John purchased a house in the central Montana community of White Sulphur Springs. Set in a high, pastoral valley, White Sulphur Springs was a small commercial hub for outlying mining camps and ranches. Its hot springs attracted Indian and European American settlers. A decade later, while working for a Canadian railroad, John was killed in a train accident before Rose's youngest brother Taylor was born. Mary supported her five children by cooking, doing laundry, and providing nursing care for area families. Her children also worked for others around town to help with the family's support.

Notwithstanding long hours helping her mother with laundry, Rose graduated valedictorian of her

1904 White Sulphur Springs High School class. Her graduation oration, titled "The Progress of the Negro Race," ended with praise for the African American educator BOOKER T. WASHINGTON and Tuskegee Institute. Gordon spent the remainder of her life living Washington's particular kind of black populism with its emphasis on self-improvement, self-reliance, education, and cordial rather than confrontational relationships with white people.

Gordon aspired to be a doctor, but lacking funds, she began nurse's training in the state capital of Helena, seventy-five miles away. She soon was forced to return home to assist her mother by contributing immediately and regularly to the family's income. She found employment as a domestic helper with area families and as a hotel clerk in the nearby community of Lewistown. In 1913 Gordon began training in physiotherapy in Spokane, Washington, before again interrupting her education to return home and assist her mother.

In her first years after school, Gordon established a lifelong pattern in which she interspersed earning whatever living the isolated community provided, pursuing as much medical training and work as she could, supporting and advocating for her family, helping neighbors, writing, and singing. In fact, when she returned from Spokane, Rose became the head of the Gordon family as most of her brothers had moved elsewhere. Most notably, her youngest brother, EMMANUEL TAYLOR GORDON, had made his way to the East Coast and ultimately to Europe as a concert tenor, nurtured by both wealthy and connected local families and the creativity of the Harlem Renaissance.

Gordon and her mother ran a restaurant and variety store in White Sulphur Springs until her mother's death in 1924. Gordon continued the business through the early 1930s, when the Great Depression hit hardest. During this period Gordon began her own life story in a memoir, "Gone Are the Days." In its 170-typescript pages, she juxtaposes descriptions of her parents' lives and her own with lively biographical portrayals of leading citizens and characters she met in Montana's formative years. In 1934 she began a fifteen-year unsuccessful campaign to publish her memoir, continuing to revise it throughout. Her archived papers include poems, plays, and other short narratives, most of which blend autobiographical and historical information.

From 1935 to 1942 Gordon received employment assistance, primarily as a Works Progress Administration seamstress. Between 1942 and 1944 she again owned and ran a café. In 1949 she received a diploma from the College of Swedish Massage in Chicago, Illinois.

From the mid-1940s until her death in 1968, Gordon practiced her medical skills most intensively. She nursed elderly community residents in their homes, cared for newborns and their mothers, and provided multiple physical therapy treatments each week, often coordinating with area physicians. She offered patients diet, exercise, and general medical and homeopathic recommendations and remained current in naturopathic equipment and thinking. In the 1950s, when White Sulphur Springs acquired a bustling sawmill, Gordon treated workers referred and paid for by the state's Industrial Accident Board. She advertised her physiotherapy services in the community's weekly newspaper and on formal printed business cards and stationery.

During that same period, Gordon assumed more clearly the mantle of community historian. She began the practice of writing letters to the editor of the White Sulphur Springs's weekly *Meagher County News* on the deaths of many longtime residents. Each began "I write to pay tribute to … ," and in each Gordon recalled and praised the individual's specific contributions to the area. She belonged to the Meagher County Historical Association, the Montana Historical Society, the local hospital guild, the Grace Episcopal Church, and the Montana Federation of Negro Women's Clubs.

In 1951, frustrated by slow attention to community problems, Gordon ran for mayor of White Sulphur Springs. She ignored an anonymous letter that threatened her with the resignation of all other city council members and employees should she be elected. She lost to the incumbent 58 to 207. A week later Gordon wrote a letter to the newspaper editor reminding the community that, as a local business owner, she had been recruited for support by politicians from around Montana, that she was entitled to file for office, and that white and "colored" soldiers were both dying in Korea for, among other things, better race relations.

At this time Gordon assumed responsibility for her younger brother Taylor, whose musical career had ended with a diagnosis of mental illness. In 1959 she brought him home from a New York state mental hospital to join her in the family home that their father had purchased seventy-five years earlier.

Gordon continued to enrich her life of responsibility by attending programs, singing at public events, baking for her neighbors, and playing her piano. She corresponded with friends, including many families for whom she had worked. Incoming and outgoing correspondence was detailed, full of fun, and focused on shared personal and community memories. She maintained a scrapbook that she began in 1903 of newspaper and magazine articles, theatrical programs, and other tidbits, often pasting over earlier enclosures.

In 1964, on the occasion of Montana's hundredth anniversary as a territory, Gordon received a certificate and recognition as a centennial pioneer in the state program Our Fair Ladies: A Centennial Review. By 1967 the *Meagher County News* regularly published two separate columns written by Gordon: "Centennial Notes" and "Rose Gordon's Recollections." In them Gordon presented significant portions of her still-unpublished autobiography.

The 1890 Montana census recorded 4,668 people in Meagher County, including thirty African Americans. The mining boom and its accompanying commercial and transportation industries accounted for both numbers. By 1950 a physically smaller and economically weaker Meagher County recorded 2,237 citizens, including one black female and one black male. In her autobiography Gordon wrote that, when she was a child, frontier Montanans appeared to treat her without prejudice, choosing instead to focus on building the new state. On 9 May 1968, following the assassination in April of Reverend MARTIN LUTHER KING JR., Gordon wrote a letter to the *Meagher County News* titled "The Battle of Pigment." In it she acknowledged that many people she met had not liked the color of her skin. She went on to say that she still found the world richer because of its many colors (alluding to both the natural world and to skin color), that she understood that everyone had a cross to bear, that soldiers of all colors "being baptized into full citizenship by their bloodshed" had earned the protection of their country, and that life was too short to focus on people who could not accept different colors.

Gordon died abruptly of upper gastronintestinal hemorrhage six months later. Montana senator Mike Mansfield joined hundreds in sending Taylor, her one surviving brother, letters and cards of condolence. Community leaders served as pallbearers at her well-attended funeral service, graced by two dozen flower arrangements. The *Meagher County News* editor wrote a poem about the woman who had paid tribute to so many others and offered a full page for letters of remembrance from others. On that page community members wrote about Gordon's unselfishness, compassion, wit, curiosity, and exuberant appreciation of others; her talent for making friends and keeping them; her great chicken dinners; and the courage with which she confronted racism. Rose Gordon, like her brother Taylor, never married.

FURTHER READING
Gordon's extensive papers are in the Emmanuel Taylor Gordon Family Papers, 1882–1980, Manuscript Collection 150, Montana Historical Society Archives, Helena, Montana.
Obituary: *Meagher County News*, 21 Nov. 1968 and 28 Nov. 1968.

MARCELLA SHERFY

Gordone, Charles (12 Oct. 1925–16 Nov. 1995), playwright and actor-director, was born Charles Edward Fleming in Cleveland, Ohio, the son of Charles Fleming and Camille Morgan Fleming. His stepfather was William Gordon. The boy never knew his biological father and often referred to himself as "part Indian, part Irish, part French, and part Nigger." With the birth of Charles, the family moved to his mother's hometown, Elkhart, Indiana, where the young Gordon went to school. Shirley Gordon Jackson, the older of his two sisters, recalled that the family then moved out of the "colored" part of town and crossed the railroad tracks to the white side of Elkhart's "Mason-Dixon line." All of Gordon's school friends were white. He was a straight-A student, "doing everything right," winning honors in dramatics, music, writing, and debate. He also received sixteen letters in sports and set a school record in the high jump.

Gordon explained that he was "Run outa town because I dated a black girl." He left for Los Angeles after graduating from high school; shortly after his arrival, he joined the army air corps special services and helped organize entertainment programs. "Everything was segregated," he remembered. "We even had separate chow halls." The day after his discharge Gordon returned to Elkhart, became involved with a local girl, Juanita Burton, and married her after she became pregnant; they had two children, but the marriage failed. After that, a period of itinerancy led to promiscuity, wantonness, and alcoholism.

In 1945 he returned to Los Angeles and worked as a police officer, but he judged himself to be a "miserable failure." Taking advantage of the GI Bill, he studied music and later drama at Los Angeles City College. Gordon and a fellow actor, Tony Carbone, drove the southern route to New York City in 1952, ignoring the warning from his teachers that there would be no work there for blacks. Three weeks after they arrived in Manhattan, Gordon landed a role as an eccentric half-caste in Moss Hart's *Climate of Eden* on Broadway. Upon joining Actors' Equity, he saw another Charles Gordon on the Equity membership list, so he renamed himself by adding his middle initial, E, to "Gordon."

After *Eden* closed, he endured the angst of the improvident actor in New York with the occasional role and the frequent binge, won an Obie (Off-Broadway award) for his performance as George in an all-black production of John Steinbeck's *Of Mice and Men*, and then experienced encounters that changed his fortunes. Although Gordone did no serious writing during the 1950s—for a time he worked as a waiter—he turned to directing in 1958 and made his debut with an ambitious production of Goethe's *Faust* for the Village's offbeat Judson Memorial Church players. He also met Jeanne Warner, a blonde nurse from Columbus, Ohio. They lived together as husband and wife, though the legality of the marriage was open to question because of inconclusive evidence of the dissolution of the first marriage. They had one child.

In 1961 Gordone landed a small role as a queen's valet in the historic Off-Broadway production of Jean Genet's *The Blacks*. He called the experience life-changing: "Living with Genet's words night after night for four years—traveling to Europe—forced me to confront the hatred and fear I had inside me about being black. It set my head straight." At various times the cast included almost every substantial black name in live theater. GODFREY CAMBRIDGE, LOUIS GOSSETT JR., and CICELY TYSON became his lifelong friends. Cambridge and Gordone formed CORE's (Congress of Racial Equality) Committee for the Employment of Negro Performers, and they picketed *Subways Are for Sleeping*. "All we wanted," he said, "was to get black performers an equal chance to audition for jobs."

During the long run of *The Blacks*, Gordone began setting down some of the vignettes for a play that would become *No Place to Be Somebody*. The play nearly died in manuscript because the Gordones at first failed to find backers. After an experimental production directed by Gordone, in November 1967, which nobody in show business attended, two years of desperation ensued. Finally, following a showcase of three weekends at the director Ted Cornell's tiny Other Stage in South Manhattan, the much-shortened play was launched on 4 May 1969 by Joseph Papp on a 248-performance run at the New York Shakespeare Festival's Public Theatre, followed by an acclaimed limited engagement at Broadway's ANTA Theatre.

No Place's power lies in the stunning interplay between Johnny Williams, angry and bitter, trying to make it as a small-time hustler, and Gabe Gabriel, angry but hopeful, a young playwright trying to find another way to be somebody. Gabe sees the futility of Johnny's course but can't find an acceptable alternative. They perform a tragic duet that Gordone laced together with flashes of what he called "black-black comedy." The *New York Times* drama critic Walter Kerr proclaimed Gordone "the most astonishing new American playwright to come along since Edward Albee." *No Place to Be Somebody* won the 1970 Pulitzer Prize. In January it started a run of nearly two years at the Promenade Theatre, on Broadway at Seventy-sixth, and was presented by two national touring companies in Los Angeles, San Francisco, Chicago, and Boston, all directed by Gordone. He was also presented at Carnegie Recital Hall in May 1970, performing his poems and short sketches in an evening titled *Gordone Is a Muthah*.

With so much success crowded into one year of his life, Gordone set a standard that few could approximate. The Pulitzer accomplishment, rooted in the 1960s upsurge in militant black theater in New York, was also a kind of disaster for so politically conservative a playwright. "There can be no black experience without the white experience," Gordone once observed. "I believe there never has been such a thing as 'black theater.' What is called black theater has, as it should, come out of the civil rights movement [but] Broadway theater has depicted blacks in sensational and stereotypical ways [without] showing any interest in the black experience" ("Yes, I Am a Black Playwright, but … ," *New York Times*, 25 Jan. 1970).

Gordone's apostasy from any constricted ethnic identity—his alienation from most African American political organizations that dealt exclusively with black urban problems—only partially explains why his playwriting career lacked a second act. His fall was inseparable from his alcoholism.

In 1982 Gordone headed west. The 1980s found Gordone in Berkeley and San Francisco, where once again he entered into a companionate symbiosis. Susan Kouyomjian, a young and innovative producer, invited him to direct Tennessee Williams's *The Night of the Iguana* at her community theater in Berkeley. He stayed, and they did fifteen plays together—from August Strindberg to Eugene O'Neill—cast untraditionally with minority actors while at once acknowledging their ethnicity and the plays' historical contexts. And he stopped drinking.

Kouyomjian remained with him for the rest of his life. They married in 1987. In summer 1987 he completed a D. H. Lawrence Fellowship at Taos, New Mexico, and that fall he accepted an invitation to lecture at Texas A&M University, where he stayed until his death, directing plays and teaching playwriting and acting in the drama and English departments. His fascination with the American West was reflected in his last play, *Roan Browne and Cherry*, which received a workshop production at the university. Gordone also wrote a series pilot for CBS television, *Heart and Soul*, but the writers' strike of 1987 prevented the project from going forward.

No Place to Be Somebody, as the reviewer Stanley Eichelbaum wrote after its Bay Area opening, "isn't just another piece that lashes out at Whitey. It's a powerful, funny, searingly theatrical and fascinating human tragi-comedy about the black man's hate-love relationship with whites and with his own race as well. For there's lots of harsh comment on black paranoia and intra-racial hatred, along with the more familiar hang-ups of black rage" ("A Powerfully Affecting Black Play," *San Francisco Examiner*, 12 Nov. 1970). Written with more coherence than the early plays of AMIRI BARAKA (LeRoi Jones) and with none of the ethnic stereotypes of Lonne Elder III, *No Place* crosses the barroom drama of William Saroyan's *The Time of Your Life* and O'Neill's *The Iceman Cometh* with the social outrage of John Osborne's *Look Back in Anger*.

FURTHER READING

Hay, Samuel A. *African American Theatre: An Historical and Critical Analysis* (1994).

Hill, Errol G., and James V. Hatch, eds. *A History of African American Theatre* (2003).

Obituary: *New York Times*, 19 Nov. 1995.

This entry is taken from the *American National Biography* and is published here with the permission of the American Council of Learned Societies.

RICHARD HAUER COSTA

Gordy, Berry, Jr. (28 Nov. 1929–), songwriter, entrepreneur, and filmmaker, was born in Detroit, Michigan, the seventh of eight children of BERRY GORDY SR. and Bertha Fuller. After Reconstruction, Gordy's paternal grandfather, who was born a slave, managed to acquire 168 acres of land where he and his wife, Lucy Hellum, raised nine children, one of

them being Gordy's father. Gordy's mother was of direct African descent on her father's side and of African and American Indian heritage on her mother's side. She was a schoolteacher in Sandersville, Georgia, and married Berry Gordy Sr. in 1918, when he returned from service in World War I.

In 1922 Gordy's parents left Milledgeville, Georgia, and settled in Detroit with their three oldest children. Unlike the majority of black migrants to the North, the Gordys owned their own home. Seven years and five children later, Berry Jr. was born on Thanksgiving Day. The Gordys were a large, close-knit family, proud and middle class by the prevailing standards of the day. Until the Depression struck, Gordy's father and older siblings were industrious enough to supply the family with its material needs, working as laborers and selling ice and produce. By 1931, however, their financial situation was so desperate that the Gordy family had lost its home and, for a brief time, was forced onto the welfare rolls.

Gordy's uncle B.A., Bertha's brother, gave him the only formal music lessons of his life. After only a year, Gordy tired of the monotony of learning scales when he discovered that he could play boogie-woogie and other popular styles by ear. By taking him to church three evenings a week and all day on Sunday, his parents exposed the young Gordy to soulful Negro spirituals and the stirring rhythms of black gospel, distinct influences on what would become the "Motown sound."

The business work ethic was deeply ingrained in the Gordy children throughout their upbringing by both by their mother, who managed an insurance and real estate business, and by their father, who worked his way up from being an apprentice plasterer to running his own plastering business. Gordy's father purchased a commercial building on the corner of St. Antoine and Farnsworth, from which at various times the family operated businesses such as Gordy Contractors, Gordy Print Shop, Friendship Mutual Life Insurance Company, and a grocery store that bore the name of BOOKER T. WASHINGTON, the African American leader who most emphasized economic development.

Young Gordy was a bright charmer who loved to be the center of attention. He was ambitious but impetuous and dropped out of Northeastern High School in his junior year to become a boxer. He had decent skills in the ring, but it was his fighting spirit and persistence that led to his appearance on the same card with JOE LOUIS in 1948, when the champ returned to Detroit to defend his title. Through

Gordy Berry Jr., president and founder of Motown records, joins his friend Smokey Robinson (left) midway through his performance at the Greek Theater in Los Angeles, California,15 June 1981. (AP Images.)

sheer determination, Gordy eked out an unimpressive victory over his opponent in the featherweight division. By the time Gordy was drafted during the Korean War in 1951, he was already looking for some other occupation at which he might gain fortune and fame. When he returned from Korea in 1953, he had a GED and a new idea for a business.

Gordy's first foray into the music industry was as part owner of the 3-D Record Mart: House of Jazz. Gordy's father put up some of the money, and Gordy's brother George invested on the condition that he be a partner. At this time Gordy was a jazz enthusiast; when patrons requested music by blues artists such as JOHN LEE HOOKER and B. B. KING, Gordy would try to persuade them to purchase music by bebop jazz artists like CHARLIE PARKER and MILES DAVIS. The record shop soon went out of business. However, Gordy learned two valuable lessons that guided him in the future: he did not like partners, and smart business decisions are as important as the music itself.

Over the next few years Gordy tried a number of jobs, from selling cookware to assembling cars at the Lincoln-Mercury plant. As he worked, he composed songs that he sent to magazines, entered in contests, and attempted to sell to performers appearing at local venues. Four of Gordy's

enterprising siblings had established a photo concession at the Flame Show Bar and helped get a song written by Gordy and Tyran Carlo to JACKIE WILSON, who recorded it as "Reet Petite" in 1957. With this triumph Gordy's confidence and determination grew.

Gordy and Carlo wrote four more hits for Wilson, including "To Be Loved," which later became the title of Gordy's 1994 autobiography. Gordy, however, was not content merely to hear his songs on the radio. By now a shrewd businessman, he realized that he could be much more successful if he owned the copyright for his songs and had his own record label to market them. In 1958 he took the first step toward realizing this goal by establishing a music publishing company, Jobete, named from the first two letters of Joy, Berry, and Terry, Gordy's children with his first wife, Thelma Coleman Berry. He married and divorced once more; ultimately, he fathered eight children with several women. To finance his company, Gordy once again had to approach his family. Despite the fact that Berry Jr. had failed in his first venture, his family believed in him, and in January 1959 they lent him eight hundred dollars. With this money he rented an eight-room house at 2648 West Grand Boulevard, where he lived with his second wife, Raynoma Liles Gordy. Family, friends, and performers helped him to transform that house into "Hitsville USA," the first headquarters of Motown, the recording company he named after Detroit, the "Motor City." Motown would grow into a conglomerate that owned several record labels, a talent management agency, and a recording studio, with subsidiaries in the television and film industries.

Gordy's ability to identify, nurture, and retain talent for as long as he did was a major factor in Motown's success. He spotted SMOKEY ROBINSON when the latter was only seventeen. The two became lifelong friends and collaborators. Gordy signed "Little STEVIE WONDER" at the age of eleven, and he hired talented writers such as Brian Holland, Eddie Holland, and LAMONT DOZIER. He brought in Maxine Powell, who ran a finishing school, to give his young performers a clean-cut, professional, telegenic look. This allowed his artists to cross over onto the pop charts with unprecedented frequency. He hired Cholly Atkins, the famed dancer of the Cotton Club and Savoy Ballroom, to choreograph the signature steps of the Temptations, the Four Tops, and the Supremes. With these professionals added to a smart and loyal business staff, Gordy created a company that worked like a team and felt like a family.

In 1961 Gordy's young company had its first number one hit when "Please Mr. Postman," by the Marvelettes, went to the top of the charts. At times as many as five of the top ten songs on the *Billboard* charts were Motown productions. By the late 1960s Motown had become a virtual hit factory, producing top songs like cars rolling off an assembly line. This music was not merely commercially successful; it also won critical acclaim as Motown artists garnered Grammy awards and other accolades while they dominated the charts. By 1972 Motown had become a powerful force in the record industry, with more than one hundred top ten songs, including thirty-one number one hits.

In the early 1970s Gordy's interests began to move in other directions. In 1972 he moved the Motown headquarters to Los Angeles. He had experimented with a few television productions such as *Diana!* and a cartoon about the Jackson 5 but he wanted to take DIANA ROSS, his biggest star and love interest, to the big screen. *Lady Sings the Blues* (1973) was his first and biggest box-office smash. He had to put up the money himself before Paramount would agree to produce this film about the life of BILLIE HOLIDAY, which ultimately received five Academy Award nominations, including a Best Actress nomination for Diana Ross. This was followed by *Mahogany* (1975), which Gordy directed himself, *The Bingo Long Traveling All-Stars and Motor Kings* (1976), *Scott Joplin* (1977), *The Wiz* (1978), and *The Last Dragon* (1985).

While Motown's record sales from the 1970s and 1980s surpassed even the remarkable figures of the 1960s, as new acts such as the Jackson 5 and the Commodores reached ever-expanding audiences, the accomplishments of the 1960s remain unparalleled in terms of their cultural impact. Motown helped to define a generation through its music. By integrating American popular music to an unprecedented degree, Gordy helped to facilitate the social and political integration of the period. He also marketed some of the early recordings of speeches by MARTIN LUTHER KING JR. and readings by black poets, and he gave MARVIN GAYE and Stevie Wonder the creative freedom to produce such politically conscious albums as *What's Going On* (1971) and *Songs in the Key of Life* (1976), respectively, as well as the controversial anti–Vietnam War single by Edwin Starr, "War" (1970).

In 1988 Gordy sold Motown Records to MCA and Boston Ventures for $61.9 million. In 1997 he sold 50 percent of his Jobete Publishing Company, with its extensive music catalog, to EMI for $135 million. In 2001 he endowed the Gwendolyn B. Gordy Fund to assist less fortunate Motown artists, writers, and musicians. Gordy turned his eight-hundred-dollar investment into hundreds of millions of dollars; in the process, he created one of the largest and most influential black companies in history.

FURTHER READING
Gordy, Berry, Jr. *To Be Loved: The Music, the Magic, the Memories of Motown* (1994).
Abbott, Kingsley. *Callin' Out around the World: A Motown Reader* (2001).
Benjaminson, Peter. *The Story of Motown* (1979).
Early, Gerald Lyn. *One Nation under a Groove: Motown and American Culture* (1995).
Smith, Suzanne. *Dancing in the Street: Motown and the Cultural Politics of Detroit* (1999).

SHOLOMO B. LEVY

Gordy, Berry, Sr. (10 July 1888–21 Nov. 1978), entrepreneur and consultant, was born in Oconee, Georgia, one of twenty-three children born to Berry Gordy, a successful farmer who owned at least 168 acres, and Lucy Hellum Gordy. He was one of nine Gordy offspring who lived to adulthood and the fifth oldest child. Gordy's maternal great-grandfather was Native American, and his maternal great-grandmother was African American. Gordy's paternal grandmother, Esther Johnson, was a slave, and his paternal grandfather, Jim Gordy, was a plantation owner.

Gordy Sr. and his family lived in a log house in Oconee. When he and his siblings (Sam, Lula, Esther, Mamie, Lucy, John, Joe, and Charlie) were old enough to attend grammar school, they worked on the family farm after the school day ended. During the summer, the Gordy children also worked one hour before they attended school. When they completed elementary school, their father required them to work on the farm for several years before they attended the high school for African Americans in Sandersville, Georgia. After Gordy's three oldest siblings completed high school, he, Mamie, and John were allowed to attend school; thus Gordy was approximately twenty-two years old when he began his secondary education. Since the high school was fifteen miles away, Gordy and his siblings stayed in Sandersville during the school week. In the afternoons, Gordy did yard work for white residents of Sandersville and earned between forty and sixty cents each day. On 31 May 1913, during a weekend visit home weeks before Gordy's twenty-fifth birthday, his father asked him to accompany him as he walked among the various crops and showed Gordy the farm's borders. A few hours later, Gordy's father died after having been struck by lightning.

The Gordy family, in addition to grieving, had to deal with unscrupulous white men who tried to steal their land. Gordy's mother, instead of asking a white man to serve as the administrator of her husband's estate, decided that she and Gordy would fill that role. Gordy began receiving bogus bills; his father had always kept receipts, so Gordy knew that the debts had either been paid or were never owed. A bank claimed that Gordy's father had borrowed $200. Gordy went to court and asked the judge to have the bank show proof that his father had borrowed the money. The bank representative had no evidence, and the case was dismissed. Gordy, in addition to being presented with bogus debts, shrewdly and obdurately refused to buy an automobile or any other products from salesmen who wanted him to go into debt and consequently put the farm at risk.

Gordy, who served briefly in the U.S. Army and received an honorable discharge, continued to manage the farm. He began selling beef from a wagon and later sold vegetables, watermelons, and chickens, as well as other produce. In 1918 Gordy married Bertha Ida Fuller, a schoolteacher. Four years later Gordy sold timber stumps and received a $2,600 check. Concerned that white people might try to swindle him, he followed his brother George to Detroit in order to cash the check. Once Gordy arrived in the city, he was so impressed with the financial opportunities that he decided to live there. Gordy was soon joined by his wife and their three children. Five more children were born in Detroit; thus the Gordys were the parents of four girls and four boys. Gordy supported his family by working as a blacksmith and at several other jobs prior to becoming a plasterer and opening his own plastering and carpentering company. In addition he and his wife opened the Booker T. Washington Grocery Store. Gordy, following in the footsteps of his father who made his children work on the farm as soon as they were old enough, made his progeny work in the grocery store even before they were as tall as the store's counter. Gordy's plastering and carpentering business was so successful that he sold the grocery store.

Gordy and his wife created a family savings fund, and members were required to contribute ten dollars each month. In 1959 Gordy's seventh child, BERRY GORDY JR., founded Motown Records in Detroit after borrowing $800 from the Gordy fund. Motown, known as "the Sound of Young America" and "Hitsville, U.S.A," transformed relatively unknown singers such as SMOKEY ROBINSON and the Miracles, the Temptations, MARVIN GAYE, STEVIE WONDER, the Four Tops, DIANA ROSS and the Supremes, the Jackson Five, LIONEL RICHIE, and other performers into legendary superstars as Motown dominated the record charts during the 1960s and early 1970s. By 1965 Gordy Jr. had purchased his father's contracting company and hired the elder Gordy for the dual positions of consultant to Motown and company liaison. Motown expanded into the film industry, and Gordy and his daughter Esther appear as extras in *Mahogany* (1975), which was directed by Gordy Jr. and starred Diana Ross and Billy Dee Williams.

In July 1978 Gordy celebrated his ninetieth birthday, and to commemorate the occasion, Ross, Gaye, Robinson, and Wonder recorded the single "Pops, We Love You." On the evening of 20 November, Gordy, who had indigestion, was visited by his daughter Anna and Gordy Jr. They spent hours talking, and the next morning, Gordy Sr., who was predeceased by his wife, died. In 1979 Motown released the album *Pops, We Love You*, which included the previously released title single and other songs performed by various Motown artists. Also that year Gordy was the posthumous recipient of the Tribute to a Black American Award from the National Council of Black Mayors. The single, album, and award are appropriate accolades for Berry Gordy Sr., the patriarch of a prominent African American family and a pioneering entrepreneur whose success paved the way for Berry Gordy Jr. to create a multimillion-dollar entertainment corporation and become one of America's most successful businessmen in the twentieth century.

FURTHER READING

Materials relating to Berry Gordy Sr. and other family members between 1928 and 1947 are housed in the Michigan Historical Collection in the Bentley Historical Library at the University of Michigan in Ann Arbor, Michigan.

Gordy, Berry, Sr. *Movin' Up: Pop Gordy Tells His Story* (1979).

Gordy, Berry, Jr. *To Be Loved: The Music, the Magic, the Memories of Motown* (1994).

LINDA M. CARTER

Goreleigh, Rex (2 Sept. 1902–1986), painter, printmaker, and educator, was born in Penllyn,

Pennsylvania. He began drawing at age five and maintained an interest in art as he grew up as a means of overcoming severe shyness related to a speech impediment. His mother died when he was fifteen and he left Philadelphia the following year and relocated to Washington, D.C., where he attended Dunbar High School from 1918 until 1920 and briefly took classes at Howard University. By 1922 Goreleigh was living in Harlem and working as a waiter. He saw the first Harmon Foundation exhibition of African American art at the International House in 1926 and was inspired to take drawing lessons at the Art Students League. In Harlem during the culturally rich New Negro era, he met a number of talented people, including the poet CLAUDE MCKAY, the painters AARON DOUGLAS and Norman Lewis, and the musician EUBIE BLAKE, who encouraged him to pursue the arts. While waiting tables in 1933 Goreleigh met the Mexican artist Diego Rivera, who invited him to observe his Rockefeller Center mural project, *Man at the Crossroads*.

Goreleigh showed in *An Exhibition by Young Negro Artists* in April 1927 organized by the writer Wallace Thurman. He also showed in the several non-juried exhibitions organized by the Society of Independent Arts in New York in the late 1920s and early 1930s, and was represented in shows at the Anderson Gallery in 1931 and 1932, the year he also participated in an invitational at Atlanta University. In 1934, under the auspices of the Works Projects Administration (WPA), the federal program supporting artists during the Depression, he worked with the painter Ben Shahn. He spent the next two years in Europe studying painting at the Atelier of Andre L'Hote in Paris, and sculpture with Leo Z. Moll in Berlin and in Copenhagen. In 1935 he had his first solo exhibition at the Strindberg Gallery in Helsinki, Finland. As a young artist in France he enjoyed brief friendships with such renowned artists as the cubists Georges Braque and Pablo Picasso. Returning to New York in 1936 he had work on view in three exhibitions, including shows at the Harmon Foundation Exhibition and Anderson Gallery in New York and at Atlanta University in Georgia. He also studied with the social realist painter Xavier J. Barile, and that same year taught at Utopia House, working at the Harlem community art center from 1936 to1938 when it was located at its original site on Lenox Avenue at 125th Street. The painter JACOB LAWRENCE and the printmaker ROBERT BLACKBURN were among his students.

In 1938 Goreleigh moved to Greensboro, where he collaborated with Norman Lewis to establish the North Carolina Art Center through the WPA and served as associate director from 1938 to 1939, the year he married a local librarian. In 1939 he had exhibitions at the Baltimore Museum of Art in Maryland, the Augusta Savage Gallery in New York, and Shaw University in Raleigh. He taught briefly at Palmer Memorial Institute in Sedalia, North Carolina, and he had his second one-person show—his first such show in the United States—at the Greensboro Public Library in 1940. Relocating to Chicago that year he and his wife arrived in time to see his work in the American Exposition of Negro Art at the Chicago Coliseum. He quickly became affiliated with the Chicago art scene, working one year as art coordinator for the Schreiner-Bennet advertising firm and attending classes at the University of Chicago from 1940 to 1941 and at the Art Institute of Chicago in 1942. That same year marked his third invitational at Atlanta University, as well as a show at the Pyramid Club in Philadelphia.

Goreleigh was director of Chicago's Southside Community Art Center from 1942 until 1945 and had a show at the American Artist Gallery in 1943. He took the helm of the Southside Center at a critical time, when federal support waned as the nation became involved in World War II and funds had to be raised from local sources.

Leaving Chicago for New Jersey late in 1945 he settled in Princeton and lived in a restored mill he named Studio-on-the-Canal. He became director of the newly formed Princeton Group Arts Center in 1947, where he oversaw art classes, concerts, exhibitions, lectures, and special events. He planned the first outdoor exhibition held at Palmer Square and held seminars and fund-raisers to support art appreciation classes and arts and crafts classes for children. Still active as an artist and maintaining strong ties with the Philadelphia arts community from which he had come, he had shows at the Pyramid Club in 1948 and 1949. Holding the post until 1953 he had shows of his own work at the Montclair Museum of Art and New Jersey State Museum in Trenton in 1950. He received the Afro-American Award for Superior Public Service in 1955, the same year he established a modest art colony at Studio-on-the-Canal, offering private instruction and teaching art classes. For a period the painter HUGHIE LEE-SMITH worked as one of his advanced painting instructors. Goreleigh produced a group of oils and watercolors inspired by the scenic landscape around his home that were exhibited at Phillips Mill in New Hope, Pennsylvania, in 1959 and at Little Gallery in Princeton in 1960. A larger body of similar work was presented in a solo exhibition at Lambertville House in New Jersey in 1961.

His exhibition history also included one-person shows at the Trenton Trust Company in 1965 and Westtown School in Pennsylvania in 1968. Additional shows were held at the Newark Museum in 1968; Studio Museum in Harlem in 1973 and 1976; Boston Museum in 1976; and Princeton University Museum in 1976.

Goreleigh became a member of the Princeton Historical Society in 1964 and the New Jersey State Council on the Arts in 1966. He received the New Jersey State Council on the Arts Award for Contributions to New Jersey in 1971 and the New Jersey State Council on the Arts Grant in 1971. In 1976 he fulfilled a lifelong dream when he earned a BS in art from Livingston College in Rutgers, New Jersey, at age seventy-three. One of his teachers had been the sculptor MEL EDWARDS. His retrospective, The Art of Rex Goreleigh, was held in 1980. He taught one semester at Montclair State College (later Montclair State University) in New Jersey in the early 1980s.

Goreleigh's work is represented in the permanent collections of the Schomburg Center for Research in Black Culture in New York, the Paul R. Jones Collection at the University of Delaware, First Baptist Church of Princeton, and several private holdings. Goreleigh was a respected artist, teacher, and mentor best known for his numerous depictions of migrant farm workers in the New Jersey area as seen in The Planters series and Tobacco Series. He was also recognized as an accomplished painter of rural and coastal landscapes.

FURTHER READING
Fax, Elton C. Seventeen Black Artists (1971).
New Jersey State Museum. The Art of Rex Goreleigh (1980).

AMALIA K. AMAKI

Gorham, Sarah Everett (5 Dec. 1832–10 Aug. 1894), traveling preacher, social worker, and missionary, was born in either Fredericktown, Maryland, or Fredericksburg, Virginia. Little is known of her life before 1880. In that year she visited relatives who had emigrated to Liberia, and then she spent a year traveling throughout that African country preaching and comforting the needy. It was on this trip that she became interested in African missionary work.

Gorham settled in Boston, Massachusetts, where she joined the Charles Street African Methodist Episcopal Church. She became active in humanitarian and volunteer work with her church, assisting needy families with food and clothing and educational and social welfare projects. Between her move to Boston in 1881 and her travels to Sierra Leone in 1888, she was employed as a social worker by the Associated Charities of Boston.

In 1888, at age fifty-six, Gorham offered her services as a missionary to the African Methodist Episcopal (AME) Church and received an appointment to Sierra Leone. According to every published history of the AME Church, she became the first woman missionary of that church appointed to a foreign field. In honor of her achievement, Sarah E. Gorham women's missionary societies—or special missions departments of the AME Church— formed throughout the country. Gorham's AME Church in Boston, for instance, organized the Sarah Gorham Missionary Society and the Bethel Methodist Episcopal Church of Indianapolis, Indiana, established the Sarah Gorham Special Missions department.

Gorham's Sierra Leone mission was sponsored in part by the AME Church's Woman's Parent Mite Missionary Society, a group organized in Philadelphia by the women of the northern conferences of the church. The Woman's Home and Foreign Missionary Society, the other female auxiliary formed in the AME Church, was established in South Bend, Indiana, in 1898 to fulfill the need that AME Bishop Henry McNeal Turner had seen in South Africa for black missionaries. This auxiliary was also founded by southern AME women who rejected northern women's leadership in the Woman's Parent Mite Missionary Society. The Women's Parent Mite Missionary Society supported the work of the church in Haiti, Santo Domingo, Barbados, Demarara, the Bahamas, the Virgin Islands, Trinidad, Jamaica, Liberia, and Sierra Leone, while the Woman's Home and Foreign Missionary Society supervised AME missions in southern Africa. Gorham also received financial support from the Ohio Conference of the AME Church.

Africa had been set apart as a foreign mission field by the General Conference of the AME Church in 1856. The first permanent AME mission in Africa was established in 1878 by Samuel F. Flegler who settled in Liberia with over 206 South Carolina emigrants. John Richard Frederick of the AME Church Conference of Providence, Rhode Island, was sent to Africa by the New England Conference of the AME Church, although most of his financial support came from the church's Ohio

Conference. He sailed on 20 November 1886 as the first officially sponsored AME missionary to Sierra Leone. Gorham arrived in Freetown, Sierra Leone, two years later in September 1888. She traveled to Magbele, one of the country's leading AME missions, situated on the banks of the Scarcies River and one hundred miles from Freetown. There she was active in the Allen AME Church, founded by Frederick. She worked among women and girls of the Temne people, the largest ethnic group in northern Sierra Leone. At Magbele she established the Sarah Gorham Mission School, which gave both religious and industrial training.

She traveled back and forth between the United States and her mission post several times over the next few years. In 1891, however, her health began to fail, and she returned to the United States to recuperate. One year later, after regaining her health, she returned to Sierra Leone. But in July 1894 she became bedridden with malaria and died the next month. She was buried in Kissy Road Cemetery in Freetown, and her tombstone bears the following inscription: "She was early impressed that she should go to Africa as a missionary and that her life['s] work should be there. She crossed the ocean five times, and ended her mission on the soil and among the people she so much desired to benefit."

FURTHER READING
Berry, Lewellyn L. *A Century of Missions of the African Methodist Episcopal Church, 1840–1940* (1942).
Keller, Rosemary Skinner, Louise L. Queen, and Hilah F. Thomas, eds. *Women in New Worlds* (1982).
Kinch, Emily C. *West Africa, An Open Door* (1917).
Parks, H. B. *Africa, The Problem of the New Century* (1899).

SYLVIA M. JACOBS

Gossett, Louis, Jr. (27 May 1936–), actor, director, and producer, was born Louis Cameron Gossett Jr. in Brooklyn, New York, to Louis Gossett, a porter, and Hellen Rebecca Wray, a maid. His parents had emigrated north from Georgia before Gossett was born. Gossett attended Abraham Lincoln High School, where he was an athlete and class president. Gossett's first acting performance was in a high school production of *You Can't Take It With You*. His performance elicited much praise, and Gossett next tried out for, and won, a role in the 1953 Broadway production of *Take a Giant Step*. He was seventeen years old.

After high school, Gossett enrolled at New York University on a basketball scholarship and became a star player. In 1958 he was drafted by the New York Knicks, but after college, instead of pursuing a career in pro basketball, Gossett decided to study acting under John Sticks and Peggy Fury at The Actors Studio, soon after landing a role in Broadway's 1959 production of *A Raisin in the Sun*. Gossett went on to star in the 1961 film production of *Raisin* to critical acclaim.

In addition to film, Gossett has enjoyed a richly varied television career. He was one of the first African American actors to play the lead in a TV series, *The Lazarus Syndrome* (1979). The year before, he had starred as Dr. MacArthur St. Clair, the chief of staff at a major hospital, in the TV movie that predated the series. That same year, Gossett earned an Emmy for his captivating portrayal of Fiddle in Alex Haley's *Roots* (1977). His great-grandmother, a strong-minded former slave who lived to be 117, inspired Gossett's portrayal of Fiddle. Gossett's numerous TV appearances during the late 1960s and throughout the 1970s included as Smitty in *The Mod Squad* (1968); as Hurricane Smith in *The Bill Cosby Show* (1970); as Sam in *The Partridge Family* (1971); as Buck Walter in *Bonanza* (1971); as Joe Sims in *Alias Smith and Jones* (1971); as Donald Knight (1974) and also as Uncle Wilbert (1975) in *Good Times*; and as Freddie in *Police Story* (1975). Gossett also served as executive producer for a dozen TV film productions, including *Father & Son: Dangerous Relations* (1993), *Run for the Dream: The Gail Devers Story* (1996), and *For Love of Olivia* (2001).

Gossett moved beyond acting and started his own production company, Logo Entertainment. The company's first production was *Carolina Skeletons* (1991), a TV movie starring Gossett and directed by John Erman, about an African American soldier who returns home years after the execution of his brother for the murder of two white girls. Gossett's character works to discover the truth behind the murders and to clear his brother's name. Logo Entertainment has produced a TV miniseries, numerous TV movies, and a theatrical film, *Managua* (1996).

An active philanthropist over the course of his career, Gossett has supported numerous charitable causes, many geared toward helping disadvantaged youth, such as The Family Tree, an organization created to help kids from broken families discover a sense of community. In 1964 Gossett, with JAMES EARL JONES and Paul Sorvino, received a grant to start a theatre company for troubled youth. Along with Father George Clements, Gossett founded

GOTTSCHALK, LOUIS MOREAU 119

Shamba Centers, with several locations around the United States, which teach African American history and culture. He also became very involved in Eracism, an anti-racism project. In 2005 Gossett sponsored One Summer of Peace, an anti-violence movement that addressed the growing gang violence in Los Angeles. He encouraged gang members to put down their weapons and instead remember their ancestors and work toward building a sense of community.

Over his long career, Gossett received numerous awards and honors. At the 1983 Academy Awards, Gossett won the Oscar for Best Supporting Actor for his role as Sgt. Emil Foley in *An Officer and a Gentleman* (1982), becoming only the third black actor to receive an Oscar. In 1983 he took home a Golden Globe for the same role, as well as the 1982 NAACP Image Award for the same film for Best Performance by an Actor. Gossett was nominated in 1977, 1979, 1981, 1984, 1987, and 1997 for the Emmy for Outstanding Lead Actor for his performances in a variety of productions. In 1991 he won a Golden Globe for HBO's *The Josephine Baker Story*. In 1998 he received another Image Award for Outstanding Supporting Actor in a Drama Series for *Touched by an Angel* (1994–2003). Gossett also won a daytime Emmy for Children's Special for *In His Father's Shoes* (1997). In 2000 Gossett won a Black Reel Award for Best Director for *Love Songs* (1999). In February 2006, he was honored with a Life Achievement Award at the Pan African Film and Arts Festival Night of Tribute.

Gossett is a testament to the infectiousness of human integrity and the efficacy of believing in one's self and community. His quiet strength inhabits his screen characters with vitality and dignity, affirming the power of character and community to resist the negativity of stereotypes and racism. His tireless work for young people and peace, and his innate talent behind and in front of the camera, demonstrate his compelling blend of social consciousness and artistic excellence that have made Louis Gossett Jr. one of the most highly respected and talented African American actors in the United States.

DEBBIE CLARE OLSON

Gottschalk, Louis Moreau (8 May 1829–18 Dec. 1869), pianist and composer, was born in New Orleans to Edward Gottschalk, a Londoner of German-Jewish extraction who emigrated to Louisiana to trade in real estate, commodities, currency, and slaves, and Aimee-Marie Bruslé, whose murkier ancestry has contributed to much confusion over her musician son's ethnic heritage. Virtually all period sources identify Gottschalk's mother as "Creole," a term "synonymous with native" in early-nineteenth-century New Orleans and embracing "all objects indigenous to Louisiana, from cabbage to cotton, and all people, regardless of hue" (Gary B. Mills, "Creole," in *Encyclopedia of Southern Culture*, 426). By the late 1800s, however, the word was reserved both for those "of 'pure' white ancestry," who were "wealthy and aristocratic" and "rooted in the Delta country of lower Louisiana," as well as for those "uniformly poor in worldly goods, quaint in customs, and mixed of blood" (Mills, 427). That Edward Gottschalk, in addition to the eight children he would have by his wife, also fathered two daughters and two sons by his free black mistress, Judith Françoise Rubio, only further obscures Louis Moreau's pedigree. The pianist-composer, in fact, has been characterized as "mulatto" or "black" in several prominent secondary sources, among them ALAIN LOCKE's *The Negro and His Music* (1936) and RAOUL ABDUL's *Blacks in Classical Music* (1977). Nevertheless, a more recent Gottschalk biographer, S. Frederick Starr, argues persuasively that Aimee Bruslé, "a Louisiana-born Catholic whose … French ancestors fled Haiti after the Haitian slave rebellion in the 1790s," was white (27).

Gottschalk began studying piano (and perhaps harmony) at age three with F. J. Narcisse Letellier, a noted singer at the Theatre d'Orléans. After a local debut in April 1841 the eleven-year-old sailed for France to further his musical studies. Rejected initially by the eminent Paris Conservatoire professor Pierre Zimmerman, who chauvinistically declared America "the country of railroads but not of musicians" (Gottschalk, 297), Gottschalk briefly took lessons with Charles Hallé before joining the piano class of Camille Stamaty. He also studied composition with Pierre Maleden. Louis Moreau's informal debut at Salle Pleyel on 2 April 1845, attended by some of the Continent's leading musicians, including Sigismond Thalberg, Hallé, and Frédéric Chopin, was the first successful inroad made by a pianist from the New World on the European musical scene.

Of equal importance was the compositional breakthrough Gottschalk made in France. There he wrote *Bamboula, Danse de nègres*, op. 2; *La savane, Ballade créole*, op. 3; *Le bananier, Chanson nègre*, op. 5; and *Le mancenillier*, op. 11, all based on Creole melodies and the first significant body of works influenced by African American and Afro-Caribbean cultures. *Bamboula*, its title referring to the African dance of the same name that Gottschalk likely saw performed in New Orleans by free and enslaved blacks, is a virtuoso piano piece notable for its setting to a cakewalk rhythm of the Creole tune "Quan' patate la cuite na va mangé li!" ("When that 'tater's cooked don't you eat it up!") included with different lyrics in William Francis Allen's, Charles Pickard Ware's, and Lucy McKim Garrison's *Slave Songs of the United States* (1867) under the song title, "Musieu Bainjo." In *Le bananier*, Louis Moreau's superimposing of another Creole melody, "En avan' Grenadie," over what would later be termed a "stride bass" anticipated by a half-century the textures of ragtime and early-twentieth-century American popular music. So well received were the pianist's performances of this New World exotica in Belgium, Italy, France, Switzerland, and Spain between 1848 and 1852 that a *Bamboula-Bananier* craze soon took hold in Europe.

Gottschalk returned to the United States in early 1853 intent on taking advantage of the artistic reputation he had established in Europe. After a critically acclaimed New York debut at Niblo's Saloon on 11 February 1853, he traveled to New Orleans for more concerts and, from there, up the Mississippi River into the Midwest and ultimately upstate New York. That summer spent in Saratoga Springs reaped a dozen new works, among them *The Banjo*, a piece vastly more compositionally developed than the many competing published works inspired by the popularity of this African instrument transplanted to the New World. Today the work is considered an accurate portrayal of the drone and downstroking style of early black-faced minstrels and street-corner musicians, both white and black, that Gottschalk heard firsthand.

When Edward Gottschalk died penniless in October 1853, the onus was now on Louis Moreau to pay off his father's debts and financially support his mother and siblings living in Paris. But with his career beginning to falter in the United States, the pianist sought engagements in Cuba, the nearest cultural center. In Havana he premiered his *Maria de la O* (now lost), "an African dance and air as heard one night by Mr. Gottschalk in the woods of Santiago performed by a band of runaway negroes" (*Daily Picayune*, 11 Mar. 1855), and *El cocoyé*, op. 80, a generically titled work based on an Afro-Cuban carnival organization's rendition of the popular, Haitian, up-tempo dance of the same name Gottschalk encountered the following July in Santiago de Cuba. The writing of *The Last Hope* that summer in Santiago, however, signaled a new phase in his compositional career for which he would be much criticized—the fashioning of melodramatic salon pieces (among them, the later piano works *The Dying Poet*, *Ricordati*, and *Morte!!*) that had a broad appeal, particularly among the pianist's female admirers, and that were more in step with the popular sentimental works being churned out daily by Gottschalk's American contemporaries.

On 28 February 1855 Gottschalk returned to New Orleans. Back in New York City by mid-June, he entered into an arrangement with William Hall & Son that called for the sheet music publisher to underwrite a December concert at Dodworth Hall in exchange for a guarantee from Gottschalk to perform those pieces to be published. The response to what was the first recital in the United States devoted almost exclusively to piano music of a single American composer was so enthusiastic that another sixteen musical evenings were planned. This, heretofore the longest concert series mounted in the New World, elevated the piano recital in the United States to a level of cachet formerly associated only with opera (Starr, 224).

Although "Gottschalk stood outside the Liszt tradition of thundering virtuosity" (Starr, 233), the Louisiana pianist's penchant for emerging onstage at each concert wearing doeskin gloves was clearly an homage to his Hungarian counterpart. Once seated, he would remove each glove finger by finger before launching into the program with the rhythmic accuracy and incisiveness, fluency of execution, clarity of touch, burnished sound, interpretive spontaneity, and improvisatory flair for which he was almost universally praised by critics and audiences. The loudest dissenting vote came from John Sullivan Dwight, editor of the Boston-based *Dwight's Journal of Music* and the period's arbiter of high musical taste, who relentlessly took Gottschalk to task for eschewing the more rigorous Germanic repertoire in favor of his own solo pieces, opera transcriptions, and collaborative works.

The arrival of Thalberg, Liszt's storied rival, on American soil soon after the Dodworth Hall concerts only enhanced Gottschalk's notoriety back home. Instead of going mano a mano in a much-anticipated piano duel, the two friends from Gottschalk's days in Paris decided to give joint recitals in Manhattan, Baltimore, Philadelphia, and Brooklyn, a series that would prove enormously successful.

His American career at its pinnacle, Gottschalk abruptly left the United States in early 1857. The catalyst appears not to have been music, however, but the public airing in the New York *Atlas* by the actress and writer Jane McElhenney, a.k.a. Ada McElhenney, Alastor, and Ada Clare, of a failed three-and-a-half-year relationship between her and Gottschalk that likely produced a son, named Aubrey Clare, never acknowledged by the pianist. Rather than suffer ongoing public embarrassment, Gottschalk elected to go into self-imposed exile in the West Indies.

Arriving in Havana on 12 February 1857, he spent the next five years on tour (some of it in collaboration with the burgeoning teenage diva Adelina Patti) in Cuba, St. Thomas, Puerto Rico, Barbados, Trinidad, British Guiana (later Guyana), Dutch Guiana (later Suriname), Martinique, and Guadeloupe. In each country Gottschalk continued a tradition he had initiated years earlier in Spain: premiering new works drawing upon indigenous folk music of the country in which he was touring. Woven into his *Souvenir de Porto Rico*, op. 31, were the syncopated Afro-Caribbean *tresillo* and *cinquillo* rhythms characteristic of the many *danzas*, fandangos, *tiranas*, boleros, and *seguidillas* he heard performed by slaves and subsistence farmers during a monthlong stay on a Puerto Rican sugar plantation. In Guadeloupe he penned *A Night in the Tropics*, the first orchestral work scored for both Afro-Caribbean and European instruments, in addition to several other important piano works based on Cuban folk sources, including *Ojos criollos* (Creole eyes), op. 37, *Souvenirs de la* Havane, op. 39, and *Responds-moi*, op. 50. On the same tour, Gottschalk enlisted the help of 650 musicians before an audience of 4,000 in Havana's mammoth Gran Teatro Tacon in the first of his "grand festivals" (Hensel, 174) modeled after monster concerts he saw mounted in Paris by his friend and supporter Hector Berlioz. That evening the *Gran galop de bravura* for two pianos was premiered, a work that would evolve into his *Grande tarentelle*, op. 67, one of the first American pieces for piano and orchestra, and the eventual subject of a 1988 poem, *Gottschalk and the Grande Tarantelle*, by the esteemed African American author, GWENDOLYN BROOKS. The journal he began keeping on this trip, some of the entries of which appeared in *La France musicale*, *L'art musicale*, and the *Atlantic Monthly*, would be published posthumously as his *Notes of a Pianist* (1881).

In early 1862 the New Orleans musician, ever loyal to his southern heritage but vehemently antislavery, was allowed to return to the United States after declaring his allegiance to the Union now embroiled in civil war. From 1862 to 1865 he performed more widely than any other artist or entertainer in America on a grueling, nonstop tour north of the Mason-Dixon Line rendered more difficult by the war. Appropriately his repertoire staple during this period was *The Union*, op. 48, a thunderous patriotic piano work dedicated to Union General George B. McClellan that quoted "The Star Spangled Banner," "Hail, Columbia," and "Yankee Doodle," and was premiered at the Brooklyn Academy of Music on a stage festooned with American flags.

In spring 1865 Gottschalk accepted a lucrative offer to tour California and the rough-and-tumble mining outposts of Nevada. However, on 16 September 1865, less than a week after the last of three highly successful concerts at Platt's Hall in San Francisco, a scandal broke that would again put the pianist on the run. Local newspapers reported that, on a double blind date two evenings before, Gottschalk and a male acquaintance named Charles Legay had deflowered two coeds from Oakland Female College. Although the college announced on 17 September that "the matters were not as bad as they might be" and that the affair amounted to nothing more than "very indiscreet conduct" (Starr, 379), Gottschalk interpreted this adverse publicity as the temporary end to his career in the United States. Disguised as "Mr. John Smith," he boarded a steamship the following day bound for Panama City.

The next four years were spent touring Peru, Chile, Uruguay, Argentina, and Brazil. At every major stop grand festivals were staged to premiere Latin American–inspired works designed by Gottschalk to awaken the nationalistic pride of a local populace beleaguered by its dictatorial government's brutality and corruption. So intense was the public's reaction to these pro-democracy affairs, the proceeds from which often going to support local education, that Gottschalk left each country a national hero. In Santiago, Chile, after a performance of the *Gran marcha solemne* (now lost), featuring the Chilean national anthem amid a backdrop of cannon fire and drums, thousands of uplifted Santiago citizens escorted Gottschalk back to the American embassy in a torch-lit procession accompanied by a battery of blaring trumpets.

Gottschalk boarded a steamship bound for Rio de Janeiro on 21 April 1869, intending Brazil to be merely an interim stop on the long journey back to New York. On 24 November 1869, however, during the second concert of a three-day festival at the Theatro Lyrico Fluminense in Rio, the pianist, feeling ill, crumbled onstage, unable to continue. Determined to perform on the final concert the next night, he managed to get himself to the hall, only to collapse again beforehand. His condition steadily deteriorating over the next three weeks in the stifling Rio heat, Gottschalk was taken inland on 8 December 1869 to the more temperate hillside town of Tijuca, where, ten days later, he died at the age of forty. Although the death certificate cited the cause as "incurable galloping pleuropneumonia" arising from an abdominal abscess stemming from an earlier bout with yellow fever, the likely culprit was a ruptured appendix (Starr, 435–436).

Thousands of Brazilians joined the funeral cortege the next day from the Philharmonic Society to São João Baptista Cemetery, where the pianist's coffin was installed in a donated private vault. After a year of legal maneuvering, Gottschalk's sister, Clara, arranged for her brother's remains to be shipped back to New York. A memorial service on 3 October 1870 at the Church of St. Stephen in Manhattan was followed by reburial at Brooklyn's Green-Wood Cemetery in a plot shared by Gottschalk's brother, Edward, who had died in September 1863. In the intervening years the sculpted angel atop the grave's once magnificent marble tombstone and the lyre-decorated iron fence surrounding it vanished. The marker's carved lettering has been virtually erased by time.

So ended the distinguished career of a seminal figure in American music. Louis Moreau Gottschalk was perhaps the first American artist to draw upon both highbrow and lowbrow, multicultural sources, and the first in a trio of African-American-inspired nineteenth-century pianist-composers (among them, the Georgia slave pianist BLIND TOM and his Midwestern musical descendant BLIND BOONE) whose works would have an enormous influence on the development of twentieth-century popular music in the United States.

FURTHER READING

The largest archive of Gottschalk materials, including copies of his published scores and autograph manuscripts, is housed in the New York Public Library for the Performing Arts, New York City.

Gottschalk, Louis Moreau. *Notes of a Pianist*, ed. Clara Gottschalk (1881); revised by Jeanne Behrend (1964, 2006).

Fors, Luis Ricardo. *Gottschalk* (1880).

Hensel, Octavia (née Seymour, Mary Alice Ives). *Life and Letters of Louis Moreau Gottschalk* (1870).

Starr, S. Frederick. *Bamboula!: The Life and Times of Louis Moreau Gottschalk* (1995); reissued in paperback as *Louis Moreau Gottschalk* (2000).

Obituary: *New York Times*, 21 Jan. 1870.

DISCOGRAPHY

Doyle, John G. *Louis Moreau Gottschalk 1829–1869: A Bibliographical Study and Catalog of Works* (1982).

Perone, James E. *Louis Moreau Gottschalk: A Bio-Bibliography* (2002).

JOHN DAVIS

Gould, William B. (18 Nov. 1837–23 May 1923), Union navy sailor in the Civil War and journalist, was presumably born into slavery, in Wilmington, North Carolina, to Elizabeth "Betsy" Moore of Wilmington, a slave, and Alexander Gould, who was white. William had at least one sibling, Eliza Mabson, who acquired her last name by virtue of a publicly acknowledged relationship with George Mabson, a white man in Wilmington. She eventually became the mother of five children by Mabson, including her son GEORGE L. MABSON, the first black lawyer in North Carolina.

Little is known about William B. Gould's early life. As a young man he acquired skills as a plasterer or mason, and he learned how to read and write, although those skills were forbidden by law to slaves. His initials are in the plaster of one of the Confederacy's most elegant mansions, the Bellamy Mansion in Wilmington. Among his young friends were GEORGE WASHINGTON PRICE JR., eventually to represent New Hanover County in the state house of representatives and the senate at the conclusion of the Civil War, and ABRAHAM HANKINS GALLOWAY, the black "Scarlet Pimpernel" of North Carolina who escaped from slavery in 1857 and returned during the war as a spy for Union forces. Galloway also served in the North Carolina legislature after the war.

On 21 September 1862 Gould and seven other "contraband" (as escaping slaves were characterized during the Civil War) from Wilmington made a dramatic dash to freedom, departing from the dock at Orange Street and rowing down to the Atlantic Ocean at the mouth of the Cape Fear River. The eight "contraband" were picked up by USS *Cambridge*, part of the North Atlantic Blockading Squadron. Five days later, Gould began keeping a diary—apparently the only diary of any former slave who joined the United States Navy. On 3 October 1862 the eight contraband joined the navy by "takeing [*sic*] the Oath of Allegiance to the Government of Uncle Samuel" (Gould, *Diary*, 3 Oct. 1862). Classified as a "boy," the lowest occupation—and the only one then open to blacks—in the navy, Gould would ultimately progress to wardroom steward.

In the fall of 1862 the *Cambridge* was assigned to inshore blockade duties. Gould described the shots coming from Fort Fisher on the North Carolina shore as "too close to be at all agreeable" (Gould, *Diary*, 17 Jan. 1863). There were other engagements. "In a brief five days [in November–December '62], she [the *Cambridge*] and two other ships in company took four blockade runners and chased a fifth ashore" (Navy Department, *Dictionary of American Naval Fighting Ships*, 2 [1963]). In the spring of 1863 the *Cambridge* was given a respite and came north to dock at Newport News in Virginia, New York, and Boston.

From the beginning of his service Gould corresponded with a wide variety of colleagues from North Carolina: Galloway, Price, Eliza Mabson, and her son George Mabson, who would serve in both the army and the navy. He also wrote to his future wife, Cornelia Williams Read, whom he had known since childhood in Wilmington. She had been purchased out of slavery in 1857 by JAMES CRAWFORD. Gould eventually reunited with her in Nantucket.

In Massachusetts, Gould, ill with the measles, left the *Cambridge*, and in October 1963 joined USS *Niagara*, one of the navy's most formidable wooden frigates. The *Niagara* proceeded first to Nova Scotia to recapture the steamer USS *Chesapeake*, which had been taken by the Confederates off Cape Cod and was being held by the British authorities in Canada. On 11 December the *Niagara* departed Gloucester, Massachusetts, in search of the *Chesapeake*, following it into LaHave and Halifax, Nova Scotia. The *Chesapeake* was taken by USS *Ella and Annie*. The *Niagara* returned to New York on 20 December. It remained there for approximately six months, during which there was a dramatic rescue of the Italian ship *Galantoumo*, in which the crewmen of the *Niagara* delivered the Italian crew and passengers from "the very jaws of death" ("Perilous Voyage of the Niagara," *New York Times*, 5 Apr. 1864).

During this stay in New York City, Gould reunited with Abraham Galloway, attended meetings on the future suffrage of North Carolina, and in June 1864 became a correspondent for the *Anglo-African*, describing his escape in that paper. Meanwhile he began a correspondence with the *Anglo-African*'s editor, ROBERT HAMILTON. Finally, Gould encountered rank discrimination against a Maryland black regiment that boarded his ship and was treated roughly by the crew. Gould characterized the crew as "scoundrels" who treated blacks "shamefully" (Gould, *Diary*, 18 May 1864).

On 1 June Gould departed for Europe, looking for CSS *Florida* and other ships, and on 24 June, while running up the English Channel, they learned of the sinking of CSS *Alabama*. The crew were as "proud of the deed as if they had done it themselves" (Gould, *A Portion of the Cruise of the U.S. Steam Frigate "Niagara,"* 1911). Active engagements followed in Spain and Portugal.

After returning to Wilmington, another of his contributions to the *Anglo-African* observed that the local black citizens were "well satisfied" with the Thirty-seventh and Thirty-ninth regiments of Colored Troops and that "the *Anglo-African* takes well" (*Anglo-African*, 1865). He also wrote an article, "Our Noble Tars Speak—How They Feel for the Freedman," which was published on 29 July 1865, in which he recounted donations by the sailors on the *Niagara* and said that they "see the necessities of thousands of our own people liberated by the victorious march of the armies of the Union through the would be Confederacy." Gould returned to Nantucket, Massachusetts, to marry Cornelia Read on 22 November 1865 in the African Baptist Church.

The couple had eight children—six boys and two girls—and made their home in Dedham, Massachusetts. There, Gould became a tradesman and contractor who worked on the construction of St. Mary's Roman Catholic Church. He was also active in the Union veterans' organization, the Grand Army of the Republic (where he served as commander of the Dedham chapter), and in the 1870s was a founder of the Episcopal Church of the Good Shepherd in Dedham, where four generations of Goulds were baptized. One son, William B. Gould Jr., served in the Spanish-American War, and five others served in World War I. In June 1918 the *Dedham Transcript* quoted a speech by William B. Gould in which he commented on his sons' service in World War I: "I have ever tried to set them a good example … and I expect to hear some good things from those boys."

William B. Gould died on 23 May 1923, predeceased by Cornelia in 1906. The following headline appeared in the *Dedham Transcript* on 26 May 1923: "East Dedham Mourns Faithful Soldier and Always Loyal Citizen: Death Came Very Suddenly to William B. Gould, Veteran of the Civil War."

FURTHER READING

The diary of William B. Gould (1862–1865) is on file at the Massachusetts Historical Society, Boston, Massachusetts, 2006. The pension papers of William B. Gould are in the National Archives, on file with William B. Gould IV and William B. Gould V.

Fowler, William M., Jr. *Under Two Flags: The American Navy in the Civil War* (1990).

Gould, William B., IV. *Diary of a Contraband: The Civil War Passage of a Black Sailor* (2002).

Gould, William B, IV. *A Portion of the Cruise of the U.S. Steam Frigate "Niagara" in Foreign Waters, Compiled from the Journal of Wm. B. Gould* (1911).

Ramold, Stephen J. *Slaves, Sailors, Citizens: African Americans in the Union Navy* (2002).

Reidy, Joseph J. "Black Men in Navy Blue during the Civil War," *Prologue: Quarterly of the National Archives and Records Administration* (Fall, 2001).

Sluby, Paul E., Sr., and Stanton L. Wormley, eds. *Diary of Charles B. Fisher* (1983).

WILLIAM B. GOULD IV

Gourdin, Edward Orval (10 Aug. 1897–22 July 1966), athlete, scholar, soldier, and judge, was born in Jacksonville, Florida, one of nine children of Walter Holmes Gourdin, a meat cutter and part Seminole Indian, and Felicia Nee, an African American woman who was a housekeeper. Little is known about his early school career, other than that he was valedictorian of his high school class in 1916. Although poor, Gourdin's parents recognized their son's talents and educational potential and, following his high school graduation, moved to Cambridge, Massachusetts, to further his career. There, Gourdin attended Cambridge High and Latin, which helped prepare him for the high academic demands of an Ivy League education.

By the time he enrolled in his freshman year at Harvard in 1917, Gourdin appears to have been a conscientious and responsible student. To pay tuition, he supported himself by working as a postal clerk. He also became a member of the Student Trainings Corps as a sophomore. It was his athletic ability, however, that distinguished him from many other students. Some sources even appear to see Gourdin's main achievements in the athletic arena, neglecting or even disregarding his high accomplishments in the field of law and in politics. Gourdin's athletic career started at Harvard, when he became the National Amateur Athlete Union's junior one-hundred-yard dash champion in 1920 and the national pentathlon champion in 1921 and 1922. At a track meet between a Harvard–Yale selection and a combined Oxford–Cambridge team in 1921, Gourdin set a new world record (twenty-five feet, three inches) in the broad jump. In 1924 he went to the Paris Olympic games and won a silver medal

in the broad jump. In that same year he received his law degree, an LL.B., from Harvard.

Gourdin married Amalia Ponce of Cambridge in 1923 and with her had three daughters and a son. While continuing to work as a postal clerk until 1927, he began his career as a Massachusetts lawyer in 1925 and also enlisted in the National Guard that year. In 1929, he passed the federal bar exam. Jobs were hard to come by during the Depression Era, but particularly hard for an African American law graduate. All the Boston law firms he applied to rejected Gourdin, who increasingly turned his attention to politics. Briefly a member of the Republican Party like many African Americans, he decided to switch his allegiance to the Democrats in the early 1930s. His political career led to many relationships with politicians and lawyers in the Boston area. Among his associates were Francis J. W. Ford, an influential lawyer whose classmate, Franklin Delano Roosevelt, had named him U.S. attorney for the district of Massachusetts in 1933. Three years later Roosevelt appointed Gourdin as an assistant U.S. attorney, a position he held until 1951.

During World War II Gourdin became the commanding officer to the 372d Infantry from 1941 until 1945. In the 1950s his appointments as a special justice of the Roxbury District Court and then as judge of the Massachusetts Superior Court made him famous as one of the first African Americans in such a position. He continued his work as an assistant U.S. attorney in Boston and had been promoted to the chief of the civil division before his promotion to the bench in 1951. In 1952 Governor Foster Forulo appointed Judge Gourdin as the Special Justice of Roxbury District Court.

The crowning moment of Gourdin's professional career was in 1958, when he was elected as the first black judge on the Massachusetts Superior Court.

Gourdin rejoined the National Guard after his discharge and retired in 1959 with the rank of brigadier general, becoming the first African American to reach that position. During the civil rights era Gourdin was at pains to maintain a position of judicial neutrality. This did not preclude his membership of the National Association for the Advancement of Colored People. He was also active in the New England Olympians (serving as its president in 1966) and in promoting social programs for youths in the predominantly African American Roxbury community. He spent his final years with his wife in Quincy, Massachusetts.

In 1999 the Jacksonville, Florida, *Times Union* ranked Gourdin as one of the one hundred greatest Jacksonville-area athletes of the twentieth century.

FURTHER READING
Edward Orval Gourdin's papers, photographs, and records are saved at Boston University's Mugar Library's Special Collections.
Abeel, Daphne. "Edward Orvil Gourdin." *Harvard Magazine.*
Mallon, Bill, and Ian Buchanan. *Quest for Gold* (1984).
Obituary: *New York Times*, 23 July 1966.

ANTJE DAUB

Gourdine, Meredith C. (26 Sept. 1929–20 Nov. 1998), physicist and engineer, was born in Newark, New Jersey. He was one of four children. His father worked at various maintenance and painting jobs and his mother was a teletype operator. After classes at Brooklyn Technical High School, Gourdine often worked long hours with his father on cleaning and painting jobs. This experience led him to focus on his studies as well as athletics in hopes of an easier life.

His talent in swimming earned him a scholarship offer from the University of Michigan, but he instead chose to attend Cornell University. He paid his own tuition early in his college career, working for a radio and telegraph firm, prior to receiving a scholarship for track and field. Gourdine competed in sprints, low hurdles, and the long jump. The six-foot-tall 175-pound Gourdine earned the nickname "Flash" as a result of both his speed and his favorite comic book superhero. He excelled at the long jump and won the silver medal in this event at the 1952 Olympic Games in Helsinki, Finland. He also won four titles at the Intercollegiate Association of Amateur Athletes of America Championships, five titles at the Heptagonal Games, and contributed to Cornell's strong performance (placing second to the University of Southern California) at the 1952 NCAA Championships.

Gourdine graduated from Cornell with a BS in engineering physics in 1953. He married June Cave, whom he met during his sophomore year. They had four children and later divorced. He served for a short time as an officer in the U.S. Navy before enrolling at California Institute of Technology (Caltech) on a Daniel and Florence Guggenheim fellowship to pursue a doctoral degree in engineering physics. In the latter years of his graduate studies, Gourdine worked at several of the leading corporations and laboratories in the defense and aerospace fields. In 1957 Gourdine joined the technical staff of the Ramo-Wooldridge Corporation in Los Angeles, and the following year he became a Senior Research Scientist at Caltech's Jet Propulsion Laboratory in Pasadena, a position he held until he completed his PhD in 1960, having written his dissertation on magnetohydrodynamic flow over solids. Gourdine then took the position of laboratory director of the Plasmodyne Corporation and in 1962 he moved to the Aeronautical Division of Curtis-Wright Corporation and became chief scientist until 1964, a year in which he served on President Lyndon B. Johnson's Panel on Energy.

Gourdine had built a considerable base of knowledge and technical and managerial skills working at some of the most innovative engineering corporations and organizations. He decided to take advantage of this and demonstrate his entrepreneurial acumen by moving back east to found the research and development firm Gourdine Systems in Livingston, New Jersey. He raised $200,000 from friends to fund the venture. It was at this company that he achieved his pioneering work in the field of electrogasdynamics, the study of the forces resulting from the motion of ions (electrically charged particles) carried by insulating gases as they move through electrical fields.

At Gourdine Systems, he and his staff pioneered many applications in electrogasdynamics. Gourdine Systems grew into a multimillion-dollar laboratory and became a publicly traded firm that at its height, in the early 1970s, employed more than 150 people. The company, however, struggled, overspending on its marketing of a spray gun product. It also suffered from a New York City law that banned industrial incinerators, a primary product and market for the firm.

Following the failure of Gourdine Systems, Gourdine formed Energy Innovations in Houston, Texas, in 1974. This firm was focused primarily on producing direct-energy conversion devices extending from early patents of Gourdine. In all, Gourdine and his research teams developed mechanisms that successfully applied principles of electrogasdynamics to solve or address many real-world problems, including the aiding of processes of electricity transmission, the conversion of low-grade coal into inexpensive high-voltage electricity, the creation of circuit breakers, sea water desalination, acoustic imaging, electrostatic painting, and the reduction of pollutants in smoke. He was granted more than forty patents pertaining to such innovative techniques and procedures in the application of electrogasdynamics.

Among Gourdine's most influential research applications in electrogasdynamics were techniques used to dissipate smoke from buildings by applying electrostatic precipitator systems that electromagnetically attracted pollutants to the ground and cleared the air above (earliest patents from 1971 and 1972), and a technique to reduce fog from airport runways (patented in 1987). This Incineride System was also commercialized for other types of air-pollution deterrent devices.

Following upon his early service to the Johnson administration, Gourdine continued to devote considerable time and energy to civic activities throughout his career. He served on President Richard Nixon's Task Force on Small Business, was a member of the Army Science Board, and a trustee of Cornell University.

Widely recognized as a leader in the field of electrogasdynamics, Gourdine was elected to the National Academy of Engineering in 1991 and inducted into the Engineering and Science Hall of Fame in 1994. Still active in research toward the end of his career, in 1994 and 1995 he also advanced techniques for focus flow heat sink in order to cool computer chips. In spite of various health problems, including a leg amputation and blindness resulting from complications of diabetes, he remained CEO of Energy Innovations until his death at the age of sixty-nine.

FURTHER READING

Carwell, Hattie, ed. *Blacks in Science: Astrophysicists to Zoologist* (1977).

Ho, James K. *Black Engineers in the United States* (1974).

United States Department of Energy. *Black Contributors to Science, Energy, and Technology* (1979).

Winslow, Eugene. *Black Americans in Science and Engineering: Contributors of Past and Present* (1974).

JEFFREY R. YOST

Govan, Sandra (28 July 1948–), educator and writer, was born Sandra Yvonne Govan in Chicago at the all-black Provident Hospital to Tanzel R. Govan, a bus driver with the Chicago Transit Authority, and Sarah D. Wilson Govan, a lunchroom manager for the Chicago board of education. Both of Govan's parents were from the South. They met and married in Louisiana, and following Tanzel Govan's service in World War II they settled in Chicago, where they raised Sandra and her older brother. Govan was born with dislocated hips and did not walk until age four. In stories about her childhood she describes a loving and strict upbringing with occasional difficulties because of physical challenges and ever-present racism. She was a precocious child who loved to read and was doted upon—as well as firmly held in line—by her neighborhood community.

Govan earned a BA in English and history at Valparaiso University in 1970, an MA in American studies at Bowling Green State University in 1972, and the PhD in American studies at Emory University in 1980. At Valparaiso the English Department chair, Paul F. Phipps, was her adviser and mentor and suggested she consider graduate school. She also took a class with John McCluskey Jr., the first African American instructor in the English Department, who greatly influenced her later focus on the Harlem Renaissance. At Bowling Green, Alma Payne, director of the American Studies Program, helped Govan to change from English to American studies. Eugenia Collier, Gloria Wade Gayles, and Helen R. Houston also played important supportive roles in her scholarly development. Govan was assistant professor of English at the University of Kentucky from 1980 to 1983 and then moved to the University of North Carolina at Charlotte, where she remained for more than twenty years, earning tenure in 1987 and attaining the title of professor in 1998.

Govan's contributions to the field of African American literary scholarship laid the groundwork upon which future scholars would build. She contributed a significant number of entries on African American writers to reference books. In particular, her research on OCTAVIA BUTLER and GWENDOLYN BENNETT—beginning with her dissertation on Bennett and continued through journal articles, essays in edited collections, and conference papers—introduced these writers to many and provided key critical lenses for interpretation. She was also among the first to bring the study of African American writers of science fiction such as SAMUEL R. DELANY to a larger critical audience. In addition to her scholarship, she was also active in creative writing, publishing poems and writing short memoir pieces.

Govan was a longtime member of the Wintergreen Women Writers' Collective, along with other notable black women writers such as TRUDIER HARRIS, Daryl Dance, PAULE MARSHALL, Karla Holloway, NIKKI GIOVANNI, and its founder Joanne V. Gabbin.

Govan experienced ongoing health issues, some related to joint disintegration that resulted in a series of joint replacements during her years at UNC Charlotte. She provided an outspoken voice for access on the campus, serving for a decade on the University Accessibility Committee (1992–2002) and working as an advocate for disabled faculty and students.

Another notable feature of Govan's career was her service to black students on the UNC Charlotte campus as a teacher, mentor, and coordinator of the federally funded Ronald E. McNair Post-Baccalaureate Achievement Program from 1994 to 2000. She received recognition for her teaching throughout her career and was named a finalist for the Bank of America Award for Teaching Excellence—the highest recognition for teaching on the UNC Charlotte campus—in 2001.

A significant portion of Govan's contribution to the field of African American literature and African Americans in academia cannot be quantified by articles, books, or awards; her unique, vocal presence helped shape conversations about black literature and the future of blacks in the academy in ways beyond the printed page. For example, one organization key to her development was the annual conference for CLA, the College Language Association, which she began attending as a graduate student and did not miss in thirty years. More generally, her attendance at a wide range of conferences, workshops, and lectures became almost legendary owing to her energetic delivery of her work. Throughout her career, and most directly in her work with the McNair program, Govan marshaled through sheer force of personality many talented African American students into a community of mentoring relationships with supportive faculty and the larger academy, helping to create and strengthen the pipeline for blacks into the halls of higher education.

MALIN PEREIRA

Goyens, William (1784–20 June 1856), was the first African American and perhaps the first of any color to become a millionaire in Texas. His life reflects substantial changes in the social and legal implications of skin color from the late eighteenth century to the mid-nineteenth century, distinct from, but closely related to, changes in the institution of slavery.

His father was a "free colored" man named William Goyens Sr. (or Goin), born in 1762, who enlisted in a company of the Tenth North Carolina Regiment May 1781–May 1782 for the Revolutionary War. After discharge from the militia, Goyens Sr. married an unknown woman referred to as "white," who was the mother of the younger William Goyens.

Goyens Sr. then remarried a colored woman named Elizabeth in 1793. Goyens Sr. received an invalid pension for North Carolina militia service in 1835, at the age of seventy-two (Research of Cindy Goins Hoelscher of Corpus Christi, Texas, published by the Gowen Research Foundation, Lubbock, Texas).

The younger Goyens first came to Galveston Bay in 1820; historians have speculated that he arrived with the privateer Jean Lafitte, who is known to have used the bay as a base of operations. He moved on to Nacogdoches, then a small city in the Mexican state of Tejas, and remained there for the rest of his life. He worked as a blacksmith and wagonmaker, accumulating savings, acquiring slaves, and hiring white wage laborers as the business grew (Greene, p. 23). He later profited by complex land deals and raising horses. He served as an Indian agent for the Mexican government and was trusted by Anglo-American settlers who had their own dealings with Indians.

Goyens married Mary Pate Sibley, from Georgia, in 1832. Like Goyens's mother, Sibley was deemed "white" by the arcane laws of the day; antislavery advocate Benjamin Lundy (who attempted to arrange for a colony of free colored people from the United States to settle in Tejas) wrote that her brothers visited the couple and approved of the marriage. People of color received land grants either directly under Mexican law or as part of the early land grant communities of Anglo-Americans under Stephen Austin. Mexican law, after independence from Spain in 1821, provided full rights of citizenship for people of African descent, including ownership of property. Like the Mexicans who had joined the revolt against the federal government in 1835–1836, people of color had many legal rights and practical advantages taken away by the laws of the early Texas Republic. Lawless actions by new waves of Anglo-American immigrants, who arrived during or immediately after the secession of Texas from Mexico, posed additional hazards to life, legal status, and property.

Goyens served in the Texas army during the revolution that broke the state away from Mexico and established an independent "Republick." Fluent in Spanish, Cherokee, and several Indian dialects, he served as interpreter at treaty meetings Sam Houston arranged with Cherokee and Comanche leaders from 1835 to 1838, which prevented an alliance between these nations and the Mexican government. Goyens later served as Indian agent for Texas. The laws of newly independent Texas forbade ownership of property by anyone deemed "colored."

That Gowens was able to keep his substantial property represents in part a historical anomaly—he was already resident and wealthy. It also shows that such laws could be selectively enforced, but generally because highly placed men accepted as white provided implicit patronage. Many who voted for general laws prohibiting permanent residence of free "colored" persons took exception to enforcement of such laws, against individuals they knew and respected personally in their local communities.

Sam Houston, the republic's first president, had ambivalent views on race, similar to Thomas Jefferson and Patrick Henry: he owned enslaved persons as household servants, but found the institution degrading and morally dubious (Anderson, p. 121). But this ambiguity was vanishing from Texas and among a newer generation of Americans. Goyens's uncertain status was emphasized by his own reference to twice being kidnapped and sold into or threatened with slavery, having each time to buy his way out. At least one of these incidents occurred while on a business trip in Louisiana.

In 1838 Goyens was reduced to humbly petitioning the Senate and House of Representatives of the fledgling "Republick of Texas" because "he is unfortunately a man of colour—and consequently his rights and interests have not in his humble opinion, been so reserved and protected by the general laws of the Republick" (Schweninger, p. 167). Although he had immigrated to the Republick in 1820 and "has ever been identified with the feelings and interests of the Anglo American population and born his humble part in their struggles," he had never made application for land grants "since he has reason to fear from the peculiar provisions of the late land law his application would be rejected." He had purchased land, but most settlers were entitled to free grants as a matter of "head right" (Schweninger, pp. 167–168).

His petition for grant of land as a Head Right was rejected. Nevertheless, in October 1838 Goyens served as a go-between for Texas militia general Thomas J. Rusk with Cherokee war chief Bowles, in connection with the "Kickapoo War." In 1840 the "Ashworth law," allowing several mixed-race couples who moved across the Sabine River from Louisiana to remain in Texas, was adopted with an amendment, approving continued residence for "all free persons of color together with their families who were residing in Texas the day of the Declaration of Independence," but did not extend protection to his ownership of land. A more general law gave free colored persons two years to leave the republic or risk being sold into slavery.

By 1841 his estate, Goyens Hill, encompassed 4,160 acres of agricultural land worth $20,600 and nine slaves. Still, he remained in constant danger of losing everything, because any man able to present himself as white could fraudulently or by naked violence take it from him. He sued whites successfully at least sixteen times, employing some of the most prominent lawyers in Texas (Greene, pp. 23–24). When he died, his estate had grown to almost 13,000 acres in four counties of eastern Texas. Two years later, in 1858, the Texas legislature passed a law encouraging free colored persons like Goyens to voluntarily choose a master and become slaves—sometimes misstated as "reentering" slavery. Many free colored persons, like Goyens, had been born free.

FURTHER READING

Anderson, Gary Clayton. *The Conquest of Texas: Ethnic Cleansing in the Promised Land, 1820–1875* (2005).

Greene, A. C. *Sketches from the Five States of Texas* (1998).

Prince, Diane Elizabeth. *William Goyens, Free Negro on the Texas Frontier* (1967).

Schoen, Harold. "The Free Negro in the Republic of Texas," *Southwestern Historical Quarterly*. April 1936–July 1937, pp. 39–41.

Schweninger, Loren, ed. *The Southern Debate over Slavery* (2001–2008).

Taylor, Quintard. *In Search of the Racial Frontier: African Americans in the American West* (1999).

Treat, Victor H. "William Goyens: Free Black Entrepreneur," in *Black Leaders: Texans for Their Times*, Alwyn Barr and Robert A. Calvin, eds. (1981).

CHARLES ROSENBERG

Grace, Charles Emmanuel (25 Jan. 1881–12 Jan. 1960), better known as Daddy Grace or Sweet Daddy Grace or by his self-proclaimed title, Boyfriend of the World, was one of the more flamboyant religious leaders of the twentieth century. He was born, probably as Marceline Manoel da Graca, in Brava, Cape Verde Islands, of mixed Portuguese and African ancestry, the son of Manuel de Graca and Gertrude Lomba. In the charismatic church that he founded and headed, however, he managed to transcend race by declaring: "I am a colorless man. I am a colorless bishop. Sometimes I am black, sometimes white. I preach to all races." Like many other Cape Verdeans, Grace immigrated to New Bedford, Massachusetts, around the turn of the century and worked there and on Cape Cod as a short-order cook, a salesman of sewing machines and patent medicines, and a cranberry picker. Also known as Bishop Grace, he may have established his first church in West Wareham, Massachusetts, around 1919, but he achieved his early success in Charlotte, North Carolina, where he held evangelical tent meetings and attracted more than ten thousand followers in the 1920s. In 1927 in Washington, D.C., he incorporated the United House of Prayer for All People on the Rock of the Apostolic Faith. The phrase "All People" was said to indicate Grace's acceptance of the poor and disinherited who were unwelcome in more conventional churches. Grace established churches up and down the eastern seaboard, eventually numbering at least five hundred thousand people in some one hundred congregations in nearly seventy cities. Most, but not all, members were African American.

In person, Daddy Grace presented a dramatic figure with his shoulder-length hair; six-inch-long fingernails painted red, white, and blue; and gold and purple cutaway coats and chartreuse vests. A master of public pageantry and showmanship, he sponsored bands and parades, outfitted his followers in uniforms, and staged colorful outdoor mass baptisms in swimming pools or with fire hoses. He promoted band music and once asked, "Why should the devil have all the good times?" He was generally surrounded by adoring followers who pinned dollar bills to his robe as he walked slowly down the aisle of one of his churches.

Many nonfollowers thought Daddy Grace an exploitative religious fraud and confidence man. The alleged escapism of his church was widely criticized, and E. FRANKLIN FRAZIER, the Howard University sociologist, condemned the church for what he called its erotic dancing while disciples, mainly female, sang, "Daddy, you feel so good." Whatever spiritual or emotional satisfactions Daddy Grace provided his people, he also supplied apartment buildings, pension funds, retirement homes, burial plans, and church cafeterias that dispensed free food. He received a considerable income, invested heavily in real estate, and personally owned some forty residences. He bought the El Dorado on Central Park West in New York City, then the world's tallest apartment building. He purchased Prophet Jones's fifty-four-room mansion in Detroit, which he had repainted red, white, and blue to the consternation of the neighborhood. In 1938 he acquired the kingdom of heaven property in Harlem of another charismatic leader, FATHER DIVINE.

The money came not only from the offerings of the faithful members of the United House of Prayer for All People but also from the numerous Grace-sponsored moneymaking enterprises that manufactured and sold such products as soap, hair pomade, vitamins, and ice cream. Followers reportedly believed these products had special powers bestowed by Daddy Grace. Healing was an important element in the movement, and Grace was widely believed by the faithful to have curative powers, particularly via buttered toast from which he had taken a bite. His *Grace Magazine*, which sold for ten cents, was also thought to be restorative when touched to the body.

Daddy Grace fused elements from the Holiness and Pentecostal religious traditions, but his church (often referred to as a sect) depended largely on his charisma. He did not himself actually assert the divinity his followers attributed to him. "I never said I was God," he once stated, "but you cannot prove to me I'm not." He did say, however, "If you sin against God, Grace can save you, but if you sin against Grace, God cannot save you," as well as "Grace has given God a vacation, and since God is on His vacation, don't worry Him." He delighted in pointing out how many times the word *grace* appears in the Bible and was fond of repeating the classic Protestant formula that salvation is by grace alone.

Grace's considerable wealth attracted several lawsuits. In 1957 Louvenia Royster, a retired Georgia schoolteacher, claimed that Daddy Grace had married her in New York in 1923 under the name of John H. Royster but had deserted her in 1928, leaving her with a daughter, now an adult. Grace responded that he was in the Holy Land at the time of the alleged marriage and had spent the night in question in the manger in which Jesus was born. The court dismissed her claim. Jennie Grace of New Bedford claimed that Daddy Grace had married her in 1909. She also was the mother of a grown daughter, whom she also said he had fathered. Whatever his relationships with these women, Daddy Grace apparently was the father of at least one child, a son, Marcellino V. Grace of Brentwood, Maryland.

The greatest legal difficulties came, however, after Grace's death, which occurred while he was visiting in Los Angeles. His finances were chaotic, and it was unclear what monies and property belonged to the church and what constituted his personal estate. There was some $25 million at issue, much of it in real estate but also including $3 million in cash in 75 banks in 50 cities and diamond-studded keys to numerous safe deposit boxes. Thirty-six lawyers became involved in the litigation. The Internal Revenue Service put a lien of $5.9 million against the estate at his death, claiming he owed that amount in back taxes, but settled in 1961 for $1.9 million. Grace was buried in New Bedford.

A fierce internal struggle for succession ensued. Bishop Walter McCollough took over the United House of Prayer after winning a lawsuit against rival contender James Walton. Much less flamboyant than Grace, McCollough concentrated on consolidating the denomination, making it more traditionally Pentecostal, and building a substantial low-income housing project. He moved the church, he said, "from the storefront to the forefront."

FURTHER READING

Davis, Lenwood G. *Daddy Grace: An Annotated Bibliography* (1992).
Halter, Marilyn. *Between Race and Ethnicity: Cape Verdean American Immigrants, 1860–1965* (1993).
Manuel, Charles. "Sweet Daddy Grace?," in *Twentieth-century Shapers of American Popular Religion*, ed. Charles H. Lippy (1989).
Sevitch, Benjamin. "When Black Gods Preached on Earth: The Heavenly Appeals of Prophet Cherry, Daddy Grace, and Father Divine," in *Black Religious Leadership from the Slave Community to the Million Man March: Flames of Fire*, ed. Felton O. Best (1998).
Obituary: *New York Times*, 13 Jan. 1960.
This entry is taken from the *American National Biography* and is published here with the permission of the American Council of Learned Societies.

RICHARD NEWMAN

Graham, Lorenz (27 Jan. 1902–11 Sept. 1989), missionary, educator, social worker, and author was born in New Orleans, Louisiana, the third child of the Rev. David Andrew Graham, a Methodist minister, and Etta Bell Graham. His father's pastorates took the family from New Orleans to Detroit, Indianapolis, Chicago, Nashville, Colorado Springs, and Spokane. Graham attended the University of Washington and the University of California at Los Angeles.

While a student at UCLA, Graham learned about the need for missionary teachers in Liberia, West Africa, and felt he was called there to serve. He left for Liberia in 1924 to teach at Monrovia College, a Christian boys' school.

Going to Africa changed Graham's life. He realized he had gone with a false concept of what African people were like. He decried the fact that all he had read or seen had described Africans in stereotypical terms as savages, at best stupid and amusing, and at worst, vicious and depraved. While in Africa he decided that he would become a writer and write stories that would describe Africans realistically as he was coming to know them and their lives.

In Liberia he met Ruth Morris, the young woman who would become his life partner. Graham and Ruth, a Christian missionary teacher, shared their dreams for the future, both desiring that their lives would be devoted to service and to humanity. Graham suffered from serious bouts of malaria and was eventually forced to return to the United States in 1928

Graham arrived in New York City in 1928 at the height of the Harlem Renaissance. He felt strongly committed to pursue a career in writing. He enrolled in writing courses at Columbia University School of Journalism, worked on his manuscripts that he started in Africa, and associated with other promising writers and poets. He had a minor acting role in the Broadway play *Harlem*. Some publishers were willing to read his manuscripts, but invariably they rejected his writing because they felt readers would not be interested in literature portraying Africans as hard working and moral people as he portrayed them.

Graham married Ruth Morris on 20 August 1929 in Richmond, Virginia, just at the onset of the Great Depression. The couple settled in Virginia where Graham took on numerous jobs while earning his Bachelor's degree in Social Sciences at Virginia Union University in Richmond from 1934 to 1936. He later did graduate work at New York University and UCLA.

Their five children provided many joys as well as challenges through the years, as Graham struggled to provide adequately for his family and realize his ambition of becoming a writer. For the next three decades the serious business of earning a living led him in several fields: educational advisor in the New Deal's Civilian Conservation Corps (CCC), manager of a housing project, social worker, and probation officer. The family moved from Virginia to New York in 1942 primarily to get out of the segregated South and give the children better educational opportunities.

But writing about Africa was in Graham's blood. His first published book, *How God Fix Jonah* (1946), was a compilation of Bible stories beautifully portrayed in the idiom of West Africa as he had heard them through the African storyteller. With a foreword by W. E. B. DuBois, *How God Fix Jonah* was hailed for its rich rhythms and complex cultural texture. That same year Graham's first novel, *Tales of Momolu (1946)*, was published providing American children with realistic stories depicting the life of a young African boy. When a newspaper reviewer wrote that an American reader would recognize the African boy as "just another fellow," Graham was ecstatic. He knew he had achieved his purpose of showing American boys and girls how similar African children are in their joys, hopes, and dreams.

Struggling to send his children to college on a social worker's salary, he continued to write books, primarily for young people, to convey his belief that "people are people"—whether white or black, born in the United States, Africa, Europe, or Asia. Through his writings he conveyed the message that people are basically alike; they have the same needs, emotions, and desires and want basic human rights and social justice.

The Grahams moved to Los Angeles, California, in 1957 where he was drawn by the desire to find work writing in Hollywood. His first big success as a writer, however, came with the publication of *South Town* (1958), a novel portraying the life of a poor, hard-working black family in the rural South who experienced racism and violence, yet remained hopeful that someday the struggle would be over. It had taken twelve years of rejections from publishers, however, because publishers repeatedly told him that the American public would not accept a story that did not conform to the popular images of blacks as poor, violent, and hopeless. *South Town* was awarded the Child Study Association of America Award (1958) and this encouraged him to write three succeeding novels over the next two decades. *North Town* (1965), *Whose Town?* (1969), and *Return to South Town* (1976) chronicle David Williams's journey from adolescence to manhood, moving from the South to the North and back to the South, while finally realizing his dream of becoming a doctor.

These novels made Graham a true pioneer in the field of literature for young adults with his sensitive portrayal of his characters showing how they led everyday lives bravely overcoming injustice and racism while determined to have a better future.

Graham received national recognition for his works. He published two other books on Africa, *I, Momolu* (1966) about the boy coming of age in Africa, and a touching picture book, *Song of the Boat* (1975), about Momolu helping his father make

a canoe. He traveled across the country to research and write *John Brown: A Cry For Freedom* (1980), a book for young adults chronicling Brown's view of the destructive aspects of slavery and his struggle for social justice.

Throughout the years of working and writing, Graham and his wife, Ruth, were actively involved in civil rights and human rights issues. In the 1960s they risked their lives in the innermost regions of Mississippi as voter registration workers. Graham lectured throughout the United States and became a popular faculty member at California State College Pomona, California. He was an active member of Poets, Essayists, and Novelists (PEN) International and served as president of the Los Angeles chapter.

Graham and Ruth Graham became world travelers. They went to Haiti as volunteer teachers and traveled throughout the Caribbean. They lectured at universities and other institutions in Europe, Asia, and Africa where they were often saluted as ambassadors of peace. In 1974 they were invited to the People's Republic of China during the celebration of that government's twenty-fifth anniversary, along with Lorenz's sister, renowned writer SHIRLEY GRAHAM DuBois, widow of W. E. B. DuBois. In 1987, at the age of eighty-five, Graham was a guest speaker at a symposium on children's literature at the University of the Western Cape in South Africa, a crowning experience in his life and career.

Graham's works brought him numerous awards, including the Follett Award, the Martin Luther King, Jr. Award for Service, and an honorary Doctor of Letters degree from Virginia Union University.

Graham died in 1989 in Los Angeles County at the age of eighty-seven. He left a legacy of commitment, service, and a fervent belief that, through hope, understanding and the power of God's love, we will all come to know that "people are people wherever you go."

FURTHER READING

Lorenz Graham's papers are housed in the Kerlan Collection, University of Minnesota, in Minneapolis, Minnesota.

Graham, Lorenz. "*Something About the Author,*" *Autobiography Series*, Vol. 5, 1988, pp. 111–145.

Obituary: *Los Angeles Times*, 15 Sept. 1989.

RUTH GRAHAM SIEGRIST

Graham, Mary Henrietta (25 Dec. 1857–2 Jan. 1890), professor and newspaper editor in chief, was born in Windsor, Ontario, Canada. Few details about her family's background have come to light, except that her mother, Sarah M. Graham, took an active part in her daughter's life and supported Mary's educational ambitions. During the 1850s and 1860s, southwestern Ontario was a hub of fugitive and free black settlements. The schools that were open to black students were either denominational, often short-lived, private schools or racially segregated public schools. These factors may have influenced Sarah Graham's decision to move to Flint, Michigan, a growing manufacturing town and rail hub about sixty-five miles north of Detroit. Flint, the seat of Genesee County, had few black residents and no school segregation ordinances.

Genesee County also had one of Michigan's most developed public school systems during the 1870s, when Mary Graham initially enrolled in elementary, or common, school. Although only organized in 1867, the system had forty-two district libraries with well over 2,100 volumes, and almost 2,500 students enrolled in Flint's schools. Schools sessions lasted ten months each year. When Mary Graham entered Flint High School in 1872, its classes were being convened in Flint's City Hall. In 1874 Mary was one of some 350 students who moved to a massive new building on Beach Street, an impressive three-story structure in the Second Empire, or French mansard, style, complete with central steam heating, an enormous clock tower, and a 2,000-pound school bell. The school's curriculum, which included classical languages, mathematics, and literature, had been certified by the faculty of the University of Michigan (UM) at Ann Arbor as offering advanced academic preparation such that its graduates would be admitted to UM, located about forty miles south of Flint, without further interview or testing. When Graham graduated from Flint High School in 1876, she was thus prequalified for admission to UM. When she applied, she was duly admitted.

The University of Michigan had been admitting women since 1870. Because Graham held a diploma from a certified Michigan high school, and the university did not request written information from applicants concerning race, her identity was probably unknown to the university's admissions officer. When Graham, accompanied by her mother, moved to Ann Arbor in July 1876, no untoward public reaction occurred, although a local newspaper did announce their arrival. Graham would enroll in the university's Literary Department in the autumn of 1876, the newspaper noted, as the university's first "colored lady" student. The university did not provide dormitories for its students at that time, and the scores of women who attended classes between

1870 and 1876 lived in privately run rooming houses or with relatives or friends. To avoid any difficulty, Graham's mother moved to Ann Arbor, along with Mary and another daughter, Sarah A. ("Bertie") Graham. She established residences on Maynard Street (1876–1877), on Huron Street (1877–1878), and finally at 4 State Street, directly across from the UM campus. The family evidently lived in an upstairs apartment, while Graham's mother operated a hairdressing salon and fancy-goods shop in the street-level store below.

Graham's academic study at UM focused on classical literary studies. She was awarded a PhB (bachelor of philosophy) degree in the spring of 1880. While Mrs. Graham and Bertie remained in Ann Arbor, providing room and board for other black women students attending UM, including the medical student Sophie Bethena Jones, Mary Graham was immediately hired as a faculty member at Lincoln University (initially, in 1866, the Lincoln Institute), the state of Missouri's teacher training institutions for African Americans, located in Jefferson City. She remained on the faculty for two years (1880–1882).

Probably while still an undergraduate in Ann Arbor, Graham had met politically active black lawyer Ferdinand Lee Barnett, an 1878 graduate of the Law School of Northwestern University. In 1878 (some sources say 1877) Barnett had founded Chicago's first black-owned newspaper, the *Conservator*. By 1880 he was already a member of the Chicago Bar Association and a leader in Chicago's black community. Graham resigned from the Lincoln University faculty, and Barnett and Graham were married in Graham's mother's home in Ann Arbor, on 14 November 1882. They moved to Barnett's home on Portland Avenue in Chicago.

The Barnetts had two sons. Ferdinand Lee Barnett Jr., a lawyer, became a state's attorney in Illinois and worked as a civil rights lawyer in private practice. Albert G. Barnett was a newspaperman who in the 1940s was an editor with the *Chicago Defender*, the city's leading black paper. After the birth of her children, Mary Graham Barnett took an increasingly active role in the *Conservator*. In 1886 she joined the newspaper's staff, and in 1888 she became its chief editor. Meanwhile her husband's political ambitions grew and were supported by stories and editorials in the *Conservator*. Barnett briefly went into law practice with an African American graduate of the University of Michigan's Law School, Samuel Laing Williams. Like Barnett, Williams and his wife, FANNIE BARRIER WILLIAMS, were political activists and members of Chicago's well-educated black elite.

Mary Graham Barnett died in Chicago in January 1890, just as her husband's political fortunes began to rise. Ferdinand Lee Barnett remarried in 1895; his second wife, who helped raise his young sons, was the crusading journalist IDA B. WELLS-BARNETT who, already famous for her antilynching reporting, began writing for the *Conservator*.

FURTHER READING

Biographical details on Mary Henrietta Graham are available at the University of Michigan's Bentley Historical Library, in the UM Alumni Association's Necrology File.

LAURA M. CALKINS

Grainger, Porter (22 Oct. 1891–c. 1955?), pianist, songwriter, playwright, and music publisher, was born in Bowling Green, Kentucky. His father, also named Porter, was a laborer (a "porter," according to a Bowling Green city directory). The family name was "Granger," without the "i," and it is not known when the pianist changed the spelling. He and a younger sister, Ursula, were living with their grandparents, Joseph (a farmer) and Patience Coleman, and with other relatives in Hickory Flat, Kentucky, at the time of the 1900 Census. By the 1930s the Grangers appear to have left the city, although Porter Grainger still had numerous relations there and remained in contact with them.

Grainger was living in Chicago, a leading center of black music and theater, when he registered for the draft during World War I. His name was entered by the clerk as Porter Parrish Granger, but he signed as Grainger. At this time he claimed to be married and requested a deferment on the grounds that he was the sole source of support for his father. He gave "composer of songs" as his occupation at this time, indicating that he had already entered show business, although compositions of his from before 1920 appear to be unknown. Grainger seems to have moved to New York around 1920. *Trow's New York City Directory* for the year 1924–1925 shows him sharing both a Harlem address and a Broadway business office with Bob Ricketts. The two men were very closely associated during this period. Together they wrote and published an instructional book titled *How to Play and Sing the Blues Like the Phonograph and Stage Artists* in 1926.

Although he was not involved in the earliest "city" or "vaudeville" blues recordings in 1920–1921, Grainger would soon become among the most prolific piano accompanists in the field, perhaps surpassed only by FLETCHER HENDERSON and CLARENCE WILLIAMS, and he was often the composer of the songs. Among the best known of the singers he worked with in the 1920s were Viola McCoy, CLARA SMITH (frequently, from 1924 to 1930), and VICTORIA SPIVEY in 1930 (Grainger also sings on the Spivey records, under the pseudonym "Harold Grey"). He also made recordings with his wife, Ethel Finnie, in 1923–1924. She is probably the Sister Ethel Grainger who recorded with J. C. Burnett in 1926. Porter Grainger also recorded with Burnett some two decades later. Whether she is the same wife he mentioned to the draft board in 1917 and in the U.S. Census in 1930 is unknown (neither is mentioned by name). Grainger also played for non-blues singers, such as the West Indian Sam Manning, on three of Grainger's own songs, in 1925 and 1926. On some of these recordings there was also a banjo and/or a violin, instruments commonly used on the earlier "jazz" recordings of this era, but they could hardly be considered either band recordings or genuine jazz recordings.

Grainger's most important collaboration was with the blues singer BESSIE SMITH. Together they recorded over a dozen sides for Columbia Records between 1924 and 1928. Several of these are memorable records, such as "Mean Old Bedbug Blues." Grainger was also Smith's accompanist at a notorious 1928 party at the apartment of Carl Van Vechten and Fania Marinoff. Supposedly, on this occasion Smith performed several blues songs with her customary power but also became drunk and struck Marinoff after the Russian-born dancer took the liberty of embracing and kissing her. Members of Smith's circle who were interviewed by Chris Albertson for his 1972 biography *Bessie* claimed that Grainger was homosexual. However, he still claimed to be married at the time of the 1930 Census and was survived by a daughter, Portia (Bastin). It is not known whether Ethel Finnie was his only wife or whether she was Portia's mother.

Grainger made at least eight records as a bandleader, including four with the Get Happy Band, in 1925. These recordings are of great interest to early jazz collectors, with appearances by such jazz greats as soprano saxophonist SIDNEY BECHET and the DUKE ELLINGTON sidemen JOE ("Tricky Sam") NANTON (trombone) and ELMER SNOWDEN (banjo). One of the four compositions, "(In) Harlem's Araby," co-written with Jo Trent and Thomas FATS WALLER, is among Grainger's finest works. He had already recorded it as a vocal soloist, with Waller at the piano, in 1924. Grainger's other combo recordings, with the Tennessee Tooters in 1924 and the Memphis Jazzers in 1929, are of lesser interest to jazz aficionados. He also recorded behind vocal ensembles, and his 1925 pairing of "Done Got Da Blues" and "I've Got a Gal and She Ain't No Good" with the Harmony Hounds are charming examples of the then wildly popular vocal quartet genre.

During the mid-1920s Grainger sometimes appeared as an onstage pianist for shows he had co-written. In 1923–1924 he toured with *Aces and Queens* and appeared in it, as a character called "Hit Keys," when the show played New York in 1925 under the title *Lucky Sambo*. In the 1920s and 1930s Grainger collaborated on a number of projects with the actor and playwright LEIGH WHIPPER, including the plays *De Board Meetin'* in 1925 and *We's Risin'* in 1927. The two had their own firm, Grainger and Whipper, on New York's West 46th Street in 1926–1927. In March 1928 he, Whipper, and the arranger and conductor Hall Johnson were employed by a theatrical consortium run by George Morris and John Gillespie. Grainger also appeared in the short Mamie Smith picture *Jail House Blues* (1929), with actors Homer Tutt Whitney and Billy Mills. His association with Mamie Smith went back to 1920, when he replaced pianist WILLIE "THE LION" SMITH in her band The Jazz Hounds. For a number of years he was Mamie Smith's regular pianist for stage shows. Oddly enough, he is only known to appear on a few of her records.

Grainger remained prolific as a theater songwriter into the 1930s and was also still involved with films. In 1930 he was engaged to write music for a series of twelve talkie shorts called "The Royal Roustabouts." In 1930 Grainger contributed to the show *Hot Rhythm*. He was one of several songwriters to contribute to *Brown Buddies*, which ran from October 1930 through 1931, and the show *Yeah Man*, with a cast including Leigh Whipper, was mounted in 1932. His revue *Harlem Swing Hotel* was performed in 1936 as a benefit for the Hope Day Nursery. Reports published in black press in the mid-1930s claiming that the popular dance known as the "Suzie Q" was based on one of Grainger's compositions are unsubstantiated.

Grainger wrote the musical arrangements for ZORA NEALE HURSTON's show *From Sun to Sun* in 1931, marking an occasional turn to more serious material in the later part of his career. In 1932 Eva Jessye's Dixie Jubilee Choir was performing his "Sorrow Song." In April–June 1936 Orson Welles used some of Grainger's music in his all-African/African American production of *Macbeth*

at Harlem's New Lafayette Theater, along with music by JAMES P. JOHNSON, Joe Jordan, and the African composer ASADATA DAFORA, a drummer from Sierra Leone. In 1939 Grainger mounted a "Panorama of Negro Folklore" at Harlem's Alhambra Ballroom, as a benefit for a Masonic order. In the sacred music arena he had already recorded spirituals with Porter Grainger's Jubilee Singers in 1926, and he made more religious recordings in 1945.

Grainger remained active in show business through the 1940s, as an entrepreneur as well as a songwriter and performer. In 1937 he was operating the Broadway Music Clinic, and in the 1940s, when he operated the Sun Tan Studios, he was advertised as a "noted coach" for vocalists. Later contributions to show business included the show *Mr. Swing* in 1940 and music for BILL ("Bojangles") ROBINSON revues at Harlem's Apollo Theater and at Robinson's own Mimo Club in 1941. Grainger also wrote material for other nightclub revues, such as one at Small's Paradise titled *By the Spell of the Moon* (1943). Grainger also participated in a few last recordings. Among these were a pair of J. C. Burnett sessions, on which Grainger played the organ, in 1945. Very little has come to light regarding Grainger's later years. Grainger, or someone else acting in his name, filed a copyright renewal application for the *How to Play and Sing the Blues* book in 1954. It is unlikely that he is identifiable with a Porter Grainger who died in Pennsylvania in 1964; this person was supposedly born in 1897, six years later than the year of birth Grainger gave on his draft registration.

Grainger was a versatile pianist, but not a flashy one. He seldom played solos on his records: a rare example is his solo on the Martha Copeland recording of "Nobody Rocks Me Like My Baby Do." As a composer and lyricist, Grainger was prolific, but few of his songs became major hits. The most durable are two songs that became blues perennials, "Tain't Nobody's Business if I Do" (Everett Robbins, co-author), and "Dying Crapshooter's Blues" (1927). In all likelihood, Grainger based both of these closely on pre-existing folk sources, common practice throughout the history of blues composition. "Tain't Nobody's Business" has been recorded by numerous artists, including Bessie Smith, ALBERTA HUNTER, Fats Waller, and the Ink Spots, and it is still revived by blues singers in the early twenty-first century. "Dying Crapshooter's Blues" was recorded by Martha Copeland, Viola McCoy, and Rosa Henderson in 1927. The song then entered the folk-blues orbit, and was frequently recorded as a folk blues, most notably by the Atlanta street singer BLIND WILLIE MCTELL. It also formed the basis for the pop standard "St. James Infirmary." Grainger's "Laughin' Cryin' Blues" was recorded by Sara Martin in 1923. "I Want a Long Time Daddy" was revived in 2002 for the show *Elaine Stritch at Liberty*. Among Grainger's many other songs were "What's the Matter Now" (1921), "Heart Breakin' Joe" (1923), "Honey" (1924, with Bob Ricketts), "Wylie Avenue Blues" (1927, Joe Davis, co-author), "Soul and Body" (1927), "Good Time Mama" (1927), "Fat and Greasy," (1936), "Give It to Him" (1937), "I've Got to Have My Ashes Hauled" (1937), "One Hour Mama" (1937), "Can't You Take a Little Joke" (1939), and "By an Old Southern River" (1943).

FURTHER READING
Albertson, Chris. *Bessie* (1972).

Bastin, Bruce. *Never Sell a Copyright* (1990).

Rust, Brian. *Jazz Records 1897–1942*, 4th ed. (1978).

ELLIOTT S. HURWITT

Grandmaster Flash (Joseph Saddler) (1 Jan. 1958–), disc jockey, producer, and pioneer of hip hop known for his use of turntables as a rhythmic instrument, was born Joseph Saddler in Barbados, an island in the West Indies. The Saddler family left Barbados in the 1960s and migrated to the Bronx, a borough in New York City. Saddler's father was an avid music fan and record collector. Risking punishment, Saddler would go behind his father's back to use his prized stereo equipment to listen to the albums, which led to his appreciation and interest in records and electronics. While attending Samuel Gompers Vocational Technical High School in the Bronx, Saddler was formally trained in electronics. This understanding later helped him manipulate the turntable and contribute to the creation of a new form of music. Growing up in the Bronx in the early 1970s, Saddler witnessed the emergence of the hip-hop culture. Graffiti was the dominant visual art form, break dancing was the latest dance craze, and the disc jockey emerged to provide musical entertainment at block parties throughout the borough. Saddler was immediately drawn to the sounds and techniques of neighborhood legends like DJ Pete Jones and Clive Campbell Herc (aka DJ KOOL HERC). Impressed by the crowd's reaction to Herc's technique of playing break beats of obscure music and Jones's reputation for blending the sounds of disco seamlessly, Saddler was inspired to try DJing himself and to adopt and expand on what he saw and heard.

His interest in DJing led Saddler to experiment with turntables and ultimately to invent a system that allowed him to transition from one turntable to another, thereby combining Jones's blending technique and Herc's concept of the break beat. He also developed several other techniques, such as the "quick mix theory," which makes a loop of a musical passage using duplicate records; "back spinning," in which the DJ focuses on a portion of the record and transitions to a second record with the same beat continuously; and the "clock theory," in which the DJ places the needle down on both records and alternates between the two. These techniques became standard practices in the art of DJing.

In 1976, Saddler joined "Mean" Jean Livingston's DJ crew. Saddler earned the reputation of being quick on the turntables and an inventor in electronics and style and eventually became known as Grandmaster Flash. While in the Mean Jean's crew, Saddler developed a friendship with Livingston's younger brother Theodore Livingston (aka GRANDWIZZARD THEODORE). The thirteen-year-old Livingston became Saddler's protégé and ultimately developed his own techniques such as scratching, or pulling the record back and forth under the needle to create a rhythmic sound.

The combined skill and innovation of Grandmaster Flash and Grandwizzard Theodore changed the sound of music and shifted the attention of the audience from the dance floor to the DJ table. Recognizing the importance of vocals in music, Grandmaster Flash worked with artists such as Keith Wiggins (aka Cowboy), Melvin Glover (aka Melle Mel), and Daniel Glover (aka Kidd Creole) to integrate vocals into his music. The group became known as Grandmaster Flash and the Three MCs, which, after adding two more members in the late 1970s, became Grandmaster Flash and the Furious Five. The skillful raps, costumes, and choreography landed them their first recording contract with Enjoy Records in 1979. Although their first recorded single, "Supperrappin'" was successful, it could not contend with the rival hip-hop group Sugarhill Gang's single "Rappers Delight." Frustrated by their lack of commercial exposure, Grandmaster Flash and the Furious Five left Enjoy Records and signed a contract with Sugarhill Records in 1980 because of the New Jersey–based record company's reputation for establishing the sound of hip hop beyond the local market.

In 1981, their first album with the Sugarhill Records, *The Adventures of Grandmaster Flash on the Wheels of Steel* included the single "Freedom," which showcased Saddler's style and technique on the turntables and which commercialized

Grandmaster Flash, discussing the beginning of his career at a news conference for the launch of Hip-Hop Won't Stop: The Beat, the Rhymes, the Life, an exhibit at the Smithsonian's National Museum of American History in New York City, 28 February 2006. (AP Images.)

scratching. As the group recorded other popular singles such as "The Party Song," "Birthday," "Genius of Love (It's Nasty)," and "White Lines," Grandmaster Flash and the Furious Five continued to mature musically, allowing for further creativity. In 1982 the group recorded their second album titled *The Message*. The title track of the album is a socially charged song that was informally adopted as the anthem of hip hop. Shortly after the album's release, a disagreement about the creative direction of their music, as well as mismanagement, led to the group's dissolution.

Following the breakup of Grandmaster Flash and the Furious Five, Grandmaster Flash signed with Elektra Records in 1985. His solo albums did not enjoy the positive public reception that Grandmaster Flash and the Furious Five had experienced. He spent much of the 1990s out of the public eye, instead working behind-the-scenes in the entertainment industry. In 1998 Flash was invited by actor and comedian CHRIS ROCK to be the music director for the HBO series

the *Chris Rock Show*. For four years Saddler used is DJing skills as the Master of Ceremonies for the show, spinning music in between segments of the show. Grandmaster Flash reemerged in the music industry when he appeared on several radio stations in New York City and produced his own satellite radio show, *The Flash Mash*, in 2001. In 2002 he performed at the Manchester Commonwealth Games Closing Ceremonies in England.

Grandmaster Flash has received many honors and awards for his pioneering role in DJing. In June 2004 he was inducted into the Bronx Walk of Fame with a plaque dedication at 161st Street. He was also awarded the Key to the City award in Cincinnati, Ohio, and he received the Blast Community Award for his contributions to urban arts and culture. Grandmaster Flash has also been honored for his talent and contributions to the music industry by the business community, including Microsoft, Black Entertainment Television, and the urban magazine *The Source*.

In 2004 and 2005, Grandmaster Flash worked with the New York City schools, educating students about the art and business of hip hop as well as the fundamentals of his craft. His knowledge and participation in the genesis of hip hop will be remembered by his donation of memorabilia to museums such as the Rock and Roll Hall of Fame in Cleveland, Ohio, and the Experience Music Project in Seattle, Washington, preserving his place and contributions to American music and history. In 2007, Grandmaster Flash and the Furious Five were inducted into the Rock and Roll Hall of Fame.

FURTHER READING

Chang, Jeff. *Can't Stop Won't Stop: A History of the Hip-Hop Generation* (2005).

Rose, Tricia. *Black Noise: Rap Music and Black Culture in Contemporary America* (1994).

Shapiro, Peter. *The Rough Guide to Hip-Hop: The Definitive Guide to Hip-Hop from Grandmaster Flash to Outkast and Beyond* (2005).

VONZELE DAVID REED

Grandmaster Melle Mel (Melvin Glover) (15 May 1962–), hip-hop pioneer, was born Melvin Glover in New York, New York. Glover gained widespread acclaim as the first self proclaimed emcee, Grandmaster Melle Mel of the hip-hop group Grandmaster Flash and the Furious Five.

Glover's exposure to hip hop came through parties known as "jams" in New York City. He and his older brother, Nathaniel "Nate" Glover, were originally break dancers (Nate would become Kidd Creole of the Furious Five). Citing Coke La Rock and Timmy Tim as his favorite DJs, the Glover brothers began imitating the DJ "shout outs" to the crowd but adding their own verses. Childhood friend Eddie "Scorpio" Morris joined Glover and his brother to start an MC group, the Furious Five, which included childhood friends Guy "Raheim" Williams and Keith "Cowboy" Wiggins. The group evolved with DJ GRANDMASTER FLASH, becoming Grandmaster Flash and the Furious Five in 1979. Glover credited the name "Furious Five" to the dynamic lyrical skill of the group members (allhiphop.com interview). "Superrapin'" became the group's first single with Enjoy Records in 1979. That year, the group moved to New York's Sugar Hill Records where they recorded the classic rap song "The Message." It debuted as Glover's first solo rap attempt in 1982. Glover's lyrical content reflected a socially conscious perspective of his surroundings. He released the singles "New York New York" and

"Survival (the Message 2)" about the grittiness and struggle for blacks in New York's inner city.

After legal battles with Sugar Hill Records over royalties and publishing rights, Flash and members Nate Glover and Guy Williams left the label and the group in 1983. Glover, Wiggins, and Morris remained with Sugar Hill Records and continued to call themselves the "Furious Five." Glover won legal rights to use the name "Grandmaster" and began calling himself "Grandmaster Melle Mel." In explaining the derivation of the name, Glover maintained that its use was simply a business move and was needed to distinguish his sound and style from Grandmaster Flash.

In 1983, as Grandmaster Melle Mel and the Furious Five, Glover recorded "White Lines/Don't Do It," an antidrug track that warned against the use and abuse of cocaine. The height of Glover's career was arguably 1984. That year he teamed with R&B songstress Chaka Khan on the single, "I Feel for You," which appeared in the 1984 feature film *Beat Street*. The record won a Grammy Award. The collaboration with Khan threw hip hop into the wider arena of mainstream R&B listeners. Glover later recorded "Beat Street," named after the 1984 film in which he had made a cameo appearance. Remaining aware of the social problems around him, Glover recorded "King of the Streets" and "Vice" in 1985. The latter also made it into the soundtrack to the popular television series *Miami Vice*. Glover also performed with the United Artists Against Apartheid, a charity project of the same year. In 1988 Glover recorded a reunion album with the Furious Five, *On the Strength*. Because of competition from new-school artists like Run-DMC, Eric B. and Rakim, and DJ Jazzy Jeff and the Fresh Prince, *On the Strength* gained little momentum and even less revenue. It was the last album produced by Flash and the Furious Five.

Glover, however, continued rapping and added acting to his entertainment resume. After the successful *Beat Street* and *Miami Vice* soundtrack recordings, Glover appeared as "Rap Man #1" in *Police Academy 6: City Under Siege* in 1989. Four years later, Glover reappeared on the silver screen. Alongside a cast of rising rap stars, Glover played the role of Delroy in 1993's *Who's the Man?*

Glover both recorded new tracks and used earlier releases for movie soundtracks in the 1990s and 2000s. Glover performed "Back on the Block" for the 1992 film *Black to the Promised Land*. "White Lines/Don't Do It" was heard on the *Basquiat* (1996) and *Gross Pointe Blank* (1997) soundtracks. He released an album with fellow Furious Five member Scorpio in 1997. The album, *Right Now*, failed to meet expectations, though the setback did not deter Glover. Glover also collaborated with the Sugar Hill Gang on the single "Ain't Nothin' But a Party," used in the 1998 *Dr. Dolittle* movie soundtrack. Glover also crossed over into performing on videogame soundtracks in 2002. Glover recorded "I'm a Star" for the videogame *Tony Hawk's Pro Skater 4*. And the classic "The Message" was heard on *Grand Theft Auto: Vice City*. In 2001 Glover teamed up with the rapper Rondo and formed the group Die Hard. Their first album *On Lock* was released the same year.

Glover remained true to his call for social reformation. His first children's book, *The Portal in the Park*, aimed to help children address their self-awareness and emotional development. The book came with a bonus CD of Glover's narration of the book through rap songs. Glover explained that his primary reason for writing the book was to show the positive side of rap music. In a 2006 interview with *Metro New York*, Glover expressed his disdain for hip-hop music and commented that it was "way too negative." The year 2006 also added a new dimension to Glover's career—wrestling. In the same *Metro New York* interview, Glover announced his completion of professional wrestling training from the Deep South wrestling school.

During the first decade of the twentieth century, Glover's groundbreaking lyrical contributions to hip hop began garnering him special recognition. Both he and the Furious Five accepted the 2005 VH1 Hip Hop Honors for lifetime achievement. "The Message" was heard on a 2005 episode of the television series *Everybody Hates Chris* and the 2006 film *Little Man*. Both the Furious Five group and Grandmaster Flash were inducted into the Rock and Roll Hall of Fame in March 2007.

Glover made a lasting impact on both hip hop and the African American community because of his versatility and vehement desire for change within American society. Glover's refusal to mold himself into the narrow category of "rapper" allowed him to progress as an entertainer. His influential lyrical delivery and incessant strides to advance himself helped him endure the various shifts and trends in hip-hop styles and contemporary popular black culture.

FURTHER READING

Creekmur, Chuck. Interview with Melle Mel, "The Original G.O.A.T.—Grandmaster Melle Mel." Available at www.allhiphop.com (2003).

Patalano, Heidi. "My Day: Wrestling with Rap, Children." Available at http://ny.metro.us (2006).

REGINA N. BARNETT

GrandWizzard Theodore (5 Mar. 1963–), DJ and hip-hop pioneer, was born Theodore Livingston in New York City. He was the seventh of eight children born to a single mother, Mary Livingston and, except for his first three months (spent in Harlem Hospital with infant meningitis), lived his life in the Bronx.

Livingston was best known for introducing the DJ technique known as "scratching" into the art of hip-hop DJing (also called turntablism). His invention or discovery of scratching came in the summer of 1975, when he was twelve years old. Already a professional DJ, he was playing records in his bedroom when his mother demanded that he lower the volume. Livingston had been preparing to tape a particular track and, not wanting to lose his place, kept his hand on the record. However, instead of holding it in one place, he moved the disc back and forth underneath the needle. The resulting "scratching" sound immediately appealed to him, and he soon incorporated the technique into his DJ performances. Scratching quickly caught on among hip hop DJs, and in the following years became an art in itself. Building upon Livingston's contribution, DJs invented dozens of scratches and created countless compositions derived solely from variations on the basic back and forth motion of the record (known as the "baby" scratch). Scratches, which were given names such as the crab, stab, flare, tear, scribble, and transformer, were distinguished not only by the movement of the hand on the record but also by the manipulation of the mixer, an essential tool for DJs that controls and shapes the sound coming from the turntables. Livingston also was credited with developing the "needle drop," a technique in which the turntable's tone arm (which holds the needle) was moved quickly and precisely to various parts of a record to repeat passages or create a sound collage. Although careful handling of the tone arm was a crucial skill, the needle drop did not develop into the virtuosic art to the same extent as scratching.

Livingston did not develop scratching and the needle drop in isolation. His contributions were part of the Bronx hip hop community of the early 1970s. He was influenced by a variety of pioneering figures, in particular DJ Grandmaster Flash (Joseph Sadler). Sadler kept his equipment at the Livingston apartment on E. 168th St. and Boston Rd. and visited regularly to practice with Livingston's older brother

"Mean" Gene (also a DJ). Livingston received a good deal of his musical education by observing the two DJs and by practicing on their equipment, as well as by observing and performing with a variety of other DJs (including KOOL HERC and AFRIKA BAMBAATAA) and MCs (rappers) in the emergent hip-hop community. The moniker GrandWizzard, given to him by his peers, reflected his ability to mix music of disparate styles and genres seamlessly at the turntables.

In the three decades following the development of scratching, Livingston worked both as a solo DJ and as part of various musical groups, including The L Brothers ("L" for Livingston), GrandWizzard Theodore and the Three MCs, and the Fantastic Five. As DJ, Livingston was featured in the 1982 hip hop film *Wild Style* and the 2001 documentary *Scratch*. In addition to his work as a performer, he was a frequent judge at DJ competitions (battles). He also taught the art of DJing at the Scratch DJ Academy in Manhattan and gave lecture-demonstrations across the globe, including China, Germany, Poland, Romania, Russia, and Switzerland.

FURTHER READING

Brewster, Bill, and Frank Broughton. *Last Night a DJ Saved My Life: The History of the Disc Jockey* (2000).

Chang, Jeff. *Can't Stop, Won't Stop: A History of the Hip-Hop Generation* (2005).

Fricke, Jim, and Charlie Ahearn. *Yes Yes Y'all: The Experience Music Project Oral History of Hip-Hop's First Decade* (2002).

Souvigner, Todd. *The World of DJs and the Turntable Culture* (2003).

MARK KATZ

Grandy, Moses (c. 1786– ?), slave and antislavery reformer, was born in Camden County, North Carolina, the youngest of his mother's children. The names of his parents are unknown. As he recounts in his *Narrative of the Life of Moses Grandy*, at least eight of his siblings were sold to other slave owners by their master, Billy Grandy. Moses Grandy remembered the day in his childhood when a younger brother was taken away to be sold and his panicked and grief-stricken mother tried to resist. According to his narrative, she was beaten unconscious, then tied to a peach tree and beaten again.

Grandy often played with his master's son, James, who was the same age as he. When Grandy was about eight years old, Billy Grandy died, and Grandy was given to James. Until James came of age, Grandy was hired out by auction at the beginning of each year. He had a series of masters, some of whom treated him comparatively well and others who starved and beat him.

When James turned twenty-one, he reclaimed his slaves. Grandy, who now freighted canal boats, gave part of his wages to James and part to his current employer, whose name was Grice. During this time Grandy married a slave belonging to Enoch Sawyer. Eight months into their marriage, his wife was suddenly sold to another slave owner. Despite Grandy's efforts, he never saw her again. The horror of this experience heightened Grandy's determination to purchase his own freedom and that of his loved ones.

Under Grice's urging, Grandy began to save up money to purchase his freedom from James, who demanded a sum of six hundred dollars. Rather than honor the deal, James took Grandy's money, tore up the receipts, and sold him to Mr. Trewitt, a canal boat operator, for six hundred dollars. Grandy began the process of purchasing his freedom over again, accumulating six hundred dollars in the next two-and-a-half years, only to be cheated again and sold to another slave owner.

Grandy eventually began working in the cornfields for Enoch Sawyer, his first wife's former owner. With a loan from his friend Captain Minner, Grandy finally and successfully purchased his freedom from Sawyer. Grandy repaid Captain Minner by returning to his work on canal boats. He also set about purchasing the freedom of his second wife and his children by working in coal yards and on ships. He settled in Providence, Rhode Island, and then Boston.

In the 1840s Grandy traveled to England to raise money to purchase the rest of his family. There he met the abolitionist George Thompson, a former member of the House of Commons. With Thompson's help Grandy began to appear at antislavery meetings to advertise his cause. In 1843 his *Narrative of the Life of Moses Grandy, Late a Slave in the United States of America*, was published in London. The following year, the narrative was published in Boston under the auspices of the American Anti-Slavery Society. In his introduction, Thompson emphasizes his preservation of Grandy's language and point of view, writing, "I have carefully abstained from casting a single reflection or animadversion of my own. I leave the touching story of the self-liberated captive to speak for itself." Grandy's narrative was a popular success, going through two English and three American editions in two years.

Grandy's life exemplifies the common tragedy of slave families, who were separated and sold off with little regard for ties of kinship. Grandy's plight also demonstrates the lack of legal rights accorded to slave marriage. In the years following emancipation, some slaves attempted to reunite with their families, only to discover that their spouses had remarried and established new families. Like the narratives of CHARLES BALL, JOSIAH HENSON, and LEWIS CLARKE, the *Narrative of the Life of Moses Grandy* is an example of an "as told to" slave narrative, a form that allowed even illiterate slaves and former slaves to publish their stories.

FURTHER READING

Grandy, Moses. *Narrative of the Life of Moses Grandy, Late a Slave in the United States of America* (1843).

Andrews, William L. *To Tell a Free Story: The First Century of Afro-American Autobiography, 1760–1865* (1986).

Starling, Marion Wilson. *The Slave Narrative: Its Place in American History* (1982).

JULIA LEE

Granger, Lester Blackwell (16 Sept. 1896–9 Jan. 1976), social scientist and former executive secretary of the National Urban League, was born in Newport News, Virginia, one of six sons of William Randolph Granger, a physician from Barbados, and Mary L. Turpin Granger, a local teacher. Granger earned his BA degree from Dartmouth College in 1918, but his dream of pursuing a law degree was derailed by the outbreak of World War I, during which he served as a lieutenant in the U.S. Army in the Ninety-second Infantry Division.

Following his military service, Granger returned to New Jersey and joined the New Jersey Urban League, where he briefly served as the industrial secretary for the Newark affiliate. In 1920 he moved to North Carolina in order to teach at the Slater Normal School in Winston-Salem and at St. Augustine College in Raleigh. Two years later Granger returned to New Jersey, having accepted a job as an extension worker at the Manual Training and Industrial School for Colored Youth in Bordentown, New Jersey, a position he retained until 1934. It was in Bordentown that he met Harriet Lane, whom he married in August 1923. During the early to mid-1920s Granger also pursued graduate studies at New York University and the New School of Social Work.

Upon his departure from the Manual Training and Industrial School for Colored Youth, Granger began work at the New York office of the National Urban League. There he headed the Workers Bureau and even became the first business manager of the League's magazine *Opportunity*. His vigorous leadership led to the creation of the Workers Councils, which promoted trade unionism among African American workers and challenged the racial discrimination they faced from their employers and the labor organizations that were set up to protect their rights. In 1938 he took a two-year leave of absence to work with the New York City Welfare Council, but he returned to the National Urban League in 1940 to serve as assistant executive secretary in charge of industrial relations. He was promoted to executive secretary in 1941, and he remained at this position for the following twenty years.

The 1940s saw Granger's increasingly active participation in the struggle against racial segregation, especially in military service and defense employment. Even while at the helm of the National Urban League, where the focus of his duties was social service, Granger participated in a number of political movements, including the March on Washington movement, which he joined in 1941. Granger's commitment to equality in military service received broad recognition in 1945, during which year he served as a special adviser on race relations to Secretary of the Navy James Forrestal and was awarded the U.S. Navy's highest civilian award, the Distinguished Civilian Service Medal. Two years later President Truman awarded Granger the Medal of Merit, expressing gratitude to Granger as a man who contributed "more than any other person to the effective utilization of Negro personnel in the service" (Ploski, 293). In 1948 President Truman personally appointed Granger to the Committee on Equality of Treatment and Opportunity in the Armed Services. This five-man committee pressed for the integration of the armed services, which was achieved in 1950.

One of the most noteworthy innovations Granger implemented during his service in the National Urban League was the creation of the Pilot Placement Project. This program was aimed at placing blacks in positions from which they were previously barred. Additionally Granger helped establish a Commerce and Industry Council and Trade Union Advisory Council, which became the nexus of business support for the League, thus ensuring cooperation from various organizations. During his time as executive secretary of the Urban League, the number of local affiliates grew from forty-one to sixty-five and the organization's budget rose from $600,000 to $4.5 million.

Granger's innumerable efforts in the sphere of social service did not go unrecognized. In 1951 he became the first African American to be nominated as president of the National Conference of Social Work, and just ten years later he was elected in Rome as the president of the International Conference of Social Work.

When Granger retired at age sixty-five from the National Urban League in October 1961, President Eisenhower praised him for his character and integrity. In the years following his retirement Granger taught at Dillard University in New Orleans, Louisiana, where he was named an Amistad Scholar in Residence. After a lifetime of public service, Lester Granger died in 1976 in Alexandria, Louisiana.

FURTHER READING

Lester B. Granger's papers are housed in the Amistad Research Center at Tulane University in New Orleans.

Parris, Guichard, and Lester Brooks. *Blacks in the City: A History of the National Urban League* (1971).

Wormley, L. Stanton, and Lewis H. Fenderson. *Many Shades of Black* (1969).

Obituary: *New York Times*, 10 June 1976.

LATICIA ANN MARIE WILLIS

Grant, Frank (1 Aug. 1865–27 May 1937), baseball player, was born Ulysses F. Grant in Pittsfield, Massachusetts, the youngest of seven children born to Franklin Grant, a farm laborer, and his wife, Frances. The family had come to Pittsfield from Dalton, Massachusetts, possibly because of Franklin's death. In any event, census records indicate that Franklin was not with the family when it relocated to Williamstown, Massachusetts, in 1870. There Frances was employed as a domestic servant while her sons assisted in keeping house and worked as waiters in a local restaurant. While the Grants were not a wealthy family they made a comfortable life in Williamstown and may have even owned their own home.

Frank Grant, however, chose to seek his fortune on the ball field. An outstanding baseball player he was already a local star when he pitched and caught for Pittsfield's amateur hometown team at the age of seventeen. The next year he moved on to play for another amateur side from Plattsburgh, New York. In 1886 he entered organized baseball with the Eastern League team from Meriden, Connecticut. The diminutive Grant, standing a little over five feet seven and weighing 155 pounds, did not look like an imposing player. Nevertheless he was a ferocious

power hitter, possessed terrific speed, and was an agile, acrobatic fielder. One New England legend even had it that Grant once scaled a telegraph pole in order to snag a fly ball. Those who saw him play were left with little doubt that he was a rare talent.

In 1886 Grant was hitting a superb .325 in thirty-three games with Meriden when the team disbanded, possibly for financial reasons. Grant and several white teammates were signed by Buffalo of the International Association. In forty-five games with the Bisons, Grant hit .340, one of the best marks on the team. At the time Grant, who had been mistaken for a Spaniard by the Buffalo *Express* because of his light skin, was one of a number of black baseball players in organized baseball, the most notable of whom were the brothers Moses and Weldy Walker. Two years earlier, in 1884, the Walker brothers had played for a Major League club in Toledo, Ohio. Because segregation had not yet become institutionalized in the sport, there was no official Negro League. While it was certainly difficult for a black man to succeed in organized baseball, it was not unheard of. The careers of men like Grant, the Walkers, the second baseman BUD FOWLER, and the pitcher GEORGE STOVEY were a testament to that rare opportunity. It was an opportunity that would soon be lost.

In 1887 the Bisons finished second in the International Association with Grant starring at second base. In 105 games he hit eleven home runs, a prodigious number for the time and tops in the league. In addition to placing among the circuit leaders in doubles and batting average, he also stole forty bases. Fans and writers began calling him the "Black Dunlap" after white second baseman Frank "Sure Shot" Dunlap of the St. Louis Browns, the nonpareil of the position in those years. Yet, despite his outstanding numbers and the growing sense that he was the finest player ever to take the field for Buffalo, Grant's position was precarious. While there was no enforced segregation in organized baseball, black players like Grant were still prime targets of the era's virulent racism. Black players suffered constant verbal abuse from the stands and opposing benches. Black pitchers couldn't count on their own white teammates to play honest defense behind them. Grant's Buffalo teammates refused to have their photo taken with him while white players on other teams went out of their way to spike him (that is, slide into him with their spiked shoes), forcing the second baseman to choose between staying out of the game or playing in near constant pain. It has been widely suggested by baseball historians and journalists that

Grant responded to these attacks by inventing the first shin guards. A shift to the outfield may have saved Grant from the spiking, but opposing pitchers continued to throw at him regularly. That same year the directors of the International League responded to the increasing call for segregation by prohibiting the signing of additional black players. Black players already under contract, like Grant or MOSES WALKER, were allowed to remain with their teams. They would not stay long. Despite another fine hitting campaign Grant was dismissed from Buffalo at the end of the 1888 season. The descent of the color line was complete. It would remain a part of organized baseball until 1947 and Jackie Robinson's arrival on the diamond in Brooklyn.

Though barred from organized ball Grant was far from finished with the sport. For the rest of his nineteen-year career, he starred on black baseball teams like the Cuban Giants, barnstorming around the country. He retired for good in 1903 after a season with the Colored Capital All-Americans of Lansing, Michigan. Little is known of Grant's life after his departure from baseball. Census data from 1910 located him in Greenwich Village, New York, living with a wife, Celia, of five years and her son, Frank Moore. He also had a number of nieces and nephews living in Massachusetts. As he had in his youth, he found work as a waiter, porter, and hotel worker.

Grant died in 1937, just a few months shy of his seventy-second birthday. His death was reported in newspaper obituaries and the legendary Negro League pitcher SMOKEY JOE WILLIAMS served as one of his pallbearers. Though impoverished at the end of his life Grant left behind a rich legacy that many years later began to receive its due recognition. He was selected by a committee of experts for induction into the Baseball Hall of Fame in 2006, joining sixteen other black baseball players and executives. Many of the same experts hold Grant to be the finest black baseball player of his era, a tremendous talent who succeeded in the face of tremendous adversity.

FURTHER READING
Hogan, Lawrence D. *Shades of Glory: The Negro Leagues and the Story of African-American Baseball* (2006).
Peterson, Robert. *Only the Ball Was White: A History of Legendary Black Players and All-Black Professional Teams* (1970).
Riley, James A. *The Biographical Encyclopedia of the Negro Baseball Leagues* (2002).

NATHAN M. CORZINE

Granville, Evelyn Boyd (1 May 1924–), mathematician, college professor, and public school reformer, was born Evelyn Boyd, the second of two girls of William Boyd, a blue-collar worker who held various jobs as a custodian, chauffeur, and messenger, and Julia Walker Boyd, a civil servant who worked for the Bureau of Engraving and Printing during the Depression. Granville received her early education in the pre–*Brown v. Board of Education* era of "separate but equal" public schools for blacks and whites. Despite the dual system, Boyd would later insist that she received a quality education in elementary and middle school, and later at Dunbar High School, one of three public high schools in the Washington, D.C., area designated for black students. Dunbar had a reputation for high academic standards and for emphasizing the importance of racial pride and personal excellence. Recalling that period, Granville writes: "My generation benefited by being brought up in a culture that prized education and stressed education as a means of improving the quality of one's life…. We listened and we learned. And we succeeded" (Granville, 2005, 273–274).

Boyd graduated Dunbar in 1941 as one of five-valedictorians. She was accepted at and attended the all-female Smith College in Northampton, Massachusetts—one of fewer than ten black students on a campus of 2,000. Though Boyd had no financial aid from the institution that first year, her aunt, Louise Walker, was determined that her niece would attend an Ivy League college and helped with the fees. Boyd also won a small scholarship from the Phi Delta Kappa sorority for black teachers. Financial support from her mother and a part-time job as a waitress helped with the remaining expenses. She pursued a major in mathematics and theoretical physics but also studied astronomy. She was elected to the Phi Beta Kappa national honor society and the Sigma Xi scientific honor society, eventually won scholarship support from Smith, and graduated summa cum laude in 1945 with honors in Mathematics.

Boyd was accepted at Yale University for graduate study, completing double master's degrees in Theoretical Physics and Mathematics in one year, 1946. She continued at Yale for the doctoral degree, conducting research under the tutelage of Einar Hille, the former president of the American Mathematical Society, in the area of functional analysis. In 1949 Boyd earned the distinction of becoming the second known African American woman to earn the doctoral degree in Mathematics.

Her dissertation was titled "On Laguerre Series in the Complex Domain."

Boyd spent a year doing post-doctoral research at New York University before accepting a faculty appointment at Fisk University, a historically black college in Nashville, Tennessee. There Boyd worked alongside Lee Lorch, a white faculty member who would eventually be exiled to Canada because of his civil and human rights activism. Boyd found herself participating in the struggle, albeit briefly. When black faculty were refused admission to the banquet of the annual meeting of the southeastern region of the Mathematical Association of America in Nashville in 1951, Boyd spoke out. She joined her colleagues and issued a letter that launched the first efforts to desegregate the meetings of the American Mathematical Society and the Mathematical Association of America. While at Fisk, Boyd also taught two black women who would later earn the doctoral degree in mathematics, VIVIENNE LUCILLE MALONE MAYES, who received her doctorate from the University of Texas at Austin in 1966, and ETTA ZUBER FALCONER, who received the PhD in Mathematics from the Atlanta-based Emory University in 1969.

Boyd would only stay at Fisk two years before returning to Washington, D.C., in July 1952 to work at the National Bureau of Standards (NBS), a federal government agency focused on refining the science of measurement and developing precise engineering standards needed for advanced technologies. At the NBS (known as the National Institute of Standards and Technology beginning in 1988), Boyd consulted with engineers and scientists on mathematical analyses of problems related to missile fuzes, the devices and arrangements that cause the missile's explosive charge to function in proper relation to the target. But Boyd's position at the NBS was short-lived as well. She left after three years and in January 1956 went to work for IBM, first in Washington, D.C., and later at a subsidiary (the Service Bureau Corporation) in New York City. Computers were in their infancy, and Boyd developed early programs for the IBM 650, a state-of-the-art system at the time.

Boyd enjoyed her work but did not like the expense of living in New York. So when IBM opened a computing center in Washington, D.C., to plan, write, and maintain computer programs for the National Aeronautics and Space Administration (NASA), she transferred. Boyd joined a team of other mathematicians and scientists writing computer programs to track vehicles in space as part of the Project Vanguard and Project Mercury space. For Boyd, developing real-time calculations in support of the satellite launchings was one of the most interesting jobs of her lifetime.

In 1960, Boyd married the Reverend Gamaliel Mansfield, a minister at a local church in Los Angeles whom she had met during a previous summer vacation. She left IBM and moved to her husband's home in California, where she joined the Computation and Data Reduction Center of the Space Technology Laboratories, continuing to do research on orbit computations from 1960 to 1961. The period saw a high demand for mathematicians and scientists to join private industries engaged in defense-related work and the newly emerging electronic computer field. Boyd took advantage of the opportunities, unique for black, female mathematicians, most of whom worked as teachers. In 1962 she joined the North American Aviation Company (NAA), which had been awarded a contract by NASA to help design the early Apollo space shuttle. At NAA, Boyd worked as a research specialist in numerical and trajectory analyses, orbit computations, celestial mechanics, and digital computer techniques. Boyd would only stay a short while with NAA before returning to IBM the following year in 1963.

In 1967 Boyd divorced her first husband, resigned from IBM, and returned to higher education as assistant professor of mathematics at California State University, Los Angeles (CSULA). The move back to academia proved a good one and personally fulfilling. In addition to teaching classes in computer programming and numerical analysis at CSULA, Boyd worked with elementary school youth in a state-sponsored mathematics improvement program (1968–1969); provided training in a National Science Foundation–sponsored elementary school teacher preparation program (1972); and coauthored a college textbook, *Theory and Application of Mathematics for Teachers*. The textbook was released in 1975, reprinted in 1978, and adopted by more than fifty colleges.

Boyd retired from CSULA in 1984 and moved to a sixteen-acre farm in East Texas with her second husband, Edward V. Granville, a Los Angeles real estate broker she had married in 1970; they had no children. She would emerge from retirement twice to teach, first at the historically black Texas College in Tyler, Texas, from 1985 to 1988; and again as the Sam A. Lindsey Professor of Mathematics at the University of Texas in Tyler from 1990 to 1997. After retiring for a third time in 1997, Granville was invited to participate in the Dow Chemical campaign to recruit students to the study of science and mathematics—an area of concern shared by private industry and government. For Granville, one solution to the problem lay in her own personal experiences, the role and influence of competent, well-trained teachers who want to teach and who care for their students. The right to a first-rate education, Granville argued, should be listed beside other civil liberties if every child is to have the tools to survive, thrive, and go as far as their talents can take them.

FURTHER READING

Granville, Evelyn Boyd. "Looking Back … Looking Ahead," in *Complexities: Women in Mathematics*, eds. Bettye Anne Case and Anne M. Leggett (2005).

Granville, Evelyn Boyd. "My Life as a Mathematician," *SAGE: A Scholarly Journal on Black Women* (Fall, 1989).

Scriven, Olivia A. "The Politics of Particularism: HBCUs, Spelman College, and the Struggle to Educate Black Women in Science, 1950–1997," PhD diss., Georgia Institute of Technology (2006).

Warren, Wini. *Black Women Scientists in the United States* (1999).

OLIVIA A. SCRIVEN

Gravely, Samuel Lee, Jr. (4 June 1922–22 Oct. 2004), naval officer, was born in Richmond, Virginia, the son and eldest child of Samuel Lee Gravely Sr. and Mary George Simon Gravely. The family resided in Fulton's Bottom, one of the city's older and poorest neighborhoods, and the elder Gravely supported his family on a modest income as a U.S. postal worker in the mail-handling department. Mrs. Gravely was a homemaker who died when Samuel was fifteen years old. The couple had four other children.

Gravely worked at various jobs and ran errands to save for college, and after graduation from Armstrong High School he enrolled at Virginia Union University in Richmond in fall 1940. Athletically talented, he aspired to become a football coach, but he put those plans on hold following the Japanese attack on Pearl Harbor on 7 December 1941. After having completed only two years of college, he enlisted in the Naval Reserve on 15 September 1942. Although he was originally assigned to be a fireman apprentice at the Great Lakes Naval Training Station at North Chicago, Illinois, he demonstrated such potential that in 1943 he was permitted to enter the officers' training program, known at that time as the V-12 program. He finished the course on 14 December 1944, thereby gaining the first Naval Reserve Officer's commission ever earned by an African American (at the rank of ensign). During the course of his training program he had had the occasion to study in New York and New Jersey and at the University of California at Los Angeles. It would not be for another eleven years after receiving his commission that he would be transferred from the reserve into the regular navy; in all, he would serve in the naval reserve and the regular navy for thirty-eight years (1942–1980).

The first African American officers endured hostility, prejudice, and even bullying with calm and determination. The potential for danger—or at least humiliation—was always present. Segregation was the rule of the day, and Gravely and other black officers were socially shunned by their white counterparts; for a time they were not allowed into the officers' clubs. Shortly after being commissioned, Gravely was subjected to the blatant discrimination that black service personnel in the South usually experienced. While on leave in Miami, Florida, he was briefly jailed on the charge of impersonating a naval officer. Reporting for active duty at Camp Robert Smalls, he was immediately named assistant battalion commander. Before long he was assigned to service onboard USS *PC-1264* and was dispatched to the combat zone. The vessel was a patrol boat with "submarine chaser" duties. The first African American naval officer to serve in a combat situation, Gravely remained on active duty until April 1946.

Gravely resumed his studies at Virginia Union University in 1946 and in 1948 graduated with a BA degree in history. He married Alma Bernice Clark in 1946, and the couple would rear three children: sons Robert Michael Gravely and David Edward Gravely and daughter Tracey E. Gravely. Following this hiatus, during which time his status was officially that of a drilling reservist, Gravely was promoted to lieutenant, junior grade, in August 1949 and recalled to active duty and assigned as a Naval Services recruiter. This coincided with and was indeed directly contingent upon President Harry S. Truman's Executive Order 9981, committing the administration to a policy of integrating the armed services.

During the Korean War, Gravely served onboard the battleship USS *Iowa*. In 1955 he was transferred from the reserve into the regular navy at the rank of lieutenant. From that point on he rose steadily through the ranks to become the first African American to make commander, then captain, then rear admiral (1971), and finally vice admiral (1976). In 1962, during the Vietnam War, Gravely was elevated to command the radar picket ship USS *Falgout* and thus became the first African American to command a fighting ship. As rear admiral he was appointed to take charge of USS *Jouett*, while his vice admiral's commission elevated him to the command of the entire U.S. Third Fleet stationed at Pearl Harbor. He retained the Fleet appointment from 1976 to 1978. He was then transferred to administrative duty as director of the Defense Communications Agency from 1978 to 1980. In the course of his naval career he was further entrusted as commanding officer of USS *Taussig* and USS *Theodore E. Chandler*. He served additional tours of duty onboard USS *Toledo* and USS *Seminole*. When not engaged in administrative tasks, Gravely devoted time to the National Naval Officers Association (NNOA), an organization designed to mentor junior officers. Gravely was prominent among those who served as "sea daddies" to provide counseling and support to the younger officers. His efforts were recognized by the NNOA when the membership voted to sponsor a scholarship for high school graduates seeking to enter a college degree program. In recognition of his long and distinguished naval career, in 1977 the Richmond City Council voted to rename Nicholson Street (where Gravely's family once resided) Admiral Gravely Boulevard. He was the recipient of the Legion of Merit, the Bronze Star, the Meritorious Service Medal, and Navy Commendation Medals.

After his retirement from the U.S. Navy in August of 1980, Samuel Gravely took up residence in Haymarket, Maryland, and was actively involved in a variety of ventures and community service activities. He served as a consultant for Automated Business Systems and Services, head of the Virginia Union University Alumni Association, chair of the board of directors of the Tredegar National Civil War Center Foundation (2000–2002), senior corporate adviser for Potomac Systems Engineering, and on the Charles Stark Draper Laboratory board of directors. He wrote about African Americans' experiences going through the V-12 program in an article, "A Few Beers Ain't All Bad" (*Naval History* 7.1 [Spring 1993]).

The admiral continued these activities despite his declining health. In October 2004 he was admitted to Bethesda Naval Hospital for treatment for an infection of the bloodstream and suffered a stroke. He died at Bethesda and was interred at Arlington National Cemetery on 17 December 2004.

FURTHER READING

"Oral History Recollections of Vice Admiral Samuel L. Gravely, Jr.," compiled by the U.S. Naval Institute (2003).

Nelson, Dennis D. *The Integration of the Negro into the U.S. Navy* (1982).

Northrup, Herbert R., et al. *Black and Other Minority Participation in the All-Volunteer Navy and Marine Corps* (1979).

Stillman, Paul, ed. *The Golden Thirteen: Recollections of the First Black Naval Officers* (1994).

Obituaries: *Richmond Free Press*, 28–30 Oct. 2004; *Richmond Times-Dispatch*, 24 Oct. 2004.

RAYMOND PIERRE HYLTON

Graves, Denyce (7 Mar. 1964–), opera singer, was born in Washington, D.C., the daughter of Dorothy Graves (later Graves-Kenner) and Charles Graves, who left the family when Graves was one year old. As a single mother in one of the poorest areas of the nation's capital, Dorothy Graves worked in a laundry and as a typist to support her three children. She also designed evening activities to protect them from the hardscrabble streets of Southwest D.C., including regular church attendance, which is where Graves began her singing career as part of a family group called the Inspirational Children of

Denyce Graves, rehearsing her role as the title character in the opera *Margaret Garner* at the Detroit Opera House, 14 April 2005. (AP Images.)

God. Graves's early interest in music made her the butt of jokes among many of the children in her neighborhood, who accused her of wanting to be white and dubbed her "Hollywood."

At W. B. Patterson Elementary School, Graves attracted the attention of the music teacher, Judith Grove, who was impressed with her determination. Grove later encouraged the young singer to apply for admission to the DUKE ELLINGTON School of the Arts. Graves's initial interest in opera was awakened during her time at the school, as she and a friend skipped class one day to listen to an album of arias by the famed soprano LEONTYNE PRICE. Graves was mesmerized and found herself thinking, "I can do that." (*Ebony*, 1 Feb. 1996) She began even more serious work on her voice and landed a scholarship to Oberlin College, well known for its excellent classical voice program. When her music teacher at Oberlin left for the New England Conservatory of Music, Graves followed and continued her vocal education there. In 1986, while still in school, Graves participated in the regional Metropolitan Opera auditions and won a spot at the national competition in New York City. Unfortunately, disaster struck before that competition as Graves began experiencing serious vocal problems, which doctors were unable to diagnose. Graves quit singing and got a job as a secretary, believing her career was over before it had even gotten started. However, she finally found a doctor who correctly diagnosed her vocal difficulties as stemming from a treatable thyroid problem. Then came an opportunity Graves later attributed to divine intervention: the Houston Grand Opera called, encouraging her to audition for its renowned young artists' program, an apprenticeship that launched many successful opera careers. Graves turned them down twice, saying she was no longer singing, before finally accepting and heading to Houston in 1988. Her time in this program gained her valuable experience as well as the attention and support of the superstar tenor Placido Domingo. Later in her career, Graves would sing opposite Domingo many times in both Saint-Saëns's *Samson et Dalila* and Bizet's *Carmen*. In 1989 Graves also met David Perry, a classical guitarist, whom she married in 1990. Though her choice to marry a white man initially caused consternation in her family, Perry was soon accepted as Graves's life and business partner and took an active role in developing her career.

The 1990s marked Graves's rapid rise to superstardom in the opera world. She began the decade by receiving the 1991 Marian Anderson Award, which recognizes artists who are also committed to improving society. While Graves sang leading roles in smaller companies prior to 1995, that October brought her Metropolitan Opera debut in the title role of *Carmen*. Following this performance, she was deluged with offers to play Bizet's sensual, provocative gypsy, and she was often regarded as *the* Carmen, performing the role regularly at most of the world's leading opera houses, including the Met, Vienna Staatsoper, Royal Opera-Covent Garden, Opéra National de Paris, Chicago Lyric Opera, Bayerische Staatsoper, and Teatro Real in Madrid. Her other signature role developed during this decade as well: Dalila in Saint-Saëns's operatic re-telling of the Biblical story of Samson and Delilah. One might question whether or not there is some racial typecasting in Graves's immense popularity in the two roles, both of them highly sexualized women who are racially or ethnically "other." In fact, Graves noted in a 1996 article that "I've had other black artists say to me, 'They will allow you to sing Carmen. It's easy for them to see you as this wild, out-of-control sexual being because that's an image they have of black women'" (*Washingtonian Magazine*, Dec. 1996). Nonetheless, Graves was usually credited with bringing particular depth to her depiction of Carmen, portraying her as an "unhappy woman afraid of love because love is a loss of power" (*Washingtonian Magazine*, Dec. 1996). And while Carmen and Dalila became signature and financially rewarding roles for Graves, she also performed a variety of other roles during the 1990s, including Charlotte in Massenet's *Werther* and Adalgisa in Bellini's *Norma*.

After her dizzying rise to fame in the nineties, 2000–2001 marked a year of both vocal and personal struggles for Graves. She suffered from excruciating cluster headaches, and began experiencing problems with her voice and eventually lost it completely, experienced bleeding, and needed surgery to remove a non-cancerous polyp. Graves sank into depression. She nevertheless managed to meet most of her professional obligations during this time, including singing at the memorial service held at the National Cathedral in Washington, D.C., following the terrorist attacks of 11 September 2001. Her renditions of "America the Beautiful" and "The Lord's Prayer" deeply moved a nation in mourning. While she recovered from her vocal problems, her marriage to David Perry came to an end, and she remarried Vincent Thomas, a French flautist, and, having been told that she would never bear children after undergoing several surgeries to remove fibroid tumors, gave birth to Ella-Thaïs Thomas in 2005.

Graves marked another career milestone in 2005 by singing the title role, written specifically for her, in the new American opera *Margaret Garner*, based on the true story of the escaped slave woman who in 1856 killed one of her children and attempted to kill the others and herself rather than return to slavery. Composed by Richard Danielpour with a libretto by the Nobel-laureate TONI MORRISON, the opera was co-commissioned by the Detroit Opera, the Cincinnati Opera, and the Opera Company of Philadelphia and enjoyed highly publicized and successful runs in each city; it also attracted some of the most diverse audiences American opera had ever seen and offered exciting, respectful roles for African American singers. Graves continued to branch out from her usual roles by playing Judith in Bartok's *Bluebeard's Castle* with the Los Angeles Opera in 2002 and Azucena in Verdi's *Il Trovatore* with the Washington Opera in 2004.

Graves was also among those rare opera singers who gained some recognition outside opera circles. An appearance on *Oprah* following the 9/11 memorial service, performances for both the Clinton and George W. Bush White Houses, profiles in such popular magazines as *Vogue* and *Essence*, a popular PBS television special titled *A Cathedral Christmas*, and an educational project called *Breaking the Rules* were all means by which Graves reached a wider audience.

FURTHER READING

Graves, Denyce, with Marilyn Molloy. "Diva," *Essence Magazine* (Sept. 1996).

Haywood, Richette L. "New Diva on the Block," *Ebony* (1 Feb, 1996).

Kellow, Brian. "Diva, Inc," *Opera News* (Sept. 2001).

Tucker, Neely. "Denyce Graves, After the Low Notes: D.C.-Born Mezzo-Soprano Reclaims the Stage, Her Life," *Washington Post*, 24 Oct. 2004.

CHRISTINA G. BUCHER

Graves, Earl (9 Jan. 1935–), entrepreneur and publisher, was born Earl Gilbert Graves in Brooklyn, New York, the oldest of the four children of Earl Godwyn Graves and Winifred Sealy, both the children of immigrants from Barbados. Graves's parents were very different people, yet both had characteristics that would influence his career. His father, an assistant manager at the Overland Garment Company, an apparel firm in New York City, was very serious and demanding, while his mother was outgoing and

involved in a host of community activities. Graves has credited his work ethic, salesmanship, and drive to his father and his involvement in various causes and organizations to the example of his mother. Growing up, Graves always looked for opportunities to make money. At age six he sold Christmas cards to neighbors. Later, while attending Morgan State University in the early 1950s, Graves worked two jobs at once. Seeing the reluctance of local white florists to make deliveries on the predominantly black campus, he started a small business selling flowers. When Graves decided to major in economics at Morgan State, his decision was ridiculed; the corporate world was not considered a viable career option for African Americans. Undeterred, Graves continued in his course of study.

After graduating from Morgan State in 1957, Graves entered the army, became a paratrooper, and eventually rose to the rank of captain in the Nineteenth Special Forces Group, the Green Berets.

Earl Graves, publisher and CEO of *Black Enterprise Magazine*, posing with his book *How to Succeed in Business Without Being White*, in New York City's Times Square, 17 April 1997. (AP Images.)

In 1960, while in the service, he married Barbara Eliza Kydd. With children on the way, Graves left the army and the couple returned to Brooklyn, where he worked as a real estate agent. Graves, who had taken a real estate course in college, sold nine houses in his first three months.

Feeling the need to become more involved in politics, Graves wrote a letter to the Democratic National Committee (DNC) and was soon volunteering for the 1964 presidential campaign. His work with the DNC led to a job as an administrative assistant to the newly elected senator Robert F. Kennedy, a position he held for the next three years.

For the first time Graves was exposed to extraordinary wealth and the power of money. If Kennedy wanted something, he was able to get it. Graves often recalled Kennedy's response when Graves informed him that former astronaut John Glenn, with whom the senator wished to speak, was on a rafting trip in Colorado. "Well, Graves," Kennedy exclaimed, "he won't be on the raft all day and when he gets off, I want to talk to him" (Graves, 119). Those in power, Graves learned, get things done. The larger lesson, a realization that drove the rest of Graves's professional life, was that money, above all other resources, can acquire the power to influence social and political causes.

After Robert Kennedy's assassination in 1968 many of his staffers were offered jobs or work-study grants, and Graves landed a seat on the advisory board of the Small Business Administration (SBA). The same year he established the consulting firm Earl G. Graves Associates (later Earl G. Graves Limited), to advise corporations about economic development and urban affairs. Around this time Graves conceived the idea to create a newsletter that would chronicle the successes of, and issues relevant to, black businesspeople and also raise awareness of the importance of black consumer power. At the suggestion of the SBA's director, Howard Samuels, Graves decided to publish a full-fledged monthly magazine, and in August 1970 *Black Enterprise* was born.

In its early days *Black Enterprise* had trouble convincing much of corporate America that African Americans were interested in business. After all, out of three thousand senior-level executives at major corporations, only three were black. Potential advertisers questioned whether there were enough stories for *Black Enterprise* to tell, and they doubted the power of the African American market to buy the pricey items the big corporations produced. As a result, the magazine initially depended on the advertising of tobacco, liquor, and low-priced automobile companies. Financial support from other sectors, such as technology and securities industries and luxury car makers, took years of effort, with Graves leading the way, before big companies came to respect African American consumers. Despite these challenges, *Black Enterprise* was profitable by its tenth issue. By bringing stories and information to the marketplace that many mainstream media outlets had been ignoring, the magazine soon established itself as a premier magazine for African Americans. In 1973 the magazine introduced one of its most popular creations, the BE 100s, an annual list of the nation's largest black-owned businesses. By 2002 *Black Enterprise* had a circulation of 475,000 and annual revenues of more than $53 million.

In addition to *Black Enterprise* and *Black Enterprise's Teenpreneur*, launched in 2002, Earl G. Graves Limited publishes a host of print and electronic material, arranges high-profile conferences for black businesspeople, and sponsors the Greenwich Street Corporate Growth Fund, a venture capital fund that supports midsized black-owned businesses. While he has remained dedicated to the magazine, Graves's entrepreneurial spirit has not been limited to publishing endeavors. In 1990 he bought the bottling franchise Pepsi-Cola of Washington, D.C. Graves sold the franchise back to the parent company in 1998 and remains active at Pepsi as the chairman of the company's Advisory and Ethnic Marketing Committee.

Because of his wide array of activities, Graves has become one of the most important champions of black capitalism. His book, *How to Succeed in Business Without Being White* (1997), part autobiography and part career guide, made the *New York Times* and *Wall Street Journal* best-seller lists. Graves has served as a trustee or on the board of directors of many companies and organizations, including Aetna Foundation, Inc., AMR Corporation (American Airlines), Federated Department Stores, Inc., Rohm and Haas Company, DaimlerChrysler AG, the Steadman Hawkins Sports Medicine Foundation, the Schomburg Center for Research in Black Culture, the Boy Scouts of America, Howard University, and the Committee for Economic Development. He has supported numerous causes, including his alma mater, Morgan State University, to which he donated $1 million in 1995. Graves served as a civilian aide to the secretary of the U.S. Army from 1978 to 1980.

In addition to more than four dozen honorary degrees, Graves has received numerous awards and honors, including the RONALD H. BROWN Leadership

Award from the U.S. Department of Commerce, the NAACP Spingarn Medal, induction into the Black College Hall of Fame, and election into the American Academy of Arts and Sciences. In 2002 he was appointed to the presidential commission charged with developing a plan for the establishment of a National Museum of African American History and Culture. Named one of the fifty most powerful and influential African Americans in corporate America by *Fortune* magazine in 2002, Graves has become a widely sought after as a speaker.

Graves has taken steps to make sure that Earl G. Graves Limited lives long into the future. Each of his three sons has taken an active role in the company, though as of 2007 Graves remained chairman of the magazine he started. In August 2000, on its thirtieth anniversary, Graves quoted FREDERICK DOUGLASS in illuminating *Black Enterprise*'s efforts: "If there is no struggle, there is no progress…. This struggle may be a moral one or a physical one but it must be a struggle. Power concedes nothing without demand."

FURTHER READING

Graves, Earl G. *How to Succeed in Business Without Being White* (1997).

Bell, Gregory S. *In the Black: A History of African Americans on Wall Street* (2001).

Edmond, Alfred, Jr. "Earl G. Graves: On the Record," *Black Enterprise* (Aug. 1995).

Weeks, Linton. "The Sweet Smell of Success," *Washington Post*, 17 June 1997.

GREGORY S. BELL

Graweere, John (c. 1615– ?), servant and legal pioneer, was born Joao Geaween in Africa, probably in Angola, and was among the first generation of Africans captured and brought to the English colony of Virginia in the late 1620s and early 1630s. At that time, indentured servants from the British Isles vastly outnumbered the few hundred Africans in the colony. Graweere worked as a servant near James City for a white colonist, William Evans. It is not clear whether Graweere was a servant for life or for a fixed term, but like most early Virginia settlers, white and black, he probably helped to cultivate and harvest his master's tobacco, which became the colony's staple export commodity in the 1620s. Court records show, however, that Evans also allowed his servant Graweere to "keep hogs and make the best benefit thereof to himself provided that … Evans might have half the increase" of any livestock Graweere was able to raise (Higginbotham, 1978,

25). Such conditions were nearly always dependent on the whim of the master, however. Unlike the case for white servants in the colonies, there were no formal contracts between black laborers and their masters in colonial Virginia.

The frontier conditions of early Virginia also ensured African settlers somewhat greater freedom in social relations than in later years. In 1635 or thereabouts, Graweere married an African-born woman, Margaret Cornish, who worked as a servant for another white colonist, Lieutenant Robert Sheppard. A few years later the couple had a child, whom they named Mihill, or Michael. By 1640 Graweere had saved enough money to purchase Michael's freedom from Sheppard, but a question soon arose as to whether the child now belonged to his own father or to his father's master, William Evans. To settle this dispute, John Graweere became one of the first Africans in America to petition the Virginia courts. In its decision, *In re Graweere* (1641), the court granted his request, though its reasons for doing so are instructive. In his petition, Graweere, who was probably not a Christian, argued that Michael "should be made a Christian and be brought up in the fear of God and in the knowledge of religion taught and exercised by the Church of England" (Higginbotham, 1978, 25). The court agreed and ordered "that the child shall be free from the said Evans and his assigns," as long as Graweere and the child's godfather (probably a white Anglican) raised Michael in the Church of England.

Religion, not race, appears to have been the decisive factor in Graweere's success in gaining his son's freedom, though an earlier legal case involving another of Lieutenant Sheppard's black servants indicates that the Virginia courts treated people of color more harshly than they did whites for the same crime. *In re Sweat* (1640) concerned a white man, Robert Sweat, who fathered the child of an unnamed black servant belonging to Sheppard. While the black woman was sentenced to the whipping post, Sweat was ordered to do public penance at the James City Church. Nonetheless, as in the case of another black Virginian, ANTHONY JOHNSON, Graweere's experiences are suggestive of the relative legal and economic autonomy that Africans enjoyed in colonial America in the first half of the seventeenth century. While certainly not equal with whites before the law, they were not yet chattel slaves for life. That change emerged gradually by the late seventeenth century, with the passage of piecemeal legislation diminishing the legal rights of African Americans, including their right to petition in court, and was consolidated in the Virginia slave codes of 1680 and 1705.

FURTHER READING

Higginbotham, A. Leon, Jr. *In the Matter of Color: Race and the American Legal Process: The Colonial Period* (1978).

Higginbotham, A. Leon, Jr. *Shades of Freedom: Racial Politics and Presumptions of the American Legal Process* (1996).

Morgan, Edmund S. *American Slavery, American Freedom: The Ordeal of Colonial Virginia* (1975).

STEVEN J. NIVEN

Gray, Fred D. (14 Dec. 1931–), civil rights attorney, was born in Montgomery, Alabama, the youngest of five children of Abraham Gray, a carpenter trained at Tuskegee Institute, and Nancy Jones, a cook and domestic with a sixth grade education. His father died when he was two years old, leaving his mother to support the family. He went to a segregated elementary school through the seventh grade, then was sent by his mother to Nashville, Tennessee, to attend Nashville Christian Institute, an African American boarding school operated by the Church of Christ. This institution channeled young men into the ministry, a profession Gray's mother hoped he would enter.

After graduating from the institute in 1947, Gray entered Alabama State College. In the course of his undergraduate career, some of his professors encouraged him to consider a career in law, yet upon his graduation in 1951 Gray did not seek admission to the University of Alabama Law School. Despite the U.S. Supreme Court decision in *Gaines v. Missouri* (1937) mandating admission of a black student to Missouri's "white" law school given that the state had failed to provide a "black" alternative, Alabama, like most of the states of the Deep South, continued to deny blacks access to its professional schools without providing an option at black state campuses.

Instead of staying in Alabama, Gray in 1951 continued his education at Case Western Reserve Law School in Cleveland, Ohio. He intended to return to Alabama to practice law but was uncertain what the bitter segregationist climate would allow in terms of a fair chance to take and pass the state bar examination. He took the Ohio bar exam in June 1951 before taking the Alabama bar one month later. He was back in his hometown when he heard that he had passed both exams.

At the age of twenty-three, Gray opened an office with no clients, no money, a few borrowed law books, and a vow to fight segregation. Within months circumstances provided him with an opportunity to

fulfill the vow. On Thursday, 1 December 1955, ROSA PARKS was arrested for refusing to give her seat on a Montgomery city bus to a white man. Gray knew Parks, and on Monday, 5 December, he went to court to represent her—the boycott in protest of Parks's arrest began that day and lasted for more than a year.

Parks was found guilty and fined, and that night a meeting at the Holt Street Baptist Church to lay plans for extending the boycott was attended by hundreds. MARTIN LUTHER KING JR. spoke and came to play an increasingly important role in the boycott movement. Eventually he too was arrested and was represented by Gray.

Efforts to negotiate a desegregation agreement with the city failed. On 2 February 1956, three days after the bombing of a black church, Gray filed *Browder v. Gayle* in federal court on behalf of four plaintiffs seeking an order striking down the bus segregation law. On 19 June 1956, two days after Gray's wedding to Bernice Hill, a three-judge panel ruled 2 to 1 that the segregation ordinance violated the Fourteenth Amendment. The decision was appealed, but the U.S. Supreme Court refused to hear the case, thereby letting it stand. Along with 1954's *Brown v. Board of Education* decision, the Montgomery bus boycott's legal resolution signaled the end of an era in which segregationists could use the courts to deny equal access.

The segregationists fought back. As the civil rights struggle in Montgomery unfolded, there was an attempt to disbar Gray. He was arrested on a charge of failing to move to the "colored" waiting area at the Montgomery airport, an attempt was made to have him inducted into the armed forces, he received threatening calls and hate mail, and he was the target of an attempted stabbing. In 1956 the state moved against the NAACP, historically a major player in the fight to end segregation. Judge Walter B. Jones, who wrote a weekly column for the *Montgomery Advisor* that bore such titles as "I Speak for the White Race," enjoined the organization from doing business in Alabama on grounds that it had failed to comply with state law by, among other things, not submitting a list of its Alabama members to the state. Gray played a major role in mounting the cases resisting Alabama's efforts to oust the organization from the state and intimidate its members. The *NAACP v. Alabama* cases culminated in U.S. Supreme Court decisions barring Alabama from further attempts to cripple the organization.

As the civil rights struggle succeeded in increasing black electoral participation in Alabama, the state legislature passed a law redrawing the boundaries of Tuskegee in such a way as to place all but four or five of the city's four hundred black voters outside municipal boundaries. The redistricting did not affect any white voters. The practical effect was to place blacks in a municipal no-man's-land, unable to have a voice in the provision of services. Along with ROBERT CARTER, Gray argued *Gomillion v. Lightfoot* before the U.S. Supreme Court, contesting the disenfranchisement of his friends and neighbors, and in 1960 the Court, in an important voting rights ruling, held that the rights of Tuskegee's blacks had been violated.

Unable to attend the University of Alabama himself in the 1940s, Gray on 15 April 1963 filed *Malone v. University of Alabama* on behalf of VIVIAN MALONE, seeking to desegregate the University of Alabama. The resulting federal order led to the famous on-campus confrontation between Governor George Wallace, who had vowed "segregation now, segregation tomorrow, segregation forever," and officials of the John F. Kennedy Administration. The governor backed down, and the university became an integrated institution. *Franklin v. Parker* led to the desegregation of Auburn University, and *Lee v. Macon* and *Franklin v. Barbour* yielded court orders requiring elementary and secondary schools to desegregate.

While Gray's cases in the 1960s paved the way to the racial future, his first major case in the 1970s harked back to the grimmest aspects of the racial past. On 27 July 1972 CHARLIE POLLARD, a black Macon County farmer, entered Gray's Tuskegee office. Pollard had read a disturbing story in the newspapers about a secret study of the effects of untreated syphilis on black men begun in the early 1930s. Even after the discovery of penicillin, a cure for the disease, the subjects had been left untreated. Pollard was one of the men in the study, and he wanted to know whether his civil rights had been violated. Their conversation led to a class action suit, *Pollard v. United States*, an eventual settlement, and at Gray's urging, an apology from President Bill Clinton.

Gray was the first African American president of the Alabama Bar Association, and he received the American Bar Association's Spirit of Excellence Award and its 2004 THURGOOD MARSHALL Award. He lectured at a number of institutions, including Case Western Reserve School of Law, Harvard Law School, the John F. Kennedy School of Government, the University of Houston, and the North Carolina Central University School of Law. In 1995 Gray published two books about his most famous cases: *Bus Ride to Justice* and *The Tuskegee Syphilis Study*.

FURTHER READING
Burns, Stewart, ed. *Daybreak of Freedom: The Montgomery Bus Boycott* (1997).

JOHN R. HOWARD

Gray, Ralph (1873–17 July 1931), sharecropper and communist martyr, was born in Tallapoosa County, Alabama, a white majority county in the state's eastern piedmont. One of fifteen children, Gray was born into a family with a strong radical tradition. His father, whose name and occupation are unknown, was the son of Alfred Gray, an African American state legislator in Perry County, Alabama, during Reconstruction who famously vowed to fight for the Constitution "until hell freezes over." A critic of both white racism and the inadequacy of the Freedmen's Bureau, Alfred Gray recognized that his outspoken militancy came at a price. "I may go to hell," he told an interracial gathering in Uniontown in 1868, "my home is hell, but the white man shall go there with me" (Kelley, 39). Ralph Gray, who was only one year old when Reconstruction ended in Alabama, grew up hearing stories of his grandfather's radicalism. But like most of his black neighbors, he also suffered from the failure and suppression of that radicalism: working long hours on his parents' farm from an early age and migrating to the rapidly industrializing city of Birmingham in search of work in the early 1890s before returning to Tallapoosa at age twenty-two, in 1895, to marry and become a tenant farmer.

Gray and his family remained in Tallapoosa until 1919, when they migrated west, first to Oklahoma and then New Mexico. In both states he found work sharecropping, and he managed to save enough money to buy a small farm upon his return to Alabama in 1929. Although he barely managed to eke out a living from his small acreage, Gray avoided debt, and as one of a small but growing number of tenant farmers who owned a car, he traveled the state in search of cheaper supplies. Hoping to increase his holdings by renting a farm from John Langley, a white Tallapoosa merchant, Gray applied for a federal loan in early 1931 only to see Langley cash the low-interest loan check and withhold his share. Gray protested the merchant's actions by filing a complaint with the state Agricultural Extension Service, prompting Langley to confront him and attempt to beat him, in the time-honored tradition of labor relations in rural

Alabama. Gray, however, beat Langley. Gray also became increasingly interested in the Communist Party's newspaper, the *Southern Worker*, whose articles on the plight of tenant farmers and share-croppers and their efforts to fight back against unscrupulous merchants and landlords struck a chord with his own experiences.

Alongside his brother Tommy Gray, Ralph Gray joined the Communist Party and helped found a Tallapoosa branch of the Croppers' and Farm Workers Union (CFWU) in April 1930. The timing was propitious, since it coincided with a decision by several landlords in the county to withdraw all cash and food advances from their tenants to try to force them to seek work in a recently opened saw-mill that the landlords also operated. The CFWU's demand that landlords restore the traditional cash advances struck a chord with Tallapoosa blacks, as did its program calling for a minimum wage of a dollar a day, the right of tenants to market their own crops, the extension of the school year for black children to nine months, and the provision of free school transportation.

By July 1931 the Grays, assisted by Mack Coad, an unemployed black Communist steelworker from Birmingham, had increased CFWU membership in Tallapoosa to eight hundred but had achieved few concrete victories other than the restoration of cash advances for a few tenants. Nevertheless, the simple fact of black political organizing, not to mention the involvement of the Communist Party, terrified the region's white power structure and made a vio-lent confrontation almost inevitable. On 15 July 1931 Tallapoosa County Sheriff Kyle Young deputized a posse of whites to break up a meeting near Camp Hill, where eighty CFWU members had gathered to discuss the case of the SCOTTSBORO BOYS, nine African American youths falsely accused of raping two white women who had been sentenced to death by an all-white jury five days earlier. After assaulting many of the unionists, both male and female, the white vigilantes moved on to the home of Tommy Gray and attacked him and his wife, who suffered a fractured skull. The beatings ended after the timely arrival of an armed and extremely angry Ralph Gray. Upon discovering copies of the *Southern Worker*, the police arrested two of the unionists for possessing Communist Party literature.

Unbowed, a crowd of 150 CFWU members gath-ered the following night at a church near Camp Hill. Expecting white vigilantes or the authorities—the two were barely distinguishable—Ralph Gray estab-lished a picket line and stood guard a quarter-mile

from the meeting. When Sheriff Young, his deputy, and Camp Hill's chief of police approached Gray, an argument ensued, and shots were exchanged. A *New York Times* report claiming that Gray fired first was based largely on police accounts. Within moments both Young and Gray were on the ground, the sheriff shot in the stomach, Gray unable to move because of several bullet wounds in his legs. While Young was rushed to a nearby hospital and a posse moved on to break up and fire on the CFWU meet-ing, Gray was left at the side of the road to die. Some comrades rescued him, however, took him home, and called a doctor. The physician responded to the call but also apparently alerted the police to Gray's whereabouts, prompting the heavily armed white posse, now 150 strong, to descend on Gray's home. There one of the posse forced a pistol into Gray's mouth and shot him dead. After burning down his home, the mob then placed Gray's brutally beaten and bullet-riddled body on the steps of the county courthouse, a clear warning to other Tallapoosa blacks of the consequences of joining the Croppers' Union or the communists.

In the days that followed, the police arrested as many as fifty-five union members, all of them black, charging most with weapons offenses but indicting five for murder. Many of the unionists were beaten by the police and white mobs, and an uncertain number were killed, though several escaped, fear-ing that the Camp Hill police chief would succeed in his professed desire to "kill every member of the 'Reds' … and throw them in the creek" (Kelley, 41). Efforts to stifle sharecropper activism briefly suc-ceeded, but the worsening plight of tenant farmers throughout the South soon led to other organizing efforts, including the founding of five chapters of a revived CFWU, now known as the Sharecroppers Union (SCU), in Tallapoosa County in August 1931. Among the SCU's first members in Tallapoosa was a young sharecropper named NED COBB, whose story was told pseudonymously by Theodore Rosengarten in the book *All God's Dangers: The Life of Nate Shaw* (1974).

As a native of Tallapoosa County, Gray gave the lie to efforts by the Alabama authorities to blame the Camp Hill violence on outside agitators seeking racial intermarriage and social equality. Like HOSEA HUDSON and other native-born southern commu-nists, Gray was far more concerned with matters of economic justice and legal and political equality. As the first black, southern communist martyr, Gray was honored in the party's literature and iconography. Most notable of these was a poem by Ruby Weems,

"The Murder of Ralph Gray," which depicted him as a Stakhanovite JOHN HENRY, "a scepter of militant Negro manhood …. His muscles swelling into a mighty challenge / Mount into a vision of a million clenched fists" (Kelley, 46). Leftist gatherings in the 1930s and 1940s even alternated Gray's name with that of the Soviet founder V. I. Lenin when singing "Give Me That Old Communist Spirit," an SCU reworking of the African American spiritual "Give Me That Old Time Religion."

FURTHER READING

Dyson, Lowell K. "The Southern Tenant Farmers Union and Depression Politics," *Political Science Quarterly* 88 (June 1973).

Kelley, Robin D. G. *Hammer and Hoe: Alabama Communists during the Great Depression* (1990).

STEVEN J. NIVEN

Gray, Simon (fl. 1835–1865), flatboat captain and lumber retailer, was probably born a slave in the mid-South in the early nineteenth century and brought to Mississippi in the 1820s after the Indian removal policies of President Andrew Jackson opened up the Deep South for exploitation by American businessmen and planters. The rich, alluvial soil of the Yazoo-Mississippi river basin offered prime opportunities for cotton cultivation, but the region, also heavily wooded with cypresses, first needed to be cleared. As a result an extensive lumber industry emerged in Mississippi in the 1830s and 1840s alongside the expansion of cotton cultivation. Slave labor was central to both enterprises. The hundreds of ambitious businessmen who flocked to Mississippi, Louisiana, and Alabama needed lumber for the plantations they hoped to construct with the vast profits to be made from cotton. They also built wood cabins for the more numerous slaves whose labors would create those profits.

Nothing is known of Gray's parents, birthplace, or early life. He first appears in the historical record in 1835, as one of several slave laborers employed by Andrew Brown, a Scottish emigrant who ran a lumber construction and sawmill business in Natchez. Brown hired Gray's services for seventy-five cents a day from the slave's owner, a blacksmith and merchant. By 1838 Brown had appointed Gray as head of a rafting crew whose job it was to transport logs down from lumber camps in the Yazoo River basin to his sawmill in Natchez. The position provided Gray with a far greater degree of freedom than that enjoyed by slaves employed in clearing forests or working on the vast Delta plantation run by Andrew Brown's partner, Stephen Duncan, who by 1850 had become one of the wealthiest men in the United States. Still Gray needed a pass from his employer to assure him free passage on the Yazoo and other rivers. Since he corresponded frequently with Brown, we know that Gray was literate, and since Brown trusted Gray with sums of money as large as $800 to pay creditors and purchase lumber and supplies, the slave was also numerate and in Brown's view trustworthy. Because the amount of lumber available upriver exceeded what could be sold in Natchez, Gray also worked with Brown's son, Andrew Jr., selling lumber by flatboat to towns and settlements located on the banks of the Mississippi and its tributaries between Natchez and New Orleans. Gray's skill in navigating these often treacherous waters and in securing a good price for Brown's lumber led to his appointment as Andrew Brown Jr.'s replacement as flatboat captain, when Brown Jr. moved to New Orleans to manage that branch of the company's expanding operations in 1844. As chief boatman Gray was responsible for a crew as large as twenty men, both slaves and white men. According to company records his relationship with the latter was usually more harmonious than with the former. Some of his fellow slaves complained that Captain Gray was an overbearing taskmaster. A typical voyage involved Gray supervising the delivery of 100,000 feet of lumber from a mill in Natchez to a lumberyard in New Orleans. His crew loaded lumber onto two small flatboats, which were tied together, before making the weeklong journey— good weather and currents permitting—to the South's largest city. Such "coasting" trips, in which Gray delivered lumber to various riverside plantations, proved more hazardous and lasted as long as two or three weeks. He was also responsible for all aspects of bookkeeping, soliciting new lumber orders, as well as collecting debts and paying the creditors of Andrew Brown and Sons lumber company. For his services Gray received a monthly salary of $8, a $5 bonus for each trip to New Orleans, and a Christmas bonus; Brown continued to pay Gray's owner seventy-five cents a day for his labors.

When Andrew Brown Jr. died in 1848, however, Gray lost a valuable ally in the company. Brown Jr.'s successor, William Key, distrusted Gray, believing that he often kept some of the money he collected on his trips. Company records also show Key's concern that Gray was shipping lumber for a competitor using Brown's boats, and that the captain intentionally missed the steamboat intended to take him back to Natchez, so as to spend more time in

New Orleans. Most of all Key resented Gray's preference for hiring as crew members "the meanest lot of white men ... I ever saw.... This thing of leaving Simon his own master has been going on too long and must be put an end to" (Moore, 475), Key complained in July 1850. Andrew Brown Sr. disagreed, however, for the following month he purchased Gray's wife and some of his children from their owner for $500 and reunited them with Simon in a house rented in Natchez at the company's expense. Three years later Gray's owner agreed to stop hiring him on a daily basis to Andrew Brown, who subsequently raised the captain's wages to $20 a month, the same salary enjoyed by white boatmen. Since his owner did not apply to the Mississippi state legislature for permission to emancipate him, Gray remained legally a slave, though he apparently tried to secure legal status as a freeman.

Gray was nonetheless free to pursue his own business interests when not needed by Andrew Brown. In the 1850s, boom times for lumber and construction in New Orleans and for the Yazoo basin river trade, he began a lucrative career trading and speculating in sand, securing enough money to purchase his own son, Washington. Or rather, since it was illegal for a slave to purchase another, Gray gave the money to Andrew Brown to purchase Washington. Beginning in 1857 Gray worked primarily in transporting and selling lumber in the swamps near the Yazoo River basin, which were at that time opening up to cotton cultivation. To that end he also directed crews in clearing cypress brakes and constructing levees. The years of working in the swampy malarial lands of the Yazoo-Mississippi Delta had begun to take its toll, although Gray was able to recuperate from malaria and rheumatism by making frequent visits to the spa town of Hot Springs, Arkansas. These treatments cost Gray almost $1,000, which, assuming he paid for them himself, indicated the continuing success of his own business ventures, and if paid for by his employer, reflected Andrew Brown's continuing faith and trust in his employee.

The capture of New Orleans by Union troops in 1862 forced Andrew Brown to move his company's operations north of Natchez to the Yazoo river basin, a move that again united Simon Gray with his family. They lived there until the fall of Vicksburg in July 1863, after which Gray no longer appears in the business records of Brown's lumber company. It is possible that he died or faced a recurrence of the rheumatism or malaria that had earlier afflicted him. But it is also conceivable that Simon Gray viewed the federal troops' military success with the same degree of hope as cotton field slaves like GEORGE W. ALBRIGHT, a spy for the Union army later elected to the Mississippi legislature. For all of the autonomy and relative prosperity that he enjoyed as a flatboat captain and trader, Simon Gray was still legally a slave who must have dreamed of freedom. The material comfort of Captain Gray's life was hardly representative of the black experience in antebellum Mississippi, but his yearning to control his work life and to unite and protect his family was no different from slaves laboring in the plantation house or in the cotton fields.

FURTHER READING
Moore, John Hebron. "Simon Gray, Riverman: A Slave Who Was Almost Free," *Mississippi Valley Historical Review* 49 (Dec. 1962).

STEVEN J. NIVEN

Gray, Wardell (13 Feb. 1921–25 May 1955), jazz tenor saxophonist, was born Carl Wardell Gray, in Oklahoma City, Oklahoma. The names and occupations of his parents are unknown. During his childhood he moved with his family to Detroit, where he attended Cass Tech High School and began his musical life, first as a clarinetist, then as a saxophonist. While still a teenager he worked in local jazz bands, in the company of fellow jazz musicians HOWARD McGHEE, Big Nick Nicholas, SONNY STITT, and others. In 1943 he joined EARL HINES's big band, with which he worked for two or three years as a tenor saxophonist, and with which he made some early recordings. This engagement, playing with a fulltime road band, led him to Los Angeles, where he played an important role in the development of the bebop jazz idiom.

While living in Los Angeles Gray made some early bebop records with the alto saxophonist CHARLIE PARKER, including "Relaxin' at Camarillo" (1947) and with the tenor saxophonist DEXTER GORDON, including a famous tenor saxophone musical battle, "The Chase" (1947). A twenty-minute concert performance by the two tenor saxophonists, "The Hunt" (1947), was another well-known tenor battle, one that Jack Kerouac referred to in his novel *On the Road*: "They ate voraciously as Dean, sandwich in hand, stood bowed and jumping before the big phonograph, listening to a wild bop record I had just bought called 'The Hunt,' with Dexter Gordon and Wardell Gray blowing their tops before a screaming audience." Gray played in BILLY ECKSTINE's big band in 1947, although he did not record with Eckstine.

In 1948 Gray joined clarinetist Benny Goodman's band, taking part in the famed swing-style clarinetist's brief attempt to move into the bebop idiom. He is heard on Goodman's "Stealin' Apples" (1948) and "Bedlam" (1949). While playing in Goodman's band he traveled to New York City. Soon thereafter he left Goodman to work with the pianist COUNT BASIE's band and appeared on "Little Pony" (1951). While in New York he also worked with the pianist TAD DAMERON and other bebop players, and in 1949 he recorded another famous piece, his blues tune "Twisted." The singer Annie Ross subsequently wrote lyrics for Gray's theme and improvised solo and recorded her version in 1952.

In 1951 Gray returned to the western United States, where he spent the rest of his life working as a freelance musician. His last recording date, with the alto saxophonist FRANK MORGAN, was in early 1955. On 25 May 1955 Gray died in or near Las Vegas, where he had gone to play an engagement with Benny Carter's band. His body was found on vacant land a few miles outside of town. His broken neck and head injuries suggested that he might have been murdered, though some of his colleagues said he was a heroin addict and might have died from a drug overdose. Las Vegas police arrested the dancer Teddy Hale on suspicion of Gray's murder, but Hale claimed that Gray broke his neck when he fell out of bed after taking heroin. Hale also said that he panicked and dumped Gray's body in the open field, unintentionally inflicting head injuries in the process. Hale was found guilty of illegally moving Gray's body and sentenced to a brief jail term. No autopsy was performed, so the exact cause of Gray's death may never be ascertained. A brief news item in the *Los Angeles Times* on 27 May 1955 stated that the Las Vegas sheriff considered Gray's death a "probable murder." Subsequent details about the incident appeared in *Melody Maker* on 4 June and 11 June 1954.

Gray was one of the first tenor saxophonists to adopt the bebop idiom pioneered by Parker, the trumpeter DIZZY GILLESPIE, and a few other players in the mid-1940s. His personal style was a blend of the smooth-toned, harmonically conservative approach of the swing tenor saxophonist LESTER YOUNG and the newer melodic and rhythmic vocabulary of Parker. The gentler, Young-derived components of his style made it easy for him to fit in with the older style of playing favored by Goodman and Basie. At the same time, however, Parker's influence was so strong that Gray even borrowed entire phrases from some of Parker's improvised solos. These borrowings appear in "Twisted" and other recorded solos. Strangely, he favored a fast and prominent vibrato (especially in ballads such as "Easy Living"), while his role models Young and Parker favored slower and less pronounced vibratos. Despite his bows to his predecessors, his playing style was nonetheless distinctive and of musical importance. His colleagues ranked him as one of the best and had he lived longer he probably would have built a reputation equal to that of Gordon, SONNY ROLLINS, and other famous bebop tenor saxophonists. His music is heard to best advantage on two recording dates under his leadership, the quartet session that resulted in "Twisted" and "Easy Living" (1949) and the sextet session that produced "Bright Boy," "Jackie," and "Farmer's Market" (1952).

FURTHER READING

Gioia, Ted. *West Coast Jazz* (1992).

Gordon, Robert. *Jazz West Coast* (1986).

Horricks, Raymond. *Count Basie and His Orchestra* (1957).

This entry is taken from the *American National Biography* and is published here with the permission of the American Council of Learned Societies.

THOMAS OWENS

Gray, William Herbert, III (20 Aug. 1941–), minister, congressman, businessman, philanthropist, was born in Baton Rouge, Louisiana, the son of WILLIAM H. GRAY JR., a minister and university president, and Hazel Yates Gray, a university dean. During Gray's early childhood, his father was president of both Florida Memorial College and Florida A&M University, and his mother was dean of students at Southern University in Baton Rouge. However, the family then moved to Philadelphia in 1949. There, Gray's father took a position as pastor of the Bright Hope Baptist Church. William H. Gray Jr.'s own father had held that post since 1925.

Gray was educated in the public school system and graduated from Philadelphia's Simon Gratz High School in 1959. Upon graduation, Gray enrolled at Franklin & Marshall College in Lancaster, Pennsylvania, and pursued his joint interest in religion and politics, even taking an internship with Democratic Congressman ROBERT N. C. NIX JR. Nevertheless, when he graduated from college, Gray entered the ministry as assistant pastor at Union Baptist Church in Montclair, New Jersey, in 1964. By 1966 he had received a Master of Divinity degree from Drew Theological School in Madison,

New Jersey, and earned a Master of Theology degree from Princeton Theological Seminary in 1970.

Throughout his work in the ministry, Gray displayed a commitment to public service and was particularly active in securing equitable housing for low-income families. He also continued his own family tradition of religious and educational dedication by lecturing at New Jersey colleges and acting as assistant professor at Saint Peter's College in Jersey City. The 1970s brought significant personal changes for Gray, who married Andrea Dash in 1971 and suffered the death of his father in 1972. William H. Gray III would represent the third generation of Grays to serve at Bright Hope Baptist Church when he took over his father's position in 1972. The Grays would have three sons, William H. Gray IV, Justin, and Andrew.

In 1976 Gray sought to enter national politics by challenging his former employer Representative Dix for the Democratic Congressional nomination. Although he lost in the primary, he was successful in a bid two years later and took his position as Democratic Representative from Pennsylvania in 1979. During his tenure he was a member of the committees on foreign affairs, the District of Columbia, and the budget, and he was a member of the Congressional Black Caucus. Gray earned a reputation as an avid negotiator who created budget consensus during the presidencies of Ronald Reagan and George H. W. Bush. Nevertheless, he consistently favored limiting the deficit by decreasing military spending and raising taxes while continuing funding for educational and social programs, classic Democratic financial priorities that would shape his later career.

While Chairman for the Budget Committee in 1985 Gray introduced a bill for economic sanctions against South Africa, prohibiting loans and restricting imports and exports with the country as long as it supported its system of apartheid segregation and racial discrimination. These sanctions were an important precursor to the Comprehensive Anti-Apartheid Act of 1986. As Democratic Caucus chairman and majority whip from 1989 through 1991, Gray was the highest-ranking African American member of the U.S. House of Representatives in the twentieth century.

Inspired by the plights of high-achieving African American high school students unable to pursue the higher educational opportunities he and his family held dear, Gray left national politics to head the United Negro College Fund (UNCF), the primary philanthropic organization funding college educations for African American students. By doing so, Gray expressed his belief in the importance of historically black colleges and universities (HBCUs) and raising private funds to send high-achieving African American students to college. As president of the UNCF, Gray established the Franklin D. Patterson Research Institute to analyze data on the achievements of primary and secondary school African American students, raised awareness and funds to provide technological equipment and training for underprivileged black children, and to improve the technological infrastructure of the UNCF's member HBCUs. Furthermore, while speaking to representatives of the Microsoft Corporation for his technology campaign, Gray met Bill Gates and persuaded him to commit an impressive $1 billion to fund UNCF endowments through the Bill and Melinda Gates Foundation. Gray served in six successive Congresses until his resignation on 11 September 1991.

Still a prominent figure in U.S. foreign affairs, Gray reentered national politics in 1994 when under pressure from the Congressional Black Caucus and others. President Bill Clinton appointed him special adviser on Haitian affairs. In 1991 Haitian president Jean-Bértrand Aristide had been overthrown in a coup and replaced by dictator Raoul Cédras. Thousands of Haitians were killed and tens of thousands fled seeking asylum in the United States during the three years of violence that followed the coup. By 1994 the United Nations Security Council adopted a resolution to support any member nation using military force to restore Aristide's democratically elected administration. A special negotiating team helped to avert additional violence by convincing Cédras to step down. In 1995 Haitian president Jean-Bertrand Aristide awarded Gray the Republic of Haiti's Medal of Honor for his role in removing the dictatorial regime.

Gray left the UNCF in 2004, but continued to preach for his Philadelphia parish. Under his long tenure, Bright Hope Baptist saw a doubling of its membership and the creation of a new church constitution in 1994 that eliminated gender barriers to church leadership positions and provided for the ordination of female deacons. In the twenty-first century Gray turned his interest and financial experience to the private sector by becoming a corporate adviser through consulting firms Amani Group and Buchanan, Ingersoll & Rooney. He acted as vice chairman of the Pew Commission on Children in Foster Care, was member of the board at Dell, JP Morgan Chase, Prudential, and Pfizer, among other corporations, and was a lifelong member of Alpha Phi Alpha fraternity, the Benevolent and Protective Order of the Elks, and the Freemasons.

FURTHER READING

Anf, Michael. "A Politician and Fund Raiser Returns to the Ministry," *Chronicle of Philanthropy* (30 Oct. 2003).

Farmer, Paul. *The Uses of Haiti* (2004).

Ragsdale, Bruce A., and Joel D.Treese. *Black Americans in Congress, 1870–1989* (1996).

Scott, Matthew S. "A Higher Calling: William H. Gray—Interview," *Black Enterprise* (Feb. 1992).

AMBER MOULTON-WISEMAN

Gray, William Herbert, Jr. (25 Sept. 1911–26 Jan. 1972), college president, pastor, and educator, was born in Richmond, Virginia, and attended public schools. He received his undergraduate degree in Education from Bluefield State College in West Virginia in 1933. The following year he earned a master's degree in Chemistry from the University of Pennsylvania. Gray began his teaching career as professor of chemistry, professor of education, principal of the demonstration schools, and field director of Extension Services at Southern University in Louisiana. In the 1930s he married Hazel Yates in Louisiana. The couple had two children, a daughter Marion and a son WILLIAM HERBERT GRAY III.

Upon the death of NATHAN WHITE COLLIER, the president of Florida Normal and Industrial Institute (FNII) in 1941, Gray was appointed president of that institution in 1942 and moved his family to St. Augustine, Florida. There he sought to improve the financial crisis of FNII, which, like other schools, faced wartime shortages in enrollment and whose financial resources had already been weakened by the Depression. Gray improved the institute's financial standing by securing the largest state war-production training program at an African American institution in Florida in the 1940s. He also began offering summer programs to renew African American teacher certificates and introduced wartime industrial trade courses, including boat building, masonry, and radio maintenance. Gray often relied on SARAH BLOCKER, the cofounder of the institution, to assist him in maintaining the stability of FNII until her death in 1943.

After only two years as FNII president, Gray covertly pursued the presidential position of Florida Agricultural and Mechanical College for Negroes (FAMC), later known as Florida Agricultural and Mechanical University, in Tallahassee, Florida.

Relying on a network of relationships with members of John D. Rockefeller's General Education Board and contacts with other prominent educators, he secured the presidency of FAMC in 1944. The position offered a better salary and benefits and required less intense fund-raising, but his appointment was made over the objections of FAMC alumni, as well as the board of trustees, faculty, and students of FNII. Most FAMC supporters considered his youth as evidence of his lack of experience despite his two-year appointment as president of FNII.

Upon becoming the fifth president of FAMC on 1 September 1944, Gray began a massive construction, expansion, and renovation program. His efforts culminated in the construction of male and female dormitories and most notably the Polkinghorne Village, a state veterans housing project of 420 units in 1948. Gray fostered strong ties with federal, state, and local officials in Tallahassee. He increased funding for the institution and used his position to discreetly oppose segregationist policies. He published articles concerning education and expressed support for black teacher organizations seeking equalization of teacher salaries throughout the South.

Among his other achievements, Gray increased student enrollment and recruited the international tennis player ALTHEA GIBSON, who later won the Wimbledon championship in 1957. Gray was also a member of the Florida Citizens Committee on Education, which ardently pursued equitable distribution of financial resources for African American institutions throughout Florida. On 11 February 1948 Gray was appointed to serve as chairman of the major nominating committee of the Southern Regional Council, an interracial organization that sought to improve race relations in the South.

Gray's abrupt resignation from FAMC, effective immediately on 7 July 1949, was accepted by the Florida State Board of Control, the educational governing body of FAMC. Gray's tenure was marked by controversial budgetary and professional decisions, including resources allocated to the institution's building programs over student scholarships and retention. His immediate departure from the state and his lack of a public explanation fueled his detractors, including FAMC alumni, state, and local legislators, to make allegations of financial irregularities and moral misconduct. Investigations by the Florida state legislature's finance committee and three Leon County grand juries over several months in 1949 failed, however, to uncover any impropriety or wrongdoing concerning personal misconduct and the FAMU budget.

Gray later sought bids for the presidency of other institutions that were ultimately unsuccessful thanks to a tainted reputation. He settled in Philadelphia in 1949 and became editor of the *Philadelphia Afro-American* and briefly wrote a column for the *Philadelphia Daily News*. In 1950 he succeeded his father as pastor of Bright Hope Baptist Church in Philadelphia, a position he held for the next twenty years. Gray's commitment to racial uplift was evidenced by his service on several Philadelphia civic boards in the 1950s and early 1960s, including director of the Industrial Race Relations Commission of the State Department of Labor and Industry, vice president of the Pennsylvania Council of Churches, director of the Citizens and Southern Bank, member of the Philadelphia Housing Authority, and executive secretary of the Police Advisory Board.

On 28 December 1964 the Philadelphia mayor James H. J. Tate appointed him to the city Civil Service Commission, where he served until his resignation on 15 December 1971. He also served on a number of educational boards during his lifetime, including as chairman of the Berean Institute and the Division of Higher Education of the American Baptist Convention at Valley Forge. Gray was also one of the founders of Cloverlay, Inc., established in 1965 to subsidize the Philadelphia boxer JOE FRAZIER's career.

After Gray died in New York City at the age of sixty, FAMU named the William H. Gray Plaza on its campus in honor of his service. His son William H. Gray III also endowed scholarships in his honor at Franklin and Marshall College in Lancaster, Pennsylvania, and at Drew Theological School in Madison, New Jersey.

FURTHER READING

McKinney, George Patterson, and Richard I. McKinney. *History of the Black Baptists of Florida, 1850–1955* (1987).

Neyland, Leedell, and John Riley. *The History of Florida Agricultural and Mechanical University* (1963).

ROSE C. THEVENIN

Greaves, Bill (8 Oct. 1926–), actor and film director, was born William Garfield Greaves in Harlem, New York, one of seven children of Garfield Greaves, a cabdriver and part-time minister, and Emily Muir. A precocious student who was active in the arts and sports, Greaves won a scholarship at the age of fourteen to the prestigious Little Red Schoolhouse in New York's Greenwich Village. Later he attended the highly competitive and academically demanding Stuyvesant High School (a science- and math-oriented magnet school that only accepted New York's finest public school students), graduating in 1943. In 1944 Greaves enrolled as an engineering student at the City College of New York, but he soon left to pursue his love of dance. He became a skilled performer in several African and African American dance troupes, including the PEARL PRIMUS Dance Troupe and the (West African) Sierra Leonean ASADATA DAFORA Dance Company.

Greaves also began studying acting and became a featured actor with the American Negro Theater, where he appeared in *Garden of Time* and *Henri Christophe*, both written by the noted playwright and Howard University theater professor OWEN DODSON. Soon Greaves competed for stage roles with SIDNEY POITIER and HARRY BELAFONTE. In 1946 Greaves landed his first film role in *The Fight Never Ends*, with the heavyweight champion JOE LOUIS. Greaves continued acting onstage with a role in *Finian's Rainbow* on Broadway in 1946, and he appeared in the films *Miracle in Heaven* (1947) and *Lost Boundaries* (1948). In 1948 he was accepted as a full member of the Actors Studio, newly founded by the legendary acting teacher Lee Strasberg. His classmates included Marlon Brando, James Dean, Anthony Quinn, Maureen Stapleton, and Shelley Winters. The following year Greaves was featured on Broadway in *Lost in the Stars*. Despite his acting career's progress, Greaves was deeply troubled by the racially demeaning roles he was offered. Disturbed by the racist images of black people in the theater and film, he turned down an insulting part as a slow-witted porter in a 1950 Broadway revival of *Twentieth Century*. He then made the pivotal decision to become a film director to control how images were used and generated. As a student at the Film Institute of City College from 1950 to 1952, he worked with the noted documentary filmmaker Louis DeRochemont.

Greaves struggled to establish himself as a filmmaker in the United States. Although McCarthyism was at its peak and no black directors were working in Hollywood, he continued to seek opportunities to develop his craft. In 1952 he got his chance with the National Film Board of Canada. Over the next eight years he worked as a writer, chief editor, assistant director, or director on more than eighty films in Ottawa, Ontario. Greaves gained invaluable experience as a documentary filmmaker in this supportive environment. One of his major documentaries, *Emergency Ward* (1958), was filmed entirely in a Montreal hospital. From 1960 to 1962 he worked as the public information officer for the United

Nations International Civil Aviation Organization, producing *Cleared for Takeoff* (1963).

Greaves also served as an acting teacher and artistic director of the Canadian Drama Studio in Montreal and Toronto. When he returned to the United States in 1963, he became a film producer and director for UN Television, an agency of the United Nations. He produced three films for UN-TV before starting his own company, William Greaves Productions, in 1964 with a five-thousand-dollar Small Business Administration loan. The American avant-garde documentary filmmaker Shirley Clarke recommended Greaves to the head of the U.S. Information Agency's Film Division. Working from the United Nations headquarters in New York, Greaves made the well-received documentary films *Wealth of a Nation* (1964), about political dissent in the United States, and *The First World Festival of Negro Art* (1966), selected by the Senegalese government as the official film of its world festival.

For National Educational Television, Greaves made his breakthrough film *Still a Brother: Inside the Negro Middle Class* (1967) and produced, wrote, and hosted the groundbreaking series *Black Journal* (1968–1970), which won an Emmy Award in 1970. This innovative public television program featured news, political and cultural commentary, and timely documentary coverage "of, by, about, and primarily for, the Black community." As the first African American executive producer in network television history, Greaves spawned a new kind of documentary television programming nationwide and mentored a new generation of African American filmmakers, including St. Clair Bourne, Stan Lathan, and Kathleen Collins.

In 1967 Greaves made his landmark film *Symbiopsychotaxiplasm: Take One*, incorporating the formal techniques of both cinema verité and narrative film. In its camera style, jump cutting, and playful editing as well as in its ironic humor and improvisation, the self-reflexive documentary is an avant-garde film with affinities to French New Wave cinema and U.S. cinema verité documentary. Critically acclaimed by the few who saw it, the film in the early twenty-first century still awaited a commercial U.S. release (though it appeared periodically after 2002 on American cable television). Greaves's sequel, *Symbiopsychotaxiplasm: Take Two*, with the independent film actor Steve Buscemi, appeared in fall 2005.

Since 1968 the prolific Greaves has written, produced, edited, and directed more than 175 films, ranging from historical documentaries to avant-garde and commercial feature films. The recipient of over eighty national and international awards for his films, including the 2004 Career Achievement Award from the International Documentary Association, Greaves also has written, produced, and directed several documentaries on African American figures in politics, literature, music, and sports, including FREDERICK DOUGLASS, IDA B. WELLS-BARNETT, LANGSTON HUGHES, MUHAMMAD ALI, and RALPH BUNCHE. In 1980 Greaves was honored, along with fellow actors such as Robert DeNiro, Marlon Brando, Al Pacino, Dustin Hoffman, Shelley Winters, and Jane Fonda, with one of the Actors Studio's first Dusa Awards. From 1969 until 1982 Greaves also occasionally taught acting classes for Strasberg at the Actors Studio and the Lee Strasberg Theatre Institute in New York and remained involved as a member of the Actors Studio's board of directors and auditioning committee. In 1981 Greaves was the executive producer of the mainstream commercial film *Bustin' Loose*, starring RICHARD PRYOR.

FURTHER READING

Contemporary Black Biography (2003).

Klotman, Phyllis R., and Janet K. Cutler. *Struggles for Representation: African American Documentary Film and Video* (1999).

Warren, Freda. "Ralph Bunche Reconsidered: An Interview with William Greaves," *Cineaste* (22 Mar. 2001).

KOFI NATAMBU

Greaves, Clinton (12 Aug. 1855–18 Aug. 1906), former slave, buffalo soldier, corporal in the U.S. Army, Indian Wars veteran, and Medal of Honor recipient, was born in Madison County, Virginia, to John Greaves and a mother whose name is unrecorded. Clinton Greaves enlisted in the U.S. Army on 21 November 1872 at Baltimore, Maryland, and on 19 March 1873 he was sent to the Western frontier to join Troop C, Ninth U.S. Cavalry Regiment, in Texas. The Ninth Cavalry was one of four black regular army regiments later given the name the "buffalo soldiers." Greaves distinguished himself in 1877 during the height of the Apache campaigns when he became one of twenty-three black soldiers to receive the Medal of Honor for his service in the Indian wars.

Clinton Greaves was a laborer in Prince George's County, Maryland, when he decided to journey to Baltimore to enlist in the army. Like many former slaves, Greaves undoubtedly thought that the army would provide better opportunities than a life as a laborer taking odd jobs where he could find them. In the case of Greaves at least, some of the army's promises of an improved life proved true. At the time of his enlistment in 1872 he was able to sign his name only with a mark, although no evidence exists concerning his ability to read. At the time of his reenlistment in 1877, however, Greaves was able to sign his full name. In his first few years in the Ninth Cavalry, Greaves learned the skills of a soldier through constant patrols and skirmishes against Indians. He proved an able soldier; he was promoted several times during this period despite repeated arrests for fighting and disorderly conduct.

By 1877 Troop C was stationed at Fort Bayard, New Mexico. In early January of that year Chiracahua Apache, Warm Springs, and Mescalero Indians began conducting raids in Arizona and New Mexico as their frustration with deplorable living conditions on the reservations grew. A small group of raiders was reported to have crossed into New Mexico from Arizona that month, and the Ninth Cavalry's Second Lieutenant Henry Wright was ordered to patrol near the Florida Mountains with Corporal Greaves, five other troopers, and three Indian scouts. Wright and his troopers soon picked up the trail of the Indians and followed it to their camp in the mountains. Observing that the raiding party consisted of an estimated forty to fifty warriors, women, and children, Wright attempted to negotiate with the Indians to avoid a pitched battle. Intense negotiations ensued but quickly reached an impasse. Greaves noticed that the women and children in the camp had vanished and that the remaining eighteen warriors were slowly encircling the scouting party. Lieutenant Wright ordered his men to break out of the encirclement.

All the troopers fired as they charged the warriors, and Corporal Greaves led the way until he ran out of ammunition and used his carbine as a club. He managed to punch a hole in the Indian lines with the help of his fellow troopers, who also engaged in fierce hand-to-hand combat or fired their carbines at close range. Charging through the opening, Lieutenant Wright and his men turned and continued to exchange fire with the warriors until their ammunition was nearly exhausted. Wright ordered a slow withdrawal toward Fort Cummings, taking eleven Indian horses with his command. Behind them they left five dead warriors with several others injured. Taking little rest, Lieutenant Wright and his troopers returned to the field for several more weeks in difficult weather conditions

and with nearly constant skirmishes against raiding parties. Troop C had little rest until the Indians were pushed out of the Florida Mountains in the spring.

In his after-action reports Lieutenant Wright lavishly praised his troopers for their conduct during the skirmish with the Indian band. He recommended four of his troopers, including Greaves, and one scout for the Certificate of Merit. For his actions in leading the detachment through enemy lines in the face of near-certain annihilation, Greaves was also recommended for the Medal of Honor. Unfortunately, higher command was not so impressed with the bravery and conduct of these men. All the troopers and the scout were rejected for the Certificate of Merit. In the late-nineteenth-century army the Certificate of Merit was often more coveted by soldiers than the Medal of Honor because the certificate came with a bonus. Still, through the continued efforts of Lieutenant Wright and pressure from other Ninth Cavalry officers, the high command finally relented and awarded Greaves the Medal of Honor for his conduct in the Florida Mountains on 24 January 1877 as well as during the ensuing campaign.

Greaves reenlisted in 1877 in the Ninth Cavalry, this time with Troop H, serving until 1883. Between 1883 and 1887 he served on the frontier in Troops A and B of the Ninth Cavalry. After he had been in the army for nearly twenty years, the hard campaigning began to take a toll on Greaves's health. Greaves developed asthma and chronic stomach pains and was not up to the rigors of active duty in the harsh environment of the West. In January 1888 he transferred to the army's General Services and was assigned to Columbus Barracks at Columbus, Ohio. He supplemented his army pay by working evenings as a porter at a local saloon, though witnesses for his pension application went to great lengths to emphasize that he was not a hard-drinking man.

Shortly after arriving in Columbus, Greaves met Bertha Williams of Appomattox, Virginia, and began courting her in 1889. Married twice before, Bertha had drifted to Ohio after separating from her second husband in Virginia some years earlier. She filed for divorce and was granted one on 25 November 1890, and she married Greaves a day later. It was his first marriage. Blaming his deteriorating health, Greaves retired from the army in January 1893 after just over twenty years of military service. He continued to live in Columbus with Bertha until his death of chronic asthma and heart disease on 18 August 1906. Bertha survived him by thirty years, living on a widow's pension and a few odd jobs that she occasionally took. She died on 3 January 1936 of pneumonia.

FURTHER READING

The National Archives and Records Administration Building, Washington, D.C., has various papers related to Greaves. See the Records of the Adjutant General's Office, United States Regular Army Returns, Ninth Cavalry, 1873–1888 (Record Group 94), and the Records of the Office of Veterans Affairs: Pension Files, Pension 11,779, Greaves, Clinton (Indian Wars).

Kenner, Charles L. *Buffalo Soldiers and Officers of the Ninth Cavalry, 1867–1898: Black and White Together* (1999).

Leckie, William H., and Shirley A. Leckie. *The Buffalo Soldiers: A Narrative of the Black Cavalry in the West*, rev. ed. (2003).

Schubert, Frank N. *Black Valor: Buffalo Soldiers and the Medal of Honor, 1870–1898* (1997).

Trask, David F. *The War with Spain in 1898* (1981).

MICHAEL F. KNIGHT

Green, Al (13 Apr. 1946–), singer, songwriter, and minister, was born Albert Leornes Greene in Dansby, Arkansas, the sixth of ten children of Robert Greene, a sharecropper, and Cora. During slavery the Greene ancestors were owned by the Benton family; after emancipation the Greene descendants continued to work the land of their former owners under an economic arrangement known as crop lien, which promised the workers a share of profits that rarely materialized. Shortly after Al's birth, his family moved into a two-bedroom shack in nearby Jacknash, Arkansas, with the hope that a new field would produce more profitable corn, cotton, and soybeans than their old farm. Jacknash had two churches: Taylor's Chapel, a fiery Pentecostal congregation, and the slightly more subdued Church of the Living God. Green's parents were very religious and attended both.

Music was the most constant influence during Green's formative years; it was heard around the house, sung in the fields, and shouted in the churches. His five older brothers had been organized into a traveling gospel quintet called the Greene Brothers. They were as much a vehicle for the musical ambitions of their father, who was the lead singer and manager, as they were a promising pastime for Al's siblings. During the late 1940s and early 1950s, a halcyon period when gospel rivaled blues for the hearts of African Americans, the Greene Brothers modeled themselves after the Dixie Hummingbirds, the Soul Stirrers (with SAM COOKE), and the Five Blind Boys of Alabama. Initially Green was too young to tour with the group around the South and the Midwest. But he diligently prepared himself for his eventual place in the group, and his father never failed to take him along on their frequent trips into town. There Green observed that while he and his brothers were given money to buy candy and soft drinks, his father ducked into the local juke joint. Green could not see the drinking within, but his ears were tantalized by the "devil's music" that blared out.

In 1955 Robert Greene decided to abandon farming and move his family to Grand Rapids, Michigan. Education was not strongly encouraged in the Greene household, but when the Greene Brothers were not performing, Al Green went to school while his father and brothers worked at a car wash. He was intelligent but lacked proper motivation, and his best subject was singing in the school choir. His slight build made him an easy mark for

Al Green, performing "Take Me to the River" at the Waldorf-Astoria Hotel in New York City during his induction into the Rock and Roll Hall of Fame, 12 January 1995. (AP Images.)

bullies; his good looks and sweet voice made him popular with girls before he became interested in returning their attention. As a result he became a loner with few friends outside of his musical acquaintances. In Michigan the tension between sacred and secular began to build in Green, just as it had in his father. In Mother Bate's House of Prayer, the matriarch of the storefront congregation pleaded for his soul in such a passionate and gripping manner that her words and visage haunted him even as he was being drawn by the seductive entreaties of DIANA ROSS that seemed to beckon him from Motown in nearby Detroit. He managed to conceal his growing love for rhythm and blues from his father for several years by singing publicly with the Greene Brothers while he secretly formed a doo-wop group called the Creation with four neighborhood crooners. When his father caught Green practicing a JACKIE WILSON song, he threw his fourteen-year-old son and the forbidden music out onto the streets. Rather than submit to his father, Green lived in the crawl space under a friend's porch.

In 1967, after Green graduated from high school, the group changed its name to Al Greene and the Soul Mates and signed a contract with a small label called Zodiac Records. By that time Green had found solace in the arms and apartment of Juanita, a local prostitute ten years his senior. Like many of his relationships with women, it was partly sexual and partly maternal. The group recorded its first single with the short-lived company, but it got no airtime. Believing that his group was the next SMOKEY ROBINSON and the Miracles, Green tried to get an interview with BERRY GORDY JR., but he could not get past the star maker's secretary. Instead, the group used Hot Line Records, which was merely the name of a music magazine envisioned by one of the group's members, as the label for their hit "Back Up Train," written by the Soul Mates Palmer Jones and Clinton Rodgers. The simple but catchy tune went to number five on the rhythm and blues charts and reached forty-one on the *Billboard* pop ratings. The group rode the crest of their hit all the way to the Apollo Theater in New York, where, with nine encores, they had their most memorable performance.

Like many one-hit wonders, the Soul Mates tried in vain to repeat their success before squabbling broke them up. By 1969 Green was on the verge of burning out as a struggling solo act when he had a fortuitous meeting at a dive in Midland, Texas, with Willie Mitchell, a bandleader, arranger, and talent scout with the Memphis-based Hi Records. Mitchell, who had worked with B. B. KING and ISAAC HAYES, recognized Green's talent and knew how to capture and market it. He surrounded Green with established musicians, such as the drummer Al Jackson Jr. and three Hodges brothers, Tennie, Charles, and Leroy, on guitar, organ, and bass, respectively. It was at this point that Al dropped the "e" from his name, as a subtle way of establishing his new identity. Their first album, *Green Is Blue* (1970), fell flat, but Hi Records remained confident. Within a few months they released a remake of the Temptations' "I Can't Get Next to You." It was an instant sensation and inspired their first hit album *Al Green Gets Next to You* (1971), which included the blockbuster "Tired of Being Alone." As owner and president of Green Enterprise, Inc., and Al Green Music, Inc., Green was now on his way to commercial and critical success.

During most of the 1970s Green came to epitomize a new sound called soul music, distinctive for its melding of the rhythm and blues pulse with many of the vocal qualities of gospel. Green had a unique range in this respect because his rich, warm timbre could sound pleading and desperate or his cries could rise into a long falsetto of ecstasy. These features were most evident in *Let's Stay Together* (1971). The title song went platinum, and his remake of the Bee Gees' "How Can You Mend a Broken Heart" became a classic, demonstrating how Green's soulful renditions could breathe new life into existing material. His next hit, *I'm Still in Love with You* (1972), also went to the top of the charts and solidified his crossover appeal. It featured a touching remake of "For the Good Times" by Kris Kristofferson and introduced a funk element in "Love and Happiness." By the end of 1972 *Rolling Stone* had proclaimed Green the rock and roll star of the year.

Unlike other male soul singers of the era, such as CURTIS MAYFIELD, STEVIE WONDER, and MARVIN GAYE, whose musical oeuvre engaged broader social concerns, Green's repertoire was almost exclusively about lovemaking. Yet he frequently included singles such as "God Is Standing By" and "Jesus Is Waiting" on his albums. In 1973 Green saw his first Grammy Award nomination for *Call Me*. Later that year, while staying at a hotel near Disneyland with his father and brothers (whom he employed as security personal), Green had a dream in which Jesus appeared to him and asked, "Are you ashamed of me?" (Green, 294).

Al Green Explores Your Mind was released early in 1974. Its most post popular cut was "Sha-La La

(Make Me Happy)," but "God Bless Our Love" and "Take Me to the River" hinted at the spiritual-sexual turmoil that was about to erupt in Green's life and music. In October 1974 Green returned to his mansion in Memphis with Mary Woodson, whom he had met during a charity concert at a women's prison, and Carlotta Williams, an airline attendant. As Green undressed to take a shower, Woodson entered the bathroom and proceeded to scald Green with a pot of boiling grits. While he lay on the floor with second-degree burns, Woodson fled to a bedroom, where she shot and killed herself. During Green's long convalescence, Hi Records released *Al Green Is Love* (1975) and his *Greatest Hits* (1975). Sales for these compilations showed that Green had a loyal fan base. However, his heart was shifting back to gospel. In 1976 Green was ordained a pastor of the Full Gospel Tabernacle Church in Memphis, a nondenominational congregation he purchased from the Assembly of God for a reputed $355,000.

In 1977 Green married a gospel singer, Shirley Ann Kyles; the couple had three children before their divorce in 1983. In his mind Green had returned to gospel after his revelation in 1973, but when he seriously injured himself after falling off a stage in 1979, he interpreted the accident as a message from God that he was still literally blinded by the lights of popular music. Although his recordings as a gospel singer did not approach in sales the thirty-five million records he reached as a soul man, Green became a legitimate gospel star with a long and distinguished career that earned him his first Grammy Award for *The Lord Will Make a Way* (1981). In 1982 he played the part of a minister in a Broadway production of *Your Arm's Too Short to Box with God* with PATTI LaBELLE, and a duet with the gospel legend SHIRLEY CAESAR brought him the second of the nine Grammy Awards he garnered by 1994. He was inducted into the Rock and Roll Hall of Fame in 1995 and the Gospel Music Hall of Fame in 2004.

As a minister Green continued to sing as much as he preached, and in the early twenty-first century he still occasionally performed some of his soul hits. He compared his life to the biblical figure of Moses, who reigned as a prince of Egypt before becoming a shepherd of God. Yet to many observers there has never been a clear line between the prince and the shepherd—at least not in the life of Al Green.

FURTHER READING
Green, Al, with Davin Seay. *Take Me to the River* (2000).

Broughton, Viv. *Too Close to Heaven* (1996).
Guralnick, Peter. *Sweet Soul Music* (1986).
Shaw, Arnold. *Black Popular Music in America* (1986).

SHOLOMO B. LEVY

Green, Calvin Coolidge (19 July 1931–10 Feb. 2011), pastor, educator, civil rights activist, was born Calvin Coolidge Green at Laneview, Essex County, Virginia, the son of James H. Green and Levalia C. Green. One of eleven children, Green spent most of his youth and adolescent years in Middlesex County, Virginia, graduating from high school in Stormont (later Saluda), Middlesex County, in 1950. Green's father worked a variety of different jobs, often as a lumberman, but also as a farm laborer and general laborer. His mother was a homemaker. Green himself worked many of the same jobs, supplementing the family income until he left Middlesex after high school.

In 1950 Green attended Virginia State College (later Virginia State University) for a semester, before leaving for financial reasons, and joined the military, spending the next two years overseas. In 1951 he fought and earned commendations in the Korean War with the First Cavalry Division. Green's experiences in the military, which remained largely segregated, opened his eyes to racial injustice and prompted his later civil rights activism. Green returned to Virginia State College in 1953, graduating in 1956 with degrees in Biology and Education. Prior to graduating, in 1954 he married Mary; the two had known each other in high school and attended Virginia State College together. They would have three sons.

Green moved briefly to Pennsylvania, teaching at Downingtown Industrial and Agricultural School for a semester before rejoining the U.S. Army and moving to Fort Sam Houston, Texas. In the summer of 1957 Green returned alone to Virginia, New Kent County, and began working as a research technician on a pioneering open-heart surgery project at the Medical College of Virginia. He left this program two years later because of job discrimination. In 1959 he took a position teaching chemistry, biology, and physics in the Richmond school system, from which he would retire in 1990. Green also furthered his own education over the years, earning a master's degree in chemistry from North Carolina Agricultural and Technical College (later University) in Greensboro and a doctorate in physiology from the Medical College of Virginia.

Green became active in the NAACP shortly after returning to New Kent County in 1957. He helped reorganize the local branch in the late 1950s and was elected president of the New Kent County branch in 1960, a position he would hold for the next sixteen years. As president of the local NAACP, Green petitioned the local school board to desegregate the county's schools. Although school desegregation began in Virginia in 1959, it had occurred in only a handful of localities around the state, and New Kent was not one of them. Predictably the board ignored Green's requests in the early 1960s. In 1964 Green learned that the NAACP hoped to use the newly passed Civil Rights Act to pressure school boards throughout the South to integrate their schools. At that time school integration was stymied, held up by "freedom of choice" and pupil placement plans in most of the South. Because New Kent County refused to integrate its schools at all, ten years after the original *Brown v. Board of Education* decision, Green volunteered to file a lawsuit against the local school board.

The lawsuit—filed in Green's youngest son's name, Charles—was developed by the state NAACP and filed in federal district court in the spring of 1965. Originally paired with a similar case from Charles City, Virginia, the case slowly worked its way through the federal court system, suffering losses at the federal district court and Fourth Circuit Court of Appeals in 1966 and 1967, respectively. Green and the plaintiffs in the *Green* case faced significant resistance for their actions. Many people, including conservative black leaders, asked them to withdraw the suit. Racial harassment and intimidation increased, and the teaching contract of Green's wife was not renewed, throwing the family into a financial crisis.

In 1967 attorneys for the national office of the NAACP chose to appeal the *Green* case to the United States Supreme Court. In hearings before the court, NAACP attorneys argued that southern school desegregation plans, including "freedom of choice" plans, were not bringing about school integration as mandated by the 1954 *Brown v. Board of Education* decision. The Supreme Court handed down its decision in *Charles C. Green v. County School Board of New Kent County, Virginia*, on 27 May 1968. Noting that "freedom of choice" plans rarely accomplished significant integration in the public schools, the court called for the development of more effective measures. Justice William Brennan, author of the unanimous opinion, explained: "The burden on a school board today is to come forward with a plan that promises realistically to work, and promises realistically to work now" (*Charles C. Green v. County School Board of New Kent County, Virginia*,

391 U.S. 430 [1968]). The decision transformed *Brown*'s prohibition of segregation into a requirement for integration, later prompting Supreme Court Justice William Rehnquist to refer to *Green* as a "drastic extension of *Brown*" (Justice William H. Rehnquist in *Keyes v. School District No. 1, Denver, Colorado*, 413 U.S. 189 [1972]).

The impact of the *Green* decision spread far beyond the borders of New Kent County. Throughout Virginia, courts ordered school boards to develop desegregation plans to conform to the decision. New Kent County integrated its school faculties and staffs in 1968, and the following year the county operated its two schools on a completely integrated basis. As a Supreme Court decision, *Green* also mandated immediate school integration nationwide. Referring to *Green*, a National Park Service study of school desegregation in the United States noted: "The results were startling. In 1968–69, 32 per cent of black students in the South attended integrated schools; in 1970–71, the number was 79 per cent" (Waldo Martin, Vicki Ruiz, Susan Salvatore, Patricia Sullivan, and Harvard Sitkoff, *Racial Desegregation in Public Education in the U.S. Theme Study* [2000]: 91). Accordingly, *The Encyclopedia of Civil Rights in America* argues that the *Green* decision "did more to advance school integration than any other Supreme Court decision since *Brown v. Board of Education*" (David Bradley and Shelley F. Fishkin, eds., *The Encyclopedia of Civil Rights in America* [1998]: 411). Green died in Richmond, Virginia, at the age of 79.

FURTHER READING

Because few written accounts of Green's life or the *Green* decision exist, court cases represent an invaluable source. See *Charles C. Green v. County School Board of New Kent County, Virginia*, 391 U.S. 430 (1968) and *Keyes v. School District No. 1, Denver, Colorado*, 413 U.S. 189 (1972).

Martin, Waldo, et al. *Racial Desegregation in Public Education in the United States Theme Study* (2000).

Salvatore, Susan. "New Kent School and George W. Watkins School," (New Kent County, Virginia) National Historic Landmark Nomination, Washington, D.C.: U.S. Department of the Interior, National Park Service (2001).

BRIAN J. DAUGHERITY

Green, Chuck (6 Nov. 1918–7 Mar. 1997), jazz tap dancer, was born Charles Green in Fitzgerald, Georgia, to parents whose names and occupations are unknown. As a young boy he stuck bottle caps to the bottoms of his bare feet and danced on the sidewalk for coins. At the age of six he won third place in an amateur dance contest in which NOBLE SISSLE was the bandleader and soon thereafter toured the South as a child tap dancer. At the age of nine he was spotted by a talent agent and taken to New York to study tap dance.

Nat Nazzaro, known as the "monster agent" by those who knew of his practice of signing vulnerable young performers to ironclad contracts, signed Green to his own contract when he was twelve years old. A few years later Green formed the team of Shorty and Slim with childhood friend James Walker, a talented comic and dancer. They studied the great comedians of the day, picking up lines of patter from such shows on the black vaudeville circuit as Pigmeat Crack Shot and Hunter Pete and Repeate. "Their act was hilarious. Chuck was a natural—so cute," the tap dancer Leonard Reed remembered, adding that Walker at the time was tall and skinny and that Green was as small as a chair. They did what was called "dumb talk comedy," a rapid rhythmic banter that was interspersed between the songs and dances. As Walker played a broken-down vibraphone that looked as if it were failing apart, Green sang, "Some people was born to be doctors ... some people were born to be kings ... I fortunately was born to swing." Then they tap-danced, with Green making graceful turns and Walker excelling in "legomania" (highly individual and unusual leg movements in jazz dancing, such as rubber-legging).

Nazarro at the time also managed Buck and Bubbles (Ford Lee "Buck" Washington and JOHN SUBLETT BUBBLES). He suggested that Green and Walker study the singing-dancing-comedy team that had bypassed the black vaudeville Theater Owners' Booking Association (TOBA) circuit to become headliners on the white vaudeville circuit; by 1922 they had played New York's prestigious Palace Theatre. Changing the name of their act to Chuck and Chuckles, Green and Walker were groomed as a "juvenile act" to Buck and Bubbles. Bubbles soon took Green under his wing, calling him "the son I never had," and offered to teach him what he knew, though it came in the form of a challenge. "Bubbles would do a step just once," Green explained, "and then say, 'you got one chance.' He was a creator. They called him the 'father of rhythm.'" Bubbles's style of rhythm tapping—in which he "loaded the bar" (put many extra beats into a bar of music) and dropped his heels, hitting unusual accents and syncopations—was revolutionary. He prepared for the

new sound of bebop in the 1940s and anticipated the prolonged melodic lines of "cool jazz" in the 1950s. "If you dropped your heels, you could get a more floating quality, like a leaf coming off the top of a tree," said Green, who became a protégé of Bubbles. "It changed the quality of the sound, gave it tonation."

Through the 1930s and early 1940s Chuck and Chuckles toured Europe, Australia, and the United States, performing in such venues as Radio City Music Hall and the Paramount, Apollo, and Capital theaters. Jobs were plentiful and their manager had the team doubling up on performances. They averaged five stage shows a day, played nightclubs until early morning, and toured nonstop with big bands across the country and abroad. By 1944 the strain of performing had taken its toll. The team of Chuck and Chuckles broke up, and Green was committed to a mental institution. When he was released some fifteen years later, he was changed—extremely introverted and seemingly in a world of his own. His friends thought it a miracle he could still dance. By experimenting with the new harmonies, rhythmic patterns, and melodic approaches of the bop musicians, Green created his own bop-influenced style of rhythm tapping that was ad-libbed, up-tempo, and ultracool. In the 1960s Green began to perform again on stage and television. He appeared with the Copasetics (a tap fraternity dedicated to the memory of BILL ("Bojangles") ROBINSON) on a show hosted by Dick Cavett on the popular educational channel WNET. On 6 July 1963 he performed at the Newport Jazz Festival as a member of the "Old Time Hoofers" with HONI COLES, Charles "Cooky" Cook, Ernest Brown, Pete Nugent, Cholly Atkins, and BABY LAURENCE. The show was introduced by the jazz historian Marshall Stearns and marked the resurgence of tap dance in popular culture.

At New York's Village Vanguard in 1964, the legendary tap dancer Groundhog faced Green in a tap challenge. "I've been waiting to battle Chuck Green for twenty years," Groundhog told Stearns. "Dancing is like gang war and tonight I'm up against one of the best." Groundhog's rapid and syncopated staccato tapping was foiled by Green's relaxed and fluid style of jazz tapping and almost dreamlike grace. In 1969 Green appeared with members of Harlem's Hoofers Club for a series of "Tap Happenings" that were produced in New York City by Letitia Jay.

Through the 1970s and 1980s, Green continued to perform with the Copasetics. Host Honi Coles introduced him as "Chuck Green, the greatest tap dancer in the world." When asked why that special title was bestowed on Green, Coles answered, "His slow dance is genius. Most dancers would fall on their face. His timing is like a musician's."

In the late 1980s Green toured Europe with The Original Hoofers, appeared as a guest soloist at the Kennedy Center Honors, and was awarded an honorary professorship at Washington University. In New York in 1987 he began teaching a weekly two-hour tap class to a dedicated cross section of New York's top professional jazz dancers. With great clarity and precision, he led his students into the complexity of his material with warmth and ease, allowing the dancer to hear and feel the weight of the rhythm and movement.

In the late 1980s and early 1990s, Green was twice honored with a New York Dance and Performance Award (the Bessies) for his innovative achievements and technical skill in dance, and for his work in *Black and Blue* (1989) on Broadway. Tall and big-footed, Green was a surprisingly light, graceful, and melodious rhythm dancer who was known for his specialty "strut" when he came on stage and for his tick-tock tap sounds. Whether dancing to such favorite tunes as "A Train" or "Caravan," Green's smooth and graceful rhythm tapping was uncluttered, even, and beautifully phrased. He has been called the "Poet of Tap."

In the "Green, Chaney, Buster, Slyde" number from the 1996 Broadway musical *Bring in 'Da Noise, Bring in 'Da Funk*, SAVION GLOVER celebrates Green as a master teacher who "was educatin' people, not entertainin'." "Chuck's dancin'," rapped Glover as he danced before a multipaneled mirror, "was like, kind of slow. Every tap was clean, you know what I'm sayin'. You hear every tap. He was, just like, on the slow type, smooth type."

Chuck Green died in Oakland, California.

FURTHER READING

The fluency of Green's tap dancing is captured in George Niremberg's documentary film *No Maps on My Taps* (1979) with "Sandman" Sims and Bunny Briggs. His free-association poetry of speech is beautifully rendered in the film *About Tap* (1987). His gentleness of spirit is immortalized in *Masters of Tap* (1983).

Obituaries: *New York Times*, 14 Mar. 1997; *New York Post*, 15 Mar. 1997.

This entry is taken from the *American National Biography* and is published here with the permission of the American Council of Learned Societies.

CONSTANCE VALIS HILL

Green, Darrell (15 Feb. 1960–), professional football player and businessman, was born in Houston, Texas, one of seven children to Leonard and Gloria Green. Leonard Green was a lab technician for Maxwell House Coffee. He attended Texas A&I (1978–1983), where he played football and ran for the school's track team and recorded the fastest time for the school in the 100 meter dash.

Green was the first round draft choice of the Washington Redskins in the 1983 National Football League (NFL) draft. During his more than twenty years in the NFL, he was regularly recognized as the fastest or one of the fastest players in the game. He was clocked at 44.3 seconds in the 400 yard dash, 20.5 seconds in the 200 meter dash, 10.08 seconds in the 100 meter dash, and 4.15 seconds in the 40 yard dash. In the summer of 2004, at the age of forty-four, he ran the 40 yard dash in 4.36 during a running demonstration at a youth summer football camp.

Green started at cornerback for the Washington Redskins in his rookie year and played for the team until his retirement in 2002. He opened his career with the Redskins by returning a punt sixty-one yards in an exhibition game. It was the first time he touched a football as a pro. In his first regular season game against the Dallas Cowboys broadcast to the nation on *Monday Night Football*, he showed his speed by running down TONY DORSETT from behind, preventing a sure touchdown. Other memorable plays include a punt return for fifty-two yards and a touchdown in the National Football Conference (NFC) divisional playoff game against the Chicago Bears in 1983. Green actually hurdled a Chicago Bear player, tearing rib cartilage in the process, on his way to the touchdown. The following week he jarred the ball loose with a hit on the Minnesota Vikings' Darrin Nelson on fourth down near the goal line to preserve a 17-10 victory for the Redskins and a trip to the Super Bowl. Green was instrumental in leading the Redskins to three Super Bowls and winning two of them. He was selected to seven Pro Bowls and was also chosen by a special panel as one of the seventy greatest Redskins of all time. Moreover in 1996 he was NFL Defensive Player of the Year, Redskins Alumni Player of the Year, and Redskins Most Valuable Player. He married Jewell Elizabeth Fenner in 1985. In 1998, Green earned a bachelor of science degree in general studies and social science from St. Paul's College in Lawrenceville, Virginia.

After his retirement from professional football in 2002, Green settled in Ashburn, Virginia, and became a prominent businessman and a champion of charitable causes. In 1988 he started the Darrell Green Youth Life Foundation, which assists in the education of children. He also founded the Darrell Green Speed Enhancement for Youth Huddle to enhance the running technique and speed of children. He served as a board member for the Baltimore-Washington 2012 Olympic bid, the NFL/NFLPA (National Football League/National Football League Players' Association) September 11th Fund, and the Loudoun Education Foundation, and he became the chairman of President George W. Bush's Council on Service and Civic Participation. The group includes Bob Dole, former U.S. senator from Kansas and the Republican presidential candidate in 1996, and John Glenn, former astronaut and U.S. senator from Ohio. Green received a plethora of awards and honors, including the 1996 NFL True Value Man of the Year, the 1996 Ken Houston Humanitarian Award, the 1997 *USA Today* Most Caring Athlete Award, and the 1997 Sprint Good Sportsmanship Award.

Green's business holdings included Intekras, an infrastructure and network management firm; Trusted Solutions Group (TSG), which offers information technology services and training, security, surveys, and cabling; Score Title and Escrow; and Sports Combine, a Web site that provides space for high school, youth, and adult teams to publish their game scores, team rosters, athlete statistics, and league standings. He received honorary doctorate of humane letters degrees from Marymount University, George Washington University, and St. Paul's College. Green and his wife, Jewel, had three children.

FURTHER READING

Attner, Paul, and Denlinger Ken. *Redskin Country: From Baugh to the Super Bowl* (1983).

Goodman, Michael E. *The History of the Washington Redskins* (2005).

O'Donnell, Chuck. "The Stat Sheet: Darrell Green," *Football Digest*, Mar. 2003.

Tandler, Rich. "The Redskins from A to Z," vol. 1, *The Games* (2002).

Torres, John Albert. *Fitness Stars of Pro Football: Featuring Profiles of Deion Sanders, Shannon Sharpe, Darrell Green, and Wayne Chrebet* (2000).

ROBERT JANIS

Green, Eddie (2 May 1933–6 July 2004), pianist, arranger, and composer, was born Clifton Edward Green Jr. in Abington, Pennsylvania, the son of Clifton Edward Green Sr., a paper hanger and carpenter, and Carrie Townes, who worked as a domestic. Self taught, Eddie Green began playing piano at five years of age and became active in music in public school. His formal secondary education ended at Abington High School when he was in the tenth grade. At age sixteen he came under the tutelage of the hard bop pianist Richie Powell and his brother, the bebop legend BUD POWELL. During this time, Green learned the essentials of jazz by listening to and absorbing the lessons of his mentors. Green also formed a band and regularly played a local African American venue in Willow Grove called the Three C's. Like many African American communities that supported young musicians and vocalists, the Three C's provided valuable mentoring between generationally separated virtuosos. Two well-known brothers emerged from Green's band, the drummer Donald "Duck" Bailey and the composer Morris "Mo'" Bailey.

Green played piano around the Willow Grove area with different local musicians, sometimes venturing into Philadelphia to play at jam sessions in the homes of other young jazz players until he went into the U.S. Army at the age of twenty in 1953. Sent to Japan after the end of the Korean War in July, Green entered an integrated unit in the Army Forces Far East. He quickly went from guard duty to playing piano in the officer's club, even though he was not able to read music at this time. He was discharged in 1955 and returned to a hard bop and organ trio-dominated jazz scene in Philadelphia.

In his early twenties Green, while employed at a grocery store, started playing club dates at world famous Philadelphia venues such as the Showboat, Spider Kelly's, and Pep's Musical Showbar, where he later led the house band for a time with the bassist Tyrone Brown and the drummer Charlie Johnson, accompanying such singers as Etta Jones and Little Jimmy Scott. From 1955 to 1958 Green attended Coombs College of Music along with the organist Jimmy Smith to sharpen his reading and composition skills. He also married Leona Smith in 1957 and the couple had one son, Steven. They divorced in 1961.

Green did not get really serious about his music, however, until a call came to play the Catskills in the early 1960s for O. C. Smith, a singing sensation who had just struck out on his own after a stint with the COUNT BASIE Band. Green played the Catskills for two years at the Concord, one of the era's grand hotels, with the noted saxophonist Hugh Brodie and the bassist Paul West. The two veteran musicians inspired Green to take creative chances with his music, and the night-after-night collective improvisational moments taught him valuable lessons. He would utilize such training when he returned to Philadelphia to work in two very different genres: the pop world of Kenny Gamble and Leon Huff's Philadelphia International Records, where he worked with LOU RAWLS and the Three Degrees, as a new jazz idiom emerged on the scene—jazz fusion.

President Lyndon Johnson's administration in the mid-1960s developed the Model Cities Program, a federal urban development initiative that required widespread citizen participation. The program was designed to address infrastructure problems in inner city neighborhoods and attempted to link social services, job training, and local cultural activity to housing and physical community development, specifically "model" inner-city neighborhoods. The year 1967 found Green, the saxophonist Odean Pope, the bassist Tyrone Brown, and the drummer Sherman Ferguson teaching together in a Model Cities program, mentoring young musicians in blighted neighborhoods. Along with awakening young hearts to the power of music, these young men were developing a new band that would break musical barriers in jazz. Along with his involvement with the band Catalyst, Green also was lending his musical expertise to the jazz guitar virtuoso Pat Martino. With Martino, he recorded three projects, appeared at Lincoln Center and Carnegie Hall, and toured every top jazz club in the country.

In 1972 a representative from the Muse label happened into a Philadelphia jazz club, the Aqua Lounge, and heard a phenomenal band that mixed avant-garde, hard bop, and soul into an exceptional brew that preceded the fusion explosion. Catalyst recorded four albums (1972–1975) that drew raves from fusion and jazz enthusiasts. Without promotional support from the record company, however, the group could not secure work and broke up in 1976. Green began driving a cab to support himself as a session player between gigs. That the group had emerged before its time was only amplified by the fact that, in 1999, Muse records re-released the Catalyst material under the title *The Funkiest Band You Never Heard!* to great international acclaim.

In 1979 Green went out on tour with Billy Paul, a vocalist who had had a hit with "Me and Mrs. Jones" in 1972 for Philadelphia International. Green played on four more albums with Paul and toured all over the world, but returned to a post-1970s Philadelphia jazz scene that had drastically changed. The disco era had decimated area venues that no longer featured jazz. The famed nightclubs of the 1950s and 1960s had long closed their doors. The 1980s witnessed Green's evolution into an elder statesman as he encouraged and worked with new, young talent in the city while playing neighborhood jazz clubs and major hotels. He became renowned for his accompaniment style with singers and horn players and for his sensitivity on the bandstand, and as a songwriter, recording artist, and performer, remained continually in demand.

In 1991 and 1994 Green recorded with the saxophonist Odean Pope and his Saxophone Choir and with the vocalist Rachelle Farrell in 1990 and 1991. His songs "Little Miss Lady," "Prayer Dance," and "Peace" were covered by many artists and became standards in some quarters. In 1996 Green recorded a critically acclaimed CD, *This One's for You*, which included his original material and inventive arrangements of revered songs like "Lift Every Voice and Sing." Critics labeled him a jazz authority at ease with his material. Just before his death in 2004, Green completed his final project, *Shades of Green*. The *Philadelphia Inquirer* cited it as the top CD jazz pick of the year.

FURTHER READING

Baszak, Mark, ed. *Such Sweet Thunder: Views on Black American Music* (2003).

SUZANNE CLOUD

Green, Elisha Winfield (c. 1818–1889), Baptist minister, was born into slavery in Bourbon County near Paris, Kentucky. As he recounted in his *Life of the Rev. Elisha W. Green* (1888), at age ten he traveled to Mason County to live with Judge Brown, his new owner, while his mother and sisters Charlotte and Harriet were divided among heirs of the Dobbyns: his sister Evaline and brother Marshall to Silas Devaugh, his brother Alvin to Thomas Perry, his brother Henry to Thomas Dobbyns, and his brother Elijah to Enoch Pepper. In 1828 J. L. Kirk of Mayslick, Kentucky, purchased Elisha and put him to work cooking, washing, spinning flax and yarn, and doing household chores until 1832, when his sister, four children, and he were sold at a sheriff's sale to his mistress and the Reverend Walter Warder, her new husband. Green experienced religious conversion and baptism on Warder's farm.

While Green battled a bout of inflammatory rheumatism, he was taught to read by the nine-year-old Alice Dobbyns. She instructed him during the evenings after she had attended school. Following a month of instruction, he had learned to copy the alphabet and penned a letter to his brother in Missouri. Green married Susan Young in 1835 but moved to Maysville in 1838, leaving her as a servant to Mrs. Sissen in Mayslick. However, Mrs. Sissen sold Susan, she thought, to Mr. Peck, but in actuality it was John P. Dobbyns, Green's master, who had bought her. Dobbyns, unable to keep Susan, sold her and her three children to John Reid, who enslaved them for ten years. Dobbyns repurchased them but financial failure forced him to resell them, fortunately this time to Green, who, thanks to the generosity of several abolitionists, bought his family's freedom for $850. Green would endure watching various family members being sold into slavery, then struggle to reclaim them, for many years to come.

A sexton in the white Baptist Church in Maysville for sixteen years, Green was granted licensure by the Church "to exercise his gifts in the public before the colored population of this city" on 10 May 1845. Two years later he received ordination and assumed his first pastorate in Flemingsburg in 1853. He preached to blacks in the white church building until he was called to a black church in Paris in 1855, yet he served longest in the black church in Maysville (Green, 3–9).

At the encouragement of the white Baptist Church in Paris, Green assumed leadership of the African Baptist Church, which was essentially "a slave to the white Baptist Church." The black church worshipped in a stable until its members could construct a small place of worship. Shortly after beginning preaching in Paris in July 1855, Green purchased his own freedom.

In 1865 the Reverend H. Adams summoned Green to Louisville in hopes of founding a black college. They helped organize the Convention of Colored Baptist Ministers of the State of Kentucky, the first assemblage of black ministers in the state. The General Association, a major arm of the convention, acquired fifty acres of land in Frankfort and sold it. With the proceeds, the association purchased property in Louisville and created the Kentucky Normal and Theological Institute, later known as the State University at Louisville, with the Reverend W. J. SIMMONS as its first president.

With the coming of the Emancipation Proclamation, Green grew optimistic that the end of slavery was inevitable. Although he disavowed the role of politician, he recognized that the unceasing defamation and degradation of blacks by the Democratic Party required united political action. Thus in 1866 he represented the black community

of Paris at the first convention of black men ever held in Kentucky. Meeting in Lexington, the convention concluded a three-day session by developing resolutions and a memorial on the right of black suffrage to be presented before the U.S. Congress. The convention also addressed resolutions to the general assembly of Kentucky.

Black Baptist churches in Kentucky organized into the Zion District Association, and delegates gathered in Bethel Baptist Church in Maysville in 1869. The association resolved to be a permanent body and elected Green moderator. Under Green's self-effacing leadership, the association experienced eleven unbroken years of increasing influence, particularly in eastern Kentucky, ultimately consolidating with the Elkhorn Association in 1879. The Elkhorn and Mount Zion District consolidated in 1880 into the Consolidated Baptist Educational Association with Green continuing as moderator.

As Green traveled between his Paris and Maysville churches, he often witnessed Jim Crow laws in action. One experience that was indelible in his memory occurred on a train ride from Maysville to Paris on 8 June 1883. The Reverend G. T. Gould, president of Millersburg Female College, and two professors boarded the train with a group of female students. Professor Bristow, desiring to have the students seated together, vehemently insisted that Green relinquish his seat. Colonel Morrow, Green's friend, offered his seat, but Bristow persisted: "I'll make this nigger [Green] get up." Nonetheless Green held his seat even as Bristow and his group pummeled him, eventually winning an assault and battery suit against President Gould and $24 in damages (Green, 37–59).

On 13 September 1880 Green lost his wife, Susan, to illness. Though immensely pained by her death, he remarried and enjoyed brief happiness with his second wife. At this juncture in his life he had ministered to Maysville Colored Baptist Church for more than thirty-nine years. He had served his congregations in Maysville and Paris diligently and unselfishly, helping many of his parishioners free relatives from slavery, acquire property, and obtain education or training. Though not formally educated and occasionally derided by young black ministers who were, he modeled the "good character" necessary for effective spiritual and political leadership during his time. As he so aptly concluded his narrative, "We old fathers have prepared the material for the building, and you [young black ministers] must do the building" (Green, 60).

FURTHER READING

Green, Elisha Winfield. *Life of the Rev. Elisha W. Green, One of the Founders of the Kentucky Normal and Theological Institute—Now the State University at Louisville; Eleven Years Moderator of the Mt. Zion Baptist Association; Five Years Moderator of the Consolidated Baptist Educational Association and Over Thirty Years Pastor of the Colored Baptist Churches of Maysville and Paris. Written by Himself* (1888).

FLOYD OGBURN JR.

Green, Ely (11 Sept. 1893–27 Apr. 1968), author, black activist, and clairvoyant, was born near Sewanee, Tennessee, to a college student, Edward H. Wicks, later a Texas attorney, and Lena Green, a fourteen-year-old kitchen servant and daughter of a privy cleaner who had been a slave. In Green's own words, he was "a half-white bastard." His mother died when he was eight, and he was reared by Mattie Davis, a sympathetic neighbor who worked as a domestic. He did not finish the second grade and was largely self-taught. His phenomenal vocabulary came about because, as he said, "I studied from every man who would talk to me."

Green's youth, up to age eighteen, was spent in Sewanee, the site of the University of the South. He worked odd jobs, such as shining shoes, carrying spring water to the third floor of dormitories, and selling peanuts at sports events. He had only indirect contact with his white family. When they came to Sewanee from Texas in the summer, he sometimes played with the children, but the adults did not openly acknowledge a relationship. A child Robin Hood, Green "borrowed" toys from white children and gave them to his black friends who had never seen such novelties.

In the nearby mountains and coves, Green hunted for small game—rabbit, squirrel, possum, and quail—all edible when cooked by "Mother Mat." He became a crack shot with rifle and pistol and learned of a firm in St. Louis that would buy cured skunk skins. He prospered but spent his earnings on friends, one of them needing expensive medicine for venereal disease. His superiority over the semi-literate "sagers" aroused their enmity, and Green was forced to leave in 1911 to avoid being killed by the group of mountain whites he had offended. He escaped by night on a railroad handcar, riding a perilous nine miles out of control down the steep tracks. He did not return to Sewanee until 1919.

At eighteen Green made his way from Tennessee to Waxahatchie, Texas, where his mother had relatives. He was befriended by the most influential man in town, the judge and banker Oscar E. Dunlap, and his family. Against the entreaties of his benefactors, Green volunteered for military service, under the misimpression that it would make him a full-fledged citizen. He became an accomplished boxer, fighting to a draw the champion at Camp Travis, Texas. Overseas he found that the American armed forces were among the most segregated parts of society, in contrast to, for example, the French, who treated their African colonials as equals. He marveled when he saw Marshal Ferdinand Foch kiss on both cheeks a black hero whom he was decorating for valor. Green was sergeant in an all-black stevedoring unit at Saint-Nazaire from 1918 to 1919.

After his army service, Green never again held a steady job but not because of any character defect. He was never charged with illegal use of alcohol or drugs or with stealing. He lived at or near the poverty line, mostly in California after a stint in Texas, where he was "too black" to get a job in the lucrative new oil fields and "too white" to find security as a Pullman porter. He worked intermittently, as a handyman, body servant, butler, chauffeur, and chef on a yacht that took him along the California coast and throughout the Caribbean. He worked for such elegant movie stars as John Barrymore, Lionel Barrymore, and Mary Pickford, usually as a caterer for parties. He broke the color line at the Lockheed plant in California, where the company was willing to hire blue-collar blacks, but the unions would not give them cards. His standing up for principles cost him merciless beatings at the hands of police, who considered him obstinate and "uppity." On one occasion he lost his front teeth and suffered a fractured cheekbone.

Throughout this period, Green wrote steadily but erratically in his "diaries"—the notes and observations he used in composing his twelve-hundred-page autobiographical manuscript. His frequent letters to his sweetheart were lost when she died while he was overseas, as were those to and from the Dunlaps, who tried in vain to keep him out of trouble and who treated him like a son. The diary he kept in the oil fields was "borrowed" by an oil speculator who used its date as evidence in a claim to a half-million-dollar piece of property. The suit was won, the promise of a reward was not kept, and the diary was not returned. Thus, Green's sole written legacy is the autobiography, with its erratic punctuation, absence of paragraph divisions, hundreds of misspellings, and scattered dots where, he said,

"I was resting my pen." This document, however, is a compelling capsule of the formerly subtle persecutions that erupted during the civil rights movement of the 1960s and 1970s. The autobiography was begun in the 1950s, two-thirds finished by 1963, and completed over the next two years. In his conversation and writing Green would harangue listeners not to use the word *Negro*—a "slave word," he said. Ironically, *black* became acceptable usage about the time Green died.

Green went to Sewanee in the summer of 1963 to visit his half brother Edward Miller, custodian of the student union. He called on the employers of his youth and was referred to the university's historiographer. The following summer he returned with a small suitcase containing his "book" in six loose-leaf folders. More than a year was required to transcribe the manuscript, which was in difficult handwriting on unnumbered pages. Edited into standard English and published as *Ely: An Autobiography* in 1966, the book covers Green's youth through his eighteenth year. The editor prevailed on the widely known author of *Strange Fruit*, Lillian Smith, to write the introduction. In what was the last essay she wrote before dying in Atlanta of cancer, she called Green a "fabulous story-teller" who was "torn between love and hate" and was always in the limbo between the races of his father and his mother.

At seventy, Green had been unknown, unpublished, and broke. Sympathetic friends typed his manuscript. He lived to see the first edition enthusiastically reviewed by more than fifty magazines and newspapers, including the *New York Times*, which called him the "Grandma Moses of American literature." The book in its four various editions has been used as a text in religion and literature classes in high school and college. The prizewinning novelist Walker Percy wrote, "The love in it and the terrible reproach … wring the heart." *Christian Century* described it as "a microcosm of the tragedy and pathos of race relations."

In 1968 the *Sewanee Review* published a chapter, "The Aristocratic Mouse," and Green and the magazine each received a prize of $1,000 from the National Endowment for the Arts. Royalties at the time of his death had reached about $4,000, but his total estate came to less than $5,000 and thus was exempt from probate. After his death another $4,000 went to his widow, Beatrice McCarroll Green, whom he had married the year before. He knew before he died that the University of Massachusetts Press had agreed to publish his complete work in one volume. This became the second of the four editions.

Green died in Santa Monica, California, and was survived by two daughters whose mothers were sisters whom Green never married. He left only one book, but in it are the raw materials of sociology, ethics, and theology. It is an epic in black history, the story of an extraordinary man constricted by an imperfect society, bad laws, and illogical customs. As the Right Reverend C. FitzSimons Allison, the thirteenth bishop of South Carolina, wrote in a review, "His is the story of injustice, grace, suffering, anger, pride, community, but above all a victory over the need to hate."

FURTHER READING

Ely Green's original twelve-hundred-page handwritten manuscript is in the Archives of the University of the South, Sewanee, Tennessee.

Green, Ely. *Ely: An Autobiography* (1966; repr. 1990).

Green, Ely. *Ely: Too Black, Too White* (1970).

Obituary: *New York Times*, 29 Apr. 1968.

This entry is taken from the *American National Biography* and is published here with the permission of the American Council of Learned Societies.

ARTHUR BEN CHITTY

Green, Eustace Edward (3 Feb. 1845–1931?), teacher, physician, public official, legislator, and lay religious leader, was born in Wilmington, North Carolina, to Mary Ann Sampson, a slave, and an unnamed white father of Scottish descent. Green was raised in Wilmington by his mother, who later married Reverend Cornelius Sampson, an African Methodist Episcopal (AME) Zion clergyman. After Wilmington's fall to invading Union forces in early 1865, Green was allowed to begin his formal education at age twenty in the local Presbyterian parochial school.

For the next two years, while working as a carpenter by day, Green attended school at night. An excellent student, he supplemented his savings with loans to enter Lincoln University in May 1867 and continued to work before being granted a scholarship in his second year. He completed his bachelor's degree in 1872, taught for a year in Lincoln's normal and preparatory schools, and completed a master's degree at Lincoln in 1875. He then accepted an appointment as deputy clerk of the Court of General Sessions and Common Pleas (Superior Court) in South Carolina's Seventh Judicial District in Laurens County, where he remained for two years. In 1877 Green was appointed principal of the Hoge Institute for African American children in Newberry County,

South Carolina, and as the county's examiner of public schools. In 1878 he was named the first principal of the larger Williston graded (public) school in Wilmington, North Carolina, a post he held until 1882, at a salary of forty dollars a month.

Green also became active in local political affairs, serving in March 1882 as a New Hanover County delegate to a statewide convention of African Americans held in Goldsboro to recruit candidates for office. In the fall of 1882 he was nominated and elected as a Republican member of the lower house from New Hanover County, one of twenty African American state legislators elected that year. Green served with distinction in the 1883 general assembly, being named to three house committees, those on Propositions and Grievances, Penal Institutions, and Education. An 11 March 1883 edition of the *Wilmington Post* called Green "one of the best representatives this county has ever had in the legislature." Green enjoyed the confidence of his local colleagues, and he was named in January 1883 as a member of the board of directors of the newly chartered Wilmington, Wrightsville & Onslow Railroad, an all–African American venture. After leaving the legislature, Green was briefly appointed as a mail carrier under the free mail delivery system.

Green found himself at a professional crossroad, so he chose to continue his own education, but in a new direction, and he entered the medical department of Howard University in Washington, D.C., in the fall of 1883. He taught in Howard's normal department during his first year, and during the summers he returned to North Carolina to teach in the state's new normal school for African American teachers at New Bern, North Carolina. After receiving an MD degree from Howard in 1886, he briefly returned to Wilmington before establishing his medical practice in Macon, Georgia, in about 1890.

Green remained in Macon for the next three decades, establishing the Central City Drug Store in partnership with Dr. T. G. Patterson. He attended a postgraduate medical course at Chicago's College of Physicians and Surgeons in 1893, and he later served for four years as president of the Georgia State Medical Association of Physicians, Dentists, and Pharmacists, organized in 1893, and later renamed the Georgia State Medical Association. Green later helped organize the National Medical Association, based in Atlanta, and he served as its president for one term.

A devoted Presbyterian layman, Green served three times as a member of the lay committee of the general assembly of the Presbyterian Church in the USA and as moderator of both the Knox Presbytery and the Atlanta Synod at Macon. The biographer Arthur Caldwell described Green as well-traveled and widely read, and as especially interested in the Bible. Green was married on 2 July 1879 to Georgianna Cherry of Tarboro, North Carolina, a stepdaughter of the former Edgecombe County legislator and merchant Henry C. Cherry. The Greens eventually had four children.

A distinguished figure with a trademark mustache, and in his later years, a goatee, Green moved to Detroit, Michigan, after retiring from his medical practice in Georgia in the early 1920s. A widower by 1930, he was last recorded in that year's federal census as living in Detroit with his daughter and her family.

FURTHER READING

Reaves, Bill. "*Strength Through Struggle*": *The Chronological and Historical Record of the African-American Community in Wilmington, North Carolina, 1865–1950* (1998).

BENJAMIN R. JUSTESEN

Green, Grant (6 June 1935–31 Jan. 1979), jazz electric guitarist, was born in St. Louis, Missouri, the son of John Green, a security guard, and Martha Smith. His year of birth appears incorrectly as 1931 in standard reference sources, but his birth certificate confirms 1935, as Green himself asserted twice in interviews. Grant played guitar in grade school. His father, a blues and folk guitarist, gave his son some early instruction, and Grant took lessons from Forrest Alcorn for one year. Otherwise he was self-taught. He explained to the writer Laurie Henshaw, "I learned mostly from listening to records of [the swing guitarist] CHARLIE CHRISTIAN—and to [the bop alto saxophonist] CHARLIE PARKER."

As a teenager Grant played gospel music in area churches. He then worked with the accordionist Joe Murphy. Green later mentioned that it was quite unusual to find an African American playing accordion, and his early experience in blending the guitar with-this instrument may help explain why he later became so comfortable working with Hammond organists. Depending on how it is played, the accordion can sound like a cousin of the Hammond organ, particularly when it is amplified through a Leslie speaker.

Green married Annie Maude Moody in the mid-1950s. They had four children. The writer Dan Morgenstern reported a comment on Green's early years: "The first thing I played was boogie woogie.... Then I had to do a lot of rock and roll. It's all the blues, anyhow." By the latter part of the decade he was playing jazz with the tenor saxophonist JIMMY FORREST, with whom he made an outstanding first album, *All the Gin Is Gone* (1959). He also worked with the trumpeter Harry "Sweets" Edison, although the date is unknown. He then performed with the alto saxophonist Lou Donaldson, who encouraged Green to move from St. Louis to New York City in the late summer of 1960 and got him involved with Blue Note Records.

Green's recordings for this label extend into the early 1970s, but he was particularly active from 1961 to 1965, recording albums with the saxophonists Donaldson, STANLEY TURRENTINE, HANK MOBLEY, and IKE QUEBEC; the trumpeter LEE MORGAN; and the organists Larry Young and Big John Patton. He also recorded numerous sessions under his own name, including *Grant's First Stand*, *Green Street* (both 1961), and *Talkin' About* (1964). During this period he performed in a number of trios consisting of organ, guitar, and drums.

From 1967 to 1969 Green was inactive because of problems with drug addiction. He participated in the Guitar Workshop at the Jazz Expo '69 show in London as a last-minute replacement for Tal Farlow, and in that year he resumed recording. He watered down his music on several of his late albums in a largely misguided attempt to reach a larger audience. As with many musicians who took this path during the 1970s, Green's efforts to assimilate rock and pop into jazz frequently sounded halfhearted. Nonetheless he had a modest hit with the title track of his album *Easy*, recorded in April 1978. In the fall of that year he was hospitalized for ten weeks for a blood clot near his heart. He refused to undergo open-heart surgery and resumed his career, performing in Los Angeles and then driving to New York City, where he died of a heart attack.

Few details of Green's life are documented, despite his stature as one of the greatest jazz guitarists. He holds a position in hard bop and soul jazz groups somewhat akin to that of the cornetist Bobby Hackett in swing and Dixieland bands. He was not an innovator but rather a musician who perfected an existing approach, improvising immaculately clean, controlled, and tasteful melodies and accompaniments. From his early career he gained a deep feeling for idiomatic blues guitar playing, which made him—in his own restrained way—as soulful as any soul-jazz musician. Yet he was also able to combine this emotive approach with the fleet and comparatively abstract lines expected of a fluent hard bop player. Few other musicians have operated in both camps so well.

FURTHER READING

Feather, Leonard. *The Encyclopedia of Jazz in the Sixties* (1966).

Feather, Leonard, and Ira Gitler. *The Encyclopedia of Jazz in the Seventies* (1976).

Green, Sharony Andrews. *Grant Green: Rediscovering the Forgotten Genius of Jazz Guitar* (2002).

Obituaries: *Michigan Chronicle*, 10 Feb. 1979; *Down Beat*, 22 Mar. 1979.

This entry is taken from the *American National Biography* and is published here with the permission of the American Council of Learned Societies.

BARRY KERNFELD

Green, Jacob D. (24 Aug. 1813– ?), slave and antislavery lecturer, was born in Queen Anne's County, Maryland. The names of his parents are unknown, but he is recorded as the property of Judge Charles Earle. In *Narrative of the Life of J. D. Green, a Runaway Slave, from Kentucky* (1864), Green recounts that as a child he was employed as an errand boy, a cowherd, and a houseboy. When he was about twelve years old, his mother was sold to a trader named Woodfork. Green never saw her again.

As a teenager Green began to attend a black church. He was taught to defer to white men and to accept abuse without retaliation. Green witnessed the brutal flogging of slaves and was himself flogged by his master for disobedience. At age seventeen Green fell in love with a young woman named Mary who was owned by Dr. Tillotson, a neighboring slave owner. This youthful affair ended with his rejection, and Green subsequently married Jane, one of Judge Earle's slaves.

Five months after their marriage Jane gave birth to a nearly white child, whose father was Judge Earle. In the next six years Green and his wife had two of their own children. Judge Earle, whose first wife had died, married Dr. Tillotson's daughter. As a condition of their marriage, Earle was required to sell any female slaves with whom he had had sexual relations. While Green was away on an errand, his wife was sold to a trader.

Green, who had been known as "one of the most devout Christians among the whole Black population" (*Narrative*, 22), now contemplated running away, despite his belief that to do so was a sin.

He stole a horse and fled to Baltimore, where he discovered that the authorities were already looking for him. After several near-captures and skirmishes with bloodhounds, Green reached Chester, Pennsylvania, where a Quaker took him into his home. Unwilling to venture farther north to Canada, Green began to work outside of Philadelphia, but when his employer went bankrupt he was arrested and sent back to Maryland.

Green was auctioned off for $1,025 and sent to Tennessee. After three years he was hired out as a servant to Mr. Steele, a gentleman who was visiting New Orleans. He managed to escape again by stowing himself aboard a ship and made it as far as Utica, New York. There he was recaptured and sent to Ohio, where he spent time in and out of prison. He was eventually sold to a man in Kentucky, where he worked as a coachman and house servant. He succeeded in escaping a third time, this time disguised as a woman. After days of traveling on train and steamboat, Green successfully reached Toronto, Canada, in 1848.

From there Green emigrated to England three years later. Like many fugitive slaves he sought asylum in the British Empire, where slavery had been abolished in 1833. He became an antislavery lecturer, speaking in schoolrooms and churches about slavery and the Civil War. In 1864 he published the *Narrative of the Life of J. D. Green, a Runaway Slave, from Kentucky, Containing an Account of His Three Escapes, in 1839, 1846, and 1848* in Huddersfield, West Yorkshire, England. After this date Green disappears from the historical record.

FURTHER READING

Green, Jacob D. *Narrative of the Life of J. D. Green, a Runaway Slave, from Kentucky, Containing an Account of His Three Escapes, in 1839, 1846, and 1848* (1864).

Andrews, William L. *To Tell a Free Story: The First Century of Afro-American Autobiography, 1760–1865* (1986).

Andrews, William L., and Henry Louis Gates Jr., eds. *American Slave Narratives* (2000).

Starling, Marion Wilson. *The Slave Narrative: Its Place in American History* (1982).

JULIA LEE

Green, Jim (1823–17 May 1891), politician, civil rights activist, black nationalist, and labor leader, was born James K. Green in North Carolina. Little is known about Jim's parents or his childhood years, but eventually he became the valued servant of a Mr. Nelson, a wealthy Hale County, Alabama, planter who owned 500 slaves. Despite Green's somewhat privileged position among the bondmen, he was never taught how to read or write, but he did master carpentry. Consequently, Green became one of the relatively few black skilled laborers in the predominantly black cotton, or Black Belt, region of Alabama who were able to use their antebellum earnings to become economically independent once they were emancipated.

Following the Civil War, Green joined the Republican-led Union, or Loyal, League and entered politics. In 1867 he represented Hale County during the state constitutional convention. The same year, he succeeded Greene County Registrar Alexander Webb, a black Republican who had been murdered following an argument with a local white. In 1868 Green was elected to the Alabama House of Representatives, where he remained until 1876. By then he had become one of the most vocal spokespersons for black self-help in Alabama.

Green was not known for being an eloquent orator, but his passion was unmatched. He was also an excellent organizer whom white Democrats detested. When in 1868 the Greene County sheriff threatened to assault Green, numerous black men marched to Eutaw, the county seat, to defend him. The same year a freedman was shot in nearby Greensboro, the county seat of Hale. Afterward, Green helped organize an all-black militia to prevent white terrorism in the Black Belt.

The early 1870s were particularly eventful years for Green. In January 1871 he and a handful of other black leaders formed the Alabama Negro Labor Union (ANLU), or Convention, ultimately one of the most influential black labor unions in the Reconstruction South. In July 1871 Green helped found the Perry County Labor Union (PCLU) or Convention. He and other officers encouraged rank-and-file members to understand the contracts that they signed and to meet every contractual obligation, an occurrence about which the Freedmen's Bureau worried constantly. A resolution was then read in which it was made clear that, despite substantial family and religious ties, each member was prepared to leave the state if pay and working conditions did not improve by 1 January 1873.

Green was an ardent supporter of the emigration scheme, which he proposed on several occasions. In 1867 he advised a group of Hale County blacks to move to Liberia, where they could live in complete freedom, according to Green. At the first meeting of the ANLU, Green recommended sending a small number of blacks to Kansas to seek opportunities there similar to those that the residents of the African American community at Nicodemus would later enjoy.

Green's labor advocacy helped his political career. In 1872 he decided to run for Congress. If elected, he would have become the second black congressman from Alabama, representing the majority black Fourth District. Unfortunately for him, several white Republicans, including the incumbent congressman Charles Hays, a white Hale County Republican, and at least one black Republican, Greene Lewis of Perry County, blocked the nomination. Lewis's motivations are unknown, but Hays wanted to return to Capitol Hill and thought Green's education and labor advocacy, self-help position, and civil rights activism, unpopular among white conservatives, could help him secure the nomination.

Over the next two years, Green's reputation grew. In the summer of 1874 he, several black, and a few white Republicans created the Equal Rights Association (ERA) of Alabama. Among other activities, the ERA sought to guarantee that a comprehensive state civil rights bill would be passed and that equality would be given to all Alabamians regardless of their color, gender, or previous condition of servitude.

ERA leaders included a number of the Alabama's most influential black and mixed-race politicians. JAMES T. RAPIER, a U.S. congressman and principal leader of the ANLU, served as president. Jim Green was vice president. Philip Joseph, a light-skinned Afro-Creole attorney and newspaper editor from Mobile, was second vice president; and Alexander H. Curtis, a prominent black Baptist from Marion in Perry County, former president of the PCLU, and the only black man to preside over the Alabama Senate during the nineteenth century, was treasurer.

Among the officers, only Green was known for his forthright activism. Black Mobilians had even accused Joseph of avoiding darker-skinned blacks, opting to associate with other Afro-Creoles and prominent whites. Rapier was a well-known moderate, and Curtis was a self-proclaimed conservative. Despite their overall outlooks, the four men agreed that segregated public facilities should not be lawful in Alabama. Though Green had championed separatist Black Nationalism in the past, he was certain that the day when black and white children would eat together, play together, and attend the same schools was fast approaching. He therefore became upset when in 1874 State Senator Alexander

White, an opportunistic white Democrat-turned-Republican, introduced a bill into the state legislature to perpetuate segregation on trains and other public conveyances.

Senator White's proposal was made during one of Alabama's most important political campaigns to date. Having lost the governor's race in 1872, Democrats in 1874 were determined to place one of their own back in the state house, and they did not mind using any means at their disposal to achieve that aim. When rhetorical appeals to white solidarity and supremacy did not work, they turned to more proven tactics, such as physical violence. In what has to be one of the most bizarre incidents of threatened violence in the state, James T. Walker, an influential attorney and conservative white Democrat, told Green that he would slit his throat because he was tired of hearing Green mispronounce words.

As the 1874 elections approached, Green decided to run for Congress a second time. In the end, Congressman Hays was re-nominated. Having secured the bid, Hays traveled from Washington, D.C., to the Alabama Black Belt to launch his campaign. His entourage included some of the fourth district's most respected black politicians, Alexander Curtis and Greene Lewis were two of them. Jim Green, then president of the Hale County Republican Central Club, was another. Because of their and other blacks' support, Hays returned to Congress, where he remained longer than any other postbellum politician from Alabama.

In 1880 a congressional committee charged with evaluating the economic, political, and social conditions of the South interviewed Green. He testified that, despite the legacy of slavery that had forbidden most slaves from receiving a formal education, black Alabamians had made significant strides since 1865. Having retired from politics in 1876, Green moved to Montgomery, where he continued to make a comfortable living as a carpenter before dying of consumption.

FURTHER READING

Bailey, Richard. *Neither Carpetbaggers nor Scalawags: Black Officeholders in the Reconstruction of Alabama, 1867–1878* (1995).

Fitzgerald, Michael. *The Union League Movement in the Deep South: Politics and Agricultural Change during Reconstruction* (1989).

Foner, Eric. *Freedom's Lawmakers: A Directory of Black Officeholders during Reconstruction* (1996).

Foner, Philip S., and Ronald L. Lewis. *Black Workers: A Documentary History from Colonial Times to the Present* (1989).

BERTIS ENGLISH

Green, John Patterson (2 Apr. 1845–30 Aug. 1940), lawyer and politician, was born in New Bern, North Carolina, the son of John R. Green, a tailor, and Temperance (maiden name unknown), free African Americans of mixed ancestry. He learned the rudiments of reading and writing at a private school for free blacks. His father died while John was a child, and in June 1857 his mother moved the family to Cleveland, Ohio.

After working as an apprentice to a harness maker in Oberlin, Ohio, Green returned to Cleveland and attended school briefly before being forced to withdraw because of the family's financial problems. He worked temporarily as a tailor, a waiter, and at other jobs. He continued to study on his own, however, and at his own expense in 1866 published *Miscellaneous Subjects by a Self-Educated Colored Youth*. Later that year, after returning from a lecture tour to promote his book, he entered Central High School in Cleveland, graduating in 1869. Also in 1869 he married Annie Walker; they had six children. That same year Green entered Cleveland's Union Law School, from which he graduated in 1870.

Green and his wife moved back to North Carolina in 1870. They remained there only a short while before settling in South Carolina, where Green was admitted to the bar and embarked on a lifelong political career in the Republican Party. In 1872 he was elected a delegate to the state Republican convention and an alternate delegate to the national GOP convention. In the fall of 1872 he returned to Cleveland and easily won election as a justice of the peace, a position that at the time had both judicial and some police powers. One of the first black elected officials in the North, Green held this post for nine years while continuing to work as an attorney. In 1877 he apparently won election to the Ohio house of representatives, but a recount gave the victory to the Democratic candidate; Green unsuccessfully claimed that the election had been stolen from him as a result of a fraudulent vote count.

In 1881 Green was renominated for a seat in the state assembly; this time he was elected. He was not reelected in 1883 but won handily when he ran again in 1889. In 1891 Green was elected to the Ohio senate from a mostly white district—an amazing feat for an African American from the North before World War I. His ability to win election to the state assembly and the state senate demonstrated both the power of the GOP and the racial liberalism of many white Clevelanders at the time. In the senate he supported funding for Wilberforce University, an institution affiliated with the African Methodist Episcopal Church, and in 1893 he helped defeat a bill designed to allow some local school districts to segregate students by race. Green became best known, however, as the sponsor of legislation establishing Labor Day in Ohio in 1893. The Ohio law served as a model for Congress when Labor Day was made a national holiday in 1894, and Green became known as "the father of Labor Day."

Throughout the 1890s Green worked closely with the prominent black Clevelander GEORGE A. MYERS, the owner of a barbershop that catered primarily to whites, in support of the Marcus A. Hanna faction of the Ohio Republican Party. Green, who did not run for reelection to the state senate in 1893, became well known as a speaker on the Republican lecture circuit. He also wrote periodically for the Afro-American News Syndicate, which distributed his articles to numerous black newspapers. In 1896 he lectured throughout the state on behalf of William McKinley and was an alternate delegate-at-large at the Republican National Convention. Green's support for McKinley led to his appointment in 1897 as U.S. postage stamp agent, a position that oversaw the printing and distribution of postage stamps. Green remained in this post until 1905, when he was named acting superintendent of finance for the Post Office Department. While holding these federal positions, he lived in Washington, D.C.

In 1906 Green left government service and returned to full-time law practice in Cleveland. Like most black lawyers in the North at the time, he drew his clientele mostly from the working class of both races. Following the death of his wife, Annie, in January 1912, he married a widow, Lottie Mitchell Richardson, in September 1912. In 1920 he published his autobiography, *Fact Stranger than Fiction*, a volume in the Horatio Alger mold that Green hoped would inspire young African Americans. After 1906 Green took little part in politics, except as an occasional speaker during election campaigns.

Green was typical of an elite group of light-skinned African American professionals and businessmen who established themselves in Cleveland and other northern cities in the decades following the Civil War. Although by objective standards their income placed them in the middle class at best, they set themselves apart from the rest of the black community through their lifestyle, institutional affiliations, and frequent association with whites of similar or higher social status. Green was among the founders of St. Andrew's Episcopal Church, Cleveland's wealthiest African American congregation, and was a member of the Social Circle, an exclusive African American club that dated to 1869. He was also the first black member of the Logos Club, an elite group that met periodically to discuss important social issues of the day. He counted as his friends many prominent white Clevelanders and even had a passing acquaintanceship with John D. Rockefeller.

Green generally believed in the value of integrated institutions, but, unlike some members of the city's African American elite (such as HARRY CLAY SMITH), he was not a leader in the fight against the rising tide of racism in the post-Reconstruction era. At a time when racial discrimination was becoming increasingly evident in Cleveland, he described the city as an "asylum from prejudice and proscription" (*Fact Stranger than Fiction*, dedication page). As a politician, Green was cautious and conservative, and he never criticized Republican leaders on civil rights issues.

During a period when the northern black population was too small to provide an independent base of support for African American politicians, Green was successful because he was a party loyalist who never rocked the boat. Even after retiring from political life, he was unwavering in his allegiance to the GOP. In 1928 and 1932 he spoke on behalf of Herbert Hoover. After most black voters switched to the Democratic Party in 1936, he remained a committed Republican. Green was struck and killed by an automobile in Cleveland after disembarking from a streetcar. He was the oldest practicing attorney in Ohio at the time of his death.

FURTHER READING

Green's papers are located in the Western Reserve Historical Society, and his substantial correspondence with George A. Myers is in Myers's papers at the Ohio Historical Society.

Green, John Patterson. *Fact Stranger than Fiction: Seventy-five Years of a Busy Life with Reminiscences of Many Great Men and Women* (1920).

Green, John Patterson. *Recollections of the Carolinas* (1881).

Davis, Russell H. *Black Americans in Cleveland: From George Peake to Carl B. Stokes, 1796–1969* (1972).

Kusmer, Kenneth L. *A Ghetto Takes Shape: Black Cleveland, 1870–1930* (1976).

Obituary: *Cleveland Gazette*, 7 Sept. 1940.
This entry is taken from the *American National Biography* and is published here with the permission of the American Council of Learned Societies.

KENNETH L. KUSMER

Green, Jonathan (9 Aug. 1955–), painter, printmaker, and illustrator, was born in Gardens Corner, South Carolina, the second of seven children of Ruth J. Green (a home manager) and Melvin Green (occupation unknown). Green is possibly the first person of Gullah descent to train at a professional art school. The Gullah are the descendants of West African slaves who lived on and near the Sea Islands of Georgia and South Carolina.

Great things were expected of Green from the time of his birth. He was born with an inner fetal membrane covering his head and for this reason was considered a "child of the Veil" (Green). In Gullah culture the Veil marks children "touched by uncommonness and magic that will bring inordinate grace to the community." Traveling to New York seeking employment, Green's mother left Green in the care of his maternal grandmother, Eloise Stewart Johnson. Green was interested in art from an early age. His first creative attempts involved paint-by-number kits, but his interest in art heightened in high school. Although he was not encouraged by his teachers, Green dreamed of pursuing a career as an artist. After completing high school, he joined the Air Force in 1973, lured by the recruiter's promise of training in illustration. Green, however, was assigned duty as a cook and stationed in Michigan, North Dakota, Colorado, and Texas. Green discovered East Grand Forks Technical College when he was stationed in Michigan. In 1974 Green began studying illustration at East Grand Forks Technical College. His professors were very enthusiastic about his talent. Green ultimately earned a Bachelor of Fine Arts in painting from the School of the Art Institute of Chicago in 1982. While completing this degree, Green worked as a security guard at the Art Institute.

After graduating from the School of the Art Institute, Green continued to work from a studio in Chicago until 1986 when he moved to Naples, Florida, and opened the Jonathan Green Studios. He returned regularly to South Carolina, where his roots inspired his images of Gullah culture, life, and daily activities. Green preferred to paint in oil using Rembrandt paints because he liked the brilliance and viscosity of the paint. Green also painted with Golden Acrylic paints because of their noted longevity and the buttery quality of the paint, especially when he traveled, as they dry quickly and could be safely shipped back to Green's studio in Naples.

Generally, Green "makes sure that the structure of his canvas or linen is of sound structure, atop that Green applies sizing, and then up to three coats of ground or acrylic. Green predominantly uses a variation of the Verdaccio style of underpainting, in which Green uses blue-grey colors to establish values for later layers. Green also outlines the figures and the landscape shapes during this phase" (Weedman, 2007). On top of the underpainting he applied four to six layers of paint to make his figures, which are highlighted and shadowed to make them look three dimensional and volumetric.

Green's large- and small-scale works took three months to a year to complete. Green had a tendency to work serially, usually painting one series at a time to maintain chromatic and compositional continuity over twelve to fifteen paintings. The "White Laundry" series of 1999 includes *Grandma's Wash, Washed Quilts,* and *Monday Wash.* Occasionally, subjects explored in earlier series are revisited because of other ideas for expression. The one theme that Green revisited over and over again is the similarity between people regardless of who or where they are.

Green was an extremely disciplined painter, working from his Naples studio approximately 43 weeks a year. He generally painted from 1:00 a.m. until 11:00 a.m., with a break until 12:30 p.m., and continued painting until 4:00 p.m. Within two years of graduating from the Art Institute, Green's paintings became popular, and once they were translated into prints, his career took off. He created original, limited edition lithographs, and art for Tide-Mark Press calendars, the covers of cookbooks, note cards, and postcards published by Pomegranate Press. Green also illustrated the following books: *Amadeus the Leghorn Rooster*(2004), *Crosby* (1996), *Father and Son* (1992), and *Noah* (1994). Green is the author of *Gullah Images: The Art of Jonathan Green,* which was published in 1996 by the University of South Carolina Press.

After 1982, Green held over fifty solo exhibitions and participated in over seventy group exhibitions. His work has been exhibited across the United States and in Germany, France, Japan, and Sierra Leone, and in 2010 it was in the permanent collections of the Morris Museum (Augusta, Georgia), the Beach Institute Museum (Savannah, Georgia), the Greenville County (South Carolina) Museum,

the McKissick Museum (Columbia, South Carolina), the Norton Museum of Art (West Palm Beach, Florida), the Philharmonic Center (Naples, Florida), and the Museum Wurtz (Kuenzelsau, Germany). Green's art also was exhibited by the U.S. State Department in the American Embassies in Japan and Sierra Leone. In 2006 twenty-two of Green's paintings inspired the ballet *Off the Wall & Onto the Stage: Dancing the Art of Jonathan Green,* which toured nationally.

Green received numerous awards, including the Annual National Arts Program Award in 2006, the Century of Achievement in Art Award from the Museum of the Americas in 2003, the King-Tisdell Foundation Award for cultural achievement in 2002, the Clemente C. Pickney Award from the South Carolina House of Representatives in 1997, and the Martin Luther King Humanitarian Award for the Arts in 1993. Green served as honorary chair for the School of the Art Institute Bare Walls, as a member of the Board of Directors of Share Our Strength, which works to combat hunger, as Vice President of the Collier County (Florida) United Arts Council in Naples, and as a board member of the Chicago Academy of Arts. Green received an Honorary Doctorate of Fine Arts from the University of South Carolina in 1996. Green was featured in the E. Morris Communications documentary *The Will to Survive: The Story of the Gullah-Geechee Nation* in 2006.

FURTHER READING

Branch, Muriel Miller. *The Water Brought Us: The Story of the Gullah-Speaking People* (1995).

Green, Jonathan. *Gullah Images: The Art of Jonathan Green* (1996).

ANNE DRISCOLL

Green, Marlon D. (6 June 1929–6 July 2009), the first African American commercial passenger airline pilot, was born in El Dorado, Arkansas, the son of McKinley Green, a domestic servant for a wealthy El Dorado dentist and oilman, and Lucy Longmyre. In 1944, due to the influence of a charismatic priest, the five Green siblings, with the exception of one brother, converted from Baptism to Roman Catholicism. Green later earned a scholarship to complete his senior year of high school at the Xavier Preparatory School, affiliated with Xavier University in New Orleans, Louisiana.

At Xavier Prep Green did well academically, graduating at the top of his class. His goal was to attend Epiphany Apostolic College, a Josephite seminary in Newburgh-on-the-Hudson, New York, and study for the priesthood. However, during his first semester he was wrongly diagnosed with a medical condition and was dismissed from the school. Seeking a new direction for his life, he decided to enter the U.S. Air Force in 1947 with the goal of becoming an aircraft mechanic.

Assigned to Wheeler Air Force Base (AFB) in Hawaii, Green found, instead of advancement, only menial assignments. While watching aviators, he developed an interest in learning how to fly and used his off-duty hours to hitch rides on aircraft to observe the pilots, all of whom were white.

In spite of his lack of a college degree, Green applied for pilot training and was accepted on the basis of his high aptitude scores. In February 1950 he was transferred to flight school at Randolph Field in San Antonio, Texas. His roommates were three white cadets, with whom he enjoyed a friendly, easy relationship with no overtones of racism or discrimination. Virgil I. "Gus" Grissom, destined to be one of America's original Mercury Seven astronauts, was a member of Green's graduating class.

Green quickly acquired the skills and knowledge necessary to pilot single-engine, propeller-driven aircraft. Given a choice of specialized training as either a jet fighter pilot or a multi-engine pilot, he chose multiengine school at Reese Air Force Base and earned a commission as a second lieutenant and his pilot's wings.

After graduation in March 1951, Second Lieutenant Green was assigned to Lake Charles Air Base near New Orleans. There, despite the prohibitions against interracial relationships and over the protests of her family in Boston, Green began dating Eleanor Gallagher, a white physical education instructor at Xavier University. Because of Louisiana's miscegenation laws, the couple was prohibited from marrying in that state, so on 29 December 1951 they said their vows in Los Angeles, where state laws allowing intermarriage had only recently been passed. The couple had six children. Green was reassigned to Lockbourne AFB in Columbus, Ohio, where he served with the Ninety-first Air Refueling Squadron.

Further assignments took Green to Mitchel AFB in Long Island, New York, and Johnson AFB in Irumagawa, Japan, where he served with the Thirty-sixth Air Rescue Squadron.

After serving in the U.S. Air Force for nine years (1948–1957), Green left the military and returned to the United States to pursue his dream of becoming a commercial airline pilot. Because of the rampant discrimination in the airline industry at that time, he was denied employment by every major airline, even though he had an impeccable flying record and over three thousand hours of multiengine experience as a-pilot, considerably more than most of the white applicants.

Green moved his family to Lansing, Michigan, where he found work as a pilot for the Michigan State Highway Department. He continued to apply for employment with the airlines and with every large corporation he thought might need pilots. None responded positively.

In June 1957 Green was invited to Denver, then the headquarters for Continental Airlines, to take a flight test. The flight test went smoothly, and Green learned that he had more than twice the number of hours as the next applicant. Yet the other five applicants, all white, were hired, and he was not. Furious and realizing he had nothing left to lose, he submitted a formal complaint to the Colorado Anti-Discrimination Commission.

After investigating, the commission determined that Continental had discriminated against Green solely because of the color of his skin and ordered the airline to admit Green to their next pilot training course. The airline, then run by the flamboyant Robert F. Six, refused—even after receiving a personal written plea from the former first lady Eleanor Roosevelt.

Continental took the matter to Denver District Court, where its lawyers argued that the airline was engaged in interstate commerce and as such was exempt from control or regulation by individual states. The court ruled in Continental's favor. At this point Green engaged the Colorado attorney T. Raber Taylor, who appealed to the Colorado Supreme Court.

While awaiting the court's decision, Green became despondent. He quit his job with the state of Michigan in October 1960, citing the unsafe condition of the aircraft he was required to fly. He and Eleanor, now with six children, exhausted their savings and were forced to go on public assistance while Green continued to search for meaningful work. His desire for an airline pilot's job was undiminished, however, and he pursued every lead, including applying to foreign airlines.

In February 1962 the Colorado Supreme Court ruled in Continental's favor. Because of the interstate nature of its business, the airline was found not to have discriminated against Green and was not required to hire him. Taylor told Green that his last resort was the U.S. Supreme Court, but taking the case to the highest Court in the land, if the Court agreed to hear the matter, would involve considerable expense.

With their spirits low and their savings depleted, the Greens considered giving up. Even though he was being paid nearly nothing for his services, Taylor pursued the case, and the U.S. Supreme Court agreed to hear *Marlon D. Green v. Continental Air Lines, Inc.*, on 28 March 1963. U.S. attorney general Robert Kennedy's Justice Department as well as the attorneys general of several states and other organizations submitted friend of the court briefs on Green's behalf.

In a unanimous landmark ruling released on 22 April 1963, the Supreme Court ordered that Continental must admit Green to a future training class. The airline, however, continued to stall.

While Green was waiting to be hired by Continental, his case caught the attention of Floyd Dominy, the outspoken, controversial head of the Bureau of Reclamation in Washington, D.C. In April 1963 Dominy hired Green to fly him around the West, where the agency was building a number of dams and water diversion projects. The Greens relocated to Denver, where the bureau's plane was housed. Green flew for the bureau until January 1965, when Continental finally admitted him to a training class. On the basis of his demonstrated abilities, he was hired first as a copilot on domestic routes, and he was promoted to captain in less than two years. He was later assigned to fly DC-10s across the Pacific.

Achieving his dream, however, came at a heavy personal price. The years of struggling against discrimination, the financial deprivation, and the pressures that attended an interracial marriage took their toll on Green and his marriage. In 1970 he and Eleanor divorced, and he moved to Southern California.

Continental's fears that a black pilot would drive customers away proved unfounded. Green continued to fly for Continental while his personal life maintained a bumpy course. He was married and divorced three more times and had another son. In August 1978 he retired after fourteen years with the airline and eventually settled in south Florida.

The failures of Marlon Green's personal life, however, cannot dim the success of his dogged determination and his groundbreaking achievement in earning an airline pilot's position against seemingly overwhelming odds. As a result of his personal struggle to become the first scheduled commercial passenger airline pilot of African American descent, Green achieved the aim of all black aviators who had come before: to be allowed equal access to economic opportunity based on skill and not limited by the color of their skin.

After retiring from Continental, August 1978 Green garnered many awards and honors from organizations such as Negro Airmen International and the Tuskegee Airmen's Association. He was presented with a Lifetime Achievement Award by the Organization of Black Airline Pilots, was inducted into the Arkansas Aviation Historical Society Hall of Fame, and is included in the Smithsonian Institution's National Air and Space Museum's Black Wings permanent exhibit. Even more importantly, he earned the gratitude of the black pilots and aircrew members who followed in his wake. He died in Denver, Colorado, at the age of 80.

FURTHER READING
Whitlock, Flint. *The Troublesome Pilot* (forthcoming).

FLINT WHITLOCK

Green, Percy, II (1935–), civil rights activist, cofounder, and chairman of ACTION (Action Committee To Improve Opportunities for Negroes) was born in St. Louis, Missouri, the eldest of four children of Percy Green I, a worker for the Independent Packing Company; his mother did not work outside the home. Three of the Green children completed college.

Raised in a predominantly black neighborhood on the near south side of the city, Green graduated from Vashon High School in 1954 and began working for McDonnell Douglas Aircraft (later Boeing) in 1956. He was drafted in 1958, served twenty-one months in the military, and returned to McDonnell Douglas in 1960. He completed undergraduate studies at St. Louis University in 1970 and earned an MSW from Washington University in St. Louis in 1976.

While working at McDonnell Douglas, Green became involved in the Civil Rights movement. He joined the Congress of Racial Equality (CORE) and eventually became chairman of its St. Louis Employment Committee.

At that time, most major St. Louis businesses did not hire blacks or only hired blacks into low-paying positions. One business targeted by CORE was the national grocer, Kroger, which had no black employees in St. Louis in 1962. CORE organized a boycott of Kroger and engaged in frequent picketing, which prompted Kroger to begin to hire African Americans and brought the protest to a successful conclusion.

CORE's next major effort targeted the St. Louis-based Jefferson Bank. Until 1963, the bank was located in a predominantly black neighborhood on the city's near north side. In 1963, however, the white owners of the bank moved the facility to a midtown location to cater to white-owned businesses. In the move, all black employees were let go and replaced, in the new facility, with white employees.

CORE members, under Green's lead, picketed the bank. The bank, in turn, received a court injunction against the protests and, soon after, nineteen members of CORE were arrested, jailed, and held pending large bail amounts. The struggle was lengthy, expensive, and, while eventually successful (the bank hired four black tellers), resulted in a split within CORE.

Green and twenty-four others came to believe, based on actions like the demonstrations against Kroger and Jefferson Bank, that confrontational, nonviolent, civil disobedience was the quickest way to achieve progress. Others in CORE, whom Green described as having grown "battle fatigued" and "intimidated" (Green Oral History, June Christian, p. 8), preferred a more negotiated approach. As a result, in 1964, Green and others split with CORE and formed ACTION.

ACTION's primary focus was to achieve "More and Better Paying Jobs for Black Men." Underpinning ACTION, in Green's view, was "a conscious social construct to try to develop the family unit and to build from that" (Green Oral History, June Christian, p. 15). To Green and ACTION, it was essential that black men, in particular, have good-paying jobs. In so doing they would earn the respect of black women and their own children. As a result, the number of black men in jail would decrease, as would the number of black women on welfare and in poverty. In turn, ACTION argued, the black family unit would strengthen. On 14 July 1964, Green and Richard Daly, a white member of the as-yet-unannounced splinter group, ACTION, climbed 125 feet up the north leg of the uncompleted St. Louis Gateway Arch to protest the exclusion of blacks from the skilled trades and contractors working on the Arch. Ultimately, more blacks were hired for the federally assisted Arch project and, based on this example, the first federal affirmative action program in the nation was created.

About one month after the Arch action, Green was laid off by McDonnell Douglas even though several white workers with comparable experience and lesser seniority were retained. Green and CORE filed complaints. They staged a "stall in" and "lock in" at McDonnell Douglas, but Green was not rehired. A year later, McDonnell Douglas advertised a position for which Green was fully qualified. He was turned down because of the "lock in" of the prior year. Green filed a complaint with the Equal Employment Opportunity Commission and, eventually, a suit in federal court under the recently enacted federal Civil Rights Act of 1964. Green's case was decided by the U.S. Supreme Court in 1973 (*McDonnell Douglas Corp. v. Green*). It became a landmark decision. In its ruling, the Court defined three criteria or tests to be used to analyze employment discrimination cases; these have been used in most such cases since.

In 1965, its focus still on black employment, ACTION approached St. Louis's major utility companies—companies with large numbers of good-paying nonprofessional jobs—and demanded that six hundred racial minorities be hired in the next ten days. Green knew this would not happen, but, he reasoned, it would shorten the talk time so they could get on with the fight—confrontational, nonviolent, civil disobedience—tactics proven successful in the past (Library of Congress, *Voices of Civil Rights*).

A protest was held outside the headquarters of Southwestern Bell Telephone. It was only a diversion, however, for when police converged on Southwestern Bell, members of ACTION chained themselves to the front door of Laclede Gas, trapping five hundred workers inside. Eventually these actions, too, were successful. Lacelde Gas instituted a policy that 40 percent of all new hires were to be black.

Other notable projects undertaken by ACTION included the "unveiling" of the Veiled Prophet, whose parade, fair, debutante ball, and secret traditions dated back to the late 1870s in St. Louis. Because the "secret," whites-only membership of the Veiled Prophet organization was known to include many of St. Louis's most prominent business and civic leaders, ACTION targeted the organization and its activities.

On the evening of 22 December 1972, during the debutante ball held in Keil Auditorium, Gena Scott, a white member of ACTION, slid down a power cable onto the stage where the Veiled Prophet was situated and "unmasked" him as Tom K. Smith, then executive vice president of Monsanto, a major corporation.

The Veiled Prophet, Gateway Arch, and utility company actions highlight several key components of ACTION's philosophy. ACTION's membership was by intent diverse and integrated, but its leadership was black and male, which Green viewed as a form of therapy. Whites would learn to accept and work under black leadership. Blacks would learn to recognize and accept strong black leadership, especially exercised by black males. Finally, there was ACTION's commitment to confrontational, nonviolent, civil disobedience.

Even though ACTION disbanded in 1984, Green remained active in St. Louis. His and ACTION's commitment to fair employment not only opened significant opportunities for blacks in St. Louis but, as a result of the Arch action and McDonnell Douglas suit, would result in the development of federal affirmative action programs throughout the nation.

FURTHER READING

Washington University: American Culture Studies Program–American Lives, available at http://amlives.artsci.wustl.edu/index.php, has several oral histories from Percy Green. Two good ones are listed below:

Christian, June. *Percy Green Oral History* (December 2005).

Lamberson, Christine. *Percy Green Oral History* (November 2003).

Lang, Clarence. "Between Civil Rights and Black Power in the Gateway City: The Action Committee to Improve Opportunities for Negroes, 1964–1975," *Journal of Social History* (Spring 2004). Available at http://findarticles.com/p/articles/mi_m2005/is_3_37/ai_n6137076/pg_8

Library of Congress. *Voices of Civil Rights: Online Exhibition* (26 May 2005). Available at http://www.loc.gov/exhibits/civilrights/cr-exhibit.html

DENNIS MICHAEL CORCORAN

Green, Sam (c. 1802–28 Feb. 1877), preacher, farmer, and Underground Railroad agent, was born into slavery on the Eastern Shore of Maryland. Although details of his early life and parents are unknown, he probably spent his childhood and young adulthood laboring for white masters in Caroline and Dorchester counties, eventually settling near the town of East New Market with his owner, Henry Nichols. Of mixed race background, possibly American Indian and African descent, Green was eventually manumitted in 1832 by a provision in Nichols's will that required Green be sold for a term of five years and then set free. Green, however, purchased his own freedom within the year.

Green married an enslaved woman named Catherine, also known as Kitty, and they had two children who survived to adulthood. Though Kitty and their children were owned by a different man, it appears that they were allowed to live with Green in his home on historic Nanticoke Indian land near East New Market. By 1842 Sam had earned enough money as a farm laborer and part-time preacher to purchase his wife's liberty. His children's freedom remained out of his grasp. Ezekiel Richardson, their owner, sold the two children to another Dorchester County resident, James Muse, in 1847, taking them out of the Green household forever.

Taught to read and write while he was still a slave, Green became a highly respected lay preacher and licensed exhorter in the Methodist Episcopal Church in Dorchester County. In spite of severe restrictions on African American ministers in the slave states throughout the antebellum period, particularly after the NAT TURNER rebellion in August 1831, Green preached to both free and enslaved African Americans in his community. White observers on the Eastern Shore of Maryland monitored black ministers closely, and Green was probably no exception. His stature within the community grew during the 1840s, however, and by the early 1850s he had taken on a leadership role among Dorchester County free blacks. In 1852 Green traveled to Baltimore as a delegate representing Dorchester County at the Convention of the Free Colored People of Maryland. The meeting was convened to discuss the present condition of civil rights and future prospects for free African Americans living in the state. The issue of emigration to Liberia was hotly debated during the convention, and it appears that Green opposed the idea. He attended the National Convention of the Colored People of the United States, held at Franklin Hall in Philadelphia in October 1855, as a delegate from Maryland. During the convention he mingled with many prominent Northern black abolitionists, including FREDERICK DOUGLASS, Jacob Gibbs, Stephen Myers, WILLIAM COOPER NELL, CHARLES LENOX REMOND, JOHN STEWART ROCK, and MARY ANN CAMBERTON SHADD CARY.

Throughout the antebellum period racial tensions escalated on the Eastern Shore of Maryland. While the free black population continued to expand due to natural increase and manumissions, the slave population experienced tremendous destabilization. Eastern Shore slaveholders found a lucrative market selling their slaves to the plantations of the Deep South, where labor needs continued to outpace existing supplies of workers. Like Green's family, many black families on the Eastern Shore included both free and enslaved family members. The constant threat of separation left many African Americans facing daily uncertainty. With the sales of loved ones a constant menace, efforts to protect those at risk became a high priority among some families. Escape to a free state was risky though often the only alternative to being sold away. Maryland's proximity to free soil, however, offered a better chance of success in reaching freedom than that in the Deep South. Slaves had been running away from Dorchester County since the earliest days of colonial settlement. During the early to mid-nineteenth century, the Eastern Shore began to experience a profound acceleration in the numbers of slaves taking their own liberty. By the early 1820s and 1830s a loosely organized network of sympathizers formed the foundation of a system that worked to aid runaway slaves in their quest to reach free soil. This network became known as the Underground Railroad, and whites and blacks in the North and the South maintained its operations.

In August 1854 Green's son Sam Green Jr., a skilled blacksmith, ran away from Muse after learning that he might be sold. Using instructions given to him by HARRIET TUBMAN, he found his way to the office of WILLIAM STILL, Philadelphia's most famous Underground Railroad stationmaster, who forwarded him to the home of Charles Bustill, another prominent African American Underground Railroad agent in Philadelphia. From there he was sent along swiftly to Chipaway, Ontario, Canada, where he joined other Eastern Shore runaways living relatively safe and free lives. Once settled in Chipaway, Sam Green Jr. wrote to his parents, telling them of his successful journey to freedom. Tragically his sister Sarah Green was unable to flee. As the mother of two young children, Sarah may have been unwilling or unable to run away with her brother. Muse, angry over the escape of Sam Green Jr. and suspicious that Sarah might run off as well, sold her to a Missouri family, cruelly separating her from her family forever.

It is not known when Sam Green first became an agent on the Underground Railroad. Sam and Kitty Green sheltered Tubman and a group of her charges in November 1856, and they may have helped Tubman and others on several occasions before this date. Tubman was born and raised in the same county, and there is a possibility that she was related to Sam through her mother, Rit Green Ross.

By mid-March 1857 rumors were circulating that Green had played a role in the escape of the Dover Eight, a group of fugitive slaves who had successfully eluded capture in a dramatic flight from Dorchester County. Green had apparently been suspected of aiding in the escape of other slaves before this, but he was so highly regarded in both the black and white communities that he was able to deflect suspicions for some time. When it was discovered that the Dover Eight passed near his home during their escape, doubts about his innocence were raised. Adding to local whites' suspicions, Green had recently returned from a trip to Canada to visit his refugee son. On 4 April 1857 the Dorchester County sheriff Robert Bell arrived at Green's house with a search warrant. Green was promptly arrested when the authorities found a Canadian map, letters from Sam Green Jr. and other Dorchester County fugitives living in Ontario, various railroad schedules, and a copy of one volume of the two-volume set of Harriet Beecher Stowe's *Uncle Tom's Cabin*.

Green was charged with illegal possession of material that could rouse feelings of "discontent" and dissatisfaction among slaves, in violation of Maryland's Act of 1841, chapter 272, which stated that if any free black "knowingly receive or have in his possession any abolition handbill, pamphlet, newspaper, pictorial representation or other paper of an inflammatory character," which could "create discontent amongst or to stir up to insurrection the people of color of this State, he or she shall be deemed guilty of felony," subject to a prison term of ten to twenty years (*Easton Gazette*, 28 Aug. 1858).

Prosecutors claimed that the maps, railroad schedules, and letters from Canada were abolitionist in nature and were used to create dissatisfaction among the local slave population. The court acquitted Green, though, ruling that those materials in and of themselves were not inflammatory publications. New charges were lodged against him, however, citing his possession of *Uncle Tom's Cabin*, and this time he was convicted. Though local newspapers acknowledged that Green never would have been charged with this particular crime if he had not been under suspicion for aiding slaves to run away, they congratulated themselves for "testing the applicability of the Act" to *Uncle Tom's Cabin* (*Easton Gazette*, 28 Aug. 1858).

At fifty-five years old, Green represented what some slaveholders resented and feared the most: a literate, well-respected, free black who may well have encouraged resistance to the slave system. Green was sentenced to ten years in the Maryland State Penitentiary, officially for "having in his possession a certain abolition pamphlet called *Uncle*

Tom's Cabin," the first and only time anyone was ever convicted for such a crime (*Easton Gazette*, 28 Aug. 1858). Beyond the expected abolitionist outrage over the conviction, the case also created a firestorm of controversy, sparking intense debate about the Bill of Rights and a free person's rights to privacy in Maryland and beyond.

Appeals were made to Maryland's governor Thomas H. Hicks, a Dorchester countian who had himself known and respected Green, to pardon Green and set him free. In spite of significant pro-Green support in the northern press, Hicks and the Maryland courts remained determined and steadfast in their decision to keep him incarcerated. An exemplary prisoner, Green was spared the more arduous physical labor required of inmates at the prison when he was assigned to work in the warden's office, presumably because he could read and write. The expenses of the trial forced Kitty Green to sell the couple's property in Dorchester County. She followed her husband to Baltimore, where she found work as a launderer. Finally, in March 1862, after continued pressure from northern abolitionists, powerful Baltimore Quakers, and Methodist Episcopal Church officials, the newly elected governor Augustus W. Bradford pardoned Green on the condition that he leave Maryland immediately. On 21 April 1862 Green walked out of prison a marginally free man.

Sam and Kitty Green soon left Maryland for Philadelphia, where Still sheltered them. In June they traveled to New York City, where Green spoke at HENRY HIGHLAND GARNET's Shiloh Presbyterian Church. During the following month Green was introduced to Stowe, who gave him a new copy of *Uncle Tom's Cabin*. The Greens spent the summer traveling to different northern communities, where they found ready audiences eager to hear Sam's story. Funds were raised throughout New England for their support as they made their way slowly to Canada and the home of their son Sam Green Jr.

The Greens returned to Dorchester County soon after the Civil War. Once again Green built a life around farming and preaching. He was an active member of the Delaware Conference of the Methodist Episcopal Church and the Centenary Biblical Institute in Baltimore. The Greens moved to Baltimore around 1874, presumably to devote more time to the institute. Sam Green died there.

FURTHER READING

Blondo, Richard A. "Samuel Green: A Black Life in Antebellum Maryland," MA thesis, University of Maryland (1988).

Larson, Kate Clifford. *Bound for the Promised Land: Harriet Tubman, Portrait of an American Hero* (2004).

Still, William. *The Underground Rail Road* (1871; rpt. 1970).

KATE CLIFFORD LARSON

Green, Shields (1836–16 Dec. 1859), fugitive slave, was hanged for his participation in John Brown's raid at Harpers Ferry. Nothing is known about his family or early life except that he was from Charleston, South Carolina, and was nicknamed "Emperor." Green escaped from slavery, leaving behind a son, and reached Canada, but then returned to the United States and sought out FREDERICK DOUGLASS. In 1859 Green met Brown at Douglass's Rochester, New York, home. According to Douglass, Brown saw "at once what 'stuff' Green 'was made of' and confided to him his plans and purposes" (*Life and Times*, 757). Green felt a kindred chemistry too. He was ready to follow Brown and accepted a position in Brown's provisional government for a nation without slavery.

On 19 August 1859, with his raid on the federal arsenal at Harpers Ferry looming large on the horizon, Brown summoned Douglass to a meeting that would decide Green's fate. Brown suggested they meet in a disused quarry pit near Chambersburg, Pennsylvania, along with Green and John Kagi, Brown's lieutenant. Brown arrived in disguise as a fisherman named Isaac Smith, wearing clothes that seemed almost a camouflage, colored like the quarry. The four sat among the rocks. Douglass was nervous, Brown was anxious, and the two disagreed as to the wisdom of Brown's plans. Brown desperately wanted to recruit Douglass and urged him to join the group already installed at the Kennedy farm in Virginia.

Douglass gave a cool reception to Brown's plea that he join the expedition, which he saw as a "trap of steel, and ourselves in the wrong side of it," as he explained in his Storer College address of 1881 (*John Brown*, 209). To Douglass, the raid seemed dangerous for raiders and liberated slaves alike, and Brown's militancy sounded too extreme. But Brown was unswerving. Douglass remembered, "He was not to be shaken by anything I could say, but treated my views respectfully" (*Life and Times*, 759). They talked throughout Saturday and Sunday, and eventually Douglass stood to leave, telling Green he could go home too. Brown was not finished. He embraced Douglass and entreated: "I will defend you with my life. I want you for a special purpose.

When I strike, the bees will begin to swarm, and I shall want you to help me hive them" (Douglass, *Life and Times*, 760). Douglass refused again and turned to go, but Green hung back. Douglass asked, "Shields, are you coming?" To his surprise, Green answered calmly, "I believe I'll go with the old man" (Douglass, *Life and Times*, 760). With Green, Brown left the "council of war," as Douglass called it, and returned to Virginia. Douglass left the quarry alone and never saw Brown again.

Green became, in Douglass's words, "one of the bravest of [Brown's] soldiers" (*Life and Times*, 760). Douglass's self-confessed attempt, in his Storer address, to "pay a just debt long due, to vindicate in some degree a great historical character … whose friendship and confidence it was my good fortune to share," was perhaps made with this painful meeting in mind. "I could live for the slave, but he could die for him," he acknowledged of Brown and by implication of Green (Douglass, *John Brown*, 205). In *The Life and Times of Frederick Douglass* (1881; rpt. 1994) Douglass describes Green as "a man of few words" whose "speech was singularly broken" but whose "courage and self-respect made him quite a dignified character." Green, he adds, was "not one to shrink from hardships or dangers" (757).

The men who followed Brown into the history books were young, idealistic, and passionate about their leader. All but two were under thirty years old, and three were under twenty-one. Numbering twenty-two, including Brown himself, the raiders were an interracial group, sixteen white and five black. Some born slaves and some born free, the black men were Lewis Sheridan Leary, JOHN ANTHONY COPELAND JR., OSBORNE PERRY ANDERSON, DANGERFIELD NEWBY, and Green. Of the five black raiders, only Anderson survived both the raid itself and execution in its wake.

Anderson wrote in *A Voice from Harper's Ferry* (1861) of the remarkable interracial dynamic of the band of raiders, calling it an "Anti-Slavery family" where "men from widely different parts of the continent met and united into one company, wherein no hateful prejudice dared intrude its ugly self—no ghost of a distinction found space to enter" (83). While preparations for the raid continued at the Kennedy farm during the summer of 1859, there was, he explains, "no milk and water sentimentality—no offensive contempt for the negro, while working in his cause" (Anderson, 83). Anderson paints a picture of an almost utopian interracial community at the Kennedy farm, with Brown at its center.

Late in the evening on Sunday, 16 October 1859, the interracial band seized the federal arsenal at Harpers Ferry, Virginia (later West Virginia). Green severed telegraph wires to the east and the west and helped capture the armory, the arsenal, and the rifle works. He went to bring in slaves from the surrounding areas as soon as the arsenal was captured, for Brown hoped they would flock to his cause and intended to arm them and spark a slave uprising across the South. The band held out against Virginia and Maryland militia for two nights until marines finally took the arsenal back on Tuesday morning. Green, who was outside Harpers Ferry when Brown and his men surrendered, asked another of Brown's men, Jeremiah Anderson, if Brown might yet get away. Hearing that all was lost, he headed for the besieged engine house and certain death.

Jeremiah Anderson fled, and Douglass later asked him, "Why then did not Shields come with you?" Anderson explained, "I told him to come; that we could do nothing more, but he simply said he must go down to de ole man" (Douglass, *Life and Times*, 761). Green was with Brown when the "ole man" was captured. An article in *Harper's Weekly* on 5 November 1859 speculated of Green: "Doubtless, at that moment he would have swapped himself and his honors to boot for the meanest field-nigger on a Georgia plantation." But Osborne Anderson insisted in *A Voice from Harper's Ferry* that "a braver man never lived than Shields Green" (106).

Brown was indicted on counts of assault, murder, conspiracy, and treason, then was convicted and sentenced to hang. He died in Charleston on 2 December 1859. Of the men who fought beside him, ten died in battle, six escaped, and five were hung. Two of the black raiders died at Harpers Ferry, and one escaped. Green and Copeland were charged with treason and sentenced to death. Remembering Green's final weeks, Anderson called the process a "mockery of a trial, sentence and execution" (112). Green was hanged on 16 December 1859, two weeks after Brown. He was twenty-three years old.

A few days later Professor James Monroe found Green's body in the dissecting rooms of the Winchester Medical College in Virginia. On Christmas Day there was a funeral service for Green at the First Church in Winchester, Virginia, and in 1860 a monument to Green and Copeland was erected in Westwood Cemetery in Oberlin, Ohio. The monument was moved to MARTIN LUTHER KING JR. Park in Oberlin in 1972. In *Douglass' Monthly*, Douglass noted that "the noble Shields Green, NATHANIEL TURNER and DENMARK VESEY stand ready to peril everything at the command of the Government" (Sept. 1861). Two years later Douglass again put Green alongside Vesey and Turner: "Remember Denmark Vesey of Charleston; remember Nathaniel Turner of Southampton; remember Shields Green and Copeland, who followed noble John Brown, and fell as glorious martyrs for the cause of the slave." He concluded with the call: "Men of Color, to Arms!" (*Douglass' Monthly*, 21 Mar. 1863).

FURTHER READING

Anderson, Osbourne P. *A Voice from Harper's Ferry* (1861, rpt. 2000).

Aptheker, Herbert. *Toward Negro Freedom* (1956).

Douglass, Frederick. *John Brown: An Address by Frederick Douglass, at the Fourteenth Anniversary of Storer College, Harper's Ferry, West Virginia, May 30, 1881*, in *Meteor of War: The John Brown Story*, ed. Zoe Trodd and John Stauffer (2004).

Douglass, Frederick. *The Life and Times of Frederick Douglass*, in *Autobiographies: Frederick Douglass*, ed. Henry Louis Gates Jr. (1994).

Hinton, Richard J. *John Brown and His Men* (1968).

Libby, Jean. *Black Voices from Harper's Ferry: Osbourne Anderson and the John Brown Raid* (1979).

Quarles, Benjamin. *Allies for Freedom: Blacks on John Brown* (2001).

Stutler, Boyd B. *Captain John Brown and Harper's Ferry: The Story of the Raid and the Old Fire Engine House Known as John Brown's Fort* (1930).

ZOE TRODD

Green, William (1820s?–?), writer and laborer, was born a slave in Oxford Neck, Maryland, to an enslaved mother named Matilda Jackson. Green lamented throughout his life that he was born too early, because his mother was freed by the terms of her owner's will three months after his birth. Because he was born to a slave mother, he was a slave by law regardless of how little time remained in her tenure as a slave. Green still had hopes of being free in his lifetime because Molly Goldsbury, his owner, bequeathed to him a gradual emancipation by which Green could be freed when he turned twenty-five years old. However, she was not alive to ensure the proper execution of her will, and when he was sold after her death, there were no explicit provisions regarding his emancipation.

In his early years, then, Green was sold from owner to owner, working as a body-servant, a waiter, and even a horse racer. Because he was surrounded by family members and friends who were emancipated, freedom was always foremost in his mind, and his imagination often dwelled on escape plans. Though Green reported in his slave narrative that he was treated more humanely than most of those enslaved in the South, he witnessed severe brutality enacted upon his family members and close friends and experienced mistreatment himself, all of which added to his certainty that he must resist his bind of enslavement. After defying his owner's insistence that he always remain on the premises of the plantation, for instance, Green was confronted by his owner, Dr. Solomon Jenkings, and threatened with whipping. Green, determined not to be beaten, fought Jenkings and won. Not to be shaken by his slave's resistance but cowardly in the face of Green's power, Jenkings attempted to trick Green into going to the jail to be whipped by a professional. Cleverly, Green avoided the punishment and ran away the same night.

Green's narrative of his escape provides some details regarding the operation of the Underground Railroad at the time of his flight, around 1840. He hid for a few days in the home of a fierce slave owner, assured that no one would ever suspect that he would run to find his safety there. After the search for him cooled, he proceeded north, across the river and through fields to several homes of people he heard had safehouses. At some homes he was only hesitantly welcomed because some abolitionists were being watched carefully to prevent their participation in the emancipation of runaways. Green however, was heartily aided and welcomed by many, black and white, and he was surprised to find such generosity in the hearts of white people. He followed the trails suggested by those abolitionists he met, which led him to an "Aunt Sarah," who helped him finally to cross to Philadelphia. He then traveled to New York City, where he felt relative safety, but still moved on to Hartford, Connecticut, and then to Springfield, Massachusetts. There he was married to Parthena Peters by the prominent abolitionist Dr. Rev. Samuel Osgood, and subsequently had at least four children. In his narrative, Green recalled fondly both Rev. Osgood and Dr. DAVID RUGGLES, also an abolitionist who led the New York Vigilance Committee, for their enthusiastic assistance in his journey out of slavery and in his life as a free person.

In 1853 Green decided to record his life story, but carefully protected the lives and work of those abolitionists who provided his route to freedom and continued to do the same for many others who sought to leave the South for the emancipation awaiting them in the North.

FURTHER READING

Green, William. *Narrative of Events in the Life of William Green, (Formerly a Slave.) Written by Himself* (1853).

LAURA MURPHY

Green, William Thomas (May 1860?–3 Dec. 1911), attorney, was born in Canada, probably in St. Catharines, Ontario. His parentage is uncertain, but it appears that he was born into the family of Thomas and Mary Green, two African Americans who had migrated to Canada. His father was a laborer; neither parent was literate.

Green's early schooling is undocumented. He may have attended St. Catharines Collegiate Institute, but no records substantiate that. In 1884 he moved to the United States, probably to Chicago; no records support his claim that he became a naturalized citizen. Three years later he settled in Milwaukee, Wisconsin. Employed as a waiter in the prestigious Plankinton House, he was at home in the upper circles of Milwaukee's black society. While he was at Plankinton House it is likely that Green benefited from the schooling that the African American head of dining services, John J. Miles, arranged for members of his all-black crew.

After moving to Madison in 1890, Green received a patronage appointment as a janitor in the state capitol. He became known to politicians, one of whom, James H. McGillian, influenced him to apply to the University of Wisconsin Law School. Green received his law degree in 1892 and, returning to Milwaukee, joined James H. Stover, also a new attorney, for a year before establishing his own practice. Green was the first—and during his lifetime the only—black attorney in Wisconsin.

Green's rise to prominence was acknowledged by his leadership role in framing and lobbying for the state's first civil rights act. When a Milwaukee black, having been refused admission to the orchestra of a theater in 1889, took the theater owner to court, the suit galvanized the city's black community. Following a call signed by Green, among others, a meeting was held during which a substantial list of grievances was compiled and those in attendance asked the governor to recommend a civil rights law. Those at the meeting also endorsed *New York Age* editor T. THOMAS FORTUNE's idea of a national convention to support black commercial and political interests and urged that civil rights become the yardstick for race support of political parties.

Milwaukee's black leaders produced a civil rights bill a month later, but it was not introduced until 1891, at which time Green, the probable author of the bill, was the only African American to testify before the assembly judiciary committee. Although he made a favorable impression, it was not sufficient to overcome the opposition, and the bill died. Back in Milwaukee the next year, Green was elected to the state Republican convention, the first African American to be so recognized. His major contribution was a platform amendment denouncing the treatment of blacks by southern whites, a ploy for which the black press chided him but which was a strategically sound maneuver to get Republicans on record against discrimination for possible later use locally. When Republicans regained control of the legislature, Green's bill passed easily with a slight reduction of penalties and was signed into law in April 1895.

Twice thereafter Green was called on to lobby against bills that would ban intermarriage. One of these, known as the Cady bill, was defeated in the legislature in April 1901; two years later Green's testimony before the assembly committee was instrumental in having the similar Williams bill killed. He argued that the bill, based on "malice, prejudice and a desire to humiliate the Negro," was essentially a reintroduction of the Black Laws that had long since been repudiated by northern states. He maintained that a law grounded in "class hatred and or race or other prejudice was never beneficial to the state."

Associated with neither BOOKER T. WASHINGTON's network nor W. E. B. DuBOIS's supporters, Green denounced prejudice and spoke out for positive action. The time had come, he told a black audience in 1902, for the Negro to "carve out his own destiny." At other times he rejected color lines drawn by whites or blacks, endorsed the gospel of work, and believed that race amalgamation—that is, the interbreeding of blacks and whites over time to create a single race—"is the only salvation for the Negro." He urged blacks in 1906 to "keep up the fight, ever and always, for our constitutional rights."

Green's law practice flourished from the beginning. "We have the best Afro-American lawyer in the country," the black Milwaukee paper boasted in 1899, "and the best part of his clients are white people." He frequently traveled to other Wisconsin cities and to Chicago on legal business. As a defense attorney, his cases ranged from petty crime to corporate negligence, from debt recovery to divorce, from civil rights to murder. One of his most famous cases involved Nina Brown, who was accused of killing her paramour. Green offered an insanity defense; the prosecutor conceded, and the judge so instructed the jury. Both officials praised Green "for the manner in which he conducted this case." Four years later, when a well-established Milwaukee black was charged with murder, Green successfully entered a plea of self-defense to win the case. In each case he single-handedly defended his client. "If I engage counsel," he explained, noting his status as the only black attorney in Milwaukee, "and we won the case, some of my people would say, 'the white man did it.'"

Although a leader in black Republican circles and a faithful campaigner, and despite near-unanimous support from the black community and measurable endorsements from whites, Green was denied opportunities to run for city supervisor, assistant city attorney, and justice of the peace. "Our well-known attorney, Green, can tell you a thing or two, when it comes to Republican promises," the Milwaukee black weekly groused in 1906.

Active in the social life of the Milwaukee African American community, Green also held leadership positions in the black Masonic order, in which he often acted as orator, master of ceremonies, toastmaster, or introducer of prominent out-of-town speakers. An impressive speaker himself, he was well versed in local history, race matters, church affairs, and Wisconsin politics. A friend's description of his court appearances depicts him as "trembling with sincerity" and then using humor to "sweep the room with laughter."

There is no record of Green's marriage; he lived in single rooms and listed himself as a widower. At a probate inquiry his only child, a son, testified that his mother was still alive. Green died in Milwaukee of kidney disease after a short illness. His funeral, the largest ever held in the city's St. Mark's African Methodist Episcopal Church, "was crowded to the doors," including "a large representation of lawyers and judges." He was, a white newspaper concluded, "one of the colored people's most ardent defenders, and always worked for the uplifting of his race."

FURTHER READING

Fishel, Leslie H., Jr. "The Genesis of the First Wisconsin Civil Rights Bill," *Wisconsin Magazine of History* 49 (1966), 324–333.
Olson, Frederick I. "Early Civil Rights Hero Honored in Sandburg," *UWM Report* 14 (1993), 15.
Obituaries: *Milwaukee Free Press* and *Evening Wisconsin* (Milwaukee), 4 Dec. 1911.

This entry is taken from the *American National Biography* and is published here with the permission of the American Council of Learned Societies.

LESLIE H. FISHEL

Greene, Belle da Costa (26 Nov. 1879–10 May 1950), library director, bibliographer, and art connoisseur, was born Belle Marion Greener, the daughter of RICHARD GREENER, a lawyer and Republican Party activist, and Genevieve Ida Fleet Greener. Her place of birth was probably Washington, D.C., where her father held a variety of jobs. But specifics concerning Greene's childhood and education are scarce because she preferred to keep them a mystery. Apparently she attended Teachers College in New York City, where the family had relocated after Richard Greener was rewarded with a patronage job for his efforts on behalf of the Republican Party. Around 1897 Belle Marion Greener's parents separated, the children staying with their mother, who within a few years changed the surname to Greene and some years thereafter altered her maiden name from Fleet to Van Vliet. During this time the Greenes fully "passed" in the white world, and Belle da Costa Greene (who claimed for herself nonexistent Portuguese forebears) never acknowledged her African lineage.

Greene's first position was librarian in training at the Princeton University Library, where she learned cataloging practices and reference services. While working there she met two men who greatly influenced her life. Her first mentor, a university librarian and bibliographer, Ernest C. Richardson, helped develop her interest in rare books; the second, Junius Spencer Morgan, an alumnus of Princeton and a collector of early manuscripts, was a nephew of the banker J. Pierpont Morgan. Knowing that his uncle was in need of someone to organize and catalog his sizable collection of manuscripts and rare books, Morgan recommended Greene. In 1905 Greene met and impressed the 68-year-old Morgan, who hired her as his private librarian. For Greene, he became a father figure who opened doors for her to the scholarly, the wealthy, and the collectors of museum-class art and books. Their instant rapport and continued mutual respect based on similar attitudes toward historical artifacts laid the groundwork for their interdependent and mutually rewarding relationship. Morgan's increasing reliance on Greene's judgment in the acquisition and management of his growing collection made possible the assembling of a valuable and extraordinary private collection of medieval illuminated manuscripts, incunabula, early bindings, autographed manuscripts, rare books, paintings, and art objects.

The new Renaissance-style Morgan Library building at Thirty-sixth Street and Madison Avenue in New York City, designed by Charles F. McKim with an elegant and ornate interior planned by Morgan, became Belle Greene's workspace for the next forty-three years. From 1905 to 1908 her main function was organizing Morgan's existing collection, but he also frequently sat with her for short chats and liked to have her read to him. From the onset she was loyal to her "boss," to the staff, and to her mission, willingly giving her best in the smallest undertaking, gaining the respect of all who worked for her or needed her assistance. Humor, humility, and an energetic personality were essential ingredients of her quest for knowledge.

As Morgan came to depend on her judgment, Greene's duties expanded to include travel abroad to locate suitable additions for his collections. Her knowledge, coupled with Morgan's financial backing, had an effect on the book markets and auction houses of two continents. From the beginning of her employment Greene was provided the means to live and work in the manner befitting an agent for a wealthy banker. In the early years at the library, she often wore Renaissance-style dresses or bustling brocades with appropriate jewelry. After 1908, when she traveled on buying trips for Morgan, she stayed at the best hotels, wore elegant clothing, including large, plumed hats, and sometimes brought her thoroughbred horse to London, England, to ride in Hyde Park.

Through Morgan Greene met in 1908 the noted art connoisseur Bernard Berenson, with whom she developed a lifelong attachment and a voluminous correspondence. Sydney Cockerell, the director of the Fitzwilliam Museum at Cambridge University, another of Morgan's acquaintances, taught her how to sharpen her critical evaluations and introduced her to European scholars from whom she could seek advice. She soon became well known and respected in museums, galleries, libraries, and upper-class homes throughout Europe. In spite of her growing expertise and acumen when evaluating rare objects she always consulted with experts before recommending a purchase to Morgan, who had the final say.

When Morgan died in 1913 Greene was devastated: "I feel as if life had stopped … it is all I can do to go on without him. He was much more than my 'boss.' He was almost a father to me" (Canfield, 152).

She did remain in charge of the library when his son J. P. Morgan Jr. inherited the collection, even though he was less involved than his father had been. She encouraged his interest in the library, and when some of the art collection had to be sold to settle the estate, Morgan relied on her to negotiate the best prices. It was at this time that she came to increasingly seek advice from Berenson, who continued to be an important influence on her intellectual pursuits as well as a friend.

With characteristic energy Greene approached war work when the United States entered World War I in 1917. In addition, her mother, who had been living with her since she first moved to New York in 1905, was joined by Greene's war-widowed, pregnant youngest sister who gave birth in her home. Several years later, when her sister remarried, she adopted her sister's child, Robert Mackenzie Leveridge, and took on the added responsibility of his education.

In 1920 Morgan decided to enlarge the collection, and Greene resumed her professional excursions to Europe. When Morgan incorporated the library in memory of his father in 1924, Belle Greene was named director, a position she held until she retired. As an endowed educational institution, the library took on a new orientation dedicated to scholarship. It was a challenge to turn a private collection into a semipublic one, and she and her staff took great interest in aiding scholars by increasing the availability and usefulness of the collection. When interviewed by Aline B. Louchheim, Greene recalled that even when it was a private collection, the elder Morgan said, "Of course, that man can come, someday they can all come." Expansion continued under Greene's direction, including an annex completed in 1928 that increased the research facilities and allowed for regular exhibitions and lectures. Large numbers of reference books were added, as well as files to accompany thousands of objects. On many of the flyleaves of books and in those files, she added annotations in her firm, clear writing as aids for researchers.

Over the decades Greene kept up a lively correspondence with scholars and friends and continued to travel to Europe for business and pleasure until 1936. By 1940 her life had begun to change radically. After an accident resulted in a broken arm she became fearful of falling and experienced other health problems. Within the next two years her mother and her older sister both died, her nephew was killed in action, and J. P. Morgan Jr. died soon after.

By 30 November 1948, when she retired because of her failing health, Greene had spent twenty-five years as executive head and a total of forty-three years amassing a collection few librarians have had the opportunity or the ability to assemble. Her first devotion and responsibility was the Morgan Library, but she was often called on to make significant contributions to other institutions, for which she was honored during her lifetime. In recognition of her public service, the governments of Belgium, France, and Italy decorated her. After World War I she was made a member of the Committee for the Restoration of the Louvain Library and was one of the first women accepted as a fellow of the Mediaeval Academy of America. She was a fellow in perpetuity of the Metropolitan Museum of Art, a consultant to the Walters Art Gallery board of trustees, and a trustee of the Art Foundation, and she was elected to the board of the College Art Association, the Library Advisory Council of the Library of Congress, the Index Society, and the editorial boards of the *Gazette des Beaux-Arts* and *Art News*.

Among the many letters of praise she received on her retirement in 1948, the one from Eric Millar, former keeper of manuscripts at the British Museum, summarizes the distinction of her contribution to the shaping of a world-class institution: "It must mean something to you to know what a monument of your taste, enthusiasm, and whole-hearted devotion to its interests you have built up to yourself in that wonderful institution, with which your name will always be associated." Greene died in New York City, where her legacy continues in the collection of the Morgan Library, which includes a 1913 portrait of her by Paul Helleu.

FURTHER READING

Information concerning Greene's parents, racial origins, and name change can be found in Jean Strouse, *Morgan: American Financier* (1999).

Canfield, Cass. *The Incredible Pierpont Morgan: Financier and Art Collector* (1974).

The First Quarter Century of the Pierpont Morgan Library: A Retrospective Exhibition in Honor of Belle da Costa Greene (1949).

Minor, Dorothy, ed. *Studies in Art and Literature for Belle da Costa Greene* (1954).

Obituaries: *Publishers Weekly*, 10 June 1950; *New York Times*, 12 May 1950.

This entry is taken from the *American National Biography* and is published here with the permission of the American Council of Learned Societies.

CONSTANCE KOPPELMAN

Greene, Beverly Lorraine (4 Oct. 1915–22 Aug. 1957), the first African American woman licensed as an architect in the United States, was born in Chicago, the only child of James A. Greene, a lawyer, and Vera Greene, a homemaker.

Greene received a Bachelor of Architecture degree from the University of Illinois at Urbana-Champaign in 1936 and a Master of Science degree in City Planning and Housing in 1937 from the same school. After graduation she was hired by Kenneth Roderick O'Neal, the first black architect to open an office in downtown Chicago (he later hired the nation's second licensed black female architect, Louise Harris Brown). In December 1942, Greene became the first officially licensed black female architect in the state of Illinois and in the nation. After working in O'Neal's office, Greene applied for and was eventually hired for a position at the Chicago Housing Authority. This was something of a milestone; until that time, few black professionals, especially architects, had been hired by the Chicago Housing Authority.

Greene wanted to go to New York to attend Columbia University to obtain an additional degree. She applied to the school, where she sought a scholarship. In 1944, not knowing the fate of her scholarship, she also applied for a position as an architect with the Metropolitan Life Insurance Company in New York City. This company was planning to build a large 8,000-unit housing complex in Lower Manhattan. The company later announced its intention to bar Negroes from living in the new Stuyvesant Town housing project. This discriminatory stance caused a big controversy at the time (the company later sponsored the Riverton Houses project in Harlem, which was all black). Greene was sure when she learned about their attitude that she—a black woman—would not be hired. It may have been to deflect criticism that she was the first architect hired for the project. She accepted the offer and moved to New York City.

Greene was later quoted in a newspaper article about her experience working at the company for only three days before quitting. By that time she had found out that she had been offered a scholarship to pursue further architectural studies at Columbia University. She attended Columbia from 1944 to 1945 and in 1945 received a Master of Science in Architecture degree. She lived on West 146th Street in Harlem.

After graduation, Beverly Greene worked for two of the leading architects in New York City:

Edward Durrell Stone and Marcel Breuer. In Stone's office, she is believed to have worked on a theater at the University of Arkansas campus built in 1951 and a portion of the Sarah Lawrence College Arts Complex in Bronxville, New York, completed in 1952.

Beverly Greene is mentioned in two books about architect Marcel Breuer as one of two talented female architects (and the only African American) who worked in his office in the 1950s. Greene is credited with work on several of Breuer's projects, including a building for New York University and the UNESCO Secretariat and Conference Hall in Paris (completed in 1958).

At some point Greene also worked in the architectural office of Isadore Rosenfield, a medical facility specialist. That office employed Conrad Johnson, another black architect who went on to establish a prominent office of his own. Greene's wide range of friends suggests that her interests extended beyond the world of architecture. According to those who knew her, Greene's New York social circle included entertainer LENA HORNE and DUKE ELLINGTON's music composer BILLY STRAYHORN.

In 1957 Greene, who was a member of the Council for the Advancement of the Negro in Architecture (CANA), was mentioned in a letter to *Ebony* magazine that talked about an exhibit of the work of black architects organized by CANA and co-sponsored by the New York Chapter of the American Institute of Architects and the Architectural League. Other black women, including New York State's first black architect, Norma Fairweather (who later became Norma Sklarek) were also CANA members. While her obituary stated that Beverly Greene designed two projects in Harlem (Unity Funeral Home, where she was later eulogized, and the Christian Reformation Church), it is not known if she did any other private architectural work.

Beverly L. Greene died at the age of 41 in 1957 at Sydenham Hospital in New York City. A memorial service held at Unity Funeral Home in Harlem was attended by friends Lena Horne, musician Billy Strayhorn, and Dr. ARTHUR LOGAN, a black surgeon and civil rights advocate. Dr. Logan's wife, Marion Bruce, a cabaret singer who later headed New York City's Commission on Human Rights, sang at the memorial service. Beverly Greene's remains were sent to Chicago where a few days later a funeral was held at a chapel in Chicago attended by her family and Chicago area friends.

FURTHER READING
"Woman Architect Blazes a New Trail for Others," *Amsterdam News*, 23 June 1945.
Obituaries: *Chicago Daily Tribune*, August 26, 1957; *Jet Magazine*, 5 September 1957.

ROBERTA WASHINGTON

Greene, Bob (14 Feb. 1936–), journalist and sports writer, was born Robert Everett Greene, in Portland, Maine. He was the elder of two children born to Ruth Madeline Fisher, a federal government administrator, and Robert "Rob" Leo Lake Greene, a U.S. Postal Service employee. Reading maps from throughout the world and planning trips for the family was one of his hobbies. Greene's sister Sheryll Lee "Shery" Greene was born in Quindaro, Kansas, where the family moved when he was young.

Young Greene grew up between Maine and Kansas, where his family lived in the Quindaro section of Kansas City. Quindaro's history as a black settlement began in the mid-1800s when runaways from slavery crossed the Missouri River to seek freedom in the West. By the 1940s, when Greene was a student of Kansas City's racially segregated schools, Quindaro had Western University (WU) and Douglass Hospital. Greene's mother was a WU student. Quindaro is now abandoned, but the life-size statue of John Brown, once the center of WU's campus, still stands in the overgrowth.

In Portland, Maine, Greene lived on Munjoy Hill in the state's oldest, continuous (free) black community in Maine, starting with a settlement of late eighteenth-century seafarers and stevedores. Nineteenth-century black men worked as stewards and cooks on steamers, including the S.S. *Portland* that sank in 1898. All of the passengers and crew of the *Portland* died, including Greene's relative Eben Francis Heuston, who had bought the house on Lafayette St., Munjoy Hill, the year before he drowned. Heuston's widow and descendants, including the Greenes, lived there until the twenty-first century.

At the time Greene was growing up, Portland's black community was Maine's largest and the only one with its own institution, Green (no relation) Memorial A.M.E. Zion Church. Portland's black community fostered their youth and sense of self-worth. Several of the young black Portlanders of Greene's era (1950s) went on to illustrious careers out of state and many were skilled athletes as well. Greene, a tall, strong youth, excelled in track and football at Portland High School and continued at Virginia State College. He also attended the University of Kansas.

Greene's journalism career began in the Midwest with the *Hoosier Herald* in Indianapolis, Indiana. He was entertainment editor for the *Kansas City Call*, sports editor at the *Leavenworth (Kansas) Times*, and then began a long career with The Associated Press (AP), where he worked in Kansas City, Missouri, Milwaukee, Wisconsin, Washington, D.C., Portland, Maine, and New York Sports. Greene interviewed presidents Harry S. Truman, Lyndon B. Johnson, and Richard M. Nixon and covered the funeral of Dr. Martin Luther King, Jr. Over a thirty-six-year career he reported on riots, floods, political conventions, jailbreaks, and sports, but writing about tennis became his expertise.

Greene began covering tennis in 1969 and the U.S. Opens in 1980. His introduction to the sport was reporting about Lamar Hunt's Handsome Eight, which helped start Open tennis. The second tournament he covered was the fourth Virginia Slims, which Billie Jean King won. Greene was named AP Tennis Writer in 1980, covering Wimbledon, the French Open, and tournaments in Switzerland, Germany, France, and Sweden as well as the United States. In 1985, he was elected president of the U.S. Tennis Writers Association and was a member of the media committees for both the International Tennis Federation and the United States Tennis Federation.

One of Greene's continued interests has been the Easter Bowl Junior Tennis Championships (EBJTC) for boys and girls competing at ages fourteen, sixteen, and eighteen, which he covered both for their hometown newspapers and nationally. Almost all of the top U.S. tennis players have played at the EBJTC. Greene was on its staff when tournaments were held in Miami and Grenelefe, Florida, and Palm Springs, California; and he was honored in 1999, when EBJTC founder Seena Hamilton praised him as "one of the most knowledgeable writers about kids and the game."

While living in Washington, D.C., in the early 1970s, Greene served on the board of directors of the Greater Washington Boys Clubs and was responsible for the National Football League Players Association holding its annual dinner in the Nation's Capital, with the proceeds going to the Boys Clubs.

Most of Greene's AP tenure was in New York City. He retired in 2001 but has continued as a freelance author for various publications at the U.S. Open, Davis Cup, Fed Cup, and men's season-ending Tennis Masters Cup, held in 2001 and from 2005 to 2008 in Shanghai, China. He writes a weekly column, "Mondays with Bob Greene," for *Tennis Grand Stand* (http://www.teamwta.com), where he is billed as the "former esteemed Associated Press tennis writer."

While Greene has become a world traveler, seeming to live out his father's interest in scouring maps and planning trips, his own avocation has been unearthing family genealogy. He began in 1991 after his oldest son asked if they had any relatives. "Who are we? Where do we come from?" wrote Greene in the introduction to his book *Maine Roots: The Manuel/Mathews/Ruby Family*. He traced his Maine ancestors back to the 1780s, making the most recent generation the eleventh in Maine.

"I've found that my family touches almost every black family that has been in Maine for any length of time," Greene wrote in *Maine Roots*. His research led him to publish "A Family Affair" newsletter and organize family reunions from throughout the country. Simultaneously he has added considerably to the overall body of knowledge about black history, particularly in Maine.

Since retiring to Maine, Greene has been a speaker about Maine black history. In 2008 he began teaching a course on Maine's black history to the Osher Lifelong Learning Institute at University of Southern Maine (USM). Greene chairs USM's Jean Byers Sampson Center of Diversity in Maine board of directors; is on the board of trustees of the Maine Historical Society; and is on the board of directors of the Greater Portland Boys and Girls Clubs Alumni Association, the Maine Freedom Trails, the Maine Philanthropy Center, and Visible Black History.

FURTHER READING

Greene, Bob. *Maine Roots: The Manuel/Mathews/Ruby Family* (1995; revised 1999, 2008).

Hoose, Shoshana, and Karine Odlin, video producers. *Anchor of the Soul: A Documentary about Black History in Maine* (1994).

Price, H. H., and Gerald E. Talbot. *Maine's Visible Black History: The First Chronicle of Its People* (2006).

Witcher, T. R. "A Sorry Free State (Quindaro)," *Pitch Weekly*, 21 Mar. 2002.

H. H. PRICE

Greene, Joe (24 Sep. 1946–), football player, was born Charles Edward Greene in Temple, Texas, one of four children raised by his mother Cleo after his father, whose name is unknown, abandoned the

Joe Greene, of the Pittsburgh Steelers, takes a break during a game against the Philadelphia Eagles, 4 November 1974. (AP Images.)

family. Greene would later credit much of his ferocity on the football field to an encounter he had with a local bully nicknamed "Old Speedy." After the bully had stolen five dollars from Greene's mother, Greene took matters into his own hands and successfully battled the bully.

At Dunbar High School, Greene was known as a strong pass rusher with a knack for slashing through blockers and getting to the quarterback. His work ethic, along with his ferocity on the field, got him noticed by several college football programs. He was recruited by several schools before finally accepting a scholarship at North Texas State University. Greene played for North Texas State from 1965 until 1968, leaving the university after two years for the National Football League. During the time Greene attended North Texas State the team, dubbed the "Mean Green" because of its green uniforms, went 23-5-1 over three seasons. It was also during this period that Greene met Agnes Craft, also a student at North Texas who he married in 1967. The couple went on to have three children. It was also during his career at North Texas State that Greene found a role model to pattern his game after. Greene attended many Dallas Cowboys games during his time at North Texas State

and he became fascinated with the fierce style of the Cowboys' veteran defensive tackle Bob Lilly. Lilly's explosive speed off the ball and his quickness was an inspiration to the young Greene, who later admitted to having patterned his whole game after Lilly's. In the 1968 college football season Greene's hard work and tenacity on the football field paid off as he was named a consensus All-American.

Greene's play at North Texas State had also drawn attention from the National Football League (NFL). In fact, he was the controversial first round pick of the Pittsburgh Steelers in the 1969 NFL Draft. Some fans and experts questioned the Steelers for choosing Greene, arguing that he had not played at a big-time school and questioning if he had the skills to compete at football's highest level. It did not help matters that before Greene arrived the Steelers were a franchise with a bleak history. They had had few winning seasons and during the 1968 season went 2-11-1. In an online profile for *Cigar Aficionado* magazine, Greene admitted that "Pittsburgh was the last place I wanted to go" after an early 1969 contract dispute drew the ire of both his coach and the Pittsburgh fans. During his early career with the Steelers, Greene showed flashes of being a dominant player by winning the Defensive Rookie of the Year award in 1969, but he also got into too many fights and was ejected from several games.

Greene's fortunes began to shift as an NFL player after he had a talk with his coach, Chuck Noll. Noll implored Greene to become a positive leader instead of a negative one. According to Greene, Noll helped him learn that he could be a great defensive player without always going for the "knockout blow." After Greene learned this valuable lesson, he was fully on his way to becoming one of the most dominant defensive linemen in NFL history.

Throughout the 1970s Greene had individual success, but also helped to anchor the most dominant team of the 1970s. "Mean" Joe Greene and the rest of the "Steel Curtain" defense helped to change the climate around the Pittsburgh Steelers. They were no longer perennial losers, but AFC Central Division Champions and eventually Super Bowl Champions. Greene anchored a defensive line that helped the Steelers win seven AFC Central Division crowns and four Super Bowls in 1974, 1975, 1978, and 1979. Greene was an important part of the defense of those Super Bowl winners and could dominate a game like few defensive linemen before or since, recording five sacks, forcing a fumble, recovering a fumble, and blocking a field goal attempt in one game against Houston in 1972.

Greene's individual achievements are legendary. He went to the Pro Bowl a record ten times during his career. He was voted NFL Defensive Player of the Year on two occasions in 1972 and 1974 and had sixty-six career sacks. Greene was known as "mean" because he did not simply seek to shed blockers or overpower them, but rather had a punishing style that wore opponents down and earned him a reputation for intimidating the opposition. Greene also developed a tactic of lining up at a sharp angle between the guard and center to disrupt blocking assignments, a strategy that has seen continued use in the NFL. Furthermore, Greene was an extremely durable player beginning his career with ninety-one straight games played and finishing his career having played in 181 of a possible 190 regular season games.

Despite Greene's on the field reputation, he insisted that he was not "mean" off the field and this side of him was showcased in a famous 1978 Coca-Cola television advertisement in which a child offers a tired Greene a Coke after he had played a game and Greene gives the child his jersey in return. This commercial was listed as one of *TV Guide*'s top ten commercials of all time. The commercial also won a Clio Award and Greene himself was honored with a Clio for best male performance in a commercial.

After his retirement following the 1981 season, Greene continued his involvement with football. He was named to the Texas Sports Hall of Fame in 1985 and the NFL Hall of Fame in 1987. In 1987 Greene was named assistant coach under legendary Steelers head coach Chuck Noll where he coached until 1991. He later coached defensive linemen for the Miami Dolphins (1993–1995) and Arizona Cardinals (1995–2003) before once again being named a special assistant to player personnel for the Steelers coaching staff in 2004.

FURTHER READING
Chastain, Bill. *Steel Dynasty: The Team that Changed the NFL* (2005).
Mendelson, Abby. *The Pittsburgh Steelers: Official Team History* (2005).
Wexell, Jim. *Tales from Behind the Steel Curtain* (2004).
DANIEL A. DALRYMPLE

Greene, Lorenzo Johnston (16 Nov. 1899–24 Jan. 1988), historian and activist, was the sixth child born to Willis Hamilton Greene, a teamster, and Harriett Coleman Greene in Ansonia, Connecticut. Lorenzo Johnston Greene attended Ansonia's public schools and participated in his high school's debate team and German club. In 1917 he became Ansonia High School's first African American graduate and the first recipient of the school's History Prize.

After working several jobs to earn money for college, Greene began undergraduate studies in medicine at Howard University in Washington, D.C. During his senior year, however, he enrolled in Greek and English history courses, which inspired him to become a historian. In 1924 he received an AB from Howard and returned to New York City to attend Columbia University's Graduate School. Greene received an MA in history from Columbia in 1926 and continued graduate studies there in pursuit of a PhD in history.

From 1928 to 1933 Greene worked with CARTER G. WOODSON, the founder and director of the Association for the Study of Negro Life and History (ASNLH) and a pioneer of black historiography. In March 1928, upon recommendation by Greene's favorite history professor, Charles Harris Wesley, Woodson hired Greene as a research investigator for the ASNLH. After briefly researching black churches, Greene became Woodson's assistant in June 1928 and conducted sociological and historical research on African American occupations for the 1930 publication *The Negro Wage Earner*.

In June 1930 Greene and four Howard University students sold books published by the ASNLH throughout the South, Midwest, and Northeast. From March through August 1931 he took a hiatus from bookselling to survey African American employment in Washington, D.C., with E. E. Lewis. The findings of their research were published in the 1932 text *Negro Employment in the District of Columbia*, co-authored with the ASNLH researcher Myra Colson-Callis. On 4 September 1931 Greene's bookselling tour ended successfully, with his having disseminated knowledge of black history to African American churches, schools, colleges, and organizations.

From 1931 through 1932 Greene completed course-work and examinations at Columbia University and was a staff member for the university's journal *Social Science Abstracts*. In addition, on behalf of the ASNLH, Greene gave lectures, conducted research, sold books, and convinced the New York City Board of Education to use the Association's books as classroom texts. His experience working for Woodson shaped the direction of Greene's life thereafter as a pioneer of black historiography.

In September 1933 Greene accepted an assistant professorship of history and political science at Lincoln University in Jefferson City, Missouri.

Humiliated upon arrival by racial segregation in the city, he immediately became involved in civil and human rights activism with the Missouri Association for Social Welfare (MASW) to desegregate schools and establish a Commission on Human Rights. In 1935 he encouraged his student Lloyd Gaines to apply for admission into the all-white University of Missouri-Columbia Law School. Denied admission, Gaines filed a lawsuit, *Gaines v. Canada*, which established a legal precedent for *Brown v. Board of Education* in 1954. In 1939 Greene and his students initiated relief efforts for Missouri sharecroppers who were evicted for demanding fair employment practices.

Greene married Dr. Thomasina Talley, an accomplished concert pianist, in 1941; their union would produce a son, Lorenzo Thomas, in 1952. In 1942 Greene received a PhD in history from Columbia University. That same year, Greene's dissertation, *The Negro in Colonial New England, 1620–1776*, a classic interpretation of Africans' contributions to the colonies and slavery's effects upon New England culture, was published. Greene's subsequent analyses of slavery in New England would be published through the 1980s in *Phylon*, *Negro History Bulletin*, the *Journal of Negro History*, and the *Journal of Negro Education*. From 1948 to 1956 he edited the *Midwest Journal* published by Lincoln University.

During 1957 to 1972 Greene served on the Missouri State Advisory Committee to the United States Commission on Civil Rights. He attended President Dwight D. Eisenhower's Commission on Children and Youth in 1960 and President Lyndon Johnson's White House Conference "To Fulfill These Rights" in 1966. Greene was vice president and president of the ASNLH from 1964 to 1966. In addition, he lobbied for legislation to desegregate Missouri's hotels, restaurants, and bowling alleys. Moreover, he worked to obtain legislation regarding open housing, fair employment practices, and improvements in mental health and foster care in Missouri. During the Black Studies movement of the 1960s and 1970s, Greene was a visiting professor and guest lecturer at several universities. He served as a consultant in Missouri, Kansas, Pennsylvania, and Illinois to develop courses and compile publications about black history and culture. At Lincoln University, Greene helped establish the first Afro-American Studies major in the state of Missouri. He also directed and secured grants for Missouri's Institute for Drop Out Prevention and Teacher Orientation to the Unique Needs of Minority Students. In 1975 he helped edit *Oral Interviews Relative to the Growth and Development of Lincoln University*.

Throughout his life Greene received many awards—such as a commendation from the U.S. Commission on Civil Rights and the Alex and Catharine Hope Award from Cole County Historical Society—for his contributions to academia, American education, and the American public. In 1971 the University of Missouri–Columbia awarded Greene an honorary doctorate of Humane Letters. He retired in 1972 as professor emeritus of history at Lincoln University. In 1973 the president of Lincoln University declared 12 February "Lorenzo Johnston Greene Day." Before he could complete several book projects, he died of a brain hemorrhage in Jefferson City. Greene established a foundation for interpreting African American history. As a public intellectual, he challenged racism, segregation, and inequality through scholarship and activism.

FURTHER READING

Greene's personal and professional papers are housed at the Library of Congress. A smaller, unprocessed collection is housed at the Western Historical Manuscripts Collection in Columbia, Missouri.

Greene, Lorenzo J. "The Black Experience in Missouri: A Personal Reminiscence," *Missouri's Black Heritage* (1993).

Greene, Lorenzo J. *Selling Black History for Carter G. Woodson* (1996).

Greene, Lorenzo J. *Working with Carter G. Woodson, the Father of Black History* (1989).

Obituary: *New York Times*, 27 Jan. 1988.

KIMBERLY M. CURTIS

Greene, Maurice (23 July 1974–), track-and-field star, was born in Kansas City, Kansas, the youngest of four children of Ernest Greene and Jackie. Maurice began participating in track events while he was a fourth grader at Quindaro Elementary School. His first race was in the All City Competition, where he won the first-place blue ribbon in three events, the 50 meters, the 100 meters, and the eraser shuttle. At Colonado Middle School, Maurice ran the 100 meters, the 200 meters, and the 4×100 meter relay. He admired the athletic feats of his older brother Ernest Greene, whose track career, though less prominent, included specialization in the 100 meters and the 200 meters.

Greene attended Schlagle High School in his hometown, where he participated and excelled in track and football. At the prestigious Kansas State, competitions Greene won the 100 meters and the

200 meters for the first time. In the summer he ran for the Kansas City Chargers, one of the state's premier private track clubs, and was given the opportunity to travel to various states to compete in track-and-field meets. During this time Greene met Al Hobson, who groomed and guided him to many Amateur Athletic Union (AAU) youth titles. Greene's running ability qualified him for the Junior Olympics, in which he ran the 100 meters and the 4×100 meter relay. He won gold in the relay but ironically did not place in the top three in any event that he later dominated. Greene still had a love for football, but in his sophomore year an argument with the football coach shifted his focus to running. In his junior year that coach was replaced, and Greene returned to the sport, playing tailback and winning a place on the all-city team. After consultation with his father and his coach, Greene declined a football scholarship to Hutchison (Kansas) Community College to concentrate on a track career. In his senior year Greene broke a national and high school record with a time of 10.2 seconds in the 100 meters.

After graduation in 1993, Greene decided to attend Park College in Parkville, Missouri, where he studied physical education but never competed for the school, focusing instead on international competition. In 1995, at the USA Outdoors Championship, Greene placed second in the 100 meters with a wind-aided time of 9.88 seconds. At the Texas Relays, Greene received a psychological boost when he defeated the great sprinter CARL LEWIS. Later that year, however, at the World Championships in Gothenburg, Sweden, Greene only managed a disappointing sixth in the 100 meters quarter final. Greene seriously considered leaving the sport. Meanwhile, in an effort to make ends met, the future sprinting star worked at menial jobs, including in fast food restaurants, in a movie theater, in a warehouse, and at a dog track.

In another personal setback, Greene in 1996 failed to qualify for the U.S. Olympic team and therefore missed the Summer Olympics in Atlanta. With the blessings of his former coach, he opted to relocate to Los Angeles and train under the renowned former champion quarter-miler John Smith, who along with the manager Emanuel Hudson headed a selective track club, HS International, informally known as Handling Speed Intelligently. Smith provided the necessary confidence for Greene's bruised ego, and Greene complied with Smith's stringent training and dietary regimen.

The watershed in Greene's career occurred in 1997, when he clocked a scorching time of 9.86 seconds at the World Championships in Athens, Greece, and won the coveted 100 meters title. More importantly, he beat the world record holder Donovan Bailey of Canada. In February 1998 Greene set a world indoor record in Madrid with a blistering dash of 6.39 seconds in the 60 meters. On ten occasions that year Greene easily went under the elusive 10 seconds mark.

During 2002 to 2004, there were doping scandals which affected some of the biggest names in track and field including members of Greene's HSI group—Tori Edwards, a former 100 meters champion. Sprinters such as Tim Montgomery, world record-holder in the 100 meters; Alvin Harrison, the 2000 Olympic silver medalist in the 400 meters and Michelle Collins, the 2003 world indoor champion in the 200 meters have been investigated by the United States Anti-Doping Agency. Amidst this controversy, Greene, who has never been accused of taking banned substances, indicated that the state of track and field seemed confusing. He admitted that he had been regularly tested for illegal drugs, sometimes more than twenty times a year, and that every vitamin he took was tested by various laboratories.

For the next few years (1997–2003) Greene was highly ranked by USA Track and Field (USATF) as one of the world's top three sprinters in the 100 and 200 meters events. Finally Greene seemed to have found his groove and commanded respect from the world's sprinting elite. The training and advice from Hudson and Smith coupled with Greene's rigid discipline and hunger for speed proved to be a winning formula. In 1999 he was a triple gold medalist at the World Championships, winning the 100 meters (9.80 seconds), the 200 meters (19.90 seconds), and the 4×100 relay, which he anchored (39.59 seconds). Greene was the first person to win both the 100 and 200 meters at this event.

At the 2000 Olympics in Sydney, Australia, Greene scorched the track in 9.87 seconds to win gold in the 100 meters along with winning the 4×100 meters relay. The winning performance was repeated as he captured the 100 meters at the Grand Prix tournaments in Zurich, Switzerland (9.94 seconds), and Rome (9.97 seconds). Additionally, in May 2000 he clocked 9.91 seconds in the 100 meters in Osaka, Japan.

During 2001 Greene struggled with tendonitis in his knee, but he convincingly won the 60 meters in the USA Indoor Championships in a time of 6.51 seconds. Additionally, he recorded a winning time of 9.90 seconds in the opening round of the U.S. Outdoor Nationals. Subsequently, with a time of 9.91 seconds, he placed first in the 100 meters in Athens, Greece. His name was etched in the record books as he won, in 9.82 seconds, for the third consecutive time the world 100 meters title. This was the third-fastest time in history and was no easy feat, since there was a headwind of 0.2 meters per second and Greene injured his left quadriceps prior to crossing the finish line. This injury abruptly ended Greene's season for 2001.

Recovered in 2002, Greene returned to the track with a vengeance as he won his third U.S. 100 meters title (9.88 seconds) and then went on to win in Rome (9.89 seconds), Athens (9.97 seconds), Monaco (9.97 seconds), and Paris (9.99 seconds). However, the juggernaut runner faltered twice—in Oslo, Norway, where he placed second (10.06 seconds), and in London, where he copped the third spot (10.06 seconds).

In 2003 Greene's knees again forced him to skip the 200 meters final at the USA Outdoors. This did not hamper him from placing first in the Adidas Boston Indoor Games (6.52 seconds), the Home Depot Invitational Outdoors (9.94 seconds), and the Mt. San Antonio College (SAC) (20.16 seconds). In 2004 Greene placed first in three major events—the Mt. SAC Relays (10.02 seconds), the Japan Grand Prix (10.04 seconds), the Payton Jordan U.S. Open (9.78 seconds), and the Home Depot (9.86 seconds). At the Summer Olympics in Athens, Greece, he placed third (9.87 seconds) in the 100 meters.

For the next two years, injuries hampered Greene but he still displayed a creditable performance and remained among the world's top ten sprinters. In 2005 at the USA Outdoors he did not complete the 100 meters final due to a left hamstring injury. During that year he placed first in the 100meters at the Reebok Grand Prix (10.08), fourth in the 100 meters at the Adidas Track Classic (10.32). In 2006, his best time was 10.35 at the Baie Mahault meet where he placed third.

In addition to his athletic achievements, Greene established the Maurice Greene Finish the Race Youth Foundation in Kansas City, a fund to benefit underprivileged but talented young persons in his hometown. In 2001 Greene was awarded the USATF's Visa Humanitarian of the Year Award. Additionally, in 2000 he was a guest on the game show *Who Wants to Be a Millionaire*, in which he won $125,000 and donated half of the prize money to the United Negro College Fund.

FURTHER READING
New York Times, 21 June 2004.

JEROME TEELUCKSINGH

Greene, Percy (7 Sept. 1897–16 Apr. 1977), journalist and publisher, was born in Jackson, Mississippi, the fourth of twelve children of George Washington Greene, a carpenter, and Sarah Stone Greene, a laundress. He was educated at the Smith Robertson School and at the high school division of Jackson College (later Jackson State University), receiving his degree in 1915; during this period he also pent one year at Jackson's black Catholic high school. He attended the college division of Jackson College from 1920 to 1922, where he was active on the football team. On 8 September 1917 he enlisted in the army and served with black troops in Company B, 25th Infantry in France. He returned to the United States on 26 June 1920.

Following his stint in the army, Greene developed an interest in business and journalism, and he wanted to study law and become an attorney. For several years in the early 1920s he worked in Jackson's United States Post Office and served as a clerk in the law office of Dr. SIDNEY D. REDMOND, a famous black Mississippi medical doctor and lawyer. However, he was prevented by segregation laws from passing the Mississippi Bar Examination. He thus concentrated his attention on journalism in the years after 1927, and abandoned his law studies in the state. Percy Greene married Frances L. Reed on 16 June 1921; they had two daughters, Frances Lorraine and Gwendolyn, both born during the decade of the 1920s.

From 1927 to 1928, Greene served as the editor of the *Colored Veteran*, published in Greenwood, Mississippi. This newspaper was devoted to the affairs of black American veterans who, because of segregation, were not allowed to join freely the American Legion, the Disabled Veterans, or the Veterans of Foreign Wars. In 1939 Greene took on the editorship of the *Jackson Advocate*, a position he would hold for nearly forty years. The *Advocate*, one of the longest running black newspapers in Mississippi history, was perhaps the most important publication in the history of blacks in the state. The paper became a leading press voice among black Mississippians in the 1940s and 1950s, with its good coverage of local and state news. However, Greene became a controversial figure in Mississippi because of his conservative stance on many issues impacting the black community in the state, including his opposition to the civil rights movement in the 1960s, and his defense of the white status quo in Mississippi during this same period. In essence, Greene remains a paradox in modern black American history.

Greene was considered a radical black by many whites in the 1940s, but he became a conservative in the 1950s and 1960s. He was a successful journalist, but he lived in the poorest state in the nation, apparently never having earned much money. And while he did accept small payoffs from the state through the Sovereignty Commission—a state agency established in the 1950s to attack the civil rights movement in Mississippi—for supporting the campaign against the civil rights movement in the state during the 1950s and 1960s, he always believed that black Americans had a right to vote and to participate in the affairs of government.

By the beginning of the 1960s Greene was one of the most despised black men in Mississippi. Many blacks were upset with him because of his pro-segregation stance and the support he received from the White Citizens' Councils (another anti-black group of leading white citizens in Mississippi), and the Sovereignty Commission.

Percy and his wife were the basic staff members of the *Advocate* for the 1960s. They had the help of four part-time staff members and eight high school students. The circulation of the paper averaged between 4,000 and 4,500 weekly copies during this period, and an average issue consisted of eight pages. Single issues of the paper were priced at ten cents, and a yearly subscription cost four dollars between 1960 and 1964, and rose to five dollars in 1965. Green was critical of the civil rights movement and its work in Mississippi, and made a major effort to attach such groups as the NAACP and the Student Non-Violent Coordinating Committee, among others. Greene praised only the National Urban League, long considered the most conservative of the major 1960s movement groups.

Greene opposed two of the decade's greatest movements, the March on Washington in 1963 and the Mississippi Freedom Summer Project of 1964. The March on Washington, Greene wrote, did not bring any "hope … to the Negro Masses [or] the little Negroes of the State of Mississippi" (*Jackson Advocate*, 24 Aug. 1963). Mississippians were told to "hope and aim for the time when responsible white and Negro leaders in the state, uninfluenced by any outside sources, begin again the great progress that we made from 1940 to 1954 in this state" (*Jackson Advocate*, 24 Aug. 1963). Greene saw only "tragedy" in the efforts

of young people who went to Mississippi in the summer of 1964 to press for political, economic, and social reforms in the state. When three civil rights workers—Michael Schwerner, JAMES CHANEY, and Andrew Goodman—were murdered on 21 June 1964 by local whites in Neshoba County, Mississippi, Greene placed the blame on the shoulders of all the summer project workers. He demanded that they return "to their own states, where much work on the Negro Question is still needed, and leave the affairs of Mississippi to the white people and Negroes of the state" (*Jackson Advocate*, 18 July 1964). Greene ignored the fact that James Chaney, a black, was from Meridian, Mississippi.

Greene did not view his work and perspectives as being a part of the traditional nature of black separatism in the United States, as promoted by MARCUS GARVEY's Universal Negro Improvement Association, Elijah Muhammad's Nation of Islam, or MALCOLM X's Organization of Afro-American Unity. Instead, his worldview was based on the ideology of BOOKER T. WASHINGTON, which encouraged the development of small black businesses and other institutions (economic separatism), but did not challenge the political and social supremacy of the white world. Greene's overall ideological position by the 1960s placed him to the right of even Washington. He became a symbol of right-wing extremism among modern black leaders because of his pro-segregationist views and his work for the Mississippi State Sovereignty Commission.

FURTHER READING
Percy Greene's personal papers are held by the Jackson State University Archives, at the central office of the Jackson Advocate, Jackson, Mississippi, and in the Aaron Henry papers, Tougaloo College Archives, Jackson, Mississippi.

Thompson, Julius E. *The Black Press in Mississippi, 1865–1985* (1993).

Thompson, Julius E. *Percy Greene and the Jackson Advocate: The Life and Times of a Radical Conservative Black Newspaperman, 1897–1977* (1994).

Sewell, George Alexander, and Margaret L. Dwight. *Mississippi Black History Makers* (1984).

Obituary: *Jet*, 5 May 1977.

JULIUS E. THOMPSON

Greener, Richard Theodore (30 Jan. 1844–2 May 1922), educator, lawyer, and diplomat, was born in Philadelphia, Pennsylvania, the son of Richard Wesley Greener, a seaman who was wounded during the Mexican War while serving aboard USS *Princeton*, and Mary Ann Le Brune. When he was nine, Greener and his parents moved to Boston but soon left for Cambridge, where he could attend "an unproscriptive school." Greener's father, as chief steward of the *George Raynes*, had taken his son on a voyage to Liverpool but then abandoned the sea in 1853 for the California gold fields. He "was taken sick, met with losses," and was never heard from again. When Greener was twelve years old, he left school to help support his mother. Although he quit one of his positions after an employer "struck" him, those whom he met while "knocking around in … different occupations" often helped educate him, sharing their libraries and tutoring him in French and Latin.

Greener's employer, Augustus E. Bachelder, helped finance Greener's education. Following Bachelder's suggestion, Greener enrolled in the two-year college preparatory program at Oberlin College in Ohio (1862–1864), where he received "considerable practice in speaking and debating," but because of "some colorphobia, shown by … classmates" he returned to New England. In 1865 he graduated from Phillips Academy in Andover, Massachusetts, and then attended Harvard, whose president, Thomas Hill, was eager to experiment in educating an African American. Although Greener received the second prize for reading aloud that year, he had been conditionally admitted to college because his background was uneven, and he especially lacked mathematical training. Because Hill wanted the experiment "fairly tried," Greener repeated his first year. At the end of his sophomore year he took the Boylston Prize for Oratory, and his senior dissertation, which defended the land rights of Irish peasants, won the first Bowdoin Prize for research and writing.

After becoming the first black person to graduate from Harvard College (1870), Greener later could not recall "many pleasant incidents" there, but he had done well scholastically and made friends with whom he felt at ease. Hailed as a member of the Negro intelligentsia, he began the decade as principal of the male department of the Institute for Colored Youth in Philadelphia (1870–1872) and ended it in the law department of Howard University, where he began teaching in 1877 and was dean from 1879 to 1880. In the interim he was principal of the Sumner High School in Washington, D.C. (1872–1873); associate editor of *New National Era and Citizen*, a publication for blacks; and a law clerk in the office of the attorney for the District of Columbia. He also taught Latin, Greek, international law, and U.S. constitutional history at the University of South Carolina (1873–1877). As acting librarian he rearranged and cataloged the university's books, completed a law degree there, and served on a commission to revise the state school system. In 1874 Greener married Genevieve Ida Fleet; five of their seven children reached adulthood. In 1876 Greener was admitted to the South Carolina bar and the next year to the bar of the District of Columbia, where he moved at the end of Reconstruction, when doors in South Carolina were suddenly closed to blacks.

Having left the South rather than surrender to white supremacists, Greener heartily endorsed the Windom Resolution (introduced in the U.S. Senate on 16 January 1879 by William Windom of Minnesota) encouraging black migration out of the South (primarily to Kansas). Fearing that the federal government would not give southern blacks the protection they needed, Greener was the spokesman for a delegation of "representative colored men" who saw Windom and called for a special, but not legally exclusive black territory. Greener, who became secretary of the Exodus Committee, met in February with a group in Cincinnati and, along with Windom, took a central role in mid-April in organizing an Emigrant Aid Association in Washington. In December he went to Kansas to see firsthand the condition of new black settlers, who were called Exodusters. Disagreeing with FREDERICK DOUGLASS, the distinguished black abolitionist, who urged blacks to stay in the South, where their freedom would depend on "right" rather than "flight," Greener brilliantly answered Douglass's objections, taking them up one by one at a congress of the American Social Science Association held in September 1877 at Saratoga Springs, New York.

Greener had been a law professor at Howard University from 1877 to 1880 when the Board of Trustees temporarily disbanded its law department for lack of students. Having held two government clerkships before teaching at Howard and having in 1878 started a law firm, Cook & Greener, he continued his law practice, became a clerk in the office of the U.S. Treasury Department's first comptroller, and remained in demand as a speaker and writer.

In 1880 Greener became involved in the case of JOHNSON C. WHITTAKER, which divided the nation and led to the dismissal of the commandant of the U.S. Military Academy at West Point. While teaching at the University of South Carolina, Greener had helped secure Whittaker's appointment to West Point, after choosing him from among two hundred possibilities as the student most likely to succeed at the academy. Whittaker entered West Point in 1876 and was the roommate of HENRY O. FLIPPER, who, in the following June, became the first black cadet to graduate from the academy. Helping Whittaker secure an education, just as his own benefactors had aided him, Greener kept in touch with his former student, who, on the morning of 6 April 1880, was found tied to his bed, bleeding and unconscious. Writing to Greener after he was accused of staging the attack and mutilating himself, Whittaker called it a "heinous plot engaged in by ... cadets" and "sanctioned by the authorities."

Greener remained by Whittaker's side for most of the early inquiry and became a leading witness and assistant counsel in the court-martial that Whittaker demanded to clear his name (establishing the precedent that a West Point cadet is an officer of the U.S. Army). Because Greener had campaigned in six states for the Republican Party and was one of the thirty members of President James A. Garfield's Inaugural Executive Committee, he had access to important officials in both the departing Rutherford B. Hayes administration and the entering Garfield one. After army officers sitting on the court-martial found Whittaker guilty as charged, their decision was reviewed and overturned in March 1882 by Judge Advocate General David G. Swaim. Although, thanks to Greener, Whittaker was reinstated at West Point, Secretary of War Robert Todd Lincoln ordered him discharged for failing an examination he had taken immediately after his attack.

In 1884 Greener campaigned vigorously in eight states for the Republican Party and in 1885 was made chief examiner of the New York City Civil Service Board, a position he held until 1889. Also in 1885 he became a trustee of the Grant Monument Association and was elected its secretary (1885–1892). A personal friend of Ulysses S. Grant, whom he had met in 1868 at Harvard and to whom, during the Grant administration, Greener had led four delegations of black and white supporters, Greener was proud to be the chief administrative official of Grant's monument association and remained a trustee for the rest of his life. A lover of art who had enjoyed browsing through books on monumental art in the libraries at Harvard, Greener considered himself "better posted [on the subject] than any member of [the Grant Monument Association], and did not hesitate to attack ... unworthy designs ... foisted on the committee." After rejecting all proposals in the first competition, the association selected a design by John Hemenway Duncan from the second competition.

"I was one of the first to point out the simplicity, dignity, and fitness of [Duncan's design]," Greener later noted, "as presenting the characteristics of the Conqueror of the Rebellion."

Greener was rewarded for campaigning for the Republican Party with a political appointment abroad. In January 1898 he turned down an appointment as consul to Bombay because of a bubonic plague epidemic there, and in July he became the first U.S. consul to Vladivostok, Russia, where he served until 1905. His tour of duty began as his country emerged as a world power from the Spanish-American War, and he witnessed both the completion of the Trans-Siberian Railroad and the Russo-Japanese War. American newspapers often complimented Greener on the excellent performance of his duties and his help to American businessmen. Few people objected to his Japanese mistress (his marriage having been dissolved years earlier, after which his mixed-race wife and their children had passed as white). The Russians liked working with him, as did the British, who had him carry on their business when they were expelled from Vladivostok because of their pact with Japan. The Chinese decorated him with the Order of the Double Dragon for aiding war victims during the Boxer Rebellion in 1900.

But Greener's decoration for services to Japan during the Russo-Japanese War went to his successor, Roger Greene, whose name the Japanese confused with his. The U.S. State Department, where blacks were sometimes referred to as "coons," refused to rectify the situation. Dismissed from the post in 1905 on charges of bad habits and dereliction of duty, Greener requested a special investigation, which was carried out by his successor. The charges were not confirmed; apparently he had been confused with another Greener living in Vladivostok. Nevertheless, back in the United States, he was denied a personal hearing over his dismissal.

In 1906 Greener moved to Chicago, where he worked as a special agent for an insurance company and championed black rights in numerous letters to newspapers and in lectures. In July of that year he joined with W. E. B. DuBois and others in the second convention of the Niagara Movement at Harpers Ferry, West Virginia. Although DuBois and his backers, who later founded the NAACP, had formed the Niagara Movement to oppose the accommodationist philosophy of BOOKER T. WASHINGTON, Greener had hoped to make peace between the two black leaders. When his efforts failed, he backed DuBois, ending a twenty-three-year friendship with Washington, and worked diligently for the NAACP.

Still brooding in 1912 over the Republican Party's treatment of him and other African Americans, Greener backed Woodrow Wilson for president and lived to see him reintroduce segregation into the federal bureaucracy. Greener, who died in Chicago, was perhaps the most gifted of those whom DuBois called the "Talented Tenth" of African Americans. But the end of Reconstruction cut short his promising career as an educator in the South, and the seven years he was away in Russia lessened his impact on race relations in the United States during a crucial period.

Greener's second daughter, Belle, after concealing her identity, had a career equal to her talents, a privilege denied to her father. Claiming she was part Portuguese, she took "da Costa" as her middle name and removed the final "r" from her last name. Enjoying books and art, as her father did, BELLE DA COSTA GREENE steeped herself in the knowledge of rare books at Princeton University Library and in 1905, at the age of twenty-six, began working for the elder J. P. Morgan. With his backing and her own expertise, she became prominent in the world of rare books and manuscripts and was responsible for acquiring much of his collection. Long called "the soul of the Morgan Library," she was its director from 1924 to 1948.

FURTHER READING

Greener's papers, photographs (accompanied by a biographical leaflet), correspondence, and writings are at the Schomburg Center for Research in Black Culture of the New York Public Library. His letters are also in the archives of Howard and Harvard universities.

Blakely, Allison. "Richard T. Greener and the 'Talented Tenth's' Dilemma," *Journal of Negro History* (Oct. 1974).

Stewart, Ruth Ann, and David M. Kahn. *Richard T. Greener: His Life and Work* (1980).

West, Emory J. "Harvard's First Black Graduates: 1865–1890," *Harvard Bulletin* (May 1972).

Obituary: *Chicago Daily Tribune*, 4 May 1922.

This entry is taken from the *American National Biography* and is published here with the permission of the American Council of Learned Societies.

OLIVE HOOGENBOOM

Greenfield, Elizabeth Taylor (c. 1817–31 Mar. 1876), singer and teacher, known as the "Black Swan," was born a slave in or near Natchez, Mississippi. Her father may have been born in Africa, and her mother, Anna, was of mixed ancestry. Various sources offer no fewer than seven different birth dates between 1807 and 1824. Greenfield's use of "Taylor" rather than "Greenfield" in certain documents suggests that her parents used this surname, but little record of them survives.

When their owner, the wealthy widow Elizabeth Holliday Greenfield, joined the Society of Friends and moved to Philadelphia, Pennsylvania, in the 1820s, Greenfield's parents were manumitted and immigrated to Liberia. Though records suggest her mother planned to return, Greenfield never saw her parents again. She lived with her mistress until she was about eight years old and then rejoined her as a nurse-companion in about 1836; she seems to have lived with relatives in the interim. Several sources assert that Greenfield's mistress cared for her, and probate records show that her will called for an annuity to be paid to Greenfield. When her mistress died in 1845, though, her will was fiercely contested, and Greenfield received only a token

Elizabeth Taylor Greenfield, an acclaimed concert singer dubbed "The Black Swan" by audiences in the United States and Britain, in a proof scheduled to appear in the *Illustrated News* on 2 April 1853. (Schomburg Center for Research in Black Culture, New York Public Library.)

sum. Her biographer Arthur LaBrew speculates that Greenfield began singing in church in the early 1830s. Though Quaker, her mistress seems to have approved of Greenfield's musical aspirations, and a family friend (probably one of the physician Philip Price's daughters) gave her some rudimentary instruction. Greenfield was singing at private parties by at least the mid-1840s, and LaBrew notes a performance in Baltimore around 1849 with the black musician William Appo. By 1850 one Philadelphia directory listed her as a "music teacher."

In October 1851 Greenfield traveled to Buffalo, New York, supposedly to hear the "Swedish Nightingale" Jenny Lind. She impressed Electa Potter, wife of the prominent Buffalo attorney Heman B. Potter, with both her voice and her carriage, and the Potters became her patrons. Their support and introductions to Buffalo's leading citizens led to a public performance on 22 October. Greenfield's "debut," which featured works by Bellini and Donizetti, was praised by Buffalo newspapers, and Greenfield, whom several reviewers compared favorably to Lind, was quickly dubbed the "African Nightingale." A comparison to another singer, "Irish Swan" Catherine Hayes, won out, though, and Greenfield became forever known as the "Black Swan."

The favorable press and promotion by the Buffalo merchant Hiram Howard led to additional performances in Rochester and Lockport and an agreement with Colonel J. H. Wood, a promoter of mixed repute and sometime-associate of P. T. Barnum. Wood set up a tour in 1852 that took Greenfield across the North; she performed in more than thirty cities, ranging from Boston and Providence to Chicago and Milwaukee. She also traveled to Ontario and to smaller abolitionist strongholds like Niles, Michigan. Her repertoire was similar to Lind's, and the press regularly compared the two. She also began to include popular American works like Stephen Foster's "Old Folks at Home." Praise for—and even amazement at—her vocal range, which reputedly encompassed more than three octaves, was consistently tempered with comments emphasizing her lack of formal training; racist newspapers referred to her as the "African crow." Nonetheless, Greenfield filled theaters, and the tour was quite successful. After a brief rest, Greenfield made arrangements for a performance in New York City and a tour of Great Britain, during which she would further her training. Buffalo citizens held a benefit concert on 7 March 1853 to help support her travel to Britain.

After the outpouring of support from both blacks and whites in Buffalo, Greenfield's time in New York City was both frightening and frustrating. The theater, Metropolitan Hall, was threatened with arson for featuring a black performer, its management barred blacks from attending, and Greenfield herself was refused entry to another theater to see the Italian contralto Marietta Alboni. Still, her performance on 31 March attracted more than two thousand people and cemented her celebrity. Soon after, Greenfield gave a second concert before an integrated audience specifically to benefit black charities.

Trouble followed Greenfield to Britain. Her British manager refused to advance her funds against future performances, and Greenfield struggled to meet basic expenses before finally withdrawing from her contract. She contacted the abolitionists Lord Shaftesbury and Harriet Beecher Stowe for aid, and they introduced her to Britain's abolitionist elite. The Duchess of Sutherland became Greenfield's patron, and Sir George Smart, composer to the Chapel Royal, began tutoring her. Greenfield's May 1853 performance at Stafford House, Sutherland's London home, led to several other performances. Sutherland and Smart eventually engineered a command performance for Queen Victoria on 10 May 1854. Victoria's praise—and her twenty-pound gift—did much to help Greenfield's spirits; however, she returned to the United States in July 1854.

Greenfield began touring the North soon after her return; in this second U.S. tour, and in her third in 1856, Greenfield returned to several of the cities from her first tour but also sought new venues—traveling as far south as Baltimore and performing more widely in Canada. Her 1854 tour included performances by the Philadelphia tenor THOMAS J. BOWERS, known as the "colored Mario." Greenfield's 1856 tour was complemented by the 1855 publication of *The Black Swan at Home and Abroad*, a sixty-four-page promotional biography that heavily emphasized her early successes and her British tour. Greenfield's final extended tour in 1863 included mainly cities in the upper North.

After 1863 Greenfield gave occasional concerts, often to benefit African American causes. She regularly sang at events sponsored by the Civil and Statistical Association of the Colored People of Pennsylvania, including lectures by FRANCES ELLEN WATKINS HARPER and General O. O. Howard. LaBrew has also found evidence that she founded a Black Swan Opera Troupe, which gave performances in Washington in 1862 and Philadelphia in 1866.

Between tours and after 1863, Greenfield lived in Philadelphia near her extended family. She achieved local note as a music teacher and was intermittently listed in city directories as a musician and a teacher (though one directory simply lists her occupation as "black swan"). Among her students she counted Carrie Thomas, the leading soprano of the original Hampton Institute Singers, and Lucy Adger, whose family achieved local prominence for their talents. A devout Baptist, Greenfield also directed the choir and sang at Shiloh Baptist Church. Upon her death in 1876 Greenfield was eulogized in newspapers across the country.

Harriet Beecher Stowe said that had Greenfield received the education given her white peers "*no singer of any country could have surpassed her*" (*Sunny Memories of Foreign Lands*, vol. 2, 139). Given such talent, as well as her unprecedented international fame, her successes as a teacher, and her pioneering efforts to promote other black musicians, Greenfield was undoubtedly, as the author and activist MARTIN R. DELANY noted, "among the most extraordinary persons of the nineteenth century" (*The Condition, Elevation, Emigration, and Destiny of the Colored People of the U.S.*, 102). In the early 1920s, several generations after Greenfield's death, HARRY HERBERT PACE established Black Swan Records, the first black-owned record label in the United States. Named in honor of the original Black Swan, the company issued the music of ETHEL WATERS and FLETCHER HENDERSON.

FURTHER READING

Contemporary newspapers' coverage of Greenfield can be found in the microfilm collection *The Black Abolitionist Papers*, ed. C. Peter Ripley (1981).

Anonymous. *The Black Swan at Home and Abroad* (1855).

LaBrew, Arthur. *The Black Swan: Elizabeth T. Greenfield, Songstress: Biographical Study* (1969).

Riis, Thomas L. "Concert Singers, Prima Donnas, and Entertainers: The Changing Status of Black Women Vocalists in Nineteenth Century America," in *Music and Culture in America, 1861–1918*, eds. Michael Saffle and James R. Heintze (1998).

Story, Rosalyn. *And So I Sing: African American Divas of Concert and Opera* (1990).

Trotter, James Monroe. *Music and Some Highly Musical People* (1878).

Obituary: *New York Times*, 2 Apr. 1876.

This entry is taken from the *American National Biography* and is published here with the permission of the American Council of Learned Societies.

ERIC GARDNER

Greenlee, Sam (13 July 1930–), poet, novelist, film producer, activist, and radio talk show host, was born in Chicago, Illinois. His father, Sam Greenlee Sr., was a chauffeur, and his mother a singer and dancer. Greenlee, who identifies himself as a second-generation immigrant from the Deep South, has claimed that he made up for his "non-education in Chicago ghetto non-schools at three universities: Wisconsin, Chicago and Thessalonikki, Greece" (Afterword, *Blues for an African Princess*). Greenlee received his BS degree in Political Science from the University of Wisconsin in 1952. He studied at the University of Chicago between 1954 and 1957 and at the University of Thessalonikki for one year (1963–1964). Greenlee professes fluency in Greek, Indonesian, and Malay and a much more limited knowledge of Arabic, French, and Italian, the languages he mastered while working as a foreign service officer in Iraq, Pakistan, Indonesia, and Greece for the United States Information Agency. The USIA awarded Greenlee a Meritorious Service Award, but he quit that job in 1965 to pursue his writing in Greece for the next several years.

In the preface to his first published novel, *The Spook Who Sat by the Door* (1969), Greenlee says: "I am a black American and I write; not necessarily in that order of importance." The order of importance may not be accidental, however, considering that black consciousness comes to the foreground in all of his written works, which, in addition to *The Spook Who Sat by the Door*, include two volumes of poetry, *Blues for an African Princess* (1971) and *Ammunition!: Poetry and Other Raps* (1975); his second novel, *Baghdad Blues* (1976); and a collection of all his poems, *Be-Bop Man/Be-Bop Woman* (1995). Films produced by Greenlee include *The Legend of Nigger Charley* (1972), *Gordon's War* (1973), and *Cornbread, Earl and Me* (1975). In the 1960s and 1970s Greenlee was a member of the black cultural-nationalist movement, cooperating with such artists and activists as NIKKI GIOVANNI and SONIA SANCHEZ.

Greenlee had problems finding a publisher for his first novel, which was seen by many as too revolutionary to be published. *The Spook Who Sat by the Door* was finally issued in 1969 in Great Britain and in 1970 in the United States. It received the London Sunday Times Book of the Year Award and would become his best-known novel. Greenlee, together with Ivan Dixon, turned the book into a movie in 1973 after encountering serious problems obtaining permission to make the film. The FBI soon saw to it that the movie disappeared from the screens and was withdrawn from distribution. Greenlee himself claims that his phone was tapped.

The protagonist of *The Spook Who Sat by the Door* espouses militant guerrilla struggle against white oppression of African Americans. Assuming the role of a mediator between the black ghetto and the white turf, Dan Freeman feigns his loyalty to white authorities only to put their vigilance to sleep and successfully launch a ghetto rebellion. Self-reliance, separatism, and group cohesion are the basic tenets of Freeman's ideology. BILLIE HOLIDAY's lyric "God bless the child that's got his own" epitomizes Freeman's separatist stand. Time and again he repeats, "We need to get our own," though he never explains to what extent his people are to be autonomous.

Greenlee's second novel, *Baghdad Blues* (1976), received limited attention and not nearly as much interest as his first novel. The main character in the novel, Dave Burrell, is an African American foreign service officer, like Greenlee in the days of his work for the government. Watching events unfold during the Iraqi revolution against the British in 1958, he does a lot of mind-searching, drawing parallels between the situation of the colonized Iraqis and black people in the United States. Commenting on his character in an interview, Greenlee said:

> It's about a Black, restless, frustrated, angry cat off the block who didn't know why he was angry or what he could do about it. He sort of grew up in Baghdad and learned a lot of things about himself in a context which was totally exotic yet at the same time similar to home. That Black cat was me…. (Burrell, 47)

While Dave Burrell's external allegiance is to the American government, spiritually he identifies with the colonized people, feeling greater affinity with them than with his foreign service colleagues.

Sam Greenlee's poetry presents a consistent philosophy and raises recurring themes. Greenlee offers an incisive look at racial relations in the United States, the disenfranchisement of his people, their response to it, and white people's role in the perpetuation of black oppression. In "prison poems" Greenlee says, "anybody / black / writing poetry / in the USA / is writing poetry in / prison" (*Blues for an African Princess*, 33). The theme of incarceration and yearning for freedom persists in his writing. In "Property Values" the I-speaker reflects on the rhetoric of cultural deprivation propagated by white liberals such as Assistant Secretary of Labor Daniel Patrick Moynihan, who sought the source of African American misfortunes in their cultural deprivation rather than racist policies

of successive administrations. The speaker ostensibly agrees with that interpretation, implicitly hinting that he knows better than that:

> I know that it's not because I'm black
> that I'm not in the race
> for goodies…. It's because
> I'm a culturally deprived member
> of the indigenous population
> of the inner city …
> which is enough to hang up anybody.
> (*Blues for an African Princess*, 9)

Greenlee himself refuses to be "hung up," responding to his situation with wry humor. This humor is visible, for example, in "Suburban Soul," in which he mocks white appropriation of black culture: "if white folks would just get a soul thing 'bout / rats and roaches, we might really be into something…. / we could ship motherfuckers to the suburbs" (*Blues for an African Princess*, 11). Not only white people but also African Americans living in the suburbs bear the brunt of Greenlee's criticism. The rift between the black middle class and African Americans in the ghetto, raised already in *The Spook*, finds its way into Greenlee's poetry as well.

A resident of Chicago's South Side, Greenlee continued to work as a radio talk show host and write and participate in poetry readings into the twenty-first century. Greenlee's whole life as well as the message underlying his work can be traced to a statement he made in 1971: "If you can content yourself with just making a living and making a living at doing something you believe in, then you stick to the real Black thing" (Burrell, 46).

FURTHER READING

Greenlee, Sam. Afterword, in *The Blues for an African Princess* (1971).

Greenlee, Sam. Preface, in *The Spook Who Sat by the Door* (2002).

Burrell, Walter. "Black World Interview with Sam Greenlee," *Black World* 20.9 (1971).

KLARA SZMÁNKO

Greenlee, William Augustus (1897–7 July 1952), National Negro League president and owner of the Pittsburgh Crawfords, was born in Marion, North Carolina, to a masonry contractor with the surname Greenlee (his mother's name is unknown). Little is known of his early life. After dropping out of college, Greenlee hopped a freight train north to Pittsburgh in 1916 and settled in the Hill District, a gathering point for immigrants of many nationalities. He operated a steam drill, drove a taxi, shined shoes, and worked as a fireman at Jones and Laughlin's Southside Steel Works before serving overseas in the army's 367th Regiment during World War I. Returning to Pittsburgh in 1919, he bootlegged liquor and entered the nightclub business.

Greenlee ran a poolroom, then the Paramount Club, a restaurant and cabaret, then the Sunset Cafe before opening the Crawford Grill, considered the Hill's classiest nightspot. The club was the center for Greenlee's numbers game, a business that he and William "Woogie" Harris, brother of the photographer CHARLES "TEENIE" HARRIS, popularized in Pittsburgh. The numbers were a lottery in which bettors wagered that a three-digit number would be the one to "hit" that day. The number was based on numbers drawn from transactions in the stock market, the commodity exchange, or a particular horse track. Greenlee and Harris turned the operation into the city's largest black-controlled enterprise during the 1930s. They made never-to-be-repaid loans to help families pay their bills, and Greenlee bankrolled many early black political efforts in Pittsburgh.

Greenlee also used the profits from numbers to become a sports patron. In 1926 he bought uniforms for the Crawfords, a popular sandlot baseball club that took its name from the Crawford Bath House, a city facility for migrants. By 1930 the Crawfords were ready to take on the Homestead Grays, then among the nation's best black professional teams. The team asked Greenlee if he wanted to run the ballclub. Greenlee accepted the offer, but according to captain Harold Tinker, "When he took the ballteam, he let us know that it was his intention not to leave it as a sandlot team. He was going to the top." Along with the Crawfords' cross-town rivals, CUMBERLAND POSEY and the Grays, Greenlee helped Pittsburgh become the center of black baseball.

Greenlee secured the Negro League veteran Bobby Williams as his player-manager and soon began recruiting the best black players in the country. Over the next few seasons he added Negro League stars OSCAR CHARLESTON, COOL PAPA BELL, Ted Page, TED "DOUBLE DUTY" RADCLIFFE, and JUDY JOHNSON to the roster. Several of his recruits were lured from the Homestead Grays. The Crawfords could boast a battery of SATCHEL PAIGE and JOSH GIBSON, possibly the finest assembled, as well as three other future Hall of Famers, Charleston, Bell, and Johnson.

As the Crawfords overtook the Grays, Greenlee built the country's foremost black-controlled stadium. Costing more than $100,000, Greenlee Field opened on the Hill in 1932 and hosted Negro League baseball, black college football, soccer matches, and boxing.

Greenlee also began to piece together the Negro National League, one of the strongest national black institutions of its time before its collapse in 1931 as the result of the Depression and the death of its founder, Andrew RUBE FOSTER. The NNL attained greater financial stability and public presence than any earlier black professional sport, and much of its success was due to Greenlee, the league's president. As the league's principal innovator during its first five years, he initiated an annual all-star game, the East-West Classic, first played in 1933 at Comiskey Park in Chicago. He also began four-team doubleheaders at Yankee Stadium in New York and Forbes Field in Pittsburgh.

In 1937 the Negro American League was formed from the Midwestern teams of the NNL. Greenlee retired as NNL president the same year, largely because of Caribbean politics. Ciudad Trujillo, a team representing the Dominican dictator Rafael Trujillo, persuaded Paige, Gibson, Bell, and a half-dozen of their teammates to abandon the Crawfords for a summer season. Trujillo's team had lost the championship the previous summer, and his minions were determined not to repeat that humiliation. Ciudad Trujillo won the island championship, and Greenlee's Crawfords never recovered from the blow.

Greenlee gave up baseball before the 1939 season, and the Crawfords, who bore little resemblance to their former selves, played a few seasons in Toledo and Indianapolis before folding. Greenlee Field was torn down in 1938 and replaced by a public housing project.

Greenlee kept a hand in the sporting scene. In 1935 he purchased the contract of a twenty-one-year-old boxer, JOHN HENRY LEWIS, who on 31 October became the first African American light heavyweight champion by winning a decision over Bob Olin. Greenlee thus became the first African American to manage a light heavyweight titleholder. Lewis later was knocked out by JOE LOUIS in the first heavyweight championship bout between two black fighters. After Lewis quit the ring in 1939 Greenlee soon tired of boxing.

Greenlee later sought to reenter black baseball. Denied a franchise in the Negro Leagues he formed the United States League (USL) in 1945. The league lasted two seasons, with franchises in Pittsburgh, Brooklyn, Chicago, Detroit, Cleveland,

Philadelphia, Toledo, and Boston. Headquartered upstairs from the Crawford Grill, the USL had the endorsement of Brooklyn Dodgers' president Branch Rickey, who offered it the use of parks controlled by the Dodgers. During this period Rickey and Greenlee held discussions regarding the effect of integration on baseball. Some have charged that the USL detracted from the NNL and the NAL and left those leagues more vulnerable to Rickey's policy of signing players without compensating their Negro League teams.

After the USL's demise, Greenlee focused on the Crawford Grill, which he made into one of the city's foremost revenue-producing restaurants. In 1950 he became ill and the following year the restaurant was destroyed by fire. By then, white numbers entrepreneurs had taken over much of his territory, and the federal government was suing him for unpaid taxes. He died in Pittsburgh. The black-owned *Pittsburgh Courier*, which splashed news of his death across its front page, called Greenlee the city's "most fabulous sports figure."

FURTHER READING

Ruck, Rob. *Sandlot Seasons: Sport in Black Pittsburgh* (1987).

Obituary: *Pittsburgh Courier*, 12 July 1952.

This entry is taken from the *American National Biography* and is published here with the permission of the American Council of Learned Societies.

ROB RUCK

Greer, Hal (26 June 1936–) basketball player, was born Harold Everett Greer in Huntington, West Virginia. After graduating from Douglass High School in Huntington, Greer would become one of the greatest high school basketball players in the history of West Virginia. He broke a significant racial barrier when he enrolled at Marshall University in his home state in 1954. He became the first African American to receive a scholarship to Marshall and the first African American to play a sport at the university. Listed at six feet two inches and 175 pounds, Greer averaged 19.2 points per game during his college career, earning all-conference honors in 1957. In his senior year of 1958 he not only made the all-conference team for a second consecutive year, but he was also named a college All-American.

Greer was known as a quick shooting guard, with a near-unstoppable mid-range jump shot. Following his graduation from Marshall in 1958, he was drafted by the Syracuse Nationals in 1958 and averaged eleven points per game as a player off the bench during his rookie season. Although that first season did not match the type of production he was accustomed to at Marshall, Greer grew into his role on the Nationals as a complement to the team's leader, future hall-of-fame player Dolph Schayes. By the 1960–1961 season, Greer became the team's second leading scorer, producing 19.6 points per game and earned his first selection to the league's All-Star game.

After playing four seasons in Syracuse, the franchise moved to Philadelphia in 1963 and was renamed the Philadelphia 76ers. By that time, Greer had replaced Schayes as the focal point of the team. During the 1963–1964 season, his first as a Philadelphia 76er, he averaged over twenty-three points per game. That season began a seven-year stretch during which Greer averaged at least twenty points per game. When the team acquired WILT CHAMBERLAIN for the 1964–1965 season, Greer returned to his role as the team's second leading scorer, but he continued making All-Star teams. In fact, Greer made ten consecutive All-Star game appearances from 1961 to 1970. Although considered by contemporaries as one of the great guards of his era, Greer was never known as a flashy player. He was often overlooked by the fans, who preferred the likes of Oscar Robertson of the Milwaukee Bucks, Jerry West of the Los Angeles Lakers, Walt Frazier of the New York Knicks, or Sam Jones of the Boston Celtics.

In the 1966–1967 season, the 76ers assembled a team that sportswriters often call the greatest in NBA history. With Greer and Chamberlain leading the way, the 76ers won sixty-eight games during the regular season and captured the NBA title, defeating the San Francisco Warriors four games to two in a best-of-seven series. Greer elevated his already outstanding play to new heights, when his regular season scoring average of 22.1 points per game rose to 27.7 during the playoffs. The following season, Greer earned MVP of the 1968 All-Star game when he scored a record nineteen points in one quarter, twenty-one overall for the game, all in only seventeen total minutes played.

The 1972–1973 season proved to be Greer's last with the 76ers. as he served as both assistant coach and part-time player. The team won only nine games. With his playing time drastically reduced, Greer retired from a team with the worst regular-season record in league history. That infamous season, however, did not diminish Greer's career achievements. He retired as the all-time highest scorer in the franchise's history, recording 21,586 points. He was also ranked in the top ten in NBA history for points, field goals attempted, field goals made, and minutes.

In 1982 Greer was elected to the Basketball Hall of Fame, and in 1985 he was elected to the Marshall University Sports Hall of Fame. The 76ers and Marshall University both retired his jersey numbers, 15 and 16 respectively. He and his wife, Mamie, settled in Scottsdale, Arizona. In 1997 he received one final honor: In celebration of its fiftieth anniversary season, the NBA named Greer one of its fifty greatest players.

FURTHER READING

Goodman, Michael E. *The History of the Philadelphia 76ers* (2002).

Lynch, Wayne. *Season of the 76ers: The Story of Wilt Chamberlain and the 1967 NBA Champion Philadelphia 76ers* (2002).

JOHN BRYAN GARTRELL

Greer, Sonny (13 Dec. 1885–23 Mar. 1982), jazz drummer, was born William Alexander Greer Jr. in Long Branch, New Jersey, the son of William Alexander Greer, an electrician for the Pennsylvania Railroad. His mother, whose name is unknown, was a seamstress. Greer was first attracted to playing as the result of his contact with Eugene "Peggy" Holland, a drummer, singer, and dancer with J. ROSAMOND JOHNSON's touring vaudeville show. His few lessons with Holland (bartered for pool-shooting tips by Greer) gave him with the basic tools he needed to teach himself drums.

His first professional jobs began in the late 1910s with Wilber Gardner and Mabel Ross, and in society orchestras contracted by Harry Yerek and WILL MARION COOK. When he was nineteen he worked with FATS WALLER and the violinist Shrimp Jones at the ocean boardwalk resort of Asbury Park, New Jersey. In 1919, while vacationing in Washington, D.C., Greer was asked to fill in as drummer with Marie Lucas at the Howard Theater, where he met DUKE ELLINGTON. While playing at the Howard, he also worked after hours at the Dreamland Café with the pianist CLAUDE HOPKINS and the trombonist Harry White. After spending several years in Washington, Greer returned to New York, where in 1923 he joined the Washingtonians, a five-piece band led by ELMER SNOWDEN that included Snowden on banjo, Otto Hardwick on saxophone, Artie Whetsol on trumpet, and Ellington on piano. With the addition of BUBBER MILEY (replacing

Whetsol) and Charlie Irvis, this group became the nucleus for the Duke Ellington Orchestra after Snowden departed. In 1928 Greer married Millicent C. (maiden name unknown), with whom he had two children.

From the early 1920s until 1951 Greer worked almost exclusively as Ellington's drummer. After leaving Ellington he freelanced in New York, playing with JOHNNY HODGES, RED ALLEN, Tyree Glenn, and Louis Metcalf. During the next decade Greer played with two ex-Ellingtonians, the saxophonist Eddie Barefield and the trombonist J. C. HIGGINBOTHAM, later fronting his own small group at the Garden Cafe in New York. He made an appearance (with Barefield and other band members) in the film *The Night They Raided Minsky's* (1968) and in that same year was featured in *Sonny*, an eleven-minute film made by Midget Productions. During the 1970s Greer played with the pianist and Ellington interpreter Brooks Kerr, recording *Soda Fountain Rag*, an album of duos with him in 1975. He was active almost until his death in New York City.

Greer's career was remarkable not only for its longevity with one of the premier jazz bands of the twentieth century but also for his complementary and unobtrusive playing style. Greer's best recordings were made in the late 1920s, when drummers, still influenced by earlier ragtime styles, were developing techniques that would be used by drummers in the coming Swing Era. Perhaps most influential in forming Greer's playing style was the Ellington stint as house band at the Cotton Club in New York. Here Greer was required to provide percussive effects for the many "Jungle" shows and productions performed nightly at the club. As a result Greer collected perhaps the largest selection of percussion instruments of any drummer during the Swing Era, as numerous photographs of him taken at this time illustrate. At times some of these instruments found their way onto recordings made by Greer, including chimes ("Freeze and Melt," 1929), temple blocks ("Arabian Lover," 1929), bells, and timpani.

At that time drum solos were de rigueur for any swing drummer, so it is surprising that extensive solos are rarely heard on recordings made by Greer. In fact his infrequent and brief solos throughout his career are notable only for the fact that his playing can be heard clearly and plainly, since he most often remains in the background of many of the recordings he made with Ellington. Recordings representative of his best playing derive mainly from the 1920s, late 1930s, and early 1940s, including "East St. Louis Toodle-oo" (1927), "Downtown Uproar"

(1937), "Chasin' Chippies" (1938), "Cotton Tail," (1940) and "Jumpin' Punkins" (1941). These exhibit Greer's adherence to contemporary drum solo techniques, including those played by Gene Krupa, Chick Webb, and COZY COLE.

FURTHER READING

Dance, Stanley. *The World of Duke Ellington* (1980).

Ellington, Duke. *Music Is My Mistress* (1973).

Tucker, Mark, ed. *The Duke Ellington Reader* (1993).

Obituaries: *Jazz Journal International* 35, no. 6 (June 1982); *Modern Drummer* 6, no. 4 (Mar. 1982); *New York Times*, 25 Mar. 1982.

This entry is taken from the *American National Biography* and is published here with the permission of the American Council of Learned Societies.

T. DENNIS BROWN

Gregg, John Andrew (18 Feb. 1877–17 Feb. 1953), African Methodist Episcopal (AME) bishop and educator, was born in Eureka, Kansas, the son of Alexander Gregg and Eliza Frances Allen. Early positive experiences in Sunday schools and the Epworth League (a Methodist youth organization) encouraged him to develop good study habits and to expect successful results from his efforts. During the Spanish-American War, Gregg signed on for service in the Twenty-third Kansas Volunteers. Within six months he had risen from the rank of sergeant to that of lieutenant. This is all the more notable because few African Americans were commissioned as officers in those days. His capacity for disciplined work blended with his proven ability to coordinate large-scale activities, and these qualities stood him in good stead through the following half century. In 1900 he married Celia Ann Nelson; they adopted one child. In 1945, four years after his first wife's death, he married Melberta McFarland.

In 1898 Gregg decided to enter the ministry and obtained a license to preach from the Kansas Annual Conference of the AME Church. That same year he entered the University of Kansas, receiving his baccalaureate in 1902. While teaching school for a year at Oskaloosa he was admitted to the Kansas Annual Conference. In 1903 he was ordained a deacon and appointed minister to Mount Olive Church in Emporia, Kansas. Shortly thereafter he volunteered to go overseas.

In 1903 Gregg became a teacher and administrator of the AME mission station in Cape Colony, South Africa, where he was a presiding elder.

After returning to the United States in 1906 he was ordained an elder and appointed minister of Bethel Church in Leavenworth, Kansas. Two years later he became pastor of Ebenezer Church in Saint Joseph, Missouri, and served that congregation for half a decade. In 1913 he accepted the presidency of Edward Waters College in Jacksonville, Florida, showing once again how much he valued education alongside spiritual guidance as an element of human improvement. This strong commitment to intellectual training among African Americans propelled him to fill the presidential chair at Wilberforce University in Ohio from 1920 to 1924; it was during this time that he was elected a bishop of the AME Church. That year he returned to South Africa to preside over his church's Seventeenth District. In 1928 he returned to America to assume responsibility for a succession of Episcopal districts: the Fifth (Kansas, 1928–1936), and the Fourth (Virginia, 1936–1948; Florida, 1949–1958). Beginning in 1948 and serving until his death he also presided over the Bishops Council.

In the early 1940s the AME Church joined the Colored ME Church and the National Baptist Convention to form the Fraternal Council of Negro Churches, and in 1943 the council nominated Gregg to represent it in a visit to the White House. President Franklin D. Roosevelt gave him the task of touring with U.S. troops in both the European and Pacific theaters. Gregg strove to boost morale among African American soldiers and to encourage racial harmony. He wrote two pamphlets, *Superlative Righteousness* (1944) and *Of Men and Arms* (1945), based on his experiences. In 1947 he was presented the Award of Merit from the secretary of the army. He died in Jacksonville, Florida.

Throughout his career Gregg displayed no outstanding gifts as a scholar, writer, or public speaker. His intellectual grasp of doctrine and administrative procedures was firm, however, and his strength lay in helping people apply the basic principles of acquired skills and moral virtues in their lives.

FURTHER READING

Obituary: *New York Times*, 19 Feb. 1953.

This entry is taken from the *American National Biography* and is published here with the permission of the American Council of Learned Societies.

HENRY WARNER BOWDEN

Gregory, Dick (12 Oct. 1932–), comedian, civil right activist, nutritionist, and actor, was born Richard Claxton Gregory in St. Louis, Missouri. He grew up on North Taylor Street with his mother, Lucille, and his five siblings. His father, Presley Sr., abandoned the family when Gregory was very young. On North Taylor Street, Gregory told jokes to the neighborhood children, jokes that would later lead to his fame as a comedian. For most of his childhood, however, he faced poverty and racism. His first brush with segregation came at an early age when he raised his hand and volunteered to give five dollars to needy children after the teacher asked his class if their parents would be able to make donations for Christmas. His teacher told him to "put your hand down, Richard, this money is for your kind." The entire class laughed at him as he ran out of the room. The Gregory family was so poor that they did not have running water. Gregory always wanted to be neat and clean, so he started taking showers at school when the track team showered in the afternoons. When the coach told him that showers were for track players only, Gregory joined the team. Not long after the coach watched him build up his speed as he ran around the field to make himself sweat so he could then take a shower, Gregory was enlisted as a Sumner High School starter. Some of his records there remain unbroken. In 1951 Gregory's cross-country

Dick Gregory, shortly after addressing a group of students at the University of South Florida, 14 April 1971. (AP Images.)

track abilities earned him a scholarship to Southern Illinois University, which he attended for two years. After the death of his mother, Gregory dropped out of school and was drafted into the army.

Because Gregory constantly made fun of his peers, his sergeant forced him to join a talent show as punishment. He won that show, and many more to follow. After leaving the army, Gregory moved to Chicago with his oldest brother, Presley, and worked as master of ceremonies at a nightclub. Within three years he was considered one of the funniest comedians in Chicago. While working the city's nightclubs, he met his future wife, Lillian Smith, whom he married in 1959. On the day of their marriage the two traveled by bus to St. Louis to live with his oldest sister, Dolores. Gregory continued to travel back and forth to Chicago to work. Their first child, Michelle, was born on Dolores's kitchen floor while everyone was at work. The couple had ten more children; one son, Richard Jr., died in 1963.

As Gregory's family grew, he continued to work the nightclub scene. His big break came when Hugh Hefner invited him to perform at the Playboy Lounge in Chicago as a replacement for the white comedian Irwin Corey. His job that night was to entertain a group of white southerners who were in town for a chicken convention. That one night turned into a six-week stint. With rave reviews, including one from *Time* magazine, and an invitation to the *Jack Paar Show*, Dick Gregory was on his way to stardom. No matter who the audience was he continued to blast segregation with humor. Between 1960 and 1961 he released three record albums: *Talk Turkey*, *Two Sides*, and *Running for President*. After receiving a call to go to Leflore County, Mississippi, because the food bank that fed mostly black people was closed, he raised money by recording and selling his fourth album, *My Brother's Keeper*.

Gregory was drawn further into the movement when he was invited by the civil rights activist MEDGAR EVERS to march with him in support of black voting rights in Jackson, Mississippi. On 12 June 1963 Evers was murdered in his driveway after returning home from a voters' registration meeting. Not long after Evers's death, Gregory began to cancel his nightclub dates so that he could march with MARTIN LUTHER KING JR. and other civil rights leaders. In 1964 Gregory flew to Moscow to protest the treatment of black soldiers for what he believed was "dating white girls." He had only been there a few days when he learned that JAMES CHANEY, Andrew Goodman, and

Michael Schwerner were missing in Philadelphia, Mississippi. The three civil rights workers were part of the "Mississippi Summer" voting rights campaign sponsored by the Student Non-Violent Coordinating Committee (SNCC). Gregory traveled to Jackson and accused Sheriff Lawrence Rainey of being responsible for the deaths of the three young men. Rainey was later arrested but was found not guilty of murdering the three men. Eventually, seven Klansmen were convicted of conspiracy in the murders of Chaney, Goodman, and Schwerner, including Deputy Sheriff Cecil Price.

Still fighting for change, in 1967 Gregory ran unsuccessfully for mayor of Chicago against the incumbent Richard J. Daley and then ran for president of the United States in 1968. He received a million and a half votes in his failed presidential bid. In the early 1970s Gregory became a vegetarian and began to focus on world hunger and malnutrition. He later developed an extremely profitable diet drink, and subsequently used that money to continue his fight against world hunger; he ran marathon after marathon to bring attention to the cause.

The world changed, but not Dick Gregory. He still marched for civil and human rights. Colleges and universities throughout the country invited him to lecture on civil rights and current events. Though diagnosed with lymphoma in 2000 he continued to walk five miles each day in Washington, D.C., where he lived part-time and hosted his own radio show; he and his wife lived most of the year in Plymouth, Massachusetts. His numerous books include *Nigger*, *Up From Nigger*, *Code Name Zorro* (with Mark Lane), *No More Lies*, and *Callus on My Soul*. In 2000 he was honored at the Kennedy Center and was inducted into Southern Illinois University's Athletic Hall of Fame.

FURTHER READING

Osborne, John. "Black Chutzpah," *New Republic*, Vol. 158 (17), 27 April 1968, 14–15.

Rahman, Ali. "A Conversation with Dick Gregory," *New York Amsterdam News*, 10 Oct. 2002.

SHELIA PATRICE MOSES

Gregory, James Monroe (23 Jan. 1849–17 Dec. 1915), educator, civil rights activist, and author, was throughout his life a brilliant and forceful figure in the push for equal rights and the higher education of African Americans. He was born in Lexington, Virginia, the elder of two sons of William Lewis and Maria A. Gladman, both free persons. After the death of her first husband, his mother later married Henry L. Gregory, a minister, who supported the family as a laborer. Maria was one of eight offspring of Claiborne Gladman and Anna Pollard. The Gladmans were prominent members of Lynchburg, Virginia's community of free African Americans (Delaney and Rhodes, 2).

In 1859, eager to be free of the repressive Virginia environment, Henry, Maria, and their young sons set out from Lynchburg for the Midwest, primarily in order to assure a good education for their boys. Residing temporarily in Indiana, Illinois, and Michigan, they settled in Cleveland, where Gregory attended the public schools. His parents must have separated during this period, for later in his life Gregory indicated that when he was age thirteen he met FREDERICK DOUGLASS in his father's home in New Bedford, Massachusetts.

Early in life Gregory showed signs of leadership ability and an active commitment to civil rights issues. In 1864, at age fifteen, he served as secretary of the organizational meeting of the Oberlin, Ohio, chapter of the National Equal Rights League, an organization formed by members of the 1864 National Convention of Colored Men to combat racial inequality. He spent a summer following the end of the Civil War back in Lynchburg as a teacher with the Freedmen's Bureau, an organization founded in 1865 to aid the emancipated slaves and destitute whites in the South.

In the fall of 1865 Gregory entered the preparatory department at Oberlin College, in Ohio, an institution unique in its time for opening its doors to free blacks. The town of Oberlin had, as a consequence, become a magnet for such families, and a community of free blacks resided there. Gregory, the only African American in his class, earned a reputation for exceptional oratory, which motivated his classmates to select him to represent them at the 1867 senior preparatory exhibition.

A major turning point in Gregory's life came about through General Benjamin Butler of Massachusetts. Eager to recommend an African American to West Point, Butler contacted General Giles Shurtleff, then a professor at Oberlin, asking him to suggest a student for that purpose. The name furnished was that of James Monroe Gregory (Simmons, 633). Subsequently, in the summer of 1867, on the heels of a bitter congressional struggle over Reconstruction, Gregory traveled to Washington, D.C. While there, he met several influential men, among them General Oliver Otis Howard, the chief figure in the founding of Howard University and its first president. Gregory soon found that his chances of entering West Point had been scuttled by President Andrew Johnson, who, resentful over his battles with Congress, refused to consider sending an African American to the academy. Gregory returned home and entered Oberlin College. However, the full impact of his visit to Washington had yet to evolve. General Howard, learning that the West Point appointment had not been approved, set the wheels in motion to convince Gregory to withdraw from Oberlin and enroll in the newly established Howard University. Gregory accepted the challenge. A. L. Barber, principal of the normal department at Howard, sent him a letter, dated 10 September 1868, urging him to attend, which ended with the words: "Do not fail to come, you will never regret it" (*Washington Bee*, 1 Jan. 1915, 1).

Eventually Gregory gained two classmates, Arthur C. O'Hear and JOSIAH THOMAS SETTLE, the three men constituting Howard's first graduating class on 13 June 1872. Gregory earned an AB degree.

Following graduation Gregory stayed on as instructor of mathematics in the preparatory department, eventually becoming professor of Latin in the college department, dean for two years, and instructor of political economy and general history (Scarborough, 6). He was also largely responsible for Howard receiving its first appropriation from the U.S. Congress in the amount of ten thousand dollars. One of his students in the preparatory department had been Fannie Emma Whiting Hagan of Williamsport, Pennsylvania, whom he married on 29 December 1873. They became the parents of four children: Eugene Monroe, James Francis, Margaret Briggs, and THOMAS MONTGOMERY GREGORY.

An intimate of Frederick Douglass, Gregory labored in the struggle for black rights. He was elected permanent secretary of the National Convention of Colored Americans, an organization over which Douglass presided, that met in Louisville, Kentucky, on 24 September 1883 "to consider ways and means for the elevation of the status of the Negro" (Simmons, 638). Gregory was an organizer and the presiding officer of the civil rights mass meeting held in Washington, D.C., on 23 October 1883, following the Supreme Court's decision that the Civil Rights Act of 1875 was unconstitutional (Simmons, 636).

In 1886 Gregory accepted an invitation from the Congregational Society of New York to speak on the higher education of blacks at its annual meeting. BOOKER T. WASHINGTON spoke on industrial education, and FANNIE JACKSON COPPIN on the education of women. In that same year Gregory was appointed a trustee of the District of Columbia public schools. In 1890 he founded and was the first executive officer of the American Association of Educators of Colored Youth (*Washington Bee*). Additionally, he was secretary of the Republican Central Committee of the District of Columbia for four years. His book, *Frederick Douglass the Orator*, a tribute to his friend and mentor, was published in 1893.

Gregory resigned from Howard University in 1895 after twenty-two years of service. A lack of rapport with President Jeremiah Rankin created such tension between them that Gregory was convinced that remaining there would be too stressful. The family moved to a house not far from the university and in 1897 departed for New Jersey, where Gregory had accepted a position as principal of the Bordentown Manual and Industrial Training School for Colored Youth. The Bordentown school was at that time very run-down with a sparse student enrollment. Then falling under the control of the State of New Jersey, responsibility for the school was passed, at Gregory's urging, to the state board of education. Concerned that the school's facilities were woefully inadequate, Gregory persuaded the state to purchase a 225-acre estate he had found was available.

The school was relocated from a few frame houses in town to a beautiful countryside site on the Delaware River that had been the property of Delia Stewart Parnell, the daughter of the commander of the ship USS *Constitution* ("Old Ironsides"). State funds were made available for the erection of additional buildings, students flocked to the campus, and under Gregory's leadership the school flourished (*Boston Guardian*, 25 Dec. 1915), offering a rare and successful combination of academic and industrial courses.

After seventeen years at Bordentown, Gregory was overtaken by recurring bouts of ill health, forcing his retirement. He died in December 1915 and was buried at Mount Auburn Cemetery in Cambridge, Massachusetts, in a family plot he had purchased while visiting his son Thomas Montgomery at Harvard.

James Monroe Gregory devoted his life to working for the betterment of African Americans, both in the classroom and in the political arena. Recognized as a consummate scholar and a skilled and dedicated teacher, he was the fourth member of his race to attain membership in the American Philological Association. Upon his death, the *Boston Guardian* newspaper stated that Gregory had been "the leading exponent of the higher education of the Negro."

FURTHER READING

Gregory's papers are included in the Thomas Montgomery Gregory Papers at the Moorland-Spingarn Research Center, Founders Library, Howard University, in Washington, D.C.

Cheek, William, and Aimee Lee Cheek. *John Mercer Langston and the Fight for Black Freedom, 1829–65* (1989).

Delaney, Ted, and Phillip Wayne Rhodes. *Free Blacks of Lynchburg, Virginia, 1805–1865* (2001).

Logan, Rayford W. *Howard University: The First Hundred Years 1867–1967* (1969).

Scarborough, W. S. "Introduction," in *Frederick Douglass the Orator*, James M. Gregory (1893).

Simmons, William J. *Men of Mark: Eminent, Progressive, and Rising* (1887).

Obituaries: "Prof. J. M. Gregory Dead," *Boston Guardian*, 25 Dec. 1915; "Prof. James M. Gregory Dead," *Washington Bee*, 1 Jan. 1915.

SHEILA GREGORY THOMAS

Gregory, Louis George (6 June 1874–30 July 1951), public lecturer, lawyer, and government administrator, was an early-twentieth-century champion or "race amity worker" for racial equality and social justice in America. A direct descendant of slavery, Louis George Gregory was born in Charleston, South Carolina. His mother, Mary Elizabeth, and his grandmother, Mary Bacot, had been enslaved on the George Washington Dargan plantation in Darlington, South Carolina. Louis Gregory stated that "my grandmother, wholly of African blood was without ceremony [Dargan's] slave [mistress] and my mother, his daughter" (Morrison, 12).

At an early age Gregory experienced racial oppression, poverty, and segregation. Gregory's father, Ebenezer George, died of tuberculosis in 1879, leaving Mary Elizabeth and her two sons, Louis and Theodore, in severe poverty. In 1885 Gregory's mother married George Gregory, who became a devoted stepfather to Louis and his brother. It is because of the older Gregory's support and involvement in his stepson's education that Louis Gregory was able to attend Fisk University. After graduating from Fisk and after a short-term teaching position, he began to study law at Howard University and graduated with his law degree in 1902. As an attorney he worked for the U.S. Department of the Treasury in Washington, D.C.

It was in the nation's capital that he became impressed with the teachings of the Bahá'í religion, which emphasized the principles of social justice, racial equality, and harmony in America. He officially joined its membership in 1909. With the intensity of such "ideals and their agitation" Gregory began his forty-year journey to promote racial unity and gender equity through speaking engagements, university lectures, his involvement with the National Association for the Advancement of Colored People (NAACP) and national race unity conferences, and through teaching the principles of his religious beliefs throughout the Midwest, the South, and the northeastern states.

In 1911 Gregory traveled to Palestine as a member of the newly developing American Bahá'í community, making him the first African American to do so officially. It was on this journey of "pilgrimage" in the Holy Land, Europe, and Egypt that he met his future wife, Louisa Matthew, a wealthy, Cambridge-educated woman from southern England. Interracial marriage was not only socially forbidden in the United States but also illegal in the majority of states at that time. Louis Gregory and Louisa Matthew, however, were legally married in New York City on 27 September 1912. Despite the obstacles of prejudice, legal sanctions, and social criticism they encountered because of their interracial union, they remained together for the rest of their lives in unity and companionship.

Upon realizing the condition of race relations in the United States, Gregory envisioned that his efforts to engage with wide-ranging groups of white Americans and African Americans on a spiritual level would "set in motion a plan that was to bring the races together, attract the attention of the country … and have a far-reaching effect upon the destiny of the nation itself" (Morrison, 132).

A man of extraordinary patience, dignity, and eloquence, Louis Gregory was a contemporary of renowned black intellectuals, educators, and political activists such as W. E. B. DuBois, his wife, Nina Gomer DuBois (a member of the American Bahá'í community), ALAIN LOCKE, Edward J. Braithwaite, A. PHILIP RANDOLPH, and WALTER F. WHITE. ROBERT S. ABBOTT, the editor and founder of the *Chicago Defender*, joined Louis Gregory in Bahá'í membership. As an eloquent speaker with relentless energy, Gregory was among the college-educated black "talented tenth" of W. E. B. DuBois's vision.

In the decades of the 1920s and 1930s Gregory was instrumental in planning the first series of "race amity" conventions in the United States. Through his association with contemporary black leadership and with affluent white patrons in Washington, D.C., such as the famous socialite Agnes Parsons, the first convention for amity between the "white and colored races in America" was held at Washington's First Congregational Church in 1921. The Washington amity convention was historically significant not only because two thousand attended in a city where racial segregation was alive and well but also because it was the first conference in the nation's capital that focused on racial accord in America. Alain Locke, the Howard University professor-scholar, philosopher, and "dean" of the arts movement known as the Harlem Renaissance, chaired one of the convention sessions. Locke, another African American Bahá'í, became a member of the Bahá'í Interracial Amity Committee. Louis Gregory believed and advocated that new ideas about race and gender were being

> set into motion [relating] to the great peace, the universality of truth, to the great law that humanity is one, even as God is one, to the elevation of the station of woman, who must no longer be confined to a limited life but be everywhere recognized as the equal and helpmeet of man (Morrison, 134).

Gregory spearheaded subsequent race amity conventions. With the heightened awareness of race unity that Gregory created through his activism, these "race amity" conventions eventually transformed into "race unity" committees in the decades of the mid-twentieth century. Gregory became the chief spokesman for racial unity as a representative of the American Bahá'í community.

Throughout his years of activism for racial equality and social justice, Gregory continued to travel and work extensively as a lecturer, writer, administrator, and community organizer promoting the cause of racial harmony through his teaching of the principles of the Bahá'í religion.

Schools, educational centers, and projects were named in his honor, including the Louis G. Gregory Bahá'í Institute and WLGI Radio Bahá'í, both in Hemingway, South Carolina. In 1995 the first Bahá'í museum in the United States opened and was named after Louis Gregory. It is located in his childhood home of Charleston, South Carolina. Predating the civil rights movement, Louis Gregory was instrumental in creating multiracial religious communities and heightened social awareness of a future American society free from racial prejudice. He died in Eliot, Maine.

FURTHER READING
Documents and articles related to Gregory are held in the Louis G. Gregory Papers, National Bahá'í Archives, Wilmette, Illinois.

"Abdul Bahá'í on Religious Unity." *Washington Bee*, 27 Apr. 1912.

"Fourth Annual Conference of the National Association for the Advancement of Colored People." *Crisis*, 4 June 1912.

Locke, Alain. "Impressions of Haifa," in *The Bahá'í World* (formerly *Bahá'í Year Book*): *A Biennial International Record* 2 (1926–1928).

Locke, Alain. "Unity through Diversity: A Bahá'í Principle," in *The Bahá'í World: A Biennial International Record* 4 (1930–1932).

Mason, Ernest D. "Alain Locke's Social Philosophy," *World Order* 13.2 (Winter 1978–1979).

Morrison, Gayle. *To Move the World: Louis G. Gregory and the Advancement of Racial Unity in America* (1982).

Ober, Harlan F. "Louis Gregory," in *The Bahá'í World: A Biennial International Record* 12 (1950–1954).

ANGELITA D. REYES

Gregory, Thomas Montgomery (31 Aug. 1887–21 Nov. 1971), educator, dramatist, social philosopher, and activist, was born in Washington, D.C., the youngest of the four children of JAMES MONROE GREGORY and Fannie Emma Whiting Hagan. His father, a professor of classics at Howard University, had been a member of the university's first college graduating class in 1872. The family lived on the university campus until Gregory was eight years old, at which time his father resigned from the faculty to head the Bordentown Manual Training and Industrial School for Colored Youth in New Jersey.

The family's 1897 move to Bordentown gave Gregory the run of a beautiful 225-acre campus on the Delaware River. A favorite time for him was Saturday mornings when he and his father traveled to Philadelphia by boat to make purchases for the school, for these shopping trips inevitably included dinner at Wanamaker's or Snellenburg's and a stage performance at the Chestnut Street Theatre.

In 1902 Gregory was sent to Williston Seminary in Easthampton, Massachusetts. Although it is probable that he encountered at least some racial prejudice there, nothing stopped him from full participation in all aspects of the life of the school. He was editor of the *Willistonian*, the school paper, and he was junior class president, Adelphi Literary Society president, a star member of the debating team, and on the football, baseball, and track teams. From Williston, Gregory entered Harvard University as a member of the class of 1910. Among his classmates were T. S. Eliot, Walter Lippman, Alan Seeger, and John Reed.

At Harvard he was a student in George Pierce Baker's 47 Workshop class, where the focus was "on playwriting techniques and a laboratory of experimental productions" (*Columbia Encyclopedia*, 6th ed.). It was here that his vision of a viable black college dramatic troupe took root. Later, in 1919, as a professor at Howard University, he founded the Howard Players and served as the group's first director. It is conceivable that his lifelong love of theater stemmed from the times that he sat in Philadelphia audiences with his father, thrilling to onstage performances by John Drew Jr. and Ethel Barrymore.

Gregory maintained essentially as full a program at Harvard as he had at Williston, running track, playing football, and debating. His record at Williston won him an immediate place on Harvard's debating team. He served on the Debating Council, was president of the debating club, and a member of Delta Sigma Rho. In addition, he participated in the first annual "triangular debates" held between Harvard, Yale, and Princeton.

After graduating from Harvard and studying briefly at Columbia University, Gregory joined the Howard University faculty as an English instructor in 1912, teaching argumentation, public speaking, and composition. In 1913 he founded the Howard University Debating Club. In 1915 he and fellow Harvard alumnus and Howard professor ALAIN LOCKE organized the Stylus Literary Society, out of which grew the *Stylus*, a publication of student poetry and prose. Gregory also contributed articles to *The Crisis*, the magazine of the NAACP, and to the *Citizen*, a Boston-based literary magazine for which he also served as an associate editor. He made three trips on southern passenger trains to document Jim Crow seating conditions for a three-part *Crisis* article, "The Jim Crow Car: An NAACP Investigation," published in 1915 and 1916 issues of the magazine.

With the entry of the United States into World War I, Gregory became a key figure in the efforts of the Central Committee of Negro College Men to secure officer training for African Americans, an intensive campaign that resulted in the establishment of the first such camp at Fort Des Moines, Iowa, in June 1917. On 29 May 1918, six months before the end of the war, he married Hugh Ella Hancock of Austin, Texas. They were the parents of six children.

By 1919 Gregory had been appointed professor of English at Howard as well as head of the department. Deeply concerned that serious black theater had gained no foothold and that the black experience was regarded mainly as material for minstrel shows, Gregory set out to change that condition. He motivated his students to write plays based on black life as they knew it to be, a concept foreign then to most blacks as well as whites. Determined that his Howard Players become involved in all aspects of theater, he secured the assistance of the nationally known acting coach Marie Moore-Forrest and the celebrated New York set designer Cleon Throckmorton. Gregory's students performed in plays they wrote and created their own costumes and sets. Plays and short stories crafted by Gregory's best students appeared in publications with which he had an association.

As the Howard Players' reputation grew, so too did the makeup of their audiences. On one occasion Secretary of War Newton Baker was seen en route to a performance of *Thaïs*, written by Paul Wilstach. *Simon the Cyrenian*, written by Ridgely Torrence, was performed for the delegates to the World Disarmament Conference.

Gregory was the catalyst for two major developments that grew out of his work with the Howard Players: the 1921 Washington, D.C., performance of Eugene O'Neill's *Emperor Jones* and the thrust toward a National Negro Theatre.

Gregory's accomplishment in building an outstanding black college theater company was rewarded by the relationships he developed with nationally known playwrights such as O'Neill. He received permission from O'Neill to put on a Players' performance of *Emperor Jones* at Washington's Shubert-Belasco Theater with CHARLES GILPIN in the lead role, for which he had won acclaim in O'Neill's New York production. It was a remarkable accomplishment, made all the more noteworthy because in racially polarized Washington it was the first and only such performance before a markedly integrated audience until decades later.

In a Department of Dramatics publication titled *The Negro Theatre*, Gregory stated: "Our immediate aim is to lay the foundation stones upon which in the future the super-structure of the Negro Theatre will be erected." He abhorred what he described as "a regrettable tendency to imitate ... the Anglo-Saxon" (*Citizen*, 46). He wrote, "America is experiencing a remarkable awakening in the drama" and then asked, "What of the Negro?" He had begun to promote the concept of a National Negro Theatre. His article "For a Negro Theatre" was published in a 1920s issue of the *New Republic*. A theater critic commented in a 1921 issue of *Life* magazine, "It is encouraging ... to find that in Howard University a movement is under way for the establishment of a National Negro Theatre." Unfortunately this groundswell of interest and support was not to continue much beyond 1924, for in that year Gregory resigned from Howard University.

Gregory decided to accept the position of supervisor of Colored Schools in Atlantic City, New Jersey. There he became active in community theater both as actor and director. He continued to contribute articles and reviews of literary works and plays to *The Crisis* and to *Opportunity* magazine. His reviews for *Opportunity* included JEAN TOOMER's *Cane*, JESSIE FAUSET's *There Is Confusion*, Llewelyn Powys's *Black Laughter*, and Paul Green's *The No 'Count Boy*. A book co-edited with Alain Locke, *Plays of Negro Life*, was published in 1927. In 1931 his article "The Negro in Drama" was published in the *Encyclopaedia Britannica*. Gregory retired in 1956. He returned to Washington in 1960 and served a one-year consultancy with the Department of State, subsequent to a recommendation by his former classmate Walter Lippman. Following his death from leukemia, he was buried at Mount Auburn Cemetery in Cambridge, Massachusetts.

FURTHER READING

The Thomas Montgomery Gregory Papers are housed in the Moorland-Spingarn Research Center, Howard University, Washington, D.C.

Gregory, (Thomas) Montgomery. "Race in Art" (conclusion), *Citizen* 1.2 (1915).

Dyson, Walter. *Howard University, the Capstone of Negro Education, a History: 1867–1940* (1941).

Scott, Emmett J. *Scott's Official History of the American Negro in the World War* (1919).

SHEILA GREGORY THOMAS

Gregory, Wilton (7 Dec. 1947–), Roman Catholic priest, liturgical scholar, and bishop, was born Wilton Daniel Gregory, in Chicago, Illinois, the son of Ethel Duncan and Wilton Gregory Sr. The maternal side of Gregory's family was part of the Great Migration of African Americans after World War I, arriving in Chicago from Oxford, Mississippi. Soon after their arrival in the North, Gregory's maternal grandmother and her sister were enrolled at St. Benedict the Moor Boarding School in Milwaukee, Wisconsin, because their mother could not care for them and find work at the same time. While at St. Benedict the Moor, Gregory's grandmother, Etta Mae Duncan, was baptized and received into the Roman Catholic Church. Even though she was not a practicing Catholic in her later life, she never lost her profound admiration and respect for the

Catholic priests and nuns who provided her with a home and an education during those several years of her childhood.

Along with his two younger sisters, Gregory was raised in a single-parent home by his mother and grandmother after his parents divorced. In 1958, when the religious women who staffed St. Carthage Grammar School in Chicago made an aggressive effort to enroll neighborhood black children in the school, Etta Mae Duncan and Ethel Duncan Gregory placed all three children there. Wilton Gregory remembered his grandmother often exhorting her grandchildren to "get an education. They can't take that away from you" (private interview, 16 June 2003). Gregory began the sixth grade at St. Carthage Grammar School, and by the end of that academic year he was formally baptized and received into the Roman Catholic Church. Gregory has attributed his attraction to the Catholic Church to the teachers and priests who staffed St. Carthage parish. After graduating from the eighth grade, he enrolled at Quigley Preparatory Seminary South, in the Archdiocese of Chicago, afterward attending Niles College (later St. Joseph's College Seminary) of Loyola University in Chicago. He completed his theological studies for the priesthood at St. Mary of the Lake Seminary and was ordained a Roman Catholic priest for the Archdiocese of Chicago on 9 May 1973.

Gregory began an active priestly ministry after his ordination, serving as an associate pastor at Our Lady of Perpetual Help parish in Glenview, Illinois, teaching at St. Mary of the Lake Seminary, and assisting Cardinal John Cody in liturgical functions throughout the archdiocese. After three years of such service, Cardinal Cody released Gregory from his pastoral duties and sent him to begin graduate studies at the Pontifical Liturgical Institute ("Sant' Anselmo") in Rome, Italy. He earned his doctorate there in 1980 with a dissertation titled "The Lector: Minister of the Word: An Historical and Liturgical Study of the Office of the Lector in the Western Church."

Upon completion of his degree, Gregory returned to Chicago and to his position as a professor at the seminary. By this time Cardinal Joseph L. Bernardin had replaced Cardinal Cody as archbishop of Chicago. Gregory was ordained an auxiliary bishop for the Archdiocese of Chicago in December 1983, making him, at the age of thirty-six, the youngest bishop in the United States at that time. He has described his years as a bishop in Chicago as one of the great periods of his life and singled out Bernardin as "an extraordinary mentor, a beloved brother in Christ, and a devoted friend." Within a year of his ordination as bishop, Gregory became involved in the preparation of a document that would help define black Catholicism in the latter part of the twentieth century. Along with nine other black Catholic bishops, he published "What We Have Seen and Heard: A Pastoral Letter on Evangelization," in September 1984. This pastoral letter asserted that the black Catholic Church community—at that time, numbering more than 1.5 million participants—had "come of age" and must be responsible for its own development and growth. The letter echoed the sentiments of Pope Paul VI in claiming that the black church had much to offer to the universal Catholic community and should no longer depend on missionary activity from other cultures for the spread and sustenance of faith.

In 1987 Gregory was chair of the Bishops' Subcommittee on Black Liturgy, which supervised the publication of another substantive contribution to black Catholic concerns. "In Spirit and Truth: Black Catholic Reflections on the Order of the Mass" carried liturgical reform into new areas of research and reflection. When the bishops' pastoral letter called for black Catholic initiatives in all aspects of religious life, the liturgy was central to their message. Gregory has stated that "as Catholics, our sacramental, ritual, life is our most precious heritage" (private interview). Once his administrative duties as bishop took up more and more of his focus and energy, Gregory devoted much of his love and care for liturgy in his preaching and presiding at rituals within his home dioceses and throughout the country, especially at regional and national gatherings of black Catholics.

In December 1993 Wilton Gregory made another sort of history within the Roman Catholic Church when he was appointed the seventh bishop of the Diocese of Belleville, Illinois. The Diocese of Belleville covers twelve thousand square miles in southern Illinois, from East St. Louis, Illinois, to Cairo, at the southernmost tip of the state, where the Ohio and Mississippi rivers meet. Gregory was the first African American cleric to be assigned to this 106-year-old diocese, with its even longer history of riots, lynchings, and systematic oppression of African Americans. In addition, upon his arrival Bishop Gregory had to confront a local crisis dealing with charges of sexual abuse among the clergy.

Restoring faith in the church, confronting racial abuses, and providing leadership for a demoralized clergy were priorities for Gregory during his early years as bishop in Belleville. He wrote a regular column, "What I Have Seen and Heard," for the diocesan newspaper *The Messenger*, in which he addressed topics such as the death penalty, prison reform, euthanasia, and physician-assisted suicide. In 2000 Gregory funded and served as principal resource for a three-part video series on racism in the Catholic Church, *Enduring Faith: A Story of African American Catholics in America*.

In 1998 Gregory was elected vice president of the United States Council of Catholic Bishops (USCCB), serving a three-year term, and was elected president in November 2001. He was the first African American bishop to serve as the coordinating administrator for the Catholic Bishops of the United States. In January of the following year, the *Boston Globe* began to publish a series of articles on sexual abuse among Catholic priests, and Gregory's tenure as president of the USCCB became almost entirely focused on that issue and its ramifications for the American Catholic Church.

In reflecting on his goals as president of the USCCB, Gregory once stated, "As bishop, as president of the conference, I hope I can get us to a point where we have a clear focus as to what must be done [about this scandal], and a means to accomplish it" (private interview), but he noted that it will take several generations for reconciliation to occur. "The reconciliation the church needs is not merely a reconciliation that is facile and quick, that is easy and too swiftly spoken … it involves the challenge of forgiving. Admission of guilt is only salvific when the response is 'you are forgiven'" (*Enduring Faith*). His personal anguish was summed up in his understanding, developed as a child in Chicago, that the Catholic Church should be at its best in caring for children. As he said, "If you love people's children, they will love you—that's what made this particular scandalous moment so devastating—because it was a violation of the children" (private interview).

In 2005 Gregory was installed as the Seventh Bishop, Sixth Archbishop of Atlanta. Gregory has held on to a belief that in every crisis there is an opportunity for growth, and he maintains that the scandal that emerged during his time as bishop, both in Chicago and in Belleville, and that eventually erupted during his presidency presented just such an opportunity within the Roman Catholic Church. He summed up his optimism by saying, "I think that there is a new and healthy dialogue and relationship being established between clergy and laity. Something new is being born … what is being born is a new relationship with our laity who are educated, who are knowledgeable, whose love for the church is deep" (*Enduring Faith*).

FURTHER READING

Davis, Cyprian. *The History of Black Catholics in the United States* (1990).

Davis, Cyprian, and Diana L. Hayes, eds. *Taking Down Our Harps: Black Catholics in the United States* (1998).

JOSEPH A. BROWN, S.J.

Grier, Eliza Anna (July 1864–14 Apr. 1902), physician, was born a slave in North Carolina. Little else is known about her early life, including the names of her parents. In 1884 she enrolled in the normal course at Fisk University, and to pay for tuition she alternated each year of study with a year of picking cotton. She graduated in 1891.

Grier taught at Paine Normal School and Industrial Institute in Augusta, Georgia, during the 1890–1891 school year, but her long-range goal was to become a physician. In 1890, just one year before her graduation from Fisk, she wrote to Woman's Medical College of Pennsylvania, inquiring about aid that was available to "an emancipated slave" who wanted to enter "so lofty a profession." No doubt Grier had heard about the school from her mentor and friend Emily Howland, a Quaker teacher and suffragette from upstate New York who had gone south to participate in educational programs for newly freed slaves.

Woman's Medical College was the first school in America that was established solely for the purpose of educating women for the medical profession. It was founded in 1850 by Quakers who did not subscribe to prevailing nineteenth-century notions about the negative effects of education on the "most important female function, the perpetuity of the race." When Grier entered Woman's Medical College in 1893, there were several medical schools that provided nurturing and supportive environments where women could study medicine without encountering the hostility and harassment that women experienced in coeducational schools. But with the Quaker tradition of liberalism and a commitment to academic excellence, Woman's Medical College was among the best in the country. It was one of only five medical colleges that required a four-year course for graduation and one of two that required a laboratory course in physiology.

Although Grier had made it quite clear in her letter to the school that she would need financial assistance, the only record of aid that she received was a $100 stipend, awarded for the 1894–1895 session. Nevertheless, Grier graduated in the class of 1897, which included another medical student of African ancestry, MATILDA ACABELLA EVANS.

After receiving her MD, Grier went to Greenville, South Carolina, and began her career as post-Reconstruction politics solidified. In the South, and often in the North, vigorous efforts were made to prevent blacks from exercising their rights as American citizens. Racial segregation—supported by the *Plessy v. Ferguson* decision in 1896—was enforced in health care facilities in South Carolina. When segregated facilities were not available, blacks simply received no medical care. In South Carolina, where blacks were dying of tuberculosis at a rate that was three times that of whites, blacks were not admitted to the only existing tuberculosis facility in the state until segregated units were constructed five years after it opened.

In this environment of intense racism and violence, Grier wrote that there were "a great many forces operating against the success of the Negro in business" (cited in Sterling, 447). Nevertheless, she was able to establish what she described as a "pretty good practice. But it was among very poor people and did not generate enough money to meet the expenses required to maintain it. In a desperate attempt to continue her work in Greenville, Grier appealed to the noted feminist Susan B. Anthony, writing to her of the need for "assistance in a financial way" during a "time of severe trial and want." But the leader of the women's rights movement was not in a position to help and forwarded the letter to the Woman's Medical College of Pennsylvania.

Grier was never able to secure the funds needed to continue the Greenville practice, and in 1901 she decided to make a new start in Thomasville, Georgia. But working with no professional or financial supports and among people who were wary of, if not hostile to, a black female physician was finally too much for Grier. In 1902 she died from the effects of a stroke, leaving a legacy of courage and tenacity in the face of overwhelming odds.

FURTHER READING

Papers are on file for Eliza Grier in Archives and Special Collections/Black Women Physicians at Drexel University College of Medicine, Philadelphia.

Beardsley, Edward H. *A History of Neglect: Health Care for Blacks and Mill Workers in the Twentieth-Century South* (1987).

Hine, Darlene Clark. "Co-laborers in the Work of the Lord," in *"Send Us a Lady Physician": Women*

Doctors in America, 1835–1920, ed. Ruth J. Abram (1985).

Peitzman, Steven J. *A New and Untried Course: Woman's Medical College and Medical College of Pennsylvania, 1850–1998* (2000).

Sterling, Dorothy, ed. *We Are Your Sisters: Black Women in the Nineteenth Century* (1997).

GERALDINE RHOADES BECKFORD

Grier, Mike (5 Jan. 1975–), professional hockey player, was born in Detroit, Michigan, where his father Bobby Grier worked as an assistant coach for the Detroit Lions professional football team. When Mike was three, however, Bobby was hired away by the New England Patriots, and the family relocated to Boston, where Grier attended local schools and planned for a life of athletics. Mike Grier's uncle is ROSEY GRIER, the professional football defensive great. The young Grier began skating at the age of four, and sometime later was excelling in a youth hockey league, where he was often the only African American on the ice. He attended St. Sebastian's School, where he again played hockey. During his senior year, he was drafted by the St. Louis Blues, but instead chose to attend college and play hockey while also working toward a degree. He matriculated at Boston College in 1993 only to find that he was too heavy to make the team.

Grier walked on during his sophomore year. He had shed twenty pounds and made the team, soon becoming a star. In 1994–1995 he scored twenty-nine goals, was named a First Team All-Star, and led the Terriers to an NCAA championship. During his junior year, he was again drafted by the National Hockey League (NHL)—this time by the Edmonton Oilers, which had obtained rights to him from the Blues—and decided to skip his senior year and go pro. The move made Grier the first African American from the United States to play in the NHL. He was preceded by the black Canadian-born NHL players GRANT FUHR and WILLIE O'REE. Grier debuted as an Oiler in 1996 and scored a notable fifteen goals in that season. Occasional incidents on the ice involving racial epithets—including one instance that led to a suspension for the Washington Capitals' Chris Simon—were not unheard of, but Grief typically downplayed such events and refused to make much of them in the sports press.

With the Oilers, Grier remained a standout, scoring eighty-one goals in six seasons. In 2002, however, he was traded to Washington, though for salary cap reasons rather than performance. He played well for Washington, but the team's big-money push for a Stanley Cup ultimately came up short, and Grier was traded to the Buffalo Sabres in 2004. Grier's main strength was as a penalty killer. He had a reoccurring problem with a dislocating shoulder—which he often popped back into place in order that he could return immediately to the ice—which eventually necessitated a surgical fix. In 2005 he scored a personal-best four game-winning goals, but he again switched teams, this time joining the San Jose Sharks as a free agent. In his first season there, he scored sixteen goals and had seventeen assists. He remained with the Sharks for a couple of years before returning to the Sabres for the 2009 season. In 2010 he played his 1,000th NHL game.

FURTHER READING

Harris, Cecil. *Breaking the Ice: The Black Experience in Professional Hockey* (2003).

JASON PHILIP MILLER

Grier, Pam (26 May 1949–), film and television actress, was born Pamela Suzette Grier in Winston-Salem, North Carolina, the second of four children of Clarence Grier, an air force mechanic, and Gwendolyn (Samuels) Grier, a nurse from rural Wyoming whose great-grandfather owned the Davis Hotel, a hotel for blacks and Chinese railroad workers. Grier's father was transferred to a military base in Swindon, England, and moved the family there when Grier was five years old. After living on American military bases in England, then Germany, the family returned to the United States in 1962 and settled in Denver, Colorado. Grier began attending Smiley Junior High School and became a track star there. She later attended the city's East High School and joined the Echoes of Youth gospel choir, where she played organ and piano with future Earth, Wind and Fire band members Philip Bailey, Larry Dunn, and Andrew Woolfolk.

Grier entered Denver's Metropolitan State College in 1967 at age eighteen with the intention of eventually becoming a doctor. During her freshman year she was offered a spot as a Denver Broncos cheerleader. Instead Grier entered the Miss Colorado beauty pageant in order to win prize money that would cover expenses for a second year of college. Although she did not win the pageant, she won the swimsuit competition and the talent segment for her singing and dancing. David Baumgarten, then head of the Agency for the Performing Arts (APA), was in the audience and suggested to Grier that she pursue an acting career in Hollywood. Grier left

Colorado for Los Angeles, where she lived in her aunt's garage and began working as a switchboard operator at APA while Baumgarten sent her to acting classes and auditions. According to the writer JAMAICA KINCAID, during those early forays in the entertainment industry in the late 1960s one of the criticisms Grier would often hear from producers who decided against hiring her was that she was not "Negro enough." Ironically Grier would soon become an icon of black power on screen.

Grier eventually got a job as a switchboard operator at American International Pictures, where she met the B movie producer and director Roger Corman. In 1969 she was cast in a minor role in his film *The Big Bird Cage*, followed by small parts in *The Big Doll House*, *Beyond the Valley of the Dolls*, and *Women in Cages*, all commonly known as "babes in bondage" or "sexploitation" films. Corman eventually cast Grier in the pivotal role of her career, as the leading character Lee Daniels in the 1972 film *Black Mama, White Mama*. A broadly based "female" version of the film *The Defiant Ones*, *Black Mama, White Mama* got Grier noticed as the gritty black heroine, an image that fit perfectly with the 1970s blaxploitation film era. Fueled by the civil rights and Black Power movements,

Pam Grier, photographed at an unknown location in 1974. (AP Images.)

these films successfully showcased black characters, normally male, that avenged white injustice and redeemed and restored the black community with fearlessness, righteous aggression, and no small dose of sexual potency. For Grier this translated into starring roles in the classic blaxploitation films *Coffy* (1973), *Foxy Brown* (1974), *Sheba, Baby* (1975), and *Friday Foster* (1975). The film historian Donald Bogle notes in *Toms, Coons, Mulattoes, Mammies, and Bucks: An Interpretive History of Blacks in American Films* (2001) that Grier was "the first black woman to rise to stardom through B movies" (251). Grier's success, influence, and iconic persona even struck a chord with white feminists. She became the first African American woman to be featured on the cover of *Ms.* magazine, in the August 1975 issue. As the 1970s came to an end Grier made the conscious career decision to move away from action films and branch out into other types of dramatic film roles. She starred opposite RICHARD PRYOR in the 1977 film *Greased Lightning*, appeared in the 1979 TV miniseries *Roots: The Next Generations*, won critical acclaim for her role opposite Paul Newman in the film *Fort Apache, the Bronx* (1981), and portrayed the Dust Witch in the Walt Disney film *Something Wicked This Way Comes* (1983, based on the novel by Ray Bradbury). She returned to action films for a major role in the hit Steven Seagal film *Above the Law* (1988).

Also in 1988, during a routine physical exam, Grier was diagnosed with cancer and given eighteen months to live. "My whole life changed," she told the reporter Rebecca Ascher-Walsh in an interview for *Entertainment Weekly* (19 Dec. 1997). "I became a different person at that point." Grier underwent treatment for two years at Cedars-Sinai Medical Center in Los Angeles. After beating the disease, Grier eased back into performing with a departure into theater. She took the lead role of the waitress Frankie in San Diego's Gaslamp Quarter Theater Company production of *Frankie and Johnny in the Clair de Lune* (1990). Soon tragedy struck again when Grier's nephew shot and killed himself because his mother (Grier's older sister) was dying of cancer. "I just collapsed onstage. I went numb and I couldn't get up," Grier revealed of her grief to the actor Michael Keaton in a 1997 interview in *Interview* magazine. "I tried not to think about it and carry on, but I couldn't," she continued. "I was tested that whole first week."

Grier did eventually carry on to even greater and more enduring career success. The actor-director MARIO VAN PEEBLES cast her in his 1993 western drama *Posse*. Next she reunited with fellow "blaxploitation" icons JIM BROWN, RICHARD ROUNDTREE, and FRED WILLIAMSON in *Original Gangstas* (1996). Her most significant role came in 1997, in the lead role of Quentin Tarantino's homage, *Jackie Brown*. It was Grier's fiftieth film and her first starring role in over twenty years, and it earned her both NAACP Image Award and Golden Globe Award nominations for best actress.

The next year Grier co-starred in the Showtime television series *Linc's* (1998) and had a supporting role as Harvey Keitel's girlfriend and assistant in Jane Campion's film *Holy Smoke* (1999). Grier also appeared in the acclaimed 2001 Showtime television miniseries *Feast of All Saints*, adapted from the novel by Anne Rice, and the series *The L Word* for the same network.

Says Mario Van Peebles of Grier's solid yet challenging thirty-plus-year career, "Pam triumphed because she didn't get bitter" (*Entertainment Weekly*, 19 Dec. 1997). The peace Grier exudes stems from her connection to her roots and heritage. "What I love about my midwestern upbringing [is] the nourishment of the body, and therefore of your mind and your soul and your spirit," she said (*Interview*, Jan. 1998). Grier, who has never been married, spent time at her ranch home in Denver, Colorado, where she found nourishment—and the strength and savvy to forge an enduring, diverse career—from nature, her animals, and good books.

FURTHER READING

Ascher-Walsh, Rebecca. "Rosy Grier," *Entertainment Weekly* (19 Dec. 1997).

Bogle, Donald. *Toms, Coons, Mulattoes, Mammies, and Bucks: An Interpretive History of Blacks in American Films*, 4th ed. (2001).

Kincaid, Jamaica. "Pam Grier: The Mocha Mogul of Hollywood," *Ms.* (Aug. 1975).

SHARON D. JOHNSON

Grier, Rosey (14 July 1932–), football player, social activist, author, singer-actor, and ordained minister, was born Roosevelt Grier on a farm in Cuthbert, Georgia, the seventh of Joseph and Ruth Grier's eleven children. At age thirteen he moved with his family to Roselle, New Jersey. Offered an athletic scholarship to Penn State University, he enrolled in 1950 and studied psychology, music, and education. His college athletic career was exceptional. Not only did he receive first-team All-American football honors in 1955, but he also set an Intercollegiate Association of Amateur Athletics of America shot-put record (fifty-eight feet) in track and field.

In 1965 Grier signed with the National Football League's New York Giants for a $500 bonus and a yearly salary of $6,500. During a long career that lasted from 1955 through 1968, Grier was a dominant defensive tackle in an era known for excellent defensive players. His size—6′5″, 300 pounds—and his agility combined with aggressiveness made him a feared and respected opponent. He performed on a line that helped the Giants to the National Football League championship in 1956. After a stint in the U.S. Army he returned to the Giants and won East Conference titles in 1958, 1959, 1961, and 1962.

Grier, in a controversial trade, was sent in 1964 to the Los Angeles Rams for John Lovotere. Grier professed bitterness over the move but never let it affect his on-field performance, and his play with the Rams became the stuff of sports legend, earning him two All-Pro titles while there. He and his teammates David "Deacon" Jones, Lamar Lundy, and Merlin Olsen were nicknamed the "Fearsome Foursome," and forty years later they remained the standard for modern defensive line play: enormous physical size combined with keen intelligence, quickness, and strength. A severe Achilles tendon injury sidelined Grier for all of the 1967 season, and the next year, after a career of 142 games, he retired from football.

Rosey Grier, defensive tackle for the New York Giants, photographed in 1963. (AP Images.)

Other careers beckoned. A published songwriter, guitarist, pianist, and singer, Grier recorded his own songs as early as 1959 and performed at New York's Carnegie Hall in 1963. In retirement Grier became a full-time entertainer and media celebrity. In 1969 he hosted his own pioneering half-hour talk show, *The Rosey Grier Show*, which featured racial issues and matters of political importance. Though brief in duration it served as a model for future public interest television shows. An unabashed liberal, Grier became active in politics. He vigorously campaigned with Senator Robert Kennedy during his 1968 bid for the presidency. Grier and his close friend, the Olympic athlete Rafer Johnson, entered the Kennedy family's inner circle. Their presence ensured an African American voice in campaign strategies and in plans for future policy making. Grier also was acting as a bodyguard for Kennedy's wife, Ethel, when Sirhan B. Sirhan assassinated Kennedy. Grier wrestled Sirhan to the ground while Johnson disarmed him. After Kennedy's death Grier launched a film career that included a notable starring role in the science fiction cult classic *The Thing with Two Heads* (1972). He made guest appearances in numerous television sitcoms, including *Make Room for Daddy*, *The Jeffersons*, *I Dream of Jeannie*, and *The Simpsons*, and dramas such as *White Shadow*, *Daniel Boone*, *Kojak*, and *ChiPs*. He appeared as the character Big Slew Johnson in the popular television miniseries *Roots: The Next Generations* (1979). He made appearances on *The Dick Cavett Show* and *The Tonight Show with Johnny Carson*. His interest and skills in needlepoint, an incongruous hobby for a 300-pound former professional football player, also kept him in the public eye, and his book *The Rosey Grier Needlepoint Book for Men* was a 1973 best seller.

Grier married Beatrice Lewis and they had one child, Denise, before divorcing. He then married Marge Grier, whom he divorced in 1978 and, after a born-again conversion to Christianity, remarried in 1980. They have one son, Roosevelt Kennedy. Grier is also the cousin of PAM GRIER, the noted television and film actress.

After Grier's religious conversion he left show business and was ordained as a minister in 1983. Based primarily in Los Angeles, he devoted himself to religious and community causes. Since 1968 he has served on the board of the Special Olympics and the Kennedy Foundation for the Mentally Retarded. He has also been on the board of directors of the Milken Family Foundation, Americans for Children Relief, Soulville Foundation, Giant Step, Teammates, and the Anti-Self-Destruction Program. He has been a consultant to Youth and Senior Citizens Affairs, the U.S. Civil Service Committee, and the Right to Read program of the former Department of Health, Education, and Welfare. He founded American Neighborhood Enterprises (ANE) and served as chairman of the board for Impact Urban America. He also founded the youth program Rosey Grier's Are You Committed? and worked with the ministry group called Lead Like Jesus. At this point in his career Grier also began to support the Republican party. In 1994 and 1995 Grier gained the national spotlight when he became the spiritual adviser for O. J. SIMPSON, a fellow pro football player and actor, during the latter's arrest and trial for the murder of his wife, Nicole Brown Simpson, and her friend Ron Goldman.

Grier's gentle demeanor for one who built his reputation in the violent world of professional football, his honesty, his fervor, and his commitment to African American social issues secured for him a respected place in American life for over fifty years. One of the first professional athletes to build a solid entertainment career as an actor and a singer, he also managed to become a prominent activist, first as a political operative and then as Christian minister, spiritual adviser, and community organizer.

FURTHER READING

Grier, Roosevelt, with Dennis Baker. *Rosey, An Autobiography: The Gentle Giant* (1986).

Roosevelt Grier file, Pro Football Hall of Fame, Canton, Ohio.

"Takin' Care of Business: Rosey Grier." *Black Sport*, 6 May 1972.

JOHN HANNERS

Griffey, Ken, Jr. (21 Nov. 1969–), major league baseball player, was born George Kenneth Griffey Jr. in Donora, Pennsylvania, the oldest of two sons of George Kenneth Griffey Sr., a major league baseball player, and Alberta ("Birdie") Littleton Griffey. Junior, as he was popularly known, often visited the Cincinnati Reds' River Front Stadium with his father, an outfielder during the halcyon days of the "Big Red Machine" (1970–1976).

At Cincinnati's Moeller High School, the left-handed throwing and batting Griffey excelled at baseball as an outfielder and football as a running back, receiving the offer of a football scholarship from the University of Oklahoma. On 2 June 1987 the Seattle Mariners selected the seventeen-year-old Griffey as the first overall pick in the free agency draft, signing him for a $160,000 bonus. Playing the 1987 season for the Mariners' Bellingham (Washington) team in the short-season Northwest League, he batted .313, hit fourteen home runs, and batted in forty runs in 182 times at bat. In January 1988 feeling depressed by the pressures to succeed and family strife, Griffey attempted suicide by swallowing more than 200 aspirin. In 1988 he moved up to the San Bernardino club in the California League, batting .338 before being sidelined with an injury, the first in a series that hampered his career. Griffey finished the 1988 season as the designated hitter with the Mariners' Vermont farm club in the Class AA Eastern League. The Seattle Mariners invited Griffey to its 1989 spring training camp as a non-roster player. A phenomenal performance in spring games landed Griffey a spot on the parent club. Junior, the youngest player in the majors at nineteen, and the thirty-year-old KEN GRIFFEY SR. became the first father and son to play major league baseball during the same regular season. Griffey led all major league rookies in batting average,

Ken Griffey, Jr., after taking a swing during the Cincinnati Reds' game against the Colorado Rockies in Denver, Colorado, 2 June 2007. (AP Images.)

homeruns, and runs batted in, before going on the disabled list for four weeks in July and August. Griffey's baseball skills and exuberance made him a fan favorite.

Griffey played 155 games in 1990, batting .300 (seventh best in the American League) and leading the team with twenty-two home runs and eighty runs driven in, becoming the first Mariner to start in the All-Star game. On 29 August 1990 the Mariners acquired Griffey Sr. from the Cincinnati Reds. Two days later the Griffeys again made history as the first father and son to play in the same lineup. Senior singled in his first at bat, and Junior, who batted next in the order, also singled. On 14 September 1990, he and his father hit back-to-back home runs, thus becoming the first father/son combo in baseball history to do so. In 1991 he had the first of eight seasons with 100 or more runs batted in, led the American League with three grand-slam home runs, set a new club record for batting average with .327, and was the leading vote recipient among American League All-Stars. In 1992 he continued to improve his offense and was second among American League outfielders with a fielding percentage of .997. In his third consecutive All-Star appearance, he was voted the Most Valuable Player. The 1993 season saw Griffey among the leaders in eleven offensive categories, ranking first in total bases (359) and extra-base hits (86); second in home runs (45), intentional walks (25) and slugging percentage (.617); sixth in runs (113), doubles (38), and on-base percentage (.408); eighth in hits (180) and walks (96); and fourteenth in batting average (.308). Griffey was again the leading vote getter on the American League All-Star squad.

In the strike-shortened 1994 campaign Griffey led the American League with forty home runs and placed among the leaders in other offensive categories. The fans sent Griffey to his fifth consecutive All-Star contest with over six million votes, eclipsing by over 1.8 million votes the major-league record set by Rod Carew in 1977. A broken wrist limited him to seventy-two games in 1995, but the Mariners made it to the postseason, where Griffey shone against the New York Yankees, hitting .391 in twenty-three at bats with five home runs, seven runs driven, and nine scored. In a losing effort Griffey batted .333 in twenty-one plate appearances against the Cleveland Indians.

The 6'3" and 205-pound Griffey put up substantial offensive numbers in 1996 with forty-nine home runs and 140 RBI. He topped this in 1997 when led the league in four categories—home runs (56), RBI

(147), slugging percentage (.646), and runs scored (125)—earning the league's Most Valuable Player award. In 1998 he again led the league with fifty-six home runs while driving in 146 runs. Griffey led the league in home runs for the third straight year, clouting forty-eight in 1999. During the 1990s fans voted Griffey to each American League All-Star team, while managers and coaches selected him each year as the recipient of the league's Gold Glove Award as one of the three best defensive outfielders.

In February 2000 Griffey returned to his hometown to play for the National League's Cincinnati Reds, accepting a below-market contract for $116.5 million over nine years. The baseball prodigy of the 1990s continued unabated into the new millennium, becoming the youngest player at thirty years and 141 days to reach 400 home runs, which he did on 10 April 2000, his father's fiftieth birthday. This was the fourth time Junior hit a round tripper on his father's birthday, including his first home run in 1989. During his first season in a Reds' uniform he played in 145 games, scored 100 runs, belted 40 round trippers, and drove in 118 runs. His season highlights included an eight RBI game on 8 July and being voted by the fans to his first National League All-Star team. While Griffey spent considerable time on the disabled list between 2001 and 2004 with a commensurate decline in productivity, he had two major achievements in the first half of the 2004 season. On 20 June, "The Kid," as he was known to many, became the twentieth major leaguer to slam 500 home runs. A feat accomplished on Father's Day with Griffey Sr. in the stands. Fans voted Griffey to his twelfth All-Star team on the strength of his twenty home runs by mid-season, but he spent nearly the entire second half of the season on the disabled list. Griffey Jr. made his 13th and final appearance in an MLB all-star game in 2007, and left the Reds in 2008. After a stint with the Chicago White Sox, he returned to Seattle for two more seasons, and retired from baseball in May 2010, with 630 home runs. That figure was, as of the end of the 2011 season, the fifth highest of all time, behind only BARRY BONDS, HANK AARON, Babe Ruth, and WILLIE MAYS. In 2009 Secreaty of State CONDOLEEZZA RICE named Griffey Jr. an American Public Diplomacy Envoy.

During the 1990s Griffey was a five-tool player capable of performing the basic baseball skills in an extraordinary manner—hitting for average, hitting for power, catching, throwing, and running. He played at a level matched by few players in the history of the national pastime.

FURTHER READING

Griffey, Ken, Jr., with Mark Vancil, and Walter Iooss. *Junior: Griffey on Griffey* (1997).

"Griffey Doesn't Spend Time Thinking About What If." *New York Times*, 12 Mar. 2005.

Leavy, Walter. "Why Ken Griffey, Jr. Gave Up Millions To Go Home Again," *Ebony* 55.9 (1981).

Shipnuck, Alan. "Junior Comes of Age," *Sports Illustrated* 81.6 (8 Aug. 1994).

PAUL A. FRISCH

Griffey, Ken, Sr. (10 Apr. 1950–), baseball player, was born in Donora, Pennsylvania. His father, Joseph "Buddy" Griffey, was a decent athlete in his own time, playing third base on the Donora All-Star team and attending Kentucky on a football scholarship. Unfortunately, he was not as dedicated to being a father. He left Griffey and his mother when Griffey was two, and Griffey did not see him again until he was nine and then not again until he was seventeen.

Ken Griffey, a left-handed right-fielder, was drafted twenty-ninth by the Cincinnati Reds in

Ken Griffey Sr., of the Cincinnati Reds, photographed in 2000. (AP Images.)

1969 at the age of nineteen. After spending almost five years in the Reds' minor league system honing his skills, Griffey made his big league debut in August 1973. The timing for Griffey's arrival could not have been better, since the team he joined would later come to be known as "The Big Red Machine" and win two World Series, one in 1975 against the Red Sox and another the following year against the Yankees. During his time with the Reds, Griffey posted an impressive .307 batting average and was named to the National League All-Star squad three times, in 1976, 1977, and 1980. The best year of his career also came in Cincinnati, when in 1976 he batted .336 and stole thirty-four bases. In 1982 Griffey was traded to the New York Yankees. Injuries began to take their toll on him, and the Yankees organization did not seem to know where to place him (in his four years with New York, he played four different positions). Griffey was traded to Atlanta halfway through the 1986 season, where he somewhat regained his swing, and he went on to play with the Reds again in 1988 and 1989, finishing his career with the Mariners in November of 1991, at the age of forty-one. At the end of his career, Griffey had amassed 152 home runs, 2,143 hits, 859 runs batted in, and 200 stolen bases.

Remarkably, when Griffey Sr. retired he was playing on the same team as his son. On 31 August 1990 Ken Griffey Sr. and KEN GRIFFEY JR. became the only father and son to play major league baseball on the same team in the same year. In their twenty-one games together, Griffey Sr. hit for a hefty .377 batting average and drove in seventeen runs. On 14 September the father-son duo hit back-to-back home runs against the Anaheim Angels, becoming the first father/son combo ever to do so in the majors.

When Griffey Jr. got his first hit against Oakland's Dave Stewart, Griffey Sr. cried. Of the season spent playing next to his son in the outfield, Griffey said, "A lot of times I look over and, this is no lie, I still see the hat too big for his head, a baggy uniform and he's got No. 30 across his chest and back. That's a father-son game I was remembering when he was just a little kid with the Reds." This commitment to and love for his sons (his son Craig also played baseball, though in the minor leagues) comes in direct contrast with Griffey's relationship with his own father.

Most of Griffey Jr.'s awards and significant game balls rest on the mantle in his father's house—all except his MVP award and his 500th home run ball (which he hit on his father's birthday). Griffey Sr.

spent most of his time as an associate in the Reds organization front office. And he still finds time to take in one of his son's games.

FURTHER READING
"The Griffeys: Major-League Baseball's First Father and Son Pair," *Ebony* 44 (Sept. 1989): 78.

BAILEY THOMAS PLAYER

Griffin, Archie (21 Aug. 1954–), football player and two-time Heisman Trophy winner, was born in Columbus, Ohio, the fourth of eight children. His father, James Griffin, worked several jobs at a time, including employment with the Columbus sanitation department and a local steel foundry; his mother, Margaret, primarily raised the family of seven boys and one girl while also running a corner store called Griffin's Grocery. The Griffins moved several times within Columbus during Archie's childhood, but the city provided the perfect backdrop for a kid who would grow to love sports.

When he was nine, Griffin was too heavy to play with his age-group football team, so he joined his brother's Larry's team even though Larry was four years older. Because of his girth and lagging speed relative to his older teammates, Griffin was tagged with the nickname "Tank" and found himself playing on both his team's offensive and defensive lines. By the time he was in eighth grade, Griffin had used a variety of techniques—running around his neighborhood in the heat of the summer clad in a cleaning bag or doing sit-ups in his father's station wagon—to slim down so he could play in a 135-pound-and-under league.

Through junior high Griffin and his family lived in the predominantly black north end of Columbus, but in 1969, as he prepared to enter tenth grade and high school, the Griffins moved to Columbus's far east side, a predominantly white area, a move Griffin would later say was made because his father simply wanted a bigger house. But it would mean Griffin would attend Eastmoor Academy High School, where blacks at the time made up less than a quarter of the school's enrollment. At first, Griffin was hesitant about attending the school—"We really felt in the minority," he would say—but he also missed his football-playing pals on the other side of town. Any inhibitions, though, subsided once he made the Eastmoor varsity football team as a sophomore. On the field and among his teammates, Griffin would say, race never seemed to matter. "You get in those situations and you are playing together with people for the same cause. We were able to develop friendships and develop a bond that was pretty terrific."

Football became a means for Griffin both to prove his athletic skills and to satisfy his father's wish that all of his children attend and graduate from college. Neither of his parents had attended college, and Griffin sensed that his father wanted his children to avoid a professional life of endless workdays. Whatever the motivation, Griffin shone himself on the field. Playing fullback, the position of his childhood hero, Jim Brown, he helped lead the Warriors to two city championships. In his senior season, he scored twenty-nine touchdowns (Eastmoor's home field was later renamed Archie Griffin Field in his honor). Along the way he caught the attention of several college football powerhouses, with schools such as Michigan, Northwestern, and the United States Naval Academy heavily recruiting him. Ultimately, though, Griffin chose to stay in Columbus and play at Ohio State—and for its legendary, if often controversial, coach, Woody Hayes. Hayes had walked Ohio State's sidelines since 1951, leading the school to three national championships. But he was also a coach known for his temper—a temper that he was not afraid to show to both players and opponents alike (Hayes would eventually lose his job in 1978 after striking an opposing player). But beyond Hayes's fiery reputation, some close to Griffin advised him not to play for the coach for pure football reasons; they feared Griffin would see little action because Hayes generally favored two-hundred-plus-pound running backs. Griffin, despite his earlier weight issues, entered the school at five foot eight inches and around 170 pounds. "But as an athlete," Griffin would say, "you feel you know your ability better than any one else, and I took it as a challenge."

The challenge only got tougher after his first game in the Buckeyes scarlet and gray uniform. In that game, against Iowa in the fall of 1972, he fumbled on his first play; Hayes immediately benched him for the remainder of the day. But the coach did not hold the mistake against the freshman for long. In the team's next game against North Carolina, Griffin, playing tailback, entered midway through the first quarter and went on to rush for 239 yards, which would stand as an Ohio State single-game rushing record for twenty-three years. He would lead the team in rushing that year, setting an Ohio State freshman record in the process, as the Buckeyes finished 9–2 and won the first of four successive Big Ten Championships. The title earned Griffin and his teammates a trip to the Rose Bowl,

the "granddaddy" of college bowl games; in fact, in his four years at Ohio State, Griffin would become the only college football player ever to start in four successive Rose Bowl games.

In his sophomore year, Griffin rushed for 1,577 yards and began a college-record streak of thirty-one games in which he would rush for more than 100 yards a game. His increased production on the field gained attention in the press box. He finished fifth in the voting for the Heisman Trophy. In his junior year, Griffin catapulted to the top of the voting when he rushed for more than 1,600 yards and scored twelve touchdowns. He was just the fifth junior in Heisman history to win the award, although none of the previous four winners ever repeated. That streak ended in 1975 when Griffin beat out such future National Football League stars as Chuck Muncie and TONY DORSETT to become the first college football player to win a second Heisman award. As of 2009 no college player had repeated that feat.

Other awards would come as well: Griffin earned All-American honors each of his final three seasons at Ohio State. He was a National College Athletic Assocation Top Five Award winner in 1975, which recognizes both athletic and academic achievement. Griffin has since been elected to the College Football Hall of Fame and the National High School Football Hall of Fame. In 1999 Griffin became the first Ohio State player to have his uniform number, 45, retired.

Beyond the numbers and awards, though, are the plaudits. Woody Hayes, who died in 1987, would call Griffin "the best football player I've ever seen." But more than Griffin's football skills impressed the coach. Prior to the 1975 season Hayes said, "Archie Griffin is the greatest back I've ever seen or coached. He's also the most popular player we've ever had, by far. In fact, we value Archie's attitude more than his football ability. Which is saying something, because he can do everything … Archie doesn't say much. He leads by example. When we go running out at halftime I keep stumbling over him because he's always down there on his knees, praying. Oh, my God, he's so honorable!" (*Sports Illustrated*, Fall 1975). For all his work on the football field, Griffin managed to graduate from Ohio State in less than four years with a degree in industrial relations. In fact, fulfilling the wish of their father, James, who died in 1991, all eight of the Griffin children graduated from college.

Following his final season, Griffin was drafted in the first round of the National Football League

(NFL) draft by the Cincinnati Bengals. His eight years as a pro never produced the numbers or recognition of his college days. He never rushed for more than 1,000 yards in a season; instead, he became more of a short-yardage receiver. So, considering his college acclaim and legacy, was Griffin a bust as a pro? Not in his eyes. "People said to me, 'What are you going to do to top your college career?'" Griffin said. "It was going to be difficult, but I'm very proud [of my pro career]." In fact, while his total rushing yardage as a pro (2,808) may seem meager compared with his college total (5,589), his average of 4.1 yards per carry is among all-time leaders in that category.

He left the NFL in 1984 and returned to his hometown—and his alma mater. He first began work in Ohio State's administrative staffing department. A year later, then-athletic director Rick Bay offered him a job in the athletic department. Over the next nineteen years, he would rise to the position of assistant director of athletics and oversee fourteen of the University's athletic teams and be involved in aspects such as budgeting, recruiting, and fund-raising. During that period, Griffin, along with his second wife, established the Archie and Bonita Griffin Foundation, a charitable fund used to develop children's programs in central Ohio. In addition, the Archie Griffin Scholarship Fund provides resources for many of the Ohio States Olympic sports teams, such as gymnastics.

In January 2004 following a nationwide search, Griffin was named president and chief executive officer of the Ohio State University Alumni Association, an organization of 123,000 members, including alumni, former students, and friends of the school.

Griffin had three children, Anthony and Andre with his first wife, and Adam, his son with Bonita.

FURTHER READING

Griffin, Archie, with David Diles. *Archie: The Archie Griffin Story* (1977).

Pennington, Bill. *The Heisman: Great American Stories of the Men Who Won* (2004).

CHARLES BUTLER

Griffin, Mary (Mazie) Campbell Mossell (10 Oct. 1885–5 June 1968), clubwoman, suffragette, and author was born in Philadelphia, Pennsylvania, to Dr. NATHAN F. MOSSELL and GERTRUDE E. H. (BUSTILL) MOSSELL. Born into one of the elite families of Philadelphia, Mazie attended Philadelphia public schools and the F. F. Jones Private School for Girls. After graduation she taught kindergarten for

one year in Darby, Pennsylvania. She married Dr. Joshua R. Griffin Jr. of Richmond, Virginia, in 1909. They had one son, Francis Raleigh.

Following in her mother's footsteps, Mazie became a writer and contributed to a variety of newspapers. Her columns were published in the *Philadelphia Tribune, Philadelphia Courant, Washington Sun,* and *Chicago Defender.* Griffin founded the Phyllis Wheatley Club in order to encourage young women to write. While Griffin also published a book, *Afro-American Men and Women Who Count,* in 1915, her true calling was in public service. As a member of one of the leading African American families in Philadelphia, Griffin participated in social uplift activities that ranged from heading the auxiliary for the Fredrick Douglass Memorial Hospital (founded by her father) to raising money for the Elizabeth C. Carter Outing Association, which raised money to send destitute inner-city youth to summer camps. During World War I, Griffin donated the use of her home as a service club for soldiers and sailors. Through her generous offer and the work of the Dunbar Service Club, Griffin continued the family tradition of combining social service work with the fight for racial equality.

On the local level, Griffin was extremely active in the women's club movement and held a variety of leadership positions, including chairwoman of the suffrage department of the Northeastern Federation of Woman's Clubs. Griffin was a vocal participant in the suffrage movement and served as one of the captains of the 1915 Philadelphia suffrage parade. Once suffrage was attained, Griffin along with others created a course of weekly lectures on citizenship, which included topics such as the historical background of voting, understanding legislation, and voting procedures. Griffin built on this success and gained national prominence during the fight for passage of the Dyer Anti-Lynching Bill in the United States Congress. As national legislative chairwoman of the National Association of Colored Women's Clubs she traveled throughout the United States lobbying congressmen and speaking publicly about the evils of lynching.

During the 1920s, Mazie Mossell Griffin became a political force among Philadelphia's African American women. Within the year Griffin integrated the previously lily-white Philadelphia Republican City Committee's Women's Auxiliary and was elected vice president of the organization. She emerged as a leader of women in the predominantly African American 30th Ward and challenged African American men for leadership of the district.

In 1921, when Philadelphia congressmen proposed a state law to secure Equal Rights for African Americans, the entire Mossell and Griffin family traveled to Harrisburg in support of the cause. By the early 1930s Mazie Mossell Griffin, like many African Americans in the urban North had become disenchanted with the Republican Party. Citing the Republican Party's poor record on civil rights, she switched her political allegiance to the Democratic Party. In doing so she followed, among others, CRYSTAL BYRD FAUSET. Fauset would become the first black woman elected to any state legislature, when West Philadelphia voters sent her to Harrisburg in 1938. In 1937 Griffin served as a political lobbyist to the Pennsylvania General Assembly and was in charge of monitoring all potential legislation that might have an impact on the African American community. By the 1940s Griffin focused her efforts on the club movement and raising money for the Fredrick Douglass Memorial Hospital. In declining health, she moved to Richmond, Virginia, to live with her son. Mazie Mossell Griffin died on 5 June 1968 in Richmond Virginia.

FURTHER READING

Mather, Frank Lincoln. *Who's Who of the Colored Race: A General Biographical Dictionary of Men and Women of African Descent, Volume 1* (1915).

Obituary: *Philadelphia Tribune*, 15 June 1968.

JENNIFER REED FRY

Griffith, Emile (3 Feb. 1938–), professional boxer and trainer, was born in St. Thomas, Virgin Islands, and moved to New York with his family, which included seven siblings, when he was thirteen years old. His father had abandoned the family prior to their move to New York and his mother had to leave the family to take a cooking job for the governor of Puerto Rico. His brothers and sisters were scattered to the homes of their mother's relatives and friends. Griffith was given to his Aunt Blanche. He hated living there and begged to go to Mandal, St. Thomas's home for wayward and orphaned boys where he was finally placed. As the oldest child he helped to reunite the family for its move to New York.

Once in New York, his first job was working in a hat factory when he was sixteen years old. He caught the eye of the fight manager Howard Albert, who hired the legendary boxing trainer Gil Clancy to work with Griffith. He fought as an amateur for two years and won the Golden Gloves in 1956 and fought his first professional fight on 2 June 1958. He defeated his opponent in a four round decision. He

went on to win twenty-one of his next twenty-three fights and then challenged the Cuban prize fighter Benny "Kid" Paret for the welterweight title at Miami Beach, Florida, on 1 April 1961. Griffith won the fight on a knockout in the thirteenth round. His name would forever be associated with Paret, not only because the two fought a total of three fights, two of which were won by Griffith, but also because Paret died as a result of a beating he took from Griffith in the third fight on 24 March 1962 in New York City. Griffith won the welterweight championship with the victory. Griffith trapped Paret against the ropes in the twelfth round and pummeled him with a succession of punches before the referee pushed him off and Paret slowly slid down the ropes to the canvas. He was counted out, fell into a coma, and died ten days later. Because of this fight, Griffith said that he didn't want to fight again. He said that he received hate mail from Cuban fans calling him a murderer as well as positive mail from fans who wanted him to continue his boxing career. He claimed that the advice and support of fans got him back into boxing on 13 July 1962 when he beat Ralph Dupas to retain the welterweight championship. However, the experience made him more of a cautious fighter who did not want to hurt anyone in the ring.

Griffith fought in both the welterweight and middleweight divisions and was only the third fighter in history to hold both the welterweight and middleweight championships. He first won the welterweight crown in 1961 when he beat Paret in their first fight and obtained the middleweight championship when he beat DICK TIGER IHETU in 1966. He fought such ring legends as Tiger twice (25 April 1966 and 15 July 1970, Griffith won both fights); Luis Rodriguez four times (17 December 1960, a win; 21 March 1963, a loss; 8 June 1963, a win; and 12 June 1964 a win); and Don Fullmer twice (6 October 1962, a win; and 20 August 1964, a loss). In fact, the fight in which he lost to Fullmer was Griffith's first try for the middleweight championship. He lost in a twelve-round decision. He also fought Nino Benvenuti of Italy three times. In the first fight, Benvenuti used his longer reach to defeat Griffith on 17 April 1967. Griffith reclaimed the title on 29 September 1967 against Benvenuti and then lost the title to Benvenuti in the third fight on 4 March 1968. He also fought Carlos Monzon twice losing by knockout on 25 September 1971 and losing a controversial decision on 2 June 1973.

Griffith and Dick Tiger were good friends and often sparred together at Gleason Gym in the Bronx in New York. Griffith credited these sessions with helping him beat Tiger. Fight fans were most impressed with Griffith's foot and hand speed. He could throw a series of short, quick punches and combinations, but often seemed to lose his concentration and focus, even during important fights. Ironically, boxing experts often accused him of not having a "killer instinct." He won eighty-five professional fights, twenty-three by knockout and lost twenty-five fights, two by knockout. He also had two draws and one no-contest and was a six time champion. He fought a total of twenty-four world championship bouts and his 339 rounds in world title fights were more than any other boxer in history. He was inducted into the International Boxing Hall of Fame in 1990. Griffith married Mercedes "Sadie" Donastorg, a dancer from St. Thomas, Virgin Islands, in 1971 and adopted her daughter, Christine. Two years after the marriage, Griffith and his wife separated.

Griffith retired from boxing in 1979 and became a trainer of professional boxers and tended bar at a pub in Jersey City, New Jersey. The boxers he trained included Wilfredo Benitez and Juan Laporte, both Puerto Ricans who became world champions.

Griffith's boxing career and the troubles he experienced coping with the death of Benny Paret was the theme of a documentary called *Ring of Fire*, which was broadcast on the USA cable channel in April 2005.

FURTHER READING
Oates, Joyce Carol. *On Boxing* (1995).

ROBERT JANIS

Griffith-Joyner, Florence (21 Dec. 1959–21 Sept. 1998), track star, was born Delorez Florence Griffith in Los Angeles, California, the daughter of Robert Griffith, an electronics technician, and Florence Griffith, a seamstress. The seventh of eleven children, her parents divorced when she was four. Dee-Dee, as she was then known, grew up in a housing project in Watts, the site of race riots in the late 1960s. She described her family life as inwardly rich, though money was so tight she sometimes ate oatmeal for breakfast, lunch, and dinner. She developed her fashion sense from her mother, who taught her knitting and crocheting, and her grandmother, a beautician, who provided instruction on hair and nails. Though she was a quiet child, her fashion tastes betrayed a nonconformist streak: a gravity-defying braid thrust to the heavens in kindergarten, a pet boa constrictor wrapped around her neck as a teen.

Her speed was apparent at a young age. Nicknamed "Lightning" by one of her sisters, Griffith was known to chase jackrabbits on visits to her father in the Mojave Desert. She began competing in meets with the SUGAR RAY ROBINSON Youth Foundation at age seven. In her early teens she twice proved a champion at the JESSE OWENS National Youth Games. After one such victory she earned congratulations from Owens himself.

The meeting did not seem to portend Olympic glory for Griffith, who spent most of her career in the shadow of others. Though she set records at David Starr Jordan High School, she could not beat fellow Los Angeles runner Valerie Brisco in championship meets. In college, first at California State University, Northridge, and then at UCLA, she worked with sprint coach Bob Kersee. In 1980 she just missed making the U.S. Olympic Team. Though she did manage an NCAA title in the 200 meters in 1982 with a time of 22.39, her hopes for Olympic gold were dashed two years later in the Los Angeles Games when her 22.04 was only good enough for a close second, yet again, to Valerie Brisco-Hooks. That silver medal seemed to cement her status as a just-less-than-great performer, especially considering the boycott by Eastern European countries, which significantly diluted the field. Even her fashion statements didn't earn universal acclaim: her self-styled glistening bodysuits did result in a new nickname—"Fluorescent Flo"—but her elaborately painted six-inch nails were cited as a reason for keeping her off the 400-meter relay, for fear that the baton pass could prove treacherous. For a while it looked like her running career might be over. She competed only sporadically, gained weight, and focused largely on her career—working in a bank by day and as a beautician at night. In time, though, she was lured back to the track, drawn by both an unquenched inner fire and an emerging family of track luminaries. In 1987 she married Al Joyner, the reigning gold medalist in the triple jump. Al's sister, JACKIE JOYNER-KERSEE, was the world record holder in the heptathlon, and the wife of sprint coach Bob Kersee. This formidable foursome set its sights on the Seoul Olympics in 1988.

Competing in a white hooded bodysuit that seemed more *Star Trek* than track star, Griffith-Joyner took her familiar second place in the 200 meters in the World Championships in Rome in 1987. In the ensuing months she intensified her training, sometimes pushing her workouts past midnight. She worked her hamstring and gluteal muscles for greater explosion out of the blocks. She adopted weightlifting advice from the new world record holder in the men's 100 meters, Ben Johnson of Canada. She claimed to have found a new ability to relax in competition, making her stride more efficient. Stronger and more focused than ever, she began to train in the sport's marquee race, the 100-meter dash, an event where she had almost no international experience.

Toting fourteen self-designed racing suits, she arrived in Indianapolis in mid-July for the U.S. Olympic Trials. Amid a midwestern heat wave that had track temperatures soaring well over one hundred degrees, she transformed into "Flo-Jo," a blazing beauty who put together some of the most breathtaking performances in the history of the sport. In one forty-eight-hour stretch she carved an indelible image: black mane flowing freely, neon nails clawing the humid air, perfectly made-up face locked in concentration, veins bulging to the surface, sculpted muscles surging relentlessly to the tape. Her outfits were "one-leggers"—dazzlingly hued spandex from shoulder to ankle with one beautifully defined leg laid bare, and brightly colored bikini briefs hugging her hips. Her speed was otherworldly. Four times she toed the line in the 100; four times she shattered Evelyn Ashford's four-year-old world record of 10.76. Though her initial heat of 10.60 was discounted because of excessive wind, the second heat of 10.49 set the standard far beyond her own lifetime. In shaving an almost incomprehensible .27 off the record (since the advent of electronic timing twenty years before, the mark had never been bested by even half that much), she provided one of track and field's most stunning moments—a time when perceived human limitations are torn asunder. It was commensurate with Roger Bannister's breaking the 4-minute mile in 1954, and BOB BEAMON's awe-inspiring long jump of 29 feet 2.5 inches in the Mexico City Games in 1968.

The record was hard to believe. Some doubted the accuracy of the wind gauge that registered 0.0, while a nearby gauge at the triple jump exceeded the legally allowed 4.47 miles per hour. Still, the stellar run was not completely out of context for the comet that had become Florence Griffith-Joyner. The next day she roared to victory in the semifinals and the finals in times of 10.71 and 10.61, both well within legal wind limits. In the 200 meters she won again, setting an American record of 21.77. That time had track enthusiasts salivating—as did her white lace bodysuit that she termed "athletic negligee."

In Seoul, the first Olympics in twelve years not to be softened by political boycott, Flo-Jo became a phenomenon the likes of which women's track had never known. Though she was required to wear the comparatively modest team uniforms, her speed was not compromised. She became the first U.S. woman ever to win four medals in the Olympics, garnering gold in the 100 (a wind-aided 10.54), the 200 (obliterating a nine-year-old world record in 21.34), and the 400 relay, and taking silver in the 1,600 relay.

In a mere ten weeks, she had put a defining stamp on her sport and become, for a moment, the most widely recognized athlete in the world. She earned recognition from all corners: the Sullivan Award as the U.S. top amateur athlete, the Associated Press Female Athlete of the Year, even the top sports personality of the year from Tass, the Soviet News Service. She was deluged with endorsements, earning her yet another nickname—"Cash Flo." She graced covers of a wide variety of sports and fashion publications. Even *Ms.* magazine weighed in with a lengthy piece, referring to her as the "Siren of Speed."

It was not, however, a complete lovefest. Pointing to her huge improvement at twenty-eight, a relatively old age for a sprinter, and to her newly chiseled physique, some in the track community accused her of using banned substances to supercharge her speed. The speculation was compounded by the fact that Ben Johnson, competing in the men's 100, had his gold medal and world-record time of 9.79 stripped after testing positive for steroid use at Seoul. The fact that Flo-Jo passed every drug test she ever took, even submitting to especially rigorous testing in Seoul, did little to silence the critics. When she retired in February 1989 to concentrate on business interests, some felt she was merely ducking the random, out-of-meet testing that was being instituted in the sport. Always, she vehemently denied the allegations.

In the decade after her glittering performances, Flo-Jo poured herself into a variety of pursuits. She gave birth to a daughter, Mary Ruth, in 1990. She set up a foundation for underprivileged children and frequently returned to Watts to talk to kids. Designing new uniforms for the Indiana Pacers fueled her passion for fashion. She cochaired the President's Council on Physical Fitness. Occasionally she entertained comeback plans, targeting the 400 in the 1992 Olympics, and, rather quixotically, the marathon in 1996. She never ran an important race, though, after her blaze to glory in Seoul.

In 1996 she was hospitalized briefly after suffering a seizure on an airplane. Given a clean bill of health, she resumed her active schedule, which included writing the book *Running for Dummies*. She never lived to see its publication, however. At the age of thirty-eight she died in her sleep in the family's Mission Viejo home. The sudden death of an apparently healthy athlete revived allegations of steroid use. Autopsy results on Griffith-Joyner, however, revealed no evidence of banned substances. She died because of a vascular problem in her brain known as a "cavernous angioma," which apparently led to a seizure, causing her to asphyxiate in bed.

Griffith-Joyner took the world records in the 100 and 200 meters with her to the grave. She was not merely the fastest woman in the world or its most glamorous athlete. She provided a new definition of the possible for the American woman, a vision where speed and strength were compatible with sexiness, where being a fast female was nothing but a compliment.

FURTHER READING

Aaseng, Nathan. *Florence Griffith-Joyner: Dazzling Olympian* (1989).
Koral, April. *Florence Griffith-Joyner: Track and Field Star* (1992).
Stewart, Mark. *Florence Griffith-Joyner* (1996).
Obituary: *New York Times*, 22 Sept. 1998.

MARTY DOBROW

Griggs, Sutton E. (1872–1930), writer and Baptist minister, was born Sutton Elbert Griggs in Chatfield, Texas, the son of Allen R. Griggs, a prominent Baptist minister; his mother's name is not known. Griggs received his elementary education in the Dallas public schools and attended Bishop College in Marshall, Texas. After graduating in 1890, he attended the Richmond Theological Seminary (later a part of Virginia Union University) and graduated after three years. After his ordination as a Baptist minister, he was given his first pastorate at Berkley, Virginia, where he remained for two years. He then moved to Tennessee, where he spent thirty years, first at the First Baptist Church of East Nashville and later at the Tabernacle Baptist Church of Memphis, where he held ministerial office for nineteen years. Griggs married Emma J. Williams of Portsmouth, Virginia, in 1897; they had no children.

After Reconstruction and the subsequent segregation and antiblack violence, Griggs, along with other African American writers such as CHARLES CHESNUTT, PAUL LAURENCE DUNBAR, W. E. B. DuBois, and BOOKER T. WASHINGTON, responded by creating works that portrayed black Americans, often emphasizing their demands for civil rights. Griggs not only wrote five novels but also published a number of political and philosophical tracts. He published, promoted, and distributed these works himself, often by selling them door-to-door. One critic, HUGH MORRIS GLOSTER, asserts that because of Griggs's strategy of taking his work directly to his audience his books were more widely read and circulated than those of Chesnutt or Dunbar. In spite of Griggs's vigorous promotion of his own work, he maintained that all his novels were financial failures.

The first, the best known, and arguably the finest of Griggs's five novels, *Imperium in Imperio*, appeared in 1899. It is, as are all his novels, a political work. The story is centered on two individuals: Belton Piedmont and the biracial Bernard Belgrave. Starting with their early childhood, Griggs traces the lives of these two characters through their contrasting social positions. Although Belton suffers intense discrimination (he is even hanged by a lynch mob but not killed), he adopts an accommodating and integrationist stance. Bernard, on the other hand, is well treated because of his white father; nevertheless, he becomes the more militant of the two. Perhaps most important, the story contains a description of a secret black government situated within the United States. The story's two protagonists wrestle with the problems of racism and segregation, as well as many of the political and philosophical ideas found in Griggs's other work.

Griggs's four other novels likewise address the themes he examined in *Imperium in Imperio*. His second novel, *Overshadowed* (1901), deals with the harsh conditions imposed on blacks through segregation, painting a gloomy picture. *Unfettered* (1902) is the story of a young biracial woman, Morlene, who falls in love with Dorlan Worthell, a courageous young black man. In this novel Griggs brings all his characteristic melodramatic and sentimental tendencies to bear. In addition he tacks on an appendix, called "Dorlan's Plan." Foreshadowing his own more didactic work, the plan runs more than fifty pages, presenting a program to elevate the black race. In *The Hindered Hand* (1905) Griggs continued his probing inquiry of race relations through themes of lynching, miscegenation, and emigration to Africa. His final novel, *Pointing the Way* (1908), offers legal action as a possible recourse for blacks, a suggestion that also appears in his later writings.

After *Pointing the Way* Griggs abandoned the novel in favor of social and political tracts. He produced nearly three dozen such works. For the most part his themes remained the same, as he discussed problems such as lynching and mob violence, inadequate employment opportunities, miscegenation, and black suffrage. One of the longest of these works, *Wisdom's Call* (1911), is a reworking of two of his earliest tracts, *The Needs of the South* (1909) and *The Race Question in a New Light* (1909). In it Griggs directed his attention toward the intelligence and capability of blacks, concluding that their judgment is sound and reliable. *The Guide to Racial Greatness*, published in 1923 and one of his better-known works, lays out a guide intended to solve many of the racial problems that Griggs detailed in his novels and tracts. As with his novels, he published these tracts himself and sold them door-to-door.

Griggs's work was, for the most part, ignored until the 1940s. Since then there has been a reexamination of his writings, with critics labeling him everything from a radical militant to an accommodationist.

Near the end of his life, Griggs returned to Texas. In Denison he served as pastor of Hopewell Baptist Church, a position his father had held. He left Denison for Houston, intending to found a religious and civic institute. He died there, however, before the realization of his plan.

FURTHER READING

Bigsby, C. W. E., ed. *The Black American Writer* (1969).
Bruce, Dickson D., Jr. *Black American Writing from the Nadir: The Evolution of a Literary Tradition, 1877–1915* (1989).
Davis, Arthur P. *From the Dark Tower: Afro-American Writers (1900 to 1960)* (1974).
Fleming, Robert E. "Sutton E. Griggs: Militant Black Novelist," *Phylon* 34 (Mar. 1973).
Gloster, Hugh M. "Sutton E. Griggs: Novelist of the New Negro," *Phylon* 4 (Fourth Quarter, 1943).
This entry is taken from the *American National Biography* and is published here with the permission of the American Council of Learned Societies.

CHRIS RUIZ-VELASCO

Grigsby, Snow Flake (13 Feb. 1899–22 Mar. 1981), civil rights advocate and trade unionist, was born in Newberry County near Chappells, South Carolina, the son of Fred Grigsby and Kitty (maiden name unknown), farmers. Named for the unusual snowfall that occurred on the day of his birth, he was known throughout his life as Snow Grigsby. He learned the lesson of fending for oneself in a family of twelve children raised by religious, education-minded, politically active parents. He embraced individualism but benefited from philanthropy and endorsed government activism. Grigsby left home to receive his high school diploma in 1923 at Harbison Junior College in Irmo, South Carolina, courtesy of the Presbyterian Church. Heading north to look for what he called "rosy opportunities," he worked menial jobs by night and attended the Detroit Institute of Technology by day. He graduated in 1927 but failed to find employment as a pharmacist. Like his father, a onetime federal mail contractor, he became a postal employee. He married Eliza Red, and they raised a son and a daughter.

Confronting racism in the face of economic depression, he began a lifetime crusade of "militant insistence" on equal opportunities for blacks, evolving from activist to unionist to political candidate. In each phase he penned pamphlets in the revolutionary tradition: presentation of facts exposed lies and alibis to produce results, whereas confrontation without research wrought "blood on the conscience" but little change.

In 1933 Grigsby's research for *X-Ray Survey of Detroit* statistically demonstrated how disproportionately few municipal jobs were held by black citizens. Following a discussion of his finding at the Bethel African Methodist Episcopal Church, he and the Reverend William Peck formed the Civic Rights Committee and descended on the city's board of education. They presented data on the paltry number of black school employees and provided dossiers of numerous black college graduates, while also revealing that whites continued to be hired. They thereby undermined both the argument that no qualified black candidates were available and the claim that budgetary limitations prevented additional hiring. Nineteen blacks were employed that day.

Thereafter, Grigsby headed the committee in what became known as formulistic protest. He sought to place blacks in the Recorder's Court and among firemen, and although he may have cost one white judge reelection he failed to succeed in either effort as he had with the school board. He proved more effective with the Detroit Edison Company, dramatically dragging thirty-two feet of records of blacks' electricity payments before company representatives and, with other black leaders, negotiating jobs for black utility workers.

Essentially, Grigsby's effort was part of the "Jobs for Negroes" campaign occurring in several Depression-racked cities, but he adopted a less intimidating tone than that of the more militant organizations in both New York and Chicago. He stressed community control over the influence of nationally established civil rights organizations and opposed pickets and marches. His criticism of apathetic black citizens and leaders of both races in *White Hypocrisy and Black Lethargy* (1937) resulted in his having few allies among them. He did not concentrate on the private sector or secure large numbers of jobs there; rather, he broke barriers in municipal employment and laid the groundwork for future advances.

In 1939 Grigsby was forced to resign from the committee so that he would not lose his government job for engaging in political activities. He may have done more than loudly protest the denial of a federal loan by the Home Owners' Loan Corporation, for there were both blacks and whites in Detroit who considered him a rabble-rouser. The Civic Rights Committee soon faded, partly because of his departure and partly because of the emergence of other, more militant organizations inspired by his example, including the United Automobile Workers, and the Second World War.

Grigsby transferred his energies to the National Alliance of Postal and Federal Employees. In 1941 he won election as the editor of its *Postal Alliance*. Over the next thirty-two years, he promoted union and racial concerns in the monthly magazine, which ultimately reached forty thousand members nationwide and every public official in Washington, D.C. During the war he advanced the Double V Campaign for victory over racism at home and fascism abroad, often through statements of others, for instance, Detroiters involved in the Sojourner Truth Housing Project controversy of 1942. In that dispute he also mobilized *Postal Alliance* staff members to lobby congressmen and federal authorities for black occupancy of the defense units. He made the publication an integral part of the biracial union and served as one of its spokesmen.

Throughout the 1950s and 1960s Grigsby expressed union concerns over automation and similar issues, while nudging postal workers toward the civil rights movement. He believed that the causes of both trade unionism and civil rights advanced equality of opportunity and human dignity; postal employees comprised "one big union," a microcosm of the Reverend MARTIN LUTHER KING JR.'s nonviolent efforts to integrate society. True to his beliefs, he rarely mentioned racial separatism and disorder.

Grigsby considered Detroit politics as important as "bread-and-butter" issues. In *Taps or Reveille?* (1956) he stressed the need for blacks to vote, yet failed nine years later in his bid for a common council seat, as did his petition for district rather than at-large elections (elections that would guarantee black representation). By the early 1970s he circulated old and new material in publications, including *Are You Aware?* and *Think!*, alerting voters to issues and to "shafting" politicians. Nonetheless, he failed to obtain primary nominations as a county commissioner in 1974 or community college trustee in 1978.

From the Great Depression to his death from cancer in Detroit, Grigsby promoted achievement and pride. He wrote pamphlets for every black generation, including *Of This We Can Be Proud* (1961) and *Brainwashed—and Ignored* (1976). He also spoke widely during the racially aware 1960s, continuing in retirement to work as a researcher and consultant. A member of St. John's Presbyterian Church, the Republican Party, and the NAACP (despite having criticized it in the 1930s), he combined a belief in individualism with collective action in an ongoing drive for self-improvement and racial justice. An "Old Warrior" lifestyle reflected his propagandist creed: "A drop of ink may cause thousands to think!"

FURTHER READING
Seymour, Ruth. "Detroit Honors Its Volunteers," *Detroit News*, 11 Feb. 1981.
Thomas, Richard W. *Life for Us Is What We Make It: Building Black Community in Detroit, 1915–1945* (1992).
This entry is taken from the *American National Biography* and is published here with the permission of the American Council of Learned Societies.

DOMINIC J. CAPECI

Grimes, Henry (3 Nov. 1935–), bassist and composer, was born Henry Alonzo Grimes in Philadelphia, Pennsylvania. His parents, Leon and Georgia Grimes, were restaurant workers who worked at a Horn & Hardart's automat. Grimes had two siblings: a sister Yvonne and a brother Leon, who was also active in music for a time.

Grimes's musical career began at Barrett Junior High School in south Philadelphia, where he began playing violin and met fellow musicians Ted Curson, Albert TOOTIE HEATH, and BOBBY TIMMONS. Grimes attended north Philadelphia's Mastbaum Technical High School, famous for its rigorous music curriculum; Grimes's classmates there included future jazz trumpet greats Curson and LEE MORGAN. Between 1948 and 1952, Grimes began playing bass and performing for Philadelphia's all-city orchestra.

Grimes moved to New York in the early 1950s to study at the Juilliard School of Music under the tutelage of bassist Fred Zimmerman. Grimes's earliest professional experiences were with rhythm-and-blues groups, including some dates with the Texas saxophonist and bandleader KING CURTIS. Shortly thereafter, Grimes began playing nightclub engagements with singer Anita O'Day. Tenor saxophonist Gerry Mulligan first heard Grimes play in O'Day's group and invited him to join his quartet in 1956. After graduating from Juilliard in 1954, Grimes worked full time for Mulligan, recording several albums for the Pacific Jazz label. Grimes also collaborated with many of the crucial pioneers of the "cool jazz" movement of the late 1950s, which emphasized restraint and control in comparison to the sometimes wild emotionalism of earlier jazz styles, experimentation with unorthodox instrumental groupings, and an openness to the influence of modernist European art music: pianist Lenny Tristano, saxophonist Lee Konitz, and trumpet player Chet Baker. In the late 1950s Grimes began what would be a long relationship with SONNY ROLLINS, touring Europe extensively with the tenor saxophone giant. Grimes appeared at the 1958 Newport Jazz Festival, playing in groups as varied as those of swing clarinetist Benny Goodman and visionary modernist pianist THELONIOUS MONK. The latter's group's performance was captured on film in Bert Stern's 1959 documentary *Jazz on a Summer's Day*.

New York City in the early 1960s was the crossroads of an extraordinary efflorescence of creativity on the part of African American jazz musicians. Grimes participated in many of the most important recording sessions, live performances, and group experiments of that fertile period. One crucial aspect of this historical moment was the reevaluation of the roles played by different instruments within jazz groups. Instruments traditionally thought of as "accompaniment" began to seize new opportunities to occupy the center of musical attention. Grimes's bass work from this period is admired for striking a delicate balance between the traditional jazz bass responsibilities (sustaining the rhythmic pulse and providing harmonic grounding for soloists), and innovative forays into new sonic areas. Even at its most experimental extremes, Grimes's playing was distinguished by a consistently rich tone and palpable mastery of the instrument. Particularly impressive and influential were his contributions to the use of *arco* (bowed) bass technique in avant-garde jazz.

In 1961 Grimes played on pianist CECIL TAYLOR's sessions for Impulse Records (later released in 1961 as Gil Evans's *Into the Hot*) and began a long musical relationship with clarinetist Perry Robinson. In 1962 Grimes and Robinson recorded *Funk Dumpling* for the Savoy label. Grimes also continued his musical relationship with Rollins in the early 1960s, a period during which the tenor saxophonist began experimenting with more adventurous forms and sounds. With the addition of trumpeter DON CHERRY to Rollins's quartet, Grimes participated in a landmark 1963 performance at the Newport Jazz Festival with Rollins's musical hero COLEMAN HAWKINS. Grimes also participated in a recording session, in February 1963, of the same group for the RCA Victor record label, although he only appears on some of the tracks of the classic album documenting Rollins's encounter with Hawkins, *Sonny Meets Hawk!*

Grimes participated in a number of historically important groups in the years between 1963 and 1967. School Days, with fellow Taylor alumnus Steve Lacy on soprano saxophone, trombonist Roswell Rudd, and drummer Dennis Charles, was later recognized as one of the most musically innovative ensembles of the early 1960s avant-garde jazz scene. Grimes also played with what was likely Rollins's most musically adventurous quartet, alongside trumpeter Cherry and drummer BILLY HIGGINS.

Perhaps the most significant of Grimes's many creative relationships with powerful tenor saxophonists was his work with ALBERT AYLER. In 1964 Grimes played on a number of sessions that would gain acclaim as Ayler's finest recordings: *Spirits Rejoice* (1965), *Witches and Devils* (1964), *Goin' Home* (1964), and *Albert Ayler Live in Greenwich Village* (1967). The raw, gospel-inflected style of Ayler's playing and the openness of his march-derived melodic motifs created an ideal forum for Grimes's gifts to find expression. Many of Ayler's recordings were released by the New York label ESP-Disk, which encouraged artists to produce uncompromising musical statements free from commercial concerns. *The Call*, a recording by the Henry Grimes Trio in 28 December 1965, was released by ESP-Disk in 1966. A remarkable document, it reflected the near-telepathic group sensitivity of Grimes, Robinson, and drummer Tom Price. The group's musical communication was bolstered by its shared accommodation of an apartment in the East Village, near "free jazz" hotspot Slug's Saloon.

Grimes moved to California in 1968. His low profile in the years thereafter led to the circulation of erroneous information regarding his whereabouts. The free jazz revival of the 1990s, in conjunction with the reissue of many classic 1960s free jazz recordings on compact disc, spurred renewed interest in Henry Grimes. In 2003, Marshall Marrotte, a music enthusiast from Atlanta, Georgia, tracked Grimes down in a residential hotel in Los Angeles by means of persistent amateur detective work. Marrotte alerted Grimes to the interest in his life and music that had been steadily growing in the years since Grimes's retirement. Bassist WILLIAM PARKER donated a bass to Grimes and featured him as a star performer at the annual Vision Festival in New York, of which he was curator. In the years since 2003, Grimes relocated to New York City and renewed contact with many of his collaborators from the 1960s, including Taylor and drummer Sunny Murray. The years since 2003 also saw Grimes working with critically acclaimed groups featuring guitarist Marc Ribot, drummer Hamid Drake, and saxophonists David Murray and Fred Anderson.

FURTHER READING

Blumenfeld, Larry. "The Ballad of Henry Grimes (And Other Recent Visions)," *JAZZIZ* 20.11 (Nov. 2003).

Goldsby, John. "Henry Grimes: A Master Returns," *Bass Player* 14.10 (Oct. 2003).

Litweiler, John. *The Freedom Principle: Jazz After 1958* (1984).

Strauss, Neil. "Left New York in '68, Plays Again Tonight," *New York Times*, 26 May 2003.

Wilmer, Valerie. *As Serious As Your Life: The Story of the New Jazz* (1977).

KURT NEWMAN

Grimes, Leonard A. (9 Nov. 1815?–14 Mar. 1873), clergyman and abolitionist, was born Leonard Andrew Grimes in Leesburg, Loudon County, Virginia, the son of free black parents, Andrew Grimes and Mary (Polly or Molly) Goings (or Goines). After being orphaned at a young age, Grimes moved to Washington, D.C. On 27 May 1833 he married Octavia Janet Colson (or Colston), and by 1845 the couple had two daughters and one son. During the 1830s Grimes worked at various jobs and may have been hired by a local slaveholder, but he eventually went into business driving hacks in Washington. In 1840 he was convicted of using his hack to help an enslaved family escape from Loudon County to Canada and was sentenced to two years in prison.

About two or three years after his release, Grimes moved to New Bedford, Massachusetts. A fourth child was born there in 1846 but died five years later. The elder Grimes had probably experienced a religious conversion to Christianity before leaving the South, because he soon became active in the Baptist church in New Bedford, probably preaching in an unofficial capacity as an exhorter. In 1848 Grimes was invited by a fledgling black church in Boston to occupy its pulpit, and in November he was ordained, under the auspices of the Boston Baptist Association, as the pastor of Twelfth Baptist Church, beginning a twenty-five-year career as one of Boston's leading clergymen and activists.

When Grimes arrived, the Twelfth Baptist Church was a small congregation without its own building. Its members had seceded in the early 1840s from Boston's first independent black Baptist church, which met at the African Meeting House in Smith Court, now a historic site on Beacon Hill. The breakaway group had remained in Smith Court, but in 1849, after Grimes's arrival, the church purchased a lot for its own building on Southac (later Phillips) Street. Grimes oversaw efforts to raise around thirteen thousand dollars for the building, which was under construction from 1850 to 1854. The new building accommodated a church that grew rapidly under Grimes's leadership. Between his arrival and 1855 the group increased from about two dozen worshippers to around 140. In the next three years that number nearly doubled, and by the time of Grimes's death the church had surged past seven hundred members.

Like other African American congregations in the antebellum North, Grimes's church was a center for community activism. The Southac Street building was frequently used for meetings on religion and reform, and Grimes became a respected leader in Boston's interracial community of abolitionists. He remained unattached to antislavery organizations, however, preferring to pursue activism through the pastorate. This enabled him to avoid, for the most part, the internecine quarrels that divided Boston's abolitionists in the 1840s and 1850s. For instance, after FREDERICK DOUGLASS and William Lloyd Garrison parted ways publicly in 1851, Grimes tried to mediate between the parties. When Douglass came to Boston in 1853, he stayed in Grimes's home. Grimes tried to persuade Garrison and WILLIAM C. NELL, both critics of Douglass by then, that Douglass regretted the rupture. Nell and Garrison were unconvinced, but Grimes continued to be ecumenical in his friendships and affiliations.

In 1853 and 1855 he attended the black abolitionist conventions that organized the National Council of the Colored People, and in 1854 he presided over meetings at his church to organize an affiliated state council in Massachusetts.

Grimes's greatest renown as an abolitionist came from his assistance to fugitive slaves. His church was reputed to have sheltered a large number of escapees from the South, lending credence to the view that Grimes had been involved in helping fugitives in Virginia as well. According to some reports, the passage of the Fugitive Slave Law in 1850 caused up to forty or sixty members of Grimes's church to flee the city, fearing capture. If so, the church recovered from the loss by continuing to grow and by dedicating itself to resisting the law. In 1851 Grimes was involved, along with his fiery parishioner LEWIS HAYDEN, in the rescue of SHADRACH MINKINS and the unsuccessful attempt to rescue Thomas Sims, both captured fugitive slaves who probably worshipped at Grimes's church.

Grimes was crucially involved in the case of ANTHONY BURNS, another fugitive slave and member of Grimes's church who was returned to the South in 1854, in spite of tumultuous protests in Boston. After Burns's arrest, Grimes quickly raised funds to purchase him from his owner. But when his owner retracted the offer to sell Burns and other efforts to free him collapsed, Burns was taken back to Virginia and sold later that year to a slave trader. Learning of this transaction, Grimes raised thirteen hundred dollars and arranged to meet the trader, buy Burns, and return him to the North as a free man. In 1855 Grimes traveled back to the Chesapeake Bay region where he had grown up to complete the sale in Baltimore.

For the remainder of the decade Grimes remained active in local antislavery efforts. On 1 January 1863 abolitionists gathered in Boston to await news of the Emancipation Proclamation, then they adjourned to Grimes's church to celebrate through the night. After the proclamation Grimes actively supported the enlistment of black soldiers in the Union war effort, telling one audience that he was himself "willing to go. He would take his Bible, and go with them; and, if need be, would not refuse to take the musket" (*Liberator*, 6 Mar. 1863). When the famous Fifty-fourth Massachusetts Regiment of black infantrymen paraded through Boston in May, Grimes spoke at the ceremonies honoring the soldiers. Thereafter he threw his energies into aiding freed people from the South, collecting donations of clothes in his church and traveling to the border states again that fall to visit emancipated slaves.

After the war Grimes continued to use his pulpit as a platform for missionary efforts, community aid, and political activism. According to one early biographer, he died suddenly upon returning to his home in East Summersville, Massachusetts, from a missionary meeting (Simmons, 662). From his days as a driver in Washington, D.C., to the day of his death, Grimes exemplified African American leaders in the antebellum period who used their personal experiences and pastoral offices as instruments of aid and activism on behalf of their communities.

FURTHER READING

Horton, James Oliver, and Lois E. Horton. *Black Bostonians: Family Life and Community Struggle in the Antebellum North* (1979).

Jacobs, Donald M., ed. *Courage and Conscience: Black and White Abolitionists in Boston* (1993).

Levesque, George A. "Inherent Reformers—Inherited Orthodoxy: Black Baptists in Boston, 1800–1873," *Journal of Negro History* 60.4 (1975): 491–525.

Simmons, William J. *Men of Mark: Eminent, Progressive, and Rising* (1887).

Von Frank, Albert J. *The Trials of Anthony Burns: Freedom and Slavery in Emerson's Boston* (1998).

W. CALEB MCDANIEL

Grimes, Tiny (7 July 1916?–4 Mar. 1989), jazz and rhythm and blues guitarist and bandleader, was born Lloyd Grimes in Newport News, Virginia. The names of his parents are unknown. Grimes told the interviewer Bob Kenselaar that he was unsure of his birth date but told the writers Stanley Dance and Arnie Berle that he was born in 1917. Other published sources give 1916 or 1915. He took up drums in a Boy Scout marching band and played regularly at a beach dancehall near Newport News until a storm and subsequent flood destroyed the hall and his drums. Around the seventh grade he dropped out of school to work jobs selling papers and shining shoes. He taught himself to play piano, and while living in Washington, D.C., he became a pianist and singer in a trio called Wynken, Blynken, and Nod. The group performed regularly on radio on *Major Bowes's Original Amateur Hour* around 1936, and worked at a club in Alexandria, Virginia.

Grimes came to New York around 1937 or 1938 and taught himself to play tiple, a miniature guitar. He then bought an unusual acoustic guitar with four rather than six strings, because the thinner fretboard fit his small hands. For his entire career he would use such an instrument, tuned to the standard guitar's four highest pitched strings (in ascending pitch, the notes D, G, B, and E). After acquiring an electric banjo, with its four strings tuned the same way, he took up electric guitar and modified it accordingly. Much later in his career he played four-string electric guitars custom-made by the Guild company.

In 1940 Grimes joined a tiple and guitar group, Cats and the Fiddle, playing guitar, singing high tenor parts, and devising unnotated arrangements. After touring to California, he left Cats and the Fiddle to join the bassist SLAM STEWART in the duo Slim and Slam as a replacement for SLIM GAILLARD, who had been inducted into the army. Stewart and Grimes then joined the pianist ART TATUM, forming a renowned trio from 1943 to 1944. Their recordings include "Cocktails for Two," "I Would Do Anything for You," "Body and Soul," "Topsy," and "Soft Winds." Accustomed to playing by ear Grimes was as ready as anyone could be for Tatum's notoriously impetuous and difficult conception of harmony and rhythm: wherever Tatum's fingers went, the guitarist followed. "It was an honor, but certainly no pleasure," Grimes said. "It was a struggle trying to keep up with him." He recalled that even the group's most intricate arrangements evolved on the bandstand, without rehearsal.

After Tatum broke up the trio to work again as a soloist, Grimes formed his own trio at Tondelayo's in New York, initially using the pianist Clyde Hart and the bassist OSCAR PETTIFORD. The alto saxophonist CHARLIE PARKER came regularly to sit in with Grimes's group. Grimes made a number of recordings in the summer of 1944, including "Blue Harlem," "Indiana," and "Hard Tack," all in the tenor saxophonist IKE QUEBEC's band. A session with the trumpeter HOT LIPS PAGE featured Grimes playing tasteful obbligato lines in support of and in alternation with Page's singing on the ballad "I Got What It Takes" and on "Lip's Blues." Three days later, three takes of Grimes's own "Tiny's Tempo" offered fine examples of his melodic improvising, which followed the swing guitarist CHARLIE CHRISTIAN's manner of blending in catchy riffs while spinning out long lines; two other titles from this session, one being "I'll Always Love You Just the Same," offered rare examples of Grimes's bland singing (an experiment that he would not repeat until 1973), but the true importance of this date for the Savoy label was in providing a forum for the first substantial studio recordings of Parker's bop soloing. Later, in November 1944, Grimes twice recorded with the

drummer COZY COLE, who featured him on a version of "Take It on Back."

During late 1944 or early 1945 Grimes moved from Tondelayo's to the Spotlite club, where he hired the pianist Al Haig, and then to the Downbeat club, where he worked alongside the tenor saxophonist COLEMAN HAWKINS and the singer BILLIE HOLIDAY. Terry Gibbs, while working as a drummer rather than a vibraphonist, also played with Grimes's band at some point during this tenure in New York clubs. Grimes returned regularly to the Downbeat through 1946, and he accompanied Holiday in her first solo concert, at Town Hall in New York in February 1946, and on several recordings, including "What Is This Thing Called Love" in 1945, and "Good Morning Heartache" in 1946. He also recorded with Quebec in 1945, the tenor saxophonist John Hardee, and his own swingtet, both 1946.

Around 1947 Grimes moved into the emerging rhythm and blues field. He had a hit that year with a version of "That Old Black Magic" with a group that included Hardee on saxophone and George Kelly on piano. Grimes's group became known as the Rockin' Highlanders when the members began wearing kilts and tam-o'-shanters as a gimmick. In 1948 they had begun a two-year stand at Gleason's in Cleveland. The Rockin' Highlanders made their first tour around 1949, returned to Gleason's until 1951, and then began extensive touring, spending summers entertaining in Atlantic City. Accounts of the band's personnel are confusing. The tenor saxophonist Red Prysock figured prominently. The pianist Sir Charles Thompson and the bassist Ike Isaacs were members early on, and Kelly (as a tenor saxophonist, perhaps doubling on piano) joined or alternated with Prysock and other tenor players. The tenor saxophonist Benny Golson was a Rockin' Highlander around 1952. "Tiny's Boogie Woogie," recorded in 1951, exemplifies instrumental dance music well on its way to what would be known as rock and roll; this title finds Grimes intentionally overdriving the amplifier to distort the speaker and thus achieve a harsher sound than in his days with swing groups. The Highlanders' recordings from the early 1950s include "Riverside Jump," "Call of the Wild," "Juicy Fruit," and "Second Floor Rear." The group disbanded in 1955 after a severe automobile accident. Grimes settled in Philadelphia, where he was inactive as a musician and separated from his wife. (Details of the marriage are unknown.)

From 1958 to 1961 Grimes occasionally organized and played on recordings for the Prestige company. The results included an album as coleader with the tenor saxophonist Coleman Hawkins, *Blues Groove*

(1958), and Grimes's own *Callin' the Blues* (1958) and *Tiny in Swingland* (1959). The pianist ERROLL GARNER then procured a recording session for Grimes on the United Artists label, resulting in what is regarded as his best album, *Big Time Guitar* (1962). Grimes performed at the Village Gate in New York in 1962. He stopped playing altogether in 1964, when he had the first of six operations on his leg.

Grimes resumed his career in New York late in 1966. In 1967 he was featured on "A Tiny Bit of Blues" on the alto saxophonist JOHNNY HODGES's album *Triple Play*. The following year he toured Europe with the tenor saxophonist Buddy Tate, the organist MILT BUCKNER, and Cole, recording in Paris. He recorded with the tenor saxophonist ILLINOIS JACQUET in 1969. He returned to Europe in 1970 with Kelly and the pianist JAY McSHANN and again recorded in France. On 14 August 1971 he participated in a concert in the Great Guitarist series at New York's Town Hall, but the resulting recording is disappointing. For a few months in 1972 he joined the pianist EARL HINES's touring band. In 1973 he gave his first performance at the Newport Jazz Festival (in New York), and he recorded the rather uneven album *Profoundly Blue*.

The year 1974 brought further performances and recordings in France, this time with the tenor saxophonist Arnett Cobb and the drummer Panama Francis. As coleader with the trumpeter ROY ELDRIDGE, Grimes recorded the album *One Is Never Too Old to Swing* (1977). Around 1979 he performed at the Nice Jazz Festival in France. The following year he had a hip replacement. After his recovery he resumed a routine of festival appearances and performances in New York clubs. He died in New York City.

Not one of jazz's extraordinary talents Grimes is remembered for his ability to deal with the complexities of Tatum's music and for his fostering of Parker's career. In rhythm and blues, he supplied, via his Rockin' Highlanders, a jazz-oriented approach to instrumental improvisation that was far meatier than the usual fare.

FURTHER READING

Britt, Stan. *The Jazz Guitarists* (1984).
Dance, Stanley. *The World of Swing* (1974).
Shaw, Arnold. *52nd Street: The Street of Jazz* (1977).
Obituary: *New York Times,* 7 Mar. 1989.
This entry is taken from the *American National Biography* and is published here with the permission of the American Council of Learned Societies.

BARRY KERNFELD

Grimes, William (1784?–1865?), slave and writer, was born in King George County, Virginia. His father was Benjamin Grymes, a wealthy Virginia planter; his mother was a slave of a neighbor, Dr. Steward, who was therefore William Grimes's first owner. Grimes (under three different names) served ten masters as a house servant, plantation worker, stable boy, and coachman in Virginia, Maryland, and Georgia. He was severely mistreated, more than once coming close to death from too much whipping. Grimes made a number of unsuccessful escape attempts: on one occasion he tried to break his own leg and on another pretended to starve himself. Cunning and combative, he several times induced his masters to sell him in order to improve his situation, with mixed results; he also entered into several bloody fights with other slaves. A superstitious man, he was frequently haunted by ghosts and was troubled by a woman he believed was a witch. But he also fervently embraced Christianity, from which he derived some solace.

Being light-skinned (he was at least three-quarters white), Grimes often passed as white at nighttime during his long residence in Savannah; this proved helpful to him in obtaining provisions for his final escape from slavery in about 1814. This he effected by hiding in a cotton bale onboard a ship bound for New York, after befriending some of the sailors. He then made his way to New Haven, Connecticut, having heard good things about the place from one of his former masters.

At first Grimes found it harder to be a freeman in Connecticut than to be a slave in Georgia. The employment he was able to procure demanded hard labor for little recompense. After saving about twenty dollars, he opened barbershops in Providence, Rhode Island, and then New Bedford, Massachusetts, both of which closed within a few months. He had better luck in Litchfield, Connecticut, where he also let and traded horses and gigs. He nonetheless was involved in a number of court cases, including several in which he claimed to have been falsely accused of crimes, and his reputation suffered thereby. As he would later write in his autobiography, "It has been my fortune most always to be suspected by the good, and to be cheated and abused by the vicious" (60).

Grimes soon moved back to New Haven, where he waited on students, sold them groceries, and lent them money. By then, however, his last master knew where he was and sent a man to threaten to send him back to slavery if he did not buy his freedom. Grimes, at this point living in Litchfield, gave up everything he owned, including his house and land, for his freedom. He was, of course, happy to be free but also bitter about freedom's cost. "I would advise no slave to leave his master," he wrote. "If he runs away, he is most sure to be taken: if he is not, he will ever be in the apprehension of it" (67).

Now entirely destitute, with a wife, Clarissa Caesar, and children to support, he wrote his autobiography in 1824 and published and sold it the following year in the hope that the proceeds would ameliorate his condition. *Life of William Grimes, the Runaway Slave* was the first book-length autobiography of a fugitive American slave and thus inadvertently helped inaugurate a genre; it was also the longest autobiography of an African American yet written. While later slave writers almost invariably depicted a heroic triumph over adversity, Grimes remained unredeemed, fearful, bitter, and disconsolate. His book concludes with one of the most profound, chilling, and complex comments on American slavery to be found in any slave narrative: "If it were not for the stripes on my back which were made while I was a slave, I would in my will, leave my skin a legacy to the government, desiring that it might be taken off and made into parchment, and then bind the constitution of glorious happy *and free* America. Let the skin of an American slave, bind the charter of American Liberty" (68).

Grimes seems to have had no exposure to antislavery thought; yet his was the first black autobiography to refer to its author as a slave in its title, and it stands as a powerful indictment not only of southern slavery but also of northern anti-black discrimination. So while Grimes pined for and praised freedom, he also stated, "I do think there is no inducement for a slave to leave his master and be set free in the Northern States" (67).

This is but one example of the apparent contradictions of Grimes's book. He professes the most profound religious faith, yet continually shows himself willing and ready to sin, and the virtue of forgiveness is noticeably absent in his narrative. He identifies as a black former slave, but he insistently repeats that he is three-quarters white. In the first sentence of his book he gives his year of birth and, still, at the end states, "I think I must be forty years of age, but don't know; I could not tell my wife my age" (68).

These contradictions probably arose from the difficulties Grimes had in defining himself, since that self had been heretofore defined by ten different owners. Throughout his book Grimes seems confused about how to present himself, for he was confronting a conundrum that every slave author faced: the necessity of asserting (or creating) an identity after having been robbed of one for most of one's life. Nowhere in the slave narrative tradition is this conundrum more evident than in Grimes's book, for no other slave autobiographer faced more difficulties in, and received less help in dealing with, his or her newfound freedom. As the slave narrative scholar William Andrews has noted, "Grimes's text signifies the possibility that the black self—as a unitive, knowable essence, as the locus of a usable past for its creators and sponsors—could not be recovered at all in the slave narrative.... The *Life* has stood as a loaded gun, ... as much a threat to the literary system of autobiography as to the social system of slavery" (80–81).

After publishing his narrative, Grimes continued his peripatetic ways, making his home in Bridgeport, Norwalk, Fairfield, Stratford Point, and finally New Haven once more, where he remained for the rest of his life, "shaving heads," cleaning clothes, working at the colleges, and selling lottery tickets. In 1855, "being more than seventy years of age," he published a second edition of his autobiography, bringing it up to date with some humorous anecdotes and doggerel. No longer bitter or reproachful, he poked fun at himself, remarking that he had "often been called one of the most remarkable personages of modern times" (84). He had eighteen children, twelve of whom survived.

Grimes's pioneering book stands today as the most complex and disconsolate of all slave narratives, but it was little read until recently and had no discernible impact on the genre. Because it is untouched by abolitionist rhetoric, it is invaluable for fully understanding the psychological effects of slavery.

FURTHER READING

Grimes, William. *Life of William Grimes, the Runaway Slave* (1825, updated 1855).

Andrews, William. *To Tell a Free Story: The First Century of Afro-American Autobiography, 1760–1865* (1986).

Taylor, Yuval, ed. *I Was Born a Slave: An Anthology of Classic Slave Narratives* (1999).

YUVAL TAYLOR

Grimes, William W. (7 Sept. 1824–28 Nov. 1891), minister and abolitionist, was born William Waugh Grimes in Alexandria, Virginia, the eldest of five children of Thomas Grimes and Elizabeth Ann Waugh. Little is known about Grimes's early life other than that he started earning a living at the age of nine, after his father died. In 1841 Grimes traveled to Washington, D.C., to see the inauguration of William Henry Harrison, and he was employed during the early part of the decade by several members of Congress, including Millard Fillmore, then a Whig congressman from New York. In 1847 Grimes married Mary Ann Brown. Following the death of President Zachary Taylor on 9 July 1850, Grimes worked in the White House for the Fillmore family; he remained there until 1855, when he left to work full time as a minister in the African Methodist Episcopal (AME) Church.

Grimes joined Union Bethel African Methodist Episcopal Church in Washington, D.C., in 1843. A decade later the AME minister Reverend A. W. Wayman licensed him to exhort, and the following year Grimes began to preach. His first assignment was on the Smyrna Delaware circuit, where he was well received by many young blacks. His popularity concerned some of the members of the community, and they accused him of holding meetings after ten o'clock at night, a violation of Delaware's 1832 black codes. When Grimes proved this accusation false, he was charged with violating an 1851 law that prohibited free blacks from moving into the state. Grimes refuted the claim, declaring that he was a resident of the District of Columbia, where he paid taxes and his family and most of his things resided; he was merely a transient in Delaware. In spite of Grimes's defense, the local squire ordered him to leave immediately. Grimes fought the order, seeking recommendations from President Franklin Pierce, several commodores of the U.S. Navy, and others, and appealed to the Delaware chief justice Samuel Harrington. Harrington read the recommendations and agreed that Grimes could stay. Over the next two years Grimes was ordained a deacon, started several congregations, paid off the debt on the old church in Smyrna, and built or renovated several other church buildings.

During Grimes's next assignment on a Maryland circuit, local whites accused him of being an agent of the Underground Railroad and using the money he raised to pay off the debts of his church to help slaves escape. They declared that if he ever set foot on Dorchester County soil again he would be hanged. Grimes refused to obey the order, and the sheriff arrested him. Grimes was brought before the state's attorney to defend his sermons, which many whites said were used to encourage slaves to flee. According to his autobiography, Grimes

Told them that I never told or persuaded a slave to run away; this was the truth. But I did not tell them that when they came to me and wanted to go, I told them how to go. I did not tell them that I was always ready to point out to them the way, and what points to make, and what places to shun. No man or woman that went by my counsel was ever taken back into slavery (16–17).

Although the sheriff did not hang him, Grimes was put on a boat to Baltimore with orders to leave the state. In spite of this threat he traveled to Easton the very next day, where he finished out his assignment unscathed.

The bishops of the AME Church recognized Grimes's talent as a minister, both in terms of the numbers of conversions he brought to the church and in terms of the amount of money he raised to build new church buildings and pay off their debts. Grimes often started new appointments with congregations in crisis, and he usually left the churches bigger and more financially secure. Often these successes came at great financial cost to himself and his family. While he served in New Haven, Connecticut, for example, the small congregation owed so much debt on the church that he did not receive any salary. All of the money collected at services went to save the building from being taken over by the sheriff. In order to feed his family, Grimes worked as a day laborer at Yale College. In other congregations he cut wood or raised crops to support his wife and five children. He was not afraid of hard work of the physical or spiritual kind.

Grimes held a key leadership role in his community, using his sermons and his churches to promote and fight for equal rights for African Americans. He played an integral role in the formation and recruitment of the Fifty-fourth Regiment Massachusetts Volunteers during the Civil War. Several local political and religious politicians recommended Grimes for chaplain's post; however, when Governor John Albion Andrew appointed both Grimes and the Baptist minister WILLIAM JACKSON to serve together, Grimes declined, proclaiming that it did not take two black ministers to fill a single position. When Grimes was transferred to the New Haven circuit, he urged his new congregants to join the Twenty-ninth Connecticut Colored Volunteers and was critical of the state government for not giving the enlisted black men the opportunity to fight. He protested the injustices occurring at the ballot box and in the schools. During the summer of 1865 he chaired a committee in New Haven to organize a state Equal Rights League. When he moved to serve a congregation in New Jersey, he held public meetings at his church in Woodbury to raise money for a lawsuit to demand suffrage for black men.

In his sixth and seventh decades Grimes showed few signs of slowing down. He continued to serve in congregations in the Northeast, taking an active role in the life of the national AME Church and in the order of Freemasons, serving as grand chaplain at the state and national levels. He preached at revivals, built new churches, and wrote his memoir, *Thirty-Three Years Experience of an Itinerant Minister of the A.M.E. Church* (1887). He died serving a congregation in Phoenixville, Pennsylvania, weeks after the dedication of its new building.

FURTHER READING
The largest source of material regarding Grimes is the *Philadelphia Christian Recorder*, the weekly newspaper of the African Methodist Episcopal Church.
Grimes, William W. *Thirty-Three Years Experience of an Itinerant Minister of the A.M.E. Church* (1887).
Obituary: *Philadelphia Christian Recorder*, 3 Dec. 1891.
KARA M. MCCLURKEN

Grimké, Angelina Weld (27 Feb. 1880–10 June 1958), poet and teacher, was born in Boston, Massachusetts, the daughter of ARCHIBALD HENRY GRIMKÉ, an attorney and diplomat, and Sarah E. Stanley. Angelina's parents separated when she was very young, and she, an only child, was raised by her father. Her mother's absence undoubtedly contributed to Grimké's reverential treatment of maternal themes in her poetry, short stories, and especially her only published play, *Rachel* (1920). Her father dominated Grimké's life until his death in 1930. His continual insistence on her personal propriety and academic achievement seemed to inhibit his daughter's self-determination as much as it inspired her to make him proud of her. Growing up in Boston, Grimké enjoyed a comfortable, middle-class life. Her distinguished family name gave her certain advantages, such as an education at better schools and frequent exposure to prominent liberal activists. But as the daughter of a white woman and a man of mixed ancestry, she was no stranger to racial tension. Her sensitivity to racism was further enhanced by her family's history. Grimké was named for her father's aunt, the social reformer Angelina Emily Grimké, who had campaigned for women's suffrage and for the abolition of slavery. Her father, the son of a slave, had dedicated his life to fighting prejudice. This heritage put enormous pressure on Grimké to carry on her family's tradition of embracing social causes. Timid and obedient as a child, she turned to writing as a release for her preoccupations: her need for a mother's attention, her diligence in living up to her father's expectations, and her inability to establish a lasting romantic partnership. Upon reaching adulthood, she remained introverted but began to use her writing as a public platform for denouncing racism.

In 1898 Grimké enrolled in the Boston Normal School of Gymnastics (which eventually became the department of hygiene at Wellesley College), graduating in 1902 with a degree in physical education. She then moved to Washington, D.C., where she taught physical education at the Armstrong Manual Training School, a vocational institution, until 1907. Apparently unhappy with both her duties and her work environment, Grimké left Armstrong to teach English at the M Street High School, having prepared herself by taking summer courses in English at Harvard University from 1904 to 1910. Grimké remained at M Street until she retired from teaching in 1926.

Although Grimké wrote most prolifically between 1900 and 1920, her first published piece, a poem titled "The Grave in the Corner," appeared in the *Norfolk (Massachusetts) County Gazette* when she was only thirteen (27 May 1893). During her postsecondary studies Grimké published more of her verse in the *Boston Transcript*. However, not all of her work was well received. The editor of the *Transcript*, Charles S. Hunt, rejected Grimké's poem titled "Beware Lest He Awakes" on the grounds that its "implied threat of a bloody rising on the part of the negro" was anachronistic. The poem, eventually published in the *Pilot* (10 May 1902), reflects the battle against racism that more typically characterizes Grimké's short fiction and her play *Rachel*. Another early poem, "El Beso," was published in the *Transcript* (27 Oct. 1909), accompanied by praise for Grimké's poetic talent.

Grimké's best-known poems include "To Keep the Memory of Charlotte Forten Grimké" (1915), about CHARLOTTE L. FORTEN GRIMKÉ, her aunt by marriage, "The Black Finger" (1923), "A Winter Twilight" (1923), "Tenebris" (1924), "For the Candlelight" (1925), "When the Green Lies over the Earth" (1927), and "Your Hands" (1927). These poems express her recurring themes of unfulfilled love and racial injustice or pay tribute to famous people. Other works feature tender depictions of children and mothers. A sense of despair pervades much of Grimké's verse, but only occasionally does her tone become strident or even moderately antagonistic.

Her surviving manuscripts suggest that Grimké had, at one time, considered collecting her poetry into a volume tentatively titled *Dusk Dreams*. The project never materialized, and the majority of Grimké's verse remains in holograph form among her personal papers. Much of this unpublished work consists of highly sentimental love poetry addressed to women by obviously female speakers. Some scholars have suggested that these lesbian overtones kept Grimké from publishing verse that might have brought scandal to her family name.

Less varied in theme than her poetry, Grimké's prose and drama focus almost exclusively on lynching and the chagrin of African American motherhood. Her short stories "The Closing Door" (1919) and "Goldie" (1920) combine these two topics in an effort to shock white readers into realizing how prejudice and racially motivated violence contribute to the disintegration of the black family. Both stories appeared in the *Birth Control Review* and were widely perceived as advocating childlessness among African Americans. The heroines of these stories fervently desire to bear children, but they sacrifice their maternal longings in order to avenge and prevent persecution of blacks by whites. The young women make this decision after they lose friends and family members to lynch mobs. Likewise, the title character in Grimké's play *Rachel* breaks off her engagement and forswears motherhood when her "adopted" children come home in tears after having racist taunts hurled at them by white children.

Grimké is primarily regarded as a poet, yet her most celebrated work is her play *Rachel*. Written in three acts, the play depicts the struggle of a young black woman and her family in dealing with the racial prejudice that constricts their lives. Grimké unabashedly uses the story as a vehicle for antiracist propaganda, subtitling it *A Play of Protest*. Even critics who have faulted Grimké's dramatic technique have been unable to deny the impact of her message. When the Drama Committee of the NAACP supported the original production of *Rachel* on 3 March 1916, Grimké became the first African American woman to have written a publicly staged drama. The play underwent at least two other stagings before its publication in 1920. It was not performed again for nearly seventy-five years, until its revival by the Spelman (College) Players in 1991.

Critics suggest that parts of *Rachel* are autobiographical. The title character's physical description matches that of Grimké. More significantly, Rachel's decision to forgo marriage and motherhood parallels a conscious choice made by Grimké. However, these similarities are largely superficial. Rachel abandons her dreams because of her heartbreak and anger over the racial injustice she sees affecting her loved ones. In contrast, Grimké's journals and poetry indicate that her homosexuality relegated her to a lonely and celibate life.

A second play, *Mara*, was discovered among Grimké's personal papers. It was apparently written in the wake of *Rachel's* popularity, but no record exists of any performances or of Grimké's attempts to have it published.

Throughout her life Grimké never enjoyed good health, which may explain in part why she eventually stopped teaching physical education in favor of English. A train accident led to a serious back injury in July 1911, and her retirement from teaching may have stemmed from physical incapacity. She nursed her father, who had retired to Washington, D.C., as he declined into death (1928–1930). She then moved to New York, where she spent the rest of her life in virtual seclusion. Her last significant publication was a selection of poems featured in COUNTÉE CULLEN's anthology *Caroling Dusk* (1927). After some thirty years of isolation, both artistic and social, Grimké died in New York in 1958.

For the most part, Grimké's published poems, stories, and her play enjoyed moderate acclaim during her lifetime. Although she lived geographically remote from the hub of the Harlem Renaissance, she earned recognition from her more prominent contemporaries, notably LANGSTON HUGHES and Cullen. She also attended literary gatherings in the Washington, D.C., home of her close friend and fellow poet GEORGIA DOUGLAS JOHNSON. Yet compared with her peers, Grimké published relatively few works. Her renown may have suffered further because of her failure to produce a collection of her poems or any other sizable volume. When she withdrew from the literary world, her works faded into obscurity, where they remained until they regained scholarly interest in the late twentieth century. Grimké's resurgent eminence as a poet stems not only from her skillful imagery and lyricism but also from her unusual perspective as a woman of color who felt compelled to suppress her sexuality.

FURTHER READING

Grimké's papers are held at the Moorland-Spingarn Research Center of Howard University in Washington, D.C.

Hirsch, David A. Hedrick. "Speaking Silences in Angelina Weld Grimké's 'The Closing Door' and

'Blackness,'" *African American Review* 26 (1992), 459–474.

Hull, Gloria T. *Color, Sex, and Poetry: Three Women Writers of the Harlem Renaissance* (1987).

This entry is taken from the *American National Biography* and is published here with the permission of the American Council of Learned Societies.

LAINE A. SCOTT

Grimké, Archibald Henry (17 Aug. 1849–25 Feb. 1930), scholar and activist, was born in Colleton County, South Carolina, near Charleston, the eldest of three sons of Henry Grimké, a lawyer and member of one of South Carolina's leading families, and Nancy Weston, a slave owned by Grimké. He was also a nephew, on his father's side, of the noted white southern abolitionists Sarah Grimké and Angelina Grimké Weld. Although Archibald was born a slave, Henry acknowledged him as his son. After Henry's death in 1852 his mother took him to Charleston, where, even though he was still legally a slave, he attended a school for free blacks.

This condition was to change with the coming of the Civil War, when, in 1860, one of Henry's adult white sons, from an earlier marriage, forced the Grimké brothers—Archibald, John, and FRANCIS J. GRIMKÉ—to work as household slaves. Archibald escaped in 1863, hiding in the home of a free Charleston family for the duration of the war.

Following emancipation, the brothers enrolled in a school for freedpeople, where Archibald and Francis in particular caught the attention of the principal, the abolitionist Frances Pillsbury. She arranged for them to continue their education at Lincoln University in Pennsylvania. They entered in 1867 and succeeded notably. They also seem to have come to the attention of their aunts for the first time. Angelina Grimké Weld, living in Massachusetts, read an article about Lincoln in the *National Anti-Slavery Standard*, an abolitionist journal that continued to publish after the war. The Grimké brothers were singled out for their talents, and Weld immediately suspected their connection with her family. She and her sister Sarah undertook the support of their newfound nephews. They enabled Francis to continue his education through Princeton Theological Seminary; he was to become a prominent Presbyterian minister, intellectual, and activist. They also helped support Archibald through Harvard Law School, from which he graduated in 1874. And they supported the youngest Grimké brother, John, but John did not do well and subsequently played little role in

his older brothers' lives. Following his graduation from Harvard, Archibald settled in Boston. In 1879 he married Sarah Stanley, the daughter of a white abolitionist minister from Michigan, and on 27 February 1880 their daughter, ANGELINA WELD GRIMKÉ—destined to become a prominent poet and writer—was born. The marriage soon became stormy, partly but not entirely on racial grounds, and dissolved in 1883. Sarah Stanley Grimké pursued a successful career as a writer and lecturer on occultism until her death in San Diego, California, in 1898.

At the same time, Grimké became involved in politics as, aided by his aunts, he developed contacts with some of Boston's leading citizens. Identifying with the reform Republicans known as "mugwumps," he entered the public arena in 1883 as editor of the *Hub*, a party newspaper addressed to African American readers. He also involved himself in movements for women's rights and for labor and tariff reform. In about 1886 he began to rethink his Republican ties, believing that the party was taking African American constituents for granted. By 1887 he had followed many of his mugwump friends into the Democratic Party. Even as he engaged in politics, he began to show an interest in scholarship, writing well-received biographies of William Lloyd Garrison (1891) and Charles Sumner (1892).

In 1894 as a reward for his political efforts, Grimké was appointed American consul to the Dominican Republic under the second administration of the Democratic president Grover Cleveland. Grimké performed his duties well and enjoyed his time in the Dominican Republic, especially since it appeared to be a society untarnished by American-style racism. He was not entirely happy when the Republican administration of William McKinley replaced him with one of its own loyalists.

Returning to the United States, Grimké divided his time between Boston and Washington, D.C., where his brother Francis and Francis's wife, CHARLOTTE L. FORTEN GRIMKÉ, were leading figures. He also became active in the American Negro Academy, the scholarly society founded in 1896. Francis Grimké had been one of the founding members, along with such major figures as ALEXANDER CRUMMELL, KELLY MILLER, and W. E. B. DuBois. Archibald Grimké became a member in 1899 and assumed the organization's presidency in 1903, serving until 1919. Speaking and writing in a wide variety of settings, he displayed a growing interest in the economic and psychological dimensions of

American racism, an interest he pursued for the remainder of his life.

At the same time, his career became intertwined with the increasingly virulent dispute between allies and opponents of BOOKER T. WASHINGTON. Like many, Grimké admired Washington's achievements but was angered by Washington's often conciliatory stance toward the racist policies and practices being put in place in turn-of-the-century America. As early as 1903 he was one of those leaders singled out by DuBois in *The Souls of Black Folk* for their misgivings about Washington's programs and prominence.

Grimké occupied a complex place in the dispute over Booker Washington's leadership. He never came to share Washington's accommodationist approach to American racial problems and could even be said to have been at the cutting edge of creating an anti-Washingtonian ideology. Nevertheless, he spent several years closely affiliated with Washington and Washington's allies. In 1905 he signed on as the District of-Columbia correspondent, writing weekly columns for the *New York Age*, edited by Washington's ally T. THOMAS FORTUNE. Grimké's columns were fiercely independent, directly challenging Washington's leadership and ideas. Still, he worked with Washington and Washington's organization in a variety of ways.

During 1906 a number of factors began to drive him away from Washington's camp, and when the 1907 creation of the Niagara Movement by DuBois, WILLIAM MONROE TROTTER, and others appeared to offer an alternative to Washington's machine, Grimké decided to join. Becoming, at the same time, editor of *Alexander's Magazine*, an important—and at one time Washingtonian—periodical, he used his position to champion the new movement.

The Niagara Movement was to undergo a major transformation over the next few years, especially as several important white reformers, also frustrated with Booker Washington's accommodationism, joined with DuBois and others in contemplating the creation of an interracial organization to fight racial oppression. This was to result in the founding of the NAACP in 1910. Grimké was peripherally involved in the founding but actively involved in the association's activities. By 1913 he had become president of the Washington, D.C., branch and a member of the national board.

The D.C. branch was especially important to the NAACP. Woodrow Wilson had been elected president in 1912 and, upon assuming office, had instituted a thoroughgoing policy of segregation and discrimination in the federal government. As head of the D.C. branch, Grimké took on a major role in challenging those policies while trying to protect black federal employees from discriminatory treatment. These efforts were to become increasingly complex after April 1917, when the United States entered World War I. Grimké opposed the war—he was put under federal surveillance for a time—and was particularly incensed when DuBois, in the NAACP's magazine *The Crisis*, urged African Americans to put aside their grievances to support the war effort. He was to be even more incensed when he learned that DuBois had been offered a military commission to help address racial problems in the armed forces. He protested as a member of the national board and led the D.C. branch to condemn DuBois bitterly.

After the war Grimké's career began to wind down. His work for the NAACP was widely appreciated, and he was awarded its highest honor, the Spingarn Medal, in 1919. At the same time, the national organization took on more of the lobbying activity that had previously been the province of the D.C. branch, lessening Grimké's role in such efforts. Plagued by ill health, he stepped down from the national board in 1923 and officially retired as president of the branch in 1925. His health failed in 1928, and he was bedridden for much of the time until his death, in Washington.

Although he was not as influential as Booker T. Washington or W. E. B. DuBois, Grimké was an important figure. His significance was recognized, and occasionally resented, by his contemporaries, as he sought to carve out an independent place in a factional setting. Often prescient in his analyses of race relations, his life was itself a challenge to the simplistic, brutal racial environment of late-nineteenth- and early-twentieth-century America.

FURTHER READING

Grimké's papers, along with those of his brother Francis Grimké and his daughter, Angelina Weld Grimké, are housed in the Moorland-Spingarn Research Center at Howard University in Washington, D.C.

Bruce, Dickson D., Jr. *Archibald Grimké: Portrait of a Black Independent* (1993).

Harlan, Louis R. *Booker T. Washington: The Wizard of Tuskegee, 1901–1915* (1983).

Lewis, David Levering. *W. E. B. DuBois: Biography of a Race, 1868–1919* (1993).

Obituary: *Journal of Negro History* 15 (1930).

DICKSON D. BRUCE JR.

Grimké, Charlotte Forten (17 Aug. 1837–23 July 1914), educator, diarist, and essayist, was born in Philadelphia, Pennsylvania, the daughter of Mary Virginia Wood and ROBERT BRIDGES FORTEN, who were free blacks. Her father, a mathematician, orator, and reformer, was the son of the wealthy sailmaker JAMES FORTEN SR., a leading African American activist in Philadelphia. Her mother, grandmother, and aunts had been among the founding members of the interracial Philadelphia Female Anti-Slavery Society (PFASS). Prominent figures such as the abolitionist William Lloyd Garrison and the Quaker poet and abolitionist John Greenleaf Whittier were friends of the Fortens. Whittier wrote a poem, "To the Daughters of James Forten."

Both privilege and misfortune marked the early life of Charlotte Forten. Although a very talented and well-educated man, Robert Forten never achieved financial stability. By the time he joined the family business, the sailmaking industry had been undermined by new steam-propelled vessels. Charlotte's mother died in 1840. Consequently, Charlotte spent most of her first years in the homes of her grandmother and of her aunt HARRIET FORTEN PURVIS, the wife of the wealthy and mixed-race ROBERT PURVIS, who led the black reform community after James Forten died. Encountering a rapidly hardening racial climate, including mob violence and black disfranchisement in Pennsylvania, Purvis in 1842 moved his household from Philadelphia to the Quaker suburb of Byberry.

The inferior and segregated Pennsylvania schools prompted Robert Forten to send his daughter to Massachusetts to complete her education. In 1853 Charlotte was enrolled in the Higginson Grammar School in Salem. Following the examples of her aunts, particularly MARGARETTA FORTEN, a teacher, and SARAH LOUISA FORTEN PURVIS, who composed poetry, Charlotte decided to teach and to devote her skills to "elevate the race." After graduating from the Higginson School in February of 1855 and the Salem Normal School in July of 1856, she began teaching at the previously all-white Epes Grammar School of Salem.

In Massachusetts, Forten joined an expanding circle of abolitionists, including African Americans CHARLES LENOX REMOND (in whose home she lived briefly) and his sister SARAH PARKER REMOND, who were agents for the American Anti-Slavery Society, and white abolitionists Maria Weston Chapman and Lydia Maria Child, leading members of the Boston Female Anti-Slavery Society. This abolitionist community supported Forten's literary aspirations. In the *Liberator* Garrison published her "Poem for Normal School Graduates" in 1856. One of her last works, "Personal Recollections of Whittier," published in *New England Magazine* in 1893, honored the poet who had immortalized her aunts more than a half century earlier. Although Forten possessed a facility for writing and would continue to publish her poems and essays in reform and literary magazines for decades to come, her ambitions as a writer were never fully realized.

Forten has become best known for the diary she began in 1854. Consisting of four volumes that record her thoughts and experiences between 1854 and 1864 and a fifth volume covering the years from 1885 to 1892, Forten's journal provides valuable insight into the experiences of the black elite. Early diary entries reveal the struggle of a young woman of African ancestry in an era when the assumption of Anglo-Saxon superiority went virtually unchallenged. Measuring herself against European standards of beauty and morality led to feelings of inadequacy and depression, which probably influenced her physical health. Severe headaches and ongoing respiratory illness interrupted her work as a teacher between 1857 and 1862, during which time she traveled back and forth between Philadelphia and Massachusetts.

When she recovered sufficiently, Forten joined the ranks of "Yankee School Marms" who traveled to the Union-controlled Sea Islands of South Carolina to educate erstwhile slaves left behind in large numbers by fleeing or absentee masters. Under the auspices of the Philadelphia Port Royal Relief Society, she became in 1862 the first African American teacher on St. Helena Island, working at a school conducted by the teacher and physician Laura Towne. Her writings from this period again reveal the tensions and contradictions in her life. She was, especially at first, enthusiastic about her mission, but her background—so very different from that of the population she served—sometimes limited her rapport with the Sea Islanders. Her relations with certain white colleagues, at the same time, were circumscribed by the racism that she suspected even some of the most well-disposed among them harbored. The death of her father, who had enlisted in the Union army and had been recruiting other African Americans, as well as her declining enthusiasm, ill health, homesickness, and poor living conditions, caused Forten to return to the North in May 1864. That same month and the next, *Atlantic Monthly* published her account of the Sea Islands.

From 1865 until 1870 Forten was secretary of the Teacher Committee of the New England branch of the Freedmen's Union Commission in Boston, serving as a liaison between the teachers who labored among the newly freed people and their supporters in the North. In 1869 her translation of a French novel, Erckmann-Chatrian's *Therése; or, The Volunteers of '92*, was published. She spent the years 1870–1873 teaching, first at Robert L. Shaw Memorial School in Charleston and later at Summer High School, a black preparatory school in Washington, D.C. Turning to a profession newly opened to women during the Civil War era, she worked as a clerk in the Fourth Auditor's Office of the U.S. Treasury from 1873 until 1878, when she left to marry Francis J. Grimké, a divinity student twelve years her junior. A short time before their marriage FRANCIS GRIMKÉ had been ordained and appointed pastor to the Fifteenth Street Presbyterian Church in Washington.

Forten's marriage to Francis Grimké completed a unique circle of black and white abolitionists. Grimké, the son of the wealthy planter Henry Grimké of South Carolina and one of his slave women, Nancy Weston, was the nephew of two of the most famous white women abolitionists of the antebellum period, Angelina Emily Grimké and Sarah Grimké, who briefly had been members of PFASS, which the Forten Purvis women had helped found. Francis Grimké conducted the marriage ceremony, an interracial union, of FREDERICK DOUGLASS and his second wife, Helen Pitts.

The death a few months after the birth in 1880 of their only child, Theodora Cornelia, cast the only major shadow on the Forten-Grimké union. Illness plagued both at various times, and to improve his failing health, Francis Grimké was assigned to Jacksonville, Florida, where from 1885 to 1889 he was minister at the Laura Street Presbyterian Church. While in Jacksonville, Forten Grimké worked with the women of this church to provide social services for the local black community. She expanded these activities by becoming in 1896 a founding member of the National Association of Colored Women, which made major contributions to education, health, and other social services and to political activism, such as the antilynching campaign conducted by IDA B. WELLS-BARNETT.

After returning to Washington, Forten Grimké assumed additional family responsibilities by helping raise her husband's niece, ANGELINA WELD GRIMKÉ, the daughter of ARCHIBALD H. GRIMKÉ and Sarah Stanley, a white woman, who had proved unable to shoulder the burdens of an interracial family. In the 1890s Archibald and Angelina Weld Grimké became permanent members of the household of Francis and Charlotte Grimké.

In Angelina, Forten Grimké found both a focus for her maternal care and affection and an opportunity to nurture a literary talent. Living up to the family tradition of social activism, Angelina Weld Grimké used her talent to promote racial justice. In 1916 she wrote the play *Rachel*, a denunciation of the widespread lynching of that period and the first play written by an African American woman to be staged and performed, two years after the death of Forten Grimké.

After a long period of invalidism that left her bedridden for sixteen months, Forten Grimké died in Washington, D.C. Angelina Weld Grimké paid a final poetic tribute to her aunt in "To Keep the Memory of Charlotte Forten Grimké," which eulogized the "gentle spirit" who was both substitute mother and bearer of the family standard of political activism and intellectual endeavor.

FURTHER READING

The best source of information about Forten Grimké's life, character, and work are her diaries in the Moorland-Spingarn Research Center at Howard University, Washington, D.C.

Billington, Ray Allen, ed. *The Journal of Charlotte L. Forten* (1953).

Cooper, Anna Julia. *The Life and Writings of the Grimké Family* (1951).

Stevenson, Brenda, ed. *The Journals of Charlotte Forten Grimké* (1988).

This entry is taken from the *American National Biography* and is published here with the permission of the American Council of Learned Societies.

CAROLYN WILLIAMS

Grimké, Francis James (4 Nov. 1850–11 Oct. 1937), Presbyterian minister and civil rights activist, was born near Charleston, South Carolina, the son of Henry Grimké, a planter, and Nancy Weston, a biracial slave. As the second son of an unrecognized dalliance that was familiar to plantations such as Caneacres, young Grimké inherited his mother's status as servant. During the Civil War his white half brother sold him to a Confederate officer whom Grimké accompanied until the end of that conflict. The end of the war brought his manumission, and a benefactor from the Freedmen's Aid Society sent him to study at Lincoln University in Chester County, Pennsylvania.

Hard work and natural talent brought Grimké recognition on the campus. A newspaper account of the young scholar's outstanding record also attracted attention from his white aunts, Angelina Emily Grimké and Sarah Moore Grimké, who had been deeply involved in antislavery activities. After learning of the existence of a heretofore unknown nephew, the reformist sisters subsidized Grimké's education and remained in contact with him for the rest of their lives. After graduating from Lincoln in 1870, Grimké studied law for a time (1870–1871, 1872–1873 at Lincoln; 1874–1875 at Howard University) but at length decided to enter the Presbyterian ministry. In 1878 he completed training at Princeton Theological Seminary and was ordained.

In 1878 Grimké accepted an invitation to become pastor of the Fifteenth Street Presbyterian Church in Washington, D.C., inaugurating a ministerial career that spanned more than half a century. That same year he married Charlotte Forten (CHARLOTTE L. FORTEN GRIMKÉ), whom he had first met at a freedman school. The couple had one child who lived for a scant few months in 1880. The city of Washington grew rapidly in the last quarter of the nineteenth century, and Grimké made his church an eminent part of that rapid development. His fame as a pulpit orator spread, and members of all denominations as well as people with diverse ethnic identities attended his sermons.

Health problems due to overwork soon intervened, however, and Grimké viewed as providential an invitation to serve a church in Florida in 1885. He followed a more relaxed routine at the Laura Street Church in Jacksonville for four years, but he was ready to return to Washington when his old church pleaded for his help in 1889. Thereafter he became an even more important figure in aesthetic and literary circles in the nation's capital. But more significant than recognition for erudition and genteel manners among the black elite, he developed a reputation for passionate advocacy in struggles for racial justice. As Jim Crow laws became more manifest and lynching increased, he moved from an accommodationist philosophy represented by BOOKER T. WASHINGTON to a more strident demand for government action in protecting the civil rights of black American citizens.

Grimké displayed powerful intellect and eloquence in his sermons. Using such standard components as biblical exposition and illustrative material from classical literature, he shaped most of his addresses into what he called "helpful" sermons. His preaching included ideas about salvation and proper doctrine, but it focused primarily on questions of social relevance. In Grimké's view the Christian ministry functioned essentially as a moral teacher, and he used contemporary issues to apply those lessons. In his day racial prejudice made itself known through lynchings, disfranchisement, and Jim Crow legislation, especially in the areas of education and public transportation. Grimké denounced those abuses and rallied African American leaders to fight racist discrimination. He repeatedly stressed self-improvement as a means of achieving equal rights with other segments of American society. He urged character formation, moral integrity, and education as elements that commanded respect. Through industriousness black citizens could, he argued, insist on parity with whites because they deserved it.

In the years around 1895 Grimké moved from being an accommodationist to being a gadfly, impatient at slow progress and insistent on faster change. He criticized Booker T. Washington for being too meek, and his prophetic ardor did not diminish with age. In 1913, for instance, he wrote Woodrow Wilson that he had hoped Wilson's "accession to power would act as a check upon the brutal and insane spirit of race hatred that characterizes certain portions of the white people of the country." After faulting the president for lack of vigor, he reminded him that "all class distinctions among citizens are un-American, and the sooner every vestige of it is stamped out the better it will be for the Republic." He finally retired from the pulpit in 1928 and lived another nine years before dying in Washington.

FURTHER READING

A collection of Grimké's personal papers, sermons, and addresses is housed in the library at Howard University in the District of Columbia.

Ferry, Henry J. "Patriotism and Prejudice: Francis James Grimké on World War I," *Journal of Religious Thought* 32 (1975): 86–94.

Ferry, Henry J. "Racism and Reunion: A Black Protest by Francis J. Grimké," *Journal of Presbyterian History* 50 (1972): 77–88.

Weeks, Louis B. "Racism, World War I and the Christian Life: Francis J. Grimké in the Nation's Capital," *Journal of Presbyterian History* 51 (1973): 471–488.

Woodson, Carter G., ed. *The Works of Francis James Grimké* (4 vols., 1942).

This entry is taken from the *American National Biography* and is published here with the permission of the American Council of Learned Societies.

HENRY WARNER BOWDEN

Gronniosaw, James Albert Ukawsaw (c. 1710–c. 1773), slave narrative author, was born Ukawsaw Gronniosaw, probably between 1710 and 1714 in Bournou (Bornu), a kingdom in what is now northeastern Nigeria. He was the youngest child of the oldest daughter of the king of Bournou. All that is known about James Albert Ukawsaw Gronniosaw is found in *A Narrative of the Most Remarkable Particulars in the Life of James Albert Ukawsaw Gronniosaw, an African Prince, as Related by Himself* (1772), one of the earliest "as-told-to" slave narratives recorded by a white amanuensis. According to this account, Ukawsaw Gronniosaw, spiritually dissatisfied with the animist faith in which he was raised, alienated himself from his friends and relatives by his constant questions challenging their faith in physical objects, as well as by his growing belief in the existence of an uncreated creator. Consequently he became increasingly "dejected and melancholy."

When an African merchant from the Gold Coast invited the adolescent Gronniosaw to return with him to his home, more than a thousand miles away, Gronniosaw seized the opportunity. There, the merchant promised, Gronniosaw could play with boys his own age, and "see houses walk upon the water with wings to them, and the white folks." On arrival at the Gold Coast, however, the local king thought him a spy and decided to behead him. Affected by Gronniosaw's obvious courage in the face of death, the king relented, choosing to sell him into slavery rather than kill him. Rejected by a French slave trader because he was so small, Gronniosaw successfully implored a Dutch captain to buy him. On the voyage to Barbados, in a scene imitated in later slave narratives, Gronniosaw watched his new master reading, and thinking the book talked to the Dutchman, he held his ear close to it, hoping it would speak to him as well. He blamed his complexion for the book's silence.

A man named Vanhorn purchased him in Barbados and took him to New York City, where he was soon sold as a domestic slave to Theodorus Jacobus Frelinghuysen, a wealthy Dutch Reform clergyman in New Jersey and friend of the English evangelist George Whitefield. Introduced to Christianity by Frelinghuysen and to reading by his schoolmaster, Peter Van Arsdalen, Gronniosaw experienced despair when he became convinced that his own sins were too great to deserve salvation. Around 1747, after reading the spiritual writings of John Bunyan and Richard Baxter, an attempt at suicide, and a three-day illness, Gronniosaw experienced his own spiritual rebirth when he recalled the words from the Bible, "Behold the Lamb of God." Gronniosaw's newfound happiness was quickly ended by the death of his master, who freed him in his will, and by recurrent spiritual doubts. As a freeman Gronniosaw worked for various members of the Frelinghuysen family, all of whom, however, died within four years of the minister's death.

Having lost his friends in America, Gronniosaw decided to go to England and above all to Kidderminster, the birthplace of Baxter. Gronniosaw's reading and his experience in meeting Whitefield in New Jersey had convinced him that the English "people must be all *Righteous.*" During the Seven Years' War, known in North America as the French and Indian War, debts forced Gronniosaw to work his way across the Atlantic, first as a cook on a privateer, and later as an enlistee in the Twenty-eighth Regiment of Foot. His lack of interest in money caused him to be cheated repeatedly. Landing at Portsmouth, England, near the end of 1762 brought Gronniosaw further disappointment when he discovered the English to be no more pious than Americans. Disillusioned, Gronniosaw went to London, where Whitefield found him housing. There he fell in love at first sight with an English weaver named Betty, who introduced him to the preaching of the eminent Baptist minister Dr. Andrew Gifford.

After about three weeks in London, Gronniosaw agreed to go to Holland at the request of some friends of his late master Frelinghuysen, to be examined about his experiences and his faith by several Calvinist ministers. While there, he was hired as a butler in the household of a very rich Amsterdam merchant, who treated him more as friend than a servant, and whose wife wanted Gronniosaw to marry her maid, an attractive young woman who had saved a good deal of money. But Gronniosaw chose to return to London after a year to be baptized by Gifford and to wed Betty, despite the objections of his English friends to his marrying such a poor widow. Although Betty normally earned a good living as a weaver, Gronniosaw and his wife and growing family soon fell on hard times because of the postwar economic depression. Through a series of Quaker contacts, Gronniosaw was able to find employment outside of London, first in

Colchester, then Norwich, and later Kidderminster. Unfortunately, much of his work was seasonal, leading to long periods of deprivation and near-starvation during the winters, with the brief exception of the time spent in Norwich, where Betty was also able to find employment before their children contracted smallpox. They experienced the generosity of benefactors like Henry Gurney, a Quaker worsted manufacturer and banker in Norwich. But they also suffered the cruelty of an unnamed Baptist minister, Quakers, and an Anglican minister, all of whom refused to give a proper burial to one of Gronniosaw's daughters, who had died of fever in Norwich. His *Narrative* closes with the "very poor Pilgrims" living in abject poverty in Kidderminster, their faith in God still intact.

Dedicated to Selina Hastings, Countess of Huntingdon, Gronniosaw's *Narrative* was first advertised in December 1772 in *Boddley's Bath Journal*. According to its preface, written by the countess's cousin, Walter Shirley, the *Narrative* "was taken from his own Mouth, and committed to Paper by the elegant Pen of a young LADY of the Town of LEOMINSTER." In 1809 the "young LADY" was identified, probably incorrectly, as Hannah More. By 1800 the *Narrative* had appeared in at least ten editions in England and America, as well as in a Welsh translation (1779) and serial publication in the *American Moral and Sentimental Magazine* in New York (1797).

The publication of Gronniosaw's *Narrative* in 1772 marked the beginning of the modern anglophone tradition of autobiographies written or dictated by slaves of African descent. As a foundational text, the *Narrative* contains many tropes, themes, character types, events, historical figures, and situations that reappear in various ways in subsequent writings by and about African British and African American figures. Perhaps most significantly, Gronniosaw's *Narrative* introduced in anglophone-African writing the trope of the "talking book," by which an illiterate African is introduced to the concept of reading. Although Paul Edwards first identified the trope in the narratives of Gronniosaw, JOHN MARRANT, Quobna Ottobah Cugoano, OLAUDAH EQUIANO, and JOHN JEA, the significance of the relationship between literacy and freedom was subsequently developed at length by HENRY LOUIS GATES JR. in *The Signifying Monkey* (1988).

FURTHER READING

Gronniosaw, James Albert Ukawsaw. *A Narrative of the Most Remarkable Particulars in the Life of James Albert Ukawsaw Gronniosaw, an African Prince, as Related by Himself* (1772).

Costanzo, Angelo. *Surprising Narrative: Olaudah Equiano and the Beginnings of Black Autobiography* (1987).

Gates, Henry Louis, Jr. "The Trope of the Talking Book," in *The Signifying Monkey: A Theory of Afro-American Literary Criticism* (1988).

VINCENT CARRETTA

Grooms, Anthony (15 Jan. 1955–), novelist, poet, and creative writing professor, was born in Louisa County, Virginia, a rural community 120 miles south of Washington, D.C., the eldest of six children of Dellaphine Scott, a textile worker and housewife, and Robert E. Grooms, a refrigerator mechanic. A clever and curious child with an affinity for the written and spoken word, Grooms was encouraged by his parents to explore his intellectual and creative desires to the fullest. Though an excellent student, the young Tony may have learned more from the social project in which he participated. In 1967 his parents enrolled him in a Freedom of Choice plan that was one of the forerunners to the racial integration of public schools in Virginia.

In 1971 T. C. Williams High School in Alexandria, Virginia, served as the only high school in that community. Following a spate of court decisions that struck down racially segregated schools, the integrated school experienced numerous challenges, not the least of which was the demotion of its white football coach to assistant and the selection of a black coach as his replacement. The 1971 football team won the state championship and achieved immortality in the film *Remember the Titans* (2000), starring DENZEL WASHINGTON and Will Patton. It was in this turbulent but transforming atmosphere of black students and students from other nonwhite backgrounds gaining entrance to historically white educational institutions that Grooms found himself as he came of age in the late 1960s and early 1970s.

By the time he had earned his BA degree in theater and speech from the College of William and Mary in 1978, the destiny Grooms saw for himself as a wordsmith, as a linguistic and cultural steward of "everyday" or "ordinary" African Americans in the South of the 1950s and 1960s, had begun to take shape. While he is best known for his fiction, Grooms emerged on the literary scene with *Ice Poems* (1988), a chapbook that revealed his fastidious use of language as well as his belief in the transforming power of verse. Following this publication, Grooms's poetry appeared in *Atlanta Magazine*,

Chattahoochee Review, *Crab Orchard Review*, *Georgia Journal*, *Catalyst*, and numerous other journals and magazines.

As his endeavors in verse revealed, Grooms did not limit himself by genre. In his debut short story collection, *Trouble No More* (1995), Grooms offered tales about southern African Americans in the 1950s and 1960s whose personalities and politics vary, and whose responses to the abuses of the segregated South are anything but homogenous. As Diptiranjan Pattanaik remarked, Grooms was interested in exploring the universal human condition through the twentieth-century African American experience. His characters' "private heroism and cowardice, commitments and betrayals, triumphs and failures show how hard it is to stereotype any group of people by their sole membership in any particular race, gender, or nationality" (*MELUS* 24.3 [Fall 1999], 194). For *Trouble No More* the liberal Southern Regional Council awarded Grooms its highly coveted Lillian Smith Award.

In *Bombingham* (2001), a historical novel, Grooms mined the historical record to bring to life both the wonderful and traumatic black experience in Birmingham, Alabama, in the 1960s. Centered on the youth-led black protest movements of the early 1960s, the novel revolves around a young man named Walter Burke. The novel opens with Burke on the killing fields of Vietnam seeking the will and words to write home to the parents of one of his buddies that their son has been killed under the most brutal of circumstances. As he tries to fashion this letter, his mind takes him back to the first war in which he was involved when, as a young boy, he, his sister, and other children risked their lives in the fight to achieve African American voting rights and political visibility.

As Grooms moved back and forth from Vietnam to Birmingham (called "Bombingham" because of the notorious spate of bombings in black communities), readers must confront their own personal and collective histories and imaginations. Somehow, in the midst of insidious oppression, Walter's family and the black community emerge from the racial maelstrom not flawless but standing with a good measure of dignity. So inspirational and insightful was this portrait of African American life that the Southern Regional Council again gave Grooms the Lillian Smith Award, making him the first person to receive the award twice.

In addition to Grooms's accomplishments as a creative writer, he gained recognition as a teacher and administrator. Standing firmly in his belief that art is the universal common denominator, Grooms celebrated the artistic endeavor as one of the most powerful means of social transformation. Having participated in similar programs in Montepulciano, Italy (2003), and Cape Coast, Ghana (2001), Grooms received a Fulbright award for study abroad in Sweden in 2005. As his body of work and teaching experience reveal, the world was Grooms's imaginative canvas.

FURTHER READING

Maurer, David A. "Professor Put Writer on His Career Path," *Daily Progress*, 7 Sept. 1992.

Melville, Sylvia. "Interview with Anthony Grooms," *Chattahoochee Review* 5.4 (Summer 2002).

O'Briant, Don. "The Practice of Writing," *Atlanta Journal-Constitution*, 19 July 1992.

JEFFREY B. LEAK

Grooms, Bruce E. (30 Mar. 1958–), U.S. naval officer, submarine commander, and Commandant of Midshipmen at the U.S. Naval Academy, was born in Cleveland, Ohio, to Gilbert Grooms, a postal worker, and his wife Julietta Grooms, a homemaker. Grooms grew up in Maple Heights, a suburb of Cleveland, and was a skilled basketball player at Maple Heights High School. However, Grooms's parents urged him to go to college, so he also focused on academics. Grooms considered several of the service academies when deciding on which college to attend, but eventually chose the naval academy to pursue a career as an aviator, as well as to play for its highly regarded college basketball program. And so, following his high school graduation in 1976, Grooms entered the naval academy as part of the Class of 1980.

Grooms came to the naval academy at an exciting time in its history: not only were racial discrimination issues largely a thing of the past, but 1976 was also the first year that the academy accepted female midshipmen and, as Grooms would later recall, most of the focus was on this groundbreaking event. Well prepared academically for the service, Grooms majored in aerospace engineering and excelled in his studies. In 1979, Grooms entered the navy's submarine program; traditionally a volunteer service, for Grooms and other members of the Class of 1980 who had chosen other areas of study, it was required. The drive toward a 600-ship navy was well under way in the late 1970s as the cold war continued, and would soon gain further support under President Ronald Reagan. Because of this build-up, the navy had a serious shortage of officer candidates in the Submarine Force. Although the experiment of drafting midshipmen into the submarine program would ultimately be considered a failure and was never repeated, the Submarine Force nevertheless made a fine catch when it selected Grooms, even if he was less than enthused by his assignment. Indeed, Grooms excelled at his nuclear studies and in March 1982 gained his first assignment as a junior officer on USS *Jacksonville* under Commander Phil Davis.

It was on the *Jacksonville*, during an around-the-world cruise and in cold war operations in the North Atlantic that Grooms learned about leadership under difficult conditions from a commanding officer with superb tactical skills, and he would later successfully apply this knowledge to his future commands. After his time on the *Jacksonville*, from 1982–86, Grooms returned to the naval academy, serving as a company officer from 1986–1988. A satisfying tour of duty, it was here that Grooms continued the development of his own leadership skills, while at the same time developing the leadership skills of the midshipmen that he mentored. One of these midshipmen was Roger Isom, who would one day become just the ninth African American naval officer ever to command a United States submarine, and who later credited Grooms with inspiring him to become a submariner. Grooms's time serving as a company officer at Annapolis was made even more enjoyable with his marriage in August 1988 to Emily J. Penn, a real estate agent.

Following this assignment, Bruce Grooms served aboard the missile boat *John C. Calhoun* as a department head from 1989–92 before gaining his masters degree in National Security and Strategic Studies at the Naval War College in Newport, Rhode Island. Bruce Grooms returned to sea in 1993, serving as executive officer on USS *Pasadena* for two years and gaining further valuable experience during two rigorous deployments to the Persian Gulf. Upon his return to the United States in August 1995, Grooms was a National Security Affairs Fellow at Stanford University and underwent further submarine command training from 1995–97.

In the fall of 1997 Grooms was named commanding officer of USS *Asheville*, thereby becoming the seventh member of the Centennial 7, the first seven black submarine commanders in the Submarine Force's first 100 years. True to his ideal of having a positive effect on the naval careers of those that served under him, Grooms did just that on *Asheville*. In addition to a number of fleet awards, Grooms's ship was also awarded the Fleet Recreation Award for the best quality of life programs, the Golden and Silver Anchor for the highest retention rate, and the Battle "E" Efficiency Award. Indeed, Grooms had a knack for dealing with people; on his first boat he recalled that it was "a successful ship partially because of the weak performers we took on from other ships. We had a Round Peg-Square Hole Club in which we believed there was a place for everyone … in the environment that was fostered people thrived. *Asheville* was a fantastic experience." Grooms's leadership and ship-handling skills were recognized by his peers in the entire Pacific Fleet when he won the Vice Admiral Stockdale Inspirational Leadership Award in 1999. Coming on the heels of Cecil Haney's 1998 Stockdale Award, the receipt of this award two years in a row by an African American submarine commander was an incredible sign of just how far the navy had come in promoting diversity.

Upon leaving the *Asheville*, Grooms's other assignments included that of Senior Inspector, Atlantic Fleet Nuclear Propulsion Examining Board (1999–2001), Senior Military Aide to the Under Secretary of Defense for Policy (2001–2003), and Commander of Submarine Squadron Six (2003–2005). In 2005 Grooms made history again when he was named the eighty-first Commandant of Midshipmen at the naval academy, the first African American ever to hold this position whose civilian equivalent is that of college dean. Grooms called his two years there "a wonderful tour and one of those jobs most people would love to have … acting as cheerleader, father confessor, and disciplinarian. My interactions with the midshipmen resulted in lifelong mentoring connections." Grooms served as the Commandant of Midshipmen at the naval academy from 2005 to 2007 before being named Deputy Director, Submarine Warfare Division, Chief of Naval Operations N87B and stationed in Washington, D.C. at the Pentagon. Elevated to flag rank on 1 June 2007, Rear Admiral Grooms moved to the Washington, D.C., area with his wife and their two sons, Geoff and Jared.

FURTHER READING

The information for this entry, including all quotations, came from the author's telephone interview with Bruce Grooms on 9 March 2007 and subsequent e-mail exchanges.

Knoblock, Glenn A. *Black Submariners in the United States Navy, 1940-1975* (2005).

Smith, Mike. "Creating Opportunities; Naval Academy Commandant of Midshipmen Molds Future Warriors," *Undersea Warfare* 7 (Winter 2006).

GLENN ALLEN KNOBLOCK

Grosvenor, Verta Mae Smart (4 Apr. 1938–), culinary anthropologist, poet, performing artist, and journalist, was born Verta Mae Smart in Fairfax, South Carolina, the daughter of Frank Smart. She grew up in Monk's Corner, South Carolina, and as a teenager moved to Philadelphia, Pennsylvania, where she attended Kensington High School. Grosvenor married twice, first to Robert S. Grosvenor and later to Ellensworth Ausby, and had two children.

Grosvenor's early life in the South Carolina Lowcountry was enormously influential in her later career, grounding her in a cultural milieu that was thoroughly Geechee (or Gullah) in language (her first language was the Creole known as Gullah), in ritual, and perhaps most importantly to her later work, in food. Geechee communities of the American South have retained African linguistic and cultural practices.

At the age of thirty-two, in 1970, Grosvenor published her culinary memoir *Vibration Cooking; or, The Travel Notes of a Geechee Girl*, an innovative work that combined recipes, personal anecdotes, and political commentary. Her use of language and melding of her own life history with recipes from her childhood and from her travels in black communities around the world made the book an unequivocal success because it fit into the period's culturally conscious African American emphasis on heritage. The book was reissued first in 1986 and then again in 1992. Also in 1970 she contributed "The Kitchen Crisis" to TONI CADE BAMBARA's anthology *The Black Woman*.

In 1972 Grosvenor published *Thursdays and Every Other Sunday Off*, a meditation on the lives of working-class black women. Throughout the decade she published both nonfiction and poetry in *Essence* and *Ebony* magazines, and in 1973 she contributed to SONIA SANCHEZ's compendium *We Be Word Sorcerers*. While nurturing her writing career, Grosvenor also ventured into work in the performing arts, joining the avant-garde jazz musician SUN RA's Solar Arkestra in 1972 and appearing in his 1974 film *Space Is the Place*. Also during the 1970s she was part of a group of black women who met regularly in New York City and called themselves the Sisterhood. Among the participants were the writers TONI MORRISON, ALICE WALKER, NTOZAKE SHANGE, and JUNE JORDAN.

In the early 1980s Grosvenor was both a script contributor and a cast member in the writer ISHMAEL REED and the director BILL GUNN's black soap opera *Personal Problems*, in which she played Johnnie Mae Brown, a nurse's aide at Harlem Hospital. *Personal Problems* was considered the first black serial in this genre.

Grosvenor continued her work with food of the African diaspora, and in 1982, while serving as a contributing editor for *Élan* magazine, she traveled to Brazil to further her research on foodways of the black Atlantic. In 1985 she took her work into the Spanish-speaking Caribbean when she joined a delegation of writers and artists sponsored by the periodical the *Black Scholar* that visited Cuba. The group included the poets AUDRE LORDE, MARI EVANS, and JAYNE CORTEZ, the writers Bambara and Rosa Guy, and the sculptor Melvin Edwards.

Throughout the 1980s Grosvenor continued to publish work on food and culture not only in *Essence* magazine but also in the *New York Times*, the *Village Voice*, *Life*, and *Redbook*, and she contributed to the writer and activist AMIRI BARAKA's 1983 volume *Confirmation: An Anthology of African American Women*. Grosvenor expanded the scope of her journalistic work into other media, appearing on numerous television programs. She focused most of her efforts, though, on building a presence on National Public Radio, working on *All Things Considered* and with the organization's Cultural Desk. While there she produced numerous pieces on African American life and culture, including her Robert F. Kennedy Award–winning "Daufuskie: Never Enough Too Soon" and "Slave Voices: Things Past Telling." She received a Dupont-Columbia Award for the 1990 program "AIDS and Black America: Breaking the Silence" and in 1991 a Communications Excellence to Black America (CEBA) Award for "Marcus Garvey: Twentieth-Century Pan-Africanist." In 1992 she received a commendation from the National Association of Black Journalists for her segment "South Africa and the African-American Experience," on the NPR program *All Things Considered* and in 1996 she won the prestigious James Beard Foundation Award for hosting "Seasonings," another NPR project but one that focused on food and culture.

In the late 1980s Grosvenor composed the "culinary folk opera" *Nyam*, a multimedia piece that tells the story of the retention, adaptation, and creative reordering of West African culinary practices in the New World. In the Gullah lexicon *nyam* means "to eat," and her opera, through song, dance, humor, and visual art, explores the multifaceted nature of black food practices on the U.S. side of the Atlantic. The opera has played to numerous audiences throughout the United States with a number of casts, including a production in 1988 at Harlem's Riverside Church that featured the famed jazz musicians Hugh Masekela and Olu Dara.

In 1991 Grosvenor contributed, as a featured performer, language consultant, and producer, to JULIE DASH's *Daughters of the Dust*, a film that tells the story of successive generations of an African American family in the Georgia Sea Islands during the late nineteenth century and early twentieth century. Later in the decade she worked on another film, Jonathan Demme and OPRAH WINFREY's 1998 film adaptation of Toni Morrison's novel *Beloved*. In this same year she also served as the narrator on the documentary project *The Language You Cry In: The Story of a Mende Song*, which tells the story of the retention of a Sierra Leonean funereal song among members of a Gullah family in Georgia. Owing to the range and depth of her work on the Lowcountry, for a significant period of time in the 1990s Grosvenor was writer-in-residence at the Penn Center, a renowned Gullah cultural center on St. Helena's Island off of South Carolina, and she also served on the state art commission's Literary Task Force. Grosvenor returned to food writing, publishing *Vertamae Cooks in the Americas' Family Kitchen* in 1996 and *Vertamae Cooks Again* in 1999.

FURTHER READING

Smart-Grosvenor, Vertamae. *Vibration Cooking; or, the Travel Notes of a Geechee Girl* (1970).

Garland, Phyl. "Vibes from Verta Mae," *Ebony* (Mar. 1971).

Publishers Weekly. *The Author Speaks: Selected PW Interviews 1967–1976* (1977).

VANESSA AGARD-JONES

Grovey, R. R. (22 Aug. 1890–1 Oct. 1961), civil rights and labor activist, was born in Brazoria County, Texas, the son of the landowners Thomas and Nellie Grovey. The oldest of four children and the only one to finish high school, he graduated from A. J. Moore High School in Waco, Texas, in 1910. He then earned a degree from Tillotson College (now Huston-Tillotson University) in Austin, Texas, in 1914. After a brief stint as a school principal, Grovey in 1916 married a Prairie View College (now Prairie View A & M University) student, Ethel Nathan, from Brenham in Waller County. The next year, following the birth of their son, the family embraced the Great Migration and moved to Houston. They considered Houston a good place to raise a family, despite the drawbacks of segregation and the tumultuous Houston Riot that engulfed the city that same year.

To be sure, the couple in some ways identified with the black soldiers of the 24th United States Infantry, who had taken up arms during the 1917 Houston Riot. They too hated racial segregation and inequality, resisting daily. Relying on what the historian Robin D. G. Kelley calls "infrapolitics," the Groveys, for example, conducted business and signed documents using their first and middle initials, followed by their last name, thereby never disclosing their full name and risking humiliation. Grovey's protest imagination went further. Tired of taking orders and feeling undervalued, Grovey in the 1920s left a skilled job as a boilermaker's helper at Houston and Texas Central Railroad and enrolled in barber school, in time opening a barbershop in the Third Ward on Dowling St. Grovey soon used his barbershop as a meeting place for the community, especially the working poor.

Motivated by ongoing conversations at his shop about the perpetual racial divide, Grovey in the late 1920s founded a political-action organization, the Third Ward Civic Club (TWCC), one that intersected civic reform with labor organizing. The organization protested wage differentials, poor city services, crime, police brutality, segregation, and led labor strikes. Grovey also sought to unite African Americans across class lines, believing that a well-executed united front in the community could mean the start of a concerted civil-rights agenda.

Racial exclusion in politics particularly frustrated many African Americans in Texas. In 1923 the state passed the White Democratic Primary law and explicitly barred African Americans from voting in local and statewide primary elections. Like other former Confederate states, Texas had a single political party—the Democratic Party. Interestingly, other southern states used Democratic political machines, which most considered private organizations and outside state control, to disfranchise African Americans through implicit means. White Texans, paradoxically, frustrated with what they considered a growing Black political threat, for example, continued voting rights in local elections, the rise of the NAACP, and direct challenges to white hegemony, including resistance to violence, adopted a maneuver that explicitly violated the constitutional rights of Blacks.

Black Texans, unabashed, took the state to court in response to the election law. The Supreme Court in *Nixon v. Herndon* (1927) and *Nixon v. Conden* (1932) ruled that these white primary laws, including a new statute passed following the *Herndon* decision, did in fact violate the 14th amendment rights of black Texans. Even after the rulings, Texas continued to discriminate against African Americans with the use of effective legal maneuvers. Black Texans like R. R. Grovey, unmoved, continued their fight.

Grovey and the TWCC worked with the newly formed Independent Colored Voter's League, which sought ways to address the statewide election abuses. Grovey and the TWCC in 1928 also joined forces with other Houstonians and formed the Harris County Negro Democratic Club in an attempt to unite African Americans against a common foe. The organization staged mass demonstrations and boycotts, published editorials in newspapers, and held debates on local radio programs. Black Texans got behind the men. Women's clubs held fundraisers, and ministers in the pulpit advocated continued defiance. The group also launched lawsuits against political officials who upheld the biased law.

Grovey in 1932 filed a lawsuit against the election judge Albert Townsend, charging the official with violating his constitutional rights when he refused to issue him a ballot. In what many considered a controversial move, with the financial backing of local Houstonians but without the assistance of the national NAACP, Grovey took the case to the U.S. Supreme Court. The national office expressed some apprehension about the suit, fearful a negative verdict could reverse the organization's efforts. A loophole—suing for damages under twenty dollars—allowed the attorneys to forgo the Texas Appellate and High Courts and take the case directly to the United States Supreme Court. This time the Court ruled in favor of the defendant, arguing the Democratic Party and other political organizations were "voluntary associations for political action ... not the creatures of the state ... [with] ... power to determine ... membership and ... [eligibility] ... in the party's primaries." Many, according to historian Darlene Clark Hine, compared the devastating ruling to the Supreme Court's *Dred Scott* decision of 1857 and blamed the defeat on Grovey and his attorneys. Determined to rewrite history, Houstonians and the NAACP continued their assault, ultimately invalidating the white primary with the *Smith v. Allwright* decision (1944).

Black Houstonians, however, turned on Grovey. Middle-class professionals in particular resented how whites and the media criticized African Americans. Blacks threatened Grovey, verbally attacked the family, and stopped patronizing his barbershop. Even members of the NAACP, according to daughter Nell Grovey Cole, branded the activist a troublemaker.

Hardly phased by the community's pretensions, Grovey continued fighting for the rights of others. Grovey and the TWCC in the late 1930s and 1940s worked almost exclusively with the Congress of Industrial Organizations (CIO) in its attempt to organize black workers. Propelled by the 1946 national steelworkers strike, Grovey and the CIO forced Houston companies to agree to a seventeen-cent wage increase. Unfortunately, the CIO acquiesced to the Hughes Tool Company's demands that job classifications based on race remain. According to the historian Michael Boston, CIO staffer Grovey, like African American company unionists who blindly supported the discriminatory practices of industrialists, failed to acknowledge the racism within the CIO; still, it could also be argued that Grovey achieved what he could within the system, and made at least a tangible improvement in wages. Only in the 1960s with the successful modern civil rights movement did wage differentials in these firms end. Grovey, who also served as chair of the NAACP legal redress committee, died in 1960.

FURTHER READING

Botson, Michael R., Jr. *Labor, Civil Rights, and the Hughes Tool Company* (2005).

Hine, Darlene Clark. *Black Victory: The Rise and Fall of the White Primary in Texas* (2003).

Pitre, Merline. *In Struggle against Jim Crow: Lulu B. White and the NAACP, 1900–1957* (1999).

BERNADETTE PRUITT

Gryce, Gigi (28 Nov. 1927–17 Mar. 1983), jazz saxophonist, flutist, and composer, was born in Pensacola, Florida, and grew up in Hartford, Connecticut. The names and occupations of his parents are not known. Gryce was the product of a highly musical family: his brother and four sisters were classically trained on a variety of instruments. In his youth Gryce attended music school in Hartford, developing his skills on flute, alto saxophone, clarinet, and piano. In 1946 he began performing in and around Hartford, both as a sideman and as the leader of his own twenty-three-piece group. In 1948 Gryce moved to Boston to attend the Boston Conservatory, where he studied composition and instrumentation with Daniel Pinkham and Alan Hovahness. In 1952 he won a Fulbright scholarship to study music in Paris, where he continued his instruction in composition with the famed composer Arthur Honegger.

Gryce returned to the United States in 1953 and quickly established his reputation on alto saxophone as a dynamic and original soloist in a bebop style similar to that of CHARLIE PARKER. In 1953 Gryce performed and recorded with MAX ROACH, CLIFFORD BROWN, and HOWARD MCGHEE in New York City; worked with the TAD DAMERON band in Atlantic City, New Jersey; and toured the United States and Europe with LIONEL HAMPTON's group for six months. While in Europe Gryce composed and recorded several original arrangements, including "Paris the Beautiful," "Capri," "Consultation," "Eleanor," "Simplicity," and "Brown Skins," which was performed by a twenty-piece orchestra featuring Clifford Brown on trumpet. In 1954 Gryce performed on recordings with DONALD BYRD, LEE MORGAN, and THELONIOUS MONK. In 1955 he led his own group, the Jazz Lab Quintet, which included Byrd on trumpet, Wade Legge on piano, Wendell Marshall on bass, and Arthur Taylor on drums. The group recorded one LP, *Gigi Gryce and the Jazz Lab Quintet* (1960), which ironically was one of Gryce's less experimental recordings but nonetheless received praise from reviewers. From 1955 through 1957 Gryce also wrote and performed with the Duke Jordan and OSCAR PETTIFORD bands. From 1959 through 1961 Gryce led a new quintet, featuring Richard Williams on trumpet, Richard Wyands on piano, Julian Euell on bass, and Mickey Roker on drums. In 1960 this fivesome recorded *The Rat Race Blues*, considered by many jazz critics to be Gryce's finest and most original album.

Through the 1950s Gryce also produced several well-known compositions, most notably "Nica's Tempo," which he wrote for Art Farmer and the Jazz Messengers; "Capri," written for J. J. JOHNSON; and "Speculation" and "Minority," which were recorded by several bebop bands in the 1950s and 1960s. In 1961 Gryce retired from performing and became a music teacher. He died in Pensacola, Florida.

Though never considered a virtuoso performer, Gryce was one of the most proficient alto saxophonists of the bebop era. His playing lent an unusual classical technique to the more "organic" structures of bop, yet he never sought to merge European music with jazz. He was best known for his writing, which included several compositions that became jazz standards, especially popular with bop and postbop groups of the 1950s and 1960s.

FURTHER READING

Cohen, Noal, and Michael Fitzgerald. *Rat Race Blues: The Musical Life of Gigi Gryce* (2002).

Hentoff, Nat. "A New Jazz Corporation: Gryce, Farmer," *Down Beat* 22, no. 21 (1955).

Horricks, Raymond. *These Jazzmen of Our Time* (1959). This entry is taken from the *American National Biography* and is published here with the permission of the American Council of Learned Societies.

THADDEUS RUSSELL

Guilford, William (5 Feb. 1844– ? Oct. 1909), harness maker, state legislator, community organizer, and barber, was born on James Spier's farm, the Hurricane Place, three and a half miles from Thomaston, Upson County, Georgia, the fourth child of GUILFORD SPEER and Viney, two of Spier's slaves. Guilford and Viney separated soon after William was born, and Guilford moved to Thomaston to operate a harness and shoe shop. William probably spent his earliest years with his mother, his three elder brothers, and several younger half siblings on the Hurricane Place, but by the late 1850s William had undoubtedly moved to the village and was learning his father's trade of harness making. In 1863 a devastating fire destroyed three-quarters of downtown Thomaston, and thereafter William probably worked in a shop organized by his father in Barnesville, Pike County, sixteen miles away.

Sometime during the Civil War, William married Lourinda, presumably a slave but whose prior history is unknown. Census sources suggest that they had eleven children, nine of whom survived childhood. The slave regime in Upson County collapsed dramatically on 19 April 1865, when Major General James H. Wilson's Union cavalry arrived and camped overnight in Thomaston on its way to capture Macon. During the subsequent military occupation, federal forces confirmed and enforced the emancipation of Upson County's slaves.

After emancipation William took his father's given name, Guilford, as his surname. In doing so he asserted his patrilineal descent and his independence from any previous owner's name; in contrast, both his mother and his father took the surname Speer. Guilford worked in Barnesville and Thomaston at trade and mercantile jobs through 1870. He had learned to read and write, although not well; another hand penned at least one of his more important letters.

Guilford organized the first anniversary Emancipation Celebration in Upson County on 29 May 1866. The Freedman's Bureau agent, one of five invited speakers, wrote that the event was "a brilliant Celebration" (National Archives, RG 105 [M798, roll 27], James W. Greene to Davis Tillson, 30 May 1866). Guilford served many years as president of the Upson County Colored Celebration Association (later the Emancipation Proclamation Committee) that organized the annual celebrations on 29 May. He was often grand marshal of the parade.

Soon after emancipation Guilford immersed himself in politics and education. In 1866 he was sales agent in Pike and Upson counties for the *Loyal Georgian*, one of Georgia's leading Republican newspapers. Guilford, his father, and other freedmen organized a short-lived Upson County branch of the Georgia Equal Rights and Educational Association in 1866. The primary goal of this association was to establish schools for freed people, and Guilford represented Upson at the Georgia Education Convention in Macon in May 1867. Guilford's efforts to establish a permanent school in Thomaston stumbled over the dual obstacles of finding a house in which to hold class and money to pay a teacher. Upson had to wait until October 1869, when the pastor of Thomaston's African Methodist Episcopal (AME) church opened a freedmen's school in the sanctuary.

When U.S. military authorities organized a statewide voter registration in 1867, Guilford was appointed one of three registrars for the Twenty-fifth District, which included Upson, Talbot, and Harris counties. He helped register over sixteen hundred men, half of them black, and gained the political opportunity to meet each potential voter.

Guilford's nomination as voting registrar prompted petitions of protest and letters of support that reveal a complex tapestry in local politics. His detractors included rural planters, self-described "old citizens," who characterized Guilford as "an extra officious individual & up-start." A petition from freedmen, including names of several well-known town tradesmen and three founders of Thomaston's AME church, declared Guilford "very unreliable and unfit for the office" (RG 393, Part 1, Entry 5783, petitions enclosed in John B. McCoy to E. Hulbert, 19 June 1867). Guilford's white backers included native-born Republicans, among them town lawyers and county officials, who declared him "well qualified and competent." Freedmen in the local Union Club supported Guilford because he had "represented the Colored people in their councils of deliberations for over twelve months" (RG 393, Part 1, Entry 5786, enclosures in Charles Wilson et al. to [John R.] Lewis and C.C. Sibley, 5 June 1867).

In October 1867 Guilford was elected to a seat representing Upson County at the state constitutional convention. He was only twenty-three years old when he arrived in Atlanta on 9 December 1867, and for the next four months he participated in this parliamentary process and met the men who would lead the state's Republican Party.

Taking full advantage of his name recognition and recent experiences, Guilford ran for county representative in the April 1868 elections but lost to John C. Drake, a former state senator and one of the most prominent white citizens of Upson County. Guilford protested to the federal military authorities that Drake was ineligible to take the required loyalty oath due to his previous support of the Confederacy. Eventually, language in the Congressional Reorganization Act of 1869 disqualified Drake, and Guilford, as runner-up in the 1868 election, took his seat in January 1870. Guilford's legislative career was short and relatively uneventful; he introduced two bills, one to organize volunteer military companies and the other to amend jury laws. Neither bill passed. Guilford wrote a letter to his constituents that was published in Thomaston's *Georgia Herald*, but the editor made fun of his poor spelling and composition.

Guilford ran for state senator in December 1870 but was defeated by the Democratic candidate, 941 votes to 779. Although he never held another public office, he promoted Republican Party politics in Thomaston for fourteen more years, attending meetings and giving speeches up to the November 1884 elections. The *Thomaston Times* (29 Nov. 1884) may have exaggerated in declaring that "the Independent and Republican parties are dead in Upson," but the local paper did not note any political activity by Guilford thereafter.

Guilford energetically applied himself to the social activities of his black community and Thomaston's AME church. Besides his work with the annual Emancipation Celebration, he managed an amateur theatrical troupe whose fund-raising performances received favorable local reviews, and he chaired a debating society.

In May 1873 Guilford opened a barbershop in Thomaston that served an all-white clientele; barbering was a trade at which he could hear all the local news and maintain acquaintance with many local white men prominent in politics and business. In later years two of Guilford's sons followed him into the barbering trade. By the 1890s Guilford had returned to his first occupation, harness making, although he sometimes barbered with his sons.

Someone at St. Mary's AME Church annotated the membership roll next to Guilford's name: "dead October 1909." The *Thomaston Times* ignored his passing. Guilford was survived by his wife, who died in 1923.

Although racial prejudice combined with his own limited education to stifle his political aspirations, Guilford had a knack and the enthusiasm for organizing cultural activities in which Thomaston's freed blacks could find community and express themselves. His living legacy is Upson County's Emancipation Proclamation Celebration, held annually in Thomaston on or about 29 May since 1866, possibly the country's longest-running celebration of freedom from slavery.

FURTHER READING

Documents relevant to Guilford's life are in the Thomaston-Upson Archives, Upson County, Ga.; the National Archives, RG 105, Records of the Assistant Commissioner for the State of Georgia, Bureau of Refugees, Freedmen and Abandoned Lands, 1865–1869, Unregistered Letters Received (M798, roll 27); the National Archives, RG 393, Part 1, 3rd Military District, Bureau of Civil Affairs, Entry 5783, Miscellaneous Letters Received, 1867–1868, and Entry 5786, Letters Received Relating to Appointments as Registrars of Voters, Apr.–June 1867; the Georgia State Archives, RG-SG-S 037-01-006, *House Journal* (1870), and Upson County newspapers, 1869–1909.

Drago, Edmund L. *Black Politicians and Reconstruction in Georgia: A Splendid Failure* (1982).

Drago, Edmund L. "Georgia's First Black Voter Registrars during Reconstruction," *Georgia Historical Quarterly* 78.3 (Fall 1994): 760–793.

Kachun, Mitch. *Festivals of Freedom: Memory and Meaning in African American Emancipation Celebrations, 1808–1915* (2003).

Wiggins, William H., Jr. *O Freedom! Afro-American Emancipation Celebrations* (1987).

DAVID E. PATERSON

Guillaume, Robert (30 Nov. 1927–), actor, was born Robert Peter Williams in St. Louis, Missouri, where he was raised with three siblings by his maternal grandmother, Jeanette. His grandmother worked as a laundress at a Catholic rectory to support her family. It is not known when he legally assumed the surname Guillaume, which is French for William. Early on, Guillaume had a passion for music; he enjoyed singing and participated in school musicals. He sang in the church choir and served as an altar boy; alternately, he spent much time hanging around pool halls and in ninth grade was expelled from parochial school due to his uncontrollable temperament. At age eighteen, in 1945 Guillaume enrolled in the United States Army; fifteen months later he resigned receiving an honorable discharge. He returned to St. Louis, completed high school, and began working various jobs to save money for college. Among the odd jobs Guillaume worked was dishwasher, salesman, and streetcar driver; yet, he maintained his passion for singing. Guillaume was in his twenties when he enrolled in night school at St. Louis University to study business administration. Soon thereafter he decided to follow his heart and transferred to the school of music at Washington University in St. Louis in order to pursue his long-held passion. Guillaume excelled in his craft at WU; as an artist-in-residence, the Hungarian opera tenor Laslo Chabay applauded his talent and helped him to win a scholarship to the 1957 Aspen Music Festival in Colorado. He made a striking impression on Russell and Roweni Jelliffe, the founders of the Karamu Theater in Cleveland, Ohio, one of the oldest interracial theaters in America, who offered him an

Robert Guillaume walks out to a standing ovation before presenting the award for best actor in a comedy series during the 51st Annual Primetime Emmy Awards at the Shrine Auditorium in Los Angeles, 12 September 1999. (AP Images.)

apprenticeship with their company. Guillaume consented and, aged thirty-one, relocated to Cleveland to make his professional debut in Karamu's production of *Carousel*. Oscar Hammerstein was present at this performance and invited Guillaume to join the Broadway review of *Free and Easy*.

Guillaume had the opportunity to tour Europe with *Free and Easy* before the production ended. He joined the touring cast with *Finian's Rainbow*, *Golden Boy*, *Kwamina*, *Othello*, and *Porgy and Bess* until landing his 1970 role in *Someplace to Be Somebody*. Previously, he had appeared on television, in *Julia*, the sitcom starring the actress Diane Carroll. In 1972 Guillaume appeared as the lead actor in *Purlie*, the musical adaptation of the Ossie Davis play *Purlie Victorious*. The following year he appeared in *Superfly T.N.T*, produced by Ryan O'Neal, who also starred as the character "Priest." By 1975 Guillaume was appearing in several hit sitcoms; among them, *Sanford and Son* with the actor RED FOXX, *The Jeffersons* with the actor SHERMAN HEMSLEY, *Good Times* with the actor JIMMIE WALKER, *All in the Family*, and *Marcus Welby, M.D.* In 1976 he won a Tony Award nomination for his portrayal of Nathan Detroit in the all-black revue of *Guys and Dolls*. As *Guys and Dolls* was coming to a close, Guillaume sought new employment; fortunately, after several auditions, in 1977 he won the role of Benson DuBois, the arrogant and condescending butler on the new ABC series, *Soap*. For his portrayal Guillaume won an Emmy Award. He became so popular in his debut series role that when *Soap* ended in 1979 he starred in the spinoff series *Benson*. In 1985, for this role he won an Emmy Award for best actor in a comedy series, Outstanding Lead Actor in a Comedy series (the first and only African American to do so as of 2010), and the Massachusetts Mental Health Association Award for projecting a positive image. His character escalated from a butler to lieutenant governor and the program ran until 1986. In 1989 he coproduced, cocreated and starred in *The Robert Guillaume Show* for twelve episodes as a marriage counselor married to a white secretary. The same year he costarred as Dr. Frank Napier in the film *Lean on Me*, starring Morgan Freeman. In May 1990 Guillaume was selected to star as the Phantom in Andrew Lloyd Weber's Los Angeles production of *Phantom of the Opera*. He was the first African American to assume the role and received rave reviews. Later that year in December his thirty-three-year-old son Jacques died after suffering from AIDS for two years. In 1991, he founded Confetti Entertainment with his

third wife in an effort to combat illiteracy through a series of multicultural educational books and videos titled *Happily Ever After: Fairytales for Every Child*. In 1994 Guillaume was the voice on Rafiki, the mandrill, in the Walt Disney animated film, *The Lion King*. In 1996 he formed Longridge Production Company to develop acting projects. He suffered a stroke in 1999 on the set of the sitcom *Sports Night*, but returned to portray Isaac Jaffe for another year. The beginning of the twenty-first century found Guillaume performing voices for animated series and appearing on network sitcoms. In 2003 he was featured in the successful film *Big Fish*, by Tim Burton, and published a biography, *Guillaume: A Life*. Guillaume has recorded a number of albums, and in May 2009 released the album *There Is Love*.

In 1999 Guillaume earned a star on The Walk of Fame in his hometown, St. Louis, and four NAACP Image Awards in 2001. In 1983 he divorced his first wife, Marlene, with whom he had two sons, Jacques and Kevin. He married Donna Brown a freelance television producer in 1984, and together they have three daughters Rachel Jeanette, Patricia, and Melissa.

FURTHER READING

"Robert Guillaume Is Recovering from Stroke and Back on 'Sports Night'" *Jet*, 11 Oct. 1999.

"Robert Guillaume Returns to the Big Screen in Sony Pictures' *Big Fish*." *Chicago Defender*, 27 Aug. 2003.

Braxton, Greg. "Singing Praises of the New Man Behind the Mask, Stage: Robert Guillaume receives adulation and a standing ovation on his first night as the Phantom." *Los Angeles Times*, 3 May 1990.

SAFIYA DALILAH HOSKINS

Guillén, Nicolás (10 July 1902–16 July 1989), poet, journalist, political activist, and Cuba's poet laureate, was born Nicolás Cristóbal Guillén y Batista in Camagüey, Cuba. His parents were of mixed African and Spanish descent; his father, a journalist and progressive senator, was murdered in 1917 while protesting against the conservative president Mario García Menocal.

Briefly a law student at the University of Havana, Nicolás soon left to become a journalist. He took after his father in populism and protest. Cuban society was victimized by sequential regimes of repression and oppression. Guillén was among the worst hit, due to his increasingly socialist ideology. His first poems and antiestablishment articles were published in the early 1920s. He and editors of the *Mediodía* newspaper were briefly jailed in 1936.

He joined the Communist Party. In 1937 he traveled to Spain for the Congress of Writers and Artists while doubling as a correspondent on the Spanish Civil War. There he met fellow writers, such as Ernest Hemingway. Upon returning home, he ran for the 1940 local elections on the Communist Party platform and lost. Blacklisted, he was refused an entry visa to the United States.

During the next fifteen years, he traveled to various countries, including France, where he met writers from Africa and the African Diaspora: Jacques Roumain (Haiti), Léon-Gontran Damas (Guyana), and Langston Hughes (United States). Thus, he was involved in the Negritude movement. The Batista regime refused him permission to return home in 1953, a decision subsequently overturned by the Fidel Castro–led Revolution of 1958.

Guillén became president of the National Union of Writers of Cuba in 1961. He won the Stalin Prize for Peace. He remained fully committed to the program of constructing a nonracial society devoid of class divisions. In the final years of his life, there were reports alleging that he suffered from torture and mental debility (cf. Carlos Moore, *Castro, The Blacks and Africa*, 1988). Guillén never protested against the Castro regime.

Guillén's early poems belonged to the Modernista movement exemplified by Rubén Darío. Soon enough, in his first collection, *Motivos de son* (1930), he asserted his presence in the Afrocubanist-negrista movement and became the main exponent of *poesía negra*. While his compatriots wrote as outsiders, Guillén wrote on Afro-Cuban experience as an insider. As stated earlier, he was a participant in the Negritude movement although, according to him, "in Cuba, the problem of *negritude* does not make sense, because it would be a kind of racism, a dispersing element rather than an agglutinating one" (quoted in Keith Ellis, *Cuba's Nicolás Guillén*, 1983, p. 226). That position underscores the revolutionary concept of eradicating racism and class oppression in Cuba. Besides, Guillén condemns the ideology, not the ideas valuing African and black culture as a springboard for national emancipation and as a means of universal liberation of all those whom Frantz Fanon calls the wretched of the earth.

Criticism of Guillén's work may be seen from two perspectives: First, the Eurocentric viewpoint emphasizing the poet's Marxist commitment and the Spanish artistic affiliation (see Ellis), and second, the Afrocentric position affirming that the whole body of his art "tells us what it is to be black in Cuba" (Martha Cobb, *Harlem, Haiti, and Havana*, 1979, p. 108). A corollary to this latter concept insists upon the African underpinnings of the poetry (Femi Ojo-Ade, *Being Black, Being Human*, 2004, pp.155–180).

In all his poems, Guillén's thoughts are centered on popular Afro-Cuban experience. He uses the rhythm of the *son*, a popular Cuban dance, as the basis for his art. He asserts, "Blacks are their most authoritative interpreters [of the *son*]" (in Angel Augier, "The Cuban poetry of Nicolás Guillén," *Phylon* 12 [1951]: 29). Beyond folk tradition, these poems implicitly address social issues. The focal point is the Havana streets populated by poor, suffering blacks. One poem, "Tú no sabe inglé," is a comical take on a man incapable of speaking English; however, beneath the humor lies criticism of American domination.

The 1931 collection *Sóngoro Cosongo* establishes the poet's overt commitment to blackness as part of the revolutionary process. For example, the black boxer is depicted as a strong symbol for his people, but he runs the risk of becoming victim of "that Broadway," America. Guillén also brings to the fore the importance of both the Harlem Renaissance and Cuban art.

West Indies Ltd. (1934) reveals further an anticapitalist stance. The title underlines the imperialist enterprise of multinationals exploiting small Caribbean countries. The poems support radical change and rebellion against foreign oppressors. Yet Guillén is aware of the potentially negative effects of racial history steeped in inequality and injustice. "Ballad of the Two Grandfathers" pitches memories of the black grandfather against those of the white, merging in the iniquitous encounter of slavery. In a cathartic conclusion, both men draw from their anguish the strength to cooperate for liberation and survival together, as they "dream, weep, sing." The collection's thrust is the Caribbean, beyond Cuba's borders, culminating in a universalistic humanism of the oppressed of all countries and climes, races and religions. The Caribbean is a microcosm of that universe: "Here there are whites and blacks and Chinese and mulattos." The other poignant message is meant for "good negroes" like Sabás, chronic beggar: "Seize your bread, don't beg for it."

The two 1937 collections directly address Guillén's Spanish roots. *España* laments Spain's entrenched dictatorship and the ouster of democracy. *Cantos para soldados y sones para turistas* contrasts the condition of soldiers dying for meaningless causes with the pranks of moneyed tourists immune to the plight of the underlings.

Other collections are *El son entero* (1947), *La paloma de vuelo popular* and *Elegías* (1958). The last text includes the thought-provoking poem "El apellido," in which Guillén questions his naming from slavery to liberation and, once again, confirms attachment to his blackness: "I am also ... the great great grandson of a slave. (Let the master be ashamed.)"

FURTHER READING

Augier, Angel. *Nicolás Guillén: notas para un estudio biográfico-crítico*, 2 vols. (1965).

Marquez, Robert, and McMurray, David Arthur, eds. *Man-Making Words: Selected Poems of Nicolás Guillén* (1972).

Williams, Lorna V. *Self and Society in the Poetry of Nicolás Guillén* (1982).

Obituary: "Nicolás Guillén, 87, National Poet of Cuba." *The New York Times*, 18 July 1989.

FEMI OJO-ADE

Guillory, Ida Lewis (15 Jan. 1929–), zydeco accordionist, band leader, and singer, was born Ida Lewis in Lake Charles, Louisiana, into a French-speaking family of rice farmers and musicians. Zydeco, from the French *les haricots* or "snap beans," is the music of Creole people from southwestern Louisiana and southeastern Texas. Ida was the fourth of seven children born to Ben Lewis, a harmonica player, and Elvina Broussard Lewis, an accordionist. Ida's mother taught her to play the accordion, while insisting it was "not a very lady-like instrument" (Ida Lewis Guillory, cited in DeWitt, p. 73) and a woman could only play at home for herself. Ida seldom heard other women musicians, except church singers.

At the local segregated one-room schoolhouse, Ida quickly learned English because students were punished for speaking Creole. During her second-grade year, her family moved to Beaumont, Texas, in search of better-paying work. In 1947 they moved to San Francisco, California. Through the cuisine and music they brought with them, they connected with other Creole migrants.

In 1947, after finishing high school, Ida Lewis married Ray Guillory. They had a daughter, Ledra, and two sons, Ronald and Myrick, nicknamed "Freeze." Ida Guillory drove a school bus part-time until Ledra, their youngest child, went to college. On school field trip runs, she brought her accordion and practiced in the bus while waiting for the students to return. After her children were all school age, Guillory began to play accordion professionally.

With her husband's blessing, his musician friends, the accordionist John Semien and his band, the Opelousas Playboys, invited her to perform with them at house parties. She also played in clubs with her brother Al Lewis (stage surname: Rapone) and his Barbary Coast Band.

At a 1975 Mardi Gras party in San Francisco, Ida Guillory was introduced as "Queen of the Zydeco Accordion and ... Zydeco Music." A *San Francisco Chronicle* article about the musicians at the party identified her as "Queen Ida," and from then on this was her stage name. She immediately received so many concert bookings that her brother Al changed the name of the Barbary Coast Band to Queen Ida and the Bon Temps Zydeco Band. He became her business manager, musical director, and lead guitarist. It was very unusual for a woman to play with, let alone front, a zydeco band. In 1976 Queen Ida performed at the Bay Area Blues Festival and released her first album on the Los Angeles jazz label GNP/Crescendo.

In 1978, after Guillory hired the agent John Ullman, she began to win national and international attention. She went on a National Endowment for the Arts–funded West Coast tour. In 1979, she was nominated for a Bay Area Music Award. She went on her first of many European tours, with her brother Willie Lewis playing the *frottoir* (zydeco rubboard) for her band, as he did until 1988. In 1983 *Queen Ida on Tour*, recorded in Denmark, won a Grammy Award. Guillory preferred to make live albums. The same year, Queen Ida and her band appeared in the movie *Rumble Fish*, directed by Francis Ford Coppola. They later appeared on the TV programs *Austin City Limits* and *Saturday Night Live*.

By 1986 they were touring six months out of the year, and Ray Guillory was employed as their road manager. In 1988 their son Myrick replaced Willie Lewis in the Bon Temps Band. In 1988 they toured Africa under the auspices of the U.S. State Department, and became the first zydeco band to perform in Japan. In 1989 they appeared in *J'ai été au bal* (*I Went to the Dance*), a Louisiana music documentary directed by Les Blank and Chris Strachwitz.

In 1990 they performed in New Zealand and Australia. During the 1990s and early 2000s, Queen Ida gradually reduced her public performances. By the late 2000s, she occasionally attended concerts, sometimes joining the musicians.

Queen Ida inspired many musicians—including her son Freeze Guillory and His Nouveau Zydeco Band and the accordionist Rosie Ledet—to keep zydeco alive and fresh. Guillory described "feeling like a teacher or missionary" toward "older" women seeking their life's purpose. "When I was a little girl, women in Louisiana were expected to raise their children, tend chickens, go to church, and bake bread. I tell older women that they are just now mature, and ... know what direction they want to go in, something they didn't know at an earlier age ... I believe it's never too late to expand your human potential" (Morrow and Winters, 2005).

FURTHER READING

Guillory, Ida, and Naomi Wise. *Cookin' with Queen Ida* (1996).

DeWitt, Mark F. *Cajun and Zydeco Dance Music in Northern California* (2008).

Morrow, John, and Kelly Winters. "Queen Ida." Vol. 51 of *Contemporary Musicians,* edited by Angela M. Pilchak (2005).

Rollins, Brian. *Let the Good Times Roll! A Guide to Cajun & Zydeco Music* (1998).

Tisserand, Michael. *The Kingdom of Zydeco* (1998).

MARY KRANE DERR

Guinier, Lani (19 Apr. 1950–), professor and civil rights advocate, was born Carol Lani Guinier, in New York City, to Ewart G. Guinier, attorney, history professor, and first chairman of Harvard's Afro-American Studies Program, and Eugenia Guinier, a school teacher. Growing up with two sisters in a Manhattan household, she graduated third in a class of fifteen hundred from Andrew Jackson public high school, where she was an editor of the school newspaper. She attended Radcliffe College/Harvard University on National Merit and New York Times scholarships, majoring in social studies, and graduated with honors in 1971. She received a J.D. from Yale Law School in 1974.

Guinier lived in a black Jewish household of "coalition builders," wherein her mother taught "her daughters how to get along with others" and to see themselves as bridge people able to "to listen closely to hear other people's anger or feelings.... It taught me not to internalize rejection," and to be able to fight back (*New York Daily News*, 10 May 1998). She learned about the danger of racial quotas from her father, who had been denied financial aid at Harvard in the 1920s because one black student had already been granted a scholarship. As a result, he was forced to drop out of Harvard and work as an elevator operator while earning a law degree from New York University (Guinier, 104).

From 1974 to 1976 Guinier clerked for the federal appeals court judge DAMON KEITH in Detroit, and in 1976–1977 she was a referee for the Wayne County Michigan Juvenile Court. In the Carter administration she worked in the Justice Department as a special assistant to Drew Days, the head of the Civil Rights Division (to which she would be nominated in 1993). Between 1981 and 1988 Guinier served as assistant counsel and chief litigator for the NAACP Legal Defense and Education Fund (LDEF) on voting rights cases under the Voting Rights Act of 1965. An adjunct professor at New York University Law School from 1985 to 1989, she became a tenured associate professor at the University of Pennsylvania Law School in 1988 and was promoted to a full professor in 1992. In 1986 Guinier married Nolan Bowie, a Philadelphia attorney and artist, and they had one son, Nikolas.

President Bill Clinton nominated Guinier, a Yale Law School classmate, to be the assistant attorney general in the Civil Rights Division of the Justice Department on 29 April 1993. The nomination became controversial because her legal writings "raise questions about racial conflict and political power in the U.S." (NBAW, 1996). Many conservative critics suggested that she advocated quotas and did not support majority rule. Though a 1993 *New York Post* column caricatured her as a "hard-hitting extremist," or "quota queen," Guinier countered in an ABC *Nightline* interview on 2 June 1993, "I do not believe in quotas. I have never advocated quotas." She explained that "I believe that the majority should rule [as] the essence of democracy. But ... consistent ... with what the Bush and even Reagan administration have said ... in some instances we have to worry ... [as] certainly [was] Madison's concern ... about the tyranny of a fixed majority." Guinier's legal articles raise issues of political equality for minorities and criticize the winner-takes-all, single-member, local electoral system, in which black candidates seldom win except in majority black districts. Her scholarship proposes a system of "proportionate interest representation," similar to some European electoral systems for representing diverse political interests. Her law review article, "The Triumph of Tokenism: The Voting Rights Act and the Theory of Black Electoral Success" (quoted in the *Congressional Record* during the debate over her nomination), argues, "For those at the bottom ... [A] fair system of political representation would provide mechanisms to ensure that disadvantaged and stigmatized minority groups also have a fair chance to have their policy preferences satisfied" (Guinier, 1991, 1135–1136).

Responding to her critics, Guinier stated in an interview, "We may aspire to a race-blind, or color-blind constitution, but we shouldn't confuse ourselves into thinking we live in a race-blind political reality." She added, "We have to stop thinking that when black people get some political power, that means white people lose political power" (National Black American Women, 1996). Her approach to preventing the tyranny of the majority echoes James Madison's concerns and John C. Calhoun's advocacy of "concurrent majorities" that require both subgroup and majority votes that in essence provide for minority vetoes (Safford, 215). *The New Yorker* countered her critics by pointing out that Guinier's writings "do not show her to be … a proponent of racial polarization, or an opponent of democratic norms. They do show her to be a provocative, interesting thinker, whose speculations could nourish what is a nascent debate in [the United States] about alternative electoral systems" (14 June 1993).

On 3 June 1993 President Clinton withdrew Guinier's nomination, noting that her writings "clearly lend themselves to interpretations that do not represent the views that I expressed on civil rights during my campaign" (*New York Times*, 4 June 1993). She held that the president and others had misinterpreted her writings, but like Clinton's refusal to let her defend herself in the press, the withdrawal prevented her from defending her writings before the Senate Judiciary Committee. Congressional Black Caucus members were so angered by Clinton's treatment of Guinier that they refused to meet with him. The White House characterized the accusations of the mishandling the nomination as a "vicious attack" by conservative groups seeking revenge for Democrats' refusal to support Reagan's Supreme Court nominee Judge Robert Bork who (unlike Guinier) had the opportunity to defend himself before the Senate Judiciary Committee. Harvard Law School's Professor Randall Kennedy called the misuse of Guinier's writings a vivid example of the "dumbing of American politics" (*Washington Post*, 4 July 1993). Later Guinier felt that the president had done her a "favor" by forcing her to develop her own voice (*Jet*, 22 July 1998). She called on Clinton to convene a summit about racial issues and has since become a leading spokesperson on racial and gender politics.

After the nomination controversy, Guinier returned to teaching at the University of Pennsylvania and began a speaking tour on the issues her nomination raised. In 1996 she co-founded, and served as president through 1999 of Commonplace, an organization devoted to improving public discussion of racial issues through local and national conversations. She was a visiting professor at Harvard Law School in 1996, and in 1998 became the first black women to be tenured as a full professor at Harvard Law school, thus resolving an issue highlighted by Harvard Law professor DERRICK BELL in 1990 when he took a "leave of conscience" until the university tenured a black woman ("Lani Guinier Is Finally Going to Harvard," 85). In 2001 she was named Bennett Boskey Professor at Harvard Law School (Cose, 25).

Guinier received Outstanding Service Awards from the Department of Justice annually from 1978 to 1980; the Champion of Democracy Award from the Center for Voting and Democracy in 1993; the Congressional Black Caucus Chair's Award in 1993; the NAACP Torch of Courage Award in July 1993; the Rosa Parks Award from the American Association of Affirmative Action in 1994; the American Bar Association Commission on Women in the Profession award in 1995; the National Women's Political Caucus's Champion of Democracy Award in 1995; and the Big Sister Award from the Big Sister organization in 1999. She received honorary degrees from the University of Pennsylvania in 1992; Northeastern Law School in 1994; Hunter College in 1994; Swarthmore College in 1996; Spelman College in 1998; Smith College and the University of Rhode Island, both in 1999; and the University of the District of Columbia in 2001. A forceful advocate for creative solutions to issues of gender and racial inequality, Lani Guinier continued to raise provocative questions concerning pressing national problems in the twenty-first century.

FURTHER READING

Branan, Karen. "Lani Guinier: The Anatomy of a Betrayal," *Ms.* 4 (Sept.–Oct. 1993).

Funderberg, Lisa. "A 'Commonplace' Conversation with Lani Guinier," *AA Review* 30.2 (1996).

"Lani Guinier Is Finally Going to Harvard," *Journal of Blacks in Higher Education* 19 (Spring 1998).

Russakoff, Dale. "Lani Guinier, in Person: Who She Is and What She Believes in Got Lost in the Furor of Her Nomination," *Washington Post National Weekly Edition* (20–26 Dec. 1993).

Safford, John. "Lani Guinier and Minority Rights, *PS: Political Science & Politics* (June 1995).

RICHARD SOBEL

Gumbel, Bryant (29 Sept. 1948–), broadcaster, was born Bryant Charles Gumbel in New Orleans, Louisiana, the second of four children to Richard Dunbar Gumbel, a World War II veteran, and Rhea LeCesne Gumbel. During his infancy Gumbel's parents moved the family from New Orleans to Chicago. Though it would ultimately benefit the entire family, the major motivation for the move was Gumbel's father's personal ambition. Richard Gumbel, a graduate of Xavier University in Louisiana, had his sights on law school. Unfortunately he was denied admission to law schools in his home state, something he ascribed to the racist climate of the South at that time. The more liberal North seemed a logical move, and he eventually pursued a law degree at Georgetown Law School in Washington, D.C., while continuing to support his family full time. Eventually becoming a Cook County Probate judge, Richard raised his family in Chicago. Both of Gumbel's parents were activists in the city's Democratic Party.

Raised in the middle-class Chicago suburb of Hyde Park, Bryant attended Catholic elementary schools. His father demanded good grades but also emphasized the pleasure of sports by frequently taking his children to Chicago Cubs and White Sox baseball games. Gumbel struggled academically but excelled at sports. This affinity would lead him to sports broadcasting as an adult.

Though his parents emphasized sports in their children's lives, they had hopes that Gumbel would pursue a career in law, following in his father's footsteps. After graduating from Bates College he worked in sales at Westvaco Corporation, a paper manufacturer in New York. Uninterested in pursuing law, Gumbel set his sights on sports writing. An article in *Black Sports* magazine became the catalyst to a promising career. Gumbel, talented and ambitious, worked his way up to the position of editor in chief of the magazine within a year of joining the staff. As a reporter and writer he spent time interviewing prominent sports personalities and gained industry respect. Unfortunately Gumbel's father died before seeing his son realize his dream. In 1972 Gumbel was hired by KNBC-TV, an NBC affiliate in Los Angeles, as an on-air sportscaster. Devastated by the loss of his father, Gumbel poured himself into his work and garnered new assignments with greater responsibility. At KNBC-TV he held the positions of weekly sportscaster, weeknight sportscaster, and sports director.

On 1 December 1973 Gumbel married his college sweetheart, June Carlyn Baranco, an artist and Baton Rouge native. The couple had two children.

In 1975, while he was working in Los Angeles, NBC Sports hired Gumbel as co-host of *Grandstand*, the network's National Football League pregame show. *Grandstand* was broadcast from New York, so Gumbel commuted between Los Angeles and New York City. He spent the next several years covering sporting events for NBC, including the Rose Bowl and a 1976 Olympic program for which he won an Emmy Award. He earned another Emmy the next year as anchor of the CBS News magazine *Public Eye with Bryant Gumbel*, followed by a Golden Mike Award sponsored by the Los Angeles Press Club.

In 1980 Gumbel was offered a minor sports reporting position with NBC's *Today Show*. He began branching out of sports and ventured into news reporting to showcase his versatility. The strategy paid off when Gumbel was asked to fill in for Jane Pauley, *Today*'s co-host, who was out on medical leave. Successful as a substitute co-host, Gumbel was tapped to fill in for *Today*'s other co-host, Tom Brokaw. By January 1982 Gumbel had replaced Brokaw, who became the *NBC Nightly News* anchor. Gumbel would be the first African American to host a nationally televised morning program. It did not take him long to earn the respect of colleagues and his viewing audience. In 1986 one thousand journalists voted him "Best Morning TV News Interviewer" in an annual *Washington Journalism Review* readers poll.

In 1989 Bryant suffered a bruise to his reputation when an internal *Today* memo he wrote was leaked to the press. In it, Bryant strongly criticized some of his colleagues on the show, including the weatherman Willard Scott and the film critic Gene Shalit. Written as a response to the executive producer's request for critiques of the show, Gumbel was horrified when his honest but harsh comments became public. The press was unforgiving, and although Gumbel and his colleagues remained professional throughout the ordeal, his reputation suffered. Nevertheless, Gumbel reestablished himself as a solid reporter and interviewer. In 1992 he took *Today* to Africa for a week of unprecedented broadcasts, one of the career accomplishments of which he remained most proud. While on location he shed light on issues largely ignored by other mainstream media outlets. For his Africa programming Gumbel received the 1993 International Journalism Award from the group TransAfrica, the U.S. Committee for UNICEf's Africa's Future Award, and Journalist of the Year Award sponsored by the National Association of Black Journalists.

In January 1997, after fifteen years on NBC's *Today Show*, Gumbel resigned to pursue other interests. Shortly after leaving he was hired at CBS to host *Public Eye with Bryant Gumbel*, a news magazine program. Because of poor ratings, the show was canceled in less than a year. In 1999, however, Gumbel was again hired by CBS to host its morning news program, *The Early Show*, where he remained until 2002. After an acrimonious divorce from his first wife, Gumbel married the model Hilary Quinlan in August 2002.

A widely respected broadcaster, Gumbel traveled the world covering historic events. In Saudi Arabia he reported on the start of the first Persian Gulf War. He also covered the tenth anniversary of the fall of Saigon from Ho Chi Minh City. Gumbel was honored with the United Negro College Fund Frederick D. Patterson Award and the Congress of Racial Equality MARTIN LUTHER KING Award. Additionally he won four Emmy Awards and three NAACP Image Awards. Gumbel received honorary doctorate degrees from a number of colleges and universities, including Bates, Xavier, Holy Cross, Providence, and Clark Atlanta.

Following his semiretirement in 1995 Gumbel hosted *Real Sports with Bryant Gumbel*, an HBO investigative series. The show received various awards, including numerous Sports Emmy Awards.

FURTHER READING

Clarke, Caroline V. *Take a Lesson: Today's Black Achievers on How They Made It and What They Learned Along the Way* (2001).

Smith, Jessie Carney. *Black Heroes* (2001).

Smith, Jessie Carney. *Notable Black American Men* (2006).

NANCY T. ROBINSON

Gumby, Levi Sandy Alexander (1 Feb. 1885–16 Mar. 1961), collector, historian, author, and social personality, was born in Maryland, the son of Levi Thomas and Louisa Morris Gumby. In 1901 Gumby and his sister were sent to live with their grandparents, and it was there, at age sixteen, that Gumby began his scrapbook collection, making his first book—a practice that he would continue throughout the rest of his life—out of wallpaper, paste, and clippings of the September 1901 assassination of President McKinley. In 1902 Gumby entered Dover State College (later Delaware State University) in Delaware and began to study law. Before completing his studies Gumby withdrew from school and

moved to New York City around 1906, where he would live until his death nearly sixty years later.

Gumby was immediately dazzled by life in the "big city" and sought to integrate himself into the urban community. During his early years in New York, Gumby held a variety of jobs to support his passion for collecting African American memorabilia and creating scrapbooks, including waiting tables at Columbia University and working as the personal butler of a wealthy banker, as a bellhop, and also as a postal worker during World War I. Gumby was also a founding member of the Southern Utopia Fraternity, an organization that provided support for young men who came to New York from the South seeking a wider variety of social, economic, and educational opportunities.

By 1910 Gumby had begun to recognize the importance of chronicling the often-ignored events of African American history and consequently began to take his role as a collector more seriously. In addition to creating scrapbooks composed of clippings, photographs, letters, and playbills, he began to collect rare books and manuscripts with the financial backing of his friend Charles W. Newman, a wealthy white stockbroker, who supported Gumby throughout the 1920s. When his growing collection of scrapbooks, rare books, and manuscripts began to overflow his apartment, with the help of Newman, Gumby rented a large studio at 2144 Fifth Avenue between 131st and 132nd streets in Harlem that became known as "Gumby's Bookstore" because of the shelves of books that lined the studio's walls. Gumby furnished his studio, a converted storefront, with a grand piano and Persian rugs as a means of impressing his guests, as well as the young men whom he liked to entertain. He used the studio to hold gatherings and receptions, sometimes renting it out for exhibitions, performances, and parties. The studio officially opened in 1926 and became a gathering place for the major literary figures of the Harlem Renaissance—a period ranging from roughly 1920 until 1935 that represented an explosion of black literary, artistic, intellectual, and cultural production—including ALAIN LOCKE, CLAUDE MCKAY, COUNTÉE CULLEN, LANGSTON HUGHES, RICHARD BRUCE NUGENT, WALLACE THURMAN, HELENE V. JOHNSON, and DOROTHY WEST, as well as artists, actors, and musicians such as PAUL ROBESON, all of whom Gumby was personally acquainted with.

At his gatherings Gumby proved a vivacious and spirited host who loved to entertain, often performing his own sexually explicit sonnets. Gumby's reputation as a host, his magnetic personality, and his keen sense of fashion garnered him nicknames such as "The Count," "Mr. Scrapbook," and "Great God Gumby," and established him as one of the most significant personalities of the Harlem Renaissance. Not only did he collect documents and materials relating to and created by Harlem Renaissance figures but his studio also served as a meeting place for those interested in the movement. Gumby's personality, coupled with his studio, helped to create a major creative and social nexus—a place in which the artistic community of Harlem at the time could thrive, as nearly every major literary or artistic figure of the Harlem Renaissance was associated with Gumby and his studio at one time or another. As Richard Bruce Nugent humorously noted in his biographical vignette of Gumby titled "On Alexander Gumby" from the collection *Gay Rebel of the Harlem Renaissance* (2002), not only did Gumby collect memorabilia, clippings, and books but he also collected artists (224).

Gumby was openly gay and his studio became a gathering place for Harlem's queer community as well as for its literary and artistic elite. The popularity of "Gumby's Bookstore" illustrates that the Harlem Renaissance was in many ways also a queer renaissance.

In 1930, inspired by other literary publications of the time such as *FIRE!!* and *Harlem* (both edited by Wallace Thurman), Gumby set out to produce his own literary journal titled *The Gumby Book Studio Quarterly*. The journal was short-lived—the first and only issue was printed in 1930–1931 and was never distributed. The stock market crash of 1929 and the Depression of the 1930s affected Gumby greatly, as Charles W. Newman lost millions and "Gumby's Bookstore" lost the support of its regular patrons, forcing Gumby to give up the studio, sell many of his books, and store his scrapbooks in the cellar of a friend's home. In 1931 Gumby was diagnosed with tuberculosis and was forced to spend nearly a year in Riverside Hospital in the Bronx and four years in Randall's Island Hospital. Throughout his hospital stay Gumby continued to work on his scrapbooks, collecting newspaper articles, cards, and photos of friends who came to visit, which he eventually incorporated into his autobiographical scrapbooks. Although Gumby was behind on his scrapbooking because of his illness, when he was released in 1934 he renewed his urge to collect and sought to rebuild and restore his collection by creating new scrapbooks and adding additional clippings and documents.

In 1950 Gumby donated his collection of 300 scrapbooks—which he titled *The L. S. Alexander Gumby Collection of Negroiana*—to Columbia University's libraries, and was subsequently hired in 1951 for a period of eight months to organize the collection. The materials in Gumby's scrapbooks, which chronicle the history of the American Negro from 1850 on, consist mainly of newspaper and magazine clippings, photos, pamphlets, playbills, autographs, letters, slave documents, and materials that Gumby personally gathered from well-known African American personalities such as Langston Hughes, Paul Robeson, and JOSEPHINE BAKER. Each scrapbook within Gumby's collection is devoted to one subject, be it an individual, an organization, or a more general topic such as "Jazz" or "Lynchings and Race Riots." Six of the scrapbooks pertain to Gumby himself and are labeled "Gumby's Autobiography." In 1952 Gumby also composed an autobiographical essay about his collection titled "The Adventures of My Scrapbooks" that was published in the *Columbia Library Columns*. Gumby continued to add materials to the collection until his death from complications due to tuberculosis. He considered his scrapbooks not just a hobby but also as a significant contribution to African American history and culture, a history that in Gumby's mind frequently remained unrecorded within mainstream narratives.

FURTHER READING

"The L. S. Alexander Gumby Collection of Negroiana" is housed in the Butler Rare Book and Manuscript Library of Columbia University in the New York City.

Gumby, L. S. Alexander. "The Adventures of My Scrapbooks," *Columbia Library Columns* 2.1 (Nov. 1952).

Gumby, L. S. Alexander. "Autobiographical Essay," *Columbia Library World* (Jan. 1951).

Kadlecek, Jo. "Black History Remains Alive in Alexander Gumby's Popular Scrapbooks," *Columbia News* (18 Feb. 2002).

Nugent, Richard Bruce. "On Alexander Gumby," in *Gay Rebel of the Harlem Renaissance: Selections from the Work of Richard Bruce Nugent*, ed. Thomas H. Wirth (2002).

Wirth, Thomas H. "Introduction," in *Gay Rebel of the Harlem Renaissance: Selections from the Work of Richard Bruce Nugent*, ed. Thomas H. Wirth (2002).

Obituary: *New York Times*, 18 Mar. 1961.

J. JAMES IOVANNONE

Gunn, Bill (15 July 1934–5 Apr. 1989), actor, playwright, screenwriter, director, and novelist, was born William Harrison Gunn in Philadelphia, Pennsylvania, the only child of William Gunn, a songwriter, musician, comedian, and unpublished poet, and Louise Alexander, an actress, theater director, and community activist. Gunn grew up in a middle-class neighborhood and attended integrated public schools in Philadelphia, graduating from high school in 1952.

After serving two years in the U.S. Navy, Gunn moved to New York City's East Village in 1954, intending to become an actor. At twenty, he won critical acclaim in 1954 for his portrayal of the young boy in the New Theatre Company's revival of *Take a Giant Step*. Throughout the 1950s and 1960s he continued to appear in plays on and off Broadway, including *The Immoralist* with James Dean and productions of *Antony and Cleopatra* and *Troilus and Cressida* in 1956 and 1957. By the early 1960s he was also regularly performing minor or supporting parts in popular television series such as *Dr. Kildare* and the *Interns*. However, the few and limited roles that Gunn was offered were not challenging enough for the intellectually restless, young artist, and he decided to become a writer as well. In 1958 Gunn began a parallel career as a playwright, writing *Marcus in the High Grass*, which was well received. Some critics, assuming he was white because the play featured an all-white cast and did not examine racial issues, hailed him as another Tennessee Williams.

In 1964 Gunn wrote his first novel, *All the Rest Have Died*, which was published by Delacorte Press. Like much of his subsequent work in theater, film, and literature, the novel has strong autobiographical elements. Influenced by the existential philosophies of French writers Jean-Paul Sartre and Albert Camus, the major protagonist in the novel (who, like Gunn, is an actor) is on a personal quest to understand and confront the specific challenges, problems, and responsibilities of life as an individual artist in a largely indifferent, materialistic, and conformist society. At that time, Gunn eschewed much of the increasingly politicized black "protest" literature of the period in favor of what he then deemed the "objectively human" dimensions of experience. This stance would change significantly over the next few years, as Gunn was confronted with, and deeply frustrated by, the pervasive racial and artistic limitations imposed by Hollywood and Broadway. In 1964 Gunn was quoted in *Variety*, complaining about the film industry's racist casting practices: "When a good part for a Negro actor comes along,

they always offer it to SIDNEY POITIER. If he turns it down, they rewrite it for a white actor" (spring 1964).

Though some incremental improvements for black actors were made by the industry in the early 1970s, experienced and accomplished black writers and actors, such as OSSIE DAVIS and BILL (WILLIAM) GREAVES, like Gunn were stifled by the limited gains. Increasingly vocal about his disappointments during this period, he stated, "[Hollywood] studios have no interest whatsoever in depicting Black culture or Black life" (*Variety*, spring 1964). As a serious and ambitious filmmaker and writer (Gunn had begun writing screenplays in 1968), he advocated that one must "begin on a commercial premise and go where you want with it" (Peterson, 1973). For Gunn, this meant trying to infuse conventional genre film projects with a new and more radical form and content. The film *Stop*, which he wrote and directed at Warner Bros., was first enthusiastically accepted in 1969, and then Warner Bros. mysteriously rejected and shelved it. Gunn went on to write two successful scripts from adapted novels for the films the *Landlord* and the *Angel Levine*, both in 1970. He longed to write and direct his own original independent film. After his bitter experience with *Stop*, he realized that a serious black filmmaker with his artistic aspirations would never be given an opportunity in mainstream Hollywood, so Gunn decided to develop his own project.

The result was the critically acclaimed 1973 film *Ganja and Hess*, which Gunn wrote, directed, and appeared in. The only one of three hundred American film entrants selected for showing during the prestigious Cannes Film Festival Critics' Week in 1973, *Ganja and Hess* ran in New York for only one week, closing just as word of mouth began to spread. The small, independent producers who released the film expected, and thought they were getting, a commercial black vampire film (their original title was the *Vampires of Harlem*). However, Gunn used the vampire genre as a structural device for a complex and critical examination of the multilayered theme of addiction (to money, sex, power, religion, drugs, and mythology) in the lives of the wealthy and intellectually sophisticated black protagonists who are or become vampires. Their addiction to blood is a metaphor for Gunn's vision of the destructive nature of bourgeois life on blacks who choose decadent materialism over humane standards of living. Despite its initial failure to reach a U.S. audience, the film was a great success in Europe, especially in France. Later many critics here and abroad chose it as one of the ten best films of the 1970s.

Unhappy with the film's marked departure from its commercial direction and its lack of economic success in the United States the producers sold *Ganja and Hess* to Heritage Films, which completely reedited, reshot, and retitled the film as *Blood Couple* (also called *Double Possession*). One original print survived and was screened in 1973 at the Museum of Modern Art in New York City, where it became part of the museum's permanent collection. This landmark event and many subsequent screenings at museums, universities, film festivals, and art institutions throughout the United States and abroad have contributed to a renewed interest in the film and in Gunn's creative output. He continued to write and direct his own plays on and off Broadway throughout the 1980s, two of which were published as books in the late 1980s, the *Black Picture Show* and *Rhinestone Sharecropping*. A talented actor and writer dedicated to African American creative independence, Gunn died of encephalitis at the age of fifty-five.

FURTHER READING

Klotman, Phyllis Rauch. *Screenplays of the African American Experience* (1991).

Monaco, James. *American Film Now: The People The Power The Money The Movies* (1979).

Peterson, Maurice. "Interview with Bill Gunn," *Essence*, 4 (October 1973).

KOFI NATAMBU

Gunn, Moses (2 Oct. 1929–17 Dec. 1993), actor and performer, was born in St. Louis, Missouri, the oldest of seven children of George Gunn, a blue-collar laborer, and Mary Briggs Gunn.

He attended local schools and had a relatively uneventful upbringing until, when he was twelve, his mother died of complications related to asthma, and the family imploded. Gunn ran away and drifted, riding the rails and generally living an unmoored life, until he at last returned to St. Louis and fell in with a foster family headed by Jewel Richie, an English teacher and diction coach. Richie recognized Gunn's nascent dramatic talents and encouraged him to pursue training and further education.

Gunn was an able student, and upon his graduation from high school he found himself with a veritable raft of scholarship offers. He attended historically black Tennessee State University (TSU) in Nashville, paused for a three-year stint in the army (1954–1957), and graduated with his Bachelor's

degree in drama in 1959. He subsequently attended the University of Kansas for two years, but left without taking a degree. He soon secured a job teaching speech and dramatics at Grambling College, a historically black college in Louisiana, but was hungry to take a crack at the New York theater scene and so relocated there in 1961 or 1962.

Gunn's first role of note was in Jean Genet's *The Blacks*, for which he was an understudy, though after some time he secured a part on the main cast. His career took off. He began to excel in Shakespearean roles especially. At the time, the New York Shakespeare Festival had begun casting its plays without consideration of race, so Gunn was able to play parts that had largely been off limits to black actors. In 1966, Gunn married Gwendolyn Landes. The couple went on to have two children. In 1967, he won his first Obie Award for a part in *Titus Andronicus*. That same year, Gunn cofounded the Negro Ensemble Company, whose alums would one day include ANGELA BASSETT, AVERY BROOKS,

Moses Gunn as Joe Kagan and Ketty Lester as Hester-Sue Terhune in an episode of *Little House on the Prairie* that aired in 1981. (AP Images.)

LAURENCE FISHBURNE, and ESTHER ROLLE. Meanwhile, Gunn was making the leap to television and motion pictures.

Gunn appeared as a gangster in both *Shaft* (1971) and *Shaft's Big Score* (1972), the popular blaxploitation films. He appeared on the *Kung Fu* (1973) television series and in the television movie *Roots* (1977). Meanwhile, he continued acting on the stage, especially relishing his roles in Shakespearean drama. He won another Obie in 1975 for his part in *First Breeze of Summer*, which was mounted by the Negro Ensemble. Among his other notable performances, he appeared in the motion pictures *Ragtime* (1981), a part that won him an NAACP Image Award; *The Neverending Story* (1984); and *The Women of Brewster Place* (1989). On the small screen, he made appearances on *Little House on the Prairie* (1977–1981), *A Man Called Hawk* (1989), and *The Cosby Show* (1989). Most of these parts were small ones, however, and Gunn was somewhat frustrated by the lack of black actors in leading roles on television and in the movies.

Gunn, like his mother, died of complications from asthma in Guilford, Connecticut, where he and his family made their home. He left behind an extensive body of work in a variety of entertainment media and is now widely considered one of the most versatile black actors of his generation.

FURTHER READING

Bogle, Donald. *Primetime Blues: African Americans on Network Television* (2001).

Hill, Errol, and James V. Hatch. *A History of African American Theatre* (2003).

Obituary: *New York Times*, 20 Dec. 1993.

JASON PHILIP MILLER

Guthrie, Robert Val (14 Feb. 1932–6 Nov. 2005), educator and psychologist, was born in Chicago, Illinois, to Lerlene C. and Paul L. Guthrie. Shortly after his birth his family moved to Richmond, Kentucky, where his father had become a principal. They moved again in 1938 when his father became principal of Dunbar High School in Lexington, Kentucky.

Guthrie played the clarinet and earned a band scholarship to Florida A&M College in 1948. There he took several psychology courses and considered becoming a psychologist. He doubted whether he could make a career in psychology but his professor, Joseph Awkward, encouraged him in this pursuit. The Korean War interrupted his studies and he enlisted in the United States Air Force. While in the service he met and married Elodia Sanchez. After his discharge he returned to Florida A&M (now University) and completed his degree in psychology in 1955.

The *Brown vs. the Board of Education* decision had forced Kentucky to integrate its colleges when Guthrie enrolled at the University of Kentucky to earn his master's degree. After completing his degree, he returned to the Air Force. According to Guthrie, "The military was the first place where I felt equal, because they had rules against racism even way back then."

During his second tour of duty, he rose to the rank of staff sergeant at the Air Force base on Baffin Island, in northern Canada. He left the Air Force in 1960 and moved with his family to San Diego. Initially he taught at San Diego High School and Memorial Junior High School, as well as part-time at San Diego Mesa College. He eventually became Professor and Chair of the Behavioral Sciences Department at Mesa College.

During this period Guthrie began work on *Psychology in the World Today*, a collection of articles he edited to accompany introductory psychology textbooks. Guthrie decided that this book would not only include articles from psychology journals but also from popular magazines like *Time* and the *New York Times Magazine*. Likewise he included articles from well-known psychologists such as B. F. Skinner and from non-psychologists such as Isaac Asimov. It was published in 1968, with a second edition in 1971.

When he attended the American Psychological Association (APA) convention in 1968, he and a group of black psychologists drew up a list of demands to the APA's Board of Directors to integrate the organization. However, Guthrie and his colleagues changed their minds and instead formed the Association of Black Psychologists (ABP), which now includes more than 10,000 members.

He was also working on his doctorate in psychology. He received his Ph.D. from U.S. International University in 1970. He was then hired by the University of Pittsburgh in the position of associate professor of psychology, later becoming the director of the Urban Psychology Program there. He left the University of Pittsburgh in 1973 to become a research psychologist at the National Institute of Education. He was promoted to associate director of the psychological sciences division of the Office of Naval Research. He returned to San Diego in 1976 to be a supervising research psychologist at the Navy Personnel Research and Development Center (NPRDC).

In the same year he published the book *Even the Rat Was White*. This groundbreaking study presented several different themes. Guthrie demonstrated how psychology was used to perpetuate racism, as well as the history of racism within the discipline of psychology. Finally he brought into the light the forgotten history of black psychology by examining the development of psychology programs at historically black colleges and universities and the personal histories of black men and women who earned advanced degrees in psychology between 1920 and 1950.

The book was met with hostility by some and indifference by many. Guthrie reported that some of his colleagues told him that it was divisive and revolutionary; however, black faculty described it as a godsend. Its initial sales were low but its popularity grew so much that it became a required book in many history of psychology classes. Due to its eventual popularity a second edition was published in 2003. Joseph White, another of the founders of ABP, remembers that the book was "a challenge to psychology to make us visible" (*Union-Tribune* obituary).

In 1981 he left the position at NPRDC to go into private practice. His retirement lasted until 1991 when he became Professor of Psychology at Southern Illinois University at Carbondale. There he headed the program in applied experimental psychology. He retired once more in 1998 and returned to San Diego. There he engaged in a private practice, Psychiatric Associates of South Bay. After his retirement Guthrie worked in a community center dispensing counseling to white and black blue-collar workers, which he called "lunch bucket psychology," and worked as an adjunct professor of psychology at San Diego State University.

In 2001 Guthrie donated his papers to the Archives of the History of Psychology (AHAP). He was the first black psychologist to do so. His donation led to a one-day conference sponsored by AHAP and the University of Akron.

Among his awards is recognition as a Special Elder by the APA National Multicultural Summit and Conference. He was also named a Fellow for Division 26 (Society for the History of Psychology) of the American Psychological Association.

FURTHER READING

Guthrie's professional and personal papers are housed at the Archives of the History of Psychology (AHAP) at the University of Akron in Akron, Ohio, http://www3.uakron.edu/ahap/online at http://www3.uakron.edu/ahap/.

Guthrie, Robert V. *Even the Rat Was White: A Historical View of Psychology* (2d. edition, 2003).

Obituaries: *San Diego Union-Tribune*, November 12, 2005 (online at http://www.apa.org/divisions/div45/images/Robert_V.pdf); *American Psychologist*, September 2006.

STEPHEN A. TRUHON

Guy, Buddy (30 July 1936–), singer and guitarist, was born George Guy to Sam Guy and Isabel Toliver, who were sharecroppers in Letsworth, Louisiana. Raised with four siblings, Buddy made his own guitar when he was seven years old. He taught himself to play by listening to the blues records his parents spun on the family's wind up record player. Guy played in the Big Poppa John Tilley Band in Baton Rouge and sat in with artists such as Lightin' Slim, Slim Harpo, and Lazy Lester in the early 1950s. Buddy was profoundly influenced by the showmanship of fellow Louisiana native Guitar Slim. It was the single note playing style of B. B. KING, however, that really influenced Buddy, and he went on to adopt King's approach of bending and shaking the guitar strings for a vocal lead guitar style.

In 1957 Guy moved to Chicago, the epicenter of electric blues music, to find better employment and to help his younger brother financially and musically. He was enthralled with the music and started sitting in around town. MUDDY WATERS, who was a dominant force in Chicago blues, fed the young and hungry Guy salami sandwiches in his car and gave him encouragement. Guy won a blues guitar battle at the Blue Flame lounge one Sunday afternoon in 1957. His frenzied interpretation of the B. B. King style wowed the audience. By the time he collected his prize, a bottle of whisky, however, it had already been drunk by his co-contestants. Magic

Buddy Guy, photographed in New York, 30 October 2006. (AP Images.)

Sam, who, along with OTIS RUSH, was a purveyor of the tough urban blues style dubbed "West Side," was impressed by Guy and urged him to come to a recording studio. Guy was offered a recording contract with Eli Toscano's Cobra record label, where Magic Sam and Otis Rush had both enjoyed hit singles. WILLIE DIXON, the great blues songwriter who had penned many hits for Muddy Waters and HOWLIN' WOLF, was temporarily estranged from Chess Records and served as house producer, talent scout, and bass player for the new label. Artistic, a Cobra subsidiary, released two singles with Guy and his band in 1958. The records were only moderately successful, and Toscano's labels folded after he was killed over gambling debts. Guy followed Dixon to Chess Records, Chicago's leading blues label, where he began doing session work. He contributed guitar parts for the legendary Chess artists Howlin' Wolf, Muddy Waters, SONNY BOY WILLIAMSON, as well as BIG MAMA THORNTON and KOKO TAYLOR. Muddy Waters's *Real Folk Blues* album featured just Muddy and Buddy Guy on acoustic guitar.

Guy recorded as a leader for Chess in 1960. "The First Time I Met the Blues," "Stone Crazy," and "Let Me Love You Baby" were marked by passionately strong vocals and guitar work. Guy played all over Chicago and Chess released several singles, though with only modest success. Buddy's reputation was built on the power of his manic live performances. In 1965 Buddy toured England with the American Folk Blues Festival, where he was viewed by a young Eric Clapton.

Forever frustrated by the lack of hit recordings, Guy teamed up with the singer and harmonica player JUNIOR WELLS. Together, they recorded Wells's seminal 1965 *Hoodoo Man Blues*, regarded as one of the most influential modern blues albums of all time. Still under contract to Chess Records, Buddy's guitar credits were attributed to "Friendly Chap." The Guy-Wells collaboration proved fruitful for many years, well into the 1970s. Guy's younger brother Phil lent his considerable guitar talents to their road band.

Rock stars such as JIMI HENDRIX and Eric Clapton were singing Guy's praises, though it was frustrating for Guy to sometimes hear others suggest that he was imitating Hendrix when he and Hendrix knew it was the other way around. Guy played all over the United States and Europe and toured Africa as well. In 1967 Vanguard released his first solo album, *This is Buddy Guy*, which was recorded live. Though Buddy regarded it as less than he was capable of, it nonetheless showcased his explosiveness as a performer.

Buddy continued to play and tour with such rock superstars as Carlos Santana, Jeff Beck, the Rolling Stones, and Eric Clapton, further cementing his reputation as one of the greatest guitar players alive. Stevie Ray Vaughan, whose incendiary style owed not a little to Buddy Guy, re-paid the favor by covering Buddy's songs, "Mary Had a Little Lamb," "Leave My Little Girl Alone," and the Willie Dixon-penned "Let Me Love You Baby" on his own hit albums.

Though Buddy had recorded many albums for several labels over the years, it was not until 1991's Grammy-winning *Damn Right I've Got the Blues* that he had a bona fide hit record. His years of hard work and the praises of many famous rock and blues guitarists finally paid off. He subsequently earned three more Grammys for his albums *Feels Like Rain* (1993), *Slippin' In* (1995), and *Blues Singer* (1993). In 1989 Guy opened the famous Chicago blues club, Buddy Guy's Legends, which remained the pinnacle of the city's blues scene into the 2000s. In addition to his Grammys, by the late 2000s he had won twenty-three W. C. HANDY Awards, *Billboard*'s Century Award, and the Congressional Medal of Arts. In 2005 he was inducted into the Rock and Roll Hall of Fame. He continued to record and play the world over into his seventies, by which time he was regarded, along with B.B. King and Otis Rush, as the last of the breed of original electric bluesmen.

FURTHER READING

Wilcock, Donald E., with Buddy Guy. *Damn Right I've Got the Blues* (1993).
Harris, Sheldon. *Blues Who's Who* (1979).
Leadbitter, Mike, and Neil Slaven. *Blues Records 1943–1966* (1968).
O'Neal, Jim, and Tim Zorn. "Interview with Buddy Guy," *Living Blues* 1.2.

MARK S. MAULUCCI

Guy, Edna (1907–1982), dancer, was born in Summit, New Jersey. The names of her mother and father are not known. An only child of poor but supportive parents, Guy developed an early interest in dance which extended to a love of reading and writing poetry. Guy loved to fantasize and no doubt dreamed of becoming a famous dancer. One of her early idols was Ruth St. Denis, an early pioneer of modern dance. St. Denis and her husband, Ted Shawn, formed the Denishawn School, which had offices in both Los Angeles and New York City.

A note sent by Guy to St. Denis during a concert intermission prompted a meeting between the two after the performance, launching a friendship that spanned several years. The note became the first of many exchanged between the two from 1923 to 1940, even after they began to work together. Given Guy's fascination with St. Denis, it is likely that she wanted to start classes as quickly as possible at Denishawn. However, after consulting with her mentor, Guy apparently agreed that she was not yet ready for dance instruction at Denishawn, although it is clear that other schools would willingly have accepted her if not for the racial prejudice prevalent in the 1920s.

For the next two years Guy continued her weekend classes with her dance teacher at the time until finally, in the fall of 1924, she enrolled in Denishawn. Guy's teachers praised her hard work and saw great promise in her abilities during her daily two-hour classes and one-hour practices, and her teachers often worked with her outside of class. She also began taking private dance lessons, where she learned such routines as *Temple Bells* and *Dancing Girl of the Delhi*. Eventually she added secretarial courses at Hunter College to her daily routine and did well in all of her studies.

In 1925 the Denishawn Dancers began a series of tours that took them around the United States and abroad. Guy stayed behind. Her devotion to St. Denis grew even more in 1926, after the death of her mother. In 1927 Guy accompanied the Denishawn Dancers on tour for the first time as St. Denis's personal assistant. Their travels sometimes took them to the southern states, where the friendship was strained by St. Denis's failure to mitigate the racially prejudiced treatment Guy received there. Still, the young dancer served St. Denis tirelessly.

As Guy grew older, however, her battles with depression prompted her to turn to St. Denis for help. St. Denis's own struggles with her marriage and professional career likely left her with little solace to offer her protégée. An argument in 1930 between Guy and a member of St. Denis's staff resulted in the two women parting ways. Guy was living with St. Denis at the time and was forced to leave amid the poverty of the Great Depression. Guy managed to support herself with odd jobs and the kindness of friends willing to offer her temporary shelter.

Although Guy had performed in numerous student recitals, she never became a part of the Denishawn Dancers. The separation from St. Denis did not stop her from auditioning, however, and apparently motivated her to pursue her own dance career. Guy met the dancer Hemsley Winfield, which proved to be a turning point in her career. In March 1931 Guy performed as a featured artist with the New Negro Art Theatre. One month later she and Winfield partnered to produce a performance billed as the "First Negro Dance Recital in America." This period also afforded Guy a chance to hear PAUL ROBESON sing, inspiring her to incorporate Negro spirituals into her dance routines.

In 1932 Guy performed five solos in her first independent concert. The performance included *African Plastique*, in which she used African-themed choreography; *Luleta's Dance*, *After Gauguin*, and two ensemble pieces titled *Gimme Yo' Hen* and *Juba*. Guy's offstage efforts to form a dance company were unsuccessful and she performed very little in 1933. A 1934 comeback did find her performing at Studio 61 at Carnegie Hall. Then, in May 1936, she participated in the First National Dance Congress and Festival. This ambitious undertaking was organized by the Dancers' Association, the New Dance League, and the Dance Guild and attracted nearly fifteen hundred people over a six-day period. Other performers included Alison Burroughs, Lenore Cox, and a group of Bahamian dancers. John Martin, a dance critic for the *New York Times*, criticized the event for being too local in scope despite its name. However, he agreed with a resolution made at the end of the congress that creative performances by black people should be both encouraged and sponsored by the community at large.

Guy's next major performance was at the Negro Dance Evening on 7 March 1937 at the Theresa L. Kaufmann Auditorium of the 92nd Street YM-YWHA. Organized by Guy and Alison Burroughs, the event proved to be a milestone in the history of American dance because all of its performers were black and included such notable modern dancers as KATHERINE DUNHAM and Clarence Yates. Buoyed by the event's success, Guy opened a dance school in New York in 1938, but since little information is available about the venture it is assumed that the school closed soon after.

Guy married Walter McCully in 1941 and the couple left New York for Enfield, New Hampshire, where they managed an inn. The 1940s brought health problems for Guy, including several heart attacks which ended any plans she may have had to continue dancing. Guy moved back to New York in the 1960s and taught at a training school for girls. She died in Fort Worth, Texas.

FURTHER READING

Emery, Lynne Fauley. *Black Dance: From 1619 to Today*, 2nd ed. (1988).

Long, Richard A. *The Black Tradition in American Dance* (1989).

Perpener, John O., III. *African-American Concert Dance: The Harlem Renaissance and Beyond* (2001).

Thorpe, Edward. *Black Dance* (1990).

PAMELA D. BLACKMON

Guy, Harry P. (7 July 1870–9 Sept. 1950), composer, arranger, and musician, was born in Zanesville, Ohio, son of Samuel Guy, a Zanesville native and laborer, and Lucy A. Hurley Guy, a homemaker. The Guys had strong roots in Ohio and held a deep appreciation for education. Harry's paternal uncle, Daniel M. Guy, an Oberlin College graduate, administered the school for African American children in Newark, Ohio. Harry graduated from Zanesville's Hill High in 1886. His sister Jessie Ruth Guy, born the next year, pursued a lifelong career as a public school teacher.

Harry began training in piano, violin, and pipe organ at age eight. Through events at his school and at the Saint Paul African Methodist Episcopal (AME) Church of Zanesville he had opportunities to meet prominent musicians, such as the tenor H. M. Wilson of Donavin's Original Tennesseans and Alexander Luca of the Luca Brothers, who directed the AME Church choir in 1865. Such men may have encouraged Guy's talent and helped him obtain advanced musical training.

After high school Guy received a scholarship to study with George Schneider, a noted pianist and teacher in Cincinnati, Ohio. While there Guy demonstrated an ability to intermix with white and black musical communities and be equally at ease with both serious and popular forms of music. He composed his first two waltz songs for Ilson & Company of Cincinnati and worked as an accompanist for the Cincinnati Opera Club, a white institution. He also accompanied the opera star Madame Marie Selika and the Fisk Jubilee Singers during their tours to the city.

In the late 1880s Guy earned another scholarship to study at the National Conservatory of Music in New York. His cello teacher was Victor Herbert. While in New York, Guy taught piano and performed in several concerts, including one at Carnegie Hall in 1890. Guy accepted a position as music instructor for Paul Quinn College in Waco, Texas, in 1894. The next year he moved to Detroit, Michigan, where on 21 July 1895 he married the soprano Julia E. Owens, daughter of George Owens, a prominent Detroit chorister. The couple had two sons, Harry Maurice Guy and another who died as a child.

Detroit at the time of Guy's arrival was a major center for musical and theatrical productions and home to several philanthropic organizations developed by the city's African American community. These included the Colored Musical Society, the Musicians' League, and the Iroquois Club, an elite association of professional men, including members of Theodore Finney's Orchestra and the Detroit City Band, a brass ensemble led by John W. Johnson. Johnson in particular mentored Guy, ensuring his active participation in the Iroquois Club and the Musicians' League. Guy often played with Finney's Orchestra and the Detroit City Band, and from 1903 to 1907 he led his own five-piece Harry P. Guy Orchestra that performed on the ferries carrying recreation seekers to and from Belle Isle. Guy also accompanied classical musicians, performed as a soloist, and from 1897 to 1909 served as music director and church organist for Saint Matthew's Episcopal Church of Detroit.

Guy's initial Detroit employment was unique for an African American. He started off as a clerk and sheet music demonstrator for stores catering mainly to a white clientele. He was first hired by the Detroit Music Company in 1896. There he began arranging music, mostly for white composers. From 1899 to 1902 Guy clerked and arranged for the Willard Bryant Band Instruments and Music store. Bryant published nearly all of Guy's early ragtime compositions, including his majestic "Echoes from the Snowball Club" (1899), the first ragtime waltz ever published.

In 1903 Guy began arranging for Detroit's Jerome H. Remick & Company, soon to become one of the world's largest sheet-music publishers. Guy created a sensationally popular song version of Neil Moret's 1901 instrumental hit "Hiawatha." He assisted Moret with songwriting techniques. He also helped Remick's Henrietta Blanke earn popularity in 1911 as "America's Waltz Queen." By 1915 Guy was a top Remick staff arranger, noted particularly for coaching (and lending money to) a new and struggling Remick composer, Richard A. Whiting. Guy became Whiting's sole arranger. Together they turned out such memorable standards as "Japanese Sandman," "And They Called It Dixieland," and the World War I hit "Till We Meet Again."

From 1916 to the early 1930s Guy freelanced from a downtown Detroit office where renowned celebrities including BERT WILLIAMS, Al Jolson, Sophie Tucker, Seymour Simons, Walter Donaldson, Eddie Cantor, Eva Tanguay, and Buddy DeSylva turned to Guy for help with songs and spot arrangements for their vaudeville shows. During this period Guy also created nonsecular arrangements for churches and universities, early jazz band scores, and orchestrations for musical revues. His known output of compositions and arrangements exceeds a hundred and sixty titles, but Guy frequently neglected to add his name to his arrangements.

After his wife's death in 1933, Guy lived in relative obscurity, mainly tutoring new musicians from his Detroit home. Helen Westin, writing for the National Sheet Music Society's *Song Sheet*, recalled the speed with which Harry P. Guy arranged and transcribed two copies of her songs in 1946. He charged a mere two and a half dollars. This included preparing her copyright applications and serving her coffee and cookies in his scrupulously clean living room. She described Guy as an affable and distinguished gentleman whose clothes, though dated, were finely tailored and spoke of quality. He was seventy-six at the time. Though frightened to leave his home because of a recent neighborhood shooting, he was vitally interested in current events, especially the upcoming Detroit Auto Fair. He died of stomach cancer at eighty and was buried in an unmarked gravesite beside his wife in the Owens family plot. On 11 October 2003 members of Detroit's Societé for the Culturally Concerned celebrated the unveiling of a headstone honoring "Master Musician Harry P. Guy," thus ensuring his inclusion on the Elmwood Cemetery's Black History Tour.

FURTHER READING

Guy compositions, photographs, and obituaries are in the Azalia Hackley Collection at the Detroit Public Library. Descriptions of Guy as a musical genius are provided in the unpublished memoirs of the Detroit historian Fred Hart Williams in the Burton Historical Collection at the Detroit Public Library.

Kenyon, Norma. "A Detroiter Named Guy, the Forgotten Man of Music," *Detroit Free Press*, 4 Sept. 1949.

La Brew, Arthur. *The Afro-American Music Legacy in Michigan* (1987).

La Brew, Arthur, and Nan Bostick. "Harry P. Guy and the 'Ragtime Era' of Detroit, Michigan," *Rag-Time Ephemeralist* 2 (1999).

Westin, Helen. "Echoes from the Snowball Club (Harry P. Guy)," *Song Sheet* (Apr. 1989).

NAN BOSTICK

Guy, Rosa Cuthbert (1 Sept. 1925?–), writer, was born Rosa Cuthbert in Diego Martin, a town in Trinidad and Tobago, West Indies, one of three children born to Henry and Audrey (née Gonzales) Cuthbert. During the late 1920s, Guy's parents emigrated to the United States, and after they found jobs and housing in Harlem, New York, Guy and her older sister, Ameze, left Diego Martin and were reunited with their parents when Guy was seven years old. By the time Guy was fourteen, both of her parents had died; Guy and her sister then resided in an orphanage and foster homes. Guy eventually left school and worked at a factory. In 1941 she enrolled in classes sponsored by the American Negro Theater (ANT) and married Warner Guy; their son, Warner Guy Jr., was born the following year. Warner Guy Sr. died in the early 1960s, a decade after the couple separated in 1950.

Also in 1950, Guy joined the Committee for the Negro in the Arts after the demise of the ANT. One year later Guy, JOHN OLIVER KILLENS, JOHN HENRIK CLARKE, Willard Moore, and Walter Christmas founded the Harlem Writers Guild (HWG), the influential workshop that attracted a significant number of African American writers during its first two decades. Although Guy studied writing with Viola Brothers Shore and took classes at New York University, the HWG played the pivotal role in her development as a writer. In 1954 Guy's one-act play *Venetian Blinds*, which included a role for her, was staged off-Broadway at the Topical Theatre. Six years later, Guy became a published author when C. L. R. JAMES, editor of *The Nation*, published two of Guy's short stories (including "The Carnival") in that Trinidadian newspaper. Apparently there are no extant copies of the aforementioned narratives. Also in 1960 Guy, MAYA ANGELOU, ABBEY LINCOLN, and Sarah E. Wright founded the Cultural Association for Women of African Heritage (CAWAH). After the 17 January 1961 assassination of the Congolese president Patrice Lumumba, Guy and Angelou persuaded CAWAH's members to spearhead the 15 February 1961 sit-in at the United Nations to protest Lumumba's murder. Additional turbulent events of the 1960s such as the bombing of the Birmingham, Alabama, church where four African American girls died, the assassinations of MALCOLM X and MARTIN LUTHER KING JR., and the riots led to Guy's traveling across the United States in order to glean the thoughts and feelings of African American youth pertaining to the traumatic decade. As a result, Guy edited and published *Children of Longing* (1970), a collection of twenty-five essays written by young African Americans. Over the decades, Guy continued her involvement with the HWG, and from 1967 to 1978 she served as the organization's president.

Guy's short stories and essays appear in a variety of anthologies and periodicals; however her acclaim as a writer is due to her talents as a novelist. She is the author of four adult novels: *Bird at My Window* (1966); *A Measure of Time* (1983); *My Love, My Love; or, The Peasant Girl* (1985); and *The Sun, The Sea, a Touch of the Wind* (1995). *My Love, My Love*, based on Hans Christian Andersen's fairy tale "The Little Mermaid," was awarded first prize at a Cabourg, France, festival in 1988, and was adapted for the stage by Lynn Ahrens and Stephen Flaherty. The musical *Once on This Island*, opened on Broadway's Booth Theatre on 18 October 1990 and closed on 1 December 1991 after 469 performances. Guy's novels, especially her young adult novels, have won a variety of awards, and *The Friends* (1973), which marked Guy's debut as a novelist for young adults, was made into a British television documentary in 1984. Guy's young adult novels include the Jackson-Cathy trilogy: the aforementioned *The Friends* (1973), *Ruby* (1976), and *Edith Jackson* (1978); the Imamu Jones trilogy: *The Disappearance* (1979), *New Guys around the Block* (1983), along with *And I Heard a Bird Sing* (1987); as well as three additional novels: *Mirror of Her Own* (1981), *The Ups and Downs of Carl Davis III* (1989), and *The Music of Summer* (1992). Most of Guy's novels, after being published in the United States, were subsequently published in London. Her novels have been translated into a variety of languages including French, German, Italian, and Japanese. In addition, Guy published the children's picture book *Mother Crocodile* (1981), which is her adaptation and translation of Birago Diop's *Maman-Caiman*. Guy's other children's books are *Billy the Great* (1991) and *Paris, Pee Wee, and Big Dog* (1984).

FURTHER READING

Lawrence, Leota S. "Rosa (Cuthbert) Guy," in Thadious M. Davis and Trudier Harris-Lopez, eds., *Afro-American Fiction Writers after 1955* (1984).

Norris, Jerrie. *Presenting Rosa Guy* (1988).

LINDA M. CARTER

Guyot, Lawrence (17 Jul. 1939–), civil rights activist and television news analyst, was born to the carpenter and builder Lawrence Guyot Sr. and the domestic worker Margaret Piernas in Pass Christian, Mississippi, on 17 July 1939. Widely known for the important part he played in organizing voter registration drives in Mississippi during the period of the civil rights movement, Guyot extended his activism beyond the sixties into the

twenty-first century, as he became a stalwart public figure on the District of Columbia political landscape. Guyot's part in the civil rights movement is less recognized than that of celebrated figures like FANNIE LOU HAMER, BOB MOSES, CHARLES E. COBB JR., STOKELY CARMICHAEL, MEDGAR EVERS, MARTIN LUTHER KING JR., and MALCOLM X, yet he was intricately involved in numerous important historical developments within the movement, and sometimes worked side-by-side with the aforementioned.

Guyot's immersion into the civil rights movement can be attributed to his early upbringing and the events that later unfolded around him at Tougaloo. Raised Catholic, Guyot matriculated through parochial schools before entering Randolph High School, where he played sports and debated. Early on Guyot learned the importance of voting, perhaps because in Pass Christian, unlike most of the places governed by Jim Crow—particularly Mississippi—African Americans faced fewer restrictions at the polls. Rather than being confronted with poll taxes, grandfather clauses, and literacy tests, there politicians actually sought out the small African American swing vote. It was not until age seventeen, while attending Tougaloo University, a small historically black college located on the northern edge of Jackson, Mississippi, that the young Guyot would encounter firsthand the wrath of the South's stringent racism. When he entered Tougaloo in the 1950s the college was at the vanguard of the civil rights battle. Quite heroically, Tougaloo opened its doors wide open to the Freedom Riders and the Student Nonviolent Coordinating Committee (SNCC)—it became a safe haven for civil rights student activists from across the country.

In 1962 Bob Moses recruited Guyot into the SNCC. Founded in 1960, the SNCC originally focused almost exclusively on coordinating the sit-in movement. By 1962, however, when Guyot joined, the SNCC began to redirect its energies toward registering voters, a strategy more suited to Guyot's political temperament and background. Guyot worked throughout Mississippi registering voters and organizing disenfranchised citizens around the concept of participatory democracy.

Like many of the civil rights workers in the South, Guyot was jailed and experienced violence at the hands of angry mobs, as well as racist law enforcement officials. The noted journalist Charles Cobb recalls that when SNCC embarked on its first Delta voter registration effort in Greenwood, Mississippi, he received a call from a worker telling of an angry mob of townspeople attacking their office. Fortunately, Guyot, Sam Block, and Luvaugn Brown escaped injury, or even death, by climbing through a back window and sliding down a television antenna. Guyot would not always have such good fortune.

Returning from a voter education training session in 1963, the noted civil rights icon Fannie Lou Hamer and a group of organizers, including fifteen-year-old June Johnson, were arrested and jailed in Winona, Mississippi. African American prisoners there were coerced into beating the party of organizers; Hamer suffered permanent kidney damage as a result. When Guyot received word of their arrests, he went to post bail but was himself arrested, severely beaten, and threatened with death. Several outside calls from supporters as far away as New York and California probably saved him from being killed; or perhaps it was the broadened media spotlight ensuing from the assassination of Medgar Evers, which occurred while he and the others were held in custody.

In 1964 Guyot was instrumental in helping to organize and coordinate the Freedom Summer Project, a voter registration drive that spanned twenty-six counties throughout Mississippi. More than one thousand students from the north traveled to Mississippi to embark on a massive voter registration project. This effort culminated in the Mississippi Freedom Democratic Party (MFDP), which was organized to challenge the seating of the segregated white delegation from Mississippi at the Democratic Convention in Atlantic City, New Jersey. With the support of Hamer and others, Guyot defeated the National Association for the Advancement of Colored People leader AARON HENRY for chairperson of the MFDP. Unfortunately, Guyot was jailed in Hattiesburg, Mississippi, for picketing in front of the courthouse two days before the convention and, thus, was unable to attend. Nevertheless, the efforts of the MFDP did lead to the integration of the Mississippi delegation from Mississippi and played a significant part in bringing about the eventual passage of the Voting Right Act of 1965. In 1966 Guyot ran unsuccessfully for Congress on an antiwar platform.

As the civil rights movement entered its descent Guyot continued his activism around a wide variety of issues facing disenfranchised citizens. After receiving a law degree from Rutgers University Law School in New Jersey in 1971, he worked with constitutional rights groups between Mississippi and the nation's capital until finally making Washington, DC, his home in 1976, after being hired by Pride, Inc. In 1981 he was hired by a former SNCC colleague, then Washington, D.C., mayor, MARION BARRY to work for the Department of Health and Human Services. Years later, when the re-airing of the award-winning *Eyes on the Prize* documentary (a documentary he appears in) was stalled by legal disputes, Guyot led in the successful effort to preserve its footage and re-air the important series. He has also led in efforts to achieve statehood for the District of Columbia, community policing and reauthorization of the Voting Rights. In 2005, Guyot began appearing regularly as a guest analyst for Fox News, mostly as a liberal commentator on the conservative talk shows *O'Reilly Factor* and the *Sean Hannity Show*. In 2005 he argued on O'Reilly's show against the media's portrayal of the Hurricane Katrina victims as "refugees" and described the Bush administration's tepid rescue as racist; and in 2010 he appeared on Hannity's show and defended the construction of a controversial Islamic mosque near the site of the 9/11 terrorist attack.

FURTHER READING

Cobb, Charles, Jr. *On the Road to Freedom: A Guided Tour of the Civil Rights Trail* (2008).

Payne, Charles. *I've Got the Light of Freedom: Organizing Tradition and the Mississippi Freedom Struggle* (2007).

Watson, Bruce. *Freedom Summer: The Savage Season That Made Mississippi Burn and Made America a Democracy* (2010).

LARVESTER GAITHER

Guy-Sheftall, Beverly (1 June 1946–), feminist scholar and educator, was born Beverly Lynn Guy in Memphis, Tennessee. The oldest of three daughters, Beverly was raised in a traditional African American extended-family household. Her mother, Ernestine Varnado Guy, separated from husband, Walter P. Guy Jr., when Beverly was eleven and moved with the children to live with Beverly's stay-at-home grandmother and her Baptist-minister grandfather. Hard work, education, independence, and self-reliance were central principles in the Guy household. "Every tub sits on its own bottom," Beverly recalls being told by her mother. She supported the three girls by working as a public school math teacher and later as an accountant at two black colleges. Beverly credits her mother with developing her earliest sense of "feminist consciousness," often urging Beverly and her sisters Francine and Carmella to respect the dignity of all women; that irrespective of marriage, a woman should always have resources—or the skills to earn resources—to call her own; and that a woman's body was hers to control (Guy-Sheftall, *Gender Talk* [2003], 9, 10, 11).

After graduating from Manassas High School in 1962 at the age of sixteen, Guy enrolled at Spelman College, a small, historically black college for women in Atlanta, Georgia where students were "expected to dress a certain way, walk a certain way, pour tea a certain way" (Zinn, 1994, 18). Guy's mother felt Spelman's good academic reputation and protective environment would nurture her eldest daughter's emotional and intellectual development. Guy pursued a major in English, with a minor in secondary education. She had intended to become a teacher. But after graduating from Spelman with honors in 1966, Guy left the familiarity of the South for a fifth year of undergraduate study in English at the all-female Wellesley College in the very white, very liberal world of greater Boston, Massachusetts. It was at Wellesley where Guy took her first women-focused course and where her interest in gender issues began to develop.

Guy returned to Atlanta in 1968 to pursue a master's degree in English at Atlanta University. Her thesis was a critical examination of William Faulkner's treatment of women in his novels. Long hours of research would further stimulate Guy's attraction to the growing field of women's studies.

While in graduate school Guy met and married Willis B. Sheftall Jr., an alumnus of Morehouse College who was studying economics. In 1969 the couple moved to Montgomery, Alabama, where Guy-Sheftall landed her first academic appointment in the English department at Alabama State University. The two returned to Atlanta in 1971; Willis to teach economics at Morehouse College and Guy-Sheftall across the street at Spelman College as an assistant professor in English. Though Spelman offered a few women's studies courses, Guy-Sheftall was disturbed that students knew little of black women writers. She was convinced that the college needed a "campus-wide program with an explicitly black feminist perspective," influenced as she was by the writings of TONI CADE BAMBARA, AUDRE LORDE, and BELL HOOKS, among others (Guy-Sheftall, "Other Mothers of Women's Studies," in *The Politics of Women's Studies: Testimony from 30 Founding Mothers*, ed. Florence Howe [2000], 153).

Guy-Sheftall's colleagues at Spelman did not universally share her enthusiasm. Many viewed feminism as something invented by privileged, middle-class, suburban white women to push their agendas. Feminism, they argued, did not speak to the condition, struggles, values or aspirations of African Americans. The irrelevancy of feminism to the African American experience was a sentiment voiced by many in the black community. Guy-Sheftall, in her own writings, would acknowledge that mainstream feminists did little to bridge the divide. Instead, she argued, reconstructed histories of "their" Movement ignored or denied the contributions of black women. Notable activists such as New York state congresswoman SHIRLEY CHISHOLM; attorney and founder of the National Organization of Women, PAULI MURRAY; and the author Michele Wallace had been largely erased from popular and scholarly narratives of the contemporary women's movement (Guy-Sheftall, *Gender Talk*, 2003, 3–4).

Despite ambivalence by some of her colleagues, Guy-Sheftall continued to advocate for curricular change. She also entered a doctoral program in American Studies at Emory University in 1976 and saw the publication of her first book, *Sturdy Black Bridges: Visions of Black Women in Literature*, an anthology co-edited with Roseann P. Bell and Bettye Parker Smith in 1979.

Guy-Sheftall's professional triumph as a published scholar was met with personal challenge. In 1980, she and her husband divorced. A year later, her mother died from breast cancer. Varnado Guy would not live to see her daughter complete the doctoral degree, which Guy-Sheftall did in 1984 with support from a Woodrow Wilson Fellowship for Dissertations in Women's Studies that she had been awarded two years prior. Guy-Sheftall's efforts to integrate women's studies and a black feminist perspective into curricular and co-curricular offerings at Spelman also began to show results. With the approval of Spelman's sixth president, Donald Stewart, and a grant from the Charles Stuart Mott Foundation, she founded and established the Women's Research and Resource Center in 1981 and inaugurated the Women's Studies minor. Both the center and the minor were the first at a historically black college. Three years later, in 1984, Guy-Sheftall worked with colleague Patricia Bell-Scott to co-found *SAGE: A Scholarly Journal on Black Women* (*SAGE* would cease publication in 1995). A 1987 grant from the National Endowment for the Humanities enabled Guy-Sheftall to establish an archives, also attached to center, to serve as repository for research by and about black women. In the fall of that year, the college appointed its African American female president, JOHNNETTA

BETSCH COLE, a cultural anthropologist who had been professor of anthropology and director of the Latin American and Caribbean studies program at Hunter College in New York City. At the announcement of Cole's presidency, the actor-comedian-educator-philanthropist BILL COSBY awarded Spelman College $20 million to construct an academic facility for the humanities and to establish the Anna Julia Cooper Professorship in Women's Studies. The endowed chair was named in honor of the twentieth-century feminist and only the fourth woman in the United States to have earned the doctoral degree by that time. Guy-Sheftall would be the first to hold the Anna Julia Cooper Professorship (Spelman College Women's Research & Resource Center, 25th Anniversary Program, 2007).

Nationally, Guy-Sheftall was becoming a regular on the academic lecture circuit. She routinely served as a proposal reviewer and project consultant for the New York-based Ford Foundation and traveled to other colleges, such as the University of Wisconsin, the University of Arizona, Smith College and Bowling Green State University, to consult on curriculum development in Women's Studies. In between teaching, research, consulting and lecturing, Guy-Sheftall continued to advocate for change at Spelman College. In 1996 she successfully petitioned to elevate women's studies from a minor to a major. In 2001 she launched the Toni Cade Bambara Writers/Scholars/Activists Program to develop students' ability to link scholarship with activism for social change. In 2002 Guy-Sheftall recruited the African American filmmaker Ayoka Chenzira to Spelman, and the two later added digital media to the programs of the center. Other program components would include women's health (added in 2005) and a lesbian, gay, bisexual and transgender program (added in 2006).

Guy-Sheftall also continued to solidify herself as a scholar, pushing the field of women's studies to acknowledge the roles and contributions of black women feminists. Her dissertation, *Daughters of Sorrow: Attitudes Toward Black Women, 1880–1920*, was published in 1991, followed by *Words of Fire: An Anthology of African American Feminist Thought* in 1995, and an anthology, *Traps: African American Men on Gender and Sexuality*, co-edited with Rudolph Byrd in 2001. Her publication *Gender Talk: The Struggle for Women's Equality in African American Communities* 2003 is a personally intimate, politically unapologetic, and "truth-telling" book co-authored with her friend and the former Spelman College president Johnnetta Betsch Cole.

Guy-Sheftall has been recognized with numerous honors for her work, including the Bronze Jubilee Award for Literature (1984); Kellogg National Fellowship (1987); Spelman College President's Award for Faculty for Outstanding Scholarly Achievement (1989); Phi Beta Kappa induction (1996); Association of Black Women Historians' Letitia Brown Memorial Publication Prize for Best Anthology (1996) and the Emory Medal by Emory University (2000).

FURTHER READING
Cole, Johnnetta Betsch, and Beverly Guy-Sheftall. *Gender Talk: The Struggle for Women's Equality in African American Communities* (2003).

Blake, John, "The Discipline of Women: Independent Mom Was Professor's Role Model," in *The Atlanta Journal and The Atlanta Constitution*, 6 Mar. 1992.

Hammonds, Evelynn M., and Beverly Guy-Sheftall, "Whither Black Women's Studies: An Interview, 1997 and 2004," in *Women's Studies Future Foundations Interrogations*, eds. Elizabeth Lapovsky Kennedy and Agatha Beins (2005).

Zinn, Howard. *You Can't Be Neutral on a Moving Train: A Personal History of Our Times* (1994)

OLIVIA A. SCRIVEN

Guyton, Tyree (24 Aug. 1955–), artist and activist, was born in Detroit, Michigan, the third of ten children of Betty Solomon Guyton and George Guyton, a construction worker. His mother reared the children on her own after George Guyton left the family, when Tyree Guyton was nine years old. Guyton grew up on the east side of Detroit in an area called "Black Bottom," one of the oldest African American communities in the city. He attended Northern High School, but he did not graduate and earned his GED at a later date.

Guyton began painting at the age of eight when his grandfather, Sam Mackey, a housepainter at the time who later became a painter of fine art, gave him the tool to create, a paintbrush. Because of his family's poverty, Guyton felt all he had was his art. He felt like he had no freedom, and he realized early on that pursuing art could be a way out of poverty. The rest of his family did not understand his interest and did not understand art; therefore, he was an object of ridicule.

Guyton joined the army in 1971. Upon returning to Detroit in 1972 when his enlistment ended, he studied art for six years at several institutions in Detroit, including the Center for Creative Studies and Marygrove College. Primarily a painter and sculptor, he studied with the painters Charles McGee and Allie McGhee.

In April 1974 Guyton married the Detroiter Mary Andrews. They were married for two years and had two children, Tyree Jr. and Towan. When the marriage ended, Guyton retained custody of the children. He had three children from other relationships: Omar, James, and Tylisa. Guyton held a variety of jobs in the 1970s and 1980s, including inspector at a Ford Motor Company automobile plant, firefighter for the City of Detroit, and art teacher. In 1986 Guyton founded the *Heidelberg Project*, an installation of environmental art on Heidelberg Street in Black Bottom, an area that had declined after urban unrest in 1967, and by 1986 had been devastated by crime due to illegal drug traffic. Guyton wanted to make a change in his community and saw the possibilities of using art as a means of reclaiming the neighborhood. He started with an abandoned house that was being used to sell drugs. He painted it, gathered discarded objects that he painted, and affixed them to the house. It was not long until the drug dealers had abandoned the property.

Tyree Guyton, photographed at the site of the *Heidelberg Project*, his two-block outdoor art gallery on Heidelberg Street in Detroit, 27 July 2006. (AP Images.)

Because of his success, and with the artistic assistance of his grandfather and his future wife, Karen Smith, who also had a formal art education, Guyton began to decorate the outside of other abandoned houses on Heidelberg Street, transforming them into urban art. Guyton used children's dolls, bicycles, tires, toilets, and tombstones. He also began clearing the weeds off an abandoned lot and assembling found objects, discarded drinking fountains, and appliances, to create freestanding sculptures. The popularity of the *Heidelberg Project* brought constant visitors to the neighborhood, and the criminals were forced to relocate. After transforming Heidelberg Street, Guyton spread his art over two more blocks. Guyton married Smith in 1987.

Two of the significant images in Guyton's art were painted polka dots and accumulated shoes. The polka dot, according to the "The Dottie Wottie House" postcard, represented "the common unifying spirit among us, and the jelly beans 'Grandpa' Mackey loved so much." Guyton painted polka dots on abandoned properties throughout the Detroit area to highlight disrepair and the fact that city government was allowing absentee landlords to let their properties deteriorate. Shoes, meanwhile, represented the worn-out shoes Guyton and his siblings had to wear while growing up, as well as his grandfather's recollections of lynching he had seen in the South: Mackey remembered only seeing the soles of the hanged victim's shoes. "Shoes come from my soul and my soul is on Heidelberg Street" (Guyton, *Hot, Raw, and Funky*, Exhibition Catalog, Detroit, Michigan, Scarab Club, 2–28 Feb. 2000).

The *Heidelberg Project* was featured in *People* in 1988, in *Newsweek*, on *NBC Nightly News*, on ABC's *Good Morning America* in 1989, and on *The Oprah Winfrey Show* in 1991. Visitors came from across North America and from as far away as Japan and Africa. Meanwhile the neighborhood children learned about art and were exposed to individuals from a variety of cultures. Some of the adult residents began to be proud of their community and played an active role in the expansion of the *Heidelberg Project*.

Yet many of the residents of Black Bottom found the decorated houses and lots disturbing. Interviewed by television and newspaper journalists, they called the installations unwanted eyesores and argued that art should be in a museum. In response, the City of Detroit repeatedly ticketed Guyton for littering.

Guyton had several solo exhibitions in the early 1990s: OMAP X1: Tyree Guyton at the Detroit

Institute of Arts in 1990; Tyree Guyton at the LedisFlam Gallery, in New York City in 1991, and at the Liberal Arts Gallery in Detroit in 1992.

In November 1991 the Detroit mayor COLEMAN YOUNG issued an order to dismantle the project. Guyton was given fifteen minutes to retrieve his artwork before four of the abandoned houses were demolished. Guyton and Mackey lost dozens of original works of art. Guyton filed a lawsuit against the City of Detroit.

In 1992, after receiving the Michigan Artist Award from Governor John Engler, Guyton began to rebuild the *Heidelberg Project* using the vacant lots cleared in the demolition, including those that were city-owned and privately owned. Because of the controversy, for Guyton to be able to use the privately owned properties was quite an accomplishment. In 1993 Guyton dropped with lawsuit at the urging of the new mayor, DENNIS ARCHER, who was publicly supportive of the project by assisting in securing several grants and contributing to *Heidelberg Project* fund-raisers. The project was resuscitated and became an empowering force in the community. In 1994 Guyton and his wife, Karen, were divorced.

Despite his backing in the statehouse, the battles with some of the residents and city government continued, and in 1999 the project not on privately owned property was destroyed. But Guyton continued the *Heidelberg Project* on a smaller scale, and lots filled with assemblages, paintings on wood, trees studded with found and other objects, and many political campaign signs remained. In 2000 Guyton married Jenenne Whitfield, the director of the *Heidelberg Project*, and became stepfather to her daughter, Chloé.

Guyton exhibited and lectured in numerous galleries and museums, including the Detroit Institute of Arts and the Charles H. Wright Museum of African American History. He was invited to create urban environments worldwide, and he traveled throughout the United States and to Australia, Brazil, Ecuador, Italy, and the Netherlands. In 2005 he won the Rudy Bruner Foundation Silver Medal for Urban Excellence.

FURTHER READING

Colby, Joy Hakanson. "The Shoe Fits at Guyton's Scarab Club Double Showing," *Detroit News*, 4 Feb. 2000.

Thomas, Mary. "Local Photographer Documents Controversial Project That Used Discarded Objects to Transform Inner-City Section of Detroit," *Pittsburgh Post-Gazette*, 19 May 1999.

Turla, Gary. "Tyree Guyton: The Heidelberg Project, Exhibition from 26 October to 27 November 1996," Detroit, Michigan.

Tyree Guyton: Hot, Raw, and Funky, Exhibition Catalog, Detroit, Michigan, Scarab Club (2–28 Feb. 2000).

Whitfield, Jenenne. "Thoughts on Tyree Guyton's Heidelberg Project," *Southern Quarterly* (Fall–Winter, 2000/2001).

CHERYL A. ALSTON

Gwaltney, John Langston (25 Sept. 1928–29 Aug. 1998), anthropologist, educator, author, and wood sculptor, was born in Orange, New Jersey, to Stanley and Mabel Harper Gwaltney and into a thriving, extended family environment that also included his brother, sister, aunts, uncles, and cousins. Gwaltney became blind by the age of two months. His mother taught him the alphabet and the names of animals with homemade cardboard shapes, encouraged him to play the piano, and gave him pieces of wood to carve as he saw fit. Throughout his life, Gwaltney carved "ritually inspired" wood sculptures, taking as his role model his great uncle Julius in Virginia. This relative was known locally for his ritual wood carving in "the tradition of the Old Time Religion … the translation into wood sculpture … of that Core Black theology … a largely undocumented and clandestine art" (Freeman, p. 70). Concerned about John's need for formal education, Mabel Gwaltney wrote a letter to First Lady Eleanor Roosevelt, a disabled children's advocate. Roosevelt actually helped enroll him in a program for visually impaired children. His grade school teachers cheered on his growing fascination with geography, as did his father, a merchant seaman full of stories about travel to Latin America, Europe, and Asia. At age ten, John discovered CBS Radio's *School of the Air* program, which regularly featured anthropologist Margaret Mead. Intensely curious about the diverse ways humans lived, he decided to pursue a career in the social sciences.

Gwaltney's mother especially encouraged him to attend college. Because she became severely ill from diabetes, he attended Upsala College in nearby East Orange, New Jersey, on scholarship. Gwaltney's mother died shortly before his graduation in 1952 with a sociology and history BA. Gwaltney then won a scholarship to the New School for Social Research in New York City on scholarship, earning his MA in political science and sociology there in 1957. Gwaltney taught at New York City's Henry George School, a private high school for students interested in the social sciences. This job helped to finance his doctoral studies at Columbia University, which started in 1959. None other than Margaret Mead became his advisor, encouraging him to conduct field research for his dissertation. Gwaltney was awarded funding from the National Institutes of Health to study the Chinantec Indians of San Pedro Yolox, a remote mountain village in Oaxaca, southeastern Mexico. One in twenty villagers had river blindness, a parasitic disease that African slaves originally spread to the Americas. Gwaltney was fascinated with this community's ability to accommodate its blind members while grappling with deep, chronic poverty. He lived alone in San Pedro Yolox over a year, returning to New York in 1966 and receiving his doctorate from Columbia in 1967. Gwaltney won Columbia's Ansley Dissertation Award. According to Mead, he gave "one of the most brilliant PhD oral examinations in my long experience" (Freeman, p. 62).

In 1969, Gwaltney joined the anthropology faculty of the State University of New York at Cortland in Cortland, New York. In 1970, his dissertation was published as *The Thrice Shy: Cultural Accommodation to Blindness and Other Disasters in a Mexican Community*. By then he had married his wife, Judith (Judy). They had one daughter, Karen. In 1971 John Gwaltney began teaching at Syracuse University on Margaret Mead's recommendation "both for his very original and brilliant mind and his extraordinary integrity" (Freeman). As a researcher, he sought out new communities: the Maroons of Jamaica, the Native American nations of the Shinnecock and Poospatuck, and the black Jews of Harlem. He was also very interested in native anthropology, the study of one's own group. Social science often pathologized and criminalized black culture. Yet Gwaltney knew from experience about "ordinary" black people's daily remarkable strength, resilience, and wisdom. To document the core elements of black culture, Gwaltney secured grants from six different funders, including the National Endowment for the Humanities and the American Philosophical Society. He gathered oral histories from hundreds of African Americans and transformed them into his most widely read and cited book, *Drylongso: A Self-Portrait of Black America*. *Drylongso* has the meaning "acceptable" or "everyday." Published in 1981, it received a Robert F. Kennedy Book Award Honorable Mention. Portions of it were reenacted on PBS television. Gwaltney's next oral history research effort became the 1986 book *The Dissenters: Voices from Contemporary America*, about Americans of diverse races and religions who took action against the status quo, including then-incarcerated Puerto Rican "*independentistas*." In this book, which was nominated for the RFK Book Award, Gwaltney simply described his research methodology. "Listening, and the very occasional appropriate questioning, are the heart and soul of the oral historian's art" (*The Dissenters*, p. xix).

Bucknell University and Upsala College awarded Gwaltney honorary doctorates. He served as a consultant on racial issues for *US News and World Report*, *Life Magazine*, and several colleges, including Swarthmore. Gwaltney advised the National Science Foundation and the American Association for the Advancement of Science on career opportunities for disabled people. He was appointed to the boards of the New York Council for the Humanities, the Smithsonian, the Association of Black Anthropologists, and the ABA's journal *Transforming Anthropology*. Gwaltney published in a wide variety of academic and popular journals, from *Practicing Anthropology* and *The American Scholar* to *Reader's Digest*.

After retiring from Syracuse in May 1989, Gwaltney devoted more time to carving and exhibiting his prize-winning wood sculptures. Shortly before his seventieth birthday, he died in Reston, Virginia, from long-standing health problems. The Association of Black Anthropologists established the John L. Gwaltney Native Anthropology Scholarship and dedicated an issue of *Transforming Anthropology* to him. It featured some of his unpublished writings, tributes to him from friends, and photos of his carvings. In his *American Anthropologist* obituary (Sept. 1999, p. 615), JOHNNETTA B. COLE praised Gwaltney as "a humanist and a visionary, who believed in the indomitability of the human spirit to rise above oppression" (Sept. 1999, p. 615). Community Change, an anti-racist organization based in Boston, Massachusetts, continued with its annual Drylongso Awards, established in 1989 to honor unrecognized citizens who challenged systemic racism.

FURTHER READING

Kessler, James H., et al. *Distinguished African American Scientists of the 20th Century* (1996).

Freeman, Michael. "On the Occasion of John Gwaltney's Retirement," *Transforming Anthropology* 7(2) (1998).

Obituary: Cole, Johnnetta B. "John Langston Gwaltney (1928–1998)," *American Anthropologist* 101 (3), 614–616 (Sept. 1999).

MARY KRANE DERR

Gwynn, Tony (9 May 1960–), baseball player, was born Anthony Keith Gwynn in Los Angeles, California, the second of three son of Charles Gwynn, a state employee, and Vendella (maiden name unknown), a mail clerk. The family moved from Los Angeles to Long Beach when Gwynn was in the fourth grade. At Long Beach Poly High School, Gwynn excelled in both baseball and basketball, making the first team All-California Interscholastic Federation in both sports. In his junior year the basketball team won the state championship, and Gwynn attracted the interest of universities such as Gonzaga and Texas Christian. After his senior year began, Gwynn considered attending several different colleges, but they all wanted him to play strictly basketball. Only San Diego State University would let him play both baseball and basketball, so after graduating from Long Beach Poly High in 1977, Gwynn matriculated at San Diego State as a highly recruited basketball point guard and baseball outfielder.

During his freshman year Gwynn chose not to play baseball, and it was only in 1979 that he first suited up for the San Diego State Aztecs baseball team. During the next three years Gwynn was a two-time All-American outfielder, and he led the Aztecs in hitting in his final two seasons. At the same time he excelled in basketball and was named to the All–Western Athletic Conference (WAC) team on two occasions. In the early twenty-first century he remained the only athlete in WAC history to be honored as an all-conference performer in two sports. On 10 June 1981 the San Diego Padres drafted Gwynn in the third round of the baseball amateur draft; on the same day he was drafted in the tenth round of the basketball amateur draft by the NBA's San Diego Clippers. Gwynn's girlfriend, Alicia Cureton, had followed him to San Diego State, where she received a track scholarship after transferring from the University of California, Los Angeles. They married on 6 June 1981 and had two children.

Choosing baseball over basketball, Gwynn signed with the Padres. At the time he joked that his reason for choosing baseball was that he was newly married and the signing bonus was greater. Later his career numbers proved a better explanation for his choice of sport. Gwynn's time in the minor leagues was short; in less than thirteen months he was in the majors. In the 1981 season he led the Rookie Northwest League's with a .331 batting average and was named the league's most valuable player. He was called up to double-A Amarillo of the Texas League for the final twenty-three games of the season and batted .462. Gwynn started the 1982 season with the Hawaii Islanders of the triple-A Pacific Coast League, where he hit .328 in ninety-two games before receiving the call; he'd made it to the show.

On 19 July 1982 Gwynn made his major league debut against the Philadelphia Phillies. At the plate Gwynn went 2 for 4 with an RBI and scored a run. He batted .289 in fifty-four games with the Padres in 1982—the only time in his career he batted under .300. In fact he only batted under .315 one more time in his career, when he batted .313 in 1988 and still won a batting title.

Gwynn's breakthrough season was 1984, a year of firsts. That year he recorded 213 hits and batted .351, which won him his first batting title. He recorded more than 200 hits five times, batted over .350 seven times (including a streak of five consecutive seasons from 1993 to 1997), and won eight batting titles, which tied him with Honus Wagner, second only to Ty Cobb's twelve. Gwynn was the first player in major league history to win four batting titles in two separate decades. The 1984 season also marked Gwynn's first all-star appearance, a feat he accomplished fifteen times in his career.

Gwynn's best season came in the strike-shortened season of 1994. That year he batted .394, the highest batting average in the National League in over sixty years and in all of baseball in fifty-three years. Gwynn's quest to become the first batter to hit .400 since Ted Williams hit .406 in 1941 ended when the season was canceled because of a players strike. Gwynn was batting .394 for the season, but even more impressive he was hitting .475 in the month of August, just before the season was canceled. Gwynn almost never struck out and was quite adept at earning a walk. With the exception of his rookie season (in which he recorded fourteen walks and sixteen strikeouts) Gwynn never struck out more than he walked in any single season. In a career that spanned twenty seasons, 2,440 games, and over 10,000 plate appearances, Gwynn only struck out 434 times.

Gwynn's attention to detail and desire to continually improve by viewing videos and studying the mechanics of his at bats is perhaps one reason he only got better as a hitter as he aged. Defying the aging process, in 1998, his sixteenth season, Gwynn had what for most would be a career year. He hit for both power and average, belting seventeen home runs, driving in 119 RBIs, and hitting .372 with 220 hits, all career highs, not including the strike-shortened season.

On 6 August 1999, in Montreal's Olympic Stadium, Gwynn became the twenty-second player in baseball history to reach 3,000 hits. Only Cobb and Nap Lajoie took fewer games to reach that benchmark, and only five players took fewer at bats. Gwynn retired with 3,141. Over his twenty-year career, his batting average was .338 and .351 with runners in scoring position. In addition to his eight batting titles and fifteen All-Star Game appearances, he won five Gold Gloves as the top defensive player at his position in the outfield and also was named the most valuable player for the Padres seven times. Gwynn helped the Padres to their only two World Series appearances, both of which they lost. Gwynn retired at the end of the 2002 season, and on 4 September 2004 the San Diego Padres retired his number, 19. Remarkably, in an age of free agency, he spent his entire career with the same team.

Gwynn rarely spoke about his community service, but his work off the field was even more impressive than his hall of fame baseball career. He was inducted to the World Sports Humanitarian Hall of Fame in 1999 and won such prestigious awards for community service as the Branch Rickey Award as the top community activist in Major League Baseball, the Lou Gehrig Memorial Award, and Major League Baseball's Roberto Clemente Man of the Year. In 1998 San Diego State University named its new baseball stadium after Gwynn. Also he and his wife began the Tony Gwynn Foundation, which helped fund local programs such as the Casa de Amparo, the Neighborhood House, the YMCA, and the Police Athletic League. After retiring, Gwynn worked as an analyst for ESPN's baseball coverage and as the head baseball coach at San Diego State, a position given to him on 21 September 2001 and which he officially took over in July 2002 (and in which he coached his son Anthony Gwynn). In 2007 Gwynn joined history's greatest baseball players in the Baseball Hall of Fame in Cooperstown, New York.

FURTHER READING
Gwynn, Tony, and Jim Geschke. *Tony!* (1986).

STEPHEN M. GENNARO

Hacker, Benjamin Thurman (19 Sept. 1935–28 Dec. 2003), naval officer, was born in Washington, D.C., to Coleman Leroy Hacker, an author, army chaplain, and Baptist minister, and Alzeda Crockett Hacker, a public school music teacher and former director of girls at Bethune-Cookman College, Daytona Beach, Florida. The Hackers placed a premium on academic excellence. In a prophetic move they named the eldest of three children after personal friends, the Morehouse College president BENJAMIN MAYS and the theologian HOWARD THURMAN.

Benjamin Hacker spent his childhood years in Daytona Beach and in Dayton, Ohio. He graduated in 1957 with a B.A. degree in science from Wittenberg University in Springfield, Ohio. In 1958 Hacker married Jeanne Marie House, a Springfield native who later became a public school teacher. Their forty-five-year marriage produced three children, Benjamin Jr., Bruce, and Anne, and seven grandchildren.

Hacker forged a remarkable thirty-year naval career, which included ten command assignments. He enrolled in the Aviation Officer Candidate School in Pensacola, Florida, in 1958. Upon graduation he was commissioned an ensign. In 1960 Hacker became a naval flight officer serving with Patrol Squadron 10 and Patrol Squadron 21. In this role he had the distinction of being the first African American naval bombardier-navigator.

Promotions followed in the 1960s. In 1963 Hacker completed the engineering science curriculum at the Naval Postgraduate School in Monterey, California. The following year Hacker was assigned to Patrol Squadron 31, Moffett Field, California, as

a P-3A aircraft flight and ground instructor. In 1966 he reported to the U.S. Naval facility in Argentia, Newfoundland, Canada, as operations officer. The next year he moved to the U.S. Naval facility in Barbados, West Indies, as operations officer. In 1968 Hacker was promoted to lieutenant commander, the equivalent of a major in other U.S. military services.

The early 1970s were historic years for African American naval personnel. In 1971 SAMUEL LEE GRAVELY JR. was promoted to the rank of admiral, the first African American to achieve flag rank. Hacker felt the U.S. Navy offered African Americans a worthwhile career path and actively sought to clear the way. In 1972 Hacker established the Naval ROTC Unit at Florida A&M University in Tallahassee, Florida, and served as its first commanding officer and as a professor of naval science.

Hacker resolved to break racial barriers by demonstrating personal leadership and excellence at all times. In 1974 he was assigned to Patrol Squadron 24, a P-3C Orion squadron stationed in Jacksonville, Florida. The P-3C Orion was a four-engine turboprop antisubmarine and maritime surveillance aircraft manufactured by Lockheed. Patrol Squadron 24 spent six months deployed in Keflavik, Iceland, patrolling the northern Atlantic. African American enlisted personnel were typically discouraged from leaving the naval base in Keflavik at that time. Hacker's commanding leadership in Keflavik helped end this discriminatory practice and opened the doors for other black naval officers to serve in Iceland. Hacker next served as director of the U.S. Navy's Equal Opportunity Division and special assistant to the Chief of Naval Personnel for Minority Affairs in Washington, D.C., from 1975 to 1977. He was promoted to captain in 1977.

In 1978 Hacker earned a M.S. degree in administration from George Washington University in Washington, D.C. Additionally he completed studies in national security policy at the Industrial College of Armed Forces, also in Washington, D.C. Later in the year Hacker was assigned to the naval air station in Brunswick, Maine, another P3 Orion squadron home, as commanding officer. In 1980 he was promoted to rear admiral, the equivalent of a brigadier general in other U.S. military service branches. This promotion signaled the first time a naval flight officer was elevated to flag rank. Hacker assumed command duties at the U.S. Military Enlistment Processing Command in Fort Sheridan, Illinois. Two years later Rear Admiral Hacker held three posts in Naples, Italy: commander, Fleet Air Mediterranean; commander, Maritime Surveillance and Reconnaissance Forces, Sixth Fleet; and commander, Maritime Air Forces Mediterranean. Hacker was responsible for fifty thousand naval personnel and for U.S. Navy air units in Greece, Italy, Spain, and Turkey.

Hacker's final military assignments were as commander, San Diego Naval Training Center, and later of the entire naval base in San Diego. He retired as the most senior African American officer in the U.S. Navy in 1988. During his thirty-year service Rear Admiral Hacker received the Defense Superior Service Medal, the Legion of Merit with three gold stars, the Meritorious Service Medal, the Navy Unit Commendation, and the Cuban Armed Forces Expeditionary Medal.

Retirement did not slow him down. He served as director of the California Department of Veterans Affairs for two years and later held various positions, such as regional senior vice president/general manager Western Region and, later, Mid-Atlantic Region for the United Services Automobile Association, from which he finally retired in 1998. Rear Admiral Hacker demonstrated his desire to preserve African American military and naval history by joining the board of directors of the Black Patriots Foundation in 1997. The foundation sought to establish a memorial on the National Mall in Washington, D.C., and to educate Americans about the 5,000 slaves and free blacks who fought in the American Revolutionary War. Hacker served on the board until his death.

Those who met Rear Admiral Hacker fondly remember his charismatic smile and rich baritone voice. He had the ability to make people feel important, and he also readily made himself available to those needing advice or encouragement. He mentored countless naval officers and enlisted many personnel over his thirty-year career. Hacker loved music, particularly jazz. He also cared deeply for family, co-hosting the Crockett-Hacker reunions with his uncle, Congressman George W. Crockett Jr.

Hacker, the first Naval Flight Officer elevated to flag rank, died of leukemia. In 2005 the Naval headquarters building in Naples, Italy, Commander Task Force 67, which Hacker once commanded, was renamed in his honor.

FURTHER READING
"Admiral Hacker Takes Command," *Ebony* (Feb. 1983).
KYRA E. HICKS

Hackley, Emma Azalia (29 June 1867–13 Dec. 1922), singer, musician, educator, and advocate for African American music and musicians, was born Emma Azalia Smith in Murfreesboro, Tennessee, to Henry Smith, a blacksmith and native of Murfreesboro, and Corilla Beard, the daughter of Wilson Beard, an escaped slave who began a profitable laundry business after fleeing to Detroit. Following the birth of Azalia, as she was called, Corilla Smith opened a school in Murfreesboro for newly freed slave children. In 1870, just after the birth of Azalia's sister Marietta, increasing hostility from local whites forced Corilla Smith to close the school. The family moved to Detroit, Michigan, where Henry Smith opened a curio shop and Corilla Smith taught school. In the early 1880s the couple separated and Corilla raised her daughters on wages earned by private tutoring. In Detroit the Smiths were the first black family in their neighborhood, and Azalia was the first African American student at Miami Avenue public elementary school. Azalia, who had been taking piano lessons since age three, began voice and violin training, and by the time she attended Detroit Central High School she was moonlighting in local orchestras and performing with the Detroit Musical Society. Three years after graduating from high school with honors, Azalia became the first African American graduate of the Washington Normal School in Detroit, in 1886. For the next eight years she taught second and fourth grades at Clinton School, a public school in Detroit.

In January 1894 Azalia Smith quit her teaching job and eloped with Denver lawyer and journalist, Edwin Henry Hackley, whom she had met several years earlier at a SISSIERETTA JONES concert. The couple settled in Denver, where Edwin Hackley was editor of the *Denver Statesman*, a short-lived but influential African American newspaper. While studying at the University of Denver School of Music, Azalia Hackley turned to civil rights activities, founding the Denver branch of the Colored Women's League and establishing, with her husband, a black fraternal organization, the Grand United Order of Libyans (or Imperial Order of Libyans). Immediately after relocating to Denver and taking her place amid the city's black elite, Hackley began editing and contributing articles to the *Statesman's* women's section, "The Exponent," which included articles "of interest to the Colored woman." including "Hygiene, Current Events, Civil Government, Importance and Compiling Facts about the Negro, English Literature and Literature on the Negro, Household Economics, Influence of Music in the Negro Home and on Youth, Practical Talks to Mothers, Physical Culture of our Girls, [and] Abolition Heroes." After experiencing first-hand the increasing grip of Jim Crow and growing antiblack sentiment, Hackley began a book on the subject, which was never published.

In 1900 Hackley became the University of Denver School of Music's first African American graduate. She was, at the time, already teaching in the school's extension department, performing with the Denver Choral Society, and directing local choral groups. A soprano equally skilled on the piano and violin, Hackley had achieved enough renown by 1901 to embark on a cross-country concert tour. At the conclusion of the tour she settled in Philadelphia, taking a post as musical director of the Episcopal Church of the Crucifixion, in part to effect a trial separation from her husband. By 1904 she had established the Peoples Chorus (later the Hackley Choral Society), an all-black group of one hundred singers. In programs that came to exemplify Hackley's musical and pedagogical approach, the chorus performed a combination of choral music, classical music, and Negro spirituals. A concert at the Philadelphia Academy of Music yielded enough money for Hackley to study in Paris with Jean de Reszke, the distinguished Polish opera singer, from 1905 to 1906 and again in 1907 and 1909. Using revenues from her concerts and other fund-raising efforts, Hackley established the Hackley Foreign Scholarship Fund, a competition and scholarship program that sponsored study abroad for African American musicians and vocalists, including Clarence Cameron White and Carl Rossini Diton.

By 1909 Hackley and her husband, who had since joined her in Philadelphia, permanently separated. That same year she published her first book, *A Guide in Voice Culture*. "This 'guide,'" Hackley offered in the book's introduction, "is neither a scientific not a literary treatise. Its sole purpose is to be *helpful*, in a *tangible* way (Hackley's emphasis). A compendium of her developing pedagogical, philosophical, and musical approach, the book offered information and advice on musicianship, breathing, posture, stage presence, elocution, and mental focus, as well as vocal production. Although she continued to perform, Hackley used her tours of black schools, colleges, churches, and organizations across the country to encourage African Americans of all background to undertake the serious study of music. Audiences flocked to hear her speak—and demonstrate—the sustaining power of beauty, art, and music. Art uplifts the soul, she preached, and black music and black musicians uplift the race. Hackley's second book, *The Colored Girl Beautiful*, an anthology of her lectures published in 1916, was written at the behest of BOOKER T. WASHINGTON, who was impressed by a series of lectures she gave at Tuskegee Institute.

Hackley was tenacious and creative in encouraging and promoting African American vocalists, musicians, and composers, arranging concerts, showcasing young talent, and raising money for their training. On tour she featured debuts and duets with other black singers and musicians, including Mary Fitzhugh, ROLAND HAYES, and R. NATHANIEL DETT and highlighted music by African American composers, including Harry T. Burleigh, Samuel Coleridge-Taylor, WILL MARION COOK, and J. ROSAMOND JOHNSON. From December 1914 through March 1915 Hackley wrote eleven articles for the *New York Age* titled "Hints to Young Colored Artists." The articles, typical of Hackley's approach, combined professional advice with life lessons. In one of her essays, "How a Professional Achieves Success," for example, she extolled, "Give to get…. Our world is what we ourselves make it…. Whatever we reap we sow."

Hackley, who described herself as a "race musical missionary," proselytized about the spiritual benefits of music and beauty. She believed in growing race pride through validating the contributions of black artists and the importance of black vernacular music, traditions, and musical production. Using a grassroots and hands-on approach, she pioneered broad and unique musical programs, devising events that combined performance, instruction, and community involvement. Dubbed the "Vocal Teacher of Ten Thousands," she traveled the country organizing large community concerts, choral groups, and massive folk festivals. At each venue she would stay in town for a week to ten days giving workshops, demonstrations, and lectures on voice culture and training local singers identified through churches and community organizations. The culminating event, featuring choral recitals by locals and Hackley performing a program of arias, classical compositions, and Negro spirituals, exposed African American audiences to opera and classical music and celebrated African American folk traditions. These events consciously bridged the gap between the African American elite and the working classes as well as the Baptist, Methodist, and Episcopal churches.

In the mid-teens Hackley established several other ventures, including the Normal Voice Institute, a school for training music teachers located in Chicago, and the Azalia Hackley Music Publishing House. Both projects were short lived. The financial failure of these projects and a mismanaged California concert tour exacerbated Hackley's flagging emotional and physical health. By the late teens she was suffering from dizziness and hearing loss, and in 1922 she died of a cerebral hemorrhage.

While a number of schools and awards have been founded in Hackley's name, her most significant legacy is the E. Azalia Hackley Collection at the Detroit Public Library, established in 1943 with a donation of more than six hundred pieces of nineteenth- and twentieth-century sheet music by African American musicians covering the years 1799 to 1922 from the Detroit Musicians Association, a branch of the National Association of Negro Musicians. The collection was subsequently expanded to include materials related to dance, drama, and the performing arts. In 1927 HALLIE QUINN BROWN profiled Hackley in her pioneering celebration of African American women *Homespun Heroines and Other Women of Distinction*. Wrote Brown:

> Some of the envious have called her a mesmerist. Her personality was one of her strongest points. While splendidly gifted by nature and while honors were showered upon her she was simplicity itself. She was the kind of a woman that mothers point to as an example for their daughters, and she was the idol of young girlhood and children. Strange to say, she was a queen among woman admirers, who everywhere adored and followed her.

FURTHER READING

Brevard, Lisa Pertillar. *A Biography of E. Azalia Smith Hackley, 1867–1922* (2001).

Brown, Hallie Quinn. *Homespun Heroines and Other Women of Distinction* (1926).

Davenport, M. Marguerite. *Azalia, the Life of Madame E. Azalia Hackley* (1947).

Detroit Public Library. *Catalog of the E. Azalia Hackley Memorial Collection of Negro Music, Dance, and Drama* (1979).

LISA E. RIVO

Haden, Mabel Rebecca Dole (17 Feb. 1904–12 Oct. 2006), activist, lawyer, and businesswoman, was born in Lynch Station, Virginia (near Lynchburg), the eighth of eleven children of Mary Elizabeth Robinson, a domestic, and John Milton Haden, a junk dealer. John Haden was almost totally absent from his children's lives, leaving it to Mary Elizabeth Haden to both rear and educate her progeny. She worked exceptionally hard scrubbing floors and clothes and serving white families to ensure that her children were provided for and received good educations. John Haden often turned to his white father for money allegedly to support the family. But Mabel recounted that her mother made the money to support the family and that her father kept the money from his junk business for himself.

Mabel was named for the white woman president of the boarding school (the Allen Home School) in Asheville, North Carolina, that she later attended. She was always reluctant to discuss her birth date, telling one interviewer, "The person who tells his age will tell anything." In the Haden household, the older children were responsible for the younger ones. Mabel's first teacher in the one-room school near the family home was her oldest sister Martha Haden. Her mother saved enough money to send Mabel and her favorite older sister Alice Haden to boarding school in Asheville. The Allen Home School for "colored girls" had been started by a group of northern white women who believed in the necessity of education of young African American women, and when she attended, Mabel had only two or three classmates who were also black. Mabel was a good student and later transferred to the Barber-Scotia School for Girls, later a college, in Concord, north Carolina. She graduated in the mid-1920s from Pittsylvania County High School in Gretna, Virginia. She took teaching jobs in the public schools of Danville, Virginia, and Campbell County, Virginia, since she could not afford to attend college. She sent her earnings back home to help the rest of the family. But she was still determined to get more education and moved to Washington, D.C., where she became a nanny for several years during the 1930s.

At this point her mother suggested Haden continue her education and prepare for college by attending night school and getting a second high school diploma. In the 1940s Haden enrolled at Howard University. One semester before she would have graduated, she ran out of money and had to withdraw. This seeming tragedy had a silver lining, however. She took a job at a Catholic social services agency as a switchboard operator, and there she met the Reverend Michael J. Ready. When he asked her about her plans, Haden told Ready she wanted to return to school but was broke. Ready told her to "choose your school, Mabel" and promised to pay her tuition.

Instead of returning to Howard, Haden enrolled at Virginia State University in Ettrick, Virginia, which was considerably less expensive, and she completed her undergraduate degree in education. In the years that followed, while she was teaching at the Neval Thomas Elementary School in Washington, she learned about Howard University's night law school classes. She enrolled and received her law degree in 1948, graduating as president of her class.

Haden began her legal practice in Washington as a criminal defense attorney, often getting her clients by sitting on what she called the "mourner's bench" in criminal court, where the lawyers for indigent clients sat waiting for the judge to assign them to cases. She opened her own office when she had saved enough money and switched from criminal to civil law. She also continued teaching into the 1950s, until she could become a full-time attorney. But that was still not enough. Even though she worked seven days a week, in 1956 she became the first African American woman to earn a master's degree in law from Georgetown University.

Over the years, Haden represented numerous clients from all over the social spectrum, from moneyed professionals to popcorn vendors. She belonged to numerous civic and political organizations, founded and became president of the National Association of Black Women Attorneys (NABWA), and won numerous awards, including the Washington Bar Association's Charles Hamilton Houston Medallion of Merit. Near the end of her life she said, "I was always climbing the hill, and now I'm tired." Her husband Russell Smith died in 2002.

FURTHER READING

Women's Legal History Biography Project, Robert Crew Library, Stanford Law School. www.law.stanford.edu/publications/projects/wlhbp/profiles/HadenMabel.html.

Obituary: *Washington Post*, 20 Oct. 2006.

LUTHER BROWN JR.

Haggler, Joseph, Jr. (20 Jul. 1921–1 Jan. 1977), Baptist minister and civil rights activist, was born Joseph Houston Haggler Jr. in Winston-Salem, North Carolina, to Vida Margaret and Joseph Haggler. In 1940 Haggler graduated from Winston-Salem State University with a B.S. degree in education. While stationed in Seattle, Washington, during World War II, Haggler was ordained by the Northwest Baptist Convention of Seattle in June 1943. After the end of the war he returned to North Carolina to become a principal and teacher in Edgecombe County and a field missionary for the General Baptist State Convention of North Carolina.

By the early 1950s Haggler had married Ophelia Durham. With the first two of their children, Joseph III and Cynthia, they moved to Metuchen, New Jersey, where Haggler became a full time minister of his own congregation. While serving there, the Hagglers had their third child, Patricia. When he first arrived in Metuchen, it had no church of its own. Haggler employed his parishioners to construct a building. The work began with the foundation and walls. The roof, which was built on the ground, had to be manually lifted and placed on top. The process of building a church was an enormous inspiration to his parishioners, but it was not the only building that Haggler accomplished. In the early 1950s he became involved with an effort to build affordable housing in New Jersey and Philadelphia in a project led by the famed suburban housing developer William Levitt.

In 1956 Haggler moved to a new congregation, taking his family to the small central Pennsylvania town of Carlisle, about twenty miles west of Harrisburg. In Carlisle, Haggler took charge of a much older ministry in a historic church located on the north side of town. Carlisle had a relatively small African American population, but it was an old one dating back to before the Civil War, when the borough had been a stop along the Underground Railroad—both a refuge for fugitive slaves and fertile ground for ruthless bounty hunters. The history of the Shiloh Missionary Baptist Church dated back to 1868 when it was formed out of the Primitive Baptist Church. Although a northern town, Carlisle had a long history of racial segregation, its schools having been fully integrated only two years before the arrival of the Hagglers.

It was at Shiloh that Haggler first became aware of the problems faced by migrant farm laborers. During the 1950s and 1960s a large proportion of migrant workers who traveled the Eastern Seaboard to harvest crops were African American. Haggler's first involvement with migrant workers came in 1959 when a family, having driven approximately fifteen miles from the orchards into Carlisle, arrived at his door looking for help. "I remember him helping these folks get a car repaired and they were at our house," recalls Joseph Haggler III. "We were not real pleased with that as kids, but [we helped] them get themselves back together so they could go back to Florida" (Oral history interview conducted by John Bloom, 13 Mar. 2001).

This incident motivated Rev. Haggler to investigate the needs of the migrant farm labor population in the local area. A small group of white residents from rural Adams County, just south of Carlisle, led by a social worker named Parker Coble, had begun to offer services such as day care to the children of migrant workers through the National Council of Churches (NCC). Since 1951 the NCC had been a leader in raising awareness of conditions for migrant farm laborers. Noting the frequency of debt peonage, along with exemption from the Fair Labor Standards Act and from federal minimum wage legislation, the NCC sponsored a variety of movements to provide migrant farm workers with services.

Haggler involved a number of his parishioners in the programs he created during summers in the early 1960s. Programs included recreational activities, reading instruction, advocacy, and child care. For many children of migrant workers, the programs offered by Shiloh volunteers were their first introduction to formal education. Mildred Jones, one of the most active volunteers from the Shiloh church, recalls that Haggler recruited her to work in one of the migrant programs that he had helped to create. "He asked me if I wanted to go over, and he probably explained to me that it was like a daycare and they needed somebody to be with the children. And they had quite a few children then because we had ... a pretty good sized staff" (Oral history interview conducted by John Bloom, 19 Feb. 2001).

In addition, Haggler became involved as an advocate for workers who were being victimized by "crew leaders," overseers who transported workers to job sites, charging them inflated prices for food and transportation, and intimidating workers with threats of violence.

After the death of Ophelia, Haggler married Marjorie H. Dean and left Shiloh for Philadelphia in 1966. There he became minister of the McKinley Memorial Baptist Church in Willow Grove, Pennsylvania, establishing the Willow Grove Community Baptist Church and the Mount Airy Baptist Church in Philadelphia, both under the direction of the Southern Baptist Convention. Haggler also remained active in civil rights issues statewide through the NAACP. He died after a long illness.

In central Pennsylvania, the vast majority of migrant farm workers are immigrants from Mexico and other parts of Latin America. Much of the work of the Shiloh Missionary Baptist Church in Carlisle was eventually replaced by state and federally funded social service agencies in Adams County. However, these agencies are a contemporary legacy of the work of the Reverend Joseph Haggler in the early 1960s.

FURTHER READING
Bloom, John. "Voices of Migrant Workers,"
    Pennsylvania Heritage (Winter 2005).

JOHN BLOOM

Hagler, Marvin (23 May 1954–), boxer, was born in Newark, New Jersey, the son of Ida Mae Hagler and Robert Sims. Most of his youth, however, was spent in Brockton, Massachusetts, where his mother and father moved with Marvin and his five siblings just a few years after Marvin's birth. Sims left the family when Marvin was a child. Like so many young men who turn to boxing, Hagler had found little to interest him in school. He dropped out during his first year in high school to pursue amateur fighting. The home of the former undefeated heavyweight king Rocky Marciano, Brockton had a history of producing champions. Hagler became acquainted with the Petronelli brothers, Goody, who served as his trainer, and Pat, who became his manager for most of his career.

Just shy of sixty amateur fights to his credit, Hagler quickly established himself as one of the best amateur middleweight fighters in the country. He consolidated his standing after winning the Amateur Athletic Union's middleweight title in 1973. Fighting mostly in Massachusetts, Hagler ran off fourteen straight victories, twelve by knockout. In August 1974, in his fifteenth fight, Hagler stepped up his level of competition considerably when he took on the former Olympic champion Ray Seales. Hagler emerged with a ten-round decision. A few months later, fighting in Seales's hometown of Seattle, the two men fought to a draw. By 1976, with twenty-five wins and one draw, Hagler began to fight outside of the limited boxing opportunities in Massachusetts. In his first out-of-state experience he lost a ten-round decision to Bobby "Boogaloo" Watts, a crafty ring veteran in Philadelphia. Less than two months later, Hagler lost a decision to another mainstay of the Philadelphia boxing scene, Willie "the Worm" Monroe. Hagler would not lose another fight for eleven years. He began 1977 by avenging his loss to Monroe with a knockout in February. He met Monroe later that year and knocked him out again. In 1978 Hagler fought and defeated the talented Bennie Briscoe, then started out 1979 with a one-round knockout of his old foe Seales. Three more knockout victories followed, leading to a fight with the reigning world middleweight champ, the tough veteran Vito Antuofermo, in November 1979. Hagler appeared to dominate much of the fight, though the champion mounted a comeback in the later rounds. Many in the audience were stunned, however, when the fight was

announced as a draw, with Antuofermo retaining his crown. Hagler, who already believed that he had been passed up for title fights in the preceding two years, was furious with the decision.

In 1980 Hagler continued his domination of the other middleweight contenders, knocking out his Philadelphia nemesis Watts in April. Hagler desperately wanted a rematch with Antuofermo, but the latter lost his title to the Englishman Alan Minter that same year. In September 1980 Hagler traveled to England to fight for the middleweight crown and demolished Minter in three rounds. For the next six years Hagler terrorized the middleweight division, defending his title twelve times. He knocked out Fulgencio Obelmejias twice and did the same to the tough but awkward Mustafa Hamsho. Hagler also got his revenge on Antuofermo, battering and cutting his opponent so badly that the fight was stopped. Only the legendary Roberto Duran, who challenged Hagler in November 1983, managed to last the entire fifteen rounds before losing a decision.

By 1985 Hagler had virtually cleaned out the middleweight division of serious challengers. Despite his accomplishments, however, he felt that he had not really established his greatness as a fighter because

Marvin Hagler pounds challenger Roberto Duran during their title fight in Las Vegas, Nevada in November 1983. (AP Images.)

of the lack of a truly defining fight against a championship caliber opponent. That opportunity came when the former welterweight champion THOMAS ("Hit Man") HEARNS stepped up to meet Hagler in April 1985. The prefight publicity organized by DON KING characterized it as "the War." At the opening bell, Hearns rushed out to meet Hagler and immediately began launching powerful shots. Never one to back down, Hagler responded in kind. The result was perhaps the most brutal three minutes in the history of middleweight boxing. Most fighters would have crumpled during such a savage assault, but Hearns and Hagler simply stood toe to toe and banged away at each other with horrifying precision. Hearns stunned Hagler early in the round and eventually opened a nasty cut on Hagler's forehead that bled for the remainder of the fight. By the end of that first round two things were evident: Hearns's best punches could not stop Hagler, and Hagler's blows were wearing Hearns down. In the second round the brutal slugfest continued, but it was clear that Hagler was getting the best of the exchanges. By the end of the round Hearns looked exhausted. In the third round, however, the drama increased. The cut on Hagler's forehead had grown progressively worse, and the bleeding continued unabated. Midway through the round, the referee called timeout to have the cut checked by the ringside physician. The doctor gave his permission for the fight to continue. Hagler emerged from his corner almost a man possessed. Sensing that the fight might be stopped at any minute, he pounced on Hearns, pummeling him across the ring and finally knocking him out with a devastating flurry.

Shortly after his victory over Hearns, Hagler legally changed his name to Marvelous Marvin Hagler. However, he fought only two more times over the next two years. In 1986 he met John "the Beast" Mugabi. The nickname was apt; Mugabi was undoubtedly one of the hardest hitters in the history of boxing and went into his fight with Hagler with twenty-six straight victories, all by knockout. Hagler took the best Mugabi could dish out and finally broke him down and knocked him out in the eleventh round. There remained but one more challenge. SUGAR RAY LEONARD had announced his retirement from boxing in 1984 and then surprised the boxing world by coming out of retirement in 1987 to face Hagler. Few people gave Leonard a chance against the bigger, stronger Hagler. In a fight that was as controversial as it was entertaining, Leonard used every trick in the book, including constant holding, to frustrate Hagler. With brief flurries designed to catch the attention of the judges, Leonard eked out enough rounds to win a split decision victory over Hagler. Hagler, who was never hurt during the fight, protested the decision long and loud and demanded that Leonard give him a rematch. When the rematch was not forthcoming, Hagler walked away from boxing forever.

In the years following his retirement from boxing, Hagler turned his attention to personal appearances at sports memorabilia shows and as a spokesperson for various products. He also began an acting career in Italy, starring in mostly low-budget action and adventure films. In 1993 he was elected to the International Boxing Hall of Fame.

FURTHER READING

Ashe, Arthur R., Jr., with Kip Branch, Ocania Chalk, and Francis Harris. *A Hard Road to Glory: A History of the African-American Athlete* (1988).

Berger, Phil. "Boxing's Angry Man," *New York Times Magazine* (22 Mar. 1987).

MICHAEL L. KRENN

Hailstork, Adolphus (17 Apr. 1941–), composer and university professor, was born Adolphus Cunningham Hailstork III in Rochester, New York, the only child of Phyllis Hailstork, a civil servant in the State of New York Estate Tax Department, and Adolphus Hailstork II, whose occupation is unknown. He grew up primarily in Albany, New York, his musical education beginning with childhood piano lessons. Hailstork also studied the organ, the violin, and voice. As a student at Albany High School, he conducted a boys' choir and began to compose music. He received his high school diploma in the spring of 1959.

Hailstork continued his musical education at Howard University. Entering in the fall of 1959, he studied composition under Mark Fax and graduated magna cum laude with a Bachelor of Music degree in 1963. In the summer of that year he received a LUCY MOTEN Travel Fellowship and went to France to study with Nadia Boulanger at the American Conservatory in Fontainebleau, following in the footsteps of an earlier generation of major American composers such as Walter Piston, Aaron Copland, Virgil Thomson, Roy Harris, and David Diamond. In 1963 he entered the Manhattan School of Music, where he earned a Bachelor of Music in composition in 1965 and a Master of Music in composition in 1966 while studying with Diamond as well as Vittorio Giannini.

Hailstork returned to Europe in 1966 to serve two years in the U.S. armed forces in Germany. In 1969 he embarked upon a teaching career by accepting a graduate assistantship at Michigan State University, where he studied with H. Owen Reed and completed his doctorate in 1971. Hailstork's first faculty position was a professorship at Youngstown State University in Ohio, which he held from 1971 to 1977. He attended the summer 1972 Electronic Music Institute at Dartmouth College in New Hampshire. In 1977, Hailstork accepted a new position at Norfolk State University in Virginia. While composing and teaching, he continued his professional development, taking part in the Seminar on Contemporary Music at the State University of New York at Buffalo in the summer of 1978 and winning a Fulbright Fellowship in 1987. In 2000 he joined the faculty at Old Dominion University in Norfolk as Eminent Scholar and Professor of Music.

Beginning with his Albany High School days and continuing through his university teaching career, Hailstork continuously wrote music. His musical comedy *The Race for Space* was performed during his senior year at Howard. His 1966 master's degree thesis at the Manhattan School, *Statement, Variations, and Fugue*, was performed by the Baltimore Symphony Orchestra. A mid-1970s series on Columbia Records devoted to African American composers featured Hailstork's *Celebration* in a performance by the Detroit Symphony Orchestra. He composed for a myriad of instrumental and vocal combinations including solo piano and organ, chamber music, concert band, orchestra, and song. Hailstork described his own compositional style as "Neo-Romantic, with a growing emphasis on using idiomatic materials of the African diaspora."

A very prolific composer with a widely varied output, Hailstork received many awards and commissions. The 1977 Belwin-Mills Max Winkler Award was presented to him by the Band Directors National Association for his composition *Out of the Depths*. *American Guernica*, which commemorated the deaths of four young girls (CYNTHIA WESLEY, ADDIE MAE COLLINS, DENISE McNAIR, and CAROLE ROBERTSON), in the 1963 bombing at the Sixteenth Street Baptist Church bombing in Birmingham, Alabama, won first prize in the Virginia College Band Directors national contest in 1983. He received the Ernest Bloch Award for choral composition for *Mourn Not the Dead* (1971). In 1992 Hailstork was proclaimed a cultural laureate of the state of Virginia, and he received the state's Outstanding Faculty Award in 1994. In 1995

a work by Hailstork for seven instruments, *Consort Piece*, was awarded first prize at the University of Delaware's Festival of Contemporary Music. He received an honorary doctorate from the College of William and Mary in 2001, the Governor's Award for the Arts in Virginia in 2000, and another honorary doctorate from Michigan State University in 2005. Hailstork married Dr. Qiu Jin, Beijing-born Director of the Institute of Asian Studies at Old Dominion University.

The 1990s and the first decade of the new millennium were an extraordinarily productive compositional period for Hailstork. Five symphony orchestras combined their resources in 1990 to commission from Hailstork a piano concerto that was performed with Leon Bates as soloist. Another commission came from the Barlow Endowment for Music for *Festival Music*, which was premiered by the Baltimore Symphony Orchestra. Hailstork's music has been performed by many major American orchestras, including those of New York, Cleveland, Philadelphia, Chicago, Baltimore, Cincinnati, and Detroit, and under top conductors such as Kurt Masur, Lorin Maazel, Daniel Barenboim, and David Lockington. In 1996 Hailstork's Symphony No. 2 was commissioned by the Detroit Symphony Orchestra. The work was recorded, along with his new Symphony No. 3, by the Grand Rapids Symphony in 2003. Other commissions came from the Opera Theatre of St. Louis, the Kansas City Lyric Opera, the Virginia Symphony, Miami University of Ohio, the Baltimore Symphony Orchestra, the Evelyn White Chorale, the Dayton Opera Company, and the Bank Street Baptist Church in Norfolk, Virginia. The Cincinnati May Festival premiered his *Earthrise* for two choirs and orchestra in 2005, followed by Cincinnati Opera's commissioning of a Hailstork opera titled *Rise for Freedom* and a first performance of his *Settlements* by the Virginia Symphony.

FURTHER READING

The Adolphus Hailstork Collection is located in the special collections of the Diehn Composers Room at Old Dominion University in Norfolk, Virginia.

Zick, William J. *Composers of African Descent, American Heritage in Classical Music* (2006).

DAVID BORSVOLD

Hairston, Jester (9 July 1901–18 Jan. 2000), choral director, composer, arranger, actor, singer, and educator, was born Jester Joseph Hairston in Belews Creek, North Carolina, the only son and first of two children born to his parents (names unknown). He was the grandson of former slaves. When Hairston was a year old the family moved to Kunersville, Pennsylvania, where his father obtained work in the steel mills. His sister was born about six months later and when she was three days old their father died of pneumonia. As a child Hairston is said to have loved music. Although he was a small-framed boy, he played basketball and football in high school and college. His church presented him with a scholarship to attend Massachusetts Agriculture College, now known as The University of Massachusetts in Amherst, Massachusetts, where his educational aspirations were to study landscaping design. After his scholarship ran out he went to work to replenish his finances. After acquiring a patron who recognized his musical gifts he returned to his colligate life, entering Tufts University in Medford, Massachusetts, as a music major. Hairston was also a member of the *Kappa Alpha Psi* Fraternity. In 1929 Hairston graduated cum laude with a baccalaureate degree in music. He then went to the Julliard School of Music in New York City. Hairston became a teacher in Harlem and trained choirs for radio and Broadway shows. He also became a member of the renowned HALL JOHNSON Choir. He worked his way up to assistant director of the choir and traveled with them to Hollywood to make a film, "Green Pastures." In 1936 Hairston had the opportunity to collaborate with Russian composer Dmitri Tiomkin on the score for the movie "Lost Horizon." He also conducted the choir for the movie. That association lasted thirty years and together they produced the music for numerous movies, with Hairston also acting as conductor for the choirs in those films. Hairston learned early the value of protecting his work and joined the American Society of Composers, Authors, and Publishers.

Hairston joined the Screen Actors Guild in 1937 and is also recognized as a founding member and one of the first African Americans to join the Guild,. Hairston married Isabel Margaret (Madge) Lancaster in 1939 and became stepfather to her nine-year-old daughter, Jeanne-Marie. They shared forty-seven years as husband and wife until her death in August 1986.

As he made further inlays into the world of Hollywood he formed his own choir. It was the first integrated choir to be used in the movies. Hairston went on to compose music that was featured as underscores for movies and television. He began working on the Amos 'N' Andy radio show and in 1951 was cast as Henry Van Porter and Leroy Smith on the television show. He went on to do extensive work on movies and television, although he did not always receive credit for his work. Although at times a daunting task, Hairston's willingness to stay the course through inequitable treatment and bigotry set him as a pioneer. He is quoted as having said, "We had a hard time then fighting for dignity. We had no power. We had to take it, and because we took it the young people today have opportunities" (*University of Massachusetts Amherst Winter 2000 Chronicle*, 19 Dec. 2000, by Chronicle staff). Hairston composed a song that was used in the film *Lilies of the Field*. If you listen closely you can hear his voice dubbed in as SIDNEY POITIER's singing "Amen!"

And that was his heart, the music. Hairston dedicated his life to the perpetuation and preservation of the Negro spiritual. He has composed or arranged over three hundred pieces of music, with the song "Mary's Boy Child" being one of the most renowned. Even toward the end of his life when a degree of dementia began setting in, Hairston was sharp as a bell when it came to music. He knew when and where each note began and ended. His animated style of conducting, his patient tutelage of his students, and his gift of extracting just what he envisioned the sound to be was brilliant. He was engaging and inspirational to all he encountered, especially the youth. He regaled them with stories of times past, bringing to light the struggles of a people that mournfully wailed to overcome, joyfully sang about the freedom at hand, adamantly chanted about equality's yearn, and reflectively rapped about the future ahead. He brought the gift of authenticity through his music, imparting insight through the candor of the stories he told.

Dr. Hairston was the recipient of honorary doctoral degrees from Tufts and at least three other universities. It is reported that he directed more choirs than any other conductor, including the famed Mormon Tabernacle Choir. Hairston has been deemed the Dean of African American choral/spiritual music. During the 1960s the United States appointed him as an Ambassador of Goodwill. He traveled the globe, sharing his talent and music. In 1991 Hairston received the 1949th star on the Hollywood Walk of Fame. Although he had achieved extraordinary levels of fame, Hairston was family oriented and took on the role of patriarch. His family has a comprehensive history that can be traced back to the days of slavery. As he traveled the country he would go through phonebooks, calling anyone named Hairston and making arrangements to meet with them. It was his goal to unite his family members, both African American and Caucasian. In an extraordinary gathering in 1989, well over one thousand African American Hairstons came together with a smaller measure of their Caucasian counterparts for a massive family reunion. They came to embrace one another and a common lineage. Hairston dedicated his life to uniting people through shared links, whether musical or familial. In 2003 independent filmmaker Richard J. Hatch completed a documentary on Hairston's life titled *Jester! The Amen Man* and Hairston's cousin Jacqueline Hairston, who has strongly followed in Hairston's footsteps and is a musician, composer, arranger, and music instructor, was commissioned in 2007 to write the inspiring story of his life.

On 18 January 2000, at the age of ninety-eight, Dr. Hairston quietly passed from this world, most probably welcomed into the next by a chorus of angels singing "Don't be weary, traveler, come along home to Jesus," the lyrics from his arrangement of "Don't Be Weary, Traveler." Lauded and acclaimed throughout the world, Hairston possessed a keen polished wit that was both charming and endearing. A Renaissance man, he used his undeniable strength, talent, and innovation to further not only himself, but also others.

FURTHER READING

Thomas, Andre J. *Way over in Beulah Lan':*
    Understanding and Performing the Negro Spiritual
    (2007).
Tomasson, Robert. "1,400 Hairstons Honor Kinship
    Born of Slavery." *New York Times*, (1989).
Wiencek, Henry. *The Hairstons: An American Family in*
    Black and White (1999).
Obituary: *New York Times*, 30 January 2000.

DISCOGRAPHY

Spirituals (1989)
An Evening with Jester Hairston (1971)

                    JANELLE F. H. WINSTON

Haizlip, Shirlee Taylor (3 Sept. 1937–), writer and television executive, was born Shirley Anne Morris Taylor in Stratford, Connecticut, the third of four children of Julian Augustus Taylor, a minister, and Margaret (Morris) Taylor. Her mother named her Shirley, after the child star Shirley Temple. Much of her mother's life as a black woman abandoned by her family who chose to "pass" as white has been chronicled and published by Haizlip. She revealed in her first book, *The Sweeter the Juice: A Family Memoir in Black and White* (1994), that she was eight years old when she "first understood that all

but one of my mother's family had become white" (13). Haizlip's entire writing career has been dedicated to the examination of the complexities of race and identity in America, as experienced through her own family life and history.

Haizlip considered her childhood to be "idyllic" and her comfortably upper-middle-class family to have lived "extraordinary lives" during that time. Luminaries such as JACKIE ROBINSON, ADAM CLAYTON POWELL, ROY WILKINS, and General BENJAMIN O. DAVIS were regular visitors to the Haizlip home. Through her father's library, Haizlip developed her love of music and reading, becoming familiar with authors such as PHILLIS WHEATLEY, FREDERICK DOUGLASS, LANGSTON HUGHES, Charles Dickens, and James Fenimore Cooper. From her mother Haizlip developed her sense of style and social grace (in addition to being a doting mother and involved minister's wife, Margaret Taylor founded the Southern Connecticut chapter of the Links).

Haizlip graduated from high school third of 125 students. She was editor of the senior yearbook, vice president of the senior class, and voted most popular. It was also in high school that she changed the spelling of her name from "Shirley" to "Shirlee" in order to differentiate herself from those who used the traditional spelling. She entered Wellesley College in 1955, where she was one of three black students in her class. They lived together in a single room because entering black students were not assigned white roommates at that time. "Most of the time I felt like an outsider," she has said of her Wellesley years (*The Sweeter the Juice*, 189). "I had maintained a special place for my colored self that did not need Wellesley for its validation, a place back home with my family and my church community" (190).

Haizlip joined the historically black Alpha Kappa Alpha (AKA) sorority. Most significantly she met Harold Haizlip, a young man from Washington, D.C., who was studying classics at Harvard University. The two married on 27 June 1959 in Yale University's Dwight Chapel, a few weeks after her graduation from Wellesley with a degree in sociology. Their courtship was chronicled in their book *In the Garden of Our Dreams: Memoirs of a Marriage* (1998).

After deciding against attending medical school and declining acceptance to Stanford and Brown University law schools, Haizlip worked as editorial director at Boston's Allergy Center from 1959 to 1961. She next did publicity and fund-raising work at the Boston Boy's Clubs in Charlestown, South Boston, and Roxbury. While working for the Boys' Clubs, Haizlip took an urban planning course through the Harvard extension program, which inspired her to apply to the Harvard Graduate School of Design.

Watching televised horrors of the civil rights movement and Vietnam war prompted Haizlip to attempt traveling to the March on Washington. That trip never happened. After miscarrying her first pregnancy in 1961, Haizlip discovered that she was pregnant again and gave birth to their first daughter, Deirdre, in August 1963. Dr. MARTIN LUTHER KING JR.'s "I Have a Dream" speech was the talk of the maternity ward. Within a week of Haizlip's return from the hospital, CAROLE ROBERTSON, DENISE MCNAIR, ADDIE MAE COLLINS, and CYNTHIA WESLEY were killed in a Sunday morning bombing in Birmingham, Alabama. A second daughter, Melissa, was born in 1965, the same year the couple moved to New York City. There Haizlip worked for the service group Liaison, where she advocated child development and civil rights issues alongside ELEANOR HOLMES NORTON and Alma Brown (wife of RON BROWN, secretary of commerce during the Bill Clinton presidency).

In 1971 Haizlip and her family moved to St. Thomas, where Harold was hired as the commissioner of education of the U.S. Virgin Islands in order to revitalize its school system. In 1974 Shirlee Haizlip began working as a production assistant at WBNB, the CBS affiliate television station of the Virgin Islands, becoming general manager shortly thereafter, the first and only woman, and only black, to hold the position among all CBS's affiliates at the time. This position was the one that "filled (her) soul," where she could be in charge, create, and initiate (*In the Garden of Our Dreams*, 208).

Haizlip returned to the United States with her husband in 1979 and a year later found work as special assistant to the president at WNET, a Public Broadcasting System station in New York City. During her tenure there she witnessed the development of such programming as *The MacNeil/Lehrer NewsHour*, *Brideshead Revisited*, *Great Performances*, and *American Playhouse*. In 1986, after almost seven productive years at the station, budget cuts at WNET meant that Haizlip was downsized out of her position. "I thought I was immune," Haizlip said in a February 1999 article in *Black Enterprise* magazine. "Instead," she added, "the layoff left me feeling ashamed and humiliated." She did not want to tell her family about this first "failure" in her life.

In 1989 Haizlip became executive director of the National Center for Film and Video Preservation at the American Film Institute in Los Angeles, where she remained until 1993. The following year she received an Honorary Doctorate of Humane Letters from the University of New Haven in Connecticut and published *The Sweeter the Juice*, her first book, which won the 1995 Bruno Brand Book Award from the Simon Wiesenthal Center. The award is given to authors of nonfiction work that promotes tolerance. In 1998 Haizlip and her husband co-wrote *In the Garden of Our Dreams: Memoirs of a Marriage* in commemoration of their fortieth wedding anniversary. By 2000 her efforts at finding her mother's estranged family were coming to fruition, and by 2002 Haizlip was able to reunite her mother, Margaret, with her only sister, Grace Morris. She chronicled this journey in her third book, *Finding Grace: Two Sisters and the Search for Meaning beyond the Color Line* (2004). "I wanted to bring the story to closure," she told Tavis Smiley on his National Public Radio program, *The Tavis Smiley Show* (28 Jan. 2004). On 24 December 2002 Margaret Taylor Haizlip Hancock passed away at a hospice in Branford, Connecticut. Through her grief, Haizlip felt satisfied to have brought the two divergent sides of her family together, as well as to "show the universality of family issues" (*Tavis Smiley*, 28 Jan. 2004).

FURTHER READING

Haizlip, Shirlee Taylor. *The Sweeter the Juice: A Family Memoir in Black and White* (1994).

Haizlip, Shirlee Taylor. *Finding Grace: Two Sisters and the Search for Meaning beyond the Color Line* (2004).

Haizlip, Shirlee Taylor, and Harold C. Haizlip. *In the Garden of Our Dreams: Memoirs of a Marriage* (1998).

SHARON D. JOHNSON

Hale, Clara McBride (1 Apr. 1905–18 Dec. 1992), humanitarian and founder of Hale House, was born Clara McBride in Philadelphia, Pennsylvania, where she grew up. Her father was murdered when she was a child, and her mother died when Clara was sixteen. She left high school without graduating, although she eventually earned her high school equivalency diploma at the age of eighty-seven. After leaving school she married Thomas Hale and moved with him to New York City. There she did cleaning, worked as a domestic, and studied business administration by taking night classes at City

College. When she was twenty-seven her husband died, leaving her with three children.

The conflict between financially supporting and physically caring for three young children spurred Hale to begin caring for children in her home. She became a licensed foster parent, taking in seven or eight children at a time. Between 1941 and 1968 she reared more than forty foster children.

Hale's work with addicted babies began in 1969, after her retirement as a domestic, when she took in the baby of a heroin addict; within months she was caring for twenty-two infants in her Harlem apartment. Her home was licensed as a child care facility and in 1970 was incorporated as the residential center called Hale House. She later moved to a five-story brownstone. Hale's prescription for caring for infants was simple: hold them, rock them, love them, and tell them how great they are.

Hale's work with and for children extended well beyond the care of infants. With her daughter, Lorraine E. Hale, she created numerous programs for children and families, including Community-Based Family, a program for troubled youngsters; Children Helping Children, an apprenticeship program for juveniles; and Time Out for Moms, a haven to which children could be brought when their parents needed relief. In addition, Hale House launched research programs on the problems of drug- or alcohol-addicted mothers and their infants, founded a home for mothers and infants infected with HIV, and established programs for housing, educating, and supporting mothers after detoxification.

In 1986 Hale was honored by President Ronald Reagan as "an American hero" in his State of the Union address and, with Lorraine, was appointed to Reagan's Drug-Free America task force. Also in 1986 the Women's International Center presented Hale with its Living Legacy Award "to honor women for their great contributions to humanity."

Mother Hale, as she was known, traced her philosophy and values to her Baptist upbringing and to the difficulties she experienced in her youth. Until shortly before her death in New York City, she kept at least one infant in her own room.

FURTHER READING
Johnson, Herschel. "Healing Baby 'Junkies' with Love," *Ebony*, May 1986.
Obituary: *New York Times*, 20 Dec. 1992.
This entry is taken from the *American National Biography* and is published here with the permission of the American Council of Learned Societies.

CHERYL LAZ

Hale, Mamie Odessa (1911–c. 1968), nurse-midwife, was born in Pennsylvania. Little is known of her family or early life. She is best known for her work with African American midwives in Arkansas during the 1940s; her efforts are credited with having reduced drastically the race-based disparities in maternal mortality in that state at mid-century. Hale trained in and practiced public health nursing in Pittsburgh, Pennsylvania, before attending the Tuskegee School of Nurse-Midwifery in Alabama. Hale, who received a certificate in midwifery from the program, was one of thirty-one African American women graduates of the Tuskegee school, only the fourth such education program in the United States. Opened in 1942 the school was also the first postgraduate nurse-practitioner course in midwifery for African American students. It awarded both master's degrees and certificates, but it closed in 1946, as did several other programs for African American nurse-midwives begun at that time, due to white opposition and reductions in federal funding.

In 1942 Hale was recruited by the Arkansas State Board of Health to work with its maternal-child health programs and particularly with African American granny midwives, so called because their ages ranged generally between sixty and eighty. Her recruitment reflected a shift in the landscape of American public health, begun after the passage of the Sheppard-Towner Maternity and Infant Protection Act in 1921, that supplied funds to aid state and local efforts to reduce infant and maternal mortality by establishing training programs and legislating medical intervention. The act expired in 1929, but the model of care it established greatly influenced later initiatives.

Although countrywide maternal mortality had declined significantly in the early 20th century, black women, especially in the rural South, were still at a great risk of death from complications of pregnancy and delivery. The Sheppard-Towner model attributed these high rates of maternal mortality among African Americans in the South both to economic conditions, as was the case in the North, and to the fact that these births were attended by granny midwives. These midwives represented a vexing dilemma for the medical establishment. On the one hand, their practices were implicated in exacerbating the problems of maternal mortality among African American women because, much like early physicians, they lacked training in hygiene and the proper treatment of pregnancy complications. On the other hand, granny midwives—also called granny doctors—were often the sole source of health care for disenfranchised African Americans in the South. In Arkansas by the 1940s black women still were two and a half times more likely than white women to die from complications of childbirth. Thus the Arkansas legislature considered several proposals to address the discrepancy between black and white maternal mortality. Most of these proposals involved severely scaling back the influence of the granny midwives in accordance with the lessons learned through the Sheppard-Towner years. However, the war caused a shortage of physicians and nurses, and the dearth of training opportunities for blacks in the state made the granny midwives a necessary tool for managing African American health care.

It was decided that Mamie Odessa Hale, a trained nurse on staff who, it was assumed, could relate to the granny midwives, would serve as a compromise for this government-initiated effort at reducing African American maternal and infant mortality. In 1945 she was promoted to the position of midwife-consultant for the Maternal and Child Health Division of the Arkansas Health Department. Her task was to implement a statewide training program for midwives, after completion of which they were to receive state certification. In her seven-session courses, conducted in churches and schools, Nurse Hale (as she was referred to by the midwives) offered instruction on current midwifery methods, including proper sterilization of delivery tools, proper hand-washing techniques, maintaining prenatal contact with clients, proper caseload size, evaluating clients' diet, prenatal care, and seeking medical supervision for cases. She encouraged the midwives to view their training as a move toward modernity. Using a transportation analogy, Hale prompted the women to become sophisticated "airplane" midwives, the airplane having recently been commercialized. Many midwives took this recommendation to heart, referring to those who stuck doggedly to the old ways as "horse-and-buggy."

Hale's teaching methods ranged from songs and demonstrations to movies and pictures, in acknowledgment of her students' high rates of illiteracy. Notably, in all of her instruction Hale incorporated an understanding of granny midwives' beliefs and demonstrated respect for their stature in the community. For example, many of the midwives saw their professional choice as a divine calling. Perhaps catering to this belief, Hale began her sessions with prayer and hymn singing and organized many of the midwifery sessions around religious themes. By

the late 1940s, as her tenure drew to a close, more than a thousand midwifery training programs followed the model that Hale established across the state of Arkansas. As a result of the success of these programs the number of maternal deaths among African American women in Arkansas fell from a hundred and twenty-eight recorded in 1930, to forty-three in 1950.

Hale and other midwife pioneers of the time served as an inspiration to a growing cohort of women, African American and others, who sought to redress this inequity by reviving the best of the granny midwife tradition. These women combined hygienic practices with the comforts of nonmedicalized birthing in settings where, as was the case in Arkansas, African American women continued to lack access to proper pre-, peri-, and postnatal care. In 1950, Hale returned to Pennsylvania and married. She later went on to work with the World Health Organization. Little is known about her later career.

FURTHER READING

Bell, Pegge J. "'Making Do' with the Midwife: Arkansas's Mamie O. Hale in the 1940s," *Nursing History Review* (1993).

Fraser, Gertrude Jacinta. *African American Midwifery in the South: Dialogues of Birth, Race and Memory* (1998).

Susie, Debra Anne. *In the Way of our Grandmothers: A Cultural View of Twentieth-Century Midwifery* (1988).

Williams, Nancy A. and Jeannie M. Whayne. eds. *Arkansas Biography: A Collection of Notable Lives* (2001).

ADRIA N. ARMBRISTER

Hale, Millie E. (27 Feb. 1881–6 June 1930), nurse, social activist, and hospital founder, was born Millie Essie Gibson in Nashville, Tennessee, one of five children of Henry Gibson, a blacksmith, and Nannie Gibson. Millie spent her childhood in Nashville, having attended Pearl Elementary School from 1888 to 1892 and graduating from Fisk University's Normal School in 1901. She moved to New York City in order to study nursing at the Graduate School of Nurses there. Later, in 1927, she received her B.A. degree from Fisk. On 20 December 1905 she married John Henry Hale, who taught at Nashville's Meharry Medical College. They had two daughters, Mildred and Essie.

Hale returned from New York committed to improving health care for Nashville's African

American community. On 1 July 1916 she founded the Millie E. Hale Hospital, which became the first year-round hospital in the city to provide health care for African Americans. The hospital, which started with only twelve beds and a staff of three, including Hale, expanded dramatically in less than a decade. By 1923 the hospital included one hundred beds and a staff of twenty-six nurses and three physicians; also by that time, the hospital staff had treated several thousand patients and its physicians had performed more than five thousand operations, with a mortality rate below 3 percent. Before long, the hospital earned a reputation for excellent medical care (Ragland, 371). Concerned with providing both medical care and social services for the African American community, Hale and her husband soon converted their own fourteen-room house to a community center, which became the site for a prenatal and baby welfare clinic and a free clinic for adults. The center also served as a place for black women to meet, attend free health lectures, and discuss ways to improve the community.

Hale was not only concerned with health care, but also recognized the importance of the physical and social development of children in her community. At Hale's urging, the hospital staff organized boys and girls into clubs and taught them healthful recreation. In 1923 Hale purchased land and built four large neighborhood playgrounds. She arranged for the hospital to host an annual youth picnic and a celebration called Boy's Week, a reception for black news carriers. She also organized free band concerts and open-air movies for children. The community lauded Hale for these efforts.

As her involvement in the Nashville black community grew, Hale led the hospital staff in the development of a suite of social services, including educational and recreational programs, home visitations, and even a relief program through which food, coal, medical care, and sometimes even monetary assistance was provided to the most needy. She particularly stressed proper health education, setting up informational meetings open to the community, and publishing a monthly newspaper.

As Hale worked tirelessly to establish and maintain the social service units of the hospital, she also developed the Nurse Training Department. The hospital received recognition from the American College of Surgeons for its outstanding services, which in turn attracted more people to its staff. By 1925 twenty-four women had graduated from its three-year nursing program and many more were enrolled. In order to address the widespread need for a social service department that could cope with the demand for health care in the community, the nursing program included a course in social service and an internship program.

In addition to her devotion to the hospital, Hale managed and maintained a local grocery store. Furthermore, she was active in community activities and organizations, including the Saint Paul African Methodist Episcopal Church, the YMCA, the Nashville Federation of Colored Women's Clubs, and the Heliotrope Literary Circle.

In 1930, after being ill for several months, Hale died of nephritis at age forty-nine, in the hospital she founded. Following her death the management of the Millie E. Hale Hospital passed to her husband. While the hospital remained open for the black community until 1938, the impact of Hale's lifelong devotion to community service has endured into the twenty-first century.

FURTHER READING

Neverdon-Morton, Cynthia. *Afro-American Women of the South and the Advancement of the Race* (1989).

Ragland, John Marshall. "A Hospital for Negroes with a Social Service Program," *Opportunity* 1 (Dec. 1923).

LATICIA ANN MARIE WILLIS

Haley, Alex (11 Aug. 1921–10 Feb. 1992), writer, was born Alexander Palmer Haley in Ithaca, New York, the son of Simon Alexander Haley, a graduate student in agriculture at Cornell University, and Bertha George Palmer, a music student at the Ithaca Conservatory of Music. Young Alex Haley grew up in the family home in Henning, Tennessee, where his grandfather Will Palmer owned a lumber business. When the business was sold in 1929, Simon Haley moved his family to southern black college

Alex Haley in his San Francisco apartment in May 1974. (AP Images.)

communities, including Alabama Agricultural and Mechanical College in Normal (near Huntsville), Alabama, where he had his longest tenure teaching agriculture. The three sons of Bertha and Simon Haley, Alex, George, and Julius, spent their summers in Henning, where, in the mid-1930s, their grandmother Cynthia Murray Palmer recounted for her grandsons the stories of their family's history.

After graduating from high school in Normal, Alex Haley studied to become a teacher at Elizabeth City State Teachers College in North Carolina from 1937 to 1939. In 1939 he enlisted in the U.S. Coast Guard. Two years later Haley married Nannie Branch. They had two children. Haley spent twenty years in the coast guard, advancing from mess boy to ship's cook on a munitions ship, USS *Murzin*, in the South Pacific during World War II. To relieve his boredom, he began writing, first love letters for fellow shipmates at first, then romance fiction, which brought many rejection letters from periodicals such as *True Confessions* and *Modern Romances*. Finally Haley sold three stories on the history of the coast guard to *Coronet*. In 1949 the coast guard created the position of chief journalist for him. Haley did public relations, wrote speeches, and worked with the press on rescue stories for the coast guard until he retired in 1959. Failing to find other work and sustained by his military pension, Haley moved to Greenwich Village to work as a freelance writer in 1959. Casting about for his subject and voice, his early articles included a feature on Phyllis Diller for the *Saturday Evening Post*. Two articles for *Reader's Digest* were better indicators of Haley's future work. One was a feature on the Nation of Islam leader ELIJAH MUHAMMAD; the other was an article about Haley's brother George, who was the first African American student at the University of Arkansas law school in 1949 and would be elected to the Kansas state legislature in the 1960s. In 1962 *Playboy* hired Haley to produce a series of interviews with prominent African Americans, including MILES DAVIS, Cassius Clay (MUHAMMAD ALI), JIM BROWN, SAMMY DAVIS JR., QUINCY JONES, LEONTYNE PRICE, and MALCOLM X. The last interview was the genesis of Haley's first important book, *The Autobiography of Malcolm X* (1965). Based on extensive interviews with the religious leader, the book was Haley's artistic creation and has won an important place in American biography. (Haley's manuscript of *The Autobiography of Malcolm X* is in private hands, but the publisher's copy is in the Grove Press Archive at Syracuse University.) Haley's marriage to his first wife ended in 1964; that same year he married Juliette Collins. They had one child before their divorce in 1972.

Haley's second important book was even more his own story. Recalling stories recounted to him by his grandmother twenty-five years earlier, Haley had begun research on his family's history as early as 1961. Backed by a contract from Doubleday, Haley began serious work on a book that was initially to be called *Before This Anger*. His research trips across the South took him to Gambia, West Africa, where a griot identified an ancestor as Kunte Kinte. In 1972 Haley founded and became the president of the Kinte Foundation of Washington, D.C., which sought to encourage research in African American history and genealogy. *Roots: The Saga of an American Family* (1976) finally appeared in the bicentennial year to great fanfare. A historical novel that invited acceptance as a work of history, it told the story of the family's origins in West Africa, its experience in slavery, and its subsequent history. A best-selling book that won a Pulitzer Prize, *Roots* had even greater impact when it was made into a gripping television miniseries. Broadcast by ABC in January and February 1977, it was seen, in whole or in part, by 130 million people. It stimulated interest and pride in the African American experience and had a much greater immediate impact than did *The Autobiography of Malcolm X*.

In 1977, however, MARGARET WALKER brought suit against Haley, claiming he plagiarized from her novel *Jubilee*. Her case was dismissed. Subsequently, however, Haley reached an out-of-court settlement for $650,000 with novelist Harold Courlander, who alleged that passages in *Roots* were taken from his book, *The Slave*. Haley acknowledged that *Roots* was a combination of fact and fiction. By 1981 professional historians were challenging the genealogical and historical reliability of the book. A third lawsuit for plagiarism was filed in 1989 by Emma Lee Davis Paul. The symbolic significance of the linkage in *Roots* of the African American experience to its African origins for a mass audience continues to be important. Yet, by the time of Haley's death, renewed interest in Malcolm X and questions about the originality and reliability of *Roots* seemed to have reversed early judgments about the relative importance of the two books.

In 1988 Haley published *A Different Kind of Christmas*, a historical novella about the Underground Railroad. When he died in Seattle, Washington, Haley was separated from his third wife, Myra Lewis, and there were legal claims of more than $1.5 million against his estate. The primary claimants were First Tennessee Bank, his first and third wives, and many creditors, including a longtime researcher, George Sims. The bank held a mortgage of almost $1 million on Haley's 127-acre farm near Norris, Tennessee. His first wife claimed that their 1964 divorce was not valid, and his third wife claimed entitlement to one-third of the estate. The executor of Haley's estate was his brother George, who had been chief counsel to the U.S. Information Agency and chaired the U.S. Postal Rate Commission. George Haley concluded that the estate must be sold. In a dramatic sale on 1–3 October 1992, Alex Haley's estate, including his manuscripts, was auctioned to the highest bidder.

His novel *Queen: The Story of an American Family*, based on the life of his paternal grandmother, was published posthumously in 1993 and was the basis for a television miniseries that aired in February 1994. A second novel, *Henning*, which was named for the small community in West Tennessee where Haley lived as a child and is buried, remains unpublished.

FURTHER READING

Haley's early interviews for Playboy, research files on Malcolm X, and forty-nine volumes of *Roots* in various languages are at the Schomburg Center for Research in Black Culture of the New York Public Library. Manuscript and research material for *Roots* are at the University of Tennessee, Knoxville.

Haley, Alex. "Roots: A Black American's Search for His Ancestral African," *Ebony* (Aug. 1976).

Bain, Robert, ed. *Southern Writers: A Biographical Dictionary* (1979).

Nobile, Philip. "Uncovering Roots," *Village Voice*, 23 Feb. 1993, 31–38.

Taylor, Helen. "'The Griot from Tennessee': The Saga of Alex Haley's Roots," *Critical Quarterly* 37 (Summer, 1995): 46–62.

Wolper, David L. *The Inside Story of TV's "Roots"* (1978).

Obituary: *New York Times*, 11 Feb. 1992.

This entry is taken from the *American National Biography* and is published here with the permission of the American Council of Learned Societies.

RALPH E. LUKER

Hall, Adelaide (20 Oct. 1901?–7 Nov. 1993), vaudeville, musical theater, and jazz singer and actress, was born in New York City, the daughter of William Hall, a white man of Pennsylvania German roots who worked as a music teacher at the Pratt Institute, and Elizabeth Gerrard, an African American. She made many jokes about her birth year; on her birthday in 1991 she declared that she was ninety years old, hence the conjectural 1901.

Hall and her sister sang at school concerts. After her father's death she began her stage career. From its debut in 1921 and into 1922 she appeared in the pioneering African American musical revue *Shuffle Along* as one of the Jazz Jasmines chorus girls; she also sang a duet with Arthur Porter, "Bandana Days." In the revue *Runnin' Wild* (1923) she introduced the song "Old Fashioned Love." At some point in 1925 she performed at the Club Alabam in New York City. In May of that year she traveled to Europe with the *Chocolate Kiddies* revue. By one account she married in 1924 her manager Bert Hicks, a Trinidadian merchant navy officer who would not allow her to tour with *Chocolate Kiddies* to the Soviet Union; elsewhere the marriage is dated 1936.

Back in New York, Hall was featured in *Tan Town Topics* (1926), and she starred in *Desires of 1927*, which toured from October 1926 to early 1927. In October 1927 she recorded two titles, including "Creole Love Call," as a guest member of DUKE ELLINGTON's orchestra. Following the death of actress FLORENCE MILLS, Hall was chosen to star on Broadway with dancer BILL ROBINSON ("Mr. Bojangles") in *Blackbirds of 1928*, in which she introduced the songs "I Can't Give You Anything but Love" and "Diga Diga Do." The show opened in May 1928 and then traveled the following year to Paris, where Hall remained, starring at the Moulin Rouge and the Lido. Dazzlingly beautiful, a formidable dancer (partnering with her tutor Robinson), and equally comfortable singing jazz melodies and risqué cabaret songs, Hall in those days rivaled JOSEPHINE BAKER as the leading African American female entertainer.

In 1930 Hall starred in *Brown Buddies on Broadway*. She toured widely in the early 1930s as a soloist accompanied by the pianist Joe Turner (not the singer of that name), Benny Payne, ART TATUM, or the guitarist Bernard Addison. In Europe she performed in the *Cotton Club Revue* of 1931, and she recorded with Turner and Francis Carter in London that year. In 1933 she recorded two titles as a leader accompanied by Ellington's orchestra.

Hall was featured in the film short *All Colored Vaudeville Show* (1935). From 1936 she lived in Europe and through her marriage to Hicks became a British citizen (perhaps in 1938), but accounts of those few years are somewhat confused. In Paris she recorded "I'm Shooting High" and "Say You're Mine" with Willie Lewis's orchestra in the spring of 1936, and Hall and Hicks opened their own club, La Grosse Pomme (The Big Apple). She also worked with Ray Ventura's orchestra in France. After touring Europe she settled in London in 1938, when she starred in *The Sun Never Sets* and recorded with FATS WALLER. Hall and Hicks opened the Florida Club, but it was destroyed by a German bomb in the Blitz. She then toured, entertaining the troops in battle zones.

After the war Hall had her own radio series. She performed in London in *Kiss Me, Kate* (1951), *Love from Judy* (1952), and *Someone to Talk To* (1956). She came to New York to work in the show *Jamaica* (1957) and then returned to London, where she and her husband opened the Calypso Club. After Hicks died in 1963, Hall's activities lessened considerably, but she performed in the show *Janie Jackson* (1968), recorded her first album, *That Wonderful Adelaide Hall* (1970), and sang at St. Paul's Cathedral in a memorial service following Ellington's death in 1974.

In 1977 Hall created a one-woman show with which she toured widely for the remainder of her life, giving concerts in New York in 1988 and 1992. She was the subject of a documentary made for BBC television, *Sophisticated Lady* (1989). Pneumonia and an infection resulting from a fall led to her death in London.

In jazz circles Hall is remembered specifically for her first session with Ellington, in which she set aside her mainstream, smooth-toned, quavering, vaudeville-style singing voice and instead delivered a wordless vocalization imitating the sound of BUBBER MILEY's growling, plunger-muted trumpet playing. More broadly, Hall was a leading actress and singer in African American musical theater who helped to introduce the genre in the 1920s and to ensure that it would be remembered at the century's end.

FURTHER READING

Chilton, John. *Who's Who of Jazz: Storyville to Swing Street*, 4th ed. (1985).

Sampson, Henry T. *Blacks in Blackface: A Source Book on Early Black Musical Shows* (1980).

Obituaries: (London) *Times*, 8 Nov. 1993; *New York Times*, 10 Nov. 1993.

This entry is taken from the *American National Biography* and is published here with the permission of the American Council of Learned Societies.

BARRY KERNFELD

Hall, Al (8 Mar. 1915–18 Jan. 1988), jazz string bass player, was born Alfred Wesley Hall in Jacksonville, Florida, the son of Henry Hall, a cement finisher, and Alene K. (maiden name unknown), a dietician.

(His birth date is often given as 18 March, but 8 March appeared on his driver's license, in his *New York Times* obituary, and in one interview.) Hall was raised in Wilmington, Delaware, from age two and Philadelphia, Pennsylvania, from about age five. His aunt Marie Gilchrist gave him his first lessons on piano, which he studied until he was fourteen. When he was eight he also took up the violin, which he went on to play in school orchestras before switching to string bass in 1932. He hoped to work in a symphonic orchestra but found that path closed to African Americans. After graduating from high school, and while performing in jazz and dance bands in Philadelphia and Atlantic City from 1933 until 1935, he continued his music education at the Mastbaum Music School, where he concentrated on string bass but took up cello and tuba as well.

Hall moved to New York City in August 1936 and joined the swing band Billy Hicks and his Sizzling Six, with which he made his first recordings in 1937 under Hicks's name and accompanying the singer Midge Williams. He married shortly after his arrival in New York, though details of the union are unknown. He worked for the reed player Campbell "Skeets" Tolbert and in 1938 began recording with TEDDY WILSON. He was a guest member of Benny Goodman's sextet on the CBS *Camel Caravan* radio show on 10 January 1939 and a founding member of Wilson's big band from April 1939 into 1940. The group was pared down to a sextet, and he remained with Wilson until May 1941, also recording in Wilson's trio, including "Rosetta" (April 1941).

Hall's second marriage dated from about 1940, though again details are unknown, except that the couple had three children and were divorced in 1950. Their first daughter was born while Hall was working in the violinist HEZEKIAH STUFF SMITH's combo in Chicago around 1941. Returning home he joined the pianist Ellis Larkins's trio (1942–1943) and KENNY CLARKE's group (early 1943). In 1943–1944 he was a staff musician at CBS radio and played on Mildred Bailey's show. Continuing to work in piano trios, he accompanied MARY LOU WILLIAMS, with whom he recorded in 1944–1945, and ERROLL GARNER, intermittently from 1945 until 1963. Also in 1944–1945 he regularly recorded in swing groups for the armed forces V-Disc label. His steady timekeeping was equally useful as a house bassist at Decca for the newly emerged rhythm and blues style and also for the newly emerged bop style, the latter including recording sessions with DIZZY GILLESPIE and CHARLIE

PARKER in Clyde Hart's group (January 1945), the Be Bop Boys under Kenny Dorham and SONNY STITT, FATS NAVARRO and Gil Fuller's Modernists, and Clarke (all 1946).

Hall contributed to the integration of black and white hiring and working practices in Broadway theater orchestras, initially in George Abbott's production of *Barefoot Boy with Cheek* (1946), in which he was the only African American musician. Concurrently he played in jazz clubs, including a period at Eddie Condon's club early in 1947 and a recording session uniting LOUIS ARMSTRONG and Jack Teagarden (10 June 1947). He also ran his own record company, Wax, from 1946 until 1948, at which time it was acquired by Atlantic. The small Wax catalog revolved around BEN WEBSTER, the pianist Jimmy Jones, the drummer DENZIL BEST, and Hall.

In 1950 he attended television school to learn to be a producer and director and then spent five years unsuccessfully fighting racism to get a job in the industry. From the 1950s through the 1970s he continued to play in Broadway shows, including *The Music Man* (1957), *Gypsy* (1959), *Fiddler on the Roof* (1964), and *Ain't Misbehavin'* (1978). He joined COUNT BASIE's big band for a few weeks in 1952 and rejoined Erroll Garner around 1953. Among his many recordings as a freelancer was a jam session under Condon's leadership (24 June 1954) including "Blues My Naughty Sweetie Gives to Me," on which Hall plays a walking bass solo (following Edmond Hall's clarinet solo). During another of his stays with Garner, he recorded "Misty" (1956). He accompanied MEMPHIS SLIM and MUDDY WATERS in concert at Carnegie Hall on 3 April 1959, the French singer Yves Montand on an American tour, and EUBIE BLAKE at the Newport Jazz Festival (both 1960) while recording within DUKE ELLINGTON's circle in sessions with Ellington and Johnny Hodges, Billy Strayhorn, Shorty Baker, Harold Ashby, and Paul Gonsalves.

Hall appeared in WABC television's "Salute to Eddie Condon" on 27 March 1965, and that same year he worked with the pianist Phil Moore. As a member of Benny Goodman's small group from May into November 1966, he participated in the Comblain-La-Tour Jazz Festival in Belgium in August; the group's performances were telecast the following year. He played in the film *The Night They Raided Minsky's* (1968). Late in 1969 he worked with the pianist HAZEL SCOTT's trio. At Carnegie Hall in May 1970 he accompanied BIG JOE TURNER, Eddie "Cleanhead" Vinson, and T-BONE WALKER, and

later that year he recorded the album *Just a-Sittin' and a-Rockin'* with Gonsalves and RAY NANCE. He played in TINY GRIMES's trio in 1971.

Around 1974 Hall married Elizabeth Hoeffner Turner, an art professor. He toured France in 1976 with the Harlem Song and Dance group. In 1978 he joined ALBERTA HUNTER at the Cookery in Greenwich Village, and with her he recorded the soundtrack to the movie *Remember My Name*. He also worked at the Village Vanguard, at Gregory's, and in his final years with Doc Cheatham at Sweet Basil, all in New York City, where he died.

Hall was among the pool of string bassists who were regularly called on as accompanists in swing, bop, and rhythm and blues groups. "The Man I Love," recorded with Garner at a prolific recording session on 7 June 1956, summarizes his art: in the first minutes (taken at a ballad tempo) he plays with a beautiful tone, rock-steady rhythm, and a tasteful selection of notes; for the remainder of the piece (as the tempo quadruples in speed) he reliably underpins Garner's bouncy swing rhythms.

FURTHER READING
The definitive source is Hall's own oral history, taken by Ira Gitler for the Smithsonian Institution on 11–22 Nov. 1978 and held on disc and in transcript at the Institute of Jazz Studies, Newark, N.J.
McCarthy, Albert. *Big Band Jazz* (1974).
Meeker, David. *Jazz in the Movies* (1981).
Obituary: *New York Times*, 21 Jan. 1988.
This entry is taken from the *American National Biography* and is published here with the permission of the American Council of Learned Societies.

BARRY KERNFELD

Hall, Amos T. (2 Oct. 1896–12 Nov. 1971), civil rights leader, lawyer, and judge, was born in Bastrop, Louisiana, to Cecil Hall, a brick mason, and the former Callie McCollough, a homemaker. Hall was educated locally and graduated from Rust College in Mississippi and Gilbert Industrial College in Baldwin, Louisiana. Hall taught primary school, in Bastrop, Lousiana, before moving to Tulsa, Oklahoma, in 1921. He married Ella, a homemaker, and they had two daughters, Adelle and Sammie.

While working as a church janitor, he acquired an old set of law books and developed an interest in law. He became a Justice of the Peace, a position which did not require a law degree, and continued to study law at night. A self-taught lawyer, he passed the bar in 1925 and was admitted to the

Oklahoma Bar Association and the Tulsa County Bar Association. Although soft-spoken, he was a dynamic advocate and articulate trial lawyer. As the attorney for the Oklahoma Association of Negro Teachers, Hall led the fight for equal salaries for teachers via the case of *Freeman v. Oklahoma City School Board* (1948). He also represented ADA LOIS SIPUEL against the University of Oklahoma Law School in the landmark case *Sipuel v. Board of Regents of University of Oklahoma* (1948), which fought the "separate but equal" edict to open higher education to African Americans in Oklahoma, and lay the foundation for *Brown v. Board of Education* (1954). Hall served as the attorney for the State Conference of Branches of the National Association for the Advancement of Colored People (NAACP). He was a close and personal friend of the future U.S. Supreme Court Justice THURGOOD MARSHALL and was a member of the National Legal Committee of the NAACP. For eleven years he served as president of the local Tulsa branch of the NAACP.

In 1946 Hall formed a partnership with the actor Spencer Williams Jr. to found the American Business and Industrial College, a GI school that instituted a six-vocation curriculum for trades such as photography and radio.

Hall was appointed special judge of the District Court of Tulsa County in 1969 and served until 1970. In 1970 he was elected associate district judge of Tulsa County and served in that capacity until his death. Judge Hall was the first African American to be elected to a countywide office and the first African American to be elected a judge in Oklahoma.

Judge Hall was very active in the Masonic order and served as grand master mason of the state of Oklahoma from 1941 to 1971. He was a member of the Xi Omega Chapter of the Omega Psi Phi Fraternity, Inc. He also served as a member of the Tulsa YMCA board and led the capital fund drive to build the Carver Youth Center. Judge Hall was an active member of the Morning Star Baptist Church of Tulsa and later of the First Baptist Church of North Tulsa. He received many honors for his more than forty years of public service, including Outstanding Citizen of Tulsa by the Tulsa Chamber of Commerce, honorary doctor of laws degree from Wiley College, and honorary doctor of humane letters from Langston University. He also received citations from the United States Treasury and the March of Dimes National Foundation. Amos T. Hall died of a heart attack on 12 November 1971 in Tulsa.

FURTHER READING
"Amos T. Hall." Vertical File, Jimmy Stewart Archives, Ralph Ellison Library, Oklahoma City, Oklahoma.
Curtis, Gene, "Only in Oklahoma: Judge Led Battle for Desegregation." *Tulsa World*, 18 Mar. 2007.
Obituary: *Jet*, 2 Dec. 1971.

ALEXANDER J. CHENAULT

Hall, Arsenio (12 Feb. 1955–), actor, comedian, and writer, was born in Cleveland, Ohio, the only child of Fred Hall, a Baptist minister, and Annie Hall. Hall entertained himself as a child by learning magic tricks and watching television talk shows. He played basketball during his teens, and the love of the sport carried over to frequent attendance at professional basketball games as an adult. His parents divorced in 1964, when Hall was nine, and he went to live with his mother, grandmother, and godmother. Hall still had a relationship with his father, but they spent limited time together because of his father's travel schedule. He attended Warrensville Heights High School near Cleveland and then Ohio University, where he was a member of the speech team. He transferred to Kent State University and graduated with a degree in speech.

After graduation he worked for Noxell Corporation, and then left for Chicago. There he won a comedy contest at the Playboy Club and found a job as the comedy emcee at the Sheba Lounge, where he introduced the acts, including the singer Nancy Wilson. She was impressed with Hall and invited him to Los Angeles to introduce him to industry representatives in the early 1980s.

Hall made his television debut on *Elvira's Movie Macabre* in 1982. He backed up Alan Thicke on the *Thicke of the Night* late-night talk show and appeared on the MTV series *The 1/2 Hour Comedy Hour* (1983), *Star Search* (1983), and *Solid Gold* during the 1986–1987 season. The *Motown Revue Starring Smokey Robinson* in 1985 featured Hall's comedy act. He performed in episodes for television shows *New Love, American Style* (1985), *The Real Ghost Busters* (1986), and *The Match Game/ Hollywood Squares Hour* (1984).

Hall's first film appearance was in a John Landis science fiction spoof, *Amazon Women on the Moon*, in 1987. The following year Hall starred alongside EDDIE MURPHY in *Coming to America*. In this film, Hall played four characters, all of which he created. Even though he wrote a portion of the script, Hall did not receive writing credit and was involved in one of the longest running civil trials in the history of the Los Angeles Superior Court, *Buchwald v. Paramount*, which challenged authorship credits and royalty payments from the film. Hall then joined Murphy in 1989 on *Harlem Nights*, in which he played a cameo role alongside Murphy, RICHARD PRYOR, and REDD FOXX. Hall hosted the *MTV Video Music Awards* in 1990 and 1991, *Soul Train's 25th Anniversary Program* in 1995, and the *28th NAACP Image Awards* in 1997.

Hall had three major television parts. The first was as host for a late-night television show, which he took over after the spot was vacated by the comedian Joan Rivers and held for a successful 13 weeks. After this he signed as the host and executive producer of his own show, *The Arsenio Hall Show*. The contract also included a three-movie deal. *The Arsenio Hall Show* was the first syndicated talk program hosted by an African American performer. The show followed the traditional format but made significant changes that included eliminating the host's desk and creating a more informal style that appealed to a young audience. He featured black actors, comedians, and musical artists at that point rarely seen on television and launched the careers of many rap and hip-hop performers. The reclusive musician PRINCE performed on Hall's show, and Bill Clinton, then a candidate for the presidency, played saxophone as a surprise guest in 1992. Hall was noted for his treatment of sensitive subject matter, including a celebration of MARTIN LUTHER KING JR. Day and shows that featured Hall's friend MAGIC JOHNSON discussing AIDS. Critics claimed Hall's interview style was overly deferential to his guests, especially those who were his friends. The talk show ran from May 1989 to January 1994. In 1997 Hall starred as a broadcaster on an all-sports network headquartered in Atlanta in the short-lived comedy *Arsenio*, costarring Vivica A. Fox. He followed this with a role in 11 episodes of the series *Martial Law* (1998–2000).

After 2000 Hall guest-starred in numerous animated features and television shows, including *The Norm Show* in 2000, *The Proud Family Movie* in 2005, and *Scooby-Doo! Pirates Ahoy* in 2006. He produced Nia Peeples's television series *The Party Machine* in 1991 and served as executive producer on two projects, *Time Out: The Truth About HIV, AIDS and You* in 1993, and *Bopha!* the following year. He also cowrote the documentary *Before They Were Kings: Vol. I*, a joint effort with D. L. Hughley, George Wallace, and CHRIS ROCK, in 2004.

Hall's television career continued. He was a guest on *Playboy* magazine shows in 2001 and 2002, *TV Land* (2004), *Sharon Osbourne Show* (2004), *Chappelle's Show* (2005), and Black Entertainment Television (2005). Hall returned to stand-up comedy, making numerous appearances on the *Tonight Show with Jay Leno*. He was listed as one of *People Magazine* and *VH-1*'s 200 Greatest Pop Culture Icons. Hall was single in 2007 and had one son, Arsenio Hall Jr., with his former manager Cheryl Bonacci.

FURTHER READING
King, Norman. *Arsenio Hall* (1993).
Littleton, Darryl J. *Black Comedians on Black Comedy: How African Americans Taught Us to Laugh* (2006).
PAMELA LEE GRAY

Hall, Charles "Buster" (25 Aug. 1920–22 Nov. 1971) pilot and member of the Tuskegee Airmen, the first black military aviation program during World War II, was born in Brazil, Indiana, the younger child of Anna and Frank Hall. Hall's parents' occupations are unknown. Hall had an older sister, Victoria. Growing up in Brazil (population 698) Hall was well liked, an outstanding athlete, and a good student.

In 1938, upon graduating from high school, Hall began classes at Eastern Illinois Teachers College (EITC), which became Eastern Illinois State University in 1957. While attending EITC, Hall played varsity football and worked in the campus restaurant to help pay the cost of school. He left EITC in November 1941 to begin aviation cadet training at Tuskegee Army Air Field in Tuskegee, Alabama. It was in flight school that Hall earned the nickname "Buster." The pilots who attended Tuskegee were unique among all other pilots who flew in World War II because they received all four aspects of training on the P-40 airplane: pre-flight, basic, advanced, and transitional pilot training. Tuskegee was the only airbase in the United States to train in that fashion. Hall graduated from the fourth flight training class on 3 July 1942.

Hall was commissioned as a second lieutenant in the Army Air Corps and was assigned to the Ninety-Ninth Pursuit Squadron, known as the "Red Tail Angels" because the tails of their planes were painted bright red. From 1943 to 1945 Hall flew with the Ninety-Ninth over Europe. The unit shot down or damaged four hundred German planes and was the only unit (black or white) that never lost a bomber they were protecting. The red tails eventually became a symbol of hope for the aircraft they escorted, because the pilots of the escorted planes knew they would make it safely back to base with the Ninety-Ninth's protection. The Ninety-Ninth also held the distinction of being the first all-black unit to go overseas. They were stationed at Fordjouna, Algeria, in May 1942.

The final phase of Hall's flight training was introduction to combat. His first experience in combat was 3 June 1943 when he flew as wingman with Lieutenants William Campbell, Clarence Jamison, and James Willey. After successfully completing the mission, the pilots were considered ready to fly. The pilots' primary duties in addition to flying bomber escorts were to strafe tanks, trains, trucks, bridges, and enemy troops.

On 2 July 1943 Hall, flying a P-40 Warhawk, was returning to base after successfully completing his eighth mission, escorting Mitchell Medium bombers to bomb Castelvetrano Airfield in Sicily. Hall was intercepted by three German Focke-Wulf 190s that were preparing to attack the planes he was escorting. Hall opened fire. The German planes began attacking Hall, forcing him to lower and lower altitudes. He was low on fuel and ammunition when suddenly one of the Germans flew into the crosshairs of his gun. When Hall shot him down, the others planes turned tail and ran. Hall became, arguably, the most famous black pilot in the world with that kill, and it was the first plane credited to the Ninety-Ninth Pursuit Squadron. Hall was congratulated by General Dwight D. Eisenhower, then Allied Supreme Commander of North Africa, and three other generals, including the head of a joint American-British unit, the Eighth Air Force Commander, and the commander of the North African Training Command. The 2 July ceremony was broadcast via radio to all Allied troops as Hall was recognized as the first black airmen to shoot down a German plane in World War II. Hall also received as a prize what was said to be the only bottle of Coca-Cola in North Africa. It had been kept in a safe to be given to the first pilot to shoot down an enemy plane.

From 22 January through 27 January 1944, Hall and the Ninety-Ninth Pursuit Squadron patrolled the beachheads of Anzio, Italy, protecting convoys of men, supplies, and equipment. On 28 January 1944 Hall led a mission in which four German planes were shot down. Hall personally shot down two of them.

The Ninety-Ninth was eventually incorporated into the 332nd Squadron on 3 July 1944 and based in Ramitelli, Italy. In total Hall flew 108 combat missions in Africa, Sicily, and Italy. Hall's record of shooting down three enemy planes was surpassed by only one other black pilot in World War II, Edward Toppins, who shot down four. During Hall's tour of duty, he was awarded the Distinguished Flying Cross, in the process becoming the first black man to win the award.

Upon returning to the United States in 1946 Hall went back to Tuskegee, where he assisted with war bond drives. He also spent time in Lubbock, Texas, to attend airplane instrument instructor school before returning to Tuskegee to become a fighter pilot instructor. Hall remained in the army until 1946, when he retired with the rank of major.

Upon leaving the Army Air Corps, he managed a restaurant in Chicago's DuSable Hotel until 1947, then worked as an insurance agent in Oklahoma City, Oklahoma, and Nashville, Tennessee. While working in Nashville Hall met and married Jeanne Ackiss in 1947. The couple moved back to Oklahoma City where Hall began work as a production control specialist in 1949 at Tinker Air Force Base. This first marriage ended in the early 1950s. Hall had a daughter, Peggy Ann, with Ida Mucker in 1957. In January 1961, Hall married his second wife, Delois Miles, with whom he had two daughters.

Hall remained at Tinker Air Force Base until 1967, when he joined the Okalahoma City Federal Aviation Administration. Hall held the distinction of being the only person hired who did not already work for the FAA. He worked for the FAA at Will Rogers Airport in Oklahoma until his death in 1971 in Oklahoma City, Oklahoma. Following Hall's death, the Tinker Air Force Base Charles B. Hall Chapter of the Tuskegee Airmen was founded. Hall's portrait was hung in the District of Columbia's Military Hall of Fame as well as in Oklahoma City's Ralph Ellison Library in 1978. The Airbase's Tinker Heritage Air Park was renamed the Major Charles B. Hall Memorial Airpark on 19 June 2002. The Airpark project was completed in 2005 with the dedication of a bronze plaque dedicated to Hall. The ceremony was attended by Hall's daughters with Delois Miles.

FURTHER READING

Francis, Charles E. *The Tuskegee Airmen: The Men Who Changed a Nation* (1997).

Gubert, Betty Kaplan. *Distinguished African Americans in Aviation and Space Science* (2002).

Holway, John B. *Red Tails, Black Wings: The Men of America's Black Air Force* (1997).

ANNE K. DRISCOLL

Hall, Edmond (15 May 1901–11 Feb. 1967), clarinetist, was born Edmond Blainey Hall in New Orleans, Louisiana, son of Edward Blainey Hall, a plantation and railroad worker, and Caroline Duhé. His father had played clarinet with a brass band in Reserve, Louisiana. Edmond's four brothers all became professional musicians. His brother Herb Hall had a distinguished career in jazz.

Edmond taught himself to play guitar and then one of his father's clarinets. He worked occasionally with such New Orleans trumpeters and cornetists as KID THOMAS VALENTINE, Lee Collins, and Chris Kelly around 1919–1920. From 1921 to 1923, while with Buddy Petit's band in New Orleans and around the Gulf Coast, he began playing alto saxophone as well. He traveled to Pensacola, Florida, with the trumpeter Mack Thomas then joined the pianist Eagle Eye Shields in Jacksonville in 1924 and brought the trumpeter COOTIE WILLIAMS into the band. In 1926 Hall and Williams joined Alonzo Ross's big band, in which Hall reluctantly played soprano saxophone rather than clarinet. Ross's De Luxe Syncopaters spent nine months in Miami and the remainder of the year touring regionally and, on the strength of recordings made while in Savannah in August 1927, were invited to the Rosemont Ballroom in Brooklyn, New York, in March 1928. The Ross band lost the job after two weeks and disbanded, with Hall and Williams joining the drummer Arthur "Happy" Ford at Happyland, a dime-a-dance hall. They parted company when Williams joined CHICK WEBB's orchestra, with Hall staying at Happyland until July 1929, when he began working in Billy Fowler's band at a dance hall in Atlantic City, New Jersey. Two months later he joined the pianist Charlie Skeets in a band that played another dime-a-dance hall in New York. By year's end CLAUDE HOPKINS had replaced Skeets and assumed the leader's position. Hopkins's group played at the Savoy Ballroom for seven months in 1931. From 1931 to 1934 it was the house band at Roseland Ballroom, from which it broadcast nationally. During this period Hall, featured on clarinet and baritone saxophone, also toured extensively and recorded regularly with Hopkins. With Hopkins's orchestra Hall left Roseland to perform steadily at the Cotton Club, again with national broadcasts several times per week, from March 1935 until around December, when Hall quit the band.

In 1936 Hall joined the trumpeter Billy Hicks and his Sizzling Six at the Savoy. He recorded with FRANKIE NEWTON and then, after John Hammond heard Hicks's band at the Savoy Ballroom in June 1937, with Mildred Bailey and BILLIE HOLIDAY, whose session included "Me, Myself, and I." Hall's solos on two versions of this delightful song are characteristically joyful and bouncy but somewhat stiff, especially in contrast to those of his fellow sideman LESTER YOUNG. His last job in big bands was as a saxophonist with LUCKY MILLINDER in late 1937. In 1938 he married Winifred "Winnie" Henry; they had no children. After rejoining Hicks, Hall joined ZUTTY SINGLETON's trio at Nick's club early in 1939 and Joe Sullivan's band at the downtown location of Barney Josephson's Café Society in October. Josephson took a great liking to Hall's clarinet playing, and no matter what the band, Hall would work at either the downtown or the uptown location for the next seven years: with RED ALLEN from late in 1940; with TEDDY WILSON from late 1941 to 1944; and with his own groups from September 1944 through the fall of 1946. From 1942 he also performed regularly in Eddie Condon's concerts at Town Hall. Recordings from this period include Singleton's "Shimme-sha-wabble" and "King Porter Stomp," Allen's "Down in the Jungle Town" (all from 1940), and his own "Jammin' in Four" and "Profoundly Blue" (from 1941). This last session may have been modeled after the sound of Benny Goodman's quartet (with MEADE LUX LEWIS's celeste serving as a parallel to LIONEL HAMPTON's vibraphone) and thus underscored the conventional wisdom that Hall's personal style on clarinet was modeled after Goodman's, although modified by Hall's persistent use of a husky tone, achieved by humming while blowing.

Hall led bands in Boston until 1950, including one with Ruby Braff and VIC DICKENSON at the Savoy. After a three-week engagement in San Francisco, he began playing at Eddie Condon's club in New York in July 1950, and recording with Condon and his colleagues. He also recorded two sessions with Vic Dickenson's septet, including "I Cover the Waterfront," "Russian Lullaby" (both 1953), "Nice Work If You Can Get It," and "Everybody Loves My Baby" (both 1954). After recording Condon's album *Bixieland* in 1955, he toured internationally with LOUIS ARMSTRONG's All Stars, performing in the movie *High Society* and the film documentary *Satchmo the Great*, both from 1956. That year the writer Max Jones described Hall as a quiet, modest man whose energies were channeled in two directions: his exuberant clarinet playing and his love for fast European cars.

The pianist Joe Battaglia observed, "Edmond got so tired and bored playing the same twenty tunes at every concert that he just had to resign" (Selchow, p. 425), and Hall quit the Armstrong band in July 1958. Having toured Africa with Armstrong in the course of filming the documentary, he moved to

Ghana in the fall of 1959, with the intent of settling there to play and teach. But he found local musicians to be uninterested and unreliable, and after three months he returned to New York. He toured Czechoslovakia as a featured soloist with local musicians in 1960 and then made wide-ranging tours of Europe, as a member of the English trombonist Chris Barber's band in 1962 and again as a soloist. He also rejoined Condon and in the summer of 1964 played with the cornetist Jimmy McPartland. Soon after performing in January 1967 at a concert at Carnegie Hall and at the Boston Globe Jazz Festival, he died at his home in Boston.

Hall sometimes played with bands associated with the revival of New Orleans jazz (for example, recording with MUTT CAREY in 1947), and he often played blues, but neither situation showed him to advantage. Rather his considerable stature as a jazz clarinetist derives from his interpretations of popular songs in a swing style, lightly touched by Dixieland jazz, as best represented on record by his work in Vic Dickenson's septet.

FURTHER READING
Jones, Max. *Talking Jazz* (1987).
Selchow, Manfred. *Profoundly Blue: A Bio-Discographical Scrapbook on Edmond Hall* (1988).
Obituaries: *Down Beat*, 23 Mar. 1967; *New York Times*, 13 Feb. 1967.
This entry is taken from the *American National Biography* and is published here with the permission of the American Council of Learned Societies.

BARRY KERNFELD

Hall, Harry Haywood (4 Feb. 1898–4 Jan. 1985), political theorist, was born Haywood Hall in South Omaha, Nebraska, the youngest of three children of Haywood Hall, a factory worker and janitor, and Harriet Thorpe Hall. When he was fifteen, racist violence in Omaha prompted the family to move to Minneapolis, Minnesota, where Hall soon dropped out of school and began working as a railroad dining car waiter. In 1915 the family moved to Chicago, Illinois, to be near extended family, and Hall enlisted in the military in 1917. He served in World War I for a year as part of an all-black unit in France, where he grew accustomed to the absence of racism. Hall married his first wife, Hazel, in 1920, but the marriage lasted only a few months. In spite of their lengthy separation, they did not officially divorce until 1932.

Hall's experiences in World War I and defending his neighborhood during the 1919 Chicago

Race Riot led to the gradual radicalization of his political views. He joined the African Blood Brotherhood (ABB), a radical organization led by CYRIL V. BRIGGS that fused Marxist class activism with Black Nationalism, in 1922. Though initially attracted to the Communist Party of the United States of America (CPUSA), Hall was convinced by his brother Otto to delay membership until the party had dealt with issues of internal racism. Following the ABB's merger with the CPUSA in 1923, Hall joined the Young Communist League and eventually applied for official membership in the CPUSA in 1925.

That same year, Hall was sent by the party to the Soviet Union to study at KUTVA, the Russian acronym for the Communist University of Workers of the East, an international school in Moscow designed to train comrades in Marxist doctrine and political organizing. In preparation for his travels, Hall officially adopted the pseudonym "Harry Haywood" (a combination of his parents' first names), on his American passport. Hall showed great promise at KUTVA in Marxist theory and was recommended for admission into the Lenin School in Moscow in 1927, to develop his skills as a future party leader. Hall was the first African American assigned to the Lenin School, which sought to develop future party administrators through courses in theory and trade union organizing. That same year, Hall married his second wife, Eketrina (or "Ina"), a young Russian woman who he had met through his social circle in the Communist Party.

During these years in the Soviet Union, Hall collaborated with Charles Nasanov on a formal Communist program to deal with the "Negro Question" in the United States. The Haywood-Nasanov thesis was adopted by the Communist International at the organization's Sixth Congress in 1928. Basing their ideas on a Stalinist definition of nationalism, Hall and Nasanov argued that the black population in the Deep South in effect constituted an oppressed nation. According to this so-called Black Belt Nation thesis, the only solution was black self-determination, even extending to the possibility of formal secession and independence from the United States. This policy was a departure from a strictly class-based understanding of racism, and the combination of traditional Marxism with nationalist black radicalism allowed the party to become a force in American race relations throughout the 1930s.

Hall left the Soviet Union in 1930 to organize for the CPUSA in New York. His return to the United

States also marked the end of his marriage with Ina, who was forced to remain in Moscow. Since Hall's divorce from his first wife did not become official until after his return to the United States, there was no formal divorce of this second marriage. Though he made several attempts to bring Ina into the United States, these efforts failed and they eventually lost contact. Upon his return to the United States, Hall served as a member of the Central Committee and in the Political Bureau (Politburo) from 1931 to 1938. Hall also became general secretary of the League for the Struggle for Negro Rights (LSNR), a group committed to organizing black workers under the guidelines of the self-determination thesis, when it was formed in 1930. But Hall also came into conflict with fellow comrades and party leaders. Ideological differences with JAMES FORD, another leading black communist, led Hall to transfer to the Chicago branch of the CPUSA in 1934. A record of questionable leadership during his service in the Spanish Civil War with the International Brigades in 1937 also led many within the party to question his future in an official capacity. Hall's position as a political commissar was perceived by many other soldiers to be a political favor from party leaders and he lacked the necessary rapport to effectively maintain discipline and morale. In the aftermath of this professional setback, Hall was stripped of his committee positions at the Tenth Convention of the CPUSA in 1938. Needing money and suffering from poor health, Hall moved to California in 1940, where he married fellow communist organizer Belle Lewis. The couple remained together for fifteen years before divorcing in 1955. Beginning in 1943, Hall served in World War II as part of the merchant marine and, after the war, worked at sea as a mess cook and as a member of the National Maritime Union (NMU).

In the midst of his declining relationship with the CPUSA, Hall began to formalize his views on the oppressed black nation in the American South. Hall's *Negro Liberation* (1948) argued that black self-determination in the Black Belt was the only solution to class and race oppression. At the same time, the CPUSA was in the process of marginalizing black self-determination in party doctrine in favor of a more traditional class analysis of American race relations. The shift away from nationalism, which had begun as early as the cooperative politics of the Popular Front period in 1935, ultimately led to the expulsion of many original black comrades. Hall was officially expelled from the CPUSA in 1958 for his nationalist ideas and his continued

support of Stalinism. During his final years in the party, Hall married Gwen Midlo. Together, they had two children, Harry Haywood Jr., in 1956, and Rebecca Lorraine Hall, in 1963.

In the 1960s and 1970s Hall became involved with the New Communist Movement, which marked a reemergence of black Marxist activism in light of Maoist third world communist struggles. His essay "For a Revolutionary Position on the Negro Question," originally written in 1957, was published by the Marxist October League (OL) in 1975. The OL's Liberator Press also redistributed *Negro Liberation* and published his influential autobiography, *Black Bolshevik* (1978). This visibility in Black Power circles made Hall an important activist and mentor for groups like the Communist Party (Marxist-Leninist) and Revolutionary Action Movement (RAM). Hall remained active in the New Communist Movement until his death in Chicago in 1985.

FURTHER READING

Harry Haywood Hall's papers are housed in the Manuscripts, Archives, and Rare Books Division of the Schomburg Center for Research in Black Culture, New York Public Library.

Haywood, Harry. *Black Bolshevik: Autobiography of an Afro-American Communist* (1978).

Dawson, Michael C. *Black Visions: The Roots of Contemporary African-American Political Ideologies* (2001).

Kelley, Robin D. G. *Freedom Dreams: The Black Radical Imagination* (2002).

Solomon, Mark. *The Cry Was Unity: Communists and African Americans, 1917–1936* (1998).

ERIC W. PETENBRINK

Hall, Juanita (6 Nov. 1901–28 Feb. 1968), singer and stage performer, was born in Keyport, New Jersey, the daughter of Abram Long, a farm laborer, and Mary Richardson. Of African American and Irish parentage, she was raised by her maternal grandparents and received training in classical music at Juilliard School of Music in New York City. Although one source mentions an earlier marriage to Clayton King, most sources state that, while still in her teens, she married the actor Clement Hall, who died in the 1920s. There were no children from the union, and Hall never remarried. Despite severely limited opportunities for African Americans on Broadway in the 1920s, Hall managed to break into the chorus of *Show Boat* in 1928 and joined the HALL JOHNSON Choir in the chorus of *The Green Pastures* in 1930. She remained with the Hall Johnson Choir as soloist and assistant director from 1931 to 1936. In 1936 Hall served as musical arranger and director for *Sweet River,* a George Abbott adaptation of *Uncle Tom's Cabin* at the 51st Street Theatre. She conducted a Works Progress Administration chorus in New York City from 1936 to 1941 and also organized the Juanita Hall Choir. She directed the latter group in a Brattleboro Theatre production of *Conjur* in Brooklyn, New York, in 1938 and also appeared in radio broadcasts with Kate Smith, Rudy Vallee, and the Theatre Guild of the Air.

Hall began to reestablish her presence on Broadway with a bit part in S. N. Behrman's *The Pirate* in 1942. This was followed by appearances in the musicals *Sing Out, Sweet Land* in 1943, *St. Louis Woman* in 1946, and *Street Scene* in 1947. In 1948 she made her-debut as a nightclub singer at New York's Old Knickerbocker Music Hall, singing, among others, songs written for her by LANGSTON HUGHES and Herbert Kingsley.

The break in her career came when Hall appeared in "Talent '48," an annual talent showcase

Juanita Hall as Bloody Mary in *South Pacific* in June 1949. (Library of Congress\Carl Van Vechten.)

sponsored by the Stage Managers Club. There she was seen by the songwriting team of Richard Rodgers and Oscar Hammerstein II, who were then in the process of writing *South Pacific.* As recalled later by Rodgers in the *New York Times,* "As soon as we heard her, Oscar and I knew that at least one part in *South Pacific* had been filled. There was our Bloody Mary—high spirited, graceful, mischievous, proud, a gloriously gifted voice projected with all the skills of one who knew exactly how to take over a song and make it hers." When she opened in the original cast of *South Pacific* in the Majestic Theatre on 7 April 1949, Brooks Atkinson commented, "Juanita Hall's bustling, sharp-witted performance is a masterpiece" (*New York Times,* 5 June 1949).

Bloody Mary became Hall's signature role for the remainder of her career. Her rendition of her big number, "Bali Ha'i," in the words of *Variety,* "virtually stole the show from its principals Ezio Pinza and Mary Martin and gave her name status" (6 Mar. 1968). The short, stocky actress walked away with both the Donaldson and Antoinette Perry (Tony) awards for Best Supporting Actress in a Musical that season. She left the show after nine hundred performances for a year of nightclub singing and then returned at the request of Rodgers. She later re-created the role in summer stock and notably for a revival at the City Center in 1957. She finally committed it to film for the movie version of *South Pacific* in 1958. Her other song from the show, "Happy Talk," eventually became her favorite for its positive outlook. According to Mary Martin, Hall had worked out the number's singular hand movements herself.

Thanks to her multiracial heritage, Hall found herself in demand for a variety of character roles. After the Tonkinese Bloody Mary, she played a West Indian brothel keeper in Harold Arlen's *House of Flowers* in 1954, appearing opposite PEARL BAILEY and DIAHANN CARROLL. In 1958 Rodgers and Hammerstein cast her as a Chinese American marriage broker in their *Flower Drum Song.* (Joshua Logan, *South Pacific's* director, had originally thought Hall was Chinese.) She also appeared in the movie version of *Flower Drum Song* (1961).

Hall made numerous television appearances on *The Ed Sullivan Show, The Coca-Cola Hour, The Perry Como Show,* and *The Dave Garroway Show.* She also sang with her Juanita Hall Choir in the movie *Miracle in Harlem* (1949). Among her other stage appearances were *Sailor, Beware* with the Lafayette Players in 1935, *The Secret Room* in

1945, and *The Ponder Heart* in 1956. She was also the recipient of a citation from Israel in 1952 for her efforts in the Bonds for Israel drive.

Suffering from failing health and eyesight because of diabetes, Hall scored her last triumph in a one-woman show, *A Woman and the Blues*, at the East 74th Street Theatre in 1966. Her program combined the blues and jazz of her nightclub acts with the showstoppers of her Broadway career. A benefit on her behalf was staged the year before her death by the Actors Fund of America. She died in Bay Shore, Long Island, and was buried in her hometown of Keyport.

Hall's interpretation of Bloody Mary set the standard for the perennially popular *South Pacific* for half a century. Hall expanded opportunities for African Americans during the American musical theater's golden age. Her versatility in roles other than as African American characters, while not exactly nontraditional casting, may have helped point the way to that later practice.

FURTHER READING

"After 21 Years," *Time*, 6 June 1949.
Anderson, Doug. "The Show Stopper," *Theatre Arts* 36, no. 10 (1952).
Rodgers, Richard. "Juanita Hall," *New York Times*, 10 Mar. 1968.
Obituary: *New York Times*, 1 Mar. 1968.
This entry is taken from the *American National Biography* and is published here with the permission of the American Council of Learned Societies.

J. E. VACHA

Hall, Jude (c. 1744–21 Aug. 1827), Revolutionary War soldier, was born a slave in Exeter, New Hampshire. His first known master was Philemon Blake of nearby Kensington, on whose farm Hall worked, who sold him to his fellow townsman Nathaniel Healey in early 1775. Hall was so distressed by the sale that he ran away from his new master and had made it as far as Amherst, New Hampshire, when the first battle of the Revolution broke out at Lexington and Concord. With the uproar caused throughout New England by the war's outbreak, Hall could have made an easy escape. However, he seems to have been filled with the patriotic spirit of the day and on 10 May 1775 enlisted as a soldier in the company of Captain Jacob Hind in Colonel James Reed's Third New Hampshire Regiment.

Hall's service in the New Hampshire militia was not unusual. While New Hampshire had a 1719 statute that prohibited blacks (along with lunatics and "Indians") from serving in the militia, the law was ignored and black soldiers were mustered, paid the same, and shared the same hardships as any other soldier. While the enlistment of black troops in other colonies, notably Massachusetts and Connecticut, was the subject of considerable debate, the same did not hold true for New Hampshire, and nearly two hundred black men that saw service in the state's forces have been documented. The legal condition under which New Hampshire's black soldiers (and sailors) performed their service was varied; some were free men, others were slaves who were freed by conscientious masters on the eve of the Revolution, and some were slaves that purchased their freedom with the bounty money they received for enlisting. Not to be forgotten are those men that served in the army, sometimes as substitutes for their masters, and were only freed when their service was over, as well as a small number of men that served but never gained their freedom and remained slaves even after the war ended. As for Hall, tradition holds that he was formally freed, presumably by Healey, after his military service was completed.

Whether or not Hall's company commander had any reservations about using black soldiers is unknown; if he did, his fears were quickly dispelled as Hall turned out to be a tough soldier. He fought with his regiment at the Battle of Bunker Hill on 17 June 1775 and was "thrown headlong by a cannonball striking near him" while stationed at the rail fence at the bottom of the hill (Sawyer, 202). Hall would continue serving in the Third New Hampshire until 13 November 1776. He then immediately re-enlisted in Col. Nathan Hale's Second New Hampshire Regiment. The reasons for this switch are unknown, but they may have been motivated by the lure of additional bounty money for an additional term of service, as well as chance to serve with men from the part of the state that Hall knew well, Kensington included. Despite the fact that Hall had run away, the town of Kensington claimed him as one of its own soldiers; so too did Amherst, where Hall had stopped his running to enlist. The two towns would later argue over the matter, further demonstrating that color was not an issue when it came to troop enlistment in the state.

Described on his regiment muster rolls as "a Negro," twenty-three years old, five feet, ten inches tall, with "black" complexion, hair, and eyes, Hall became a battle-hardened veteran and served with his regiment at least through 1782. He particularly distinguished himself in the Battle of Monmouth in June 1778, gaining the nickname "Old Rock" in fighting that took place in 100° heat (Nell, 119). Later in the war he served garrison duty with his regiment in the area of West Point, New York. From January to February 1783 Hall was absent on leave and may have returned to Exeter or Kensington, New Hampshire, to spend time with his future wife, Rhoda Paul. Whether or not Hall returned to serve with the New Hampshire Battalion until its disbandment in January 1784 is unknown but likely. It would not be until 1786 that he was paid in full for his seven years of nearly uninterrupted military service.

As with many veterans, both black and white, times were tough for Hall after the war, and he suffered through many economic and physical hardships, the latter no doubt aggravated by his years of grueling service. Living in and around the former Revolutionary War capitol of Exeter, which had a small but well-established population of free blacks, Hall was warned out of town a number of times—indicating his severe poverty. In 1786 he married Rhoda Paul and they would have ten children. Life for their children was equally difficult; three of the Hall's grown sons were kidnapped and sold into slavery, two of whom were never heard from again. For a time the family lived in a cabin in the woods near Exeter, close to a body of water called Jude's Pond, and Hall was known as a skilled fisherman. The family's financial situation eased somewhat in 1818 when Hall began receiving a small pension for his military service. After his death, Rhoda Hall moved to Maine and collected a widow's pension until her death in 1844.

Jude Hall's service as a soldier in the American Revolution is representative of the valuable service performed by large numbers of patriotic black soldiers from New England. Though his own future freedom was not assured, Hall and others like him fought as if they were indeed free men. In the case of Hall, his influence would continue beyond his own lifetime; during the Civil War two of his grandsons, Moses (Third U.S. Colored Regiment) and Aaron (Fifty-fourth Massachusetts Regiment) Hall would enlist as soldiers, undoubtedly spurred on by the legendary service of their grandfather.

FURTHER READING

Knoblock, Glenn A. *"Strong and Brave Fellows": New Hampshire's Black Soldiers and Sailors of the American Revolution, 1775–1784* (2003).

Nell, William C. *The Colored Patriots of the American Revolution* (1855).

Sawyer, Roland D. *The History of Kensington, New Hampshire* (1946).

GLENN ALLEN KNOBLOCK

Hall, Julia R. (1 Oct. 1865–28 Apr. 1918), physician in several capacities at the Howard University medical school, as well as in private practice and public service in Washington, D.C., was born in Dandridge, Tennessee, on the Cumberland plateau east of Knoxville.

The names of her parents, and her own maiden name, have not been established. The 1900 census records that her father was born in Massachusetts, and her mother in Tennessee, but the 1910 census that both were born in Tennessee. She came to Washington in 1889 with her husband, Reverend Jeremiah L. Hall, who is never mentioned in any subsequent reference to her life and work. An 1890 city directory lists him living at 1919 ½ 8th St. NW, in the District of Columbia.

Julia Hall entered Howard University College of Medicine in 1889 and graduated in 1892. She was the twentieth of 278 women who received medical degrees from Howard between 1872 and 1967. She was the first woman gynecologist on the staff of Freedman's Hospital (associated with Howard's medical college) beginning in 1894. During this time, she was also a member of the university's Boarding Hall Committee, as well as matron and university physician, instructor on hygiene, and professor of Diseases in Children. For some years she supervised a dormitory in Miner Hall, where the 1900 census shows she was accompanied by a housekeeper, a cook, and thirteen female students.

Hall opened a private medical practice at 1517 M Street, Washington, D.C., directly across the street from the Metropolitan AME Church, with the hours 8:00 to 10:00 am and 4:00 to 6:00 pm listed in *Union League Directory* of the District of Columbia in 1901. She was appointed physician to the Board of Children's Guardians of Washington, D.C., on 6 January 1894, continuing this work at least through 1913. The agency employing her later became the District of Columbia Board of Charities, after a consolidation of departments. Initially the position paid a salary, but after 1906 Hall was "called to attend the wards of the board as a physician on the basis of services rendered," up to a maximum of $100 per month. ("Reports of the Board of Children's Guardians," *Report of the Government of the District of Columbia—1908*, p. 701).

The board noted as early as 1898 that "To Dr. Julia R. Hall, the regular physician of the board, is due much praise for the skillful, painstaking, and conscientious manner in which she has performed the duties assigned her. She has more than complied with the demands made upon her, and has, on several occasions, voluntarily served as a nurse, in addition to her duties as physician, but without extra compensation" (*Report of the Commissioners of the District of Columbia*,1898, p. 402).

Dr. Hall's practice is briefly illuminated by an article that appeared in both the *Archives of Pediatrics*, volume 23, and *Transactions of the American Pediatric Society*, volume 17, acknowledging a case history furnished by Dr. Hall to the author, concerning an orphaned child named Lizzie who was born blind and died in 1905 at the age of eleven with a diagnosis of porencephalus. Her report to the Board of Charities for 1913 lists 522 wards under treatment, an additional 100 physical examinations, 70 vaccinations, and 810 separate cases requiring treatment. Total visits during the year were 2,100. Of eighty or so diseases in a very detailed accounting, bronchitis stands out as the most common, with pertussis, tonsillitis, measles, mumps, indigestion, eczema, coryza, and constipation, all common ailments among her patients.

By 1910, Hall no longer lived on campus, having moved to 513 Florida Avenue, NW, where two grown daughters, Willard and Frana, had joined her. Both were District of Columbia public school teachers, and both had been born, like both their parents, in Tennessee. There is no record of either daughter living with Hall during her years at Howard. A young lady named Willard E. Hall, born in June 1886 in Tennessee, was listed in the 1900 census living at Scotia Seminary, in Concord, North Carolina. Established by the Presbyterian Church, U.S.A., in 1867 as "an institution for the training of Negro women," Scotia's initial goal was to "prepare teachers and social workers to improve the lot of the freedman and to provide a pool of leaders." Like many historically black colleges, Scotia accepted boarding students for precollege levels of education as well.

In her final years, Julia Hall lived at 913 S Street NW, but the circumstances of her death are unrecorded. Willard Hall married James H. Cowan, a teacher at Dunbar High School, Washington, D.C. Their son, Dr. James R. Cowan, served as New Jersey State Commissioner of Health, and as U.S. Assistant Secretary of Defense for Health and Environment under Presidents Richard M. Nixon and Gerald R. Ford.

FURTHER READING
Howard University, *Catalog*, March 1896–March 1897.
District of Columbia Board of Commissioners. *Report of the Government of the District of Columbia* (1908).
Lamb, Daniel Smith. *Howard University Medical Department: A Historical, Biographical, and Statistical Souvenir* (1900).

CHARLES ROSENBERG

Hall, Lloyd Augustus (20 June 1894–2 Jan. 1971), chemist, was born in Elgin, Illinois, to Augustus Hall, a Baptist minister, and Isabel Hall. In the 1830s his paternal grandfather had been a founding member and later pastor of the first African American church in Chicago, Quinn Chapel African Methodist Episcopal (AME). Hall developed an interest in chemistry while attending East High School in Aurora, Illinois, where he was a debater and athlete, competing in football, baseball, and track.

After receiving a number of scholarship offers, Hall chose to attend Northwestern University in Evanston, Illinois. He graduated with a B.S. in Chemistry in 1916. He continued his studies in chemistry, taking graduate courses at the University of Chicago. During World War I he served in ordnance as a lieutenant, working on explosives in a Wisconsin weapons factory. He suffered from racial harassment at this factory and requested, and was granted, a transfer after which things improved. He experienced discrimination in the civilian sector as well; he was offered a job at Western Electric over the phone that was rescinded when he showed up for work and the hiring authority saw that he was African American.

In 1916 Hall secured a position in the Chicago Department of Health Laboratories and within a year was promoted to senior chemist. He married Myrrhene E. Newsome in September 1919. He became chief chemist of Boyer Chemical Laboratory in Chicago in 1921. He had become interested in food chemistry by this time, and the following year he was named president and chemical director at Chemical Products Corporation, a laboratory consulting services firm. Hall continued running this consulting operation while working at Griffith Laboratories beginning in 1924, a firm started by his former lab partner at Northwestern. The following year he became chief chemist at Griffith and by 1929 was working exclusively for this firm, where he would stay for the next three decades.

Hall became a leader in the field of food chemistry. He developed a technique that addressed a long-standing problem in the preservation and curing of meat. Meat packaged for sale would spoil because the curing agent, nitrogen (nitrates and nitrites), penetrated meat more quickly than the preservative agent, sodium chloride, and dissolved prior to the preservation agent taking effect. Hall utilized a process called flash-drying that resulted in the formation of sodium chloride crystals that enclosed the nitrate and nitrites; upon the crystals' dissolving, the sodium chlorite would penetrate the meat first and give it a longer shelf life. This had a revolutionary impact on the meat packing industry by allowing for greater flexibility and reducing the amount of spoiled meat.

Hall later developed an effective method to sterilize spices to rid them of yeasts, molds, and bacteria. Spices could be sterilized by heating them to temperatures greater than 240 degrees Fahrenheit, but this resulted in the degradation of the flavor of common spices, such as cloves, cinnamon, and paprika. Hall invented the technique of using ethylene oxide, a chemical used as an insecticide, to kill the germs in spices. He eliminated moisture from the spices by using a vacuum chamber and introduced the ethylene oxide in the chamber to permeate and sterilize the spices. This technique had a profound effect on meat processing. It also had broader applications for other types of sterilization and was used to sterilize bandages, dressings, and sutures, as well as for various industrial applications.

Hall also broke new ground by using antioxidants to prevent rancidity in foods with fats and oils. Such foods go rancid upon oxidation, the fats reacting with oxygen. Hall discovered that some chemicals in vegetable oils act as antioxidants. Using these chemicals with salt, he created an antioxidant salt that could protect foods with fats and oils from spoilage.

Hall published extensively on the topic of food chemistry, and was granted more than 100 domestic and foreign patents for his discoveries. Both his scientific and organizational work proved influential in getting the field of food chemistry off the ground during the interwar period and after. Hall was a charter member of the Institute of Food Technologists, a professional organization founded in 1939. He also served as the editor for its journal, *The Vitalizer*. Hall was a recognized member of the broader field of chemistry and was named chair of the Chicago chapter of the American Institute of Chemists in 1954; he became the first African American member of the organization's national board of directors the following year.

After Hall retired from Griffith in 1959 he continued to consult in the field of food chemistry for the United Nations (UN) and other organizations, and worked in both national and international settings. He served as an advisor to the UN's Food and Agricultural Organization, conducting research and engaging in education efforts in Indonesia in 1959. President John F. Kennedy appointed Hall to be a member of the American Food for Peace Council, a position that he held from 1962 to 1964.

During the second half of the 1960s Hall retired from his active consulting career and moved with his wife to Altadena, California. He continued to be involved in community work until his death.

FURTHER READING

Haber, Louis. *Black Pioneers of Science and Invention* (1970).

McMurray, E. J., ed. *Notable Twentieth-Century Scientists* (1995).

Sammons, Vivian O. *Blacks in Science and Medicine* (1990).

JEFFREY R. YOST

Hall, Primus (29 Feb. 1756?–22 Mar. 1842), Revolutionary War veteran and community activist, was by his own account born in Boston to Delia Hall, a domestic servant, and PRINCE HALL. Most of what is known about Primus's early life comes from his application for a military pension in the 1830s. When he was one month old, he reported, he was "given" to Ezra Trask, a shoemaker in Essex County, Massachusetts. At age fifteen Primus decided he did not want to pursue shoemaking and convinced Trask to release him from service. Upon receiving a certificate of freedom the young man sought his own fortune for several years, working as a farmer and truckman in Salem (a leading commercial port and one of the largest cities in colonial America) until the Revolutionary War broke out.

Pay receipts and other military records document several stints of Revolutionary service under the name Primus or Priam Trask between January 1776 and October 1780. Initially stationed near Boston until the British siege ended, Hall subsequently marched to New York and New Jersey, where he was present at the Battles of Harlem Heights, White Plains, Trenton, and Princeton before receiving an honorable discharge from the Continental army. He reenlisted into militia service in the fall of 1777 and served in the Saratoga campaign. Later he served briefly at Newport, Rhode Island, building forts alongside the French. In March 1781 Hall introduced himself to Timothy Pickering, quarter-master general of the Continental army, whom he served as a steward until the following year.

Few facts survive about Hall's private life after the war. Through his work as a soap boiler he acquired enough money to buy property in Boston's West End, where most of the city's black community was concentrated. He was married to Phebe Robson from 1784 until her death in 1808. Boston records list a marriage between Primus Hall and Martha Gardner in 1809. Hall's last marriage was in 1817 to Anna (or Ann) Clark, who outlived him. He was also survived by two children, Ezra Trask Hall and Isannah Trask Hall, named after his childhood master and mistress.

Hall's activism in Boston began soon after the war. In 1787 he, Prince Hall, and other black men petitioned the Boston city council for a separate school for black children. When the request was denied Primus Hall briefly opened up space in his own house for a private school. In 1806 the African School moved into the new building of the African Baptist Church, which Hall also helped found. Continuing to advocate African American education into the 1830s, Hall supported initiatives to establish a college and an orphanage for blacks. He also publicly took stands against slavery, both in the Revolutionary and antebellum periods. He joined Prince Hall and others in petitioning the Massachusetts legislature to intervene on behalf of three free black men in Boston kidnapped into slavery in 1788. Later he was a leader of Boston's African Abolition Freehold Society and a supporter of William Lloyd Garrison, the city's leading white abolitionist.

In 1835 Hall applied for a military pension. The War Department contested his claim on the grounds that he was "emancipated," not "free-born," and that he had served as a "waiter," not a "soldier." In response Hall insisted that Ezra Trask had treated him as a ward, apprentice, and even adopted son, but never as a slave. His comrades-in-arms testified that Hall had been involved in military operations, but the commissioner of pensions was not persuaded. Undaunted, Hall and his lawyer petitioned Congress to override the War Department's bureaucracy. In 1838 the House of Representatives passed a bill declaring that Hall merited a pension for his "faithful service of eighteen months as a revolutionary soldier, not merely in camp duty ... but in the field of battle, where his bravery and good conduct ... would have done honor to any man."

When Hall died a few years later, his obituary highlighted his veteran status: "Mr. Hall ... was in the habit of recounting scenes of the Revolutionary War, especially the capture of Gen Burgoyne and the surrender of Lord Cornwallis, at both of which he was present." Another posthumous account of Hall described how he gave up his bed to George Washington one night in the Continental army camp. When Washington discovered that Hall had no place to sleep, he insisted that the two of them share the bed, "and on the same straw, and under the same blanket, the general and the negro servant slept until morning" (*Godey's Lady's Book*, June 1849).

Reprinted in WILLIAM COOPER NELL's *Colored Patriots of the American Revolution* (1855) and elsewhere, this story about Hall represented him as an obedient servant to the father of the republic. An alternative interpretation of Hall's life might center on his insistence on acting as an equal citizen in his own right. Even as he encountered the racism of the early republic, Hall capitalized on the possibilities of his situation. Though he worked for a time as a servant, he sought out an employer (Pickering) whom he deemed an honest man. Though his efforts to establish an "African" school would be undone by a later push to integrate Boston schools, he advocated black education at a time when "separate" was as close as African American children could get to "equal." And though Hall proudly told tales of his Revolutionary service, he did not hesitate to challenge his government when it failed to live up to what he perceived as the Revolution's ideals of liberty and equality.

FURTHER READING
The National Archives holds papers relating to Hall's military pension application.
Horton, James Oliver. "Generations of Protest: Black Families and Social Reform in Ante-Bellum Boston," *New England Quarterly* 49 (1976).
Levesque, George A. "Before Integration: The Forgotten Years of Jim Crow Education in Boston," *Journal of Negro Education* 48 (1979).
Minardi, Margot. "Freedom in the Archives: The Pension Case of Primus Hall," *Dublin Seminar for New England Folklife Annual Proceedings* 2003.
Obituary: *Semi-Weekly Atlas* (Boston), 26 Mar. 1842.
                                          MARGOT MINARDI

Hall, Prince (1735–4 Dec. 1807), abolitionist and founder of the first black Freemasonic lodge, probably received his manumission from William Hall, a Boston leather-dresser, and his wife, Susannah, in 1770. No extant material confirms Hall as the Barbados son of a white father and a mother of mixed racial heritage, as most of his published biographies state, or as an emigrant to Boston any time before 1760, or as a preacher in a Cambridge church. The slave released by William Hall, only described as Prince, probably went on to become Prince Hall, a Boston leather worker, who, having organized the first black Freemasonic lodge, garnered respect from Boston luminaries and deference from his northern black peers and organized one of the country's oldest African American institutions.

Marriage records show that one or several Prince Halls had several wives. Hall, while a servant to William Hall, married Sarah Richie, also a servant, on 2 November 1763. Sarah Richie died in 1769. The next year, Boston authorities reported that a Prince Hall had married Flora Gibbs, of Gloucester, in Gloucester. In 1783 a Prince Hall married Affy Mondy or Moody. The esteemed Bostonian, Reverend John Eliot married a Prince Hall and a Naby or Nabby Ayrault in 1798. Six years later, the Reverend Joseph Eckley married Prince Hall and Zilpha or Sylvia Johnson. Pension records reveal that this last wife, Sylvia, became the arbiter of the Hall estate, which included Masonic paraphernalia. By virtue of political status and employment, the husband of Flora Gibbs, noted as being free and a leather dresser, was probably the founder of black Freemasonry. In applying for a pension as a Revolutionary War veteran, PRIMUS HALL disclosed his status as a child of Hall, and remembered that his father, free at the time of his birth in 1756, had married a Delia Hall. Perhaps, the Masonic Prince Hall entered into all of these unions; however, it is unlikely and the circumstances surrounding these marriages remain unclear.

In contrast to his early years, Hall left a remarkably full and exceptional record after the Revolutionary War. Between 1780 and 1801 Boston tax assessors identified Hall and his son Primus in fifteen annual tax lists. Officials identified Hall as "Freemason," "Worshipful Grand Master," "blkman," "Master Mason," and "Bl[ac]k Freemason & Master of Lodge" (Boston Taking Books, 1780–1801). In 1785 tax assessors noted the death of a different Prince Hall. In 1788 town records listed Primus Hall as "Prince's Son," and in 1789 listed, presumably Primus or perhaps another son, as "Prince Hall Junr, Bl[ac]k son to [Prince Hall]" (Boston Taking Books, 1780–1801). Tax assessors listed Hall as a leather dresser and as a huckster, a peddler of various goods. James Ross,

a drum major in the Continental army wrote a bill certifying that by 24 April 1777, his regiment had received five drumheads from Hall. By 1800 Hall had amassed enough wealth to be one of the few black Bostonians who owned property.

Hall demonstrated his commitment to black Bostonians through thirty years of activism. On 6 March 1775 he and fourteen other men of color either entered into or gained advanced degrees in Freemasonry. As the leader of this group, Hall spoke to and for a larger black community. In 1777 Hall and others petitioned the Massachusetts legislature demanding the end of slavery in the Bay State. In 1784, after maintaining a correspondence with English Freemasons and relying on the services of both black and white seamen, he conveyed a request to the Grand Lodge of London for a charter that would formally recognize the African Lodge he had formed about eight years earlier. Again utilizing a network of sailors, Hall received the actual document in 1787, officially turning his African Lodge into "Lodge No. 459," the first of its kind.

Forming the first black Lodge comprised only part of a pragmatic and uniquely expansive political strategy. Less than a year earlier, on 26 November 1786, Hall had written to the governor of Massachusetts, James Bowdoin, pledging the support of the black Masons to any state-supported moves against Shays's Rebellion. The pledge undoubtedly sought to affirm the loyalty of the Commonwealth's black residents, but it solicited no known response. However, undeterred, Hall astutely always considered, in simultaneity, multiple and seemingly contradictory agendas. Perhaps this explains why the very next year Hall and approximately seventy-two others requested that the Massachusetts General Court support an African emigration plan, and why, just months later, Hall and a group of thirty-four Boston blacks, including some of the emigrationist petitioners, asked the town selectman to open a school for black youth. In 1788 he complained in several New England newspapers about the kidnapping of three blacks from Boston, one of whom was a brother Freemason. The reaction of Hall and Boston blacks to the illegal seizure helped spur the Massachusetts legislature to pass, in March, 'An Act to prevent the Slave-Trade, and for granting Relief to the Families of such unhappy Persons as may be Kidnapped or decoyed away from this Commonwealth.'

Hall and JOHN MARRANT, a black itinerant Methodist preacher, produced the only extant eighteenth-century black Masonic texts. Marrant, born free in 1755 in New York, preached to Native

Americans in the southern states and blacks in Nova Scotia, and arrived in Boston in 1789. Later that year, at the behest of Prince Hall, he gave a public sermon on the anniversary of the Masonic patron, St. John the Baptist, a standard Masonic practice. Marrant, a Calvinist, asserted that the bonds of brotherly affection arose from providential design and that "this we profess to believe as Christians and as Masons." (Marrant, 79). Prince Hall delivered and published his own similar speeches in 1792 and most notably in 1797. Beginning a millennial tradition followed by future black abolitionists, Hall invoked in 1792 what would become a touchstone reference for black Christians, Psalms 68:31. He pressed his audience to listen and "Hear what the great Architect of the universal world saith," that "*Aethiopia shall stretch forth her hands unto*" him (Hall, 10). Hall maintained that God would eventually rescue "Aethiopia," Africans and their enslaved descendents, from bondage and debasement. Hall had exhorted black Freemasons to forebear the burdens of racial injustice. Hall, also bitterly rebuked the racial discrimination endured by African Americans as unchristian. The "iron hand of tyranny and oppression" had destroyed happy families, Hall exclaimed in his 1797 address, and dragged the unwilling from Africa and deposited them in "a strange land and strange people, whose tender mercies are cruel" and expressed through "the iron yoke of slavery & cruelty" (Hall, 4). Marrant and Hall worked to recover an African past in the Bible and contemporary Masonic histories. Just as important, they set the agenda for future black abolitionists and fraternal members by imagining a future free of slavery, devoid of racial oppression, and defined by opportunity.

Hall forwarded copies of his lectures to William Bentley, an influential white Congregationalist minister and Freemason in Salem. He also dispatched copies to the London Grand Lodge, the Prince of Wales, and the king of England. Bentley had remarked favorably on the influence of Hall among African Americans, acknowledging him as one of the most widely known and active black post-Revolutionary leaders. Moreover, his founding of black Freemasonry gave institutional roots to later black activism. The lodge he had founded would attract those who would become the city's leading black abolitionists, particularly DAVID WALKER, the important antebellum polemicist and abolitionist, JOHN T. HILTON, LEWIS HAYDEN, and many others. Not only did Hall work to secure social, political, and economic freedoms for African Americans

but he also began a Freemasonic Lodge that, today, is one of the few American lodges, white or black, that possesses its original charter. Since the death of its founder in 1807, Prince Hall Freemasonry continued to thrive in the United States and spread throughout the African Diaspora.

FURTHER READING

Hall, Prince. *A Charge Delievered to the Brethren of the African Lodge On the 25th of June, 1792. At the Home of Brother William Smith, In Charlestown* (1792).

Bullock, Stephen C. *Revolutionary Brotherhood: Freemasonry and the Transformation of the American Social Order, 1730–1840* (1996).

Brooks, Joanna. *American Lazarus: Religion and the Rise of African-American and Native American Literatures* (2003).

Marrant, John. *A Sermon Preached on the 24th Day of June 1789, Being the Festival of St. John the Baptist* (1789), in *Face Zion Forward: First Writers of the Black Atlantic, 1785–1798*, eds. Joanna Brooks and John Saillant (2002).

Sherman, John. "More About Prince Hall: Notes and Documents," *The Philaethes* 15.3 (June 1962).

Wesley, Charles H. *Prince Hall, Life and Legacy* (1977).

CHERNOH M. SESAY JR.

Hall, William Henry (1823–1901), activist and entrepreneur, was born to free parents in Washington, D.C. Nothing is known of his parents or his early life. However, although he trained as a barber, Hall reportedly spent two years at Oberlin College and considered the ministry before moving to New York in 1845, where he ran a restaurant called the "El Dorado" on Church Street, and became active in both black Masonic organizations and the fight for black suffrage. However, at the end of the decade, like many other Americans, Hall headed west to seek gold in California.

He had some success as both a miner and a merchant and returned to New York in late 1851. He married Sarah Lavina Bailey in New York City on 16 March 1852 in a ceremony whose "splendor," according to an item copied in the 1 April 1852 *Frederick Douglass's Paper*, was "without parallel in 'the history of colored society in New York.'" The young couple moved back to California and settled briefly in Oroville. Hall served as the Butte County delegate to the first California Colored Convention in 1855, chaired the 1856 and 1857 conventions, served as a member of the State Executive Committee, and, along with Frederick Barbardoes and C. Wilson, authored a pamphlet coming out of the 1857 Convention, *Address of the State Executive Committee to the Colored People of the State of California.* Hall worked closely with leading black Californians, ranging from PETER WILLIAMS CASSEY and JEREMIAH BURKE SANDERSON to MIFFLIN WISTAR GIBBS and WILLIAM HENRY YATES on issues of black testimony, equal education, and broader civil rights. His convention speeches, among other public addresses, made him one of the better-known black orators of the region.

Hall was in San Francisco by the late 1850s and-ran a successful billiard parlor and saloon. The Halls had their first of eight children in 1857, and by 1860 Hall owned $600 in real estate. By 1870 his property was valued at over $7,000 and he had returned to barbering, a trade he would practice until his death. The acquisition of wealth did not stop his political activism; in fact, in the spirit of black self-determination and economic self-sufficiency, he saw the two running parallel. He helped found the California Savings and Land Association in 1859 and the San Francisco Literary Institute in 1861. He was a trustee of the failed Livingstone Institute (an attempt to found a secondary school for blacks in northern California) and he was a member of the Brannan Guard (a black drill club). Hall gave the keynote address at the 1 January 1864 Emancipation Celebration in San Francisco; the speech, which was published in the *Pacific Appeal*, praised Lincoln, called John Brown a "sainted soul," noted Harpers Ferry as his generation's Bunker Hill, and asserted the need for equal rights.

He continued to be active on the Executive Committee and was a key force in organizing the 1865 Colored Convention. He also wrote regularly for the California black press, including both the *Elevator* and the *Pacific Appeal*—sometimes under his own name and sometimes under the pseudonyms "Uncas" and "Pericles," which invoked, respectively, a 17th century Mohegan chief and an Athenian statesman and general, both of whom were famous for their military prowess and oratory. He remained in demand as a speaker throughout the 1860s and 1870s. The black citizens of Virginia City, Nevada, invited him to given the keynote at their celebration of the passage of the Fifteenth Amendment in 1870.

Much less is known of Hall's life after Reconstruction, though he continued to live with his large family in San Francisco. Most sources list his death as taking place in 1901 in San Francisco, but he is absent from the 1900 federal census.

FURTHER READING
Lapp, Rudolph. *Blacks in Gold Rush California* (1977).
Wheeler, B. Gordon. *Black California* (1993).

ERIC GARDNER

Hamer, Fannie Lou (6 Oct. 1917–14 Mar. 1977), civil rights activist, was born Fannie Lou Townsend in Montgomery County, Mississippi, the twentieth child of Lou Ella (maiden name unknown) and Jim Townsend, sharecroppers. When Hamer was two, the family moved to Sunflower County, where they lived in abject poverty. Even when they were able to rent land and buy stock, a jealous white neighbor poisoned the animals, forcing the family back into sharecropping. Hamer began picking cotton when she was six; she eventually was able to pick three to four hundred pounds a day, earning a penny a pound. Because of poverty she was forced to leave school at age twelve, barely able to read and write. She married Perry "Pap" Hamer in 1944. The couple

Fannie Lou Hamer at the Democratic National Convention, Atlantic City, New Jersey, in August 1964. (Library of Congress.)

adopted two daughters. For the next eighteen years Fannie Lou Hamer worked first as a sharecropper and then as a timekeeper on the plantation of B. D. Marlowe. Hamer appeared destined for a routine life of poverty, but two events in the early 1960s led her to become a political activist. When she was hospitalized for the removal of a uterine tumor in 1961, the surgeons performed a hysterectomy without her consent. In August 1962, still angry and bitter over the surgery, she went to a meeting in her hometown of Ruleville to hear JAMES FORMAN of the Student Nonviolent Coordinating Committee (SNCC) and JAMES BEVEL of the Southern Christian Leadership Conference (SCLC). After hearing their speeches on the importance of voting, she and seventeen others went to the courthouse in Indianola to try to register. They were told they could only enter the courthouse two at a time to be given the literacy test, which they all failed. On the trip back to Ruleville the group was stopped by the police and fined one hundred dollars for driving a bus that was the wrong color. Hamer subsequently became the group's leader. B. D. Marlowe called on her that evening and told her she had to withdraw her application to register. Hamer refused and was ordered to leave the plantation. Because Marlowe threatened to confiscate their belongings, Pap was compelled to work on the plantation until the harvest season was finished. For a time, Hamer stayed with various friends and relatives, and segregationist night riders shot into some of the homes where she was staying. Nevertheless, she remained active in the civil rights movement, serving as a field secretary for SNCC, working for voter registration, advocating welfare programs, and teaching citizenship classes.

Hamer gained national attention when she appeared before the credentials committee of the 1964 Democratic National Convention in Atlantic City, New Jersey, on behalf of the Mississippi Freedom Democratic Party (MFDP), an organization attempting to unseat the state's regular, all-white delegation. Speaking as a delegate and cochair of the MFDP, she described atrocities inflicted on blacks seeking the right to vote and other civil rights. She spoke of the abuse she had suffered at the Montgomery County Jail, where white Mississippi law enforcement officers forced black inmates to beat her so badly that she had no feeling in her arms. Hamer and several others had been arrested for attempting to integrate the "whites only" section of the bus station in Winona, Mississippi, during the return trip from a voter registration training session in South Carolina. After giving her dramatic testimony, she wept before the committee. Although her emotional appeal generated sympathy for the plight of blacks in Mississippi among the millions watching on television, the committee rejected the MFDP's challenge.

That same year Hamer traveled to Ghana, Guinea, Nigeria, and several other African nations at the request and expense of those governments. Still, her primary interest was in helping the people of the Mississippi Delta. She lectured across the country, raising money and organizing. In 1965 she ran as an MFDP candidate for Congress, saying she was "sick and tired of being sick and tired." While many civil rights leaders abandoned grassroots efforts, she remained committed to organizing what she called "everyday" people in her community, frequently saying she preferred to face problems at home rather than run from them. In 1969 she launched the Freedom Farm Cooperative to provide homes and food for deprived families, white as well as black, in Sunflower County. The cooperative eventually acquired 680 acres. She remained active, however, at the national level. In 1971 she was elected to the steering committee of the National Women's Political Caucus, and the following year she supported the nomination of Sissy Farenthold as vice president in an address to the Democratic National Convention.

After a long battle with breast cancer, Hamer died at the all-black Mound Bayou Hospital, thirty miles from Ruleville. Civil rights leaders ANDREW YOUNG, JULIAN BOND, and ELEANOR HOLMES NORTON attended her funeral.

FURTHER READING

Hamer's papers are in the Amistad Research Center at Tulane University, the Mississippi Department of Archives and History, and the Wisconsin State Historical Society. Other papers and speeches are in the Moses Moon Collection at the National Museum of American History of the Smithsonian Institution and the Civil Rights Documentation Project at the Moorland-Spingarn Research Center at Howard University.

Dittmer, John. *Local People: The Struggle for Civil Rights in Mississippi* (1995).

Lee, Chana Kai. *For Freedom's Sake: The Life of Fannie Lou Hamer* (1999).

Mills, Kay. *This Little Light of Mine: The Life of Fannie Lou Hamer* (1993).

Payne, Charles M. *I've Got the Light of Freedom: The Organizing Tradition and the Mississippi Freedom Struggle* (1995).

Obituaries: *Washington Post,* 17 and 19 Mar. 1977.

This entry is taken from the *American National Biography* and is published here with the permission of the American Council of Learned Societies.

MAMIE E. LOCKE

Hamid, Sufi Abdul (6 Jan. 1903–30 July 1938), religious and labor leader, was born, according to his own statement, in Lowell, Massachusetts. According to the Harlem historian ROI OTTLEY, however, Hamid was born in Philadelphia, Pennsylvania. At various times he also claimed to have been born in different places in the South. Little is known about his early life, including his parents' identities. According to Ottley, his original name was Eugene Brown. In an interview with writers from the Works Progress Administration, Hamid claimed to have been taken to Egypt at the age of nine, then to Athens, Greece, where he received his schooling through the university level. According to the interview, he returned to the United States in 1923 and began to work for the William J. Burns Detective Agency in St. Louis, Missouri, and Memphis, Tennessee. Hamid soon left that job and moved to Chicago, where he joined the Ahmedabad movement, an Islamic organization based in India. Around this time he changed his name to Bishop Conshankin. In 1928 he left the Ahmedabad organization and formed the Illinois Civic Association, which led several boycotts of white-owned businesses that, though operating in black areas of Chicago, refused to hire African Americans. Sponsored by the *Chicago Whip*, a black newspaper, and J. C. Austin, a minister of a black Baptist church, the organization successfully waged boycotts with the slogan "Don't buy where you can't work." The group claimed credit for the hiring of eighteen hundred African Americans in Chicago from 1928 to 1930.

In 1930 Hamid moved to New York City, changed his name to Sufi Abdul Hamid, and began to call for boycotts of white-owned businesses in Harlem that did not employ African Americans. He founded the International Islamic Industrial Alliance, a boycott organization that later changed its name to the Negro Industrial and Clerical Alliance. Through 1932, however, most of Hamid's political work took place atop stepladders on the streets of Harlem, where he became famous for his orations demanding jobs for African Americans in the stores along the neighborhood's main commercial thoroughfares. Sporting a turban, cape, and riding boots, Hamid was one of Harlem's most colorful characters. Although his soapbox oratory was laced with references to the Koran and various Asian religions, his message was economic organization, and it gained him a significant following in a section of New York that suffered from an unemployment rate that was higher than 50 percent throughout the Depression.

During the summer of 1933 Hamid organized the picketing of small stores in the area of 135th Street. Several of the store owners capitulated and hired African Americans as clerks. Emboldened by this success, Hamid in the spring of 1934 moved his campaign to the large chain and department stores on 125th Street, Harlem's commercial and cultural axis. In May he organized a picket line around Woolworth's after the manager refused to hire members of the Negro Industrial and Clerical Alliance as sales clerks. Hamid's successes spurred other black leaders in Harlem, among them ministers, various black nationalists, and communists, to mount their own boycotts. He was invited to join a coalition of groups in leading a boycott of Blumstein's department store but was soon expelled after insisting that any newly hired black sales clerks should be made members of his organization. After his expulsion he began to appeal to African Americans to "drive Jewish businessmen out of Harlem." Hamid was accused by the Communist Party of being a "black Hitler" and of taking money from merchants who agreed to hire black workers. Similarly, mainstream black ministers and newspapers denounced Hamid for his anti-Semitism, and he was often accused of embezzling dues money from the Negro Industrial and Clerical Alliance.

In the fall of 1934 a group of Jewish businessmen met with Mayor Fiorello La Guardia to complain that Hamid was conducting a race war against Jews in Harlem. In October he was arrested on charges of "spreading anti-Semitism in Harlem." Following four days of conflicting testimony he was acquitted. A few weeks after his acquittal Hamid changed the name of his organization to the Afro-American Federation of Labor.

In January 1935 Hamid was arrested, reportedly for publishing and selling a pamphlet without a license, and was sentenced to ten days in jail. By this time the Harlem boycott movement had ebbed, and after his release Hamid declared that he would return to studying and teaching black magic and mysticism. He continued to speak atop his stepladder on Harlem streets and to operate a headquarters that housed a grocery store and the remnants of the Afro-American Federation of Labor, and his organization continued to picket stores in an attempt to force them to hire African Americans.

But Hamid's rhetoric often veered into a mystical racialism, and his group became increasingly isolated. In July 1935 one of Hamid's targets, the Lerner Company, won a court injunction against the activities of the Afro-American Federation of Labor, effectively disbanding the organization. The company had argued that Hamid's aim was to drive white people—and Jews in particular—out of Harlem. Hamid then dropped out of public view for more than two years, during which time he reputedly studied Asian religions. He was briefly married to Madame STEPHANIE ST. CLAIR, who ran the numbers racket in Harlem in the 1930s. In 1938 she was sentenced to prison for shooting at him.

That same year Hamid formed the Temple of Tranquility, a quasi-religious organization and economic cooperative in Harlem. The organization established a cooperative wholesale fruit and vegetable market as well as a parking garage and an automobile service station. Hamid died later that year in an airplane crash.

Hamid was an important catalyst behind the Harlem boycott movement of the early and mid-1930s, one of the defining events in New York's black community during the Great Depression. He was also one of the first African American leaders to be embroiled in a controversy concerning anti-Semitism, an issue that vexed relations between African Americans and Jews for the rest of the twentieth century.

FURTHER READING

An interview with Hamid and various conflicting biographical accounts are included in the "biographical sketches" section of the Negroes of New York, 1936–1941, project of the Writers' Program of the Works Progress Administration, on microfilm at the Schomburg Center for Research in Black Culture, New York City.

McKay, Claude. *Harlem: Negro Metropolis* (1940).

Muraskin, William. "The Harlem Boycott of 1934: Black Nationalism and the Rise of Labor-Union Consciousness," *Labor History* 13 (Summer, 1972), 361–373.

Naison, Mark. *Communists in Harlem during the Depression* (1983).

Ottley, Roi. *"New World A-Coming": Inside Black America* (1943).

This entry is taken from the *American National Biography* and is published here with the permission of the American Council of Learned Societies.

THADDEUS RUSSELL

Hamilton, Grace Towns (10 Feb. 1907–18 June 1992), legislator and activist, was born Grace Towns in Atlanta, Georgia, the second of five children of George Alexander Towns, a professor of English and pedagogy at Atlanta University, and Nellie McNair, a graduate of the same institution. Both of her parents placed a high premium on education, civic involvement, and political activism. George Towns was a protégé and friend of W. E. B. DuBois, publicly supporting his clashes with BOOKER T. WASHINGTON and independently striving to increase the ranks of African American voters. Nellie Towns, meanwhile, volunteered extensively in the community; she worked with the First Congregational Church and the Young Women's Christian Association (YWCA), and she helped found the Gate City Free Kindergarten Association, which assisted children of the black working poor. In this environment, the young Grace Towns grew up with senses of relative privilege and social obligation.

For a time, Towns was privately tutored, but from grade school through college she attended Atlanta University. She was a dedicated member of many student groups, but she devoted most of her time to the YWCA. In 1926 she was elected vice president of the YWCA's National Student Division, becoming the first black woman to hold such a prestigious post. After receiving her B.A. in 1927, Towns matriculated at Ohio State University, where she was awarded an M.A. in Psychology in 1929. Her time in Ohio proved difficult; after the comparatively friendly environs of her childhood home, the widespread racial hostilities and segregation of Columbus distressed her.

Towns returned to Atlanta, where she taught briefly at the Atlanta School of Social Work and then at Clark College. On 7 June 1930 she married Henry Cooke "Cookie" Hamilton, who was an administrator and professor at LeMoyne Junior College in Memphis, Tennessee, so Grace Towns Hamilton moved to that city and joined the college's faculty as an instructor in psychology. She gave birth to the couple's only child, Eleanor, in 1931.

As a young couple, the Hamiltons were forced to cope with the strains of a two-career marriage. Grace continued to teach at LeMoyne while her husband moved to the University of Cincinnati to pursue a Ph.D. In 1935 she took a job supervising a Works Progress Administration (WPA) survey titled *The Urban Negro Worker in the United States, 1925–1936* and was hired to serve on the YWCA's National Student Council. Because of their busy and split lives, she and her husband sent Eleanor to live with Hamilton's parents in Atlanta. The family would remain apart until 1941, when Hamilton and her husband returned to their home city; he secured an appointment at Atlanta University and she soon headed the Department of Education and Psychology at Morehouse College. Hamilton continued her work with the YWCA before becoming the director of the Atlanta Urban League (AUL) in 1942.

Hamilton was one of the first women to hold a prominent position in the National Urban League (NUL) system, and under her leadership the AUL took on the daunting tasks of improving housing, school funding, health care, and voting rights for Atlanta's African American residents. Her first and greatest achievement was the creation of at least seventeen residential subdivisions for middle-class blacks, who until that point had few suitable housing options in the city. Hamilton believed that her first mission was to educate Atlanta's white public, and she made a habit of collaborating with the city's white elites, insisting that their support was essential for any community change. Given Atlanta's turbulent political climate and white hostility to racial integration, Hamilton put aside demands for desegregation in favor of more gradualist goals. This shift put her at odds with NUL policy, and she was forced to resign her post in 1960.

Hamilton spent the next several years involved in a variety of civic roles. She returned to the national board of the YWCA, opened her own community relations consulting firm, and conducted interviews for Eli Ginzberg's book *The Middle Class Negro in the White Man's World*, which was published by Columbia University Press in 1967. Around the time that Hamilton was conducting these interviews, in the early '60s, she began to attract broad public attention. Atlanta's new mayor, Ivan Allen Jr., appointed Hamilton to the city's Fund Appeals Review Board and Citizens Advisory Committee for Urban Renewal, and ultimately made her director of the Atlanta Youth Council. At the same time, Georgia Governor Carl Sanders chose her to serve on a variety of state-level committees.

In 1965 a federal district court ordered the reapportionment of all legislative districts, and Atlanta's Fulton County, where Hamilton resided, received an eightfold increase in representation. Hamilton became a favorite to run for office. In May of that year, she won the Democratic primary race for the new 137th legislative district. Facing no opposition in the general election, she became the first black woman to hold a seat in the Georgia house of representatives. She was also the first black woman to hold such a prominent elected seat anywhere in the Deep South.

Hamilton remained in the Georgia legislature for almost twenty years. The zenith of her legislative career was during the late 1960s and early 1970s, when Hamilton fought successfully for the development of a new Atlanta city charter, one that made the city's government more workable and racially representative. Most of her work focused on similar quests for governmental restructuring in an effort to increase black representation. Yet Hamilton was increasingly marginalized by local black leaders, who disagreed with her position on various issues related to redistricting. Hamilton tended to take a broad view of governmental organization, seeing the preservation of individual "black" seats as less important, which went against the stance of almost every other black leader. Their disagreements came to a head after the 1980 census, when Hamilton took the side of white leadership against African Americans who wanted Atlanta redistricted to the advantage of blacks. Hamilton lost her bid for reelection in the 1984 Democratic primary to Mabel Thomas, a twenty-six-year-old graduate student.

From 1985 to 1986 Hamilton served on the Georgia Advisory Committee to the U.S. Civil Rights Commission, which would be her final public position. After her husband's death in 1987, her own health deteriorated, and for the last few years of her life she rarely left home. She died in her sleep at Atlanta's Briarcliff Nursing Home.

FURTHER READING

Mullis, Sharon Mitchell. "The Public Career of Grace Towns Hamilton: A Citizen Too Busy to Hate," Ph.D. Diss., Emory University (1976).

Spritzer, Lorraine Nelson, and Jean B. Bergmark. *Grace Towns Hamilton and the Politics of Southern Change* (1997).

SUSAN J. MCWILLIAMS

Hamilton, Robert (1819–28 April 1870), abolitionist, political activist, and journalist, was born in New York City, the son of Hannah (1793–1864, maiden name unknown) and William Hamilton. William Hamilton, a freeborn black, was a carpenter by trade who set a stellar example for the New York black community as a strong leader in the fight for political and civil equality. William Hamilton was a staunch supporter of William Lloyd Garrison and the *Liberator* but stopped short of adopting Garrison's doctrine of pacifism. This aspect of

William Hamilton's abolitionist ideology made a deep impression on his son Robert—one that lasted a lifetime. During the riotous summer of 1834 in New York when "the mob spirit was in the city," Robert recalled that his father took him to a hardware store, purchased a pistol, and instructed him to use it if attacked by the rampaging mob. "Boy as we were," Robert later wrote in 1863, "we highly appreciated the act and remember it with pride to this day" (*Weekly Anglo-African*, 24 Jan. 1863).

During the antebellum years Robert Hamilton worked on behalf of a number of issues of concern to the black community, which included the circulation of petitions to repeal the repressive statute that disfranchised most black men in New York State. In the effort to thwart the Fugitive Slave Law of 1850, he became a member of the Committee of Thirteen which protected black New Yorkers from slave catchers. In 1856 he sat on the executive committee of the American League of Colored Laborers, "established to encourage and assist black businesses and vocational education throughout the North" (Ripley, vol. 5, p. 28). Hamilton taught music for many years in local public schools, and he incorporated his musical talents into his activist agenda. He was always ready to comply with requests for a song at political gatherings, which included the "war meetings" organized in New York state and other Northern black communities, when Governor John Andrew of Massachusetts began recruitment for the North's first black regiment, the 54th Regiment of Massachusetts Volunteer Infantry. In an advertisement in the *Weekly Anglo-African* newspaper announcing "A Grand Congratulation Banquet and Old Folk's Reunion" to celebrate the Emancipation Proclamation, Hamilton was listed as the "Literary and Musical Manager." He noted in the ad that "Liberty songs" were preferred for those wishing to participate as singers during the festivities (*Weekly Anglo-African*, 7 Feb. 1863).

Robert Hamilton was also the much-beloved chorister of the Zion Church Singing Association of the African Methodist Episcopal Zion Church of New York City. This denomination had been founded at the end of the eighteenth century by a handful of black men who refused to accept the discriminatory policies of the John Street Methodist Church where they had been members. JAMES VARICK and William Hamilton were among the founding fathers of the new denomination, and the AME Zion Church (Mother Zion) became, within the black population of New York City, what the African Methodist Episcopal Church

(Mother Bethel) was to the black population of Philadelphia.

When Robert's brother THOMAS HAMILTON founded the *Weekly Anglo-African* newspaper in July 1859, an ideal forum was created from which the brothers could disseminate a variety of ideas and strategies for the benefit of the black community at large. And when, because of financial difficulties, Thomas sold the *Weekly Anglo-African* in March 1861, Robert founded a newspaper of the same name in July of that year, noting the community's need for a press "devoted specially to the best interests of the colored people in this and other countries" (*Weekly Anglo-African*, 27 July 1861). The Hamiltons succeeded so well in achieving this goal that the AME Zion Church designated the *Weekly Anglo-African* its official organ, a truly suitable honor to bestow on the newspaper whose owner and editor was the son of such an influential founding member of Mother Zion.

Very early during the Civil War, Robert Hamilton took the lead in organizing the contraband relief efforts of Northern black communities. In November 1861 he led a committee to solicit donations of clothing for the freedmen at Fortress Monroe, Virginia. These ongoing relief efforts yielded hundreds of dollars' worth of clothing, shipped not only to Fortress Monroe but also to freedmen encampments at Port Royal and Beaufort, South Carolina, and in Washington, D.C.

Despite the horrors and dislocations of the war, Robert Hamilton professed a special affection for military life, and perhaps this was because he believed—as did FREDERICK DOUGLASS—that if black men proved themselves brave defenders of the Union, equality in political and civil life would soon follow. His wish to obtain firsthand information on the lives of black soldiers in camp was one motive for his decision to travel to the Union-occupied South in September 1863. One of his most lengthy visits was spent in the Norfolk and Portsmouth region of southeastern Virginia, where he had many opportunities to observe not only black soldiers but also the progress of freed people. Hamilton's editorial correspondence to the *Anglo-African* describing his experiences in the South at the height of the war surely ranks among the most informative collection of documents from that critical time.

Hamilton traveled not only through the Union-occupied South but also to cities of the West, including Cincinnati, Chicago, Detroit, and Kalamazoo. He curtailed his tour for a short while in the fall of 1864, when he returned to New York to serve as a delegate to one of the most critical of the national conventions of colored men, held in Syracuse, New York, 4–7 October 1864.

The nation was indeed in crisis with war raging during a presidential election year and the fate of blacks poised in the balance.

When the war ended Hamilton was still on the road, and while traveling in Tennessee he learned of the assassination of President Lincoln. Some weeks later his brother Thomas, at home in New York managing the daily business of the newspaper, died of typhoid fever on 29 May 1865. With the death of Thomas, Robert Hamilton lost his most trusted associate. Within just seven months of Thomas's death the *Weekly Anglo-African*, which the brothers had so brilliantly employed in the service of their people, would be gone as well.

In a letter to John L. Sibley, chief librarian at Harvard University, Robert Hamilton confided that on Christmas Day 1865 "I was taken sick … and having no person connected with me in business, I was compelled to suspend the publication. I am slowly recovering and hope to be about next week when the publication will be resumed" (31 Jan. 1866, Houghton Library, Harvard University). The *Anglo-African* did not survive, however, and the last extant issue of the newspaper is 23 December 1865. Hamilton devoted his life to the uplift of black people everywhere, but his memory faded into obscurity as a new generation of black leaders assumed the challenges of Reconstruction following the Civil War.

FURTHER READING

Bell, Howard Holman, ed. *Minutes of the Proceedings of the National Negro Conventions 1830–1864* (1969).

Dann, Martin E., ed. *The Black Press, 1827–1890: The Quest for National Identity* (1972).

George, Carol V. R. *Segregated Sabbaths: Richard Allen and the Emergence of Independent Black Churches, 1760–1840* (1973).

Jackson, Debra. "A Black Journalist in the Confederate South: Robert Hamilton's Travels in Civil War Virginia," *The Virginia Magazine of History and Biography* (forthcoming 2008).

Jackson, Debra. "A Cultural Stronghold: The *Anglo-African* Newspaper and the Black Community of New York," *New York History* (Fall 2004).

Ripley, C. Peter, ed. *The Black Abolitionist Papers*, vol. 3: *The United States, 1830–1846* (1991) and vol. 5: *The United States, 1859–1865* (1992).

Walls, William J., Bishop. *The African Methodist Episcopal Zion Church: Reality of the Black Church* (1974).

Wilder, Craig Steven. *In the Company of Black Men: The African Influence on African American Culture in New York City* (2001).

DEBRA JACKSON

Hamilton, Thomas (1823–29 May 1865), journalist and abolitionist, was born in New York City, the youngest son of the abolitionist and political activist William Hamilton and Hannah (1793–1864, maiden name unknown). William Hamilton, a freeborn black, worked as a carpenter and was a respected, influential member of the New York City black community. His son Thomas followed this example and became a prominent member of the community in his own right.

As a young boy Thomas Hamilton learned the newspaper business by working in the neighborhood of "Printing House Square," the lower Manhattan area where many newspaper offices were located. Hamilton first worked as a carrier and in many other capacities for a variety of newspapers, including the *Colored American*. The journalist PHILIP A. BELL offered posthumous praise when he recalled that Hamilton went from the offices of the *Colored American* and worked "as mailing clerk on the *Evangelist* … and subsequently on the *National Anti-Slavery Standard*…. He was one of the most rapid [address] writers we ever knew, and his memory of names was remarkable. He would write the wrappers for the large editions of the *Standard* and *Independent* without referring to his books" (*Elevator*, 8 June 1872).

This youthful experience prepared Hamilton for his first publishing venture, the *People's Press*, launched when he was just eighteen years old. *People's Press* survived a mere two years but certainly provided the training and experience for his next and most important journalistic contributions. In January 1859 Hamilton introduced the *Anglo-African Magazine*, which was followed by the *Weekly Anglo-African* newspaper in July of the same year. The *Anglo-African Magazine* was a monthly literary journal featuring essays, poetry, and political commentary by some of the most gifted black intellectuals of the day, including the Reverend J. W. C. PENNINGTON, FRANCES ELLEN WATKINS HARPER, FREDERICK DOUGLASS, MARTIN R. DELANY, J. SELLA MARTIN, and MARY ANN SHADD CARY, founder and editor of her own newspaper, the *Provincial Freeman*, in Canada West.

Hamilton strongly felt the need for a press devoted to the interests of black people but could not afford the luxury of committing his time solely to the expensive enterprise of managing both the magazine and the newspaper. In the federal census of 1860 Hamilton was listed as a "Book Binder," an occupation at which he undoubtedly worked to keep both the *Anglo-African Magazine* and the *Weekly Anglo-African* afloat. In addition to the financial resources needed to support his journalistic output Hamilton had a large family to support, with two children from a first marriage and those by his second wife, Matilda. The dependents recorded in the 1860 census were: Matilda, age thirty-seven; William, age fifteen; Mary, age thirteen; Ellen, age eight; Thomasinia, age four; Eileen, age two months.

To generate more income Hamilton also engaged in the presumably lucrative sideline of bookselling and offered a wide selection by both white and black authors; these included histories, biographies, and autobiographies of people of African descent, commentaries on the African slave trade, and books on temperance. Hamilton also sold medicinal products which could be had, along with the books, at the *Anglo-African* offices located near Printing House Square at 48 Beekman Street.

Despite Hamilton's best efforts, both the *Anglo-African Magazine* and *Weekly Anglo-African* newspaper were ventures far too costly to sustain, and as a result of these financial burdens the magazine survived just over a year, until March 1860. Lack of financial resources also temporarily claimed the life of the *Weekly Anglo-African*, when Hamilton sold the newspaper in March 1861 in the hope that someone "having more capital than he possessed" could better manage the paper (Jackson, p. 336). With the welfare of the black community in mind, Hamilton's brother ROBERT HAMILTON began another newspaper using the same name in July 1861, and a *Weekly Anglo-African* (commonly referred to by contemporaries as the *Anglo*) was again under Hamilton management. Brothers Thomas and Robert worked to make the newspaper the most influential black paper in the North during the critical Civil War years.

At the outbreak of the war the *Anglo* became an invaluable source of information for the black community. The paper reprinted regular reports from the various theaters of battle—many written by black soldiers stationed all over the South—and also kept the community informed on the general needs of escaping slaves as they sought protection behind Union lines. Although news on the progress of the war commanded a great deal of space, Hamilton always made room in the *Anglo*'s editorial columns for the exposure of discrimination and injustice on the home front. His condemnation of the segregationist policies of the Eighth Avenue Railroad called on New York City's black community to get up a "monster" petition for submission to the state legislature. Hamilton noted with encouragement that "Such a petition, backed up by an efficient lobby attendance at Albany, and by such newspaper influence as we can command, might do the work effectually" (*Anglo-African*, 7 Nov. 1863).

The daily management of the *Anglo* became increasingly onerous for Hamilton. His brother Robert left New York in the fall of 1863 to travel throughout the Union-occupied South; Thomas was therefore in sole charge of all responsibilities relative to the production of the paper, including writing editorials and selecting items for publication from the voluminous correspondence regularly received at the *Anglo* office. He eventually succumbed under the strain and died, at the age of forty-two, of typhoid fever at his home in Jamaica, Long Island. Hamilton was survived by his wife, Matilda, their six children, and two children by a former marriage.

Thomas Hamilton died at the height of his productivity as a journalist, and at a time when his powerful pen and voice would have made a profound difference in a nation just emerging from civil war. One can only imagine the contribution he might have made on behalf of black men—many of them Union veterans—as they struggled against disfranchisement in postbellum New York. Yet his contribution to black life during the antebellum and war years had been immense. The publishing efforts of Thomas Hamilton gave voice to New York's black community during the crises of urban racial violence and the revolution that was the Civil War and Emancipation.

FURTHER READING

Anglo-African Magazine (Jan. 1859, facsimile pub., 1968).

Bullock, Penelope L. *The Afro-American Periodical Press, 1838–1909* (1981).

Dann, Martin E., ed. *The Black Press, 1827–1890: The Quest for National Identity* (1972).

Jackson, Debra. "A Cultural Stronghold: The Anglo-African Newspaper and the Black Community of New York," *New York History* (Fall 2004).

Ripley, C. Peter, ed. *The Black Abolitionist Papers*, vol. 3: *The United States, 1830–1846* (1991) and vol. 5: *The United States, 1859–1865* (1992).

Obituary: *Weekly Anglo-African*, 10 June 1865.

DEBRA JACKSON

Hamilton, Virginia Esther (12 Mar. 1936–19 Feb. 2002), children's author, was born in Yellow Springs, Ohio, the youngest of five children of Kenneth James Hamilton, a farmer, and Etta Belle Perry Hamilton, a housewife. She was named for the home state of her maternal grandfather, Levi Perry, a slave who as a child had escaped from the state by crossing the Ohio River. An inveterate storyteller, Hamilton's grandfather would tell his children and grandchildren the story of his escape in order to relate to them their history and to keep them mindful of their freedom. Her family was full of storytellers, and Hamilton became convinced early on that she would one day be a writer of stories herself. Hamilton has stated that her childhood was a happy one, and she was encouraged to follow her dreams. Her childhood was spent helping her mother with the farm, listening to the stories told by family members, and reading as many books as she could from the local library. She attended nearby Antioch College on a full scholarship, enrolling in 1957. There she studied literature and creative writing and was soon recognized as a talented writer. After three years at Antioch, she transferred to Ohio State University for one year, and then studied at the New School for Social Research in New York. It was there she met a poet named Arnold Adoff. They married in March 1960, eventually having two children: a daughter, Leigh, and a son, Jaime Levi. Hamilton and Adoff lived in New York for several years, with Hamilton working at several different jobs as a nightclub singer, a receptionist, and a cost accountant.

While she had been a storyteller and writer for years, meeting a friend from her Antioch College days served as the catalyst for her prolific publishing career: Janet Schulman, an editor at Macmillan, encouraged Hamilton to submit a manuscript of some of the stories she had written in college. One of these stories became the basis for her first novel, *Zeely*, a children's novel (1967). The book was published at a time when many African Americans were exploring their roots and the theme of "black is beautiful" became a source of pride for many; *Zeely* fit well within the theme. The book, about a young girl who becomes convinced that a local woman is an African princess, broke ground for its depiction of blacks in a children's book. The people in Hamilton's book were not impoverished or suffering, and *Zeely* was not a "problem story."

The success of her first book led quickly to the publication of her second one, *The House of Dies Drear*, the following year. A different genre than

her first book, *Dies Drear* won the Edgar Allan Poe Award for best juvenile mystery of the year. The ability to successfully shift genres and painstaking historical research, such as the research that went into *Dies Drear*, would be hallmarks of Hamilton's prolific career. On average, she would publish a book a year until her death, and she would go on to win almost every major award given in the field of children's literature.

After ten years in New York City, Hamilton and her family moved back to Yellow Springs, Ohio, where they would settle on a plot of the land that had been in her family for generations. She followed her first two successes with *The Planet of Junior Brown* (1971), the story of a boy growing up in New York, followed three years later by perhaps her most acclaimed book, *M.C. Higgins, the Great* (1974). This book won the John Newbery Medal, making Hamilton the first African American to receive the award. *M.C. Higgins* also won the Boston Globe–Horn Book Award as well as the National Book Award. No other book has ever won all three of these awards in the same year. In 1975, Hamilton received a John D. and Catherine T. MacArthur Fellowship, the first children's book author to do so. In 1984, Kent State University honored her by creating the Virginia Hamilton Conference, held every April to recognize the growing field of multicultural children's literature.

Hamilton's versatility as a storyteller drove her to keep trying new genres and techniques. She ventured into science fiction with the Justice Cycle series: *Justice and Her Brothers* in 1978, *Dustland* (1980), and *The Gathering* (1981). She wrote a ghost tale, *Sweet Whispers, Brother Rush* in 1982, and then began gathering and writing folk tales, both historical and fantasy, publishing an illustrated collection of these in *The People Could Fly* in 1985. The title story is about a slave teaching his fellow slaves how to escape their lives by literally flying away. She followed with two more folk-based collections: *In the Beginning: Creation Stories from around the World* in 1988, and *Many Thousand Gone: African Americans from Slavery to Freedom*, in 1995.

In 1992, she received one of the most prestigious awards given in the field of children's literature, the Hans Christian Andersen Author Award. This is given every other year by the International Board on Books for Young People to a writer whose body of work has made a lasting impact on the world of children's literature. Exploring the limits of traditional folk tales, Hamilton published a collection of stories with strong female protagonists called *Her*

Stories: African American Folktales, Fairy Tales, and True Tales (1995), which won the Coretta Scott King Award. The same year Hamilton was honored with the Laura Ingalls Wilder Award, a bronze medal given to American authors or illustrators who have made, over many years, a significant contribution to children's literature.

Hamilton has been recognized for awakening an interest in multicultural books for children and for setting an example of vivid storytelling, as well as for her diversity in theme and genre. She is credited with creating the thematic genre of "liberation literature," in which individuals pursue their own freedom struggling against even the worst of circumstances. These individuals whom she wrote about were historical, well-known figures such as *W. E. B. DuBois: A Biography* (1972), *Paul Robeson: The Life and Times of a Free Black Man* (1974), and *Anthony Burns: The Defeat and Triumph of a Fugitive Slave* (1988) and her accounts of their lives were meant to inspire readers.

Hamilton also wrote about the struggles of lesser-known historical figures and about the struggles faced by children every day. Her compassion and understanding for those struggling for their own autonomy shone through her writing, even leading some critics to compare Hamilton's writing with that of Toni Morrison.

FURTHER READING

Mangal, Melina. *Virginia Hamilton* (2002).

Marinelli, Deborah, A. *Virginia Hamilton* (2003).

Mikkelsen, Nina. "But Is It a Children's Book? A Second Look at Virginia Hamilton's *The Magical Adventure*," *Children's Literature Association Quarterly* 11 (Fall 1986).

Mikkelsen, Nina. *Virginia Hamilton* (1994).

Nodelman, Perry. "The Limits of Structures: A Shorter Version of a Comparison between Toni Morrison's *Song of Solomon* and Virginia Hamilton's *M.C. Higgins the Great*," *Children's Literature Association Quarterly* (Fall 1998).

Trites, Roberta Seelinger. "'I Double Never Ever Lie to My Chil'ren': Inside People in Virginia Hamilton's Narratives," *African American Review* 32 (Spring 1998).

Obituary: *Booklist*, 15 Mar. 2002.

AMY SPARKS KOLKER

Hamlet, James (c. 1818–?), first man to be returned to slavery under the Fugitive Slave Act of 1850, was born James Hamilton Williams in Baltimore, Maryland, the slave of Mary Brown. Little is known of Hamlet's parents, but he claimed during his brief trial that he was the son of a freewoman and thus had never been a slave at all. A purported escaped slave, Hamlet left Baltimore for New York City in 1848, where he worked as a porter in the Tilton and Maloney general store. Before his capture and return to slavery, he lived in the city of Williamsburg (present-day Brooklyn) with his wife and two children, whose names are unknown. While in Williamsburg, Hamlet was an active member of the African Methodist Episcopal Zion Church and a devoted husband and father. It is not surprising that Hamlet chose New York as a safe haven for his family. In the two decades preceding the passage of the 1850 Fugitive Slave Law, New York's black population rose to 13,815, a fact suggesting that many escaped slaves and freed blacks considered the city a refuge from the slaveholding South.

By the fall of 1850, however, Hamlet's refuge was about to turn into a nightmare. On 18 September 1850 Congress passed the Fugitive Slave Law, a part of the Compromise of 1850 that made California into a free state and defined as territories New Mexico and Utah, leaving the possibility of slavery open to the residents of these regions. The most dire component of the Compromise of 1850, however, was its amendment of the Fugitive Slave Act of 1793. The Fugitive Slave Act of 1850 provided federal jurisdiction, complete with special courts and administrators, for the return of escaped slaves replacing state jurisdiction. The consequences of this move from state power to federal power meant that crossing over into another state would no longer provide immunity or a safe haven for escaped slaves, who could be returned to slavery by any person. The new Fugitive Slave Law also meant that any person who hid or otherwise aided and abetted an escaped slave or did not turn a known escaped slave over to federal authorities was committing treason and could be both fined and imprisoned. On 26 September 1850, only eight days after the passage of the new law, James Hamlet became the first person to be returned to slavery under its provisions. Hamlet was arrested at 58 Water Street, his place of work, by the U.S. marshal Benjamin H. Tallmadge, after the U.S. commissioner Alexander Gardiner issued a warrant for his arrest. Hamlet's former owner, Mary Brown, had enlisted the help of Thomas J. Clare, a renowned slave catcher, as well as the New York City's Union Safety Committee, an organization formed to assist slave owners in retrieving their "property." Brown sent written testimony along with a power of attorney with Clare to the Circuit Court of the U.S. New

Effects of the Fugitive-Slave-Law.

Holy Bible.

Thou shalt not deliver unto the master his servant which has escaped from his master unto thee. He shall dwell with thee. Even among you in that place which he shall choose in one of thy gates where it liketh him best. Thou shalt not oppress him.

Deut XXIII.15.16

Declaration of independence.

We hold that all men are created equal. that they are endowed by their Creator with certain unalienable rights. that among these are life, liberty and the pursuit of happiness.

James Hamlet, the first man to be returned to slavery under the Fugitive Slave Act of 1850. This abolitionist poster protests his recapture. (Library of Congress.)

York Southern District claiming that James Hamlet was her property and accusing him of running away. She also sent her son, Gustavus Brown, to offer oral testimony in support of her case that Hamlet was actually her slave and not a freeman at all.

Upon his arrest, Hamlet was taken to the old city hall where he was given a summary hearing—which meant that he could be tried, convicted, and deported the very same day of his capture. Hamlet claimed during his defense that he was not a slave because his mother was free and so he had "entitled himself to freedom," but since blacks were not allowed to testify under the new law, his statements were inadmissible (Quarles, 197). The New York abolitionists tried to prevent his deportation by offering legal counsel, but the attorney arrived too late, and Hamlet was rushed back to Baltimore, all within the space of a few hours. Immediately upon his return to Baltimore, Brown advertised the sale of Hamlet in the *Journal of Commerce*, claiming that he was a "steady, correct and upright man" (Tappan, 5).

News of Hamlet's arrest spread rapidly across New York in both abolitionist and religious circles. Many New Yorkers, both white and black, were outraged by what they considered to be unconstitutional treatment with respect to Hamlet's trial, and five days later the black abolitionist leader the Reverend CHARLES BENNETT RAY of the Mother African Methodist Episcopal Zion Church informed 500 people during a sermon that $800 had been raised by abolitionists to purchase Hamlet's freedom, a controversial move since many abolitionists argued that slavery constituted a theft and that slave owners should never be compensated. On 5 October 1850 thousands of people, Whigs and Democrats, Free-Soil and Liberty Party men, along with black and white abolitionists gathered at the park next to the New York City Hall to welcome Hamlet home. Before Hamlet took the stage that day, the crowd heard speeches by the black abolitionists WILLIAM PETER POWELL, the Reverend John P. Raymond, and ROBERT HAMILTON. When Hamlet took the stage alongside his wife, he was too overcome with gratitude to speak and so simply waved around a handkerchief that had been dampened by his tears. Hamilton apparently said of Hamlet's silence, "he is a free man—that is a speech itself" (Quarles, 198).

After the meeting in the park, Hamlet was escorted home to Williamsburg by nearly 200 people. Though little else is known of Hamlet's life, including the exact date of his death or what his activities may have been after his capture and release, his life has become a symbol of the struggle by abolitionists against the injustices of the Fugitive Slave Law. As a result of the Hamlet case and the federal government's drive to enforce the new law, New York's black population dropped from 13,815 to 12,574.

FURTHER READING
Johnson, James Weldon. *Black Manhattan* (1930).
Middleton, Stephen. *The Black Laws: Race and the Legal Process in Early Ohio* (2005).
Quarles, Benjamin. *Black Abolitionists* (1969).
Tappen, Lewis. *The Fugitive Slave Bill, Its History and Unconstitutionality: With an Account of the Seizure and Enslavement of James Hamlet, and His Subsequent Restoration to Liberty* (1850, repr. 2006).
MARLENE L. DAUT

Hamlin, Albert Comstock (10 Feb. 1881–29 Aug. 1912), politician, was born in Topeka, Kansas, the son of Andrew Jackson Hamlin and Fanny (maiden name unknown), former slaves who had migrated from Tennessee. Like many of the so-called exodusters, the Hamlins moved on to Oklahoma Territory in 1890 and began to farm in Logan County. Educated in Topeka and in Logan County, Albert Hamlin continued to work the family's farm after his father's death in 1891. In 1899 he married Katie Weaver; the couple had five children.

Logan County's population was nearly one-quarter black in 1900. African Americans were especially numerous in such settlements as Langston, an all-black town, and Guthrie, the territorial capital. Hamlin took advantage of such opportunities as their numbers still afforded black Oklahomans, serving on the school board and as a trustee of Springvale Township, where his farm was located. In 1907 Oklahoma became a state, and the next year Hamlin ran for a seat in the legislature. The local black leadership was hardly united in support of his candidacy, however. Convinced that

African Americans should be politically independent, the two prominent editors of black newspapers in the county rarely deigned even to mention Hamlin in their columns, no doubt put off by his loyalty to the Republican Party. Nevertheless he won his race by a better than two-to-one margin, becoming the only African American to sit in the second legislature.

Hamlin's election as the new state's first black legislator was the most conspicuous manifestation of the black electoral power that increasingly turned white Democrats' thoughts to disfranchisement. With little choice but to accept the more formalized segregation likewise being visited upon the state, Hamlin evidently sought as a legislator to ensure that if "separate but equal" was to prevail, the latter condition truly be enforced. He helped carry through the legislature a $35,000 appropriation to establish a state school for blind, deaf, and orphaned black children and secured passage of a resolution calling on Oklahoma's Jim Crow railroads to provide genuinely equal accommodations for black patrons. A member of the African Methodist Episcopal (AME) Church, he also pressed Sabbatarian legislation, and a bill he sponsored banning theatrical performances and baseball games on Sunday passed the legislature in amended form.

Hamlin's 1910 reelection bid came to naught. Supporters claimed he won a majority of several hundred votes but was "counted out" by local officials. Less than two years later Hamlin died of unknown causes at his Logan County farm. He lived long enough to see a literacy restriction on the franchise, together with a "grandfather clause" grafted onto the Oklahoma Constitution. More than half a century passed before another African American sat in the state's legislature.

FURTHER READING
Teall, Kaye M., ed. *Black History in Oklahoma: A Resource Book* (1971).
This entry is taken from the *American National Biography* and is published here with the permission of the American Council of Learned Societies.
PATRICK G. WILLIAMS

Hammon, Briton (fl. 1747–1760), slave narrative author, wrote the earliest slave account published in North America. Practically nothing is known about him other than what he stated in the account of his life's events between 1747 and 1760. While living as a slave in New England in 1747, Hammon undertook a sea voyage that turned out to be a thirteen-year odyssey featuring numerous perils and repeated captures by American Indians and Spaniards. *A Narrative, of the Uncommon Sufferings, and Surprizing Deliverance of Briton Hammon, a Negro Man,—Servant to General Winslow, of Marshfield, in New-England, Who Returned to Boston, after Having Been Absent Almost Thirteen Years*, published as a fourteen-page pamphlet, was printed and sold in 1760 by Green and Russell, a Boston publishing firm that was bringing out popular Indian captivity narratives.

This remarkable story of sea adventures, treachery, and multiple captivities is believed to be the first autobiographical slave narrative on record. It is not clear whether Hammon's work was actually written by him. More than likely it was dictated to a writer who faithfully transcribed the slave's spoken tale. The ungrammatical and plain style of the text and the lack of much editorializing in the main body of the account seem to indicate that Briton Hammon's words were written down almost exactly as he delivered them. However, the beginning and ending sections of the narrative do point to the probability that a white recorder stylistically embellished Hammon's work with traditional eighteenth-century religious statements and personal expressions of humility.

Hammon's journey commenced on the "25th Day of December, 1747," when, with his master's permission, the adventurous slave left Marshfield, Massachusetts, on a sea voyage. The next day he set sail from Plymouth on a ship bound for Jamaica and the "Bay" of Florida. After a month's journey, the ship arrived in Jamaica for a short stay and then sailed up the coast of Florida for the purpose of picking up "log wood." The vessel left Florida at the end of May, and in the middle of June it ran aground a short distance from shore, off "Cape-Florida." There, the captain's refusal to unload some of the cargo of wood so as to free the ship proved fatal. In two days' time a large group of Indians in canoes, flying the English colors as a ruse to trick the captain and his crew, attacked and murdered everyone on the ship except Hammon, who saved himself by jumping overboard. But the Indians soon took him out of the water, beat him, and told him they were going to roast him alive. However, much to Hammon's surprise, they treated him fairly well as their prisoner.

Hammon remained with the Indians for five weeks, until he managed to get to Cuba aboard a Spanish vessel whose captain he had previously met in Jamaica. The Indians pursued their escaped captive to Havana and demanded that he be returned to them. The governor of the island refused, but paid the Indians ten dollars to purchase Hammon. After working in the governor's castle for about a year, Hammon met up with a press gang that demanded he serve aboard a ship sailing to Spain. Upon his refusal Hammon was put into a dungeon and held there for four years and seven months, during which time he tried without success to make the governor aware of his imprisonment.

Finally, through the efforts of friends, Hammon's situation came to the attention of the governor, who ordered him released and returned to his service. For the next several years Hammon worked for the governor in his castle and later for the bishop of Havana. During this time the long-suffering prisoner made three attempts to escape, and on the last one he succeeded. After a bit of difficulty he managed to be taken aboard an English ship that was about to sail for Jamaica and then on to London.

Upon his arrival in England, Hammon signed up for service on a succession of British naval vessels, one of which engaged in a battle with a French warship. During this encounter he "was Wounded in the Head by a small Shot." After serving several months at sea, Hammon was discharged on 12 May 1759 to the Royal Hospital for Seamen at Greenwich, England, after "being disabled in the Arm." Hammon soon recovered, and over the next few months he worked as a cook on several ships. After suffering a bout of fever in London, Hammon signed aboard a vessel sailing for Boston. On the passage over the Atlantic Ocean he became delighted to learn that his-"good Master" General Winslow, who had allowed Hammon to leave New England thirteen years before, was one of the passengers aboard ship. After the happy reunion Winslow remarked that Hammon "was like one arose from the Dead, for he thought I had been Dead a great many Years, having heard nothing of me for almost Thirteen Years" (Hammon, 13).

At the ending of Hammon's narrative, he thanks the "Divine Goodness" for being "miraculously preserved and delivered out of many Dangers," and attests to the fact that he has "not deviated from Truth" (Hammon, 14). The ending corresponds to the spiritual declaration at the beginning of his narrative, and both sections seem to be tacked on by someone else to give the story a religious framework. These, in addition to the many religious references Hammon himself inserts in his story, impart a spiritual autobiographical character to the work. The title of Hammon's book was similar to those of other published Indian captivity accounts, and at times his text seems to echo the phraseology and religious references of those accounts.

Hammon's work is believed to be the first of thousands of slave narratives written in America. His story follows the pattern of spiritual striving and of escape from physical captivity (in Hammon's case, Indian and Spanish bondage but not American slavery) that is an essential element of the many slave narratives that were published in the late eighteenth and early nineteenth centuries. In the immediate decades after Hammon's publication, there appeared several notable slave narratives including those by JAMES ALBERT UKAWSAW GRONNIOSAW (1772), OLAUDAH EQUIANO (1789), and BROTEER (VENTURE SMITH) (1798). All that is known about Hammon's life after his return to New England in 1760 is that his short tale of captivity and escape became a well-known personal account in eighteenth-century America.

FURTHER READING
Hammon, Briton. *A Narrative, of the Uncommon Sufferings, and Surprizing Deliverance of Briton Hammon, a Negro Man,—Servant to General Winslow, of Marshfield, in New-England, Who Returned to Boston, after Having Been Absent Almost Thirteen Years* (1760).

Andrews, William L. *To Tell a Free Story: The First Century of Afro-American Autobiography, 1760–1865* (1986).

Costanzo, Angelo. *Surprizing Narrative: Olaudah Equiano and the Beginnings of Black Autobiography* (1987).

Foster, Frances Smith. *Witnessing Slavery: The Development of Ante-bellum Slave Narratives* (1979).

ANGELO COSTANZO

Hammon, Jupiter (11 Oct. 1711–?), poet and preacher, was born on the estate of Henry Lloyd on Long Island, New York, most probably the son of two of Lloyd's slaves, Rose and Opium, the latter renowned for his frequent escape attempts. Few records remain from Hammon's early life, though correspondence of the Lloyd family indicates that in 1730 he suffered from a near-fatal case of gout. He was educated by Nehemiah Bull, a Harvard graduate, and Daniel Denton, a British missionary, on the Lloyd manor. Except for a brief period during the Revolutionary War, when Joseph Lloyd removed the family to Hartford, Connecticut, Hammon lived his entire life on Long Island, in the Huntington area, serving the Lloyds as clerk and bookkeeper. There is no surviving indication that Hammon either married or had children. The precise date of his death and the location of his grave remain unknown, although it is known that he was alive in 1790 and had died by 1806.

Hammon is best known for his skill as a poet and preacher. Early in the spiritual Great Awakening of the 1730s and 1740s he was converted to a Wesleyan Christianity, and his poems and sermons reflect a Calvinist theology. Within the framework of these religious doctrines Hammon crafted a body of writing that critically investigates slavery. His first published poem, "An Evening Thought," appeared as a broadside on Christmas Day 1760. Embedded within the religious exhortation is a subtle apocalyptic critique of slavery in which the narrator prays that Christ will free all men from imprisonment:

> Now is the Day, excepted Time;
> The Day of Salvation;
> Increase your Faith, do not repine:
> Awake ye every Nation.

The poem ends by calling on Jesus to "Salvation give" and to bring equality to all: "Let us with Angels share." Hammon couples a protest against earthly injustice with his religious conviction that all men are enslaved by sin.

Hammon's next publication, "An Address to Miss Phillis Wheatley," appeared in Hartford on 4 August 1778. The language of the poem offers PHILLIS WHEATLEY, then the most prominent African in America, spiritual—and thereby literary—advice. From the position of elder statesman Hammon attempts to correct what he sees as the pagan influences in Wheatley's verse:

> Thou hast left the heathen shore; Thro' mercy
> of the Lord, Among the heathen live no more,
> Come magnify thy God. Psalm 34:1–3.

Typical of eighteenth-century American poetry, and primarily influenced by Michael Wigglesworth, Hammon's verse portrays America as a site for spiritual salvation since it is free of the corruption of the Old World. The poem seizes on biblical passages in order to fashion an argument that he hopes will convince Wheatley to write more religious verse. Hammon's next piece, *An Essay on the Ten Virgins*, advertised for sale in Hartford in 1779, is now lost.

Hammon exhorts his "brethren" to confess their sins and thus receive eternal salvation in his 1782 sermon *Winter Piece*. Its call to repentance and the proclamation of man's inherent sinfulness is consistent with other sermons of this era. Another prose essay, *An Evening's Improvement*, was printed in Hartford in 1783, and in it Hammon continues his protest against the institution of slavery. Published along with the sermon is Hammon's greatest poem, "A Dialogue, Entitled, the Kind Master and the Dutiful Servant," wherein he directly questions the unequal relationship between slave and master by emphasizing that before God, only sin divides Man:

Master
My Servant we must all appear,
And follow then our King;
For sure he'll stand where sinners are,
To take true converts in.
Servant
Dear master, now if Jesus calls,
And sends his summons in;
We'll follow saints and angels all,
And come unto our King.

The end of the poem disrupts the dialogue structure as the voice of the servant blends into that of the poet's. In the last seven stanzas Hammon instructs all in how to attain peace and harmony:

Believe me now my Christian friends,
Believe your friend call'd Hammon:
You cannot to your God attend,
And serve the God of Mammon.

Here Hammon argues that materialism (Mammon), a code for economic slavery, prohibits salvation because it leads an individual away from religious contemplation.

Hammon's final and most widely read piece, *An Address to the Negroes in the State of New-York*, was first printed in 1787 and then republished by the Pennsylvania Society for Promoting Abolition in 1806. In it Hammon speaks most directly against slavery. Within the body of his address Hammon argues that young African Americans should pursue their freedom even though he, at age seventy-six, does not want to be set free. Hammon calls for gradual emancipation: "Now I acknowledge that liberty is a great thing, and worth seeking for, if we can get it honestly; and by our good conduct prevail on our masters to set us free."

Hammon argues that earthly freedom is subordinate to spiritual salvation and that the need to be born again in the spirit of Christ overpowers all else, for in death "there are but two places where all go ... white and black, rich and poor; those places are Heaven and Hell." Eternal judgment is what ultimately matters; thus Hammon urges his fellow African Americans, in their pursuit of freedom, to seek forgiveness through repentance and to place spiritual salvation above mortal concerns.

Hammon remained unknown from the early nineteenth century until 1915, when literary critic Oscar Wegelin, who rediscovered Hammon in 1904, published the first biographical information on him as well as some of his poetry. Although Hammon apparently was not the first African American writer (evidence suggests he was predated by one LUCY TERRY poem), his canon makes him one of America's first significant African American writers.

FURTHER READING

Blackshire-Belay, Carol Aisha, ed. *Language and Literature in the African American Imagination* (1992).

Inge, M. Thomas, et al., eds., *Black American Writers*, vol. 1 (1978).

O'Neale, Sondra A. *Jupiter Hammon and the Biblical Beginnings of African American Literature* (1993).

Ransom, Stanley Austin, Jr., ed. *America's First Negro Poet: The Complete Works of Jupiter Hammon of Long Island* (1970).

Wegelin, Oscar. *Jupiter Hammon: American Negro Poet* (1915).

This entry is taken from the *American National Biography* and is published here with the permission of the American Council of Learned Societies.

DUNCAN F. FAHERTY

Hammonds, Evelynn Maxine (2 Jan. 1953–), feminist scholar, historian, physicist, engineer, and advocate for minorities and women in science, was born in Atlanta, Georgia, the oldest of two girls of William Emmett Hammonds, a postal worker, and Evelyn Marie Hammonds, a reading specialist and elementary school teacher. At age nine, Hammonds's father gave his daughter a chemistry set. For Hammonds, the chemistry set, along with later gifts of a microscope, and building sets, sparked an interest in science that would be encouraged by both parents. The events also set her on a path that would force her to think more critically about her own identity and the struggles and contributions of blacks and women in science.

Growing up in Atlanta, Hammonds attended all-black public elementary schools. This would change in 1967 when, as a fourteen-year-old ninth-grade student, she was bused to a predominantly white school as part of a program to end segregation. In high school, Hammonds took advanced science and mathematics courses to increase her chances of getting into college. However, after participating in a summer mathematics program for high school students at the Atlanta-based Emory University, Hammonds would soon discover how underprepared she, and the only other two black students in the program, was to handle the material. Hammonds felt that she had been cheated with an inferior education because she was black and because she lived in the South. Angered but determined to achieve her career goals, Hammonds voluntarily took another year of science and mathematics.

After graduating from Southwest High School in 1971 as a National Merit Scholar, Hammonds enrolled at Spelman College, also in Atlanta, in the newly established Dual Degree Program in Engineering. When Evelynn Hammonds applied to Spelman College, she wrote in her college essay that, "I believe in honesty and truth, the worth of mankind and the right of each individual to pursue his own goal" (Spelman College Office of Alumnae Affairs). While Spelman was not Hammonds's first choice, attending the historically black college for women enabled her to come "to terms with what it was going to mean to be a female and be a serious scientist" (Sands, 242). Hammonds began to think in these terms after hearing SHIRLEY JACKSON, the first African American woman in the United States to earn a Ph.D. in physics, give a talk on campus. The Jackson talk prompted a discussion among students about whether women could be serious scientists. Some of Hammonds's female classmates at Spelman felt that, as a female scientist and engineer, she was not behaving appropriately.

Hammonds's experiences as an aspiring black female scientist didn't get any better once she began her engineering coursework at the Georgia Institute of Technology in 1973. Many felt that black students were only there because of affirmative action. A male lab partner questioned Hammonds's ability to run an experiment but expected that she would simply take notes. A faculty member, impressed by Hammonds's neat handwriting, asked whether she had ever considered becoming a secretary. Hammonds was one of three black women who entered Georgia Tech that year as part of the dual degree program. She would be the only black woman to finish. In 1976 she graduated with bachelor's degrees in physics and electrical engineering from Spelman College and the Georgia Institute of Technology, respectively.

When Hammonds began graduate study at the Massachusetts Institute of Technology (MIT) on a fellowship from Xerox in 1976, she again faced feelings of isolation and inferiority, fueled by a climate of racism and sexism. "I'd sit there in the back of the room [at MIT] and hear professors and fellow students talk about how the woman was dressed, and not ever talk about the content of her presentation" (Sands, 245). An adviser reviewed Hammonds's transcript, noted that she had received one of her undergraduate degrees from a black college in the South, and advised her to take freshman physics. Hammonds viewed the comments as racist, sexist, and insulting.

Hammonds would stay at MIT for three-and-one-half years, take a leave and ultimately finish with the master's degree in physics in 1980. When it came time to prepare for her comprehensive qualifying exams as part of the doctoral requirements, Hammonds was at a crisis. "I didn't know if I really wanted to go on. I questioned whether I really wanted to be a physicist" (Sands, 247).

After graduating MIT, Hammonds landed a job with Polaroid and her career took off doing computer software engineering. But she was never quite fulfilled. She would drive past MIT feeling as though she had failed. A friend later told Hammonds about the doctoral program in the history of science at Harvard University. Working as a systems engineer, Hammonds wondered about the impact of technology on peoples' lives and found the program at Harvard appealing. "After one semester, I knew this was for me" (Harvard, 62). In 1991 Hammonds won a fellowship from the Ford Foundation to complete her doctoral dissertation, and in 1993 was awarded the Ph.D. in the history of science, the first African American woman to earn the degree in the discipline from Harvard.

Ironically, in 1992, shortly before earning the doctoral degree, Hammonds would return to MIT, the institution that had caused her so much pain and anxiety; she would assume her first tenure-track faculty appointment as assistant professor in the history of science. This time, her achievements flourished. In January 1994 she and MIT colleague, Robin W. Kilson, organized a national conference to address the status of black women in higher education, titled "Black Women in the Academy: Defending Our Name 1989–1994." What was envisioned as a small gathering to share experiences, research, and network, turned into a path-breaking event in which women, such as attorney Lani Guinier, who had been nominated by former President Bill Clinton to become assistant attorney general but later withdrew her nomination, discussed their often hard-wrenching experiences. Two years later, in 1996, Hammonds saw the publication of her first book, *Gender and Scientific Authority*. In 1997 she was promoted to associate professor and won tenure a year later. In 1999 her second major publication, *Childhood's Deadly Scourge: The Campaign to Control Diphtheria in New York City*,

1880–1930, was released. In 2000 Hammonds won a million-dollar grant from the New York City–based Andrew W. Mellon Foundation to establish the Center for the Study of Diversity in Science, Technology and Medicine. That following year, she traveled to Germany as a visiting scholar at the Max Planck Institute for the History of Science. By 2002 Hammonds was promoted to full professor, becoming one of less than twenty black faculty members at MIT to achieve such a rank.

Hammonds's accomplishments and growing national reputation would not go unnoticed. In May 2002 Harvard University offered and Hammonds accepted a joint appointment as professor of the history of science and of Afro-American studies (later, renamed African and African American studies). She was only the fourth black woman tenured within the faculty of arts and sciences at Harvard.

Two years following Hammonds's appointment at Harvard, the university erupted into a highly publicized controversy regarding remarks the university's president, Lawrence Summers, made about innate biological differences that prevent women from achieving in science. The faculty was also concerned with the declining number of females winning tenure since Summers's term in office. In February of 2005 Hammonds was named to head a task force to address this issue (Hemel, 1). In July 2005 she was appointed senior vice provost to ensure diversity in faculty appointments, promotion, and tenure. Three years later, in June 2008, Hammonds was appointed Dean of Harvard College.

Although Hammonds ceased her scientific work, she continued to have influence as a scholar and as an advocate for blacks and women in the field.

FURTHER READING

Hammonds, Evelynn M. "Seeing AIDS: Race, Gender and Representation" in *The Gender Politics of HIV/AIDS in Women: Perspectives on the Pandemic in the U.S.* (1997).

Harvard University. "Harvard Portrait: Evelynn Hammonds," *Harvard Magazine* (Jan.–Feb. 2003).

Hemel, Daniel J. "Plan Calls for Task Force to Tackle Women's Issues," *Harvard Crimson* (Feb. 2005).

Sands, Aimee. "Never Meant to Survive, A Black Woman's Journey," in *The Racial Economy of Science: Toward a Democratic Future* (1993).

Williams, Clarence B. *Technology and the Dream: Reflections on the Black Experience at MIT, 1941–1999* (2001).

OLIVIA A. SCRIVEN

Hampton, Carl B. (17 Dec. 1948–27 July 1970), founder and chairman of People's Party II, was born Carl Bernard Hampton in Houston, Texas, the son of Louis Hampton and Pearline Gayton. His parents' occupations are unknown. Carl Hampton's life and death were typical of the many idealistic black youths that came of age during the turbulent 1960s. Like many of his restless contemporaries, Hampton was dissatisfied with the social and economic condition of black Americans.

The passage of the 1964 Civil Rights Act and the 1965 Voting Rights Act were great victories for the civil rights movement. However, these political triumphs did not mean an immediate improvement in the poverty-stricken lives of many blacks. The legislation had no affect on police brutality, nor did it mean any rapid change in housing or employment conditions. Urban rebellions, many sparked by poor police-community relations, flared from California to New York from 1964 to 1968. Furthermore the assassination of MARTIN LUTHER KING JR. increased the anger, frustration, and hopelessness of urban dwellers.

Some of these men and women began to call for a "revolution" in the United States to secure the "self-determination" of American blacks. The founding of the Black Panther Party by HUEY P. NEWTON and BOBBY SEALE deeply influenced Hampton. Newton and Seale called for armed self-defense against perceived police misconduct. They also thought of themselves as allies with African, Asian, and Latin American revolutionaries. The Panther political philosophy was known as the ten-point program and platform. This document called for, among other things, full employment, housing, education, freedom for all prisoners, all-black juries for black defendants, and a United Nations–supervised plebiscite to determine the national destiny of black Americans.

Panther radicalism resulted in the deaths of many of its members and the incarceration of others. Ironically the party's travails increased its appeal to some black youths because its adherents were viewed as uncompromising militants who refused to bow to superior government force.

Hampton was one of these adherents. He traveled to the Panther Party's national headquarters in Oakland, California, in 1969 and attempted to join the organization. The Panthers, however, were not accepting members at that time because they were attempting to eliminate police infiltrators and increase internal discipline. Hampton was undaunted by this refusal, and he stayed on to work with the party as a community volunteer. He learned Panther ideology and organizing tactics during his stay in Oakland and returned home to implement the lessons. The Black Panther Party was not organizing in Houston at that time, and Hampton formed his own group called People's Party II. The Houston group sold the Black Panther newspaper and adopted its political philosophy. The People's Party also carried out a program of uniting with other ethnic organizations in the city.

The Chicago branch of the Black Panther Party, under the leadership of FRED HAMPTON (no relation), organized a Rainbow Coalition in 1969. The Chicago Rainbow Coalition consisted of the Puerto Rican Young Lords Party, the white Young Patriot Party, and the Black Panther Party. The Panthers considered this organization an attempt to unify different racial organizations around a common radical platform. Carl Hampton helped organize a Houston version of the Rainbow Coalition that included the white John Brown Revolutionary League, the Hispanic group known as MAYO, and the Black Panther Party.

Hampton's organizing efforts in the Houston ghetto encountered resistance from the police. Local police had an armed encounter with Hampton on 17 July 1970, when they attempted to stop a People's Party member from selling Panther newspapers in the middle of the street. The youth retreated to the party office, and Hampton along with another member intervened on behalf of the paper seller. The police and the People's Party members displayed weapons, but neither side fired at that time. However, a warrant was later sworn out for Hampton on weapons and assault charges. The volatile situation escalated when a local activist, completely unrelated to the People's Party, gave an inflammatory speech before the city council and "banned" the police from the area of the incident. The activist claimed the group was armed and would fight any police who dared to approach its headquarters. Other members of the community, fearing the results of a confrontation, fruitlessly attempted to convince Hampton to surrender. Hampton refused because he feared he would be killed in police custody. His fears were based on the fact that five other black men had died in police custody over the previous seven months in Houston.

The end came quickly. People's Party II held a street rally on the night of 26 July 1970 to protest the arrest of two supporters and the increased police presence in the area. After the rally Hampton was alerted to a report of "armed white men" on the roof of an adjacent church. The men were members of the Houston police force. Hampton, armed with a shotgun, went to investigate and was immediately shot by the police. A young woman named Maggie Lee Hicks, who was described by the press as both his wife and his girl friend, carried him to the hospital, but his abdominal wound was too severe. Hampton died at Ben Taub General Hospital that night. Three others were wounded and fifty-two arrested in the sporadic violence during the evening.

A coalition of community groups formed and called for the ouster of the police chief but to no avail. Ironically, after Hampton's death his organization finally became part of the Black Panther Party. Hampton, like some other activists of the era, sacrificed his life in the belief that he was working on behalf of the black community. Tragically, like so many of the others, he is all but forgotten in the early twenty-first century. He was not a glamorous man, but he was just as dedicated and competent as any of the better-known figures of his day.

FURTHER READING
Barlow, Jim. "Police Say Militants Began Houston Fight," *Dallas Morning News*, 28 July 1970.
"Black Amnesty among People's Party II Goals." *Houston Chronicle*, 27 July 1970.
"Black Leader Dies at Second Run-In." *Dallas Morning News*, 28 July 1970.
"Carl Hampton: Assassinated July 28, 1970." *Fallen Comrades of the Black Panther Party* (1973).
"*Chronicle* Lensman Is Beaten by Six Blacks." *Houston Chronicle*, 28 July 1970.
"Gunfire Erupts in Houston: Two Blacks Wounded." *Dallas Morning News*, 27 July 1970.
Rosenblatt, George, and Steve Singer. "Police, Gunmen Exchange Fire; Fifty-two Are Arrested," *Houston Chronicle*, 27 July 1970.
"Short Issues Statement Explaining Shootings." *Houston Chronicle*, 27 July 1970.
Wright, Thomas. "Who 'Fingered' Carl Hampton?" *Sepia* (Nov. 1970).

PAUL ALKEBULAN

Hampton, Fred (20 Aug. 1948–4 Dec. 1969), chairman of the Chicago branch of the Black Panther Party (BPP) for Self-Defense, was born in Chicago, Illinois, and raised in Maywood, a suburban community located to the east of the city. Hampton's parents, migrants from Louisiana, had secured work at the Argo Starch Company. Hampton was an excellent athlete, and his athletic accomplishments were exceeded by his academic prowess. The Chicago area youth displayed his mental prowess via his matriculation from high school with honors in 1966.

Coming of age in the racially charged crucible of Chicago politics, Hampton, a prelaw student at Triton Junior College, witnessed the civil rights movement in the South as a potential solution to his worsening urban environs. As a teen, Hampton adopted a posture of nonviolent, civil disobedience and assumed leadership of the National Association for the Advancement of Colored People's West Suburban Branch Youth Council in Chicago. However, by the late 1960s, the civil rights movement's failure to secure tangible gains for urban African Americans caused a titanic shift in group goals from integration to Black Nationalism. Hampton's political ideology followed suit.

On 15 October 1966 in Oakland, California, HUEY P. NEWTON and BOBBY SEALE created the BPP for Self-Defense. The BPP soon came to serve as an activist alternative to nonviolent civil disobedience. The BPP's militarism attracted followers in urban environs such as Chicago, Cleveland, and Harlem. In late 1967 the Chicago Black Panther Party (C-BPP) was formed by Bob Brown and BOBBY L. RUSH.

By November of 1968, the year that Hampton joined the C-BPP and quickly assumed a position as a primary instructor of group ideology and revolutionary theory, MARTIN LUTHER KING JR. had failed in his struggle to eradicate northern urban poverty and been silenced by an assassin's bullet. The teenaged Hampton quickly assumed the Chicago chairman's position—a rank that allowed its possessor to sit on the national-level policymaking central committee. However, Hampton's ascension had a downside. Along with other BPP leaders, he became a major target of FBI Director J. Edgar Hoover's Counter Intelligence Program (COINTELPRO).

Among the BPP's most charismatic leaders, Hampton was cited in FBI memorandums as potentially a "Black Messiah" capable of politicizing and unifying divergent revolutionary and gang-affiliated blacks behind a revolutionary program. Ongoing surveillance, including wiretaps, fraudulent letters, and agent provocateurs (or informers), only solidified Hoover's determination to eliminate Hampton's leadership.

Plans to subdue Hampton flowed from the FBI's "Racial Matters" squad. Integral to the Bureau's surveillance activities was the advent of agent provocateurs. William "Gloves" O'Neal would be the bureau

agents' most reliable informer after joining the BPP and earning a trusted position as the head of director of chapter security and Hampton's bodyguard. O'Neal, seeking to avoid incarceration for interstate car theft and impersonation of a federal officer, arranged to work off his charges by becoming an informant/agent provocateur within the BPP. Once inside the BPP, O'Neal quickly became the group's director of security.

One reality for national-level Black Power figures such as Hampton was the risk of coordinated local, state, and federal attack and entrapment. Occasionally, the Chicago Police Department superseded the FBI in its pursuit of Hampton. For example, Chicago officers attacked the Panthers' Monroe Street office, destroying Panther provisions intended for its free breakfast/lunch programs and health clinic. Officers set fire to the supplies and boarded up the Panther office. Despite such measures, the Panthers refused to close up their office. Law enforcement officials discerned that the only permanent solution to the Panther problem was the removal of Chicago leader Hampton.

Toward removing Hampton from the C-BPP, FBI agents ordered informant O'Neal to build a criminal case against the Panther leader. As a general principle, Hampton refused to participate in illegal activities. However, he did fail to obey the law on one hot summer day when he took $72 worth of ice cream from a vendor as a treat for neighborhood children. The police arrested Hampton for this transgression; he was later convicted and sentenced to a prison term of two to five years. A reasonable jurist released Hampton several weeks later on an appeal bond. However, Hampton's release and quick return to his chairman status within the C-BPP led opponents to seek his permanent removal.

FBI agents began making specific requests of their inside informant, O'Neal. The Bureau's informant was to provide both a map of Hampton's dwelling and a legitimate reason to raid the house. O'Neal, knowledgeable of the Panthers' weapons cache and the layout of Hampton's dwelling, easily fulfilled both requests and, thereby, laid the foundation for an unprecedented assassination of C-BPP leader Hampton on 4 December 1969.

After teaching his usual political education class on 3 December, Hampton returned home and discovered that O'Neal had prepared a late dinner for the returning Panthers. After serving dinner and refreshments, O'Neal left. A fatigued Hampton retired to his bedroom and telephoned his mother; she later recalled that her son drifted off to sleep in the middle of their final conversation. At 4 A.M. on 4 December, fourteen officers mobilized on Monroe Street and prepared to storm Hampton's residence. Armed with O'Neal's detailed map, officers stormed Hampton's residence at 4:45 A.M. and found a slumbering Mark Clark in the front room. Clark was executed at point-blank range by raiding officers. Clark's shotgun fell from his lifeless grip and discharged as it hit the floor. Police immediately unleashed a savage attack on the wall that stood between them and their target. Satisfied that no one could have survived their attack, they entered the room to claim Hampton's lifeless body.

Amazingly, the barrage of bullets had failed to kill the still-slumbering Hampton who had only been struck in the shoulder. A subsequent coroner's report would shed much light upon why Hampton never stirred from his sleep to seek cover from the gunfire. The C-BPP chairman had been drugged with secobarbitol, a powerful barbiturate by none other than informant O'Neal. Hampton's fiancée, Deborah Johnson (Akua Njeri) later recalled that as she stood outside the bedroom, one officer remarked that Hampton was barely alive; moments later, two shots rang out killing Hampton. Autopsy reports relate that Hampton's official cause of death was two bullets to the back of his head. Incredibly, the Panthers in the house who survived the raid were charged with aggravated assault and attempted murder and were held on $100,000 bail.

Chicago law enforcement administrators and public officials initially praised the police for their actions and blamed the Panthers for the shooting. Only after progressive Chicagoans, a congressional investigation, and inquisitive reporters questioned such statements would irrefutable proof arise that Hampton and Clark had been executed by police officers during that early morning raid—this version of events proving weightier than the accounts of law enforcement officers. Ballistics experts proved that of the one hundred shots fired in Hampton's dwelling only one had come from a gun belonging to the Panthers. That round came from Clark's shotgun after he had been shot at point-blank range.

Despite their obvious culpability in the murders of Hampton and Clark, the raiding officers were never prosecuted. The estates of Hampton and Clark were given a monetary settlement by the city of Chicago a decade after the incident. Chicago's inability to produce another individual possessing the charisma, strength, honor, intelligence, and courage of Hampton led to the C-BPP's eventual demise in the 1970s. In 2004 Chicago's city council, at the behest of Alderwoman Marlene C. Carter, designated 4 December "Fred Hampton Day" in his honor. In March 2006 controversy erupted when Alderman Madeline Haithcock's sought to honor Hampton's charitable work by naming a section of West Monroe Street, the site of Hampton's murder, "Chairman Fred Hampton Way." Alderman Haithcock's resolution led Chicago Police Department Superintendent Phil Cline to counter that if Hampton were afforded such consideration, each Chicago Police Department officer killed in the line of duty should be likewise honored. Mayor Daley remarked that the aforementioned actions would force the city to honor firefighters killed in the line of duty in a similar fashion, actions that the Mayor strongly resisted. The attempt to honor the racially polarizing legacy of Hampton ultimately failed.

FURTHER READING

Churchill, Ward, and Jim Vander Wall. *Agents of Repression: The FBI's Secret Wars Against the Black Panther Party and the American Indian Movement* (2002).

Foner, Philip S., ed. *The Black Panthers Speak* (2002).

Jones, Charles. *The Black Panther Party Reconsidered* (2005).

O'Reilly, Kenneth. *Racial Matters: The FBI's Secret File on Black America, 1960–1972* (1989).

JAMES THOMAS JONES III

Hampton, Henry (8 Jan. 1940–22 Nov. 1998), film and television producer, writer and social entrepreneur, born in St. Louis, Missouri, the only son of Julia Veva and Dr. Henry E. Hampton, a prominent physician and surgeon. Hampton's parents were leaders in efforts to change a city that was still racially segregated in the 1940s. They joined the Catholic Church because of its commitment to desegregation and enrolled their children, Henry and his two sisters, Veva and Judi, in Catholic schools. The young Hamptons were the first black students to be enrolled at an all-white suburban parochial school.

The Hamptons created a family environment that emphasized the arts (trips to Sunday Symphony were a regular occurrence) and intellectual accomplishment. Both parents were strong-willed and held their children to high standards of personal behavior and academic achievement. Henry's older sister, Veva, went on to Wellesley College, attended medical school, and became a clinical psychiatrist and associate dean of students at New York University Medical School. His younger sister, Judi, graduated from Columbia University and maintained a public relations and leadership mentoring practice in New York City and Boston.

As a child Hampton was vigorous, outgoing, and an accomplished athlete until he contracted polio at the age of fifteen. The disease left him with a paralyzed leg. He filled the spaces between intense physical therapy sessions with a steady diet of reading, a habit that was to stay with him all of his life.

When he graduated from St. Louis University High School in 1957 Hampton enrolled at the College of the Holy Cross, but after a year he found the college's regimen not to his liking. He returned to St. Louis and entered Washington University, majoring in English literature and pre-med, and graduating in 1961.

Encouraged by his parents, Hampton entered McGill University Medical School in 1962, but left soon after to enroll in Boston University with the intention of pursuing an advanced degree in writing and literature. His life took another, more dramatic turn, however, when in 1963 he took a job as editor for the Adult Programs Department of the Unitarian Universalist Association (UUA). Less than a year after going to work for the UUA, another position opened and he was tapped to become the denomination's director of information. At twenty-four, he became one of the first African American professionals to hold a major post in a mainstream Protestant denomination.

In 1965 he went as part of a team from the UUA in response to Dr. MARTIN LUTHER KING JR.'s appeal for support of the Freedom Marchers who had been brutally attacked in Selma, Alabama. There Hampton saw first-hand the work, dedication, and courage of ordinary citizens doing extraordinary things. As a writer and photographer for the denomination's publications he covered the highlights of the now-famous march from Selma to Montgomery, which led to the Voting Rights Act of 1965 and helped to change the political contours of the South. He also experienced the loss of a close friend, a young white minister, Reverend James Reeb, who had traveled with him to Selma and who had been set upon and killed by a group of white thugs. The Selma experience left an indelible mark upon Hampton and he reported later that it was while marching across the Edmund Pettus Bridge that he resolved to tell the story of the civil rights movement.

In 1968 Hampton left the UUA to form a production company and develop his own voice through the medium of independent filmmaking. He called his company Blackside, Inc., and over the next twenty years it became the largest and most significant African American-owned film production company in America.

For the first few years Blackside, Inc., concentrated on producing industrial training and government-sponsored films. An example from this period was a film designed to attract minority youths to the health care professions called *Code Blue*. Then, beginning in the early 1980s, Hampton reorganized his company to produce history-oriented, first-person documentaries. This set the stage for the landmark public television series *Eyes on the Prize* (1987), which told the story of the civil rights years in America as seen through the eyes of those who lived it.

Eyes on the Prize was created through a rigorous process that was a reflection of Hampton's desire to tell the story fair and square. Each fact needed to be proven at least three times. If there was another side, it needed to be represented. Each program, produced by individual teams mixed by race and gender, was subjected to review by a faculty that included historians and authors, among them Clay Carson, David Garrow, Vincent Harding, Darlene Clark Hine, Gerald Gill and Howard Zinn. Wherever possible, the story was to be seen through the eyes of the people who were there and told by them, not by a narrator.

The result was a breakthrough film documentary and *Eyes on the Prize* drew one of the largest audiences in public television history (over twenty million viewers) and won over forty prestigious awards, including six Emmys. The series was reproduced and made available to schools and colleges across the country; it became a widely used tool for teaching contemporary history and the process of change in democracy.

Hampton followed the *Eyes on the Prize* model in producing a string of distinguished and award-winning documentary series, including *The Great Depression* (1993), *America's War on Poverty* (1995), and *I'll Make Me A World: A Century of African American Art* (1999). He also produced one episode for the Public Broadcasting System's *The American Experience* series, "Malcolm X: Make It Plain" (1994).

In late 1992 Hampton was diagnosed with lung cancer and given two months to live. However, participation in an experimental treatment program involving the radiation of his bone marrow enabled him to survive and continue to lead his company's creative efforts for the next seven years. He finally succumbed to complications from a blood disease, believed to have stemmed in part from his original cancer treatment and post polio syndrome.

Hampton was active on the boards of many organizations, most notably Boston Center for the Arts, of which he was a founder, the Revson Foundation, and Facing History and Ourselves. He was a founding trustee of the Philanthropic Initiative and from 1987 to 1997 he served as a juror for the DuPont-Columbia Awards for radio and television journalism.

The Museum of Afro-American History in Boston commanded a major commitment of his time, talent and resources until the time of his death. He served as chair of its board for two decades, from 1970 to 1990 and partnered with Ruth Batson (the co-founder of Metco, an innovative program to desegregate Boston schools by busing students to suburban schools) in building support for the museum and preserving its home in the African American Meeting House, a historically significant building on Boston's Beacon Hill.

Hampton was also the recipient of many awards, among them the first Heinz Family Foundation Award (1993) and the Charles Frankel Prize from the National Endowment for the Humanities (1990), as well as honorary doctorates from Tufts University ([1995), Boston College (1993), Brandeis University (1993), and his alma mater, Washington University in St. Louis (1989).

In 2002 Washington University established the Henry Hampton Collection which houses his archive and contains 58,000 plus items, including 570 hours of original footage and 730 of stock footage as well as manuscripts, photographs, interview logs, and many other artifacts. In addition to preserving and promoting this collection for educational and scholarly use by students, faculty, filmmakers, and the wider public, the university is constantly adding to it with the work of others, many of whom worked with Hampton. The collection, devoted to promoting an understanding of how democratic societies change and grow, is a permanent and fitting tribute to a man who devoted his life to this process.

FURTHER READING

The Henry Hampton Collection, housed at Washington University, contains over 35,000 items related to Hampton's Blackside, Inc.

Hampton, Henry, and Steve Fayer. *Voices of Freedom: An Oral History of the Civil Rights Movement* (1990).

Williams, Juan, and Julian Bond. *Eyes on the Prize: America's Civil Rights Years, 1954–1965* (1988).

Obituary: *New York Times*, 24 Nov. 1998.

G. ROBERT HOHLER

Hampton, James (8 Apr. 1909–4 Nov. 1964), visionary and folk artist, was born in Elloree, South Carolina, to an itinerant minister father, also named James, who abandoned the family when Hampton was young, and a mother whose name is unknown. Indeed, as is the case with many visionary or outsider artists, little is known about Hampton himself. He left the rural South around 1931 to join his older brother, Lee, in Washington, D.C., where fully half of the newly arrived black residents also came from South Carolina. Hampton worked as a short-order cook until he was drafted into the army in 1943 as a noncombatant. He served in with the 385th Aviation Squadron in Texas, Hawaii, and in Saipan and Guam, and upon his discharge in 1945 he returned to Washington. In 1946 he found employment with the General Services Administration as a night janitor. He lived in the Shaw neighborhood (named after a nearby school named for Robert Gould Shaw), a crowded, thriving center of black life located in the northwest section of the city. His brother Lee died in 1948 after a short illness.

Hampton attended but did not join the local churches. Interestingly, he labeled many pieces of his masterwork *The Throne of the Third Heaven* with the name of A. J. Tyler, who was the minister of Mt. Airy Baptist Church, as well as the phrases "Monument to Jesus," and "Tyler Baptist Church" (Hartigan, 37). Around 1950 Hampton rented a former stable on Seventh Street, a location that appears in the writings of JEAN TOOMER and LANGSTON HUGHES.

Hampton's artistic life work was *The Throne of the Third Heaven of the Nations (sic) Millennium General Assembly* (c. 1950–1964), a 400-foot representation of his faith in his eventual salvation. This elaborate construction, largely held together with tinfoil, was built from discarded furniture, toys, paper, light bulbs, glass jars, and other scraps that Hampton collected over a period of about fourteen years. Hampton assembled this mixed-media assemblage in a garage he rented in northwest Washington, D.C. Hampton's intricate construction at first glance appears as random and tightly packed as a junk-store window. A tiny legend, "Fear Not," is perfectly centered over the assemblage, which spreads out in symmetrical swaths below it. The various objects reveal themselves to include a "mercy seat," an altar, pulpits, and offertory tables. While it lacks the charming or playful qualities of much American folk art, *The Throne of the Third Nation* does embody another common "outsider" characteristic: serenity achieved through the construction's remarkable symmetry and unity. The effect of the tinfoil "skin" is a surprising grandeur and solidity. Like the construction itself, the many labels and plaques that provide the text for *The Throne of the Third Heaven* are intricate and difficult to decipher, though their forms are familiar. Art historians and cryptographers have closely examined the 180 separate objects of *the Throne of the Third Heaven*, and Dennis J. Stallings, who has closely studied a similar cryptic document known as the Voynich manuscript, has identified a "Hamptonese" alphabet of thirteen vowels and eighteen consonants. Yet scholars have not been able to crack Hampton's coded script, which bears resemblance to the Greek and Semitic alphabets. Although Hampton may have been emulating "protective spirit writing," a vernacular practice that is an African retention, such writing is not a discrete, organized language, but a distortion of an idiomatic script. Others have theorized that Hampton's text is the material evidence of an idiolect that he developed in an altered state of consciousness and that his script is based on the pidgin language Chamorro, which he could have learned while stationed on Guam. The Smithsonian National Museum of American Art has microfilmed Hampton's 112-page notebook, "The Book of the 7 Dispensations by St. James," as well as sixty-three loose sheets that contain drawings of tablets for commandments, and what may be plans for the throne. Hampton's choice of materials may have been inspired by African Diaspora cultural practices in the South, where graves have been decorated with light bulbs and tinfoil. As early as age twenty-two, Hampton experienced mystical visions that he recorded on scraps of paper and incorporated in the assemblage. The assemblage also reflects the second stage of Hampton's life, as an "immigrant" to urban D.C., where storefront churches provided the poor black population with pageantry and ritual, and evangelists like CHARLES M. ("SWEET DADDY") GRACE preached salvation from a white satin throne.

Hampton died of cancer in a Washington, D.C., Veterans Administration hospital. His work finally came to the attention of the public and of museum officials, and *The Throne of the Third Heaven* became part of the permanent collection of the Smithsonian American Art Museum. The noted art critic Robert Hughes has called it "the finest work of visionary religious art produced by an American" (Hartigan, 34).

FURTHER READING
In addition to the installation at the Smithsonian American Art Museum, Hampton's 112-page

encrypted notebook, *St. James: The Book of the 7 Dispensations*, is available on microfilm at the museum. Other writings on loose sheets of paper and on a clipboard are also preserved on microfilm.

Gould, Stephen Jay. "James Hampton's Throne and the Dual Nature of Time," *Smithsonian Studies in American Art.* Vol. 1, No. 1 (1987).

Hartigan, Lynda Roscoe. "Going Urban: American Folk Art and the Great Migration," *American Art* (Summer 2000).

INGRID SCHORR

Hampton, Lionel Leo (20 Apr. 1908–31 Aug. 2002), vibraphone pioneer, philanthropist, and big band leader, was born in Louisville, Kentucky, to Charles Edward, a railroad worker, and Gertrude Morgan, a waitress. Lionel's father was sent to France as a combat soldier during World War I and was soon declared missing in action. When his family could not learn of his whereabouts, they presumed that he had been killed. Mrs. Hampton had returned

Lionel Leo Hampton poses in his New York City in April 1988. (AP Images.)

to her parents in Birmingham, Alabama, where Lionel was entrusted to his grandparents, Richard and Louvenia Morgan. Lionel considered them to be his parents after his mother remarried and started a new family. After achieving fame Lionel had a brief reunion with the father he thought he had lost three decades earlier when a fan told him of an elderly man who had been blinded in the war and living in a Veterans Administration hospital in Ohio, who told everyone that he was the father of that great jazz musician Lionel Hampton.

When Lionel was a child Louvenia was the person he called "mother," and she had a profound influence on the course of his life. She was a well-known healer and evangelist in the local Church of God in Christ. There young Lionel was inspired by both the message and the music, which was played with a raucous fervor that seemed to lift the congregants out of their seats and into a state of rapturous bliss. In particular he was moved by the female drummer at the church who seemingly played the instrument until she reached a spiritual ecstasy that could be seen, heard, and felt. With Louvenia's encouragement, Lionel began learning to play the drums in the church. In 1916 his family became part of the great black migration to the North when it moved to Chicago in search of better economic opportunities. Louvenia tried to run a sanctified home while her son, Uncle Richard, manufactured alcohol in their basement and ran a popular speakeasy during Prohibition that was visited by such musicians as LOUIS ARMSTRONG and BESSIE SMITH (Uncle Richard's love interest until she died in a tragic car accident in which he was driving). Lionel found a strange harmony between the sacred and the profane and even recalled frequent conversations between Louvenia and Al Capone, who would call to check on production; Louvenia would pray for Capone when he was sick or in trouble. Later Hampton credited Capone with employing many black musicians at his clubs who could not find work at more "respectable" establishments.

Eventually Louvenia feared that the city's vices might overcome Lionel, so she sent him to Holy Rosary Academy, a Catholic boarding school in Wisconsin for black and Indian children. One of the nuns, Sister Petra, was a virtuoso on the drums, and she gave Lionel some of his first formal lessons in proper drumming technique and music theory. When the school was forced to close just over a year later, Lionel was able to read music and left with a basic understanding of several percussion instruments including the xylophone. Back in Chicago he attended St. Monica's School and got a job delivering papers for the *Chicago Defender* because he knew that its owner, the influential black publisher ROBERT SENGSTACKE ABBOTT, sponsored a band for his delivery boys called the Chicago Defender Youth Band. There he received valuable ear training from bandmaster Major N. Clark Smith. While at St. Elizabeth's High School, Uncle Richard bought Lionel a xylophone, his first drum set, and introduced him to club patrons such as JELLY ROLL MORTON, KING OLIVER, and MA RAINEY.

As a teenager Hampton began to play drums in a band formed by an older neighbor, saxophonist LES HITE. In 1927 Hite went to Los Angeles, California, got a gig with Reb's Legion Club Forty-Fives, and then invited Hampton to join him. Though not yet eighteen, Hampton left Chicago, promising Louvenia that he would finish high school in Los Angeles. When Hampton arrived he became a drummer in Reb's band, with whom he made his first recording, "My Mammy's Blues," in 1924. He then joined Paul Howard's band Quality Serenaders and made several recordings on the Victor label. With the Serenaders, Hampton was at times a drummer, pianist, and vocalist who intentionally tried to get laryngitis so that he could sound more like Louis Armstrong. He performed on such tracks as "California Swing," "Cuttin' Up," and "New Kinda Blues." During an intermission at the Antique Club in 1929 he met his future wife and business manager Gladys Riddle, who used the name Gladys Neal. She had attended Fisk University, had a head for business, saw great potential in Hampton's music, and, among other things, encouraged him to enroll in a high school completion course at the University of Southern California. At the start of the Depression, Hampton worked odd jobs and helped Hite start a group until they landed a permanent engagement as the house band for a popular nightclub and became known as Frank Sebastian's Cotton Club Orchestra. When Armstrong played there they accompanied him. After one sensational performance Armstrong told Hampton, "You swings so good, Ima call you Gates" (Hampton, 37). Armstrong invited Hampton to record with him on the Okeh and Columbia labels. On 16 October 1930, Armstrong noticed a fairly new instrument in the corner of the NBC recording studio that had never been used on a jazz recording. Hampton explained that it was called a "vibraharp," others referred to it as a "vibraphone." Essentially it was an electrified xylophone made of metal keys that allowed it to produce clear bell-like tones. The station used it to sound out their call letters and signal intermission during its radio programs. Hampton had never played it before, and while he was experimenting with it Armstrong asked him to play something. Hampton chimed out EUBIE BLAKE's "Memories of You," which they had been working on; Armstrong liked it, and they recorded it.

Hampton was beginning to develop a reputation as a talented and versatile musician and as an entertaining performer. He billed himself as the "World's Fastest Drummer"; he would literally dance on top of his drums, leap onto tables, hurl his sticks or mallets into the air, and engage in antics with the audience. Later, during the bebop and cool jazz eras, musicians such as MILES DAVIS and THELONIOUS MONK regarded such behavior as undignified for true artists and unnecessary distractions from the music.

Hampton had always experienced music as a participatory activity, and whether it was performed in a church or a club its goal was to get those who heard it to swing. With Gladys's help he started the first of many bands he would lead over the years. They generally received critical praise but made little money. Most significantly, Hampton and his early bands were subjected to the most demoralizing forms of racism on the road—particularly in southern states.

One night in August 1936 Benny Goodman came to see Hampton, who was performing regularly at the Paradise Nightclub in Los Angeles. Goodman joined Hampton on stage; they jammed together for two consecutive nights, after which Hampton was asked to record the next day with the Goodman trio, which consisted of Gene Krupa on drums and the black pianist TEDDY WILSON. "Moonglow" and "Dinah" were such tremendous hits that Goodman offered Hampton a one-year contract to join his group—which Hampton mistakenly thought referred to Goodman's all-white big band.

Gladys and Lionel were married in 1936 on their way to New York to accept Goodman's offer. Over the next four years Hampton achieved fame as a member of the Benny Goodman Quartet—which was one of the first major interracial jazz bands. Hampton was paid and treated well; Goodman demanded that he and Wilson receive the same accommodations as white band members, even in the South, and in New York provided limousines to take them back to Harlem. Goodman had hired FLETCHER HENDERSON to arrange for his big band and later added the black musicians COOTIE WILLIAMS and CHARLIE CHRISTIAN to form his sextet. Hampton believed that the racial barriers they broke down in music paved the way for JACKIE ROBINSON in sports and ultimately to the opening of American society.

In 1939 Hampton composed "Flying Home" for Goodman; it later became Hampton's theme song. It was then, at the height of the swing era, that Hampton decided to form his own big band. The legendary musicians who played with "Hamp's Orchestra" include COLEMAN HAWKINS, DIZZY GILLESPIE, DEXTER GORDON, QUINCY JONES, ILLINOIS JACQUET, NAT KING COLE, WES MONTGOMERY, and CHARLES MINGUS. In 1942 he picked up Ruth Jones, a young vocalist whose name he changed to DINAH WASHINGTON when she joined his band. He was one of the first to hire women as instrumentalists and in 1945 integrated his own band when he hired the white saxophonist Herbie Fields. His impressive discography lists over two hundred recordings, many of them classic compositions such as "Hamp's Boogie Woogie," "It's Gotta Be Me," "Hey! Ba-Ba-Re-Bop," "Jivin' the Vibes," and "Midnight Sun." He recorded most with Decca, Victor, and his own label Glad-Hamp.

Hampton became politically active in the 1940s. He worked for Richard Nixon, then a young congressman from California, and supported him all the way to the White House. When asked, he said "Nixon was a true friend of black people.... Nixon really looked after blacks, but it wasn't in direct ways that people could understand" (Hampton, 154). He campaigned for Nelson Rockefeller in New York, had a close and personal relationship with George H. W. Bush, and served as head of the Black Republicans Committee for the Reagan-Bush ticket. In reference to Ronald Reagan he said, "There is no such thing as racism when it comes to the governor" (Hampton, 167).

Hampton was flamboyant onstage but socially and politically conservative in temperament. He could be bold, as when he flew to London in 1956 to take part in a benefit for 156 dissidents arrested in South Africa (which included Nelson Mandela) and went to Ghana in 1958 to celebrate its independence, but in the United States he preferred to work behind the scenes on tangible projects. Improving housing in Harlem was one of his chief concerns. He helped to raise $750,000 to build 350 apartments called the Lionel Hampton Houses and then another 205 units called the Gladys Hampton Houses, in honor of his wife, who died in 1971.

As recorded music, radio, and television variety shows quenched the public's appetite for live danceable music in the United States, the big bands died out. Hampton's bands enjoyed an exceptional longevity by touring often in Europe, where they were immensely popular, and in Israel, with which he cultivated a special relationship. When rock and roll became the craze Hampton asked, "Where did it come from? Black musicians. But it was white musicians who became famous for it. They took the rhythm and blues and turned it around and called it rock and roll" (Hampton, 128). Through the 1980s and 1990s he remained in demand with a much-reduced band, played a lot of reunions and jazz festivals, and collected accolades for being a living legend. He was inducted into the Jazz Hall of Fame (1986), became the United Nations music ambassador to the world (1985), received the Kennedy Center lifetime achievement award (1992), and earned the National Medal of the Arts from President Clinton (1997). When Hampton died at the age of ninety-four he was proud of the role he had played in establishing the vibraharp as a serious jazz instrument and of his musical legacy, but he was melancholic over the possibility that the cultural network of bands and artists that had produced so many great jazz musicians was dying out.

FURTHER READING

The Lionel Hampton Center at the University of Idaho, Boise, has the largest collection of extant material pertaining to his life and career. Additional documents from the years 1936 to 1940 can be found with the Benny Goodman Papers in the Irving S. Gilmore Music Library at Yale University, New Haven, Connecticut.

Hampton, Lionel, with James Haskins. *Hamp: An Autobiography* (1989). (Contains an extensive discography.)

Feather, Leonard, and Ira Gitler, eds. *The Biographical Encyclopedia of Jazz* (1999).

Gioia, Ted. *The History of Jazz* (1997).

Obituaries: *New York Times*, 1 Sept. 2002; *Boston Globe*, 1 Sept. 2002.

SHOLOMO B. LEVY

Hampton, Pete (7 Aug. 1871–13 Mar. 1916), song and dance entertainer, musician, and variety actor, was born in Bowling Green, Kentucky, the son of Ambrose Hampton, a carpenter, and Lou (Luann) Hampton. The family lived on a property which Luann had bought seven years after the end of Civil War with 100 percent financing, payable by work to be performed by Ambrose and an obligation of the seller (W. Cook) to find enough work for them in order to pay for their home. The stage singer and comedian ERNEST HOGAN, seven years

Pete's senior, lived in the neighborhood. Nothing is known of Hampton's childhood, education, or musical training, but by age eighteen he was earning his first money in a quartet of singing banjo players, performing for a "medicine doctor" at Columbus, Ohio. By 1896 Hampton was working with a partner under the name of Hampton and Johnson, doing a banjo act for two seasons with Al G. Field's Real Negro Minstrels, performing a show called *Darkest America*. Hampton and Johnson then went with Mahara's Minstrels and P. T. Wright's Nashville Students (1897). In 1898 they did vaudeville acts in New York until both joined John W. Isham's Royal Octoroons (1900) as comedians. Hampton then became associated with BERT WILLIAMS and GEORGE WALKER, and he is shown on the roster of the *Sons Of Ham* company (1900) and the *In Dahomey* company (1902), where he met the then-chorus girl LAURA BOWMAN. Hampton and Bowman had a common-law marriage until Hampton died. They sailed with the eighty-one-member *In Dahomey* company to England in 1903. During the boat trip to Europe Hampton taught Bowman to play the banjo, and that was when they started to call themselves "Hampton & Bowman." Hampton wrote the music for "Lindy, Lindy, Sweet as the Sugar Cane" and Bowman contributed the lyrics—this tune was later sold to the team of Johnson & Dean, and published in Budapest. The *In Dahomey* show opened at the London Shaftesbury Theatre and was an immediate success. Pete Hampton was one of the stars. While on an extended tour upcountry, in July 1904, he was made a Master Mason at the Waverly Lodge in Edinburgh. After *In Dahomey* ended, Hampton and Bowman briefly returned to the United States to join a new show called *The Southerners*, while simultaneously training for a second European *In Dahomey* production. However, back in London in 1905, Hampton, a baritone, and Bowman, a soprano, joined with the tenor William Garland and the bass Fred Douglas to form "The Quartet from In Dahomey," later known as "The Darktown Entertainers." With Garland also playing piano and Bowman playing banjo, mandolin, and guitar, they toured with engagements in Germany, Bohemia, Austria, and Russia. Hampton and Bowman also toured with Garland and Douglas's revue *A Trip to Coontown*, with a cast of eighteen black artists.

Over the next seven years Hampton and Bowman (in Germany often spelt "Baumann") criss-crossed Europe with annual engagements in Germany and the United Kingdom, but also in the Austro-Hungarian Empire (1907, 1911, 1912), Switzerland

(1907, 1912), Italy (1907), Belgium (1909, 1910), France (1910), and Russia (1910), visiting the United States in 1910. In March 1909 Hampton made a film appearance for the Warwick Cinephone Films company; it was a short film in which he was the sole actor/singer, performing "Hannah, Won't You Open That Door?" in synchronization with a disc record, and which is believed to be the first appearance of a black artist in a British film.

With war looming in Europe, Hampton (now aged forty-two) and Baumann (now aged thirty-two) returned to the States in 1913. They opened at the Howard Theatre, Boston, and toured the east coast. Mostly they worked in clubs rather than vaudeville, as the Bowman Trio (Pete Hampton, Laura Bowman, and Will Garland). Three years later Hampton died of cancer of the stomach. His wife and partner, Laura Bowman, left vaudeville and pursued a career as a dramatic actress, performing on the legitimate stage, in film, and on the radio.

Having grown up in the African American minstrel tradition, Hampton must have been an above-average comedian, actor, singer, instrumentalist, and dancer by the time he reached Europe. His talents were recognized and within a few years he (and Bowman) had made over a hundred recordings—both flat disc (Ariel, Beka, Berliner, Favorite, Grammavox, Nicole, Neophone, Odeon, Pathé, Popular, and Zonophone) and cylinders (Clarion, Edison, Electric, Premier, and Sterling)—more than any other African Americans in the United States or elsewhere. Those on which he is accompanied by Burt Earle, a finger-style or plectrum banjoist, are among the very first examples of "racially mixed recordings" involving Americans. European listeners were impressed by such offerings as the stomping "Mouth Organ Coon," his own composition on which he played the harmonica with both his mouth and his nose, and intrigued by his virtuoso African American performance style. His influence as a vocalist was such that Jack Charman, one of the most popular British recording artists of the Edwardian era, used the name "Pete Hampton" on record labels after the real Hampton had returned to the United States.

FURTHER READING

Green, Jeffrey P. "'In Dahomey' in London in 1903", *The Black Perspective in Music*, Vol. 11, No. 1 (Spring 1983).

Heier, Uli & Lotz, Rainer E. *The Banjo on Record* (1993)

Le Roi, Antoine. *Achievement—The Life Of Laura Bowman* (1961).

Lotz, Rainer E. *Black People: Entertainers of African Descent in Europe and Germany* [with audio CD] (1997).

Obituary: *New York Age*, 16 Feb. 1915.

RAINER E. LOTZ

Hampton, Slide (21 Apr. 1932–), jazz trombonist, composer, and rhythm and blues arranger, was born Locksley Wellington Hampton in Jeannette, Pennsylvania, into a musical family. His father Cliff Hampton played saxophone and drums and led a family band that played big band music at political and social functions, and his mother played the piano. Cliff Hampton chose the trombone for his son because that instrument was not yet represented in the family band. Slide Hampton was left handed, a rarity among trombone players. By the late 1940s the Hampton family band had played such illustrious venues as Carnegie Hall (where in the 1990s Hampton was a consultant to the Carnegie Hall Jazz Band, now known as the Jon Faddis Orchestra of New York), the Apollo Theater, and the Savoy Ballroom, where the band spent two weeks in residence. Along with some of his brothers, Hampton attended the McArthur Conservatory of Music in Indianapolis, Indiana. The conservatory, whose founder Ruth McArthur was affiliated with Crispus Attucks High School, was in existence from 1946 to 1963 and was important in the black community. Hampton counted the trumpeter LOUIS ARMSTRONG as his primary musical influence.

Hampton joined Buddy Johnson's band in 1953. He subsequently played with LIONEL HAMPTON (no relation) and Maynard Ferguson, for whose band he contributed many popular arrangements. Though his personal relationship with Lionel Hampton was full of tension, Slide Hampton met many great musicians in the band. He also played in the bands of ART BLAKEY, Mel Lewis, THAD JONES, and MAX ROACH. He then joined DIZZY GILLESPIE's band. Gillespie became a great musical and personal influence, and Hampton's later career was tied closely to Gillespie's.

In the early 1960s Hampton stopped playing the trombone briefly and became the musical director for the rhythm and blues singer Lloyd Price. From 1964 to 1967 Hampton worked for Motown Records, becoming musical director for such prominent and popular acts as the Four Tops and STEVIE WONDER. In this capacity he was in charge of their live performances. In 1968 Hampton returned to the trombone and played with Gillespie's band and then Woody Herman's. After a tour of England, Hampton settled in France and remained there until 1977. In Europe he worked with such famous expatriate musicians as Art Farmer, DON BYAS, and DEXTER GORDON. Hampton claimed that he made more money for one concert in France than it was possible to make in a month in the United States. He was also appreciative of the arts subsidies of the French government, which made it easier to make a living in France than in the United States.

Upon his return to the United States, Hampton started teaching, holding master classes at Harvard, the University of Massachusetts, and DePaul University. As a gesture toward promoting the trombone, he founded the World of Trombones, a group that featured nine trombones and a rhythm section. They released *The World of Trombones* in 1979, and a reconfigured group released *Spirit of the Horn* in 2003.

Hampton's other albums of note include *Slide Hampton and His Horn of Plenty* (1959), *Sister Salvation* (1960), *Somethin' Sanctified* (1961), *Two Sides of Slide Hampton* (1962), *A Day in Copenhagen* (1969), *The Fabulous Slide Hampton Quintet* (1969), *Roots* (1985), and *Dedicated to Diz* (1993). In 2004 he recorded *Slide Plays Jobim*, on which he plays his own arrangements of the work of the Brazilian composer Antonio Carlos Jobim.

In 1986 Hampton appeared in an episode of *The Cosby Show* ("Russell's Trombone") alongside such great musicians as Tommy Flanagan, Tito Puente, ART BLAKEY, JIMMY HEATH, and Percy Heath. He was a founding member of Dizzy Gillespie's United Nations Orchestra (1988), which he later co-directed with Paquito D'Rivera. His work with Gillespie continued when he arranged Gillespie's score for the film *The Winter in Lisbon* (1991) and was the musical director of Gillespie's seventy-fifth birthday celebration festivities. In 2004 Hampton became the director of the Dizzy Gillespie All Star Big Band.

Hampton received a Grammy Award in 1997 for Best Instrumental Arrangement Including Vocal(s) for his work on the singer DEE DEE BRIDGEWATER's album *Cotton Tail* and another in 2004 for Best Instrumental Arrangement for the album *Past, Present, and Future* by the Village Vanguard Jazz Orchestra. In 2005 Hampton was awarded a prestigious Jazz Master Fellowship by the National Endowment for the Arts.

FURTHER READING

Applebaum, Larry. "Before and after with Slide Hampton," *Jazz Times* (Oct 2003).
Atkins, Clarence. "Slide Hampton Thrills Them at the Five-Spot," *Amsterdam News* (July 1993).
Bradley, Jeff. "Odyssey in Brass: Slide Hampton Has Run the Gamut with His Respected Trombone," *Denver Post* (Dec. 1998).
National Endowment for the Arts. "Jazz Masters on Tour," http://arts.endow.gov/national/jazz/artists_tour/ hampton.html.

PAUL DEVLIN

Hancock, Gordon Blaine (23 June 1884–24 July 1970), educator and social reformer, was born in Ninety-Six Township, Greenwood County, South Carolina, the son of Robert Wiley Hancock, a minister, and Anna Mark, a teacher. Both parents had been born into the last generation of slavery, and both eagerly sought the new opportunities available to freedom's first generation. Robert, born in 1862, had left South Carolina at an early age to study in Jamaica Plain, Massachusetts. He returned to the South in 1876 to train as a bookkeeper in Ninety-Six, worked briefly in a foundry in Anniston, Alabama, and in 1880 established a farm and a ministry in Ninety-Six. Anna, born in 1863, had been educated in the freedmen's schools of Greenwood County, and in 1879 she became the first black teacher in Ninety-Six. Gordon hardly knew his mother, however, because she died of hypertension at the age of twenty-three in 1886. Robert Hancock later married Georgia Anna Scott, who became stepmother to Gordon and his sister Ethel and with whom Robert had six more children.

Perhaps the most powerful event of Gordon Hancock's young life occurred in November 1898 in the neighboring town of Phoenix when he was fourteen years old. In response to the efforts of local blacks to vote and the alleged killing of a white man, an armed white mob killed perhaps as many as thirty-five African Americans in Phoenix and the surrounding area. Other blacks, Hancock later recalled with horror, were brought out to the woods, chained to logs, and beaten, some to death. Among those who were beaten but survived the Phoenix riot was the father of BENJAMIN MAYS, who later became president of Morehouse College.

Gordon, like his siblings, was educated in a one-room schoolhouse near Ninety-Six and by a private tutor. He also studied widely in his father's personal library and received a teacher's certificate in 1902, the year his father died. Only sixteen at the time, Hancock moved into the home of an uncle and taught in nearby black public schools of Edgefield and China Grove. There he discovered that South

Carolina's separate schools were far from equal; in 1900, for example, the state spent $5.55 to educate each white pupil but only $1.30 for each African American. Outraged by the inadequate provision for black students, Hancock organized parents in China Grove to demand better treatment and succeeded in extending the school term from two months to five months. Hancock's teaching experiences persuaded him to "seek training to help Negro people" (Gavins, 10).

To that end, Hancock enrolled at Benedict College in Columbia, South Carolina, graduating with an AB in 1911. Also that year he was ordained as a minister at the Bethlehem Baptist Church in Newberry, South Carolina, and he married Florence Marie Dickson, who taught home economics at Benedict. The couple had no children. The following year Hancock received a bachelor's degree in Divinity from Benedict and was appointed principal of Seneca Institute, a small, ill-equipped black boarding school located 150 miles northwest of Columbia. By the time Hancock left the institute in 1918, he had more than doubled enrollment, raised salaries, and greatly improved the school's reputation. Although he modeled his school on sound Washingtonian principles of self-reliance and moral uplift, his public speeches against racial discrimination earned him a reputation among Seneca's whites as something of a radical. Upon hearing that he was to be lynched, Hancock hurriedly left South Carolina to study at Colgate University in Hamilton, New York. Colgate awarded Hancock a B.A. in 1919 and a BD the following year. He then enrolled at Harvard University to study sociology. He received his master's degree from Harvard in 1921, having written a thesis on community tensions between blacks and Roman Catholic Irish immigrants in Boston. Although he completed much of the course work at Harvard for a Ph.D. and also did postgraduate research at Oxford and Cambridge Universities in England, he did not finish his doctoral dissertation.

Upon graduating from Harvard in 1921, Hancock was appointed professor at Virginia Union University in Richmond, where he established the university's first department of economics and sociology. Although he had been offered a position at a northern white university at a salary three times the twelve hundred dollars offered by Virginia Union, Hancock turned it down out of a belief that "educated Negroes born in the South should not run away and leave the submerged Negro to fight it out as best he can" (Gavins, 20). Over the next decade Hancock played a major role in improving Virginia

Union's academic reputation. He published more than twenty scholarly articles and promoted the study of the social consequences of industrialization and urbanization in Richmond, whose black population grew rapidly after 1920. In 1925 he became pastor of one of Richmond's three leading churches, Moore Street Baptist, and broadened its outreach to the poor by providing a nursery, evening classes, and job training advice.

Between 1928 and 1965 Hancock penned a weekly column, "Between the Lines," for the *Norfolk Journal and Guide* that was syndicated in more than one hundred newspapers nationwide by the Associated Negro Press. These columns, which drew on Hancock's scholarly research on the problems of unemployment, poverty, crime, social dislocation, labor strife, and racial violence in the urbanizing South, earned him the nickname the "Gloomy Dean." The acerbic journalist GEORGE SCHUYLER, who penned a column for the *Pittsburgh Courier*, was a frequent critic who attacked Hancock's "constant yapping" about jobs (Gavins, 62). Hancock retorted by dismissing the northern-born-and-bred Schuyler as a "black Nordic" who knew nothing of the struggles of black southerners (Gavins, 63).

Hancock was not always gloomy. He enthusiastically embraced any and all organizations dedicated to improving the lot of African Americans. He was active in the NAACP, the Urban League, and the Virginia Commission on Interracial Cooperation, among many other organizations. Most notably he founded the Torrance School of Race Relations at Virginia Union in 1931, a visionary plan to establish a major center of new academic thinking on race and race relations that he hoped would sponsor workshops on issues like the psychology of racism and promote interracial cooperation between black and white colleges. The early years of the Great Depression were an unpropitious time for such schemes, however, and many of his black colleagues on the Virginia Union faculty viewed the Torrance School as a waste of the university's precious resources.

A reorganization of the university in 1934 ended Hancock's tenure as head of economics and sociology and led him to focus on issues beyond Virginia Union. Chief among these was his "Back to the Farm" campaign in the early 1930s. Along with KELLY MILLER, NANNIE BURROUGHS, and P. B. YOUNG, Hancock believed that blacks could best survive the Depression by remaining on southern farms or returning to them. Most black thinkers and educators, especially those based in the urban

North, opposed the idea and viewed Hancock as out of step with the modern African American. The historian RAYFORD LOGAN noted that "back to the land" for most blacks meant a return to sharecropping. W. E. B. DuBois sniped that a six-month stint on a tenant farm in Georgia would cure Hancock and his allies of their romanticism about the land. The black sociologists IRA DE REID and ABRAM HARRIS similarly dismissed the usefulness to the black poor of Hancock's Double Duty Dollar plan, in which he urged African Americans to spend their money in black-owned businesses. Hancock's call for black economic solidarity was not, however, greatly different from various "buy black" campaigns in the Depression-era North.

Throughout the 1930s Hancock was an ambivalent supporter of President Franklin D. Roosevelt's New Deal and kept his distance from the more radical solutions to the Depression proposed by the likes of the National Negro Congress and the Communist Party. Not a member or confidant of Roosevelt's Black Cabinet, he endorsed the Republican hopeful Wendell Willkie in 1940.

Increasingly Hancock focused on finding southern solutions to the southern race problem and looked to the Virginians P. B. Young, MAGGIE LENA WALKER, and LUTHER P. JACKSON and the North Carolinians C. C. SPAULDING and CHARLOTTE HAWKINS BROWN as his main allies. He also began working more closely with white racial moderates and liberals in the South-wide Commission on Interracial Cooperation, and in 1942 Hancock and Jesse Daniel Ames, a white anti-lynching reformer, agreed to coordinate a series of race relations conferences. Hancock was director of the first, held in Durham, North Carolina, in October 1942 and attended only by southern blacks, mostly educators, business leaders, and ministers. The conferees released a statement of principles for southern postwar race relations, the Durham Manifesto, which directly challenged both the principle and the practice of segregation but couched its opposition to Jim Crow in moderate language to appease southern whites. Following a conference of southern whites led by Ames in Atlanta in April 1943, an interracial gathering of southerners met at a collaboration conference in Richmond in October 1943. Despite Hancock's efforts to have a fully integrated meeting, the large black and much smaller white delegations chose to seat themselves separately by race, and much of the debate was rancorous. Contrary to many northern observers who criticized Hancock's accommodationism, it was he who most upset the white delegates by insisting that if the South wished to avoid outside interference in its affairs, then the South itself would have to pursue more progressive race relations policies.

Out of these conferences an interracial organization, the Southern Regional Council (SRC), eventually formed in 1944, though white liberals at first predominated in leadership positions. Hancock joined it in part because the SRC's emphasis on race relations, education, and research on the economic consequences of segregation closely resembled the institute he had tried to establish in Richmond in 1931. In the 1950s Hancock urged the SRC and other southern organizations to pursue a more aggressive desegregation agenda and welcomed the upsurge of southern-based activism with the emergence of the Southern Christian Leadership Conference in the 1950s and the Student Nonviolent Coordinating Committee in 1960. The emergence of a new generation of southern-based leaders also marginalized Hancock, who became professor emeritus at Virginia Union in 1952 and retired his pastorate at Moore Street Baptist in 1963. He received five honorary degrees: doctorates in divinity from Benedict College (1925) and Virginia Union (1963) and doctorates of law from Shaw University and Benedict College (both 1952) and Colgate University (1969).

Hancock died of cancer at his Richmond home in July 1970. Historians have been kinder to the Gloomy Dean than many of his contemporaries, primarily for his role in furthering interracial cooperation in the South and establishing the SRC.

FURTHER READING
Hancock's papers are in the Duke University Special Collections Library, Durham, N.C.

Gavins, Raymond. *The Perils and Prospects of Southern Black Leadership: Gordon Blaine Hancock, 1884–1970* (1977).

Sullivan, Patricia. *Days of Hope: Race and Democracy in the New Deal Era* (1996).

Obituary: *Norfolk Journal and Guide*, 8 Aug. 1970.

STEVEN J. NIVEN

Hancock, Herbie (12 Apr. 1940–), jazz pianist and composer, was born Herbert Jeffrey Hancock in Chicago, Illinois. His father owned a neighborhood meat business, allowing his son to grow up in relatively comfortable middle-class circumstances. After receiving a piano for his seventh birthday, Hancock began his initial training not in an African American music form but in the classical European canon. Showing prodigious talent for his instrument, he advanced quickly and, at the age of eleven, was chosen to play the first movement of Mozart's Fifth Piano Concerto with the Chicago Symphony Orchestra. He became interested in jazz, however, after hearing a boy his age improvise at a student talent show. Impressed by his peer's spontaneous compositions, he further educated himself in the language and idiom of jazz by imitating and transcribing the music of George Shearing, OSCAR PETERSON, and ERROLL GARNER. Later he attended Grinell College, majoring in both music and electrical engineering. His combined study was prophetic; electricity and music's cross-germination would later flower in much of his oeuvre.

In 1961 the trumpeter Donald Byrd invited him to join his group and record for Blue Note Records in New York City. Francis Wolff, owner and producer of Blue Note, was impressed with the young pianist and offered him a contract. In 1962 Hancock released his debut album, *Takin' Off*. The album garnered significant recognition for Hancock, in part because one track "Watermelon Man" became a hit single for the percussionist MONGO SANTAMARIA. Stimulated by a brief period as a sideman with ERIC DOLPHY, Hancock soon opened himself up to the emerging avant-garde, adding another component to his harmonically rich, R&B influenced style. His third album, *Inventions and Dimensions*, is, in essence, a free jazz record, albeit one that adopts its absence of predetermined form while retaining the piano language of Bill Evans. In 1963 Hancock

Herbie Hancock performs in Basel, Switzerland, in November 2006. (AP Images.)

was hired by MILES DAVIS to play on a portion of his album *Seven Steps to Heaven*. The rhythm section, including the bassist Ron Carter and the *wunderkind* drummer TONY WILLIAMS, became the core of Davis's second quintet. Williams exerted a strong influence on Hancock, prompting him to appreciate the music of contemporary composers John Cage, Elliot Carter, and Karlheinz Stockhausen (one of the pioneers of early electronic music) as well as the new jazz of ORNETTE COLEMAN and JOHN COLTRANE. For the next four years the group pushed hard bop to its limit, abstracting harmony and time to a point at which its source was almost unrecognizable. The rhythm section itself was especially revolutionary, shifting the texture or tempo of a tune at a moment's notice, creating a swelling flux to challenge the soloist. The band made four albums for Columbia between 1965 and 1967: *ESP*, *Miles Smiles*, *Sorcerer*, and *Nefertiti*.

During the same period Hancock participated in numerous sessions as a sideman and led five albums of his own. He continued to associate himself with the avant-garde surrounding Blue Note, playing with Sam Rivers, Grachan Moncur III, and Bobby Hutcherson. His albums *Empyrean Isles* and *Maiden Voyage* are particularly notable. They employ a similar feel to Davis's group, but each song forms a coherent tone poem as well as collectively integrating into a concept album. In 1966 Hancock wrote and performed the soundtrack for Michelangelo Antonioni's *Blowup*, the first of many works he composed for film.

At the end of the sixties Miles Davis began to experiment with electric instruments and introduced Hancock to the Fender Rhodes electric piano. As the trumpeter began looking for a new sound by altering his personnel, the pianist left to venture on his own, although he would still play on Davis's pioneering fusion albums *In a Silent Way*, *A Tribute to Jack Johnson*, and *On the Corner*. Seeing new possibilities in electronic instruments, he began to delve deeply in their use in his own music. At the urging of BILL COSBY, Hancock moved to Warner Bros. and recorded three albums, two of which were with his Mwandishi group (so named because the musicians all took Swahili names). The band incorporated elements of fusion—including a quickly multiplying number of synthesizers—and the avant-garde, joining chaotic outbursts with ambient and groove sections. Hancock next joined Columbia Records, but finding mixed critical response and little commercial success, he made only one more album with Mwandishi. Disillusioned with the burden of constant innovation and the highbrow approach of his music, he sought a different direction. Encouraged by his recent devotion to Nichiren Buddhism and its chanting practice, Hancock decided to fully embrace the funk elements of SLY STONE and JAMES BROWN in his next endeavor. The result, *Headhunters*, hit home with a younger audience and generated massive sales, becoming the first jazz record to go platinum.

Throughout the 1970s Hancock continued to make jazz-funk records in the style established by *Headhunters*, including *Thrust*, *Man Child*, and *Flood*. After a reunion of the Miles Davis quintet without its leader at the 1976 Newport Jazz Festival, however, he returned to recording acoustic music. The group named itself V.S.O.P. and recorded three albums with Freddie Hubbard in the trumpet chair. Later Hancock toured and recorded piano duets with Chick Corea. His passion for technology continued at the end of the decade in his disco-inflected albums *Feets Don't Fail Me Now*, *Mr. Hands*, *Magic Windows*, and *Lite Me Up*.

Hancock found commercial success again in 1983 with *Future Shock*, whose single "Rockit" traveled high in the pop charts and won a Grammy Award for "Best R&B Instrumental Performance." The album was innovative, embracing hip hop through the use of turntable "scratching" as well as appealing to an emerging audience through a new technological medium: the music video. Indeed the mid-eighties were a high point for critical appreciation of his work. He repeated his success with the follow-up album *Sound System*, receiving another Grammy. In 1986 Bertrand Tavernier cast him alongside the saxophonist DEXTER GORDON in his popular film *Round Midnight*. Hancock also wrote the soundtrack, for which he was awarded an Oscar.

Miles Davis, who had been guiding force in much of jazz's evolution since the late forties, died in 1991. In memoriam, Hancock, who had left Columbia, recorded an album with Carter, Shorter, Williams, and Wallace Roney titled *A Tribute to Miles*. This would prove to be his last recording with Williams, who would pass away at the end of the decade. After the renewed use of hip hop in *Dis Is Da Drum*, his next album, *The New Standard*, sought to continue expanding jazz's limits, interpreting songs by Nirvana, PRINCE, STEVIE WONDER, and the Beatles (among others), just as jazz had the Broadway songbook for much of its history. In 2005 he released *Possibilities*, an album of duets with pop musicians, in conjunction with Starbucks' music label Hear.

FURTHER READING

Heckman, Don. "Watermelon Man: Herbie Hancock," *Down Beat* (21 Oct 1965).

Pond, Steven Frederick. *Head Hunters: The Making of Jazz's First Platinum Album* (2005).

Sidran, Ben. *Talking Jazz: An Oral History* (1995)

MICHAEL SCHMIDT

Hancock, Hugh Berry (1855–21 Jan. 1910), teacher, politician, and businessman, was born in Austin, Texas. His mother, Eliza, a slave of mixed race, was owned by John Hancock, a lawyer, judge, state legislator, and U.S. congressman whom Hugh knew to be his father. When he was five years of age and the Civil War was threatening, Hugh and his mother were sent by John Hancock to Oberlin, Ohio, a thriving community of whites and free blacks. This not only placed them in a safe environment but also guaranteed Hancock an education, as Oberlin College and its preparatory department welcomed all. For younger children there was the village elementary school.

Hancock was one of many offspring of white fathers and former slaves for whom Oberlin was a safe haven from the hostilities and limitations of life in the South. Black residents of Oberlin in the 1800s included entrepreneurs, teachers, and elected officials. The town was also a stop on the Underground Railroad. It was in this environment that Hancock spent his formative years.

Oberlin, while no utopia, was a place where blacks and whites lived side by side, and education was a primary focus. Hancock saw members of his race graduating from high school and college and going on to lead independent lives. He was exposed to the stirring orations of abolitionists, such as JOHN MERCER LANGSTON.

Following elementary school Hancock became a student in the Oberlin College preparatory department, where records show him as being registered from 1872 to 1873. Although there is no documentation that he attended the college, his family stated that he was a student there.

Hancock's father wanted to send him to law school, but Hancock turned down the opportunity. He had other ideas and ambitions. He had met Susie James, an Oberlin student also from Austin, and the two made plans for a life together, marrying on 19 November 1879 in Austin. Initially, they lived in Bastrop, a primarily agricultural area outside of Austin where members of the Hancock family owned houses and land. Hancock taught school there before deciding to take advantage of other opportunities.

Sponsored by a friend of his father, Hancock became the proprietor of the Black Elephant Saloon at 424 East Sixth Street and the H. B. Hancock Saloon at 404 East Sixth Street, both in downtown Austin. By the early 1890s he owned two additional saloons, at 302 Colorado and 212 West Live Oak.

The earliest record of Hancock's involvement in local politics appears in an 1882 issue of the *Statesman* of Austin, which announced that he might be a candidate for county collector. Instead, a short while afterward, the paper announced that the mayor had appointed him health inspector. He served at least one term on the Austin City Council, from 1893 to 1894, and was obviously still in politics in 1896 when he was commended for being "the shrewdest of the shrewd" (*Austin Daily Statesman*, 10 Sept. 1896). To date, however, no records have been discovered that provide further information regarding his political career nor an account of issues that he raised or supported or opposed while on the council.

In 1886 a house Hancock had commissioned to be built at 1010 Bois d'Arc was completed, and by 1887 he and Susie were the parents of three daughters. In 1896 another daughter, their last child, was born. The Hancock home was located in the Robertson's Hill area, and there they lived for approximately fourteen years. Legal documents specify that they sold the house in 1903, although the 1900 U.S. federal census indicates that they had already set up housekeeping in Evanston, Illinois.

It is not known why the Hancocks left Austin for Evanston. Their youngest daughter always believed it was because a sister had committed the unthinkable by eloping with someone her parents considered unacceptable, casting shame upon the family. That, however, does not seem to be a powerful enough reason for their father to have abandoned Austin. A grandson recounted hearing that one or two of Hancock's saloons had been set on fire, suggesting that perhaps Hancock's life and the well being of his family had been threatened. Hancock's father, who surely had served as a source of protection, was no longer living, and it is likely that the friend who sponsored Hancock in business had passed on as well.

The 1890s saw segregation in Texas widely supported by both state and local government. There had been ongoing efforts to turn back the clock on black civil rights, and acts of violence were far from uncommon. There was an average of eighteen lynchings annually during that period. And while blacks constituted a large segment of the Texas Republican Party, by 1898 conservative whites were regaining control. Hugh and Susie Hancock undoubtedly witnessed a rising tide of injustice and oppression that they no longer had the resources to hold back.

The move away from Austin did not present Hancock with the kinds of opportunities he had enjoyed in Austin, and instead initiated a time of frustration and struggle. In Evanston he was employed as a saloon keeper, but the family did not remain there for long. In 1904 they were living in Portland, Oregon. Toward the end of 1905 Hancock convinced his wife to travel on to Nevada, to the silver-mining boomtown of Tonopah, where he tried his hand at prospecting. In Nevada he discussed moving to Idaho, but Susie had decided that she and their daughters could no longer endure a life of uncertainty and instability, and she took them back to Texas.

Hancock died in Pocatello, Idaho. The *Pocatello Tribune* of 26 January 1910 stated: "Mr. Hancock … at one time was held in the highest esteem by the people of Austin, Tex…. [A]nd in the zenith of his power, financial and political, he was elected a member of the board of aldermen, and chairman of the congressional district, a position which he filled with credit and distinction for ten years."

On 13 June 1982 the Texas Historical Commission designated the house built for Hugh Hancock and his family in Austin a Texas Historic Landmark.

FURTHER READING

Barr, Alwyn. *Black Texans: A History of Negroes in Texas, 1528–1971* (1973).

Cheek, William, and Aimee Lee Cheek. *John Mercer Langston and the Fight for Black Freedom, 1829–65* (1989).

SHEILA GREGORY THOMAS

Handcox, John (5 Feb. 1904–18 Sept. 1992), songwriter and labor activist, was born to George and Vinna Handcox on their farm near Brinkley, Arkansas. Unlike many African Americans in the rural South at this time, the Handcox family owned their own land. However, it was not very productive, so they had to rent land on which to grow cotton, the area's dominant crop.

Because of his responsibilities, young Handcox could not devote much time to education. Five months a year were all that most farm children in Arkansas could spare to attend school, a schedule dictated by the cotton-growing season. But Handcox thrived there, mainly because of his interest in poetry. His father bought him a book by the poet PAUL LAURENCE DUNBAR, who became Handcox's model for his own writing. Often he was asked to recite his work during school events, and when he graduated from the ninth grade, the end to his formal education, Handcox gave the keynote speech.

Unfortunately, the relatively good times the family enjoyed soon came to an abrupt end. In 1921 Handcox's father died, killed by a team of runaway mules. Without his efforts, their fortunes rapidly decreased. When they finally lost their land, the only option available was tenant farming. In this situation, a renter provides the landowner a percentage of the crops raised, usually a fourth of the cotton. Handcox tried to hold his family together, moving them in 1924 to the Delta region of Arkansas where the land was richer. But even there tenant farming offered little opportunity for advancement. Often, landowners in this area also acted as their tenants' sole cotton agent and storekeeper. So they set both the prices for the cotton and at the commissary, frequently resulting in their tenants falling into debt. With his marriage to Ruth Helen Smith in 1927 and the coming of his own four children, Handcox had a larger family to fend for even as the tenant system limited his income.

After a decade of struggle Handcox had enough of tenant farming and started his own business venture. He had always supplemented his farm income in various ways before this time, such as bottling his own soft drinks and selling them to local workers. But in 1935 he took up fishing as his sole job. Within a month, he cleared more money than he had in a year as a cotton farmer.

His new job allowed him a freedom of movement he had never enjoyed before. Along his established route, he would sing out his catch and sell it by the pound. Moving about the community, Handcox heard about others who were also frustrated with the tenant farming system but who had joined together to make a change. In 1934 two members of the Socialist Party and eighteen tenant farmers, both black and white, came together in a Tyronza, Arkansas, schoolhouse to form the Southern Tenant Farmers Union (STFU). They had been advocating for tenant farmers' rights ever since. After learning about this union, Handcox immediately joined and soon become involved with its activities by distributing the newspaper *The Sharecropper's Voice* and by trying to get others to become members. He also began writing lyrics about the tenant farmers' plight and setting them to the tunes of southern gospel hymns, resulting in such famous labor songs "Raggedy, Raggedy" and "Roll the Union On."

His union activity did not come without danger. Powerful landowners and the local police resisted the STFU's efforts, and violence against various members often occurred. Many were threatened, some were beaten, and a few were even murdered. Handcox barely escaped this fate when a friendly white neighbor warned him that anti-union locals had plans to lynch him. After his family begged him to leave, he traveled to Memphis, Tennessee, where the STFU had its headquarters.

There he wrote more songs, which were printed in the union's various newspapers, and waited for other opportunities to help. After training at the STFU's collaborative farming project at Hillhouse, Mississippi, he traveled to southeast Missouri and assisted with organizing efforts there. Although he only stayed in the region a few months, his songs remained long afterward. When the famed Missouri Bootheel Roadside Demonstration occurred in 1939, drawing national attention to the labor struggles of tenant farmers, participants sang his songs.

In early 1937 Handcox left the South during a fund-raising trip to various urban centers in the North. Encouraged by H. L. Mitchell, the secretary of and driving force behind the STFU, Handcox dropped by the Library of Congress where Charles Seeger recorded six of his songs and two of his poems for the Archive of Folksong.

Soon after returning from this organizing trip, Handcox left the union, for both economic and personal reasons. He met up again with his family in Oklahoma, where they had moved to avoid the tensions in Arkansas. Soon they relocated to Salinas, Kansas, where they joined two of Handcox's brothers. Together they ran a rooming house for workers constructing a military camp.

Because of the growing war effort, good jobs became available on the west coast, and many black and white workers from the South drifted there during the early 1940s. In November 1942 Handcox moved his family to San Diego, California. He got work as a carpenter and later at an aircraft plant.

By the early 1950s, Handcox had again taken up fishing as one of his employments. He sold fish, fruits, and vegetables at a small market that he and some of his brothers ran. During this time period, he separated from his wife. They finally divorced in 1954 and a year later he married his second wife, Dollie, in a ceremony in Las Vegas. Together, they ran a restaurant. This partnership came to an end in 1961 when his second wife met another man and filed for divorce, which hurt him deeply.

Handcox's various business ventures and romantic relationships became the focus of his life in California from the 1940s through the 1970s, because he did not participate in politics to any great degree or do much songwriting. But in the early 1980s he came back into contact with former STFU members and even attended a reunion in Memphis, where he met labor singer Joe Glazer. Through Glazer's efforts, Handcox traveled to Washington, D.C., in 1985 to perform his songs and poems at the Labor Heritage Foundation's Great Labor Arts Exchange. During this visit, he also recorded a marathon interview for the Smithsonian's Center for Folklife and Cultural Heritage. For the next few years, he was an eager and welcome participant at a number of labor and folksong gatherings across the nation.

In 1992 John Handcox died of cancer, leaving behind his common law wife, Lanie Ruth Glass. His body was donated to the School of Medicine at the University of California at San Diego, as in accordance with his will, where he wrote, "Let it be said that I not only donated my life to helping others, but my death too" (Schroeder and Lance, p. 205).

FURTHER READING

John Handcox's longest interview is housed in the Ralph Rinzler Archives at the Center for Folklife and Cultural Heritage, Smithsonian Institution, Washington, D.C.

Honey, Mike, and Pat Krueger. "John Handcox: Union Song Writer." *Sing Out!* Vol. 35, No. 3, 1990, pp. 14–21.

Miller, Marjorie. "Footprints: John Handcox, Songwriter." *Southern Exposure*, Jan./Feb. 1986, pp. 17–22.

Schroeder, Rebecca B., and Donald M. Lance. "John L. Handcox: 'There Is Still Mean Things Happening,'" in *Songs about Work: Essays in Occupational Culture*, Archie Green, ed. (1993).

DISCOGRAPHY

John L. Handcox: Songs, Poems, and Stories of the Southern Tenant Farmers Union (2004).

MARK ALLAN JACKSON

Handy, W. C. (16 Nov. 1873–28 Mar. 1958), blues musician and composer, was born William Christopher Handy in Florence, Alabama, the son of Charles Bernard Handy, a minister, and Elizabeth Brewer. Handy was raised in an intellectual, middle-class atmosphere, as befitted a minister's son. He studied music in public school, then attended the all-black

Teachers' Agricultural and Mechanical College in Huntsville. After graduation he worked as a teacher and, briefly, in an iron mill. A love of the cornet led to semiprofessional work as a musician, and by the early 1890s he was performing with a traveling minstrel troupe known as Mahara's Minstrels; by mid-decade, he was promoted to bandleader of the group. Handy married Elizabeth Virginia Price in 1898. They had five children.

It was on one of the group's tours, according to Handy, in the backwater Mississippi town of Clarksdale, that he first heard a traditional blues musician. His own training was limited to the light classics, marches, and early ragtime music of the day, but something about this performance, by guitarist CHARLEY PATTON, intrigued him. After a brief retirement from touring between 1900 and 1902 to return to teaching at his alma mater, Handy formed his first of many bands and went on the road once more. A second incident during an early band tour cemented Handy's interest in blues-based music. In 1905, while playing at a local club, the Handy band was asked if they would be willing to take a break to allow a local string band to perform. This ragged group's attempts at music making amused the more professional musicians in Handy's band until they saw the stage flooded with change thrown

W. C. Handy in New York City in November 1949. (AP Images.)

spontaneously by audience members and realized that the amateurs would take home more money that night than they would. Handy began collecting folk blues and writing his own orchestrations of them. By 1905 Handy had settled in Memphis, Tennessee. He was asked in 1907 by mayoral candidate E. H. "Boss" Crump to write a campaign song to mobilize the black electorate. The song, "Mr. Crump," became a local hit and was published five years later under a new name, "The Memphis Blues." It was followed two years later by his biggest hit, "The St. Louis Blues." Both songs were actually ragtime-influenced vocal numbers with a number of sections and related to the traditional folk blues only in their use of "blue" notes (flatted thirds and sevenths) and the themes of their lyrics. Many of his verses were borrowed directly from the traditional "floating" verses long associated with folk blues, such as the opening words of "St. Louis Blues": "I hate to see that evening sun go down." In the mid-1920s early jazz vocalist BESSIE SMITH recorded "St. Louis Blues," making it a national hit.

In 1917 Handy moved to New York, where he formed a new band, his own music-publishing operation, and a short-lived record label. He was an important popularizer of traditional blues songs, publishing the influential *Blues: An Anthology* in 1926 (which was reprinted and revised in 1949 and again after Handy's death in 1972) and *Collection of Negro Spirituals* in 1939. Besides his work promoting the blues, he also was a champion of "Negro" composers and musicians, writing several books arguing that their musical skills equaled that of their white counterparts. In 1941 he published his autobiography, *Father of the Blues*, a not altogether reliable story of his early years as a musician.

By the late 1940s Handy's eyesight and health were failing. In the 1950s he made one recording performing his blues songs, showing himself to be a rather limited vocalist by this time of his life, and one narrative recording with his daughter performing his songs. His first wife had died in 1937; he was married again in 1954, to Irma Louise Logan. He died in New York City. His autobiography was reissued after his death. In 1979 the W. C. Handy Blues Awards were established, to recognize excellence in blues recordings.

Handy may not have "fathered" the blues, as he claimed, nor did he write true "blues" songs of the type that were performed by country blues musicians. But he did write one of the most popular songs of the twentieth century, which introduced blues tonalities and themes to popular music. His influence on stage music and jazz was profound; "St. Louis Blues" remains one of the most frequently recorded of all jazz pieces.

FURTHER READING

Handy, W. C. *Father of the Blues: An Autobiography* (1941, repr. 1991).

Dickerson, James. *Goin' Back to Memphis: A Century of Blues, Rock 'n' Roll, and Glorious Soul* (1996).

Southern, Eileen. *The Music of Black Americans: A History* (1971, repr. 1983).

This entry is taken from the *American National Biography* and is published here with the permission of the American Council of Learned Societies.

RICHARD CARLIN

Haney, Cecil D. (1 Dec. 1955–), U.S. naval officer and submariner, was born in Washington, D.C., the son of Jesse, a taxicab driver and a worker at a bus terminal, and Ella Diggs, a seamstress. Haney had long nurtured an interest in joining the army, but his perspective began to change when he was in high school. Prior to graduating from Eastern High School in Washington, D.C., in 1974, he worked as a math aide for the NAVSEA Systems Command where, as he later recalled:

> I was a computer card puncher. However, my boss, an O-6 captain, had vision, and I learned all the various computing languages. One day he asked me what I was going to do after graduating and I told him I wanted to join the army.... Well, his jaw dropped and he asked me why I wanted to do that.... He really opened my eyes and caused me to look at all the service academies. (interview, 9 Feb. 2007)

That is just what Haney did, subsequently applying and gaining acceptance at West Point, the U.S. Naval Academy, and the Coast Guard Academy. In the end, Haney chose the navy because he was "still into pounding the ground and thought the Marines would be my choice. However, I also realized that with the Naval Academy I had other options" (interview, 9 Feb. 2007). Haney entered the Naval Academy in 1974 as part of the class of 1978.

By the time Haney entered the naval academy, racial conditions for African American midshipmen had vastly improved. Haney recalled that "during that time frame, quite frankly there was enough of a mixture that nothing overt happened.... One thing that did occur was the comradeship that developed among my classmates and initial roommates, both white and black" (interview, 9 Feb. 2007). As a result, Haney's time at the academy was positive. As for choosing his navy career path, Haney had an interesting journey:

> I was fired up about joining the Marines and went down to Fort Benning to jump out of a perfectly good airplane. It really was a good time, and I earned my airborne wings. However, I injured my feet on a jump and my dad voiced concerns that made me think about other options. I later worked with the yard patrol craft and the more I thought about it, I became excited about floating on the ocean. In looking at the facts of underwater duty, I liked working with the intricate machinery and was impressed with the small crew and how professional they were.... That sold me! (interview, 9 Feb. 2007)

Gaining acceptance into the navy's nuclear power program, Haney subsequently graduated from the naval academy in 1978 with a B.S. in Ocean Engineering.

In 1978 Haney married Bonita ("Bonny") Kay Thompson. The couple had three children, Thomas, who followed his father's footsteps and became a junior engineer at Naval Air Systems; Elizabeth; and Joseph.

Haney attended Nuclear Power School in New York State and prototype training with many members of his graduating class. Following this intensive training period, Haney experienced his first submarine duty aboard the missile boat USS *John C. Calhoun* as a junior officer. Here he qualified in submarines to earn his gold "dolphins" and served on five deterrent patrols. To become a fully "qualified" (submarine vernacular for "trained") submariner, all members of a crew, including officers, had to learn every aspect of a boat's entire operational systems. When fully trained, a man received his dolphins, a uniform insignia unique to the Submarine Force—officer dolphins are gold; enlisted men's are silver. Haney subsequently served on the submarine tender USS *Frank Cable* as radiological controls officer and completed his surface warfare qualifications between July 1983 and July 1985. In addition to duty that took Haney aboard submarines to manage and facilitate repairs, he also had the thrill of "driving this big surface ship in and out of port." He followed this duty by completing postgraduate studies for a master's degree in both Engineering Acoustics and System Technology at the Naval Postgraduate School in 1988 and subsequently served on the USS *Hyman G. Rickover* from April 1988 to June 1991 as engineering officer. From 1991 to 1993 Haney served

on the new Fast Attack submarine USS *Asheville*, joining her at the end of her building phase to put the ship into commission as executive officer. Haney had excellent commanding officers and further honed his leadership skills. Following duty as assistant squadron deputy, Submarine Squadron 8, and shore duty at Naval Reactors, Haney gained his first command when he was named skipper of the USS *Honolulu* in June 1996.

Upon taking command, Haney became the fifth African American officer to command a submarine, joining a group that would one day be called the Centennial 7, the first seven black submarine commanders in the Submarine Force. The elevation to command of such men as Haney and his predecessors C. A. Pete Tzomes, Tony Watson, William Bundy, and his fellow 1978 Annapolis classmate Melvin Williams Jr., is not only a tribute to their hard work and professional dedication but also a sign of just how much the navy had done to overcome its history of racial discrimination. Following the adage of an early 1970s navy recruiting campaign that stated, "You can be Black and Navy too," these men proved that this ideal was now no longer just a slogan.

Haney's tour of duty in command of *Honolulu* was extremely successful; his squadronmate Bruce E. Grooms remembered him as the best skipper in the squadron. When Haney won the prestigious and peer-nominated Vice Admiral Stockdale Leadership Award in 1998, Grooms recalled that "every now and again someone comes along who, man oh man, is so good that he deserves it. We had consensus in the crowd for Cecil. He was legitimate!" (interview, 9 Mar. 2007). The mild-mannered Haney, however, downplayed the award:

> The achievement was nothing compared to what Stockdale himself went through in Vietnam.... On being named to Honolulu I was extremely grateful and thankful and mindful of the immense responsibility. I looked at it like being the coach of a team; the neat thing about it is, as captain, unlike a sports coach, you have to participate in the sport with your shipmates. A submarine is an intricate piece of machinery and requires an integrated team.... My passion in this business is teamwork, helping other sailors to grow in their careers, while you yourself grow. I had a fortunate ship in Honolulu, a great crew, and we maintained a high level of performance for two deployments. Nothing compared to this experience. (interview, 9 Feb. 2007)

Haney's duty after serving on *Honolulu* was equally exemplary. He earned a third master's degree in 2000, this one in National Security Strategy from the National Defense University and served in the Pentagon as congressional appropriations liaison officer for the secretary of defense ("A remarkable education in how the military is funded" (interview, 9 Feb. 2007)) from 2000 to 2002. He also served as commodore, Submarine Squadron One from 2002 to 2004, and as Pacific Fleet deputy chief of staff for plans, policy, and requirements from 2004 to 2006. In October 2006 Haney was assigned to the New London Naval Submarine Base as commander, Submarine Group 2, in charge of the North Atlantic attack submarine forces based out of New London and Norfolk, and the training and certification of new construction and overhaul at New London and the Portsmouth Naval Shipyard.

Rear Admiral Cecil Haney lived in Connecticut with his wife, Bonny, and their children Elizabeth and Joseph. Haney fondly recalled his navy years by stating that "the overseas experience and all I've learned … the teamwork piece … it has been a remarkable twenty-eight plus years" (interview, 9 Feb. 2007).

FURTHER READING

The quoted material herein comes from the author's interviews with Rear Admiral Haney in person on 9 February 2007, and follow-up via phone on 14 March 2007, as well as the author's interview with then Captain Bruce Grooms on 9 March 2007.

Knoblock, Glenn A. *Black Submariners in the United States Navy, 1940–1975* (2005).

United States Navy. Biographies. *Rear Admiral Cecil D. Haney Commander, Submarine Group 2*, available online at http://www.navy.mil/navydata/bios/navybio. asp?bioid=317.

GLENN ALLEN KNOBLOCK

Hansberry, Lorraine Vivian (19 May 1930–12 Jan. 1965), playwright, was born in Chicago, Illinois, the daughter of Carl Augustus Hansberry, a real estate agent, and Nannie Perry, a schoolteacher. Throughout her childhood, Lorraine Hansberry's home was visited by many distinguished blacks, including PAUL ROBESON, DUKE ELLINGTON, and her uncle, the Africanist WILLIAM LEO HANSBERRY, who helped inspire her enthusiasm for African history. In 1938, to challenge real estate covenants against blacks, Hansberry's father moved the family into a white neighborhood where a mob gathered and threw bricks, one of which nearly hit Lorraine. Two years later, after he won his

case on the matter of covenants before the Supreme Court, they continued in practice. Embittered by U.S. racism, Carl Hansberry planned to relocate his family in Mexico in 1946 but died before the move.

After studying drama and stage design at the University of Wisconsin from 1948 to 1950, Hansberry went to New York and began writing for Robeson's newspaper *Freedom*. She also marched on picket lines, made speeches on street corners, and helped move furniture back into evicted tenants' apartments. In 1953 she married Robert Nemiroff, an aspiring writer and graduate student in English and history whom she had met on a picket line at New York University. Soon afterward, she quit full-time work at *Freedom* to concentrate on her writing, though she had to do part-time work at various jobs until the success of Nemiroff and Burt D'Lugoff's song "Cindy, Oh Cindy" in 1956 freed her financially to write full-time. She also studied African history under W. E. B. DuBois at the Jefferson School for Social Science.

Lorraine Hansberry, author of *A Raisin in the Sun*, in New York City in April 1959. (AP Images.)

In 1957 Hansberry read a draft of *A Raisin in the Sun* to Philip Rose, a music publisher friend, who decided to produce it. Opening on Broadway in 1959, it earned the New York Drama Critic's Circle Award for Best Play, making Hansberry the youngest American, first woman, and first black to win the award. This play about the Youngers, a black family with differing personalities and dreams who are united in racial pride and their fight against mutual poverty, has become a classic.

Although Hansberry enjoyed her new celebrity status, she used her many interviews to speak out about the oppression of African Americans and the social changes that she deemed essential. Her private life, however, remained painful and complex. Shortly after her marriage, her lesbianism emerged, leading to conflicts with her husband and within herself, difficulties exacerbated by the widespread homophobia that infected even the otherwise progressive social movements she supported. At some point amid her public triumph, she and Nemiroff separated, though their mutual interests and mutual respect later reunited them. In 1960 she wrote two screenplays of *A Raisin in the Sun* that would have creatively used the cinematic medium, but Columbia Pictures preferred a less controversial version that was closer to the original. Accepting a commission from NBC for a slavery drama to commemorate the Civil War centennial, Hansberry wrote *The Drinking Gourd*, but this, too, was rejected as controversial. During this busy year she began research for an opera titled *Toussaint* and a play about Mary Wollstonecraft; started writing her African play, *Les Blancs*; and began the play that evolved into *The Sign in Sidney Brustein's Window*. In 1961 the film *A Raisin in the Sun* won a special award at the Cannes Film Festival.

In 1962 Hansberry wrote her post–atomic war play, *What Use Are Flowers?*, while publicly denouncing the House Un-American Activities Committee and the Cuban "missile crisis" and mobilizing support for the Student Nonviolent Coordinating Committee (SNCC). The following year she began suffering from cancer but continued her support for SNCC and, at JAMES BALDWIN's invitation, participated in a discussion about the country's racial crisis with Attorney General Robert Kennedy.

During 1964 Hansberry and Nemiroff divorced, but because of her illness they only told their closest friends and saw each other daily, continuing their creative collaboration until her death. She named Nemiroff her literary executor in her will. From April to October 1964 she was in and out of the hospital for therapy but managed to deliver her "To Be Young, Gifted and Black" speech to winners of the United Negro College Fund writing contest and to participate in the Town Hall debate on "The Black Revolution and the White Backlash." In October she moved to a hotel near the site of rehearsals for *The Sign in Sidney Brustein's Window* and attended its opening night. Despite its mixed reviews, actors and supporters from various backgrounds united to keep the play running until Hansberry's death in New York City.

FURTHER READING

The Hansberry Archives, which include unpublished plays, screenplays, essays, letters, diaries, and two drafts of an uncompleted novel, are held at the Schomburg Center for Research in Black Culture of the New York Public Library.

Carter, Steven R. *Hansberry's Drama: Commitment amid Complexity* (1991).

Cheney, Anne. *Lorraine Hansberry* (1984).

Nemiroff, Robert. *To Be Young, Gifted and Black: Lorraine Hansberry in Her Own Words* (1969).

This entry is taken from the *American National Biography* and is published here with the permission of the American Council of Learned Societies.

STEVEN R. CARTER

Hansberry, William Leo (25 Feb. 1894–17 Oct. 1965), historian of Africa, was born in Gloster, Mississippi, the son of Harriet Pauline Bailey and Eldon Hayes Hansberry, a professor at Alcorn A&M College in Mississippi. His father's personal library inspired him to pursue history as a career. According to Hansberry, by the time he entered Atlanta University in 1914 he had become "something of an authority on the glory that was Greece and the grandeur that was Rome."

A second major influence on Hansberry was W. E. B. DuBois's book, *The Negro*, published in 1916. For the first time, Hansberry learned about the societies and achievements of Africans in ancient and medieval times. Unable to pursue the subject in depth at Atlanta University, he transferred to Harvard University, where he studied anthropology and archaeology and received a B.A. in 1921 and an M.A. in 1932. Although Harvard did not offer courses on Africa, it had reference works on the subject, and the courses in anthropology and archaeology inspired Hansberry to commit himself to the study of the ancient heritage of Africa. He later pursued postgraduate study at the University of Chicago and Oxford University.

Upon receipt of the BA, Hansberry announced that he would promote and facilitate the teaching of "Negro Life and History, in order to bring

to the attention of teachers and students the significance of ancient African civilization." When he
joined the Howard University faculty in 1922, he
inaugurated the first program in African studies in
the United States, and possibly the world. This program included several courses in African history
and culture and a number of symposia. In 1925, for
example, he organized a conference at which twenty-
eight papers were read, including several by his
students from Panama, Guyana, Colombia, and the
United States.

During the 1920s Hansberry formulated a "plan
for expanding a pioneer project in collegiate education," which included the preparation of teaching
materials, publication of source books, and a program to promote interest in Africa through general
publications, visual aids, and lectures. Hansberry
believed that Howard University, as a predominantly
and historically black institution, should undertake
this initiative. In letters and reports to the president
and dean at Howard in 1935 he noted, "No institution
is more obligated and no Negro school is in a better
position to develop such a program as Howard. No
institution has access to specialized libraries—the
Moorland Collection [at Howard], and city reposi-
tories; nowhere else are the thought and planning
put forth; no better courses exist anywhere else;
there are no better trained students anywhere ... to
[enable Howard to] distinguish itself as a leader in
the general cause of public enlightenment."

Hansberry knew his ideas were "at odds with
prevailing notions about Africa's past." This was a
period when Africa was subjected to European colonial rule justified by negative stereotypes, including the myth that "Africa had no history." Several
of Hansberry's colleagues ridiculed his efforts as
"professionally unsound" and "without foundation
in fact," and he thus received only limited financial
support from his university. He was discouraged
from proceeding with an application to join an
archaeological expedition to Sudan, at least partly
because a trusted white adviser at the Museum
of Fine Arts in Boston confessed in a letter to
Hansberry on 2 February 1932 that he would "hesitate long before taking an American Negro on my
staff." Finally, in 1937, Hansberry received a fellowship to study at Oxford under a renowned archae-
ologist who conducted an expedition to Nubia, but
again he was denied a place on the expedition. That
same year he married Myrtle Kelso, with whom he
would have two children. Subsequent proposals to
the Rosenwald and Carnegie foundations in 1947
were also rejected.

Racism was surely at work in these disappointments, but there was another factor as well.
Hansberry knew more about his subject than anyone else; few nonexperts were prepared to judge his
plans. As Earnest A. Hooton, chairman of Harvard
University's anthropology department, wrote on
17 September 1948: "I am quite confident that no
present-day scholar has anything like the knowledge
of this field (prehistory of Africa) that Hansberry
has developed. He has been unable to take the Ph.D.
degree ... because there is no university or institution ... that has manifested a really profound interest in this subject." Finally, in 1953, Hansberry, then
fifty-nine years old, received a Fulbright Research
Award, which allowed him to study and conduct
fieldwork in Egypt, Sudan, and Ethiopia. By this
time African studies had begun to gain acceptance at U.S. universities and foundations. In fact,
Howard University established its program in 1954
while Hansberry was in Africa, but even after his
return to the university several of his colleagues,
who remained skeptical about the objectivity of his
research and the quality of African-history scholarship generally, succeeded in minimizing his role in
the program. But in addition to teaching at Howard
he joined the faculty part-time at the New School
for Social Research in New York in 1957 to teach
early African civilization.

Hansberry's interest in Africa extended beyond
the university. In 1927 he read a paper on African
archaeology at the Fourth Pan-African Congress
in New York. In 1934 Hansberry, Malaku Bayen
(the first Ethiopian student at Howard University),
William Steen (one of Hansberry's African American
students), and others organized the Ethiopian
Research Council to promote interest in Ethiopia.
When Italy invaded Ethiopia in 1934, the council
served as an information center and coordinating
body for contributions to the Ethiopian cause. After
the defeat of the Italians in 1941, Hansberry helped
to recruit African American technicians for the
Ethiopian government. The result was that several
African Americans served Ethiopia with distinction as teachers, journalists, aviation pilots, and
technicians.

Hansberry was a founding member of the
Institute of African-American Relations, whose
objective was to further people's understanding of
Africa. Located in Washington, D.C., that organization became the Africa-American Institute, which
established Africa House, a center for African student activities; Hansberry served as chairman of
its governing council. Among the guests hosted

by Africa House were Prime Minister Sylvanus Olympio of Togo, President Sékou Touré of Guinea, and Alioune Diop, director of the International Society of African Culture. Hansberry published a number of articles on Africa, and two volumes of his lectures and essays were published after his death. Those publications confirm Hansberry's commitment to the reinterpretation of the history of African peoples. His works foreshadowed the current controversies concerning Egyptian influence on ancient Greek culture, the need for reorientation of curricula and publications to include African peoples and their cultures, and the ultimate goal of a humane approach to the study of all peoples.

After his retirement in 1959 as an associate professor, two internationally renowned scholars visiting the United States, Kenneth Diké of Ibadan University in Nigeria and Thomas Hodgkin of Oxford University, examined Hansberry's research and recommended that it be published. Unfortunately Hansberry died in Chicago before he could complete that project.

Throughout his career Hansberry gave untiringly of his time to students and took a particular interest in African students whom he believed had an obligation to return to their countries to apply their skills in support of their native heritages and countries. He helped them obtain scholarships, emergency financial aid, and employment; he also helped several of them enter professional schools and corresponded with African parents regarding their children's welfare. Hansberry raised thousands of dollars for the Committee on Aid to African Students, including contributions from Liberian president W. V. S. Tubman and Ethiopian emperor Haile Selassie. During the 1950s he helped to found the African Students Association of the United States and Canada, which monitored issues and addressed problems relating to African students.

Hansberry's greatest contribution was as a teacher. Students in several African and Caribbean countries recalled him as a great teacher and mentor, and one former student reported in 1958 that he had started a "Hansberry Club" at Queens Royal College in the West Indies. Williston H. Lofton, Hansberry's colleague at Howard University, wrote, "Along with W. E. B. DuBois and CARTER G. WOODSON, Hansberry probably did more than any other scholar in these early days to advance the study of the culture and civilization of Africa." His student and the first president of Nigeria, Nnamdi Azikiwe, said, "You [Hansberry] initiated me into the sanctuaries

of anthropology and ancient African history." In *The World and Africa* DuBois wrote, "Mr. Hansberry, a professor at Howard University, is the one modern scholar who has tried to study the Negro in Egypt and Ethiopia."

FURTHER READING

Harris, Joseph E. "William Leo Hansberry: Pioneer Afro-American Africanist," *Presence Africaine* 110 (1979).

Spady, James G. "Dr. William Leo Hansberry: The Legacy of an African Hunter," *Current Bibliography on African Affairs* 3 (Nov. 1970).

This entry is taken from the *American National Biography* and is published here with the permission of the American Council of Learned Societies.

JOSEPH E. HARRIS

Haralson, Jeremiah (1 Apr. 1846–1916?), politician, was born a slave on a plantation near Columbus in Muscogee County, Georgia. Sold twice before becoming the property of Jonathan Haralson of Selma, Alabama, a lawyer and the head of the Confederate Niter Works, the self-taught Haralson remained in Dallas County as a freedman following the Civil War. There he married Ellen Norwood in 1870, and their son Henry (who later attended Tuskegee Institute) was born.

Unsure about the future of the Republican Party, Haralson entered politics in 1867 as a Democrat. A gifted orator who combined humor and wit with a discussion of serious issues, he campaigned in 1868 for Democratic presidential candidate Horatio Seymour, who, he said, "represented the true principles of philanthropy and national government" (Selma *Times*, 4 Nov. 1868). When Democrats failed to attract support from newly enfranchised blacks, Haralson switched his party allegiance in 1869. He and fourteen other Republicans signed an open letter urging Selma's BENJAMIN TURNER, a former slave, to run for Congress, and in 1870 Haralson served as chairman of the Republican district convention that nominated Turner. Campaigning across the predominantly black First District at Turner's side, he played a significant role in the election of Alabama's first black congressman. When in 1870 Haralson failed to receive the Republican nomination to run for a seat in the state house of representatives from Dallas County, he bolted the party and ran as an independent, winning by more than a thousand votes. Two years later he won a seat as a Republican in the state senate, where his most important achievement was the introduction of a civil rights bill. In its original form—reported in the *Southern Argus* on 14 February 1873, five days before it was introduced—the bill provided blacks and whites with "equal and impartial enjoyment of any accommodation" on common carriers and in theaters, places of public amusement, hotels, cemeteries, and common schools. Persons convicted of violating the proposed statute faced a fine of $500 to $1,000 and a jail sentence of up to one year. By any test, it was a radical measure, although it was quickly amended to eliminate the clause pertaining to schools. The amended bill passed the senate on 4 April by a vote of 18 to 9 but failed when the legislature adjourned before the house of representatives could act.

Despite his sponsorship of civil rights legislation Haralson faced increasing opposition within his own party. Some Republicans were suspicious of his earlier support for the Democratic Party; others criticized him because some of his white supporters opposed equal rights for blacks; and still others accused him of corruption, or of entering politics for personal gain. There was probably little truth to the latter accusations, although Haralson sometimes humorously boasted of eliciting a $50 "loan" from railroad officials to support a bill prior to his

Jeremiah Haralson, c. 1916. The Alabama legislator was killed by wild beasts near Denver, Colorado, about 1960. (Library of Congress.)

ever having run for office, and he was indicted for but eventually acquitted of stealing a bale of cotton worth $100. The factionalism that developed within Alabama's Republican Party pitted Haralson and the white former gubernatorial candidate William Hugh Smith in one camp against the black leader JAMES RAPIER, Third District congressman Charles Pelham, and U.S. senator George Spencer in another.

The factions resulted more from the fight for patronage positions (internal revenue, post office, and customs appointments) and the struggle to attract black voters than from strict ideological differences. For his part Haralson often appealed to racial pride in his speeches, as when he told an audience that he would never look twice at a white woman unless, of course, she were rich, and when he said that he was proud to be of pure African background, in contrast to his white and mixed-blood opponents. He also appealed to racial fears, warning the audience at a convention in New Orleans in 1872 for example that if Grant were not elected, former slaves would be exterminated in a race war. Neither Smith nor members of the opposition faction condoned such appeals.

Haralson also became involved in the black labor union movement in Alabama during Reconstruction. At a convention in Montgomery in January 1871, he was chosen president of the newly formed Alabama Negro Labor Union, an organization seeking ways to make freedmen into landowners and provide additional money for black education. The union had little success, however.

In 1874 Haralson ran against the white Liberal Republican incumbent Fredrick G. Bromberg as the regular Republican candidate for a seat in the U.S. House of Representatives from the First Congressional District. Although Bromberg enjoyed strong Democratic support Haralson's appeal to racial pride and his support for a strongly worded civil rights bill won the day. After taking his seat in the Forty-fourth Congress on 4 March 1875, he was informed that his election was being contested. Haralson asked his former owner to write letters on his behalf to the Confederate veterans in the Democratic-controlled House, and he won the contest, but his congressional career was lackluster. Serving until 3 March 1877 he was appointed to the Committee on Public Expenditures; introduced several bills, resolutions, and petitions; and voted in favor of amnesty for former Confederates. He never rose to speak before the House, however, and none of his bills was enacted into law.

During the spring of 1876, having been selected to head the Alabama delegation at the Republican National Convention in Cincinnati, Haralson conferred with President Ulysses S. Grant at the White House about patronage appointments and possible presidential candidates. Although the Spencer faction also sent a delegation to Cincinnati, the convention seated Haralson and his followers.

With the support of Smith, Haralson launched his reelection bid during the summer of 1876 in the newly gerrymandered Fourth Congressional District, which consisted of five overwhelmingly black counties (Dallas, Hale, Lowndes, Perry, and Wilcox). Former congressman James Rapier, who rented plantations in Lowndes County, also sought the nomination, and at the nominating convention Rapier won. Outraged, Haralson ran as an independent. In the end, although the two black candidates together garnered more than 60 percent of the vote, they were defeated by the white Selma sheriff Charles Shelley, the Democratic standard-bearer. Haralson contested the election, and in 1878 Congress declared him the victor, but the Forty-fifth Congress adjourned before he could be seated. The indefatigable Haralson ran for Congress again in 1878 but was "counted out" when Democratic election officials refused to accept the returns from Selma's two black wards. In 1884 a split in the Republican vote again allowed a Democrat to defeat him.

As recognition of his prominence in the Republican Party, in 1879 Haralson was appointed collector of customs at the port of Baltimore by Rutherford B. Hayes. Later he found employment as a clerk in the Interior Department, and in 1882 he was appointed to a position in the Pension Bureau in Washington, D.C. He resigned the latter post in August 1884 to run for Congress in Alabama. After his defeat he moved to Louisiana, where he engaged in farming, and then in 1904 to Arkansas, where he served briefly as a pension agent. He returned to Selma in 1912 before moving again, first to Texas then to Oklahoma and finally to Colorado, where he was reportedly engaged in a mining venture when, about 1916, he was killed by a wild animal in the mountains near Denver.

FURTHER READING

Bailey, Richard. *Neither Carpetbaggers nor Scalawags: Black Officeholders during the Reconstruction of Alabama, 1867–1878* (1991).

Fitts, Alston, III. *Selma: Queen City of the Black Belt* (1989).

Schweninger, Loren. *James T. Rapier and Reconstruction* (1978).

This entry is taken from the *American National Biography* and is published here with the permission of the American Council of Learned Societies.

LOREN SCHWENINGER AND
ALSTON FITTS III

Hardin, William Jefferson (1831–1890), legislator, was born in Russellville, Kentucky, the illegitimate son of a free mixed-race woman (name unknown) and a white father. Hardin claimed that his father was the brother of Ben Hardin, a Kentucky politician and congressman, but the fact cannot be verified. Raised in a Shaker community in South Union, Kentucky, Hardin's educational and social opportunities were unusual for a person considered black in the antebellum period.

Following the completion of his own education, Hardin became a teacher for "free children of color" in Bowling Green, Kentucky, but soon left the teaching profession and traveled in the midwestern states and Canada. In 1850 he returned to Kentucky, where he married Caroline K. (maiden name unknown) and fathered one child. Sometime between his marriage and the outbreak of the Civil War, Hardin moved his family to Iowa.

Leaving his first family in Iowa, Hardin relocated in Denver, Colorado Territory, in 1863 and took up a number of occupations, including stock speculator, poolroom manager, and barber. During the fall of 1864 he acquired a certain local prominence in Denver and nearby mining towns by giving unpaid lectures on the contributions of noted blacks in history, especially General Toussaint L'Ouverture, a revolutionary leader in the French colony of St. Domingue (later Haiti). Because of his speaking ability and experience, Hardin became the chief spokesman for the Colorado black community when it agitated for equal suffrage in 1865.

When Congress gave Colorado permission to write a state constitution in 1865, Hardin and other black leaders attended the convention as spectators and demanded equal suffrage for black men. The convention, however, chose to put the issue to a public vote at the same time that the constitution was submitted for popular approval, and black suffrage was rejected by an overwhelming majority. In response Hardin, HENRY O. WAGONER, and Edward Sanderlin began a campaign to block Colorado's admission into the Union until equal suffrage was granted. They petitioned Governor Alexander Cummings to request a change in the territorial suffrage laws and to crusade against statehood until the constitution was amended to give all men the right to vote. Hardin appealed to Horace Greeley, editor of the *New York Tribune*, and to U.S. Senator Charles Sumner to oppose statehood as long as the restriction remained. Greeley paid little attention to Hardin's request, but Sumner did mention the Colorado restriction in several of his speeches on equal suffrage in the Senate.

Colorado failed to achieve statehood with its 1865 constitution and did not enter the Union until 1876. Possibly as a result of the suffrage issue, James Ashley, a radical Republican from Ohio, introduced a bill on 15 May 1866 giving black men in all territories the right to vote. The bill passed the House of Representatives but failed in the Senate during the 1866 session. Senator Benjamin Wade reintroduced the bill during the next session; it quickly passed the Senate and House, becoming law without President Andrew Johnson's signature on 31 January 1867. It was implemented for the first time during municipal elections held in Colorado in April 1867, and blacks voted without incident.

From 1867 to 1873 Hardin was an important political figure in Denver's black community and the territorial Republican Party, and his ability to deliver the black vote gained him a patronage appointment as weigher at the Denver Mint. Success may have been his undoing, for by 1873 both blacks and whites in Denver had turned against him. He angered blacks when he criticized their celebrations of emancipation as "disgraceful nigger frolics" and "utterly depraved and degraded" (*Rocky Mountain News*, 2 and 6 Aug. 1867). Whites and Republican politicians rebuffed Hardin in 1873, when his first wife, Caroline, arrived in Denver accusing him of bigamy for his recent marriage to Nellie Davidson, a white milliner, and declaring that he fled to Colorado in 1863 to avoid conscription into the Union army. Although Hardin claimed his marriage to Caroline was not legal because she was a slave and he was underage at the time, officials at the mint fired him. Threatened with legal action, he and Nellie fled to Cheyenne, Wyoming Territory.

Hardin took up barbering again in Cheyenne but did nothing to bring attention to himself until he successfully ran for the territorial legislature in 1879, becoming the first black man elected to a western legislature and the only black to serve in the Wyoming territorial and state lawmaking body. He held his seat for two sessions and served on a number of committees, but he did not initiate or champion any notable legislation. Even though he seems to have been well respected, Hardin chose not to seek reelection in 1882 and for unknown reasons left Wyoming Territory. He lived for a short time in Park City, Utah, and then moved to Leadville, Colorado, where he died of natural causes.

FURTHER READING

Berwanger, Eugene H. "William J. Hardin: Colorado Spokesman for Racial Justice, 1863–1873," *Colorado Magazine* 52 (Winter, 1975).

This entry is taken from the *American National Biography* and is published here with the permission of the American Council of Learned Societies.

EUGENE H. BERWANGER

Hardman, Della Brown Taylor (20 May 1922– 13 Dec. 2005), art educator and newspaper columnist, was born in Charleston, West Virginia, to Captolia Monette Casey Brown, a teacher, and Anderson H. Brown, the owner of a meat market and a real estate broker. When Hardman was twenty months old her mother died in childbirth. Two months later Hardman's twin sister died. Her aunt Della Brown, for whom she was named, helped raise her. Education played a central role in Hardman's life from an early age. Both Hardman's mother and aunt were teachers, and Hardman was encouraged to do well in school. She graduated from Garnet High School in 1940 and enrolled in West Virginia State College, a historically black college in suburban Institute, West Virginia.

Following her graduation from West Virginia State with a B.S. in Education in 1943, Hardman moved to Boston. She took classes at the Massachusetts College of Art and earned an M.A. at Boston University in 1945. That same year Hardman married Francis C. Taylor, a jazz musician with whom she had three children. The couple spent the next few years living in Boston, where Hardman worked as a photo department assistant at Harvard University's Fogg Art Museum from 1952 to 1954 and taught art in the Boston public schools from 1954 to 1956.

In 1956 Hardman returned to West Virginia and accepted the position of associate professor in the art department of her alma mater, West Virginia State College (later University). Over the next three decades Hardman transformed the college's small art department into a vibrant center of study where she herself taught both art history and studio art classes. While teaching at West Virginia State, Hardman exhibited her own ceramic and textile arts, traveled extensively, appeared on radio and television programs to discuss arts issues, and gave lectures at institutions around the world. Hardman's commitment to education manifested itself through her continued involvement in community leadership activities. She was a member of many national organizations, including the National Art Education Association, and of local institutions, serving for many years as a trustee of the Charleston Art Gallery and from 1979 to 1987 as a commissioner on the West Virginia Arts and Humanities Council.

In 1978 Hardman's husband died, and eight years later, in 1986, she retired from West Virginia State University and moved to Martha's Vineyard, an island off the southern coast of Massachusetts. Retirement for Hardman, however, did not mean absenting herself from society. She soon began volunteering with many local organizations, including the local library. She also continued in her role as teacher, leading art classes at the local community center.

In 1987 Hardman married her high school boyfriend Leon Hardman. Next she returned to the classroom, this time as a graduate student at Kent State University in Ohio, beginning as a part-time student in 1984. In 1994 at the age of seventy-two Hardman received a Ph.D. in Education. Her dissertation, "William Edouard Scott Remembered: Lessons from a Remarkable Life," explored the life of an artist whom she had actually briefly met in 1940 while living in Charleston. After completing her doctorate, Hardman returned to Martha's Vineyard, where she continued to teach studio and art history classes. She also kept up her own art, painting watercolors outdoors in good weather and weaving inside at her loom in bad.

Hardman lived in a town on Martha's Vineyard called Oak Bluffs, which was the center of African American life on the island. In 1997 she wrote the preface to a volume of collected newspaper articles about the history of blacks on Martha's Vineyard, *African Americans on Martha's Vineyard*. In it she traced how her trips to the island began as a teenager, spending summer vacations there with her aunt, and continued through her adulthood. By that time Hardman had become a staunch member of the community about which she wrote. A year later, in 1998, she began writing a weekly newspaper column in the *Martha's Vineyard Gazette*. Hardman took over the "Oak Bluffs" column following the death of DOROTHY WEST, a Harlem Renaissance author and Oak Bluffs resident. Each week Hardman addressed the island community, discussing local events and her own life.

Hardman wrote her column for seven years, until her death in Martha's Vineyard. In her lifetime Hardman's contributions to her community did not go unrecognized. Over the years she received awards from some of the many organizations to which she gave her time and energy. In 1994 West Virginia State University named its art gallery the Della Brown Taylor Art Gallery in honor of her years of dedicated service. That same year the Martha's Vineyard NAACP gave her its Humanitarian Award. In 1998 she was inducted into the National Black College Alumni Hall of Fame. West Virginia State University honored Hardman again in 2000 when it named her an Outstanding Art Alumna. In 2005, 29 July was designated Della Brown Hardman Day in Oak Bluffs.

FURTHER READING

Hardman, Della Taylor. "Preface," in *African Americans on Martha's Vineyard* (1997).

West Virginia's Women Commission. *American Sampler: West Virginia's African American Women of Distinction* (2002).

Obituaries: *Martha's Vineyard Gazette*, 16 Dec. 2005; *Boston Globe*, 18 Dec. 2005.

ANGELA SIDMAN

Hardwick, Toby (31 May 1904–5 Aug. 1970), jazz alto saxophonist, was born Otto J. Hardwick in Washington, D.C., to parents whose names and occupations are unknown. A younger neighbor of DUKE ELLINGTON, Hardwick may have worked locally as a string bassist from as early as age fourteen. He attended Dunbar High School. Ellington got Hardwick started on C-melody saxophone around 1920, and his career followed Ellington's: local jobs, many involving the banjoist ELMER SNOWDEN; two attempts to establish themselves in New York, first without Snowden in March 1923 in Wilbur Sweatman's vaudeville band and again at midyear with Snowden and his Black Sox Orchestra at Baron Wilkins's Exclusive Club; and an engagement at the Hollywood (later the Kentucky) Club, where Snowden's Washingtonians evolved into Ellington's orchestra. During the Washingtonians' years Hardwick concentrated on playing alto saxophone while doubling on violin and string bass.

As a young man Hardwick was unreliable because of heavy drinking and extended romantic affairs. According to Ellington, "Lots of chicks wanted to mother him—so every now and then he'd submit! It meant he was in and out of the band rather unpredictably" (Dance, 58). Hardwick acquired his nickname, Toby, in Atlantic City, New Jersey, during one such absence. Nonetheless Hardwick was the one constant element in Ellington's reed section as the orchestra grew in size in the mid-1920s. His alto saxophone led the band in ensemble passages (although evidently HARRY CARNEY sometimes took this role after first working with the band in the summer of 1926), and Hardwick contributed solos on many of Ellington's important early recordings, playing in a sweet, pretty manner on "Immigration Blues" (1926) and "Black and Tan Fantasy" (1926 and 1927), and in a jaunty, florid style on "The Creeper" (1926) and "Jubilee Stomp" (1928). Like most professional reed players he doubled on clarinet and other saxophones: soprano, baritone, and bass; "Birmingham Breakdown" (1927) features solos on alto and baritone saxophones. Several of these titles exist in more than one recorded version, but Hardwick's contributions do not vary appreciably from one to the next. With Ellington he composed "Hop Head" and "Down in Our Alley Blues" (1927).

Hardwick nicknamed JOE NANTON "Tricky Sam" because of his manual dexterity, and later in life ROY ELDRIDGE "Little Jazz" due to his physical stature, RAY NANCE "Floorshow" (because of his flair for presentation), and BILLY STRAYHORN "Swee' Pea" (after the character in the Popeye comic strip). He loved to have fun, and he was curious about the world. He realized the first ambition throughout his career in music; he undertook the second in 1928. Ellington had no intention of leaving the Cotton Club, so Hardwick quit in the spring of 1928 and left for Europe, where he joined NOBLE SISSLE's orchestra, among others.

Back in the United States the following year he briefly joined CHICK WEBB's big band. According to Hardwick, he led a band full-time for three years, from 1930 to 1932, mainly at the Hot Feet Club in Greenwich Village, where CHU BERRY, Garvin Bushell, and FATS WALLER were among his sidemen. In 1931 at a benefit performance featuring a "battle of the bands," Hardwick's ensemble was judged to have defeated Ellington's. After the demise of the Hot Feet Club, the band continued to perform with JAMES P. JOHNSON and then COUNT BASIE as Hardwick's pianist. He then ceased band leading and rejoined Snowden at Smalls' Paradise in Harlem. Bushell though claims that in 1930 the bandleader was Snowden, with Hardwick playing lead alto saxophone, and that the musicians quit the Hot Feet Club as a group that same year. John Hammond recalled Hardwick in Snowden's band in 1931. Standard sources on Waller, Johnson, and

Basie shed no further light on this period. In any event Hardwick performed in Snowden's band in the movie short Smash Yo' Baggage (1932).

In the spring of 1932 he rejoined Ellington. As BARNEY BIGARD explained, "Toby wasn't an improvising musician, but he played some beautiful things. He was a melody boy. He used to have all the first parts, because JOHNNY HODGES couldn't read so well at that time" (Dance, 87). By this point Ellington's orchestra had many soloists superior to Hardwick, and his importance came in focusing the band's sound in passages for reeds and for the full ensemble. During the next fourteen years he was a soloist on only a few significant recordings, including the last phrases of "Sophisticated Lady" (1933), which he wrote in collaboration with Ellington and the trombonist LAWRENCE BROWN; "In a Sentimental Mood" (1935), at the beginning and again before the first trumpet solo; and "All Too Soon" (1940), in the opening theme intertwining Hardwick's soprano saxophone and Brown's muted trombone. In 1945 a recording session by SONNY GREER and the Duke's Men produced fine versions of "Mood Indigo" and "The Mooche" on which Hardwick figured prominently.

Tired of traveling constantly from one venue to the next, Hardwick left Ellington in May 1946 and retired from music to work on his father's tobacco farm in southern Maryland. Later he became a hotel shipping clerk. He suffered a long illness, and after the death of his wife, Gladys (details of his marriage are unknown), he died in a nursing home in Washington, D.C.

FURTHER READING
Dance, Stanley. The World of Duke Ellington (1970).
Schuller, Gunther. The Swing Era: The Development of Jazz, 1930–1945 (1989).
Tucker, Mark. Ellington: The Early Years (1991).
Obituaries: Washington Post, 7 Aug. 1970; New York Times, 8 Aug. 1970.

This entry is taken from the American National Biography and is published here with the permission of the American Council of Learned Societies.

BARRY KERNFELD

Hardy, David (7 June 1942 – 14 Jan. 2011), journalist and activist, was born David Walker Hardy in Plainfield, New Jersey, one of four children born to John Hardy Sr. and Abigail Hardy. He graduated from Fairleigh Dickinson University in 1964 and soon after began his professional stint as a sports writer for the

Courier News in Plainfield, New Jersey. Hardy's first brush with notoriety occurred in July 1967, when he covered the Plainfield riots for the *Courier News*. Because of his in-depth knowledge of the civil unrest in Plainfield, Hardy spoke on 21 September 1967 before the National Advisory Commission on Civil Disorders (Kerner Commission), which was assembled by President Lyndon Johnson to investigate and find solutions for the racial tensions and violence plaguing numerous American cities. He was also featured alongside Richard Hughes, New Jersey's governor, on an episode of *Face the Nation* to discuss the turbulent events. In September 1967 Hardy was hired as a sports writer by the *New York Daily News* only to be quickly shuffled to the news department when the editor Mike O'Neill refused to have a black journalist cover sports for the paper. He remained at the *Daily News* until 1969, when he took a position with the *Washington Post*.

After spending two years with the *Washington Post*, Hardy resumed working for the *Daily News* in 1972, where he focused almost exclusively on probing the political ins and outs of Hudson County, New Jersey. One of his standout investigations focused on David Friedland, the former New Jersey senator who, while awaiting his sentencing for corruption and racketeering, fled the United States, staged his own death in the Bahamas, and was subsequently apprehended by authorities and imprisoned. Hardy's coverage of the Friedland case garnered him an Investigative Reporting Award in 1986 from the New York Bureau of the United Press International as well as a Pulitzer Prize nomination. He was further feted by the Society for Professional Journalists in 1987.

Hardy's lasting impact however, is not as a result of his journalistic endeavors but rather for his role in the groundbreaking racial discrimination suit he and three other African American journalists (Causewell Vaughan, Joan Shepard, and Steven W. Duncan) filed against the *Daily News* in 1982. The "Daily News Four" as they were commonly referred to, accused the newspaper of discriminating against minority employees in issues of promotions and raises, and claimed that qualified black journalists were routinely passed over for plump assignments in favor of less experienced, less qualified white coworkers. Moreover, those who filed grievances or openly challenged the discriminatory practices were punished with demotions and transfers to less desirable locations. Hardy was himself eventually transferred to the *Daily News's* New Jersey headquarters.

The case went to trial 9 February 1987, with Hardy emerging as the lead plaintiff and most vocal critic of the paper's deeply ingrained racial bias. During his testimony Hardy noted that he had, for example, been passed over for covering Abscam, the FBI's undercover operation targeting several members of the U.S. Congress, despite having obtained key information regarding the investigation. The proceedings quickly turned personal, with Hardy bearing the brunt of the criticisms. Thomas C. Morrison, the newspaper's lawyer, countered Hardy's statements by depicting him as volatile and unbalanced, and by downplaying his professional achievements and accusing him of shoddy journalistic practices. On 15 April, following nine weeks of testimony, the jury ruled in favor of the plaintiffs, finding that between 1979 and 1982 the *Daily News* had discriminated against Hardy and his coworkers. They were eventually awarded $3.1 million in damages, with Hardy pocketing the largest percentage. As part of the agreement, the *Daily News* pledged to promote African Americans currently working for the newspaper and to actively recruit and employ minorities.

Hardy continued to work at the *Daily News* until 1993, when he lost his position after Mortimer Zuckerman purchased the newspaper and eliminated over 30 percent of the existing staff. Following his departure from the *News,* Hardy wrote for the Dorf Feature Service, a subsidiary of the *Star-Ledger* (Newark, New Jersey). Before his death on 14 January 2011 from a heart attack, Hardy was employed part-time by the Vamoose Bus Co. while spending much of his free time writing a monograph chronicling his many years as a journalist and his ongoing battle against racial discrimination in the newspaper industry. Hardy had two children, a son, David Jr., and a daughter, named Daly. On 4 May 2011 the New York Association of Black Journalists honored Hardy with a lifetime achievement award accepted on his behalf by his son and his sister, Jacqueline Casey.

FURTHER READING

Hornblower, Margot. "Jury Finds *Daily News* Discriminated against Blacks." *Washington Post,* 23 Apr. 1987.

Newkirk, Pamela. *Within the Veil: Black Journalists, White Media* (2000).

DÁLIA LEONARDO

Hardy, Isaac (?–10 Sept. 1813), a sailor during the War of 1812, was a crewman aboard the brig *Niagara* during the Battle of Lake Erie. Little is known of Hardy's life prior to the war, except that he was a free man and resident of Philadelphia when he was married to his wife, Diane, by Reverend JOHN GLOUCESTER of the First African Presbyterian Church in Philadelphia sometime between 1807 and 1813. Hardy, his name also given as "Harely," was almost certainly working as a sailor prior to the war and probably sailed on vessels operating from the port of Philadelphia. It is unknown when Hardy enlisted in the United States Navy, but it was likely sometime in 1812 to early 1813; with the commencement of the war the merchant shipping trade in the Northeast came to a sudden halt and many sailors, black and white, were suddenly unemployed. Driven by the necessity of earning a wage and surely by a measure of patriotism as well, men like Hardy often joined in the fight against the British by joining the navy or serving in armed merchant ships known as privateers.

The service of African American sailors, men like Hardy, JOHN JOHNSON, and ANTHONY WILLIAMS, is an important but little known aspect of a war that is often referred to as America's second war for independence. Black sailors were well established in America's merchant fleet prior to the war and served side by side with white sailors in almost every shipboard position with but little discrimination, and even black captains and ship owners were not unknown. Thus it was that their service, both in the navy and on privateers during the War of 1812, was both commonplace and vital; although records are lacking, it is estimated that black sailors made up anywhere from 10 to 20 percent of naval crews during the war. Isaac Hardy's service as an ordinary seaman is an indicator of his prior maritime experience; those rated in the navy as ordinary seamen were judged to possess basic sailor skills and, as the saying goes, "knew the ropes." Below this position among the enlisted men in the navy's hierarchy were those of landsmen, a newly enlisted sailor with no prior experience, and that of ship's boy, a position held by inexperienced youths under the age of eighteen. Although we know nothing of Isaac Hardy's prior naval service, if any, his experience should have made him a welcome addition to the newly formed naval squadron on Lake Erie under the command of Oliver Hazard Perry. Ironically, although Perry would complain in general of the color and caliber of the sailors sent to man his newly formed Lake Erie squadron, these men, sailors like Isaac Hardy, would not only prove Perry wrong in his assessment, but also in the process of doing so gave America one of its most celebrated victories of the war.

By July 1813 Hardy was assigned to the Great Lakes theater of operations, serving aboard the twenty-gun brig *Niagara*, which, along with Perry's flagship, the twenty-gun *Lawrence*, comprised the majority of the strength of the Lake Erie squadron. On 10 September 1813 Perry and his fleet sailed out of Put-In-Bay on western Lake Erie to confront a British sail spied on the horizon; the Battle of Lake Erie that developed that day would subsequently decide which side controlled the lake and the surrounding territory. In the events to follow, it was Perry's flagship that bore the brunt of the fighting for two hours, while the commander of the *Niagara* inexplicably held his ship out of the battle. The fight developed into a stalemate, with the *Lawrence* slugging it out broadside for broadside with the combined power of the British fleet, but when Perry's flagship was reduced to a wreck topside, with many of its crew dead or wounded, the American commander made a decisive move. Handing over command of his ship to a surviving officer and lowering his "Don't Give Up the Ship" battle flag, he was subsequently rowed under fire to the as yet unbloodied *Niagara*, raised his battle flag once again, and took over command. Armed with a new ship and a fresh crew, Hardy among them, Perry sailed boldly forward to join the battle once again. Undoubtedly inspired by Perry, the men of the *Niagara* proved themselves equal to the task, and although the crew endured heavy fire, succeeded in turning the tide and capturing all but one of the ships of the British fleet. When the battle was over, the British were effectively swept from control of Lake Erie while the Americans gained a badly needed victory. As for the men of the *Niagara*, the brig suffered many wounded, and two men were killed outright; one of these men was ordinary seaman Isaac Hardy, the only known African American to be killed in action during the battle.

After the War of 1812, Hardy's widow, Diane, lived in Philadelphia and was a resident there in 1820 when she was represented by Peter Sprout, a lawyer who also represented Lake Erie veteran Jesse Williams, to settle the affairs of her late husband. Although Sprout was likely hired so that Diane Hardy could obtain the share of the prize money from the navy due her husband that resulted from the sale of the captured British fleet, he also inquired of Pennsylvania governor William Findlay whether she was entitled to receive the silver medal authorized by the state in early 1814 and intended to be presented to veterans of the Battle of Lake Erie "in Compliment of their Patriotism and bravery"

(Montgomery, p. 247). Although it is unknown whether Diane Hardy ever received the medal, which was to be inscribed with her husband's name and was of two dollar weight, she subsequently applied for a government pension based on the service and ultimate sacrifice of her husband.

FURTHER READING

Altoff, Gerard T. *amongst my best men: African-Americans and the War of 1812* (1996).

Montgomery, Thomas, ed. *Pennsylvania Archives, Sixth Series*, Vol. IX (1907).

GLENN ALLEN KNOBLOCK

Hare, Nathan (9 Apr. 1933–), scholar, activist, psychologist, and coordinator of the first Black Studies program in an American university, was born in Slick, Oklahoma, one of five children of Seddie Henry Hare, a sharecropper, and Tishia Lee Davis Hare, a civilian janitor in the Navy. As a child he moved between California and Oklahoma, before settling on the family farm in Slick once his mother could afford to purchase it with her savings. His father left the family home when Hare was nine. The young Hare showed promise in two careers, boxing and academia, but was encouraged by teachers at L'Ouverture High School to attend college. Though he continued to box, Hare graduated from Langston University in Oklahoma in 1954 with an AB in Sociology. It was at Langston that he met Julia Reed, whom he would marry in 1956. Hare continued to show promise in both fields, reaching the state semi-finals of the Oklahoma Golden Gloves competition, while also winning a Danforth Fellowship to continue his education. This he did, earning an M.A. and a Ph.D. in Sociology from the University of Chicago in 1957 and 1962 respectively.

It wasn't until his first teaching position that Hare was forced to choose between his two passions. In 1961 Hare became Assistant Professor of Sociology at Howard University in Washington, D.C., where the dean required him to decide on either boxing or teaching. Hare chose to teach. He desired to work at Howard University because it was famed for being "the cream of the crop" for black education, and as such there existed the highest possibility for instituting the greatest change. Hare wanted to use his skills to fight for social change, and rather than attempting to work with the grassroots masses, he believed that since it was Howard students who would become future black leaders, it was they who needed guidance and "the courage to be black." Furthermore, Hare hoped that if Howard

students became "more concerned and aware, then other black college students would emulate them" and that this generation "might go on to have an impact on the entire race" (Nathan Hare interview, 10 Sept. 2005). He was an avid supporter of the emerging Black Power movement, and inspired his students with his radical ideas. At Howard, Hare taught a student by the name of Stokely Carmichael, a young leader of the Black Power movement and later chairman of Student Nonviolent Coordinating Committee (SNCC), who, upon a return visit to his Alma Mater, described the young professor as his "mentor." Supporting the trend towards Black Nationalism on campus, Hare helped to establish in 1967 the Black Power Committee, and became its spokesman. The purpose of the committee, according to Hare, was "the overthrow of the Negro college with white innards and to raise in its place a militant black university which will counteract the whitewashing black students now receive in Negro and white institutions." The committee also aimed to bring the black community together, claiming that their membership comprised of "black students, black professors, black women and black prisoners of the ghetto" (*Washington Post*, 23 March 1967). The belief in a black-orientated education and community support was one that would remain with Hare throughout his life. More radical than the majority of faculty, particularly the older black professors, Nathan Hare brought considerable controversy to the Howard campus and in 1967 was dismissed. The *Negro Digest* blamed Nathan Hare's dismissal on "his militant pro-black activities" but Hare believed that it was his criticism in a newspaper article of the university's president, James Nabrit, that led to his removal.

Upon leaving Howard, Hare pursued a number of ventures, including a brief return to boxing and a position as chairman of the Washington Committee for Black Power in September 1967. This committee aimed to mobilize the Washington black community, register voters, and reinstate Nathan Hare as a professor at Howard University. Instead, in 1968, the president of San Francisco State College, Dr. Robert Smith, appointed Hare as Black Studies Coordinator to develop the first program of Black Studies in the country. Critics suggested, however, that the recruitment of Hare was a political decision, rather than an academic one, designed to appease the increasingly militant Black Student Union.

Despite the criticism, Hare designed a pioneering degree-granting Department of Black Studies that involved not just "the blackening of white courses" but the stimulation of the individual and the community. He rejected accusations of separatism as irrelevant and erroneous. Integration meant tokenism, Hare claimed, and neither separatism nor integration could be ends in themselves. Rather the goal was education, and the elevation of the whole, not the "plucking of the most promising members from a group while failing to alter the lot of the group." For Hare, educational relevance and the "black perspective" were pivotal to any comprehensive program of Black Studies. Among other components, Hare was keen that the program would make an effort not only to educate the student but also to advance the community through a pragmatic, interdisciplinary approach that would focus on applied fields of knowledge. The qualifications required to teach would be reconsidered, so that the "white" Ph.D. was no longer necessary and positions could be opened up to black teachers without these degrees. However, a series of incidents on the college campus, including the suspension of teaching assistant and Black Panther member George Murray, led to a five-month long strike and the closing of the campus. Hare would take part in the strike, and support the demands of the students. After a tumultuous year that saw much violence and tension, Hare was informed on 29 February 1969 that he would not be reappointed as the department chair for the following year. The new Black Studies Department, without Hare as its chair, would be the first of its kind in the United States.

Still frustrated by the failures of black education, Hare teamed up with Robert Chrisman and Allen Ross in November 1969 to found the *Black Scholar*, a journal devoted to black scholarship and research to find solutions to the problems facing African Americans. He wrote extensively for the journal, reissuing his call for a "Black University" and educational relevance.

In 1975, Hare left the *Black Scholar* and obtained a Ph.D. in Clinical Psychology from the California School of Professional Psychology. He remained focused on the fate of the black community, however, turning his attentions to the black family and gender relationships. This led him to establish in 1979 *The Black Think Tank* with his wife, Dr. Julia Hare, a lecturer and social commentator, publishing the journal *Black Male-Female Relationships* and issuing reports on black sexuality, rebuilding the black family and raising children. The journal eventually ended, but the Hares would continue to develop their consultancy firm, which focused on issues affecting the black family. Between them

they have published extensively on the topic. In particular, they have campaigned for a rite of passage movement for black boys, and for black churches, black college groups, and the black middle class to come together in the raising of children and the advancement of their race. Controversially, the Hares' have been consistently opposed to homosexuality, believing it to be a threat to the black family. While not opposed to gay rights and freedoms, they have claimed that homosexuality is an identity crisis that could and should be cured to prevent the destruction of black family stability. Primarily, the Black Think Tank continued Hare's lifelong dedication to the elevation and education of the African American community, and in 2002 he received the Joseph S. Himes Award for Distinguished Scholarship from the Association of Black Sociologists.

FURTHER READING

The records and papers of Nathan Hare are not publicly available. A study of his time at Howard exists in an unpublished dissertation by Verity J. Harding, "Black Power on the Black Campus: The Radicalization of the Howard University-Student Movement, 1963–1968," Oxford University, 2006.

Anderson, Talmadge. *Introduction to African American Studies: Cultural Concepts and Theory* (1993).

Norment Jr., Nathaniel. *The African American Studies Reader* (2001).

Rojas, Fabio. *From Black Power to Black Studies: How a Radical Social Movement Became an Academic Discipline* (2007).

VERITY J. HARDING

Hargrave, Frank Settle (27 Aug. 1874–11 Mar. 1942), physician and surgeon who specialized in pulmonary medicine, was born in Lexington, Davidson County, North Carolina. He was the son of Henry M. and Laura Hargrave, farmers, and one of fourteen children; he attended local public schools in Lexington before attending the state normal school in Salisbury, North Carolina. Hargrave received a B.S. from Shaw University in 1901 and an MD from Leonard Medical School. Founded in 1885, Leonard Medical School was one of the first medical schools in the United States to have a four-year curriculum. It also was the first four-year medical school to train African American doctors and pharmacists in the South. Hargrave practiced medicine in Winston-Salem, North Carolina, from 1901 to 1903 before relocating his private medical practice to Wilson, North Carolina, where he practiced from

1903 to 1924 and established the Wilson Hospital and Tubercular Home. Hargrave married Bessie E. Parker, of Wilson, North Carolina, in 1907.

In May 1905 Silas and Charity Lucas conveyed a sixteen-room house to Hargrave, who turned it into the first private hospital for African Americans in the South. He envisioned a larger private hospital and tubercular home that would include a nurse training school for African Americans. By 1912 Hargrave had enlisted the support of two other prominent African American citizens of Wilson, James D. Reid and SAMUEL HYNES VICK. In October 1913 Hargrave conveyed the property to Vick, Reid, and himself for fourteen hundred dollars.

These three gentlemen constituted the board of trustees of the Wilson Hospital and Tubercular Home. They hired the Wilson architectural firm of Benton and Moore to design a suitable hospital building on the property where the sixteen-room house once stood. African American masons were especially prominent in the building of the hospital, which remained the only such facility in this section of eastern North Carolina during the early twentieth century.

In the late 1890s and early 1900s increasing numbers of African Americans settled in and near Wilson for employment opportunities, but health care for African Americans did not keep pace with the population growth. Even though a white hospital, the Wilson Sanitorium, had been operating since 1896, African Americans received care only from Dr. Benjamin Woodard, the first African American physician in Wilson, until Hargrave established his hospital in 1905. It is estimated that while there was one white doctor for every three hundred whites, there was only one black doctor for every nine thousand blacks in the state. On 10 September 1912 the *Wilson Daily Times* declared that "this sanatorium will probably be the first private institution of its kind exclusively for tuberculous Negroes in the South, and indeed in the United States. In the entire South, with its millions of Negroes and with their enormous death rate from tuberculosis, there are not, all told, more than two hundred beds for colored consumptives, and most of these are in the public institutions, where through fear, superstition and politics they are not used."

Data on the actual number of African American hospitals that existed before 1920 is scarce and often inaccurate, but the *Negro Year Book and Annual Encyclopedia of the Negro* listed the Wilson Hospital and Tuberculosis Home as one of six hospitals and

nurse training schools for African Americans that existed in North Carolina in 1913.

The Wilson Hospital and Tubercular Home established by Hargrave was unlike the other five hospitals, which were founded and financed by prominent white philanthropists from North Carolina or were affiliated with established religious or educational institutions. In essence, the Wilson Hospital and Tubercular Home was the only known private hospital established by African Americans for African Americans with tuberculosis in North Carolina during the early twentieth century.

In 1912 the North Carolina Medical, Dental, and Pharmaceutical Association elected Hargrave president, and the same year he was elected a member of the executive board of the National Medical Association (NMA), the nation's oldest and largest organization representing African American physicians and health professionals. In 1914, without opposition, Hargrave became president of the NMA. He also served for six years as president of the Lincoln Benefit Society, headquartered in Wilson, North Carolina, a fraternal insurance organization chartered by the North Carolina legislature in 1914. The organization established councils in the principal towns and cities of the state. The Lincoln Benefit Society provided insurance rates that were low enough to be in reach of the citizens of the African American community.

Despite several unsuccessful attempts to receive funding through the North Carolina legislature during its formative years, the Wilson Hospital and Tubercular Home continued operating until 1929. Between 1918 and 1924 the hospital suffered from financial difficulties, and when the mortgage debt was not retired in 1924, Hargrave was able to purchase the hospital for seven thousand dollars. But in 1929 the hospital was sold to a group of civic leaders. The fact that Hargrave was able to sell this historic hospital to an interest group of civic leaders rather than allow the hospital to close is significant, given that many black hospitals in the South did not survive.

In 1924 Hargrave moved to Orange, New Jersey, where he established his medical practice. From 1927 until his death in 1942, he served as chairman of the Committee on Medical Education for the National Medical Association. He was also a member of the North Jersey Medical Association and the Essex County Medical Society and was active in the New Jersey Tuberculosis League.

In 1930 the Wilson Hospital and Tubercular Home became Mercy Hospital, and it continued operation until 1964, when the city of Wilson built an integrated public hospital. In 1930 Hargrave received a master of arts, honoris, from his alma mater, Shaw University.

Hargrave also had political ambitions and served as a New Jersey assemblyman for nine terms, from 1929 until his death in 1942. In addition, he served as chairman of the Committee on Public Health for four terms, 1936–1938 and 1939–1940. He authored a bill creating a battalion of African American men in the state militia and another creating the Migrant Welfare Commission, of which the New Jersey governor Morgan F. Larson appointed him chairman. Hargrave was also the first president of the New Jersey Colored Republican League, which was established in 1936.

Hargrave's early religious affiliations included the Jackson Chapel First Baptist Church, one of Wilson's largest and most prominent African American churches. Hargrave was also a prominent and active member of the North Carolina Baptist State Colored Convention in Wilson and served on its executive committee for eleven years. When he moved to New Jersey, Hargrave became a deacon of the Union Baptist Church of Orange and served as superintendent of its Sunday school. Hargrave was also a member of the Young Men's Christian Association, the fraternal organizations of the Knights of Pythias, and the Masons. He died in 1942 at the age of sixty-seven at his home in Orange. Hargrave was survived by his wife, Bessie, two brothers, Dr. Henry P. Hargrave of New York and James Hargrave of Lexington, North Carolina, and three sisters, Fannie Mason, Rose Ellis and Flossie Douglass, all of Lexington, North Carolina.

FURTHER READING

Bainbridge, Robert C., and Kate Ohno. *Wilson Historic Buildings Inventory, Wilson, North Carolina* (1980).
"Frank S. Hargrave," in *Manual of the Legislature of New Jersey* (1942).
Kenney, John A. *The Negro in Medicine* (1912).
Valentine, Patrick M. *The Rise of a Southern Town, Wilson, North Carolina, 1849–1920* (2002).
Obituaries: *New York Times*, 12 Mar. 1942; *Afro-American*, 21 Mar. 1942; *Journal of the Medical Society of New Jersey* (June 1942); *National Medical Association Journal* (July 1942).

E. RENÉE INGRAM

Harlan, Robert (12 Dec. 1816–4 Sept. 1897), businessman and politician, was born a slave in Mecklenburg County, Virginia, the son of a slave woman of mixed race. His father was reputedly his owner, James Harlan (1800–1863), a white lawyer, Kentucky politician, and the father of the first justice John Marshall Harlan (1833–1911). However, modern DNA analysis of male descendants from both families revealed no match. While still young, Robert Harlan arrived in Kentucky, where he began attending the public schools that were closed to black children. It seems that the boy's mixed-race heritage was not readily apparent, but he was expelled when the authorities learned of it. He continued his education at home, where James Harlan's older sons tutored him in their lessons despite his status as one of several slaves owned by James Harlan.

Robert Harlan began his business career as either a barber or a shopkeeper in Harrodsburg, Kentucky. He also hired out his time. He may have invested his earnings in a racehorse at this time. Harlan moved in 1840 to Lexington, where he lived as a freeman although he was still legally a slave. In late 1840 he posted a marriage bond with Margaret Sproule, of whom little is known save for the fact that she is generally believed to have been free. She died in 1845 leaving behind three surviving daughters. All accounts agree that Harlan made his fortune at age thirty-two by joining the thousands of Americans who traveled to California following the news of the discovery of gold in 1848. But before he left Kentucky, Harlan went to the Franklin County courthouse, where on 18 September 1848 James Harlan presented him with a deed of emancipation. The county clerk described Robert Harlan as six feet tall with straight black hair and blue-gray eyes. The clerk of the court also collected from his former owner a $500 bond to ensure that the new freedman would not become dependent upon the state for charity. Far from becoming a ward of the state, Harlan returned from California with a fortune of some $45,000 earned from running a store at a time and place where goods were rare and dear. He almost certainly then paid James Harlan the $500 for the bond, which had been taken out at the time of his emancipation. This payment explains the accounts of Robert Harlan having returned to Kentucky to buy his freedom for $500. This act did not signal an absolute break from James Harlan's family. Robert Harlan's wealth allowed him to send one of James's daughters a piano upon her marriage, and he remained in contact throughout his life with John Marshall Harlan, a fellow Republican Party member.

Harlan moved across the Ohio River to the free state of Ohio and the town of Cincinnati, where he would live for most of the rest of his life. He invested in real estate by building houses and owned a share of the photographic studio and gallery of JAMES PRESLEY BALL. As was common in the northern states, public education was racially segregated, and Harlan supported the creation in 1858 of the first school in the city for black students. He was elected a trustee of the "colored schools" in elections in which only black men could vote. He was also elected to serve as a trustee for the Colored Orphan Asylum. But after ten years in Cincinnati, Harlan grew tired of the racial prejudice he faced and traveled to England with his family, living there from 1858 to 1868 and thereby missing the travails and triumphs of black Americans during the Civil War. In England, Harlan continued to indulge his taste in racehorses and in gambling. He returned home just as Congress approved the Fifteenth Amendment to the U.S. Constitution, which gave black men the right to vote when the amendment was finally ratified in 1870.

Harlan made a lifelong commitment to the Republican Party and served as a delegate to local and state committees for years. Like many black Republicans, he had some success within the party but eventual reservations about its dedication to civil rights. He sought, unsuccessfully, the party nomination as candidate for the state legislature in 1871. A year later he ran unsuccessfully for Cincinnati City Council. He had more success at the federal level through patronage positions that recognized his influence among black voters. He was appointed a special mail agent in 1873 during President Ulysses Grant's administration; he was, according to a newspaper account, the only black in the old Northwest to be chosen for a federal appointment. Perhaps because he had been so rewarded by the party, Harlan rejected in 1873 the complaints of PETER HUMPHRIES CLARK, a public-school teacher and black Cincinnati leader, that the party was not doing enough to better the position of blacks. He became known as Colonel Bob Harlan after he raised a state militia battalion and received a commission from Governor Rutherford B. Hayes in 1875. Only in 1877, with the end of Reconstruction and the removal of all federal troops from the South, did Harlan take the Republican leadership to task and complain to Senator John Sherman about the party's failure to better the condition of blacks. Harlan ran unsuccessfully for the Ohio State house in 1880 and lost, but he was rewarded by President Chester A. Arthur with the post of special agent to the Treasury Department in 1881. In 1886 he again ran for the state legislature and won despite attempts

to defraud him of votes. During his term Harlan supported the Arnett Bill, sponsored by BENJAMIN WILLIAM ARNETT, which aimed to overturn the Black Laws that banned racial intermarriage and integrated public schools. When he died in 1897 the *Cincinnati Enquirer* pointed to his life as an example "of what thrift and enterprise can accomplish when properly applied."

Colonel Harlan remarried at some point and fathered a son, Robert Jr. Because the Y chromosome is passed intact from father to son, it became possible to discover if James Harlan was Robert Harlan's father through an analysis of the blood of their descendants. Such a connection had long been rumored. A 15 October 1881 article report in the *Cincinnati Daily Gazette* suggested that Colonel Harlan, "on the paternal side, is a son of one of the best Kentucky families." Oral history passed down through Robert Jr.'s wife's family also declared a connection. In 1999 blood samples were gathered from the sole living direct male descendant of Robert Harlan and from three distant cousins descended from the same male line as James Harlan. While the three cousins matched, Robert's descendant did not.

FURTHER READING
Gordon, James W. "Did the First Justice Harlan Have a Black Brother?," *Western New England Law Review* 15 (1993).

Lane, Roger. *William Dorsey's Philadelphia and Ours: On the Past and Future of the Black City in America* (1991).

Simmons, William James. *Men of Mark, Eminent, Progressive and Rising* (1887, repr. 1968).

Obituary: *Cincinnati Enquirer*, 22 Sept. 1896.

LINDA PRZYBYSZEWSKI

Harleston, Edwin Augustus (1882–21 Apr. 1931), painter and civil rights activist, was born in Charleston, South Carolina. "Teddy," as he was called, was one of six children of Edwin Gailliard Harleston and Louise Moultre. Harleston's father, born in 1852, was one of eight children of the white plantation owner William Harleston and his slave Kate. Edwin Gailliard Harleston had worked as a rice planter but returned to Charleston and his family's Laurel Street home in search of a better living for his-wife and children. There he ran a produce-transporting business for a few years and then brought his nickname "Captain" along when he left boating in 1896 to set up the Harleston Brothers Funeral Home with his brother Robert Harleston, a former tailor. The segregated funeral business meant they would have no competition from whites. Most of Captain's sons were uninterested in joining the business after their uncle Robert left, however, and it fell to Edwin Augustus Harleston to put aside his own dreams of art for the family business.

For his elementary education Edwin attended the Morris Street School, the first public school for African Americans in Charleston, where he was taught by white teachers. In 1897 Harleston's mother died shortly after the stillbirth of her sixth child; Captain Harleston's sister and her husband moved from Beaufort to Charleston to help care for the Harleston children. Edwin left public school and began to blossom in the college preparatory program at the Avery Institute. With a scholarship in hand, he participated in chorus as well as several clubs, found a lifelong mentor in his English teacher Mattie Marsh, and graduated class valedictorian in 1900. He presented the principal with a portrait of Abraham Lincoln as a farewell gift. At Atlanta University, a black college with a predominantly white faculty, Harleston considered teaching and later medicine as possible careers. He took public speaking and the typical drawing classes, became a starter on the football team, and most likely heard a sociology lecture or two by the faculty member W. E. B. DuBois. During his college years, Harleston supported himself by working summers on the Hudson River Day Line. When he graduated in 1904, he won a fellowship for graduate study. In 1905 he pursued graduate studies in sociology and chemistry at Atlanta University. His application for admission to Harvard for 1906 was accepted, and he was scheduled to enter that fall as a junior, with a career in medicine in mind. (It was standard practice at the time for Harvard to demand that white students from less prestigious colleges and African American students in general enter studies at a lower level in order to bring their educations up to Harvard standards.)

When Harleston arrived in Boston in the fall of 1906, however, he found that he was more interested in art, and instead of matriculating at Harvard, he enrolled at the new Boston School of the Museum of Fine Arts, becoming the only African American in a class of 232. To earn money for his art studies, Harleston, along with his roommate, sold postcards, but short finances caused him to take a year off (1907–1908) to work on a cargo line between Boston and Canada. During this year Harleston's race consciousness was raised by activist black organizations and newspapers in his new surroundings. Here was the budding of what later became his civil rights activism. His savings enabled Harleston to return to the Boston School in 1908, where he studied under William Paxton and Frank Benson and was awarded a scholarship for free tuition in 1911. He had finished most of the required courses by the end of 1912, when he decided to leave school. The reasons for his departure—whether the resignation of a mentor or pressing family matters—remain unclear.

Harleston returned to Charleston and a third-floor apartment over the newly expanded Harleston and Mickey Funeral Home. Harleston's father had a skylight installed to encourage his artist son; however, the family business allowed no free time during his first year and caused many interruptions in the years that followed. In 1913 he began a long-term romance with Elise "Little Liza" Forrest. They married seven years later. Harleston's 1916 self-portrait shows the strain of balancing two lives: a picture in a white shirt with a black bow tie of the thirty-three-year-old frustrated artist who a year later became a certified embalmer and sank even deeper into the work of the funeral home. Nonetheless, Harleston attempted to drum up commissions for portraits. The man who as a teenager had presented his high school principal with a portrait of Lincoln now in 1917 sent the president of a life insurance company, where his college friend Truman Gibson was vice president, a portrait of his mother. The ploy did not work, but Gibson used his contacts to get Harleston a commission for a portrait of one of Atlanta's black leaders.

Harleston's attempt to find work as an artist coincided with his groundbreaking work with the National Association for the Advancement of Colored People. The northern-based NAACP had been unsuccessful in its earlier attempts to expand its statewide organizations into the South, but worsening conditions for African Americans nationwide changed its fortunes. The NAACP protests and picketing throughout the spring and summer of 1915 against the release of D. W. Griffith's racist film *The Birth of a Nation* enhanced the organization's reputation in a year that saw nearly one hundred blacks lynched, which was, according to DuBois in the *Crisis*, the highest number of lynchings in more than decade. Under Field Secretary JAMES WELDON JOHNSON, the NAACP made a new push into the South to set up chapters for eventual state organizations, and Harleston helped establish the Charleston chapter. On 27 February 1917 the twenty-nine African American professionals in the new Charleston chapter applied for a charter. Harleston became its first president and soon afterward led the campaign that forced the public school system in Charleston to hire African American teachers.

On 15 September 1920 in Brooklyn, New York, Harleston married his longtime sweetheart Elise Forrest. The previous year Harleston had financed her training as a photographer in New York so they could work together in a studio. Although the couple had no children, they raised as their own child their niece, Gussie Edwina, whose parents had succumbed to tuberculosis in 1921, when she was just four years old. In 1922 the Harlestons opened their joint studio, featuring portraits in oils, charcoal, and photography. Harleston used Charleston as a base from which he traveled to New York and Washington, D.C., to exhibit his work. His work in a realistic style influenced by his wife's photography began to gain recognition. He produced commissioned portraits of a former president of Atlanta University, the philanthropist Pierre S. du Pont, and the president of the Atlanta Life Insurance Company as well as his 1924 The Bible Student. He was also featured in a 1924 article in Opportunity, the new Urban League arts and letters periodical.

Harleston continued his training in art. He spent the summers of 1924 and 1925 studying outdoor painting at the Art Institute of Chicago. These years were part of the creative energy fueled by the Harlem Renaissance, and like other African American artists during this time, Harleston benefited from the new interest and support shown in contests sponsored by the Urban League and the NAACP and exhibitions funded by the Harmon Foundation. His drawing A Colored Grand Army Man, based on a photograph by his wife, Elise, won the seventy-five-dollar first prize in the Spingarn Competition of the NAACP in 1925, and his oil portrait Ouida won the 1931 Joel Spingarn Award in the annual competition sponsored by the NAACP's periodical the Crisis. Harleston was chosen to assist the graphic illustrator AARON DOUGLAS in painting the Black History murals for the library at Fisk University, completed in October 1930. Shortly afterward, in February 1931, Harleston's The Old Servant was awarded the ALAIN LOCKE Prize for portraiture at the Harmon Foundation Exhibition.

The third decade of the twentieth century not only ushered in new attention to African American art but also groped toward a definition of its unique gifts. Harleston saw little of the fourth decade. In April 1931 his father died of pneumonia, and Harleston, who is said to have kissed his dead father goodbye, succumbed to the same disease on 10 May

1931. Although his work was praised posthumously, Harleston's realistic portraiture style was at odds with the new styles and sensibilities erupting in these Harlem Renaissance years. Nonetheless, critics such as the art historian JAMES AMOS PORTER argued against opinions that dismiss too quickly such art as outside these shifting trends. Porter noted that traditional painters like Harleston, LAURA WHEELER WARING, PALMER C. HAYDEN, and HENRY OSSAWA TANNER were indeed "concerned with the Negro [subject]" in the opening decades of the twentieth century and moreover that Harleston's "unforgettable renderings of The Old Servant and The Negro Soldier [were] both rich in sensuous and psychological values and done before 1925" (p. 34). The reevaluation of Harleston's art continues. Five of Harleston's paintings, including his portrait of Douglas, are owned by the Gibbes Museum of Art in Charleston.

FURTHER READING

McDaniel, Maurine Aku. Edwin Augustus Harleston, Portrait Painter, 1882–1931 (1994).

Porter, James A. "Four Problems in the History of Negro Art," Journal of Negro History 27, no. 1 (Jan. 1942): 9–36.

Reynolds, Gary A., and Beryl J. Wright. Against the Odds: African-American Artists and the Harmon Foundation (1989).

Riggs, Thomas, ed. The St. James Guide to Black Artists (1997).

MARY ANNE BOELCSKEVY

Harmon, Leonard Roy (21 Jan. 1917–13 Nov. 1942), World War II sailor and Navy Cross winner, was born in Cuero, Texas, the son of Cornelius and Naunita Mabry (White) Harmon. Little is known about Harmon's early years, although apparently his parents were sharecroppers. He graduated from Daule High School and also had a job working for the historic William Frobese home in Cuero.

Growing up in a town close to the Texas Gulf Coast, perhaps Harmon felt the call of the sea. It is more likely, however, that he joined the navy for economic reasons; the country was just emerging from the Great Depression, and jobs were still hard to come by. The navy offered a steady job with pay, housing, and an opportunity to see the world. Whatever his reasons, Harmon journeyed to Houston and enlisted for service in the navy on 10 June 1939.

Upon enlisting, Harmon was sent to Norfolk, Virginia, for basic training as a mess attendant at a camp known as Unit K-West. While it is unknown what Harmon's expectations were upon joining the navy, he would soon learn the truth. African Americans who joined during this time were restricted to serving only in the steward's branch of the service as mess attendants, a rating reserved for black recruits, with no regard for aptitude or educational experience. This job consisted of serving the officer cadre and was consistent with tasks often performed by African Americans in civilian life. A mess attendant served his officers by preparing and serving their meals, making their beds and cleaning their quarters, acting as chauffeurs, and even shining their shoes. While Harmon's reaction to being assigned to such segregated duty is unknown, the fact that an uncle had been a Pullman car porter for the Southern Pacific Railroad performing similar duties may have tempered his expectations. Life in boot camp at Norfolk was not unlike that in the segregated South, and African American sailor recruits such as Harmon and DORIE MILLER likely were used to such conditions. The camp was headed by a white lieutenant, while the instructional duties were carried out by chief stewards who were either black or Filipino. In addition to being taught their regular mess duties, the men also learned the traditional marching and drill routines. Weapon training was virtually nonexistent, for mess attendants were not viewed as fighting men.

Following his training, by late 1939 Harmon was sent for duty to the cruiser *San Francisco* (naval hull designation: CA-38). In addition to his regular duties, he had tasks specific to battle conditions; these were to assist the hospital corpsmen, help to give first aid, and act as a stretcher bearer for wounded men. Harmon was a big man, standing nearly six feet tall and weighing 195 pounds, and, as one shipmate commented:

[He] had a good disposition, a good mind, carried himself with a friendly dignity that made you feel comfortable to be around him. He was a much liked and respected hombre in Officer's Country by both the brass and his fellow workers.... One could say he had the rank, the muscle and no-nonsense friendliness so useful in keeping the uncomplicated Navy of those times running smoothly. (Holbrook, 11)

By 1942 Harmon advanced to mess attendant first class, being a senior man in his department. On the night of 12–13 November 1942, he would take part in one of the key naval battles in World War II, the Battle of Guadalcanal. The effort to hold this island at all costs took a tremendous toll and was the crucible of the campaign in the Pacific. Serving as the flagship of a cruiser and destroyer task-force, the *San Francisco* engaged a force of Japanese battleships, cruisers, and destroyers. As the battle raged on, the *San Francisco* was hit more than forty times by enemy salvos, and Captain Cassin Young was killed, as were many others. Harmon, assigned to a first-aid station, was a busy man aiding hospital corpsmen. During the course of the fighting he was topside with the corpsman Lynford Bondsteel near an open hatchway. Both men realized that one incoming round was heading their way and made a dash for safety. Harmon, however, was quicker than his shipmate and reached the hatchway first. A lesser man might have ducked for safety, but not Harmon. Instead, he grabbed Bondsteel and sent him through the hatchway ahead of him. Bondsteel reached the top stairs of the hatch when the enemy shell exploded. Harmon almost made it but was only partly inside when he was killed instantly in a hail of shrapnel. Bondsteel survived due to Harmon's heroism. The *San Francisco*, too, would survive the battle but took heavy casualties. Two other mess attendants, Charles Allen Jackson and Herbert Madison, also died in the fighting. Once the battle was over, Harmon and seventy-six shipmates who lost their lives were buried at sea.

For his actions during the Battle of Guadalcanal, Harmon was awarded the Navy Cross, the navy's second highest award for valor. In some cases awards for valor to African American combatants were downgraded to a lesser degree because of race bias, but this was not the case with Harmon—there was no disputing his heroism. It was men like Harmon who proved that African Americans deserved a proper place in the navy as fighting men, and his actions helped open up opportunities for black sailors in later years. The importance of Harmon's service and sacrifice is highlighted by the fact that he is the first African American to have a navy ship named after him. The secretary of the navy, a white southerner, Frank Knox, ordered such, and in July 1943 the destroyer-escort *Harmon* (DE-678) was launched. Harmon is remembered in his hometown, which erected a historical marker in Cuero Municipal Park in his honor. The navy further perpetuated his memory, naming the bachelor enlisted quarters at the Naval Air Station in North Island, San Diego, Harmon Hall.

FURTHER READING

A portion of Leonard Roy Harmon's personal military records held by the National Personnel Records Center in St. Louis are available under the Freedom of Information Act and its guidelines.

Heber, Holbrook A. "Leonard R. Harmon: The First Black to Have a Navy Warship Named in His Honor," *The Pacific Ship and Shore Historical Review* (repr. 1988).

Knoblock, Glenn A. *African American Casualties in the Navy, Coast Guard, and Merchant Marine in World War II* (Forthcoming).

Miller, Richard E. *The Messman Chronicles: African-Americans in the U.S. Navy, 1932–1943* (2004)

GLENN ALLEN KNOBLOCK

Harney, Ben R. (6 Mar. 1871–1 Mar. 1938), ragtime pianist, singer, and songwriter, was born Benjamin Robertson Harney to Margaret Draffen and Benjamin Mills Harney, a Union army captain, teacher, and engineer. There is conflicting information on his place of birth. His listings in the census cite Kentucky, and his death certificate specifies Louisville, which agrees with information given by his Louisville publisher, Bruner Greenup. However, the *Louisville Herald* of 27 April 1916 says he was from Middlesboro, Kentucky, his marriage registry from 1897 specifies he was born "on board steamer," and his father's military pension record gives Memphis, Tennessee, as his birthplace. There is no information available about Harney's childhood or education, but the 1880 census shows that his parents had divorced and he was living in Anderson County, Kentucky, with his mother and her parents; his father was living alone in Louisville. Harney is thought to have some black ancestry despite a family background, going back to the early 1800s, that includes individuals with such prominent positions in society that an African American connection would seem unlikely. On the paternal side was a college president, military officers, a Kentucky state senator, and a popular novelist. His maternal grandfather was a lawyer and a Kentucky state representative. However, Harney is reported to have told black musicians that he was passing for white. This was the testimony of the pianists WILLIE "THE LION" SMITH and EUBIE BLAKE. Blake said that everybody knew that Harney was passing (conversation with the author, 30 Aug. 1979). Photographs of Harney, which reveal a swarthy complexion, suggest the possibility of mixed race, but not conclusively. Harney seems to have worked with black associates during most of his career, which was highly unusual at that time but still does not prove the case. In an effort to reconcile the prominence of his family in white society with his reported claim to have been passing, it has been proposed by Vernon Johnson that Harney was a Melungeon, belonging to a multiracial group stemming from intermarriages between whites, African Americans, and Native Americans and residing primarily in the Southern Appalachian area in the states of North Carolina, Tennessee, Virginia, and southeast Kentucky (the area of Middlesboro). Though Melungeon's suffered discrimination and, despite light skin, were considered non-white, his family may have evaded discovery. Harney's middle name, Robertson, has aroused interest in this regard because it is a common surname among Melungeons. While no conclusive proof of Harney's African American or Melungeon membership can be offered, we are left with the unusual and widely reported fact that he claimed to be "passing" and worked most of his career with African Americans.

In 1890 Harney was listed in the Louisville directory as an usher in the Masonic Theatre, and in 1891 he lived in Middlesboro, Kentucky, near the borders of Tennessee and Virginia, where he worked as a post office clerk. He claimed that it was in Middlesboro that he first heard music that inspired his early ragtime compositions. Around this time he also appeared on the vaudeville stage, playing piano, singing, and dancing. In 1893 he offered his song "You've Been a Good Old Wagon but You've Done Broke Down" to a Louisville music publisher, Bruner Greenup. Since Harney was musically illiterate Greenup had the music notated by John Biller, a local musician, and the music was published in 1895 with composer credit given to both Harney and Biller. The melody of the first section resembles "Froggie Goes A-Courtin'" and a number of Appalachian folk songs, and all three sections of the song feature syncopations that were soon to become associated with ragtime, a musical style just then emerging from the black subculture. The lyric is in the style of the prevailing "coon song," which depicts African Americans in a disparaging manner.

Harney's performances attracted attention in the vaudeville world, and his New York debut in January 1896 was a sensation, leading to appearances at the city's major vaudeville houses. Notices describe him as an excellent pianist (an appraisal echoed by the jazz piano greats JAMES P. JOHNSON and Willie Smith), a singer with a gruff voice, a dancer, and a Negro impersonator. A review of Harney in the *Brooklyn Eagle* of 6 June 1896 uses what may be the earliest printed reference to the term "rag time" (as opposed to the partial term "rag," which had surfaced in a musical context by 1894): "He invents and plays what he calls *rag time* airs and dances, the effect of syncopations being to make the melody ragged."

This article also refers to an unnamed woman—"a brunette from South Carolina"—joining his act as a singer and dancer. In September 1896 he added a third member to his act, a black man called Strap Hill. Hill originally pretended to be an audience member who would heckle from his seat before being invited to the stage, where he joined in with the singing and dancing.

M. Witmark, a major Tin Pan Alley music publisher, took notice of Harney and bought the rights to his "Good Old Wagon," reissuing it in 1896 with a cover banner proclaiming Harney as "the original introducer of the now popular 'rag time' in Ethiopian songs." Witmark also published Harney's "Mister Johnson, Turn Me Loose" (1896), which became a hit when sung by the musical comedy star May Irwin and was frequently used by ragtime's detractors to typify what they considered the new style's degraded character. In 1897 Harney became the first to issue a ragtime instruction manual, his "Ben Harney's Rag Time Instructor" (notated by Theodore H. Northrup), which uses such well known tunes as "Annie Laurie" and hymns "Old Hundred" and "Come Thou Fount" to demonstrate how to "rag"—syncopate—existing music. In performances he ragged more ambitious classic material, such as Mendelssohn's "Spring Song" and Rubinstein's Melody in F. His final important publication was "Cake Walk in the Sky" (1899), issued in both instrumental and vocal versions. The vocal version has an alternate text of "ragtime words" that attempts to capture the essence of Harney's singing style in which he used nonsense syllables, similar to the scat singing introduced by LOUIS ARMSTRONG more than two decades later.

Throughout the late 1890s Harney performed onstage with Strap Hill and a Canadian-born singer and dancer named Edith Murray, who had appeared previously in several major Broadway shows as a specialty dancer. She and Harney married on 1 January 1897 in Streator, Illinois; they had no children. In 1899 her name appeared on the cover of his song "Tell It to Me," and in 1901 he dedicated to her his song "I'd Give a Hundred if the Gal Was Mine," but she seems to have left his show soon afterward and was performing with others. It is not known when or if they divorced. Her replacement was Jessie Haynes, whose picture appears on the cover of another Harney song, "The Only Way to Keep a Gal, Is to Keep Her in a Cage" (1901). She worked with Harney at least until 1918 and continued traveling with him throughout the rest of his career. They married around 1916 and had no children. Blesh and Janis, the first modern authors to write about Harney, refer to her has "Jessie Boyce" (211–213, 228–230) but this seems to be an error.

Harney's stardom faded after the beginning of the twentieth century. His style of performance had gone out of fashion in the major American cities, but he continued performing as a touring artist for the next three decades, traveling widely throughout the United States, Canada, Australia (in 1911), and reportedly to other places in the Pacific and several times to England. During much of this period he continued to receive outstanding reviews, but his outdated style made it impossible for him to retrieve the stature he had once had in places like New York and Chicago.

Harney was recorded only once, this on a non-commercial field recording made around 1925 by the folklorist Robert Winslow Gordon, later to become head of the Archive of American Folksong for the Library of Congress. Harney sings, without accompaniment, something similar to the first strain of "Good Old Wagon," but mostly with lyrics from several other songs. A heart attack in 1930 ended Harney's career, and for most of his remaining eight years he and his wife lived in Philadelphia, Pennsylvania, reportedly in a boardinghouse in a black neighborhood, where he died of chronic nephritis.

FURTHER READING

Berlin, Edward A. *Ragtime: A Musical and Cultural History* (1980).

Berlin, Edward A. *Reflections and Research on Ragtime* (1987).

Berlin, Edward A. "Reflections on the Ben Harney Mystery," *Mississippi Rag* (Sept. 1997).

Blesh, Rudi, and Harriet Janis. *They All Played Ragtime* (1971).

Johnson, Vernon. "Kentucky's Ben Harney: Black or White?" *Mississippi Rag* (July 1997).

Tallmadge, William H. "Ben Harney: The Middlesborough Years, 1890–93," *American Music* 13.2 (Summer 1995).

Whiteoak, John. *Playing Ad-Lib: Improvisatory Music in Australia 1836–1970* (1999).

EDWARD A. BERLIN

Harper, Frances Ellen Watkins (24 Sept. 1825–20 Feb. 1911) poet, novelist, activist, and orator, was born Frances Ellen Watkins to free parents in Baltimore, Maryland. Her parents' names remain unknown. Orphaned by the age of three, Watkins is believed to have been raised by her uncle, the Reverend William Watkins, a leader in the African Methodist Episcopal (AME) Church and a contributor to such abolitionist newspapers as *Freedom's Journal* and the *Liberator*. Most important for Watkins, her uncle was also the founder of the William Watkins Academy for Negro Youth, where she studied. A well-known and highly regarded school, the academy offered a curriculum included elocution, composition, Bible study, mathematics, and history. The school also emphasized social responsibility and political leadership. Although Watkins withdrew from formal schooling at the age of thirteen to begin work as a domestic servant, her studies at the academy no doubt shaped her political activism, oratorical skills, and creative writing.

After leaving school Watkins worked as a seamstress and as a child caretaker for a family who owned a bookstore. While in their employ, she continued her studies independently, reading liberally from her employers' book stock. Watkins's first poetry appeared in local newspapers while she was still a teenager. In 1846, at the age of twenty-one, she published her first book, a collection of prose and poetry titled *Forest Leaves*. No known copy of *Forest Leaves* has survived, though the scholar Frances Smith Foster has speculated that

Frances Ellen Watkins Harper, c. 1898 (Library of Congress.)

the volume probably contained poems and prose on subjects as varied as "religious values, women's rights, social reform, biblical history and current events" (Foster, 8). Although Watkins had the advantage of a better education than that of many of her peers, she was not immune to the racial hostilities of the antebellum years. The Compromise of 1850 complicated the lives of Watkins and her family. Among the many components of this federal legislation was the Fugitive Slave Act, which required that all citizens participate in the recovery of slaves and imposed severe penalties on those who refused. The family lived in the precarious position of being free blacks in Maryland, a slave state, at a time when federal legislation increasingly challenged black freedom. This undoubtedly shaped Watkins's feelings that all blacks—slave and free, wealthy or poor—had a duty to the welfare of their fellow African Americans, a theme that emerges frequently in her literature.

In 1850 Watkins's family was forced by local officials to disband their elite school for blacks and sell their home. Watkins moved to Ohio and began working as a teacher at the Union Seminary near Columbus. Why she chose to go to Ohio while some of her family members remained in Baltimore and others relocated to Canada is unknown. But in 1853 the State of Maryland forbade free blacks to enter the state. The penalty was enslavement. During this period in which Watkins was unable to return to her home state, a free black man was arrested and enslaved for entering Maryland. The man died soon after the ordeal. In a letter to WILLIAM STILL, Watkins cast this man's death as the beginning of her own commitment to abolitionism: "Upon that grave I pledged myself to the Anti-Slavery cause" (Still, 786).

Soon after this incident in Maryland, Watkins moved to Philadelphia, Pennsylvania, where she lived in a home that functioned as an Underground Railroad station, one of a series of homes used to assist fugitive slaves in their escape. While there, she published several poems in response to Harriet Beecher Stowe's *Uncle Tom's Cabin*: "Eliza Harris," "To Harriet Beecher Stowe," and "Eva's Farewell." The poems appear to have been widely circulated. "Eliza Harris" appeared in at least three national papers. Building on the pathos of Stowe's representation of the escape of the nearly white slave Eliza, Watkins makes the national implications of Eliza's condition explicit:

Oh shall I speak of my proud country's shame?
Of the stains on her glory, how give them their
  name?

How say that her banner in mockery waves—
Her "star spangled banner"—o'er millions of
    slaves?
(Foster, 61)

In 1854 Watkins initiated her career as a public speaker in New Bedford, Massachusetts, delivering a lecture titled "The Education and the Elevation of the Colored Race." Soon after, she was enlisted as a traveling lecturer for the Maine Antislavery Society and became an admired and much sought-after lecturer. In a letter that same year, Watkins reports lecturing every night of the week, sometimes more than once in a day, to audiences as large as six hundred people. In a period of six weeks in the fall of 1854 she gave thirty-three lectures in twenty-one cities and towns. Contemporary newspaper accounts describe her as an eloquent and moving speaker. The *Portland Advertiser*, for example, characterized her lectures by saying that "the deep fervor of feeling and pathos that she manifests, together with the choice selection of language which she uses arm her elocution with almost superhuman force and power over her spellbound audience" (Boyd, 43). Also in 1854 Watkins published *Poems on Miscellaneous Subjects*, which included poems on antislavery and equal rights. It appears that the publisher was confident that the book would be well received. Y. B. Yerrington and Sons of Boston published the book in Philadelphia and Boston. Both editions were reprinted in 1855, and by 1857 the publisher claimed that they had sold ten thousand copies of the book.

In 1860 Watkins married Fenton Harper, and together they purchased a farm outside Columbus, Ohio. The couple had a daughter, Mary. Although little is known about the marriage, Foster has described this period as a "semi-retirement" from Watkins's public life (18). Soon after her husband's death in 1864, Harper returned to New England and resumed her lectures. After the Civil War, she began lecturing in the South. She was particularly concerned with the future of the newly freed people. This trip would greatly influence Harper's literature. Three of her books, in particular, are concerned with Reconstruction efforts: a serialized novel, *Minnie's Sacrifice* (1869); a book of poetry, *Sketches of Southern Life* (1871); and her most famous novel, *Iola Leroy* (1896).

Significantly, the vision of a new nation that emerges in Harper's literature is not only one of racial equality but also one in which gender equality is represented as crucial to the fulfillment of the American creed of liberty. Harper participated in many women's organizations, including the American Women's Suffrage Association, the National Council of Women, the Woman's Christian Temperance Union, and the First Congress of Colored Women in the United States. Her status as both a woman and an African American, however, placed her in a complicated position, particularly as early white feminists, such as Susan B. Anthony and Lucretia Mott, used racist propaganda to assert the importance of women's suffrage over black male suffrage.

Harper, along with FREDERICK DOUGLASS, participated in the 1869 American Equal Rights Association meeting to debate the proposed Fifteenth Amendment, which would grant suffrage to black men. Harper supported the vote for black men: "When I was at Boston there were sixty women who left work because one colored woman went to gain a livelihood in their midst. If the nation could handle one question I would not have the black woman put a single straw in the way if only the men of the race could obtain what they wanted" (Boyd, 128). Harper continued her activism on behalf of African American and women's rights well into the 1890s, becoming the vice president of the National Council of Negro Women, which she had helped found in 1896.

Little is known about Harper between 1901 and her death in Philadelphia in 1911. Indeed, though she was a well-known public figure throughout much of the nineteenth century, many of the details of her life and work remain unknown. The rediscovery in the early 1990s of three of her novels—*Minnie's Sacrifice* (1869), *Sowing and Reaping* (1876–1877), and *Trial and Triumph* (1888–1889)—all published in the African Methodist Episcopal Church periodical the *Christian Recorder*, suggests that there is probably much more to know about the life and career of one of the most prolific and popular black writers of the nineteenth century.

FURTHER READING

Frances E. W. Harper's papers are housed at the Moorland-Spingarn Research Center of Howard University and at the Schomburg Center for Research in Black Culture of the New York Public Library.

Boyd, Melba Joyce. *Discarded Legacy: Politics and Poetics in the Life of Frances E. W. Harper, 1825–1911* (1994).

Foster, Frances Smith. "Introduction," in *A Brighter Coming Day: A Frances Ellen Watkins Harper Reader* (1990).

Still, William. *The Underground Rail Road* (1872).

CASSANDRA JACKSON

Harper, Michael Steven (18 Mar. 1938–), poet, was born in Brooklyn, New York, to Walter Warren Harper, a postal worker and supervisor, and Katherine Johnson, a medical stenographer. His family were readers, and his mother taught him to read before kindergarten. His first book was *A Thousand and One Nights*, and LANGSTON HUGHES's poems hung on the walls of their home (Lloyd, 119). In an interview Harper told the *Callaloo* editor Charles Rowell that "My family had enormous grace and energy, most of it captured around the kitchen table. Discussion, argument, and discourse about everything, from politics, to sports, to music, was a daily occurrence" (Rowell, 785). When Harper was thirteen his family moved to West Los Angeles. The move was traumatic for Harper, and he spent his first summer in Los Angeles sitting up, sick with asthma and athlete's foot, while the houses of black families were being bombed close by (Rowell, 782).

Harper entered Susan Miller Dorsey High School in 1952 and graduated in 1955. A self-described loner, Harper held a newspaper route and explored the city and its people via public transportation, as he had in New York. During these years he was a good test taker but remained unengaged at school, where he received little encouragement. His family was supportive and hoped he would be a doctor, but he did not share this ambition. Nonetheless, he pursued a premedical curriculum at City College of Los Angeles and Los Angeles State College.

During college Harper was affected by reading John Keats, William Butler Yeats, and RALPH WALDO ELLISON, and by a course called the Epic of Search, taught by Irwin Swerdlow. Henri Coulette and Wirt Williams, both Iowa graduates, taught Harper about modernist poetry and fiction and encouraged him to apply to Iowa. Another important teacher for Harper was the novelist Christopher Isherwood, who brought his friends W. H. Auden and Aldous Huxley to class to talk with students and encouraged Harper to send out his writing. Harper also noted that Isherwood's thoughts on the relationship between art and politics in the 1930s influenced his own wariness in the 1960s because "you could sell your independence to a slogan if you were not extremely careful" (Rowell, 784). Harper also worked for the U.S. Postal Service in Los Angeles during college, an experience he credits with teaching him "about narrative … how to tell a good tale, and what to withhold and what to announce" (Rowell, 786).

Harper moved to Iowa to attend the Writers' Workshop in January 1961, in part to avoid the draft. There he felt culturally and racially isolated and had run-ins with Philip Roth, but he connected with a few of his fellow students, including the painter Oliver Jackson and the poet Lawson Inada. He spent a year at Iowa, then returned to Los Angeles to student-teach at Pasadena City College. In 1963 he completed an M.A. in English at Iowa.

From 1964 to 1970 Harper held teaching positions at Contra Costa College, Reed College, Lewis and Clark College, and California State College–Hayward. In 1965 he married Shirley Ann Buffington; they divorced in 1998. They had a daughter and four sons, two of whom died from hyaline membrane disease/respiratory distress syndrome.

In 1970 Harper published his first book, *Dear John, Dear Coltrane*, which GWENDOLYN BROOKS pulled out of a pile of nonwinning submissions for a University of Pittsburgh poetry contest. This book launched Harper's career and earned him a position at Brown University, where he began teaching in 1970. He published fourteen collections of poetry, including *Nightmare Begins Responsibility* (1974), *Images of Kin: New and Selected Poems* (1977), *Healing Song for the Inner Ear* (1985), and *Songlines in Michaeltree: New and Collected Poems* (2000). He also coedited the important anthologies *Chant of Saints: A Gathering of Afro-American Literature, Art and Scholarship* (1979) and *Every Shut Eye Ain't Asleep: An Anthology of Poetry by African Americans Since 1945* (1994), as well as edited the collected poems of STERLING ALLEN BROWN. Honored numerous times throughout his career, Harper received a Guggenheim in 1976 and was poet laureate of Rhode Island from 1988 to 1993.

Harper dedicated many of his poems to friends, family members, and historical figures who compel him, and he conjured and communed with them through the work. It is in the poems that readers catch glimpses of his children's births, the deaths of his sons, and his relationship with his wife; of his Chippewa great-great-grandmother and preacher great-grandfather; of his grandfather facing down a white mob; of friendships with ROBERT EARL HAYDEN and Sterling Brown; of heroes like JACKIE ROBINSON, JOHN COLTRANE, and John Brown. The poems incorporate Harper's personal and intellectual biography, but these details of a life also become metaphors, acts of conservation and reclamation. Harper has said that "I wanted to put into literature what I didn't see when I studied the 'masters'; I came away with questions about the American classics that made me want to write what was missing" (Rowell, 791). Many would say that

Harper has reached his goal, and that he is one of the most important American writers of his time.

FURTHER READING
Many works by and about Harper, including some rare materials, are part of the Harris Collection, John Hay Library, Brown University.

Pettis, Joyce. "Michael Harper," in *African American Poets: Lives, Works, and Sources* (2002).

"Michael S(teven) Harper," in *Contemporary Authors Online* (2004).

Antonucci, Michael. "The Map and the Territory: An Interview with Michael S. Harper," *African American Review* 34:3 (Fall, 2000).

Lloyd, David. "Interview with Michael S. Harper," *Triquarterly* 65 (1986).

Rowell, Charles H. "Down Don't Worry Me: An Interview with Michael S. Harper," *Callaloo* 13:4 (Fall, 1990).

Smith, Valerie, ed. *African American Writers* (2001).

JENNIFER DRAKE

Harper, Minnie Buckingham (15 May 1886–1978), the first African American woman legislator in the United States, was born in the town of Winfield, Putnam County, West Virginia. The Buckinghams were a large, extended mixed-race family with roots in England and in the West Indies, and branches in West Virginia and Ohio. Harper grew up with ten brothers and sisters and was educated in the West Virginia public school system.

As a young woman, Harper, along with one of her sisters, found work as a schoolteacher. In 1916 she gave birth to a son, George Ivan Edward "Buck" Buckingham. When George was six years old, Minnie Buckingham married Ebenezer Howard Harper, a man twenty-two years her senior, who was one of the leading African American men in West Virginia.

Originally from Virginia and born during the Civil War, Ebenezer Howard Harper had graduated in 1899 from Howard University in Washington, D.C., and had become a lawyer. After moving to West Virginia, he also farmed and was a dealer in real estate.

During the early decades of the twentieth century, McDowell County was a coal mining hub that had attracted a fairly large number of African Americans. Mining was hard work and hazardous, but it was a relatively well-paying job compared to other wages for manual labor at the time, and one that was open to black workers. Consequently, McDowell County became known as a place where African Americans could prosper and even achieve a measure of social mobility despite the limitations of a segregated society. As a result, opportunities existed for African American men from the county to be elected to positions of some influence and political power. Ebenezer Howard Harper was one of them. His thriving McDowell law practice led him to distinguish himself as a well-respected elected official, serving as Republican state committeeman from 1912 to 1916 and McDowell County committeeman from 1920 to 1924. Harper also served in the state legislative sessions of 1917, 1925, and 1927. The Harpers made their home in Welch, West Virginia, in comparatively comfortable circumstances among the miners who contributed to Harper's political base. Upon their marriage, Harper had adopted Minnie's son as his own. As a boy, through the influence of his father, George was able to serve as a pageboy in the West Virginia state legislature. Unfortunately, during his third legislative term, Ebenezer Howard Harper became seriously ill with diabetes and had to have one of his leg amputated. After a lingering sickness he succumbed to the disease on 22 December 1927 in a Huntington, West Virginia, hospital.

Shortly after his death, on 12 January 1928, the West Virginia governor Howard M. Gore appointed Minnie Harper to fill the unexpired term of her late husband, and she thereby became a representative in the house of delegates from McDowell County. She was unanimously recommended for the position by the McDowell County Republican Party's executive committee.

It was understood that Harper's position would function as an honorary placeholder, and she did not run for elected office in the next round of state legislative elections, held later in 1928. Nevertheless, in the course of her duties, she served on the house committees on federal relations, railroads, and labor. As a pioneer in the entry of African American women, and indeed of women in general, into the political life of the United States, she "provided the inspiration and possibly the motivation for other women of color to embark on their own legislative journeys" (Drew Ross, *Newsletter of the West Virginia Legislature*, 7 Feb. 2007).

After leaving the spotlight of public service, Harper received a number of offers to endorse various foods and other commercial products, but turned them all down. As difficult as it must have been to be a groundbreaking African American woman political figure in an era of severe racial inequality, it was also certainly difficult at that time for a woman who had had a child out of wedlock to be considered respectable; one can speculate that fear of media scrutiny and censure may have been a reason she shunned publicity despite her historical achievement.

After returning to private life, Harper lived in relative seclusion in the towns of Keystone and Welch, West Virginia, until her death at the age of ninety-one.

FURTHER READING
Phillips, Jo Boggess. *The Women Pioneers of the West Virginia State Legislature, Institute for Public Affairs Policy Monograph Series No. 6* (1997).
West Virginia State Legislative Handbook (1928).

JORJET HARPER

Harpo, Slim (11 Jan. 1924–31 Jan. 1970), blues musician, singer, was born James Moore in Lobdell, Louisiana, West Baton Rouge Parish. He was the eldest child of parents who died while he was in high school; consequently orphaned, Moore became head of the household and dropped out of the tenth grade in order to support his family. Initially, he earned money by performing manual labor, working as a longshoreman. As a child, Moore had taken an interest in music and taught himself to play harmonica in a neck rack; upon the death of his parents, he was able to utilize this musical talent to supplement the income he generated from manual labor by performing at juke joints, picnics, rent parties, and even on street corners. Moore traveled throughout Southern Louisiana playing his harmonica, earning the moniker, "Harmonica Slim." He gained local notoriety for playing and singing "swamp blues," a rural Louisiana blues distinct from other subgenres for its laid back rhythm and lighthearted lyrics. In the late 1940s Moore began performing full-time with his brother in-law, Lightnin' Slim, a swamp blues guitarist who had also garnered local notoriety. In 1948 Moore married Lovelle Casey.

By the 1950s, Moore would accompany his brother-in-law to Crowley, Louisiana, to observe and eventually take part in his recording sessions at the studio owned by J. D. Miller, a swamp blues A & R (artists and repertoire, or talent scout) and aficionado. Moore impressed Miller with his sound and was recorded playing in the background on six singles performed at the studio until 1957, when he recorded his own first record, "I'm a King Bee," for Excello Records, founded by Ernie Young in Nashville, Tennessee. Miller informed Moore that the alias "Harmonica Slim" was being used by another recording artist on the West Coast and advised that he assume another name prior to release of his first record; subsequently, he substituted "Harmonica" in his moniker for the commonly used nickname for the harp—also known as a slim harp—and devised the name Slim Harpo. His first record was thus released in 1957 and became an instant success for both songs on the album, "I'm a King Bee" and the song on the opposite side, "I Got Love If You Want It." The same year, the rockabilly artist Warren Smith recorded the song for his own repertoire. Harpo composed lyrics to his songs with the accompaniment of his wife; however, Miller fraudulently added his name to the list of authors, thereby receiving credit and royalties, as he customarily did with other artists who recorded in his Louisiana studio.

In 1961, Harpo released two more hits from the Crowley studio: "Rainin' in My Heart," which was a Billboard Top 40 hit and a top 20 pop chart hit, and "Don't Start Cryin' Now." In 1964 he recorded "Little Queen Bee." In 1966 he released, "Baby Scratch My Back," which was a number one hit on the Billboard R&B charts. Lazy Lester was among those musicians who regularly accompanied Harpo at recording sessions. The same year Harpo performed at the Apollo Theater in New York. In 1967 he released "Tip On In" and "Tee-Ni-Nee-Ni-Nu," both hits on the R&B charts from Excello. Also that year, he performed concerts and at clubs throughout Chicago with Lightnin' Slim, and by the late 1960s they were performing together at Whiskey a Go-Go in Los Angeles, and later with English blues musician John Mayall at the Filmore East in New York, and the Electric Circus in Toronto. At the same time Harpo was performing he also maintained a trucking business. He has been compared to the artist JIMMY REED, yet more laid back; among his favorite artists were BLIND LEMON JEFFERSON, MUDDY WATERS, B. B. KING, and HOWLIN' WOLF.

Harpo has been the muse for a number of British blues and rock bands who paid tribute to his artistry by recording his songs. Among those bands are most notably the Rolling Stones, who in 1966 performed their version of Harpo's 1957 hit single "I'm a King Bee" on their debut album and, in 1972, "Shake Your Hips." The Kinks recorded "Got Love If You Want It," as did the band Pretty Things, who also recorded "Rainin' in My Heart." The Moody Blues took their name from the Harpo hit and they recorded his song "Shake Your Hips." Van Morrison sang "Don't Start Cryin' Now." The country recording artist Hank Williams Jr. had a hit record with his version of "Rainin' in My Heart." Pink Floyd, Them, The Fabulous Thunderbirds, The Yardbirds, and ZZ Top also recorded songs first recorded and made famous by Harpo.

Though he had been healthy throughout his life, on 31 January 1970 he died without warning of a heart attack in Baton Rouge, Louisiana, as he was preparing to embark on a tour of Europe. He was buried at Mulatto Bend Cemetery in Port Allen, Louisiana. The Baton Rouge Blues Foundation established the Slim Harpo Awards to honor prominent blues artists or aficionados for their support of blues culture in Louisiana, annually. Among past Slim Harpo Award recipients are BUDDY GUY, Clarence "Gatemouth" Brown, Dr. John, Sonny Landreth, Silas Hogan, and Tony Joe White. In 2008 "I'm a King Bee" was inducted into the Grammy Hall of Fame.

FURTHER READING

Broven, John. *South to Louisiana: The Music of the Cajun Bayous* (1983).

Koster, Rick. *Louisiana Music: A Journey from R&B to Zydeco, Jazz to Country, Blues to Gospel, Cajun Music to Swamp Pop to Carnival Music and Beyond* (2002).

"New York Beat," *Jet,* 21 Apr. 1966.

SAFIYA DALILAH HOSKINS

Harrington, Oliver W. (14 Feb. 1912–2 Nov. 1995), cartoonist, was born Oliver Wendell Harrington in New York City, the son of Herbert Harrington, a porter, and Euzenie Turat. His father came to New York from North Carolina in the early 1900s when many African Americans were seeking greater opportunities in the North. His mother had immigrated to America, arriving from Austria-Hungary in 1907, to join her half sister. Ollie Harrington grew up in a multiethnic neighborhood in the South Bronx and attended public schools. He recalled a home life burdened by the stresses of his parents' interracial marriage and the financial struggles of raising five children. From an early age, he drew cartoons to ease those tensions.

In 1927 Harrington enrolled at Textile High School in Manhattan. He was voted best artist in his class and started a club whose members studied popular newspaper cartoonists. Exposure to the work of Art Young, Denys Wortman, and Daniel Fitzpatrick later influenced his style and technique. About that time, toward the end of the Harlem Renaissance, he began to spend considerable time in Harlem and became active in social groups there. Following his graduation from Textile in 1931, he attended the National Academy of Design school. There he met such renowned artists and teachers as Charles L. Hinton, Leon Kroll, and Gifford Beal. During his years at the academy, Harrington supported himself by drawing cartoons and working as a set designer, actor, and puppeteer. In 1932 he published political cartoons and *Razzberry Salad,* a comic panel satirizing Harlem society. They appeared in the *National News,* a newspaper established by the Democratic Party organization in Harlem, which folded after only four months. He then joined the Harlem Newspaper Club and was introduced to reporters such as TED POSTON, HENRY LEE MOON, and ROI OTTLEY of the *Amsterdam News,* as well as Bessye Bearden of the *Chicago Defender* and her son ROMARE BEARDEN. In 1933 Harrington submitted cartoons to the *Amsterdam News* on a freelance basis. During the next two years he also attended art classes at New York University with his friend Romare Bearden. In May 1935, he joined the staff of the *News* and created *Dark Laughter,* soon renamed *Bootsie* after its main character, a comic panel that he would draw for more than thirty-five years. Harrington remarked that "I simply recorded the almost unbelievable but hilarious chaos around me and came up with a character" (*Freedomways* 3, 519).

When the Newspaper Guild struck the *News* in October 1935, Harrington, while not a guild member, supported the strike and would not publish his cartoons until it was settled. During the strike he became friends with journalists BENJAMIN JEFFERSON DAVIS JR. (later a New York City councilman) and MARVEL COOKE, who were members of the Communist Party. While probably not a party member, he maintained active ties to the left from that time. Harrington soon returned to freelance work and taught art in a WPA program. Edward Morrow, a Harlem reporter and graduate of Yale University, and Bessye Bearden encouraged him to apply to the School of the Fine Arts at Yale, which accepted him in 1936. Supporting himself with his *Bootsie* cartoons (which he transferred to the larger-circulation *Pittsburgh Courier* in 1938), scholarship assistance, and waiting on tables at fraternities, Harrington received a bachelor of fine arts degree in 1940. He won several prizes for his paintings, although not a prestigious traveling fellowship at graduation, which he believed was denied him because of his race.

In 1942, after working for the National Youth Administration for a year, Harrington became art editor for a new Harlem newspaper, the *People's Voice*, edited by ADAM CLAYTON POWELL JR. He also created a new comic strip, *Jive Gray*. In 1943 and 1944 he took a leave from the *Voice* to serve as a war correspondent for the *Pittsburgh Courier*. While covering African American troops, including the Tuskegee Airmen, in Italy and France, he witnessed racism in the military to a degree he had not experienced before. In Italy he met WALTER WHITE, executive secretary of the National Association for the Advancement of Colored People (NAACP).

In 1946 White, who was attempting to strengthen the NAACP's public relations department following racial violence against returning veterans, hired Harrington as director of public relations. But by late 1947 the two had become estranged and Harrington resigned to become more active politically. With the *Bootsie* cartoons and book illustration work again his principal source of income, and

after ending a brief wartime marriage, he joined a number of political committees in support of the American Labor Party and Communists arrested in violation of the Smith Act. In 1950 he became art editor of *Freedom*, a monthly newspaper founded by Louis Burnham and PAUL ROBESON. He also taught art at the Jefferson School for Social Sciences, a school that appeared on the attorney general's list of subversive organizations. Informed of his ties to the school, the FBI opened a file on Harrington.

By early 1952, with some of his friends under indictment and others facing revocation of their passports, Harrington left the United States for France. Whether he had knowledge of the FBI investigation is unclear, but by the time he reached Paris, the Passport Office there had been instructed to seize his passport if the opportunity arose. Meanwhile, Harrington settled into a life centered around the Café Tournon with a group of expatriate

Oliver W. Harrington, artist correspondent, sketching Anti-aircraft Section Chief Sgt. Carl K. Hilton, of Pine Bluff, Arkansas, in 1944. (Library of Congress.)

artists and writers that included RICHARD WRIGHT and CHESTER HIMES. Himes called Harrington the "best raconteur I'd ever known." His *Bootsie* cartoons and illustration work continued to provide income, and he traveled throughout Europe. For a short time, following a brief second marriage in 1955, he settled in England, but he returned to Paris in 1956 as the Algerian War was worsening. The war divided the African American community, and Harrington became embroiled in a series of disputes with other expatriates. His visit to the Soviet Union in 1959 as a guest of the humor magazine *Krokodil* again attracted intelligence officials.

Saddened by the death of his close friend Richard Wright, and with his income dwindling due to financial difficulties at the *Courier*, in 1961 Harrington traveled to East Berlin for a book illustration project and settled there for the remainder of his life. He submitted cartoons to *Das Magasin* and *Eulenspiegell* and in 1968 became an editorial cartoonist for the *Daily Worker*, later *People's Weekly World*. His press credentials enabled him to travel to the West, and many of his old friends, including Paul Robeson and LANGSTON HUGHES, visited him in East Germany. In 1972 Harrington returned for a brief visit to the United States; in the 1990s he visited more regularly. In 1994, after the publication of two books of his cartoons and articles raised interest in his work, he was appointed journalist-in-residence for a semester at Michigan State University. He died in East Berlin. He was survived by his third wife, Helma Richter, and four children: a daughter from his second marriage, a son from his third, and two daughters from relationships with women to whom he was not married. Harrington's complex personal life, as well as his politics, was sometimes a motive for his travels.

Harrington was often referred to as a "self-exile," but he never described himself that way. "I'm fairly well convinced that one is an exile only when one is not allowed to live in reasonable peace and dignity as a human being among other human beings" (*Why I Left America*, 66). Remembered as the premier cartoonist of the African American press for three decades and a central figure in the expatriate community in Paris in the 1950s, he battled racism through his art, his writings, and an alter ego named *Bootsie*.

FURTHER READING

Harrington, Oliver H., and Thomas M. Igne. *Dark Laughter: The Satiric Art of Oliver W. Harrington* (1993).

Harrington, Oliver H., Thomas M. Igne, et al. *Why I Left America and Other Essays* (1993).

Stovall, Tyler. *Paris Noir: African Americans in the City of Light* (1996).

Obituary: *New York Times*, 7 Nov. 1995.

This entry is taken from the *American National Biography* and is published here with the permission of the American Council of Learned Societies.

CHRISTINE G. MCKAY

Harris, Abram Lincoln, Jr. (17 Jan. 1899–16 Nov. 1963), economist, author, and educator, was born in Richmond, Virginia, the son of Abram Lincoln Harris, a butcher, and Mary Elizabeth Lee, both descendants of slaves freed before the Civil War. After completing his secondary education in the public schools of Richmond, Harris enrolled at Virginia Union University, where he earned a B.S. in 1922. In 1924 he received an M.A. from the University of Pittsburgh.

Harris then joined the faculty of West Virginia Collegiate Institute (later West Virginia State College), where he taught economics. He remained there until 1925, at which time he began a short stint as executive secretary of the Urban League in Minneapolis. Also in that year, Harris married Callie Ellen McGuinn; they had no children and divorced in 1955. After his year with the Urban League, he went to work as a researcher for Columbia University's department of banking in 1926. Harris then embarked on a relationship with Howard University that would continue until 1945, beginning in 1927 as an assistant professor. He briefly left Howard, obtaining a Ph.D. in Political Economy from Columbia in 1930 on a Social Science Research Council Fellowship, but returned that same year to serve as chairman of the university's economics department. In 1936 he achieved full professor status.

Harris had earned his Ph.D. with a dissertation titled "The Black Worker," which dealt with the difficulties blacks had in reaching social and economic equality within the U.S. labor force. With his coauthor Sterling D. Spero, Harris published the work under the title *The Black Worker: The Negro and the Labor Movement* (1931; repr. 1968), and wrote in the preface that the book was intended as a study of "the relation of the dominant section of the working class to the segregated, circumscribed, and restricted Negro minority." The authors were not particularly optimistic about their findings and seemed to sense a troublesome future for working blacks.

They made it clear, again in the preface, that they considered their text "neither a good will tract on race relations nor an attempt to offer a program for the solution of a vexing problem." The book was highly critical of most American trade unions and also of the dominant black leadership of the day. Harris and Spero lamented the ways in which the black worker had lost his place as "an industrial labor reserve" in order to become "a regular element in the labor force of every basic industry."

In 1934, in addition to his teaching duties, Harris served on the Consumers Advocacy Board of the National Recovery Administration. He also continued his research and writing. Following the success of *The Black Worker*, he produced *The Negro as Capitalist* (1936), in which he continued a critical analysis of the various reform programs under discussion for improving the conditions of blacks in the workforce. One such program called for a consumer boycott of white businesses operating in the black community. The rallying cry of this strategy was "Don't buy where you can't work." Harris dismissed the idea of a boycott, contending that, because most white stores were merely family-run operations that employed no outside help, any economic pressure would likely cause more harm than good. "What would be more natural than a retaliatory movement of whites demanding that Negroes be employed only by those white capitalists whose income is mainly derived from Negro patronage?" he wrote. "Nationalism, whether racial or otherwise, has never found, nor has it ever sought, validity in sheer economics."

A related reform program looked to the development of black business enterprise. Harris rejected this strategy as well, arguing that black capitalism was a bad idea because black businesses were, for the most part, too small in comparison with white businesses and thus could not compete efficiently. Harris also disapproved of the economic program put forth earlier in the century the by black leader BOOKER T. WASHINGTON. He felt that Washington's plan, which involved an increase in industrial training for blacks, was futile in a developing economy in which independent small-business men were to have smaller roles and white trade unions regulated the opportunities for jobs. Harris instead supported a reform program in which both black and white workers united to form a stronger labor movement meant to achieve practical goals. He believed that only under this program were the interests of whites—as well as blacks—furthered, and he felt that only when the interests of white labor were advanced would the white trade union leadership be persuaded to act in a manner beneficial to the black worker.

In 1946 Harris accepted a position at the University of Chicago, where he taught economics and philosophy. Having been interested in the subject of economic philosophy throughout his career, he performed a series of studies in which he analyzed the methods of economic reform espoused by such philosophers as Karl Marx, Werner Sombart, Thorstein Veblen, and John R. Commons. Harris went on to write numerous articles in which he ultimately denounced their proposals and instead came to adopt the theories of the English philosopher and economist John Stuart Mill. In 1958 Harris published *Economics and Social Reform*, in which he wrote, "Progress consists not primarily in material improvement but in moral-aesthetic cultivation.... innovations and social reform must ... be effected within a framework of common moral principles, loyalties and political obligations." Mill's philosophy, he added, "upholds the ideal of a kind of classless society, that is, one in which all divisions except those of taste, interest, and ability are nonexistent."

Harris was working on a book dealing in more depth with Mill's philosophy at the time of his death in Chicago. He was survived by his second wife, the former Phedorah Prescott, whom he had wed in 1962.

FURTHER READING

Darity, William, Jr., and Julian Ellison. "Abram Harris, Jr.: The Economics of Race and Social Reform," *History of Political Economy* 22.4 (1990).

Obituaries: *New York Times* and *Chicago Tribune*, 17 Nov. 1963.

This entry is taken from the *American National Biography* and is published here with the permission of the American Council of Learned Societies.

FRANCESCO L. NEPA

Harris, Barbara (12 June 1930–), Episcopal bishop, was born Barbara Clementine Harris in Philadelphia, Pennsylvania, the middle child of Walter Harris, a steelworker, and Beatrice Price, who worked as a program officer for the Boys and Girls Club of Philadelphia and later for the Bureau of Vital Statistics for the Commonwealth of Pennsylvania. Barbara was born the day after St. Barnabas Day, and her family attended St. Barnabas Church; hence they named her Barbara.

Harris graduated from the Philadelphia High School for Girls in 1948 and then attended the Charles Morris Price School of Advertising and Journalism. Upon completion of the program, she began a twenty-year career as a public relations consultant for Joseph V. Baker Associates, a black-owned national public relations firm headquartered in Philadelphia, eventually becoming president of the company. While in this office, she entered into a brief marriage, which ended in divorce. In 1968 Sun Oil recruited her as a community relations consultant. She stayed with Sun Oil for twelve years, rising to the position of manager of their public relations department. Her career was groundbreaking, and she worked hard to dismantle barriers for both women and African Americans in a predominantly white male profession. Harris, however, found her life's work not in the corporate world, but in the church. Always active in her church, she taught Sunday school and sang in the choir. She brought her friends to church with her no matter how late they had stayed out on Saturday

Barbara Harris was ordained as the first woman bishop in the history of the Episcopal Church at the Hynes Convention Center in Boston, Massachusetts. (AP Images.)

night. She encouraged the parish of St. Barnabas to start a youth group and later initiated and took charge of a group for young adults. For fifteen years she volunteered with the St. Dismas Society, visiting prisons to conduct services on weekends and to counsel and befriend prisoners. During the summer of 1964 she helped register black voters in Mississippi, and the following year she took part in the march led by MARTIN LUTHER KING JR. from Selma to Montgomery, Alabama.

Even in the church Harris witnessed and experienced discrimination, and she came to recognize the need for change. In 1968 the General Convention of the Episcopal Church called a special convention in South Bend, Indiana, to address the concerns of African Americans in the church. As a direct result of the efforts of that convention, which Harris attended, the church began a long—and still unfinished—journey toward eliminating discrimination in the church.

In 1968 Harris transferred her membership to the more activist Episcopal Church of the Advocate in North Philadelphia. The rector, the Reverend Paul Washington, was a staunch fighter for justice who believed that the church should be the vehicle for transformation in the community. In the 1960s he hosted several controversial meetings, including an August 1968 Black Power convention that included such leading activists as STOKELY CARMICHAEL and H. RAP BROWN and that drew both thousands of people and the attention of the FBI.

On 29 July 1974 Harris led the procession into the Church of the Advocate for the controversial ordination into the priesthood of eleven women, "the Philadelphia Eleven." Two years later, after intense debate, the ordination of women as priests was sanctioned by the General Convention of the Episcopal Church. Harris soon began to hear the call to ordination herself. Because she could not just leave her career to attend seminary on a full-time basis, the Diocese of Pennsylvania made arrangements for her to attend classes at Villanova University from 1977 to 1979, and to study with clergy in the area. After several years she took the General Ordination Examinations required of all seminary graduates and passed with flying colors. She was ordained a deacon in 1979 and a priest in 1980.

After her ordination Harris served at the Church of the Advocate and then spent four years as priest in charge at the Church of St. Augustine of Hippo, in the Philadelphia suburb of Norristown, breathing new life into a congregation that had been moribund and on the verge of closing. During this period she also served as a chaplain to the Philadelphia County Prison, continuing her ministry to prisoners, giving particular attention to the "lifers," the long-term prisoners who seldom had visitors and were largely forgotten. In 1984 Harris became the executive director of the Episcopal Church Publishing Company. The primary publication of the company was the *Witness*, a liberal magazine with a history of speaking out on current issues. Harris proved to be a catalyst for the magazine's emphasis on issues of racism, sexism, classism, and heterosexism, both in the church and in society. Harris regularly contributed a hard-hitting, outspoken column titled "*A Luta Continua*" ("The Struggle Continues"), which brought her to the attention of a national and international audience.

In the spring of 1987 the Diocese of Massachusetts held a conference on women in the episcopate, with many ordained women in attendance. Harris was one of the speakers and made a great impact on all those who were present. The following spring the diocese began the process of identifying those clergy who would stand for election later that year as suffragan bishop, an assistant to the diocesan bishop, and there was talk of adding women to the list of candidates. The Episcopal Church met in convention and tried to pass a resolution to appease those opposed to the election of a woman bishop, but when the Diocese of Massachusetts released the names of the candidates, Barbara Harris was one of two women on the list. That summer the Archbishop of Canterbury hosted the Lambeth Conference, a gathering of Anglican bishops held every ten years. There was much concern and debate over the Massachusetts election, for fear that electing a woman might cause a division in the Anglican Communion and endanger ecumenical relations with the Roman Catholic Church.

Harris went to the Lambeth Conference as a member of the press corps in her role with the Episcopal Church Publishing Company and was continually bombarded by participants and the other press members. To some she became a symbol of all that was wrong with the Episcopal Church, or at least with its "liberal" element. Objections to Harris's election were raised on a number of fronts—her nontraditional education and theological training, her status as divorced (an objection not raised in regard to males also being considered), her liberal social activism—but certainly the greatest impediment in the minds of many was simply the fact that she was a woman. The conference, however, ultimately allowed for the consecration

of women by ruling that national churches had the right to choose their own bishops.

The Massachusetts election took place on Saturday, 25 September 1988, and Harris was stunned and surprised to be elected on the fifth ballot. Her strength and her faith were now going to be tested. The next step was for a majority of Episcopal dioceses to consent to the election. Although this was nominally a vote on whether the election was in accord with the church constitution, it was in reality based on the person and not the process. Harris's credentials, her qualifications, and her writings were again questioned. However, consent was obtained, and she subsequently got the necessary number of votes in the House of Bishops.

Harris was consecrated bishop on 11 February 1989. The day was glorious; Boston's Hynes Auditorium was packed with more than eight thousand clergy and laypeople, representing the diversity and breadth of the Episcopal Church. As was expected, there were formal protests during the service. After the protests, Harris's mother walked over to her and said: "Don't worry, baby, everything will be all right. God and I are on your side." The Right Reverend Barbara Clementine Harris served as suffragan bishop in Massachusetts for more than thirteen years, consistently carrying out her ministry of compassion, healing, and reconciliation and always speaking out for justice on behalf of the marginalized in our society. Harris has received sixteen honorary doctorate degrees from a broad range of colleges, universities, and seminaries and has traveled around the world sharing the good news. After retiring in November 2002, she agreed to serve part-time in the Diocese of Washington as an assisting bishop.

The debate over the role of women in the church grows quiet at times, but it has not gone away. The role of women was again called into question at the 1998 Lambeth Conference, which also saw heated discussions on homosexuality. The specter of schism in the Episcopal Church in the United States was again raised at the General Convention in 2003 in the debate over the confirmation of the openly gay canon Gene Robinson as bishop of New Hampshire. At the convention Harris reminded those present of the similar fears felt in 1989 and pointed out that the Anglican Communion remains intact. Delivering a sermon in her home parish the day after her own election as bishop in 1988, Harris expressed in metaphor the significance of that event, a metaphor that, applied more broadly, captures the difficulty of bringing about change in the face of long-standing beliefs and attitudes: "A fresh wind is indeed blowing. We have seen in this year alone some things thought to be impossible just a short time ago. To some, the changes are refreshing breezes. For others, they are as fearsome as a hurricane."

FURTHER READING
Bozzuti-Jones, Mark Francisco. *The Mitre Fits Just Fine: A Story about the Rt. Rev. Barbara Clementine Harris, Suffragan Bishop, Diocese of Massachusetts* (2003).

NAN PEETE

Harris, Charles H. "Teenie" (2 July 1908–12 June 1998), photojournalist, was born in Pittsburgh, Pennsylvania, the youngest of three sons of William A. and Ella Mae (Taliaferro) Harris. His parents operated the Masio Hotel on Wylie Avenue in Pittsburgh's famed Hill District neighborhood. During the early twentieth century, the Hill District was the mecca of African American life in Pittsburgh. The neighborhood attracted poor and working-class blacks as well as the elites of the sports and entertainment worlds, for it was an area where blacks freely socialized, shopped, worshipped, owned businesses, and lived without having to confront many of the harsh realities of the segregated city. It was this exposure to the richness of black life that influenced Harris's forty-year career as a photojournalist and portrait photographer.

Harris got his nickname at the age of two from a female relative who called him "Teenie Little Lover." It was later shortened to "Teenie." Harris came of age during the Great Depression when half of Pittsburgh's black labor force was unemployed. The underground "numbers" lottery was the Hill District's financial backbone and one of Harris's older brothers, William "Woogie" Harris, was a major numbers operator. In 1921 Harris completed the eighth grade at the Watt School (later Robert L. Vann Elementary School), and his first job as a teenager was running numbers for his older brother.

Fearful of being arrested, Harris abandoned numbers running and purchased his first professional camera—a Speed Graphic—in the early 1930s. He opened Harris Studio on Centre Avenue in the Hill District with $350 borrowed from his brother William. Harris was self-taught (with a few tips from the *Pittsburgh Courier* photographer Johnny Taylor) and began photographing visiting celebrities for the black-owned Washington, D.C.-based *Flash!* pictorial magazine. In 1936 he started working as a freelance photographer for the

Pittsburgh Courier, at the time one of the country's most influential and largest circulation black newspapers. Harris accepted a full-time staff photographer position with the *Courier* in 1941 and worked for the newspaper until his retirement in 1975.

Harris produced photographs that offered a unique glimpse into African Americans' dignity, struggle, and achievements; he had unparalleled access to the black community in Pittsburgh and also photographed celebrities such as DR. MARTIN LUTHER KING JR., LENA HORNE, MUHAMMAD ALI, John F. Kennedy, and Eleanor Roosevelt. His most compelling pictures were the candid snapshots of these newsmakers as well as his photographs of everyday black life in Pittsburgh. His intimate portraits of constables, coal miners, steel workers, cab drivers, waitresses, businessmen, and mechanics offered a view into the lives of black workers. He captured images of families, couples, dapper gentlemen and sophisticated ladies in their Sunday best, peaceful protests against discrimination, children buying war bonds, church socials, cotillions, parades, integrated Boy Scout meetings, and nightlife that countered the negative stereotypes of the black community often represented in the white press and Hollywood cinema.

Harris documented the darker side of urban black life as well. Some of his photos showed families living in the squalor of slum housing, a victim of racial hate literature, and the bodies of dead men sprawled on a barroom floor and slumped across a railing. Harris also took family portraits and pictures of servicemen in uniform for their parents and loved ones. Harris's skills were not limited to still photography. He also shot footage of people on the streets using his movie camera.

Harris's reputation as an instinctive photographer earned him another nickname—"One Shot"—from Pittsburgh Mayor David L. Lawrence, because he customarily took only one photograph of a person or event while other photographers snapped numerous shots. Harris would later say that because of the *Pittsburgh Courier's* limited resources, he didn't have any flash bulbs to waste on multiple shots. He also photographed people outside of Pittsburgh. During the *Courier's* popular "Double V Campaign" during World War II, he photographed black soldiers at Fort Bragg. Throughout the war, Harris' photos helped gain international support for the Double V Campaign, which advocated for victory against fascism abroad and victory in America against racial discrimination and inequality. In the late 1940s, Harris, along with the *Courier* staff writer

Edna Chappell, produced a groundbreaking series of articles and pictures about Pittsburgh-area businesses that discriminated against blacks. Harris was the first African American photographer to join the Pittsburgh chapter of the Newspaper Guild.

Best known for his photography, Harris was also a founding member of the Pittsburgh Crawfords baseball team. He played for the team from the mid-1920s, when it was a champion sandlot baseball club, until 1930 when the Crawfords entered the Negro League. Thereafter, Harris photographed the Crawfords and the Homestead Grays, the Pittsburgh area's other Negro League team. He continued to photograph black players after Major League Baseball integrated in 1947. One of his favorite subjects was his close friend ROBERTO CLEMENTE, the star outfielder for the Pittsburgh Pirates major league baseball team in the 1970s.

Harris was also a devoted family man. His first marriage to Ruth Butler in 1927 produced a son, Charles A. Harris. The marriage dissolved several years later. Harris didn't remarry for twelve years until he met Elsa Elliott. Together, they had four children: Ira, Lionel, Crystal, and Cheryl. The marriage lasted for fifty-three years until Elsa's death in 1997.

To supplement the income he earned as a photojournalist and studio photographer, Harris moonlighted for an insurance company, where he documented fires and accidents. By the early 1950s, he had closed his portrait studio on Centre Avenue and moved the business to his home. A talented sketch artist, he would later specialize in coloring black and white portraits by hand. As his career flourished, he was courted by other newspapers offering more money, but decided to stay at the *Courier* and close to the people it served. Harris retired from the paper in 1975.

Harris did not have a pension and relied on $700 a month from Social Security benefits. His precarious economic situation and trusting nature made him vulnerable to the unscrupulous dealings of a stranger who arrived at Harris's home one day in 1986. Harris, who was seventy-eight years old and functionally illiterate, agreed to a licensing and distribution deal of his photographs with the man. The pact was struck on a handshake. Harris signed over his life's work to the man for $3,000 and the promise of royalties. He never saw a cent more than the initial payment and the man refused to return Harris's collection, which included nearly 100,000 photographs and negatives, which one historian called the most comprehensive visual record of any

single African American urban environment. In the years to follow, Harris sought legal representation but his lack of funds made it nearly impossible to secure counsel. Just months before his death by stroke in 1998, a law firm took up his case pro bono, and Harris sued for noncompliance with the 1986 contract. In 2000 the case went to court and a jury awarded Harris's family $4.4 million, which they waived in order to have the photographs and negatives returned to them. The Carnegie Museum of Art in Pittsburgh purchased the archives from Harris's estate in 2001, and in 2003 sought community assistance in identifying many of the subjects in Harris's photographs. The Carnegie planned a 2008 exhibit and publication of Harris's photographs, to be followed a national tour.

FURTHER READING

Crouch, Stanley. *One Shot Harris: The Photographs of Charles "Teenie" Harris* (2002).

Spirit of a Community: The Photographs of Charles 'Teenie' Harris (2001).

Willis, Deborah. *Reflections in Black: A History of Black Photographers 1840 to the Present* (2000).

MICHELLE K. MASSIE

Harris, E. Lynn (20 June 1957–23 July 2009), novelist and activist, was born Everette Lynn Williams in Flint, Michigan, the son of Etta Mae Williams and James Jeter, factory workers. When he was three, he moved with his mother to Little Rock, Arkansas, where they resided with Ben Odis Harris, his mother's new husband. The Harris family eventually had three other children, all girls. Until age twelve, Harris believed he also was one of Ben Harris's biological children.

The Harrises lived modestly and, on occasion, turbulently. While Etta Harris worked two factory jobs and attended classes at Capital City Business College, work for Ben Harris, a sign painter and sanitation truck driver, was scarce. The frustration led to heavy drinking, and when Ben Harris drank, he was often verbally and physically abusive toward his wife and son. Harris's three sisters were usually spared their father's wrath, while Harris, a soft, capricious, and talkative little boy, infuriated his stepfather, who often called him "a little sissy."

Unwilling to tolerate more abuse, Etta Harris divorced her husband in 1969. That same year Harris, bookish and small, entered Booker Junior High School, where he tried out for football and was cut the first day. He became the class clown instead, and while his popularity soared, his grades plummeted. It was around this time that he became aware of his same-sex attraction, although he had not yet acted upon this inclination. Harris continued his disruptive behavior when he transferred to the integrated West Side Junior High School for his eighth-grade year. At his new school he assumed a tough-guy persona, which resulted in a minor assault on a teacher and suspension. The threat of having to repeat the eighth grade, however, caused Harris to make an abrupt about-face. The next year he was on the school newspaper staff. It was at this time that Harris had his first gay encounter. A relationship with a track and football athlete two grades his senior lasted the semester.

In 1970 Harris entered Hall High School, where he continued to excel scholastically. At the end of his sophomore year, Harris spent the summer with his Uncle Clarence, who surprised him by introducing him to his biological father, James Jeter. Harris was warmly and lovingly accepted by Jeter, Jeter's wife, and their four children. But the intended father-son relationship was cut short when Jeter was killed in a car accident the following summer. Jeter's wife died of alcohol-related complications a year later. Harris never saw his siblings on his biological father's side again.

During his junior year, in 1972, Harris was selected to attend Arkansas Boys' State, a one-week summer program sponsored by the American Legion designed to prepare young men for leadership roles in government. Graduates had included future U.S. president Bill Clinton and future Arkansas governor Mike Huckabee. A week after Boys' State, Harris flew to Washington, D.C., to participate in a six-week government agency employment program for academically gifted low-income African American students from around the country. In Washington, D.C., Harris encountered urban life and an active gay community for the first time. A field trip during the program took him to New York City for the first time also. There he saw his first Broadway show, MELVIN VAN PEEBLES's *Don't Play Us Cheap*.

Returning to Hall for his senior year, Harris received scholarship offers from Vanderbilt, Princeton, and the University of Arkansas. He accepted the Arkansas offer and in 1973 began studies at the University of Arkansas at Fayetteville. Free of adult supervision, Harris began to party and drink heavily, and he rarely attended classes. His first semester GPA, 1.30 out of a possible 4.00, seriously jeopardized his scholarships, but as he had done in the past, he refocused and turned his life around.

In 1977 Harris became the first black student to edit the university's award-winning yearbook, *Razorback*, and, according to *Jet* magazine, he became the first black to head a yearbook at a major southern university. He was also the first black male cheerleader for the Arkansas Razorbacks and president of his fraternity. The next year Harris was selected for *Who's Who in American Colleges and Universities*. After graduating with honors with a degree in journalism, Harris was recruited by IBM. For the next thirteen years he sold computers while living in Dallas, Washington, D.C., and Atlanta.

Harris was inspired to write his first novel, *Invisible Life*, when he saw a segment of *The Oprah Winfrey Show* that focused on closeted gay men. The writing was cathartic for the new author, who was able to reveal many things about himself through his fictional characters. After several rejections from publishers and agents, Harris decided to self-publish his book. Once the books were printed, he sold copies from the trunk of his car, at social gatherings, at African American bookstores and book clubs, and at black beauty salons. Less than a year later, by July 1992, he had sold all five thousand copies.

Harris's success did not go unnoticed by the mainstream houses. In 1994 Doubleday republished *Invisible Life* under its Anchor Books banner. It was an instant best-seller. Several books exploring middle-class black male homosexuality followed in quick succession, all of them making various best-seller lists. His second effort, *Just as I Am* (1994), was named Novel of the Year by Blackboard African-American Bestsellers, Inc. His first *New York Times* best-seller was *And This Too Shall Pass* (1996). *If This World Were Mine* (1997) was nominated for the NAACP Image Award and won the James Baldwin Award for Literary Excellence. It also landed on the *New York Times* best-seller list, as did his next four books: *Abide with Me* (1999), *Not a Day Goes By* (2000), *Any Way the Wind Blows* (2001), and *A Love of My Own* (2002). Harris's writing style is both folksy and sophisticated, and his stories are consistently about finding love in both the heterosexual and the homosexual contexts. Though there are many sexual encounters in his stories, he seems to be too much of the southern gentleman to go into graphic details. The romantic consistently trumps the carnal, and his ability to render same-sex love in a mainstream style, the depiction of friendship between gays and straights and between men and women (plus an underlying spirituality) made him popular in a multitude of communities.

In 2003 Harris published his memoir *What Becomes of the Brokenhearted*, a candid examination of his bouts with drugs and alcohol, failed love affairs, self-esteem issues, attempted suicide, therapy, coming to terms with his homosexuality, and the liberating effects of writing. As a result Harris, through his canon, has given voice to black gay, bisexual, and questioning men.

In 2000 Harris was inducted into the Arkansas Black Hall of Fame. In 2000 and 2001 he was named one of fifty-five Most Intriguing African Americans by *Ebony* magazine. Harris became a frequent college lecturer, a visiting professor in the English Department of his alma mater, and a novelist with millions of books in print.

While on a book tour in Los Angeles, Harris died in his hotel room, the apparent cause being heart disease. He was 54. At the time of his death, he had become a highly regarded activist and philanthropist in the black and black gay communities. His reader-friendly work has probably done more to advance the discussion of black gay and lesbian life within the black community than any other work since the writings of JAMES BALDWIN and AUDRE LORDE.

FURTHER READING

Harris, E. Lynn. *What Becomes of the Brokenhearted* (2003).

Carbado, Devon W., Dwight A. McBride, and Donald Weise. *Black like Us: A Century of Lesbian, Gay, and Bisexual African American Fiction* (2002).

STANLEY BENNETT CLAY

Harris, E. Victor (10 June 1905–23 Feb. 1978), baseball player, coach, and manager, was born Elander Victor Harris in Pensacola, Florida, the son of William Harris and Frances Calloway. Victor attended elementary school in the South until his family moved to Pittsburgh, Pennsylvania, in 1914. In 1922 he graduated from Schenley High School and in 1923 signed a professional baseball contract with the Cleveland Tate Stars. He played briefly with the Cleveland Browns and the Chicago American Giants of the Negro National League (NNL) before returning to Pittsburgh in 1925 as a member of the Homestead Grays, a team owned and managed by CUMBERLAND POSEY, Pittsburgh's most successful black businessman of the time. Harris spent twenty-two of the next twenty-four years in the Grays organization.

Having grown to five feet ten inches and 164 pounds, Harris batted left-handed and threw right-handed. A skillful outfielder and a lifetime .314 hitter he was best known as an aggressive base runner who would not hesitate to spike an opposing infielder. In his early playing days he was noted for a hot temper. Infielders on his own team asked him to be less aggressive so that they would not bear the brunt of opposing players' retaliation, and the umpire Jimmy Ahern once filed an assault charge against Harris. The charge was later dropped, and Harris matured; however, one of his temper tantrums would later prove fateful. A barnstorming club the Grays lacked a permanent home stadium. In a 1930 game at Pittsburgh's Forbes Field, Posey used portable lights for an experiment in night baseball. The Grays' catcher was injured in the first game of a doubleheader, and Harris refused to catch the second, convinced that he would not be able to see under the lights. Posey turned to an eighteen-year-old rookie, JOSH GIBSON, who would become one of the greatest players in the Negro Leagues, and with whom Harris would have a sometimes stormy relationship.

A salary dispute after the 1933 season led Harris to accept the overtures of GUS GREENLEE, who owned the Pittsburgh Crawfords of the NNL, the Grays' cross-town rival. Harris played left field and batted .360 that season on a team that featured Gibson, JUDY JOHNSON, OSCAR CHARLESTON, and SATCHEL PAIGE. When Posey allowed the Grays to join the NNL, Harris rejoined the club as player-manager for the 1935 season. Like many black players in the Jim Crow era, Harris often found work hard to come by in the off-season. In 1935 he managed the Newark Eagles in a series of exhibition matches in Puerto Rico. Harris returned to the Grays for the start of the 1936 season; that year he married Dorothy Smith, with whom he went on to have one daughter and one son. The next season Harris's team captured the first of nine straight NNL crowns. The next year Harris enjoyed one of his best seasons as a player. He hit .380 and was selected to hit leadoff in the annual East-West All-Star game, the most prestigious event in black baseball; Harris played or managed in nine of these games. The 1938 Grays—sporting talent such as Gibson, BUCK LEONARD, Sam Bankhead, and Edsell Walker—won more than 80 percent of their games and is thought by some to be the greatest team in Negro League history. In 1939 the Grays repeated their mastery of the NNL, and Harris played with a team of Negro League stars on an exhibition tour of Cuba in the off-season.

As a manager Harris displayed a different temperament than he exhibited as a youthful player. He was known for being quiet and demanding, and he was a strict disciplinarian. When Gibson returned to the Grays from a two-year stint in the Mexican League (1940–1941), Harris did not hesitate to pull him from the lineup because of Gibson's drinking problem. COOL PAPA BELL complained that Harris put him in the outfield every day in 1945, even though Bell suffered from arthritis. But Harris got results. The Grays' string of pennants did not end until 1946, though Harris did not manage the 1943 and 1944 teams, having taken time off to work in a defense plant. He continued to play in the outfield as well as manage and was selected to play in East-West games in 1942, 1943, and 1947. His 1948 Grays team again won the pennant, after which they quit the NNL and became once again an independent barn-storming team (they disbanded a short time later).

By then change was in the air, as JACKIE ROBINSON had broken professional baseball's color barrier in 1947 when he joined the Brooklyn Dodgers. Major league teams began to raid black talent and attendance at Negro League games sagged and marginally profitable teams folded. Harris spent 1949 as a coach for the Baltimore Elite Giants. In 1950, his last year in organized baseball, Harris managed the Birmingham Black Barons, whose star outfielder, WILLIE MAYS, would sign with the New York Giants.

Most Negro League teams collapsed after 1950, and the forty-five-year-old Harris was forced to seek other employment to support his family. No African American would manage in the major leagues until 1975. Harris eventually drifted to Pacioma, California, where he was a head custodian for the Castiac Union Schools. He died in Mission Hills, California.

FURTHER READING

Holway, John. *Voices from the Great Black Baseball Leagues* (1975).

Peterson Robert. *Only the Ball Was White* (1970).

Riley, James. *The All-Time All-Stars of Black Baseball* (1983).

This entry is taken from the *American National Biography* and is published here with the permission of the American Council of Learned Societies.

ROBERT E. WEIR

Harris, Eddie (20 Oct. 1936–5 Nov. 1996), jazz saxophonist, pianist, and composer, was born in Chicago, Illinois, to Walter Harris and Alice Harris. When his parents moved to the city in 1913, his father, originally from Cuba, worked in the stockyards, while his mother, a native of New Orleans, worked as a laundress. Harris lost his father when he was young and was raised by his mother. He began singing with South Side church choirs when he was five and also began taking piano lessons from his cousin, Bernice Benson.

Like many African American musicians in Chicago, Harris attended DuSable High School. He studied with the band director Walter Dyette, whose students included jazz musicians like Johnny Griffin and GENE AMMONS as well as Harris's classmates the bassist Richard Davis and the saxophonist John Gilmore. Dyette first taught Harris the marimba and the vibraphone and later the clarinet. But Harris was more interested in sports and good times. He rebelled against Dyette's strict discipline and was expelled from the band twice before transferring to Hyde Park High School. Harris hoped to attend a southern university on a sports scholarship, but his mother was worried about racial tensions in the South, so he chose instead to study music at Roosevelt University in Chicago.

Harris first performed professionally as a substitute for Gene Ammons's pianist at Chicago's Pershing Hotel. He would later lead his own group at the Pershing opposite AHMAD JAMAL's trio. Throughout the 1950s Harris played with Chicago's best jazz musicians as well as with visiting greats like LESTER YOUNG and ROY ELDRIDGE. He performed mostly mainstream jazz then. Nevertheless, his angular melodies and tight, controlled sound distinguished him from his fellow tenor saxophonists, especially other African American saxophonists like JOHN COLTRANE, who favored a rougher, more assertive tone and a more ecstatic approach to improvisation. Some criticized his playing, calling him the "black Stan Getz." Harris, however, had his own understanding of the tradition and possibilities of jazz. He felt that his fellow saxophonists were following in the footsteps of earlier players like CHU BERRY and COLEMAN HAWKINS, while he was emulating the very different sound of Lester Young as well as that of the trumpet. He sometimes said he was going for a brass effect and his search for that sound eventually led him to experiment with hybrid instruments, combining parts from both saxophones and trumpets.

In the late 1950s Harris was drafted into the army, and first served as an electrician; with the help of the trumpeter and composer Don Ellis, however, he quickly transferred to the Seventh Army Symphony Orchestra and Soldier's Show Company and performed throughout Germany and France with up-and-coming jazz musicians like the pianist Cedar Walton and the saxophonist and composer Don Menza. While in the military he also studied classical saxophone at the Paris Conservatory. After the army Harris lived briefly in New York City, where he performed frequently and supplemented his income accompanying dance classes. In the eyes of his peers he was quite successful, but he grew dissatisfied with the New York scene and returned to Chicago in 1960.

Living in Chicago allowed Harris to have more of a family life; he spent time with his mother, and he married Sarah Elizabeth Turner, with whom he had two daughters, Lolita Maria and Yvonne Marie. Living in Chicago also allowed Harris to expand his musical palette. There he found an African American working-class aesthetic that embraced a range of musical practices. The city had been home to Louis Armstrong, the gospel musician Thomas Andrew Dorsey, Chess Records, and the experimentalist Sun Ra. Audiences expected to be entertained by musicians who could play in a variety of styles. Harris, an experimenter himself, thrived in this eclectic environment. After turning down an offer to tour Europe with Quincy Jones, he embarked on a variety of projects and found commercial success. His 1961 album, *Exodus to Jazz*, on Chicago's Vee-Jay label, featured his arrangement of Ernest Gold's theme from the movie *Exodus*; this became jazz's first gold record. While pursuing commercial success, Harris also continued to explore the artistic possibilities of improvisation. With Muhal Richard Abrams he helped start the famous Workshop Band that gave rise to the Association for the Advancement of Creative Musicians, perhaps the most important organization of the black musical avant-garde.

In the 1960s Harris recorded jazz infused with the sounds of gospel, funk, and experimental improvisation. His composed and improvised melodies drew heavily on the blues as well as his modern "intervalistic" approach, making his best recordings simultaneously danceable, humorous, and artistically challenging. On *The In Sound* (1965) and *Mean Greens* (1966), Harris worked with a mainstream group that included the pianist Cedar Walton, the bassist Ron Carter, and the drummer Billy Higgins. Later in the decade he experimented with the electric saxophone and the Varitone signal processor. This work can be heard on *The Tender Storm* (1966), *The Electrifying Eddie Harris* (1967), and *Free Speech* (1969). Harris's impromptu performance with Les McCann at the 1969 Montreux Jazz Festival resulted in the live recording *Swiss Movement* that became a hit with both jazz and R&B audiences.

In 1969 Harris moved to Los Angeles and composed music for *The Bill Cosby Show* from 1969 to 1971. He also released several funk-oriented albums that featured his saxophone-trumpet hybrids. Throughout the decade he sought to cross musical, cultural, and commercial boundaries: he performed in Ghana and appeared in the African documentary *Soul to Soul* in the early 1970s; he recorded *E. H. in the UK* with the British rock musicians Steve Winwood and Jeff Beck; and he released two comedy albums in the mid-1970s. In 1971 he published *The Intervalistic Concept for All Single Line Wind Instruments*.

In the mid-1980s Harris embraced a more mainstream approach to jazz, recording with acoustic groups for European labels. Recordings like his 1990 Enja release *There Was a Time (Echo of Harlem)* helped reaffirm his standing as a serious jazz artist. At the same time, a new generation of funk-influenced musicians and acid jazz artists like Martin, Medeski, and Wood were rediscovering his work. In 1994 John Scofield featured Harris on his album *Hand Jive*, and this led to their performance together at the 1995 Chicago Jazz Festival.

Toward the end of his life, Harris suffered from several health problems, including bone cancer and kidney disease, but he remained musically active. Though criticized by jazz purists for, at times, turning away from the prevailing artistic standards of bebop and instead drawing on the popular sounds of funk and electrified instruments, he left behind a diverse body of work that at its best combined funky accessibility and artistic sophistication, a legacy that influenced musicians into the twenty-first century.

FURTHER READING

Bourgoin, Suzanne M. *Contemporary Musicians: Profiles of the People in Music, Volume 15* (1996).

Dorn, Joel. Introduction and interview with Eddie Harris accompanying *Artist's Choice: The Eddie Harris Anthology* (1993).

Tesser, Neil. "Blowing His Horn: A Requiem for Innovation; Inventor, and Brilliant Stylist Eddie Harris," *Chicago Reader* (29 Nov. 1996).

JOHN HARRIS-BEHLING

Harris, Emma E. (9 Oct. 1875?–1938) a singer who lived for over thirty years in Russia, both under Tsar Nicholas and during the first decades of the

Soviet Union, was born in Augusta, Georgia, according to her 1901 passport application. Some accounts give her year of birth as 1870. Multiple passport applications give 1875. Census records suggest she may have been the daughter of John and Ann Harris, who in 1880 were illiterate tenant farmers in Carnesville, Franklin County, northwest of Augusta. The subsequent history of her older brothers, Andrew J. and Henry Harris, and younger sister Lulu, are unknown.

In 1892 Harris married Joseph B. Harris (no relation), moving with him to Brooklyn, where she worked as a domestic and directed a Baptist church choir. She went to Europe in May 1901 as a member of the "Louisiana Amazon Guards," a singing group assembled by the German promoter Paule Kohn-Wöllner. The troupe also included Fannie Wise, Ollie Burgoyne, Virginia Shepherd, and Coretta Alfred. After a few weeks they severed ties with Kohn-Wöllner, appearing during the next eighteen months in Germany, Bohemia, Austria, Hungary, and Denmark. Several of the singers, including Harris, then sang with the "Creole Belles," led by Georgette Harvey, in Russia during 1904–1905 (Southern, p. 306). Joseph Harris died in New York in 1907.

After the failure of the 1905 revolution, the "Emma Harris Trio" (with Fannie Smith and Corretta Alfred), performed for several more years in large cities in Russia. There are a number of versions of Harris's life in Russia. Most appear to be based on what she told American visitors to the Soviet Union, in the early 1930s. The most detailed published accounts have been presented by the writer LANGSTON HUGHES, the black Bolshevik HARRY HAYWOOD HALL, and the expatriate and foreign correspondent HOMER SMITH. Harris also gave several interviews after her return to the United States.

When Smith returned to America, while Alfred married a Russian theater director, Harris continued touring as a concert singer, marrying her manager, Ivanovitch Mizikin, in 1911. In 1913 they established a residence in Kharkov, purchasing a chain of theaters, which Mizikin managed while Harris continued concert tours. She seems to have lived well, later telling Hughes, "I used to have me six servants and a boot boy. Now, best I can do is one old baba older'n me, part time" (Hughes, p. 85). Stories recounted by Americans who met her later in Soviet Russia, that she had been mistress of a grand duke, or in charge of a high-class house of prostitution, appear to be conjectural.

Mizikin was drafted when Germany declared war on Russia in 1914. Harris sold their property in Kharkov, buying a fifteen-room mansion in Moscow. She recounted turning it into a *pension*, which among other guests housed American Red Cross officials staying in Moscow, and for a brief time, the news reporter Walter Duranty. According to Heywood, shortly after the Bolshevik Revolution of October/November 1917, the house had been raided by the Cheka, the revolutionary secret police. Many Tsarist officers and "White Guards" found there were shot following brief interrogations. Harris was set free, after being warned about the company she was keeping, and informed the only reason she had not been shot was that she was a Negro woman.

Harris recounted, after returning to the United States, that she had been in a crowd in Red Square addressed by Vladimir Ilyich Lenin in March 1918, shortly after the Brest-Litovsk treaty with Germany and Austria. Extending his hand directly to her, Lenin said, "The ideal of Communism is to open the road for all the downtrodden races of the world. For you, comrade, especially, as we regard your race the most downtrodden in the world. We want you to feel when you come to Russia that you are a human being" (Writers Project, p. 2).

During the civil war of 1917–1919, she served as a nurse with the American Red Cross, and also the Red Army in the Ukraine. She served as an interpreter and taught English to Soviet officials, and assisted her husband, who had survived the war and become a director for the Soyuse Film Company. Divorcing Mizikin in 1929, she worked in a silk factory, becoming forewoman, and toured the country as a speaker for the International Labor Defense. She philosophically told Hughes, "I'm like a cat with nine lives, honey. I always land on my feet—been doing it all my life wherever I am. These Bolsheviks ain't gonna kill me" (Hughes, p. 84). She was heard cheerfully repeating jokes in public that implied it would be a great thing if Stalin died—which even before the purge trials most Russians wouldn't dare repeat.

Known to Russians as "Tovarisch Emma," she made public appearances denouncing American race prejudice in fluent Russian, hailing the workers of the world, the Soviet Union, and Stalin. After speaking to massive rallies on behalf of the SCOTTSBORO BOYS, she expressed genuine concern in personal conversations, "They ought to turn them colored boys loose." When a theatrical troupe arrived from the United States to make a movie, tentatively titled *Black and White*, she welcomed them at the train station with the exclamation, "Lord a'mighty, my people don' arrived."

In almost the same breath as she expressed sympathy with the Scottsboro Boys, Harris often muttered, "I want to go home." Harris offered Hughes a counterpoint to the notion of a vast conspiracy to sabotage Soviet industry, and transportation, "Man, last night there was a wreck right in the depot—one train going out, another coming in, both on the same track. These thick-headed comrades don't know how to run no trains."

Harris knew how to work the black markets, obtaining scarce food to serve up southern home cooking for the "Negro worker comrades" and aspiring actors, once or twice a month. She had several months to get to know the film troupe due to delays in filming. After Hughes dissected the film script for its ignorance of American culture, efforts to revise it were never completed, partly because the Soviet government found diplomatic recognition by the United States more valuable than a film denouncing American racism.

Harris returned via Hamburg to New York in 1933, arriving on 31 August on the S.S. *Milwaukee*, after establishing citizenship in Riga, Latvia, 17 August of the same year. Four years later she regretted returning, telling an interviewer in 1937, "Lenin was right. There is work for me in the Soviet Union as a human being. I don't relish the idea of dying here—a maid or a home relief client" (Writers Project, p. 6). She was unsuccessful at raising funds to return, and died a few months after the interview.

FURTHER READING

Haywood, Harry. *Black Bolshevik* (1978).

Hughes, Langston. "The Mammy of Moscow." In *I Wonder As I Wander: An Autobiographical Journey* (1994).

Lotz, Ranier E. "The Louisiana Troupes." *The Black Perspective in Music* 11, no. 2 (fall 1983): 134–137.

Smith, Homer. "Emma: Mammy of Moscow." In *Black Man in Red Russia: A Memoir* (1964).

Southern, Eileen. *The Music of Black Americans: A History* (1997).

Writers' Program (New York). *Negroes of New York Collection* (1936–1941).

CHARLES ROSENBERG

Harris, Franco (7 Mar. 1950–), professional football player and entrepreneur, was born in Fort Dix, New Jersey, to an African American father, Cad Harris, and an Italian mother, Gina Parenti. Franco, one of eight children, had three brothers (Mario, Kelly, and Pete, who played safety at Pennsylvania State University in 1977–1978, when he was named a first-team All American, and in 1980) and four sisters (Daniela, Alvara, Marisa, and Luanna). His parents met in Italy near the end of World War II and eventually settled in the United States. Harris was a star running back at Rancocas Valley Regional High School in Mount Holly, New Jersey. Graduating in 1968, Harris attended Pennsylvania State University on a football scholarship. As a freshman at Penn State, Harris, who was 6 feet, 2 inches, and 220 pounds, earned playing time primarily as a fullback, blocking for the All-American running back and future National Football League (NFL) second-round draft pick Lydell Mitchell. In his career as a Nittany Lion, Harris rushed 380 times for 2,002 yards (a 5.3-yard average) and scored 24 touchdowns. Upon graduating in 1972 with a B.S. degree in Food Service and Administration, Harris was selected by the Pittsburgh Steelers as the thirteenth overall selection of the 1972 NFL draft. In his rookie season he earned Associated Press and United Press International Rookie of the Year honors by rushing 188 times for 1,055 yards (5.6 per carry) and scoring 13 touchdowns (10 rushing).

Franco Harris taking a break between plays. (AP Images.)

While he did not possess the speed of JIM BROWN, considered by many the NFL's best running back, Harris had a similar ability to change direction and cut quickly to avoid defenders. The most memorable event of Harris's rookie season came in a divisional play-off game against the Oakland Raiders, when he made what the Pittsburgh sportscaster Myron Cope named "the Immaculate Reception." With only twenty-two seconds remaining in the game and Oakland holding a 7–6 lead, Pittsburgh quarterback Terry Bradshaw tried to pass the ball downfield on fourth down and ten yards to go to John "Frenchy" Fuqua. Oakland safety Jack Tatum broke up the pass, however, sending the ball away from Fuqua and toward the turf. Just before it hit the ground, Harris, who had been trailing the play, snagged the ball around his shoe tops at the Raiders' forty-two yard line and ran downfield into the Oakland end zone with five seconds remaining in the game. Pittsburgh's sideline celebrated, Oakland's protested, and at first game officials did not know what to rule. They consulted as a group and decided that the ball had not been deflected from Fuqua to Harris, which would have meant that two consecutive offensive players touched the ball and thereby made the play invalid, but in fact from Tatum to Harris. As a result the play was ruled a touchdown. In the early twenty-first century, controversy still swirled around the play, one of the most frequently rebroadcast and dramatic conclusions to a game in league history.

While he was named an all-pro only once, in 1977, Harris made nine straight Pro Bowls from 1972 to 1980 and set a record (surpassing the legendary Brown) by rushing for more than one thousand yards in eight consecutive seasons. Along with fullback Rocky Bleier, Harris led a potent running attack that gained large chunks of yardage and kept the opponent's offense off the field, making the team's daunting defense that much more effective. Harris led the Steelers to four Super Bowl victories (1974, 1975, 1978, and 1979). In 1975 he became both the first African American and the first Italian American to be named most valuable player of the Super Bowl by rushing 34 times for 158 yards and a touchdown in the Steelers' 16–6 win over the Minnesota Vikings in Super Bowl IX. An integral part of those great Steelers teams, Harris set a Super Bowl career record of 101 carries for 354 yards. In addition his four Super Bowl rushing touchdowns tied for the second-most in NFL history. While critics frequently pointed out Harris's tendency to run out of bounds instead of

trying to plow through tacklers for extra yards, his effective running style drew legions of fans among Pittsburgh's Italian American population, the most ardent of whom donned army helmets with Harris's number 32 on them and called themselves "Franco's Italian Army."

In all Harris played thirteen seasons in the NFL (twelve with the Steelers and one with the Seattle Seahawks). He set or tied more than two dozen records during his career and totaled 12,120 rushing yards on 2,949 carries (4.1 yards per carry) and 91 rushing touchdowns. In June 2007 his total rushing yards stood as the eleventh-most in NFL history, and his rushing touchdown total stood as the tenth-most. In addition he caught 307 passes for 2,287 yards and 9 touchdowns. Although his jersey was not officially retired, no Steelers player wore his number 32 between 1983, when Harris left the team, and 2007. He was inducted into the Pro Football Hall of Fame in Canton, Ohio, in 1990, his first year of eligibility. In 1993 he was inducted into the New Jersey Hall of Fame, which honors notables from all fields who were born in New Jersey, and in 1999 he ranked eighty-third on the Sporting News's list of the one hundred greatest football players.

After his retirement in 1984, Harris enjoyed success in the food service industry. He first established a small distribution company called Franco's All Naturèl, and in 1990 he founded Super Bakery, Inc., with the intent of making it "the leader in bakery nutrition" (Pennsylvania State University). The U.S. Department of Agriculture deemed two of his products, Super Donuts and Super Muffins, suitable for school lunch programs, and Super Bakery's products were sold to the military and in all fifty states to schools as well as to the general public. In addition in 1996 Harris purchased Baltimore's Parks Sausage Company, the first publicly held black-owned business in the United States, in an attempt to preserve an important piece of African American history after the company had to shut down due to heavy debts. For his efforts Harris received the Byron "Whizzer" White Humanitarian Award, the NFL Man of the Year Award, the American Academy of Achievement Golden Plate Award, the National Urban League's Whitney M. Young Award, and the National Multiple Sclerosis Volunteer of the Year Award. He also remained close to Penn State University. In 1981 he was named a Penn State Distinguished Alumnus and in 2001 received the university's School of Hospitality Management's Alumnus of the Year Award. In 2006 he received the Alumni Fellow Award from the Penn State Alumni

Association. He established an endowed scholarship at the university for students in the School of Hospitality Management and was an advisory board member of the school's Center for Food Innovation.

FURTHER READING

Dubner, Steven J. *Confessions of a Hero-Worshiper* (2003).

Kowet, Don. *Franco Harris* (1977).

DANIEL DONAGHY

Harris, James H. (c. 1828–28 Jan. 1898), Civil War soldier and Medal of Honor recipient, was a native of St. Mary's County, Maryland. Though nothing certain is known of Harris's early life, he was likely born into slavery and may have remained enslaved until the Civil War. Harris enlisted in the Union Army on 14 February 1864, joining the 38th U.S. Colored Troop Regiment (USCT) at Great Mills, Maryland, stating his age as thirty-six years and his occupation as that of a farmer. A number of USCT regiments recruited men, many of them formerly enslaved, from the Tidewater region of Maryland and Virginia. Among the other new recruits of these regiments were fellow St. Mary's County resident WILLIAM H. BARNES, as well as CHRISTIAN FLEETWOOD, ALFRED B. HILTON, and CHARLES VEALE (4th USCT), Decatur Dorsey (39th USCT), and MILES JAMES (36th USCT). All of these men, like James Harris and a number of others, would also earn the Medal of Honor in the near future. Perhaps due to his maturity, he being slightly older than many of his fellow recruits, Harris early on demonstrated leadership skills and abilities. He was promoted to corporal on 25 July 1864 and subsequently to sergeant on 10 September 1864, just weeks before the battle that would gain personal recognition not only for him, but also for the men of the USCT regiments as a whole.

By the fall of 1864, elaborate trenches and fortifications were built by the Confederates to keep the Union Army at bay around their capital of Richmond, Virginia. However, General Ulysses Grant was prepared to win at all costs; he had the manpower to sustain heavy losses, as demonstrated at the bloody Battle of Cold Harbor earlier that year. Among the troops available to Grant late in the war were the soldiers of the U.S. Colored Troop regiments, consisting of free blacks and former slaves. By the war's end, nearly 179,000 free blacks and former slaves, men like James Harris, had served in USCT regiments and eventually constituted 10 percent of the Union Army's manpower and suffered over seventeen hundred casualties. While the issue of using such troops was a controversial one and the fighting effectiveness of the black man was questioned by many, the ensuing Battle of New Market Heights would soon dispel all such doubts.

Late September 1864 found the men of the 38th USCT stationed near New Market Heights just south of Richmond, Virginia, on the James River. As the southern anchor in the Confederate chain of fortifications surrounding Richmond, New Market Heights was a keystone in the Confederate defense. The Battle of New Market Heights was to be a two-pronged assault against Confederate forts on both sides of the James River. The northern attack began on the morning of 29 September 1864 and would prove to be the Union's only success in a battle that lasted two days and cost five thousand casualties. Despite heavy fire and fierce hand-to-hand combat that led to 50 percent casualties in some regiments, black troops led the way when their officers were shot down and overwhelmed the Confederates at Fort Harrison, the only fort to be captured of four that were the Union's objectives in the battle. Among the first three men to enter the enemy works was Sergeant James H. Harris, along with fellow 38th USCT soldiers Sergeant EDWARD RATCLIFF and Private William H. Barnes, as well as Private JAMES GARDINER of the 36th USCT. Wounded in the fight, Harris was subsequently awarded the Medal of Honor, along with twelve other USCT soldiers.

Following the Battle of New Market Heights little is known of James H. Harris's life for certain. He continued his military service for several more years, being reduced to private for unknown reasons in July 1865 and subsequently mustered out of the service with the disbandment of his regiment at Indianola, Texas, on 25 January 1867. Harris later returned to his home state, though his exact residence is unknown. Federal Census records for 1880 indicate that Harris may have been the same man who lived at Harris Lot, in Charles County, Maryland, just south of Washington D.C., working as a farmer with his wife Ally and children Mary and Henry. Upon his death, Harris was buried in the Arlington National Cemetery, where a Medal of Honor headstone marks his final resting place.

FURTHER READING

Hanna, Charles W. *African American Recipients of the Medal of Honor* (2002).

GLENN ALLEN KNOBLOCK

Harris, James Henry (1830/1832?–31 May 1891),
teacher, editor, public official, state legislator, and
gifted orator, was born in Granville County, North
Carolina, of unknown parents. Indeed, little is
known for certain of his childhood. By some reports,
he was born free; by others, he was freed from slavery in 1848, in connection with a trade apprenticeship. Decades later, in 1883, he listed himself in his
legislative biographical sketch (Tomlinson, 70) as
"self-educated," although he may have studied at
Oberlin College in Ohio as an adult.

In 1850 Harris still lived with his employer,
Charles Allen, a white carpenter and upholsterer,
near Oxford, North Carolina. He married Isabella
Hinton in Wake County, North Carolina, on
3 December 1851; little is known of his wife, and
it is believed that they had no children. Harris
soon moved to Raleigh to open his own upholstery business, but he left the state in 1856 for Ohio,
reportedly settling in Oberlin, near a group of
other North Carolinians. By 1862 he was traveling
in Canada and Africa, visiting African American
émigré settlements in Liberia and Sierra Leone.
What motivated him to make these journeys and
how they were financed are unknown.

James Henry Harris, c. 1900. (Library of Congress.)

After contracting a serious fever in Africa, he
moved to Indianapolis, Indiana, in 1863, where he
helped recruit volunteers for the Twenty-eighth
Regiment, U.S. Colored Troops, at the request of
Governor Levi P. Morton.

In mid-1865 Harris returned to North Carolina
to teach for the New England Freedmen's Aid
Society and to raise funds for destitute freedmen.
He also entered Republican political life, serving in
the state's general assembly and as a Raleigh alderman. In the opinion of the late-nineteenth-century
writer Jerome Dowd, Harris was "the most prominent and influential colored man of the Republican
party of our state" (Dowd, 70). Harris turned
down the post of U.S. minister to Haiti, offered by
President Andrew Johnson in 1867, and a year later
he declined the Republican nomination for the
Fourth District seat in Congress.

Two years later, Harris's first active campaign for
Congress failed, although he contested his loss to
the Democrat Sion H. Rogers before the U.S. House
of Representatives, which eventually seated Rogers
in 1872. Harris was then appointed by President
Ulysses S. Grant as deputy U.S. tax collector, and he
also served as a Grant presidential elector that year.
Grant, however, did not carry North Carolina.

He was a fixture at Republican national conventions for two decades, first serving as a Fourth
District delegate in 1868 and every four years thereafter until his death. On the national level, Harris
served as deputy president of the National Equal
Rights Convention in the late 1860s, as president
of the National Convention of Colored Men in
1869, and as vice president of the National Black
Convention in 1877. At home he was a delegate to
the North Carolina Freedmen's Convention in 1865,
president of the state Equal Rights League in 1866,
and a speaker for the Republican Congressional
Committee in 1867. An organizer of the Union
League in North Carolina, he toured northern
states in 1868 with Judge Albion W. Tourgée to raise
funds for North Carolina's destitute.

In early 1868 Harris represented Wake County
as one of ten black delegates at the convention
that rewrote the state's constitution. In April 1868
Harris was elected as a Republican to the state legislature from Wake County, serving until 1870; he
was re-elected to that post in 1882. Harris chaired
the influential house Committee on Propositions
and Grievances (1868–1870) and later served on the
house Committee for Internal Improvements and
Railroads. Between house terms, he represented
the Eighteenth District (Wake County) in the state

senate from 1872 to 1874, serving on the senate Committee for Deaf, Dumb and Blind Asylum.

Described by a white chronicler of the time as "well posted in political matters" (Tomlinson, 71) and possessing "rare mental faculties which have made him conspicuous despite an imperfect education," Harris enjoyed a wide following as a legislator (Dowd, 70).

His most notable moment, perhaps, came in January 1870, in a speech supporting a proposal to reorganize the state's militia, intended to suppress intimidation of African Americans by the Ku Klux Klan. "I ask only justice and appeal to you now as men, as upright, honest and just men, as human beings, to pass this measure for the protection of the innocent," Harris declared. "While we [African Americans] are willing to submit to the laws, we are not willing to bear the shackles of political slavery" (*North Carolina Standard*, 18 Jan. 1870). His position on the militia issue was not universally popular, and Harris was angered by one Raleigh newspaper's willingness to compare his Union League activists to Klan terrorists and lynch mobs.

With the backing of most African American legislators, the bill passed. In 1869 Harris also introduced a successful bill prohibiting the use of disguises, aimed specifically at the Klan.

Harris, a shrewd investor, was also prospering personally, having acquired four thousand dollars in real estate near Raleigh by the time of the 1870 federal census. But his success did not dampen his generosity for others. Throughout his career, Harris backed many social causes, particularly education for freedmen, prison reform, and protection for women and orphans. He also built a settlement for fourteen needy families on his property. In 1877 he was elected president of the State Colored Education Convention. He generally pursued a moderate political course, although he encouraged African Americans to fight vigorously for political rights and legal equality. He was not afraid to oppose popular measures on principle. In 1879 Harris opposed mass migration by the state's black farmers to Indiana and Kansas, despite a new law forcing tenants to pay all debts before receiving crop payments; he later opposed emigration by southern blacks to Africa.

In 1878 Harris revived old hopes of congressional service by moving to Warren County, in the "Black Second" District, where he was drafted as an independent Republican candidate by those opposing the party's regular nominee, JAMES EDWARD O'HARA. Harris drew nearly four thousand votes

away from O'Hara, narrowly tipping the election to the white Democrat W. H. Kitchin.

Harris returned to Raleigh in 1880 where he remained influential politically. First appointed a Raleigh alderman in 1868, and reelected in 1875 and 1877, he served a fourth term in 1887 and also served as a local tax assessor and justice of the peace. An active parishioner of St. Ambrose Episcopal Church, Harris also supervised the state's Deaf and Dumb Asylum for African Americans for four years. During the 1880s he edited and published the *North Carolina Republican* and wrote for Raleigh's *Gazette*. Sometime after 1883, Harris was married a second time, to Bettie Miller of Raleigh. They were the parents of one daughter, Florence, who died in 1889, and a son, David. Harris's last known public address came at the Negro State Convention in August 1890.

Harris moved to Washington, D.C., in 1891 but died there soon afterward of natural causes and was returned to Raleigh for burial. In a front-page article, the 2 June 1891 Raleigh *News and Observer* described him as a "prominent Republican politician" with oratorical skills "unusually gifted for a colored man." In 1975 a state highway historical marker was erected in his honor, near the site of his Raleigh home.

FURTHER READING

The James H. Harris Papers are located in the North Carolina State Archives, Division of Archives and History, in Raleigh.

Anderson, Eric. *Race and Politics in North Carolina, 1872–1901: The Black Second* (1981).

Crow, Jeffrey J., Paul D. Escott, and Flora J. Hatley. *A History of African Americans in North Carolina* (1992).

Dowd, Jerome. *Sketches of Prominent Living North Carolinians* (1888).

Foner, Eric. *Freedom's Lawmakers: A Directory of Black Officeholders during Reconstruction* (1993).

Kenzer, Robert C. *Enterprising Southerners: Black Economic Success in North Carolina, 1865–1915* (1997).

Tomlinson, J. S. *Assembly Sketch Book, Session 1883, North Carolina* (1883).

Obituaries: Raleigh, NC, *News and Observer*, 2 June 1891.

BENJAMIN R. JUSTESEN

Harris, John Benjamin (15 Jan. 1927–), consumer markets specialist and business school professor, was born in Chesterfield County, Virginia, to Thomas D.

Harris Jr. and Georgia Laws Carter. Thomas Harris was a messenger for the Atlantic Coast Line Railroad and also worked as an embalmer, and Georgia Carter Harris was a homemaker. Thomas stressed the importance of education for his three children, tutoring them in math, anatomy, and English after dinner. Harris attended Kingsland Elementary School (one of the black primary and secondary schools funded by Sears, Roebuck philanthropist Julius Rosenwald to improve education for black southerners) in Chesterfield County, Virginia, and D. Webster Davis High School, the Virginia State College laboratory school, in Petersburg, Virginia. While in high school, Harris earned a certificate in barber practice and science. He cut soldiers' hair on the nearby Fort Lee army base to help pay for his education at Virginia State College.

Harris's education at Virginia State was interrupted by World War II, when he joined the army air force. In 1946 he left the 2532d Army Air Force Pilot School at Randolph Field, Texas, to join the Reserve Officers' Training Corps and returned to school at Virginia State; two years later he was commissioned as a second lieutenant. After graduation he was recalled and served in the Korean War, after which he rose to the rank of captain. He earned four bronze campaign stars.

While at Virginia State, Harris gave careful consideration to his future career. As a barber, he earned substantially more than the average student, and he knew that continuing in this area would be lucrative. Simultaneously, through cutting hair, he was exposed to some of the most prominent African Americans in Virginia, including leading businessmen, professors, and the university president. Through this exposure and the influence of his parents, he decided to pursue a more traditional professional field, such as law or economics.

Close to graduation at Virginia State, in August 1950, Harris met with Professor George G. Singleton, the chair of the business department, to discuss his future. Singleton pointed out that Harris could not attend graduate schools in Virginia in either law or economics, because all the professional schools were exclusively for whites. Singleton also explained, however, that Virginia would pay for him to study these fields elsewhere. In the late 1930s the National Association for the Advancement of Colored People had successfully sued the State of Maryland because the University of Maryland law school excluded African Americans, and the state did not provide an alternative option for law school for these students. In the hope of staving off

similar lawsuits, several southern states, Virginia included, began paying fees for black students who attended graduate schools in other states. Knowing this, Singleton suggested that Harris attend his own alma mater, New York University (NYU), to earn a master's in business administration. While jobs in economics were scarce for African Americans in 1950, Harris's father concurred with Singleton, suggesting that employment opportunities would open up in the near future, and that Harris should prepare by seeking out the best education he could. After his service in Korea, he attended NYU.

One of the requirements of NYU's MBA program was to work within the industry he had chosen to study, in this case, marketing. Harris "pounded the streets for a month" and applied for more than one hundred positions but was unable to obtain employment within the white marketing firms of New York. Harris said of NYU, "I received a superb education but no help in placement" (Harris interview). Business opportunities were still segregated in 1950s New York, so, with the help of a friend who was a police officer, Harris began to look for a job within the large, black-owned businesses in Harlem. He learned that the Woodside Hotel, on Seventh Avenue between 145th and 146th streets, needed an assistant manager. Along with the Hotel Theresa and the Braddock Hotel, the Woodside was one of the few places in New York that catered to the black elite. Harris got the job and while working there met JOE WILLIAMS, LIONEL LEO HAMPTON, COUNT BASIE, DUKE ELLINGTON, JACKIE ROBINSON, LENA HORNE, ELLA FITZGERALD, SARAH VAUGHAN, and numerous black business professionals. He finished his MBA in 1955, writing his thesis on "Consumer Advertising to the Washington, D.C., Negro Market."

On 2 September 1950 Harris married RUTH COLES HARRIS, who later became the first black female certified public accountant in Virginia, and they had two children, John Benjamin Jr. and Vita Michelle. Upon finishing his MBA, Harris returned to Virginia to be with his family. After a brief period working in advertising for the Richmond *Afro-American* newspaper, 15 June to 15 September, he was hired as an assistant professor of business and economics as well as the director of publicity for Virginia Union University in September 1955. In 1968 he moved to his alma mater, Virginia State College, now renamed Virginia State University, to teach marketing.

In the late 1960s the civil rights movement finally brought about the changes in career opportunities that Harris, his parents, and his mentors had anticipated in the early 1950s. At long last, major corporations became interested in the African American market, and Harris had the educational background and professional expertise to fill the newly recognized niche. One of his close friends, William J. Haskins, had become vice president of the National Urban League, and he arranged for Harris to serve as a consultant on African American marketing to many major corporations. During the late 1960s and early 1970s Harris was in demand by major corporations, which sought his expertise on black consumer tastes. While his family stayed in Richmond, he spent several summer breaks working for corporations: he was a special projects officer for IBM in New York; an advertising planner for the Eastman Kodak Company in Rochester, New York; a markets adviser to the vice president at Pillsbury in Minneapolis; an assistant account executive at Benton & Bowles Advertising Agency in New York; and an assistant brand manager at the Procter & Gamble Company in Cincinnati.

Harris's expertise was also in demand by the government, and he served three Virginia governors. In 1972 Harris was appointed by Governor A. Linwood Holton as special assistant to the governor for minority business enterprise. He was only the second African American to be appointed to serve in the executive branch by a Virginia governor. In this role, he was instrumental in the development of the nation's first state Office of Minority Business Enterprise. Harris was reappointed by two other governors: Mills E. Godwin Jr. (in May 1974) and John N. Dalton (in September 1978). The federal Office of Minority Business Enterprise (OMBE) had been established by Richard Nixon, whose 1968 presidential campaign, coming on the heels of the Civil Rights Act of 1964, emphasized the importance of "black capitalism." While Nixon rejected the Great Society programs of the Lyndon Baines Johnson administration, he focused on black entrepreneurship, promoting "black capitalism" and setting off on a campaign to create "100 Black Millionaires." The OMBE fit Nixon's views regarding improving opportunities for African Americans.

In his ten years working for the state, during which time he took a leave from academia, Harris was involved in more than $1 billion worth of business activity between the state and the minority business sector, including ensuring that minority-owned contractors participated in highway contracts and that black-owned banks became depositories for Virginia. Harris also served on the Southern Growth Policies Board, which addressed economic issues in seventeen southern states, from 1971 to 1977, including two years as treasurer. As a member of the board, he met with most of the governors of the southern states, including visits to the mansions of the Alabama governor George Wallace and the Georgia governor Jimmy Carter. In 1974 he was seated next to Rosalynn Carter when Governor Carter announced, at a dinner in Atlanta, that he would seek the U.S. presidency. Harris immediately gave Mrs. Carter one dollar and told her that he wanted to be the first to contribute to Governor Carter's campaign.

Harris's expertise was also in demand on the federal level. He served on Nixon's Minority Socio-Economic Staff for Minority Enterprise, and in 1978 he testified before the White House Conference on Balanced National Growth and Economic Development. In 1980 he participated in the White House Conference on Small Business.

After leaving the state government in 1982, Harris returned to his position as a marketing professor at Virginia State. Because there were so few opportunities in marketing and advertising for black students, classes and programs in marketing at black colleges had been rare through the 1970s. Harris pushed the state to develop these programs and persuaded it to add a marketing degree program to the business school at VSU in the 1980s. In 1985 he earned the Outstanding Teacher Award from the VSU chapter of the Student National Business League. In the early 1990s he established a chapter of the American Marketing Association at the school.

Harris never stopped seeking opportunities to learn and share his knowledge: he earned certificates in various marketing and business fields from Stanford, Howard, Princeton, Virginia State, and Case-Western Reserve universities as well as Claremont-McKenna College and the University of Chicago. In 1974 he was chosen as a Howard University West Africa American Fellow—one of thirty professors from historically black colleges who were chosen to study in West Africa. He served on the Virginia Governor's Advisory Board of Economists from 1990 to 1998 and retired from academia in 1996.

FURTHER READING

Some information in this article comes from author interviews with John Benjamin Harris conducted in January and March 2004.

Kotlowski, Dean J. *Nixon's Civil Rights* (2002).

Tushnet, Mark V. *The NAACP's Legal Strategy against Segregated Education, 1925–1950* (2005).

Weems, Robert E., Jr. *Desegregating the Dollar: African American Consumerism in the Twentieth Century* (1998).

THERESA A. HAMMOND

Harris, Little Benny (23 Apr. 1919–11 Feb. 1975), jazz musician and composer, was born Benjamin Michel Harris in New York City to parents about whom little is known, although an unconfirmed report claimed that his father was a Panamanian Indian named Cholmondeley, not Harris. At the age of twelve Harris began playing French horn and E-flat mellophone in a band sponsored by the *New York Daily Mirror*. After taking up the trumpet he toured with a band in Pennsylvania at age fifteen, but he was fired for paying too much attention to girls. Harris described himself as a tough kid who boxed professionally.

In 1937 he met DIZZY GILLESPIE, who two years later found him a job in TINY BRADSHAW's big band. Around that time Harris got to know CHARLIE PARKER, who at some point lived at Harris's family home, and he subsequently made Gillespie aware of Parker's fine recordings of 1941–1942 with JAY MCSHANN's band. After playing in EARL HINES's big band from early 1941 until June of that year, Harris joined the alto saxophonist Pete Brown's sextet at Kelly's Stable in New York, and he then played with Benny Carter's small group and big band. Early in 1943 he rejoined Hines, whose band by then included Gillespie and Parker.

Compared to his famous friends Harris was a lesser light in the development of the bebop style during informal sessions at Minton's Playhouse and Monroe's Uptown House in Harlem. According to Al Tinney, the pianist at Monroe's, Harris was obsessed with the song "How High the Moon." From this obsession came a bop theme, "Ornithology" (based on "How High the Moon"), which Harris and Parker probably wrote in collaboration.

Harris left Hines in August 1943 to work with DON REDMAN's big band and then quickly returned to Hines, but his lip muscles were not strong enough to keep up with the rigorous playing schedule, and this stay was another brief one. In 1944 he played alongside THELONIOUS MONK in COLEMAN HAWKINS's group at the Yacht Club on Fifty-second Street, played and recorded in Boyd Raeburn's orchestra, and in December recorded a few titles with a group led by the pianist Clyde Hart. These recordings include Harris's bop theme "Little Benny" (based on "I Got Rhythm"), which was later retitled "Crazeology" in a version by Parker, "Bud's Bubble"

in a version by BUD POWELL, and "King Kong" on a reissue of Hart's session. Early in 1945 Harris played in OSCAR PETTIFORD's bop group at the Spotlite in New York. He began a brief period with JOHN KIRBY's swing sextet in June, and with DON BYAS in November he made three more recordings as a soloist: "How High the Moon," "Donby," and "Byas-a-Drink." "Donby," based on "Perdido," begins with a thematic pattern composed by Harris and subsequently heard on many renditions of "Perdido" and alternate melody lines based on its chord changes. At year's end he played at Manhattan's Three Deuces with the alto saxophonist Johnny Bothwell.

Little is known of Harris after this time. He performed at an all-star bop session in 1948, played in Gillespie's big band in 1950, and worked with Parker in 1952. He traveled to Sacramento, California, and in 1961 to San Francisco, where he expressed bitterness over having been deprived of composer royalties that he now recognized were his due. He died in San Francisco.

The jazz entrepreneur Monte Kay and the writer Max Harrison support an assessment of Harris by the saxophonist BUDD JOHNSON: "his thoughts were always ahead of his chops; he knew more than he could play." The critic Jim Burns offers a more skeptical view, arguing that Harris scarcely deserves credit for unrealized thought and that his significance rests solely on his composing a few well-known themes. His recordings as a soloist support this view: Harris was no more than a competent player, with a pleasant tone, a modest and clean sense of melody, and a gentle sense of swing. He shared with Parker a fondness for inserting quotations from diverse melodies into his solos, but he did so crudely compared with Parker's genius.

FURTHER READING
Feather, Leonard. *Inside Bebop* (1949).
Hadlock, Dick. "Benny Harris and the Coming of Modern Jazz," *Metronome* (Oct. 1961).
Patrick, James. "Al Tinney, Monroe's Uptown House, and the Emergence of Modern Jazz in Harlem," *Annual Review of Jazz Studies* 2 (1983).
This entry is taken from the *American National Biography* and is published here with the permission of the American Council of Learned Societies.

BARRY KERNFELD

Harris, Louise "Mamma" (1891?–?) labor organizer, was born in Richmond, Virginia, to parents whose names and occupations are unknown. Harris left school at the age of eight to work as a childcare worker and later as a cook for white families in Richmond.

Little is known about her life until she reached her forties and began working as a stemmer at the Export Tobacco Company in Richmond, quickly noting the unhealthy working conditions, long hours, and low pay. The average salary for a tobacco laborer in Richmond was approximately six dollars per week, some factories had no cap on the number of hours worked per day, and workers had nothing but kerchiefs wrapped around their faces to protect against tobacco dust that filled the factory. Upon hearing that the Congress of Industrial Organizations (CIO) was organizing workers, she brought sixty women from Export to the next union meeting and volunteered her services. Labor organizers in the Tobacco Workers International Union, the union that oversaw white workers in cigarette factories, refused to deal with the African American stemmers and laborers. Through grassroots organizing and the help of activists from the Southern Negro Youth Congress, Richmond workers struck out on their own to organize the independent Tobacco Stemmers and Laborers Union (TSLU) in 1937. Inspired by the success of TSLU workers at other Richmond plants, Export workers attempted to organize and negotiate for improved conditions. In August of 1938, when management flatly refused to allow a union shop at Export, seven hundred of the one thousand workers employed there went on strike for eighteen days, supported financially by the CIO, the Southern Aid Society, and various churches. In addition to providing financial support, hundreds of white women from Garment Workers Union marched alongside the primarily female, African American tobacco workers, causing a stir in the local press. Nevertheless, Harris attributed their success to the hundreds of black tobacco workers who shocked Richmond's elite by marching en masse for better treatment. She gave particular credit to the marching women, stating, "You can out talk the men. But us women don't take no tea for the fever" (*New Republic*, 4 Nov. 1940). The women would not be swayed.

These organizing efforts marked a change in the relationship between black workers and white employers in Richmond. The city's tobacco industry exemplified labor in the Jim Crow South, where law and tradition relegated black workers to the dirtier and most dangerous jobs with less pay than white workers. Strikers like Harris challenged not only the segregated structure of the tobacco factories, but the very foundation of racial segregation.

The strike succeeded in securing better wages for workers and a cap on hours, though in the 1940s the unions faltered as tobacco companies chose to close stemming plants and eliminate thousands of jobs, replacing would-be members of the TSLU with stemming machines.

After a 1940 interview by TED POSTON in the *New Republic*, "Mamma" Harris disappeared from public records. Poston quotes Harris memorably on her immediate response to tobacco-factory work: "[I]t took me just one day to find out that preachers don't know nothing about hell. They ain't worked in no tobacco factory" (*New Republic*, 4 Nov. 1940). Her resistance to exploitation is emblematic of the thousands of black women laborers in the South who banded together to demand better pay, better working conditions, and respect.

FURTHER READING

Jackson, Augusta V., "A New Deal for Tobacco Workers," *The Crisis* (October 1938).

Korstad, Robert R. *Civil Rights Unionism: Tobacco Workers and the Struggle for Democracy in the Mid-Twentieth-Century South* (2003).

Korstad, Robert R. "Louise 'Mamma' Harris," in Darlene Clark Hine, et al., *Black Women in America: An Historical Encyclopedia* (1993).

Love, Richard. "In Defiance of Custom and Tradition: Black Tobacco Workers and Labor Unions in Richmond, Virginia, 1937–1941," *Labor History* (1944).

Poston, Ted. "The Making of Mamma Harris," *New Republic* (Nov. 1940).

ALICE KNOX EATON

Harris, Lyle Ashton (6 Feb. 1965–), photographer, was born in the Bronx, New York, to Thomas Allen Harris, a counselor to troubled youth, and Rudean, a chemistry professor. He grew up with his stepfather, Pule Leinaeng, who was a translator and broadcaster for the United Nations antiapartheid radio broadcasts. Raised in a middle-class home, he lived briefly with his mother and brother, the filmmaker Thomas Allen Harris, in Dar es Salaam, Tanzania, as "many African-Americans were traveling to Africa in the post civil rights era." The split of Harris's parents seemed to have been a precipitating event in Harris's awareness of his gay identity. When the brothers were going to church with their grandparents and during their parents' breakup, they began a ritual of reconstructing their sense of self by dressing up in drag on the weekends. Harris eventually transformed this childhood play with the body and self-image into a major creative outlet in adulthood. His early experiences with photographs included those amassed by his grandfather Albert Johnson as the unofficial documentarian of the African Methodist Episcopal (AME) church that Lyle, Thomas, and his grandmother, Joella Johnson, attended when the brothers were young. Harris also began some early experimentation with photography as a teenager.

Initially an economics major, Harris graduated with a B.A. in Art from Wesleyan University in Middletown, Connecticut, in 1988. He made his first series of photographs in 1987, *The Americas*, while still an undergraduate. Even at this early stage Harris was primarily interested in using himself as the photograph's primary subject. In most of his works, this interest in external symbolization of internal identity took the form of a self-portrait made up in some fashion. These self-portraits were often undertaken in conjunction with a second figure, male or female, whose gender or race was also transformed by makeup or costume. In other works, his exploration of sexual identity was less obvious, such as *Middletown* (1987/1988), which depicted him as a silhouette standing in a doorway in Middletown's downtown, reflecting his interest in the boundaries separating interior identity and exterior conditions.

Upon graduating from Wesleyan, Harris enrolled in the MFA program at the California Institute of Arts in Valencia, graduating with a degree in Photography in 1990. In 1991 Harris participated in the American Photography Institute Graduate Seminar at the Tisch School of the Arts at New York University. His formal education culminated in his acceptance into the Whitney Museum of American Art's independent study program in 1992. From 2000 to 2001 Harris was a fellow at the American Academy in Rome, where he began to explore Marguerite Yourcenar's novel *Memoirs of Hadrian* (1951), which became the title and subject of a photographic series in 2002.

Harris's consistent use of himself in a masquerading, self-fashioning form of self-portraiture in order to address issues of race and sexual difference might be seen as a variation of the postmodern photography of Cindy Sherman; in her early work she similarly transformed her own body to critique predominant gender expectations. But Sherman's masquerades, designed to show how her identity as hidden behind a set of societal codes, never revealed her identity in a personal manner. Harris's masquerades, however, not only pointed to the malleability of identity in general but also employed the personal expression and intimacy of self-portraiture. Harris viewed "autobiography as liberation strategy" (Bright, 249). Because Harris so transformed himself through costume and makeup from image to image—changing his identity from black to white, from male to female—his work regularly confronted manners of statically defined gender and race. The fluidity of these categories indicates the relationship between Harris's notion of gender and that of the literary theorist Judith Butler. Butler's theory suggested that gender identity is neither stable nor fixed but instead is communicated through reiterative performance of historical cultural codes.

Equally important for Harris's work, however, is that self-fashioned identity and autobiography have been prime modes of creative expression in the African diaspora, a phenomenon analyzed by HENRY LOUIS GATES JR. and the French postcolonial psychoanalyst Franz Fanon. Harris found helpful Fanon's statement that, "In the world through which I travel I am endlessly creating myself" (*Black Skins, White Masks*, 229). Rather than opposing personal exploration with social meaning, Fanon proposed that the underlying effect at the root of racism and colonialism could only be addressed through a psychoanalytic interpretation of the African diasporic subject. Harris's personal play with gender and race are therefore more than individual expressions but confront wider social expectations of the black male in particular. His photographs examine the fetishized black male body, twisting the stereotype of its dangerous sexuality by dressing up in campy police uniforms and ballerina tutus. Thus, Harris simultaneously elicits desire for the young, athletic black male body while undermining its fixed heterosexual nature. Further, in a series of photographic explorations called *Brotherhood, Crossroads and Etcetera*, done in collaboration with his brother Thomas in 1994, the two men appear nude, kissing, with a gun wedged between them. Here, Harris explores the boundaries of fraternal love and plays against hypermasculine images produced in the Black Power movement and rap culture. Regarding *Venus Hottentot 2000* (1994), a photograph produced in collaboration with the photographer and multimedia artist Renée Cox, Harris explained: "This reclaiming of the image of the Hottentot Venus is a way of exploring my own psychic identification with the image at the level of spectacle. I am playing with what it means to be an African diasporic artist producing and selling work in a culture that is by and large narcissistically mired in the debasement and objectification of blackness" (Read, 150).

Harris's work was exhibited internationally, at the Palazzo delle Papesse Centro Contemporanea, Siena (2005), the Seville Biennale (2006), the Whitney Museum (2007), and the Venice Biennale (2007). Harris was represented by CRG Gallery in New York, where he had a solo show in 2003. He has also had solos shows at Jack Tilton Gallery, New York (1994, 1996); Thomas Erben Gallery, New York (1997); the Corcoran Gallery of Art, Washington, D.C., (1998); Galerie Analix Forever, Geneva, Switzerland (1998); the Aldrich Museum of Contemporary Art, Ridgefield, Connecticut (1999); Baldwin Gallery, Aspen, Colorado (2002); Galerie Nathalie Obadia, Paris (2004); and Rhona Hoffman Gallery, Chicago (2005). Additionally, Harris's work is in the collections of the Whitney Museum of American Art; the Museo de Arte Contemporaneo de Castilla y Leon, Spain; the Walker Art Center; the Los Angeles County Museum of Art; and the Museum of Contemporary Art, Los Angeles.

FURTHER READING

Bright, Deborah, ed. *The Passionate Camera: Photography and Bodies of Desire* (1998).
Fanon, Frantz. *Black Skins, White Masks* (1952).
Harris, Lyle Ashton. *Lyle Ashton Harris, Selected Photographs: The First Decade* (1996).
Read, Alan, ed. *The Fact of Blackness* (1996).
Smalls, James. "The African-American Self Portrait: A-Crisis in Identity and Modernity," *Art Criticism* (2000).
Smith, Anna Deavere. *Lyle Ashton Harris* (2003).

RANDALL K. VAN SCHEPEN

Harris, Patricia Roberts (31 May 1924–23 Mar. 1985), cabinet member and ambassador, was born in Mattoon, Illinois, the daughter of Bert Fitzgerald Roberts, a Pullman car waiter, and Hildren Brodie Johnson, a schoolteacher. After graduating from a Chicago high school, she entered Howard University, from which she graduated, summa cum laude, with an AB in 1945. In 1943, while a student at Howard, she joined the nascent civil rights movement and participated in a sit-in to desegregate a cafeteria lunch counter in Washington, D.C. In 1946, while attending graduate school at the University of Chicago, Roberts was also program director of the local YWCA. In 1949 she returned to Washington, where she pursued further graduate study at American University until 1950. From 1949 to 1953 she served as an assistant director in the Civil Rights

Agency of the American Council on Human Rights. She was married in 1955 to the attorney William B. Harris, who encouraged her to enter law school (the marriage was childless), and she earned a J.D. degree at the George Washington University Law Center in 1960. Recognized early in her youth as an outstanding and diligent student, Harris graduated first of ninety-four in her class.

In 1960 Harris moved to the Department of Justice, where she worked for a year as a trial attorney in the Appeals and Research Section of the Criminal Division. She left the Justice Department to become a member of the faculty of Howard University School of Law, eventually reaching the rank of associate professor. It was that position she left in 1965, when President Lyndon B. Johnson named her U.S. ambassador to Luxembourg. Senate confirmation made her the first African American woman to serve in an ambassadorial post. After leaving the diplomatic corps in 1967, Harris returned to Howard University as a full professor, serving until 1969, when, as a result of student and faculty conflicts, she resigned to enter private practice. She remained active in the civil rights movement and served on the executive board of the NAACP Legal Defense Fund from 1967 to 1977.

Having served in professional and voluntary positions at the national and local levels to promote adequate and safe housing and shelter for the poor, including chair of the Housing Committee of the Washington Urban League (1956–1960), vice president of the Brookland Civic Association (1962–1965), and member of the board of directors of the American Council on Human Rights, Harris was nominated by President Jimmy Carter in 1977 to become secretary of the Department of Housing and Urban Development (HUD). During her Senate confirmation hearing before the Committee on Banking, Housing, and Urban Affairs, on 10 January 1977, she challenged Senator William Proxmire's suggestion that she might not be attuned to the problems of the poor. Harris responded:

> Senator, I am one of them. You do not seem to understand who I am. I'm a black woman, the daughter of a dining car waiter. I'm a black woman who even eight years ago could not buy a house in some parts of the District of Columbia. Senator, to say I'm not by and of and for the people is to show a lack of understanding of who I am and where I came from.

Once confirmed by the Senate, Harris brought control and order to the department, which had been criticized for ineffective, inefficient, and inconsistent management. Although some characterized her as having an abrasive manner, Harris proved to be hardworking and focused, determined to address the problems of the poor. With her she brought experience in providing minorities with improved access to better housing, a higher standard of living, and greater economic opportunities. In particular she directed an effort to prevent discrimination against women who applied for mortgage loans.

When President Carter reshuffled his cabinet in the summer of 1979, Harris left HUD and was named secretary of Health, Education, and Welfare (HEW). Soon after she was confirmed by the Senate, HEW became the Department of Health and Human Services, which Harris directed until the end of the Carter administration.

Harris returned to the practice of law in Washington, D.C., in 1981. The following year she ran for mayor of the District of Columbia but lost the race to MARION S. BARRY JR., having failed to convince voters that the city needed an administrator rather than a politician. In the end, however, perception of Harris as a member of the middle class contributed to her defeat.

Harris was a member of numerous organizations, including Phi Beta Kappa, and was the recipient of many awards and honorary degrees and the author of many articles and publications. She was recognized as a skilled, competent, and effective leader in both the public and the private arena. She died of cancer in Washington, D.C.

FURTHER READING

Calkin, Homer L. *Women in the Department of State: Their Role in American Foreign Affairs* (1978).

Obituary: *New York Times*, 23 Mar. 1985.

This entry is taken from the *American National Biography* and is published here with the permission of the American Council of Learned Societies.

JUDITH R. JOHNSON

Harris, Ruth Coles (26 Sept. 1928–), the first African American female certified public accountant in Virginia, was born Ruth Hortense Coles in Charlottesville, Virginia, to Bernard Albert Coles, a dentist, and the former Ruth Hortense Wyatt, a teacher. As a child she enjoyed playing "office" with her older sister and she excelled in school, graduating as valedictorian of her class at Jefferson High School when she was only fifteen years old. She entered Virginia State College for Negroes and majored in business administration. Despite graduating again

as valedictorian Harris received only one job offer, as a bookkeeper for a meatpacking plant in Cleveland. Her accounting professor, George G. Singleton, encouraged her to instead attend New York University for graduate school in accounting. In the 1940s African Americans could not attend graduate professional schools in the Commonwealth of Virginia, but to avoid lawsuits contending that the state did not provide "separate but equal" graduate education opportunities, Virginia paid tuition for black students to attend programs out of state. Although Harris wanted to become a certified public accountant, she knew that she would have a difficult time finding a position in the field. Singleton encouraged her to pursue graduate education despite these limitations.

Harris entered NYU in 1948. Because of her strong dislike of the city she did not consider staying there after completing her degree requirements, believing that few opportunities existed for professionally trained African Americans. When the president of Virginia Union University, a predominantly black college in Richmond, learned that Harris was pursuing a graduate degree in New York, he requested to interview her for a teaching position during an upcoming trip to the city. She was offered a position, earned her master of business administration in accounting and management in 1949, and began teaching at Virginia Union at the age of twenty. On 2 September 1950 she married Virginia State College classmate JOHN BENJAMIN HARRIS. They had two children, John Benjamin Jr. and Vita Michelle.

Although Harris had not intended to become a teacher, she fell in love with the work. When Harris joined the university, few business courses were offered and, despite the fact that her major had been accounting, she was needed to teach a wide variety of courses, including finance, typing, and business law. Harris was head of the commerce department from 1956 to 1969 and, when the school of business administration was founded in 1973, Harris became its first director. She served in that position until 1981 and as chairperson of the accounting department from 1987 to 1997, at which time she retired.

Although Harris focused on teaching, she did not give up her quest to become a certified public accountant. In order to earn the certificate she had to pass the difficult examination—only about 25 percent of examinees pass the examination on the first try—plus meet an experience requirement, something that in 1960s Virginia was all but impossible for a black woman. However, from an old classmate at Virginia State she learned that, though it was not publicized, Virginia informally allowed seven years of teaching experience to replace the requirement of working for a CPA firm. After having taught for over a decade she applied to take the examination. Accommodations, however, in Virginia Beach, where the exam was to be held, also proved to be a problem since the local hotels refused to rent rooms to African Americans. Unlike the white examinees who stayed overnight across the street from the test site, Harris was forced to stay twenty miles away in Norfolk. This obstacle made Harris even more determined to pass the test and prove that excluding her was a mistake. Typically, examinees found out whether they passed the examination through a letter from the examining board. This is not how Harris discovered that she had passed. Instead, one day she received an unexpected phone call from a reporter who wanted to know how it felt to be the first African American female to pass the CPA examination in Virginia. The story ran not only in the local paper but was also picked up across the country. In 1963 it was still a novelty for a black woman in a southern state to achieve such a professional distinction. Through this achievement Harris followed in the footsteps of her sister, BERNADINE COLES GINES, who in 1954 had become the first African American female CPA in New York.

After passage of the Civil Rights Act of 1964, opportunities finally opened up within mainstream accounting firms and major corporations. In 1966 Harris was invited to work as an accountant for International Business Machines during the summer. In 1972 she spent the summer working for Price Waterhouse & Co., one of the major public accounting firms that had not hired African Americans at the time Harris finished graduate school. She enjoyed the opportunity to gain experience that she could share with her students. Still discrimination clouded Harris's academic life. In 1967 the American Institute of Certified Public Accountants co-sponsored, along with the Carnegie Corporation, a study of accounting curricula and published the book, *Horizons for a Profession: The Common Body of Knowledge for Certified Public Accountants*. Each of the fifty states held a conference for educators to discuss the book's implications, and Harris attended the meeting held in Virginia. Not only was she the only African American at the meeting but she was also the only woman. During the course of the event the men seated with Harris enthusiastically discussed the upcoming Accounting Educators' Conference. Harris soon learned that the Virginia

Society of CPAs sponsored this annual event, but she had never heard of it despite the fact that she had been an accounting professor in Virginia for eighteen years. She pointed this out to the others at her table and later that year, for the first time, professors at the historically black colleges in the state were invited to attend the conference.

Harris remained interested in advancing her credentials, and after her children left for college she considered earning a Ph.D. There were no Ph.D. programs in accounting at any of the nearby universities, so with her husband's encouragement she commuted fifty miles to the College of William and Mary to pursue a doctorate in Higher Educational Administration. With a fellowship from the United Negro College Fund, she completed her degree in 1977, with a dissertation titled "A Method of Evaluating a Planning-Programming-Budgeting System." Harris took special pride in the fact that she taught two of the first one hundred African American CPAs. Over time opportunities opened up for her students. But even as late as the 1970s she found that local employers were reluctant to hire her graduates. While many of her students joined major public accounting firms, they were offered positions in Chicago or New York or other northern cities, rather than in the local Richmond offices. Race and gender both played a role in employment. When the Internal Revenue Service began interviewing Virginia Union seniors, it refused to hire female candidates, maintaining that their employees had to travel frequently and that this would not be suitable for women.

During the 1970s the American Institute of Certified Public Accountants funded an expansion of the library's business collection, sponsored summer conferences for faculty at historically black colleges and universities (HBCUs), and facilitated summer internships for students. The American Assembly of Collegiate Schools of Business, which accredits business schools, also sponsored programs to help HBCUs upgrade their business-school offerings by organizing curricula review through pairing unaccredited with accredited schools.

Harris accumulated numerous teaching and leadership awards. In the 1990s she was selected by Virginia Power for its Strong Men and Women: Excellence in Leadership award, she earned an Honorary Doctor of Humane Letters from Virginia Union University's Sydney Lewis School of Business, was selected for the Distinguished Career in Accounting Award by the Virginia Society of Certified Public Accountants, and was chosen for the Outstanding Faculty Award from the Commonwealth of Virginia's Council of Higher Education.

Late in her career Harris also served on numerous committees, including the board of directors for Virginia Society of CPAs and on the American Institute of CPAs Minority Recruitment Committee. Virginia Governor Charles Robb appointed her to Virginia's Interdepartmental Committee on Rate-setting for Children's Facilities, where she was selected by her fellow committee members to serve as its first chair. Upon Harris's retirement in 1997 the Ruth Coles Harris Endowed Scholarship fund was established for students at the Virginia Union University Business School.

FURTHER READING

Some of the information from this entry was gathered from interviews with Ruth Coles Harris on 16 Nov. 1998 and in Feb. and Mar. 2005.

Hammond, Theresa. *A White-Collar Profession: African American Certified Public Accountants Since 1921* (2002).

Middleton, Otesa. "Professor Broke Barriers: Harris Retiring after 48 Years at VUU," *Richmond Times-Dispatch*, 29 Apr. 1997.

THERESA A. HAMMOND

Harris, Trudier (27 Feb. 1948–), writer and professor of African American literature and folklore, was born in Mantua, Greene County, Alabama, to Terrell Harris Sr., a farmer and craftsman, and Unareed Burton Moore Harris, a farmer, domestic, janitor, and cook. The fourth daughter among nine children, Harris lived with her family on an eighty-acre cotton farm until age six, when her father—who was twenty-nine years older than her mother—died suddenly. Her early childhood was shaped by the rhythms of a self-sufficient farming life, including growing fruit and vegetables and raising hogs and chickens for food, canning and making sausage, and picking cotton.

The death of Harris's father forced her mother to sell the farm and move the children—whom she succeeded in keeping with her and together despite relatives' attempts to separate them to be raised by others—to the city of Tuscaloosa. While the family suffered from lack of money, accepting charity and welfare to get by, Harris credited her mother with working a series of low-paying jobs to keep the family going. In her memoir, *Summer Snow: Reflections from a Black Daughter of the South* (2003), Harris chronicled a childhood rich in black vernacular speech, neighborhood characters, church

community, and her siblings' and her own academic and athletic success. On the other hand, the larger context of her childhood world was fierce segregation and racism, which lay behind several of Harris's experiences. She recalled several molars pulled by a charity dentist (necessitating many thousands of dollars' worth of dental work in her adulthood), being offered five dollars for sex at age twelve by a white young man in a car in her neighborhood, and the decided lack of planning for college by her high school guidance counselor. In high school and college Harris played the same role as many black children and young adults during the 1960s, participating in civil rights training, joining in demonstrations against restrictions imposed by white authorities, and working for voter registration.

Harris graduated from Stillman College magna cum laude in 1969, with a major in English and a minor in social studies. Somewhat emotionally prepared for the experience of a majority-white academic environment by a summer internship the preceding year at University of Indiana at Bloomington, where she was one of a few black students, Harris completed her M.A. and Ph.D. (in American literature and folklore) at Ohio State University in 1973. Her first appointment, as assistant professor of English at the College of William and Mary, lasted six years, during which time she began publishing articles on African American literature and folklore in journals such as *College Language Association* and *Black American Literature Forum*. Harris was a leader in academia's recognition of African American literature and folklore and was part of the 1970s wave of black faculty doing research on African American culture within predominantly white institutions of higher education.

Harris was appointed associate professor of English at the University of North Carolina at Chapel Hill in 1979; she was promoted to professor in 1985 and named J. Carlyle Sitterson Professor of English in 1988. These were extremely productive years for Harris: she published three single-author books, edited three and co-edited three volumes for Gale's *Dictionary of Literary Biography* series, and published numerous articles. In particular, her book *Fiction and Folklore: The Novels of Toni Morrison* (1991), one of the first book-length critical analyses of TONI MORRISON's work, shaped the direction of scholarship on the most written-about black author of the decade. She received fellowships from the National Endowment for the Humanities, the Bunting Institute, and the Ford Foundation. In 1993 Harris left Chapel Hill and assumed the position of Augustus Baldwin Longstreet Professor of American Literature at Emory University in Atlanta, where she remained for three years.

Upon her return to the Sitterson chair at UNC Chapel Hill, Harris founded the GEORGE MOSES HORTON Society for the Study of African American Poetry in 1996, a scholarly group that maintained a Listserv and convened every other year in Chapel Hill for a conference. Over her career Harris served on a number of editorial and advisory boards for scholarly journals and series, including *Black American Literature Forum, Callaloo, Dictionary of Literary Biography, Journal of American Folklore,* and *South Atlantic Review.* In 1997 and 1998 Harris published (as co-editor) two important texts that served to codify and perpetuate the study of African American literature and culture: *The Oxford Companion to African American Literature* (1997) and *Call and Response: The Riverside Anthology of the African American Literary Tradition* (1998).

During the 1990s and the turn into the twenty-first century, Harris added commentary and memoir to her repertoire of publications, authoring a series of reflections about her experiences (collected in *Summer Snow*) and a newspaper column in the *Chapel Hill News.* She was a longtime participant in the Wintergreen Women Writers' Collective.

Harris's teaching fostered a generation of informed scholars in African American literature and culture. In 2000 she received the William C. Friday/Class of 1986 Award for Excellence in Teaching, and in 2005 she was awarded the University of North Carolina Board of Governors Award for Excellence in Teaching. Her contributions to the establishment and growth of African American literary criticism as a field of study place her in the first rank of scholars of her generation.

FURTHER READING

Harris, Trudier. *Summer Snow: Reflections from a Black Daughter of the South* (2003).

Black Issues in Higher Education, 21 Apr. 1994.

Zug, Charles G., III. "Trudier Harris, Scholar, Folklorist and Teacher," *North Carolina Folklore Journal* 45.2 (Summer–Fall 1998).

MALIN PEREIRA

Harris, Wynonie (Mr. Blues) (24 Aug. 1913–14 June 1969), rhythm and blues singer known as "Mr. Blues," was born in Omaha, Nebraska, to the fifteen-year-old Mallie Hood Anderson. (His birth year is often incorrectly given as 1915.) Harris saw his father, a Native American named Blue Jay, only

once in his life. Luther Harris married Mallie and became Wynonie's stepfather. Wynonie Harris attended Omaha public schools, leaving Central High before graduation. By the time Harris was nineteen, he had fathered two children. His first child, a daughter named Mickey, was born to Naomi Henderson on 19 October 1932. His second was a son, Wesley, born to Laura Devereaux on 13 August 1933. Harris's third child was a daughter, Adrianne Patricia (Pattie), born 20 May 1936 to the teenage Olive ("Ollie") E. Goodlow. The couple married on 11 December 1936; they had no more children.

Harris began his career as a dancer, partnering with Velda Shannon in the early 1930s. They performed at various Omaha venues on weekends, soon becoming a regular attraction at Jim Bell's Harlem, where Harris began singing blues. By the time the club closed in late 1936, Harris had become one of Omaha's top entertainers. Harris left Omaha for Los Angeles in 1939. He began singing regularly at Central Avenue's Club Alabam, where in 1941 he became master of ceremonies. During this time Harris acquired the moniker "Mr. Blues." Harris claimed (yet to be substantiated) to have appeared as a dancer in several films, *Cabin in the Sky* (1942), *Stormy Weather* (1943), and *Hit Parade of 1943.*

Harris's engagement at the Club Alabam established his reputation in Los Angeles and the surrounding area. He became known for his racy songs, dancing, and risqué performance style. The blues singers BIG JOE TURNER (the major early influence on Harris's style) and T-BONE WALKER frequently played Los Angeles. Cutting contests involving Harris and one or both other singers were often billed as "battles of the blues." Harris also appeared at clubs and theaters in San Francisco, Oakland, and Richmond.

By late 1943 Harris began touring outside California. The bandleader LUCKY MILLINDER hired him in April 1944 after losing his vocalists Judy Carol and Trevor Bacon. Harris remained with Millinder for only six months but recorded with him "Who Threw the Whiskey in the Well" for Decca Records in May. Decca released this record in April 1945, and it reached number one on *Billboard*'s black rhythm and blues chart in early June. It "crossed over" to the white pop charts in mid-July, peaking at number seven.

After leaving Millinder to pursue a solo career, Harris returned to Los Angeles and the Club Alabam. He and Johnny Otis (the house bandleader) recorded together July 1945. Later that year Harris recorded with the jazz bands of ILLINOIS

JACQUET, Jack McVea, and OSCAR PETTIFORD. By this time, his wife and daughter had joined him in Los Angeles. Harris returned to the studio July 1945—his first solo session—this time recording for Aladdin Records with a small combo led by Otis. Harris was fired from the Club Alabam because of the risqué nature of his live shows. In December, nonetheless, he was back on stage, this time at New York's Apollo Theater.

In high demand as both a touring and recording artist, Harris recorded several sides for Bullet Records in the spring of 1946. In October 1946 Harris's manager, Harold Oxley, finalized an arrangement with the New York–based Universal Attractions, giving Harris more opportunities to tour nationally.

In early 1947 Harris began performing regularly at Harlem's the Baby Grand. His new manager, Jimmy Evans, sent him on tour with the trumpeter HOT LIPS PAGE. Harris returned to New York and was engaged at Small's Paradise. After his Aladdin contract expired, Harris signed with Syd Nathan's King Records, which specialized in rhythm and blues, rock and roll, and country. In mid-December Harris made his first King recordings, including the hit "Good Rockin' Tonight." Released in March 1948, this song became a rock and roll classic, covered by Elvis Presley only a few years later. With another top ten hit, Harris was now a rhythm and blues star. He moved his family from Los Angeles to New York. His marriage to Ollie soon faltered, and Harris met Gertrude ("Ice Cream") Sloan, who soon joined him in his Addisleigh Park house in St. Albans, Queens. Harris continued to perform in Harlem and Brooklyn nightclubs and theaters. Over the next four years, he toured nationally and continued to record. In 1952 Ollie left New York and later filed for divorce.

The mid-1950s marked a downturn in Harris's career. He had built a recording career as a "blues shouter," performing up-tempo, dance blues songs with double-entendres. By the 1950s the recording industry shifted as a new record-buying public emerged. Rhythm and blues became popular with white teens, especially the music of younger artists CHUCK BERRY, FATS DOMINO, and LITTLE RICHARD. Prior to the mid-1950s, Harris had built his career primarily as a live act, but recording had become increasingly important to a popular entertainer. Disc jockeys began to shy away from playing his records because of their adult themes, and Harris's recording sales declined.

Harris, his career now in decline, tried to pursue management and promotion, booking engagements for the R&B vocalist Varetta Dillard. In late 1954, Harris's son Wesley Devereaux (by then twenty-one and a professional musician) joined him in New York. Through Harris, Wesley and his group, the Sultans, briefly secured work as backup singers with King Records and recorded their own sides as the Admirals. After an unsuccessful venture as a promoter and booking agent, Harris managed a Brooklyn bar. In late 1955 his contract with King Records ended, and in October 1956 Harris signed with Atco, an Atlantic Records subsidiary headed by Herb Abramson. Atco and Harris's manager briefly tried to repackage him as a rock and roll singer. Harris continued to appear in New York–area clubs, though he would no longer achieve his earlier level of success. Experiencing serious financial problems, Harris resumed work as a bar manager. His last attempts to revive his career were made during the summer of 1957 and the next year, when he rerecorded several of his earlier hits for Roulette Records. In 1958 Harris lost his house and separated from Ice Cream.

In late 1963 Harris returned to Los Angeles, where he found nightclub work singing his old songs. By this time the quality of his voice had seriously declined. He also had trouble finding musicians who could play behind him. Musical styles had changed, and Harris's jump blues now seemed dated. In August of 1964 Harris made three recordings with the Chicago-based Chess Records (released posthumously). After a brief stint as a bookie, Harris worked as a singer and bartender. Sometime around 1965 or 1966 he opened an open-hours club. His last performance was at the Apollo Theater in November 1967. In September 1968 Harris was diagnosed with throat cancer, which he battled for nearly a year.

Although by the mid-1950s his career as a recording artist had effectively ended, Harris's legacy is as a bridge between rhythm and blues and rock and roll. He began his career at the beginning of the R&B era, just as this style branched from jazz. Among his contemporaries are R&B artist LOUIS JORDAN. A master of the blues "shouting" style popularized by singers such as Big Joe Turner, Harris had sixteen top ten hits, including "Wynonie's Blues," "Drinkin' Wine Spo-Dee-O-Dee," "I Want My Fanny Brown," and "Bloodshot Eyes." He had three number one hits: "Who Threw the Whiskey in the Well," the rock and roll classic "Good Rockin' Tonight," and "All She Wants to Do Is Rock." He recorded with Lucky Millinder, Johnny Otis, Jack McVea, Oscar Pettiford, Todd Rhodes, and LIONEL LEO HAMPTON. His labels included Decca, Aladdin, Hamp-Tone, King, and Roulette.

FURTHER READING

Collins, Tony. *Rock Mr. Blues: The Life and Music of Wynonie Harris* (1995).

Harris, Sheldon. *Blues Who's Who: A Biographical Dictionary of Blues Singers* (1979).

Harris, Wynonie. "Women Won't Let Me Alone," *Tan* (Oct. 1954).

GAYLE MURCHISON

Harrison, Faye Venetia (25 Nov. 1951 –), anthropologist, was born in Norfolk, Virginia, to James and Odelia Blount Harper Harrison. Her maternal grandparents, Arthur and Tola Harper, came originally from rural North Carolina. Tola Harper, the daughter of slaves, taught in a one room schoolhouse there. During the 1920s, they moved to Norfolk to improve their children's opportunities. When Faye was seven, she discovered a closet full of *National Geographic* magazines in her family's new house. She read them repeatedly, marveling at the diversity of human cultures and wondering how they became different. As early as fifth grade, she excelled at school. Her teachers especially respected and encouraged her serious, perceptive questions about human societies. By high school, she was so fascinated by Latin America and the Caribbean that she learned French, Portuguese, and Spanish. One of her teachers tutored her in Spanish-language literature. A sorority awarded her a scholarship for a language study trip to Puerto Rico.

After arriving at Brown University in Providence, Rhode Island, in 1970, she determined that anthropology was the best discipline for pursuing her questions about human cultures, especially those of the global African diaspora. She was permitted to take graduate-level anthropology classes. For her senior thesis, she conducted an independent research project on immigrants from the African Atlantic island nation of Cape Verde. She achieved her bachelor's degree in Anthropology from Brown in 1974. On a Samuel T. Arnold Fellowship, she spent the next year researching Jamaican immigrant teens in the multiracial Brixton community in London, England.

In 1975 Harrison was awarded a fellowship to the anthropology program at Stanford University, where she was mentored by the noted black anthropologist and sociologist ST. CLAIR DRAKE. After writing a thesis about her Brixton research, Harrison achieved her master's degree in 1977. She won Danforth, Wenner-Gren, and Fulbright-Hays fellowships to conduct her doctoral research in the poorest areas of Kingston, Jamaica. Her findings on the informal economic activities of urban blacks challenged stereotypes of unemployed, idle slum dwellers. She earned her Ph.D. in Anthropology from Stanford in 1982.

On 17 May 1980, she wed William Louis Conwill, a counseling psychologist and educator. The couple had three sons, Giles, L. Mondlane, and Justin.

Harrison combined her teaching career with activism inside and outside academia, sometimes communicating her ethnographic findings through theater and dance performances. She was an assistant professor at the University of Louisville (1983–1989). There she became involved with the Alliance Against Women's Oppression and the Kentucky Rainbow Coalition. She was invited to become an associate professor of anthropology at the University of Tennessee-Knoxville (UTK) in 1989 and remained there until 1997. She was an anthropology adjunct associate professor, State University of New York at Binghamton (1996–1998) and professor of anthropology and women's studies graduate director, University of South Carolina–Columbia (1997–1999). She returned to UTK as a professor of anthropology (1999–2004). The University of Florida–Gainesville appointed Harrison professor of anthropology and African American studies (2004–2005), then director of the African American studies program (2007–).

In addition to teaching and research, Harrison undertook many other professional activities that challenged and transformed the legacies of racism, sexism, and colonialism within anthropology. She edited or wrote books that became widely included in anthropology curricula, especially her *Outsider Within: Reworking Anthropology in the Global Age* (2008). Her other books include *Semiproletarianization and the Structure of Socioeconomic and Political Relations in a Jamaican Slum* (1982), *Black Folks in Cities Here and There* (editor, 1988), *Decolonizing Anthropology* (editor, 1997), *African American Pioneers in Anthropology* (coeditor with Ira E. Harrison, 1999), and *Resisting Racism and Xenophobia* (editor, 2005).

She served as president, Association of Black Anthropologists (1989–1991); associate editor, *Urban Anthropology* (1992); and chair, International Union of Anthropologists and Ethnological Sciences and its Commission on Women (1993–). She won such honors as the Prize for Distinguished Contributions to the Critical Study of North America, Society for the Anthropology of North America (2004); the Zora Neale Hurston Award for Mentoring, Service, and Scholarship, Southern Anthropological Society (2007); and a Mellon Fellowship, University of Cape Town (2011).

Harrison has argued that "it has always been important for me to have some concrete grounding in a social-justice community and to bring principles of social justice into my academic work" (*Outsider Within,* pp. 295–296). Through her commitment to these priorities, Harrison influenced many other anthropologists to "liberate the discipline from the constraints of its colonial legacy and post- or neocolonial predicament," "rise to the growing challenge of ethically and politically responsible research," and "promote a genuine multicultural dialogue in the study of humanity" (*Outsider Within,* pp. 1, 2).

FURTHER READING

Bailey, Martha J. *American Women in Science: 1950 to the Present: A Biographical Dictionary* (1998).

College of Liberal Arts and Sciences, University of Florida. "Faye Venetia Harrison: Biographical Sketch." <http://www.clas.ufl.edu/users/fayeharr/ images/Bio.pdf> Accessed 4 Mar. 2011.

Kessler, James H. *Distinguished African American Scientists of the 20th Century* (1996).

Petrusso, A. "Faye Venetia Harrison." In *Notable Black American Scientists,* edited by Kristine Krapp (1999).

Wayne, Tiffany K. *American Women of Science Since 1900* (2010).

MARY KRANE DERR

Harrison, Hubert Henry (27 Apr. 1883–17 Dec. 1927), radical political activist and journalist, was born in Concordia, St. Croix, Danish West Indies (now U.S. Virgin Islands), the son of William Adolphus Harrison and Cecilia Elizabeth Haines. Little is known of his father. His mother had at least three other children and, in 1889, married a laborer. Harrison received a primary education in St. Croix. In September 1900, after his mother died, he immigrated to New York City, where he worked low-paying jobs, attended evening high school, did some writing, editing, and lecturing, and read voraciously. In 1907 he obtained postal employment and moved to Harlem. The following year he taught at the White Rose Home, where he was deeply influenced by the social worker Frances Reynolds Keyser, a future founder of the NAACP. In 1909 he married Irene Louise Horton, with whom he had five children. Between 1901 and 1908 Harrison broke "from orthodox and institutional Christianity" and

became an "Agnostic." His new worldview placed humanity at the center and emphasized rationalism and modern science. He also participated in black intellectual circles, particularly church lyceums, where forthright criticism and debate were the norm and where his racial awareness was stimulated by scholars such as the bibliophile ARTHUR SCHOMBURG and the journalist JOHN E. BRUCE. History, free thought, and social and literary criticism appealed to him, as did the protest philosophy of W. E. B. DuBois over the more "subservient" one of BOOKER T. WASHINGTON. Readings in economics and single taxism and a favorable view of the Socialist Party's position on women drew him toward socialism. Then in 1911, after writing letters critical of Washington in the *New York Sun,* he lost his postal job through the efforts of Washington's associates and turned to Socialist Party work.

From 1911 to 1914 Harrison was the leading black in the Socialist Party of New York, where he insisted

Hubert Henry Harrison, intellectual and political activist, known as "The Father of Harlem Radicalism." (Schomburg Center for Research in Black Culture, New York Public Library.)

on the centrality of the race question to U.S. socialism; served as a prominent party lecturer, writer, campaigner, organizer, instructor, and theoretician; briefly edited the socialist monthly the *Masses*; and was elected as a delegate to one state and two city conventions. His series on "The Negro and Socialism" (*New York Call*, 1911) and on "Socialism and the Negro" (*International Socialist Review*, 1912) advocated that socialists champion the cause of the African American as a revolutionary doctrine, develop a special appeal to blacks, and affirm their duty to oppose race prejudice. He also initiated the Colored Socialist Club (CSC), a pioneering effort by U.S. socialists at organizing blacks. After the party withdrew support for the CSC, and after racist pronouncements by some Socialist Party leaders during debate on Asian immigration, he concluded that socialist leaders put the white "Race First and class after."

Harrison believed "the crucial test of Socialism's sincerity" was "the Negro," and he was attracted to the egalitarian practices and direct action principles of the Industrial Workers of the World (IWW). He defended the IWW and spoke at the 1913 Paterson Silk Strike with Elizabeth Gurley Flynn and "Big Bill" Haywood. Although he was a renowned socialist orator and was described by author Henry Miller as without peer on a soapbox, Socialist Party leaders moved to restrict his speaking.

Undaunted, Harrison left the Socialist Party in 1914 and over the next few years established the tradition of street-corner oratory in Harlem. He first developed his own Radical Lecture Forum, which included citywide indoor and outdoor talks on free thought, evolution, literature, religion, birth control, and the racial aspects of World War I. Then, after teaching at the Modern School, writing theater reviews, and selling books, he started the Harlem People's Forum, at which he urged blacks to emphasize "Race First."

In 1917, as war raged abroad, along with race riots, lynchings, and discrimination at home, Harrison founded the Liberty League and the *Voice*, the first organization and newspaper of the militant "New Negro" movement. He explained that the league was called into being by "the need for a more radical policy than that of the NAACP" (*Voice*, 7 Nov. 1917) and that the "New Negro" movement represented "a breaking away of the Negro masses from the grip of the old-time leaders" (*Voice*, 4 July 1917). Harrison stressed that the new black leadership would emerge from the masses and would not be chosen by whites (as in the era of Washington's

leadership), nor be based in the "Talented Tenth of the Negro race" (as advocated by DuBois). The league's program was directed to the "common people" and emphasized internationalism, political independence, and class and race consciousness. The *Voice* called for a "race first" approach, full equality, federal antilynching legislation, labor organizing, support of socialist and anti-imperialist causes, and armed self-defense in the face of racist attacks.

Harrison was a major influence on a generation of class and race radicals, from the socialist A. PHILIP RANDOLPH to MARCUS GARVEY. The Liberty League developed the core progressive ideas, basic program, and leaders utilized by Garvey, and Harrison claimed that, from the league, "Garvey appropriated every feature that was worthwhile in his movement." Over the next few years Garvey would build what Harrison described as the largest mass movement of blacks "since slavery was abolished"—a movement that grew, according to Harrison, as it emphasized "racialism, race consciousness, racial solidarity—the ideas first taught by the Liberty League and *The Voice*."

The *Voice* stopped publishing in November 1917, and Harrison next organized hotel and restaurant workers for the American Federation of Labor. He also rejoined, and then left, the Socialist Party and chaired the Colored National Liberty Congress that petitioned the U.S. Congress for federal antilynching legislation and articulated militant wartime demands for equality. In July 1918 he resurrected the *Voice* with influential editorials critical of DuBois, who had urged blacks to "Close Ranks" behind the wartime program of President Woodrow Wilson. Harrison's attempts to make the *Voice* a national paper and bring it into the South failed in 1919. Later that year he edited the *New Negro*, "an organ of the international consciousness of the darker races."

In January 1920 Harrison became principal editor of the *Negro World*, the newspaper of Garvey's Universal Negro Improvement Association (UNIA). He reshaped the entire paper and developed it into the preeminent radical, race-conscious, political, and literary publication of the era. As editor, writer, and occasional speaker, Harrison served as a major radical influence on the Garvey movement. By the August 1920 UNIA convention Harrison grew critical of Garvey, who he felt had shifted focus "from Negro Self-Help to Invasion of Africa," evaded the lynching question, put out "false and misleading advertisements," and "lie[d] to the people magniloquently." Though he continued to write columns and book reviews for the *Negro World* into 1922, he was no longer principal editor, and he publicly criticized and worked against Garvey while attempting to build a Liberty Party, to revive the Liberty League, and to challenge the growing Ku Klux Klan.

Harrison obtained U.S. citizenship in 1922 and over the next four years became a featured lecturer for the New York City Board of Education, where the Yale-educated NAACP leader WILLIAM PICKENS described him as "a plain black man who can speak more easily, effectively, and interestingly on a greater variety of subjects than any other man I have ever met in the great universities." In 1924 he founded the International Colored Unity League (ICUL), which stressed that "as long as the outer situation remains what it is," blacks in "sheer self-defense" would have to develop "race-consciousness" so as to "furnish a background for our aspiration" and "proof of our equal human possibilities." The ICUL called for a broad-based unity—a unity of action, not thought, and a separate state in the South for blacks. He also helped develop the Division of Negro Literature, History, and Prints of the New York Public Library, organized for the American Negro Labor Congress, did publicity work for the Urban League, taught on "Problems of Race" at the Workers School, was involved in the Lafayette Theatre strike, and lectured and wrote widely. His 1927 effort to develop the *Voice of the Negro* as the newspaper of the ICUL lasted several months. Harrison died in New York City after an appendicitis attack. His wife and five young children were left virtually penniless.

Harrison, "the Father of Harlem Radicalism," was a leading black socialist, the founder and leading force of the militant "New Negro" movement, and the man who laid the basis for, and radically influenced, the Garvey movement. During a heyday of black radicalism he was the most class-conscious of the race radicals and the most race-conscious of the class radicals. He critically and candidly challenged the ruling classes, racists, organized religion, politicians, civil rights and race leaders, socialists, and communists. During his life, though well respected by many, Harrison was often slighted. In death his memory was much neglected, not least by "leaders" who had felt the sting of his criticism. He was, however, a political and cultural figure of great influence who contributed seminal work on the interrelation of race and class consciousness and whose book and theater reviews drew praise from leading intellectuals of the day. Historian

J. A. Rogers stressed that "No one worked more seriously and indefatigably to enlighten his fellowmen; none of the Aframerican leaders of his time had a saner and more effective program—but others, unquestionably his inferiors, received the recognition that was his due."

FURTHER READING

Hill, Robert A., ed. "Hubert Henry Harrison," in *The Marcus Garvey and Universal Negro Improvement Association Papers*, vol. 1 (1983).

Jackson, John G. *Hubert Henry Harrison: The Black Socrates* (1987).

James, Portia. "Hubert H. Harrison and the New Negro Movement," *Western Journal of Black Studies* 13, no. 2 (1989): 82–91.

Perry, Jeffrey B., ed. *A Hubert Harrison Reader* (2001).

Samuels, Wilford D. "Hubert H. Harrison and 'The New Negro Manhood Movement," *Afro-Americans in New York Life and History* 5 (Jan. 1981): 29–41.

This entry is taken from the *American National Biography* and is published here with the permission of the American Council of Learned Societies.

JEFFREY B. PERRY

Harrison, Juanita (1890–?), world traveler and writer, was born in Mississippi. Little is known of her early childhood except that her formal education ended at age ten. Like many African American girls of her generation, Harrison found employment as a domestic in the homes of white families. At age sixteen she left the South, traveling as far north as Canada and even making her way deeper south to Cuba, where she learned Spanish and French. Sometime during these years of work and travel, Harrison saw a magazine article depicting temple spires in a foreign land. That image fueled her lifelong desire to travel around the world.

While working in Denver, Colorado, Harrison managed to save $800 toward fulfilling her dream. Unfortunately the bank holding her savings failed. Harrison was left with just enough money to travel to California. There she secured a position with the family of George Dickinson, a real estate broker who invested Harrison's monthly salary. His efforts established for Harrison an income of $200 a year. That income would enable her to make her dreams of world travel a reality.

On 25 June 1927 Harrison boarded the SS *Sierra Ventana* in New York with two suitcases. The largest held two blue dresses, two white dresses, and appropriate accessories for working as a domestic overseas. A smaller suitcase held, among other things, two jars of sour cucumber pickles to ward off seasickness. She was thirty-seven years old.

Harrison chose a momentous decade in which to begin her journey. For African Americans it was a time of cultural awakening, of the New Negro. Many people migrated from the South to northern communities like Harlem in New York City. With church support, academic scholarships, and in some cases independent wealth, African Americans were also traveling overseas to explore life in other countries. Harrison stands apart from most other African American travelers of the period for traveling without a sponsor, without significant financing, and without a planned itinerary.

Though she traveled alone, with limited funds, and without a concrete itinerary, Harrison capitalized on her strengths, including her inquisitive nature, her skills as a domestic, and her acquisition of a YMCA membership. The YWCA directory ensured that she always had an address to seek out lodging in whatever country she chose to visit. Even if no rooms were available she could still meet with other women and learn about local culture, politics, and work opportunities.

As evidenced by the contents of her luggage, Harrison was fully prepared from the outset of her journey to work for wages to supplement her small income. As she worked, she talked with people of all races and classes, garnering invitations and suggestions for future travel. While in Paris, just six months after leaving the United States, Harrison took a momentous position with Mrs. Felix Morris. It was Mrs. Morris who suggested that a written account of Harrison's trip might be of interest to other people. She pointed to her daughter Mildred, a writer, as someone Harrison could look to for help. Harrison would later refer to Mrs. Morris as "the only American mother that I like" (Harrison, 292).

Eventually Harrison left Mrs. Morris to continue her travels throughout Europe, the Middle East, the Far East, North Africa, and Asia. She was an observant traveler. Aided by her olive complexion and long dark hair, which she often wore in two braids hanging down her back, Harrison was able to immerse herself in the culture of the countries that she visited. Unlike many Americans traveling abroad, she not only paid attention to what local people wore but also how they wore it and when. She also tried to speak the languages. She easily passed as European, Asian, and even Arab.

Eight years and twenty-two countries later, Harrison returned to the United States, settling in Honolulu, Hawaii. With the help of Mildred Morris she compiled her letters and diary entries into the book *My Great Wide Beautiful World*. *Atlantic Monthly* published two advance installments in 1935. Macmillan released the book in 1936. The publisher chose not to edit Harrison's writing significantly.

Even with its poor grammar and punctuation, Harrison's writing reflects her great intelligence and wit. With a simple style she paints vivid pictures of daily life for women. She astutely but without any apparent prejudice highlights differences between people defined by race, caste, class, and gender. In Bethlehem she noted that "there will never be any content here as long as there are Moslems and Jews. They are not really mean to each other I can see but they have no love for each other." She spiced up her accounts of culture and politics with understated comments about her liaisons with men and their reactions to her, a free-spirited American woman of color.

Using money from her *Atlantic Monthly* earnings, Harrison purchased a seven-by-seven-foot orange tent which she pitched in a vacant lot near Waikiki Beach. She called her new home Villa Petit Peep, a small home into which local children could peep with her blessing. Harrison's journey around the world began during a time of great social change. Having made her home near Pearl Harbor, her journey ended with her at the center of the next great change about to envelop the world.

In closing *My Great Wide Beautiful World*, Harrison wrote of having "nursed the joys" of life. Since no known documents record her life following her journey's end in Hawaii, it is unclear if she continued to live by this philosophy. What is known is that during a time when African Americans were just on the cusp of moving beyond Jim Crow oppression, Harrison embarked on a journey the likes of which few men or women of any race had the courage to do. She was a pioneering woman and stands as a model of perseverance.

FURTHER READING

Harrison, Juanita. *My Great Wide Beautiful World* (1936), with an introduction by Adele Logan (1996).

Roses, Lorraine Elena, and Ruth Elizabeth Randolph. *Harlem's Glory: Black Women Writing, 1900–1950* (1996).

Woods, Kathiine. "Juanita Harrison Has Known Twenty-two Countries," *New York Times*, 17 May 1936.

CYNTHIA STAPLES

Harrison, Paul Carter (1 Mar. 1936–), playwright and director, author, and educator, was born in Greenwich Village, New York, to Thelma Inez Harrison and Paul Randolph Harrison. Although he was reared in the North and nurtured by the spirit of the Harlem Renaissance, his roots are from below the Mason-Dixon Line, in North and South Carolina.

In the South the Harrison family was strongly immersed in Gullah culture and MARCUS GARVEY's Back to Africa movement. Harrison's grandfather, in fact, was a major leader of and played an active role in the Garvey movement in North Carolina. The household was also greatly involved in the African Methodist Episcopal (AME) Church in the Carolinas, and much of the mystical curiosity in Harrison's work can be attributed to his grandmother's spiritual influence. He was embraced by this richness as a young man, and it created the resonating aura of self-determination that was very much a force in his life. Harrison's work later reflected this upbringing in the language that he created for theater and in his interest in black cultural representation on stage.

Upon entering New York University (NYU) as an undergraduate in the early 1950s, Harrison had access to esteemed poets and musicians such as AMIRI BARAKA and THELONIOUS MONK. Monk had a great effect on Harrison's style and work ethic. As a psychology major, he had planned on a career as an academic, but his passion led him toward the stage. Ultimately the things that lured Harrison to the theater were the recitation, poetry, and performance that were influenced by the jazz culture of the time exemplified by such artists as the poet and trumpeter TED JOANS.

From NYU, Harrison transferred to Indiana University, where he encountered discrimination much as his contemporary, the author and activist JAMES BALDWIN, did on his visit from Harlem to the South. For Harrison this encounter was an eye-opener that led him back to New York after his graduation.

Upon his return to New York, Harrison entered the New School for graduate studies and became inspired by a lecture he heard on phenomenology and Gestalt psychology, which appealed to his sense of totality in theater, such that theater did not have to be linear and did not have to have causality. He soon began developing stage language that conveyed ritual and spectacle. Although Harrison was not interested in realism, the production of LORRAINE HANSBERRY's *A Raisin in the Sun* in 1959 launched many possibilities for black writers to make a sustainable living from their art. This breakthrough encouraged Harrison to explore his gift for writing and directing theater.

In 1962 Harrison postponed his studies to visit Europe, most notably the island of Ibiza, Spain. There he focused on writing plays that examined the black psyche. He completed his first work, *The Postclerks*, during this time and decided to remain in Europe to write and direct for the theater, thereby forgoing the completion of his doctorate.

While living in Amsterdam, Harrison married the actress Ria Vroemen, and they had a daughter, Fonteyn, in 1963. Harrison's first book, *The Modern Drama Footnote*, was published that same year. In 1967 Harrison wrote the play *Tabernacle*, with a twenty-character, all-black male cast; the play proved difficult to produce in Amsterdam because of the scarcity of black actors. Simultaneously, he became caught up in the civil rights movement, which led him to write the plays *Experimental Leader* and *The Civil Rights Movement: Dialogue from the Opposition*.

Upon invitation, Harrison returned to the United States to begin a teaching career at Howard University. There he taught such talented future actors as Phylicia Ayres-Allen Rashad and DEBBIE ALLEN. In fact, his students, he later recalled, inspired him to stay in the United States. The growing market for black theater, television, film, and literature was undoubtedly influential as well.

In 1972 Harrison wrote *The Drama of Nommo: Black Theater in the African Continuum*. Throughout this work, as well as in his other writings, a common theme emerged that he described as ethnic authenticity. Black art must identify and maintain its Africanness; it must not merely mock and imitate Western forms of expression and be labeled "black" simply because a black person created it. The product itself must be essentially and identifiably African. To this end the Negro Ensemble Company produced his ritual musical *The Great MacDaddy* in 1973, which won him an Obie Award. A year later he wrote *Kuntu Drama* (1974).

Between 1976 and 2003 Harrison served Columbia College, Chicago, as professor and playwright-in-residence, as chairman of theater and music, and finally as professor emeritus. During his tenure at Columbia he received several awards for his contribution to theater, including from the Rockefeller Fellowship and the National Endowment of the Arts.

In 1977 Harrison married the Los Angeles County prosecutor Donna Wills, but their marriage dissolved in 1979. More than ten years later he met a kindred spirit in the corporate finance banker Wanda Malone, and they married in 1988. A year later he wrote *Totem Voices: Plays from the Black World Repertory* (1989). He also has written, edited, and coedited numerous books and essays, including "Performing Africa in America: African Continuity" (*Theatre Journal* 57, no. 4, Dec. 2005) and *Black Theater: Ritual Performance in the African Diaspora* (2002). He has compiled several photographic texts, including *In the Shadow of the Great White Way: Images from the Black Theatre* (1985) and *Black Light: The African American Hero* (1993), with an introduction by the actor DANNY GLOVER. He wrote, directed, consulted on, and developed a reconceptualization of AUGUST WILSON's *King Hedley II* as a Greco-Yoruba ritual drama.

FURTHER READING

Much of the information gathered came from interviews with Paul Carter Harrison in the summer of 2006.

RACHEL WESTLEY

Harrison, Samuel (15 Apr. 1818–11 Aug. 1900), Congregational minister and civil rights advocate, was born in Philadelphia, Pennsylvania, to William and Jennie Harrison, slaves of John Bolton from Savannah, Georgia. His widowed mother, a family servant, was freed in 1821, and they moved to New York City with the Bolton family. Harrison attended school until he was nine years old, at which time his mother sent him to Philadelphia to get away from his alcoholic stepfather and become apprenticed to an uncle who was a shoemaker. His mother later left her husband and also moved to Philadelphia. At the age of seventeen, Harrison attended meetings at the black Second Presbyterian Church and soon joined the church.

Desiring more education, Harrison went to school in the morning and worked in the shoe shop in the afternoon. In 1836, with the help of the American Education Society, he attended the Peterboro Manual Labor School, founded by Gerrit Smith, a leader in the abolitionist movement. He offered his black students a classical education in return for four hours of daily work. After the school closed in 1836, Harrison enrolled in the Preparatory School of Western Reserve College in Hudson, Ohio. He took classes in Greek, Latin, philosophy, and theology, and worked as a shoemaker to help pay his way. He graduated in 1839 and returned to Philadelphia.

Harrison worked at Judah Dobson's bookstore but soon started his own shoe shop. He also taught Sunday school, became involved in temperance work, and joined the Demosthenian Institute, a literary society offering weekly debates and lectures. In 1840, at the age of twenty-two, Harrison became reacquainted with Ellen Rhodes, an orphan he had known before he was a teenager, and they married that same year. They eventually became the parents of thirteen children. In 1847 he moved to Newark, New Jersey, and became an assistant to the Reverend ELYMAS PAYSON ROGERS, a classmate from Peterboro. Harrison soon gave up his shoe business, and under the care of the Presbytery of Newark studied theology and did missionary work. The Reverend Dr. Brinsmade gave him theology books and secured a teacher. In 1848 he worked at mission churches in the suburbs of Newark and in Orange. In 1848 he was licensed to preach. He also wrote articles for a daily newspaper in Newark, often about black men being taxed but not having the right to vote. In the fall of 1849 Rogers arranged for Harrison to meet with a small church in Pittsfield, Massachusetts, which soon invited him to become its pastor. Second Congregational Church, founded in 1846, held services with the help of ministers from New York and Connecticut. Family stories about the founding of the church say that the black people could only sit in the balcony of the First Congregational Church and that they could not take Communion.

Between 1852 and 1857 Harrison received calls from Portland, Maine, Hartford, Connecticut, and Troy, New York, but the people at Second Church did not want to let him go. In the fall of 1858, with financial help from several of Pittsfield's prominent citizens, Harrison moved into his own home. Harrison continued his ministry and his shoe trade in Pittsfield until July 1862, when some dissension occurred in the church and he resigned from the pulpit. He became a spokesperson for the National Freedmen's Relief Society, which was raising funds to assist the freed blacks in the Sea Islands of South Carolina.

In July 1863 the Massachusetts governor John A. Andrew asked Harrison to go to South Carolina to carry the sympathy of the state to the 54th Massachusetts Regiment, which suffered the loss of its commanding officer and many of its men after the disastrous attack on Fort Wagner on 18 July 1863. With the recommendation of Dr. Mark Hopkins, the president of Williams College, Andrew appointed Harrison chaplain of the regiment on 8 September 1863. Harrison received Hopkins's endorsement since the previous year Harrison had given a lecture at Hopkins's church, titled "The Cause and Cure for the War," in which he called for the recruitment of black soldiers. Harrison reported to Morris Island on 12 November 1863 and was mustered into the U.S. Army. On 1 January 1864 he and the troops celebrated the first anniversary of the Emancipation Proclamation. When, by federal order, the paymaster was to give all black soldiers (including the chaplain) less than half the pay accorded to white privates, the men refused for eighteen months to take any pay at all. After some time in South Carolina, Harrison's health deteriorated, and he resigned in March 1864. In April 1864 Attorney General Edward Bates wrote to Abraham Lincoln, seconding Andrew's and Secretary of War Edwin M. Stanton's position that Harrison and other black chaplains should receive their full pay. Harrison eventually received his full pay but only after prolonged protests. Harrison remained ill for some time but later returned to work on behalf of the Freedmen's Relief Society. In October 1864 he was a delegate to the National Convention of Colored Men in Syracuse, New York.

In 1865 Harrison went to the Union Congregational Church in Newport, Rhode Island. Feeling that Newport could not sustain more than one black church after the summer season since the blacks, mainly servants, came to the summer homes with their wealthy employers and left at the end of summer, he looked for another situation. In December 1866 he went to the Sanford Street Congregational Church in Springfield, Massachusetts, as acting pastor. He remained there until 1870, at which time he became pastor of the Fourth Congregational Church in Portland, Maine. In 1872 the Second Congregational Church in Pittsfield asked him to return. He accepted, resuming the pastorate in April. He had kept his house and moved his family back into it. He served for many years as chaplain of the W. W. Rockwell Post 125, Grand Army of the Republic, located in Pittsfield. His wife, Ellen, died on 27 December 1883, and two years later he married Sarah J. Adams Davis. For all of his life Harrison was known as an impassioned speaker and writer on behalf of racial equality and the civil rights of African Americans. He died in Pittsfield and is buried in the Pittsfield Cemetery.

FURTHER READING

The Berkshire Athenaeum, Pittsfield, Massachusetts, in its Local History Collection and vaults, has a small collection of Harrison materials and books.

Emilio, Luis F. *A Brave Black Regiment: The History of the Fifty-fourth Regiment of Massachusetts Volunteer Infantry, 1863–1865* (1894).

Harrison, Samuel. *An Appeal of a Colored Man to His Fellow-Citizens of a Fairer Hue, in the United States* (1877).

Harrison, Samuel. *Pittsfield Twenty-Five Years Ago. Sermon. Second Congregational Church, Pittsfield, Mass. January 11th and 18th, 1874* (1874).

Harrison, Samuel. *Rev. Samuel Harrison. His Life Story. Told by Himself* (1899).

Wills, David W., and Richard Newman, eds. "Reverend Samuel Harrison: A Nineteenth Century Black Clergyman," in *Black Apostles at Home and Abroad* (1982).

RUTH EDMONDS HILL

Harris-Stewart, Lusia "Lucy" (10 Feb. 1955–), collegiate basketball player, was born Lusia Harris in Minter City, Mississippi, to Willie and Ethel Harris, whose occupations are unknown. The tenth of eleven children, Lusia attended Amanda Elzy High School, an all-black school in Greenwood, Mississippi, and in 1973 she was selected Miss Elzy High. Of the five daughters in her family, Lusia was the only one to play collegiate basketball. At six feet three inches she was the prototypical center in modern women's basketball.

Harris's career coincides with the rise of women's basketball during the 1970s. Although she was shy in person, she distinguished herself at every point of her college career, both on the court and off. Her major accomplishments paved the way for other individual female athletes such as CHERYL MILLER and also contributed to women's basketball programs more generally.

Success did not come easy for Harris as a youth. She was considered a "big child" and for years was embarrassed by her height, standing nearly a foot taller than many of her peers in Minter City. Harris first played organized basketball at the junior high school level, but was not a coordinated player at the time. With the encouragement of high school coach Conway Stewart, over time Harris learned how to use her tall frame to her advantage.

Melvin Hemphill, a recruiter and admissions counselor, recruited Lusia to enroll in Delta State University in Cleveland, Mississippi, in 1973. At the time, the women's basketball program, known as the Lady Statesmen, was rebuilding. Because the game was deemed too strenuous for women, women's basketball at the school had been dormant for forty-one years until Margaret Wade, a Delta State alumna, became coach. Delta State resurrected its basketball program in 1973, and at age sixty, Wade met the challenge of developing a national basketball program. Harris was a key figure in the team's rebuilding. Unlike many other women's programs at the time, the Delta State athletic administration fully supported the team. Fans traveled as far as New York City to see the team play in national venues, including Madison Square Garden.

Because the National Collegiate Athletic Association (NCAA) did not accept women's teams, a group of female administrators and coaches formed the Association of Intercollegiate Athletics for Women (AIAW) in 1972. The AIAW sponsored its own collegiate basketball tournament each year. During Harris's rookie year (1974), the team lost only two games but was not invited to play in the AIAW tournament. Chagrined, the team was more determined than ever and had an undefeated season the following year. As part of the Delta State team, Harris was a three-time Kodak All-American player (1975, 1976, and 1977) and led her team to three consecutive AIAW national championships. During those three years, the Lady Statesmen had an overall record of 109-6. Over her college career, Lusia Harris earned a career 2,981 points, 1,662 rebounds, and averaged 25.9 points per game.

The team's success brought notoriety and attention to the school, and it is quite possible that the success of the women's team encouraged more black students to enroll at the institution. Delta State was a predominantly white institution and Harris was the only African American on her team and often was the only-black student in her classes. In 1975, during her junior year, her peers voted her homecoming queen, making her the first black homecoming queen ever at the university and also the first black woman to receive such an honor at a nonhistorically black college in Mississippi.

Harris also had an influence on women's basketball globally. In 1975 she played on the World University Team, and she earned a gold medal as a member of the 1975 U.S. Pan American Team. Harris was one of only twelve players selected for the first ever women's Olympic basketball team in 1976 under the leadership of UCLA women's head coach Billie Moore and Louisiana State University coach Sue Gunter. Harris led the United States team in both scoring (fifteen points per game) and rebounding (seven per game) as the team earned a silver medal in Montreal. She solidified her place in history when she scored the game's first points.

In 1977 Lusia Harris received the Broderick Award that goes to the nation's best collegiate basketball player and she won the Honda Broderick Cup, awarded to the best collegiate athlete in any sport. Also that year, the New Orleans Jazz drafted Lusia in the seventh round of the NBA draft, making her the first woman to be drafted into the NBA. Although she was honored by the selection, Lusia, who was seven months pregnant at the time, declined a trial invitation and never played in the league. Harris-Stewart graduated with a B.A. in Physical Education and, upon graduation in 1977, worked for seven years in the admissions office to recruit students to attend Delta State. Four of those years, she worked as an assistant basketball coach for the women's basketball team. She then became the head coach of women's basketball at Texas Southern University in Houston. After receiving her master's degree in Health and Physical Education in 1984, Lusia Harris-Stewart became a high school special education teacher and high school coach at Greenwood High School in Greenwood, Mississippi.

Lusia Harris-Stewart and Nera White were the first women inducted into the National Basketball Hall of Fame as players in 1992, and in 1999 Harris-Stewart was an inaugural inductee into the Women's Basketball Hall of Fame.

FURTHER READING

Mississippi Oral History Program of the University of Southern Mississippi 748.2. Interview with Luisa Harris-Stewart (18 Dec. 1999).

Moran, Malcolm. "9 Lifetimes of Memories Wander into Hall of Fame," *New York Times* (12 May 1992).

Reily, Ross. "A Female Powerhouse," *Sun Herald* (30 Jan. 2005).

LA'TONYA REASE MILES

Harsh, Vivian Gordon (27 May 1890–17 Aug. 1960), librarian, was born in Chicago, the daughter of Fenton W. Harsh and Maria L. Drake Harsh, two graduates of Fisk University. Vivian attended Forrestville Elementary School and completed Wendell Phillips High School in 1908. In 1909 she took the first step toward what would become her life's career—a position, as a clerk, at the Chicago Public Library (CPL). Harsh pursued her education by matriculating at Simmons College Graduate School of Library and Information Science (Boston). In 1921 she earned a degree in Library Science and three years later was appointed the head of a local branch of the CPL, becoming Chicago's first black librarian. She joined the Association for the Study of Negro Life and History (ASNLH), which allowed her to remain abreast of literary developments in black history. Thanks to a fellowship from the Rosenwald Foundation, she pursued advanced studies in library science at the University of Chicago and Boston and Columbia universities.

In the early 1920s, Dr. George Cleveland Hall, the chief of staff at Provident Hospital, and other black leaders asked the CPL for a new local branch and Harsh convinced Julius Rosenwald, a white philanthropist, to donate funds for its construction on Chicago's South Side. In 1917 Rosenwald, chairman of the board of Sears, Roebuck, and Company, had founded the Rosenwald Fund that financially helped public schools, Jewish charities, and black institutions. As the new library branch was being built, the CPL appointed Harsh as its new director. In the summer of 1931 Harsh toured various black collections throughout the country and became particularly impressed by the Schomburg Collection of the New York Public Library, which would later inspire her to open a black collection in Chicago.

Vivian Gordon Harsh, a pioneering bibliophile. (Austin/Thompson Collection, from the Woodson Regional Library, Chicago.)

On 18 January 1932 the new South Side CPL branch, named for George Cleveland Hall, was dedicated with Vivian as the head librarian. The George Cleveland Hall Library was the first CPL branch to be built for the South Side black community. Having a strong interest in the preservation of black history, Harsh developed a Special Negro Collection with three hundred books donated by the widow of Charles Bentley, a local dentist, and by friends from the ASNLH. Despite lack of support from the main CPL, Harsh worked tirelessly to expand her library's black collection. She solicited book donations and even used her own money to acquire new materials. She also secured grants from several institutions, including the Rosenwald Foundation.

In 1933 Harsh instituted the Book Review and Lecture Forum, a series of semimonthly meetings with black authors as featured guests. RICHARD WRIGHT, LANGSTON HUGHES, ZORA NEALE HURSTON, ALAIN LOCKE, and ARNA BONTEMPS were among the intellectuals who attended those forums. In 1936 Harsh contributed to the planning of the ASNLH convention in Chicago. From the 1930s to the 1950s she nurtured the Chicago Renaissance, a great flowering of artistic and literary activities, by hosting emerging writers, musicians, and intellectuals at George Cleveland Hall.

During the Depression George Cleveland Hall served as the informal headquarters of the Illinois Federal Writers' Project (IFWP) sponsored by the Works Progress Administration (WPA). The WPA, created by President Franklin D. Roosevelt in 1935, involved projects funded by Congress and was designed to provide employment opportunities to the unemployed. One such project was Negro in Illinois, a study of African American life and culture, to which more than one hundred writers contributed. In 1942 the IFWP was discontinued and about one hundred boxes containing the incomplete Negro in Illinois study were turned over to George Cleveland Hall's Special Negro Collection.

Harsh retired in November 1958 after expanding the Special Negro Collection to more than two thousand items. Never marrying, she died two years later in Chicago, mourned by hundreds of library patrons. In 1970 the CPL renamed the black collection at George Cleveland Hall the Vivian G. Harsh Collection of Afro-American History and Literature. Five years later the Harsh Collection, which had become the largest repository of black historical materials in the Midwest, was relocated to the Carter G. Woodson Regional Library in

Chicago. Harsh's work as a pioneer collector and curator of black documents has significantly contributed to preserving the rich history of African Americans in the Midwest.

FURTHER READING

Hine, Darlene Clark, ed. *Black Women in America*, vol. 2 (2005).

Slaughter, Adolph J. "Historian Who Never Wrote," *Chicago Defender* (Daily Edition), 29 Aug. 1960.

DAVID MICHEL

Hart, Billy (29 Nov. 1940–   ), jazz drummer, was born William W. Hart in Washington, D.C., to William Alfred Hart and Ira Loretta Hart, both government workers who had met at Howard University. Primarily a self-taught musician, Hart played in rhythm and blues groups while still in high school. As the house-band drummer at Washington's Howard Theatre, he accompanied major soul acts such as OTIS REDDING, JOE TEX, the Impressions, the Isley Brothers, Sam and Dave, and SMOKEY ROBINSON and the Miracles when they toured through town.

Although such established names as the above are accepted as classic, coequal entertainers, societal conditions in the late 1950s restricted black artists from performing at the top venues in Las Vegas, Miami Beach, or even at Radio City Music Hall in New York. However, there was a circuit of older theaters in the bigger cities where blacks could appear before large audiences: the legendary Apollo Theater in New York City's Harlem, the Uptown Theater in North Philadelphia, the Royal Theater in Baltimore, the Regal in Chicago, and D.C.'s aforementioned Howard Theatre.

Hart's primary local influences on drums were Ben Dixon and Harry "Stump" Saunders. From 1958 to 1960 Hart began attending jam sessions hosted by the saxophonist Buck Hill, the best-known local D.C. jazz musician at that time. Because of Hill's personal relationships with other jazz artists, the unknown and relatively inexperienced Hart enjoyed playing with the established "star" saxophonists GENE AMMONS and SONNY STITT. At these sessions, he also encountered the pianist-vocalist SHIRLEY HORN, who would be one of his first steady jazz employers. Meanwhile, the guitarist Charlie Byrd was exposing Washingtonians to the new exotic Brazilian sounds of bossa nova at his club, the Showboat Lounge. Because of his straight eighth note work with pop-oriented acts at the Howard Theatre, Hart ended up being called—rather than a traditionally "jazzy" D.C.-area drummer—to work with João Gilberto,

Antonio Carlos Jobim, Bola Sete, and Luiz Bonfá. Hart also played with the pianist BOBBY TIMMONS at the Bohemian Caverns and did a brief stint with the Montgomery Brothers in 1961.

When the organist Jimmy Smith came to town, Hart was suggested for that job as well. In the early 1960s Hart accompanied Shirley Horn to San Francisco for an engagement, and while in California received a call from Smith to join him in Paris. Billy Hart ended up remaining with the busy organist for more than three years, from 1964 to 1966. A video taped in a London television studio on 30 May 1965 reveals the typical organ-trio format (organ, guitar, and drums) doing a spirited version of "Who's Afraid of Virginia Woolf?," which was originally recorded by Smith in a big band setting in 1964 with the Oliver Nelson Orchestra.

At this point in his career, Hart wished to relocate permanently to New York City because the saxophonist JOHN COLTRANE and the growing avant-garde movement based there was a magnet for young musicians. But his earlier spell with the Montgomery Brothers then paid off in a two-year stint with the famed guitarist WES MONTGOMERY. After Montgomery's unexpected death in 1968, Hart did indeed move to New York, where he immediately found work with the saxophonists PHAROAH SANDERS and EDDIE HARRIS. Hart's collaborative efforts with Sanders produced the classic recording *Karma* on 14 February 1969, which featured the memorable spiritual chant "The Creator Has a Master Plan." Hart is credited as "William Hart" on the album jacket.

The bassist Buster Williams, whom Hart had met while working with the vocalist BETTY CARTER nearly a decade earlier, then recommended him for the drum position in the former MILES DAVIS keyboardist HERBIE HANCOCK's new group, Mwandishi. Creating a unique identity to match their music, the members of Mwandishi (Swahili for "composer") took Swahili names. Hart's was Jabali ("rock"), and in the ensemble's almost three years of existence, they recorded and released a 1970 eponymous debut, the album *Crossings* in 1972, and *Sextant* in 1973. Commercially unviable, the inevitable financial and emotional exhaustion led the producer David Rubinson to ponder the following in the album liner notes for Herbie Hancock's *Treasure Chest*, May 1974: "How can one explain to … Billy Hart that the efforts of a lifetime must be rewarded only by week-in, week-out struggle?"

Despite that disappointment, Hancock also introduced Hart to the pioneering trumpeter Miles Davis, which enabled Hart to participate in the early June 1972 recording sessions for Davis's *On the Corner*. This would prove to be Davis's most controversial project. Where previously the mercurial Davis's new directions had often fragmented the jazz audience, fans and critics alike were unanimous in their mutual vilification of this work. By the late 1990s, in retrospect, it began to be viewed as visionary. Incidentally, on 12 June 1972, a piece was recorded titled "Jabali," although Davis never released it.

By the ealy 1970s Hart had become one of the most active drummers in jazz. In 1970 alone, he played on the former Coltrane pianist McCoy Tyner's *Asante*, the Viennese pianist Joe Zawinul's *Zawinul*, and the saxophonist Wayne Shorter's *Odyssey of Iska*. The McCoy Tyner connection bore fruit with another two-year stretch of work starting in 1973 and culminating with Tyner's evocative 1974 release *Sama Layuca*. Hart then switched gears and worked with the mainstream tenor saxophonist Stan Getz from 1974 to 1977. Again demonstrating his characteristic versatility, Hart's first recording as a bandleader, 1977's *Enchance*, is very progressive, with a band he assembled consisting of accomplished musicians who were all leaders in their own right.

Through the 1980s and 1990s Hart worked with collectives such as Quest, Great Friends, the New York Jazz Quartet, the Jazztet, the Mingus Dynasty, Saxophone Summit (also known as "The Three Tenors"), and the percussion ensemble Colloquium III, and he occasionally led his own four-, five-, and six-piece groups for Manhattan jazz clubs and recordings. As a sideman, Hart appeared on more than five hundred recordings. In 1988 he authored a play-along instructional book, *Jazz Drumming*. In 1992 he became assistant professor of jazz percussion at Western Michigan University and later joined the faculty at Oberlin College in Ohio. He was also an adjunct instructor at the New England Conservatory of Music and taught privately through New York University and the New School.

FURTHER READING

Donohue-Greene, Laurence. *All about Jazz—Billy Hart: A Hart of a Drummer* (2006).

Holden, Stephen. "Billy Hart and Friends," *New York Times,* 29 June 1986.

Rubinson, David. *Treasure Chest* (album liner notes, May 1974).

Tingen, Paul. *Miles Beyond: The Electric Explorations of Miles Davis* (2001).

JIM MILLER

Hart, William H. H. (31 Oct. 1857–6 Jan. 1934), professor, lawyer, activist, and entrepreneur, was born in Eufaula, Alabama, the son of Jennie Dunn and Henry Clay Hart, an Alabama slaveholder who had been born in Rhode Island. From 1867 to 1874 Hart attended Eufaula's American Missionary Association School, where he became involved in the black voting rights movement. Hart was a youth activist who spoke publicly in opposition of local government. This behavior drew attention to him and caused great concern for his safety. Fearful and impoverished, Hart left Alabama and gradually traveled to Washington, D.C., entirely on foot.

In 1876 Hart enrolled at Howard University. He graduated in 1880 with a Preparatory Department certificate and continued his studies, graduating with a B.A. degree in 1885, an LLB in 1887, an M.A. in 1889, and an LLM in 1891. During his time as a law student Hart worked for New York Senator William M. Evarts as a private secretary. This personal association would benefit him greatly over the years. Hart joined Howard University's law school faculty in 1890, specializing in teaching criminal, corporate, and tort law. His starting salary was $1,500 per year. Hart embarked on a fund-raising campaign for the establishment and annual maintenance of Howard's first law building, eventually securing an annual congressional appropriation of funds for that purpose. The law building was named for Senator Evarts in recognition of his support.

In 1889 Hart became the first black lawyer appointed special U.S. district attorney for the District of Columbia. His association with Evarts is credited for access to this post. Hart also served as Assistant Librarian of Congress from 1893 to 1897. He was selected chair of Howard's criminal law department in 1890 and dean of agriculture in 1897. That year Hart also founded the Hart Farm School and Junior Republic for Dependent Colored Boys. A rural education and farming facility on seven hundred acres on the Potomac River near Fort Washington, Maryland, the school sat on land that Hart purchased from Senator Evarts. He served as principal at the school, which was capable of housing two hundred children. In 1903 a Hart Farm student named Walter Mackenzie deliberately set fire to four large barns on the property. The ensuing damage was estimated at $10,000 but the school continued operations.

In 1904 Hart was arrested for violating Jim Crow laws in a groundbreaking interstate travel case. Hart directly challenged the legitimacy of interstate travel segregation. He purchased a train ticket on the Pennsylvania Railroad for continuous travel from New York City to Washington, D.C. The train was scheduled to make several stops. When it entered Maryland a conductor asked Hart to move to the car then designated for people of color. When he refused to move Hart was arrested, charged, and convicted of a "separate-car law" violation. Hart was fined $5 but won an appeal to a higher court, where his conviction was overturned.

Hart was a staunch social activist who had a penchant for protest. This applied to both his professional and personal lives. On 27 March 1905 in the District of Columbia the forty-seven-year-old Hart applied for a license to marry the twenty-one-year-old Mary M. Onley. Hart believed that citizenship overrode racial classification and that nationality was the prominent distinction of citizens. Therefore, in matters of government, race should not matter. As a result Hart demanded that the government clerk register the mixed-race couple as white in the marriage record book. After argument, Hart prevailed. The two were married by a justice of the peace and registered as they requested that same day. They made their home in Washington, D.C., where Hart had a thriving law practice. They had two children, Clementine and William H. H. Hart Jr.

On 11 July 1905 Hart and twenty-eight other black intellectuals from fourteen states met secretly on the Canadian side of Niagara Falls to discuss forming an organization in support of civil rights. This was the birth of the Niagara Movement. The founders drafted the Niagara Movement's Declaration of Principles, which detailed concerns and remedies in the areas of progress, suffrage, civil liberty, economic opportunity, education, courts, public opinion, health, employers and labor unions, protest, the color line, Jim Crow cars, soldiers, war amendments, oppression, the church, agitation, help (one of the official principles of the Niagara Movement, defined as making efforts to recognize the contributions of abolitionists and others toward the cause of equal opportunity), and duties. The Niagara Movement, formally incorporated on 31 January 1906, would struggle organizationally until developing into the NAACP in 1910.

Confrontational by nature, Hart often ruffled the feathers of colleagues and business associates. In 1903 he was arrested for assaulting a police officer and represented himself in that case. In another instance the U.S. government, which contracted the services of the Hart Farm School, severed ties with Hart because of his unwillingness to compromise on a settlement in a financial dispute. The

school was closed because of what some deemed a minor conflict. Even his association with Howard University would end in controversy. After thirty-two years of service Hart left Howard University's law school in 1922, under circumstances apparently caused by his short temper and his arguments with others.

Hart remained active in theater, music, and entrepreneurial pursuits in the District of Columbia area, culminating with the opening reception on 26 April 1925 of the newly acquired location for the Hart Allied Associations, which Hart founded. The company was formed to serve the local African American community with a bank, the Hart Life Insurance Company, a lyceum offering educational instruction, and a community forum through which public discussion and questions would be heard. The outcome of this venture is unknown. Hart was also a member of the District's Bethel Literary and Historical Association, and he was a founder of the FREDERICK DOUGLASS Memorial and Historical Association. Little more is known about Hart at the late stages of his life except that although he lived a life of great professional success, he was lonely and despondent over personal matters in his final days. William H. H. Hart died at his daughter's home in Brooklyn, New York, and was buried unceremoniously in Harmony Cemetery in Washington, D.C.

FURTHER READING

Logan, Rayford, and Michael R. Winston. *Dictionary of American Negro Biography* (1983).
Smith, J. Clay. *Emancipation: The Making of the Black Lawyer 1844–1944* (1993).
Obituaries: *Washington Post*, 10 Jan. 1934; *Journal of Negro History* (Apr. 1934).

NANCY T. ROBINSON

Hartley, Henry Alexander Saturnin (18 Dec. 1861–c. 1935), pharmacist, physician, man of letters, and licensed preacher in the British Methodist Episcopal Church and African Methodist Episcopal (AME) Church, was born in Port of Spain, Trinidad, to Stephen and Eleanor Jones Hartley. His mother, who was born in Bridgetown, Barbados, on 7 June 1830, was of Creole origin. She was confirmed at St. Michael's Cathedral, an Anglican church, on 6 January 1849, and moved a few months later on 27 June 1849 to Port of Spain. Her husband, whom she married at the Church of the Holy Trinity on 27 December 1860, was a merchant's clerk. A physician from Paris, France, named Louis Saturnin witnessed the couple's wedding and also the baptism on 5 February 1862 of their only son, Henry, who was Saturnin's namesake.

Not quite four years later, on 26 January 1866, Hartley's father died. To make ends meet Hartley's mother did embroidery and fancy needlework. Pious and frugal, she managed to share some of her small earnings with others who were less fortunate. Hartley had his confirmation on Palm Sunday, 28 March 1875, and attended Queen's Royal College, the leading secondary school in Trinidad, whose education was founded upon a thorough acquaintance with ancient Greek and Latin. In December 1878 Hartley passed his Cambridge examination at Queen's Royal College and in the following year decided that he would not study as he had planned for the Anglican ministry at Codrington College in Barbados. From 1880 to 1882 he worked off and on doing various jobs at the post office and railroad. He spent 1883 seeing the world and on 25 June 1883 married Naomi Locke, who had been born in London, England, on 19 May 1864. She died in childbirth less than ten months later on 13 April 1884 in Paris, France.

Returning to Trinidad after the loss, Hartley worked as a pharmacist and studied theology in his spare time. He was licensed to preach by the British Methodist Episcopal Church a month later on 1 September. The AME Church granted him the same privileges a month later, and on 15 June RICHARD HARVEY CAIN, bishop in the AME Church, made him a deacon. On 10 July 1887 Hartley became an elder in the British Episcopal Methodist Church. The two churches were—with the exception of Ontario—in the process of merging, and Hartley wanted credentials from both.

Hartley's career with the church did not run smoothly. In 1886 he was appointed to the Bethel AME Church on Board Street in Bridgeport, Connecticut, and seemed to enjoy life on the East Coast. After receiving an order of transferal to Arkansas in June 1887, he quit the AME Church and moved to Ontario, where he renewed his ties with the British Methodist Episcopal Church. About a year later Hartley rejoined the AME Church and was sent to St. Phillip's Church in St. John, New Brunswick. There on 13 August 1888 he delivered a panegyric in honor of his mother, who had died the month before. In December 1888 he married his second wife, Katherine Cunliffe, and published in the following year a small volume, *Classical Translations*, with a firm called J. & A. McMillan in St. John. The 134-page volume presented a collection of Hartley's translations from selected Greek and Latin authors. Cicero, Horace, Catullus, Tibullus, Propertius, Ovid, Martial, and Aesop were among them as well as three French writers, André Chénier, Alfred de Vigny, and Jean Reboul. He dedicated the book to Leonard Tilley, the lieutenant governor of New Brunswick (1873–1878 and 1885–1893) and sent a complimentary copy of the volume along with a postcard explaining his gift dated November 1889 to Charles W. Eliot, the president of Harvard University. In 1890 Hartley was transferred to St. Mark's Church in Amherst, Nova Scotia. While there he published his second book, *Ta Tou Pragma Emou Biou, or Some Concerns of My Life* with the Daily Press. In this 310-page book he presented certain episodes of his life, employing classical allusions and Latin quotations. The volume, which he dedicated to his mother, also contains various documents about him and his family as well as four line drawings of himself, his mother, and his first wife.

On 18 June 1891 the *Christian Recorder* reported the following comments of Hartley on race: "Rev. Henry Hartley, DD, made an address before the Baltimore Preachers Meeting Monday morning, June 8. Subject, 'The persecution of the Jews in Russia as compared with the treatment of the colored people in the United States.' The doctor said that the race prejudices were common among all people, but he thought that the semi-civilized nations were more excusable for their hate and persecution than the more enlightened nations. The doctor did not think that there was any race feeling in Russia in regard to the Jews, but because they refuse to use their money in the development of the Russian government, they are persecuted. But the prejudice of the white people against the colored people in this country is owing to color and previous condition."

But Hartley missed his congregation in St. John, and when a certain number of his new parishioners expressed their dissatisfaction with him to the presiding elder of the Nova Scotia Conference, he resigned. For the next several years he studied law and medicine while lecturing at various places in Maritime Canada. He also involved himself with several black associations such as the Order of Good Templars and the black lodge of Odd-Fellows. In 1906 he earned an MD at Laval University in Quebec City and in 1910 was admitted to the Nova Scotia Medical Society. He then returned to Port of Spain and spent his remaining years as a physician.

Within and without the church, Hartley's career was marked with moments of controversy. He was clearly a fearless and outspoken man, but one who was often misunderstood. In June 1884 in Port of

Spain he was enmeshed in a case of police brutality when he attempted to stop Detective John Lord from beating a drunken man on Abercrombie Street and was himself attacked by another officer. In November 1889 Hartley tried to pacify a ghost at Lower Cove in St. John by speaking to it in Latin and reading psalms to it in Latin. A few weeks later he gave a sermon titled "Spiritual Manifestations" at St. John, contending that spiritual forms were sent by the divine and could appear on earth. The incident with its elements of Shango-Yoruban belief in the spirit world common to the isle of Trinidad suggest that the apparent turmoil in Hartley's life may in fact stem from the fusion of cultures (African, Greco-Roman, Anglican, and Catholic) in his life. Such an intercultural synthesis would later influence the life and work of his fellow Trinidadians Eric Williams and C. L. R. JAMES, and shape the aesthetic vision of DEREK WALCOTT.

FURTHER READING

Hartley, H. A. S. *Ta Tou Pragma Emou Biou, or Some Concerns of My Life* (1890).

Fingard, Judith. "A Tale of Two Preachers: Henry Hartley and Francis Robinson and the Black Churches of the Maritimes," *Journal of the Nova Scotia Royal Historical Society* 5 (2002).

Hartley, H. A. S. *Classical Translations* (1889).

Hartley, H. A. S. "The Nova Scotia Annual Conference," *Christian Recorder*, 22 Aug. 1889.

MICHELE RONNICK

Hartman, Johnny (3 July 1923–15 Sept. 1983), singer, was born John Maurice Hartman in Chicago, Illinois, the youngest of the six children of John Hartman, a civil service employee for the city of Chicago, and Louisa Barner. At DuSable High School in Chicago, Hartman took singing lessons and sang with the school band and the glee club. His vocal skills were already evident at this time, and at sixteen he won a college scholarship to the Chicago Musical College. U.S. entry into World War II at the end of 1942 forced him to interrupt his studies. Hartman joined the military in 1943 and had his first semiprofessional experiences singing with the U.S. Army's Special Services Division. By the time of his discharge in 1945, Hartman was determined to become a professional singer.

Hartman's first break came in 1947, when he joined EARL "FATHA" HINES and His Orchestra. When Hines's group disbanded in 1948 Hartman joined DIZZY GILLESPIE, who had formed his own bebop band that year. Hartman remained with Gillespie for eighteen months, and by the time the band broke up in 1950, he seemed poised for stardom. The following year RCA Victor Records signed Hartman to a recording contract. However, the company's high hopes for the young baritone and his own aspirations to stardom were not realized. His association with the label lasted only one year and produced sixteen forgettable recordings, none of which became a hit. For several years after his departure from RCA, Hartman had no recording contract and could find little profitable work in the United States. Fortunately, though, he discovered that the market for a singer of his caliber was healthy in England, so he departed for London, where he found steady concert and television work. After two years in the country, British immigration requirements forced him to return home, where, despite his promising start, he was all but forgotten.

Two more years passed before another break came his way: the opportunity to make his first album in 1956. *Songs from the Heart*, a twelve-song set of romantic standards, was recorded for Bethlehem Records and featured Hartman's mature baritone accompanied by a superb quartet. Later in 1956 he recorded another album for Bethlehem, *All of Me*, this one with full orchestral backing. Although these albums represent some of Hartman's best work, they failed to establish him as a major national star, and another three years passed before he recorded again. Even though his career had failed to reach the heights he had expected and well deserved, Hartman did find personal happiness during this period. In 1958 he met and married Theodora Boyd, a dancer, and their twenty-five-year marriage produced two daughters.

The high-water mark in Hartman's career came in 1963, when the legendary jazz saxophonist JOHN COLTRANE suggested that he and Hartman make an album together. In its own way the invitation was astonishing, most of all perhaps to Hartman himself. Not only was Coltrane among the leading jazz musicians in the world, but he had never recorded with a vocalist before (nor did he do so again). That Coltrane initiated the contact that resulted in one of the most beautiful ballad albums ever recorded evidences the high regard in which he held the forty-year-old baritone. On 7 March 1963 Hartman and Coltrane's quartet assembled at the legendary engineer Rudy Van Gelder's studio in Englewood Cliffs, New Jersey, and recorded six songs, most of them in one take. The resulting album, titled simply *John Coltrane and Johnny Hartman* and issued on the Impulse label, became Hartman's finest and best-known work.

Like almost everything else in Hartman's life, however, the album had both positive and hindering effects on his career. On the one hand, the record's producer, Bob Thiele, worked with Hartman on his next four albums over as many years (1963–1967). On the other hand, it confirmed Hartman's reputation as a jazz singer, a label that limited his audience to a niche market and his performance venues to small black clubs in Philadelphia, Pennsylvania, Baltimore, and Washington, D.C., rather than the fancy, high-paying nightspots of New York and Las Vegas into which most mainstream singers were booked.

During the remainder of the 1960s and in the early 1970s, Hartman found more work abroad than he did in the United States. He spent much of 1968 in Australia, where he was a frequent performer on television and on concert stages. In 1972 he traveled to Japan, where he made two albums on Capitol's Japanese label with the Tokyo-based jazz trumpeter Terumasa Hino. One of those albums was a tribute to Coltrane, who had died in 1967. When he returned home later in 1972, Hartman did his best to appeal to a younger audience by recording two albums containing some of the pop tunes of the day, songs like "Raindrops Keep Falling on My Head" and "By the Time I Get to Phoenix." For the most part these efforts rang hollow and represented some of the worst recordings of his career. Hartman closed out the decade inauspiciously with a trickle of recordings and a few television appearances.

As the new decade dawned and Hartman's sixtieth year approached, he seemed to be coming into his own at last. In 1980 he recorded a superb album of standard love songs titled *Once in Every Life* for Bee Hive Records, and the album earned him his first Grammy nomination. Interestingly he seemed finally to embrace his reputation as a jazz singer. The genre had become trendy with young, upscale audiences, and Hartman was invited to play some of the fanciest clubs in New York. In his review of a 1982 performance at the Blue Note, the *New York Times* writer John S. Wilson noted that Hartman's anomalous reputation in the jazz world as a middle-of-the-road romantic baritone seemed to be giving way to a "jazzlike groove," including on one song "something approaching scat singing, which is unusual for Mr. Hartman" (C6).

Suddenly, after some thirty-five years in the business, Hartman was in demand. In early 1983 he was poised to merge his own lifelong interest in the Great American Songbook with his popular reputation as a jazz singer when Stash Records signed him to record an album of Harold Arlen songs with his old boss Gillespie. Before he could do so, however, he fell ill. After canceling a series of performances in London, Hartman returned to the United States and was diagnosed with lung cancer. In September, just two months after his sixtieth birthday, he died at Memorial Sloan-Kettering Cancer Center in New York.

Hartman's name might have remained a mere footnote in the history of American song, known only to a comparatively few jazz purists, were it not for Clint Eastwood's extensive use of his songs in the 1995 film adaptation of *The Bridges of Madison County*. The popularity of the film and its two soundtrack recordings, which feature Hartman prominently, made him known to a wider audience and ensured the subsequent release of virtually his entire recorded canon on CD. Still, given his prodigious talent and long tenure and the fact that singers as diverse as Tony Bennett and ELLA FITZGERALD had named him among their favorite vocalists, one must wonder why he is not a star of the first magnitude, a famous name known to millions. His anomalous place in the history of popular music accounts in part for his relative obscurity. "Hartman has few of the qualities that one usually associates with jazz singing," wrote Joel E. Siegel in a 1980 review in the *Washington Post*. "But his baritone is so rich, so precise and musical that jazz musicians … have welcomed him into their brotherhood" (B10). Perhaps his own pursuit of the elusive "mainstream," where some of his crooner idols like Frank Sinatra and NAT KING COLE swam, prevented him from embracing jazz as warmly as he was embraced by it. With the passage of time, however, he finally won. He is generally regarded as a great interpreter of standard American love songs.

FURTHER READING

Siegel, Joel E. "The Jazz of Johnny Hartman," *Washington Post*, 30 Jan. 1980.

Wilson, John S. "Jazz: Johnny Hartman Sings," *New York Times*, 23 July 1982.

Obituaries: *New York Times*, 16 Sept. 1983; *Jet* (3 Oct. 1983).

LEONARD MUSTAZZA

Harvard, Beverly (8 July 1950–), chief of police and security director, was born Beverly Joyce Bailey in Macon, Georgia, the youngest of seven children. She attended school in Macon, where she was an excellent student. In 1972 Harvard earned a B.A. in Sociology with a minor in psychology from Morris

Brown College in Atlanta. In 1973 she married Jim Harvard, whom she had met while they were both students at Morris Brown. They would have one daughter, Christa. Harvard graduated from the Federal Bureau of Investigation's (FBI) National Executive Institute. She held two honorary doctor of law degrees from Morris Brown and University of South Carolina.

After graduation from college, Harvard worked in communications. Out of this work she developed a genuine interest in law enforcement, but her career as a police officer was the result of a bet she made with her husband. According to Harvard, her husband agreed with a friend who asserted that only large women were suited for the police force. Harvard bet her husband $100 that she could graduate from the police academy. During that time, women and African Americans often met a hostile reception in the white, male-dominated profession of law enforcement. Also around that time, Atlanta elected its first black mayor, MAYNARD JACKSON. Subsequently, Harvard graduated from the police academy.

Following her graduation from the police academy, Harvard was hired by the Atlanta Police Department as a beat officer, where she was assigned to street patrol. She served as an affirmative-action specialist in the Atlanta Department of Public Safety from 1979 to 1980. Also in 1980 she earned an M.S. in Urban Government and Administration from Georgia State University in Atlanta. That year she became director of public affairs for the department, a position she held for two years. From 1982 to 1994 Harvard was deputy chief of police in three divisions: career development, criminal investigations, and administrative services. In 1983 Harvard became the first woman in the Atlanta police department to graduate from the FBI's National Academy in Quantico, Virginia. She won the Outstanding Atlantan award in 1983. In 1985 she was chosen as Alumna of the Year by Morris Brown College in 1985 and as Atlanta City Government's Woman of the Year.

In April of 1994 Harvard became acting chief of police for the city of Atlanta. On 26 October 1994 Mayor Bill Campbell announced Harvard's promotion to chief of police. Not only was Harvard one of the few female police executives in the United States (joined by Betsy Watson in Houston and Austin, Texas, and Penny Harrington in Portland, Oregon), at this time she became the first African American woman to head a major police force. In 1995 she was named one of Atlanta's Top 100 Powers to Be by *Atlanta* magazine and one of five Women

of the Year named on CBS's *This Morning* television program in 1995.

One of her first challenges, which came in early 1995, was to prepare the city's police force for Freaknik, the black spring break—an annual festival bringing in approximately one hundred thousand college students from predominantly black colleges to Atlanta. She also coordinated all levels of security during 1996 Summer Olympic Games. There was a deadly pipe bomb explosion in Atlanta's Centennial Olympic Park on 26 July. The police did not find the perpetrator, and the investigation was widely criticized. Harvard retired from the Atlanta Police Department in June of 2002 after 29 years on the force, including eight years as police chief. In 2002 she was appointed deputy security director at Atlanta's Hartsfield International Airport.

Harvard received many awards, citations, and honors during her career. She was a member of the International Association of Chiefs of Police, National Organization of Law Enforcement Executives, and Georgia Association of Chiefs of Police. She was a member of the board of trustees for Leadership Atlanta, the board of directors of the American Red Cross, and the Council on Battered Women. She served on the Commission on Accreditation for Law Enforcement Agencies and also served as an advisory board member of the National Center for Women & Policing.

Harvard also had a high profile in the media. She appeared on numerous television broadcasts and was featured in many magazines and newspaper articles. She appeared on NBC's *Today* show, CNN, and Black Entertainment Television. She was also profiled in major magazines and newspapers, including *Time, U.S.News & World Report, Newsweek, Ebony, Harper's Bazaar, George, McCall's, Girl's Life, Scholastic News, Jet, Women Looking Ahead, Christian Science Monitor, New York Times,* and *USA Today.*

SHERRI J. NORRIS

Harvey, Bessie (11 Oct. 1929–12 Aug. 1994) self-taught folk artist, was born Bessie Ruth White in Dallas, Georgia, the seventh of thirteen children of Homer White, a chef and a barber, and Rosa White, a seamstress. Harvey's father died when she was young, and her mother became an alcoholic. She quit school after the fourth grade to help care for her siblings. As a young child she learned how to make "something out of nothing" (Harvey). For example, she would make a car out of a box and tin cans and then pretend to go places in it. Harvey married at age fourteen, but after experiencing marital difficulties, she left her husband and moved to Knoxville, Tennessee. Later, the family moved to Alcoa, Tennessee.

The self-taught, visionary Christian artist began sculpting in 1974 at the age of forty-five. Harvey had no formal training as an artist, but she intuitively created spirit figures from roots, tree limbs, and plywood. Paint, cloth, beads, shells, hair, and other items she had around her house were also used to embellish her sculptures. Her second marriage was to Carl Henry, a native of Blount County who worked as a custodian at Maryville College. He fished with her and helped her look for pieces of wood with patterns that could be the basis for her spirit figures. Henry was one of the few people who accompanied her as she worked. She usually preferred to be alone with her sculptures. Harvey and her husband raised eleven children.

While working at Blount Memorial Hospital in Maryville, Tennessee, Harvey made dolls for some of the patients. Judy Higdon thought Harvey's work was unique and interesting. She made pictures and slides of the art and took them to Cavin-Morris Gallery in New York and Gaspari Gallery in New Orleans. Both of these galleries became interested in Harvey's work. Harvey had never imagined that her passion for creating figures would eventually earn her a place among notable artists.

Harvey was forty-five years old when her mother died in 1974. After her mother's death, Harvey began to imagine faces in wood paneling. It was then that she became serious about her art and spent more time making pieces. She believed that the natural wood pieces she found around her home were waiting to be "released." She felt that God inspired her work by telling her what each piece of wood should become. It was felt by some that Harvey's art was worth much more than she was earning from it. She told her daughter, Faye Dean, the following: "People aren't taking advantage of me; they are taking advantage of themselves. As long as God makes trees, I can make art." She was satisfied with getting $500 for a piece, which was enough to pay her mortgage; yet she knew a collector might sell the same piece for as much as $10,000. Bill Arnett, a wealthy Atlanta collector of African and African diasporic art, included her work in his collection. But Harvey didn't begin making art with the intention of profiting financially from it; she wanted to share her work with young people and help them understand its meaning and the ways in which art can be interpreted. Dean felt that Harvey's art was

her way of grieving for her deceased mother, since Harvey never attended her funeral; her feelings came out through her work.

In her neighborhood and her church, St. John Baptist Church in Alcoa, Harvey was known as "Ms. Bessie." According to a neighbor, Janice Allen, she was especially fond of children and was known to interrupt her sculpting work or to preempt an interview with a reporter if a child needed something. She often told stories and recited poetry that she wrote to entertain her family and friends.

In 1987 artist Mark Garrett met Harvey and was stunned by the first piece that he had ever seen of hers: a seven-foot-tall figure of Adam and Eve. It was a single forked branch with the fork serving as the legs, with Adam on one side and Eve on the other. This anatomically correct piece was achieved by using black paint, wood putty, plastic rubies, pearls, and real hair.

Harvey dreamed of starting a museum to help black children remember history and learn how far God had brought their race. She did not live to see this become a reality. However, two weeks before her death in 1994, Harvey learned that she had been chosen for the Governor's Award in the arts, presented by Tennessee Governor Ned McWherter; two of her daughters received the award in her honor at a ceremony at the governor's mansion. Shortly after her death, the city of Alcoa named one of its streets Bessie Harvey Avenue in her honor—it was the first street Harvey had ever lived on in Alcoa. The city also proclaimed her birthday, 11 October, Bessie Harvey Day. The city also had plans for a memorial park in her honor on the property where her first house stood. A family friend, Lorraine Garrett, was overseeing this project. Joyce McCroskey, a personal friend, sculptress, and community activist, had Bessie pose for a sculpture of Polly Toole, a black slave who saved important papers from a fire in the courthouse during the Civil War. The statue is in the Blount County Court House.

During Harvey's twenty-year career, it is estimated that the number of works she produced ran into the thousands. She had risen to the forefront of American art before her death, and her work could be found in museums across the country and Europe, including the Whitney Museum of American Art and the Smithsonian Institute's National Museum.

FURTHER READING

Cogswell, Robert. "Two Tennessee Visionaries: Bessie Harvey and Homer Green," *Folk Art Messenger* (Fall 1994).

Oppenheimer, Ann. "Outside the Mainstream: Folk Art in Our Time: A Weekend to Remember," *Folk Art Messenger* (Summer 1988).

Yelen, Alice Rae. *Passionate Visions of the American South: Self-Taught Artists from 1940 to the Present* (1993).

SHIRLEY M. CARR CLOWNEY

Harvey, Clarie Collins (27 Nov. 1916–27 May 1995), businesswoman, civil rights and peace activist, and United Methodist Church leader, was born Emma Augusta Clarie Collins in Meridian, Mississippi, the only child of Malachi C. and Mary Rayford Collins, owners of a funeral home and insurance business. The Harveys lived comfortably, despite the impositions of Jim Crow segregation. Collins began her education at two of the South's most important black institutions: Tougaloo College and Spelman College—the renowned Atlanta school for African American women—where she completed her B.A. degree in Economics in 1937. She went on to attend Indiana Institute of Mortuary Science, in 1942 becoming one of the first African Americans to receive a degree in Mortuary Science. She continued her education and in 1950 received an M.A. in Personnel Administration from Columbia University and then attended New York University's Graduate School of Business Administration.

On 1 August 1943 Collins married Martin Luther Harvey of Hampstead Long Island. Harvey was an African Methodist Episcopal Zion minister and for twenty-seven years was dean of student affairs at Southern University in Baton Rouge, Louisiana. There were no children born from this union, and the Reverend Harvey died on 23 March 1976. During their marriage the Harveys worked together on religious, civic, and civil rights activities. In 1964 Harvey and her husband were members of the Mississippi Advisory Committee to the U.S. Commission on Civil Rights and were the first husband-and-wife team to serve as board members on the Southern Regional Council, a thirteen-state southern human relations institution in Atlanta, Georgia, and one of the oldest civic organizations in the country.

The Harveys lived prosperous lives that allowed them to join an elite group of Mississippi black millionaire families. With her wealth and education, Harvey could have chosen to live an uneventful life, but she instead chose to use her money, businesses, and influence to work on behalf of what she saw as "an opportunity for Christian witness and ministry" (Harvey, 186). Her Christian faith has been the primary inspiration that has under girded all of her subsequent activities. She became a peace activist, leading businesswoman, civic and civil rights champion, and an advocate of higher education. Her paths crossed those of presidents, world leaders, and prominent women involved in civil rights, and she handled the funeral of the slain civil rights leader and luminary MEDGAR EVERS in June 1963 and worked on peace issues with the civil rights icons CORETTA SCOTT KING, DOROTHY HEIGHT, Virginia Naeve, and many others.

Some of her remarkable achievements as a Christian activist included serving as a Young Women's Christian Association (YWCA) student delegate to the 1939 World Conference of Christian Youth in Amsterdam, Holland (later called the World Council of Churches). The next year she helped establish a branch of the YWCA in Mississippi. In 1962 she joined women from ten countries at the seventeenth National Disarmament Conference in Geneva, Switzerland, followed by her participation in The World without the Bomb Peace Conference in Accra, Ghana. In 1963 Harvey and twenty-five other American women members of the Women's International Strike for Peace (later Women's Strike for Peace) met in Rome to support Pope John XXII's call for world peace. The women's group met with diplomats and heads of state and had an audience with the pope. From 1971 to 1974 Harvey was chosen as the first African American to lead the largest women's organization in the world, Church Women United, with more than 30 million members. With more than two thousand auxiliaries in the United States, Church Women United, founded in 1941, started the International World Day of Prayer and through its mission connects Catholic, Orthodox, and Protestant women in 170 countries of the world.

Harvey's civil rights, business, educational, and religious activities often overlapped, as in the case of her civil rights group Womanpower Unlimited, founded in 1961, "which consisted of Christian, Jews, atheists, anybody, Black and white who would stick their neck out" (*Washington Post*, 4 July 1971). The group aided the Freedom Riders who arrived in Mississippi to desegregate public accommodations between 1961 and 1966, providing them with bail money, food, clothing, and shelter. After the death of her parents, Harvey became president of Collins Funeral Home, Inc., and Collins Insurance Companies in Jackson, Mississippi, where she nurtured and built these businesses into multimillion-dollar industries that supported the economic development of the community in Mississippi and helped fund her causes throughout the world. In 1955 she was cofounder of the State Mutual Savings and Loan Association, a black enterprise that became a multimillion-dollar institution. Even as late at 1978, she was still establishing new businesses, founding the Unity Life Insurance and Industrial insurance company.

Her influence spread widely. In 1968 she was elected chairman of the Hinds County Community Service Association and in 1973 became secretary of the board of trustees of Atlanta University Center, Inc. In 1974 she received the Churchwoman of the Year Award from the Religious Heritage of America, and on 30 December 1974 the Mississippi governor William Waller declared Clarie Collins Harvey Day in Mississippi. In 1976 she was awarded the International Upper Room Citation to honor her leadership in the fields of human rights and worldwide Christian fellowship, the first black American to receive it and the fourth woman to be so honored. On 15 May 1977 Spelman College awarded her the first honorary degree in its ninety-six-year history, doctor of humane letters. She also received a doctor of humanities from Rust College in Mississippi. She served as a trustee for a number of academic and civic institutions such as Tuskegee Institute (1972–1984), the Martin Luther King Jr. Center for Social Change (1971–1979), and Rust College (1958–1970). In 1979 she received the Elmer L. Fowler's America's Heritage and Freedom Award, and the Business Woman of the Year Award from the Jackson chapter of the National Business League. From 1980 to 1982 she was secretary for the Mississippi Ethics Commission. She also wrote or coauthored many publications on her professional life, business management, and often on her personal life, including *From Caterpillar to Butterfly* (1978), detailing her church work and her fund raising work to establish the Mary Rayford Collins Library at Atlanta University on behalf of her mother, the first black female librarian in Mississippi. Her book *Stars at Your Fingertips* (1977) offered selections from her late husband's sermons.

FURTHER READING

An interview with Clarie Collins Harvey by John Dittmer and John Jones is kept in the Mississippi Department of Archives and History, Jackson, Mississippi.

Hankins, Rebecca, and Elizabeth Van. *Clarie Collins Harvey Papers: Finding Guide* (1990).

Harvey, Clarie, and Martin Luther Harvey. *Stars at Your Fingertips* (1977).

"Pioneers of Progress: Clarie Collins Harvey," *Black Enterprise* (June 1980).

"A Social Outcast and an Ex-Con Lead Church Women," *Washington Post*, 4 July 1971.

REBECCA L. HANKINS

Harvey, Georgette Mickey (1882–17 Feb. 1952), actress and singer, was born Georgette Mickey in St. Louis, Missouri. Her parents' names are not known, but they were reputedly shocked when their daughter, who had learned to sing in the church choir, left home in 1902 to tour with ERNEST HOGAN's *Rufus Rastus*. Harvey's deep contralto voice, striking looks, and dynamic personality ensured her rapid success. In 1904 she formed her own troupe, the Creole Belles, with whom she toured the United States and Europe, including England, France, Germany, and Belgium. They returned to America and became a sought-after vaudeville act. Tom Fletcher reports that the "Miss Georgette Mickey" became "Harvey" about this time, but no other reference to a marriage or any other cause for the name change has been found (179).

Harvey and her company returned to Europe in 1911, performing in England, Scotland, Ireland, the Scandinavian countries, and Russia. The troupe was especially welcomed in the cabarets and nightclubs of Russia, enjoying tremendous popular and financial success under Harvey's astute management. The troupe eventually broke up, but Harvey remained, enjoying even greater success as a solo act. She was living in a glorious style in St. Petersburg when the Revolution of 1917 forced her to flee. She managed to get on the last train bearing refugees out of the country but was caught and sent to Siberia, where she remained for a year and a half, watching her fortune depreciate. Landing with virtually nothing in Shanghai, Harvey ended up teaching English in China and Japan for two years; she was engaged for a time by a wealthy Japanese family as an interpreter, with whom she traveled throughout Japan and to Egypt and South Africa before earning enough to return to the United States around 1920.

Back in the states, Harvey formed another quartet and quickly reestablished her reputation, first as a recording star for Black Swan records and then in musical and dramatic roles on the New York stage. She made her Broadway debut in NOBLE SISSLE and EUBIE BLAKE's *Runnin' Wild* (1923), and when asked to create the role of Maria in the Theatre Guild's *Porgy* (1927), she insisted that the producers hire the three other members of her troupe as well. Harvey re-created the role of Maria in the 1929 revival of the play as well as in the musical version, *Porgy and Bess*, which premiered in 1935. In 1934 Harvey appeared as Binnie in the Theatre Union's controversial *Stevedore*, a play inspired by labor riots in East St. Louis and Detroit and a dock strike in New Orleans. This drama, in which Harvey uttered the memorable line "I got him! That red-headed son of a bitch!" was attacked by Congress as communist propaganda. The company gave benefit performances for the League of Struggle for Negro Rights, the Actors Fund, and the Scottsboro Defense Fund. Two years earlier Harvey had performed in a benefit to aid the national committee for the defense of the SCOTTSBORO BOYS, nine young black men falsely accused of rape in Alabama.

In 1939 Harvey starred with ETHEL WATERS and FREDI WASHINGTON in the celebrated *Mamba's Daughters*, the first nonmusical Broadway vehicle with a black female star and the first Broadway production designed by a black scenic designer, PERRY WATKINS. Ethel Waters had met the play's authors, Dorothy and Dubose Heyward, at one of Harvey's famous parties, this one for *Porgy's* director, Reuben Mamoulian. Harvey was one of several notable black actresses to portray the mother in the American Negro Theatre's *Anna Lucasta* (1944). She also performed in an adaptation of Tolstoy's *The Power of Darkness* by ABRAM HILL, who also directed. Other stage credits include *Solid South* (1930), *Savage Rhythm* (1931), *Ol' Man Satan* (1932), *The Party's Over* (1933), *Dance with Your Gods* (1934), *Lady of Letters* (1935), *The Hook-up* (1935), *Pre-Honeymoon* (1936), *Behind Red Lights* (1937), *Brown Sugar* (1937, with a young BUTTERFLY MCQUEEN), *Pastoral* (1939), *Morning Star* (1940, opposite the Yiddish star Molly Picon), the revival of *Porgy and Bess* (1942), and *Lost in the Stars* (1949).

Harvey also performed on Carlton Moss's radio series *Careless Love* (1930–1931), the radio series *A New World A'Comin'* (1944), and in four films: *The Social Register* (1934), *Chloe, Love Is Calling You* (1934), *The Middleton Family at the 1939 New York World's Fair* (1939), and *Back Door to Heaven* (1939). She was also active in the Negro Actors' Guild, serving as an officer of the executive board from 1939 to 1946 and as executive secretary in 1945. Harvey died at Harlem Hospital after a long illness. She had become a legend in the African American theatrical community, remembered by her peers for her sensational life, her adventurous spirit, her dynamic personality, and the remarkable range of her artistic achievements. Harvey once reported that she had written a memoir

titled "Soap Suds to Champagne," but its whereabouts is unknown.

FURTHER READING

A clippings file on Harvey as well as clippings files related to productions in which Harvey appeared may be found in the Billy Rose Theatre Collection, New York Library for the Performing Arts. Additional material (clippings, correspondence) is available in the Carl Van Vechten Papers, Moorland-Spingarn Collection of Howard University, and in the Black Theatre Scrapbook, Leigh Whipper Papers, and Negro Actors Guild files, both at the Schomburg Center for Research in Black Culture, New York Public Library. An audio recording of the *New World A'Comin'* program in which Harvey starred is held by the Schomburg Center.

Fletcher, Tom. *100 Years of the Negro in Show Business: The Tom Fletcher Story* (1954).

Wirth, Thomas H., ed. *Gay Rebel of the Harlem Renaissance: Selections from the Work of Richard Bruce Nugent* (2002).

Obituary: *New York Times*, 18 Feb. 1952.

CHERYL BLACK

Haskins, James S. (19 Sept. 1941–6 July 2005), writer and educator, was born in Demopolis, Alabama, to Henry Haskins, a funeral business worker, and Julia Brown Haskins, a homemaker. With the South still deeply segregated and blacks unable to use the public libraries, Haskins relied on his mother to buy solo volumes of an encyclopedia from the local supermarket to sate his literary appetite before a white friend of his mother's started to check out books from the library on his behalf. He attended a segregated elementary school in Demopolis, and though he credited the love of his family and friends for his future humanitarianism, Haskins later recalled that "Alabama in the forties was a terrible place.... For the most part, it seemed to me my childhood was a constant series of being told where to go and what to do in order to not aggravate the white power structure" (in Allen). Following his parents' separation when he was twelve, Haskins left with his mother for Boston, where he attended Boston Latin School, the oldest public school in America.

Upon high school graduation, Haskins returned to his home state to attend Alabama State University. Fervently taking part in the fight for civil rights, he was arrested at a protest in downtown Montgomery his freshman year, and was expelled from the university. He transferred to Georgetown in Washington,

DC, on a scholarship and received his B.S. in Psychology in 1960. He reenrolled in Alabama State, and earned his B.A. in History two years later, before getting his masters in Social Psychology from New Mexico in 1963. Moving to New York City, Haskins sold ad space for the *Daily News*, traded stock for Smith Barney & Co. on Wall Street, and worked in an antipoverty program, before becoming a special education schoolteacher for fifth-graders in P.S. 92 in Harlem in 1966. He recorded his struggles with his new job and the children in a journal and soon published it, on the advice of a friend, as his first book, *Diary of a Harlem Schoolteacher*.

The diary, which came out in 1969, was the first in what would be a prolific career. Sensing a new responsibility, "so children wouldn't grow up thinking that blacks had never done anything in the history of the world except be slaves" (*St. Petersburg Times*, 2 October 2005), Haskins turned his attention to children's books and biographies. He debuted in the genre in 1970 with *Resistance: Profiles in Non-Violence*, which discussed the concept of peaceful protest. Haskins began writing a vast spectrum of children's books: biographies on previously underrepresented African American political figures, activists, artists, entertainers, athletes, war heroes, ghost stories, slavery and freedom, and the civil rights movement. He won the Coretta Scott King Award, presented to an African American author for outstanding contribution to literature for children and young adults for his *The Story of Stevie Wonder* (1977), and won honors from the award committee in five other years.

Along with becoming a preeminent children's author, Haskins also moved from elementary schools to the university level. He was a visiting lecturer at New York's New School for Social Research and SUNY New Paltz from 1970 to 1972; visiting lecturer at Purdue University from 1973 to 1976, and an associate professor at Staten Island Community College from 1970 to 1977. Following the publication of his critically acclaimed adult-oriented *The Cotton Club* about the famed Harlem nightclub, he joined the faculty of the University of Florida, where he taught English and children's literature in Gainesville for the rest of his career.

In the 1980s, Haskins widened his scope of work to include the Count Your Way series, a collection of books that introduced children to the cultures and languages of diverse countries, and series on Black Theater and Black Music. He served as adviser on Francis Ford Coppola's blockbuster 1984 movie *The Cotton Club*, inspired by his book of the same name,

and proudly noted in an interview that "this movie employed more blacks than any other movie in history—900 to 1,000 of them" (Associated Press, January 1985). In 1994, he won the Washington, D.C., Children's Book Guild Award. By the end of his career, Haskins had written almost 150 titles for children and adults.

Haskins married Kathleen Benson, with whom he coauthored more than twenty books, in 1966. They had two daughters, Margaret and Elisa, and a son, Michael. Following Haskins's death by complications from emphysema in 2005, his vast collection of literature, papers, and transcripts on African American cultural studies were bequeathed to the University of Florida. The school posthumously announced a Visiting Scholar Fellowship for African-American Studies in his name. Prolific to his final day, Haskins posthumously won the Jane Addams Children's Book Award for Younger Children with his biography of the civil rights leader and president of the Savannah chapter of the NAACP, Westley Wallace Law, published in 2006.

FURTHER READING
Haskins, Jim. *Diary of a Harlem School Teacher* (1969).
Allen, K. Alycia. "Portrait of a Freedom Writer," *Applause: Gainesville's Entertainment Magazine*, 11 Mar. 1983.
Gale Research. *Something about the Author*, vol. 132 (2002).

ADAM W. GREEN

Hastie, William Henry (17 Nov. 1904–14 Apr. 1976), civil rights attorney, law school professor, and federal judge, was born in Knoxville, Tennessee, the son of Roberta Childs, a teacher, and William Henry Hastie, a clerk in the U.S. Pension Office (now the Veterans Administration). He was a superb student and athlete. His father's transfer to Washington, D.C., in 1916 permitted Hastie to attend the nation's best black secondary school, the Paul Laurence Dunbar High School, from which he graduated as valedictorian in 1921. He attended Amherst College, where he majored in mathematics and graduated in 1925, valedictorian, Phi Beta Kappa, and magna cum laude. After teaching for two years in Bordentown, New Jersey, he studied law at Harvard University, where one instructor adopted the custom of saying after asking a question of the class, "Mr. Hastie, give them the answer" (Ware, 30). He worked on the *Law Review* and earned an LLB in 1930.

Hastie returned to Washington, D.C., in 1930, passed the bar exam, and began his legal career as a practitioner and an educator. He joined the firm of CHARLES HAMILTON HOUSTON and Houston's father, William L. Houston, which then became Houston, Houston, and Hastie. He also joined the law faculty at Howard University, where his first students included THURGOOD MARSHALL and OLIVER HILL. He took a year away to study again at Harvard, where he shared an apartment with his friend ROBERT WEAVER and earned his SJD in 1933. He returned to Howard, where, when he was working in Washington, he taught until 1946. At the same time he became active in civil rights. His students researched current civil rights cases, participated in rehearsals of arguments on those cases, and attended the Supreme Court to watch Hastie and other civil rights giants argue cases. In 1935 he married Alma Syphax; they had no children before they divorced. In 1943 he married Beryl Lockwood; they had two children.

Hastie believed that, in the pursuit of justice, people should "struggle as best they know how to change things that seem immutable" (Ware, 147). In 1933 he was a founding member in Washington, D.C.,

William Henry Hastie, civil rights attorney and the first black federal judge in U.S. history, c. 1940s. (Library of Congress/National Association for the Advancement of Colored People Records.)

of the New Negro Alliance, part of the "don't buy where you can't work" movement of the 1930s. He took a case in which a local court issued injunctions against African Americans picketing at chain store outlets that, though operating in black areas, hired only white clerks. He argued the case in trial court and in federal appeals court but lost both attempts. He was unavailable to argue the case before the Supreme Court, which, convinced by the arguments Hastie and other attorneys had mounted, ruled in *New Negro Alliance v. Sanitary Grocery Co.* (1938) that the Norris-LaGuardia Act barred injunctions against peaceful labor-related picketing.

A champion of equal opportunity and racial integration, Hastie worked with the National Association for the Advancement of Colored People (NAACP) on major civil rights cases elsewhere, among them the 1933 *Hocutt* case in North Carolina, in which a black applicant unsuccessfully challenged the whites only admissions policy of the University of North Carolina. He also participated in cases that sought equalization of teachers' salaries, including the 1939 *Mills* case in Maryland and the 1940 *Alston* case in Virginia, both of which the NAACP won. With Marshall he argued cases before the Supreme Court that secured victories against the white Democratic primary in *Smith v. Allwright* (1944) and against segregated interstate transportation in *Morgan v. Virginia* (1946). In 1945 he presided at a conference in Chicago on segregated housing that the NAACP called to plan litigation against the constitutionality of restrictive covenants. A series of appointments with the federal government began in November 1933, when Interior Secretary Harold L. Ickes recruited Hastie as assistant solicitor. In that capacity Hastie helped draft the Organic Act of 1936 for the Virgin Islands, which established a fully elective legislature and broadened the electorate to include residents regardless of their property, income, or gender. Hastie, like Weaver, was an early member of what became known as President Franklin D. Roosevelt's "black cabinet." His performance at the Interior Department led to his appointment in March 1937 to a four-year term as district judge in the Virgin Islands, the first black federal judge in U.S. history. He resigned from his judgeship in early 1939 to become dean of the Howard law school. He took leave of the deanship in June 1940 to become civilian aide to Secretary of War Henry L. Stimson, in charge of handling matters of race in the military. In 1942

President Roosevelt also named Hastie a member of the Caribbean Advisory Committee, to advise the Anglo-American Caribbean Commission, established to foster the wartime social and economic cooperation of British and U.S. possessions in the Caribbean. Though Hastie's work in the War Department earned him the title "father of the black air force" (Ware, 133), he resigned his position there in early 1943 in frustration over his limited effectiveness in curtailing racial segregation and discrimination in the military. For his efforts and his resignation over what he called the army air force's "reactionary policies and discriminatory practices," he won the NAACP's Spingarn Award in 1943.

Hastie resumed his work at Howard University, and he presided at a rally in 1944 for a permanent Fair Employment Practices Committee. In 1946 President Harry S. Truman nominated him for the governorship of the Virgin Islands. The only African American who had previously served as governor of any U.S. jurisdiction was P. B. S. PINCHBACK, who served for a month as acting governor of Louisiana after being elected to the state senate during Reconstruction. Hastie had a rough time dealing effectively with public affairs in the islands, but he tried to enhance Virgin Islanders' self-government. He fostered a civil rights law that prohibited discrimination on the basis of race or color.

In 1948 Hastie briefly returned to the mainland, where he campaigned effectively in black communities in support of President Truman's reelection bid. In 1949 Truman appointed him to the U.S. Court of Appeals for the Third Circuit. Hastie took his seat as a recess appointment in December 1949, the first black federal judge with life tenure. Confirmed in 1950, he served as appeals judge until 1968, then as chief judge until he retired in 1971, and as senior judge thereafter. He wrote the decisions in more than four hundred cases. He was considered for a Supreme Court appointment as early as 1954 and as late as 1967, when President Lyndon Johnson nominated Hastie's former student Marshall instead.

A member of the board of directors of the NAACP Legal Defense and Educational Fund from 1941 to 1968, Hastie continued to give public lectures on civil rights. He also served on the boards of trustees of Amherst College and Temple University. Cool and suave, committed yet dignified, Hastie died in Norristown, Pennsylvania. He excelled as a law school professor and dean, as a civil rights attorney and leader, and as a pioneer black officeholder in the federal government.

FURTHER READING

The William H. Hastie Papers at the Law School Library, Harvard University, are available on microfilm. The Beck Cultural Exchange Center in Knoxville, Tennessee, has a collection of Hastie's papers, books, and memorabilia and maintains a permanent Hastie exhibit. Other materials are at Howard University and in the NAACP Papers at the Library of Congress.

McGuire, Phillip. *He, Too, Spoke for Democracy: Judge Hastie, World War II, and the Black Soldier* (1988).

Rusch, Jonathan J. "William Henry Hastie and the Vindication of Civil Rights," *Howard Law Review* 21 (1978): 749–820.

Ware, Gilbert. *William Hastie: Grace under Pressure* (1984).

Obituaries: *New York Times* and *Washington Post*, 15 Apr. 1976.

This entry is taken from the *American National Biography* and is published here with the permission of the American Council of Learned Societies.

PETER WALLENSTEIN

Hastings, Alcee Lamar (5 Sept. 1936–), politician, was born in Altamonte Springs, Florida, to Julius and Mildred Hastings, both of whom took domestic work. Determined that the young Hastings should have a complete education, they moved out of the state in search of more profitable employment, leaving Alcee in the care of a grandmother.

Hastings attended schools in nearby Sanford, Florida, before matriculating in 1954 at Fisk University in Nashville, Tennessee, where he pursued degrees in zoology and botany. He graduated in 1958. Soon, however, Hastings became interested in legal studies. In 1958 he enrolled at Howard University in Washington, D.C., and in 1963 graduated with a J.D. from Florida A&M in Tallahassee, Florida. Shortly thereafter he took up a law practice.

Hastings had an interest in elective office, so in 1970 he mounted a campaign for a seat in the U.S. Senate, but went down to defeat in the Florida primary. After serving two years as a circuit court judge in Fort Lauderdale (1977–1979) President Jimmy Carter appointed Hastings to the federal bench in Florida's Southern District. He was the first African American in Florida to hold such a seat. In 1981, however, Hastings was accused of soliciting a bribe in exchange for granting lenient sentences to organized crime figures. He was acquitted—largely on a technicality—but it was only the beginning of the controversy and alleged criminality surrounding Hastings.

The bribery case against Hastings refused to go away. An investigative arm of the Eleventh Circuit Court of Appeals continued to look into the matter, finally issuing a recommendation to the U.S. Congress that Hastings be removed from the bench. In 1988 the Congress took up this recommendation, voting overwhelmingly to impeach and convict. Hastings, for his part, rejected this action, arguing that his constitutional rights had been violated, inasmuch as he had been tried by a Senate committee and not by the full body of the Senate itself. A similar case before the Supreme Court, dealing with the impeachment of Walter Nixon, a federal judge from Mississippi convicted for perjury, *Nixon v. United States* (1993), found that the Court had no jurisdiction in such matters, and Hastings's removal was upheld.

Despite this disgrace Hastings did not wait long to climb back into the political ring. Following a failed bid for Florida's secretary of state, in 1990 he mounted a campaign to capture Florida's newly drawn Twenty-Third Congressional District, and this time he was successful, scoring something of a surprise victory in the primary and then cruising to victory in what was a heavily Democratic district. In that seat Hastings pursued a progressive agenda—improvements to the nation's public school system, curbs against employment discrimination, and bans on assault weapons, among other such positions. During the controversial and deeply divisive presidential cycle of 2000, won by Republican George W. Bush after the U.S. Supreme Court halted a full recount of the presidential vote in Florida, Hastings argued that voters in his district had been effectively disenfranchised by Republican dirty tricks, and he hinted at "backroom deals" struck by the Dade County election board. Believing that the presidential electoral vote in Ohio was also illegitimate—because of voting machine irregularities that allegedly favored the Republicans—Hastings and thirty other liberal House members voted against certifying the presidential election results.

Hastings served as a member of the Congressional Black Caucus and in 2006 was nearly appointed to lead the House Permanent Select Committee on Intelligence until controversy over his past led Speaker Nancy Pelosi to choose another appointment.

Controversy was not confined to Hastings's past. On occasion, he made public utterances that rankled opponents and supporters both. During the 2008 presidential election cycle, his comments that "Anybody toting guns and stripping moose don't care too much about what they do with Jews and blacks," in regard to the Republican vice presidential candidate Sarah Palin, whose image as an outdoorsy moose hunter became one of the fixtures of her public image during the campaign, led to a hasty, if somewhat half-hearted, retraction. That same year, 2008, Hastings easily won reelection, his eighth term representing Florida 23. In 2009 he again raised eyebrows when, in defense of hate-crimes legislation, he read a long list of sexual fetishes on the floor of the House and into the congressional record.

The twice-divorced Hastings had three children. In 2009, he sat on the House Rules Committee and the Subcommittee on Terrorism/HUMINT, Analysis, and Counterintelligence, and was chair of the Subcommittee on the Legislative and Budget Process.

FURTHER READING
Freedman, Eric. *African Americans in Congress: A Documentary History* (2008).
Johnston, David. "Hastings Ousted as Senate Vote Convicts Judge," *New York Times*, 21 Oct. 1989.

JASON PHILIP MILLER

Hathaway, Donny (1 Oct. 1945–13 Jan. 1979), singer, musician, songwriter, arranger, and producer, was born in Chicago, Illinois, the son of Drusella Huntley. He moved to the "ghetto" of St. Louis, Carr Square Public Housing Project, at a young age and was raised by his grandmother, Martha Pitts, who also went by the name Martha Crumwell, an accomplished gospel singer and guitarist. A child prodigy, Hathaway sang with his grandmother in the church. He was known as "The Nation's Youngest Gospel Singer" at the age of three (*Everything Is Everything*, 1970).

He learned to play the piano, and soon classical music and jazz also became an integral part of his musical upbringing. He attended Vashon High School, and upon graduation in 1964 he won a fine arts scholarship to study music at Howard University in Washington, D.C. At Howard he met his future singing partner, ROBERTA FLACK. He also roomed for three years with another notable singer, Leroy Hutson. Needing money while in college, Hathaway joined a jazz group called the Ric Powell Trio and started performing around the D.C. area.

The word quickly spread about Hathaway's prodigious talent. Tempted by a multitude of job offers from the music industry, Hathaway left school after only three years. He quickly developed into a much-sought-after songwriter, arranger, session musician, and producer. He worked with major talents such as the Staple Singers, JERRY BUTLER, Carla Thomas, ARETHA FRANKLIN, Woody Herman, and LENA HORNE.

However, it was CURTIS MAYFIELD who signed him to a contract with his emerging Curtom label. He considered him "a young genius" and was impressed with the breadth and depth of Donny's musical knowledge. "You could just talk to him over the phone and play him a piece of music, and he could call out every chord and every movement" (Werner, 157).

Hathaway worked for a short time at Curtom as a backup singer, arranger, songwriter, and house producer. In 1969 he cut his first single, a duet with June Conquest called "I Thank You Baby." After he left Curtom, Hathaway met with the legendary saxophonist and bandleader KING CURTIS at a music industry convention and secured a recording contract with Atlantic Records. In 1969 Hathaway released his debut single with the label Atco Records, a division of Atlantic Recording Corporation, "The Ghetto, Pt. 1," a song he cowrote with Leroy Hutson. Initially only a minor hit, it is now regarded as one of the seminal tracks in the shift to the more politicized soul typified by Mayfield's work. This paved the way in 1970 for the release of his critically acclaimed debut album, *Everything Is Everything*, featuring a stunning version of NINA SIMONE's "To Be Young, Gifted, and Black."

The producer and arranger Arif Mardin found out firsthand how deeply this album affected people when he went to record a live album with Donny Hathaway in Los Angeles. Arriving at the club for the rehearsal, he discovered a line of black people circling several times around the block with tickets, waiting to enter three hours before the show. He recalled his conversation when he called the office: "Something's going on here, I said. The electricity was unbelievable. Then during the live performances at the Troubadour, they knew every song. He opened his mouth and the audience went berserk" (George, 125–126). Seeing Hathaway wearing his trademark apple hat and hypnotizing the fans with his smoky yet velvety and melismatic voice, Mardin was amazed at how Hathaway could build a bridge between penetrating social commentary and soulful balladry. He viewed Hathaway as one of the leaders in expanding the harmonic language of rhythm and blues:

"Donny was a pioneer in that direction vocally as well as in his writing" (George, 126).

Hathaway released his second album, *Donny Hathaway*, in 1971. It became a major hit showcasing his formidable ability to be a musical interpreter. Two of the most memorable covers were Leon Russell's "A Song for You" and Van McCoy's "Giving Up." During that same year he recorded James Taylor's "You've Got a Friend" with his former classmate, Roberta Flack. It became a hit and set the stage for them to feature their magical and seamless blending of vocals on a full album of duets called *Roberta Flack and Donny Hathaway* (1972). The album was highlighted by one of the year's biggest songs, "Where Is the Love." The ballad shot to number one on the R&B charts, hit the top five on the pop charts, won a Grammy, and helped the album go gold. Hathaway also did a solo cover on "For All We Know," which many fans regard as one of the most hauntingly beautiful ballads he ever recorded.

Later in 1972 Hathaway released his brilliant *Live* album, a recording energized by the audience response. He also branched out into soundtrack work, scoring the film *Come Back Charleston Blue* (1972) and composing the theme song for the TV series *Maude* from 12 September 1972 to 22 April 1978. It was a huge year for Hathaway, especially when his wife, Eulaulah, had their daughter, Lalah, who would eventually forge her own career as an excellent singer.

Unfortunately, Donny's remarkable success was crippled by severe bouts of depression that resulted in periodic hospitalization and caused his partnership with Flack to deteriorate. Nevertheless, in 1973 Hathaway released *Extension of a Man*, which featured an ambitious and eclectic array of tunes. It was some of his finest work and included the inspirational song "Someday We'll All Be Free."

Sadly, due to the depression, Donny never released another album. He largely withdrew from the music industry, playing occasionally in small venues. After several years, he was able to reconcile with Roberta Flack, and they collaborated on the huge hit "The Closer I Get to You," which appeared on Flack's album *Blue Lights in the Basement* (1977).

The pair began work on a new album of duets when a disoriented and depressed Hathaway committed suicide, plunging to his death from the fifteenth floor of the Essex Hotel in New York. Devastated, in 1980 Flack released the two cuts the pair had finished, "Back Together Again" and "You Are My Heaven," on her album *Roberta Flack Featuring Donny Hathaway*. Both songs became posthumous hits.

Donny Hathaway recorded only three solo studio albums, but his influence on the musical world was phenomenal. Artists ranging from rock to hip-hop to neoclassical soul cite Hathaway's influence on their music. The musical expressions and significant contribution this pioneer and gifted artist gave to the world will always be treasured.

FURTHER READING

Bogdanov, Vladimir, et al., eds. *All Music Guide to Soul* (2003).

George, Nelson. *The Death of Rhythm and Blues* (1988).

Werner, Craig. *Higher Ground: Stevie Wonder, Aretha Franklin, Curtis Mayfield and the Rise and Fall of American Soul* (2004).

DISCOGRAPHY

Everything Is Everything (Atlantic 1970).

Donny Hathaway (Atlantic 1971).

Live (Atlantic 1972).

Extensions of a Man (Atlantic 1973).

The Best of Donny Hathaway (Atlantic 1978).

A Donny Hathaway Collection (Atlantic 1990).

These Songs for You, Live (Atlantic 2004).

WAYNE L. WILSON

Hathaway, Isaac Scott (4 Apr. 1874–12 Mar. 1967), sculptor, illustrator, ceramicist, and entrepreneur, was born in Lexington, Kentucky, the first of three children born to the Reverend Hathaway and Mrs. Hathaway. Hathaway's mother died when he was only two years old, and his father and grandmother raised him and his two sisters, Fannie and Eva.

A trip with his father to a local museum inspired Hathaway to become an artist. Walking through the museum's galleries, which were filled with busts of famous white American heroes, Isaac noticed the absence of many African Americans, such as FREDERICK DOUGLASS. He asked his father why they were absent, and the elder Hathaway simply stated that there were no trained African American sculptors to sculpt prominent African American people. The young Hathaway determined to change this by becoming a trained artist.

Hathaway began his career as an artist at Chandler College in Lexington and continued it at Pittsburg Normal College in Pittsburg, Kansas, where he studied ceramics. He studied both art and sculpture in the art department of the New England Conservatory of Music in Boston and the Cincinnati Art Academy in Ohio. He also studied ceramics at the State University of Kansas at Pittsburg and at the College of Ceramics of the State University of New York at Alfred.

In addition to pursuing training in a variety of artistic media, Hathaway taught art to elementary school students in Kentucky. Fellow artists convinced him to start his own business. He meshed his artistic talents and his entrepreneurial skills to establish his first company, called the Afro-Art Company; the name was later changed to the Isaac Hathaway Art Company. Hathaway produced busts of prominent African Americans, including Frederick Douglass, GEORGE WASHINGTON CARVER, BOOKER T. WASHINGTON, and PAUL LAURENCE DUNBAR. He was the first artist to make death masks of famous African Americans. In 1915 he gained even more recognition as an artist and educator when he founded the Department of Ceramics at Tuskegee Institute in Alabama, thereby making ceramics a part of the college curriculum in the United States.

Hathaway broke racial barriers by having his work displayed in academic and government institutions. He contributed molded plaques and masks of both black and white figures that could be displayed on the walls of universities and churches. His busts and sculptures were in the homes of President Franklin D. Roosevelt, Vice President Henry Wallace, and the automotive industry's Ford family, also at Harvard University. Hathaway created bronze metal pieces as well.

In 1946 President Harry S. Truman authorized a commission by the U.S. Mint of a fifty-cent piece; Hathaway was also chosen to design the George Washington Carver commemorative fifty-piece coin in 1951.

Hathaway's wife was Umer G. Hathaway; her maiden name and the years of their marriage are not known. Although he was a forgotten artist at the time of his death in 1967 at age ninety-two, the nonprofit Isaac Scott Hathaway Museum was established in his hometown of Lexington in 2002 to develop a traveling exhibit for schools and civic groups. The museum is also considering the purchase of Hathaway's works and papers and the documenting of other famous African Americans from Lexington.

FURTHER READING

Guelzo, Allen. *Lincoln's Emancipation Proclamation: The End of Slavery in America* (2004).

"Isaac Scott Hathaway," in *African Americans in the Visual Arts: A Historical Perspective*, available online at http://www.cwpost.liunet.edu/cwis/cwp/library/aavaahp.htm.

RENÉE R. HANSON

Havens, Richie (21 Jan. 1941–), musician, activist, author, painter, and sculptor, was born Richard Pierce Havens in Brooklyn, New York, the oldest of nine children. He grew up in the Bedford-Stuyvesant neighborhood. His father, Richard Havens, worked as a metal plater and dreamed of becoming a professional pianist, eventually learning to play a number of instruments. Richie's mother, Mildred, a bookbinder and casual singer at home, encouraged her young son when he started singing background vocals at the age of twelve for local groups. All kinds of music were played in the Havens home; Richie's grandmother listened to Yiddish, gospel, and big band music; his mother enjoyed country music, and his father loved jazz. He joined the doo-wop singing group the Five Chances at age fifteen and performed the next year with the Brooklyn McCrea Gospel Singers, a group that sang hymns for neighborhood churches. Havens learned to play the Indian sitar in 1958 and used it on many of his recordings.

Still in his teens, Havens left high school in 1961, went to live in Greenwich Village, and supported himself by painting portraits and singing folk music. Havens played guitar in Greenwich Village clubs including the Bizarre, the Fat Black Pussycat, and Café Wha! He employed an unorthodox method of

Richie Havens plays at an anniversary Woodstock concert in Bethel, N.Y., in 1999. (AP Images.)

using his thumb to bar chords in an open tuning and gained a following in the Village. Havens thought of himself as part of the Beatnik Generation and later named Fred Neil, Bob Camp, Bob (later known as Hamilton) Gibson, NINA SIMONE, and Dino Valente as early influences. When Warner Brothers began signing a group of folk artists in the early 1960s, Havens received a recording contract from the label, but he did not finish the demo and his record deal was not extended. He did record several albums for Douglas International Records. Havens played at the 1965 Newport Folk Festival and sang and acted in the off-Broadway play *Bohickee Creek* alongside a young JAMES EARL JONES in 1966.

Havens signed another contract with Verve Folkways (later Forecast records) in 1967, and his album *Mixed Bag* was released soon after. The anti-war song "Handsome Johnny" became known on the folk circuit, and Havens's distinctive rhythm-style strumming guitar on a remake of Bob Dylan's "Just like a Woman" drew attention to him as he performed in nightclubs. Performances at the Monterey Pop Festival in 1967 and the 1968 Miami Pop Festival continued to build his reputation. In 1968 he appeared on *The Ed Sullivan Show*, (then called *The Toast of the Town*) performing songs from his albums.

His second album for Verve Folkways, *Something Else Again* (1968), gained Havens a place on the *Billboard* charts, but it was his appearance at the Woodstock Music and Art Fair in August 1970 that brought him national fame. Havens was scheduled to go on at midday following some better-known performers, but these groups were delayed (or in some cases prevented from arriving) due to huge crowds at the festival. Havens ended up performing an extended three-hour set to a huge audience hungry for live music. The crowd called for an encore and Havens claimed that he had run through his entire repertoire, so he improvised a song, "Freedom," that incorporated several hymns and his distinctive guitar styling. The song resonated throughout the largely antiwar, antidraft crowd, many of whom craved freedom from government intervention in their lives. Havens, building on his fame from the Woodstock Festival, performed at the Isle of Wight Festival in England in the same year.

Havens also started his own Stormy Forest Records in 1970, for which he released albums in between contracts with the major labels; also that year his music was used in the film *Woodstock* (1970). He appeared on *The Tonight Show with Johnny Carson* from 1970 to 1973. In 1971 Havens recorded "Here Comes the Sun," written by George Harrison of the Beatles, and the song became a top-twenty pop single, helping to propel his *Alarm Clock* album into the top thirty. He received three gold records for the sales of his albums *Alarm Clock*, *The Great Blind Degree* (both 1971), and *Richie Havens on State* (1972). Havens acted on the stage in the original production of the Who's *Tommy* (1972) and in the motion pictures *Ali, the Fighter* (1971), *Catch My Soul* (1974), and *Greased Lightning* (1977). Havens continued to record, signing a contract with A&M in 1976 and making two albums, *The End of the Beginning* and *Mirage*, the next year. In 1978 his music was used for the Academy Award–winning film *Coming Home*. He signed with Elektra in 1980 and recorded *Connections*, followed by *Simple Things* in 1987. During the 1980s and 1990s his music was used in films and television including the TV shows *Hearts of Fire* (1987) and *Street Hunter* (1990), and in the films *Wired* (1989) and *Navy Seals* (1990). He was a performer at the Earth Ball during Bill Clinton's inaugural festivities in 1993 and sang at Bob Dylan's Thirtieth Anniversary Concert the same year. Rhino Records rereleased a number of his recordings in the 1990s. He was also active in other areas of education and began recording songs for children in the 1990s. His song "The Light of the Sun" was featured on the collection *Put On Your Green Shoes*, released by Sony Kids Music in 1993.

He relaunched Stormy Forest in 2000 and not only reissued earlier albums but also released new material on two CDs, *Wishing Well* and the self-produced *Grace of the Sun*. Havens was a cofounder of the Northwind Undersea Institute, an oceanographic museum for children on City Island in the Bronx and the National Guard, an educational program that taught students ways to effect ecological change in their own communities.

Richie Havens was awarded the American Eagle Award in 2003 by the National Music Council for his contributions to American music and his dedication to social responsibility. Haven also established a studio for painting, sculpture, and photography located in the Monroe Center for the Arts in Hoboken, New Jersey. In the first decade of the twenty-first century, his music appeared in the films *Collateral* (2004) and *The Pursuit of Happyness* (2006). He remained active into the twenty-first century as both a performer and an activist, extending his legacy as one of the most distinctive folk artists of his generation.

FURTHER READING

Havens, Richard, and Steve Davidowitz. *They Can't Hide Us Any More* (1999).

Rees, Dafydd, and Luke Crampton. *Rock Movers & Shakers* (1991).

PAMELA LEE GRAY

Havis, Ferd (15 Nov. 1846–25 Aug. 1918), businessman and politician, born in rural Arkansas, was the slave son of his owner, John Havis, a white farmer in Bradley and Jefferson counties, and an unnamed slave mother. Most often known simply as Ferd, his name appears in some records as Ferdinand. After the Civil War, he was educated in Freedmen's Bureau schools in Pine Bluff, Arkansas, where he lived for the rest of his life.

A successful entrepreneur, Ferd Havis began his career as a barber, but quickly expanded his interests, eventually operating both a saloon and retail whiskey distributorship in Pine Bluff, as well as owning tenement houses and two thousand acres of farmland in Jefferson County. He married his first wife, Dilsey, in the mid-1860s, and they had one daughter, Cora; Dilsey Havis died in 1870. In 1871 he was elected to the first of five terms as a Pine Bluff town alderman. An active Republican, he also served one term in the Arkansas House of Representatives (1873), but resigned to become Jefferson County's tax assessor, holding that post until 1877. A colonel in the Arkansas state militia, he was appointed by the Republican governor Elisha Baxter, whom Havis supported during the Brooks-Baxter "war" of April–May 1874—a sometimes-violent political dispute between armed supporters of Baxter and his fellow Republican challenger Joseph Brooks. African Americans fought for both sides in the dispute, which resulted in two hundred deaths. Following intervention by the federal government and adoption of a new state constitution, Baxter stepped down in late 1874, conceding rule to Democrats and ending Reconstruction in Arkansas, and becoming the state's last Republican governor for a century.

Havis continued to play an influential role in Republican Party circles, serving as an at-large delegate to the Party's 1880 national convention and joining an unsuccessful group seeking a third term for the former president Ulysses S. Grant. Havis served for twenty years as chairman of Jefferson County's Republican Party and became vice president of the Arkansas Republican Party in 1888. In 1882 Havis was elected county clerk of Jefferson County, a post he held until 1892, and served as a congressional district delegate to national party conventions in 1884 and 1888.

While his political record remained strong, his personal record was tarnished by legal difficulties. Havis regularly kept his popular local tavern open well past midnight on Saturdays, technically violating a Pine Bluff ordinance against "breaking the Sabbath," and paid a small, regular weekly fine in court in 1882 (Morgan, p. 135). Later arrested and fined after pleading guilty to selling whiskey on Sunday, Havis was also investigated by a grand jury in 1883 for allegedly seeking double reimbursement of personal expenditures, but was never indicted.

His second wife, Geneva Havis, died of natural causes in August 1886, after bearing a daughter, Ferdie P. Havis. In November 1887, Havis married his third wife, Ella M. Cooper, who became the mother of his three youngest children: daughters Viessy and Alma L., and Havis's only son, Felton.

In 1889 Havis made an unsuccessful bid as the Republican candidate for the state's U.S. Senate seat, opposing the Democratic incumbent James Henderson Berry, but the heavily Democratic Arkansas legislature reelected Berry. Havis continued to be active in Republican circles, serving as a district delegate to the 1896 national party convention, alongside his longtime ally, the former U.S. Senator Powell Clayton. Both supported the Republican nominee William McKinley, who then appointed Clayton as U.S. minister to Mexico the following year.

With Clayton's support, President McKinley nominated Havis in February 1898 as Pine Bluff's postmaster, but Havis's controversial past and strong opposition by white Democrats to black officeholders in Arkansas doomed his nomination. Even some local black leaders believed his nomination unwise, given his past record. The Senate voted to reject Havis as postmaster, after its Committee on Post Offices and Post Roads considered scandalous charges of gambling and immorality and editorial opposition by the *Pine Bluff Press Eagle* and reported adversely on the nomination in late March (Morgan, p. 296).

In later years, Havis broke with Clayton over "lily-white" policies within the state's Republican Party in 1910. Although continuing to attend national Republican conventions (1904, 1912) as a district delegate, Havis paid increasingly more attention to business and civic affairs than to politics, and was active to the end in the African Methodist Episcopal (AME) Church and the Masons. The "Colored Millionaire" of Pine Bluff, as Havis was referred to locally, died there at age seventy-one.

FURTHER READING

Foner, Eric. "Ferdinand Havis." In *Freedom's Lawmakers: A Directory of Black Officeholders During Reconstruction* (1993).

Graves, John William. "Negro Disfranchisement in Arkansas." *Arkansas Historical Quarterly*, Aug. 1967.

Morgan, Marian Bernette. "Ferdinand Havis." In *Arkansas Biography: A Collection of Notable Lives* (2000).

BENJAMIN R. JUSTESEN

Hawes, Hampton (13 Nov. 1928–22 May 1977), pianist and composer, was born Hampton B. Hawes Jr. in Los Angeles, California, the son of Hampton B. Hawes Sr., a Presbyterian minister. The name of his mother, who played piano in her husband's church, is unknown. When Hampton was eight, he learned how to play piano by watching his sister, who was training to become a concert pianist, and by listening to records by his favorite jazz musicians. His intense study of such prominent jazz pianists as FATS WALLER and EARL "FATHA" HINES during the 1930s and early 1940s had a profound influence on him during his youth. He began playing regularly while attending Polytechnic High School. He later recalled going straight from his high school graduation ceremony to a jazz gig with the CECIL JAMES MCNEELY (Big Jay McNeely) band. Throughout the 1940s Hawes played at a wide range of clubs on black Los Angeles's legendary Central Avenue with other extraordinary musicians, including DEXTER KEITH GORDON, WARDELL GRAY, and Teddy Edwards. Hawes made his first recording with Gordon and Gray in 1947.

In 1948 Hawes spent a brief period in New York, where for the first time he heard many of his idols in the emerging revolutionary music called bebop. After a month of playing in a number of Harlem jazz club jam sessions with bebop musicians, Hawes joined a band making a road tour of the Deep South, where he experienced extreme racial segregation for the first time. The sheer danger, injustice, and humiliation of this experience left a deep and lasting impression on the nineteen-year-old. He returned to Los Angeles, where he finally got an opportunity to play with his idol CHARLIE PARKER in the trumpeter HOWARD B. MCGHEE's band at the Hi-De-Ho Club on Central Avenue. Hawes had first heard Parker play live at Billy Berg's club in Hollywood in December 1945 and was astonished, as was nearly every other musician in Los Angeles at that time, by Parker's stunning virtuosity, originality, and intensity.

From 1950 to 1952 Hawes continued to play and develop his burgeoning skills in a number of well-known Los Angeles jazz bands, including those of Red Norvo, Shorty Rogers, and McGhee. In 1951 Hawes made a record in a band with Rogers. Hawes, who was quickly gaining a national reputation as an outstanding bop pianist with a fast, fluid, and dynamic style, also worked in the house rhythm section of the famous Lighthouse Club in Hermosa Beach, California, backing up many of the major national figures in the bebop movement. Unfortunately, Hawes had become addicted to heroin by this time, an ongoing condition that had a negative and fateful impact on his life.

In 1952 Hawes was drafted into the army, where his heroin habit worsened and he was put in military prison for various drug offenses. Finally released from the army in early 1955, after spending most of his military service in Korea and Japan, Hawes returned to playing music in Los Angeles and formed his own trio in the summer of 1955. This small group—with Red Mitchell on bass and Chuck Thompson on drums—quickly became a national sensation in jazz circles as critics and musicians alike sang the praises of Hawes's now fully mature and virtuosic piano style and his visionary leadership of the trio.

With a small new jazz record label in California called Contemporary Records, Hawes and his trio made a highly influential and innovative series of recordings from 1955 to 1958, including the famous "All Night" sessions with a quartet that included the guitarist Jim Hall. The recordings made Hawes a major star of the period and put him in demand by such important musicians and composers as CHARLES MINGUS, Harold Land, and Art Pepper, all of whom Hawes recorded with during this time. In 1958 Hawes made another excellent recording with the saxophonist Land titled *For Real!*, which was the last recording Hawes made for five years.

In 1958, at the height of his fame and influence, Hawes was arrested and convicted for the possession and use of heroin and sentenced to ten years in prison. As he languished in prison, he reflected on what he felt was the severity of his sentence and protested its excessiveness. After several legal appeals were rebuffed by California courts, Hawes confounded his attorney and prison officials when he insisted on applying for a presidential pardon. Everyone in the prison administration as well as

various lawyers told Hawes he was being completely unrealistic in making such an unorthodox, last-ditch appeal. Hawes waited a full year before the proper papers arrived and he was able to secure a pardon attorney to represent his clemency case. In late 1962 he wrote an impassioned plea directly to President John F. Kennedy, pointing out the unjust legal details of his conviction and sentence. Hawes waited nearly nine months for a reply, then President Kennedy granted him executive clemency on 6 August 1963. Hawes was finally free after five years in jail.

Returning to active playing upon his release, Hawes continued to tour with his trio and to record with Contemporary and many other labels in the United States, Europe, and Japan. He also began experimenting with electric piano and synthesizing other forms of music, including rock, rhythm and blues, and funk, with his own bop and hard-bop styles. In 1974 Hawes wrote, with Don Asher, *Raise Up Off Me*, a critically acclaimed and extremely candid biographical memoir, which was recognized as one of the most historically significant jazz biographies of the 1945 to 1975 period. His book won the prestigious ASCAP–Deems Taylor music writing award in 1975. Throughout the 1970s Hawes performed at many national and international festivals and continued to record. He died of a cerebral hemorrhage in his hometown of Los Angeles, California, at the age of forty-eight.

FURTHER READING

Hawes, Hampton, and Don Asher. *Raise Up Off Me* (1974).

Bryant, Clora, ed. *Central Avenue Sounds: Jazz in Los Angeles* (1998).

Gioia, Ted. *West Coast Jazz: Modern Jazz in California, 1945–1960* (1992).

KOFI NATAMBU

Hawkins, Augustus Freeman (31 Aug. 1907–13 Nov. 2007), congressman, was born in Shreveport, Louisiana, the son of Nyanza Hawkins, a pharmacist who moved his family to Los Angeles in 1918 when Hawkins was eleven years old, and Hattie Freeman. Thereafter Los Angeles remained Augustus Hawkins's home. He graduated from Jefferson High School and from the University of Southern California with a degree in Economics in 1931. Only five feet four inches tall and so light-skinned that he was often mistaken for white, Hawkins entered electoral politics at an early age. In 1935, after leaving a job selling real estate, Hawkins was elected to the California State Assembly. Running as a Democrat and a proponent of Upton Sinclair's End Poverty in California (EPIC) program, he defeated a longtime incumbent. Once in office Hawkins became a committed New Deal liberal, supporting Franklin Roosevelt and eschewing socialism and other radical prescriptions to end the Great Depression.

As the only African American state legislator for much of his twenty-eight years in office (1935–1963), Hawkins was a voice for California's burgeoning black population throughout the 1940s and 1950s. In the 1940s, prior to the desegregation of the military, he protested the segregation of the California National Guard and called for fair housing laws. After becoming the powerful chairman of the state legislature's Rules Committee, Hawkins compiled an impressive legislative record on an array of issues. Authoring more than one hundred bills, Hawkins was responsible for slum clearance, workingman's compensation, low-cost housing, and disability insurance, as well as the construction of the Los Angeles Sports Arena and the facilities that house the law and medical schools at the University of California, Los Angeles.

By the late 1950s Hawkins had gained national renown for authoring and shepherding civil rights legislation through the California State Assembly.

Augustus Freeman Hawkins in 1962. (Library of Congress.)

With the active support of Governor Edmund Brown, California was one of the first states to enact employment and housing legislation that barred discrimination based on race, religion, and national origin. Because of his political success and the growing clout of African Americans within the state Democratic Party, the legislature drew a congressional district especially for Hawkins, which consisted of large swaths of black Los Angeles. In 1962 Hawkins became the first African American elected to the U.S. Congress from west of the Mississippi, a seat that he held until his retirement in 1991.

In Congress Hawkins remained a committed New Deal Democrat who worked quietly yet effectively for civil rights, employment, and education legislation. Hawkins cemented his congressional legacy during his first term in the House by authoring Title VII of the 1964 Civil Rights Act, which barred discrimination based on sex and race in employment. In addition, he authored or was a significant force behind the passage of the 1964 Civil Rights Act Amendment and the Minority Institutional Aid Act. The former established the Equal Employment Opportunity Commission, while the latter specifically earmarked funds for historically black colleges.

In 1971 he led the fight to exonerate the 167 African American soldiers implicated in the 1906 Brownsville Affair. Though that race riot in Brownsville, Texas, was instigated by an unsubstantiated series of racially charged incidents, President Theodore Roosevelt summarily cashiered three companies of African American soldiers out of the army to quell the controversy. After Hawkins read a book on the subject and investigated the incident for himself, he introduced legislation to clear the soldiers. Though the bill failed even to get out of committee, it prompted the Pentagon to investigate and absolve all 167 soldiers of committing any wrongdoing.

In 1984 Hawkins followed ADAM CLAYTON POWELL JR. as just the second African American to chair the House Committee on Education and Labor. As a chairman, Hawkins did not limit his legislative interests to racial matters; he explained to an interviewer, "Racializing an issue defeats my purpose, which is to get people on my side." Many members of the Congressional Black Caucus criticized him for his mild manner, but an African American congressional colleague, WILLIAM HERBERT GRAY III, said of the diminutive Hawkins, "He was 40 feet tall in legislative accomplishments and public service." Among the laws he authored in his congressional career were the 1988 School Improvement Act, the 1973 Comprehensive Employment and Training Act (CETA), and the 1978 Humphrey-Hawkins Full Employment and Balanced Growth Act.

The 1988 School Improvement, or Hawkins-Stafford, Act for the first time tied student performance to state funding. Under Hawkins's legislation, if student performance on standardized exams lagged for a prolonged period, the state could intervene and force failing schools to reform. In 1973 CETA, a bill that was designed to offer job-training programs to the unemployed, had been passed. In 1978 Hawkins convinced President Jimmy Carter to expand CETA, which consequently employed more than seven hundred thousand Americans in public service jobs. Hawkins followed that bill with the signature legislation of his career, the Full Employment and Balanced Growth Act. Though this legislation did not create any programs, it established maximum employment as a national goal and mandated that the chairman of the Federal Reserve testify before the Senate Banking Committee twice a year. In effect, the legislation made the Federal Reserve more accountable to public opinion and reestablished job creation as the centerpiece of any Democratic economic policy.

As a widely respected and accomplished congressman, Hawkins won reelection handily every term, never failing to capture at least 80 percent of the vote. Despite his popularity and good health, in 1991 at the age of eighty-three he retired. As the first black congressman from California and the West, Hawkins left behind a significant legacy. Moreover, he represented the New Deal liberal tradition that emphasized job creation and educational opportunity over racial or identity politics. He died in Washington, D. C., at 100 years of age.

FURTHER READING

The congressional papers of Augustus Hawkins are housed in the department of special collections of the library at the University of California, Los Angeles.

Eaton, William. "Hawkins Retiring—but Not Quitting Politics," *Los Angeles Times*, 23 Dec. 1990.

Hill, Gladwin. "16 Men Battling in California for Eight New Seats in House," *New York Times*, 20 Oct. 1962.

JEFF BLOODWORTH

Hawkins, Coleman (21 Nov. 1904–19 May 1969), jazz tenor saxophonist, was born Coleman Randolph Hawkins in St. Joseph, Missouri, the son of William Hawkins, an electrical worker, and Cordelia Coleman, a schoolteacher and organist. He began to study piano at age five and the cello at seven; he then eagerly took up the C-melody saxophone he received for his ninth birthday. Even before entering high school in Chicago, he was playing professionally at school dances. Recognizing his talent, his parents sent him to the all-black Industrial and Educational Institute in Topeka, Kansas. His mother insisted that he take only his cello with him. During vacations, however, Hawkins played both cello and C-melody saxophone in Kansas City theater orchestras, where the blues singer MAMIE SMITH heard him in 1921.

Smith hired Hawkins to tour with her Jazz Hounds, and he traveled and recorded with the group until June 1923, at which time he moved to New York City. There he played with a variety of groups and in numerous jam sessions. In August 1923 he recorded "Dicty Blues" with a FLETCHER HENDERSON group, and in early 1924 Henderson hired him for his new band. Although Hawkins

Coleman Hawkins performs at the Newport Jazz Festival in July 1963. (AP Images.)

doubled on both clarinet and bass saxophone for Henderson, he increasingly concentrated on the tenor and soon developed a style that revolutionized saxophone playing. At first he employed the technique that was all but universal among saxophonists at the time, slapping his tongue against the reed and producing sharp, staccato notes. Gradually, though, he adopted a more legato style. He was also influenced by the trumpeter LOUIS ARMSTRONG during Armstrong's brief stay with the Henderson band and by the complex harmonic improvisations of the young pianist ART TATUM, whom he heard in 1926. By 1927 Hawkins was the band's featured soloist and was playing only tenor sax. His solo on "The Stampede" (1926) is a dramatic example of his growth, displaying a full, smooth tone and rhythmic assurance. Hawkins also played with other small groups during the late twenties and early thirties; his solo on "One Hour" (1929) with the Mound City Blue Blowers, for instance, showcases his rich tone and powerful emotionalism. He made several outstanding recordings with the trumpeter RED ALLEN, including the classic "It's the Talk of the Town" (1933). By now the master of his instrument, Hawkins had fully developed his harmonic approach to improvisation, a marked contrast to the more melodic, scalar approach of the tenor saxophonist LESTER YOUNG and others. Hawkins thought about the implications of each chord as it came, adding notes or changing them to create sweeping melodic lines. By then he was a jazz celebrity, but success began to take its toll on his personal life when he and his wife, Gertrude (they had married in 1923), separated.

Hawkins left Henderson in 1933 and arranged a deal with the English impresario Jack Hylton to tour England. He planned to take only a six-month leave but remained overseas until 1939, traveling and performing constantly. Noteworthy recordings include 1935 sessions with a Dutch group known as the Ramblers and a 1937 Paris session with Benny Carter on alto saxophone and trumpet and the Belgian guitarist Django Reinhardt.

When Hawkins returned to New York City in July 1939, his fans greeted him ecstatically. He planned to form his own big band, but musicians of his caliber were more interested in leading their own groups than in joining his. So he put together a small group to play at Kelly's Stable, then on West Fifty-first Street. On 11 October, only six days after opening there, he cut four sides at a recording date for RCA Victor. Almost as an afterthought, and with no rehearsal, he concluded the session with one of the most celebrated and influential performances in jazz history, "Body and Soul."

Hawkins had already experimented a number of times with three- and four-minute ballad improvisations, and he recorded two side-long solos in London accompanied only by the pianist Stanley Black. Although he often spoke of the spur-of-the-moment nature of his choice, it could not have been a complete surprise, since he had been playing an extended late-night version of "Body and Soul" at Kelly's. Now, in one sixty-four-bar improvisation with only minimal rhythm accompaniment, he created a solo that the composer-critic Gunther Schuller described as "a melodic/harmonic journey through a musical landscape without any fault lines." He flirts with the original melody for the first few bars, then quickly moves away, developing his own related harmonic ideas and gradually raising the pitch and intensifying the rhythm and dynamics with each extended group of phrases. By the final bars his initially warm, vibratoless sound becomes almost strident, intensified by a wide, pulsing vibrato. The recorded performance was a best-seller, and it has since become the ultimate touchstone of great tenor playing.

Hawkins toured with his own big band in early 1940, but he lacked the showmanship essential to such a venture, and the group folded. In May 1940 he cut a series of recordings for the Commodore label with a group called the Chocolate Dandies that included three of the best swing players of the era: trumpeter ROY ELDRIDGE, drummer SID CATLETT, and Benny Carter. A few months later he met the young Delores Sheridan in Chicago, and they were married in October 1941. Hawkins moved back to New York in early 1942 to spend more time with his family, which by the end of the decade had grown to include three children. Among his recording highlights during the middle 1940s were three sessions for Signature records and the legendary 1944 Keynote recordings. He also began a long and satisfying relationship with Norman Granz's Jazz at the Philharmonic tours.

Unlike other swing players, Hawkins warmly embraced the modernist bop movement. In February 1944 he led a band that included DIZZY GILLESPIE on trumpet and MAX ROACH on drums in the first bop recordings; later that year he included the pianist THELONIOUS MONK in a recording session. Throughout his life Hawkins offered younger players encouragement and advice, often talking with them on the phone for hours and inviting them to his apartment to examine and listen to his extensive collection of classical records, books, and scores. At the same time he continued to strongly influence swing-oriented contemporaries such as BEN WEBSTER, DON BYAS, Herschel Evans, BUDD JOHNSON, and many others.

By 1947 the club scene on Fifty-second Street was dying, and Hawkins left for a series of engagements in Paris, returning to Europe in 1949. The artistic highlight of this period was his recorded solo improvisation "Picasso," a revolutionary venture for the time. He continued to record extensively during the 1950s and to perform continuously in Europe and the United States, and he initiated a performance relationship with Roy Eldridge that was to last, off and on, for the next fifteen years. Two of their best albums together were *The Big Challenge* and a collection of emotionally powerful ballads, *The High and Mighty Hawk*. Once again, though, the demands of his career affected Hawkins's personal life. In 1958 he and his second wife separated, and the sense of order and balance that had come to characterize his life seemed to dissipate.

For a few years his career hardly missed a beat. He appeared on the television programs *The Sound of Jazz* (1957) and *After Hours* (1961), toured South America in 1961, played a series of dates with Eldridge at the Museum of Modern Art, and recorded several landmark albums, including a 1962 session with DUKE ELLINGTON and the classic *Further Definitions* (1961), a small band effort led by Benny Carter and featuring four leading saxophonists. Hawkins also maintained a home base at the Club Metropole, often playing there with Eldridge. Although dismayed by the appearance of free jazz— the first modernist movement he could not understand or enjoy—he recorded with some of the more traditionally grounded modernists such as SONNY ROLLINS and JOHN COLTRANE, both of whom were profoundly influenced by Hawkins's playing.

A fear of aging had always possessed Hawkins, and it seemed to overcome him in the early 1960s. He steadily withdrew, eating less and drinking more; he was fired from several jobs because he could not get along with other players or because of his drinking. He lost a frightening amount of weight, and by early 1966 his physical appearance, once a source of great personal pride, began to deteriorate. In February 1967 he collapsed while playing in Toronto, but he refused to be hospitalized and returned two nights later to complete the engagement. He embarked on a thirteen-week tour of Canadian and American cities, but he often played poorly. He collapsed again on stage in Oakland, California, on 30 June and was never healthy again. For the most part he remained in his New York apartment, his children and second wife visiting and trying to care for him. When the writer-producer Dan Morgenstern met him at the Chicago airport in April 1969, he was stunned by the saxophonist's emaciated appearance; Hawkins collapsed there while waiting for a car. He performed a moving version of "Yesterdays" for a television show, but it was all he could manage. The pianist at the session, Barry Harris, took Hawkins back to New York, and when Hawkins failed to show up for a rehearsal Harris asked that an apartment-house security guard check on him. Hawkins was found crawling across the floor of his apartment, dragging his horn. He was taken to Wickersham Hospital, where he died.

Hawkins brought the tenor saxophone into the mainstream of jazz and popular music, and he helped pioneer a then-modernist approach to improvisation, based on chords rather than melody. He profoundly influenced tenor saxophonists of his own generation, served as a mentor to the bop movement, and was a model and inspiration to some of the most important later players, particularly Sonny Rollins and John Coltrane. His musical presence could be overwhelming, and listening to his recordings can be a moving experience. More than most of his jazz contemporaries, finally, Hawkins was a man of the world, driven by a deep sense of intellectual curiosity. He listened to music of every kind, and he loved Bach most of all, especially Bach's mastery of improvising on a theme. "It's just music-adventure," he once noted. "That's what music is, adventure."

FURTHER READING

Chilton, John. *The Song of the Hawk: The Life and Recordings of Coleman Hawkins* (1990).

Harrison, Max, Charles Fox, and Eric Thacker. *The Essential Jazz Records*, vol. 1 (1984).

James, Burnett. *Coleman Hawkins* (1984).

McCarthy, Albert. *Coleman Hawkins* (1963).

Schuller, Gunther. *The Swing Era: The Development of Jazz, 1930–1945* (1989).

Obituary: *New York Times*, 20 May 1969.

This entry is taken from the *American National Biography* and is published here with the permission of the American Council of Learned Societies.

RONALD P. DUFOUR

Hawkins, Connie (17 July 1942–), basketball player, was born Cornelius Hawkins in Brooklyn, New York, the fifth of six children of Isaiah Hawkins, a sometime railroad employee, and Dorothy Hawkins, a nursery school cook. When many affluent residents of Brooklyn's Bedford-Stuyvesant section moved to the suburbs after World War II, Hawkins's family stayed behind in a coldwater flat. His father left the family when Hawkins was nine years old, and his mother was stricken with blindness during Hawkins's teenage years. Hawkins typically had only one shirt, one pair of pants, and taped-together shoes with cardboard covering holes in the soles, until basketball boosters began providing him with clothes and spending money during his sophomore year of high school—a common occurrence at the time.

Hawkins learned basketball on the highly competitive playgrounds of Brooklyn and adjacent Queens. Known for spectacular individual play, he could jump high enough to dunk by age eleven and could score on reverse swoops by age fifteen; but he also became an excellent team player. As a six-foot-five-inch junior at Brooklyn's Boys High School during the 1958–1959 season, Hawkins was described by his coach as a good jump shooter, a remarkably able passer, and the school's best defensive player. College coaches in the area called that team New York City's best-ever high school team. During his senior year, Hawkins averaged twenty-six points per game. That season's Public School Athletic League (PSAL) championship game, played in March 1960, was the lowest scoring in league history. The Bronx's Columbus High School team passed and dribbled the ball for most of the game without shooting. Boys High School team won by a score of 21–15.

The Boys High Kangaroos won forty games, lost none, and won the PSAL championship in Hawkins's junior and senior years. He won All-State honors both years, was a first-team *Parade* magazine All-American as a senior, and was named the Most Valuable Player in the All-American East-West high school game in June 1960. Hawkins was so well known to rabid basketball fans that by 1960, when his Brooklyn All-Stars team went to play in Harlem's Rucker Park summer tournament, their game had to be cancelled because the crowd was too large.

Hawkins's post-high school basketball career began on a disappointing note. He was expelled from the University of Iowa in May 1961 before playing in a single varsity game then banned from the National Basketball Association (NBA). Needing money to pay his dorm fees during his freshman year, Hawkins borrowed $200 (quickly repaid by his brother) from a former NBA player, Jack Molinas, who had been banned from the league in 1954 for betting on NBA games. Again involved in betting and point shaving, Molinas had befriended Hawkins while he was still in high school, playing playground basketball with him, taking him (and his girlfriend) with cash.

Hawkins began his professional basketball career in the fall of 1961 with the Pittsburgh Renaissance of the newly formed American Basketball League (ABL), organized by Harlem Globetrotters owner Abe Saperstein, and quickly established himself as one of the game's most dynamic and distinctive players. With his huge hands, long arms, and extraordinary leaping ability, the six-foot-eight-inch Hawkins could do things no player his size had ever done before. He could leap high above the basket for rebounds and had extraordinary shot-blocking abilities; he could also hold and wave the ball in his hand, throw the ball the length of the court to teammates, and swoop and glide from the free-throw line to the basket for unique finger rolls and dunks. He was largely ahead of his time in treating basketball as a free-flowing action-reaction game.

Hawkins's way of playing was particularly suited to the ABL, which featured such innovations as the three-point shot, a thirty-second shot clock, bonus foul shots after five team fouls, and a red-white-and-blue basketball. Only nineteen years old, Hawkins was named the ABL's Most Valuable Player for the 1961–1962 season. He was averaging 27.9 points and 12.8 rebounds per game when the ABL ceased operations after sixteen games of the 1962–1963 season.

In 1963 Hawkins married Nancy Foster. The couple would have three children.

Hawkins soon joined Saperstein's Harlem Globetrotters, where for three seasons beginning in February 1963 his skills were displayed in front of much larger audiences. The Globetrotters often appeared on the *Ed Sullivan Show*, and their flashy style of play—which included clowning that Hawkins would later call "actin' like Uncle Toms" (Wolf, 168)—proved far more popular than the NBA's more conservative style of play. One televised Globetrotter game in January 1966 earned a 16.2 Nielsen rating, while a competing game between the Boston Celtics and Philadelphia Warriors (featuring NBA superstars BILL RUSSELL of the Celtics and the Warriors' WILT CHAMBERLAIN) received a 3.2 Nielsen rating.

In November of 1966 Hawkins, still banned by the NBA, filed a triple-damage federal antitrust suit in Pittsburgh against the NBA, its commissioner

Walter Kennedy, and all of its teams. The NBA tried to move the case to New York twice, where the league's representatives hoped to find jurors less friendly to Hawkins, but its motions failed both times. After the NBA lost its second transfer motion in 1969, the NBA agreed to settle Hawkins's suit.

While his suit was pending, Hawkins had been playing in another new professional league, the American Basketball Association (ABA), which had its inaugural season in 1967–1968. He led the Pittsburgh Pipers to the ABA championship in 1968 and, just as he had been in the ABL, Hawkins was named the ABA's Most Valuable Player during the league's first season. When the Pipers moved to Minnesota for the 1968–1969 season, Hawkins and the team were less successful. A knee injury limited him to forty-seven games, and the Pipers lost in the first round of the ABA championship playoffs. Despite the loss, Hawkins was named an All-ABA forward.

Under a provision of his 1969 settlement with the NBA, the Phoenix Suns won a coin flip for the NBA rights to Hawkins. Hawkins was then able to sign a five-year $410,000 guaranteed contract with the Suns. He also received a $250,000 signing bonus, had $35,000 of his legal fees paid, and received a $600,000 annuity that would pay him $30,000 each year once he turned forty-five.

Finally fulfilling his long-held dream of playing in the NBA, Hawkins led the Suns to a 39–43 record and the 1969–1970 NBA playoffs during his first season with the team. Hawkins helped the team improve on the previous year's win-loss record of 16–66, and he was named an All-NBA forward. Phoenix forced the Los Angeles Lakers into seven games in their best-of-four playoff series before finally being defeated.

Hawkins played three more seasons for the Suns and was a three-time NBA All-Star. The Suns improved to 48–34 (the fourth best record in the NBA that season) in 1970–1971 and 49–33 (seventh best in the league) in 1971–1972. The Suns traded Hawkins to the Los Angeles Lakers in October 1973, where he played two more seasons before finishing his NBA career with the Atlanta Hawks in 1976.

The stylistic forerunner of JULIUS ERVING, EARVIN MAGIC JOHNSON JR., and MICHAEL JORDAN, Hawkins was elected to the Basketball Hall of Fame in 1992 and became a community relations representative for the Suns that same year.

FURTHER READING

Axthelm, Pete. *The City Game: Basketball from the Garden to the Playgrounds* (1999).

Green, Ben. *Spinning the Globe: The Rise, Fall, and Return to Greatness of the Harlem Globetrotters* (2005).

Greenfield, Jeff. "The Black and White Truth About Basketball," in *Signifyin(G), Sanctifyin', and Slam Dunking: A Reader in African American Expressive Culture* (1999).

Lipsyte, Robert S. "Boys High Beats Freeze, Takes Final, 21–15," *New York Times*, 18 Mar. 1960.

Mallozzi, Vincent M. *Asphalt Gods: An Oral History of the Rucker Tournament* (2003).

Pluto, Terry. *Loose Balls: The Short, Wild Life of the American Basketball Association* (1990).

Rosen, Charley. *The Wizard of Odds: How Jack Molinas Almost Destroyed the Game of Basketball* (2001).

Tuckner, Howard T. "On the Boys at Boys," *New York Times*, 17 Mar. 1959.

Wolf, David. *Foul! The Connie Hawkins Story* (1972).

STEVEN B. JACOBSON

Hawkins, Edler Garnett (13 June 1908–19 Dec. 1977), Presbyterian minister and civil rights advocate, was born on 13 June 1908 to Albert and Annie Lee Hawkins in the Bronx, New York. He attended public schools in New York and, after graduating from high school around 1935, Hawkins enrolled in Bloomfield College in New Jersey, an affiliate of the northern Presbyterian Church. The Presbyterian Church founded Bloomfield College in Newark in 1868 as a German Theological Seminary for German-speaking ministers. The College moved to Bloomfield in 1872 and by 1923 became a four-year college with approximately 1,300 full-time students. Hawkins graduated magna cum laude from Bloomfield with a Bachelor of Arts degree in 1936. At age thirty-five, in 1938, Hawkins earned a Bachelor of Divinity from Union Theological Seminary in New York City. Presbyterians had founded Union Theological Seminary in 1836 and admitted students from a wide range of Protestant sects. Since 1910, the Seminary collaborated with Columbia University becoming a seat for liberal, or, in the terminology of the time, neo-orthodox Protestant faith. Edler Hawkins's theological education shaped his response to the problem of the oppressed in the South Bronx and elsewhere. His liberal theology was evident in his secular or humanistic orientation, favoring the "feeding and clothing of the poor," rather than comforting the spiritually hungry or fretful. He saw the "kingdom of God" as earth bound in which all men would be brothers and not as a doctrinal rapture restrictive to the "saints" in a sense; it was a Social Gospel that Hawkins embraced. On 30 January 1944

Hawkins married Thelma Burnett. Their marriage produced two daughters.

In 1938, straight out of Seminary, Hawkins was appointed pastor of St. Augustine Presbyterian Church located on 165th Street and Prospect Avenue in the Bronx; he was the church's first Presbyterian minister. When another denomination, which had been using the church, went elsewhere, it left only nine members in the congregation. At the time, few African Americans embraced Presbyterianism, but under Hawkins's guidance, St. Augustine membership grew by leaps and bounds and by 1961 its congregants were predominantly black with a few Puerto Ricans. Pastor Hawkins was concerned about his Puerto Rican congregants because of their propensity to worship in family groups, and to leave as families. Although about one hundred Puerto Ricans attended the church, few joined St Augustine. Hawkins wanted an integrated church, but had to settle for starting a separate Spanish-speaking ministry under the leadership of Julio Garcia, assistant pastor to Pastor Hawkins. In a generation, Garcia had said, they might join the mainlanders in an integrated church. The church members did come together as one church on Maundy Thursday (Holy Thursday) and Easter Sunday. The Puerto Rican churchgoers were theologically evangelical and socially conservative and did not embrace the liberal theology of Pastor Hawkins. They were Catholics who in later generations would be called "charismatic" Catholics, espousing many forms of Protestantism.

During Hawkins's early tenure at Saint Augustine, he quickly gravitated to civil rights activism and a range of other issues associated with a gospel of good works. Since the 1940s a sidewalk "slave market" had existed where black domestic servants, notably maids, waited for hours in fair and inclement weather to be hired by white employers for an hour or a day without the regular references and paperwork. Many of those hired were illiterate migrants recently from the South who feared employment agencies that required the formal process. Hawkins and other blacks successfully pressured city government agencies to set up two offices in different parts of the city with hosts that served coffee and tea and retained the informal hiring practices while according black women domestics a degree of dignity.

The Presbyterian Church was among the first to denounce segregation as an appalling evil. In the 1960s, the Presbyterian Church called some missionaries from abroad to work on picket lines and inner city Freedom Schools; they had much experience with working with suppressed and brutalized people and could devote sufficient time to work on what was now the number one goal of the Church—civil rights and social justice. Hawkins challenged the white leadership of his denomination in May 1960 with a limited contest between himself and Herman Turner, a white moderate from Atlanta, Georgia, for the titular leadership of the northern Presbyterians. Turner enjoyed some prestige with northern and southern Presbyterians with his advocacy of the "Atlanta Manifesto," which called for communications between black and white on race relations. Turner squeaked through with a two-vote margin of victory. He immediately appointed Hawkins as his vice moderator. These were exciting times for good race relations. The moderator position only lasted a year; Edler Hawkins was eager to try again. By running for moderator of the 3,000,000-member Presbyterian Church, Reverend Hawkins's name and image were etched in the minds of Presbyterians throughout the northern tier of the United States. In May 1964, Edler Hawkins ran and won the position as moderator of the Presbyterian Church. Forever after, Hawkins was defined by this singular moment of triumph: the first black moderator of the Presbyterian Church, U.S.A. *Time* magazine pondered the wider implications of Hawkins's victory: "The United Presbyterians have a knack for breaking race barriers without catering to either politics or sentimentalism." A church that was 95 percent white was under no pressure to change, but it saw desegregation as a holy responsibility. Now Hawkins would show a face of color to white Presbyterians throughout the United States and Europe and reassure his black brethren in Africa of the justice of their church universal. In his one year as moderator, Hawkins championed ecumenism and civil rights and even slammed Victorian modesty, rejecting many aspects of sexual language and whatever else was considered profane, as a barrier in reaching young people. Earlier in the 1950s Hawkins had been fully involved in youth work including after school tutoring, youth fellowships, and day camps and a summer camp; "Bohatam," a merging of two names of pastors who were good friends and co-founders of the small camp that did not survive Pastor Hawkins's tenure at Saint Augustine.

After Hawkins's service as moderator, he continued his work as full-time pastor of St. Augustine and made many appearances on a variety of television and radio programs. In 1970, he gave up his pastorate and crossed the Hudson River to teach Black Studies and Moral Philosophy at Princeton

Theological Seminary. On 18 December 1977, Hawkins died of an apparent heart attack. He was survived by his wife, Thelma, and two daughters, Ellen and Renee. Within months of his death, his friends established a foundation in his name and renamed a portion of East 165th Street near Prospect Avenue in his honor.

FURTHER READING

Eleven linear feet of his personal papers are housed in the Atlanta University Center's Robert W. Woodruff Library Archives.

Cone, James H. *For My People: Black Theology and the Black Church* (1984).

Graham, W.F. *The Constructive Revolutionary* (1971).

Martin, Andrew, ed. *An Encyclopedia of African American Christian Heritage* (2002).

Wilmore, Gayraud S. *Black and Presbyterian: The Heritage and the Hope* (1998).

CLAUDE HARGROVE

Hawkins, Edwin (1 Aug. 1943–), gospel music singer, composer, and pioneer of contemporary gospel music, was born in Oakland, California, one of eight children of Dan Lee, a longshoreman with the Port of Oakland, and Maime Hawkins, a homemaker. Both the piano and the church were central fixtures of daily life for this close-knit family during the World War II era. The Hawkins family would gather around the piano for hours of impromptu singing, playful harmonizing, and group rehearsing. Edwin sang in the youth choir and played piano for the family singing group. Throughout his adolescence, he was well known in Bay Area church circles and had become the Minister of Music at Ephesians Church of God in Christ (COGIC) in Berkeley. His musical influences were diverse and included Perry Como, the McGuire Sisters, JAMES CLEVELAND, the Caravans, and the CLARA WARD Singers. His early years were spent continuously honing his craft, composing songs, rearranging hymns, performing concerts, and directing ensembles.

In 1967 Hawkins and fellow COGIC devotee, Betty Watson, organized a Bay Area contingent for an upcoming COGIC national choir competition. That July, their Northern California State Youth Choir won second prize at the COGIC Youth Congress. For a fund-raising drive, they recorded an album so the proceeds from it could support their activities as a community choir. Decades later, referring to this recording, *Let Us Go Into the House of the Lord*, Hawkins recalled: "We went [into the recording sessions] with the intention of just recording a pure gospel album that we knew was a little bit different from the ordinary, but we didn't think it was that much different" (Heron, 18 September 2001). Most others who heard the album, however, thought it was extraordinary. A warehouse worker at the record's pressing plant put one of the five hundred copies into the hands of a disc jockey at an obscure rock-and-roll radio station in San Francisco. He took a liking to one song in particular, "Oh Happy Day," and played it in daily rotation, prompting disc jockeys across northern California to do the same. Unlike anything previously heard in a gospel recording, Hawkins's vocal arrangements and instrumentation fused the pop, classical, R&B, and jazz styles of his day. This song was an aberration in gospel music. Moreover, the tune itself was infectious. Soon, it was heard all across the nation and, after seven million copies had been sold, the song could be heard throughout the world.

"Oh Happy Day" was originally penned by Englishman Philip Doddridge in the eighteenth century. Some two hundred years later, Hawkins, armed with a "knack for rearranging hymns" (*New York Beacon*, Mar. 1999), reimagined it for a forty-six-voice urban youth ensemble. His 1969 version had a twelve-bar blues format, a boogie-woogie feel, and a driving backbeat. While such styles were common in Pentecostal and "sanctified" churches, for most listeners, it was rare to hear a gospel music recording with such highly percussive, spirited, and stylized arrangements. From its humble origins as a two-track, live recording session at Berkeley's Ephesians COGIC, "Oh, Happy Day" burst forth as the highest-selling gospel single, the most popular gospel song worldwide, and a staple song of American popular culture. Yet, the recording was initially met with opposition by those in Hawkins's own religious community who disapproved of its appearance on secular radio stations. Some pastors in the Bay Area circulated a petition to get the song dropped from mainstream radio airplay, complaining that it sounded too "worldly" (Hawkins interview, 20 October 2006). As a result, the song brought about a distinction between "traditional" and "contemporary" gospel styles, which became standard categorizations in gospel music.

Remarkably, Hawkins's contribution to the "contemporary" musical genre he created extended beyond the "Oh Happy Day" phenomenon. For decades following the 1969 hit, Hawkins and his collection of exceptional singers and musicians—the Edwin Hawkins Singers—continued to be leading promoters of the genre. They were prominent ambassadors for the contemporary gospel genre, over the years expanding its base and giving it international representation. The Edwin Hawkins Singers received the American recording industry's highest honors, winning Grammy Awards in 1970, 1971, 1980, and 1983. They were inducted into the Gospel Music Hall of Fame in 2000 and completed successful concert tours throughout Europe and Japan. In 1982 Hawkins, along with his brother Walter (a gospel music dynamo in his own right), cofounded the *Edwin Hawkins Music & Arts Love Fellowship Conference* to provide culturally relevant professional instruction in the areas of gospel music performance, songwriting, music ministry, choir decorum, fashion design, music business, and communications.

In 1996 Hawkins collaborated with the Swedish Gospel choir, Svart Pa Vitt, on a recording project and a ten-city U.S. concert tour. In 2005 Hawkins was commissioned to write a theme song for the United Nations' World Environment Day and composed "United Nations: Together We Can," a song that raised awareness and funds for global environmental concerns. In January 2006, along with the other members of the Hawkins Family singing group, another beloved group in gospel that Hawkins was a key member of, publishing giant Broadcast Music, Inc., honored the Hawkins Family with the prestigious Trailblazers of Gospel Music Award. For his outstanding pioneering contributions to gospel music, Hawkins is duly fêted throughout the world as the godfather of contemporary gospel music.

FURTHER READING

Abbington, James, ed. *Christ Against Culture: Anticulturalism in the Gospel of Gospel, Spencer, in Readings in African American Church Music and Worship.*
Darden, Bob. *People Get Ready! A New History of Black Gospel Music* (2004).

MELINDA E. WEEKES

Hawkins, Erskine (26 July 1914–11 or 12 Nov. 1993), trumpet player and swing bandleader, was born Erskine Ramsay Hawkins in Birmingham, Alabama, the son of Edward Hawkins, a soldier, and Carey (maiden name unknown), a teacher. Hawkins's father was killed in World War I while serving in France. His mother exposed her five children to music and Erskine began his musical education at age five, initially playing drums and later moving on to alto saxophone, baritone saxophone, and trombone. From age eight until age twelve he played

in four- and five-piece bands during the summer. These performances took place at Tuxedo Park, just outside Birmingham, where local musicians often gathered. He would later make the location famous with his hit "Tuxedo Junction." It was Erskine's music teacher, S. B. Foster, a trumpet player (referred to affectionately as "High-C" Foster), who persuaded him to take up the trumpet.

In 1930 Erskine earned an athletic scholarship to the Alabama State Teachers College in Montgomery, where he followed in his mother's footsteps by pursuing a bachelor of science degree, while taking private music lessons. Within a few weeks he discontinued his athletic endeavors and turned his attention to the school's jazz band. Initially he was accepted into the school's second tier band, the 'Bama State Revelers, where he was reunited with several childhood friends from Birmingham. They included Haywood Henry on clarinet and saxophone, Wilbur "Dud" Bascomb on trumpet and his brother Paul on saxophone, Avery Parrish on piano, and Bob Range on trombone, many of whom later joined the Erskine Hawkins Orchestra. After several weeks Hawkins was moved up to the school's top-tier band, the 'Bama State Collegians. Shortly thereafter several of his bandmates were also promoted. At the time, J. B. Sims was the leader of the 'Bama State Collegians, who played several nights a week. The experience proved helpful to their development and soon they earned some professional gigs and gained local popularity. The profits went directly to the school, which allocated to the band members, many of them scholarship students, a small portion of the revenue for spending money.

The Collegians attracted the attention of a booking agent named Joe Glaser, who got the group a gig at the Grand Terrace Ballroom in Chicago. In 1934 the band did a tour of one-night stands, traveling as far as Asbury Park, New Jersey. The Asbury Park show proved important. Several New York luminaries, including John Hammond, Benny Carter, and Frank Schiffman, the owner of the Apollo Theatre and the Harlem Opera House, came especially to hear Hawkins. In 1935 Schiffman offered the Collegians an extended engagement at the Harlem Opera House, where they were well received. That same year-Hawkins married Florence Browning. Because of their success at the Harlem Opera House and Hawkins's spectacular trumpet playing, the band garnered immediate bookings, even if it was not as polished as some of New York's top dance bands.

The band signed with its first manager, known only as "Feet" Edson, who had convinced its members to remain in New York rather than return to school. The band recorded its first album that year for the U.S. Vocalion label; it recorded several subsequent sessions for Vocalion from 1936 through 1938, billed as Erskine Hawkins and His 'Bama State Collegians. However, now signed to formal management, and with all the members of the Collegians no longer attending school, the group had to relinquish use of that name. The band also did shows at the Apollo Theatre and eventually got a steady gig at the Ubangi Club in Harlem that lasted two years. In 1936 the group did a stint at the Savoy Ballroom, alternating with CHICK WEBB's orchestra. At the Savoy Hawkins became acquainted with the club's owner, Moe Gale, who was a well-connected booking agent, and in 1937 Hawkins signed a management contract with him. Gale engineered a recording contract for the band with RCA Victor's Bluebird label and established the band as a main attraction at the Savoy, where it became a fixture until the club's closing in the 1950s. Under new management and with a new record contract, the band was now billed as Erskine Hawkins (the 20th-Century Gabriel) and His Orchestra. During its prime the group did long stints at the Copacabana and the Blue Room and toured extensively through the South, the Midwest, and California.

In 1939 the band recorded arguably its greatest hit, "Tuxedo Junction." Initially, the tune was never intended for recording. As legend has it the band was in the studio and needed to record one more track to complete the session. The players decided to expand the short riff they used at the club to signal the alternating band to the bandstand (the Savoy had two bands that would rotate, each doing forty-minute sets), haphazardly naming it "Tuxedo Junction," in honor of the trolley stop near Tuxedo Park where Hawkins had played when he was young. The tune became an instant hit, selling over a million copies. Soon thereafter Glenn Miller recorded "Tuxedo Junction," selling even more records than Hawkins; later Gene Krupa recorded it as well.

In 1940 Hawkins scored another major hit with "After Hours," a tune that came about when another song, "Fine and Mellow," which featured vocals, proved to be too long. Several choruses of solo piano were cut. Later the choruses were used as the basis for an instrumental and given the name "After Hours" by RCA Victor's producers. The bluesy track, which prominently featured Avery Parrish, the band's pianist, influenced many pianists of that generation. In 1945 the band scored another hit with "Tippin' In."

In 1947 Hawkins was awarded an honorary doctorate of music from the Alabama State Teachers College. In 1950 he was granted a legal separation from his first wife. Later he married Gloria Dumas (the date of their marriage is unknown). He had no children in either of his marriages. That same year Hawkins's contract with RCA Victor was terminated; he then took part in three recording sessions with the Coral label. He signed with Decca in 1954. His band however continued to dwindle. By the time the band recorded an album for the label in 1961, there were only six members. Hawkins continued leading small bands, and in 1967 was contracted by the Concord Hotel at Kiamesha Lake, New York. This engagement lasted over twenty years, keeping Hawkins playing into his seventies; he also continued making frequent festival appearances.

A reunion was arranged and recorded by Platinum Records, for which Sam Lowe (former Hawkins band member and arranger) now worked as an A&R man. Those present included Dud and Paul Bascomb and Haywood Henry from the original band. In 1989 Hawkins was awarded a Lifework Award for Performing Achievement from the Alabama Music Hall of Fame. He died in his home in Willingboro, New Jersey; the date appears variously as 11 or 12 November.

Erskine Hawkins and His Band never enjoyed the success with white audiences of groups such as the JIMMIE LUNCEFORD band. The Hawkins band, however, is remembered best for providing impeccable swing for dancers, tasteful arrangements, and a sense of camaraderie and teamwork. Undoubtedly this tone was set by Hawkins, who often allowed his soloists, especially his first-chair trumpeter Wilbur "Dud" Bascomb, to solo as much as he did.

FURTHER READING

Deffaa, Chip. *In the Mainstream: 18 Portraits in Jazz* (1992).

Fernett, Gene. *Swing Out* (1970).

Gold, Gerald. "Erskine Hawkins Blows," *New York Times*, 10 Apr. 1988.

McCarthy, Albert. *Big Band Jazz* (1977).

Obituary: (New Jersey) *Sunday Star Ledger*, 14 Nov. 1993.

This entry is taken from the *American National Biography* and is published here with the permission of the American Council of Learned Societies.

BRIAN FORÉS

Hawkins, Jalacy J. "Screamin' Jay" (18 July 1929–12 Feb. 2000), singer, composer, and actor, was born in Cleveland, Ohio. One of seven children, Hawkins was placed in an orphanage by his mother while still an infant, and information about his parents is scant, though Hawkins believed his father to be of Middle Eastern descent. Accounts vary as to how he spent his childhood. By some accounts he was adopted by a member of the Blackfoot tribe at eighteen months, by others that he spent his childhood in the foster care system. Hawkins was a musical prodigy, playing the piano by age three, reading music by age six, and playing the saxophone by age fourteen. He did not graduate from high school; however, he did attend the Ohio Conservatory of Music for one year in 1943, where he studied opera. His goal of becoming an opera singer endured his entire life. He was also a boxer, winning the Cleveland Amateur Golden Gloves Diamond Contest in 1947 and becoming middleweight champion of Alaska in 1949; however, music and entertainment were ultimately the focus of Hawkins's life.

In 1943 or 1944 Hawkins enlisted in the U.S. Army, serving in the Pacific during World War II and later in Korea. Much of Hawkins's ten years in the military was spent working in the Special Services division as an entertainer, with which he performed in Germany, Japan, Korea, and the United Kingdom.

Hawkins left the military in 1952 and joined TINY GRIMES and the Rockin' Highlanders as a vocalist, chauffeur and jack-of-all-trades. In 1952 with Grimes he recorded his first single record, "Why Do You Waste My Time/Canadian Boogie." Hawkins also performed with such jazz musicians as Jimmy Sparrow, James Moody, and Lynn Hope. He briefly worked with FATS DOMINO in 1954, but was fired when he upstaged Domino during a show. It was also in 1954 that Hawkins launched his solo career with the song "Baptize Me in Wine" for Apollo Records.

It was not until September 1956, however, when Hawkins rerecorded the song "I Put a Spell on You" for Columbia Records, that his career took off. An earlier version had been recorded for release on the independent label Grand, but had not been issued. This second version of the song was recorded while Hawkins and the members of his band were extremely drunk. Rather than singing the lyrics, Hawkins essentially screamed and grunted them. The result was a record which was banned by many radio stations, but which sold more than 1 million copies. The song became Hawkins's trademark and was eventually rerecorded by singers such as NINA SIMONE, Bette Midler, Marilyn Manson, and NOTORIOUS B.I.G., as well as by bands such as the Animals, the Who, and Credence Clearwater Revival. Versions of the song would eventually be used in television commercials by McDonald's, Burger King, and Pringles potato chips.

In the late 1950s Hawkins began to wear bizarre costumes and props onstage, including a loincloth, spear, and shield, a bone through his nose, and hair combed straight up. This costume caused Hawkins to be denounced by the NAACP, who which felt that Hawkins was pandering to the basest stereotypes of black people. Hawkins also sported rubber snakes and a smoking skull (called Henry), and he sometimes began his act by being carried onstage in, and then popping out of, a coffin. Other special effects included flames shooting from his fingertips. Over the course of his career, Hawkins and those who worked with him were burned many times. In 1976 Hawkins suffered secondary burns and even experienced temporary blindness, something that caused him to take a two-year break from touring.

The 1950s were a fruitful decade for Hawkins, but the 1960s were difficult. From 1960 to 1962 Hawkins spent twenty-two months in prison for indecent exposure. After his release, he moved to Hawaii, where he formed a short-lived partnership with Shoutin' Pat (Patricia) Newborn. The two recorded *Ashes/Nitty Gritty* for Chancellor Records. The partnership ended in 1963 when Hawkins married his second wife, Virginia Sabellona. It does not appear that they had any children. Newborn was so enraged by the wedding that she stabbed Hawkins repeatedly, puncturing his lungs and diaphragm. Hawkins toured in Europe for much of the decade and experienced great success there. In 1965 his recording of "I Hear Voices" reached number fourteen on the British rhythm and blues charts. Hawkins continued to record throughout the 1970s, 1980s, and 1990s. For almost two decades he performed drunk, believing that the only way he could sing his songs was to be as intoxicated as he was when he recorded the second version of "I Put a Spell on You." However, in 1974 he quit drinking only to discover that he could perform as well sober. In 1978 Hawkins appeared in the movie *American Hot Wax*. By the 1980s Hawkins was touring Britain and interest in him had picked up again in the United States. In 1981 he was the opening act for the Rolling Stones at Madison Square Garden in New York, but it was not until the movie director Jim Jarmusch used "I Put a Spell on You" in his film *Stranger Than Paradise* (1983) that Hawkins returned to fame in the United States. He appeared in three other movies during the 1980s, including *Joey* (1985), *Two Moon Junction* (1988), and Jarmusch's *Mystery Train* (1989). Hawkins also ran a booking agency in California called Hawkshaw Talent Company. He continued to record and tour the world in the 1990s, making appearances on television and in four more films, including *A Rage in Harlem* (1991) and *Smoke* (1995).

By the early 1990s Hawkins had become increasingly frustrated at having to scream out songs rather than being seen as a serious musician, but, ironically, it was the royalties from "I Put a Spell on You" that provided much of his income. In 1993 Hawkins moved to France, where he would live for the rest of his life, and began playing concerts throughout Europe and Japan. In 1998 he received a Pioneer Award at the Ninth Annual Rhythm and Blues Foundation Awards.

By 2000 years of health problems had caught up with Hawkins, and he died at age seventy in Neuilly-Sur-Seine, a suburb of Paris, when he suffered multiple organ failure following surgery for an aneurysm. Hawkins was survived by his ninth wife. He married Anna Mae Vernon in the 1950s and his second wife, Virginia Saballeno, in 1963. He also appears to have married in 1987, 1991, 1992, and for the final time in 1998. Divorce dates are shaky at best with the exception of the marriage in 1992, which appears to have ended in 1994. By his own estimate, Hawkins fathered fifty-seven children including Suki Lee Ann (1950), Debra Roe (date of birth unknown), Irene Hawkins (1951), Jalacy Jr. (1953), Janice Paris (1956), Helen Perez (1957), and Melissa Ahuna (1968). Over the course of his career Hawkins wrote and recorded at least forty-six singles, including a disco version of "I Put a Spell on You." The song was named one of the 500 Songs That Shaped Rock and Roll by the Rock and Roll Hall of Fame in 1995.

FURTHER READING

Colman, Stuart. "Repeating Echoes with Screamin' Jay Hawkins," *Now Dig This* 205 (2000): 26–29.
Hightower, Laura. "Screamin Jay Hawkins," in *Contemporary Musicians,* vol. 29 (1991).

ANNE K. DRISCOLL

Hawkins, Ted (28 Oct. 1936–1 Jan. 1995), singer and songwriter, was born Theodore Hawkins Jr. in Lakeshore, Mississippi, the son of an alcoholic prostitute. Little is known of his father, who left soon after Hawkins's birth. In 1949, having been expelled from grade school, Hawkins was sent to the Oakley Training School in Raymond, Mississippi, a school for juveniles who committed petty crimes. At Oakley, Hawkins was encouraged to pursue his interest in music, and he began to sing regularly in a vocal group at the school. He was mesmerized by a visit to Oakley from the noted New Orleans jazz pianist PROFESSOR LONGHAIR, who recognized Hawkins's nascent talents and encouraged him to accompany him by hamboning (also called patting juba)—beating out complex rhythms by clapping and slapping various parts of the body.

At age fifteen Hawkins was caught breaking into a Harley-Davidson showroom and was sent to Parchman penitentiary for thirty-one months and nine days. His mother died of cirrhosis while he was serving his term, and upon his release in 1957 he decided to leave Mississippi. He jumped on a freight train from Biloxi that he hoped was heading north, but it took him east to Tallahassee, Florida. Over the next few years, by hopping freights, hitchhiking, and walking, he traveled through Chicago, Buffalo, Philadelphia, and Newark before finally settling briefly in Geneva, New York. There the cold, damp climate soon forced him to move on. As legend has it, he asked an assistant at the Geneva Greyhound station where he might go to get warm and was prompted to purchase a one-way ticket to Los Angeles, California.

Hawkins's early musical leanings were heavily influenced by his religious faith and his participation in a number of church-based singing groups. However, soon after his release from Parchman he heard the voice of SAM COOKE for the first time. "His voice did something to me," he later recalled. Indeed, it inspired him to such an extent that on his arrival in Los Angeles he wandered into the RCA offices and attempted to win a contract to sing Cooke's songs. In the first of what turned out to be many setbacks in Hawkins's dealings with record labels, he was told that he would be better served writing and developing his own material. His first attempts at composition resulted in "Baby," a track that was released as a single by John Dolphin's Money label in 1966. Despite its being a radio hit across southern California, Hawkins received none of the royalties.

In a sense RCA was right to insist that Hawkins stretch himself beyond Sam Cooke covers. Once he had recovered from the disappointment of the Money debacle, Hawkins concentrated upon honing his skills as a street musician, and he emerged with a vocal talent and style that was every bit as inimitable as Cooke's. Hawkins's mix of gospel, blues, folk, country, soul, and stripped-down a cappella versions of traditional standards was performed with an ease that belied the extent of his talents. Passersby in downtown Los Angeles were quick to recognize those talents, and Hawkins was soon moved on by local police worried by the size of the crowds that repeatedly formed around him. He moved to Venice Beach, where he performed on and off for four decades.

Visually, Hawkins was as unique as his blend of musical styles. He would fold his imposing frame of six feet four inches to sit on a milk crate that he carried around with him to remind him, he claimed, of his humble origins. Next to the crate he placed a small square of hardwood on which he would hammer out rhythms with a metal heel inserted into his loafers. He had his name inlaid into the head of his acoustic guitar, which, like many Delta musicians, he tuned to an open C chord. Unlike others, though, Hawkins played with a leather glove on his left hand and an oversize acrylic thumbnail on his right.

After the failure of his first single, his street performing was interrupted by episodes of nervous breakdown, depression, and rumored drug addiction, and he was incarcerated for spells in jails and mental institutions. In 1971 Hawkins was singing outside a liquor store when he was spotted by a local DJ who mentioned Hawkins's talents to the producer Bruce Bromberg. Bromberg was sufficiently impressed to record an LP of material, but only a single, "Who Got My Natural Comb," saw the light of day in the 1970s. It was not until 1982 that the full album, Watch Your Step, was released on Rounder Records.

Clues to Hawkins's whereabouts in the decade between the album's recording and release litter the sleeve. The front cover photo shows him performing while surrounded by the barred windows and walls of the California State Medical Facility in Vacaville, and the sleeve notes include special thanks to the Los Angeles County probation department, a member of the public defender's office, and a local deputy. Watch Your Step also includes backing vocals from Hawkins's third wife, Elizabeth, whom he had married soon after arriving in Los Angeles. His previous two marriages had been youthful and short-lived: the first was abruptly annulled by the bride's mother, and the second lasted only two months before his wife died of cancer.

When it was finally released, Watch Your Step received a coveted five-star review from Rolling Stone magazine, but commercial success was not forthcoming, and Hawkins went back to Venice Beach. In Europe, however, and particularly in the United Kingdom, the response was much more positive. In 1985 a session that Hawkins had recorded in Nashville, Tennessee, was released in Holland as a double LP, On the Boardwalk. In England, Hawkins's genre-defying talents were first picked up by the eclectic DJ John Peel, whose repeated playing of Watch Your Step caught the attention of fellow DJ Andy Kershaw. Kershaw persuaded Hawkins to move to the United Kingdom in 1986. That same year Rounder released a second LP, Happy Hour, and Hotshot Records released On the Boardwalk: The Venice Beach Tapes in the United Kingdom. Both garnered lavish reviews, with Kershaw proclaiming Hawkins to be "the greatest living soul/blues writer and singer." The Manchester Guardian's respected music reviewer Robin Denselow declared of Happy Hour, "This is true soul."

After four years of relative success across the Atlantic, with tours around Europe and in Japan, Hawkins returned to Los Angeles. His transatlantic success did not travel with him, however, and he soon returned to Venice Beach. In 1992 Hawkins performed at the second of a series of local benefit gigs for the homeless, Gimme Shelter. This appearance led to the stateside success that Hawkins had craved for so long. He was signed by DGC Records, and with a major label behind him he entered the studio to record The Next Hundred Years. It stands as Hawkins's great work, not simply because its production values are more polished than his previous recordings but also because it showcases the full range of his abilities. The record includes staples from his Venice Beach repertoire, such as a version of Webb Pierce's "There Stands the Glass," alongside new interpretations and compositions. In a nod to the days when he used to travel from Lakeshore to Biloxi, Mississippi, to fish for crabs, the album includes the definitive version of Jesse Winchester's "Biloxi," in which Hawkins's voice moves from rich, soulful textures reminiscent of Sam Cooke to a brutal onslaught as gritty as the Venice Beach sand. Although critics often concentrate on the quality of Hawkins's voice, the album also draws attention to Hawkins's wider musicianship. As Dave Marsh recalls on the sleeve notes, Hawkins sang his version of John Fogerty's "Long as I Can See the Light" a cappella, intending for sparse backing tracks to be layered on by a session band at a later stage. When they came to do so, they found Hawkins's original, unaided pitch to be perfect and his timing to be metronomic.

For just two years after *The Next Hundred Years* Hawkins reached an audience that had previously been denied access to his majestic musical talents. Tours and royalties gave Hawkins and his family a financial security that had never been obtainable from the tip jar on Venice Beach. On 29 December 1994 he suffered a massive diabetes-related stroke and died on New Year's Day.

FURTHER READING

Guralnik, Peter. Liner notes to *Watch Your Step* (WOLP 1).

Kershaw, Andy. Liner notes to *Ted Hawkins: The Kershaw Sessions* (SFRSCD 013).

Marsh, Dave. Liner notes to *The Next Hundred Years* (DGC-24627).

GEORGE LEWIS

Hawkins, Thomas R. (1840–28 Feb. 1870), Civil War soldier and Medal of Honor recipient, was born free in Cincinnati, Ohio. Details of Hawkins's early life are unknown, but by 1863 he would join the Union army in Philadelphia, Pennsylvania, and soon he became an accomplished soldier. By 1863, two years into the war, President Abraham Lincoln and the Union army faced a dilemma. Despite victories, albeit at a high cost, at Antietam, Gettysburg, and Vicksburg, Northern states found it increasingly difficult to raise their quotas of men for the Union army. It may have been Chaplain George Hepworth of the 47th Massachusetts Regiment who summed up the situation best when he wrote in late 1863, "We needed that the vast tide of death should roll by our own doors and sweep away our fathers and sons, before we could come to our senses and give the black man the one boon he has been asking for so long—permission to fight for our common country" (Quarles, 183). The federal government finally acquiesced in early 1863, and efforts to recruit black regiments were soon under way. One of the unsung men influential in championing the use of black troops was Adjutant General Lorenzo Thomas; his successful efforts in the Mississippi Valley led to the War Department's formation of the Bureau of Colored Troops beginning in May 1863. Many (if by no means all) civic and business leaders in Philadelphia were enthusiastic about the formation of black regiments and offered their tireless support and raised thousands of dollars to promote recruitment efforts. Possibly

residing in Philadelphia by the summer of 1863, Thomas Hawkins may have been among those black Philadelphians that passed a resolution at a public meeting, declaring that "looking only to the future, and asking merely the same guarantees, the same open field and fair play that are given to our white fellow-countrymen, desire here and now to express our willingness and readiness to come forward to the defence of our imperiled country" (Quarles, 187–188). At Camp William Penn, on the outskirts of the City of Brotherly Love, ten black regiments would soon be raised and trained to serve in the Union army, among them the 6th U.S. Colored Troop Regiment.

We have but few details concerning Hawkins's military career. Though he was born in Cincinnati, it is unknown if he was a resident there in the early years of the war; if so, he may have served in the Black Brigade, a unit of free blacks conscripted to build miles of fortifications around that city in fall 1862 for a Confederate invasion that never materialized. By the summer of 1863 Hawkins was in

Thomas R. Hawkins, c. 1870. (Library of Congress. Daniel Murray Collection.)

Philadelphia and enlisted for service in the 6th U.S. Colored Troop (USCT) Regiment, Company C. This regiment was trained at Camp William Penn from its inception through 12 September 1863, and afterward was sent to Fortress Monroe, across the James River from Norfolk, Virginia, and then into battle in October. Included as part of Colonel Edward A. Wild's African Brigade through much of the remainder of 1863 and through May 1864, Hawkins and the men of the 6th USCT took part in numerous operations in North Carolina and Virginia, but saw little fighting. Because of his aptitude and leadership abilities, Hawkins was promoted to sergeant major, in charge of carrying his unit's regimental colors in battle. Such a position was not only one of honor but it was also important in helping to rally soldiers at key vantage points and proved a morale booster during times of battle. As long as a regiment's flags were flying high, victory was deemed possible. For a soldier to see the colors fall oft times meant that disaster was at hand. Indeed, carrying the national flag and regimental colors into battle was so important that a number of black soldiers in the Civil War received the Medal of Honor for "rescuing" the colors, among them WILLIAM HARVEY CARNEY, CHARLES VEAL, ALEXANDER KELLY, and ALFRED B. HILTON.

In May 1864 the men of the 6th USCT were assigned to General Benjamin F. Butler's Army of the James and placed on the siege lines before the Confederate capital of Richmond. There, the unit took part in the action at Petersburg on 15 June 1864 and gained full battlefield experience. The men would continue siege operations until they took part in the Battle of New Market Heights on 29–30 September 1864. In fierce hand-to-hand combat, black soldiers in several USCT regiments were assigned the task of helping to capture four key enemy forts in the Confederate line of fortifications around Richmond. The battle started in the early dawn hours of 29 September and lasted two days, resulting in 5,000 Union casualties. Only one position, Fort Harrison, was captured by Union forces, accomplished by the men of four black regiments, including Hawkins and his 6th USCT. Indeed, of the eighteen black soldiers serving in the Union army during the war to win the Medal of Honor, sixteen would do so in the action at New Market Heights, including Hawkins and his fellow 6th USCT color sergeant, Alexander Kelly.

Following this action, during which he was severely wounded, Sergeant Major Hawkins was treated at the Union hospital at Fort Monroe and then discharged from the army on 20 May 1865. Tradition states that Hawkins, upon his discharge, was presented with the regimental colors in appreciation of his excellent service. However, unlike many black sergeants who were recognized for their heroism at New Market Heights, it would be five years before Hawkins received the Medal of Honor. In the intervening time, Hawkins's activities are not fully known. He would later work for the government in Washington, D.C., probably at the Freedmen's Bank or possibly the War Department, and likely came in contact with another veteran of New Market Heights, the Medal of Honor winner CHRISTIAN ABRAHAM FLEETWOOD, who also worked for the government. Hawkins was finally awarded the Medal of Honor on 8 February 1870 for "rescue of the regimental colors" (Medal of Honor citation), perhaps with the help of Fleetwood, but would die just twenty days later due to the effects of his war wounds. Hawkins's gallant service, though not as well publicized as that of other black Civil War heroes, is remembered today in his hometown of Cincinnati, where the Hawkins House of Honor, a veterans' facility, was dedicated in his honor in 1993.

FURTHER READING

Civil War Medal of Honor Recipients. "Medal of Honor Citations," available online at http://www.army.mil/cmh/html/moh/civwaral.html.

Quarles, Benjamin Arthur. *The Negro in the Civil War* (1989).

GLENN ALLEN KNOBLOCK

Hawkins, Tramaine (11 Oct. 1951–), singer, was born Tramaine Aunzola Davis in San Francisco, California, the daughter of Lois Ruth Davis and Roland Duvall Davis. Her mother was a gospel singer. At age four she moved with her family to Berkeley, California. Davis had grown up attending the Ephesian Church of God in Christ, where her maternal grandfather, Bishop E. E. Cleveland, was pastor, and her aunt Ernestine Cleveland Reems was an evangelist. Davis was raised practicing the C.O.G.I.C. faith, a Holiness-Pentecostal religion and the second-largest African American denomination. Together with her friends Mary McCreary, Elva Mouton, and Vaetta Stewart, she was part of a singing group called the Heavenly Tones and in 1966 recorded her first single, "He's All Right," on the Music City label. The same year, the King of Gospel Music, JAMES CLEVELAND, produced their album *I Love the Lord*, and the Heavenly Tones embarked on a small California tour. Three years later, the group accepted an invitation from Stewart's brother, Sylvester, to sing background for his funk band Sly and the Family Stone under the name The Little Sister Band. Soon thereafter, she left the band to begin a solo career. In 1968 she sang with the Edwin Hawkins Singers Choir, recording the globally successful gospel single, "Oh Happy Day."

Davis moved to Los Angeles, California, in 1970 to perform with Andraé Crouch and the Disciples. She sang lead on the group's single, "Christian People," for which they were nominated for a Grammy Award. In the early '70s she was also a member of Honey Cone, a group that recorded the R&B hit "Want Ads," which was sampled by the gospel group Mary Mary in 2005 for their song, "Heaven." Also in the '70s, Davis returned to the San Francisco Bay Area and briefly rejoined the Edwin Hawkins Singers. Davis married Edwin's brother, the pianist and composer Walter Hawkins, who also lead the Love Center Ministries, where she sang and recorded with Walter Hawkins and the Love Alive Choir beginning in 1975. The choir's best-selling album was the debut, which yielded such hits as "Changed" and "Going Up Yonder." In 1980 Tramaine Hawkins won her first Grammy Award for her performance of "The Lord's Prayer"; also that year she made her solo debut with the album *Tramaine*, for which she was nominated for a Grammy Award. Her subsequent album, *Determined*, was also nominated for a Grammy Award in 1983. Hawkins's 1986 album, *The Search Is Over*, reached number two on the gospel charts with singles that topped the dance charts, like "Child of the King," "In the Morning Time," and "Fall Down (Spirit of Love)," which was a huge success in the clubs. However, some in the Christian community considered her secular cross-over sensation controversial. *Freedom* was cowritten and produced by The Jacksons and released in 1987; and *The Joy That Floods My Soul* reached number five on the gospel charts in 1988. She won another Grammy Award in 1991, this time for Best Traditional Soul Gospel Album, for her 1990 work, *Tramaine Hawkins Live*. In 1991 Hawkins performed the opening number at the American Music Awards along with the host MC Hammer from a song on his best-selling album, *Too Legit to Quit*, titled "Savior Do Not Pass Me By." The same year she appeared in the Philadelphia theater production *God's Trombones* along with the veteran actor OSSIE DAVIS and appeared in the Chicago and Baltimore productions of *The Gospel Truth*. Furthermore, she made her television debut on the ABC network's *Gabriel's Fire*, as a featured guest

with the actor JAMES EARL JONES. In 1994 Hawkins released the album *To a Higher Place*, and did not release another album or a single until she appeared on the 2000 song "Highway," by the gospel trio Trin-i-tee. However, in 1999 she had been inducted into the Gospel Hall of Fame. Finally in 2001 she released, *Still Tramaine*. In 2005 Hawkins was invited to perform at the funeral service for the civil rights activist, ROSA PARKS. She also performed on a tribute album for Parks with the gospel artists Vanessa Bell Armstrong and Daryl Coley, *A Celebration of Quiet Strength*. In 2007 she earned three Stellar Awards, the gospel music industry's most prestigious accolade: the James Cleveland Lifetime Achievement Award, for those who have made a major impact in the development and advancement of the genre; Female Vocalist of the Year; and Traditional Female of the Year, for her 2007 release, *I Never Lost My Praise*. The same year Hawkins sang at the funeral service for Cleveland.

Tramaine and Walter Hawkins had two children; a son, Walter Hawkins Jr., and a daughter, Trystan Hawkins. Tramaine Hawkins is married to Tommy E. Richardson Jr., a retired educator, and has one stepson, Damar Richardson. She refers to herself as "Lady Tramaine."

FURTHER READING

Carpenter, Bill. *Uncloudy Days: The Gospel Music Encyclopedia* (2005).

Darden, Bob. *People Get Ready! A New History of Black Gospel Music* (2005).

"Tramaine Hawkins Lifts Souls with *I Never Lost My Praise*." *Jet*, 16 Apr. 2007.

SAFIYA DALILAH HOSKINS

Hawkins, Virgil Darnell (1907–11 Feb. 1988), activist and lawyer, was born in Leesburg, Florida, and graduated from high school in 1930. He then attended Lincoln University in Pennsylvania, but soon left because of the hardships of the Great Depression. Hawkins married Ida (maiden name unknown) and returned to Florida to sell insurance, and sometimes took on teaching positions. Hawkins was later a resident of Daytona Beach, Florida, and received his bachelor's degree from Bethune-Cookman College in 1952.

Seeking a law degree, Hawkins applied to, and was rejected from, the University of Florida Law School. At this time, the University of Florida in Gainesville, like other Southern universities, was segregated and barred African Americans from being admitted. After his application was rejected, Hawkins then filed a lawsuit against the law school in 1949 (along with five other black applicants), with the help of the attorneys of the National Association for the Advancement of Colored People (NAACP). Because of the efforts of the NAACP, segregated graduate and professional schools in the South were slowly opening up to blacks, particularly with the 1950 Supreme Court decisions, *Sweatt v. Painter*, concerning HEMAN SWEATT's application to the University of Texas Law School and *McLaurin v. Oklahoma State Regents*, involving a similar challenge to the Jim Crow University of Oklahoma Law School by George W. McLaurin. The decisions found that these segregated institutions of higher education had violated the 14th Amendment's guarantee of equal protection regardless of race. In 1954 the Supreme Court handed down another landmark decision, *Brown v. Board of Education*, ruling that public schools across America could no longer be segregated. The Supreme Court then decided in 1955, in *Brown II*, that desegregation of public schools must occur gradually and "with all deliberate speed." Yet, it was initially unclear how *Brown* could be applied to higher education. Virgil Hawkins's case against the University of Florida Law School was still making its way through lower district- and state-level courts, and in 1956, the Supreme Court ruled on Hawkins's case. The Court ruled that Hawkins must be admitted to the University of Florida and decided that graduate and professional schools should be integrated immediately; in effect, the infamous "with all deliberate speed" of the *Brown II* implementation decree did not pertain. This brought greater clarification and urgency to the process of desegregating universities across the South.

Despite this important legal victory, and even with his dogged persistence in pursuing litigation over nine years, Hawkins was never admitted to the University of Florida Law School. In 1958 the university agreed to desegregate, but as part of the settlement, Hawkins himself would not be admitted. University of Florida officials believed Hawkins did not meet admission criteria because he failed various entrance examinations, and was morally questionable because he bounced a $25 check. Hawkins decided to leave Florida again, and earned his law degree in 1965 from the New England School of Law in Boston, an unaccredited institution.

Hawkins's clashes with the state of Florida were far from over though. Because the New England School of Law was unaccredited, the state of Florida refused to allow Hawkins to take the state bar exam to obtain his law license, which would have allowed him to practice law in Florida. In 1976, eleven years after Hawkins obtained his law degree, the Florida State Supreme Court ruled Hawkins could practice without taking the bar exam. At this point, Hawkins was 70 years old, suffered from diabetes and high blood pressure, and represented clients in Leesburg, Florida, who were often too poor to pay. These circumstances made practicing law complicated for Hawkins, and he made some mistakes, including misappropriating $15,000. Faced with ethical complaints and unable to afford a lawyer of his own, Hawkins resigned from the Florida bar in 1985. Before he could be reinstated, Hawkins died of kidney failure in February 1988. Hawkins was reinstated to the Florida state bar posthumously in October 1988 (which appeared to be the first time this occurred), and the legal aid clinic at the University of Florida was named in honor of Hawkins. In 2001 the University of Florida also awarded Hawkins an honorary degree posthumously, the first time in its 150-year history.

It has been widely recognized that Hawkins was instrumental in the fight to desegregate the University of Florida, as George Allen, the second African American admitted to the school's law school, said, "We were only admitted because Virgil had opened the door. If Virgil had not filed the lawsuit, we would never have been admitted to the University of Florida" (quoted in Wallenstein, p. 43).

FURTHER READING

Klarman, Michael, *From Jim Crow to Civil Rights: The Struggle for Racial Equality* (2006).

Wallenstein, Peter, ed. *Higher Education and the Civil Rights Movement: White Supremacy, Black Southerners, and College Campuses* (2009).

Obituary: *New York Times*, 15 Feb. 1988.

KRISTAL L. ENTER

Hawkins, Walter Lincoln (21 Mar. 1911–20 Aug. 1992), chemical engineer and professor, was one of two children born in Washington, D.C., to William Langston Hawkins and Maude Johnson Hawkins. Walter Hawkins's father was from Wisconsin and came to Washington with a law degree but spent most of his career as a civil servant in the U.S. Census Bureau. His mother taught general science in the city's public school system. Walter's inclination toward the sciences began with the simple experiments his mother conducted to entertain the children. "Linc," as he preferred to be called, spent a good amount of his playtime building gadgets. From simple radio sets to more complex contraptions, he was fascinated with how things worked.

He attended Dunbar High School, where many of the faculty members were highly skilled black PhDs. Hawkins credited this intellectually challenging environment with providing the inspiration for his choice of a career in chemistry and engineering. One highly influential teacher was CHARLES RICHARD DREW, who is best known for his pioneering work in blood preservation. His physics teacher, "Pop" Wellis, invented a component of an automobile, the self-starter. As part of the terms of his patent, he received a new car every year, and to the young Hawkins this was quite a role model to follow. The family expected that he and his sister would go to college, and Dunbar's lively community of scholars provided a solid example of what could be accomplished with a college degree.

One of Hawkins's high school friends applied to the chemical engineering program at Rensselaer Polytechnic Institute in Troy, New York. Hawkins also applied to this program, and in the fall of 1928 he was accepted. They were the only blacks in the school. Though he wanted to take more courses in chemistry and in research, the program was highly focused.

His years there were not without turmoil. For instance, one day Hawkins was the last student to file into a class where the instructor was giving a pop quiz, the grade of which counted for a large percentage of the final course grade. As the students took their seats, the instructor called a question out to him. In the confusion, Hawkins was unable to respond to the sole question for the quiz and the instructor gave him a failing grade. Despite this and other discouraging encounters, he received his Chemical Engineering degree in 1932.

For the entire graduating class, however, there were only two campus interviews and no jobs. With little to look forward to, Hawkins returned home and eventually decided to continue his education by pursuing graduate studies at Howard University. He enrolled that same year. Even though he never had a course in that area of study, he became enthralled with organic chemistry and polymer chemistry. Hawkins's curiosity would direct his future research. When he arrived at Howard, the chemistry department had been under the direction of PERCY LAVON JULIAN, who had been at Howard since 1928. Julian became an important influence on Hawkins during his graduate training. The work of GEORGE WASHINGTON CARVER and ERNEST EVERETT JUST greatly impressed Hawkins

as a young graduate student as well. In 1934 Hawkins received his master of science degree from Howard University. Unable to find steady employment, however, he was kept on at Howard for the next two years as a research associate. Hawkins worked odd jobs during the days and spent nights and weekends in the lab doing research.

Taking a gamble that career opportunities might develop and with just enough money to enroll for one year of study, Hawkins applied to and was accepted in the Ph.D. program at McGill University in Montréal, Canada. He enrolled in 1936, and his thesis adviser at McGill was Hubert Winning. Although he took a number of courses in materials science, it was the polymer chemistry class he took with Professor Herman Mark that proved to be the most useful to him. Hawkins won a fellowship for his second year and completed his Ph.D. in 1938.

Hawkins, having long been interested in teaching, taught at McGill for three years. It was during this time that he met Lilyan Varina Bobo, and they married in 1939. On the recommendation of Percy Julian, Hawkins was planning to begin postdoctoral work in Vienna, when, just as the arrangements were being concluded, Hitler invaded Austria. Travel between the United States and Canada would become more difficult once World War II began. Hawkins would continue to search for postdoctoral positions and would eventually win a national research fellowship at Columbia University in the early 1940s.

After Columbia he joined Bell Laboratories, in 1942, as the first African American scientist on the staff. He was immediately put to work on war-related research, such as trying to find a synthetic substitute for quartz crystals used in electronics and communications. As the new applications for polymers began to unfold, Hawkins began to focus his energies on natural and synthetic polymer research. British scientists were certain that the rapid oxidation and degradation of substances such as polyethylene rendered them unsuitable for long-term use in a variety of applications. For example, communication cables were normally coated with copper wire, and polymers presented the ideal low-cost alternative, since it was made from waste materials and had great strength and flexibility. But it would not last longer than one or two years. Hawkins began researching how to extend the life of these products, and his discoveries led to a number of patents that saved billions of dollars and tons of natural resources.

Hawkins would have a great deal of success at Bell Labs. He eventually became the head of plastics chemistry research and development and the assistant director of the Chemical Research Laboratory. He retired from Bell Labs in 1976.

Hawkins received numerous awards and honorary degrees. Among his most cherished were the Percy Julian Award, the International Medal of the Society of Plastics Engineering, and the National Medal of Technology. In addition to his esteemed work in research and development, Hawkins was an active leader in efforts to expand the nation's pool of scientific talent, as first chairman of the American Chemical Society's Project SEED (Summer Educational Experience for the Disadvantaged)—created to promote chemistry among economically disadvantaged youth—and in his service as a board member of several educational institutions.

FURTHER READING

Pearson, Kim E. "Pioneering Black Bell Labs Engineer Still at Work at 71," *The Crisis* (1983).

Sammons, Vivian O. *Blacks in Science and Medicine* (1990).

"Two Esteemed Rensselaer Graduates: Garnet Baltimore and W. Lincoln Hawkins," *Issue & Views* (Fall 1992).

ROBERT JOHNSON JR.

Hawkins, William Ashbie (2 Aug. 1862–2 Apr. 1941), Baltimore attorney, civic leader, political activist, and champion of legal challenges to racial segregation laws, was born in Lynchburg, Virginia, the son of Susan Cobb Hawkins and Robert Hawkins, a minister. Hawkins graduated in 1885 from the Centenary Biblical Institute (later Morgan College). In March of the same year he married his first wife, Ada McMechen (1867–?) of Virginia, in a Baltimore service led by the Reverend Benjamin Brown, a church activist and pastor of the Sharp Street Memorial Methodist Episcopal Church, of which Hawkins was a lifelong member. William and Ada Hawkins had two daughters, Aldina Hawkins (Haynes) (1885–1940) and Roberta Hawkins (West) (1891–?).

Hawkins worked as an educator while studying law at the University of Maryland, but he was forced to leave the college when white students petitioned to exclude blacks. He graduated from the Howard University School of Law in 1892 and established his practice in Baltimore, where he spent the rest of his career. He wrote pamphlets on the law and edited the Baltimore *Spokesman* from 1893 to 1895 and the *Baltimore Lancet* from 1902 to 1905. Hawkins also provided legal counsel to the Baltimore *Afro-American* newspaper. He was

admitted to the Maryland state bar in 1897. Deeply involved in Baltimore black civic life, he became a supreme chancellor for the region in the fraternal order the Knights of Pythias.

Hawkins identified himself politically as an Independent-Republican and worked to counteract racism within the Republican Party. He backed his fellow Howard University graduate George M. Lane when Lane became the first African American candidate for mayor of Baltimore. In March 1897 Lane and Hawkins joined pioneering black attorneys of the city, together with other black Republican leaders, at Samaritan Temple to create the Committee of 100. This group, disillusioned by racial discrimination in Republican politics, held a series of mass meetings in which Hawkins served as an orator, and the group promoted an alternative slate of black candidates for municipal and state office. Until white Republican opposition broke down his support Hawkins was a favored nominee for state legislative office. The group's efforts were stymied just prior to the fall elections when the Lane-headed ticket was omitted from the ballot because of questioned qualifying petitions.

Hawkins spearheaded a series of civil rights cases in Maryland. In 1898 he argued before the Maryland Court of Appeals on behalf of a black youth barred from attending a private mechanical arts school, presenting a sophisticated constitutional argument that foreshadowed those that would be used in the following century. In 1905 he took on as a like-minded junior partner his brother-in-law George W. F. McMechen (1871–1961), a Morgan College graduate who earned his law degree from Yale University in 1899. Their firm, Hawkins and McMechen, continued until Hawkins's death. McMechen became the first black member of the Baltimore school board, and a building at Morgan State University is named for him.

Hawkins was a supporter of the Niagara Movement and became a local leader in the National Association for the Advancement of Colored People (NAACP). He drew on his fraternal connections to help build the NAACP branch in Baltimore, beginning in 1912. In the decade of the 1910s Hawkins took on an activist role in a series of significant NAACP legal challenges to state and city segregation practices, challenges that he bankrolled from his own funds. Key among these were his successful challenges of residential segregation ordinances.

In 1911 Hawkins took on the issue of poor conditions faced by blacks in public transportation, specifically Chesapeake Bay ferryboats and the trains of the Baltimore, Chesapeake, and Atlantic Railway. Although the case did not come to fruition, exposure of the issue spurred the Public Service Commission to improve facilities and services for blacks. *State v. Gurry* (1913) was another key case that confronted racial covenants. Hawkins's legal activism was capped by his 1917 amicus curiae brief filed on behalf of the Baltimore NAACP before the U.S. Supreme Court in *Buchanan v. Warley*, an NAACP test case that originated in Louisville, Kentucky, in which legal staff successfully argued that Louisville's restrictive ordinance hampering the ability of blacks to buy, build, or reside in properties in white residential areas was a violation of the Fourteenth Amendment to the U.S. Constitution. Although Hawkins had his differences with the legal committee, the case was a major victory for the NAACP legal campaign.

Hawkins's NAACP cases were among the many argued by members of the African American National Bar Association that struck at the core of local Jim Crow laws, black codes, and restrictive covenants and led the way to the landmark Supreme Court rulings of the civil rights era. Outside the courts Hawkins and McMechen both personally challenged residential desegregation. While McMechen moved in 1910 to the boundary of the fashionable Madison section of the city, prompting protest meetings by white residents, Hawkins tested restrictions promoted by a white citizens committee in the Govans neighborhood of north-central Baltimore. In April 1921 Hawkins married his second wife, Mary E. Sorrell Hawkins (known as Mamie). The couple had no children, and they resided in a house on Arlington Avenue in Govans.

Hawkins continued to challenge the established Republican Party. He was an unsuccessful Independent candidate for the U.S. Senate in 1920. In the early 1920s black progressives who opposed MARCUS GARVEY and the anti-integrationist Black Power stance of the Universal Negro Improvement Association (UNIA) launched a "Garvey Must Go" campaign. In a group letter sent in January 1923 to the attorney general of the United States advocating suppression of the Garvey movement, the black journalist CHANDLER OWEN, the NAACP leader WILLIAM PICKENS, and others claimed that threats were made by Baltimore UNIA division members against Hawkins after he criticized Garvey in a speech. They listed the incident among other alleged incitements to violence on the part of the UNIA.

Hawkins became very ill from heart disease in 1940, and he died after seven months of confinement in Provident Hospital. He was survived by his wife, Mamie, his daughter Roberta, and Roberta's two children, Cromwell Ashbie Hawkins West (later known as Carlos Ashbie Hawk Westez, or RED THUNDER CLOUD) and Ada West (Williams), who became a professor at the University of Maryland. Hawkins is buried in the historic Mount Auburn Cemetery in south Baltimore. Originally called the City of the Dead for Colored People, it is the oldest owned and operated African American cemetery in the city, founded by trustees of Hawkins's church in order to supply a burial place of dignity for African American residents when no other alternatives existed.

FURTHER READING

NAACP legal campaigns are documented in the Arthur Spingarn Papers and the Papers of the National Association for the Advancement of Colored People at the Library of Congress. The Robert W. Schoeberlein collection in the Maryland State Archives Special Collections includes information on the early history of the Baltimore branch of the NAACP.

Hawkins, W. Ashbie. "A Year of Segregation in Baltimore," *Crisis* 3 (Nov. 1911).

Carle, Susan D. "Race, Class, and Legal Ethics in the Early NAACP (1910–1920)," *Law and History Review* 20, no. 1 (Spring, 2002).

Mills, Barbara. *Got My Mind Set on Freedom: Maryland's Story of Black and White Activism* (2002).

National Association for the Advancement of Colored People. "Baltimore Branch," *3d Annual Report* (Jan. 1913).

Smith, J. Clay, Jr. *Emancipation: The Making of the Black Lawyer, 1844–1944* (1993).

Obituary: Baltimore *Afro-American*, 12 Apr. 1941.

BARBARA BAIR

Hawthorne, Edward William (30 Nov. 1921–7 Oct. 1986), physician, physiologist, and educator, was born near Port Gibson, Mississippi, the son of Edward William Hawthorne, a minister, and Charlotte Bernice Killian, a teacher. As a child Edward endured a bout with polio at the age of seven and the untimely death of his father. After graduating from Dunbar High School in Washington, D.C., he entered Fisk University in Nashville, Tennessee, and later transferred to Howard University in Washington, D.C., where he earned a B.S. in biology in 1941 and an MD in 1946. As an intern at Freedmen's Hospital in 1946–1947 he developed an interest in cardiac research. He went on to earn an M.S. in 1949 and a Ph.D. in 1951, both in physiology, at the University of Illinois, Chicago. In 1948 he married Eula Roberts; they had five children.

Hawthorne's appointment in 1951 to the faculty of Howard University marked the beginning of a lifelong career in teaching, research, and administration. At Howard he helped to devise a graduate-level program in physiology at the master's and, ultimately, doctoral levels. He was instrumental in building a cardiovascular research laboratory and in establishing a core research unit—the Cardiovascular Renal Research Group—that attracted and trained many African American cardiovascular physiologists. He headed the physiology department for eleven years, from 1958 to 1969, and also served as assistant dean, from 1962 to 1967, and associate dean, from 1967 to 1970, of the College of Medicine. In 1969 he became chairman of the newly constituted department of physiology and biophysics, a position that he relinquished in 1974 to serve as dean of the Graduate School of Arts and Sciences.

Hawthorne once referred to his research as "a personal vendetta against ignorance" ([Howard University] *Capstone*, 14 Oct. 1986). This commitment remained intact despite the lingering effects of childhood polio, which by the mid-1970s had confined him to a wheelchair. An acknowledged leader in the field of cardiovascular-renal physiology he pioneered the use of electronically instrumented techniques to record heart function in conscious, non-tranquilized animals. One of his research projects, "Movements of the Mitral Valve," was supported by the National Institutes of Health (NIH) and involved a collaboration between Howard University and Tuskegee Institute during the 1960s and 1970s. In this project, which was codirected by Hawthorne and Walter C. Bowie, professor of physiology and pharmacology at Tuskegee, the scientists attached instruments to the hearts of horses to measure mitral valve movements, changes in heart size and shape, and rates of blood flow in the coronary vessels. Such measurements would have been difficult if not impossible to take in smaller, more commonly used laboratory animals because of the size of the measuring instruments involved. Heart surgery in humans having evolved to the point at which diseased valves could be replaced, Hawthorne and his colleagues aimed to advance knowledge about the relationship of valve closure to the tension of connecting cords, the shortening of the papillary muscles, and the pressure of blood inside the heart chambers.

Using a mathematical model Hawthorne developed an innovative theoretical framework for heart research. His findings demonstrated subtle changes in the size and shape of the left ventricle, as well as functionally related modulations in aortic pressure, during the contraction and expansion phases of the cardiac cycle. On this basis he proposed the nonprolate ellipsoid as a geometric analogue for the shape of the left ventricle. This and other pioneering research on ventricular and peripheral vascular function brought him widespread recognition.

A fellow of the American College of Cardiology (elected 1969) Hawthorne was active in national and state associations concerned with cardiac care and research. The NIH and other federal agencies frequently called on his expertise as a consultant and adviser. His participation in the American Heart Association included terms as vice president (1969–1972) and as a member of the Task Force on Heart Association Responsibilities in Poverty Areas. He was a member of the research committee (1963–1967) and of the board of directors (1966–1971) of the Washington (D.C.) Heart Association. He had numerous other professional affiliations and was active in a number of predominantly black medical and scientific associations, including the John A. Andrew Clinical Society (president, 1965–1966), Alpha Omega Alpha, Alpha Phi Alpha, and the Association of Former Interns and Residents of Freedmen's Hospital (executive secretary, 1957–1969; president, 1971–1972). He also served on the editorial board of the *Journal of Medical Education* from 1969 to 1972. In 1980 he was elected to membership in the Institute of Medicine of the National Academy of Sciences. A symposium on myocardial hypertrophy, sponsored in part by the National Aeronautics and Space Administration, was held in his honor at the Heart House Auditorium, American College of Cardiology, in 1984. Hawthorne died in Washington, D.C.

FURTHER READING

Selected materials are available at the Health Sciences Library and the Moorland Room, Moorland-Spingarn Research Center, Howard University.

Obituaries: *Washington Times*, 9 Oct. 1986; Howard University Medical Alumni Association *MedicAnnales* 38 (Nov. 1986).

This entry is taken from the *American National Biography* and is published here with the permission of the American Council of Learned Societies.

KENNETH R. MANNING

Hayden, Lewis (1811–7 Apr. 1889), fugitive slave, abolitionist, and entrepreneur, was born in Lexington, Kentucky, the son of slave parents whose names are not known. Separated from his family by the slave trade at age ten, he was eventually owned by five different masters. The first, a Presbyterian clergyman, traded him for a pair of horses. The second, a clock peddler, took Hayden along on his travels throughout the state, exposing him to the variety of forms that the "peculiar institution" could take. About 1830 he married Harriet Bell, also a slave. They had three children; one died in infancy, another was sold away, and a third remained with the couple. Hayden's third owner, in the early 1840s, whipped him often. These experiences stirred his passionate personal hatred for bondage. He secretly learned to read and write, using the Bible and old newspapers as study materials. By 1842, when he belonged to Thomas Grant and Lewis Baxter of Lexington, he began to contemplate an escape. Because his last owners hired him out to work in a local hotel, he had greater freedom than most slaves, which made it easier to flee. In September 1844 Lewis, Harriet, and their remaining son were spirited away to Ohio and then on to Canada West (now Ontario, Canada), by local teachers and Underground Railroad agents Calvin Fairbanks and Delia Webster.

Following their flight to freedom, the Haydens lived for six months among other refugees in the village of Amherstburg, Canada West. Haunted by memories of those still in bondage, they resettled in the small but thriving African American community in Detroit. This heightened their risk of recapture but placed them at the center of a major base of operations of the Underground Railroad. Hayden immersed himself in efforts to build community institutions; he organized a school and church and toured New England during the fall and winter of 1845–1846 to raise funds for the struggling congregation. Finding Boston a larger vehicle for his antislavery efforts, he relocated his family there by July 1846. He then traveled for nearly a year as a lecturing agent of the American Anti-Slavery Society, carrying the abolitionist message to dozens of towns in New York, New Jersey, and southern New England. In 1848 he opened a clothing store on Cambridge Street in Boston that soon developed into a thriving business. Hayden was, by 1855, "probably the wealthiest black in Boston" (Runyon, 121).

After the passage of the Fugitive Slave Act of 1850, Hayden worked tirelessly to fight its enforcement. He lectured fellow Bostonians on the need for "united and persevering resistance to th[e] ungodly anti-republican law." As a member of the executive board of the Boston Vigilance Committee, which was created to aid and protect fugitive slaves in the city, he often functioned as a liaison between local white and black activists, including members of the Twelfth Baptist Church, to which he belonged. He personally fed and housed hundreds of runaway slaves and used his clothing store to outfit many more. "His Beacon Hill residence," noted one scholar, "was the main Boston depot on the Underground Railroad, harboring at least a quarter of all the fugitives who passed through the city" (Runyon, 140–41). On one occasion, Harriet Beecher Stowe visited the Hayden home and found thirteen escaped slaves on the premises. Protecting refugees from bondage often became a public matter. Hayden openly resisted the law in the case of WILLIAM CRAFT and ELLEN CRAFT in 1850, the rescue of SHADRACH MINKINS from federal custody in 1851, and the attempted rescues of Thomas Sims in 1851 and ANTHONY BURNS in 1854. In the Craft case, he stacked kegs of gunpowder in his basement and threatened to ignite it if slave catchers attempted to enter the house to capture the couple. He was arrested but not convicted for his prominent role in the Minkins and Burns incidents. In 1855 his testimony before the Massachusetts legislature helped prompt the passage of a strong personal-liberty law to protect fugitive slaves in the state.

The panic of 1857 brought financial reversals and forced Hayden to move his clothing business into a smaller store, which was soon destroyed by fire. In the midst of this personal crisis, he continued his antislavery radicalism. He hosted John Brown during several visits to Boston between 1857 and 1859, was privy to his insurrection plans, and even raised funds for the effort. Hayden was appointed to the office of messenger to the Massachusetts secretary of state in July 1858. This provided some financial comfort and offered a vantage point from which to influence key officials in the state government. After the administration of President Abraham Lincoln sanctioned the enlistment of African American troops in the middle of the Civil War, Hayden successfully lobbied Governor John A. Andrew to organize the Massachusetts Fifty-fourth Colored Infantry Regiment, the first black unit in the North. He then raised volunteers for the regiment and two other black units in Canada West and the northern United States.

When the war ended Hayden found new outlets for his energies. He focused much of his attention on the Masonic movement among African

Americans. Named grand master of the Prince Hall Lodge in Boston and deputy grand master of the National Grand Lodge, he traveled through Virginia and the Carolinas in 1865 to organize new lodges among the former slaves. After returning to Boston, he delivered dozens of lectures and penned several pamphlets attacking racial discrimination among the Masons and defending the legitimacy of black Masonic lodges, including *Caste among Masons* (1866), *Grand Lodge Jurisdictional Claims; or, War of Races* (1868), and *Masonry among Colored Men in Massachusetts* (1871). Active in Republican Party politics, Hayden was elected in 1873 to the Massachusetts senate. In the 1880s he successfully campaigned for the erection of a monument in Boston to CRISPUS ATTUCKS, a black hero of the American Revolution. In their later years Lewis and Harriet Hayden contributed much of their personal wealth to local cultural institutions, including the Massachusetts Historical Society and the Boston Museum of Fine Arts. They posthumously donated five thousand dollars to establish a scholarship for black students at Harvard and particularly for those at the Harvard Medical School. After his death in Boston, abolitionists and prominent African Americans lionized Hayden as one of the heroes of the antislavery struggle.

FURTHER READING

Horton, James O., and Lois E. Horton. *Black Bostonians: Family Life and Community Struggle in the Antebellum North* (1979).

Levesque, George A. *Black Boston: African American Life and Culture in Urban America, 1750–1860* (1994).

Ripley, Peter C., ed. *The Black Abolitionist Papers 1830–1865* (5 vols., 1985–1992).

Robboy, Stanley J., and Anita W. Robboy. "Lewis Hayden: From Fugitive Slave to Statesman," *New England Quarterly* 46 (1973).

Stowe, Harriet Beecher. *A Key to Uncle Tom's Cabin* (1853).

This entry is taken from the *American National Biography* and is published here with the permission of the American Council of Learned Societies.

ROY E. FINKENBINE

Hayden, Palmer (15 Jan. 1890–18 Feb. 1973), painter, was born Peyton Cole Hedgeman, the fifth of thirteen children in Widewater, Virginia, to James Hedgeman, an illiterate professional hunter and tour guide for fishermen, and Nancy Hedgeman.

Hayden began to draw at the age of four, but he also loved music and longed for a fiddle. He later illustrated these two passions in the painting *Midnight at the Crossroads* (n.d.), a self-portrait as a boy holding a fiddle, wondering which path to take.

As a teenager, Hayden was part of the Great Migration of African Americans moving to the North and arrived in Washington, D.C., in 1906, where he worked in a drugstore, and then was a roustabout and did graphic design for the Ringling Brothers Circus. In 1912 Hayden joined the U.S. Army 24th Infantry Regiment in New York, with a letter of reference from a timekeeper at the Catskill water conduit, where Hayden had worked as a sandhog in a shaft. The timekeeper wrote Hayden's name erroneously, but the artist left it as it was, afraid to tell recruiters about the mistake. While serving in the Philippines, Hayden received a commendation for mapmaking. He wanted to study in Europe in 1915, but because World War I was going on, he reenlisted with a detachment of black cavalrymen (part of the Tenth Cavalry) stationed at West Point, where he was responsible for taking care of horses. While there, he took a correspondence course in drawing.

Honorably discharged from the army in 1920, Hayden worked for the postal service and began taking summer art classes at Columbia University, which he would continue for four years, receiving average grades. He exhibited landscapes and illustrations of Hiawatha at the Society of Independent Artists in New York on a regular basis, beginning in 1922. In 1924 Hayden got a job as a custodian from Victor Pérard, an art instructor at Cooper Institute (later Cooper Union). He also cleaned homes part-time, including those of the wealthy Alice Miller Dike, and worked for two summers for Asa Randall of the Commonwealth Art Colony in Boothbay Harbor, Maine.

After Hayden's first solo exhibition of fifteen landscapes and marine studies at the Civic Club in 1926, Dike encouraged him to enter a painting—a Maine waterfront scene titled *Boothbay Harbor*—to the Harmon Foundation competition. When it won first prize of a gold medal and $400, Dike gave him $3,000 to go to Europe.

Hayden studied privately in Paris and traveled throughout Brittany while in France from 1927 to 1932. He retained a rather flat, somewhat naive painting style throughout his career, almost exclusively depicting African American folk culture in a celebratory, caricature-like manner, as in *Bal jeunesse* (c. 1927), modeled after the Bal Nègre nightclub in Paris. He painted black families, workers, churchgoers, soldiers, and heroes from memory, inspired by dreams, folktales, and legends.

Hayden exhibited harbor scenes, watercolors of Breton peasants, and images of rural blacks at Galerie Bernheim-Jeune (1927), for which he received a favorable review; the Salon des Tuileries (1930); and two paintings at the American Legion (1931). He enjoyed a lively social life abroad, and *Nous quatre à Paris* (c. 1928–1930) simultaneously invokes the card-playing motif often explored by Paul Cézanne and the leisure activities of African American expatriates, including the painter HALE A. WOODRUFF, and the writers COUNTÉE CULLEN, ERIC WALROND, and CLAUDE MCKAY. Yet *Nous quatre à Paris* is genre portraiture, for the four black male card players are rendered abstractly and are informed by the strong volumes of West African ritual sculpture and modernist modes indebted to it. Another figurally abstract genre painting, *The Janitor Who Paints* (c. 1931) was inspired by Cloyd Boykin, a friend who painted in his Harlem basement apartment; this painting was later published in ALAIN L. LOCKE's *The Negro in Art* (1940). Hayden also produced a series of watercolors depicting African dancers from the Ivory Coast whom he saw perform at the Colonial Exposition of 1931 in Paris. His well-known painting *Fétiche et Fleurs* (c. 1932), with its Fang sculpture head and Kuba textile reinvigorating the still life genre, reflects both the influence of African art on modern European painting and Alain Locke's call for racially representative art. It won the Mrs. John D. Rockefeller Jr. Prize from the Harmon Foundation, but Hayden never produced another still life like it.

Back in New York, Hayden worked for the easel division of the Federal Arts Project of the Works Project Administration from 1934 to 1940, when he was disqualified for marrying an employed white schoolteacher, Miriam Hoffman of Des Moines, Iowa. The couple had no children. Hayden had a solo exhibition at the New Jersey State Museum in 1935. In 1936 he took a second trip to Paris, and Bernheim-Jeune exhibited his work again the following year. At this time his work, such as *Midsummer Night in Harlem* (1936), which featured minstrel-like representations of blacks on a crowded urban street, shared much in common with commercial images of blacks in Europe. Like several of Hayden's compositions, *Midsummer Night in Harlem* was ironic and satirical, but critics like JAMES AMOS PORTER decried its unrealistically colored, dark-skinned figures with exaggerated facial features and deemed the artist's work ludicrous. Others championed these images and found humor in Hayden's representation of African American working-class and folk subjects. Themes throughout Hayden's career concerned old-time religion, the rural South (milking time, hog killing, berry pickers, etc.), rites of friendship and courtship, and music (piano, banjo, and guitar playing and singing). Hayden's work was included in two group exhibitions in 1940, at Rockefeller Center Galleries in New York and Tanner Art Galleries in Chicago. Five years later it appeared at the Albany Institute of Art and History.

In 1944 Hayden traveled to Big Bend Tunnel in the Berkshires of West Virginia to gather material for his *Ballad of John Henry* series, which he had first begun in Paris in the early 1930s. In 1947 Argent Galleries of New York exhibited these twelve paintings of the black steel-driving legend, Hayden's best-known work. The Frick Fine Art Gallery at the University of Pittsburgh would display it more than two decades later, in 1969.

Hayden's New York circle included ELLIS WILSON, JOSEPH DELANEY, BEAUFORD DELANEY, SELMA HORTENSE BURKE, and ROBERT HAMILTON BLACKBURN, artists who met in 1947 to discuss the problems of African American artists.

Just days before Hayden's death, he received a Creative Artists Public Service Program Foundation commission to paint a black soldier series from World War I until the end of segregated military units. Hayden's work has been exhibited at Atlanta University, Fisk University, the Oakland Museum of Art, the California Museum of African American Art in Los Angeles, and the Smithsonian American Art Museum.

FURTHER READING

Driskell, David Clyde. "The Flowering of the Harlem Renaissance: The Art of Aaron Douglas, Meta Warrick Fuller, Palmer Hayden and William H. Johnson," in *Harlem Renaissance: Art of Black America* (1987).

Gordon, Allan M. *Echoes of Our Past: The Narrative Artistry of Palmer C. Hayden* (1988).

Leininger-Miller, Theresa. "Painting Seascapes and "Negro Characters": Palmer Hayden in Paris, 1927–1932," in *New Negro Artists in Paris: African American Painters and Sculptors in the City of Light, 1922–1934* (2001).

Sélig, Raymond. "L'oeuvre de Palmer Hayden," *La Revue du Vrai et du Beau* (27 Apr. 1927).

THERESA LEININGER-MILLER

Hayden, Robert Earl (4 Aug. 1913–25 Feb. 1980), poet and teacher, was born Asa Bundy Sheffey in Detroit, Michigan, the son of Asa Sheffey, a steel mill worker, and Gladys Ruth Finn. Early in his childhood, his parents separated, and he was given to neighbors William and Sue Ellen Hayden, who also were black, and who reared and renamed him. Hayden grew up in a poor, racially mixed neighborhood. Extremely nearsighted, unathletic, and introverted, he spent much of his youth indoors reading and writing. When he was eighteen, he published his first poem. Hayden attended Detroit City College from 1932 to 1936; worked for the Federal Writers' Project of the Works Progress Administration (WPA) from 1936 to 1938; published his first volume of poetry, *Heart-Shape in the Dust*, in 1940; and, studying with W. H. Auden, completed an M.A. in English at the University of Michigan in 1944. In 1946 he began teaching English at Fisk University in Nashville, Tennessee.

During his twenty-three years at Fisk, he published four volumes of poetry: *The Lion and the Archer* (with Myron O'Higgins, 1948), *Figure of Time* (1955), *A Ballad of Remembrance* (1962), and *Selected Poems* (1966). These were years of demanding college teaching and creative isolation, but they were brightened by a Rosenwald Fellowship in 1947; a Ford Foundation grant to write in Mexico in 1954–1955; and the Grand Prize for Poetry in English at the First World Festival of Negro Arts in Dakar, Senegal, in 1966. At a writers' conference at Fisk, also in 1966, Hayden was attacked by younger blacks for a lack of racial militance in his poetry. Hayden's position, however, first articulated in 1948, was that he did not wish to be confined to racial themes or judged by ethnocentric standards. His philosophy of poetry was that it must not be limited by the individual or ethnic identity of the poet. Although inescapably rooted in these elements, poetry must rise to an order of creation that is broadly human and universally effective. He said, "I always wanted to be a Negro, or a black, poet … the same way Yeats is an Irish poet." He was trying, like William Butler Yeats, to join the myths, folk culture, and common humanity of his race with his special, transcendent powers of imagination. Hayden's Baha'i faith, which he adopted in the 1940s, and which emphasized the oneness of all peoples and the spiritual value of art, also helped sustain him as a poet. In the late 1970s he said, "today when so often one gets the feeling that everything is going downhill, that we're really on the brink of the abyss and what

good is anything, I find myself sustained in my attempts to be a poet … because I have the assurance of my faith that this is of spiritual value and it is a way of performing some kind of service."

In 1969 Hayden joined the department of English of the University of Michigan at Ann Arbor, where he taught until his death. During these years he published *Words in the Mourning Time* (1970), *The Night-blooming Cereus* (1973), *Angle of Ascent: New and Selected Poems* (1975), and *American Journal* (1978, rev. ed., 1982). He was elected to the American Academy of Poets in 1975 and appointed consultant in poetry to the Library of Congress from 1976 to 1978, the first African American to be selected.

Shifting from a romantic and proletarian approach in *Heart-Shape in the Dust* to an interest in rich language and baroque effects in *The Lion and the Archer*, Hayden's mature work did not appear until *A Ballad of Remembrance*. *Ballad* presents the first well-rounded picture of Hayden's protean subjects and styles as well as his devotion to craft. *Selected Poems* extends this impression and is followed by— *Words in the Mourning Time*, which responds to the national experience of war, assassination, and racial militance in the late 1960s. Hayden's next volumes *The Night-blooming Cereus*, the eight new poems in *Angle of Ascent*, and *American Journal*— reveal an aging poet yielding to his aesthetic nature and his love of art and beauty for their own sake.

An obsessive wordsmith and experimenter in forms, Hayden searched for words and formal patterns that were cleansed of the egocentric and that gave his subjects their most objective aspect. Believing that expert craft was central, he rejected spontaneous expression in favor of precise realism, scrupulous attention to tone, and carefully wrought verbal mosaics. In Hayden's poetry, realism and romanticism interact, the former deriving significantly from his interest in black history and folk experience, the latter from his desire to explore subjective reality and to make poetry yield aesthetic pleasure. As Wilburn Williams Jr. has observed: "Spiritual enlightenment in his poetry is never the reward of evasion of material fact. The realities of the imagination and the actualities of history are bound together in an intimate symbiotic alliance that makes neither thinkable without the other." Some of the major themes of Hayden's poetry are the tension between the tragic nature of life and the richness of the imagination, the past in the present, art as a form of spiritual redemption, and the nurturing power of early life and folk memories. His favorite subjects include the spirit of places, folk characters, his childhood neighborhood, and African American history.

In the debate about the purpose of art, Hayden's stance, closer to the aesthete than the propagandist, has exposed him to criticism. Yet the coalescence in Hayden's poetry of African American material with a sophisticated modernism represents a singular achievement in the history of American poetry. His poetry about black culture and history, moreover, reveals the deepest of commitments to his own racial group as well as to humanity as a whole.

Hayden was married in 1940 to Erma Morris, with whom he had one child. He died in Ann Arbor.

FURTHER READING

Hatcher, John. *From the Auroral Darkness: The Life and Poetry of Robert Hayden* (1984).

Williams, Pontheolla T. *Robert Hayden: A Critical Analysis of His Poetry* (1987).

This entry is taken from the *American National Biography* and is published here with the permission of the American Council of Learned Societies.

ROBERT M. GREENBERG

Hayden, Scott (31 Mar. 1882–16 Sept. 1915), ragtime pianist and composer, was born in Sedalia, Missouri, the son of Marion Hayden and Julia (maiden name unknown). Born in the birthplace of the famed ragtime pianist SCOTT JOPLIN, Hayden began composing ragtime works as a student at Lincoln High School, influenced by a schoolmate, ARTHUR MARSHALL, who was another nascent ragtime pianist. Both Marshall and Hayden became devoted pupils of Joplin's. Joplin and Hayden became a composing pair when Joplin began to court Hayden's widowed sister-in-law, Belle, at around the turn of the century. After Joplin's marriage to Belle, Hayden and his wife, Nora Wright, followed the Joplins to St. Louis, sharing a home with them from about 1901 to 1905. At that time, with the death of his wife in childbirth, Hayden moved to Chicago, married Jeanette Wilkens, and became an elevator operator.

Hayden and Joplin collaborated on four published rags, all presumably written during the duo's shared time in St. Louis. "Sunflower Slow Drag," published by John Stark in 1901, is said to have been written while Joplin was courting Belle Hayden. Its third theme is credited to Joplin, with the balance purportedly written by Hayden. At the time it was second in popularity only to Joplin's own "Maple Leaf Rag," and it is believed to be the first rag recorded on a piano roll (Aeolian 8479). Hayden's sections are designed to show off his pianistic skills, whereas Joplin's are more varied in texture, moving through a wider range of keys, and shows more sophisticated writing.

"Something Doing," published by Val A. Reis Music Co. in 1903, is their second masterpiece. It is one of the most melodic of the early rags, with the first three sections probably Hayden's and Joplin most likely responsible for the fourth section since it features a style of syncopation that was common in Joplin's other works of this time.

The duo's other two collaborations, "Felicity Rag" and "Kismet Rag," were published by Stark in 1911 and 1913, respectively, and were probably "trunk pieces" (earlier pieces, pulled from a trunk) that either the publisher or Joplin discovered and had printed. "Felicity" again probably features a trio section by Joplin, whereas "Kismet" seems to be derived from floating ideas found in other common folk rags of the time. Hayden died of pulmonary tuberculosis.

FURTHER READING

Blesh, Rudi, and Harriet Janis. *They All Played Ragtime*, 4th ed. (1971).

Jasen, Dave, and Trebor Jay Tichenor. *Rags and Ragtime: A Musical History* (1978).

This entry is taken from the *American National Biography* and is published here with the permission of the American Council of Learned Societies.

RICHARD CARLIN

Hayes, Bob (20 Dec. 1942–18 Sept. 2002), football player and Olympic sprinter, was born Robert Lee Hayes in Jacksonville, Florida, the son of George Sanders, who operated a shoeshine parlor, and Mary Hayes, a domestic. When he was growing up Bob resented having to work for his father, particularly after starting high school, because his father would not allow him to participate in sports. Coaches at his son's high school convinced George Sanders to let Bob compete, and he joined the football team in May 1958. A gifted athlete, Bob was on the field for every play, playing both offense and defense, returning kicks, and serving as kicker and punter. He also played basketball and baseball and ran track, and by his senior year he was offered numerous scholarships and a professional baseball contract. Like many black athletes in Florida, he longed to play for legendary coach Jack Gaither at Florida A&M.

Hayes got his wish. Although he did not play his freshman year in Tallahassee, by the 1962 season he had become the starting halfback and returned kicks. After his first full season as a starter, he was named a Southern Intercollegiate Athletic Conference (SIAC) all-star. His success continued for his remaining collegiate seasons. After the 1963 season Hayes was named the conference athlete of the year and again made the SIAC all-star team. Following his senior year Hayes was one of four black athletes to integrate the Senior Bowl. He played with the future National Football League (NFL) legend Joe Namath and was coached by Tom Landry, his future coach with the Dallas Cowboys.

Though Hayes excelled in football, he gained international recognition as a sprinter. Hayes had a unique style. Unlike most sprinters of the time, who were tall and lithe, Hayes was muscular and compact, particularly in the legs. When he ran he turned his toes inward, pigeon-toed, and used the brute force of his legs to propel himself. One sportswriter described him as not so much running a race as beating it to death.

Regardless of his style, there was no question about his speed. On 1 June 1961 at the National Association of Intercollegiate Athletics (NAIA) Championships in Sioux Falls, South Dakota, Hayes tied the world record for the 100-yard dash at 9.3 seconds, the first of many records that Hayes tied or broke in his college track career. During the 1962 and 1963 track seasons Hayes established himself as a consistent world-class sprinter, including going undefeated in 1963, setting world records in the 400-meter relay in July 1962, the 70-yard dash in February 1963, and the 100-yard dash in June 1963.

At the 1964 Summer Olympics in Tokyo, Hayes entered as the favorite in the 100-meter dash. In the finals Hayes won the gold medal with a world-record-tying 10.0 seconds. His race was all the more spectacular because he wore a teammate's shoe that was a size too big. The next day neon signs in the Ginza proclaimed: "Bob Hayes—World's Fastest Human." Hayes won a second gold medal in the 400-meter relay. This race was perhaps more impressive than his individual gold medal because Hayes's leg was timed (unofficially) at 8.6 seconds. His incredible speed propelled the U.S. team to a world record time of 39.0 seconds.

Following the Olympics, Hayes returned to Florida A&M to finish the football season before signing a contract with the NFL's Dallas Cowboys, who had drafted him in December 1963 as a futures choice. Shortly before leaving for his first training camp in 1965 he married Altamease Martin, and they had one child before divorcing in 1972.

Initially coach Landry was unsure how to use Hayes, but once Landry understood Hayes's speed, he became a starting wide receiver and earned the nickname "Bullet." During his rookie season he amassed forty-six receptions for 1,003 yards and twelve touchdowns, all Cowboys rookie records, and he was a reserve Pro Bowl selection.

Hayes continued to be a premier receiver through most of his ten seasons with the Cowboys, from 1965 to 1974. When the Cowboys won Super Bowl VI over Miami in 1972, Hayes became the first athlete to win an Olympic gold medal and a Super Bowl ring. By this time, however, Hayes's numbers were dropping. The turning point came after the 1968 season when quarterback Don Meredith retired. Hayes credited Meredith with making him a better player, and his productivity after Meredith left the game was never the same. The Cowboys soured on Hayes during the 1974 players' strike. Landry benched Hayes and then traded him to the San Francisco 49ers in 1975. Hayes played sparingly for half a season before being released.

Hayes finished his football career with 371 receptions, 7,414 yards, and seventy-one touchdowns. Along the way he established twenty-two Cowboys franchise records, and his 20.0 yards/reception average placed him in the top-ten all time in the NFL. Hayes's arrival in the NFL changed the game. Before, teams usually ran simple man-to-man coverage. His speed forced teams to adopt complex zone coverage to account for his presence, so even when he was not the target of a play, he opened up the field for running backs and other receivers. When he joined the NFL most people wrote him off as just another sprinter trying to play football, but they forgot that he was a football player first.

After football Hayes co-founded and served as vice president of Dycon International, a company that designed voice-activated computers for telephone solicitation. In 1976 he entered the U.S. Track and Field Hall of Fame and married Janice McDuff; the couple had three children. His life appeared to be going well until he was arrested for selling drugs to an undercover police officer in April 1978. Though he claimed that he was innocent, that he never touched drugs and was trying to help a friend, he pled guilty, hoping, unsuccessfully, to avoid jail time. On 14 March 1979 he began serving two five-year sentences, but he was released early, on 27 February 1980, for good behavior.

After jail Hayes battled alcohol problems and faced difficulty finding employment. The Cowboys owner Clint Murchison and the former quarterback

Roger Staubach tried to help Hayes, and after six years of struggle Hayes completed rehab in January 1986. He returned to Tallahassee to complete his college degree, graduating with a B.A. in special education from Florida A&M in 1993. In September 2001 the Cowboys owner Jerry Jones selected Hayes for the Cowboys Ring of Honor, a recognition that Hayes recalled as one of the proudest moments of his life. He died from liver and kidney complications resulting from prostate cancer just a year later. Many consider Hayes one of the best players not in the Pro Football Hall of Fame, believing that his drug and alcohol problems have prevented his induction.

FURTHER READING

Hayes, Bob, with Robert Pack. *Run Bullet Run: The Rise, Fall, and Recovery of Bob Hayes* (1990).

Lipman, David, and Ed Wilks. *The Speed King: Bob Hayes of the Dallas Cowboys* (1971).

Obituaries: *Dallas Morning News, Los Angeles Times,* and *New York Times,* 20 Sept. 2002.

MICHAEL C. MILLER

Hayes, Charles A. (17 Feb. 1918–8 Apr. 1997), politician and trade unionist, was born in Cairo, Illinois, the eldest son of Nevada Bell and Charles Hayes Sr., the latter a farm laborer. Charles Arthur Hayes spent his formative years in Cairo, graduating from that city's Sumner High School in 1935.

After high school, Hayes took a job stacking lumber at E. L. Bruce Company, a leading manufacturer of hardwood flooring. Hayes quickly rose to the more skilled position of machine operator and became active in efforts to organize a union. In 1939, these efforts resulted in the founding of Local 1424 of the United Brotherhood of Carpenters and Joiners of America. A few months later, Hayes was elected president, marking the beginning of a long career as a labor organizer.

During World War II, Hayes, like thousands of African Americans, migrated north to Chicago in search of better employment opportunities. In 1942 Hayes took a job at the Wilson & Co. meatpacking plant but was disappointed to find that company officials and union leaders colluded in keeping black workers confined to the lowest-paid unskilled positions. In 1943, Hayes joined the grievance committee of Local 25 of the United Packinghouse Workers of America (UPWA) and over the next four years helped to organize over thirty-five hundred workers at the Wilson plant into a UPWA local, resulting in the elimination of segregation and discrimination in hiring and promotion.

During the late 1940s and early 1950s, Hayes rose up quickly through the ranks of the UPWA in Chicago from field representative (1948–1954) to district director (1954–1968). In this capacity, Hayes extended his struggles to eliminate segregation and discrimination beyond the shop floor and into the communities surrounding the stockyards.

As the civil rights movement gained steam, Hayes endeavored to forge ties between local struggles in Chicago and the national movement's organizations and leadership. In 1955, Hayes joined Dr. MARTIN LUTHER KING Jr. in the Montgomery bus boycott. Over ten years later, Hayes was on the committee that secured King's 1966 visit to Chicago as a part of the Southern Christian Leadership Conference's first northern campaign.

In the wake of King's visit, Hayes focused on expanding the economic and political power of black workers in Chicago. Hayes was instrumental in the formation of the Black Labor Leaders of Chicago, an organization that provided union training programs for black workers, and in the 1972 creation of the National Coalition of Black Trade Unionists. In the political realm, Hayes was a staunch supporter of HAROLD WASHINGTON's campaigns for mayor of Chicago in both 1977 and 1983. After securing the mayoral victory in 1983, Hayes took Washington's vacant congressional seat representing a district that included Chicago's predominantly African American South Side.

During his ten years in office, Hayes continued the fight to improve the welfare of the working-class and poor black residents of his district who were laboring under the dual effects of deindustrialization and cuts in social welfare programs. A staunch critic of the economic policies of the Reagan administration, Hayes worked hard as a member of the Congressional Black Caucus and the House Education and Labor committees, sponsoring bills that would reduce unemployment, provide job training, and create public works programs. Hayes was also a leader in the struggles against the apartheid regime in South Africa, participating in protests at the South African embassy in Washington, D.C., in November 1984, and introducing legislation to impose economic and diplomatic sanctions. Hayes's political career came to an end in 1992 when he lost a reelection bid to BOBBY RUSH, a former Black Panther Party member, in the primary. Hayes appeared set to win the primary until allegations surfaced that the congressman had overdrawn checking accounts at the House bank. An investigation by the Justice Department cleared Hayes of any criminal wrongdoing the following year. Hayes died in Chicago after a long and successful career as a trade unionist and politician committed to eliminating discrimination and protecting the rights of black workers.

FURTHER READING

Ehrenhalt, Alan, ed. *Politics in America: Members of Congress in Washington and at Home* (1985).

Halpern, Richard, and Roger Horowitz. *Meatpackers: An Oral History of Black Packinghouse Workers and Their Struggle for Racial and Economic Equality* (1999).

Office of History and Preservation, Office of the Clerk. *Black Americans in Congress, 1870–2007* (2008). http://baic.house.gov/member-profiles/profile. html?intID=69 (14 Mar. 2010).

Ragsdale, Bruce A., and Joel D. Treese. *Black Americans in Congress, 1870–1989* (1990).

Obituary: *New York Times*, 13 Apr. 1997.

KERRY PIMBLOTT

Hayes, Isaac (20 Aug. 1942–10 Aug. 2008), musician, songwriter, producer, and actor, was born in Covington, Tennessee, to unknown parents. Before Hayes had turned two, his father had left the family home and his mother had passed away in a mental institution. Hayes was raised by his maternal grandparents, who sharecropped for a living until, at the age of seven, Hayes, his sister, and his grandparents moved to Memphis. Over the next several years, Hayes lived in a variety of places in North Memphis. Impoverished, at times the family had to split up, and at the worst point Hayes was sleeping in junk cars at a garage. Largely a self-taught musician, during and immediately following his school years, Hayes apprenticed with a number of ensembles that variously worked the school, amateur hour, and nightclub circuit singing doo-wop and gospel and playing blues and jazz saxophone, and rhythm and blues piano. Upon graduating from Manassas High School in 1962, Hayes auditioned at the recently opened American Recording Studio in North Memphis. In late 1962 he released his first 45 rpm single, "Laura, We're on Our Last Go-Round"/"Sweet Temptations," on the Youngstown label.

It was as a member of the session musician Floyd Newman's band that Hayes first worked at Stax Records in late 1963. With the Stax "house" band keyboard player BOOKER T. JONES being away at college, Hayes was asked to play piano and organ on studio recordings by Stax artists such as OTIS REDDING, RUFUS THOMAS, Eddie Floyd, and Carla Thomas. While working as a session musician at Stax, Hayes began writing songs with DAVID PORTER.

The first two Hayes and Porter compositions that were released were "Can't See You When I Want To" and "How Do You Quit (Someone You Love)," performed by David Porter and Carla Thomas, both issued in the first two months of 1965. In 1966 Hayes and Porter began to hit the charts regularly, writing and producing hits such as "Soul Man," "Hold On! I'm A Comin'," and "B-A-B-Y" for Stax artists such as Sam and Dave, Carla Thomas, Johnnie Taylor, Mable John, and the Soul Children.

Despite his prodigious ability to craft hit songs for others, Hayes never lost sight of his desire to record as a solo artist in his own right. To that end he cut a solo album, *Presenting Isaac Hayes*, in a trio format in early 1968. His second album, 1969's *Hot Buttered Soul*, forever changed the fortunes of both Hayes and Stax Records and the sonic possibilities of rhythm and blues. Its four songs were five, nine, twelve, and nearly nineteen minutes long, respectively. Such playing times were simply unknown in black popular music. The longest song, Jimmy Webb's "By the Time I Get to Phoenix," opened with an extended spoken "rap." Immensely popular, it began a craze for such raps by a wide variety of rhythm and blues artists. Hayes's singing voice was a smooth low baritone that betrayed little overt gospel influence. In the era of soul, this was a radical departure that paved the way for subsequent artists such as BARRY WHITE. Each song on *Hot Buttered Soul* was draped in an incredibly elaborate and dramatic orchestral arrangement that had absolutely no precedence in popular music.

Hayes followed *Hot Buttered Soul* with the similarly styled *The Isaac Hayes Movement* and *To Be Continued* (1970). All three albums were made up of extended and extensive reworkings of pop and R&B songs that had been hits for others. Whether Hayes tackled the Beatles' "Something" or JERRY BUTLER's "I Stand Accused," the original tunes were so substantially reinterpreted that, for all intents and purposes, Hayes had rewritten them. The formula proved to be so immensely successful that with each album he achieved the unprecedented feat of reaching the upper echelons of the pop, R&B, jazz, *and* easy listening charts. Proving unequivocally that black artists could record album-length works that would sell in the millions, Hayes was the catalyst for a complete transformation of the political economy of black music. In the process, he paved the way for the first wave of R&B album masterpieces by STEVIE WONDER, MARVIN GAYE, CURTIS MAYFIELD, and Funkadelic as 1960s soul gave way to a plethora of newly created R&B styles in the early 1970s.

Isaac Hayes performs at the Michigan State Fair in Detroit in August 2002. (AP Images.)

In 1971 Hayes was commissioned to write the score for GORDON PARKS SR.'s *Shaft*, one of the first so-called blaxploitation flicks. The resulting double album and the "Theme from *Shaft*" single kick-started disco and the phenomenon of the black soundtrack, earned Hayes both Academy and Grammy awards, and boosted his position as an African American icon to the point of his being proclaimed a "Black Moses"—the nickname stuck. Sporting a bald pate and gold chains, Hayes became an important symbol of black achievement and possibility.

After parting company with Stax in 1974, Hayes recorded for ABC and then Polydor through 1980, placing fourteen more singles on the R&B charts. With the exception of an album for Columbia in 1986 which produced the top ten R&B hit "Ike's Rap," a 1992 single with Barry White, and a pair of albums for Virgin in 1995, Hayes spent most of the 1980s and the first half of the 1990s developing an acting career, starring in movies such as *Escape from New York* (1981) and *I'm Gonna Git You Sucka* (1981) and appearing semi-regularly in *The Rockford Files* in the late seventies. Though Hayes was largely absent from the music industry, many of his funkier recordings were extensively sampled by rap artists as Hayes became a musical hero with extensive influence on artists who were not even born when he originally created his most important work.

In 1997 Hayes landed the part of the voice of Chef in the animated late-night series *South Park*. When the show became popular with the teenage set, Hayes once again achieved prominence as a contemporary icon of popular culture. In 1989 the Smithsonian Institute spent two days honoring the compositions of Isaac Hayes and David Porter; in 1999 Hayes received an R&B Foundation Pioneer Award; and in 2002 Isaac Hayes was inducted into the Rock and Roll Hall of Fame. In 2008 Hayes died of a stroke in Memphis. He was 65.

FURTHER READING

Bowman, Rob. *Soulsville U.S.A.: The Story of Stax Records* (1997).

Guralnick, Peter. *Sweet Soul Music* (1986).

ROB BOWMAN

Hayes, Roland (3 June 1887–31 Dec. 1976), singer, was born in Curryville, Georgia, the son of William Hayes and Fanny (maiden name unknown), tenant farmers and former slaves. Young Roland worked as a field hand from an early age alongside his mother and two brothers. William Hayes had become an invalid following an accident when Roland was an infant, and he died when Roland was twelve. Although neither parent could read or write, Fanny Hayes was determined that her children would get an education. However, Roland was able to attend local country schools, which were inferior and segregated, for only a few months at a time, when he was not needed in the fields. At the age of fifteen, he and his family moved to Chattanooga, Tennessee, as part of his mother's plan to have her sons educated. The three boys were to alternate school and work a year at a time, with one brother working to help support the family while the two others studied. Hayes found employment as a laborer in a machine shop, and despite the harsh working conditions—in one of several accidents, hot iron splashed on his feet and left permanent scars—he

Roland Hayes in 1954. (Library of Congress. Photographed by Carl Van Vechten.)

rose to foreman. When his turn came to take a year off and attend school, he decided against it because he was making more than his brothers could earn. He therefore stayed at the machine shop and was tutored in the evenings by a local black teacher.

Like many of his fellow workers, Hayes often sang as he labored. At his church, his distinctive tenor voice attracted the attention of the choir director, W. Arthur Calhoun, an African American who was taking a year off from his studies at Oberlin College Conservatory in Ohio. Calhoun persuaded Hayes to sing in the choir and offered to help him develop his voice. Fanny Hayes refused to let Calhoun give her son singing lessons, believing that black musicians were trashy riffraff. Calhoun persisted, and one day he took Hayes to the home of a prosperous white man who owned a phonograph. When the man played operatic recordings, including performances by the Italian tenor Enrico Caruso, Hayes was overwhelmed—he later described it as a mystical experience—and vowed that despite his mother's opposition he would become a singer.

With Calhoun's encouragement, Hayes set out for Oberlin, but when he reached Nashville he realized he did not have enough money to continue the journey to Ohio. He enrolled instead at Fisk University, an all-black institution in Nashville, where he was placed in the preparatory division. Hayes studied at Fisk for four years and took singing lessons there; he supported himself by working as a servant. Suddenly, in 1910, he was dismissed from the school—apparently because he had begun singing for organizations off campus and had not received the required permission from school authorities to do so.

The dejected Hayes moved farther north, to Louisville, Kentucky, and became a waiter in a men's club. His voice again attracted attention, and he was asked to sing at various gatherings. Hayes had remained in touch with his singing teacher at Fisk, and in 1911 he was asked to join the university's famous performing group, the Fisk Jubilee Singers, in a concert appearance in Boston. Putting aside his bitterness, Hayes agreed. After the concert, he decided to stay in Boston, which became his home for the remainder of his life.

Hayes worked first as a hotel bellboy and then as a messenger at an insurance company while continuing his vocal studies with Arthur J. Hubbard, a teacher of some renown. When his brothers married, Hayes moved his mother to Boston. She lived with him there, and he supported her on his small wages. Their home was a tenement room, where they used packing boxes for furniture. Fanny Hayes was now supportive of her son's decision, and her encouragement, combined with Hubbard's, fueled Hayes's determination to be a great singer.

In 1917, with the help of Hubbard, Hayes rented Symphony Hall in Boston to give a recital—the first black musician ever to do so. His performance of Negro spirituals, lieder, and continental art songs was a notable success, and it launched his career. However, opportunities for black concert singers in the United States were limited, and Hayes knew that a climb to prominence would take time. After four years of local appearances, he had saved enough money to go abroad. In 1921 he gave several recitals in London, including a command performance for King George V and Queen Mary at Buckingham Palace. He then went on to appear in Paris, Vienna, and Prague, taking voice lessons in those cities.

Upon his return to the United States after a triumphal year in Europe, Hayes was hailed as a musical sensation. Singing a repertoire of spirituals, folk and art songs, and occasional operatic arias, he began what was to become a series of concert appearances throughout the United States and Europe during the next four decades. In addition to giving recitals, Hayes appeared with the Boston, Philadelphia, and Detroit symphonies, the New York Philharmonic, and leading orchestras in Paris, Amsterdam, Vienna, and Berlin. Many noted musicians of the twentieth century, including Ignace Paderewski, Sergei Rachmaninoff, Pablo Casals, Fritz Kreisler, and Nellie Melba, championed Hayes, who became the first black to be recognized as a serious musician on the American concert stage.

A deeply religious man throughout his life, Hayes believed that God had given him his voice for a purpose: to express the soul of his race. His success served as an example to younger black singers, and his encouragement of MARIAN ANDERSON, PAUL ROBESON, and others helped launch their careers. Although some critics considered Hayes the equal of Lauritz Melchior, Giovanni Martinelli, and other renowned operatic tenors who were his contemporaries, his race deprived him of a career in opera. Black performers began to appear on the American operatic stage only after Anderson's debut with the Metropolitan Opera in 1955, and by then Hayes was in his late sixties.

Hayes refused to become embroiled in discussions about racism, even after a widely publicized incident in 1942 when he and his family were arrested in a shoe store in Rome, Georgia, after they sat in chairs reserved for whites. "I am not bitter," he said after his release. "I am only ashamed that this should happen in my native state. I love Georgia."

Hayes continued to perform in public until the early 1960s. To mark his seventy-fifth birthday in June 1962, he gave a recital at Carnegie Hall in New York City, and in a ceremony at city hall he was honored by Mayor Robert F. Wagner and a number of distinguished black performers, including Robeson, Anderson, and LEONTYNE PRICE.

Hayes was married to Helen A. Mann (the exact date of the marriage is unknown); they had one daughter, who later became a concert singer under the name Afrika Lambe. The family maintained a home in Brookline, Massachusetts, a Boston suburb, as well as a six-hundred-acre farm in Curryville, Georgia, which included his birthplace. One of Hayes's most valued possessions was the original phonograph from Chattanooga on which he heard operatic music for the first time. During his lifetime he received numerous awards, including the NAACP's Spingarn Medal and eight honorary degrees. Hayes died in Boston.

FURTHER READING

Brooks, Tim, and Richard K. Spottswood. *Lost Sounds: Blacks and the Birth of the Recording Industry, 1890–1919* (2004).

Hare, Maud Cuney. *Negro Musicians and Their Music* (1936).

Hayden, Robert C. *Singing for All People: Roland Hayes, A Biography* (1995).

Helm, Mackinley. *Angel Mo' and Her Son* (1942).

Stidger, William L. *The Human Side of Greatness* (1940).

Obituary: *New York Times*, 2 Jan. 1977.

This entry is taken from the *American National Biography* and is published here with the permission of the American Council of Learned Societies.

ANN T. KEENE

Haynes, Daniel (6 June 1889–29 July 1954), actor, singer, and minister, was born in Atlanta, Georgia, the son of Charles Haynes, a bricklayer, and Mary ("Mollie") Leech, an office cleaner. Haynes was educated in the Atlanta public schools and graduated from the African Methodist Episcopal (AME) Church–affiliated Morris Brown College.

Haynes worked as a porter in Atlanta and as an itinerant preacher before securing a job in the records division at the Standard Life Insurance Company in Atlanta around 1915. Founded by Heman Edward Perry in 1913, Standard was one of the nation's few black life insurance companies, and Haynes gained valuable business experience working with one of the most active black entrepreneurs in America. While at Standard, he also met HARRY HERBERT PACE, the company's secretary-treasurer, with whom he would later work in New York. Haynes registered for the draft in 1917 and, according to one source, served in military intelligence during World War I.

In 1920 Haynes married Rosa B. Sims, also a graduate of Morris Brown College, and they moved to New York City, where he began working as a bookkeeper for the Pace and Handy Music Company. Harry H. Pace and W. C. HANDY, the company's founders, wrote and published sheet music, which they sold to white-owned record companies. When Pace split with Handy to found the Pace Phonograph Corporation and Black Swan Records, Haynes joined him as chief bookkeeper. Working with Pace placed Haynes in an environment in which he was able to meet some of the most influential musicians and composers of the day, including FLETCHER HENDERSON and WILLIAM GRANT STILL, as well as performers who would soon make their mark, such as ETHEL WATERS and ALBERTA HUNTER. His interaction with these great performers no doubt influenced him musically and aided him when he began his own performing career a few years later.

Black Swan Records ceased production in 1923, and little is known about Haynes's employment at this time. He may have worked as a part-time minister, having been licensed to preach in the AME Church in 1920. Some accounts indicate that he owned a small publishing business in Brooklyn, New York, in this period.

Haynes's performing career began in 1927, when friends in the theater enlisted him to serve as the understudy to the famed actor CHARLES SIDNEY GILPIN in the Broadway production of *The Bottom of the Cup*. When Gilpin's illness prevented him from performing, Haynes assumed the lead role on opening night. Although the play was poorly reviewed, Haynes's performance was well received by critics. He went on later that year to play the lead role of a minister in *Earth* and appeared in the musical revue *Rang Tang*, which starred the vaudeville team of Flournoy Miller and Aubrey Lyles and featured the well-known stage and film actress EVELYN PREER. Haynes was also JULES BLEDSOE's understudy in the hit Ziegfeld production of *Show Boat* during its original run from 1927 to 1929, briefly assuming the lead in 1928.

Haynes achieved considerable fame when the white film director King Vidor cast him in the lead role of the Metro-Goldwyn-Mayer film *Hallelujah* (1929), which told the story of the rise and fall of a farmer-turned-revivalist preacher. The second all-black-cast film produced by a major Hollywood studio and Vidor's first sound film, *Hallelujah* became the focus of lively and heated discussion in the black press about the impact of film images of black religious life on African Americans' political and social opportunities. Haynes participated in these discussions, writing in the *New York Amsterdam News* about his sense of the film's realistic portrayal of black southern life and expressing gratitude to Vidor for providing a significant opportunity for black performers. Some African American commentators agreed with Haynes, but many insisted that the film's representation of black religion emphasized childish emotionalism. *Hallelujah*'s interpretation of African American religious practices, they argued, confirmed some white Americans' belief in the inherent and permanent backwardness of black people. Even as critics and audience members debated the film's political significance, most agreed that the performances, especially those of Haynes and his costar NINA MAE MCKINNEY, were strong and memorable.

Despite the positive reviews, it remained difficult for Haynes to find consistent work in Hollywood, where there were few parts for African American actors, and he returned to the stage in a number of capacities. His recording on Victor Records with the Dixie Jubilee Singers of Irving Berlin's "At the End of the Road" from *Hallelujah* led him to a brief career as a singer, including serving briefly as a featured singer with the HALL JOHNSON Choir, which specialized in singing African American spirituals. He returned to Broadway in 1930 when the white playwright and director Marc Connelly cast him in the parts of Adam and Hezdrel in his Pulitzer Prize–winning play *The Green Pastures*, a dramatization of stories from the Hebrew Bible set in an all-black context. The play was wildly successful, running on Broadway for more than a year and providing Haynes and the other cast members with steady work during its national and international tours beginning in 1931, and its return Broadway run in 1935. Haynes found small parts in a number of Hollywood films following his work in *The Green Pastures*, including in *Escape from Devil's Island* (1935), King Vidor's *So Red the Rose* (1935), Fritz Lang's *Fury* (1936), and *The Invisible Ray* (1936). He also appeared as Ferrovius in the Federal Theatre Project's production of George Bernard Shaw's *Androcles and the Lion*, which ran from 1938 to 1939.

Haynes retired from performing around 1939 and turned to a full-time career in the ministry. Ordained as an AME minister in 1941, he served as pastor of a number of churches in Brooklyn, Long Island, and Kingston, New York. He retired as pastor of St. Mark's AME Church in Kingston in 1952 and died of a heart attack in July of 1954.

Haynes's contributions as an actor intersect with his lifelong religious commitments. A compelling performer with a commanding presence, Haynes became one of the most significant dramatic interpreters of African American religious life in American theater and film in the 1920s and 1930s.

FURTHER READING

Ottley, Roi and William Weatherby, eds. *The Negro in New York: An Informal Social History, 1626–1940* (1967).

Weisenfeld, Judith. *Hollywood Be Thy Name: African American Religion in American Film, 1929–1949* (2007).

Obituary: *New York Times*, 30 July 1954.

JUDITH WEISENFELD

Haynes, Elizabeth Ross (30 July 1883–26 Oct. 1953), social scientist, politician, and community leader, was born in Mount Willing, Lowndes County, Alabama, the daughter of Henry Ross and Mary Carnes. Elizabeth's parents were hard workers who amassed some wealth through the purchase of land that eventually grew to become a 1,500-acre plantation, though little else is known about them beyond their commitment to their only child's well-being and success. Ross attended the State Normal School in Montgomery and later won a scholarship to Fisk University, where she was awarded an AB degree in 1903. She taught school in Alabama and Texas for several years after graduation, and during 1905 and 1907 she attended summer school at the University of Chicago.

In 1908 Ross was invited to work with "colored students" for the student department of the national board of the Young Women's Christian Association (YWCA). In this position, she traveled extensively throughout the country to college campuses and cities where branches of the Y were established for African Americans to evaluate their programs and commitment of resources. She paid special attention to the conditions under which the female students lived and noted that many had to work to pay for school. She was also alert to the leadership potential of these young women. On one occasion, when Ross met an exceptional young woman, she indicated that the student was "worthy of being kept in mind as a possible Association worker somewhere." Ross continued to work in this capacity for the YWCA until December 1910, when she married Dr. GEORGE EDMUND HAYNES at the Fisk University Chapel.

The first African American to graduate from the New York School of Philanthropy (later the Columbia University School of Social Work), Dr. Haynes was cofounder and first executive director of the National League on Urban Conditions among Negroes (renamed the National Urban League in 1920). After their marriage, Elizabeth Haynes resigned from her position as "special worker" with the YWCA but continued to work in a volunteer capacity. In 1910 Dr. Haynes accepted a position at Fisk University to establish a department of social work, and Haynes began to volunteer her time to various social service organizations throughout Nashville. They had one child.

In 1918 Dr. Haynes accepted a position as director of Negro Economics, a division of the Department of Labor in Washington, D.C.; Elizabeth Haynes became his assistant director. She was also a "dollar-a-year" worker for the Labor Department's Women in Industry Service (later the Women's Bureau). In addition, from January 1920 to May 1922 she served as domestic service employment secretary of the United States Employment Service. During this time she became one of the leading authorities on issues of African American women and labor. Haynes believed that African Americans' economic independence would "some day enable them [Negro women and girls] to take their places in the ranks with other working women." In her publication "Two Million Negro Women at Work" (1922), written while Haynes was with the Women's Bureau, she identified domestic and personal service, agriculture and manufacturing, and mechanical industries as the three main areas in which the majority of women were engaged. Haynes also recognized a need for the "standardization of domestic service" and for "domestic-training schools in connection with public employment agencies." In 1923, while pursuing a master's degree in sociology at Columbia University, Haynes wrote an outstanding analysis of domestic working women for her thesis titled "Negroes in Domestic Service in the United States," in which she also surveyed the living conditions, health, social life, and organizational affiliations of these domestic workers.

In 1924 Haynes was elected the first African American member of the YWCA National Board, a position she held until 1934. A highly segregated organization fraught with racial tension, the YWCA resisted full integration of African Americans and allowed white women to set policies and determine the involvement of African American women and girls. Nevertheless, Haynes was committed to interracial harmony and social justice and decided to work for planned change from within the organization.

After the war, the Hayneses had moved to New York City in 1921. Haynes worked with her husband while he served as secretary of the Department of Race Relations of the Federal Council of the Churches of Christ in America from 1922 to 1946. During this time, she also became deeply involved in the politics of the Harlem community. In 1935 she served as the co-leader of the Twenty-first Assembly District and as an executive member of Tammany Hall. Haynes believed that the time was right for women to become "contenders for the choicest official plums." She stated that she had "no fears in urging the women of this country, irrespective of race, to awake, register, vote, work and enlarge the fight for equality of opportunity in jobs, [and] in office for women." Identifying with the New Deal wing of the Democratic Party, Haynes worked to ensure more Works Projects Administration involvement for African Americans, cheaper rents, better schools and housing, decent hospitals, and honest relief for the needy.

Haynes joined the Alpha Kappa Alpha Sorority in 1923. She worked diligently for this women's group and was described as a "guiding light and an inspiration" for building "more stately mansions for womanhood." Haynes was involved in numerous organizations and clubs that focused on equal access to opportunities for women. She was a member of the National Association of Colored Women and served as chair of the Industry and Housing Department. Her memberships also included the Harlem Branch of the YWCA, the Mary F. Waring Club, the National Advisory Committee on Women's Participation in the New York World's Fair, the Dorrence Brooks Ladies' Auxiliary, No. 528 of the Veterans of Foreign Wars (VFW), the New York Fisk University Club, and Abyssinian Baptist Church.

Governor Herbert H. Lehman appointed Haynes to serve on the New York State Temporary Commission on the Conditions of the Urban Colored Population in 1937; the commission was designed to study the economic and social conditions of urban African Americans in the state. She was also appointed by Mayor Fiorello LaGuardia to serve on the New York City Planning Commission.

Committed to an accurate historical record of her people, Haynes wrote several books, including *Unsung Heroes* (1921), which she said was written to tell of the "victories in spite of the hardships and struggles of Negroes whom the world failed to sing about." In 1952 she published *The Black Boy of Atlanta*, the story of Major RICHARD ROBERT WRIGHT, a community leader and banker. A "race woman" who dedicated her life to the uplift and complete involvement of African Americans in every sphere of American life, Haynes was a pioneer in many ways and never lost sight of her goals and her commitment to the African American community. Her belief that women were ignored, discouraged, and humiliated in society provided the impetus for much of her work and became a hallmark of her struggle. Haynes died in New York City.

FURTHER READING
Several manuscript collections contain information on Haynes, including the Schomburg Center for Research in Black Culture and the archives of the National Board of the YWCA, both in New York City. The James Weldon Johnson Memorial Collection at Yale University and the Moorland-Spingarn Research Center at Howard University contain biography files.
Giddings, Paula. *When and Where I Enter* (1984).
Obituary: *New York Times*, 27 Oct. 1953.
This entry is taken from the *American National Biography* and is published here with the permission of the American Council of Learned Societies.

IRIS CARLTON-LANEY

Haynes, George Edmund (11 May 1880–8 Jan. 1960), sociologist and social worker, was born in Pine Bluff, Arkansas, the son of Louis Haynes, an occasional laborer, and Mattie Sloan, a domestic servant. He was raised by devout, hardworking, but poorly educated parents. His mother stressed that education and good character were paths to improvement. She moved with Haynes and his sister to Hot Springs, a city with better educational opportunities than Pine Bluff. Haynes attended Fisk University, completing his B.A. in 1903. His record at Fisk enabled him to go to Yale University, where he earned an M.A. in Sociology in 1904. He also won a scholarship to Yale's Divinity School but withdrew early in 1905 to help fund his sister's schooling.

In 1905 Haynes became secretary of the Colored Men's Department of the International (segregated) YMCA, traveling to African American colleges throughout the nation from 1905 to 1908. During this period he encountered Elizabeth Ross (ELIZABETH ROSS HAYNES), a Fisk alumna and sociologist who later became the first secretary of Negro youth with the YWCA. Haynes married Ross in 1910; they had one son. Haynes studied for two summers at the University of Chicago, then left his YMCA work in 1908 to do graduate study in sociology at Columbia University and at its social work affiliate, the New York School of Philanthropy (later the Columbia University School of Social Work). In 1910 he became the first African American to graduate from this social work school, and two years later he became the first African American to earn a Ph.D. at Columbia. His doctorate was in economics and his dissertation, *The Negro at Work in New York City* (1912), became his first book. It called for greater attention to urban

George Edmund Haynes, social worker and sociologist, founder of the National Urban League. (University of Massachusetts, Amherst.)

blacks, whose population was continuing to grow. While in New York Haynes worked with groups seeking to aid African Americans in cities. One group was the National League for Protection of Colored Women (NLPCW), which was established in 1906 by merging branches of the Association for the Protection of Colored Women that had been formed in 1905 in cities such as New York and Philadelphia. The league sought to protect African American women who migrated northward to cities from being exploited by unscrupulous recruiters. Another group with which Haynes worked was the Committee for Improving the Industrial Conditions of Negroes in New York (CIICNNY), which was also formed in 1906. This group sought to expand employment opportunities for African Americans and hired Haynes to do research through interviewing prospective employees.

Frances Kellor and Ruth Standish Baldwin, leaders in the NLPCW and the CIICNNY, shared Haynes's concern that many more black social workers needed college training and internships in agencies. Haynes hoped to have blacks work as equals with whites rather than having groups dominated by whites working on problems affecting African Americans. Along with Kellor and Baldwin, Haynes proposed that the CIICNNY expand its work to train and intern black social workers. When the CIICNNY declined, Haynes and Baldwin in 1910 led the effort to form a third group, the Committee on Urban Conditions among Negroes (CUCAN).

Overlapping leadership, membership, and programs led to a federation of all three groups in 1911 as the National League on Urban Conditions among Negroes, a title shortened in 1920 to the National Urban League. Haynes became its first executive secretary (1911–1917). The Urban League regards Haynes as its founder and considers its starting date 19 May 1910, when the CUCAN was formed. Haynes was a moderate leader, more militant than BOOKER T. WASHINGTON but not as strident as W. E. B. DUBOIS.

As part of his overall career design, Haynes had moved to Fisk University in the fall of 1910 to teach economics and to set up a sociology department to train black social workers for internships in cities. He had hired EUGENE KINCKLE JONES in April 1911 as assistant secretary of CUCAN to direct day-to-day operations in New York. Haynes commuted to New York every six weeks and spent his summers there, but eventually Jones won over the board and staff, becoming coexecutive with Haynes in 1916 and becoming the executive secretary in 1917, with

Haynes given a subordinate role. Urban League leaders increasingly deemed a full-time executive imperative, a need Haynes never met.

In a face-saving move, Haynes took a federal post in 1918, leaving first the Urban League, and later, Fisk. His post, which he held until 1921, was the director of Negro Economics, a special assistant to the secretary of labor. His main task was to allay friction arising from blacks migrating to factory jobs in the North. His research in this position resulted in another book, *The Negro at Work during the World War* (1921).

From 1921 until he retired in 1946, Haynes worked for the Federal (later National) Council of Churches, heading the council's Race Relations Department. In 1923 he founded Race Relations Sunday, and in 1940 he initiated Interracial Brotherhood Month. His department fostered interracial conferences, clinics, and committees, and he published two more books, *The Trend of the Races* (1922) and *The Clinical Approach to Race Relations* (1946). In 1930 and again in 1947 Haynes conducted surveys in Africa on behalf of the YMCA, writing his final book, *Africa: Continent of the Future* (1950).

Haynes also wrote numerous articles and engaged in many civic activities. He organized and administered the Harmon Foundation Awards for black accomplishment from 1926 to 1931. He lobbied for antilynching laws and worked hard to save the SCOTTSBORO BOYS (nine black youths unjustly charged—and some sentenced to lengthy jail terms—in Alabama for an alleged rape), forming the American Scottsboro Committee (1934). He helped form and chaired the Joint Committee on National Recovery (1933–1935) to secure a fair share of New Deal programs for African Americans. Together with A. PHILIP RANDOLPH, he fought from 1937 to 1940 to prevent communists from taking control of the National Negro Congress. Haynes served on a commission addressing the need for a state university in New York and on the board of the state university system (1948–1954) when it was set up.

During the 1950s Haynes was at the City College of New York, teaching courses on black history, interracial matters, and Africa in world affairs. After his first wife died in 1953, Haynes married Olyve Love Jeter in 1955; they had no children. He died in New York City.

FURTHER READING

Haynes's personal papers are in the George Edmund Haynes Collection at Yale University. Additional papers are in the Erastus Milo Cravath Library

at Fisk University in Nashville, Tennessee. The National Urban League's Archives (covering 1910 to 1965) are in the Manuscripts Division of the Library of Congress. Haynes's work with the Race Relations Department of the National Council of Churches is documented in the council's archives in New York City.

Brooks, Lester, and Guichard Parris. *Blacks in the City: A History of the National Urban League* (1971).

Weiss, Nancy J. *The National Urban League, 1910–1940* (1974).

Obituary: *New York Times,* 10 Jan. 1960.

This entry is taken from the *American National Biography* and is published here with the permission of the American Council of Learned Societies.

EDGAR ALLAN TOPPIN

Haynes, Lemuel (18 July 1753–28 Sept. 1833), Congregational minister, was born in West Hartford, Connecticut, the son of a black father and a white mother, both unknown, and both of whom abandoned him at birth. He was indentured at five months of age to a white family named Rose through whom he absorbed strong Calvinist theology and evangelical piety. He was educated in the local schools, but, a serious and diligent child, he also taught himself by the light of the fireside at night; he later said, "I made it my rule to know more every night than I knew in the morning." In 1783 he married Elizabeth Babbit, a white schoolteacher who had proposed to him; they became the parents of ten children.

Haynes fulfilled his indenture and came of age just as the American Revolution was beginning. He signed up as a minuteman in 1774 and joined militia troops at Roxbury, Massachusetts, following the Lexington alarm. He joined the Continental army in 1776, marched to Ticonderoga, New York, and was mustered out because he contracted typhus. Haynes remained a lifelong patriot, an admirer of George Washington, an ardent Federalist, and an outspoken critic of Jeffersonianism. He may even have been a member of the secretive Washington Benevolent Society. Haynes, who had poetic aspirations, is thought to be the author of a broadside poem (1774?) lamenting the death of Asa Burt, who was killed when a tree fell on him. He was the author of a patriotic ballad, "The Battle of Lexington" (1775?), which remained unpublished until 1985, after it was discovered by Ruth Bogin in the Houghton Library at Harvard. Although it demonstrates more sincerity than talent, the poem is not entirely without merit: "Freedom & Life, O precious Sounds / yet Freedome does excell / and we will bleed upon the ground / or keep our Freedom still."

Deciding on the ministry as a career, Haynes turned down an opportunity to attend Dartmouth College and instead studied privately with local ministers. He was licensed to preach in 1780, served the Granville, Connecticut, church for five years, and was ordained to the Congregational ministry on 9 November 1785 by the Association of Ministers in Litchfield County. Haynes was apparently the first African American ordained by a mainstream denomination in the United States. He moved to Torrington, Connecticut, where the congregation included the parents of John Brown. In the tradition of Jonathan Edwards and George Whitefield, Haynes was a New Light Congregationalist who favored revivalism but recognized and was critical of its excesses.

In 1788 Haynes became minister of the west parish in Rutland, Vermont, a conservative congregation he served for thirty years. An effective preacher, he was often invited to speak at ordinations, funerals, and public events. He later recalled that he preached 5,500 sermons in Rutland, 400 of them at funerals. He and the congregation

Lemuel B. Haynes, Revolutionary War veteran, poet, and Calvinist preacher. (Schomburg Center for Research in Black Culture, New York Public Library.)

remained a center of Calvinism in the midst of the Vermont frontier's rationalism of Thomas Paine and Ethan Allen.

In 1805 Haynes preached a sermon that made an impact far beyond his local circle. In the brief but witty response to the visiting Universalist Hosea Ballou, Haynes satirically linked Ballou to the Garden of Eden's serpent, which, as the title of his homily claimed, also promised "Universal Salvation." The sermon was printed, and then reprinted, as late as 1865, until more than seventy editions had been issued throughout the Northeast.

Haynes's humor extended beyond religious satire. When the house of the Reverend Ashbel Parmelee burned down, Haynes asked Parmelee if he had lost his sermon manuscripts in the fire. When Parmelee told him that he had, Haynes asked, "Well, don't you think that they gave more light than they ever had before?" Haynes once inadvertently walked into a hotel dining room where a private party was celebrating Andrew Jackson's election to the presidency. Handed a glass of wine and invited to offer a toast, Haynes lifted his glass to the new president and said "Andrew Jackson: Psalm 109, verse 8," then put down the glass and went on his way. When someone later looked up the Bible verse he discovered that it read, "Let his days be few and let another take his office."

Eased out of the Rutland church when he was sixty-five, Haynes moved to Manchester, Vermont, where he became involved in a sensational murder case. Two brothers, Stephen and Jesse Boorn, were in prison, having been convicted of the murder of their mentally unstable brother-in-law, Russell Colvin. Colvin's body had not been found, but he had disappeared, and several clues (a found button, a bone unearthed by a dog) pointed to the brothers' guilt. Haynes befriended the Boorns and became convinced of their innocence. Colvin surfaced in New Jersey just before the brothers were to be executed and was brought back to Manchester in a moment of great local drama. Haynes wrote an account of the case, *Mystery Developed* (1820), which had all the shape of a short story, and he preached a sermon, *The Prisoner Released* (1820), which warned against convicting a person on the basis of circumstantial evidence. The British novelist Willkie Collins later read about the case and used the dead/alive theme in his story *John Jago's Ghost*. Haynes moved once again in 1822, serving the Granville, New York, church, just across the border from Vermont, until his death there.

Haynes has been remembered chiefly as a Revolutionary War veteran and has even been omitted from some accounts of African American history, perhaps because he never lived among black people. Because his religious interests have long since been out of fashion, Haynes the theologian and preacher has been ignored, despite the remarkable publishing history of *Universal Salvation*. Haynes has often been criticized for his failure to speak out against slavery, but recent discoveries of Haynes material may alter that situation. In addition to Haynes's poem on Lexington, Bogin also found an unpublished manuscript, dating from about 1776, titled "Liberty Further Extended." Composed by the young Haynes, probably while he was in the Continental army, it argues, on the basis of natural rights, for an expansion of the Revolution to encompass the liberation of the nation's African slaves. "Men were made for more noble Ends than to be Drove to market, like Sheep and oxen," Haynes wrote. "Even an affrican, has Equally as good a right to his Liberty in common with Englishmen." The incomplete manuscript was not published until 1983. A more recent discovery, by David Proper, reveals that Haynes preached the funeral sermon in 1821 for LUCY TERRY, the earliest known African American poet. A contemporary newspaper account states that Haynes read a poem that seems to be his own composition and that includes the lines "How long must Ethaopia's murder'd race / Be doom'd by men to bondage and disgrace?"

Haynes clearly was more race-conscious than has been realized; he even identified himself, the author of "The Battle of Lexington," as "a young Mollato." In a Fourth of July speech in 1801 marking the twenty-fifth anniversary of American independence, Haynes contrasted European monarchy with American Republicanism and spoke of the plight of "the poor Africans among us." "What has reduced them to their present pitiful, abject state?" he asked. "Is it any distinction that the God of nature hath made in their formation? Nay, but being subjected to slavery, by the cruel hands of oppressors, they have been taught to view themselves as a rank of being far below others."

FURTHER READING

There is no collection of Haynes's papers, but copies of his printed sermons and addresses are in the Congregational Library, Boston, Massachusetts; the American Antiquarian Society, Worcester, Massachusetts; Union Theological Seminary, New York City; and other depositories.

Newman, Richard. *Black Preacher to White America: The Collected Writings of Lemuel Haynes, 1774–1833* (1990).

Newman, Richard. *Lemuel Haynes: A Bio-bibliography* (1984).

Saillant, John D. "Lemuel Haynes and the Revolutionary Origins of Black Theology, 1776–1801," *Religion and American Culture* 2 (Winter, 1993): 79–102.

This entry is taken from the *American National Biography* and is published here with the permission of the American Council of Learned Societies.

RICHARD NEWMAN

Haynes, Marques Oreole (3 Oct. 1926–), basketball player, was born in Sand Springs, Oklahoma, the son of Matthew, a laborer, and Hattie Haynes. When Marques was four his father left the family so that he was raised by his mother and two older brothers and a sister. Since Oklahoma was a segregated state, Haynes attended segregated schools. His introduction to basketball began when he accompanied his sister, Cecil, to her basketball practices. As an elementary school student Haynes walked over to Booker T. Washington High School and watched his older brother, Wendell, compete. By his junior year in high school Haynes made the varsity team which won the National Negro High School tournament played in Tuskegee, Alabama, in 1941. He played well enough to win a spot on the all-tournament's second team. At Booker T. Washington High School Haynes played football and basketball. In his senior year Haynes starred on a team that won the state basketball championship.

After graduating from high school in 1942, Haynes attended Langston University, a small historically black institution in Langston, Oklahoma. With thirty dollars from the Baptist Church and a partial athletic scholarship, Haynes began an athletic adventure that would take him around the world many times. At five feet eleven inches and 150 pounds, Haynes was gifted with extraordinary quickness and coordination. At Langston, Haynes quarterbacked the football team and directed the basketball team from his guard position. By the time Haynes reached Langston, he had developed the dribbling skills that would make him famous. He could dribble between his legs, behind his back, and nobody could steal the ball from him. In competition coaches frowned on fancy dribbling and Zip Gayles, Langston's coach, was no different. Haynes avoided the urge to demonstrate his dribbling skills until his junior year. In a game against Southern University in Baton Rouge, Louisiana, he decided to put on a show. Haynes thought Southern had needlessly embarrassed some of its opponents in the early games of the Southwest Conference tournament. When Langston and Southern met in the tournament finals, Haynes decided that if the opportunity presented itself, he would have some fun at Southern's expense. In the final minutes of the game, with Langston leading by a comfortable margin, Haynes dribbled for two minutes as the Southern players tried in vain to steal the ball from him. Everybody loved the show except his coach.

During Haynes's four years of collegiate competition, Langston compiled an impressive 112–3 record, which included a 74–70 victory over the Harlem Globetrotters. Haynes scored twenty-six points in that contest, and on the strength of that performance, the Globetrotters signed him to a contract worth $250 a month to play with the Kansas City Stars, a Globetrotters farm team.

The Globetrotters were the brainchild of Abe Saperstein, a Jewish immigrant who moved to Chicago with his family in 1907. Part hustler, part entrepreneur, Saperstein fell in love with sports, especially basketball. At five feet three inches, he had limited athletic ability but was a born promoter. In 1929 the Harlem Globetrotters were born, and by 1946 the all-black squad was about to become the most recognizable basketball team in the United States. After putting on a dribbling display against the Mexican All-Stars in Chihuahua, Mexico, in which Haynes kept the ball away from his opponents for over seven minutes, Saperstein recognized that he had a special talent. In January 1947 Saperstein promoted Haynes to the Globetrotters, with whom he would establish himself as the "world's greatest dribbler." Haynes and GOOSE TATUM, "the clown prince of basketball," quickly became the Trotters' two biggest attractions.

The Globetrotters were entertainers. When basketball fans heard "Sweet Georgia Brown," a whistled version of which was the team's theme song, it immediately triggered a picture of the Globetrotters' famous ball-handling routine. Nonetheless, the Trotters could also play serious basketball. On 19 February 1948 the Globetrotters played the Minneapolis Lakers. The game, supposedly between America's best white team and best black team, has assumed legendary proportions. The Lakers were in the first year of the franchise's history and played in the National Basketball League. The team already boasted two future Hall of Famers, George Mikan and Jim Pollard. Before 17,823 spectators at the Chicago Stadium Ermer Robinson hit a long one-handed shot as the buzzer sounded to give the Trotters a 61–59 victory. Marques Haynes scored fifteen points and played a flawless floor game. During the game Haynes and Mikan twice got tangled up in jumping for a rebound and twice Marques crashed to the floor in great pain. He fractured one of his vertebrae, which ended his season. The African American community on Chicago's South Side celebrated the victory into the early hours of the morning. The Trotters triumph was a source of great pride. The excitement generated by the first Globetrotters–Lakers meeting was a promoter's dream. On 28 February 1949, 20,046 people jammed the Chicago Stadium and watched the Trotters top the Lakers a second time, 49–45. The Lakers, however, won the next six meetings of the series.

On 31 October 1953 Marques Haynes, in a contract dispute, left the Globetrotters. His decision also reflected a growing dissatisfaction with Saperstein's patronizing attitude toward his players. Instead of taking advantage of opportunities to play in the National Basketball Association, Haynes started his own traveling team, the Fabulous Magicians, in 1953. Playing all around the world, the Magicians could play as many as 250 games a year. By 1968 Haynes earned $75,000 a year from basketball alone.

In 1972, Haynes returned to the Globetrotters as a player coach. In 1979, he joined ex-Globetrotter MEADOWLARK LEMON's Bucketeers. In 1981, he rejoined the Globetrotters for two years, and then revived the Magicians, ending his barnstorming career with them in 1988. On 2 October of that year Haynes became the first Globetrotter enshrined in the Basketball Hall of Fame. Marques Haynes was one of America's greatest basketball ambassadors. He was blessed with great athletic ability and used it to entertain millions around the world.

FURTHER READING

Bortstein, Larry. "Marques the Legendary Merlin on Any Court," *The Sporting News*, 9 Jan. 1971.

Christgau, John. *Tricksters in the Madhouse: Lakers v. Globetrotters, 1948* (2004).

Green, Ben. *Spinning the Globe: The Rise, Fall, and Return to Greatness of the Harlem Globetrotters* (2005).

Litsky, Frank. "King of the Court Clowns," *Boy's Life* (Feb. 1968).

DOLPH GRUNDMAN

Haynes, Martha Euphemia Lofton (11 Sept. 1890– 25 July 1980) was a public school teacher, college professor, community civic leader, philanthropist, and the first known African American woman in the United States to earn a Ph.D. in Mathematics. She was the elder of two children born in Washington, D.C., to William S. Lofton, a prominent middle-class dentist and civil rights activist, and Lavinia Dey Lofton, a kindergarten public school teacher. Haynes's parents divorced when she was seven, and she and her younger brother Joseph were raised by their mother, whose devout Catholicism would shape Haynes's nearly fifty-year career as an educator and activist.

Haynes's educational promise was revealed early. She graduated as class valedictorian from the M Street High School in 1907 and the Miner Normal School in 1909. She earned a bachelor of arts in Psychology (with course work in mathematics) from Smith College in Northampton, Massachusetts, in 1914. She married Harold Appo Haynes in 1917 before continuing her educational studies. The two had known each other as teenagers, growing up in the same Washington, D.C., neighborhood. Her husband had earned an undergraduate degree in electrical engineering from the University of Pennsylvania in 1910. Later, both attended the University of Chicago, where they each earned master's degrees in Education in 1930. It would be another thirteen years before Haynes (three years before her husband) earned a Ph.D. in Mathematics in 1943 from Catholic University in Washington, D.C., with a dissertation titled "Determination of Sets of Independent Conditions Characterizing Certain Special Cases of Symmetric Correspondences."

Haynes did not practice professionally as a mathematician but pursued a path in education. She taught for forty-seven years in D.C. public schools and also at the college level. She taught first grade at Garrison and Garfield schools; mathematics at Armstrong and Dunbar high schools; and English at Miner Normal School (originally established in 1851 by Myrtilla Miner to provide educational opportunities for African American girls and later renamed Miner Teachers College). After becoming a professor of mathematics at Miner Teachers College in 1930, she established that institution's first formal mathematics department. In 1955, a year following the U.S. Supreme Court's landmark *Brown v. Board of Education* decision ruling that separate public school systems were not equal, the all-black Miner Teachers College merged with the all-white Wilson Teachers College to become the District of Columbia Teachers College (now known as the University of the District of Columbia).

Haynes taught and remained head of the department for almost thirty years, until her retirement in 1959. That same year the Catholic diocese awarded her one of the church's highest honors, the papal medal *Pro Ecclesia et Pontifice* for her service to the church and community.

Following her retirement, Haynes devoted herself more fully to activist causes to end poverty and the segregationist policies that increased educational disparities based on race and socioeconomic status. One of Haynes's most politically charged efforts was as a member of the District of Columbia Board of Education, a tenure which ran from 1960 through 1968. Even though she had been educated in the district's public school system, excelled academically, and was able to compete in college, she argued that the area's "track system" discriminated against black and poor students and unfairly locked them into vocational programs instead of college-oriented academic programs. She supported a lawsuit filed and successfully argued by the civil rights leader Julius W. Hobson in which he charged the school system with racial and economic discrimination. In June 1967 Judge J. Skelly Wright abolished the track system for its de facto segregation.

Outside of the field of education, Haynes worked through the Catholic diocese and affiliated organizations throughout much of the 1960s to continue her activist role. She helped found the Catholic Interracial Council of the District of Columbia and supported Fides House, a charity organized by faculty and students at her alma mater, the Catholic University, to provide social services, assistance and educational help to residents in a poor neighborhood in D.C. From 1964 to 1966 she served as the first vice president of the Washington Archdiocesan Council of Catholic Women. She also sat on the board of Catholic Charities and was a member of the D.C. branch of the National Conference of Christians and Jews, the Urban League, the National Association for the Advancement of Colored People (NAACP), the League of Women Voters, and the American Association of University Women.

On 25 July 1980, at the age of ninety, Haynes passed away at the Washington Hospital Center after suffering a stroke. In honor of her commitment to the Catholic faith and to her belief in education, she bequeathed $700,000 to the Catholic University of America, which was used to establish the Euphemia Lofton Haynes Chair in the department of Education.

FURTHER READING

The Haynes-Lofton Family Papers, Collection Number ACUA 131, are held by the Catholic University of America, American Catholic History Research Center and University Archives, Washington, D.C.

Jay, James J. *Negroes in Science: Natural Science Doctorates, 1876–1969* (1971).

National Science Foundation, Division of Science Resources Statistics. *Women, Minorities and Persons with Disabilities in S&E: 2004*, NSF 04–317 (2004).

Scriven, Olivia A. "The Politics of Particularism: HBCUs, Spelman College, and the Struggle to Educate Black Women in Science, 1950–1990," Ph.D. diss., Georgia Institute of Technology (2006).

Obituary: *Washington Post*, 1 Aug. 1980.

OLIVIA A. SCRIVEN

Haynes, Roy (13 Mar. 1925–), jazz drummer, was born Roy Owen Haynes in Boston's Roxbury neighborhood to Gustavus and Edna Haynes. Before starting a family, Gustavus and Edna had emigrated from Barbados to Boston, where Gustavus worked for Standard Oil Company, and Edna was a strict churchgoer. Haynes was the third of four sons; his younger brother, Michael, became a prominent Baptist minister who served in the Massachusetts state legislature from 1964 to 1970.

The family's churchgoing activities brought Haynes into contact with music at a young age. Despite some early violin lessons, he gravitated toward the drums at age seven. Around this time, his older brother Douglas—a serious jazz fan who was friendly with many musicians—introduced Haynes to Jo JONES, the legendary drummer best known for his work with COUNT BASIE. Jones's propulsive use of the high hat cymbal and stripped-down authority had a major influence on Haynes, laying the groundwork for the younger drummer's style. Haynes began performing around the Boston area in 1944, playing with the bands of FRANKIE NEWTON and Sabby Lewis. In 1945 he was offered a job with LUIS CARL RUSSELL's big band in New York City. Russell, a New Orleans veteran who had worked with LOUIS ARMSTRONG and KING OLIVER decades earlier, taught his young drummer the discipline necessary to drive an ensemble and the willingness to adapt to the moment.

A mere two years later, Haynes was holding down the drum chair in the band of LESTER YOUNG, widely considered to be the most innovative and poetic saxophonist of the swing era. Young's loose, impressionistic style called on Haynes to both tend to the pulse and respond to the leader's aphoristic musings, setting the mold for the playing that would make Haynes into one of jazz's most respected and in-demand percussionists. By 1949 he was firmly allied with the advance guard of the bebop movement, largely because of his active approach to the chores of timekeeping. After brief stints with MILES DAVIS and BUD POWELL, Haynes found himself backing up CHARLIE PARKER, bebop's principal architect. His three years with Parker cemented Haynes's preeminent status, evidenced by the fact that he was able to turn down DUKE ELLINGTON and have it become a private joke between the two. However, Haynes did find time to lead a group of his own, which featured SONNY ROLLINS and Kenny Dorham.

After his time with Parker, Haynes joined the backing band of SARAH VAUGHAN. Despite his reputation as one of the music's most progressive, inventive drummers, Haynes relished the challenge to provide restrained, tasteful accompaniment to Vaughan's nuanced vocals. In addition, it provided him steady employment at a time when rock and roll's ascendancy had dramatically transformed the life of the working jazz musician. As Haynes toured the world with Vaughan, he was also able to set up a comfortable life for his wife, Jesse Lee Nevels Haynes, and their three children, one of whom is the well-known cornetist Graham Haynes. And while much of his time and energy were devoted to Vaughan's band, Haynes was able to periodically sneak away for sessions or shows with the likes of the Young disciple Stan Getz, who sought out Haynes's services on a semi-regular basis throughout the fifties and sixties.

Haynes left Vaughan in 1958, beginning a decade of inspired freelance work that many consider his greatest recorded legacy. Appearances on seminal sessions by THELONIOUS MONK, ERIC DOLPHY, OLIVER NELSON, as well as a standing invitation to sub for Elvin Jones in the epochal JOHN COLTRANE quartet, proved Haynes to be the rare artist who grows more revolutionary with age, as his fluid sense of rhythm proved extremely compatible with the post-bop stylings of Coltrane, Eric Dolphy, ANDREW HILL, and RAHSAAN ROLAND KIRK.

Perhaps best described up to this point in his career as a musician's musician (and a drummer, to boot), Haynes also began to forge a reputation as a bandleader in his own right. Much like ART BLAKEY before him, Haynes worked with up-and-coming players as a way of both passing on his wisdom and keeping himself current. In 1960 he began working with a group that included the pianist Kenny Barron; his Hip Ensemble, which lasted from 1969 to 1973, dabbled in jazz-rock and helped establish the tenor George Adams and the trumpeter Hannibal Peterson. Throughout the rest of the seventies and eighties, Haynes also worked steadily with old friends like the pianists Tommy Flanagan and Chick Corea and with admirers like guitarist Pat Metheny

In the 1980s Haynes led a quartet or quintet whose sensibility ran the gamut of his career, from sumptuous ballads and bluesy swing to boppish complexity and avant-expressionism. Haynes became a headliner at festivals at home and abroad, proving himself to be a piece of jazz history who played with the fire and ferocity of a young man trying to prove himself. And after a half century of flying under the radar, Haynes found himself consistently winning critics' and fans' polls, and receiving the National Endowment of Arts's Jazz Master fellowship in 1995.

FURTHER READING

Ratliff, Ben. "Roy Haynes: Attention Getter, on the Beat and Off," *New York Times*, 10 Mar. 2006.

Stephenson, Sam, "Jazzed about Roy Haynes," *Smithsonian Magazine* (Dec. 2003).

DISCOGRAPHY:

Dolphy, Eric. *Far Cry* (New Jazz, 1960).

Haynes, Roy. *Fountain of Youth* (Dreyfus, 2004).

Haynes, Roy. *Out of the Afternoon* (Impulse! 1962).

Powell, Bud. *Amazing Bud Powell, Vol. 1* (Blue Note, 1949).

Vaughan, Sarah. *Sarah Vaughan with Clifford Brown* (Emarcy, 1954).

NATHANIEL FRIEDMAN

Haynes, Thomas (c. 1868–c. 1930s), cofounder of Boley, Oklahoma, the largest all-black town in the United States, was the eldest child of Matthew and Dottie Haynes and was born in Red River County, Texas. Very little is known about Haynes's childhood and young adulthood. He was the eldest of more than twelve brothers and sisters, grew up on a farm, and had very little education during his formative years. By 1900 his parents had moved to Paris, Texas, a small city, which increased the educational opportunities available to Haynes's younger siblings, but whether the move took place early enough to allow Haynes to attend city schools is unknown. In the late 1880s or early 1890s, Haynes married and started a family. In 1899, shortly after his wife, whose name is unknown, passed away, he moved to Oklahoma City, Oklahoma Territory, to

begin anew. He was soon joined by his daughters, Winnie and George Ella, and his son Matthew.

Haynes worked briefly as a laborer in Oklahoma City, but soon headed east to Creek Nation, Indian Territory (now eastern Oklahoma), where he rented a homestead and built a sod dugout for himself and his children near tracks being laid for the Fort Smith and Western Railroad. To make ends meet, he sold cordwood and boarded African American railroad employees. Believing the area would be an excellent place for a black settlement, Haynes attempted to establish a town named Oxford. This venture failed because at the time federal law prohibited Native Americans and their former slaves from selling land they owned. When this law changed in 1903, Haynes joined with two white men, Lake Moore and John Boley, and James Barnett, a freedman descended from slaves of Creek Indians, to establish Boley, Oklahoma. The town was founded near the tracks of the Fort Smith and Western Railroad on land owned by James Barnett's daughter, Abigail. A coin flip determined that the town would be named in honor of Boley instead of Haynes.

Boley was officially opened for settlement on 26 September 1903, and Haynes served as town site manager and chief promoter. Through his energetic efforts, the town grew quickly. By 1907 Boley's all-black population was about 824, and three years later it had grown to 1,334. These numbers did not include the people who built their homes outside the official city limits or the 3,000 to 5,000 black farmers who bought or rented farms in the countryside surrounding Boley. During Boley's early years, Haynes subleased lots to settlers while he worked on gaining permission from the federal government to purchase the land. He was finally able to get the town incorporated on 18 May 1905. He was primarily occupied with selling real estate to newcomers, but he was also involved in the development of many other businesses and organizations in Boley. Notable among his achievements were helping to establish the Boley Commercial Club and the Boley Businessmen's League, which was affiliated with the National Negro Business League. He was a cofounder and major stockholder in the Farmers and Merchants Bank of Boley and served as vice president of the bank for several years. Haynes helped found the Boley Telephone Company and briefly owned the town's major newspaper, the *Boley Progress*. He was also on the board of directors of the Abraham Lincoln Life Insurance Company based in Muskogee, Oklahoma, and he helped incorporate the Boley Agricultural and

Business College in 1912. Although he was heavily involved in town life, Haynes also maintained a farm where he grew cotton. In addition to establishing Boley, Haynes founded the black town of Vernon, Oklahoma, in 1910 (named after William T. Vernon), and was involved in the creation of Bookertee, Oklahoma, in 1917 (named after BOOKER T. WASHINGTON). Haynes helped organize the first city council and represented his ward for several years. He was a member of the Republican Party and, before blacks were disfranchised in Oklahoma in 1910, he was active in county politics. In 1907 and 1908 he served as an elected delegate to county Republican nominating conventions. In 1916 he was part of a lawsuit that demanded that blacks be given the opportunity to register to vote.

While living in Boley, Haynes married Julia Allen, and the couple raised a son named Robert in addition to his three children, Winnie, George Ella, and Matthew. Haynes was joined in the town by at least two of his siblings, Dennis and Levi. In the 1920s, however, Haynes and much of his family moved to Los Angeles, California, where he continued to make his living selling real estate. The date of his death is unknown.

FURTHER READING

Crockett, Norman. *The Black Towns* (1979).

Hamilton, Kevin. *Black Towns and Profit: Promotion and Development in the Trans-Appalachian West, 1877–1915* (1991).

MELISSA NICOLE STUCKEY

Hayre, Ruth Wright (26 Oct. 1910–30 Jan. 1998), educator, activist, administrator, and philanthropist, was born Ruth Wright in Atlanta, Georgia, the daughter of Richard Robert Wright Jr., the editor of the *Christian Recorder* and president of Wilberforce College, and Charlotte Crogman Wright. Hayre's grandparents strongly influenced her life's interest in education. Her paternal grandfather, RICHARD ROBERT WRIGHT SR., who was born a slave, founded and served as president of Georgia State College (formerly Georgia State Agricultural and Industrial College) as well as Citizens and Southern Bank, a black-owned bank in Philadelphia. Hayre's maternal grandfather, William H. Crogman, was the principal of Edmund Asa Ware High in Augusta, Georgia, the first high school for blacks in the state. Hayre's grandmothers each received education degrees from normal schools.

When she was fifteen, Hayre graduated two years early with honors at the top of her class from West Philadelphia High School for Girls and received a mayor's scholarship to the University of Pennsylvania, where she earned both her undergraduate (BA, 1930) and graduate degrees (AM, 1931; PhD, 1949; LLD, honorary, 1989) in education. Her tenure at West Philadelphia High School for Girls, though brief, inspired her to make a difference. Black students made up 5 percent of the school's population, but there was not a black teacher in the school.

Hayre began a distinguished career in the field of education after completing her studies. Her teaching career began in 1930 at Arkansas State College for Negroes (also known as Arkansas Agricultural and Mechanical College), where she met a fellow faculty member, Talmadge Hayre, whom she married in 1937. While at Arkansas State, she served briefly as principal before leaving for a teaching position in Dayton, Ohio, where she earned three times the salary she had earned in the Jim Crow South. After a brief sojourn in Washington, D.C., Hayre returned to Philadelphia in 1939 when her husband received an appointment as an assistant professor of science at Cheyney State College (originally the Institute for Colored Youth).

Hayre taught English at Sulzberger Junior High School as the second black teacher in an integrated Philadelphia school. In 1946 she became Philadelphia's first African American senior high school teacher. At William Penn High School (for girls), she was promoted from teacher to vice principal (1953) and then to principal (1955). Each promotion was a first for African Americans in Philadelphia. As the newly appointed principal, Hayre realized that she needed to change the curriculum and student and teacher attitudes. She, along with the chair of the English department, Ben Schleifer, developed a program called WINGS (Work Inspired Now Gains Strength), encouraging students to discover their talents. The WINGS program received many accolades and recognition from groups, foundations, and the school district.

After eight years at William Penn, in 1963, the Philadelphia Board of Education appointed Hayre to be the first black superintendent in the public school system. Her district was the largest and most complex of what was then an eight-district system. In her twelve years as District Four superintendent, she oversaw facility upgrades and calls for change and more inclusion of black history within the curriculum. Hayre retired from her position in 1976 but kept her hand in education by accepting a brief adjunct professorship at the University of Pennsylvania Graduate School of Education.

Hayre's retirement was short-lived. On 2 December 1985 she received an appointment to the Philadelphia Board of Education. The board unanimously elected Hayre president five years later. She was the first woman to hold this position. In 1991 the board reelected her. As soon as she became president, Hayre faced the challenge of responding to the growing AIDS epidemic. Activists demanded that not only the use of condoms be included in the high school sex education curriculum but also that Philadelphia high schools distribute condoms to students. When she found a divided board of education, Hayre decided it was the school district's responsibility to educate about sexual health and distribute condoms to students.

In addition to her career as an educator and administrator, Hayre became a philanthropist. In 1988 she created the Tell Them We Are Rising Fund at Temple University—named after a statement by her grandfather, Richard Robert Wright, about the Emancipation Proclamation. She promised 116 sixth-grade graduates from two North Philadelphia schools (Kenderton Elementary and Robert Wright School—named after her grandfather) free college tuition if they graduated from high school and attended an accredited two- or four-year institution or post–high school program. The program included weekly activities and tutoring sessions, educational trips for participants and their families, as well as detailed mentoring programs. Of the 116 elementary school graduates, sixty graduated from high school, thirty-nine entered two- and four-year colleges, and twelve went to technical school. Six successfully graduated with a bachelor's degree.

The Tell Them We Are Rising program was successful. A Temple University study found that participants, compared to their peers (a cohort of students from the same school one year prior), were more successful academically. Only 33 percent of participants dropped out of high school compared to the previous year's figures of 48.7 percent. Finally, 5.2 percent of participants were on the honor roll compared to 3.5 percent of students the prior year.

Like her parents and grandparents, Hayre dedicated her career to a belief that education was essential. She referred to her giving back as a "worthwhile coda to a lifelong educational adventure" (Hayre, xii).

FURTHER READING

Hayre, Ruth Wright, and Alexis Moore. *Tell Them We Are Rising: A Memoir of Faith in Education* (1997).

Obituary: *Philadelphia Inquirer*, 31 Jan. 1998.

NOAH D. DREZNER

Haywood, G. T. (15 July 1880–12 Apr. 1931), pastor and denominational leader, was born Garfield Thomas Haywood in Greencastle, Indiana, the second son and third child of Benjamin and Penny Ann Haywood. In 1883 Haywood's family moved to Indianapolis, where his father worked in a foundry. Haywood attended elementary school and spent two years at Shortridge High School where he also studied art. He joined a Baptist church and later worked as Sunday school superintendent in local Baptist and Methodist congregations. His art training led him to draw charts and sketches to explain the Bible and to work as a cartoonist for two of the most prominent black newspapers of the day, the *Freeman* and the *Recorder*, both based in Indianapolis. On 11 February 1902 he married Ida Howard of Owensboro, Kentucky, with whom he had one child, Fannie Ann Haywood.

In 1908 Haywood attended the Apostolic Faith Assembly, an interracial Pentecostal church in Indianapolis pastored by Henry Prentiss, a black Pentecostal minister. Pentecostalism from the beginning encouraged interracial worship and the membership of the Azusa Mission, the mother Pentecostal church in Los Angeles, was racially mixed. Under Pastor Prentiss, Haywood spoke in tongues as he received the baptism of the Holy Spirit and later joined the Apostolic Faith Assembly. In early 1909 he took over the pastorate when Prentiss resigned. At the time his home church had thirteen members. He later named it "Apostolic Faith Assembly Tabernacle"—still later changed to "Christ Temple of the Apostolic Faith."

In 1910 Haywood began publication of the *Voice of the Wilderness* using a printing press he had set up in his living room. The following year he joined the Pentecostal Assemblies of the World (PAW), a loose interracial fellowship founded in Los Angeles in 1906 by J. J. Frazee, a white Pentecostal minister. The PAW was unincorporated and only met annually. Because early Pentecostalism promoted interracialism, Haywood was allowed to participate in the activities of the predominantly white Assemblies of God (AOG), founded in 1914. However, this body's stand on the Oneness movement, a major doctrinal controversy, would lead Haywood to sever his informal relationship with the AOG. The Oneness movement claimed that there is one Person on the Godhead, that that person is Jesus Christ, and that every Pentecostal should be baptized in the name of Jesus only, as opposed to that of the Father, Son, and Holy Spirit. In 1915 Haywood was rebaptized in Jesus' name and then he rebaptized his entire congregation. When the AOG rejected this form of Pentecostal unitarianism, Haywood became more active in the PAW, which had fully endorsed the Oneness movement and was responsible for drawing more northern blacks to the PAW.

As a local pastor Haywood welcomed school-teachers, school principals, and lawyers as church members. His church carried a pump organ, a piano, a choir, and granted women access to the pulpit. Even among his own parishioners, Haywood was sometimes severely criticized because many in the Pentecostal movement believed the use of musical instruments and choirs in worship was not allowed by the New Testament. Another sector asserted that women's ministry should not include the pastorate, and thus they wanted to prohibit women from that form of ministry. Despite these criticisms Christ Temple grew and by 1915 the membership reached 400. By the end of the 1920s it had jumped to 1,000, which forced the church to move six times until it built a larger building in 1924 at the cost of $80,000. Haywood's congregation was also distinctive because of its racial makeup: the membership was 60 percent black and 40 percent white. To encourage such integration Haywood made sure that the leadership of various church departments, such as the Sunday school, choirs, deacon boards, and missionaries, was also interracial. After World War I large progressive black churches in the North, called "institutional churches," had begun to address the social needs of blacks. Haywood joined this trend in the 1920s by purchasing a building and turning it into Saints Home, a house for senior citizens.

Haywood's influence was not limited to his local church. The PAW became more interracial when it merged with the General Assembly of Apostolic Assemblies, a white oneness group, in 1918. The presence of a large number of whites in the PAW did not hinder the continuing denominational promotion of Haywood. In 1919 he helped incorporate the PAW and subsequently was appointed to the positions of general secretary (1920), executive vice chairman (1922), presbyter (1923), and chairman of the foreign missions department (1924). In late 1924 blacks and whites within the PAW once again began to separate along racial lines. Southern whites had

complained that they could not attend PAW annual conventions, which were usually held in northern cities. Furthermore they became indignant that Haywood, a black minister, was co-signing their ministerial certificates. As a result three groups of whites left in 1925 and formed the Pentecostal Ministerial Alliance, the Apostolic Churches of Jesus Christ, and Emmanuel's Church in Jesus Christ. In January 1925 the still interracial but predominantly black PAW reorganized. Haywood was elected the first presiding bishop, a position he held until his death.

As PAW's general leader Haywood contributed much to its organizational survival and development, nurtured interracialism, and supported world missions. As a black person in such a high position he commanded respect from both blacks and whites. Haywood believed in interracialism and through church publications encouraged the denominational constituents to work together regardless of race. He wrote numerous booklets on the oneness view that he promoted widely through preaching and teaching, making him the most outstanding exponent of Oneness Pentecostalism in America. He also wrote a number of well-known songs, including "I See a Crimson Stream of Blood" and "Jesus the Son of God," which are used outside the PAW. As presiding bishop, Haywood was also in charge of foreign missions. He assisted white and black foreign missionaries in China, the Philippines, Japan, India, Hong Kong, South Africa, Egypt, and other countries. Haywood's legacy lives on through Christ Temple and the PAW, which remained interracial at the beginning of the twenty-first century and boasted an American membership of more than 1 million.

FURTHER READING

Goff, James R., Jr., and Grant Wacker, eds. *Portraits of a Generation: Early Pentecostal Leaders* (2002).

Golder, Morris E. *The Life and Works of Bishop Garfield Thomas Haywood* (1977).

Tyson, James L. *The Early Pentecostal Revival: History of Twentieth-Century Pentecostals and the Pentecostal Assemblies of the World* (1992).

DAVID MICHEL

Hazard, Newport (c. 1780?–?), was a sailor in the War of 1812 who fought in the Battle of Lake Erie under Commodore Oliver Hazard Perry. The details of Hazard's life are largely lost, although some speculation as to his identity may be made from surviving records. That Hazard was a slave is almost certain, although whether he was born a slave or forcibly brought to America from Africa is unknown. Hazard's first name of "Newport" is a common one of the day for enslaved men in New England and is a likely indicator that he was sold as a slave at Newport, Rhode Island, a major port in the slave trade, early in his life. Two candidates present themselves as to Newport Hazard's identity: he may be the man, born sometime between 1727 and 1761, listed as a "Negro" in the 1777 Rhode Island Military Census and living in the household of Steven Hazard of South Kingstown. If so, he probably remained a slave for many years, because Steven Hazard still owned slaves as late as 1790. The possibility also exists that the Newport Hazard who fought in the War of 1812 was considerably younger, perhaps born in the 1780s. Records indicate that on 24 December 1791 Thomas G. Hazard of Newport purchased from the town council of Jamestown, Rhode Island, "a certain negro boy named Newport Martin, now the property of Rebeckah Martin" (Thomas G. Hazard papers). Because it was customary for slaves to bear the last name of their master, it seems quite likely that Newport Martin soon became known as Newport Hazard; that he was a valued and even loved member of the Hazard household is indicated by the fact that Thomas Hazard's daughter Ruth left Newport and several of the slaves in their household various personal items in her last will and testament. Although the younger Newport Hazard would seem the most likely man to have fought in the War of 1812, a lack of any further documentation leaves the matter an open question.

Newport Hazard, whatever his background, was an experienced sailor prior to the war, perhaps serving as a free man in any of the numerous ships that sailed out of Rhode Island ports or maybe as a slave in a vessel owned by a seafaring branch of the Hazard family, of which there were several. He may have been one of the thousands of sailors, black and white, that became unemployed when America's commerce on the high seas was brought to a halt with the advent of war. Many of these men subsequently sought service in the navy or on privately armed merchant vessels, with the intent not only to earn a wage, but also to join in the fight against Great Britain. By 1813 Newport Hazard was an ordinary seaman in the navy, serving in the gunboat fleet stationed at Newport under Master Commandant Oliver Hazard Perry. Given their common family name and the fact that Perry was a native of Newport, it may even be speculated that the two men were somehow acquainted.

Hazard's rating of "ordinary seaman" indicates a basic knowledge of seamanship and thus some prior voyaging experience; enlisted ratings below that of ordinary seaman were that of landsman, a man with absolutely no prior sailor knowledge or experience, and that of ship's boy, a position held by both black and white youths under the age of eighteen. Newport Hazard's maritime background was not unusual, because black sailors were important in manning America's merchant vessels and saw extensive service both abroad and in the coastal trade. This importance extended to naval service in the War of 1812, during which African American sailors composed anywhere from 10 to 20 percent of a given ship's crew. However, because of a lack of documentation resulting from lost or missing records, black sailors, men such as Hazard, JESSE WALLS, and HANNIBAL COLLINS, have been given but scant attention for the role they played and the overall contribution of African American participants in the war has been largely forgotten.

Newport Hazard arrived in the Great Lakes theater of operations at Erie, Pennsylvania, in March 1813, one of 150 men who volunteered to leave Newport to serve with Perry in his newly formed Lake Erie squadron. He was assigned to serve in Perry's flagship, the twenty-gun brig *Lawrence*, and it is on this vessel that Hazard's participation in the war has been documented. After finishing the construction of his fleet and gathering more men, Perry was finally able to venture forth out onto the lake to confront an enemy fleet that, although smaller, was manned by experienced men of the vaunted Royal Navy. On the morning of 10 September 1813 the American squadron was at Put-In-Bay when an enemy sail was spied, and it was later that day that the historic Battle of Lake Erie was fought. The flagship *Lawrence*, with Hazard and fellow black sailor Jesse Williams aboard, led the line of battle according to Perry's plan, but soon it became clear that something went wrong. While the *Lawrence*, with Perry's "Don't Give Up the Ship" battle flag flying, led the way, the other twenty-gun brig in his squadron, the *Niagara*, inexplicably held back and stayed out of action. Thus it was that Perry and the men of the *Lawrence* bore the brunt of the battle for two hours; exchanging broadsides for broadsides with the strongest ships of the British fleet, the *Lawrence* paid a horrible price. The dead and wounded, of which Hazard was one, littered the decks of the *Lawrence* and the brig was badly damaged, but inspired by Perry, the men continued to fight and gave as good as they got. Just when all seemed lost, with the *Lawrence* in extremis, Perry made a bold move and transferred his command to the *Niagara* behind the line of battle. Armed with a new ship and a fresh crew, Perry quickly sailed forth to again confront the British fleet, and with this audacious and risky move soon turned the tide toward victory. When the fighting was over, Perry's squadron had captured the enemy fleet almost intact and thereby swept the British from control of Lake Erie and left the American army in control the surrounding territory. It would prove to be one of the most decisive battles of the war.

Hazard, ordinary seaman, was wounded during the Battle of Lake Erie and was subsequently one of the crewmen of Perry's squadron listed as being owed a portion of the prize money that resulted from the capture and sale of the enemy ships in 1814. After this, Hazard disappears from the pages of history, the details of his subsequent life unknown.

FURTHER READING
The bill of sale of Newport Martin, dated 1791, is located in the "Thomas G. Hazard papers" MSS 1026, in the collection of the Rhode Island Historical Society.

Altoff, Gerard T. *Amongst My Best Men: African-Americans and The War of 1812* (1996).

GLENN ALLEN KNOBLOCK

Healy, Eliza (23 Dec. 1846–13 Sept. 1919), Roman Catholic nun, was born a slave in Jones County, Georgia, the daughter of Michael Morris Healy, a well-to-do plantation owner, and Eliza Clark, one of his slaves. Michael Morris Healy was a native of Ireland who had immigrated to Jones County near Macon, Georgia, where, after acquiring land and slaves, he became a prosperous planter. Eliza Clark had nine surviving children by Michael Healy, who acknowledged his children and carefully made provisions for their eventual removal outside of Georgia, where at that time the manumission of slaves was virtually impossible.

Eliza Healy's mother died in the spring of 1850 and her father in the summer of the same year. By that time her five older brothers and one older sister had already been sent north to be educated. The youngest three children, including Eliza, were successfully brought out of Georgia and sent to New York.

Although he was a Catholic, Michael Healy did not have his children baptized. In the North, however, several of the Healy children pursued vocations in their father's faith. The three youngest siblings, including Eliza, were baptized in New York in 1851. Their eldest brother, JAMES HEALY, was at that time a seminarian in Montreal. In 1854 in Paris he was ordained a priest for the Diocese of Boston and in 1875 became the second bishop of Portland, Maine, and the first African American bishop in the United States. Two other brothers also became Roman Catholic priests. PATRICK HEALY was ordained a Jesuit priest in 1865 and became president of Georgetown University in Washington, D.C., in 1874. A third brother, (Alexander) SHERWOOD HEALY, served as a priest for the Diocese of Boston beginning in 1858. A fourth brother, MICHAEL HEALY, chose a secular path; he became a sea captain in the U.S. Revenue Cutter Service.

Both Eliza and her younger sister, (Amanda) Josephine, studied in schools operated by the sisters of the Congregation of Notre Dame in Montreal. At the same time, their older sister, Martha, was professed a nun in the same community in 1855. (Martha left the community with a dispensation from her vows in 1863.) After finishing her secondary education in 1861, Eliza, with Josephine, rejoined other members of the Healy family in the Boston area. About a dozen years later both sisters chose to lead the religious life.

Eliza was twenty-seven when she entered the novitiate of the congregation of Notre Dame in Montreal in 1874, and she made her first profession in 1876. Following the custom of the sisters of the Congregation of Notre Dame, she received the religious name of Sister Saint Mary Magdalen. In the beginning of her religious life, she taught in various schools operated by the Congregation of Notre Dame in Canada. She was superior of a convent for the first time in Huntington, Quebec, from 1895 to 1897, during which time her administrative gifts first became apparent. She returned to the mother house of the Sisters of Notre Dame in Montreal, where she was put in charge of English studies and then served as a teacher in the Normal School from 1900 to 1903.

Sister Saint Mary Magdalen served longest at Villa Barlow in St. Albans, Vermont. From 1903 to 1918 she was superior and headmistress of the school, and during that time she completely restored and reorganized the school and community. The annals of the congregation recount the precarious financial situation at Villa Barlow when she took over; the community was almost ready to abandon the site: "She had to struggle against the parish and even the diocesan authorities. Her wisdom enabled her to unravel the complicated problems, to assure the resources, to pay the debts, and to make this ... mission one of our most prosperous houses in the United States." Sister Saint Mary Magdalen also paid close attention to issues of health and hygiene for both the pupils and the sisters in her charge.

In 1918 she was sent to be superior of the Academy of Our Lady of the Blessed Sacrament on Staten Island, New York. In a few months she was able to improve the financial situation of the college, but her stay was brief. Her health declined rapidly, and she returned to the mother house in Montreal, where she died of heart disease the following summer.

Notices on Sister Saint Mary Magdalen by members of her community describe her as an indefatigable and somewhat demanding superior with a gift for business and organization. Her leadership qualities and her spirituality, such as her devotion to prayer, were especially remarked on by the sisters who had lived with her. Her relationship with the other sisters was described in the annals: "The sisters loved this superior, so just, so attractive, so upright! ... she reserved the heaviest tasks for herself ... in the kitchen, in the garden, in the housework.... She listened to everyone, ... was equal to everything ... spared herself nothing ... so that nothing was lacking to make the family life [of the community] perfect."

While none of the Healy siblings ever spoke publicly about the issue of race, it remains at the heart of the family's story. Both Bishop Healy and his brother Alexander were visibly black, but Patrick Healy's racial identity was not well known outside of the Jesuit order. None of the priest brothers involved themselves with the black Catholic community. In the same way, it seems that their gifted and dedicated sister lived out her life of leadership and service far removed from the world of her mother and the harsh circumstances faced by those of her mother's African heritage.

FURTHER READING

Information about Healy can be found in the archives of the Sisters of the Congregation of Notre Dame in Montreal, Canada.

Fairbanks, Henry G. "Slavery and the Vermont Clergy," *Vermont History* 27 (1959).

Foley, Albert S. *Bishop Healy: Beloved Outcaste* (1954).

Foley, Albert S. *Dream of an Outcaste: Patrick F. Healy, S.J.* (1989).

O'Toole, James M. *Passing for White: Race, Religion, and the Healy Family, 1820–1920* (2002).

This entry is taken from the *American National Biography* and is published here with the permission of the American Council of Learned Societies.

CYPRIAN DAVIS

Healy, James Augustine (6 Apr. 1830–5 Aug. 1900), Roman Catholic bishop, was born in Jones County, Georgia, the son of Michael Morris Healy, a planter, and his slave Eliza Clark. James's early years were spent in the insular world of Healy's 1,600-acre plantation. When he reached school age, James and his brothers Hugh and PATRICK HEALY were placed by their father in a Quaker school in Flushing, New York. Eventually all nine of the Healy siblings, including MICHAEL HEALY and ELIZA HEALY, left Georgia for the North.

In 1844 Healy and his brothers transferred to the College of the Holy Cross in Worcester, Massachusetts, a new Jesuit school established by Bishop John Bernard Fitzpatrick of Boston. Healy thrived in his new environment, excelling academically and experiencing a spiritual awakening that led to his decision to enter the priesthood in 1848. The Jesuit novitiate was in Maryland, a slave state, so with the help of Fitzpatrick, Healy in 1849 entered the Sulpician Seminary in Montreal, Canada. After receiving his M.A. two years later, Healy entered the seminary of St. Sulpice in Issy, France, where he worked toward becoming a professor of theology and philosophy. However, following the deaths of his parents in 1850 and of his brother Hugh in a freak accident in 1853, Healy felt called to return to the United States. In Notre Dame Cathedral in Paris on 10 June 1854, Healy became the first African American to be ordained a Roman Catholic priest. He then returned to Boston, where he became an assistant pastor of the Moon Street Church and an administrator of the House of the Guardian Angel, a home for orphaned boys. Fitzpatrick soon brought Healy onto his staff and gave him the responsibility of organizing the chancery office. In June 1855 Healy officially became the first chancellor of the Diocese of Boston, loyally serving Fitzpatrick and learning from him the subtleties of Catholic leadership in New England's anti-Catholic environment.

In 1857, after Fitzpatrick became ill, Healy took over many of the bishop's duties. Plans to build a new cathedral were delayed because of the Civil War, and in 1862 Healy became the rector of a makeshift cathedral that had been a Unitarian church. As the war climaxed, he helped found the Home for

Destitute Catholic Children, bringing in the Sisters of Charity to run it in 1865.

After Fitzpatrick's death in 1866, the new bishop, John Joseph Williams, appointed Healy as the pastor of St. James Church, the largest Catholic congregation in Boston. If Healy was concerned that as a southerner of African descent he would be unacceptable to the predominantly Irish parishioners, he kept this concern to himself, and he soon won over the congregation through firm spiritual leadership and a tender affection for those in need. As one parishioner said, if Healy "had any such thing as an inferiority complex concealed about his person, his Irish congregation never discovered it, for he ruled them—and they were not easy to rule" (Foley, 109).

A highlight of Healy's years as the pastor of St. James was the establishment in 1867 of the House of the Good Shepherd, a refuge for homeless girls. However, his success as an apologist for the Catholic Church before the Massachusetts legislature in March 1874 was perhaps his most impressive achievement. The legislature was considering the taxation of churches and other religious institutions, and Healy defended Catholic institutions— including schools, hospitals, and orphanages—as vital organizations that helped the state both socially and financially. He also eloquently condemned the laws that were already in place, which were generally enforced only on Catholic institutions.

Healy's success in the public sphere and his exemplary service as pastor of St. James led to his election by Pope Pius IX as the second bishop of Portland, Maine, in February 1875. Again he was concerned that the color of his skin would undermine his authority, particularly in regard to the fifty-two priests of the diocese. His fears, however, were never realized. Although Healy's personal history was the source of some intrigue and prejudice among his flock, his ability and pastoral excellence reduced the matter to a nonissue. He took firm control of the diocese, which covered all of Maine and New Hampshire and was growing rapidly as a result of Irish and French Canadian immigration. Relying on the savvy of John M. Mitchell, a prominent local lawyer well schooled in Maine's political and social intricacies, Healy helped unify his parishes in an era when Catholics were often divided by ethnic differences.

Healy oversaw the founding of sixty parishes, eighteen schools (including American Indian schools), and sixty-eight charitable institutions within the diocese. In 1884, at Healy's suggestion, the diocese was divided by state lines, and a separate Diocese of Manchester, New Hampshire, was established. Healy helped set up his former chancellor, Denis Bradley, as its first bishop. He also oversaw the establishment of the state's first Catholic college in 1886, as St. Mary's College in Van Buren opened its doors. Under Healy dozens of religious congregations were established, many of French Canadian origin. By 1900 the Sisters of Mercy, the Sisters of the Congregation of Notre Dame, the Dominicans, the Marist Brothers, and the Christian Brothers were all established in various educational and institutional positions throughout the state.

While the quality of Healy's career proves that a person's race is not the essential characteristic by which he or she can be judged, his desire to avoid the issue led to several lost opportunities to condemn the sin of racism on a national stage. Even after the Third Plenary Council of Baltimore in 1884, which placed Healy on the newly formed Commission on Negro and Indian Missions, he refused to participate in organizations that were specifically African American. Three times, in 1889, 1890, and 1892, Healy declined to speak at the Congress of Colored Catholics. His legacy as the first African American Catholic bishop is at least partially diminished by this reticence.

Although Healy was haunted by racism throughout his life, he never allowed it to affect his duties. His graceful attitude toward the problem is exemplified by an encounter he had with a young parishioner during the sacrament of penance. The teenage girl, unaware that her confessor was Healy himself, admitted that she had "said the bishop was as black as the devil." Healy responded: "Don't say the bishop is as black as the devil. You can say the bishop is as black as coal, or as black as the ace of spades. But don't say the bishop is as black as the *devil!*" (Foley, 145).

Healy was a religious leader whose intelligence, spiritual conviction, and dedicated service inevitably defined him and created a devoted, if not wholly color-blind, following. He died in Portland, Maine.

FURTHER READING

Healy's papers are at the library of the College of the Holy Cross, Worcester, Massachusetts; the Archives of the Archdiocese of Boston; and the Archives of the Diocese of Portland, Maine.

Foley, Albert S. *Bishop Healy: Beloved Outcaste* (1954).

Lucey, William Leo. *The Catholic Church in Maine* (1957).

Merwick, Donna. *Boston Priests, 1848–1910: A Study of Social and Intellectual Change* (1973).

O'Toole, James M. *Passing for White: Race, Religion, and the Healy Family, 1820–1920* (2002).

Obituary: *Portland Express*, 6 Aug. 1900.

This entry is taken from the *American National Biography* and is published here with the permission of the American Council of Learned Societies.

JAY MAZZOCCHI

Healy, Michael (22 Sept. 1839–30 Aug. 1904), Coast Guard officer and Alaska pioneer, was born Michael Augustine Healy in Jones County, Georgia, to Michael Morris Healy, an immigrant from Ireland, and Eliza Clark, a mixed-race slave owned by Michael Morris Healy. Michael was the sixth of nine surviving children born to his parents, who, though never legally married, maintained a common-law relationship for more than twenty years, neither one of them ever marrying anyone else. Michael Morris Healy was barred by Georgia law from emancipating either his wife or his children, but he treated them as family members rather than as slaves, even as he owned fifty other slaves. He was a successful cotton planter and amassed the resources to send his children north before the Civil War, which he did as each approached school age, beginning in 1844. The children exhibited a wide range of complexion, but most of them, including young Michael, were light-skinned enough so that anyone who did not know the family's story remained unaware of their racial heritage, presuming them to be white.

Michael followed his older brothers to the College of the Holy Cross in Worcester, Massachusetts, in 1850. They had flourished there, and three of them made the decision to become Catholic priests. JAMES HEALY, the first African American ordained as a Roman Catholic priest, eventually became the bishop of Portland, Maine; another, PATRICK HEALY, the first African American to earn a Ph.D. and to be ordained a Jesuit priest, served as president of Georgetown University; (Alexander) SHERWOOD HEALY, was the rector of the Cathedral of the Holy Cross in Boston. Two sisters, (Amanda) Josephine and ELIZA HEALY, became Catholic nuns, serving in convents and schools in the United States and Canada. Michael, however, had no interest in a religious career. Instead, he ran away from Holy Cross and by 1855 had found work in the maritime trades, serving on a succession of merchant vessels as a deckhand, mate, and, finally, second or first officer.

In September 1863 Healy enlisted in the United States Revenue Cutter Service (USRCS), the precursor of the modern-day coast guard. A year later he applied for an officer's commission, and, with the help of his brother James, who had connections among several important Republican politicians in Boston, he was appointed a second lieutenant. No mention of his racial background was made during the appointment process; had he been identified as having African American ancestry, he would almost certainly have been prevented from securing an officer's rank. Instead, officials of the USRCS were allowed to think that he was white. Shortly afterward, in January 1865, he married Mary Jane Roach, the daughter of Irish immigrants to Boston; they would eventually have one son.

For the next several years Healy had a series of routine assignments on USRCS cutters based in Newport, Rhode Island, New Bedford, Massachusetts, and New York City, rising to the rank of first lieutenant. In the summer of 1874 he was assigned to the USRCS fleet based in San Francisco, charged with patrolling the waters off Alaska, which the United States had purchased from Russia a few years earlier. The USRCS was the only government agency enforcing law and order in the northern Pacific, the Bering Sea, and the Arctic Ocean. Cutters made annual summer cruises in those waters, conducting basic exploration and scientific work, assisting commercial vessels, policing the whaling fleet, apprehending smugglers, and helping both settlers and natives. In March 1883 Healy was promoted to the rank of captain, becoming the first African American captain in the USRCS, a distinction he would not have claimed, and did not claim, for himself.

In 1886 Healy was given command of the ship *Bear*. The fame of the vessel and her captain grew steadily over the next decade as they went about their regular tasks. Exploration was high on the list. Twice, with the *Bear* anchored offshore, Healy sent exploring parties in launches upriver in search of overland routes to Alaska's northern slope. Although no practical routes were identified, the explorers cataloged much of the flora and fauna of inland Alaska for the first time, which Healy later published in two widely respected reports. Healy supervised efforts to protect wildlife, focusing particularly on attempts (not wholly successful) to prevent the overhunting of seals on the open seas. He provided regular assistance to the diminishing American whaling fleet concentrated above the Arctic Circle, which frequently entailed freeing whaling ships trapped in the ice and rescuing seamen stranded by shipwreck. Healy's contact with Inuit and Aleut natives culminated in his unusual plan to introduce domesticated reindeer into Alaska in the hope of improving native self-sufficiency. Beginning in 1891 he sailed repeatedly back and forth, buying reindeer from natives in Siberia who had been herding them for centuries, transporting the animals on the cutter, and establishing herds for the Alaska natives, among whom such herding had been unknown. By disrupting the illegal traffic in liquor and guns, Healy also attempted to curb the abuse of natives by white settlers from the United States.

Healy's endeavors earned him a wide reputation. Ask anyone in the Arctic "Who is the greatest man in America?," the *New York Sun* claimed in 1894, and the swift answer would be, "Why, Mike Healy." His picturesque career was the stuff of novels, and, in fact, he appeared in a fictionalized but reasonably accurate portrayal in James Michener's best-selling 1989 book, *Alaska*. Eventually, however, Healy's stern, no-nonsense approach to law enforcement and his aggressive personality—for which he had been nicknamed "Hell-Roaring Mike"—proved his undoing. After several minor complaints were lodged against him, Healy was tried before a court-martial in San Francisco in 1890, charged with the cruel treatment of prisoners in his custody.

The trial became a rallying cry for temperance forces, who accused Healy of having been drunk at the time. While he was acquitted of all charges on that occasion, he was less fortunate six years later, when he was tried again, this time for abusive treatment of his own men and public drunkenness. At his 1896 trial Healy was found guilty. Although he could have been dismissed from the USRCS, his punishment was less severe. Instead, he was placed in the indeterminate status of "waiting orders," and he was made to suffer the embarrassment of being dropped to the bottom of the list of captains in the service, which was normally arranged by seniority. Neither in his trials nor in the newspaper accounts of them was his racial background raised as an issue; it apparently remained unknown, even to his opponents, who probably would have used it against him had they been aware of it.

Shortly after the turn of the century, Healy briefly achieved a kind of redemption when he was once again given command of USRCS ships. Healy retired from the service in the fall of 1903 and died the following summer. Today, his trailblazing position as the first black captain of the USRCS is celebrated, and in 1997 the coast guard commissioned an icebreaker named for him, recognizing that distinction. In his own lifetime, however, Healy exemplified the desire of some African Americans to pass in order to have successful careers in the white community.

FURTHER READING

Healy's logbooks and other records relating to his USRCS career are in the coast guard records at the National Archives and Records Administration, Washington, D.C.

O'Toole, James M. *Passing for White: Race, Religion, and the Healy Family, 1820–1920* (2002).

Strobridge, Truman R., and Dennis L. Noble. *Alaska and the U.S. Revenue Cutter Service, 1867–1915* (1999).

JAMES M. O'TOOLE

Healy, Patrick Francis (2 Feb. 1834–10 Jan. 1910), Jesuit priest and university president, was born in Jones County, Georgia, the son of Michael Morris Healy, an Irish American planter, and Eliza Clark, an African American woman he had purchased. The senior Healy deserted from the British army in Canada during the War of 1812 and by 1818 had made his way to rural Georgia, where he settled, speculated in land, and acquired a sizable plantation and numerous slaves. Healy acknowledged Eliza as "my trusty woman" in his will, which provided that she be paid an annuity, transported to a free state, and "not bartered or sold or disposed of in any way" should he predecease her. Healy also acknowledged his nine children by Eliza, although by state law they were slaves he owned, and he arranged for them to leave Georgia and move to the North, where they would become free.

After first sending his older sons to a Quaker school in Flushing, New York, Michael Healy by chance met John Fitzpatrick, then the Roman Catholic bishop coadjutor of Boston, who told him about the new Jesuit College of the Holy Cross opening in Worcester, Massachusetts. Patrick, along with three of his brothers, was enrolled in Holy Cross in 1844. A sister, Martha, was sent to the Notre Dame sisters' school in Boston. Patrick graduated in 1850, the year after his older brother JAMES HEALY was literally the first person to receive a diploma from the fledgling college. At Holy Cross the Healy brothers' race was fully known and generally accepted without incident. In one poignant letter, however, Patrick Healy wrote: "Remarks are sometime made which wound my very heart. You know to what I refer ... I have with me a younger brother Michael. He is obliged to go through the same ordeal."

Although none of the Healy children were baptized until coming north, brothers James, Hugh, Patrick, and Sherwood were baptized at Holy Cross in 1844, and by 1851, all of the Healy children had been baptized. So it is not surprising that Patrick Healy decided to emulate his friends and protectors and enter the Society of Jesus. He matriculated at the order's novitiate in Frederick, Maryland, where his light skin apparently kept him from being identified as African American and thus in school contrary to the law. After making his Jesuit vows in 1852, Healy taught at St. Joseph's College in Philadelphia, Pennsylvania, and was then assigned back to Holy Cross, where he taught a variety of courses. In 1858 he was sent to Georgetown University in Washington, D.C., to continue his own studies in philosophy and theology, but soon he was abruptly reassigned to Rome, probably because his race had become an issue. His brother James, who had decided to enter the secular priesthood, attended the Sulpician seminaries in Montreal and Paris because it was not possible for a black person to be enrolled in an American school.

Patrick Francis Healy became president of Georgetown University in Washington, D.C., in 1874. (Library of Congress.)

Patrick Healy's delicate health did not long tolerate the weather in Rome, so he was sent to the Catholic University of Louvain in Belgium. He was ordained to the priesthood on 3 September 1864 by Bishop Lamont in Liége and then stayed on at Louvain to complete a doctorate in philosophy. He received his degree on 26 July 1865, apparently the first African American to earn a Ph.D. He returned to the United States the next year, after further spiritual training in France, and was assigned to teach philosophy at Georgetown.

Healy took his final vows as a Jesuit on 2 February 1867, the first African American to do so. If the illegitimacy of his birth made his ordination problematic, church officials overlooked this fact, as they did in the case of his brother James, who had become in 1854 the first African American ordained to the Roman Catholic priesthood. Patrick Healy moved quickly through the administrative ranks at Georgetown, becoming prefect of studies, or dean, and then vice president. When the president, the Reverend John Early, died unexpectedly in 1873, Healy was named acting president. Following confirmation by authorities in Rome, he was inaugurated the twenty-ninth president of Georgetown on 31 July 1874.

Patrick Healy's influence on Georgetown was so far-reaching that he is often referred to as the school's "second founder," following Archbishop John Carroll. Healy did, in fact, transform a small nineteenth-century college into a major twentieth-century university. He modernized the curriculum by requiring courses in the sciences, particularly chemistry and physics. He expanded and upgraded the schools of law and medicine. He centralized libraries, arranged for scholastic awards to students, and created an alumni organization. The most visible result of Healy's presidency was the construction of a large building begun in 1877 and first used in 1881. The imposing Healy Hall, with its two-hundred foot tower, contained classrooms, offices, and dormitories; its Belgian Gothic style was clearly reminiscent of Louvain. Paying for the building became somewhat problematic, however, when stories of Healy's race, never a secret, circulated through Washington.

Healy's influence extended beyond Georgetown as he mixed in the nation's capital with presidents of the United States and other government officials as well as the parents of Georgetown students. He served as head of the Catholic Commission on Indian Affairs. He preached often in Catholic churches in the Washington area, including St. Augustine's, an

African American parish. He was present at the cornerstone laying of this church in 1874 and at the dedication of its new building in 1876. He spoke at congressional hearings in opposition to taxes on religious and educational institutions.

Healy's health was never robust, and he apparently suffered from epilepsy, which grew more serious with age. Upon the advice of his physician, he retired from the Georgetown presidency on 16 February 1882. Several assignments followed, but they existed largely in name only: St. Joseph's Church, Providence, Rhode Island; St. Lawrence Church, New York City; and St. Joseph's College, Philadelphia. In fact, in retirement he traveled extensively through Europe and the United States, often in the company of his brother James. He spent his last two years in the Georgetown infirmary, where he died, survived only by his sister ELIZA HEALY.

Patrick Healy's brothers and sisters led equally significant lives. James became bishop of Portland, Maine. (Alexander) SHERWOOD HEALY became a professor of moral theology and accompanied the Boston archbishop John J. Williams to Vatican I as his personal theologian. Eliza became Sister Mary Magdalen, a superior in the Notre Dame sisters. MICHAEL HEALY, the only sibling not to follow a religious vocation, became "Hell-Roaring Mike," captain of a U.S. revenue cutter in the Arctic and North Pacific.

FURTHER READING

Healy's papers, including his diaries, are in the Georgetown University Library.

Curran, Robert Emmett. *The Bicentennial History of Georgetown University*, vol. 1: 1789–1889 (1993).

Foley, Rev. Albert. *God's Men of Color* (1955, 1970).

O'Toole, James M. *Passing for White: Race, Religion, and the Healy Family, 1820–1920* (2002).

This entry is taken from the *American National Biography* and is published here with the permission of the American Council of Learned Societies.

RICHARD NEWMAN

Healy, Sherwood (24 Jan. 1836–21 Oct. 1875), Roman Catholic priest and educator, was born to Mary Eliza Clark, a slave, and Michael Morris Healy, an immigrant from Ireland and a Georgia plantation owner. In 1829, Michael and Eliza entered into an unconventional union, a de facto marriage that was not recognized by law since it was illegal for blacks and whites to marry. Among their children was Alexander Sherwood, the fourth of ten children

born to them on the Healy plantation near Macon, Georgia. Legally, Sherwood and all of the Healy children were born into slavery, though their father never intended for them to remain on the plantation. Instead, he sought out possibilities for them in the North where they could be educated and escape from their status as slaves. At the age of eight, Healy arrived in Worcester, Massachusetts, to enter the grammar school of Holy Cross College. After his departure to the North, he would never again return to his childhood home of Georgia. At Holy Cross, it was expected that all students would participate in religious activities, and in November 1844 Healy and three of his brothers were baptized by a priest at the college. They took their new faith seriously, gaining a sense of identity from their religious practice.

Despite excelling as a student, Sherwood did not graduate from Holy Cross; instead, he moved to New York in 1850 to join his brother Hugh, who was seeking a career in business. After working as a warehouse clerk, he decided to follow his older brothers JAMES AUGUSTINE HEALY and PATRICK FRANCIS HEALY, who were studying to be Roman Catholic priests. In time, five of the Healy children entered the priesthood or religious life. James, the eldest, was the first African American to be ordained for service by the Catholic Church, and he became bishop of the Diocese of Portland, Maine. Patrick joined the Society of Jesus (the Jesuits) and became the president of Georgetown University in Washington, D.C. Two Healy daughters, Josephine and ELIZA HEALY, entered religious communities for women. At the age of sixteen, in 1852 Healy began studies for the priesthood at the Sulpician Seminary in Montreal, Canada. He later transferred to the Sulpician Seminary in Paris and finally to Apollonia College, a more prestigious school in Rome. He was ordained on 15 December 1858 in the Cathedral of Notre Dame in Paris, the second African American to be ordained as a Catholic priest. Recognized for his intellectual capabilities, he was invited to pursue graduate studies and went on to earn a doctor of divinity degree from Apollonia. He subsequently transferred to the Lateran University in Rome where he studied church law, achieving a doctorate in that discipline in 1860.

At the conclusion of his time in Rome, Healy's superior, Bishop John Bernard Fitzpatrick, recognizing his talent, suggested his name as a candidate to lead the North American College, then being founded in Rome as the preeminent seminary for the training of American clergy. Healy, however, was not aware that he was being considered as a candidate for the position. When the decision was made it was clear that he was passed over because of his race; Fitzpatrick confided to another bishop that Healy's color showed "distinctly in his exterior" and worried he would not be respected by the seminarians he was to have authority over. He returned to America in 1860 and became chaplain of a large orphanage near Boston, the House of the Angel Guardian. As his appointment was not demanding, he was free to pursue other priestly activities at the prompting of his bishop. Because of his musical training, he was called upon to sing at special liturgical services. He also served as acting chancellor of the diocese when his brother James was away in Europe. Primed for a life in education and administration, Healy became professor of moral theology, sacred music, and liturgy in 1864 at St. Joseph's Seminary in Troy, New York, a newly opened regional seminary for the training of clergy. During his years at the seminary, Healy had become the trusted advisor of Fitzpatrick's successor, Bishop John J. Williams. Healy traveled with Williams to the Second Plenary Council of Baltimore (1866) and the First Vatican Council in Rome (1869–1870) as the bishop's personal theologian.

Though he lived in tumultuous times, Healy showed little interest in discussions of slavery, the Civil War, or the plight of African Americans in the Reconstruction South. In the midst of the American bishops' discussion over attempts to evangelize freed slaves, Healy was silent. Though most of the Healy children had light skin which enabled them to pass for white, Sherwood Healy was the one who most clearly looked African American. Despite this, he seemed to ignore his own racial heritage, likely seeing it as a liability in his ministry as a priest. As he was leaving Rome at the conclusion of the First Vatican Council, Healy's health deteriorated significantly. Upon his return to Boston, he was diagnosed with typhus fever. Confined to his bed and unconscious for hours at a time, last rites were administered to him and he prepared himself for death. He slowly recovered from his ailment, however, and by the fall of 1870 he was well enough to accept an appointment as rector of the Cathedral of the Holy Cross in Boston. As rector, Healy supervised the construction of the new cathedral in Boston's South End. He served with distinction for five years before taking up an assignment as pastor of St. James Church in Boston, one of the largest parishes in the city and a recognized stepping-stone to the episcopacy. Healy's brother, James, had left the pastorate of St. James Church to become bishop of Portland, Maine. Healy's service there, however, lasted only a few months as he died of unknown causes just short of his fortieth birthday. As one of the first African Americans to be ordained to the priesthood, Healy is remembered for his noteworthy contributions as a seminary professor, pastor, and administrator in the Catholic Church.

FURTHER READING

Davis, Cyprian. *The History of Black Catholics in the United States* (1990).

Foley, Albert. *God's Men of Color: The Colored Catholic Priests of the United States, 1854–1954* (1955).

O'Toole, James M. *Passing for White: Race, Religion, and the Healy Family, 1820–1920* (2002).

Obituaries: *Boston Globe*, 22 Oct. 1875; *Boston Pilot*, 30 Oct. 1875.

DAVID J. ENDRES

Heard, J. C. (8 Oct. 1917–27 Sept. 1988), jazz drummer, was born in Dayton, Ohio. His father was a factory worker; further details of his parents are unknown. Heard told the interviewer Peter Vacher that he actually was named J.C. by his parents, and he invented the given names James Charles to satisfy authorities who would not believe that the initials should stand alone. He was raised in Detroit from infancy. A tap dancer by age five, he taught himself to play drums. At about age ten he won an amateur tap dancing contest, and the prize was the opportunity to tour with JODIE "BUTTERBEANS" EDWARDS and Susie Hawthorn. Five weeks into the tour, the drummer fell ill, and Heard took his place for the remainder of the show's run.

A year or two later Heard acquired his own set of drums. As a teenager he worked with bands throughout Michigan. After playing with Milt Larkin's band, he joined the pianist TEDDY WILSON's big band in New York in April 1939. In June 1940, at the end of this affiliation, Heard made several recordings with the singer BILLIE HOLIDAY under Wilson's direction, including "Laughing at Life." He then joined the tenor saxophonist COLEMAN HAWKINS's big band, which broadcast from the Savoy Ballroom in July and August. From December 1940 to the summer of 1942 he played at Café Society with Wilson's sextet, and during this period he again recorded with Wilson, including a trio version of "I Know That You Know" (April 1941). Heard also played briefly with the alto saxophonist Benny Carter's big band at the Savoy (January 1941), performed in the film short *Boogie Woogie Dream* (1941), and made further recordings with Holiday (August 1941 and February 1942).

In the fall of 1942 Heard traveled to Los Angeles to replace COZY COLE in the singer CAB CALLOWAY's big band. He remained with Calloway until September 1945, while also working with the pianist COUNT BASIE's big band in the spring of 1944 and recording with the tenor saxophonist IKE QUEBEC (several sessions, 1944–1946), the alto saxophonist CHARLIE PARKER and the trumpeter DIZZY GILLESPIE in the vibraphonist Red Norvo's group (June 1945), and Parker in the pianist Sir Charles Thompson's All Stars (September 1945).

After working in late 1945 in the sextet of the trombonist BENNY MORTON, who had been a fellow member of Wilson's groups, Heard formed his own group at the downtown location of Café Society. In January 1946 this sextet included the trumpeter George Treadwell, the trombonist DICKY WELLS, the saxophonist BUDD JOHNSON, the pianist Jimmy Jones, and the bassist Al McKibbon. Later group members were the trumpeter Joe Newman, the trombonist Dicky Harris, and the saxophonist ALBERT ("Big Nick") NICHOLAS, with the singer ETTA JONES added as well. Apart from his own group, Heard recorded "Mr. Drum Meets Mr. Piano" in a duo with the pianist PETE JOHNSON and "J.C. from K.C." as a soloist in Johnson's group in a session during January 1946, and small group versions of "52nd Street Theme," "A Night in Tunisia," and "Anthropology" with Dizzy Gillespie the following month.

Heard claimed to have played in the first Jazz at the Philharmonic concert with NAT KING COLE, but discographies identify the drummer as Lee Young (LESTER YOUNG's brother). In any event he performed regularly with Jazz at the Philharmonic in 1946. Heard substituted for JO JONES in Basie's group in the summer of 1947, and for the 1947 movie *The Kiss of Death* he found himself in the rare position of recording the soundtrack for Jones, who appears on screen; Heard's performing in Jones's stead was, in itself, a testimony to his stature as a jazz drummer.

Heard worked with the bassist OSCAR PETTIFORD in the pianist ERROLL GARNER's trio at the Three Deuces club in New York in April 1948 and continued with the group after the pianist George Shearing subsequently took Garner's place. Around 1949 Heard briefly replaced Cozy Cole in LOUIS ARMSTRONG's All Stars when Cole broke his arm; Heard may be seen performing with a related Armstrong group on an episode of the television series *Eddie Condon's Floor Show* (3 September 1949). He recorded with the pianist EARL HINES's trio in June 1950.

Heard toured with Jazz at the Philharmonic in the early 1950s, but during concerts in Japan in November 1953 he received such a lucrative offer that he decided to leave this all-star group to remain in Japan. He acted in movies, appearing once as a black samurai warrior; he hosted a television show through an interpreter; he led a jazz group that included the pianist Toshiko Akiyoshi; and he worked with a big band, the Sharps and Flats. He toured widely, playing in Hong Kong, Saigon, Manila, and Calcutta, while also continuing to perform in Japan, where he married Hiroko (maiden name unknown); they had a son. After working in Australia as a singer, dancer, and drummer, he brought his family to New York late in 1957.

A European tour with the pianist SAM PRICE in October 1958 included performances in England and at a jazz festival in Cannes. Heard worked alongside Hawkins and the trumpeter ROY ELDRIDGE at the Metropole club in New York (1959). He played in Wilson's trio (1961) and then held residencies in New York and toured with the pianist DOROTHY DONEGAN (1962–1963). In 1964 he joined Norvo's small group at the Sands Hotel in Las Vegas and the London House in Chicago. He led his own quintet, which included the hard-bop musicians tenor saxophonist Harold Land, trumpeter Carmell Jones, and pianist PHINEAS NEWBORN, at Memory Lane in Los Angeles in 1965. After further work in California, he settled in Detroit early in 1967 and gradually developed a big band for local touring and student workshops around Michigan.

In the mid-1970s Heard toured the Hilton Hotels circuit, leading a four-piece group that included the Detroit-based trumpeter Marcus Belgrave. While in France for performances at the Nice Jazz Festival in 1978, he also appeared on the tenor saxophonist ILLINOIS JACQUET's album *God Bless My Solo*. He toured Europe annually in the 1980s while continuing to work in the Detroit area, and in 1985 he performed on a jazz festival cruise ship. He died in Royal Oak, Michigan.

Heard was one of those accomplished drummers who was little known to the general public but much in demand within the community of jazz musicians: toward the end of his career a European fan sent him a list of 1,100 albums on which he had performed. The vast majority of his work was as a reliable and sensitive accompanist in swing groups (both big and small), but the recordings from 1946 with Johnson and Gillespie demonstrate that when the occasion demanded, he was also comfortable and accomplished as a soloist and as a bop musician.

FURTHER READING

Chilton, John. *Who's Who of Jazz: Storyville to Swing Street*, 4th ed. (1985).

Gillespie, Dizzy, and Al Fraser. *To Be, or Not … to Bop: Memoirs* (1979).

Shaw, Arnold. *The Street That Never Slept* (1971; repr. in 1977 as *52nd Street: The Street of Jazz*).

Obituary: *New York Times*, 30 Sept. 1988.

This entry is taken from the *American National Biography* and is published here with the permission of the American Council of Learned Societies.

BARRY KERNFELD

Heard, Marian Nobelene Langston (7 Nov. 1940–), president and chief executive officer of Oxen Hill Partners, a nationally known organization specializing in leadership development programs and brand enhancement strategies, was one of five children and the second daughter born to Ural Noble Langston, a construction worker, and Indiana Billingslea, a homemaker, in Canton, Georgia. Both Langston and her older sister, Patricia Ann were born in what was affectionately known as the "the Little House," a wonderful three bedroom home built in the rear and to the side of the home owned by her paternal grandparents, Noble Langston and Roxie Upshaw. Her grandparents lived in "the Big House," which was a lovely stucco and brick home that faced the highway that ran through the town of Canton.

When Marian was a year old, her parents moved to Stratford, Connecticut, where they had three more children, each one carrying a middle name in honor of a family member. In Connecticut, her father worked as a Crane Operator at the Bridgeport Brass Company; but with five children, he also had to work part-time as a construction worker on the massive project to build the Connecticut Turnpike. Marian's mother was always active in church and charitable groups including the Church Women United and the Salvation Army. In later years, she worked at General Electric Company in the wire and cable division.

Langston attended Birdseye Elementary school, Center School, Johnson Junior High School, and Stratford High School. She loved school, and her parents supported their children's scholarship in special ways, such as waiving all chores if they received good grades. Langston spent many hours in the library reading. In school, she achieved honors every term and was elected as class officer in each of her classes. In the 1950s girls only ran for class secretary, but Langston ran for class vice president. This

decision resulted in a special meeting with the class advisor who encouraged her to run for class secretary. Refusing the advisor's suggestion, Langston won the election by a landslide. During high school, she was president of the Smart, Strong Ladies Club, member of the National Honor Society, the Student Council, and the top student in the secretarial program. After graduating high school in 1958, she attended Butler Business School, graduating in 1960. From 1958 to 1963, she performed secretarial work for Mitchell Brothers, one of the largest manufacturers of sleepwear in America.

The year before she began college in 1961, Langston met her future husband, Winlow McQuade Heard. His first cousin introduced them upon Heard's arrival in Connecticut after serving in the air force. On their first date, Heard asked Langston to marry him. After three years of work, at the suggestion of a friend, Langston applied to and was admitted to the University of Bridgeport in 1962 where she earned an associate's degree in Executive Secretarial Studies in 1963. Langston and Heard were married in August of that same year, and the union would produce two sons and four grandchildren.

She later attended the University of Massachusetts at Amherst, 1974–1976, where she earned a bachelor's degree in Business and Management and Springfield College, 1976–1978 where she earned a master's degree in Education with a specialty in Leadership and Community Development.

Marian Langston Heard's entrepreneurial and leadership skills helped her professional career thrive. While attending high school, she formed Heard Typing Service in 1954 where she typed term papers for college students, bulletins for local churches, reports for local civic and service clubs such as the Lions, the Civitans, the Rotary, and the Junior League. After marriage, from 1963 to 1966, she worked for Warner Brothers, a producer of women's apparel. Leaving Warner Brothers in 1966 to have her first child, Langston Heard started her second business as a distributor for Dart Industries selling Coppercraft Guild home products including jewelry, crystal, and home-decorative items. This business was founded during the upswing in popularity of direct sales and network marketing endeavors. Over five years, Langston Heard soon had twenty-eight people employed with her and won top prizes including a trip to Spain, which Dart Industries sponsored. Later in 1972, Langston Heard was asked to lead the Greater Bridgeport Child Care Initiative in Bridgeport, Connecticut. She also started Heard Enterprises in 1972, which later comprised Oxen Hill Partners and a real estate management division. Subsequently, Langston Heard worked for the United Way in Bridgeport from 1974 to 1992, beginning as the childcare coordinator and finishing as the president and chief executive officer, the first black in the country to hold that title. She left the United Way of Fairfield County in Bridgeport to head the United Way in Boston in 1992. As chief executive officer of the United Way of Massachusetts Bay in Boston and also the president and chief executive officer of the United Ways of New England, Langston Heard retired in 2004 after serving the system for more than thirty years. Under her leadership at the United Ways, Langston Heard's organization won top prize for a Youth Substance Prevention Project given by newscaster Tom Brokaw with a citation from President George H. W. Bush to kick off the United Way campaigns. She also received recognition for launching "Success by 6," a program aimed at ensuring that every child is ready to succeed by age six.

During her tenure with the United Way, 1990–1995, Langston Heard was asked to serve as the founding president and chief executive officer of the Points of Light Foundation. President Bush asked her to develop this foundation to support the call for volunteers to address the social problems facing the United States. She served two terms as National Board Chairman, 1996–1999. Langston Heard took leave from the United Way to serve as president and chief executive officer of the president's Summit for America's Future Convention held in Philadelphia in 1997, cochaired by former presidents Bush and Bill Clinton with participation by all living presidents. As a result of this summit, groups at the local and national level made commitments to increase their focus on youth and support more mentoring and tutoring programs. Several companies signed on to support volunteer programs within their organizations and increase their funding for youth-related efforts. To kick off the mentoring and tutoring efforts, a historic event was held in Philadelphia and hosted by Oprah Winfrey. Many of the ideas reviewed at these meetings were implemented at the local level. Previously, in 1990, Langston Heard became a founding board member of MENTOR/National Mentoring Partnership.

In her retirement in 2004, Langston Heard joined the speaking tour of Bishop T. D. Jakes's program called "God's Leading Ladies." In addition, she wrote one book that was sold at these conferences. Langston Heard held sixteen honorary doctorate degrees, and she served as president and chief executive officer of Oxen Hill Partners, the company she cofounded in 1972.

FURTHER READING

"CEO to CEO," *Association Management* (Mar. 2004).
Heard, Marian Langston. *The Complete Leader* (2004).

JULUETTE BARTLETT PACK

Heard, Nathan Cliff (7 Nov. 1936–16 Mar. 2004), author, professor of creative writing, actor, television host, and key figure in the black crime fiction movement of the 1960s and 1970s, was born in Newark, New Jersey, the son of Gladys Pruitt Heard, a blues singer, and Nathan E. Heard, a laborer. Heard was raised by his mother and maternal grandmother, and, at the age of fifteen, he dropped out of high school. Heard spent much of the 1950s and 1960s in reform school and then in New Jersey State Prison at Trenton for armed robbery and parole violation.

Like his fellow African American crime writers Chester Himes and Donald Goines, Heard began his literary career while behind bars. It was while he was serving eight years in prison for armed robbery in the early 1960s that Heard began reading the fiction of the *Tarzan* author Edgar Rice Burroughs and other pulp writers. Heard broadened his interest in literature when a fellow inmate named Harold Carrington introduced him to the works of Langston Hughes, James Baldwin, Jean Genet, Samuel Beckett, Amiri Baraka, and Norman Mailer. Before being sent to prison, Heard had only read two books voluntarily: biographies of Lou Gehrig and Babe Ruth. After learning that a Fresno publisher named Sanford Aday was offering a $2,000 advance for book manuscripts, Heard was inspired to write novels while still in prison. His first effort was *To Reach a Dream*, the story of a street hustler who attempts to con his way out of the Newark ghetto by seducing a wealthy suburban black woman. Reminiscent of James Cain's classic noir *The Postman Always Rings Twice*, *To Reach a Dream* is at once an indictment of the American prison system and a protest against the postwar containment of working-class blacks in American inner cities. Despite its popularity among fellow inmates, Heard shelved the novel in the early 1960s and began writing what would become his first published novel, *Howard Street*.

Howard Street, the novel that established Heard's literary career, was published shortly before his release from prison in 1968. While Heard was finishing out the final years of his prison sentence for parole violation, his mother had passed the manuscript along to a lawyer named Joel Steinberg, who was impressed by the book and submitted it to Dial Press. A blunt portrayal of the Newark street life that Heard had experienced as a young man, the novel sold more than a half million copies. Though the critic Christopher Lehmann-Haupt denounced *Howard Street* as a "pot-boiler in blackface," most responses toward the novel were positive. In *Negro Digest*, NIKKI GIOVANNI called the novel "a masterpiece," while the contemporary author CLAUDE BROWN stated that Heard was "the reincarnation of RICHARD WRIGHT and a nightmarish William Faulkner of the American ghetto." The power of *Howard Street* derived from Heard's sympathetic representations of inner-city African Americans—the pimps, pushers, addicts, and gang members, all trying to survive and make meaning out of the harsh realities of Newark's postindustrial urban landscape. It remains a classic of the street genre of fiction that burgeoned in the civil rights period.

Based on the success of *Howard Street*, Heard secured a number of academic and professional opportunities. Between 1969 and 1970 he served as a guest lecturer of creative writing at California State University, Fresno, where he won the Most Distinguished Teaching Award. From 1970 to 1972 he was an assistant professor of English for Rutgers University. After the academic jobs dried up, Heard tried to support his three children, Melvin, Cliff, and Natalie, through a series of odd jobs. In the early 1970s he hosted the local television program *New Jersey Speaks*, sang in local nightclubs, and even played a pimp named Big Pink in the 1973 cult classic *Gordon's War*. In the late 1970s he wrote speeches for the Newark mayor Kenneth A. Gibson and was a regular contributor to the *New York Times*.

Throughout this period, Heard continued to write fiction. After reworking the manuscript of *To Reach a Dream* for publication in 1972, Heard embarked on *A Cold Fire Burning* (1974), a novel which, like Chester Himes's first book *If He Hollers, Let Him Go* (1945), staged the political and social dilemmas of American race relations through the narrative of a failed interracial romance. In 1977 Heard published what was regarded by most critics as his weakest novel, *When Shadows Fall*. An experimental book in which Heard conceded to the conventions of fast-paced pulp fiction, *When Shadows Fall* examines the American drug scene through the intertwining stories of a white musician named J. B. White and a prostitute named Big Red. Heard's final novel, *House of Slammers* (1983), was considered by many his best work. Based on an actual prison

strike Heard led while incarcerated in Rahway, *House of Slammers* featured lengthy debates about the penal system and graphic representations of the brutalities of prison life in America. Although seen by some as excessively didactic, H. Bruce Franklin, a cultural historian and literary critic, stated in his watershed study of American prison fiction that it was "arguably the most important novel yet published about the American prison."

Following in the tradition of urban realists like Richard Wright, Chester Himes, ROBERT BECK, CLARENCE COOPER JR., and Donald Goines, Nathan Heard represented the black American ghetto life from the perspective of an insider. The critic Richard Yarborough described Heard's work as "depict[ing] with stark and brutal frankness the violence, frustrations, thwarted dreams, and tragedies of black ghetto experience." Although Heard's books had gone out of print before his death of complications from Parkinson's disease in 2004, his work remains a testament to the everyday lives of black American street culture.

FURTHER READING

Beaumont, Eric. "The Nathan Heard Interviews," *African American Review* 28.3 (Autumn, 1994).

Franklin, H. Bruce. *The Victim as Criminal and Artist: Literature from the American Prison* (1978).

Giovanni, Nikki. "Review of Howard Street," *Negro Digest* 18 (Feb. 1969).

Lehmann-Haupt, Christopher. "Review of Howard Street," *New York Times*, 13 Dec. 1968.

Yarborough, Richard. "Nathan Heard," in *Dictionary of Literary Biography*, vol. 33: *Afro-American Fiction Writers after 1955* (1984).

JUSTIN DAVID GIFFORD

Heard, William Henry Harrison (25 June 1850–12 Sept. 1937), clergyman, politician, educator, and diplomat, was born a slave on the plantation of Thomas Jones in Elbert County, Georgia. William's mother died when he was nine, and he was obligated to rear his younger siblings while working as a plowboy. His education during his last years of enslavement (1860–1865) was in Sunday school in Elberton, Georgia. Legally prohibited from learning to read or write, he learned largely by memorizing Bible passages. But when he was fifteen the Civil War ended, and Union troops appeared. As he wrote in his memoir, *From Slavery to the Bishopric in the A.M.E. Church* (1924): "Freedom had come, and I came to meet it" (28). Freedom also meant the end of his Sunday school education, but Heard's father had earned enough money as a wheelwright to pay for William's lessons in spelling, reading, and arithmetic. From 1865 to 1867 Heard studied with private teachers and for six weeks attended classes at a "Negro school" in Elberton. In the fall of 1867 he proceeded to teach in a public school at one dollar per student per month. He also studied grammar, mathematics, and history, quickly earning a second-grade teaching certificate.

Heard was soon active in Reconstruction-era Republican Party politics. In 1872 he became chairman of the Elbert County Republican Party and ran for the state legislature. In January 1873 he moved to Mount Carmel, South Carolina, where he taught at the local high school for four years and continued his political involvement. In 1876 he was elected to the South Carolina Senate representing Abbeville County and also served as deputy U.S. marshal at the polls, guarding against ballot tampering. A few days after the election he was kidnapped by Democrats, bound, and taken to Elbert County, Georgia, for the night. He made his way back to Augusta, where he "made an affidavit of the vote of my precinct, which gave the State to Hayes and Wheeler" (*From Slavery to the Bishopric*, 43). He served as a South Carolina state senator until 1877, at which time federal troops withdrew and Republican Reconstruction ended.

Heard had won a scholarship to enter the University of South Carolina freshman class of 1876, but in 1877, with the Democrats returning to power, the university was closed to blacks. His legislative career was over, his educational opportunities were closed, and he was blacklisted as a teacher "because of politics." He returned to Georgia, opening a school at the African Methodist Episcopal (AME) Church of Athens. In Georgia, Heard entered Clarke University and then Atlanta University (1878–1879) as well as reading law with an Athens attorney. But in May 1879 he underwent what he later called a "regeneration" experience: "at a protracted meeting in Athens, Georgia, April and May, 1879, ... I reached the conclusion that open confession of my sins and acknowledgement of Christ as My Saviour was the thing to do.... After some time standing on my feet, being unable to speak, FAITH CAME, my mouth flew open and I shouted for joy" (*From Slavery to the Bishopric*, 64–65). He became an exhorter (a preacher who was not ordained) for three months and then, after preaching a trial sermon, received a local preacher's license. His ministerial career consumed him for the rest of his life.

Over the next fifteen years Heard served a number of AME churches: Johnston, Georgia (1880–1881),

Atlanta (1881–1883), Aiken, South Carolina (1883–1885), Charleston (1885–1888), Philadelphia, Pennsylvania (1888–1889, 1890–1892), Lancaster, Pennsylvania (1889–1890), Wilmington, Delaware (1892–1894), and Harrisburg, Pennsylvania (1894). He became noted for his ability to build his church's congregation, increase its financial resources, and, in some instances, construct new edifices. Until 1883 he supported himself as a federal railway postal clerk, but in order to take up the Aiken pastorate he gave up his postal job.

Heard was serving the Mount Zion church in Charleston when a devastating earthquake destroyed seven-eighths of the city's houses on 31 August 1886. Heard worked to ensure that black victims received their share of the relief money. His church having suffered considerable damage, he traveled to Philadelphia, Baltimore, New York, and Boston for assistance. This trip to the North, Heard later wrote, "opened up a new world to me" (*From Slavery to the Bishopric*, 47). One aspect of his new vision was the injustice of Jim Crow railroad cars. As a result, in October 1887 he argued successfully before the newly created Interstate Commerce Commission that the Georgia Railroad had a legal obligation to provide equal accommodation for passengers of color.

In February 1895 President Grover Cleveland appointed Heard U.S. minister to Liberia, an appointment that he accepted only after it was agreed that he could continue his church-related activities. He became, then, superintendent of the Liberia Annual Conference and in March 1895 sailed for Europe. In London he visited the British Museum and later observed that "The Pharaohs and Rameses [*sic*] are here to be seen, and no one can mistake them for Caucasian; they are African. These mummies are the exact likenesses of those old kings and show that they belong to the Hamitic race" (*From Slavery to the Bishopric*, 49). In Liberia, Heard pursued his church work. The American Colonization Society was interested in developing a public school system in Liberia and increasing Liberian-American shipping. Under the organization's auspices Heard had led two hundred former slaves from Savannah, Georgia, to Liberia. The group then purchased land and built the first AME church in Monrovia—later known as Elias Turner Memorial Chapel.

In 1896 Heard returned to the United States for two months to attend the AME General Conference at Wilmington, North Carolina, as delegate from Liberia. His subsequent return to Liberia via France afforded him an opportunity to observe race relations there. "This country is the highest in its recognition of man without regard to color of any I have ever visited…. Prejudice … among the Latin races is not so apparent as on this side of the Channel among the English-speaking people. America puts her virus into these people from New York weekly, and they seem to be easily inoculated, so that in certain parts of London and Liverpool the prejudice is as great as in New York" (*From Slavery to the Bishopric*, 58–59). In 1898, at the end of his tenure in Liberia, Heard published *The Bright Side of African Life*, an effort, he wrote, to "cause the sun to shine" on the facts of Liberia, "to show the present and future grandeur of this black Republic." The book reflected his realism and optimism. "There is vast wealth," he remarked, "in her bowels and forests—iron, silver, coal, gold and other metals. There are no woods in the world superior to the rosewood and mahogany…. The fruits of all tropical climes abound here" (60). He argued that Liberia's future "depends on the men who stand at the head of affairs…. She needs strong, patriotic men at the helm of State. It is a wonder she has existed so long as a nation under existing circumstances, but strong men have held her in the place of national recognition" (96).

His diplomatic service behind him, Heard devoted the years from 1898 to 1908 to church work. He led Zion Mission, Philadelphia, (1898–1899), was presiding elder of the Long Island District (1899–1900), moved to the Philadelphia Annual Conference (1901), and served for four months in Phoenixville, Pennsylvania. In August 1901 he was transferred to the Allen Temple of Atlanta, where he served as pastor until 1904, increasing church membership and decreasing its debts. Such was his standing by this time in his life that BOOKER T. WASHINGTON commented in 1902 that efforts to get 100,000 African Americans to move to the Congo would succeed only if Heard were one of the leaders behind the plan.

At the 1904 General Conference, Heard was elected secretary-treasurer of the Connectional Preachers' Aid and Mutual Relief Society and from 1904 to 1908 traveled nationwide, without additional salary, in that capacity. "I attended every Annual Conference in the A.M.E. Church. Yearly I spent four months on the road, two and three nights in a week curled up on a bench in a 'Jim Crow' car" (*From Slavery to the Bishopric*, 60). In 1908 Heard was elected the thirty-fifth bishop of the AME Church. He was assigned to the Thirteenth District in West Africa, comprising the Liberia, Sierra Leone, and Gold Coast Conferences, and served there from 1909 to 1916.

Returning to the United States in the midst of World War I, Heard continued to serve as bishop in the Mississippi/Louisiana district (1916–1920) and the Middle Atlantic/New England district (1920–1937). In 1924 he published his memoir, a book embodying his faith and positive outlook: "Men make progress without opportunity," he wrote, "and they ought to be encouraged to use the opportunities they have to make greater progress…. I am sending forth these words of a life lived in the midst of privation, ignorance, and slavery, hoping that they may be a means in this enlightened day, of helping those who have a better opportunity and who are encouraged to use those opportunities" (*From Slavery to the Bishopric*, 15, 17). Heard also participated in the formation of new churches in Roselle, New Jersey (1924), and Pembroke, Bermuda (1935).

A man of seemingly infinite energy, Heard traveled at age eighty-seven once again to Europe to attend the World Conference on Faith and Order in Edinburgh, Scotland (August 1937). In Edinburgh he was refused a room at a hotel because, according to the hotel's manager, "some American tourists show antipathy to Negroes" (*New York Times*, 9 Aug. 1937). Heard instead found a small hotel and declined the invitation of the archbishop of York to stay with him. After the conference Heard returned to his home in Philadelphia on 23 August 1937. He died less than three weeks later at Hahnemann Hospital, Philadelphia. His wife, Josephine Delphine Henderson Heard, whom he had married in 1882, had predeceased him in 1921. During his lifetime Heard had risen from slavery to the pinnacle of leadership in his church. Ambitious, optimistic, loyal to the Republican Party, he dedicated his career to education, his religious faith, and the uplifting of his people.

FURTHER READING
Materials related to Heard's diplomatic career can be found in the records of the State Department, Dispatches from U. S. Ministers to Liberia, 1863–1906. M 170, rolls 11–12, National Archives, Washington, D.C.

Heard, William H. *The Bright Side of African Life* (1898; rpt. 1969).

Heard, William H. *From Slavery to the Bishopric in the A.M.E. Church* (1924; rpt. 1969).

"Catholics Reject Bid to Church Parley." *New York Times*, 8 Aug. 1937.

New York Age, 22 Oct. 1887.

"Simon Decries Hotel Snub to U.S. Negro in Scotland." *New York Times*, 9 Aug. 1937.

Obituary: *New York Times*, 13 Sept. 1937.

KENNETH J. BLUME

influenced the jury's decision to award him ownership of the north half of the plantation and confirm
Prendergast's ownership of the south half. Hearne
found it odd that she had given her lawyer half of
her plantation to defend her half, but he, in losing
the case, managed to keep his half and lose her half.
The court ordered Prendergast to retain possession
of the entire plantation for the purposes of adminis-
trating the estate according to the provisions of the
will. He subsequently allowed the estate's debts to go
unpaid, neglected making annual accountings, and
sued Hearne, his own client, to perfect his title to
the south half of the plantation.

By the late 1870s Prendergast's collusion with
his so-called tenants to defraud Hearne out of
income from the estate evolved into a scheme to
cheat her out of all her remaining interest in it.
Sam's cousin's son, Henry Lee Lewis, in collusion
with Prendergast purchased at discounts the Hall
judgment and the estate's unpaid debts. When
Prendergast dismissed the appeal of the Hall judgment, Lewis became the owner of the north half
of the plantation. But Prendergast had never once
consulted Hearne, whom he characterized as an
ignorant freedwoman, about her legal options in
any of the litigation in which she was involved.

Hearne hired her longtime nemesis Hamman
to sue Prendergast. In a remarkable lawsuit that
mingled multiple claims, including attorney malpractice, fraud, breach of fiduciary duty, failure to
make required accountings, as well as trespass to
try title, Hamman described his client's disadvan-
tages when dealing with a sophisticated lawyer and
businessman like Prendergast in the hope that fair-
ness would prevail over a narrow ruling of the law.
Behind the scenes Prendergast and Lewis tried to
get Hearne to sign a release to all her interest in
the plantation. She steadfastly refused, even though
their tendered consideration for a compromise
agreement increased as the trial date approached.

The court ruled against Hearne. Her appeal was
dismissed on a legal technicality. After a final fleec-
ing of the estate's remaining assets, Prendergast
petitioned to end his administration. He never submitted a final accounting. In retrospect, although
divested of her entire lawful inheritance, many of
Hearne's actions had been reasonable given the
limited choices available to her. At one point she
came tantalizingly close to setting a precedent in
the virtually underdeveloped Texas case law dealing with attorney malpractice and misconduct. But
the manipulation by whites of a judicial system
insensitive to providing justice to those denied it

under the application of the common law exposed
the limits during Reconstruction to what could
possibly have been achieved in the way of securing
genuine legal equality not only for Azeline Hearne
but also for millions of other former slaves.

There is no record or collective memory of when
Hearne died. The last known reference indicating
that she was still alive suggests that she probably
reached her sixtieth birthday. By then, and previously for over a decade, she relied on her cherished
network of black friends and acquaintances for
her survival. If she died in the Robertson County
bottomlands, which was extremely likely, then her
neighbors would surely have buried her next to
Sam on the Brazos River plantation near the ruins
of the original manor house that he had built in the
early 1850s.

FURTHER READING

The case files initiated in Robertson County regarding
Azeline Hearne are located the county courthouse
in Franklin, Texas. They are filed in the Office of the
District Clerk under "Civil [and Criminal] Cases
Disposed Of. June 26, 1843– [Papers filed in civil
cases instituted originally and by appeal in district
court]."

Baum, Dale. *Counterfeit Justice: A Texas Freedwoman's
Story* (forthcoming).

DALE BAUM

Hearns, Thomas (18 Oct. 1958–), boxer, was born
Thomas Hearns in Memphis, Tennessee. His mother,
Lois Hearns, was a boxing promoter in Detroit, but
no other information about his immediate family is
known.

Hearns began his boxing career with a splendid
record as an amateur fighter. With more than 155
fights before turning professional, Hearns suffered
just eight losses. In 1977 he won both the Golden
Gloves and National AAU championships in the
welterweight division. That same year, Hearns, who
had moved to Detroit to train in the Kronk Gym,
turned professional. During the next two and a half
years, Hearns reeled off twenty-eight straight victories. What surprised most boxing observers, however, was the fact that Hearns, generally regarded
as more of a boxer than a puncher, knocked out
twenty-six of those opponents, often within the
first three rounds. Most were journeymen fighters, but he knocked out Harold Weston, the former
welterweight champion Bruce Curry, and Angel
Espada for the USBA welterweight title. In 1980
Hearns was matched against the hard-punching

WBA welterweight champ Pipino Cuevas. In just two rounds, Hearns destroyed the Mexican fighter and claimed the championship. He defended the title three times, and then in 1981 was matched against the WBC welterweight champion SUGAR RAY LEONARD for the world welterweight championship. It was one of the fights of the decade, not only because it matched two fighters at the absolute peak of their abilities but because also Hearns and Leonard seemed such different fighters and personalities. Leonard was boxing's golden boy, an Olympic gold medalist whose good looks seemed made for television. He was also confident to the point of arrogance, sometimes taunted and played with opponents in the ring, and had earned the scorn of some boxing purists as more flash than substance. Hearns, on the other hand, was quiet and unassuming, preferring to let his fists do his talking. A fan favorite, he was a warrior who preferred a knockout to a decision. The fight took place on 16 September 1981. For much of the early part of the fight, Hearns scored repeatedly with jabs and hard right hands, damaging the area around Leonard's left eye. The

injury caused severe swelling and a detached retina that would eventually lead to Leonard's first retirement from boxing. The brutal pace of the fight, however, began to take its toll on Hearns, who tired in the later rounds. Leonard, summoning up courage that many fight fans had believed he lacked, battered Hearns into submission in the fourteenth round and won the bout by TKO.

Hearns regrouped after the devastating defeat and decided to move up in weight and campaign as a junior middleweight. In 1982 he challenged one of the slickest boxers in the sport, Wilfredo Benitez, for the junior middleweight title. Hearns, utilizing his boxing skills, outpointed Benitez over fifteen rounds to win his second world championship. His next significant fight came in 1984 when he fought the legendary Roberto Duran. Duran was a rugged and highly skilled competitor who had rarely been knocked down, much less knocked out. In the second round, one vicious right hand from Hearns put Duran down and out for the count. The destruction of Duran set up one of the anticipated fights of the 1980s, when Hearns moved up in weight once again

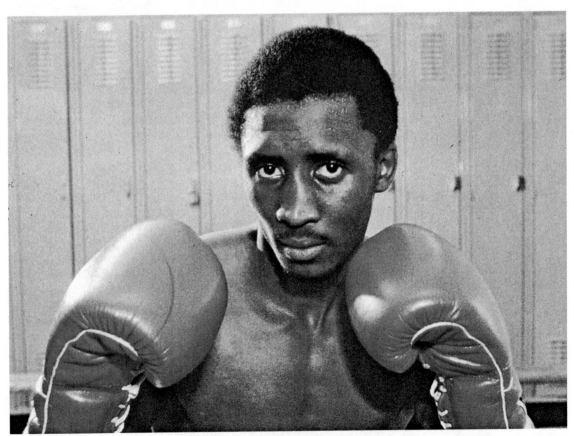

Thomas Hearns in 1980. (AP Images.)

to challenge the undisputed middleweight champion of the world, Marvelous MARVIN HAGLER.

The fearsome Hagler had been champion since 1980 and had defended his crown ten times, nine by knockout. On 15 April 1985 the two men met in a Las Vegas matchup promoted by DON KING, in what was to become one of the greatest middleweight title fights of all time. The lead-up to the fight had attracted much media attention, and Hearns's taunts had sparked outrage from Hagler's camp. From the moment the fight began, it was clear that there would be no preliminary jabbing and feinting. Hearns and Hagler began throwing vicious punches from the outset. Hearns landed some hard shots, and Hagler suffered a cut that quickly developed into a vertical gash above his eye. However, by the end of the first round it was obvious that in terms of sheer firepower, Hagler was winning the war. Round two picked up where the first round left off, with both men looking to land damaging blows with each punch. Hagler's punches were more effective, however, and Hearns began to wilt under the constant pressure. In the third round, Hagler stalked Hearns and finally landed a series of devastating punches that put Hearns down and out. Although the fight lasted less than three rounds, the Hearns-Hagler match ranks near the top of boxing history in terms of intensity and brutality.

Hearns did not fight again for nearly a year after his war with Hagler. He won the North American Boxing Federation middleweight championship with a quick knockout of James Shuler in March 1986. In 1987 he surprised everyone by moving up to challenge the light heavyweight champion Dennis Andries, knocking him out in the tenth round to take hold of his third world championship. Just a few months later, he dropped back down to middleweight and wrested the WBC title from Juan Domingo Roldan. In June 1988 Hearns was stunned by Iran Barkley, who knocked him out in the third round and took the middleweight championship belt. A few months later, Hearns added the less meaningful World Boxing Organization super middleweight title by beating James Kinchen. In 1989 Hearns finally got a rematch with Leonard, this time for the latter's WBC super middleweight belt. Hearns seemed in control for most of the fight, knocking Leonard down twice. But Leonard hurt Hearns in round five, and a barrage of punches by Leonard late in round 12 had Hearns reeling against the ropes. At the conclusion of the fight the judges ruled it a draw, much to the disappointment of the crowd and Hearns, who felt he earned a decision win. Even Leonard admitted

that he and Hearns were now "one and one" in their fights against one another.

In the next decade Hearns fought just a handful of significant fights. He beat Virgil Hill in 1991 for the WBA light heavyweight title, but lost it the next year to his old nemesis Iran Barkley. In 1999 Hearns defeated Nate Miller for the International Boxing Organization's cruiserweight title. In a bizarre ending to his fight with Uriah Grant in 2000, Hearns was forced to retire in his corner after he severely turned his ankle during the bout. Into the twenty-first century, with extremely slurred speech testifying to damage sustained during his long boxing career, Hearns defied the advice of nearly the entire boxing community in keeping open the possibility of returning to the ring for one last shot.

FURTHER READING

Ashe, Arthur. *A Hard Road to Glory: A History of the African-American Athlete since 1946* (1988).
Sugar, Bert Randolph. *Boxing's Greatest Fighters* (2006).

MICHAEL L. KRENN

Heath, Gordon (20 Sept. 1918–28 Aug. 1991), actor, musician, and theater director, was born in New York City the only child of Cyril Gordon Heath, an immigrant from Barbados, and Hattie Hooper. At age six Gordon enrolled in the Ethical Culture Society school in Manhattan, a well-known private and progressive educational institution. His musical education began at age eight when an aunt gave him violin lessons. Although he studied other instruments, he was most drawn to the guitar. In high school Gordon won prizes in both art and music and began performing in amateur theater groups, earning first place in a municipal drama competition. After his high school graduation he earned scholarships to two music schools and briefly attended the Dalcroze Institute before deciding to pursue an acting career instead.

When he joined New York radio station WMCA in 1945, Heath became the first black staff announcer at a major radio station in the United States. Many critics commented throughout his radio and theater career that Heath possessed a magnificent voice. In 1945, at age twenty-seven, Heath scored a major Broadway success starring in the play *Deep Are the Roots*, written by Araud d'Assue and James Gow and directed by the legendary theater and film director Elia Kazan. Heath played a black World War II military hero who returns to the Deep South after the war and falls in love with the daughter of a wealthy white family for whom his mother works as a housekeeper. Heath's dynamic performance was highly praised by drama critics around the country.

When the play closed after an impressive fourteen-month run, Heath traveled to London to reprise his role in a West End production, also directed by Kazan, once again receiving critical acclaim. A great commercial and critical success in both the United States and Europe, Heath seem assured of further stardom, but the virulent racism and discrimination of the period stymied his career prospects. Instead of more opportunities, he was rebuffed, and quality work on the American stage or screen was nearly impossible for him to find. As a result, when the London run ended Heath remained in England, appearing in, writing, and directing other stage productions.

In 1948 he settled in Paris, which he considered far more hospitable to African Americans. He also found Paris more accepting of his homosexuality and his relationship with his white lover, Lee Payant, a fellow actor whom he had met in New York in the early 1940s. Like so many other black and white American expatriates fleeing racism and homophobia, Heath found a haven in the cosmopolitan and progressive artistic atmosphere of Paris. In 1949 Heath and Payant became co-owners of L'Abbaye, a Paris nightclub so named because it was behind the abbey church of St. Germain des Prés. For nearly thirty years the pair entertained appreciative audiences, playing guitar and singing duets of American and French folk songs.

Throughout the 1950s Heath continued to act in many classical and modern theatrical productions in France and throughout Europe, including a critically acclaimed London performance as Othello in 1950 and again in a 1955 BBC television production. In 1957 Electra Records released an album of Heath's duets with Payant titled *An Evening at L'Abbaye*, comprising seventeen songs, five in French. Heath and Payant also recorded an album in 1954 titled *French Canadian Folk Songs*, and in the same year Heath released a self-titled solo album. Meanwhile Heath appeared in many other British television productions, starring in a revival of *Deep Are the Roots* in 1950, Eugene O'Neill's *Emperor Jones* in 1953, and an adaptation of Alan Paton's novel *Cry, the Beloved Country* in 1958. Despite the continued positive reception of his performances onstage and on television, Heath did not receive any offers for major parts in movies either in the United States or in Europe. He narrated John Halas and Joy Batchelor's animated film of George Orwell's *Animal Farm* in 1956 and contributed small supporting roles in a number of movies in France over the next three decades. Heath and Payant also dubbed many films.

In the 1960s Heath turned his talents to directing, working for a decade with the Studio Theatre of Paris, an English-language company that staged plays by Thornton Wilder, Arthur Miller, and Bertolt Brecht, among others. Heath also began appearing periodically on the American stage, performing as Faust in *Faustus* at Howard University in 1962 and writing and directing plays for a number of college and university theater companies. Throughout the 1970s Heath continued working with the Studio Theatre of Paris, serving as a mentor to many aspiring actors and directors in Europe and the United States.

In December 1976 Heath was devastated when Payant, his lover and partner of more than three decades, died of cancer. Anguished by his loss he could not bear continuing to work at L'Abbaye alone and returned to live in the United States, where he acted, directed, and taught in college and repertory theater productions for the next five years. Eventually Heath decided to return to France, where he found a new partner, Alain Woisson. In the mid-1980s Heath was commissioned to write a biographical memoir of his childhood, adolescence, and early adulthood and his experiences as a black expatriate artist, teacher, and intellectual in Paris after World War II. The book *Deep Are the Roots: Memoirs of a Black Expatriate* was published posthumously by the University of Massachusetts Press in 1992 to excellent reviews. Heath died of an AIDS-related illness in 1991.

FURTHER READING

Heath, Gordon. *Deep Are the Roots: Memoirs of a Black Expatriate* (1992).

Obituaries: *New York Times*, 31 Aug. 1991; *Independent* (London), 13 Sept. 1991.

KOFI NATAMBU

Heath, Jimmy (25 Oct. 1926–), jazz saxophonist, composer-arranger, and teacher, was born James Edward Heath, one of four children, in Philadelphia, Pennsylvania, to Percy Heath Sr., an auto mechanic and amateur clarinetist, and Arlethia, a hairdresser who sang in the church choir. His brothers Percy and Albert (TOOTIE HEATH) also went on to become noted jazz musicians. His parents bought their first home in 1945 on the south side of Philadelphia, and it became a place for musicians to gather, make music, and have meals.

Heath was sent to Wilmington, North Carolina, to attend school when he was fourteen. This was where his grandparents lived and owned a local food market. It was during this time that he began to pursue music, playing an alto sax his father sent him as a Christmas present. Just five feet three inches tall, Heath was considered too small to play competitive sports and found an outlet in jazz music. For work, he was a clerk at his grandparents' store and did deliveries across town on his bicycle. As his musical skills improved, Heath joined the high school marching band. He thrived on private lessons but attributed years of listening to Benny Clark and JOHNNY HODGES as a direct influence on his decision to become a professional musician.

In 1945, a year or two after graduating from high school, Heath took one of his first jazz band jobs with the Nat Towles Band in Omaha, Nebraska. By the age of twenty-one, he had formed his own band in Philadelphia, including JOHN COLTRANE, Benny Golson, and RAY BRYANT. Heath worked often with his brother Percy, practicing and playing together on gigs. CHARLIE PARKER would sit in occasionally and got to know Heath, fondly naming him "Little Bird." Sometime around 1949 or 1950 he joined DIZZY GILLESPIE's Big Band. Seeking his own sound, Heath moved to the tenor saxophone in 1951, and by doing so he increased his work opportunities. That same year, Heath performed in the first International Jazz Festival in Paris with HOWARD B. McGHEE, also sharing the stage with ERROLL GARNER and SLAM STEWART. Like many jazz musicians of this era, Heath was exposed to drugs and ended up in jail on a related charge from 1955 to 1959. He picked up right where he had left off musically in 1959, playing with MILES DAVIS's band in New York.

In 1959 Heath met Mona Alice Brown, an art student at the Rhode Island School of Design. Brown had grown up near Atlantic City, New Jersey, and was a big fan of jazz. Heath's brother Percy introduced them, and they hit it off right away. They were married in 1960 in Philadelphia, and later relocated to Flushing, New York. Mona worked as a teacher's aide and as a full-time mother to their two children: a daughter, Roslyn, and a son, Jeffrey. Heath also had a son, James Mtume, and grandson, Faulu Mtume, with a previous partner.

By the time Heath was thirty-three he was playing in New York City, often with Miles Davis, Kenny Dorham, and Gil Evans. During the 1960s he recorded with MILT JACKSON and Art Farmer,

including the famous tunes "Gingerbread Boy" and "CTA." A 1960 album, *Really Big*, was a breakthrough for Heath and helped build his acclaim, both as a musician and as a songwriter. One standout song on that album was "Big P," written for his big brother, Percy. In 1975 Heath and his brothers, Percy and Tootie, formed the Heath Brothers. Touring around the world, the brothers released seven albums over a three-decade span.

During his career, Heath performed most often with small groups. He was featured on more than one hundred record albums. He authored more than 125 compositions, many of which have become jazz standards. Heath also ventured into writing longer musical compositions, including seven suites and several string quartets. He premiered his first symphonic work, "Three Ears," in 1988 in New York with Maurice Peress conducting. In 1992 BILL COSBY produced a big band swing album, *Little Man Big Band*, with Heath as the lead musician and composer. The release demonstrated Heath's status as a journeyman and widely respected musician. The album featured Heath with strong backing by many members of the American Jazz Orchestra, a true big band performance on a grand scale for the sixty-five-year-old Heath.

Heath was known as a detail-oriented musician and a skilled songwriter. He grew up in the swing era but diversified his skills as a hard bebop player, exploring various musical styles and taking wide ranging roads in his own experimentation in jazz. Heath used his honed creativity and improvisational skill throughout his career in many musical styles and genres, including swing, bebop, or even classical music.

Heath was hired in 1987 as the first professor of jazz music at the Aaron Copland School of Music at Queens College in New York. Heath was able to do this full-time while continuing to perform, compose, and tour. He stayed at Queens College for eleven years.

Heath received a number of awards and accolades, including Grammy nominations for his work (1980, 1994, 1995). He was named a Jazz Master by the National Endowment for the Arts (2003), received an honorary doctorate from Juilliard School of Music (2002), and was honored with more than a dozen other acknowledgements.

FURTHER READING

Heath, Jimmy. *I Walked with the Giants: An Autobiography of Jimmy Heath* (2007).

JAMES FARGO BALLIETT

Heath, Percy (30 Apr. 1923–28 Apr. 2005), jazz musician and Tuskegee airman, was born in Wilmington, North Carolina, to Arelethia and Percy Heath Sr. Heath was raised in Philadelphia, Pennsylvania, as well as in his parents' native North Carolina, and graduated from Williston High School in Wilmington. The Heaths were a musical family; his mother, a hairdresser, sang in a church choir, and his father, an automobile mechanic, was an amateur clarinetist. Heath studied violin as a child and sang in the church choir. Both of his younger brothers, JIMMY HEATH and Albert TOOTIE HEATH, were also well-known accomplished jazz musicians. During World War II, Heath volunteered for the army, but was rejected (which Heath attributed to racism). He was eventually drafted into the U.S. Army Air Corps and became a fighter pilot with the Tuskegee Airmen, an elite group of black fliers, from 1943 to 1945. He did not fly combat missions.

After the war, Heath returned to Philadelphia, where his family had moved. In 1946 he enrolled at the Granoff School of Music in Philadelphia to study the double bass. In addition to his formal training, Heath studied with the bassist CHARLES MINGUS. Heath was a quick learner and within six months began to play with the Hollis Hoppers trio, then joined the house jazz band at the Down Beat nightclub in Philadelphia. He joined HOWARD MCGHEE's sextet with his brother Jimmy, playing in Chicago, Detroit, and New York City. In 1948 they performed at the International Jazz Festival in Paris, France.

In 1949, Heath moved to New York City with his white girlfriend June, because they could not get a marriage license in Pennsylvania. They married and had three sons. He and his brother Jimmy, a saxophone player and composer, joined DIZZY GILLESPIE's group in 1950. In 1952 Percy Heath became a founding member of The Modern Jazz Quarter (MJQ) with MILT JACKSON, JOHN LEWIS (1920–2001), and KENNY CLARKE. The MJQ lasted from 1952 until 1952. In 1954 Heath won the New Star award from *Down Beat*. The quartet, dressed elegantly in suits or tuxedos, played "chamber jazz," based on classical music, quoting Bach, which became known as "third stream" jazz.

Percy then formed the Heath Brothers Quartet, with Jimmy on saxophone, Al "Tootie" on drums, and Stanley Cowell on piano. While Percy was mostly a background player for the MJQ, rarely playing a solo, he was much more prominent with the Heath Brothers, playing melodies and solos, often with a cello tuned like a bass, which he referred to as a "baby bass." He also played the piccolo bass.

The Heath Brothers' music was not as structured or disciplined as the MJQ. The MJQ re-formed in 1981, and continued to play until 1997, having issued over forty recordings. The brothers disbanded in 1983 after recording their last album *Brother and Others*, until reuniting in 1997 with *As We Were Saying* on the Concord Records label. Albert joined the MJQ when their drummer died.

In 2002 the National Endowment for the Arts (NEA) honored Heath as a Jazz Master, the highest honor for a jazz musician in the United States. Other awards include Maria Fisher Award given by the Thelonious Monk Jazz Institute to "to an individual who has made essential and valuable contributions to jazz education and the jazz tradition," and France's Cross of Officer of Arts and Letters. It was not until 2004 that he released an album on which he was the lead musician, on the Daddy Jazz label, adding to more than two hundred jazz albums on which he played his lifetime. The solo album *A Love Song* garnered excellent reviews.

When Heath tired of life on the road, the MJQ finally disbanded. Heath performed occasionally with his brothers, but preferred fishing where lived in Montauk on Long Island, New York. Even while traveling with the MJQ, he often brought his fishing rod with him. He was awarded an honorary degree from Berklee College of Music in Boston, Massachusetts, in 1989, and in 2002 Heath received an honorary Doctor of Fine Arts from the University of North Carolina at Wilmington, and was awarded a star on their Walk of Fame. During his career, he played with most jazz greats, including Dizzy Gillespie, JOHN COLTRANE, MILES DAVIS, Charlie Parker, and THELONIOUS MONK, playing bebop, hard bebop, and cool jazz. He also performed for both Presidents Nixon and Clinton at the White House. His name, along with his brothers', is on a brass plaque on Broad Street in Philadelphia. Heath died of bone cancer on Long Island, the last surviving member of the Modern Jazz Quartet. A memorial plaque to Heath was erected at Turtle Cove by the water in Montauk, honoring him as "The Fiddler."

FURTHER READING

Condit, Rick. The Heath Brothers: Giants of Jazz. *Jazz Education Journal* 35, no. 5 (March–April 2003).

Snyder, John, and David Schroeder. *Jimmy and Percy Heath* [DVD] (2007).

Obituaries: *New York Times*, 29 Apr. 2005; *Los Angeles Times*, 30 Apr. 2006.

JANE BRODSKY FITZPATRICK

Heath, Tootie (31 May 1935–), jazz drummer, was born Albert Heath in Philadelphia, Pennsylvania, to Percy Heath Sr., an auto mechanic and clarinetist, and Arlethia, a hairdresser who sang in the church choir. He was the younger brother of the bassist Percy Heath and the saxophonist JIMMY HEATH, who would also go on to become world-famous jazz musicians. From the 1940s through the 1960s, Philadelphia, like Detroit and Newark, New Jersey, was a pivotal center in the history of jazz, spawning many talented musicians. More artists were based in Philadelphia during this time than any other city, except perhaps New York. Tootie's brother Jimmy was instrumental in the mid-1950s East Coast development of "hard bop," a style that combined the harmonic complexity of the-alto saxophonist CHARLIE PARKER and the trumpeter DIZZY GILLESPIE with a more accessible blues-oriented approach that was influenced by black gospel music.

Tootie Heath moved to New York City in 1957 and first recorded on the saxophonist JOHN COLTRANE's debut as a leader, *Coltrane*. Following that milestone, Heath joined the trombonist J. J. JOHNSON's band from 1958 to 1960, and then, in 1960 and 1961, worked with the Art Farmer / Benny Golson Jazztet, featuring Golson on saxophone, Farmer on trumpet, and the pianist Cedar Walton. Testifying to this unit's timeless sound, the Jazztet's material recorded between 16 September 1960 and 9 January 1961 has been rereleased and repackaged so often as to guarantee its availability to the public into perpetuity. Radio broadcasts from Manhattan's famous Birdland club on 15 and 22 October 1960 and 29 July 1961, plus another on 1 July 1961 from Newport, Rhode Island, generated additional public awareness. A live album was recorded at the Birdhouse in Chicago on 15 May 1961. The Jazztet reunited intermittently for tours and recordings, including Japan in 1982 and Italy in-1983.

Always active as a freelance drummer, Heath also worked regularly with the trumpeters NAT ADDERLEY and Kenny Dorham, the guitarist WES MONTGOMERY, and the pianists BOBBY TIMMONS, Mal Waldron and Tommy Flanagan. On 4 June 1963 he recorded with the pianist McCOY TYNER and the bassist Jimmy Garrison, both fellow Philadelphians and members of Coltrane's classic quartet, on Tyner's *Today and Tomorrow*. As a member of the Riverside Records rhythm-section stable, he recorded with a veritable "who's who" of jazz stars. In 1965 Heath expatriated to Stockholm and secured an engagement with the pianist Kenny Drew in the house band at the Montmarte Jazzhus in Copenhagen. There, for three years from 1965 to 1968, he performed frequently with the tenor saxophone titans DEXTER GORDON and Johnny Griffin and backed visiting American jazz legends such as the saxophonists BEN WEBSTER, COLEMAN HAWKINS, and LESTER YOUNG. Heath's tenure at this storied jazz club was depicted in Niels Lan Doky's 2005 documentary film *Between a Smile and a Tear*.

Upon Heath's return to the United States in 1968, the pianist HERBIE HANCOCK was preparing his first sextet projects after leaving his position in the high-visibility "second great quintet" led by the trumpeter MILES DAVIS. Another former Davis sideman, the bassist Ron Carter, recommended Heath to Hancock. In the liner notes for April 1969's *The Prisoner*, inspired by the recently martyred Reverend Dr. MARTIN LUTHER KING JR., the keyboardist/composer noted Heath's contribution: "Tootie is playing things I never heard him play before; he uses the drums as a total involvement and he can really swing … very tasty, very flexible and his big ears listen to everything!" The follow-up to this critically acclaimed work was *Fat Albert Rotunda*, an evolution of the theme music requested by the comedian BILL COSBY for a television special, which was released in 1970.

Hancock was a guest artist on Heath's first recording as a leader, *Kawaida* (1969), a reference to ancient Egyptian Maatian moral teachings and philosophy. Just as Hancock had taken the Swahili name "Mwandishi" (composer), Heath began using "Kuumba" (creativity) for himself, and entered into a steady working relationship with the saxophonist/flautist YUSEF LATEEF from 1970 through 1974. *Kwanza* ("the first" or "first fruits"), another recording led by Heath, was released in 1973, and because of his insatiable interest in the origins of various music from cultures around the world, he studied with master percussionists from Ghana, Nigeria, and Jamaica.

After Tootie Heath spent another year freelancing in Europe, the Heath Brothers officially started performing worldwide as a "jazz family," beginning between 1975 and 1978, continuing throughout the 1980s and 1990s, and recording seven albums together. The drummer moved to Los Angeles in 1976, the same year he appeared on the Spanish pianist Tete Montoliu's recording *Tootie's Tempo*. Heath later participated in the music for the 1980s television situation comedies *Easy Street* and *Frank's Place*. A veteran of more than six hundred recordings, including those of the Riverside (Records) Reunion Band, the pianist Billy Taylor, the saxophonists Harold Land, RAHSAAN ROLAND KIRK, and ANTHONY BRAXTON, the vibraphonist MILT JACKSON, and the Modern Jazz Quartet, Heath also became producer and leader of the Whole Drum Truth, an all-percussion jazz ensemble featuring the legendary drummers Ben Riley, Ed Thigpen, BILLY HART, Charli Persip, and Louis Hayes. Heath joined the faculty of Stanford University's Jazz Workshop in 1986, in addition to holding many other artist-in-residence positions at UCLA, CalArts, Santa Monica College, and the 2002 Monterey Jazz Festival. He taught music appreciation classes in Southern California African American high schools and received the DUKE ELLINGTON Fellowship Medal from Yale University in 2003. In 2005 the Bay Area filmmaker Jesse Block, with the music aficionado Danny Scher, produced a seventy-three minute tribute starring the Heath siblings, *Brotherly Jazz: The Music and Stories of Percy, Jimmy & Albert "Tootie" Heath*, which was shown at the California Film Institute's Mill Valley Film Festival. Tootie and his brother Jimmy were honored by Lincoln Center's Jazz from Coast to Coast series at New York City's Rose Theater on 10–11 March 2006 in a program titled *Philadelphia: City of Brotherly Jazz*.

FURTHER READING
Feather, Leonard. *Encyclopedia of Jazz* (1978, 1984).
Wong, Herb. Liner notes for *The Prisoner* (1969).
JIM MILLER

Hector, Edward (Ned) (c. 1744–3 Jan. 1834), Revolutionary War veteran, was born a freeman and lived in the Norristown, Pennsylvania, area. Though nothing is recorded of Hector's life before the war, his experiences during the war indicate he may have made living as a drayman. Nicknamed "Ned," Hector began his service in the Revolution on 10 March 1777 when he joined the company of Captain Hercules Courtenay in Proctor's Third Pennsylvania Artillery Regiment as a wagoneer. Though it is often recorded that Hector was a private in his artillery regiment, it is more likely that he was a civilian hired by the army to help provide transportation services. The team of horses he worked with in the artillery company, pulling wagons loaded with guns and ammunition, may have been his own property.

Hector was present with the Third Pennsylvania Artillery during the Battle of Brandywine, fought during the American campaign to defend Philadelphia. His regiment was located near Chadd's Ford on 11 September 1777 when British forces made a determined advance and caused American forces to retreat. When the Third Pennsylvania was ordered to abandon its position, Hector made a defiant stand, stating, "The enemy shall not have my team; I will save my horses, or perish myself." With these words, Hector loaded a stack of abandoned muskets in his wagon and escaped with his wagon while under fire. At Brandywine, General Washington's army lost 1,200 men and eleven artillery pieces. Edward Hector's actions, though seemingly small, were surely one of the battle's only positive outcomes; it was later reported that the arms Hector rescued were the only supplies salvaged from his unit's retreat.

Although Hector played but a small part in the Revolutionary War, his service is indicative of the overall contribution made by African Americans to the war efforts in a variety of capacities. Just as soldiers like OLIVER CROMWELL and SALEM POOR served with valor, so, too, did Hector and countless others. Even more important is Hector's service as a wagoneer; uncounted African Americans served in such civilian positions augmenting the Continental army to keep the machinery of war on the move. Though they were not considered soldiers in the true sense of the word, men like Edward Hector were exposed to equal dangers nonetheless, acting as, and dying like, soldiers.

After the Battle of Brandywine in 1777, Hector's life fades into obscurity. He lived in a cabin in Conshohocken for many years and later petitioned the Pennsylvania legislature for a military pension, but to no avail, no doubt due to the fact that he was not considered a regular soldier. Eventually, the legislature granted Hector a payment of forty dollars for his heroic service. When Hector died, the *Free Press* of Norristown printed his obituary, stating that "Obscurity in life and oblivion in death are too often the lot of the worthy—they pass away, and no 'storied stone' perpetuates the remembrance of their noble actions" (Kaplan, p. 55).

FURTHER READING
Kaplan, Sidney, and Emma Nogrady Kaplan. *The Black Presence in the Era of the American Revolution* (1989).
GLENN ALLEN KNOBLOCK

Hedgeman, Anna Arnold (5 July 1899–17 Jan. 1990), civil rights and women's rights activist and government administrator, was born Anna Arnold in Marshalltown, Iowa, to Marie Ellen Parker and William James Arnold II. The granddaughter of slaves, Arnold grew up in Anoka, Minnesota. Her parents, particularly her father, stressed the importance of education, religion, and discipline. She attended Hamline University in St. Paul, Minnesota, from 1918 to 1922. She majored in English and pursued her studies with a passion that marked the way she lived her life. In 1919 she attended a lecture given by W. E. B. DuBois, who had just returned from the Pan-African Conference held in Paris. This was her initial exposure to the African freedom struggles.

In the spring of 1922 Arnold became Hamline University's first black graduate. Shortly afterward she boarded a train for Holly Springs, Mississippi, and began her teaching career at Rust College. On her trip to the South, she confronted the realities of the Jim Crow transportation system when she was forced to change trains halfway through the ride.

Rust College was a vibrant place, but its resources were stretched to the limit. During her two years in Holly Springs, Arnold began to grasp the devastating impact of racism. At the same time she learned about black history from Dr. J. Leonard Farmer, the dean of Rust College and the father of the future civil rights leader JAMES FARMER. Frustrated by her inability to effect change, Arnold returned to the North in 1924, eager to work in a world she believed was more tolerant about race relations. But she quickly became disillusioned. Unable to secure a teaching position in a predominantly white school, Arnold realized that racism in the North was often more subtle, but just as devastating as it was in the South.

On the advice of a friend, Arnold sought a job with the YWCA and soon began work with the African American branch in Springfield, Ohio. But she became increasingly angry about the way racism divided resources along the color line. Searching for a community and a place to belong, she made her way to the Northeast, first working at the African American branch of the Jersey City YWCA and then settling in Harlem. She served as the Harlem YWCA's membership secretary and participated in the branch's stimulating cultural and educational programs. In 1933 she married Merritt Hedgeman, an interpreter and singer of black folk music and opera, and the couple made their home in New York City.

Ironically, the Depression enabled the relative newcomer to get a city administration job. Starting in 1934 she worked with the Emergency Relief Bureau (later the Department of Welfare), first as a supervisor and then as a consultant on racial problems. By the late 1930s Hedgeman had resigned from the Department of Welfare to assume the directorship of the African American branch of the Brooklyn YWCA. Yet, even while she held that position, she organized the Citizens' Coordinating Committee to advocate for city jobs for black workers. Through her efforts and leadership, black New Yorkers secured the first 150 provisional appointments the city had ever given the black community.

In 1941 Hedgeman helped A. PHILIP RANDOLPH with his first March on Washington effort. As World War II drew to a close, Randolph asked Hedgeman to be executive director of the National Council for a Permanent Fair Employment Practices Commission (FEPC). She spoke at rallies with other civil rights advocates and led strategy meetings on how to move legislation through Congress. Despite the pressure to maintain the FEPC, Congress eliminated the program.

Hedgeman's work with the FEPC however, had attracted national attention. Congressman WILLIAM DAWSON of Chicago brought her on board the National Citizens for the Re-Election of President Truman campaign. For her commitment to the Democratic Party, she received a high-level federal appointment as assistant director of the Federal Security Agency, which later became the Department of Health, Education, and Welfare.

In 1953 Hedgeman traveled to India at the request of Ambassador Chester Bowles. She spent three months there as part of a social work delegation, and she lectured, met with students, and studied. Shortly after her return from India, President Eisenhower took office, and Hedgeman, a Democratic appointee, left Washington. Settling back in New York City, she immediately became involved in Harlem politics. Hedgeman became the first African American in Mayor Robert F. Wagner Jr.'s cabinet in 1954. Her responsibilities included serving as the mayor's adviser and as a representative to the United Nations. In 1958 Hedgeman resigned from Wagner's administration and turned her energies to the private sector. She did not stay out of politics for long.

Local insurgents in the Bronx approached Hedgeman to run for the U.S. Congress in 1960. Although she was defeated in the primaries, she continued her activism locally and overseas. In July 1960 she flew to Ghana to deliver the keynote address for the First Conference of African Women and Women of African Descent. While there she met with the African leaders Kwame Nkrumah and Patrice Lumumba.

Hedgeman aggressively pursued civil rights, again working closely with A. Philip Randolph as a major architect of the 1963 March on Washington. The only woman on a nine-member organizing committee, she challenged the male leaders, insisting that women be recognized for their tremendous contributions to the movement and that at least one woman be put on the official program.

As the Civil Rights Bill of 1964 made its way through Congress, Hedgeman, then the assistant director of the Committee on Race Relations for the National Council of Churches, helped coordinate the lobbying effort to get the stalled bill out of the Senate. Years of experience had taught her that the only hope of moving the president or Congress on race issues was through sustained public pressure.

In 1965 Hedgeman was asked to run for New York City Council president. She suffered a defeat but maintained her commitment to electoral politics. In 1968 she ran for office one last time, for the New York State Assembly. Her opponent, the incumbent CHARLES RANGEL, beat her in the primaries. Even as she fought for civil rights and pursued elected office, Hedgeman worked for women's equality. She was among the National Organization for Women's earliest members and served on its board of directors.

Hedgeman, who published autobiographies in 1964 and 1977, received an honorary doctorate from Hamline University and numerous awards for her work on race relations. She died in Harlem Hospital in January 1990.

FURTHER READING

Hedgeman's papers are at the Schomburg Center for Research in Black Culture of the New York Public Library. The Schlesinger Library at Cambridge, Massachusetts, holds a transcript of an unpublished interview conducted in 1978 as part of the Black Women Oral History Project.

Hedgeman, Anna Arnold. *The Gift of Chaos: Decades of American Discontent* (1977).

Hedgeman, Anna Arnold. *The Trumpet Sounds: A Memoir of Negro Leadership* (1964).

Obituary: *New York Times*, 21 Jan. 1990.

JULIE GALLAGHER

Hegamin, Lucille (29 Nov. 1894–1 Mar. 1970), blues singer, was born Lucille Nelson in Macon, Georgia, the daughter of John Nelson and Minnie Wallace. In her youth Hegamin sang in church, and she also sang ragtime tunes and popular ballads at theaters in Macon. At about age fifteen she joined Leonard

Harper's touring company until it was stranded near Chicago. As the "Georgia Peach," Hegamin found steady work in that city from 1914 to 1917, presenting popular songs in nightclubs, cafés, and restaurants. Among her piano accompanists were Bill Hegamin, whom she married around 1914, Tony Jackson, and JELLY ROLL MORTON. She followed Morton, her husband, and many other entertainers to the West Coast, performing in Los Angeles, San Francisco, and Seattle from 1918 to 1919.

Around November 1919 the Hegamins settled in New York City, where they performed in cabarets. Lucille gained further prominence through appearances in Happy Rhone's occasional all-star shows of dance and entertainment at the Manhattan Casino in Harlem on 30 April and 25 September 1920 and on 22 April 1921; at this third show she was billed as the Chicago Cyclone, perhaps owing to her vocal ability to fill a large casino in the era before microphones. Around November 1920 her recording career got under way with the pairing of "The Jazz Me Blues" and "Everybody's Blues." Hegamin was the second blues singer to record, after MAMIE SMITH. On the strength of the popularity of this disc, the Hegamins began a tour of Pennsylvania, West Virginia, and Ohio in May, now billed as Lucille Hegamin and her Blue Flame Syncopaters. In the course of this tour "Arkansas Blues," which she had recorded in February, was released. It became her biggest hit, with the Arto label's master eventually being leased by and issued on ten other 78-rpm labels.

Hegamin held an engagement at the Shuffle Inn in Harlem from November 1921 to January 1922, and at the Manhattan Casino on 20 January she participated in a blues contest won by TRIXIE SMITH. From February through May Hegamin toured in the second of three companies presenting *Shuffle Along*, the pioneering African American musical comedy created by FLOURNOY E. MILLER, Aubrey Lyles, NOBLE SISSLE, and EUBIE BLAKE. Smith was one of the stars, taking the position that the legendary FLORENCE MILLS held in company number one.

After the second company of *Shuffle Along* was disbanded in May, Hegamin began touring with her own Jazz Jubilee band, directed by the pianist J. Cyril Fullerton. With the demise of Arto records—despite her blues hits—Hegamin worked briefly for Paramount and then initiated a four-year association with the Cameo label, for which she recorded "Aggravatin' Papa" (Sept. 1922), "He May Be Your Man, But He Comes to See Me Sometimes" (Oct. 1922), "Some Early Morning" (June 1923), and "Rampart Street Blues" (Oct. 1923).

The marriage to Bill Hegamin ended in 1923. Lucille toured that fall with a musical comedy, *Creole Follies*, and also in a duo with Fullerton on the Keith circuit from December 1923 through 1924. In January 1925 she was at the Cotton Club in New York, broadcasting on WHN radio three times weekly to the accompaniment of Andy Preer and his Cotton Club Syncopators. She resumed touring with Fullerton, working from February as a duo, from November 1925 to February 1926 with Fullerton leading a band, and then once again as a duo. Hegamin and singer ADELAIDE HALL were co-stars of *Lincoln Frolics* at Harlem's Lincoln Theater in March 1926. After further touring with Fullerton, Hegamin starred in shows at the Club Alabam in Philadelphia for four months in 1927; the accompanying band was led by George "Doc" Hyder. Later that year she appeared in the *Shufflin' Feet* revue at the Lincoln, and in 1928 she was at Harlem's Lafayette Theater in *The Midnight Steppers*.

Hegamin toured with Hyder in the late 1920s, and she sang with CLAUDE HOPKINS's Savoy Bohemians at the Lafayette for New Year's celebrations in 1930 and 1931. Her career ended at the Paradise Café in Atlantic City, where she appeared from 1933 to 1934. From 1934 into the 1950s she worked as a nurse. Details of a second marriage, to a Mr. Allen, are unknown. In August 1961, accompanied by the pianist WILLIE "THE LION" SMITH's band, Hegamin recorded four tracks on the album *Blues We Taught Your Mother*, and the next year she recorded the album *Basket of Blues*. Her last performance was at a benefit for Mamie Smith at the Celebrity Club in New York in 1964. She died in New York City, but despite her past fame and recent rediscovery, no obituary appeared in the *New York Times*.

Hegamin had a genuine feeling for the blues, but like her predecessor, Mamie Smith, she sang with a wholesomely full timbre and enunciated lyrics with clarity, sometimes throwing in exaggerated vaudevillian gestures as she did so. In contrast with the rough and unpretentious geniuses of the classic female blues style, MA RAINEY and BESSIE SMITH, Hegamin's sophisticated presentation fit reasonably well into the mainstream of American popular music. Thus it is not surprising that she would have been invited to record sooner than they, thereby establishing her position as a historical figure of note. Today Hegamin is largely forgotten and her recorded legacy unavailable, except to specialists in the areas of vaudeville and early blues.

FURTHER READING

Kunstadt, Len. "The Lucille Hegamin Story," *Record Research*, no. 39 (Nov. 1961); no. 40 (Jan. 1962); no. 41 (Feb. 1962); and no. 43 (May 1962).

Stewart-Baxter, Derrick. "Blues," *Jazz Journal* 20 (July 1967).

Stewart-Baxter, Derrick. "Blues: Lucille Hegamin, Part 2" (Aug. 1967).

Obituary: *Jazz Journal* 23 (June 1970).

This entry is taken from the *American National Biography* and is published here with the permission of the American Council of Learned Societies.

BARRY KERNFELD

Height, Dorothy (24 Mar. 1912–20 Apr. 2010) was born Dorothy Irene Height in Richmond, Virginia, the daughter of James Height, a building and painting contractor who became active in Republican politics, and Fannie Burroughs, a nurse and household worker, both twice widowed with children from earlier marriages. As a child, Height loved to read, liked challenges, and always kept busy. When she was four, she and her family moved to Rankin, Pennsylvania, a small borough of Pittsburgh, during the Great Migration. Fannie participated in the black women's club movement through the Pennsylvania Federation of Colored Women's Clubs, and Height

Dorothy Height, responds to a question at a forum in Washington, D.C., to launch a national economic initiative, February 1988. (AP Images.)

recalled going with her mother to every state and national meeting and hearing the imperative of "uplifting the race."

Rankin was an ethnically diverse community, and Height attended school with Germans, Croatians, Jews, Italians, Poles, and children of other ethnicities. Growing up, she generally experienced very little prejudice. Her first brush with racism, however, occurred when she was eight years old, when Sarah Hay, one of her Irish Catholic friends, refused to play with her one day because she was a "nigger." As she grew older, Height would have other, more intense racist encounters. As a student she proved to be exceptional. In addition to excelling at academics, she won several speech contests and had a passion for music, even cowriting the alma mater for her high school. She graduated from Rankin High School in June of 1929, after which she studied social work and psychology at New York University (NYU). While in college Height worked as a proofreader for the *Negro World*, MARCUS GARVEY's widely circulated newspaper. In 1932, after just three years, she finished her B.A. and one year later earned an M.A. in Educational Psychology, also from NYU. Her college years paralleled the Harlem Renaissance and had allowed her to meet and hear presentations by W. E. B. DuBois, PAUL ROBESON, COUNTÉE CULLEN, LANGSTON HUGHES, and others. After finishing college Height began a long career as a social worker. Her first job, for which she was paid twenty dollars a month, was with the Brownsville Community Center in Brooklyn, where she addressed the community's high delinquency and unemployment rates. Soon after, she became an investigator for the Home Relief Bureau of the New York City Welfare Administration, earning $27.50 a week. She also worked with other community leaders to quell the Harlem riots of 1935. This riot began after a young African American stole a knife from a Harlem store. Rumors spread that he had been beaten to death, so crowds formed, accusing the white merchants of discrimination in employment and the police of brutality. The ensuing violence resulted in the death of three African Americans and the destruction of more than $2 million in property.

During this time Height worked with the United Christian Youth Movement of North America (UCYMNA), became president of the New York State Christian Youth Council, chaired the Harlem Youth Council, and attended the UCYMNA-sponsored World Conference on Life and Work of the Churches in Oxford, England, where she worked with BENJAMIN MAYS and his wife, Sadie. Over time Height's sphere extended to Africa, where she worked with Africans in Sierra Leone, Ghana, Nigeria, and Guinea. Eventually the U.S. State Department noticed her work and appointed her to its advisory panel on Africa.

Inspired by the Oxford conference, Height helped organize the World Conference of Christian Youth, a global conference of young Christians held in Amsterdam in August 1939. Several months later Height resigned from the Home Relief Bureau and took a job as assistant executive director of the New York YWCA. The New York World's Fair brought thousands of young African American women to the city in 1939 in search of employment. In helping these young women, Height learned of the "Bronx slave market," where women waited on street corners for jobs as domestics, only to be exploited, physically and financially, by employers. Height fought, unsuccessfully, to have this practice abolished. She also fought to secure antilynching legislation, eliminate segregation in the armed forces, and reform of the criminal justice system.

At the third annual meeting of the National Council of Negro Women (NCNW), held in November 1937, Height met the NCNW's founder, MARY MCLEOD BETHUNE, and the keynote speaker, First Lady Eleanor Roosevelt. Shortly thereafter, Bethune appointed Height to the NCNW's resolutions committee, and in 1938 she worked with Roosevelt on the World Conference of Youth, held at Vassar College in Poughkeepsie, New York. Years later, in 1961, Height worked with Roosevelt again after President John F. Kennedy appointed her to the President's Commission on the Status of Women. As Height later recalled, "It was a privilege to know Mrs. Roosevelt and Mrs. Bethune, two extraordinary women" (93).

Height continued her work with the YWCA, taking a position as executive director of the Phillis Wheatley YWCA in Washington, D.C., in the fall of 1939. Five years later she returned to New York, becoming secretary for interracial education on the YWCA's national board, a position she felt would better allow her to "make a contribution to the national effort to end racism and segregation" (107). Height helped the YWCA adopt its first Interracial Charter in 1946, a very difficult task in light of the resistance on the part of many white southern YWCA branches. In 1965 she became the director of the YWCA's Office of Racial Justice, a position she held until her retirement from the organization in 1977. In 2000 President Bill Clinton became the first recipient of the YWCA Dorothy I. Height Racial Justice Award.

Dorothy Height had joined the Delta Sigma Theta Sorority in 1939. Two years later she became chair of its social action program, and from 1947 to 1956, she served as president of the sorority. Over the years she moved the Deltas' annual convention from a church basement to the Kiel Auditorium in St. Louis, Missouri. Height developed the organization's Job Opportunity Project and began the Delta bookmobile project in Georgia, an effort that led the state to start providing rural and poor children with library services.

In 1957, two years after the death of Mary McLeod Bethune, Height became the NCNW's fourth president, a position she held continuously since. Over the next four decades, under Height's leadership, the NCNW created the Bethune Museum and Archives, the first national archive on black women, and published the organization's first book. She also established the annual Black Family Reunion Celebration and an anonymous debtors' program to help young black women with their finances; both programs were designed to strengthen the black family. The NCNW, which became tax-exempt in 1966, confronted unemployment, hunger and malnutrition, the problems of poor housing and public health and participated in the March on Washington, voter education drives in the North, and numerous civil rights projects in Mississippi during the 1960s. Height herself participated in almost every major civil and human rights event, working closely with MARTIN LUTHER KING JR., ROY WILKINS, WHITNEY YOUNG, and A. PHILIP RANDOLPH among others.

In 1995 Height spearheaded the purchase of the NCNW's national headquarters, the historic Sears House on 633 Pennsylvania Avenue, in Washington, D.C. The NCNW, which includes more than 4 million women, shares its headquarters with the Dorothy I. Height Leadership Institute and the National Centers for African American Women. According to Height, the NCNW's "great strength has been that it builds leadership skills in women by emphasizing self-reliance, unity, and the commitment to working collaboratively" (271).

Height received the Citizens Medal Award from President Ronald Reagan in 1989, the Presidential Medal of Freedom, the nation's highest civilian award, from President Bill Clinton in 1994, and the Congressional Gold Medal from President George W. Bush in 2004. In 2003 Height authored a memoir titled *Open Wide the Freedom Gates*, which was adapted for the successful stage musical, *If This Hat Could Talk*. In her memoir she reminded readers that while American leaders travel the world selling democracy and expressing concern for human rights, "many here at home still cannot enjoy the simplest benefits guaranteed by the Constitution because of endemic, institutionalized racism. Institutionalized racism is more than debilitating—it is disastrous for the nation. It is long past time to end it, completely, everywhere" (268–269). Height died at Howard University Hospital in Washington at the age of 98.

FURTHER READING

Height, Dorothy. *Open Wide the Freedom Gates: A Memoir* (2003).

Giddings, Paula. *In Search of Sisterhood: Delta Sigma Theta and the Challenge of the Black Sorority Movement* (1988).

Obituary: *New York Times*, 20 Apr. 2010.

DAVID H. JACKSON JR.

Hemings, Sally (1773–1835), slave and Thomas Jefferson's mistress, whose given name probably was Sarah, was born in Virginia, the daughter of the slave Elizabeth "Betty" Hemings and, allegedly, John Wayles, a merchant and planter. (Family members spell the surname both *Hemings* and *Hemmings*.) After Wayles's death in 1773, Betty Hemings and her children became the property of Thomas Jefferson and his wife, Martha Wayles Skelton Jefferson. From an early age Sally Hemings was a personal servant of Jefferson's daughter Mary (later Maria), whom she accompanied to France in 1787, when Sally was fourteen and Mary nine.

It is not known whether Sally, while in Paris, lived at Mary's convent school or at Jefferson's residence on the Champs-Elysées, where her brother James Hemings was *chef de cuisine*. Jefferson's expenditures during her two-year residence in Paris indicate that Sally received further training in the skills of a lady's maid, and she acted in that capacity for Jefferson's older daughter, Martha, when the latter began going out in Parisian society in 1789. She intermittently received a small monthly wage during this period.

Jefferson, his two daughters, and his two slaves returned to Virginia at the end of 1789. Despite her long association with Jefferson's younger daughter, Sally Hemings remained at Monticello after Maria Jefferson's marriage and departure in 1797. Her son Madison Hemings remembered that she took care of Jefferson's chamber and wardrobe and did "such light work as sewing, &c." Jefferson's records reveal only that she was one of the "house-maids," that she bore six children, two of whom died as infants, and that, at Jefferson's death in 1826, she was still a slave, valued in the appraisal of his property at fifty dollars.

There is no certain information on Sally Hemings's status after Jefferson's death. It seems likely that she was unofficially freed by Jefferson's daughter Martha Randolph, whose 1834 will asked that "Sally" be given her "time." This may have been intended to legitimize an existing situation. She appears in an 1833 "List of Free Negroes & Mulattoes" with her son Madison, who recalled that his mother lived with him in Charlottesville until her death.

Madison Hemings, freed in Jefferson's will, related his life story to an Ohio journalist in 1873. It is this account, selectively accepted by historians, that contains most of what is known about the Hemings family. Madison Hemings is the main source for the allegation that John Wayles was the father of Sally Hemings and five of her siblings. He also stated that he and his own brothers and sisters were Thomas Jefferson's children, the result of a relationship that began in Paris. When his account was published in 1873, the story of a possible sexual relationship between Jefferson and Sally Hemings had long been part of the public discourse. It had been transformed from local gossip to national news in the fall of 1802, when an article in the Richmond *Recorder* began, "It is well known that the man, *whom it delighteth the people to honor*, keeps, and for many years past has kept, as his concubine, one of his own slaves. Her name is sally." The author was James Callender, a disgruntled convert to the Federalist cause after his former heroes on the Republican side failed to "reward" him with a postmastership. Other Federalist writers quickly incorporated the tale in their attacks on President Jefferson and his administration. Jefferson himself was silent on the issue. In accordance with his practice in regard to personal attacks, he never publicly denied a connection. One private letter, which might be interpreted as a denial, remains ambiguous. His own family members were consistent in their disbelief but made their denials privately.

For the rest of the century the allegation that the author of the Declaration of Independence kept his own children in slavery was taken up by critics of Jefferson's party, his region, and his country. Skeptical British travelers, highlighting the hypocrisy of the American experiment, repeated and embellished the story, and antislavery activists of the antebellum period used the relationship to emphasize the exploitation of the slavery system.

In the meantime, more quietly, a belief in their Jefferson ancestry passed from generation to generation of Sally Hemings's descendants. Their side of the story was first given wider circulation in 1974 in *Thomas Jefferson: An Intimate History* by Fawn M. Brodie, one of the very few Jefferson biographers to accept the Hemings-Jefferson connection. At the center of Brodie's psychological portrait is an enduring relationship between master and slave, romantic rather than exploitative. It is her version that captured and has held the public imagination since that time.

In the absence of solid evidence to prove or refute its existence, the possible relationship between Thomas Jefferson and Sally Hemings was the subject of vigorous and shifting debate for almost two centuries. The story became a convenient symbol for some of the anomalies of American history and complexities of American society, and African Americans in the twentieth century viewed its denial by historians as symbolic of the negation of oral traditions—often the only possible link to their ancestors in slavery. The results of DNA testing of Hemings and Jefferson descendants, published in the fall of 1998, strongly indicate, however, that Jefferson was the father of Hemings's youngest son, Eston, and perhaps all her known children. While the debate has turned to issues of family and master-slave relations, the findings have in effect deepened the enigma of Jefferson's character. Even more elusive, however, is the figure at the heart of the controversy, Sally Hemings herself.

FURTHER READING

Brodie, Fawn M. *Thomas Jefferson: An Intimate History* (1974).

French, Scot A., and Edward L. Ayers. "The Strange Career of Thomas Jefferson: Race and Slavery in American Memory, 1943–1993," in *Jeffersonian Legacies*, ed. Peter S. Onuf (1993).

Gordon-Reed, Annette. *Thomas Jefferson and Sally Hemings: An American Controversy* (1997).

Justus, Judith. *Down from the Mountain: The Oral History of the Hemings Family* (1990).

Peterson, Merrill D. *The Jefferson Image in the American Mind* (1960).

This entry is taken from the *American National Biography* and is published here with the permission of the American Council of Learned Societies.

LUCIA C. STANTON

Hemphill, Essex (16 Apr. 1957–4 Nov. 1995), poet, editor, and performance artist, was born Essex Charles Hemphill in Chicago, Illinois, the second-oldest of five children of Mantalene Hemphill from Columbia, South Carolina. Little is known about his father. Hemphill was raised in Anderson, Indiana, Columbia, South Carolina, and southeast Washington, D.C. From an early age Hemphill was aware of both his homosexuality and the homophobia among his peers. He described the oppressive situation of his youth in the introduction to *Brother to Brother*: "The male code of the streets where I grew up made this very clear: Sissies, punks, and faggots were not 'cool' with the boys" (xv). Hemphill started writing in 1971 at age fourteen. That same year he had his first homosexual affair with an older white man from his Washington neighborhood.

Though Hemphill grew up in a situation with hardly any visible black gay men who could have been role models, he decided to explore the dimensions and intersections of race and sexuality both politically and artistically and was one of the first openly gay black artists. Radically addressing white supremacist attitudes and racist stereotypes of black men within the white-dominated gay subculture, as well as homophobic attitudes within the black community, Hemphill became an important protagonist of the black gay culture of the 1980s.

After graduating from Ballou High School in Washington, D.C., Hemphill studied English and journalism at the University of Maryland and got his degree in English at the University of the District of Columbia. In 1978 he and another student from the University of Maryland founded the *Nethula Journal of Contemporary Literature*. During a poetry reading at Howard University in 1980 Hemphill publicly came out as a gay man. He became known to Washington audiences in 1983 when, together with Wayson R. Jones and Larry Duckette, his longtime companion, he formed the poetry performance group Cinque. They first performed at the Enik Alley Coffeehouse in northeast Washington, an important venue for African American lesbian and gay artists. Two years later he self-published his first chapbook, *Earth Life* (1985), which he funded entirely with his own savings. His career as a writer accelerated in 1986 when he received a fellowship in poetry from the National Endowment of the Arts (NEA) that enabled him to publish *Conditions* (1986), his second book of poems, with editorial assistance from JOSEPH BEAM. That same year his work appeared in *Gay and Lesbian Poetry of Our Time* and *In the Life*, an influential anthology of texts by black gay writers edited by Joseph Beam.

In 1987 his poetry was included in *Tongues Untied*, an anthology of poems by five black gay poets. The title refers to the poem "Tongue-Tied in Black and White" by MICHAEL S. HARPER and was chosen because Harper "expounds on how the mores and language of a dominant culture can stifle the creativity of peoples within that culture" (*Tongues Untied*, 5). Two years later the filmmaker MARLON RIGGS chose "Tongues Untied" as the title for his influential documentary on black gay identity. In *Tongues Untied* (1989) Riggs combined poetry, performances, and personal testimony to reflect on the situation of black gay men in the United States. It is one of three internationally acclaimed and controversially debated films in which Hemphill and his poetry would appear. He also performed his poetry for the soundtrack of *Looking for Langston* (1989), a filmic meditation on LANGSTON HUGHES and the Harlem Renaissance directed by the black British filmmaker Isaac Julien. In the United States some parts of the film were censored by the executor of the estate of Langston Hughes to prevent a connection of Hughes's name and homosexuality. The third film featuring Hemphill and his poetry is Riggs's *Black Is ... Black Ain't* (1994), a personal and radical examination of black gay experiences in the age of AIDS. Owing to these films, Hemphill became known internationally.

In 1991 Hemphill edited *Brother to Brother: New Writings by Black Gay Men*. The book was originally conceived and planned by Joseph Beam as a companion anthology to *In the Life*. After Beam's death from AIDS-related complications in 1988 Hemphill completed the work with the support of Beam's parents, Dorothy and Sun Beam, in their home in Philadelphia. Like *In the Life*, the anthology includes texts by important black gay artists of the 1980s, such as Assotto Saint, Craig G. Harris, and MELVIN DIXON, and was awarded the Lambda Literary Award. That same year, Hemphill's work was included in the anthologies *The Road before Us: 100 Gay Black Poets* (1991) and *Hometowns: Gay Men Write about Where They Belong* (1991).

Hemphill's collection *Ceremonies: Prose and Poetry* was published in 1992. Its poems and essays cover a wide range of topics concerning the situation of black gay men in the United States, such as the intersections of the categories blackness and gayness, white gay racism, homophobia among some black nationalists, and AIDS. Hemphill's pointed critique of racist representations of black men in the work of the white gay photographer Robert Mapplethorpe in his essay "Does Your Mama Know About Me?" led to controversial debates within the gay community. *Ceremonies* was awarded the National Library Association's Gay, Lesbian, and Bisexual New Author Award.

In 1993 Hemphill was a visiting scholar at the Getty Center for the History of Art and the Humanities in Santa Monica, California, and he received a Pew Charitable Trust Fellowship in the Arts and the Emery S. Hetrick Award for community-based activism from the Hetrick-Martin Institute. That same year his poem "Vital Signs" was published in the anthology *Life Sentences: Writers, Artists, and AIDS* (1994), revealing his positive HIV status to the public. Apart from books and anthologies, Hemphill's work appeared in numerous journals, among them *Black Scholar, Callaloo, Obsidian, Painted Bride Quarterly, Gay Community News,* the *James White Review,* and *Essence.* Hemphill died from AIDS-related complications at the age of thirty-eight in Philadelphia, Pennsylvania. Because of its outspokenness on black gay topics, Hemphill's work remains a source of inspiration for younger generations of black gay men.

FURTHER READING

Hemphill, Essex. Introduction to *Brother to Brother: New Writings by Black Gay Men* (1991).

Hemphill, Essex. *Ceremonies* (1992).

Glave, Thomas. "(Re-)Recalling Essex Hemphill: Words to Our Now," *Callaloo* 23.1 (2000): 278–284.

Nero, Charles I. "Fixing Ceremonies: An Introduction" in Essex Hemphill, *Ceremonies* (2000).

Reid-Pharr, Robert F. "A Child's Life," in *Black Gay Man* (2001).

SIMON DICKEL

Hemphill, Jessie Mae (13 Oct. 1933–22 July 2006), blues and gospel singer and multi-instrumentalist, was born Jessie Mae Graham to James Graham and Virgie Lee Hemphill, both farmers, near Senatobia in Northern Mississippi. Her parents separated when she was four years old, and James Graham, a blues pianist, moved to Memphis. Virgie Lee Hemphill, who soon abandoned farming for work as a domestic servant, was from an extended musical family. She and her sisters, Rosa Lee and Sydney Lee, learned to play from their father, Sid Hemphill, a blind musical polymath, known to play fiddle, guitar, piano, flute, pan pipes, banjo, and fife. The elder Hemphill, born in 1876 and blind from an early age, was recorded by the folklorist Alan Lomax in 1942

and 1959 and was widely known as a musician and bandleader in the local area.

Although she received only a meager education in rural Mississippi's underfunded and segregated public school system, Hemphill benefited from a rich musical education through her family and community. When she was seven years old she won a local dance contest by besting an older teenager, and at nine years of age her aunt, Rosa Lee Hill (who also recorded as a blues singer), gave her a guitar that her grandfather used to tune so she could play along with him. Hemphill sang in church, and by the age of 11 was playing bass and snare drum. She also listened to her mother's blues records, especially one by SONNY BOY WILLIAMSON II (Rice Miller). FRED McDOWELL, and Johnny Woods, stars of the 1960s folk-blues revival, were neighbors of the Hemphills. Playing with her family at Fourth of July picnics, fish frys, and other occasions, Hemphill became well known locally for her proficiency and versatility as a drummer.

Increasingly coming into conflict with her mother's second husband, Hemphill moved to Memphis soon after she turned 15. There she worked a variety of jobs, including domestic servant, cafeteria worker, and grocery-store clerk. She married L. D. Brooks in 1952, but the marriage did not last. During this time she performed irregularly in Memphis, West Memphis, and Helena, Arkansas, primarily as an instrumentalist or group member, not as a bandleader (although she may have occasionally performed solo). Living in Memphis also gave Hemphill many opportunities to see and meet musicians like B. B. KING, HOWLIN' WOLF, JOHNNY ACE, and Bobby "Blue" Bland.

In the mid-1960s Hemphill moved to Como, a largely African American township near Senatobia, to care for her mother. By 1967, when blues chronicler GEORGE MITCHELL made field recordings and conducted interviews with her, her mother had died and most of Hemphill's ambitions seemed to center around leaving Mississippi because of continuing segregation and racial prejudice.

However, Hemphill remained in Como, working for low wages while playing guitar and writing songs. After her grandfather and aunt died, she became concerned with keeping her family's musical tradition alive, which brought a focus and purpose to her playing. In 1973 she was recorded by Dr. David Evans, an ethnomusicologist from Memphis State University. While nothing came of these early recordings, Hemphill and Evans stayed in contact, and in 1979 Evans again recorded her, this time in a new recording studio built on the Memphis State University campus.

Hemphill's first recordings were released as singles by Memphis State's High Water label, and in 1981 she released an album called *She Wolf* on the French label Vogue. Although the album was not distributed in the United States, it was well received in Europe. Hemphill toured Europe several times, playing festivals there and in the United States. She was popular with audiences and was a critical success as well. She recorded more songs for Vogue and for the Australian label A Go Go.

In 1984 and 1985 Hemphill recorded again with Evans, and in 1987 and 1988 she won the W. C. HANDY Award for Best Female Traditional Blues Artist. In 1989 she was filmed for the Robert Mugge–Robert Gordon documentary *Deep Blues*, playing bass drum in an ensemble with fife player Napoleon Strickland. In the film she can also be seen performing solo on guitar in a sequence filmed in the Holly Springs, Mississippi, juke joint owned by local blues legend Junior Kimbrough. In 1991 Hemphill received another Handy Award, this time for Best Country Blues Album—Historical Style for the LP *Feelin' Good*, which was also produced by Evans and issued on the High Water label.

The music on these recordings was a remarkable blend of modern electric blues and hill-country guitar, fife, and drum styles. Hemphill's playing resembled that of JOHN LEE HOOKER, and some of her songs echoed the style of Howlin' Wolf, a connection she celebrated by adopting the nickname "She Wolf" and writing a song with the same name. Her minimalist, rhythmically compelling style at times sounded rudimentary, but it required discipline and commitment to play well. Similarly, her insistence on placing fife and drum rhythm patterns in the context of blues songs represented a conscious combination of usually distinct blues idioms. Many of Hemphill's early recordings featured David Evans on second guitar as well as overdubbed snare and bass drum played by Hemphill herself. On other recordings, she played bass drum or tambourine with her foot while playing guitar, and sometimes she accompanied her vocal with a one-stringed "diddley" bow. Only a few songs, recorded later, featured a full rhythm section.

During her performing years, Hemphill's presentation of herself, both onstage and offstage, was as distinct and uncompromising as her music. She often wore low-cut, gold-sequined dresses or shirts and cowboy hats. She was often known to carry a pistol as well. She sometimes wore her hair in two long braids and wore Native American bells on her ankles and, at times, spurs on her boots. All of this helped to make her a unique and noteworthy performer, although her style was more than a little at odds with a blues market dominated by rock-oriented bands playing virtuoso guitar solos over shuffle rhythms and 12-bar structures.

In 1993 Hemphill suffered a stroke that left her unable to play guitar, effectively ending her performing and recording career. She spent the next several years living a marginal existence in a trailer outside of Senatobia, Mississippi, subsisting on support from a small network of blues musicians and fans who organized the Jessie Mae Hemphill Foundation in 2004. That year, several friends and supporters organized a small celebration of her life and music, at which she sang a few gospel songs. The event was recorded, filmed, and released in 2004 under her name, on both CD and DVD, as *Dare You to Do It Again*. After Hemphill's death in 2006, the foundation rededicated itself to the documentation, preservation, and support of the musical traditions of the Mississippi hill country.

FURTHER READING
"Jessie Mae Hemphill," *Living Blues* (Mar.–Apr. 1985).
Mitchell, George. *Blow My Blues Away* (1971).

DISCOGRAPHY
Dare You to Do It Again (CD 219 1003, DVD 219 1004).
Feelin' Good (LP Highwater 1012) (CD HMG 6502).
Get Right Blues (Inside Sounds 519).
She Wolf (LP Vogue 513501) France, (CD High Water 6508).

ERIC D. JOHNSON

Hemphill, Julius (24 Jan. 1938–2 Apr. 1995), alto and tenor saxophonist, composer, and teacher, was born in Fort Worth, Texas, into a family about which little is known. What is known is that the Hemphill family included several ministers, a fact that fostered within Hemphill a religious belief that music represented an act of giving. Hemphill studied music in high school, focusing initially on the baritone saxophone, and later trained formally with John Carter, a jazz musician, composer, and music teacher, and graduated in 1956. He attended both North Texas State University in Denton, Texas, and Lincoln University in St. Louis, Missouri, between 1970 and 1972, studying alto and tenor saxophone, harmony, orchestration, and arrangement. He did not graduate from either institution, feeling that the classical world was not prepared for an African American. Besides his formal training, Hemphill gained professional experience playing with rhythm and blues bands in Fort Worth.

In 1964 Hemphill entered the U.S. Army and, after his two-year stint ended, he began playing with IKE TURNER on a national tour with Turner's group. In 1966, he married, and in 1967 Hemphill moved to St. Louis, his wife's hometown where the Hemphills would eventually have two sons. He helped to revitalize St. Louis's once thriving jazz scene through the Black Artists Group (BAG), which he founded with the local musicians Hamiett Bluiett and Oliver Lake and many other musicians, poets, writers, painters, actors, and dancers. Much of St. Louis's homegrown talent had left to play in New York, Los Angeles, and Chicago where more work was available. Jazz performance spaces had almost disappeared. BAG reenergized and promoted the African American artistic community. In 1968 BAG successfully lobbied for an Arts Council grant, which launched a community center providing musical training for children and adults, as well as performance spaces for BAG productions. This thriving artistic atmosphere played a significant role in Hemphill's career as a musician and composer over the next three decades.

Firmly committed to establishing complete artistic and economic control of his work, Hemphill founded Mbari Records in 1972 to record, publish, and distribute his work as a musician and composer. This emphasis on political, cultural, and economic self-determination was an integral part of BAG and many other 1960s and 1970s black artists and cultural activists. Equally influential was the radical, pioneering innovations of black avant-garde musicians and composers such as alto saxophonist, trumpeter, and violinist ORNETTE COLEMAN, also of Fort Worth, pianist-composer CECIL TAYLOR, and tenor saxophonists and composers JOHN COLTRANE and ALBERT AYLER. The aesthetic influence of these musicians and other free jazz players was apparent in many of Hemphill's own original compositions of the early 1970s when critics outside the Midwest began to notice his work for the first time. One of his major compositions was *Dogon A. D.*, recorded in 1972 and later reissued by Arista's Freedom Records division. Hemphill continued pursuing his intense interest in multimedia and theater productions, making innovative contributions to the 1972 production of *Kawaida*. By the mid-1970s he appeared often on the college performance circuit and toured throughout the United States and abroad and had attained a solid reputation as an avant-garde composer and performer.

In late 1972 the BAG formally disbanded and Hemphill relocated to Brooklyn, New York, with his wife and two sons. He continued his eclectic output as a musician over the next decade, adapting some of his work for the film the *Orientation of Sweet Willie Rollbar* (1974), headlining New York's African American cultural performances, and even playing on the rhythm and blues group Kool and the Gang track "Hustler's Convention" (1973). Hemphill also recorded two albums as his alter-ego persona, Roi Boye, for the 1977 releases *Blue Boye* and *Roi Boye and the Gotham Minstrels*. In 1977 he reunited with his old BAG partners Bluiett and Lake. Together with David Murray, they formed the World Saxophone Quartet (WSQ), with which Hemphill remained until 1990. As WSQ's primary composer, Hemphill's work enjoyed its greatest national and global exposure. In the 1980s Hemphill received critical acclaim for his WSQ work and his composition "Steppin'," was added to the prestigious *Smithsonian Collection of Classic Jazz*.

A car accident in 1982 somewhat impaired Hemphill's mobility, but he remained both a prolific composer and a dynamic player. In 1990 he left the WSQ and formed the Julius Hemphill Sextet. He composed commissioned multimedia collaborations, including *Long Tongues: A Saxophone Opera*, which premiered in Washington, D.C., in 1989. Through spoken words, dance pieces, photo montages, and music, the piece told the four-decade story of the Bohemian Caverns Jazz Club. Hemphill also worked on the *Last Supper at Uncle Tom's Cabin: The Promised Land*, which toured the United States and Europe in 1990 and 1991. Other commissioned works led Hemphill to work with groups as diverse as the Arditti String Quartet on "One Atmosphere (For Ursula)" in 1992, the Richmond Symphony in "Plan B" in 1993, and "A Bitter Glory" with the Walker Art Center and the American Music Theater Festival in 1994.

In 1991 Hemphill returned to recording, releasing *Fat Man and the Hard Blues* with his sextet on the Italian label Black Saint Records. He also released a live album of his performance with the cellist Abdul Wadud in 1992 called *Oakland Duets*. The final album released by his sextet during Hemphill's life, *Five Chord Stud*, was released on Black Saint Records in 1993. In March 1993 Hemphill underwent open heart surgery and treatment for his severe diabetes (his right leg was finally amputated as a result). He made one of his final appearances in a public performance from his wheelchair at the New York Jazz Festival in 1994.

Recovering from a prolonged bout with cancer and increasing problems with diabetes, Hemphill died at the age of fifty-seven.

FURTHER READING

Down Beat, June 1975.

"Julius Hemphill." *Contemporary Musicians* 34 (2002).

The Nation (7 Mar. 1994).

Village Voice, 25 April 1995; 8 December 1998.

Obituary: *St. Louis Post-Dispatch*, 4 Apr. 1995.

KOFI NATAMBU

Hemsley, Sherman (1 Feb. 1938–24 July 2012), actor and singer, was born in Philadelphia, Pennsylvania, to unknown parents. Although records of his early life lack information about his education, Hemsley did participate in elementary school plays and had early aspirations of becoming an actor. Although he served in the U.S. Air Force and was later employed with the U.S. Postal Service, Hemsley always held fast to his dream. Having attended the Philadelphia Academy of Dramatic Arts during his tenure with the postal service, he became an active member of local dramatic organizations, began acting in various children's theater productions, and starred in *Black Book*, a regional television comedy series in the mid-1960s.

In about 1966 Hemsley secured a transfer to a post office in New York. At the same time he began to study acting with the actor and director Lloyd Richards.

In New York Hemsley discovered a nurturing environment in which to hone his skills in the recently founded Negro Ensemble Company (established in 1967). In 1967 Hemsley earned a position with VINNETTE CARROLL's Urban Arts Corps, an organization devoted to African Americans in every aspect of theatrical arts, and in 1968 he made his Off-Broadway debut in *The People vs. the Ranchman*.

Sherman Hemsley in August 1986. (AP Images.)

In 1970, as part of the cast for a successful Broadway musical adaptation of OSSIE DAVIS's play *Purlie Victorious*, Hemsley shined in the role of Gitlow Judson. It was during one of these performances that he first caught the attention of the television writer and producer Norman Lear. Approached by Lear, Hemsley was unwilling to abandon his commitment to *Purlie* for a role on the new CBS sitcom *All in the Family*. However, Lear was convinced that Hemsley was the only man for the part, and he reserved the role. In 1973 Hemsley joined the show, claiming his part as George Jefferson, an upwardly mobile, crass, militant, and arrogant neighbor of the bigoted Archie Bunker (played by Carroll O'Connor). For two years ISABEL SANFORD and Mike Evans had appeared on the show as Louise and Lionel Jefferson, George's wife and son. In 1975, only two years after Hemsley made his first television appearance on the show, he starred in his very own sitcom opposite his television wife, Sanford, in a spin-off CBS network series, *The Jeffersons*. *The Jeffersons* featured the first predominantly African American cast on television in two decades, preceded only by *Amos 'n Andy* (1951–1953). Striking a contrast with the satirical hardships suffered by the characters in the previous show, George Jefferson, once a janitor, was now a self-made millionaire and owner of several dry cleaning businesses in New York. Before his success the family lived in a blue-collar Queens neighborhood next door to the Bunkers. Now the Jeffersons lived in a posh high-rise building on Manhattan's affluent Upper East Side. Among the Jeffersons' new neighbors were an interracially married couple, Tom and Helen Willis (Franklin Cover and ROXIE ROKER), often victims of George's racial epithets. Bringing balance to George's diatribes was the Jeffersons' flippant housemaid, Florence (Marla Gibbs), who welcomed any opportunity to serve George a tongue lashing. *The Jeffersons* ran until 1985. Throughout its run the show and cast members were nominated for several Emmy, Golden Globe, and NAACP Image awards. For his portrayal of George Jefferson, Hemsley won an NAACP Image Award in 1976 and 1982; in 1983 he won a Golden Globe Award.

In 1986 Hemsley moved to NBC to star in *Amen*, network television's first sitcom with religion as a backdrop. Playing the part of Deacon Ernest Frye, Hemsley yet again portrayed an egocentric and irreverent character. The show would run through 1991, earning Hemsley another NAACP Image Award in 1987.

In 1991 Hemsley joined the Walt Disney Television/ Jim Henson Production *Dinosaurs* on ABC. The show's "cast" was made up entirely of animatronics. Set in 600,000,003 b.c. with the Sinclair family as its focal point, *Dinosaurs* was essentially a satire of sitcoms featuring human casts. Hemsley provided the voice of B. P. Richfield, a tyrannical and carnivorous Ceratopsian, a role he filled until the last episode in 1994. During this time he also made guest appearances on a number of television shows, including *Hangin' with Mr. Cooper* (1993), *Designing Women* (1993), *Townsend Television* (1993), *Burke's Law* (1994), *Thunder in Paradise* (1994), and *Lois and Clark: The New Adventures of Superman* (1993). From August 1996 to May 1997 Hemsley again starred in his own sitcom, *Goode Behavior*, in which he portrayed Willie Goode, a newly paroled con artist sentenced to house arrest. In 1989 Hemsley appeared as himself in MICHAEL JACKSON's music video, "Liberian Girl." In 1992 Hemsley released a rhythm and blues album, *Dance*, featuring his vocals.

In the early 2000s Hemsley continued to make guest appearances on a variety of television shows, along with participating on game shows, including *Who Wants to Be a Millionaire?* (1999), *Hollywood Squares* (2003), and *The Great American Celebrity Spelling Bee* (2004). In 2005 he made his reality television debut on *Being Bobby Brown*, costarring Brown's wife, the singer and actress Whitney Houston, and followed in 2006 with *Living in TV Land* and *Surreal Life 6*.

Hemsley made his film debut in 1979 in *Love at First Bite*, after which he regularly worked in film. Hemsley's film credits include *The Misery Brothers* (1995), *Sprung* (1997), *Senseless* (1998), *Screwed* (2000), *Hanging in Hedo* (2007), and *For the Love of a Dog* (2007).

In 2012, Hemsley died at his home in El Paso, Texas. He was 74 years old.

An inspiration to generations of actors, Sherman Hemsley's work has been consistently reflective of evolving mores in society and changing trends in entertainment. As America danced with issues of race, sex, and class in the political arena, Hemsley portrayed a successful and ambitious African American whose own prejudice reflected that of whites while demonstrating that ignorance had no color. Never before had an African American been portrayed on television for such a long run as a character in defiance of whites and white America.

FURTHER READING

David, Marc, and Robert J. Thompson. *Prime Time, Prime Movers: From "I Love Lucy" to "L.A. Law,"* *America's Greatest TV Shows and the People Who Created Them* (1995).

Hunt, Darnell M. *Channeling Blackness: Studies on Television and Race in America* (2005).

Smith, Ronald L. *Who's Who in Comedy: Comedians, Comics and Clowns from Vaudeville to Today's Stand-ups* (1992).

Obituary: *New York Times*, 24 July 2012.

SAFIYA DALILAH HOSKINS

Henderson, Edwin B. and Mary Ellen Henderson

(24 Nov. 1883–3 Feb. 1977) and (18 Sept. 1885–4 Feb. 1976), Edwin Bancroft Henderson, physical educator, author, civil rights activist, and sports pioneer and his wife, Mary Ellen Meriwether Henderson, educator and civil rights activist, were married for sixty-five years. Each worked for educational equality and social justice for African Americans for over fifty years. Both were born in Washington, D.C. Edwin was the eldest son of William Henderson, an employee of the Federal Bureau of Engraving, and Louisa Mars Henderson, who owned and operated a grocery store. Mary Ellen was one of four children born to James Henry Meriwether, an attorney and Mary Louise Robinson Meriwether, a teacher and activist. Edwin and Mary Ellen met at Miner Teachers College in Washington, D.C., where both were studying to become teachers. Edwin graduated in 1904 and Mary Ellen in 1905. They were married in 1910, and moved to Edwin's family home in Falls Church in Northern Virginia.

Edwin dedicated his life to fighting for equality in athletics and education. He attended the Sergeant Dudley School of Physical Training at Harvard University for three summers (1904, 1905, and 1907) where he became the first black male to receive certification in physical education in 1907. While at Harvard, he learned to play basketball, a game that had originated in Springfield, Massachusetts, a few years earlier in the early 1890s. He saw the game as a vehicle that blacks could use to prove their equality to whites and would be part of a college education and focused his efforts on the promotion of interscholastic athletics. An avid basketball player, Edwin is credited with being the first (1904) to introduce the game on a wide scale organized basis to African Americans in the Washington, D.C., area. Henderson promoted athletics in the schools and the surrounding African American community. He organized the Washington 12th Streeters and they competed against black teams along the east coast and from across the country, ending with the best teams competing in the Colored Basketball World

Championship. In 1909–1910, as captain, Henderson led the team to win the Colored Basketball World Championship. The following year, Henderson petitioned Howard University to take his 12th Streeters YMCA team, minus himself, as its first varsity team. Howard accepted the team and again they won the Colored Basketball World Championship for the 1910–1911 season.

Edwin B. Henderson is best known for laying the groundwork and creating the infrastructure so that African Americans could participate in organized athletics. He established the Interscholastic Athletic Association of the Middle Atlantic States (1906), the Public School Athletic League for the segregated colored schools of Washington, D.C. (1905), and the Eastern Board of Officials for African American athletic competitions (1905). In 1923 he earned a doctorate from The Central Chiropractic College in Washington, D.C. A prolific writer, Edwin wrote over 3,000 editorial letters, which were published in newspapers across the country. He used these letters as a platform to fight segregation and discrimination. He authored several books that spread awareness about the emergence of black sports. His groundbreaking works include, *The Official Spaulding Handbook* (1910–1913), *The Negro in Sports* (1939; revised in 1949), and *The Black Athlete: Emergence and Arrival* (1969). In 1933, he earned a masters degree from Columbia University.

Mary Ellen was an outstanding teacher in Washington, D.C. Upon her marriage, she left the classroom because married women were not permitted to teach in the district at the time. Edwin continued to work in Washington, while Mary Ellen helped run the family farm, took care of their two sons, Edwin and James, and played piano at the two local black churches. In 1919, the black community implored Mary Ellen to re-open the local school for blacks. The school was closed because there was no teacher. After school officials found a caregiver for her toddler son, Mary Ellen agreed to re-open the two-room frame colored school. She served as principal, recruited another teacher, and taught fourth, fifth, sixth, and seventh grades in one room. The building was overcrowded, lacked running water, indoor toilets, and was heated by a potbellied stove. The students used cast off books from the white schools and had few supplies. Nearby, white children were being educated inside brick buildings with indoor plumbing, running water, central heat, janitorial services, and school bus service. Despite these difficult conditions of segregation, Mary Ellen taught with vitality and enthusiasm and her

students were noted for being well prepared when they attended eighth grade in Washington, D.C.

Mary Ellen worked to improve learning conditions for her students. From 1919, when she began teaching, records indicate Mary Ellen appeared regularly before the school board for thirty years appealing for the construction of a new school for black children. The community held fund-raisers and contributed the money toward the construction of the new school for their children. Often Mary Ellen appealed for supplies or books and took community spokespersons with her to school board meetings. After decades of persistence without results, she changed her tactics. Mary Ellen launched a study into the disparity between white and black school facilities, focusing on the learning environment and resources in the 1936 school budget. This study showed that 97.3 percent of the budget for Fairfax County went to educate white students, while only 2.7 percent went toward educating African American students.

Mary Ellen's work led to the formation of an interracial committee in Fairfax County, Virginia. Ultimately the school board agreed to build the first new school for African American children in the area. In 1948 the James Lee School was constructed on the same site where the two-room schoolhouse stood, land donated by African American land owner James Lee. Following Mary Ellen's success, her strategy was used as the model for educational redress throughout the nation.

In 1915, when their hometown of Falls Church, Virginia, proposed passing an ordinance to segregate all African Americans to a designated area of town, the Hendersons were among those who challenged the law. Edwin, along with Joseph Tinner, a stone mason and outstanding orator in the community, founded the Colored Citizens' Protective League (CCPL). The group pooled their resources and hired two attorneys. The CCPL succeeded not only in defeating the segregation ordinance, but also in advancing numerous civil rights endeavors. The organization later became the first rural branch in the nation of the NAACP. Dr. Henderson, held offices at the local and state levels in the NAACP, as well as other civil rights organizations, and his wife was the leading recruiter of members in the state. The couple was highly active at the state and local levels. Their stand made them the target of hundreds of threatening phone calls, letters and a cross burning on their front lawn. These extraordinary individuals not only affected their community, they helped shape the nation.

After retirement, the Hendersons moved to Tuskegee, Alabama, to live with their youngest son, James, a professor at Tuskegee University and his family. Edwin B. Henderson received many honors, including being inducted as a charter member into the Black Athletes Hall of Fame in 1974.

In recognition of Mary Ellen's dedication to educational equality, a new school was named in her honor in 2005 in Falls Church, Virginia: the Mary Ellen Henderson Middle School. In 2007 presidential artist, Simmie Knox, painted a portrait of Mary Ellen Meriwether, which hangs in the new school. A museum quality traveling exhibit was created in her honor as well.

FURTHER READING

Knock, Patricia I. *A Century of Just Women: Northern Virginia's African American Women, 1900–1999* (2001).

Kuska, Bob. *Hot Potato: How Washington and New York Gave Birth to Black Basketball and Changed America's Game Forever* (2004).

Oti, Donna. "Ned and Nell: E.B. and Mary Ellen Henderson Impact a Community and a Nation," *Homes of Color Magazine*, vol. 5, issue 6, November/December 2006.

Wiggins, David K., and Patrick B. Miller. *The Unlevel Playing Field: A Documentary History of the African American Experience in Sports* (2003).

EDWIN B. HENDERSON II AND
NIKKI GRAVES HENDERSON

Henderson, Fletcher (18 Dec. 1897–29 Dec. 1952), musician, was born Fletcher Hamilton Henderson Jr. in Cuthbert, Georgia, the son of Fletcher Hamilton Henderson Sr., a Latin and mathematics teacher, and Ozie Lena Chapman, a pianist. His middle-class family disapproved of jazz and blues, and Henderson studied piano with his classically trained mother. He graduated from Atlanta University in 1920 with a chemistry degree and then moved to New York City to pursue postgraduate studies. For a short time he was a laboratory assistant in a chemical firm, but with few opportunities for black chemists he became a part-time song demonstrator for the Pace-Handy Music Company. He subsequently worked as house pianist and recording manager for Black Swan Records, where his duties included accompanying ETHEL WATERS and BESSIE SMITH and arranging tours for Waters and the Black Swan Troubadours. He married Leora Meoux in 1924; they had no children.

Henderson eventually began to lead his own small groups in engagements at clubs and dances. He successfully auditioned for an opening at the Club Alabam on West 44th Street in late 1923, and the following summer the band took up residence at the Roseland Ballroom, which Henderson used as a base for the next decade. At first the group was little more than an ordinary dance band, playing watered-down blues and pop tunes. But Henderson also hired the best talent he could find, including COLEMAN HAWKINS on tenor saxophone and DON REDMAN as musical director. Redman's arrangements in particular had a profound and lasting influence on big band jazz. He separated reed and brass sections and played them off against each other. One section would play the melodic lead, for instance, and the other would answer during pauses, or else it would punctuate the playing with brief, rhythmic figures. In the group's recording of "Copenhagen" in late 1924, the music moved from one section or soloist to another twenty-four times in three minutes. Still, the band at this stage played stiffly, with little jazz feeling.

Also in 1924 the group's style took another major step forward when Henderson hired LOUIS ARMSTRONG. Although Armstrong stayed with the band for only a short while, his lyrical style and propulsive sense of swing strongly influenced Henderson's men, who now began to play with more feeling and a more inventive sense of melody. During the next two years they broke through to become the first great big band in jazz history. Their recording of "Stampede" in May 1926 marks an early peak. Hawkins in particular was vastly improved over his initial recordings, playing with a powerful expressiveness and a rich, full-bodied sound. The trumpeter REX STEWART contributed fiery solos, while Redman himself was writing fuller, better-integrated section passages. Recordings show the band continuing to improve over the next nine or ten months. Then in March 1927 Redman left to co-lead McKinney's Cotton Pickers. Henderson gradually lost interest in the band, his focus further blurred by an auto accident in the summer of 1928 in which he suffered head injuries. Between 1927 and 1930 the group made only a dozen or so recordings, mostly ponderous efforts that showed a steady deterioration from the advances of 1926 and early 1927.

Henderson's own weakness as a leader proved to be the last straw. In 1929 the band went to Philadelphia to rehearse for a musical review. The director, Vincent Youmans, brought in about twenty white musicians, mostly string players, to augment the band, and he suggested that an outside conductor also be hired. Henderson agreed, and the new conductor began to fire Henderson's players, giving their positions to white musicians. Henderson said nothing. Disillusioned, most of the musicians never worked for him again.

Henderson rebuilt the band, and by 1931 they were recording again. This time the group was more of a showcase for individual players, built on exchanges between the sections and the soloists. The young saxophonist Benny Carter contributed swinging, spare arrangements; Walter Johnson on drums and JOHN KIRBY on bass provided strong rhythmic support. Carter's composition, "Keep a Song in Your Soul," is a fine example of the band's playing from this period. In December 1932 the band recorded an arrangement of "King Porter Stomp" that mightily swung, the solos seamlessly integrated with the ensembles. Hawkins's playing was masterful, and he dominated the band for the next two years before leaving for England. Henderson also had become his own arranger, turning to sparer arrangements than Redman's that created a light, unpretentious sound. His tunes were set in unusual keys, and his tempos more consistently swung. The band's 1934 recording of "Wrappin' It Up" perfectly illustrates this style, one which influenced the entire big band era. The piece opens with a call-and-response pattern; as the brass section states a fanfare, the saxophones respond, and the two sections engage in a brief exchange. In the first chorus the saxes state the main theme, and the brasses comment, joined at one point by the trumpets. The pattern continues through the arrangement, creating one of the early swing era masterpieces.

Unfortunately, by this time Henderson had lost much of his drive. He dissolved the group in 1934, and in 1935 he sold the arrangements for "Wrappin' It Up" and several other pieces to Benny Goodman, who used them to help fuel the swing craze of the later 1930s.

Henderson's last great band was a 1936 ensemble that included the trumpeter ROY ELDRIDGE. Throughout the 1930s he also maintained a close relationship with his brother HORACE W. HENDERSON, who often served as pianist and arranger for the band and later led an important group of his own. Henderson worked briefly as an arranger for Goodman in 1939, and he failed several times to establish new bands. In 1950 he wrote music for the short-lived New York show *The Jazz Train* and led the accompanying band. He settled in that same year at Cafe Society in New York with a sextet. He

suffered a stroke in December and another in 1952, dying from a heart attack in New York City.

Henderson's influence on jazz and particularly on the development of big bands was pervasive and lasting. Although personally withdrawn and lacking leadership qualities, he was a superb judge of talent, an excellent pianist, and an outstanding musician. Through the musical innovations he introduced in his various groups he profoundly influenced the work of DUKE ELLINGTON, Goodman, COUNT BASIE, and other big bands of the swing era, thereby laying an important foundation for an entire genre of jazz playing.

FURTHER READING
Henderson's personal papers are located at the Amistad Research Center at Tulane University.
Allen, W. C. *Hendersonia: The Music of Fletcher Henderson and His Musicians: A Bio-discography* (1973).
Schuller, Gunther. *Early Jazz: Its Roots and Musical Development* (1968).
Schuller, Gunther. *The Swing Era: The Development of Jazz, 1930–1945* (1989).
Shapiro, Nat, and Nat Hentoff, eds. *The Jazz Makers* (1957).
Obituary: *New York Times*, 31 Dec. 1952.
This entry is taken from the *American National Biography* and is published here with the permission of the American Council of Learned Societies.

RONALD P. DUFOUR

Henderson, Horace W. (22 Nov. 1904–29 Aug. 1988), jazz and popular arranger, bandleader, and pianist, was born in Cuthbert, Georgia, the son of Fletcher H. Henderson Sr., a teacher, and Ozie Lena Chapman. He studied piano formally from about age fourteen to seventeen, at which time he left home to finish high school at the preparatory school of Wilberforce University in Ohio and then attend the university. In 1924 he visited his older brother, the bandleader FLETCHER HENDERSON, in New York City during summer vacation. Upon his return he formed an eight-piece school orchestra called Horace Henderson's Collegians. The band played local dances; the trumpeter Freddie Jenkins was an early member.

In the summer of 1925 the Collegians traveled to New York City, where Fletcher secured a job for them at the Bamville Club in Harlem. The alto saxophonist Benny Carter joined the band in Pittsburgh, Pennsylvania, on its way back to school and remained with Henderson into 1926 (though Carter did not, as often reported, attend Wilberforce). Following Carter's departure from the band, the cornetist REX STEWART joined, having deemed himself incapable of replacing LOUIS ARMSTRONG in Fletcher's orchestra. The saxophonists Elmer Williams, Castor McCord, and Ted McCord were also members during this period.

While at Wilberforce Henderson studied music for two years, disappointing his father by earning a bachelor of arts rather than a degree in science. He then followed his brother into a musical career. During these years Henderson borrowed freely from Fletcher's musical library, and his band often worked under Fletcher's name. Carter rejoined the band for a residency at the Savoy Ballroom, beginning in February 1928, and largely took over the band during the summer while Henderson played with the bandleader Sammy Stewart in Chicago, Illinois, and on tour in Ohio.

Henderson reorganized his band, now known as the Stompers, in Ohio in October 1928. The group included the trumpeter ROY ELDRIDGE, a teenager he had discovered in Pittsburgh. The Stompers toured throughout 1929 with many changes in membership, most notably the replacement of Eldridge by Jonah Jones. The band was routinely billed under Fletcher's name.

Henderson formed a third new band for a ballroom engagement at the Dunbar Palace in New York City from 1930 into 1931. With the trombonist Sandy Williams in the band, Henderson's men battled Fletcher's at the Dunbar on 19 October 1930. One published account rated the battle a tie, which attests to the quality of Henderson's ensemble. Apart from his band he recorded as pianist with the Chocolate Dandies in December 1930 and in Fletcher's big band, which recorded two of his compositions and arrangements, "Hot and Anxious" and "Comin' and Going," in March 1931. After a period of difficulty finding work, Henderson remained as pianist and arranger for his own group but gave the band's direction over to DON REDMAN for a job at Connie's Inn in Harlem early in 1932. The association with Redman proved uncomfortable, but Henderson remained in the band until the spring of 1933. In November 1932 he played in the pit orchestra at Loew's State Theater in New York as the pianist in DUKE ELLINGTON's orchestra, under Ellington's direction.

From about May 1933 to November 1934 Henderson worked with Fletcher's big band as pianist and writer. Under Henderson's nominal leadership the band recorded several titles on 3 October 1933, but his recorded contributions under Fletcher's name were more significant. These include his 1933 arrangements of "Yeah Man!" "Queer Notions," and "Nagasaki," as well as the original compositions and arrangements of 1934, "Big John's Special" and "Rug Cutter's Swing." After a well-publicized dispute between the brothers the band appeared under either Henderson's or Carter's direction at the Apollo Theater in November 1934, while Fletcher led a new band at the Harlem Opera House; accounts of this incident are conflicting and unclear.

Henderson supplied a few arrangements to Benny Goodman early in 1935 and joined Vernon Andrade's orchestra during that spring and summer. He rejoined Fletcher intermittently during 1935 and full time in January 1936 at the Grand Terrace in Chicago. The band's big hit of this period—the saxophonist CHU BERRY's riff tune "Christopher Columbus," recorded in March—is one of several arrangements credited to Fletcher but claimed by Henderson. Fletcher's biographer Walter C. Allen speculates that the misattribution was made when Fletcher supplied these arrangements to Goodman, who presumed they were Fletcher's own; in an oral history taken for the Smithsonian Institution, Horace gives an account of bringing "Christopher Columbus" into the band after hearing Berry perform it with a small group.

In July 1937 Henderson left to lead his own band for a year at Swingland in Chicago. The band was televised on CBS and expected to embark on a successful tour, but the tour failed because of poor management. During a fourteen-month stand at the 5100 Club in Chicago, Henderson's big band included the trumpeter Emmett Berry, the tenor saxophonists Dave Young and Elmer Williams, and the trumpeter and violinist RAY NANCE. (Nance is featured on a February 1940 recording of Henderson's composition "Kitty on Toast," which Nance subsequently brought into Duke Ellington's repertoire.) After a brief stay at the Tropical Room in Chicago, Henderson reorganized and improved his group by retaining Berry but otherwise taking over most of Nat Towles's big band. In New York City in October 1940 they recorded an acclaimed but seldom heard session that produced "Smooth Sailing" and "You Don't Mean Me No Good."

Henderson remained in New York from late 1940 into 1941 as house arranger for the bandleader and saxophonist Charlie Barnet, for whom he wrote "Charleston Alley" and "Ponce de Leon," recorded by Barnet in 1941. Henderson claimed to have discovered the singer LENA HORNE at the Apollo Theater in Harlem and to have brought her into Barnet's band; in her autobiography Horne credits the Apollo choreographer Clarence Robinson and makes no mention of Henderson, but their stories are otherwise consistent, and it seems plausible that he transmitted Barnet's request to Robinson. Henderson also wrote arrangements for Jimmy Dorsey's big band around this time. Horace served as a substitute in Fletcher's band early in 1942 and returned with his own band to Swingland, renamed the Rhumboogie, only to be drafted into the army in November 1942. As a sergeant in charge of musical activities at Camp Des Plaines in Joliet, Illinois, he directed a forty-five-piece field band and three dance bands until he was discharged for being over age in August 1943.

A civilian again, Henderson rejoined Fletcher, serving as pianist, musical director, and arranger. During this period JIMMIE LUNCEFORD's big band recorded his composition and arrangement "Jeep Rhythm" (Feb. 1944). While in California in May 1944, Henderson left Fletcher to form a small group. Horne was grateful for the boost that Henderson had given to her career, and although he occasionally worked with Fletcher on tour from 1945 to 1947, he mainly served as Horne's accompanist, arranger, and road manager for a tour of RKO theaters and army camps and for engagements in Chicago and New York City. At this last venue the stellar band accompanying Horne comprised the trumpeter Dick Vance, the trombonist BENNY MORTON, the reed players EDMOND HALL and EARL BOSTIC, the pianist Henderson, the guitarist Al Casey, the bassist BILLY TAYLOR, and the drummer SID CATLETT. When Horne left for Europe in 1947 Henderson took a job in Idaho leading a quartet. He led a band that included the trumpeter Teddy Buckner in Los Angeles, and in 1949 he replaced the pianist Bobby Tucker as BILLIE HOLIDAY's accompanist.

Henderson was based in Minneapolis, Minnesota, in the early 1950s but then began leading bands regularly in Las Vegas, Nevada, including one featuring the trumpeter and singer Clora Bryant. He led small combos and in 1962 briefly tried to revive his late brother's big band in Long Beach, California. He lived in Glendale, California, until about 1964 and then moved to Denver, Colorado, continuing to lead bands. At the time of a 1975 interview he was still playing regularly, but as an electric organist, having taken up the instrument around 1969. In the interview he hotly denied resentment of Fletcher's achievements and charges of his having filched some

of Fletcher's scores, as had been reported by Allen and others. He said he idolized his older brother, who had put him through college and freely shared big band arrangements. Henderson died in Denver, survived by his wife, Angell, and a daughter from a previous marriage. Details of his marriages are unknown.

Henderson obviously had a fine ear for talent, to which the careers of Carter, Eldridge, Nance, and Horne testify. Although not a renowned pianist he played with a better sense of swing than Fletcher—hence his usefulness as a sideman, taking Fletcher's place in many performances—and he was better able to adapt to changing styles. He is most important as an arranger and writer. His own preference was for his arrangement of COLEMAN HAWKINS's composition "Queer Notions," an aptly titled piece that explores whole-tone scales and features an unusual accompaniment based mainly on an oscillation between two dissonant chords. But the eccentricities of this piece are unrepresentative of Henderson's work, which is otherwise firmly based on conventions of the big band era. "Yeah Man!" (1933; recycled as "Hotter then 'ell" in 1934) features perhaps his most memorable use of the classic device of trading an idea between sections of the big band, as the instruments toss back and forth a chord that slides downward. "Big John's Special" is his best-known piece, subsequently made into a toe-tapping anthem of the swing era by Goodman, who presented it in the Let's Dance radio broadcasts of 1935, used it as the encore at his celebrated Carnegie Hall concert in January 1938, and recorded a studio version in May 1938.

FURTHER READING
Information about Henderson can be found in the oral histories at the Institute of Jazz Studies in Newark, N.J.
Allen, Walter C. *Hendersonia: The Music of Fletcher Henderson and His Musicians: A Bio-discography* (1973).
McCarthy, Albert. *Big Band Jazz* (1974).
Schuller, Gunther. *The Swing Era: The Development of Jazz, 1930–1945* (1989).
Obituary: *New York Times*, 16 Sept. 1988.

This entry is taken from the *American National Biography* and is published here with the permission of the American Council of Learned Societies.

BARRY KERNFELD

Henderson, Joe (24 Apr. 1937–30 June 2001), jazz saxophonist, composer, and educator, was born

Joseph Arthur Henderson in Lima, Ohio, the son of Dennis Lloyd Henderson, a worker in a steel mill, and Irene Farley. Henderson was one of fifteen children, and much of his introduction to the world of jazz came as a result of the musical interests of his many siblings. An older brother, James T., was an especially important influence: his collection of jazz recordings sparked Joe's curiosity, and James eventually helped Joe, then around nine, to transcribe a solo by LESTER YOUNG. Joe was precocious from the beginning. By the age of sixteen he was performing professionally, and he had already penned what eventually became his best-known jazz composition, "Recordame."

After graduating from high school, Joe Henderson left Lima for Frankfort, Kentucky, to study music at Kentucky State College. He moved to Detroit just a year later, pursuing opportunities to study saxophone performance and music theory at the Teal School of Music, as well as flute and double bass at Wayne State University. Around this time he married and had a son. In keeping with his nickname "the Phantom"—a nickname that he received much later for his intense privacy and for his mysterious tendency to disappear for extended periods of time—nothing is known of either relationship. It was in Detroit that Henderson began to establish himself as a promising young sound on the saxophone. After mining some formative affiliations with local musicians like Donald Byrd and YUSEF LATEEF, he began leading his own combo in 1959.

Henderson's career, like those of so many other jazz musicians in the postwar era, then took a detour in military service. After enlisting in 1960, Henderson joined an army band in Fort Benning, Georgia, and was subsequently invited to tour, doubling on bass and tenor sax, with a jazz ensemble that entertained troops stationed around the world. By the time that Henderson was discharged he was ready to make the jump to the New York City scene; his travels had enabled him to cultivate as early as the age of twenty-five a mature sound and an original approach to the saxophone.

Although Henderson expressed throughout his career a considerable amount of displeasure in being compared to the tenor saxophonists JOHN COLTRANE and SONNY ROLLINS, his status as a legend in the jazz canon makes such comparisons somewhat inevitable. Henderson shared much of Rollins's propulsive rhythmic sense and Coltrane's affinity for the tonal extremes of the saxophone, but Henderson's combination of harmonic sophistication and technical freedom was something

new altogether. Many critics have characterized Henderson's distinctive conception, borrowing the title of one of his early albums for the Blue Note label, as "in 'n out": he seamlessly combined hard-swinging, gutbucket inside phrases with outside harmonic flights; a cavernous tone in the lower registers of the saxophone with light, flutelike sonorities in the horn's altissimo reaches; and fiery, experimental incantations with passages of haunting tenderness and elegance.

It was this style that caught the ears of the trumpeter Kenny Dorham upon Henderson's arrival in New York in the summer of 1962. After an almost storybook debut sitting in at a club with DEXTER KEITH GORDON—immortalized in Dorham's liner notes to Henderson's first album, *Page One*—Henderson gained an underground notoriety among New York jazz musicians and was in the Blue Note recording studio eight months later for Dorham's *Una Mas*. The Henderson-Dorham nexus proved significant. As co-leaders of a collective quintet they released a series of classic albums for Blue Note under Henderson's name—*Page One* (1963), *Our Thing* (1963), and *In 'n Out* (1964)—while Henderson's exceptional quartet performance on *Inner Urge* (1964) hinted at the directions that he would take through the early 1970s on the Milestone label, without Dorham. The Blue Note and Milestone recordings also featured several compositions from Henderson's pen: "Recordame," "Inner Urge," "Isotope," "The Kicker," "Black Narcissus," and "Mamacita." All these songs became jazz standards, and he revisited them frequently throughout the remainder of his career.

In the meantime Henderson found himself in constant demand as a sideman, making remarkable contributions to albums by GRANT GREEN, LEE MORGAN, ANDREW HILL, BOBBY HUTCHERSON, McCOY TYNER, and Freddie Hubbard. In spring 1964 Henderson replaced Junior Cook in HORACE SILVER's longtime quintet; he toured with Silver for a little more than two years, recording along the way one of the best-selling albums in jazz history, *Song for My Father*. He also spent time playing with MILES DAVIS's quintets in 1967, with HERBIE HANCOCK's groups in 1969, and with the fusion band Blood, Sweat, and Tears in 1971.

Perhaps troubled by commercial shifts in the jazz recording industry, Henderson left New York for San Francisco in 1972. Around this time he married a woman named Linda (further details of this relationship are unknown) and began teaching saxophone to students in the San Francisco Bay Area.

Henderson distanced himself from the New York scene in the late 1970s and early 1980s only to return with a pathbreaking 1985 recording, *The State of the Tenor*, which captured a series of live pianoless trio performances at New York's Village Vanguard club. Henderson's masterly playing there—which both echoed and expanded on Sonny Rollins's seminal pianoless trio recordings at the same venue almost thirty years earlier—seemed to confirm his status as a true jazz innovator.

It was not until 1992, however, that Henderson achieved such acclaim. The Verve label's release of Henderson's *Lush Life*, an album made up entirely of compositions by BILLY STRAYHORN, was met with an unprecedented combination of critical approval and financial success—both a symptom of and an impetus for the so-called neoclassical movement in jazz that held sway throughout the 1990s. *Lush Life* remains Henderson's most famous recording, and arguably his finest; it won a Grammy Award for Best instrumental Jazz Album. Over the next five years Verve issued four more albums featuring Henderson's interpretations of standard material, two of which also won Grammys: *So Near, So Far* (Henderson on Miles Davis), *Joe Henderson Big Band* (Henderson on Henderson himself), *Double Rainbow* (Henderson on Antonio Carlos Jobim), and *Porgy and Bess* (Henderson on George Gershwin). His playing on these albums is consistently inspired.

In 1998 an emphysema-related stroke forced Henderson to stop playing in public, and he died of heart failure three years later in San Francisco. Kenny Dorham dubbed Henderson the "astronaut of the tenor sax" in 1963. This unconventional description certainly proved prescient: nearly all contemporary saxophonists strive to reach the colossal heights of his work.

FURTHER READING

Dorham, Kenny. Liner notes to *Page One* (Blue Note B2-84140).
Martin, Mel. "Interview with Joe Henderson," *Saxophone Journal* (Mar./Apr. 1991).
Obituary: *New York Times*, 3 July 2001.

BRIAN P. HOCHMAN

Henderson, Luther (14 Mar. 1919–29 July 2003), composer, arranger, orchestrator, conductor, and pianist, was born Luther Lincoln Henderson Jr. in Kansas City, the second child and only son of Florence Black, a public school teacher, and Luther Lincoln Henderson Sr., a professor of education, both of whom had musical aspirations.

In 1923 the family moved to New York City. Living first on Strivers Row and then in Sugar Hill, Henderson found himself surrounded by the rhythms and sounds of 1920s Harlem. His love of music embraced both jazz and classical. After hearing Ignace Paderewski at Carnegie Hall, his passion for the piano increased and the neighborhood children nicknamed him Paddy.

Luther also loved to read, and even at a young age he was a moralist, a philosopher, and a seeker of commonality and acceptance. He attended Evander Childs High School, along with his best friend Mercer Ellington, son of renowned composer and bandleader Duke Ellington. His high school graduation speech, titled "A Black Man's Plea," concludes with the hope "that someday the unholy barrier of prejudice will crumble and fall and that white man and his black brother will live in mutual amity and goodwill, born out of the understanding and appreciation of each one's contributions to our common life, our common heritage and our common destiny."

While in high school, Henderson had a working jazz trio and in 1934 won one of the famed amateur contests at the Apollo Theater. However, having scored 100 percent on his Geometry Regents exam, he decided to become a mathematician. Tuition at City College was free and he enrolled as a math major in 1936. Attending school by day and playing music at night, it took two years before Luther realized that his love lay elsewhere and persuaded his parents to pay his tuition at the Institute of Musical Art, later known as the Juilliard School of Music.

Studying the classics in school while making a living performing with the Leonard Ware Trio, Henderson soon married Tealene Alma Berry and they had two sons. He graduated in 1942 with a Bachelor of Science degree in music education, the only African American student in his class. He had no interest in becoming a school teacher, so he continued to play in jazz clubs and began writing band arrangements for Duke Ellington. In 1943 he also wrote dance arrangements for KATHERINE DUNHAM's Tropical Revue.

During World War II Henderson served as an arranger for the Navy Band stationed at Great Lakes Naval Station in Illinois and staff orchestrator for The U.S. Navy School of Music. He continued to write for Ellington's band and when he was discharged in 1946 he began work on his first theater project, Ellington's Broadway musical, Beggar's Holiday. Soon he was working on symphonic orchestrations for Ellington, who having given himself the nickname "Tentacles," called Henderson "my classical arm" and hired him to work on "Harlem," "New World A-Comin'," "Night Creature," and "A Drum Is a Woman." He also orchestrated "Three Black Kings," staged by the Dance Theater of Harlem. Henderson's musical love affair with all things Ellington was lifelong, despite the hurt of being denied recognition for his work.

From 1947 to 1950 Henderson worked as pianist and musical director for LENA HORNE. After that, singers flocked to him, wanting him to write their shows for nightclub performances and recordings, a trend that continued for decades with artists such as Bea Arthur, Robert Goulet, DIAHANN CARROLL, Nancy Wilson, Goldie Hawn, and Florence Henderson. M.S.. Horne even called him back thirty years later to work on her one-woman show, *Lena Horne: The Lady and Her Music.*

The 1950s also brought opportunities in television. Albeit off camera because of his skin color, it was Henderson who orchestrated and conducted for *Playhouse 90: The Helen Morgan Story,* starring Polly Bergen. His music was also heard on television programs such as *The Ed Sullivan Show, The Bell Telephone Hour,* and specials for the pop stars of the day including Dean Martin, Carol Burnett, Andy Williams, and Victor Borge.

Henderson's civil rights activism was low key but he felt the issues profoundly. His papers include a thank you note from SAMMY DAVIS JR. for his participation in the 1956 Civil Rights Rally at Madison Square Garden. His close friends included Marian and ARTHUR LOGAN and Rachel and JACKIE ROBINSON. In 1963 they all staged "An Afternoon of Jazz," raising $14,000 for MARTIN LUTHER KING JR. and the Southern Christian Leadership Conference. The fund-raiser became an annual tradition, later supporting the Robinson Foundation and other causes.

Divorced from his first wife, Henderson married actress Stephanie Lebeau in 1956 and they had a daughter. In 1958 he was back on Broadway writing dance arrangements for *Flower Drum Song,* and in the forty-plus years that followed he arranged and composed music for some of Broadway's greatest hits, including *Funny Girl, No No Nanette, Purlie!, Ain't Misbehavin',* and *Jelly's Last Jam,* starring such performers as Barbra Streisand, Laine Kazan, Robert Guillaume, SAVION GLOVER, Andre Deshields, Tonya Pinkins, and GREGORY HINES.

His second wife died in 1967. Work had slowed and Henderson became a single father with lots of debt and tax problems. With occasional work on a few shows (most notably *Purlie!* and *No No Nanette),* Henderson continued to write arrangements for record dates and coach singers. He worked on the annual Oldsmobile industrial shows for more than thirty years, which helped to pay the bills. In 1972 he married Margo Stamos, one of his vocal students; they had no children and she died in April 1979.

In 1978 the success of *Ain't Misbehavin',* a Broadway show celebrating the songs of FATS WALLER, marked a professional and financial turning point—for the first time he was entitled to a percentage of the show's profits.

In the spring of 1980 actress/director Billie Allen, a longtime friend, asked him to write the music for her production of *The Crystal Tree* at the AMAS Playhouse. A long, dormant romance was rekindled and that winter she joined him in Paris during an overseas run of *Ain't Misbehavin';* they were married in February 1981.

Growing up black in America, embracing both jazz and classical music—one an American art form that has yet to be fully appreciated and the other a field not truly open to blacks at that time—was not a path to fame and fortune. So Henderson carved his own inroads. One of his greatest pleasures was his twenty-year association with the Canadian Brass; his 150-plus classical and jazz arrangements written for them continue to be played by school brass ensembles nationwide.

Henderson acknowledged Ellington as a defining force in his life, and he identified his 1999 Classic Ellington project with Sir Simon Rattle and the Birmingham Symphony in Great Britain as the high point of his career. He was eighty years old and had waited nearly sixty years for such an opportunity; its success gave rise to a reprise in America at Carnegie Hall in 2000. Offers for other symphonic projects, including a commission from the Berlin Philharmonic, were finally coming in, but it was too late. Luther was fighting cancer.

Honors came late in life. He was twice nominated for Broadway's Tony Award—in 1992 for Best Score (Musical) for *Jelly's Last Jam* and in 1997 for Best Orchestrations for *Play On!* In 2002 Henderson and his wife received a VIV Pioneer Award for excellence in black theatre. The following year when his wife told him that he had just been named as a recipient of a National Endowment for the Arts Jazz Master Fellowship, an honor that pleased him greatly, Henderson said one word: "Recognition." He had little energy to say more; a few weeks later, his battle was over. He was eighty-four years old when he died in New York.

In 2006, to commemorate his legacy and give aid to students of color with musical aspirations, his widow, Billie Allen-Henderson, established the Luther Henderson Scholarship Fund, now endowing scholarships at the Juilliard School.

FURTHER READING

Luther Henderson's early papers are housed in the Manuscripts, Archives and Rare Books Division, Schomburg Center for Research in Black Culture in New York City. His later papers are housed in the Music Division, Library of Congress, Washington, D.C. There is also an Interview of Henderson by Eugene Holley, Jazz Oral History Program Collection, Archives Center, National Museum of American History, Smithsonian Institution.

Obituaries: *New York Times*, 1 August 2003; *Jet*, 18 August 2003.

DEVRA HALL LEVY

Henderson, Rickey (25 Dec. 1958–), baseball player, was born Rickey Henley in Chicago to John Henley and Bobbie (maiden name unknown). Henderson's birth itself prefigured a life devoted to being fast: he was born in the backseat of his parents' Oldsmobile en route to the hospital. When his son was only two years old John Henley left the family, never to be seen or heard from again. After John left, Bobbie Henley moved the family back to her hometown of Pine Bluff, Arkansas, where they lived on Rickey's grandmother's farm, giving Rickey a country upbringing that greatly influenced him. When Rickey was eight, Bobbie Henley left for California to establish herself, with the hope of eventually bringing her children to the West Coast. He and his brothers stayed on the farm with their grandmother. While working as a nurse in California, Bobbie met and married Paul Henderson, who adopted all of her five boys (born to three different fathers) and gave them all the name Henderson. The couple had two more children together, both girls. When Rickey Henderson was ten years old the entire family, including his grandmother, moved to Oakland, California, to live with his mother and stepfather. When the Henderson marriage eventually split up, Bobbie and her mother continued raising the children in Oakland.

While attending Oakland Technical High School, Henderson excelled at four sports and was all-city in both baseball and football. During his senior year he received football scholarship offers from twenty universities and was close to accepting an offer to study at Arizona State University because it had strong programs in both the sports that he loved. While at Oakland Tech, Henderson met Pamela Palmer, who became his lifelong partner. On 8 June 1976, while he was still in high school and before he was even eighteen, Henderson was selected in the fourth round of the amateur draft by his hometown Oakland Athletics. On the advice of his mother, who told him that he was too smart for football and who feared that he would get injured, Henderson signed with Oakland and reported to the minor leagues immediately rather than wait and go to college in the fall.

Henderson reported to the A's single-A farm team in Boise, Idaho, in the middle of the 1976 season, and in forty-six games he hit .336 with twenty-nine stolen bases in thirty-six attempts. In 1977 Henderson led the California League with ninety-five stolen bases (the record at the time), while batting .345 and scoring 104 runs. On 26 May 1977 Henderson became the fourth professional player to steal seven bases in one game. His speed and base-stealing abilities soon made him famous.

On 24 June 1979 at the age of twenty-one Rickey Henderson made his major league debut. In his first game, against the Texas Rangers, Henderson went 2 for 4 and stole his first base in the majors. He went on to steal thirty-two more bases that season (leading the team) and bat .274. In 1980, after Billy Martin came on board as the A's manager, Henderson led the league in stolen bases, stealing 100, the first of three times that he would do so. His 100 stolen bases broke Ty Cobb's American League record of ninety-six, which had stood for sixty-five years. Between 1980 and 1991 Henderson led the American League in stolen bases every year except the 1987 season, when he played in only ninety-five games because of a hamstring injury—yet he still managed to steal forty-one.

From early on it was clear that there was something different about Henderson: an extra jump in his step, a little more flash than was found in most players. Henderson's trademarks—the headfirst slide on stolen bases, the stutter step at each base during a home-run trot, the swatting of his glove from over his head to his leg on easy fly balls—made him popular with fans, but this flashiness had its downside. Henderson earned a reputation as a selfish player, a hotdogger, and a highly egotistical athlete who was focused only on his own statistics. Whether true or not, this reputation was perpetuated by the media, with whom Henderson had what could at best be regarded as a turbulent relationship.

On 5 December 1984 Henderson was traded by the Oakland Athletics to the New York Yankees in a seven-player deal. Even though he missed the first ten games of the 1985 season, his first year with the Yankees was one of his greatest statistically. Henderson hit .314, scored 146 runs, had a .419 on-base percentage and a .516 slugging percentage, and became the first American League player to hit twenty homers and steal fifty bases in a season. Between 1985 and 1989 Henderson's career blossomed in New York. He led the league in stolen bases three times, scored more than 100 runs, and made the all-star team in each of his four seasons in New York.

On 21 June 1989 the Yankees traded Henderson back to the A's. Between 1989 and 1993 Henderson had the most successful stint of his career, winning two World Series championships, one with Oakland in 1989 and one with Toronto in 1993. Henderson was the MVP of the American League in 1990, and on 1 May 1991 he stole his 939th base to pass LOU BROCK as baseball's all-time stolen-base leader. Henderson returned to Oakland as a free agent after the 1993 season and again five years later, with stints in San Diego and Anaheim in between.

Oakland always held a special place for Henderson, where he played 1,704 games, with 1,768 hits, 1,270 runs, 167 home runs, and 867 stolen bases. When he left Oakland after his fourth stint in 1998, Henderson was the A's career leader in almost every offensive category. From 1998 until 2003 he played for the New York Mets, the Seattle Mariners, the Boston Red Sox, and the Los Angeles Dodgers. Henderson began the 2004 season playing for the Newark Bears, the Dodgers' triple-A farm team, with the hope of returning to the majors one more time. At forty-two Henderson was still competing at a high level, with a love for baseball and competition as strong as it had been when he was drafted at the age of seventeen.

In assessing Henderson's career in 2003, the San Diego Padre player TONY GWYNN said, "To me, Rickey has done more in this game than just about anybody who has played it, with the exception of HANK AARON and maybe Pete Rose to a certain degree. At the end of this season, he could be the all-time leader in three categories, and that just doesn't happen." As the 2004 season began, Henderson was the major league career leader in runs scored, walks, and stolen bases—three of the most important categories for the leadoff hitter. He also hit the most leadoff homers in history, had 3,000 hits, and was an all-star ten times. He led the American League in stolen bases twelve times, including during the 1999 season when he was thirty-nine years old. He won a Gold Glove in 1981, a league MVP in 1990, and two World Series titles. Henderson's total of 1,406 career stolen bases in the Major Leagues is almost five hundred better than that of any other player. Over the course of his career he stole bases at an incredible 81 percent rate, and he averaged a stolen base every 2.19 games or 7.79 at-bats. He is widely considered the greatest leadoff hitter of all time.

FURTHER READING

Henderson, Rickey, with John Shea. *Off Base: Confessions of a Thief* (1992).

Weir, Tom. "Inside Rickey's World, He Marches to Own Beat," *USA Today*, 26 Sept. 2001.

STEPHEN M. GENNARO

Henderson, Stephen McKinley (31 Aug. 1949–), actor, director, and educator, was born in Kansas City, Missouri, to Elihue Henderson and Naomi Johnson. His father was employed at various jobs, one of which was making ice cream for the DeCorcey company of Kansas City, Kansas, after military service during the Korean conflict left him partially disabled. His mother was a hairstylist for a funeral home, a nightclub waitress, and finally a receptionist for Swope Park Community Medical Center.

Henderson attended school in Kansas City, Kansas, prior to integration. After graduating from Sumner High School in 1967, he briefly attended Lincoln University in Jefferson City, Missouri, a historically black institution founded by the Black Cavalry. After a year as a member of Lincoln's resident stage ensemble, the Stagecrafters, Henderson moved to New York City and joined the Juilliard Drama Division, where John Houseman, Michel and Suria Saint-Denis and other distinguished theater professionals were establishing a tradition of classical training. Henderson was at Juilliard from 1968 to 1970, during which time he was introduced to AMIRI BARAKA, a central figure in the Black Arts Movement. Henderson transferred to the North Carolina School of the Arts (NCSA), where he served as president of the student government. He received additional training at the Rose Bruford Academy outside London in the summer of 1971. After receiving a BFA in Acting in 1972 from NCSA, Henderson worked professionally before entering Purdue University Graduate School, where he served as director of the Black Drama Workshop for Purdue's Black Cultural Center from 1974 to

1976. He received his M.A. in Theatre Arts from Purdue in 1977. Henderson married Pamela Reed Henderson in 1978 and had a son, Jamal Stephen Henderson, in 1981.

Henderson was a resident member of the Loretto-Hilton Repertory Company (now the Repertory Theatre of St. Louis). This was a turning point in his development as an actor. As a direct result of that association, he took part in the Dublin Theatre Festival in 1981, where he performed in the Loretto-Hilton company's production of Athol Fugard's *The Island*. The company then went on to perform the play for several years throughout the Midwest. Other training included work with William Esper at his New York studio in the summer of 1991, and later in his career, the Teachers Development Intensive at the Actor's Center and work with Lloyd Richards as a Fox Foundation fellow from 2003 to 2005.

Henderson has enjoyed a distinguished career as an actor, an early example of this is his role in Harold Scott's production of LORRAINE HANSBERRY's *A Raisin in the Sun* from 1982 to 1987. The cast was assembled through several regional productions and then brought to New York City by the Roundabout Theatre Company in 1984. The subsequent Kennedy Center production with ESTHER ROLLE and Delroy Lindo was an important production for the Eisenhower Theater, because it broke existing box office records. When the Public Broadcasting Company's *American Playhouse* broadcast this work with Rolle and DANNY GLOVER, the director BILL DUKE used the entire cast from Harold Scott's stage production.

Other highlights in Henderson's acting career include performances in AUGUST WILSON's *Jitney*, which began his collaborative relationships with both Wilson and Marion McClinton. He originated the roles of Turnbo in *Jitney* and Stool Pigeon in *King Hedley II*, both under the direction of McClinton; for the former he won a 2000 Drama Desk Award for Outstanding Ensemble Performance. Other notable productions included *The Last Days of Judas Iscariot* for the LAByrinth Theater Company at the Public Theater in New York City, the HBO movie *Everyday People* (2004), and the Broadway productions of *Dracula, the Musical* and *Drowning Crow*. He also acted in Signature Theatre Company's 2006 production of *Seven Guitars* in the first installment of its season in honor of August Wilson.

As a director, Henderson's accomplishments include *ALI!* by Geoffrey C. Ewing and Graydon Royce, which was his New York City directing debut. The play, an homage to the legendary boxer

MUHAMMAD ALI, ran Off-Broadway during the 1992 season, transferring from the John Houseman Studio to the Sheridan Square Theatre. The production garnered two Audelco Awards honoring outstanding achievement in African American theater Off-Broadway and an Obie Award for Ewing's Outstanding Performance. In the summer of 1993 Henderson traveled to London to direct *ALI!* for the Mermaid Theatre. The play also was revived for the National Black Arts Festival in 1994 and the Olympic Arts Festival in Atlanta in 1996. Henderson also directed *The Meeting* by Jeff Stetson for the St. Louis Black Repertory Theater. This production was presented at Kennedy Center as part of its 1993–1994 Imagination Celebration in the Theater Lab.

Henderson joined the faculty of the theatre and dance department of the State University of New York at Buffalo as an assistant professor in 1987 and received tenure as an associate professor in 1993. He headed the acting program from 1994 to 1998 and served as department chair from 1999 to 2000. Henderson was installed on the faculty of the Actor's Center in June of 2006 and has had multiple residencies with various organizations through the years.

Among Henderson's many awards are an Obie Award, the Drama Desk Award, the Audelco Award, a FOX Foundation Fellowship, an NAACP Theater Award, a Distinguished Alumnus Award from Purdue University, a Los Angeles Drama Critics Circle Award, a Helen Hayes Nomination, a citation from the XXVI Olympiad, and numerous regional awards in the Buffalo area.

Stephen McKinley Henderson has made a lasting impact on the American theater on several levels. Though renowned as an actor and director, he may very well have made his greatest contribution as a teacher.

FURTHER READING

Hay, Samuel A. *African American Theatre: An Historical and Critical Analysis* (1994).

Rand, Ronald, and Luigi Scorcia. *Acting Teachers of America: A Vital Tradition* (2007).

MERON LANGSNER

Hendon, Ernest (12 Feb. 1907–16 Jan. 2004), laborer and sharecropper and unwitting participant in the infamous Tuskegee syphilis experiment, was born Ernest L. Hendon in Roba, Alabama, to North and Mary Reed Hendon, sharecroppers. The family resided in rural Alabama, where Ernest Hendon spent his childhood working the family farm.

Hendon studied agriculture at the Macon County Training School. When his father died in 1933, Hendon helped his mother raise his nine siblings: Willie Harvey, Mary Lou, Johngiene, Mable, Louie, Girlie, Lydar, Willion, and North. The family was poor, enduring days of laboring under unforgiving weather conditions, tending small plots of land and picking cotton.

Like many others in his community, Hendon suffered from mysterious physical ailments that often went undiagnosed and untreated. With limited financial or social resources, and in the midst of the oppressive and segregated South, there was little opportunity for medical attention in sharecropper communities. Travel to seek out a doctor often proved hazardous and fruitless. In 1932 a well-timed event took place: a bus carrying medical professionals from Tuskegee arrived in Hendon's community. Residents were offered free medical treatment for their undiagnosed ailments, generally referred to as "bad blood," and Hendon, along with hundreds of his neighbors, took the opportunity to be medically assessed.

As a result, 623 poor black men signed up to participate in a medical study that, they were told, would do them good. They were impressed by the personal attention bestowed on them by the doctors and nurses who conducted examinations and performed medical tests. The nurses—who were determined to make the men feel comfortable and unthreatened—enthralled them. Nurses like Eunice Rivers formed emotional attachments with her patients to encourage their willing participation. Participants were promised free hot meals and transportation to and from the hospital in Tuskegee. They enjoyed shopping trips in town—an extravagance that they rarely experienced otherwise.

Participants were told that they had blood disorders and would receive various benefits from the government if they consented to participation in a medical study that required examination and treatment of their blood. The men found comfort and trust in the U.S. Health Department's sanction of the study. What the men did not know was that the study's actual goal was to examine the effects of untreated syphilis, a sexually transmitted disease. At the time, syphilis was more common among blacks in Alabama than anywhere else in the South. Many who had the disease did not know it, and those who did not have it were unsure what was wrong with them.

Many of the men enrolled in the study had syphilis, but Hendon was one of those who did not. None of the men was informed of their diagnoses, nor were they privy to the true purpose of the experiment. They simply understood that they would be providing themselves, their families, and the medical research community a great service through their participation. The study of bad blood was, in fact, the infamous Tuskegee syphilis experiment. Feeling safe in the hands of U.S. government–endorsed medical professionals, these men consented to various injections, blood draws, the ingestion of liquids and pills, and the administration of painful spinal taps. What seemed an added benefit of the program was the offer of free burial insurance; unfortunately, it was just another ruse to cover up the experiment's directive.

The real purpose of the study was to examine the pathology of untreated syphilis before and after death. Thus the medications administered to patients were nothing more than placebos; Hendon himself received aspirin and iron tonics. Those who actually had syphilis remained untreated and suffered severe ill effects, deformities, or death. Many unknowingly passed the disease on to their wives and children, some of whom died as a result. Although penicillin became an effective treatment for syphilis in the 1940s, the drug was deliberately withheld from participants in the study by order of the U.S. government.

In 1941, still unaware of the Tuskegee experiment's true purpose, Ernest Hendon moved from his native Alabama to Cleveland, Ohio, in search of a better life. He established himself in the community's religious life by joining the Mount Herman Baptist Church. Hendon took a job as a laborer at the General Chemical Company. But just three months after settling in his new home, Hendon was drafted into the U.S. Army, and he reported to Camp Perry in Ohio. He served for three years during the war, with tours of duty in Germany, France, and England. After an honorable discharge, Hendon returned to his home in Cleveland. He regained his job at General Chemical and remained there until his retirement in 1969. Then, with a desire to revisit his deep-seated agricultural roots, Hendon returned south. He moved back to Roba, Alabama, his birthplace, and immersed himself in gardening, his personal passion.

In 1972 the Tuskegee syphilis experiments were exposed publicly. A whistleblower from the United States Public Health Service leaked information about the true nature of the experiment to an Associated Press reporter. As a result, the study hastily ceased operation. Unfortunately, many years had already passed, and the experiment had caused irreparable harm to its participants.

Led by the civil rights lawyer FRED D. GRAY, Hendon and the remaining Tuskegee survivors filed a class-action lawsuit against those responsible for the study. Although the government maintained innocence in the affair, it offered a cash settlement to the plaintiffs of $10 million; Hendon received $37,500. Many years later, through a formal ceremony, a concession of guilt from the government was finally offered. On 16 May 1997, on behalf of the U.S. government, President Bill Clinton publicly apologized to the Tuskegee study participants and their families. The well-documented act of contrition states: "No power on earth can give you back the lives lost, the pain suffered, the years of internal torment and anguish. What was done cannot be undone. But we can end the silence.... What the United States government did was shameful, and I am sorry."

Though late, the apology was well received by Hendon. Too ill to attend the ceremony, Hendon was represented in Washington, D.C., by his brother North while he watched at home via satellite. In 2002 the Alabama House of Representatives also expressed its regret for the study, and Hendon told reporters that he hoped this type of thing would never happen again. At the time of his death in 2004 Hendon was the last living survivor of the Tuskegee experiments. A member of the Sweet Pilgrim Missionary Baptist Church, Hendon never wed and had no children.

FURTHER READING

Baker, Shamim M., Otis W. Brawley, and Leonard S. Marks. "Effects of Untreated Syphilis in the Negro Male, 1932 to 1972: A Closure Comes to the Tuskegee Study, 2004," available online at http://www.usrf.org/urovideo/Tuskegee_2004/Tuskegee_study.pdf.

Gray, Fred D. *The Tuskegee Syphilis Study: The Real Story and Beyond* (2002)

"The Worship and Victory Celebration Honoring the Life of Mr. Ernest L. Hendon," Sweet Pilgrim Missionary Baptist Church funeral program (21 Jan. 2004).

Obituary: "Ernest Hendon, Last Tuskegee Syphilis Study Survivor, Dies," *Jet* (23 Feb. 2004).

NANCY T. ROBINSON

Hendricks, Barbara (20 Nov. 1948–), opera singer and human rights advocate, was born Barbara Ann Hendricks in Stephens, Arkansas, one of five children born to Malvin Leon Hendricks, a Christian Methodist Episcopal minister, and Della Mae Graham Hendricks, a teacher. Traveling often to churches where the Reverend Hendricks was assigned, the family eventually settled in Little Rock, Arkansas, where Barbara Hendricks graduated with honors from Horace Mann High School in 1965.

Although she grew up singing spirituals in church and classical motets in school choirs, Hendricks had never envisioned a career in music for herself. Rather, at the age of sixteen, she entered Lane College in Jackson, Tennessee, where she excelled in math and science, and later transferred to the University of Nebraska at Lincoln, with plans to pursue a career in medicine. But when one of the university officials heard her sing at a civic function and recommended she attend the Aspen Music Festival, Hendricks abandoned plans for a summer of scientific research and headed to Aspen, Colorado. There, she encountered the most significant influence on her musical life, the Russian-born mezzo-soprano Jennie Tourel, who would become her only voice teacher. Tourel persuaded Hendricks that she was talented enough to have a career in music, and invited her to continue her studies with Tourel at the Juilliard School of Music in New York. Convinced that music was her true calling, Hendricks, only twenty years old, completed her bachelor of science in Mathematics and Chemistry in 1969 and headed to New York to begin her musical training.

Hendricks won several prizes for her singing during her time at Juilliard, including first prize at the Liederkranz competition and second prize at the Naumburg competition in New York. She also participated in the celebrated master classes led by the soprano Maria Callas at the school. Hendricks spent her summers in Europe with Jennie Tourel, where she continued her studies and entered vocal competitions, taking the Grand Prize at the Concours International de Paris in 1972 and eventually making her recital debut at the Salle Gaveau in Paris in 1973. Two events marked the end of Hendricks's formal musical education: she received her bachelor of music in voice from the Juilliard School in 1973, and Tourel died of cancer later that year.

Hendricks's first professional performances in 1974 included her European operatic debut in the title role of Cavalli's *La Calista* at the Glyndebourne Festival. She made her debut recording the following year as Clara in the first complete recording of Gershwin's opera *Porgy and Bess*, with Lorin Maazel and the Cleveland Symphony. Her

Carnegie Hall and Town Hall recital debuts soon followed, but Hendricks's breakthrough performance came in the 1976 world premiere of David Del Tredici's *Final Alice*, with Sir Georg Solti and the Chicago Symphony Orchestra. An excellent showcase for Hendricks's agile, silvery soprano and personal charisma, *Final Alice* was hailed as a watershed of neo-Romantic composition, and critics felt that the work's "huge success was largely due to [Hendricks's] personality and skill" (*Chicago Tribune*, 8 Oct. 1976). Hendricks went on to perform *Final Alice* with the Boston, Philadelphia, and Cleveland symphonies, and the New York and Los Angeles Philharmonic orchestras.

On the heels of the success of *Final Alice*, Hendricks made her Salzburg Festival debut in 1977 under the baton of James Levine, and debuted the following year at the Deutsche Oper Berlin as Susanna in *Le Nozze di Figaro*, opposite Dietrich Fischer-Dieskau and with Daniel Barenboim conducting. In 1978 Hendricks married Martin Engström, the Swedish-born manager of her European engagements, and moved to Europe. The couple had two children, Sebastian Amadeus and Jennie Victoria.

Throughout the 1980s, Barbara Hendricks made debuts at the world's major opera houses, including Covent Garden, the Paris Opera, La Scala, with the conductor Riccardo Muti, and in 1986 as Sophie in Strauss's *Der Rosenkavalier* at the Metropolitan Opera. During the same period she toured and recorded with leading conductors, most notably Leonard Bernstein and Herbert von Karajan, who compared Hendricks's interpretive abilities favorably to those of Maria Callas. A lyric soprano admired for her direct and unaffected singing, Hendricks also established a reputation as one of the leading recitalists of her generation, appearing at all the major concert halls in Europe, the United States, and Japan. In 1986 Hendricks became the youngest person to receive the title of Commandeur des Arts et des Lettres from the French government.

Though she was already widely respected artistically, Hendricks's burgeoning celebrity reached new heights when she made her film debut in 1987 as Mimi in Puccini's *La Bohème*, directed by Luigi Comencini. Hendricks chose to use her fame to further the cause of human rights when she accepted an appointment as goodwill ambassador by the United Nations High Commission for Refugees in 1987. Though the goodwill ambassador program was initiated as a public relations effort to raise consciousness about the plight of refugees worldwide, Hendricks invested her humanitarian role with the same commitment and passion that characterized her operatic roles, visiting refugee camps throughout Africa and Southeast Asia and performing in peace concerts in the former Yugoslavia in the early 1990s. Hendricks was recognized for her humanitarian and cultural contributions with several honorary degrees and awards, including membership in the Royal Swedish Academy of Music in 1990, and receiving the Chevalier de la Légion d'honneur from the French president François Mitterrand in 1993.

In 1994 Hendricks undertook her second film role, as Anne Truelove in a cinematic production of Stravinsky's *The Rake's Progress*, and expanded her musical repertoire with her debut at the Montreux Jazz Festival. She acquired her Swedish citizenship in 1994, but Hendricks's marriage to Martin Engström ended in divorce in 1996. Hendricks married Sven Ulf Englund in 2003.

As she continued to perform internationally in operas and recitals, and to add to her discography of more than eighty recordings, Barbara Hendricks redefined the traditional profile of an opera singer with the unusual breadth of her cultural activities. In 1998 she established the Barbara Hendricks Foundation for Peace and Reconciliation to support the prevention of conflicts internationally and to facilitate reconciliation when conflict has occurred. She broke ground in 1999 when she became the first opera singer to serve as a member of the jury at the Cannes International Film Festival. And in recognition of nearly two decades of service to the cause of refugees, Hendricks was named honorary ambassador for life by the United Nations High Commissioner for Refugees.

FURTHER READING
"Barbara Hendricks: A Passion for Opera and Human Rights," *Ebony* (May 1990).
McFarland, Dennis. "Singer with a Gift to Be Simple Lends Others the Gift to Be Free," *New York Times*, 12 May 1991.
Scherer, Barrymore Laurence. "Mimi with a Method: On Becoming Barbara Hendricks," *Opera News* 53 (Aug. 1988).

NAT CHARLES

Hendricks, Barkley (16 Apr. 1945–), artist and educator, was born in Philadelphia, Pennsylvania, to Ruby Arlene Powell, a homemaker, and Barkley H. Hendricks, a carpenter who worked at the Philadelphia Navy Yard. Barkley L. Hendricks "didn't like school" (unpublished interview, 2005), preferring to sketch and draw in his spare time, but once he entered high school, his teachers encouraged his art studies. Another outlet for his talent was the high school yearbook, for which he was both editor and illustrator. Outside school he created chalk and pastel markings on city walls, which he later called "pre-aerosol graffiti" (unpublished interview, 2005).

In 1963 Hendricks enrolled in the Pennsylvania Academy of the Fine Arts in Philadelphia, the oldest art school in the country. At the time, there were few black students or faculty. He can easily recall fellow students Lou Sloan and Raymond Saunders. Although he noted some incidents of racism, Hendricks was the first African American to win the Cresson (1966) and the Scheidt (1967) scholarships for study and travel abroad. His encounter with monumental European figure painting led to the formation of his signature style of the late 1960s and 1970s. His voyages in Africa led to self-discovery and a continuing interest in politics there.

Returning to Philadelphia in the fall of 1967, Hendricks continued his part-time job with the Philadelphia Department of Recreation as a roving arts and crafts specialist. Observing city playgrounds, especially basketball courts, he formulated some artistic concepts based on the geometry of balls, hoops, and foul lines, creating a series of basketball-themed paintings. Simultaneously, he was painting large-scale portraits of friends in an almost iconic manner. Recognition came quickly, and he was given his first solo show at the Philadelphia Art Alliance (1968). Another solo show followed two years later at the Kenmore Gallery, one of only two galleries in Philadelphia featuring African American art in the late 1960s.

Hendricks decided to widen his exposure and seek further art education outside of Philadelphia. After serving in the National Guard (1968–1973), he applied and was accepted into Yale University's B.F.A. program in 1970, one of four or five African Americans to gain entry. At Yale he studied painting with professors Bernard Chaet, Josef Albers, and Lester Johnson and advanced photography with renowned photographer Walker Evans. Inspired by Evans's focus, Hendricks began to tote around a Polaroid camera so he could shoot at will and print out immediately. His photo subjects included New York's streets, the Port Authority bus terminal, and the subway. He found camaraderie in the darkroom with photographers Harrison Branch and Reggie Jackson. Hendricks held a teaching assistantship at Yale in his second year and taught painting at the Pennsylvania Academy from 1971 to 1972. He began to receive critical notice, participating in group shows in New York, Philadelphia, and at the Butler Institute in Ohio. Studying, teaching, and exhibiting simultaneously, he obtained his B.F.A. and M.F.A. from Yale in just two years (1970–1972).

Hendricks joined the faculty of Connecticut College in the fall of 1972 as an assistant professor. The position had opened up in response to recent protests at Connecticut College and elsewhere about the lack of black studies programs and black professors. The first African American on a tenure track in the department, he was appointed Professor of Art Studio with a specialization in portraiture, the figure, and landscape in 1978.

Since the 1970s Hendricks worked in a variety of styles and media. He gained immediate recognition for his larger-than-life oil portraits of African Americans, many of them his friends. Although clearly related to the photo-realist painting movement, they were possibly the first modern expressions of black self-affirmation and cultural authority. Titles and minute details conveyed powerful personas, such as *Miss T* (1969). With her afro, aviator-style glasses, dark bell-bottom pantsuit, and chain belt, she communicated both a sense of fashion and intelligent introspection. In portraits such as *Slick* (1977) and *Ralph and Alvin* (1974), Hendricks used contemporary fashion, intense gazes, and a stark white or gold background as a means of iconic representation of the slogan "Black Power."

Women and the female body were a recurrent theme in Hendricks's oeuvre. Susan Weig, Hendricks's wife (they married in 1983), served as his model and assistant. The female anatomy was boldly paraded in large paintings, subtly displayed in nude photographs, tenderly re-created in contour drawings, and provocatively suggested in symbolic imagery. Feminine surrogate objects also found their way into assemblages and multimedia work. High-heel shoes and circle "virgin" pins represented nostalgia for his adolescent past and expressed his long-term interest in fashion.

In the early 1980s Hendricks began to travel regularly to Jamaica, where he created landscape painting in different formats including the *tondo* (oval) and scroll. Travel also facilitated the opportunity to show his works abroad (Whitechapel Gallery, London, 2005).

Never formally aligned with any political groups or organizations, Hendricks declared his art a movement in itself. He considers the term "African American art" "myopic" and prefers to think of himself and his art in the broader context of world art history (unpublished interview, 2005). Since the 1970s he presented hidden or undesirable parts of America in his black and white photographs. Drawn to the Nigerian musical revolutionary Fela Kuti, he created a series of paintings and photographs for the multimedia show *The Black President* at the New Museum in 2003. He demonstrated his opposition to the racism of the Ku Klux Klan by documenting them in a series of photographs, which were shown at the Whitney Museum in 2006. He similarly protested Nazism by creating glittering swastikas for the Hera Art Gallery in 1993, then taking them home and burning them, a one-time event that he photographed. Those photographs lived on in slide lectures.

Music was a strong force in Hendricks's life. He played the trumpet, bongos, congas, and castanets and was involved with two bands. Since his student days he collected jazz music, often at Third Street Jazz in Philadelphia. As "Professor Dred" (for his dreadlocks), he broadcast a jazz and blues radio show at Connecticut College called *Scenes in the City.* Combining his admiration for jazz musicians with his vocation, he photographed a number of legends, including MILES DAVIS, NINA SIMONE, and GIL SCOTT-HERON.

By 2010, Hendricks had more than twenty-five solo exhibitions at American museums, including the Studio Museum, Harlem (1980), and the Pennsylvania Academy of the Fine Arts (1985). He was among the first black artists to exhibit at the Whitney Museum of Art (1971) and also participated in their high-profile exhibition, Black Male (1994). A highlight of his career was the nationally touring retrospective exhibition Barkley L. Hendricks: Birth of the Cool (2008), which introduced and recontextualized his paintings to a new generation eager to revisit the culture of the 1970s. For his trailblazing accomplishments he was honored by the National Institute of Arts and Letters (1972), the American Academy of Arts and Letters (1971, 1977), and the Connecticut Commission on the Arts (1991).

FURTHER READING

Campbell, Mary Schmidt. *Barkley Hendricks* (1980).
Hendricks, Barkley L., and Cynthia Haveson Veloric. Unpublished interview (2005).
Kramer, Hilton. "Art: To the Last Detail," *New York Times*, 17 June 1977.
Kramer, Hilton. "Portraiture by Hendricks," *New York Times*, 11 March 1980.
Mangan, Doreen. "Barkley Hendricks and His Figurative Drama," *American Artist*, July 1976: 34–38, 68–70.
Schoonmaker, Trevor, ed. *Barkley L. Hendricks: Birth of the Cool* (2008).
Smith, Roberta. "Barkley Hendricks," *New York Times*, 28 Oct. 2005.
The Barkley L. Hendricks Experience (2000).

CYNTHIA HAVESON VELORIC

Hendrix, Jimi (27 Nov. 1942–18 Sept. 1970), rock guitarist, singer, and songwriter, was born into a working-class family in Seattle, Washington, the son of James Allen Ross Hendrix, a gardener, and Lucille Jetter. Named Johnny Allen Hendrix at birth by his mother while his father was in the service, his name was changed to James Marshall Hendrix by his father upon his return home. Self-taught as a left-handed guitarist from an early age, Hendrix played a right-handed guitar upside down, a practice he maintained throughout his life since it allowed for unusual fingering patterns and quicker access to tone and volume controls. His early influences ranged from the jazz guitarist CHARLIE CHRISTIAN to blues guitarists and honking rhythm and blues saxophone soloists. He attended elementary school in Vancouver, British Columbia, and

Jimi Hendrix in 1970. (AP Images.)

Seattle and went to Garfield High School in Seattle. In his senior year he left high school to become a paratrooper with the 101st Airborne Division of the U.S. Army. At Fort Campbell, Kentucky, Hendrix formed a rhythm and blues band, the Casuals, with bassist Billy Cox, who would rejoin him years later at the height of his fame. Following his discharge from the army in 1962, he moved to Nashville, where he played with some locally successful rhythm and blues groups and recorded a demonstration tape with the soul guitarist Steve Cropper, one of many guitarists to have an influence on Hendrix's maturing style. After a brief tour in 1963 with LITTLE RICHARD, Hendrix was in great demand as a sideman, performing with a number of established figures and groups such as SOLOMON BURKE, IKE and TINA TURNER, JACKIE WILSON, B. B. KING, and, later, the Isley Brothers and Curtis Knight. In 1963–1964 Hendrix's guitar playing was increasingly influenced by traditional bluesmen such as ROBERT JOHNSON, T-BONE WALKER, B. B. KING, MUDDY WATERS, and especially ALBERT KING, although the relatively few available recordings from this period reveal only that he was a fluent and idiomatic rhythm and blues guitarist and capable sideman.

Leading his own group, Jimmy James and the Blue Flames, in a Greenwich Village club in late 1965, Hendrix began to exhibit increasing signs of an original, even eccentric approach that incorporated feedback and other electronic sounds as an integral part of his style as well as overt sexual posturing and a further development of the showmanship techniques (such as playing his guitar behind his back and with his teeth) that he had displayed while touring with the Isley Brothers. Among the influences that took root in this period were Bob Dylan, whose mannered vocal style and sometimes mystical and visionary lyrics Hendrix admired, and the guitar playing of Mike Bloomfield, the inventive lead guitarist for the Paul Butterfield Blues Band.

Impressed by Hendrix's formidable technique, distinctive playing style, and charismatic stage presence, Chas Chandler, the former bass guitarist of the British rock group the Animals, convinced Hendrix to return with him to England to launch a new career. Under Chandler's guidance, the new Jimi Hendrix Experience, also featuring the bassist Noel Redding and the virtuoso drummer Mitch Mitchell, quickly became a favorite on the British and European pop scenes, releasing its first single, "Hey Joe," in December 1966 and its first album, *Are You Experienced?* (Reprise 6267), in September 1967.

Consisting mostly of original songs, the album was characterized by extensive multitracking and electronic manipulation of sound (for example, phase shifting, tape reversed effects, and a variety of feedback sounds), the result of a collaboration between Hendrix and the recording engineer Eddie Kramer. The album demonstrated that Hendrix's virtuoso guitar style had by this point successfully assimilated and adapted techniques from an unusually wide variety of sources ranging from soul guitarists to traditional and contemporary urban bluesmen and even jazz players such as WES MONTGOMERY. His vocal style had developed into a highly individualistic blend of mannerisms derived from blues, soul, and Dylan's half-spoken narrative style.

The *Are You Experienced?* album and associated singles did much to propel Hendrix to the forefront of the emerging British psychedelic rock movement. He was one of the few black performers associated with that style. His popularity in the United States was guaranteed by his electrifying performance at the prestigious First International Monterey Pop Festival in June 1967, in which he burned his guitar and destroyed his equipment onstage.

Hendrix released his second album with the Experience, *Axis: Bold as Love* (Reprise 6281), in January 1968. This album exhibited an even more elaborate use of multitracking and electronic manipulation than the first, with some songs demonstrating more complex structures and more ambitious and visionary lyrics, some of which appear to have been inspired by drug experiences. In 1968 he was named Artist of the Year by both *Billboard* and *Rolling Stone* magazines.

Following *Axis*, Hendrix began various attempts to expand the basic "power trio" format of the Jimi Hendrix Experience. The double album issued in September, *Electric Ladyland* (Reprise 6307), employed various other artists along with Redding and Mitchell and was the most intricately textured to date. Some songs, however, such as the hit single version of Dylan's "All along the Watchtower," showed an unusually straightforward, almost austere style, and others, such as "Voodoo Chile," suggested a return to the earlier urban blues style of Muddy Waters.

After the release of this album, Hendrix continually expressed the desire to shed his "psychedelic wizard" reputation and further develop his musical style, speaking on a number of occasions of his interest in jazz and his eagerness to perform with major jazz figures such as MILES DAVIS, who had shown some interest in Hendrix's music. Hendrix disbanded the Experience in 1969, envisioning a fluid "Electric Sky Church" made up of various musicians performing in different styles. His performance at the August 1969 Woodstock Festival, in which Billy Cox, a friend from his army days, replaced Noel Redding on bass, included a particularly dynamic and violent performance of the "Star-Spangled Banner" that became famous as a demonstration of his unique guitar style. Under some pressure from black militants to make outspoken political statements, Hendrix shied away from active involvement in politics but did launch an all-black trio, the Band of Gypsys, featuring the bass player Billy Cox and the drummer/vocalist Buddy Miles, which in 1970 released an album of tracks (*The Band of Gypsys*, Capitol 0472) from a concert at the Fillmore East in New York City. But Hendrix remained dissatisfied, and the group quickly disbanded, with Hendrix walking offstage during a performance in early 1970. Hendrix was briefly rejoined by the original members of the Experience, but Noel Redding was soon replaced by Cox once again. In this period, Hendrix devoted considerable time to planning for and working in his new studio, Electric Lady Studios. His final live performances were erratic, with Hendrix sometimes appearing to be out of control or distant. He died in London in his sleep, asphyxiated following a presumably accidental overdose of sleeping pills. By then he had become a figure of gigantic proportions in the pop music world, not only as the first major black artist in the psychedelic style, but as a guitarist and composer whose work was considered strikingly original and distinctive.

Despite his great fame, his influence on later rock musicians was expressed more in terms of inspiration than direct imitation. Few if any of his followers appeared able to duplicate many of Hendrix's guitar-derived or studio-generated electronic effects with the finesse that he had demonstrated. His compositional approach was sufficiently unique that his songs were largely inimitable as well. But the Hendrix legacy remains strong, if for no other reason than because he is seen as a musical free spirit who expanded the potential of the electric guitar and the boundaries of rock music in general in the late 1960s to a degree matched by few others.

FURTHER READING

Henderson, David. *Scuze Me while I Kiss the Sky: The Life of Jimi Hendrix* (1980).

Hopkins, Jerry. *Hit and Run: The Jimi Hendrix Story* (1983).

Knight, Curtis. *Jimi: An Intimate Biography of Jimi Hendrix* (1974).

Tarshis, Steve. *Original Hendrix* (1982).

Welch, Chris. *Hendrix: A Biography* (1972).

Obituary: *New York Times,* 19 Sept. 1970.

This entry is taken from the *American National Biography* and is published here with the permission of the American Council of Learned Societies.

TERENCE J. O'GRADY

Henry, Aaron E. (2 July 1922–19 May 1997), civil rights activist, was born to sharecroppers in Coahoma County in the Mississippi Delta. When Henry was five years old, his birth parents died, and he went to live with his maternal uncle and his wife, Ed and Mattie Henry, whom he considered his parents thereafter. He spent his early years on the Flowers Plantation in Coahoma County before the family moved to Clarksdale and he could attend the black Coahoma Agricultural High School, graduating in 1943.

As with many men who played major roles in the civil rights movement, including his fellow Mississippians MEDGAR EVERS and AMZIE MOORE, Henry's World War II experience in the segregated military affected him profoundly. He remembered that his fellow black servicemen knew little about the rich African American history, crediting his teachers for supplementing the curriculum with black history lessons. When he returned home from his station in Hawaii, Henry recalled, "Ex-soldiers told their friends and families things that they had seen in their travels and the word had spread that conditions in Coahoma County had not been ordained by God" (Henry, 70).

While studying pharmacology, thanks to the GI Bill, at Louisiana's Xavier University from 1946 to 1950, Henry spent his precious spare time in student activism, serving for two years as president of the student body. In 1947 he was the first African American to vote in the Democratic primary in Coahoma County (Henry, 65). After Xavier, he returned home to Clarksdale, married Noelle Michael, and opened the Fourth Street Drug Store in 1950, and their daughter Rebecca was born shortly afterward.

Henry served as the founding secretary in the Regional Council of Negro Leadership in December 1951 in the all-black Mississippi Delta town of Mound Bayou, where he sharpened his leadership skills and made useful contacts. He remained active in the RCNL until it disbanded in the early sixties.

The Mississippi Progressive Voters' League, the most active group in Clarksdale at the time, focused on black-voter registration, working with the system rather than trying to amend the inequalities. Dissatisfied with the league's approach, and following the rape of two black girls by a local white man that went unpunished, Henry helped to found the Clarksdale NAACP branch in 1952. He recognized that the organization's legal experience and national audience could offer better protection to the struggling black citizens in Mississippi. As the president of the branch for nearly three decades, Henry was at the forefront of civil rights activities in Clarksdale and in the Delta. He was elected president of the Mississippi Conference of the NAACP in 1959, which propelled him onto the national stage during Mississippi segregationists' most defiant years.

Henry's friendly and approachable personality guaranteed his success. Affectionately called "Doc," Henry conversed as easily with prominent national leaders (such as the presidents Kennedy and Johnson, the NAACP executive secretary ROY WILKINS, and MARTIN LUTHER KING JR.) as he did with sharecroppers and domestics. Focused on the goal of racial equality, he sought the aid of multiple civil rights and philanthropic organizations, much to the chagrin of the national NAACP. Trying to mediate with the Mississippi governor Ross Barnett, who refused to meet with the NAACP in 1961, Henry cofounded, in 1961, the Council of Federated Organizations (COFO), encompassing the NAACP, the Student Nonviolent Coordinating Committee (SNCC), the Southern Christian Leadership Conference (SCLC), and the Congress of Racial Equality (CORE). Pooling multiorganizational resources, COFO coordinated civil rights activity statewide, starting in 1962 with voter registration drives.

Henry juggled his responsibilities at the state level with the civil rights movement progressing in Coahoma County. He ran his drugstore in downtown Clarksdale, a meeting and resting place for activists. As a well-known figure, he attracted the big movement names to the Delta, particularly to Clarksdale. When they came, they either stayed with him or at the home of the branch secretary VERA MAE PIGEE. His visibility provoked occasional attacks on his business and his home. He was arrested thirty-three times for his civil rights activities, and his wife, Noelle, was fired after ten years teaching in the county schools. In March 1962 Henry was arrested on trumped-up morality charges, but the U.S. Supreme Court eventually cleared him years later. Even when the city judge sentenced him to two weeks of garbage duty following an arrest in July 1963, he cheerfully posed for press photographs. He remained undeterred.

COFO's statewide actions included the 1963 Freedom Vote, in which nearly 80,000 disenfranchised blacks of voting age cast freedom ballots for Aaron Henry's gubernatorial candidacy and for the Reverend Edwin King as lieutenant governor. The campaign dispelled the myth that blacks had no interest in the vote or its outcome. Meanwhile, in Clarksdale, Henry filed *Rebecca E. Henry v. Clarksdale Municipal Separate School District* in April 1964, whose Fifth Circuit Court ruling finally brought about desegregation of the public school system in 1970. Also in April 1964, under Henry's leadership, COFO founded the Mississippi Freedom Democratic Party (MFDP) to challenge the regular Mississippi delegation to the Democratic National Convention. Dissension between moderates like Henry and more radical SNCC members came to a head when Democratic Party leaders forced a compromise and gave only two "at large" nonvoting seats to MFDP delegates, leaving the regular delegation untouched. Unable to work with the MFDP's radicalism, COFO eventually dissolved, and Henry ultimately unified Mississippi's Democratic Party, paving the way for the election of a black candidate to the state legislature, the first since Reconstruction.

Despite radicals' criticism, Henry's relative conservatism and his consummate tact earned him universal respect. He advised the Johnson White House on issues concerning African Americans, particularly in the South, accepting a committee position in 1965 within the Department of Agriculture dealing with programs designed for the underprivileged. This "conservative militant" (Henry, xiv) pushed to make sure that Mississippi's poor benefited from federal poverty programs under the War on Poverty priority. Controversially, he maneuvered to replace the Child Development Group of Mississippi, run mostly by civil rights activists, with the more moderate Mississippi Action for Progress in 1966, in order to ensure less conflict from white supremacists. This move further alienated him from his former allies in the civil rights movement who were critical of his willingness to compromise with the white power structure. Henry operated within the political realm and used political savvy and diplomacy to hover just under the media radar, working hard politically to achieve his objectives.

His goals were far-reaching. In 1963 he challenged the relicensing of the WLBT-TV 3 Jackson, Mississippi, station for failure to sell him and other black candidates equal airtime and to give fair coverage to civil rights issues. Sixteen years later President Jimmy Carter applied pressure on the Federal Communications Commission to recognize racist practices in the media, forever changing the broadcasting industry. Ironically, Henry later attracted investors and became chairman of the board and primary stockholder in the station's owners, Civic Communications Corporation.

As the most visible black civil rights leader in Mississippi with years on the front lines, Henry affiliated with numerous organizations. For example, he was a vice president and board member of the national NAACP while also maintaining leadership positions in the Southern Christian Leadership Conference, the Southern Regional Council, the Mississippi Council on Human Relations, the National Caucus for Black Aged, and the Federal Council on Aging. His popularity propelled him to public office, as a congressman in the Mississippi House of Representatives for Coahoma County from 1980 to 1996.

When Henry died, President Bill Clinton sent condolences to his daughter, Rebecca. Noelle Henry had passed away in 1994. Tributes flooded in from throughout the country, and President Jimmy Carter was an honorary pallbearer. The huge funeral and memorial service, starting in Coahoma County and ending in Jackson, was a fitting farewell to the unique Mississippian who managed to earn respect from friend and foe alike. His genuine loyalty and love for the Magnolia State kept him true to his ultimate desire for equal rights, and he left a lasting legacy that changed Mississippi's social, political, economic, and racial landscape.

FURTHER READING

Henry's personal papers are archived at the Mississippi Department of Archives and History, Jackson, Mississippi. A detailed conversation between Aaron Henry and the SNCC activist Jerry DeMuth at Henry's Clarksdale home on 3 August 1964 is housed at the State Historical Society of Wisconsin in Jerry DeMuth's files. The Mississippi Department of Archives and History in Jackson, the archives at the University of Southern Mississippi in Hattiesburg, and the Ralph Bunche Oral History Collection at Howard University Library in Washington, D.C., also hold various interview transcripts.

Henry, Aaron, ed., and completed posthumously by Constance Curry. *Aaron Henry: The Fire Ever Burning* (2000).

Dittmer, John. *Local People: The Struggle for Civil Rights in Mississippi* (1994).

Hamlin, Françoise N. "'The Book Hasn't Closed, The Story Isn't Finished': Continuing Histories of the Civil Rights Movement," Ph.D. diss., Yale University (2004).

Payne, Charles. *I've Got the Light of Freedom: The Organizing Tradition and the Mississippi Freedom Struggle* (1995).

Obituary: *New York Times*, 21 May 1997.

FRANÇOISE N. HAMLIN

Henry, Ernie (3 Sept. 1926–29 Dec. 1957), jazz saxophonist, was born Ernest Albert Henry in Brooklyn, New York. His parents' names and occupations are not known, but his father played piano and his sister was a piano teacher and church organist. Henry studied piano at age eight, violin at age ten. At age twelve he picked up the alto saxophone, which was to be his primary instrument for the rest of his life. Brooklyn at the time was home to a number of young jazz musicians, including the drummer MAX ROACH, the baritone saxophonist Cecil Payne, and the pianist Randy Weston. This community of young musicians helped foster Henry's development, and he would work with Payne throughout his professional career.

After serving in the army Henry began his professional career and joined the musician's union (local 802) in 1947. On 27 August 1947 he made his recording debut, recording four tunes with the vocalist Kenny Hagood for Savoy records. That same year Henry worked at the Onyx Club on Fifty-second Street in Manhattan with the pianist, composer, and arranger TAD DAMERON. At the time Fifty-second Street was the center of bebop, the new movement in jazz. Dameron's band also featured the outstanding bebop trumpeter FATS NAVARRO. On 26 September 1947 Dameron recorded four of his compositions (two takes of each) with Henry and Navarro for Blue Note records. Henry's performances that day were uneven. On both takes of "The Squirrel," a medium-tempo twelve-bar blues, his phrasing was awkward and his saxophone technique uncertain. However, on both takes of "Our Delight," a moderately fast bebop tune, his solo exhibited mastery of the difficult chord progression. The influence of the saxophonist CHARLIE PARKER was unmistakable; however, this did not diminish the talent that Henry showed, since every young saxophonist of the day was greatly influenced by Parker.

By the summer of 1948 Henry joined the big band of the trumpeter DIZZY GILLESPIE, arguably the greatest star of bebop. Henry sat next to Cecil Payne, his acquaintance from Brooklyn, in the reed section. During a July 1948 concert at the Pasadena Civic Auditorium, Gillespie featured Henry for the first sixteen bars of THELONIOUS MONK's composition "'Round Midnight," recorded and released on GNP records. Henry's intensely personal and soulful interpretation of the melody received a tremendous ovation from the capacity crowd. In October 1948 Henry recorded with Navarro and the trumpeter HOWARD MCGHEE for Blue Note records. Henry's solo on McGhee's blues "The Skunk" was masterful. His earlier awkwardness was gone and his unique bluesy style was emerging. Henry left Gillespie in 1949. From 1950 to 1952 he worked with the saxophonist ILLINOIS JACQUET, recording with Jacquet for Verve. Henry did not have a featured solo. He then sank into obscurity. Many bebop jazz musicians became addicted to narcotics, and Henry was no exception. To complicate matters, he was battling high blood pressure.

Orrin Keepnews, a record producer for Riverside, believed that Henry lacked self-confidence. On the recommendation of the pianist Randy Weston, one of Henry's old Brooklyn acquaintances, Keepnews in 1956 went to hear Henry at a jam session in Brooklyn. Henry had also been endorsed by the pianist Thelonious Monk, Riverside's newest and biggest star. Keepnews signed Henry immediately. On 23 August 1956, after nearly ten years of sideman roles and obscurity, Henry made his recording debut as leader. For the date, which included the trumpeter Kenny Dorham, the pianist Kenny Drew, and the drummer Arthur Taylor, Henry wrote three original compositions and chose one standard, "Gone with the Wind." A week later Henry returned to the studio with the same ensemble to record two more original compositions and another standard, "I Should Care."

By now Henry's personal style had fully emerged. He was never a technically sophisticated player, and thus he avoided doubling the time on slower tempos and rarely played long phrases on fast tempos. The strident quality of Henry's tone, along with a penchant for sustained bent notes, gave his playing an emotional, urgent quality. This approach was most effective when playing the blues, as can be heard on Henry's minor key composition "Cleo's Chant" from the 30 August date. Henry's recording of "I Should Care," from the same day, displayed his remarkable sensitivity when playing ballads.

By December 1956 Henry was back to steady work with Dizzy Gillespie's big band, which at the time was packed with young talent including LEE MORGAN, Benny Golson, and WYNTON KELLY. On 23 September 1957 Henry recorded four tunes for Riverside with an eight-piece group. The personnel included four of his band mates from the Gillespie band: Morgan, Golson, Kelly, and MELBA LISTON. The date also reunited him with Cecil Payne. A week later Henry recorded with Kelly, the bassist WILBUR WARE, and the drummer PHILLY JOE JONES. The resulting album, titled *Seven Standards and a Blues*, would be his masterpiece. In this recording the quartet format allowed him to explore fully the personal voice he had created.

But the blood pressure condition that Henry had been battling worsened. After a performance with Gillespie, Henry died in his sleep at his parents' home in Brooklyn. Although Henry had been off drugs the previous year, Cecil Payne believed that he died of a drug overdose. He recalled in *Jazz Monthly* in May 1964 that Henry had bought "a bag" of heroin on a subway and consumed a third of it.

Henry was a tragic figure in jazz. Though not a major innovator, he developed a unique and personal musical voice at a time when few of his contemporaries had done so. His Riverside recordings are among the best of the years immediately following Charlie Parker's death, and they bore promise of still greater things to come.

FURTHER READING

Ansell, Derek. "The Forgotten Ones: Ernie Henry," *Jazz Journal International* (Sept. 1987).

Cooke, Jack. "Fading Flowers—A Note on Ernie Henry," *Jazz Monthly* (July 1961).

Obituary: *Down Beat*, 2 Feb. 1958.

DISCOGRAPHY

Salemann, Dieter. *Ernie Henry* (1988).

This entry is taken from the *American National Biography* and is published here with the permission of the American Council of Learned Societies.

SAM MILLER

Henry, Thomas W. (1 Jan. 1794–13 April 1877), minister and blacksmith, was born in Leonardtown, Maryland, the son of Jane and Thomas Henry, slaves of Richard Barnes, the largest slave owner in the district. It is thought that Henry's maternal grandmother, Catherine Hill, had been purchased by the Barnes family on a return trip from England and the Caribbean. Thomas's parents were domestic servants of the Barnes family, which owned tobacco plantations and other business interests. Before his death in 1804, Richard Barnes had stated in his will that his slaves were to be freed; one unusual stipulation he added that suggests a special closeness with these individuals was that the manumitted slaves take the name Barnes.

Thomas, however, did not gain his freedom until almost twenty years after his master's death, because John Thomson Mason, a nephew of Richard Barnes and the executor of his estate, exploited a growing number of legal restrictions passed by the state of Maryland to make manumission difficult, limit the number of free blacks residing in the state, and prevent them from competing with whites for jobs. Using the pretext that the fifteen-year-old Thomas, who would later reject the name Barnes in favor of his family name, Henry, was too young to be on his own, Mason hired him out to a Dutchman, Daniel Rikehardt, in Hagerstown, Maryland, who treated him poorly. Slaves often used tactics short of violence or escape to improve the conditions of their servitude. In this case, Henry agitated until he won the right to hire himself out to anyone willing to pay Mason for his services.

In 1819 Abraham King, a Hagerstown blacksmith, took Henry on as an apprentice. King, a German Methodist, developed such a mentoring relationship that Henry remembered him as being "not a master, but a father" (Henry, 7). Until this point, Henry considered himself to be a Catholic. None of his owners had been Catholic, but since about twenty percent of Maryland's Catholics were slaves, Jesuit priests in the area took an interest in the religious instruction of the local black population. Through their teaching of the Bible and the catechism, Henry received the rudiments of his early education.

One evening the King family took Henry to a Methodist revival across the Potomac River in Virginia. The preacher there convinced Henry that as a Catholic he was "trusting in the arm of flesh." Henry described his conversion experience as if being snatched from over an open well and placed on solid ground. In 1821, as an adult and having a trade, Henry went to Saint Mary's County to obtain his freedom papers. While there, Henry participated in the burial of a murdered cousin by reciting a few biblical verses he had memorized; this was his first experience as a lay minister. He returned to Hagerstown, where he continued to work for the King family as a free man, but for several years after the funeral, he felt dogged by a calling to preach.

In *Slaves without Masters* (1981), Ira Berlin describes the complexities of life for free blacks such as Henry. Free African Americans in Maryland could not vote, could not testify in court against white people, were subject to curfews, and were prohibited from owning guns, dogs, or boats; moreover, their marriages were not usually recognized. Thus in 1821 Henry found himself in a peculiar position when he married Catherine Craig, who lived across the street but was enslaved to Jacob Powles. Powles and his family were devout Christians, and they insisted that Henry live with Catherine. Over a period of years Henry was able to purchase his wife's freedom and that of two of their children for nine hundred dollars; however, Powles sold Henry's two older children when, despite a desperate struggle, Henry was unable to earn enough to save them as well.

When Henry became a member of the Methodist Episcopal Church, black worshipers were segregated in most congregations. In 1828 he became an exhorter, and shortly thereafter Reverend James Reed "pronounced me as being capable of preaching the Word of God according to my feeble ability" (Henry, 16). His license to preach as a lay minister was made permanent by Reverend James A. Sewell after an examination in which Henry was asked, among other things, "How much godly sorrow a person must have, to work an evangelical repentance. I told him that I did not know, but I thought he must have enough to forsake sin and hate it" (Henry, 17). Henry became an itinerant minister serving the spiritual needs of black people within a twenty-mile radius of Hagerstown.

It is significant that in 1832 he held a camp meeting in the woods near Ringgold Manor, in Washington County, Maryland, because on that site in 1818 a white minister, Reverend Jacob Gruber, was arrested for preaching a fiery antislavery sermon to several hundred black and white listeners. Gruber's right to free speech was successfully defended by Roger B. Taney, who later became chief justice of the U.S. Supreme Court and wrote, in the infamous 1857 *Dred Scott* decision, that a black man "had no rights which a white man was bound to respect." Henry was aware of the historic and political importance of this site when he preached there.

Two events prompted Henry to leave the Methodist Episcopal Church. The first involved the plight of a female slave who was suddenly sold by the steward of the church, separating her from her young, mixed-ancestry (black and white) son. When black members approached the church elder, he said, "I have nothing to do with any man's property" (Henry, 19). In 1834, on being told that black ministers were not allowed to preach in a nearby church, Henry decided to join the African Methodist Episcopal (AME) Church, which RICHARD ALLEN founded as an independent black Methodist denomination a generation earlier. In 1837 Henry was made an AME deacon and elevated the following year to the office of elder. Over the next four decades he helped to bring the ministry of the AME Church from its origins in urban centers of the North to the outlying areas of Maryland and Pennsylvania. He incorporated the Ebenezer AME congregation in Hagerstown and built near Ringgold Manor the Daughter of Bethuel Church (which burned down in a suspicious fire). During one period in 1846 he ministered three churches in the Washington, D.C., area simultaneously: Union Bethel, Israel Bethel, and Allen Chapel AME Church.

Henry was once arrested during a church service for violating a law passed after the NAT TURNER rebellion of 1831 prohibiting African American gatherings. Fortunately for Henry, the law stipulated that such meetings could take place if a white man was present. Since the congregation had obtained the favors of a supportive white gentleman who was present that day, Henry had to be released. Henry was not only a minister and a blacksmith; he was also a conductor on the Underground Railroad, and his home and churches were regarded as places of refuge for escaping slaves and abolitionists. This reputation placed his life in jeopardy following John Brown's raid on Harpers Ferry, Virginia, in 1859 because "Thomas Henrie" (sic) was described in letters belonging to John Brown as a reliable friend. Henry had never met Brown or advocated violent revolution, though he later described Brown as "that good old saint" who was "led by a supernatural hand" (Henry, 51). Henry was nonetheless implicated in the conspiracy and, like FREDERICK DOUGLASS, only narrowly escaped capture.

By the time of his wife's death in 1857, Henry had a family of nine or ten children. In 1860 he married Sarah A. Butler, the widow of the Reverend John Butler (*Christian Recorder*, 14 Mar. 1863). After the Civil War, Henry returned to Maryland with his wife and became the pastor of Mount Gilboa AME Church in Baltimore. He purchased land and built a home, which he expected to rent to the church as a parsonage. In 1867 he retired briefly from the ministry at age seventy-three, anticipating living on a promised yearly pension of one hundred dollars and income from rental of the parsonage. When both failed to materialize, Henry returned to serve as the minister of Allen Chapel in Washington, D.C., while taking legal action against Mount Gilboa. In 1872 Henry published his *Autobiography of Rev. Thomas W. Henry, of the A.M.E. Church.*

Prior to his death in 1877, Henry had seen DANIEL ALEXANDER PAYNE and others push through a series of reforms designed to raise the educational caliber of AME ministers. Henry, however, remained convinced that the future of the church relied on attracting more men like him: inspired through divine revelation, committed to social action, and willing to work where the needs were the greatest. Services for Henry were held in Hagerstown, where "thousands of the citizens of Hagerstown, Williamsport, Clear Springs, white and colored, rich and poor, big and little, thronged the church and graveyard, all anxious to do honor to this good and great man" (*Christian Recorder*, 10 May 1877).

FURTHER READING

Legal records and primary documents can be found at the Maryland State Archives and the Washington County History Society in Hagerstown, Maryland. An original copy of the *Autobiography of Rev. Thomas W. Henry, of the A.M.E. Church* (1872) and related material can be found at the Moorland-Spingarn Research Center at Howard University.

Libby, Jean, ed. *From Slavery to Salvation: The Autobiography of Rev. Thomas W. Henry of the A.M.E. Church* (1994).

Payne, Daniel Alexander. *History of the African Methodist Episcopal Church*, vol. 1 (1891).

Quarles, Benjamin. *Allies for Freedom: Blacks and John Brown* (1974).

Obituary: *Hagerstown Mail Weekly*, 4 May 1877.

SHOLOMO B. LEVY

Henry, Warren Elliott (18 Feb. 1909–31 Oct. 2001), physicist, was born in Evergreen, Alabama. His father, Nelson Henry, and his mother, Mattye McDaniel Henry, were public school teachers who had graduated from Tuskegee Institute. Education was deeply valued in the Henry household, and Warren's parents brought him along to the classroom and encouraged him to study long hours during his adolescent and teenage years. He became interested in science early in life, though he did not have the opportunity to take any science courses until his senior year, when he transferred to Alabama State Normal, a school in Montgomery that concentrated on preparing future elementary school teachers. Following in his parents' footsteps, Henry worked his way through Tuskegee Institute as a night watchman and at a pharmacy, receiving a bachelor of science degree in 1931, majoring in mathematics, English, and French. He also completed course work in chemistry and physics, and worked summers on the Tuskegee experimental farm helping with studies of fertilizers and insecticides.

Soon after graduation, he served as a teacher and principal of a segregated high school in Ardmore, Alabama. During the summer of his third year, he enrolled in a summer program at Atlanta University in order to stay informed on scientific developments. By the end of the summer he had been offered a scholarship to Atlanta University's graduate school to study chemistry. During his time in graduate school, Henry taught part-time at Spelman College. In 1937 he completed his M.S. degree in Organic Chemistry. Following graduate school, Henry visited numerous laboratories in a number of major industrial cities of the upper Midwest and Northeast. He enrolled in an advanced chemistry course at University of Chicago and was invited to pursue a doctoral degree in the chemistry department. Early in the program he worked at various jobs to make ends meet, but was given a teaching assistantship and tuition waiver for his final two years and received his doctorate in 1941, defending a dissertation on resistance thermometry and experimental techniques for using alternating current to measure small temperature differences.

After graduating, Henry returned to Tuskegee as a professor. His broad training at the University of Chicago enabled him to teach courses in both chemistry and physics. With the latter, he taught physics to students training to be army air corps officers that later formed the 99th Pursuit Squadron and became the famed Tuskegee Airmen serving in World War II. In the summer of 1943 Henry was offered and accepted the position of associate professor of physics and chemistry at Spelman College beginning in the fall term. He retained this post for three years, despite taking several leaves. Prior to starting this appointment he visited research laboratories at Harvard and the Massachusetts Institute of Technology (MIT). He impressed Dr. P. R. Bell of MIT's renowned Radiation Laboratory, and after

returning to Spelman soon accepted an offer from Bell to join the Radiation Lab to conduct classified war-related research on radar systems. Henry invented a video amplifier that worked more efficiently than any existing devices.

Following a year at MIT, Henry returned to work as a postdoctoral fellow at the University of Chicago's Institute for the Study of Metals on superconductivity projects. He conducted influential research discovering principles and durability of particular alloys for use in military jet aircraft, and taught physics courses. Henry served as the adviser to a half dozen undergraduate physics majors. In 1948 he moved to the Washington, D.C., area to conduct research at the Naval Research Laboratory (NRL) on solid-state physics and superconductivity and to teach evenings at Howard University. At the NRL he worked as a physicist for the next dozen years with teams of scientists that studied and made numerous advances in the knowledge and application of superconductors and magnetism. This included directing the group that installed the high-field Bitter Magnet.

In 1960 Henry left the NRL to take a position as senior staff scientist at the Lockheed Missile and Space Company in California. He later transferred to become senior staff engineer, using his expertise in magnetism to help advance the state-of-the-art missile guidance systems and detection systems employed to identify the location of enemy submarines. He also helped to lead a research group that built a device that could measure magnetic fields in space, and contributed to the design of a hovercraft developed for night fighting in the Vietnam War. Broadly speaking, his work at both the NRL and Lockheed had important applications in space technology, oceanography, cryogenics, and electronics.

Henry returned to Howard University in 1968 to teach physics and was soon given tenure and the status of full professor in the physics department. He also taught engineering courses on nuclear systems, drawing on his lengthy practical experience as a successful engineer in the defense industry. His work, such as his demonstration of the proof of non-interacting paramagnetic ions, is frequently cited in leading physics, chemistry, and material science textbooks. Henry retired in 1977 but stayed active at Howard University, and remained a major force in helping black science and engineering students in their junior and senior years to gain the practical experience necessary to advance their career opportunities (working with a program called Minorities Access to Research Careers). He frequently gave talks and seminars on research methods and tools, including library resources at Howard. Henry was married to Jeanne Sally (Pearlson), and had a daughter named Eva Ruth.

Henry's list of honors was extensive and diverse. He published extensively in both physics and chemistry scholarly journals. He received an honorary doctorate from Lehigh University, the Carver Award (1978) from Tuskegee, was a fellow of the American Association for the Advancement of Science, and received the award for Outstanding Black Physicist from the ad hoc committee for the Afro-American Awards Program in 1975. He was without question one of the leading African American scientists and contributed greatly to education, industry, and national defense.

FURTHER READING

McMurray, E. J., ed. *Notable Twentieth-Century Scientists* (1995).

Sammons, Vivian O. *Blacks in Science and Medicine* (1990).

JEFFREY R. YOST

Henson, Josiah (15 June 1789–5 May 1883), escaped slave and preacher, was born in Charles County, Maryland, on a farm owned by Francis Newman. As a child Henson frequently saw his parents abused and severely beaten. On one occasion, as a punishment for defending his wife, Henson's father was sentenced to a physical mutilation that left him permanently scarred. Although he was raised without religion, Henson was immediately converted to Christianity after his first exposure to it at a revivalist camp meeting. As a young boy, he was sold to Isaac Riley.

Because of his unusual strength and intelligence, Henson was made superintendent of the farm at a young age. He managed the plantation well, doubling the annual crop production. One day during an argument at a neighboring farm, Henson defended his master in an argument with the other plantation's overseer. In revenge, the overseer and three of his slaves waylaid Henson one evening soon afterward, beating him and shattering his shoulder blade. For the rest of his life, he could not raise his arms above shoulder level. At age twenty-two Henson married another slave (name unknown); they had twelve children.

Isaac Riley, the master of Henson's plantation, went bankrupt in 1825 and was forced to sell his farm and to transfer his twenty slaves to his brother's farm in Kentucky. After making Henson

swear to their safe passage, Riley entrusted him with the care of the slaves. The route to Kentucky took the party through Ohio, a free state, where many implored Henson to allow them their freedom, but Henson kept his word and brought them intact to their new owner. In 1828 Henson became a preacher for the Methodist Episcopal Church. He then attempted to buy his freedom from his owner. A price of four hundred dollars was settled on, but at the last minute the owner reneged on his agreement, deciding instead to sell Henson to a new owner in New Orleans. Journeying south with his master's son, who had instructions to transact some business and then to sell Henson before the return voyage, Henson's trepidation grew as he saw the terrible conditions in which slaves in the Deep South lived. Midway through the journey, the master's son developed a serious fever, rendering him weak and helpless, and he begged Henson to bring him home safely. Though he could easily have deserted his young master and made a bid for freedom, Henson remained to escort the son back to his father. His loyalty met with neither reward nor gratitude. Henson's growing desire for freedom, augmented by outrage at this ingratitude, propelled him to escape with his wife and four young children in the summer of 1830. In two weeks he had reached Cincinnati; from there he sailed to Buffalo, New York; and, in October, he crossed the U.S. border into Canada.

Henson settled in Dresden, Ontario, near Lake St. Clair and south of the Sydenham River, and he became a preacher. His oldest son, then in school, taught him to read. Quickly establishing himself as a leader in the Afro-Canadian community, Henson made several trips back to the United States and across the Mason-Dixon line to help other slaves escape. During the Canadian Rebellions of 1837–1838 Henson served the British as a captain in a troop of Afro-Canadian volunteers. With the support of sponsors from England and America, Henson began laying the foundations for an Afro-Canadian community and industrial school. The British American Institute, begun in 1842, encompassing two hundred acres of wooded land, was intended as a refuge for escaped slaves. However, the community never grew large or self-sufficient enough to survive, and by the end of the Civil War almost all of the colony's remaining members had returned to the United States. In 1849 Henson published his autobiography, *The Life of Josiah Henson, Formerly a Slave, Now an Inhabitant of Canada, as Narrated by Himself*. Reprinted in 1858, its name was changed to *Truth Stranger than Fiction: Father Henson's Story of His Own Life*, and the next edition was titled *"Truth Is Stranger than Fiction": An Autobiography of the Rev. Josiah Henson* (1879). Both later editions contain a foreword by Harriet Beecher Stowe.

On three journeys to England, in 1849, 1851, and 1876, Henson received much attention from members of high society there, including the archbishop of Canterbury. He was honored at a private party given in 1851 by Prime Minister Lord John Russell and invited by Lord Grey to travel to India to supervise cotton plantations. Soon after his return from England, Henson met Stowe. After *Uncle Tom's Cabin* was published in 1852, the public began to believe that Henson's life story was the basis for the character of Uncle Tom in the novel. Following the death of his first wife, Henson married a Boston widow. His final trip to England, a preaching and lecturing tour in 1876, was highlighted by Queen Victoria's personal gift of her photograph encased in a gold frame. Henson died in Dresden, Ontario.

Henson's life story is that of a daring early leader of slaves and escaped slaves, a man of high moral principles who endured great suffering. Although the British American Institute was small and unsuccessful, Henson's work as an ambassador to England for African Americans did much for their perception overseas. His greatest achievement was the example he offered of a man born into slavery, illiterate and handicapped by vicious physical abuse, who gained his freedom, learned to read, and became a preacher and a leader of a community of escaped slaves.

FURTHER READING

Pease, William, and Jane Pease. *Black Utopia: Negro Communal Experiments in America* (1963).
Stowe, Harriet Beecher. *A Key to Uncle Tom's Cabin* (1853).
Winks, Robin. *Blacks in Canada: A History* (1971).
Obituary: *New York Tribune*, 6 May 1883.

This entry is taken from the *American National Biography* and is published here with the permission of the American Council of Learned Societies.

ELIZABETH ZOE VICARY

Henson, Matthew Alexander (8 Aug. 1866–9 Mar. 1955), Arctic explorer, was born in Charles County, Maryland, to Lemuel Henson, a sharecropper, and his wife, Caroline Gaines. As best as can be determined from the conflicting accounts of his life,

Matthew's mother, Caroline, died when he was just two years old. His father then married Nellie, a neighbor with whom he already had a child. A few years later Lemuel died, leaving Matthew in the care of his abusive stepmother. Shortly after his eleventh birthday, Matthew left his five siblings and fled to Washington, D.C., where he worked for food and lodging at a restaurant owned by Janey Moore, whom he called "Aunt Janey." He may have attended the N Street School in Washington before a seaman known as Baltimore Jack captured his imagination with tales of adventure upon the high seas.

At age twelve Henson signed on as cabin boy on the *Katie Hines*, a three-masted sail and steam vessel. Over the next six years, the ship took Henson around the globe several times. During these voyages Captain Childs instructed Henson in reading, writing, history, and the nautical skills required for him to advance from cabin boy to able-bodied seaman. After Childs's death in 1883, Henson signed on to the *White Seal*, a Newfoundland fishing schooner, but he found the working conditions so vile and the attitude of the white crew so hostile that he sought alternative work on land. He lived in Boston, Providence, and New York City before becoming a clerk at Steinmetz and Son, a Washington, D.C., haberdashery. In the spring of 1887 Robert Peary, a young naval engineer, entered the store to buy a sun helmet. Peary was leading a party to map a canal route connecting the Atlantic and the Pacific through Nicaragua, and he asked if Henson would be interested in coming along as his "personal servant." Henson, whose thirst for adventure was as great as Peary's, accepted. This was the first of many voyages that Henson took with Peary over the next twenty-two years.

During seven months in the tropics of Nicaragua, a relationship of trust and respect developed between Henson and Peary. On their return from Nicaragua, Peary helped Henson get a job as a messenger at the League Island Navy Yard, which provided him not only with a steady income but a pension as well, benefits that were difficult for African Americans to obtain. In April 1891 Henson married Eva Helen Flint, a member of Philadelphia's black middle class. He had financial security and a family, both of which he put at risk when he agreed to accompany Peary on a quest for the North Pole. Henson accompanied Peary on seven Arctic expeditions. The first took place in 1891–1892, with the goal of traversing Greenland. They returned to Greenland in 1893–1895 to map the region but failed to reach the ice cap. The next two voyages, in

Matthew Alexander Henson, right, received the gold medal of the Geographic Society of Chicago from Cmdr. Eugene F. McDonald, Jr. in March 1948. (AP Images.)

1896 and 1897, were expeditions to take a thirty-ton meteorite to the United States. During their longest polar expedition, from 1898 to 1902, Henson, who had recently divorced, entered into a relationship with an Inuit woman, Akatingwah, and they had a son, Anaukaq. The party returned to the United States without the grail they sought. They claimed to have set a new distance record of 87°6' N during a 1905–1906 attempt but were turned back by ice floes and water. Finally, a determined effort in 1908–1909 got Peary, at least, into the history books.

When they first set sail from Brooklyn in 1891, Henson had more experience at sea than any other member of the crew. Some of the white officers complained of Henson's "freedom and insolence." John Verhoeff, a southerner who expected subservience from blacks, clashed with Henson so intensely that on one occasion Commander Peary's wife, Josephine Peary, suggested the two men simply "fight it out." Peary developed confidence in Henson's loyalty, dedication, and ingenuity, though he himself initially subscribed to the common stereotype that blacks are better suited for warm climates. After their final mission, however, one member of the team, Donald MacMillan, stated flatly in *National Geographic* that Henson "went to the Pole with Peary because he was easily the most efficient of all Peary's assistants."

His intelligence, adaptability, and personal demeanor helped to make Henson indispensable to their mission. The Inuit called Henson *Mahri-Pahluk*, "the kind one." Henson himself writes that "I have been to all intents an Esquimo, with Esquimos for companions, speaking their language, dressing in the same kind of clothes, living in the same kind of dens, eating the same food, enjoying their pleasures, and frequently sharing their grief" (Henson, 4). Henson's close relationship with the Inuit was invaluable because they provided the expedition not only with labor and supplies, but also with knowledge and skills necessary for its very survival. For example, Europeans often used tents, whereas igloos provided better shelter and did not need to be transported. Similarly, explorers often wore woolen clothing and used Alpine skis, though the animal skins and shoes of the Inuit were more effective.

Henson was responsible for building the sledges and training the crews in their operation, engaging the Inuit who accompanied them and who manufactured their clothing, and even selecting the dogs. He participated in gathering scientific data, such as temperature and water depth, and he was cook, carpenter, hunter, and translator, as well as photographer—though most of his pictures were confiscated by Peary, who required all the members of his expeditions to sign nondisclosure agreements.

During their first voyage in 1891, Peary broke his leg and was almost completely dependent on Henson through the winter, when temperatures dropped to fifty degrees below zero. In 1898, during their fifth expedition, Peary lost eight toes to frostbite; Henson used his own body to warm Peary and saved his life by transporting him to safety. These were dangerous missions on which six men died; four Inuit died of Western diseases against which they had no immunity, Verhoeff mysteriously disappeared, and Ross Marvin was murdered by a member of his sledge crew. Under such extreme circumstances, Henson might best be described as Peary's Arctic engineer, manager, and partner. However, the bonds of necessity that held the two together on the ice gave way to conventional divisions of race and class whenever they returned to "civilization."

After eighteen years of sacrifice and repeated disappointment, Peary, at age fifty-three, and Henson, at forty-three, found themselves 175 miles from the top of the world with four Inuit—Ooatah, Egingwah, Seegloo, and Ooqueah. At intervals Peary had members of his crew return to base, leaving a cache of supplies for those who forged ahead. Henson suspected that Peary would ask him to trail behind on the last leg of the journey. Thus, on 6 April 1909, when Peary instructed him to stop just short of the North Pole, Henson claims that he inadvertently overshot his target and camped at the pole forty-five minutes before Peary arrived. Peary disputed this claim, and his relationship with Henson became much more distant after their return. Henson wrote that "for the crime of being present when the Pole was reached Commander Peary has ignored me ever since" (Henson, 151).

The recognition that Henson should have received for his role in the discovery was delayed in coming, first because of a spurious claim by Dr. Frederick Cook that he had beaten them to the pole, and then by lingering doubts that Peary miscalculated or fabricated his coordinates. But by all calculations the expedition reached an area that can be considered generally, if not precisely, the North Pole. Peary received numerous accolades and awards and was promoted to rear admiral, allowing him to retire with a pension of almost eight thousand dollars a year. In contrast, Henson found himself working as a handyman in a Brooklyn garage for sixteen dollars a week and moonlighting at the post office. His second wife, Lucy Jane Ross, had to work to supplement their income. Henson tried to make a living on the lecture circuit, and he published his autobiography, *A Negro Explorer at the North Pole* (1912), but there was little public interest in either.

BOOKER T. WASHINGTON and administrators at several black colleges held dinners or presented Henson with honorary degrees, and more than twenty years after his greatest accomplishment, he was made an honorary member of the Explorers Club and an honorary member of the Academy of Science and Art of Pittsburgh. In 1913, by order of President William Howard Taft, Henson was given a position as a messenger at the U.S. Customs House in New York, which he held until the mandatory retirement age of seventy. However, repeated efforts to present Henson with a National Medal of Honor were blocked until 1944, when Congress authorized a medal honoring *all* the men of the Peary expedition. At Henson's funeral ADAM CLAYTON POWELL JR. asserted that the "achievements of Henson are as important as those performed by Marco Polo and Ferdinand Magellan." In 1988 Henson and his wife were reinterred at Arlington National Cemetery near the site of Robert Peary's grave.

FURTHER READING

The main body of Henson's papers is located in the Matthew Henson Collection at Morgan State University in Baltimore, Maryland.

Henson, Matthew. *A Negro Explorer at the North Pole* (1912).

Counter, S. Allen. *North Pole Legacy: Black, White & Eskimo* (1991).

Miller, Floyd. *Ahdoolo: The Biography of Matthew A. Henson* (1963).

Robinson, Bradley. *Dark Companion* (1947).

Obituary: *New York Times*, 10 Mar. 1955.

SHOLOMO B. LEVY

Herbert, Bob (7 Mar. 1945–), newspaper columnist, was born in Brooklyn, New York, to parents who owned a number of upholstery businesses. When he was still quite young, the family relocated to Montclair in the suburbs of New Jersey. Though his mother and father appear not to have themselves been active in local politics, Herbert nevertheless enjoyed a fairly political upbringing: the doings of government and current events were frequent topics of conversation around the house and at the dinner table. He attended local schools and might have gone on to take up the family business (as at one time seemed nearly a certainty) except that he was drafted, serving in Korea until the end of the war there in 1953.

Upon returning to the United States, Herbert decided to pursue a career in journalism. He returned to New Jersey, where, though untrained in the profession, he contacted the editor of the *Star-Ledger* in 1970 and was amazed to be offered a job as a reporter. Herbert spent the next few years learning the ins and outs of professional journalism. In 1973 he was made the paper's night editor, a position that ultimately won him a job offer from the much larger *New York Daily News* in 1976. He served with the paper as an editor and reporter until around 1985. Meanwhile, he was developing a reputation as a passionate advocate of liberal causes, with a particular focus on class and race issues. When he left the *Daily News* he began working as an editorial columnist. His stature grew to the point that he was able to make the move to local television, where in 1990 he helped to found and frequently appeared on *Sunday Edition*, a public-affairs broadcast.

He likewise decided to formalize his journalistic training. He attended Empire State College, in the SUNY system, from which he graduated with a bachelor's in Journalism in 1989. In 1993 he was hired by the *New York Times* to write a twice-weekly opinion column. From this perch, Herbert continued to be a strong (and rare) voice for avowedly liberal politics and public policy. In a media dominated by conservative voices—Herbert proved a reliable, thoughtful (some have argued dull), and persuasive voice for progressive concerns throughout the tumultuous Bill Clinton and George W. Bush presidential administrations. He was a staunch opponent of the war in Iraq and remained deeply skeptical of the coercive (and, in many cases, objectively illegal) elements brought to bear in the so-called War on Terror. With a special concern for the plight of the urban poor and of minorities, he frequently held that climbing unemployment statistics in the United States were undercounting the effect of long-term unemployment on those least able to find adequate representation and redress in Washington.

Among his many activities, Herbert sat on the Pulitzer Prize committee for spot reporting in 1993. In that same year, he was hired by NBC News to serve as national correspondent and made occasional appearances on that network's family of news broadcasts, including the *Today Show*. His book of essays *Promises Betrayed: Waking Up from the American Dream* (2005) expressed concerns about the direction of the country—the overreach by elements of U.S. law enforcement, the growth of the surveillance state, the use of torture as an instrument of U.S. foreign policy—under the George W. Bush administration. He taught journalism at a number of institutions in New York City, including Brooklyn College. He was the recipient of an American Society of Newspaper Editors award for excellence in newspaper writing and a 2009 Ridenhour Courage Prize for especially courageous pursuit of issues related to social justice and the public good. As of 2010 Herbert was resident in Manhattan with his wife, Suzanne (maiden name unknown), and remained one of the clearest liberal voices in the U.S. print media

FURTHER READING

Herbert, Bob. *Promises Betrayed: Waking Up from the American Dream* (2005).

Frank, T. A. "Why Is Bob Herbert Boring? The Perils of Punditry for the Powerless." *Washington Monthly*, Oct. (2007): 16–21.

"Meet Bob Herbert." *The New York Times*. Video interview, available from http://select.nytimes.com/packages/khtml/2005/09/19/opinion/20050919_HERBERT_FEATURE.html

JASON PHILIP MILLER

Herc, DJ Kool (16 Apr. 1955–), disc jockey, hip-hop innovator, musician, and producer, was born Clive Campbell in Kingston, Jamaica, the eldest of six-children of Keith Campbell, a community activist and head foreman at a wharf garage from Kingston, and Nettie Campbell, from Port Maria, a city on the northern coast of Jamaica. As a child Clive Campbell fell in love with the active dancehall reggae culture of Jamaica and would often follow the local disc jockeys to watch them set up their sound systems before performances. Political instability in Kingston led the Campbell family to move to the affluent city of Franklyn Town. In search of financial and educational opportunities for her family, Nettie Campbell migrated to the United States and worked as a dental technician while studying nursing in New York. She frequently sent money to her family in Jamaica along with records of the new sounds of JAMES BROWN and Motown coming out of the United States. During the early 1960s Nettie worked in New York City, all the while trying to convince the rest of her family to migrate to the United States for a better future. In November 1967 Clive Campbell became the first to join his mother in New York, and was later followed by the rest of the Campbell family. At the age of twelve, he entered West Bronx, New York, to live in his mother's apartment at 611 East 178th Avenue. His athletic abilities in basketball and his broad physique earned him the nickname "Hercules," which helped him gain respect among his peers and overcome his background differences. To avoid the active gang culture in New York, Campbell became involved in the graffiti art revolution that was the first expression of hip-hop culture.

When he was a young teenager, Campbell's mother would often take him to house parties, where he was able to learn different musical styles and observe the new sound systems. He began to borrow sound systems from his friends and started his own house party business, even as he continued to add to his record collection. His father, too, was an avid record collector and became active in the music scene as a sponsor for a local rhythm and blues band. In fact, he became the soundman for the group and purchased a brand-new Shure Professional Audio system but did not know how to assemble the equipment. One

DJ Kool Herc speaks at a news conference at the Smithsonian's National Museum of American History in February 2006. (AP Images.)

day after school, Campbell figured out how to work his father's sound system. No longer dependent on his friends' equipment, his career as a professional disc jockey began.

Campbell developed his own disc jockey style on his father's sound system and augmented the system by adding speakers from old television sets. One day his sister Cindy developed a plan to make money for school clothes by organizing a party in the apartment complex recreation center with Clive as the disc jockey. On 11 August 1973 Campbell became DJ Kool Herc, the packed recreation center overflowed into Cedar Park, and his sound became the foundation of hip-hop. DJ Kool Herc combined Jamaican dancehall roots with American soul and funk sounds, such as James Brown. Herc recognized that the crowd would often go wild during the break of a song, when the vocals and melody would drop out and the beat would run alone. He began to choose his records based primarily on

their instrumental breaks. He took this new style one step further and begin to use the microphone to call out to his friends in the crowd similar to the "toasting" style in Jamaican dancehalls; this innovative musical style soon became quite popular throughout the Bronx.

Kool Herc performed indoors and out, at house parties, block parties, and in public parks, tapping into light posts for the power to run his enormous sound system. Seeking to extend the excitement of the break, Herc developed a technique he called "the Merry-Go-Round," in which he loaded two copies of the same record on two different turntables and cued back and forth between them to repeat the brief breaks and turn them into extended loops of rhythmic grooves. This extension of the break section of the song contributed to a new disc jockey style of urban youth music known as hiphop. Herc was the original disc jockey of this new genre. He also pioneered the DJ/MC/break crew triad with his collective the Herculords, featuring the rapper Coke La Rock, and by designing a massive sound system inspired by Jamaican dancehall performers who used huge speakers on vehicles to ride around the neighborhoods playing music. Billing the system as the Herculoids, Herc delivered a sound that was both enormous and clear, even outdoors.

By 1976 Kool Herc had become a local celebrity, moving from public parks and recreation centers to some of the most popular nightclubs in the Bronx. He was followed by an ardent group of young dancers, who became known as B-boys or break boys and whose wild, acrobatic style of dance was referred to as break dancing. Disc jockeys from all over New York ventured to the West Bronx, later referred to as the Boogie Down Bronx, to observe, mimic, and expand upon this new musical style. Soon a new generation of DJs had elaborated on Herc's style and made it their own, among them AFRIKA BAMBAATAA, GRANDMASTER FLASH, and GRAND WIZZARD THEODORE. Within a year, however, Herc's audiences had begun to diminish as the proliferation of crews and styles intensified the competition for crowds.

In 1977 Kool Herc was stabbed as he prepared for a show at a club called the Sparkle. After the stabbing and a later drug addiction, he largely withdrew from the hip-hop scene. He did return to hip-hop occasionally, through various appearances in the United States and Europe, and participate in the reconstruction of hip-hop's early history through oral history projects and interviews. Though he remained a cult figure into the 2000s, DJ Kool Herc is widely credited as the "father of hip-hop."

FURTHER READING

Brewster, Bill, and Frank Broughton. *Last Night a DJ Saved My Life: The History of the Disc Jockey* (1999).

Chang, Jeff. *Can't Stop, Won't Stop: A History of the Hip-Hop Generation* (2005).

Light, Alan, ed. *The Vibe History of Hip Hop* (1999).

Rose, Tricia. *Black Noise: Rap Music and Black Culture in Contemporary America* (1994).

KATRINA D. THOMPSON

Hercules, Felix (1888–1943), radical Pan-Africanist, journalist, and Baptist minister, was born Felix Eugene Michael Hercules in Venezuela but grew up in Trinidad, where his father was a civil servant. As a student at the Queen's Royal College in Port of Spain, Hercules showed his political awareness in a racially organized British colony by founding the Young Men's Coloured Association.

On leaving school he became a civil servant and then a schoolteacher in the town of Maparima. Hercules married a woman named Millicent Beatrice in Trinidad and had several children, including Frank, who in the 1940s moved to the United States and became a novelist and nonfiction writer. During World War I Hercules moved to Britain and studied for an intermediate B.A. degree at London University. Not untypical of the black migrant experience, he soon became disillusioned by his experiences of the "color bar" in Britain, an obstacle that fuelled his radicalism. Hercules was acquainted with John Eldred Taylor, a Sierra Leone businessman, and accepted the offer to edit his monthly journal, *African Telegraph*. In his brief period as editor Hercules made the *Telegraph* more outspokenly Pan-Africanist. He condemned racial discrimination in Britain and in the overseas colonies. But some of his harshest condemnation was directed at the violence inflicted on wounded black soldiers of the British West India Regiment by white racist servicemen whose racial taunts provoked serious unrest in a Liverpool hospital in 1918. Early in 1919 there were serious race riots in various British cities and towns, including Liverpool, London, and Cardiff, which served further to strengthen the determination of Hercules and other black leaders to secure racial unity in the face of provocative discrimination. Hercules had already become general secretary of the Society of Peoples of African Origin (SPAO), a Pan-African welfare body founded by Taylor in 1918. A little later he also served as associate secretary of the African Progress Union, another Pan-Africanist body founded in December 1918. He appears to have been instrumental in the two organizations merging in 1919.

In early July 1919 Hercules arrived in Jamaica at the start of a tour of the West Indies that included Trinidad, British Guiana, and Grenada. His aim was to enquire into social and economic conditions in the British Caribbean colonies and also to recruit members for the SPAO. Hercules's activities in Britain had been subject to official surveillance; in the West Indies he was also closely monitored by the police and called a Bolshevik, a label that he vehemently denied. A dynamic orator, his speeches led colonial governments to fear that he would incite further unrest. In fact the post-war disturbances among workers, peasants, and returned soldiers in many parts of the British Caribbean were caused by unemployment, inflation, and official disregard for the social and economic welfare of the people. Some indication of Hercules's indignant Pan-African fervour is provided by a speech he gave to a largely middle class, urban audience on 11 September 1919 in Port of Spain, Trinidad. During it he denounced the indignities suffered by the natives of South Africa and by black people in Britain stating that, "there was no single quarter of the globe and no flag under which people of African descent received fair play and that measure of justice to which they were entitled." The answer to this, he argued, was that "people of African origin, regardless of pigment, should acquire racial consciousness … they should get to know each other and act in sympathy and unison," and "they should strive to acquire a measure of economic independence, by which alone they would be able to fight their present disabilities" (*Argos* [Port of Spain, Trinidad], 13 Sept. 1919). When Hercules attempted to return to Trinidad in December 1919 he was refused permission to land by the governor. Hercules proceeded to Grenada and then took ship to New York.

Hercules's activities in Britain and the Caribbean are well documented, and he is widely recognized among British and Caribbean scholars as a significant figure in Pan-African politics at the end of World War I. However, his life in the United States, where he lived from 1920 until his death, is less well known. Indeed, several historians have stated that "we lose sight" of Hercules when he leaves the Caribbean in 1920 (Elkins, 320). Early that year, Henry Baker, the U.S. consul to Trinidad, sent a telegram to the State Department, trying but failing to have Hercules deported as politically undesirable should he arrive in the United States. Upon his arrival in New York, Hercules was briefly detained by officials but admitted when he stated that he did not agree with MARCUS GARVEY's racial ideas and the policies of the United Negro Improvement Association (UNIA). According to a press report he had come to the United States in order to examine the social, political, and economic realities of black people living in Africa, the West Indies, and the United States. Two weeks after his arrival in the city Hercules was introduced to a meeting of Garvey's UNIA in Liberty Hall, although he disliked Garvey's autocratic methods. On 8 February 1920 he spoke at Rush Memorial Church on "The Right of the Negro Races to Self-Determination." While in New York, Hercules helped found the short-lived "African International League, an organization for the uplift of the Negroes of the World," which according to its headed notepaper had an international headquarters in London. Hercules planned a newspaper to be called "United Africa" to promote the League, but this never appeared. Little is known of the League, although one of its proposals was to buy a 1,500-acre farm in British Guiana and to market the produce grown there. In early 1921 Hercules wrote to Sir John Harris, parliamentary secretary to the Anti-Slavery Society, in London that he hoped to return to Britain in late May to found and edit a Pan-African magazine and to help organize a hostel for Africans. As far as is known he did not return to Britain.

Hercules's writings and speeches indicate that as a young man he held Christian beliefs. In London he was involved in a hostel run by the Student Christian Movement and he occasionally addressed missionary meetings. Frank Hercules stated that his father was an "Afro-West Indian conservative goaded into a crusade contradictory of (to) his natural temper, by a social philosophy at fundamental odds with the inherent nature of colonialism" (Carol P. Marsh, "Frank E. M. Hercules," in *Dictionary of Literary Biography* vol. 33, *Afro-American Fiction Writers after 1955*, eds. T. M. Davies and T. Harris [1984]: 115). At some point in the United States, Felix Hercules moved from the political platform to the pulpit and was ordained as a Baptist minister. Although he continued to have a reputation as a passionate speaker on matters of race and civil rights, his energies were largely directed to pastoring churches in Illinois, Arkansas, and Tennessee. Hercules died in Chicago.

FURTHER READING

Elkins, William F. "Hercules and the Society of Peoples of African Origin," *Caribbean Studies* 11.4 (1971).

Fryer, Peter. *Staying Power: The History of Black People in Britain* (1984).

Hill, Robert, ed. *The Marcus Garvey and United Negro Improvement Association Papers*, vol. 2 (1983).

DAVID KILLINGRAY

Herenton, Willie Wilbert (23 Apr. 1940–), educational administrator and the first black mayor of Memphis, Tennessee, was born in Memphis to Willie Witherspoon Herenton and Ruby Lee Harris. His parents separated, and he was raised in a single-parent family. As a youth, Herenton had aspirations to being a boxer and took the Kentucky Golden Gloves, several southern AAU championships, and four Tri-State Boxing Championships in his class (flyweight) by the time he graduated from high school in 1958. He turned down a boxing scholarship to the University of Wisconsin and moved to Chicago briefly to pursue the sport professionally and then decided education offered greater stability and opportunities. He returned to Memphis and completed a college degree at LeMoyne-Owen College in 1963. There he met and married Ida Jones, with whom he had three children. They divorced in 1988. He fathered a fourth child in 2004.

Herenton began a career in education teaching in one of Memphis's elementary schools. After earning a graduate degree from the University of Memphis in 1966, he became at twenty-eight the youngest public-school principal in city history. After taking a doctorate in education from Southern Illinois University in 1971 and a Rockefeller Foundation fellowship in 1973–1974, Herenton was hired as deputy superintendent and then superintendent of Memphis City Schools, a position he held from 1979 to 1992. Memphis represented the country's fifth-largest school district, with over ten thousand employees and a $300 million budget. Under his leadership the system completed the Memphis Inner-City School Improvement Project.

Memphis city gained a narrow black majority in the 1980 census. Black electoral participation as candidates and voters increased through the decade. After ten years of stability but no real representational change in city government, the 1991 election was a watershed, with six black candidates elected to the city council and superintendent Herenton successfully challenging a two-term incumbent in the mayoral race. The city's first black mayor was elected on a 142-vote margin in an election polarized dramatically along racial lines.

During his eighteen-year mayoral tenure Herenton championed Second Chance, a successful training and employment program for ex-felons. The city developed fiscally sound governance that operated within budget, and hundreds of police officers were added to the city force. His service also saw rising business investment capped by a $1.3 billion downtown renovation. However, the city also experienced a dramatic rise in violent crime over the same period. The growth of a controversial mayoral entourage and political appointments of individuals with questionable experience and backgrounds generated angry public sentiment and one failed recall attempt. Despite early success with his initiatives and programs, the outspoken and increasingly confrontational mayor continued to employ language and tactics regarded as racially divisive. His tenure in office became pocked by widespread public dissatisfaction, controversy, and corruption allegations. Mayor Herenton's successful first term attracted significant support from white voters for his first reelection, but by 1999 electoral challenges to his leadership began in earnest and city politics became progressively more divisive. Herenton was reelected with smaller and smaller electoral percentages as his campaign tactics of an overtly and sometimes stridently racial political rhetoric sacrificed the biracial electoral pluralities that had predominated in city politics after the 1960s. From a field of thirteen candidates Herenton was elected to an unprecedented fifth term as Memphis mayor in October 2007 under bylaws that certified the election without a runoff on Herenton's majority of 42 percent of the total votes.

Mayor Herenton left office in 2009 amid a storm of controversy and under federal investigation (later dropped) for mixing public and private interest while in office. On 20 March 2008, shortly after his fourth reelection, he announced that he would resign as mayor effective 31 July and intended to seek the vacant superintendency of Memphis City Schools. Within a week he qualified the announced departure, stating that he would not resign unless he was guaranteed the school superintendency. In the same press conference he claimed that he had pursued a fifth term specifically to "protect" the city from the other mayoral frontrunners, which included a Jewish candidate and female city councilwoman. When July came he failed to step down as previously announced and instead vowed to serve the full term, which would end in

2011. However, in April 2009 Herenton formed an exploratory committee toward a possible candidacy in the 2010 U.S. congressional election as a Democratic primary challenger of Tennessee 9th Congressional district incumbent Steve Cohen. On 25 June 2009, Herenton again announced his retirement as mayor, effective 10 July, but then on 6 July announced he would delay departure until the end of the month. He left the Memphis mayoral office on 30 July 2009. Memphis City Council Chairman Myron Lowery was appointed mayor pro tem, but Herenton quickly filed as a candidate for the October 2009 special mayoral election, which concluded with the election of A. C. Wharton.

FURTHER READING

Herenton, Willie W. "A Historical Study of School Desegregation in the Memphis City Schools, 1954–1970." Ph.D. dissertation, Southern Illinois University (1971).

Pohlmann, Marchus D., and Michael P. Kirby, *Racial Politics at the Crossroads: Memphis Elects Dr. W. W. Herenton* (1996).

Wright, Sharon D. *Race, Power, and Political Emergency in Memphis* (2000).

RICHARD SAUNDERS

Herman, Alexis Margaret (16 Jul. 1947–), politician, was born to Alex Herman and Gloria Capronisin Mobile, Alabama. Her father, a mortician and a prominent political activist, sued the Democratic Party in an effort to allow blacks to vote and is credited as the first black elected in the South since Reconstruction when he became a wardsman. Her mother, Gloria, was a reading teacher.

Religion most shaped Herman's youth. Her Roman Catholic parents shunned segregated state education and enrolled her in parochial schools. At the time, these were still segregated, but employed white priests and nuns whose tutoring was, in Herman's recollection, colorblind. Her father once took her high school class on an unusual field trip: to a meeting of the Alabama Citizens Council, the front for the Ku Klux Klan. She graduated from Most Pure Heart of Mary High School in 1965. Shortly thereafter, Herman attended Edgewood College in Madison, Wisconsin, and Spring Hill College in Mobile, Alabama. Ultimately, she graduated from a historically black Catholic college, Xavier University of Louisiana, where she graduated in 1969 with a Bachelor of Arts in Sociology.

After graduating college, Herman returned to Mobile to work for Catholic Charities in nearby

Pascagoula, Mississippi, lobbying for the city shipyard to train African American laborers. She was later recruited by a high school classmate to relocate to Atlanta to work for the liberal civil rights organization, the Southern Regional Council, to work on a project persuading corporations to hire college-educated African American women for jobs that had been filled by exclusively by whites. In Atlanta, she worked on the mayoral campaigns of MAYNARD H. JACKSON, the city's first African American mayor and his successor, ANDREW YOUNG. During this time, from 1973 to 1974, she was introduced to Georgia Governor Jimmy Carter while he was campaigning for the presidency. Following Carter's election, Herman was appointed Director of the U.S. Department of Labor Women's Bureau. At age twenty-nine, she was the youngest person to serve in that capacity.

After her tenure in the Carter Administration, she founded a consulting firm, A.M. Herman & Associates, specializing in minority hiring issues. Herman remained in Democratic Party politics working on Washington, D.C.'s Mayor MARION BARRY's reelection campaign and JESSE JACKSON's 1984 presidential bid. While working on the Jackson's 1988 campaign, Herman was introduced to Democratic activist RON BROWN, a former National Urban League executive and Jackson campaign manager. Brown later became Chairman of the Democratic National Committee in 1989, appointing her Vice Chairman and Chief of Staff. Herman's primary role was organizing the 1992 Democratic National Convention in New York City where Bill Clinton won the party's nomination for the presidency.

When Clinton was elected President, Herman served as deputy director of his Presidential Transition office and was later appointed head of the White House Office of Public Liaison becoming only the second African American woman to serve as an assistant to the President of the United States. In that capacity, Herman's primary role was garnering public support for the Clinton Administration's policies. Herman was criticized throughout her tenure for using a historically nonpolitical role as a means of drafting public policies to gain political support of traditionally Democratic ethnic groups. Her role was scrutinized in what was known as "White House Coffees," White House gatherings organized by the Democratic National Committee for contributors with the President to support Clinton's reelection efforts.

President Clinton, after securing reelection in 1996, nominated Herman to succeed Robert Reich as Secretary of Labor—the first African American and fifth woman to be nominated for that post. Secretary-Designate Herman's nomination was initially opposed by congressional Republicans and labor unions. Herman's nomination was held up in the Republican-controlled Senate for nearly three months. Her tenure as head of the White House Office of Public Liaison, plus financial interests in a Washington real estate project that earned her $500,000 (although she invested no money), and her eight-month delay in divesting ownership of a minority business consulting firm after White House lawyers advised her the firm could constitute a conflict of interest, were all scrutinized. She was ultimately confirmed by the U.S. Senate 85–13 after President Clinton made a concession to congressional Republicans that he would not issue an executive order that gave labor unions preferential treatment on federal construction contracts. Herman was sworn into office by Vice President Al Gore on 9 May 1997.

As Secretary of Labor, Herman was lauded for her mediation during the 1997 UPS workers strike—the nation's largest strike in over twenty years. During the fifteen-day strike, UPS lost $650 million in revenue. UPS workers represented by the Teamsters Union (185,000 people) walked out on the UPS company, disrupting the delivery of millions of packages throughout the country every day for more than two weeks. As a result of Herman's efforts 10,000 UPS part-time jobs became full-time positions and the Teamsters union gained control of pension funds and paid about $10 million in strike benefits to members who got $55 a week for manning the picket lines. Secretary Herman's handling of the UPS strike cemented the support of the organized labor movement that was skeptical of her nomination. Additionally, under her tenure, the Department won the largest settlement ever in a discrimination settlement for individuals with disabilities with American Airlines paying nearly $1.7 million to ninety-nine people who were denied jobs in Nashville, Tennessee, and Detroit.

Much of Secretary Herman's tenure was plagued by allegations of misconduct for nearly two years. The U.S. Department of Justice appointed an Independent Counsel to investigate allegations that she accepted illegal funds in exchange for assisting a business associate while she served as director of the White House Office of Public Liaison during President Clinton's first term. Secretary Herman was the fifth cabinet member to come under investigation by an Independent Counsel; President Clinton testified on her behalf. She was ultimately cleared of any wrongdoing during her last year in office, 2000.

Secretary Herman was often mentioned as a leading candidate for White House Chief of Staff in a prospective Gore Administration, had the vice-president succeeded Clinton in 2001. She served as a member of Gore's planning team during the contentious Florida election recount, but the U.S. Supreme Court's ruling in *Bush v. Gore* suspended that recount and handed the presidency to Republican George W. Bush. After leaving government, Herman was hired by the Coca-Cola Company in 2001 as chairwoman of the Human Resource Task Force that oversees the company's diversity efforts. She also chairs Toyota Motors' North American Diversity Advisory Board.

Additionally, Herman serves as Chair and Chief Executive Officer of New Ventures, Inc., where she advises corporations on how to bring diversity to the workplace. A recipient of more than a dozen honorary degrees from major colleges and universities around the country, Herman serves on the Board of her alma mater, Xavier University of Louisiana. She is also a member of the Board of Directors of Cummins Inc., MGM/ Mirage Inc., the Presidential Life Insurance Corporation, and the Advisory Committee for Public Issues for the Advertising Council.

Former Secretary Herman is still active in Democratic politics and played an influential role in BARACK OBAMA delivering the keynote address at the 2004 Democratic Convention. She had served as cochair of the Democratic National Committee's Rules and Bylaws Committee since 2005. As cochair Herman led the process that decided the fate of the disputed Florida and Michigan delegates during the contentious 2008 Democratic presidential primary between Sen. Barack Obama and Sen. Hillary Rodham Clinton.

FURTHER READING

Cook, Nancy. "Who's Who on the Rules and Bylaw Committee." *NPR*, 02 June 2008.

Ifill, Gwen. *The Breakthrough: Politics and Race in the Age of Obama* (2009).

Wines, Michael. "Friends Helped Labor Nominee Move Up, then Almost Brought Her Down," *New York Times*, 15 March 1997.

JAMAL DONALDSON BRIGGS

Hernandez, Aileen (23 May 1926–), labor union organizer and officer, businessperson, educator, and activist, was born Aileen Clarke in Brooklyn, New York, to Jamaican immigrants Ethel Louise Hall Clarke, a theatrical costume maker and seamstress, and Charles Henry Clarke Sr., an art supply business worker. Their lessons of bravery, persistence, and nondiscrimination served Hernandez and her brothers well as they grew up in Bay Ridge, a majority-white Brooklyn neighborhood. Hernandez was valedictorian of her public grammar school class. In 1943 she graduated from Bay Ridge High School as salutatorian and won a scholarship to Howard University. Outraged by the more blatant segregation in the nation's capital, she picketed Jim Crow facilities with the campus NAACP chapter. Hernandez edited the college newspaper and penned a college issues column for the *Washington Tribune*. After graduating from Howard magna cum laude in Sociology and Political Science in 1947, she was briefly an exchange student at the University of Oslo, Norway.

After leadership training at the labor college of the International Ladies' Garment Workers' Union (ILGWU), Hernandez worked for the union's Los Angeles office as shop organizer and assistant educational director (1951–1959) and Pacific Coast regional public relations and education director (1959–1961). She wed Alfonso Rafael Hernandez, a Mexican American garment worker, in 1957. Recognizing her talents with Los Angeles's primarily Latina garment workers, in 1960 the U.S. State Department sent her on a speaking tour of South America. After divorcing her husband in 1961, she continued to use her married surname. The same year, she also earned an M.A. in public relations with highest honors from California State University and coordinated the future U.S. senator Alan Cranston's winning campaign for state controller. The next year she was appointed deputy chief of the California Fair Employment Practice Commission. In 1964 the federal Civil Rights Act banned employment discrimination on the grounds of race, color, sex, religion, and national origin and mandated establishment of the nationwide Equal Employment Opportunity Commission (EEOC). In 1965 President Lyndon Johnson named Hernandez one of the original five commissioners. The sole woman appointee, she charged the EEOC with neglecting sex discrimination. Hernandez resigned from the EEOC shortly after speaking at the Third National Conference of Commissions on the Status of Women, Washington, D.C., in June

1966. In the hotel room of *The Femmine Mystique* author and former labor journalist Betty Friedan, Hernandez met with other conference goers who distrusted the EEOC to carry out its full mission. They wanted instead a national nonprofit group to fight for women just as civil rights groups fought for black persons. This meeting marked the founding of the National Organization for Women (NOW), which grew so rapidly in size and visibility that many Americans equated it with feminism itself. NOW soon became predominantly white and middle to upper class, as well as focused on abortion rights advocacy. These changes caused some women of color, working-class women, and feminist-identified abortion opponents to feel excluded from NOW. Yet NOW's earliest founders and leading participants included, along with Hernandez, such distinguished women activists of color as PAULI MURRAY, SHIRLEY CHISHOLM, and even FANNIE LOU HAMER and Graciela (Grace) Olivarez, both impassioned abortion opponents.

In 1966 Hernandez also moved to San Francisco and established her own urban affairs consulting firm, Hernandez and Associates. At NOW's first national organizing conference in 1967, she was elected executive vice president in absentia. She succeeded Betty Friedan, NOW's first president, in 1970. Hernandez and Chisholm testified before a U.S. Senate subcommittee in favor of a constitutional Equal Rights Amendment (ERA), one of NOW's most treasured goals. Although Friedan had been opposed to integrating lesbian concerns into NOW's agenda, Hernandez opened the door to the organization's prominent, enduring advocacy of sexual minorities. She was friends with Del Martin and Phyllis Lyon, the white same-sex couple who cofounded the pioneering lesbian rights group Daughters of Bilitis. The group supported and identified with both women's and African Americans' liberation struggles, thus attracting the support of black, feminist-identified women such as LORRAINE HANSBERRY. Hernandez encouraged Martin and Lyon to educate NOW members about the role of lesbians and lesbian rights in women's liberation. As a result, NOW's 1971 national conference adopted its first resolution ever affirming lesbian rights as an appropriate concern for the organization.

Hernandez resigned her post the same year, feeling stymied in her efforts to forge similar alliances between racial and ethnic minority rights organizations and NOW. Many women of color agreed with Hernandez that NOW's mostly white,

middle-to-upper class membership and agenda overemphasized individualistic concerns to the exclusion of broader, deeper social and economic problems. Still hoping for change, Hernandez created a racial/ethnic minority task force within the organization. By 1979 she had resigned from NOW altogether, urging other members of color to do the same unless the organization transformed itself on matters of race.

Hernandez earned respect and recognition for her founding and other leadership roles in numerous other social-action groups, including the National Committee against Discrimination in Housing, Black Women Organized for Action, the American Academy of Political and Social Science, the American Civil Liberties Union, Black Women Stirring the Waters, the Urban Institute, Death Penalty Focus, Common Cause, the Ms Foundation for Women, and the youth leadership training project Conscious Action Together. She lectured and taught at several California public universities. Hernandez was named an honorary doctor of humane letters by Southern Vermont College; a Nobel Peace Prize nominee (2005); a KQED-San Francisco Local Hero for Women's History Month (2006); and an honoree by the National Women's History Project (2006).

While apparently believing that NOW had made some progress toward her goals in inclusiveness, Hernandez still saw a great need to expand feminism far beyond "an upper-class white women's movement" and "get into the general society" (*Ms. Magazine*, July/Aug. 1994, 56). To her this expansion remained indispensable to "com[ing] up with a society in which everyone has the chance to be who they should be" (*Ms. Magazine*, Feb./Mar. 2001, 55). In 2005 Hernandez was a featured speaker at the NOW Foundation's Women of Color and Allies Summit. As she entered her eighties, she continued as president and CEO of Hernandez and Associates, advising clients like the City of Los Angeles, United Parcel Service (UPS), and the University of California. In mid-2007 she remained the volunteer chair of the California Women's Agenda, a grassroots network of more than 600 members that implemented the twelve-point action plan adopted by 189 countries at the 1995 United Nations Fourth World Conference on Women in Beijing, China.

FURTHER READING

The Schlesinger Library on the History of Women in America, Harvard University, holds some archival materials on Aileen Hernandez. These are located primarily in the National Organization for Women Records and in the individual papers of other early NOW leaders like Pauli Murray and Betty Friedan.

Hernandez, Aileen C. *The First Five Years, 1966–1971* (1971).

Hernandez, Aileen C. *National Women of Color Organizations: A Report to the Ford Foundation* (1991).

Hernandez, Aileen C. *The Women's Movement, 1965–1975* (1975).

Gallo, Marcia M. *Different Daughters: A History of the Daughters of Bilitis and the Rise of the Lesbian Rights Movement* (2006).

Giddings, Paula J. *When and Where I Enter: The Impact of Black Women on Race and Sex in America* (1984).

Teipe, Emily, "Aileen Clarke Hernandez," in *Dictionary of World Biography: Twentieth Century* (1999).

MARY KRANE DERR

Hernandez, Nestor, Jr. (23 Aug. 1960–13 May 2006), documentary photographer and educator, was born in Washington, D.C., to Nestor Hernandez Sr., an interior decorator and photographer, and Marion Johnson. Hernandez's mother died when he was eight years old. Hernandez attended St. John the Baptist Elementary School and Roosevelt High School in D.C. While he was a teenager, he learned photography through a journalism program at the Lemuel A. Penn Career Development Center in Northeast Washington, D.C. He attended what was later Clark Atlanta University in Atlanta, Georgia, where he took additional courses in photography.

In 1980 Hernandez returned to Washington, D.C., and took a position as photographer-in-residence at the Capital Children's Museum. Most of his professional career was spent with the Children's Museum. He worked there as the staff photographer until 1991, when he became its director of Youth Photography Programs. While with the museum, he was also a freelance photojournalist for several community and national newspapers, including *DC City Desk*, *Bulletin Board Newspaper*, the *Metro Herald*, the *Brookings Review*, *El Pregonero*, and the *Latin Trade Report*.

In 1989 he settled in the Mount Pleasant neighborhood of Washington, D.C., home to many Latino immigrants. Of Afro-Cuban descent himself, he developed a strong interest in documenting the local Afro-Latino community and later broadened his scope to include the African diaspora. He was the project photographer for several exhibitions and books, including *Afro-Latino Voices*, which documented Latinos of African descent throughout the United States. From 1991 to 1993 Hernandez was also the director of the photography program at Bancroft Elementary School, a position that allowed him to teach young people the necessary skills to document their community and led to two major exhibits about Mount Pleasant. Much of Hernandez's work during this period focused on Afro-Latino culture, and some of his most poignant images were displayed as part of a group show titled *Hidden Faces: AIDS in the Latino Community*, held at the El Centro de Arte in December of 1994.

Throughout his life, photographing children was central to Hernandez's work. From 1993 he served as project director for the award-winning Shooting Back program, which was designed to give at-risk youth exposure to photography and to empower them to record images of their own home environment. He also taught a photography course to at-risk seventh graders at the Option School, which became a public charter school. In 1994 he became the chief photographer for the D.C. public school system, yet retained his ties to the Children's Museum for the rest of his career. He developed several programs involving school children participating as both subjects and photographers, and he remained with the D.C. public school system until 2002.

His solo show *Black Pearls: African-American Boys and Girls*, organized in July of 1995 at the Ramee Art Gallery in Washington, was the first of many shows in which he exhibited his striking black-and-white photographs of children at play. In 1999 he received the Children's Book Award from the African Studies Association for *Master Weaver from Ghana* (1998), which included his photographs resulting from a month-long study of traditional weavers and spinners in that West African nation.

The show that propelled Hernandez to city-wide recognition was *Forever Young: A Portrait of the Black Child* at the Capital Children's Museum: Eighty black-and-white photographs of children from the United States, Ghana, and Cuba were paired with compelling verse by poet Laini Mataka.

Hernandez enjoyed sharing his love for making images, and during the last years of his life he devoted his time to cultural-exchange ventures that linked like-minded photographers from around the world. Between 1978 and 2003 he made 18 trips to Cuba, connecting with his extended family. In 1993 he took photographers and teachers to Cuba to work with children as part of a collaborative arts project. During his trips in 2001 and 2002 he invited other American photographers to accompany him to meet and discuss photography with their Cuban peers. The exchange culminated in *Cuba Now! Images of Cuba by Cuban and American Photographers*, a major group show held at the Sumner School and Museum in Washington in 2003. The images featured presented a decidedly different and up-close portrayal of Cuban life and culture.

Hernandez was active in local photography organizations, including the Fotocraft Camera Club, the Greater Washington Council of Camera Clubs, and the Exposure Group/African American Photographer's Association. He received numerous awards for the work he submitted to juried club and citywide competitions and served as Fotocraft's president from 1990 to 1998. He was the recipient of the Photographer of the Year Award by the Exposure Group in 2001 and a Distinguished Leaders Award from District of Columbia Public Schools. He received an Outstanding Emerging Artist Award from the mayor's office and an Artist Fellowship Grant from the city's Commission on the Arts and Humanities in 2003.

Hernandez regularly exhibited his photography. In addition to local shows, his work was exhibited in galleries, museums, and other venues along the East Coast and in Havana, Cuba and Accra, Ghana. Some of his photographs were acquired for the permanent collections of the Casa de Africa museum and Galería de Arte René Portocarrero in Cuba, the Asafo Gallery in Ghana, the Cuban Art Space in New York, and the Smithsonian Anacostia Museum in Washington, D.C.

Hernandez's last venture was a joint project with *Port of Harlem* magazine. "Our Children, Our World" featured photography by children from Ghana, Cuba, Washington, D.C., and Gary, Indiana. Following its successful run in Washington, D.C., the exhibit opened in Gary in 2006 as an official event celebrating Gary's 100th anniversary. Hernandez died in 2006 of lung cancer.

FURTHER READING

Willis, Deborah. *Reflections in Black: A History of Black Photographers, 1840 to the Present* (2000).
Obituary: *Washington Post*, 26 May 2006.

DONNA M. WELLS

Hernández, Rafael (24 Oct. 1892–11 Dec. 1965), popular and classical musician, composer, and orchestra conductor, was born Rafael Hernández Marín in Barrio Tamarindo, Aguadilla, Puerto Rico. He was one of four children of Miguel Angel Rosa and María Hernández. (There is no information regarding the reason why he was given only his mother's last name.) Rafael's parents were cigar makers, and at a young age the boy learned the craft. However, it was his godmother, Eloísa Yumet, who introduced him to the world of music. At first Rafael resisted, explaining that he wanted to be a *tabaquero* (cigar maker), in keeping with family tradition. Nonetheless he became a music student under the direction of José Ruellán Lequerica and Jesús Figueroa. He learned to play the trumpet, trombone, violin, guitar, and piano. At age sixteen Rafael organized a band to play at the Casino de Los Artesanos, a club for blacks. It was at this time, in 1912, that Hernández wrote his first piece, a *danza* titled "Maria Victoria."

In 1915 Rafael and his family moved to San Juan, Puerto Rico. Despite his youth he was hired as a trombonist for the San Juan Municipal Band under the direction of Manuel Tizol. He also played with a symphonic ensemble and with a popular group called Sombras de la Noche (Night Shadows). In 1917 he sold his first waltz, "Mi provisa" (the name came from the letters of the names of the band members' girlfriends: *Pro*videncia, *Vi*centa, and Ro*sa*), for twenty-five cents. That same year, with the American entry into World War I, Hernández enlisted in the U.S. Army and became a trombonist in the band of the 396th U.S. Infantry Regiment, the Puerto Rican unit. During his time with the armed forces Hernández toured Europe entertaining the troops. While in France he composed "Oui Madame," a song about a French girl he met there.

After the war Hernández went back to Puerto Rico and later moved to New York, where he began playing for the LUCKEY ROBERTS Band. At the same time, he organized the Orquesta Hispanoamericana, a popular Latin music band. In 1921 Robert Arthur Pratchett, distribution director for Paramount Pictures in Cuba, offered Hernández the position of orchestra director in the popular Teatro Fausto in Havana. Hernández resided in Cuba for several years and composed many of his famous songs there, among them "Cachita" and "Capullito de alelí" (Carnation bud), the latter won a top prize in the Juegos Florales, a renowned literary, artistic, and musical competition of Spanish origin. The song was recorded by the great Cuban group El Trío Matamoros and became internationally famous.

In 1925 Hernández moved back to New York and founded the group Trío Borinquen. That same year they signed a contract with Columbia Records and recorded over thirty songs. A few years later, at age thirty-eight, while living in Harlem, he composed "Lamento Borincano" (Borinquen lament), the work that would become one of his most prominent pieces. This song explores the feelings of a *jibarito* (country boy); the *jibarito* is joyful because he has a crop to sell in town, but the joy turns to sorrow when he discovers that no one will purchase his produce because everyone in town is terribly poor. The lyrics depict the horrible economic conditions of Puerto Rican farmers at the time of the Great Depression. In 1930 Hernández joined Pedro Ortiz Dávila (Davilita), Rafael Rodríguez, and Francisco López Cruz to form the Conjunto Victoria.

In 1932 Rafael was offered a radio spot in Mexico City, along with a three-year contract. He became a well-known radio personality and made friends with the most prominent artists in Mexico, among them the composer Agustín Lara and the actor Mario "Cantinflas" Moreno. Hernández appeared with Cantinflas in several movies during Mexico's golden age of film, among them *El gendarme desconocido* (The unknown cop) and *Aguila o sol* (Heads or tails).

During his time in Mexico, Hernández decided to enhance his musical knowledge by enrolling in Mexico's National Conservatory, receiving a degree in harmony, composition, and counterpoint. As part of his graduation requirements he composed "Danza Capricho no. 7," a classical piece. With Hernández conducting, the piece was played for the first time by the Mexico Symphony Orchestra. Among his most enduring songs, "Preciosa" (Precious) is considered by many to be Puerto Rico's second national anthem. "Campanitas de cristal" (Crystal bells) and "Perfume de gardenias" (Gardenias' perfume) were penned in Mexico. It was there that he fell in love with and married María Pérez in 1940. The couple had four children.

The Hernández family moved back to Puerto Rico in 1947. Later Hernández began playing in the Puerto Rico Symphony Orchestra, played his music live on a program broadcasted by WKAQ TV, and was musical adviser of WIPR, the government radio station.

As part of his interest in civic service he took part in organizing the Baseball Little Leagues of Puerto Rico. In 1956 he was elected honorary president of the Composers and Authors Association of Puerto Rico.

Hernandez was invited to the White House in 1961 to attend a ceremony honoring the Puerto Rican governor, Don Luis Muñoz Marín. One of Hernández's rumbas, "El Cumbanchero," was so famous that President John F. Kennedy greeted Hernández saying, "How are you, Mr. Cumbanchero?"

Back in Puerto Rico, the Interamerican University of Puerto Rico conferred upon Hernández the degree of Doctor Honoris Causa in humanities in 1965. He died that same year after a long battle with cancer; his remains are interred in the Santa María Magdalena Cemetery in Old San Juan.

In his lifetime Rafael Hernández created over 3,000 musical compositions in various genres and styles including children's songs and patriotic hymns; however, he is best remembered for his romantic *boleros*. His pieces continue to be recorded and interpreted by many musicians.

FURTHER READING

Santiago-Valiente, Wilfredo. "Remembering Rafael and Victoria Hernández," *El Boricua* (Apr., May, and June 2005).

M. MARGARITA NODARSE

Herndon, Alonzo Franklin (26 June 1858–21 July 1927), barber and businessman, was born in Social Circle, Georgia, the son of a white father (name unknown) and a slave mother, Sophenia Herndon. Born on a farm in Walton County, forty miles east of Atlanta, he was a slave for the first seven and a half years of his life and, in his own words, "was very near it for twenty years more." After emancipation, he worked as a laborer and peddler to help his family eke out a living in the hostile rural environment, where he was able to acquire only a few months of schooling. In 1878, with eleven dollars of savings, Herndon left his birthplace to seek opportunities elsewhere.

Settling in Atlanta in the early 1880s, he obtained employment as a journeyman barber and soon purchased his first barbershop. He began to build a clientele composed of the city's leading white lawyers, judges, politicians, and businessmen. By 1904 Herndon owned three establishments; his shop at 66 Peachtree Street, outfitted with crystal chandeliers and gold fixtures, was said to be the largest and best barbershop in the region. According to the *New York World*, Herndon and his all-black staff were "known from Richmond all the way to Mobile as the best barbers in the South." Herndon's success in barbering was spectacular, and, as his earnings grew, he invested in real estate in Atlanta and in Florida.

In 1905 Herndon entered the field of insurance, placing his growing resources behind a failing mutual assistance association set up initially by a local minister to benefit his congregation and other black Atlantans. Herndon and several other men reorganized the association and incorporated it as the Atlanta Mutual Insurance Association. With Herndon playing a pivotal role as president and chief stockholder, the company expanded its assets from five thousand dollars in 1905 to more than four hundred thousand dollars by 1922 and achieved a reputation for safety and reliability. The firm reorganized as the Atlanta Life Insurance Company in 1922, and that same year achieved legal reserve status, a position enjoyed by only four other black companies at that time. With the added status of having met the state of Georgia's requirements for capitalization, Herndon was able to increase the size and variety of policies offered by the company and by 1924 had expanded its operations into seven other states. More than any other individual, he set the Atlanta operation on the way to becoming one of the largest insurance enterprises among African Americans in the country.

Herndon's growing wealth and business position placed him among a group of progressive African Americans in Atlanta and elsewhere involved in economic, social, and civic endeavors to advance blacks. Although not widely heralded as a race leader, he was deeply interested in the economic and social welfare of African Americans. He was particularly influenced by the ideas of BOOKER T. WASHINGTON and others who espoused hard work, thriftiness, and business development as means of race progress. In 1900 he was among the founding delegates of the National Negro Business League formed to promote entrepreneurship among African Americans. In 1913, in an address at Tuskegee Institute, Herndon insisted on the necessity of cooperative business efforts among African Americans, extolling the possibilities of amassing capital and providing job opportunities for youth. He told the audience, "My aim has been for several years to get as many of our people together to cooperate in business and along all lines as possible."

Herndon also demonstrated his concern for progress among African Americans in areas other than business. He shared, on some level, many of the aims of black leaders such as W. E. B. DuBois for social and political advancement. He was among the twenty-nine African Americans from throughout the country who assembled in 1905 near Buffalo, New York, to organize the Niagara Movement, the forerunner of the NAACP. In Georgia he and other African American leaders signed a memorial to protest disfranchisement measures passed by the state legislature in 1907. Herndon made donations to a host of local institutions and charities devoted to uplifting and advancing the black community.

Herndon's influence as businessman and civic leader was distinctly felt in Atlanta. He rose from slavery to become the head of a growing black enterprise and overcame poverty and illiteracy. In addition to Atlanta Life, located on Atlanta's famed Auburn Avenue, which was described by *Fortune Magazine* (Sept. 1956) as "the richest Negro Street in the World," Herndon's investments ranged from the first black-owned cemetery and loan association to the first black-owned bank and drugstore. A visible reminder of his entrepreneurship is the three-story Herndon Building, which he built to help facilitate the settlement and growth of black businesses and professionals in the community.

Herndon married twice. His first marriage, in 1893, was to Adrienne Elizabeth McNeil, a professor at Atlanta University who died in 1910. This marriage produced Herndon's only child, Norris, who succeeded him as chief executive of the company and for forty years continued its solid growth as a respected enterprise. The second marriage, in 1912, was to Jessie Gillespie, a Chicago businesswoman. Both marriages had far-reaching impact on his life, bringing culture, refinement, and education into his household and enhancing his community standing and business position.

After Herndon's death in Atlanta, the *Atlanta Independent*, a local black-owned paper, praised him as a man "who was as great in the uses of his wealth as he was in accumulating it." Writing in *Crisis* magazine (Sept. 1927), DuBois described him as "an extraordinary man [who] illustrates at once the possibilities of American democracy and the deviltry of color prejudice." Also noting Herndon's status as the wealthiest black man in Atlanta, DuBois wrote, "This representative of Negro America lies dead today and buried in a separate Negro cemetery, which he helped found, but if ever an American 'burst his birth's invidious bar' that man was Alonzo Herndon."

FURTHER READING
The Herndon Family Papers, consisting of photographs, letters, business receipts, and other items, are in the Herndon Home, a house museum in Atlanta.

Henderson, Alexa Benson. *Atlanta Life Insurance Company: Guardian of Black Economic Dignity* (1990).

This entry is taken from the *American National Biography* and is published here with the permission of the American Council of Learned Societies.

ALEXA BENSON HENDERSON

Herndon, Angelo (6 May 1913–9 December 1997), Communist organizer and political prisoner, was born in the tiny southern Ohio town of Wyoming, the son of Paul Herndon, a coal miner. His mother, Harriet, was of a mixed-race background and worked as a domestic. According to an early version of Herndon's autobiography, his name was recorded in the family Bible as Eugene Angelo Braxton Herndon. During Herndon's youth, the family experienced poverty, which grew worse after his father died. Fundamentalist Christianity helped family members endure such hard times, and at the age of nine Herndon underwent a deep religious experience and joined a local church. Shortly after he turned thirteen, Herndon and an older brother left home for Kentucky, where they worked in a coal mine for a while before heading farther south to Alabama.

Over the next several years Herndon found employment at various construction and mining sites in the Birmingham area, though he also encountered pervasive racism and witnessed the clear economic exploitation of African American workers. Upset by these degrading conditions, he became frustrated with the reluctance of black Alabamians to fight back against their mistreatment. As the teenager matured and developed a political consciousness, he came to view the emotional religion of his youth as an inadequate philosophy for the harsh realities of daily life. During the summer of 1930 Herndon attended an integrated rally held in Birmingham by the Unemployed Council, a national organization dominated by members of the Communist Party, and he was excited by the group's willingness to challenge white supremacy and economic inequality. A subsequent arrest by the local police convinced him that he had discovered the right path for himself and other African Americans. Toward the end of the summer, at the age of seventeen, Herndon formally joined the Communist Party. The new secular religion of communism had replaced the fundamentalist Christianity of his youth.

The young convert eagerly plunged into a variety of Communist projects in Alabama, working tirelessly to organize miners and sharecroppers into unions and to develop a mass campaign around the nine wrongfully imprisoned SCOTTSBORO BOYS. His enthusiasm for the Communist cause did not go unnoticed by the authorities, however, and he was subjected to several additional arrests and beatings. Believing that such harassment lessened Herndon's effectiveness, the party reassigned him to Atlanta during the winter of 1931–1932 to revitalize the Unemployed Council there.

Soon after Herndon arrived in Atlanta, the city and county governments plunged into a deep financial crisis, endangering the area's limited relief program but also presenting the Communists with an excellent opportunity to attract members. As economic conditions steadily worsened during 1932, the Unemployed Council expanded its work among the jobless. In response to an announcement of further cuts in relief payments, Herndon successfully organized, on 30 June, an unprecedented protest by more than a thousand white and black workers in front of the Fulton County Courthouse. Unnerved by the demonstration, county commissioners immediately restored some of the previously eliminated funds. Meanwhile, the police department stepped up its surveillance of local radicals and eventually arrested Herndon on 11 July. Eleven days later a grand jury indicted him under an 1866 anti-insurrection law, which had revised an 1833 statute prohibiting slave revolts. Prosecutors specifically charged the young Communist with "attempting to incite insurrection against the state of Georgia," a capital offense. The severity of this charge clearly indicated that local officials viewed Herndon's interracial efforts as a dangerous threat to the existing social order.

In January 1933 Herndon received his day in court. He turned over the handling of his case to the International Labor Defense (ILD), which retained two local African American attorneys, BENJAMIN JEFFERSON DAVIS JR. and John Geer, to defend him. This bold but risky decision reflected Herndon's and the ILD's determination to confront white supremacy directly and unequivocally. During the trial, prosecutors tried to create an atmosphere of hysteria, warning that communism directly threatened Georgia's political and economic stability. The prosecution specifically accused Herndon of circulating inflammatory literature and attempting to establish a radical movement whose ultimate aim was to overthrow the established government. Defense attorneys countered that there was no proof that the nineteen-year-old activist had taken any specific steps to organize an actual revolt and that the prosecution was based on fear of communism and interracial cooperation. Herndon willingly took the stand to justify his actions. He told the jury that, in reality, he was being tried because he had dared to organize black and white workers together. The young defendant further argued that capitalism deliberately encouraged racism "in order to keep the Negro and white divided" (quoted in Martin [1976], 52). Finally, Herndon warned that although the state had the power to send him to prison, there would be more "Angelo Herndons to come in the future." His courageous but inexpedient testimony failed to impress the all-white, twelve-man jury, which found Herndon guilty and sentenced him to eighteen to twenty years in prison.

While Davis and Geer prepared an appeal to the state supreme court, the ILD launched a national mass campaign on behalf of Herndon, arguing that he was a political prisoner who had been unjustly convicted because of his radical beliefs. The ILD's persistence eventually built the case into a national cause célèbre. In May 1934 the state supreme court rejected the appeal. The ILD then recruited several specialists in constitutional law to argue the case before the U.S. Supreme Court. Meanwhile, Herndon remained behind bars in Atlanta until August 1934, when the ILD finally gained his release on bail.

Once he was free, Herndon embarked on several national speaking tours, increasing public awareness of his case. The ILD helped him compose a short autobiographical booklet describing his conversion to communism and his trial, which the organization published under the title *You Cannot Kill the Working Class*. In May 1935 the Supreme Court turned down his appeal on technical grounds and sent the case back to the state courts. After Herndon surrendered to Georgia authorities, his lawyers initiated another round of legal maneuvers. In December a superior court judge unexpectedly ruled in Herndon's favor, temporarily striking down the insurrection law, but the state supreme court restored the conviction in June 1936.

While his attorneys prepared for another full hearing before the U.S. Supreme Court, Herndon remained free on a second bond and continued his public appearances in the North. With the assistance of a ghostwriter, he drafted a full-length autobiography, *Let Me Live*, which Random House released in early 1937. In April of that year Herndon finally received vindication. By a 5 to 4 vote, the U.S. Supreme Court declared the insurrection law, "as construed and applied," to be unconstitutional and overturned his conviction. In concluding that the Georgia statute was "an unwarranted invasion of the right of freedom of speech," the Court moved closer toward acceptance of the so-called clear and present danger test for laws restricting First Amendment rights, an important constitutional shift.

His permanent freedom finally assured, Herndon returned to New York City, where he initially took a public role in many Communist activities and occasionally wrote articles for the *Daily Worker*. In 1938 he married Joyce M. Chellis, a native of Alabama. In the early 1940s he assisted RALPH ELLISON in founding and editing the short-lived *Negro Quarterly: A Review of Negro Life and Culture*. On two occasions he successfully thwarted efforts by New York City's selective service director to revoke his draft deferment. Like many other Communists, Herndon gradually became dissatisfied with the party during the war, and by the mid-1940s he had quietly left its ranks. He subsequently moved to Chicago and took a job as a salesman, discussing his past with only his closest friends. In 1967 he tentatively agreed to speak with a historian researching his trial but then changed his mind. Two years later the *New York Times* and Arno Press published a reprint of *Let Me Live*, as part of a series on African American history and culture. Despite revived interest in his earlier political activism, Herndon refused to make any public appearances, declined requests for interviews, and continued to live a very private life.

FURTHER READING

Herndon, Angelo. *Let Me Live* (1937).

Herndon, Angelo. *You Cannot Kill the Working Class* (1934).

Martin, Charles H. *The Angelo Herndon Case and Southern Justice* (1976).

Martin, Charles H. "The Angelo Herndon Case and Southern Justice," in *American Political Trials*, ed. Michal R. Belknap (1994).

Thomas, Kendall. "'Rouge et Noir' Reread: A Popular Constitutional History of the Angelo Herndon Case," in *Critical Race Theory*, eds. Kimberle Crenshaw et al. (1995).

CHARLES H. MARTIN

Herndon, Norris B. (15 July 1897–7 June 1977), insurance executive, was born Norris Bumstead Herndon in Atlanta, Georgia, the only child of the actress and educator Elizabeth Adrienne Stephens McNeil and the entrepreneur and philanthropist ALONZO FRANKLIN HERNDON. Herndon's father, born a slave in nearby Walton County, Georgia, in 1858, was one of the most successful and respected black businessmen in the United States. In the 1880s Alonzo opened the Crystal Palace, an upscale barbershop on Peachtree Street that was reputed to be one of the largest and most elegant barbershops in the world. In 1905 Alonzo organized the Atlanta Mutual Insurance Association, which became one of the richest and most respected black-owned insurance companies in the United States. In 1922 the company changed its name to the Atlanta Life Insurance Company.

Alonzo hoped his son would take the reins of his business empire, but Herndon, who was close to his mother, instead shared her passion for the theater. However, always anxious to please his father, Herndon majored in Business at Atlanta University and then received a master's in Business Administration from Harvard University in 1921. His mother died from an unexpected illness in 1910 and Norris was raised by his maternal grandmother. Though his business dealings kept him busy, Alonzo tried to stay close to his only child through letters and by paying close attention to his upbringing. As a young man, Herndon worked hard to please his father and kept the Palace's financial books during his father's frequent absences, but his father often criticized his son's lack of business ambition and attention to detail. In 1921 Alonzo appointed his son vice president of the insurance company. It may have been difficult for Herndon to perform in the shadow of his famous father, but Herndon provided strong and able leadership for the Atlanta Life Insurance Company after his father's death in 1927.

Herndon represented a new generation of leadership in the black insurance field. Early black insurance companies evolved largely through an interdependent relationship with other black cultural institutions and prevailing social conditions. For example, black insurance companies trace their lineage to eighteenth-century mutual aid societies but owe their initial success to Jim Crow, the systematic institutionalization and legalization of racism and supremacist ideology. In the early 1880s the Grand United Order of True Reformers took the significant step from fraternity to formal entrepreneurship by starting the first incorporated black bank and offshoot businesses, including an insurance company, department store, undertaking business, hotel, and newspaper under the cofounder WILLIAM WASHINGTON BROWNE. During the same period, white insurance companies cut benefits, raised premiums, or refused to cover blacks at all. Black insurance companies enjoyed unprecedented, but not exclusive, access to the black business market. Also, because of Jim Crow, secret and mutual aid societies were one of the few places for blacks to gain business training and experience.

Herndon grew Atlanta Life largely through acquisitions of failing or smaller black- and white-owned insurance companies. He earned a reputation as a conservative, fiscally savvy executive. The company experienced its greatest growth under his leadership. For example, Herndon more than quadrupled the company's assets to $85 million. He continued race-based appeals but assured the company's future through business development and organization strategies that mirrored those of large, white-owned corporations. In the 1950s he took on an activist role by hiring black teachers fired for membership in the NAACP, posted bail for students jailed for participation in sit-ins or protests, and opened the company's doors for civil rights groups' meetings. When he retired in 1973, the company had nearly $350 million worth of policies in force. Herndon retired in 1973. He never married.

Herndon continued his family's philanthropy, giving millions to civil rights organizations, black colleges, and other black community organizations. In 1950 Herndon established the Alonzo F. and Norris B. Herndon Foundation, Inc., to facilitate his philanthropic giving and to secure his family's legacy. The nonprofit corporation supports religious, charitable, and educational causes, and it continues the century-old tradition of the Herndon family's philanthropic activities. Since 1983 the foundation primarily maintains the Herndon mansion as a public museum. The Herndon Home and Museum were registered as a National Historic Landmark in February 2000. Herndon died of heart disease in Atlanta.

FURTHER READING

Henderson, Alexa B. *Atlanta Life Insurance Company: Guardian of Black Economic Dignity* (1990).
Merritt, Carole. *The Herndons: An Atlanta Family* (2002).

SHENNETTE GARRETT

Heron, Giles (9 Apr. 1922–27 Nov. 2008), athlete, photographer, and poet, was born Gilbert Heron in Kingstown, Jamaica. Though he was a talented photographer, particularly of sporting events, and a notable poet, publishing a collection titled *I Shall Wish Just for You* as late as 1992, Heron's fame derives from neither. He remains best known as a pioneering nonwhite sportsman in the United Kingdom in the 1950s and as father to the eclectic, prolific, and hugely influential jazz musician and wordsmith GIL SCOTT-HERON.

Heron came to attention as an association football, or "soccer," player for the Detroit Corinthians, although he had previously turned out for the Canadian Air Force, Detroit Wolverines, and Chicago Sting. Standing just below five feet ten inches and weighing just under 178 pounds, Heron had the speed and agility that gave him the perfect characteristics for football's target man and goal scorer, the center forward. In the summer of 1951 one of Britain's largest and most successful football clubs, Glasgow Celtic, undertook a tour of North America. In part it was an opportunity for Celtic to raise its profile in the United States and to brandish the Scottish Football Association Cup that it had won earlier that season, but it was also a useful scouting mission.

Not coincidentally, it was while they were on that tour that a scout alerted the Celtic manager Jimmy McGrory to Heron's talents, and Heron was invited to trials in Glasgow that August. He proved sufficiently skilled and was offered a contract at the club with immediate effect. When he scored in his debut against Morton in the Scottish League Cup with a sixteen-yard drive and had another goal disallowed, Heron received favorable press reports, including one from the *New York Times*, a paper not normally noted for its soccer reporting. In Glasgow his exploits in what turned out to be a 2 to 1 victory over Morton earned Heron instant popularity with the Celtic faithful, as well as the sobriquets "Black Flash" and "Black Arrow" on account of his fleet-footedness and the directness with which he attacked his opponents' goal.

In 1952 Heron's form earned him a place on Jamaica's national team. He was selected in his favored position of center forward for a match against the traditional powerhouse of Caribbean football, Trinidad. Heron's international career coincided with an upsurge of political overtones in Caribbean sport in general, and in football and cricket in particular. In line with other nonwhite nations across the globe, the Caribbean nations were becoming increasingly disenchanted with their colonial status, and the sports field provided a vivid arena for expressing nascent nationalism. The secretary of Trinidad's football association was Eric James, brother of the radical thinker and writer C. L. R. JAMES, and when Trinidad's team toured Great Britain in 1953 it was an occasion for reinforcing those nationalist claims.

Heron's international career marked the end of his days as a Celtic player, although not for any political reasons. In May 1952, having recently returned from the Caribbean, he was released from his Celtic contract. He had played in five games in Celtic's distinctive green and white hoops, four of them in the Scottish FA Cup and one in the league, and had scored two goals. The brevity of that career belies its broader significance, for Heron was the first Caribbean footballer to play in Scotland; popular folklore often credits him with being the first to play professionally anywhere in Britain, but he was beaten to that distinction by his fellow Jamaican, Lloyd Lindbergh "Lindy" Delapenha, who played for Arsenal as an amateur immediately after World War II before going on to sign professionally with Portsmouth and then Middlesboro.

Both Heron and Delapenha were themselves preceded by players from other nonwhite countries outside the Caribbean, notably Arthur Wharton, an outstanding goalkeeper who played his first game in the 1883–1884 season and who was born in the Gold Coast (later Ghana); Tottenham Hotspur's Walter Tull, who was the son of immigrants from Barbados; and Stoke City's Hong Y Soo, who was born in China. Indeed, Heron was preceded at Celtic in the 1930s by the Calcutta-born Salim Bachi Khan, whose fierce shot was driven by bandaged rather than booted feet but who never graduated beyond the Parkhead reserve team.

Almost inevitably, given the rarity of nonwhite players in the British game, Heron's career at Celtic provoked a racist reaction in certain quarters. There were conflicting accounts of his ability to control the ball, which was fundamental for a center forward. Some of those accounts appear to have been motivated by a desire to discredit a nonwhite player, but the game in Scotland was also notoriously physical in the postwar years, which did not lend itself to the Black Flash's fluid and dynamic style of play. Many commentators on the Scottish game, which was infamous for its pockets of sectarianism, have since posited the belief that Celtic players in general were unfairly treated by referees in the postwar era, both because Celtic was a Catholic team and because its players were rarely—if ever—cast as underdogs, at least in terms of Scottish domestic football.

Certainly, Heron himself believed that he was harshly treated by match officials. Even in his short career, for example, he was sent off in a game against Stirling Albion reserves and was banned from playing for a week as a consequence. As the historian Phil Vasili accurately surmised, however, Heron's short stay at Celtic in all probability had less to do with racism than it had to do with the quality of the other members of the squad at McGrory's disposal. The Black Flash was soon replaced on the Celtic team by the newly arrived Jock Stein, a man whose contribution to Celtic as both player and manager has passed into footballing legend.

Once released from his contract at Celtic, Heron attempted to continue his playing career but could not find a club of similar stature that was willing to sign him. So instead he plied his trade with two clubs that could not hope to scale the heights that he had experienced at Celtic's Parkhead ground: first at Third Lanark in Scotland and then south of the border with England's Kidderminster Harriers. With a sense of anticlimax Heron returned stateside to play with the Detroit Corinthians. In 1956, despite his previous clashes with match officials, Heron completed his training and qualified as a referee.

Just as Arthur Wharton had excelled at other sports—notably cricket, which he played professionally, and cycling, at which he broke many records—Heron's sporting achievements were not confined to soccer. Before he embarked on his career in Britain his muscular frame and upper-body strength saw him through to the semifinals of the U.S. Golden Gloves competition and confirmed his potential as a boxer, and he also excelled at the 440-yard and then 400-meter run.

After the end of his professional sporting career Heron continued to write poetry. In 1949 his son Gil Scott-Heron was born. The memory of the Black Arrow's feats in the British football leagues has been granted extra life by the antics of much of the audience for Gil's U.K. tours. In deference to his father's trailblazing past, many people attend Gil's concerts wearing the distinctive green-and-white hooped shirts of Celtic. Famously, when asked about his own football allegiances in light of his father's achievements, Scott-Heron, ever the mischievous radical, claimed support for Celtic's archrivals, Glasgow Rangers.

Heron died in Detroit at the age of 82.

FURTHER READING

Vasili, Phil. *Colouring over the White Line: The History of Black Footballers in Britain* (2000).

Woolnough, Brian. *Black Magic: England's Black Footballers* (1983).

Obituary: *The Guardian,* 19 Dec. 2008.

GEORGE LEWIS

Herriman, George Joseph (22 Aug. 1880–25 Apr. 1944), cartoonist, was born in New Orleans, Louisiana, the son of George Herriman Jr., a tailor, and Clara Morel. There is uncertainty about Herriman's ethnic background. His birth certificate identified him as "Colored," his parents were listed in the 1880 New Orleans federal census as "Mulatto," but his death certificate noted that he was "Caucasian." During his lifetime, friends often thought he was Greek or French because of his Adonis-like appearance, and he has been called a "Creole." The family moved to Los Angeles when Herriman was a child, and his father opened a barbershop and then a bakery.

Herriman attended St. Vincent's College, a Roman Catholic secondary school for boys. When he finished school in 1897 he followed his artistic bent and began to contribute illustrations to the *Los Angeles Herald.* After the turn of the century he moved to New York City and began to contribute cartoons to *Judge, Life,* and other humorous periodicals and comic strips to various newspaper syndicates, including several sequential series such as *Musical Mose, Professor Otto and His Auto, Acrobatic Archie,* and *Two Jolly Jackies* for the Pulitzer Syndicate and *Major Ozone's Fresh Air Crusade, Alexander the Cat, Bud Smith,* and *Rosy Posy* for the World Color Printing Company. In 1902 he returned briefly to Los Angeles to marry Mabel Lillian Bridge, his childhood sweetheart; they had two children. The great variety and skill of Herriman's numerous efforts soon attracted the attention of William Randolph Hearst, who hired him for several of his papers, including the *Los Angeles Examiner.* Herriman lived in Los Angeles from 1905 until 1910, when Hearst brought him back to New York City to draw for the *New York Evening Journal.* Here Herriman created his first widely successful feature, which would become known as *The Family Upstairs,* a domestic comic strip about the Dingbat family and their noisy neighbors in the apartment above. On 26 July 1910 this study in urban paranoia was interrupted by the appearance of the family cat, which is hit in the head by a rock thrown by a mouse. Therein lay the genesis for Herriman's most successful strip, *Krazy Kat*, which began as an independent feature on 2 July 1911.

In the world of *Krazy Kat*, Ignatz the Mouse is the object of Krazy Kat's affection, but instead of returning this love, Ignatz is disposed to hit the cat in the head with a brick. The cat naively believes that these clouts are meant as tokens of love. Meanwhile, the benevolent presence of Offissa Pup, himself in love with Krazy, operates to thwart Ignatz and keep the mouse behind jailhouse bars as much as possible. This situation of fully unrequited and androgynous love (Krazy's sex changes from time to time) is acted out against a surrealistic shifting background in the Arizona desert, while the characters speak a poetic dialogue and richly mixed dialect unique in literature outside the fiction of James Joyce or the poetry of e. e. cummings. Both cummings and T. S. Eliot wrote in praise of *Krazy Kat*, which has remained the most admired comic strip in newspaper history. No other strip has matched its genius in humorous whimsy, abstract style, and metaphoric power.

Several series of animated cartoons have been based on *Krazy Kat*, two stage ballets have been inspired by it, Jay Cantor has used the characters in a novel under the same title, and any number of modern artists have created paintings and sculptures in homage to Herriman. While Herriman produced *Krazy Kat* on a daily basis, he also created other comic strips, most notably *Baron Bean*, *Stumble Inn*, *Us Husbands*, and *Embarrassing Moments* (or *Bernie Burns*). He illustrated the anthologies of Don Marquis's columns about the poetic cockroach Archy and the feline vamp Mehitabel, giving an indelible visual stamp to the characters almost as endearing as Marquis's comic verse.

In 1922 Herriman settled permanently in Hollywood. He has been described as a handsome, slender, short man with twinkling gray eyes and curly black hair, given to wearing a Stetson hat. He once wrote of his creation, "Be not harsh with 'Krazy.' He is but a shadow himself, caught in the web of this mortal skein." A shy and private man, and more given to visual than verbal communication, he seldom commented on his art. He died in Los Angeles.

At the time of his death Herriman had penciled a week's worth of *Krazy Kat* comic strips, which were to remain uninked on his drawing board. Given the limited circulation of the feature by then, Hearst permanently retired the strip rather than allow other artists to continue it. Legend has it that

Krazy Kat was a personal favorite of Hearst's, and no one could have imitated the Herriman style and whimsy, anyway. Like Pablo Picasso in painting, Herriman changed the visual style of his art form and influenced generations of cartoonists to come; like James Joyce in fiction, he stretched the traditional limitations of language; and like Samuel Beckett in drama, he captured the absurdities of efforts to communicate on the larger stage of life.

FURTHER READING
Inge, M. Thomas. *Comics as Culture* (1990).
McDonnell, Patrick, Karen O'Connell, and Georgia Riley de Havenon. *Krazy Kat: The Comic Art of George Herriman* (1986).
Marschall, Richard. *America's Great Comic-Strip Artists* (1989).
O'Sullivan, Judith. *The Great American Comic Strip* (1990).
This entry is taken from the *American National Biography* and is published here with the permission of the American Council of Learned Societies.

M. THOMAS INGE

Herron, Carolivia (22 July 1947–), writer and educator, was born in Washington, D.C., to Oscar Smith Herron and Georgia Carol Johnson Herron. She was an enthusiastic reader as a child and her parents encouraged her to pursue an education in literature. After graduating from Coolidge High School, she earned her bachelor's degree in English at Eastern Baptist College in 1969, a master's degree in English from Villanova University in 1973, and a master's degree in Creative Writing and a doctorate in Comparative Literature and literary Theory from the University of Pennsylvania in 1985.

Herron's great interest in literature led to her position as an assistant professor of Afro-American studies and comparative literature at Harvard University from 1986 to 1990 and as founder of the multimedia company Epicenter Literary Software in 1988. She then taught English literature at Mount Holyoke College for the next two years, while writing her first novel, *Thereafter Johnnie* (1991). This semiautobiographical text focuses on the successful African American middle-class Snowdon family in Washington, D.C., and their problems when confronted with racial tension, miscegenation, and incest. While writing the book, Herron examined the sexual abuse she suffered during her childhood. She also assessed her fondness of African American folk legends, Greek epics, and biblical verses. Upon its release, *Thereafter Johnnie* received great praise for being a capturing narrative. Herron was also heralded as one of the great contemporary female African American writers and was compared to TONI MORRISON and ALICE WALKER.

During 1991 Herron also edited the *Selected Works of Angelina Weld Grimké* and explored many teaching opportunities. For the next several years, she was a visiting scholar at Brandeis University; Hebrew College of Brookline, Massachusetts; and Marien N'Guabi University in Brazzaville, Republic of the Congo. In 1996 she became a faculty member at California State University at Chico and returned to writing. Her children's book *Nappy Hair* was published in 1997. The narrative focuses on the unruly hair of a young African American girl named Brenda and is written in a call-and-response format. Herron was again lauded for her flowing narrative style, realistic vision, and celebration of African American heritage.

Some people though blamed the book for using "nappy" as a pejorative word and thought the book should present African American hair in a more positive manner. The book also made headlines when the public school teacher Ruth Sherman introduced the book to her third-grade students at P.S. 75 in Brooklyn, New York, in 1998. Many parents complained that "nappy hair" was racially offensive and called for the book to be removed from the classroom. Herron commented that the book celebrates natural Afro hair and shows resistance to the dominant standards of beauty. In this sense, she finds that the book embraces the significant messages of "black is beautiful" and "black pride." Many of the critics agreed with Herron, and she received the Marion Vannett Ridgway Award, Paterson Prize for Books for Young People, and Reading Magic Award for *Nappy Hair*.

Herron's next publication was the picture book *Always an Olivia: A Remarkable Family History* (2007), in which a young child listens to her great-grandmother Olivia describe their family's African and Jewish heritage and migration from Spain and Portugal. The story bears many similarities to Herron's life. Herron's great-grandmother told her that her own great-grandmother had been Jewish. Herron also developed a keen interest in the Jewish religion and converted from her Baptist upbringing to Judaism in 1995. Herron describes her long journey to Judaism and becoming a founding member of Jews of African Descent in her unpublished memoir *Peacesong*.

In 2000 Herron left California State University, Chico, to work full-time at the Epicenter Literary Software in Washington, D.C. She stressed the company's commitment to encourage intercultural connections by creating programs that promote cultural diversity and oral and scribal traditions. For instance, one program sets Greek epics to rap music. Another program is called "The Storytelling Lab" and highlights the African American literary experience with family stories. The company's most significant achievement has been PAUSE (Potomac Anacostia Ultimate Story Exchange), a tutoring and writing program for elementary students in public schools in the Washington, D.C., area.

In addition to writing and doing multimedia projects, Herron also guest lectures and makes public appearances. Her topics are usually about African American literature, comparative epic tradition (Europe, Africa, and the Americas), and Jewish Africana, but she has also incorporated her enthusiasm of *Star Trek* into her teaching by offering the short course Race in *Star Trek* and the Epic Other at several colleges.

FURTHER READINGS

Herron, Olivia. "Olivia Herron." In *Notable Black American Women* (2002).

Keizer, Arlene R. *Black Subjects: Identity Formation in the Contemporary Narrative of Slavery* (2004).

Scapp, Ron. *Teaching Values: Critical Perspectives on Education, Politics, and Culture* (2002).

DORSIA SMITH SILVA

Heth, Joice (c. 1756?–19 Feb. 1836), slave woman, was exploited by P. T. Barnum to launch his career as a showman. Little is known about Heth's early life, and most of what is known of her later years is suspect. Perhaps no other woman in American history, white or black, experienced the brand of public exposure inflicted upon Heth. As an aged and crippled slave woman, she was exhibited for profit by slaveholders who disregarded her suffering. Barnum, the noted showman and huckster, holds the distinction of being the last one of those individuals before her death on 19 February 1836. In a feature story years after Barnum's demise, a 15 July 1923 *Los Angeles Times* headline characterized Heth as the "The Freak that Made Barnum Famous." The reporter, Morris Robert Werner, stated that she had "Thick, bushy, average gray hair [that] added to her value as a monstrosity" (X4). Benjamin Reiss's *The Showman and the Slave* (2001) poignantly records the enduring association of Heth and Barnum, forever linking the two in a twisted but remarkably revealing historical discourse.

Heth first came to Barnum's attention through a 15 July 1835 *Pennsylvania Inquirer* advertisement shown to him by Coley Bartram, in which she was billed as a "negress" slave of Augustus Washington (George Washington's father), a 116-year Baptist Church worshiper, and a 100-year resident of Paris, Kentucky—a "must see" side show attraction. Her status as a human relic was supposedly documented by a 5 February 1727 bill of sale for a 54-year-old slave woman, signed by George Washington's father. It is evident that the succession of dates and numbers in the bill of sale were contrived as key elements in the subterfuge. In order for Heth to have been 161 years of age in 1835, she would have been born in 1674 and 54 years of age in 1728, which is what the document stipulated.

The contract that transferred an African woman by the name of Joice Heth to P. T. Barnum was confusing, but legal. On 10th June 1835 John D. Bowling and R. W. Lindsay of Jefferson County, Kentucky, contracted to showcase Joice Heth across the United States for a period of twelve months. Subsequently, Bowling transferred all his rights to Coley Bartram, who later transferred his rights to Lindsay. On 6 August 1835, Lindsay executed a bill of sale transferring the "rights, title interest and claim for the African woman Joice Heth aged 161" to P. T. Barnum and William P. Saunders for the sole purpose of exhibition for the unexpired time of the twelve-month agreement dated 10 June 1835. For unknown reasons Saunders later pulled out of the agreement. Barnum, with a quick eye for what would amuse and entertain most Americans, seized the opportunity to enrich himself at the expense of an aged slave. Barnum later embraced the tricks of an experienced and unethical showman, waging an advertising campaign that made Heth one of the most publicly subjugated females of the nineteenth century. Filled with pride and excitement, Barnum wrote in his 1873 revised autobiography, *Struggles and Triumphs*, "I had at last found my true vocation. Indeed soon after I began to exhibit Joice Hethe, I had entrusted her to an agent and had entered upon my second step in show line" (76). All of the posters, flyers, news clippings, as well as a well-crafted, bogus biography circulated across the Northeast excited interest in the nation's oldest black woman who supposedly played a role in the life of George Washington.

Barnum may well have subjected Heth to cruel treatment. Because Heth was advertised as weighing only forty-six pounds, were her teeth removed to render her emaciated and authenticate the claim? Complicating the image Barnum and his associates created of Heth, Levi Lyman, Barnum's assistant, wrote and widely distributed a tract, *The Life of Joice Heth, the Nurse of General George Washington (the Father of Our Country,) Now Living at the Astonishing Age of 161 Years, and Weights Only 46 Pounds* (1835), which depicted her as the pipe-smoking wife of Peter and industrious mother of fifteen children. Later he admitted that for profit Barnum had concocted the woman's background as well as the time spent with George Washington's family. Ultimately, Barnum's weekly gross receipts climbed to over twelve hundred dollars.

In his first autobiography Barnum says that he was "favorably struck with the appearance of the old woman" (1855, 148). In his second autobiography he stated that when Joice Heth arrived in New York, she "was apparently in good health and spirits"(1873, 74). In both publications he completely overlooked the fact that her frame was bent with paralysis, her arms and fingers were deformed, she was blind, she suffered from a severely damaged eye socket, and she possessed no teeth. Even in death, Joice Heth could not escape the exploitive grip that Barnum had over her life. Reiss states that "Heth [was]one of the first true American media celebrities, … ultimately—as a corpse and then as a memory" (2001). He goes on to say that "she became an advertisement for Barnum and this new mass media even more than they advertised her" (2001). Further, even in death Barnum robbed Joice Heth of dignity. In a profit-driven scheme supposedly to verify her age, hundreds of spectators paid fifty cents to Barnum to witness the dissection of her body by Dr. David L. Rogers in a New York City saloon.

FURTHER READING

Barnum, P. T. *The Life of Barnum, the World-Renowned Showman: To Which Is Added, The Art of Money Getting; Or, Golden Rules for Making Money* (n.d.).

Barnum, P. T. *The Life of P. T. Barnum, Written by Himself* (1855).

Barnum P. T. *Struggles and Triumphs* (1873).

Life of Joice Heth, the Nurse of Gen. George Washington, Now Living at the Astonishing Age of 161 Years, and Weighs Only 46 Pounds (1835).

Reiss, Benjamin. "P.T. Barnum, Joice Heth, and Antebellum Spectacles of Race." *American Quarterly* 51.1 (1999).

Reiss, Benjamin. *The Showman and the Slave: Race, Death, and Memory in Barnum's America* (2001).

Werner, M. R. "The Freak That Made Barnum Famous," *Los Angeles Times*, 15 July 1923.

GLORIA GRANT ROBERSON

Heuston, Francis (1764–1 June 1858), Revolutionary War veteran, sailor and farmer, was born in 1764 in Nantucket, Massachusetts. That year Nantucket's census counted the number of blacks for the first time. Heuston was one of only fifty African Americans on the island. Many of the blacks counted were slaves, but there was also a small free black community on Nantucket. It is unclear if Heuston was born free or enslaved.

The location and year of Heuston's birth were reported to a local newspaper by his daughter, Lydia Bowe, upon his death. She also reported that he served on an American fighting ship during the Revolutionary War when he was a boy and that he continued to work as a mariner for the next two decades.

Other information regarding the remainder of Heuston's long life is supported by many documents. For instance, free black mariners carried American Seaman Protection Documents certifying their identity. When Heuston docked at Wiscasset, Maine, in about 1800, he carried seaman's papers with him.

He settled in Brunswick on the Maine coast, buying a farm on the shores of Merrymeeting Bay. He married Mehitable (Griffin) Swain (1781–1851), widow of William M. Swain (?–1806). Mehitable brought four children to the marriage. Between 1808 and 1825, the Heustons had eight children of their own.

While not the first African American to settle on Merrymeeting Bay in Brunswick or adjacent Bath, Heuston was the black community's patriarch. He took his civic duties seriously, voting in every election. He was respected by his neighbors, black and white, as a successful farmer and a man of honor and humor.

The respect of Heuston's white neighbors did not extend to the schoolroom, however. In 1826 white residents petitioned the town to "set off the colored people of School District 14, into a district by themselves." Instead, the town voted to segregate the school by sending white students in the summer and winter, and the black students in spring and fall. Despite this arrangement, Brunswick's superintendent of schools would later note the African American students, including Heuston's children, continued to thrive in their studies.

Heuston helped the black community in material ways. His name is found on several deeds as the seller of nearby farmland to blacks in both Brunswick and Bath, showing he eased the way for new arrivals by acting as an intermediary in the real estate transactions.

As was common in rural areas in the nineteenth century, Heuston's family burying ground was located on his farm. Although the farm itself is no longer owned by his descendants, the small cemetery still stands as a testament to the African American community on Merrymeeting Bay. Its gravestones remind us of Heuston's family connections and the care he took of his neighbors. When his friend Samuel Freeman died and the Freeman family could not afford burial arrangements, rather than see the family embarrassed by applying to the town for aid, he paid fees already incurred by the town and buried Freeman in Heuston Burying Ground.

Gravestones show us the names of some of Heuston's children, grandchildren, and great grandchildren. Granddaughter Ann Caroline Lewis's (1841–1851) epitaph reveals one of Heuston's sons-in-law was notable nineteenth-century black Mainer, Robert Benjamin Lewis (1798–1858), sailor, author, and inventor. At least two of Heuston's grandsons, Francis (1844–1864) and Marcellus Gardiner (1847–1883), mirrored their grandfather's service to their country when they participated in the Civil War. Both enlisted in Company C, 43rd United States Colored Infantry in 1863. Francis died in Philadelphia, Pennsylvania, but Marcellus was mustered out after two years of service. He is interred in the family cemetery. Heuston's family lived nearby until the mid-twentieth century, when great-grandson Austin Hopkins (1880–1954) died and was buried in the family cemetery next to his mother, Helen (1847–1926).

Maine's agricultural census taken 12 September 1850 lists Heuston's holdings as thirty acres of improved agricultural land, ten unimproved, the entire forty acre farm having a cash value of $800. Other farms in Brunswick at the time ranged from thirty acres valued at $450 to two hundred twenty acres valued at $7000. Heuston's farm implements and machinery were valued at $30. He owned one horse, one milk cow, two working oxen and owned two other cattle. He also had one swine. His livestock was valued at $170. His crops included six bushels of rye and two and a half bushels of Indian corn.

It was not unusual for nineteenth-century farmers to have a second trade, be it bricklayer, shoemaker, or butcher. Heuston supplemented the family income by occasionally working on a coasting ship, delivering supplies along the Maine shores. He was well-known in the cargo trade for his superior physical strength.

In 1850 Heuston and his neighbors conducted the rescue of slave Clara Battease (1821–1913). Many Maine shipping and merchant families had connections to Southern families. Maine ships did, after all, transport southern cotton north or slaves west from Africa. Clara was brought north to care for the Tupper children when the Tupper family came to Bath to visit relatives. The Bath census taken in July and August shows Clara "Burtson," age twenty-four, and five Tupper children, in the home of D. Helen White. The night before the Tupper family was to return to Georgia, Clara escaped the house to a waiting hack and was transported into hiding in an East Brunswick home. It is interesting to note that one of the nearby farmers who purchased land through Heuston was John MacDonald, who also operated a hack.

The Brunswick census taken in September shows Clara has become twenty-eight-year-old "Mary Scott," born in Georgia, residing in the home of Francis and Mehitable Heuston. Mary gave birth to a daughter, Emma, on 28 October 1850. After Mehitable's death, Heuston wed Mary. The couple had four children together, one of whom, Francis Eben (1856–1898), was killed when the steamship S. S. *Portland* sank off Cape Cod, Massachusetts.

Heuston actively farmed up to the day of his death at age ninety-four. That day, when planting his crops, he returned to the house for more seed and collapsed at the entryway. He was, appropriately, buried in the family burying ground on his farm.

FURTHER READING
Bolster, W. Jeffrey. *Black Jacks: African American Seamen in the Age of Sail* (1997).
Price, H. H., and Gerald E. Talbot. *Maine's Visible Black History: The First Chronicle of Its People* (2006).

BARBARA A. DESMARAIS

Hewlett, James (fl. 1821–1839), actor and singer, is a person about whom little early information is known. He told an interviewer in 1825 that he had been born in Rockaway, Long Island, New York, but JAMES MCCUNE SMITH who had known the Hewlett boy suggested that he might have been born in the West Indies. The 1830 census indicated that he was older than thirty-six, and the 1825 interviewer states that he had been a servant to a well-known actor

who died in 1812. This all suggests that he was born in the early- or mid-1790s. It also is not known whether he was born slave or free. A number of his ancestors were Euro-Americans, however, as his light skin tone was frequently remarked upon.

As a young man Hewlett worked on boats as a steward, acting as servant to the officers and passengers, probably out of New York City. He also acquired considerable skill as a tailor, which provided him with his day job during his acting career. It seems that Hewlett was an adult when he began acting in 1821. His first appearance on the public record is an uncredited one. In the summer of 1821, Mordecai Noah, the editor of a New York City newspaper called the *National Advocate*, sought to amuse his readers with an account of a visit to a backyard garden cabaret, which was run by a West Indian named William A. Brown for the benefit of black New Yorkers who were not admitted to any of the other such gardens in the city. Noah quoted at some length the chatter among the patrons, one of whom boasted of a talent for singing very like what Hewlett would later show.

This garden was replaced early in September of that year by a theater that performed in a room of Brown's house. Noah attended its first performance, a staging of Shakespeare's *Richard III*. Noah described the actor playing Richard as small, dark-skinned and a waiter: not Hewlett but apparently a man named Charles Taft, also known as Charles Beers. Hewlett took over the role of Richard for the second performance, a week later, and was the star of the company until March 1823, taking the leading male roles as well as singing and sometimes dancing.

In its first season this company changed its performing venue three times, but nonetheless it was successful enough that Brown had a playhouse built for it on Mercer Street in 1822. It was at first known as the African Theatre, later as the African Company, and then as the American Theatre. Adverse circumstances undercut its success, however, and by March 1823 Hewlett had left the company to work as a traveling performer. He briefly returned in June 1823 to recreate his role of King Shotaway in the *Drama of King Shotaway*, a play composed by Brown. By the summer of 1823 Brown's theater had failed and the African Company had disbanded. Hewlett used the playhouse in January 1824 for a one-man show.

At some time during the winter of 1822–1823, an English actor named Charles Mathews attended Brown's theater and evidently spoke with Hewlett. Mathews was a comedian whose specialty was one-man shows consisting of sketches of incidents from his travels and exhibiting his skill in mimicking dialects and making quick changes from one character to another, including costume changes. He was touring the United States in order to earn money, but also to collect material for a new show. Hewlett took his attention as a sign of respect and began to offer his interpretation of some of Mathews's sketches. But in May 1824 reports reached New York that Mathews was performing a new one-man show based on his trip to America and had included in it a ridiculous sketch of a supposed incident at the African Theater. Hewlett was deeply hurt at having been deceived and used. He immediately left for England to confront Mathews over the insult and also to find work in English theaters. He succeeded in neither and returned so deeply discouraged with his future prospects as a performer that he returned to his old occupation as a steward, signing on to a cargo ship that left New York in February 1825 for a nine-month voyage to the West Indies and the Mediterranean. The last eleven weeks of this trip were spent crossing the Atlantic, a hellish ordeal of living on rotting salt meat and moldy biscuits while being forced to serve as a tool in the persecution of one of the two passengers on the boat by the other. When the boat finally reached New York, the persecuted passenger sued the boat's captain; fortunately, a city paper printed an extensive report of this trial, including a long summary of Hewlett's testimony, which provides a glimpse of his personality.

Once back in New York, Hewlett threw himself again into his career as a performer. He appeared in Greenwich Village in November 1825 in a performance that ended in a brawl among the spectators. He was in Brooklyn in December. Then he put together a company of supporting actors—perhaps veterans of Brown's company—permitting him to present entire scenes from Shakespeare. The company offered a series of performances in Philadelphia in January 1826, including one at which he was accompanied by FRANCIS JOHNSON and his band.

Despite his resentment of his shabby treatment by Mathews, that name had drawing power, and Mathews's practice of making an evening's entertainment out of a variety of songs and one-man sketches so suited Hewlett's own talents that he continued to offer his shows as "imitations" of Mathews. And even though he failed in his attempts to get bookings in England, he began to bill himself as "the New-York and London Coloured Comedian."

Hewlett continued to perform about the northeast for the remainder of the decade, no doubt much more often and more widely than can now be traced. His career as a performer seems to have peaked in 1831, when he announced a show in New York City in which he would have the services of a full band, with "Mrs. Hewlett" at the pianoforte. His name is not seen again until 1834, when he was arrested for petty theft and sentenced to six months in jail. He was interviewed by MARTIN R. DELANY in 1836; Delany referred to his performing career as something in the past. In 1837 a young, white woman, identified as his wife (though not the wife who took the piano chair in the 1831 concert), was arrested for a petty theft; later that year, Hewlett was himself arrested for another theft, and sentenced to two years in prison in New York City.

In 1839 Hewlett revived his career, at least temporarily, by getting a booking to give his usual program of songs and recitations in the new "Royal Victoria Theatre" at Port of Spain, Trinidad. He was not well received, and nothing further is known of his career. When Delany published his remarks on Hewlett in 1852, he noted that he had died a few years before, in New York City.

Given the sad fact that most of the reports of Hewlett's performances were written by people who were hostile to him, trying to be funny, or some combination of the two, it is hard to know how to judge his real abilities. He danced; in his second appearance with the African Theatre he danced in a pantomime and choreographed and danced in a ballet. Later, he did occasional popular dance steps, such as a hornpipe, but otherwise seems to have done little to develop this aspect of his talent.

As an actor, he regarded Richard III as his signature role, so much so that in 1827 he commissioned an engraved portrait of himself in costume. He also appeared in scenes from a number of other Shakespearean tragedies, in other classic English plays, and in more recent melodramas and comedies. He was not trained in the actor's craft, though, and Delany's judgment that Hewlett was a man who "was not well educated" and was hindered in interpreting serious roles, but who "possessed great intellectual powers" and was "a great delineator of character" seems likely to be sound (Thompson, 212). Descriptions of Hewlett's performances in tragic roles seem to suggest greater enthusiasm than subtlety, while accounts of his work in comedy show considerable stage presence.

When appearing in his one-man shows, he usually offered his renditions of soliloquies and speeches as "imitations" of the style of some famous current actor. His idol was the English actor Edmund Kean, whom he had a chance to see in New York in 1820 or 1821. Kean was famous, or infamous, for his intensely emotional Shakespearian performances. Hewlett also offered imitations of Thomas Abthorpe Cooper, an English actor who emigrated to New York in 1796. He represented a restrained and dignified style of acting—stilted and dull, to the admirers of Kean. If Hewlett was able to capture the essential qualities of both styles, then he was a careful observer and a skilled performer.

Hewlett sang well; an otherwise unfriendly report of one of his shows allowed that "he sung a tarnal sight better" than those in the audience who joined in (Thompson, 150–151). As a singer, he also usually offered his songs as imitating the style of a famous singer. The descriptions of these singers indicate more similarities among their singing styles than obtained among the actors he imitated. They all worked in the high end of the tenor range and aimed for beauty of sound rather than emotional force.

Hewlett was obviously a talented, determined, and resourceful man. He lived in an unjust society that did not allow him to fully develop his talents when young or to display them when mature. Nonetheless he was an active and successful performer for at least ten years before adversity brought him down.

FURTHER READING

McAllister, Marvin. *White People Do Not Know How to Behave at Entertainments Designed for Ladies & Gentlemen of Colour: William Brown's African & American Theater* (2003).

Thompson, George A., Jr. *A Documentary History of the African Theatre* (1998).

White, Shane. *Stories of Freedom in Black New York* (2002).

GEORGE A. THOMPSON JR.

Hickman, Daniel (1 Nov. 1841–17 Nov. 1917), slave, pioneer minister, coroner, and politician, was born in Scott County, Kentucky. As a slave he was a carriage driver and house slave. It was against the law for slaves to learn to read and write, which was sometimes punishable by death, but Daniel took the risk. He learned by secretly listening to and watching his master read. He saved scraps of printed paper and taught others to read and in doing so almost lost his life after he was discovered by his master. After emancipation the Freedman's Bureau established schools to educate the formerly illiterate slaves. It was then that he could take full advantage of his freedom and spend time improving his reading skills.

In 1862, while still a slave, Hickman became a Christian, and in 1866, after emancipation, he became a minister and the pastor of the Owens Baptist Church, the Big Eagle Baptist Church, and the Mount Olivet Baptist Church in Dry Run, Kentucky. Daniel had married Williana Lewis while they were still both slaves; however, to legalize a slave marriage they were required to remarry with witnesses and have it recorded at the courthouse. They did so on 24 May 1867 in Georgetown, Kentucky. To their union ten children were born. Three of their daughters became schoolteachers.

Although emancipation afforded legal freedom, former slaves were still subjected to economic, social, and political oppression. With little or no land to call their own, they felt trapped in an endless system of oppression and servitude. When the Homestead Act provided public lands in the West for interested and brave homesteaders, the town promoters W. R. Hill and the Reverend P. Roundtree came to Scott County, Kentucky, to encourage homesteading in western Kansas and the settlement of an all-black town called Nicodemus. Hickman assisted in organizing a body of members at the Mount Olivet Church that joined the organized colony and traveled to Nicodemus with Hill and Roundtree. This group of colonists numbered about 150 and included Hickman, his wife and children, Williana Hickman's brother Austin Minor, and other families. They left Scott County by rail on 1 March 1878 and arrived at Ellis, Kansas, on 3 March. After two weeks in tents at Ellis, the group was led by Hill, with compass in hand, for two days before reaching the town site of Nicodemus. The Hickman family homesteaded west of Nicodemus, near what became known as Hill City. There they reared their children and established a new home on free soil.

Religion was important to the colonists. After enduring the harsh realities of slavery, they believed God had brought them safely to the promised lands of Kansas. In 1879, under the leadership of Hickman and Rev. Bell, the Mount Olive Baptist Church at Nicodemus was organized. Hickman and Rev. Bell set out among the colonists and distributed Sunday school and church literature from the American Baptist Publishing Society of Philadelphia. Hickman then organized the First Baptist Church in Hill City, an almost all-white membership. He turned the membership over to a white minister named Rev. Grahan and then in 1897 organized the Second Baptist Church at Hill City, of which he was pastor until 1903. During his ministry he also assisted in organizing the WaKeeney Baptist Association twenty-three miles south of Hill City.

During the mid-1880s, when Graham County, was being organized, a county seat fight broke out between the settlers of Millbrook and those of Hill City. Hickman, as a leader in the community and with much influence, was offered $1,000 to persuade Nicodemus voters to vote for the town of Millbrook. He refused, and in retaliation the other commissioners locked him in a secret room for over a week. His wife contacted a friend, Saul Hutton, who found him, kicked the door in, and finally freed Hickman. When the votes were tallied, Hill City had won the county seat election, and Hickman was elected the first county coroner. He served for two years. He was also elected the chairman of the Graham County Commissioners and served seven years, from 1886 to 1893.

In 1903 Hickman moved his family to Topeka, where he worked as custodian at the state capitol. He continued to work as a custodian until his health failed and he was forced to resign. He accepted a pastorship at a church in nearby Junction City, but his health continued to decline until he was forced again to resign. His career of fifty-one years as a Christian minister had finally ended. During the years that followed his health continued to decline. After his death in Topeka his wife had his body returned to Nicodemus and laid to rest in the Mount Olive Cemetery in the shadow of his former church, the first church built in Graham County. His daughter Anna Todd Comer wrote in tribute to him: "He was a man of rare temperaments. A man of God, decisive and firm, true to his trust, country, his race, and his friends" ("Lula Craig Manuscript").

Hickman left his mark on the high plains of Kansas by living a life of true freedom and was a proven example of community leadership while establishing Christian churches throughout the area. He had endured slavery and was subjected to white religious hypocrisy, but through his own religious conviction, he, like Moses, led souls to the promised land, to the free soil of Kansas.

FURTHER READING
The "Lula Craig Manuscript," Spencer Research Library, Kansas Collection, University of Kansas, Lawrence, includes Annie Comer Hickman's "A Tribute to My Father, Rev. Daniel Hickman." "Biographical Sketch of Rev. Daniel Hickman" is in the Manuscript Collection, Kansas State Historical Society, Topeka. Annie Comer Hickman's "Rev. Hickman's Activities in the Early Life of Graham County" is in the archives of the Graham County Historical Society.
"She Helped Settle Second Colony of Nicodemus," *Topeka Daily Capital* (29 Aug. 1937).
U.S. Department of the Interior, National Park Service. *Promises Land on the Solomon: Black Settlement at Nicodemus* (1986).
Obituary: *Reveille New Era*, 29 Nov. 1917.

ANGELA BATES

Hicks, Charles B. (c. 1840–1902), show business entrepreneur, minstrel company owner and manager, interlocutor, singer, and comedian, claimed to have been born a slave in Baltimore, Maryland. Nothing is known of his parents.

The minstrel show was, by some measures, the most popular form of public entertainment during the mid-nineteenth century. For African Americans pursuing careers in show business, there were few alternatives to blackface minstrelsy, leading to the perplexing situation of black performers perpetuating white caricatures of blacks. Some African Americans were disdainful of minstrel shows in general and especially those staged by performers of their own race (since they gave "aid and comfort to the enemy," according to JAMES MONROE TROTTER, a chronicler of black musical achievement in the 1870s). Nevertheless, the best black minstrel companies were enormously popular with black as well as white audiences. After attending a performance of the Georgia Minstrels, even the erudite Trotter, whose self-professed mission was to promote African American accomplishments in classical music, confessed that the troupe offered "some of the most pleasing music of the time" (Trotter, p. 274).

The troupe that impressed Trotter, the Georgia Minstrels, was originally formed by Charles B. Hicks, the first successful black minstrel show entrepreneur. Very little is known about Hicks before he burst onto the entertainment scene in the 1860s. He claimed to have been born into slavery in Baltimore, Maryland, probably around 1840. Between 1865 and 1891, Hicks led various black minstrel troupes through the United States, Canada, Europe, Australia, and New Zealand, both as an owner and as a manager of troupes owned by others. He also was a respected interlocutor, comedian, and singer. During the final decade of his life, he managed a circus touring Asia.

Hicks described himself as an octoroon, and another period source characterized him as "almost white." Possibly passing for white, he learned his craft working with white minstrel troupes before suddenly appearing on the national scene in the 1860s with some of the earliest black companies. He first appears in the press in 1865 with Brooker & Clayton's Georgia Minstrels—a troupe he apparently helped to launch—which was owned by the white impresario W. H. Lee. The company was formed in Indianapolis, Indiana, though it was advertised as being composed of former slaves from Macon, Georgia. Brooker & Clayton's Georgia Minstrels quickly attracted large audiences curious to see "bona fide" former slaves perform. According to a *Chicago Tribune* review: "The entertainment was without a doubt one of the best ever offered to a Chicago populace, comprising excellent selections, presented in a most laughable manner, yet devoid of the forced effort apparent in too many burnt cork companies. The troupe is comprised entirely of real colored men, all freed from the bonds of slavery during the recent war." Hicks both managed and performed with the company.

In 1866 Hicks formed a new troupe, the Original Georgia Minstrels, under his ownership. Over the next several years, Hicks-owned Georgia Minstrel troupes toured the middle-Atlantic and New England states. Hicks preferred to play in smaller cities, which were starved for top quality entertainment, though he made occasional forays into Boston, New York, and Philadelphia. He also made brief excursions into Canada and a short trip to Panama.

Hicks took a scaled-down company to Germany in 1870. Apparently failing miserably with German audiences, he took his performers to England, where they hooked up with Sam Hague's Slave Serenaders, a largely American troupe that had relocated permanently to England. The combined troupe successfully toured England, Ireland, Scotland, and Wales.

Hicks returned to the United States in 1871 and formed a new troupe of Georgia Minstrels. He sold his rights to that company in 1872 to the minstrel performer N. D. Roberts, who soon afterward sold his ownership of the troupe to a white tavern owner, Charles Callender. Callender proved to be a masterful show business entrepreneur, and Callender's Georgia Minstrels became one of the most popular and respected minstrel troupes of the later nineteenth century. This was the company Trotter saw perform. Hicks remained with Callender as advance man until about the end of 1874 and then left to form other companies between 1875 and 1877.

Hicks scored his greatest successes not in the United States, but in New Zealand and Australia. He made his first tour of those countries beginning in 1877 with Hicks's Georgia Minstrels, composed of performers he lured away from the white promoter J. H. Haverly. Blackface minstrelsy was nearly as popular in Australia and New Zealand as it was in the United States, and Hicks initially found eager audiences at every city and town on the tour. The fact that the troupe was composed entirely of African Americans added to its appeal: "The novelty of colour, the news of their success in other parts of the colony, and the tinge of romance about their history, all served to draw an immense crowd to witness the first performance," wrote a reviewer in the *The Lyttleton Times* of Canterbury, New Zealand. Australia and New Zealand were artistically liberating for Hicks and his performers, who were not limited to presenting scenes of plantation slavery in positive and nostalgic terms and who occasionally staged dramatic theatrical productions, which was all but unheard of for black actors in the United States.

Audiences began to wane in the third year of the tour. Hicks left the troupe to act with a theatrical company briefly before returning to America in 1880. He spent several years managing troupes for others—mostly white-owned companies, but also a troupe owned by the famous black comedian, Billy Kersands. In 1886 Hicks partnered with A. D. Sawyer to form Hicks and Sawyer's Consolidated Colored Minstrels. Hicks and Sawyer soon parted ways, each forming troupes called Hicks and Sawyer's Consolidated Colored Minstrels. Hicks soon disbanded his troupe and took a series of performing jobs. He formed a new company called the Hicks-Sawyer Minstrels (prompting Sawyer, who was not involved, to threaten a lawsuit) for another tour of Australia and New Zealand in 1888.

The new troupe, which Hicks's referred to as the "Big Black Boom," also was a hit. The performances were well attended and frequently elicited gushing—though often culturally insensitive—reviews. "From first to last Hicks' Minstrels showed that they were decidedly different from anybody else's minstrels," wrote a reviewer for the *Australian Star*. "They do not sit around the stage in the usual orthodox fashion, but come on with a flourish of trumpets and a clang of brass music. ... There is a splendid band, a host of excellent vocalists, 'funny coons' that would make a mute at a funeral smile, dancers that seem built on wires, and acrobats that can rival any yet seen here."

The tour was a popular success, but the troupe disbanded in late 1889 or early 1890. Hicks, as well as many of the other performers, remained in Australia. He briefly took a staff position with Gaylord's Wild West show and may have formed minstrel troupes for individual performances and brief tours in 1890 and 1891 (he continued to report performances to the show business newspaper, *The New York Clipper*, as if the original troupe were still intact). In 1891 he joined the Harmston & Son Circus and Wild West as general manager for a tour that took him to Java, India, and China. He briefly returned to America in 1894 to assemble a troupe of white performers, Col. Hick' Oriole Troupe of Vaudeville Performers, to take to China. In 1895 he rejoined Harmston's Circus. Hicks died in Surabaya, Java, in 1902.

Charles Hicks's influence on blackface minstrelsy is evidenced by the fact that "Georgia Minstrels" became almost a generic term for African American troupes, adopted by many of the most successful companies well into the twentieth century. Hicks's various troupes were launching pads, or at least important career stepping-stones, for many leading African American entertainers of the postbellum era including the banjo virtuoso Horace Weston, singer Wallace King, and comedians Bob Height and BILLY KERSANDS. After the 1888–1889 tour the singer and dancer Irving Sayles remained in Australia, where he became a beloved vaudeville star.

Hicks was a savvy businessman with a flair for publicity. His various companies were extremely popular, even to the point that, when playing in Washington, D.C., in 1869, he had the power to demand that "colored persons [be] admitted to every part of the house" (black patrons typically were relegated to the upper balcony). Nonetheless, he struggled to make a profit in America, in no small part due to the challenges of conducting business as a black man. Hicks lacked ready access to financing to tide him over in the bad times and to expand his company to take full advantage of good seasons. He also was locked out of the business networks that benefited white minstrel troupe owners. But though he faced significant business and financial handicaps, he was one of the very few black entrepreneurs of the nineteenth century to be viewed as serious competition by white minstrel company owners.

FURTHER READING

Abbott, Lynn, and Doug Seroff. *Out of Sight: The Rise of African American Popular Music, 1889–1895* (2002).

Hill, Errol G., and James V. Hatch. *A History of African American Theatre* (2003).

Southern, Eileen. "The Georgia Minstrels: The Early Years." In *Inside the Minstrel Mask: Readings in Nineteenth-Century Blackface Minstrelsy*, eds. Annemarie Bean, James V. Hatch, and Brookes McNamara (1996).

Trotter, James. *Music and Some Highly Musical People: Containing brief chapters on: A Description of Music, the Music of Nature, a Glance at the History of Music, the Power, Beauty, and Uses of Music. Following which are given sketches of the lives of remarkable musicians of the colored race. With portraits, and an appendix containing copies of music composed by colored men* (1878).

DAVID K. BRADFORD

Hicks, Robert (Bob) (11 Sept. 1902–21 Oct. 1931), guitarist and singer, was born in Walnut Gove, Georgia, the second of three children of Charlie Hicks, a sharecropper, and Mary Harris Hicks. He was a popular performer in the Atlanta area, and the best-selling blues artist on the Columbia record label during the late 1920s.

Hicks was not from a musical family. He first learned to play the guitar from a neighbor, Savannah "Dip" Weaver, the mother of Curley Weaver, who also gained fame as a blues musician. Musicologists speculate that the guitar technique Dip Weaver taught Hicks was adapted from a regional banjo style. This distinctive way of playing would characterize Hicks's guitar performances throughout his brief but productive career.

Hicks's older brother, Charlie, also was a musician. Charlie moved to Atlanta in 1924, and Robert followed the next year. The Hicks brothers along with the harmonica player Eddie Mapp performed at house parties in and around the city.

Robert was unable to support himself solely as a musician, so he worked a series of odd jobs before landing a comparatively stable position in 1926 at Tidwell's Barbecue in Buckhead, an affluent suburb.

In addition to cooking and serving at the restaurant, Hicks sometimes entertained customers with his singing and guitar playing. While performing at Tidwell's, he was discovered by Columbia Records' talent scout Dan Hornsby. Hornsby decided to use Hicks's job as a gimmick, having him dress in chef's clothing for publicity photos, and giving him the name Barbecue Bob.

Hicks's first Columbia record, "Barbecue Blues," was recorded in Atlanta on 25 March 1927. It sold well, and he traveled to New York to record its follow-up, "Mississippi Heavy Water Blues," and seven other sides in June 1927. "Mississippi Heavy Water Blues" also was a hit, establishing Hicks as an important artist for the label. Over the next three years he would record more than sixty sides for Columbia, usually in Atlanta when the company's mobile recording studio would pass through the city. He became the most heavily recorded musician within the vibrant Atlanta blues scene, and Columbia's most popular blues recording artist.

Hicks was an influential musician in what is known today as Piedmont blues. Geographically, the Piedmont is the region east of the main Appalachian Mountains, stretching from New Jersey in the north to central Alabama in the south. Culturally and musically, "Piedmont" usually refers to an area from about Richmond, Virginia, to Jacksonville, Florida. The Piedmont tradition is notable for its strong ties to nineteenth-century string band and rural ragtime styles. Piedmont guitarists, including Hicks, are renowned for their syncopated finger picking techniques.

Hicks specialized in 12-string guitar, an instrument popular with Piedmont musicians, but not widely played outside the region. He sometimes played bottleneck style, using a hard object rather than his fingers to note the strings, and always with an idiosyncratic banjo-like "frailing" technique. While he was at the center of the urban Atlanta blues scene, he is often viewed today as a country blues musician with a repertoire and a performance style that drew heavily from rural music.

Hicks's popularity and influence may have helped to land recording deals for his circle of friends. This group included his brother Charlie, who recorded widely as Charley Lincoln and Laughing Charley; his childhood friend, the singer and guitarist Curley Weaver; the harmonica whiz Eddie Mapp, who recorded only one side under his own name before being stabbed to death at age twenty; and the singer Nellie Florence, who recorded two sides in 1929 and was likely an old girlfriend. Charlie Hicks, Mapp, and Weaver are now recognized, alongside Robert Hicks, as among the most significant southeastern musicians of the era.

Hicks usually recorded as a solo performer, though he made a few recordings with his brother, Charlie, and his close circle of friends. The Hicks brothers recorded four sides, of which a pair, "It Won't Be Long Now, Parts 1 & 2," are widely regarded as blues classics. In 1930 he participated in a session for the QRS label with the guitarist Curley Weaver and the young harmonica player Buddy Moss, which were issued as the Georgia Cotton Pickers. According to the blues researcher Bruce Bastin, "If any music conjures up the atmosphere of a country juke, it must be these sides" (Bastin, p. 110). Hicks also performed as an accompanist on the two recordings by Nellie Florence.

Hicks died in March 1931 from pneumonia, brought on by a bout with influenza, at his father's home in Lithonia, Georgia.

FURTHER READING

Bastin, Bruce. *Red River Blues: The Blues Tradition in the Southeast* (1995).

Oliver, Paul. *The Story of the Blues* (1997).

DAVID K. BRADFORD

Higginbotham, A. Leon, Jr. (25 Feb. 1928–14 Dec. 1998), jurist and civil rights leader, was born Aloysius Leon Higginbotham in Trenton, New Jersey, the son of Aloysius Leon Higginbotham Sr., a laborer, and Emma Lee Douglass, a domestic worker. While he was attending a racially segregated elementary school, his mother insisted that he receive tutoring in Latin, a required subject denied to black students; he then became the first African American to enroll at Trenton's Central High School. Initially interested in engineering, he enrolled at Purdue University only to leave in disgust after the school's president denied his request to move on-campus with his fellow African American students. He completed his undergraduate education at Antioch College in Yellow Springs, Ohio, where he received a B.A. in Sociology in 1949. In August 1948 he married Jeanne L. Foster; the couple had three children. Angered by his experiences at Purdue and inspired by the example of Supreme Court Justice THURGOOD MARSHALL, Higginbotham decided to pursue a legal career. He attended law school at Yale and graduated with an LLB in 1952.

A. Leon Higginbotham, Jr., legal scholar and Chief Judge of the U.S. Court of Appeals for the Third Circuit in Philadelphia. (Evelyn Brooks Higginbotham.)

Although Higginbotham was an honors student at Yale, he encountered racial prejudice when he tried to find employment at leading Philadelphia, law firms. After switching his sights to the public sector, he began his career as a clerk for the Court of Common Pleas judge Curtis Bok in 1952. Higginbotham then served for a year as an assistant district attorney under the future Philadelphia mayor and fellow Yale graduate Richardson Dilworth. In 1954 he became a principal in the new African American law firm of Norris, Green, Harris, and Higginbotham and remained with the firm until 1962. During the same period he became active in the civil rights movement, serving as president of the local chapter of the National Association for the Advancement of Colored People (NAACP); he was also a member of the Pennsylvania Human Relations Commission. Between 1960 and 1962 Higginbotham served as a special hearing officer for conscientious objectors for the United States Department of Justice. In 1962 President John F. Kennedy appointed him to the Federal Trade Commission, making him the first African American member of a federal administrative

agency. Two years later President Lyndon Johnson appointed him as U.S. District Court judge for the Eastern District of Pennsylvania; at age thirty-six, he was the youngest person to be so named in thirty years. In 1977 President Jimmy Carter appointed him to the U.S. Federal Court of Appeals for the Third Circuit in Philadelphia. He became chief judge in 1989 and remained in the position until his retirement in 1993.

As a member of the federal bench, Higginbotham authored more than 650 opinions. A staunch liberal and tireless defender of programs such as affirmative action, he became equally well known for his legal scholarship, with more than one hundred published articles to his credit. He also published two (out of a planned series of four) highly regarded books that outlined the American struggle toward racial justice and equality through the lens of the legal profession: *In the Matter of Color: Race and the American Legal Process, the Colonial Period* (1978), in which he castigated the founding fathers for their hypocrisy in racial matters, and *Shades of Freedom: Racial Politics and Presumptions of the American Legal Process* (1996).

Higginbotham also taught both law and sociology at a number of schools, including the University of Michigan, Yale, Stanford, and New York University. He enjoyed a long relationship with the University of Pennsylvania, where he was considered for the position of president in 1980 before deciding to remain on the bench. Following his retirement in 1993, Higginbotham taught at Harvard Law School and also served as public service professor of jurisprudence at Harvard's John F. Kennedy School of Government. In addition, he served on several corporate boards and worked for the law firm of Paul, Weiss, Rifkind, Wharton, and Garrison in both New York and Washington.

Although most of his career was spent outside the public limelight, Higginbotham came to the forefront of public attention in 1991 when he published an open letter to the Supreme Court nominee CLARENCE THOMAS in the *University of Pennsylvania Law Review*. Castigating Thomas for what he viewed as a betrayal of all that he, Higginbotham, had worked for, Higginbotham stated, "I could not find one shred of evidence suggesting an insightful understanding on your part of how the evolutionary movement of the Constitution and the work of civil rights organizations have benefited you." Although widely criticized for his stance, Higginbotham remained a critic of Thomas's after he joined the Supreme Court and later attempted to have a speaking invitation to Thomas rescinded by the National Bar Association in 1998.

In his later years Higginbotham filled a variety of additional roles. He served as an international mediator at the first post-apartheid elections in South Africa in 1994, lent his counsel to the Congressional Black Caucus during a series of voting rights cases before the Supreme Court, and advised Texaco Inc. on diversity and personnel issues when the firm came under fire for alleged racial discrimination in 1996. In failing health, Higginbotham's last public service came during the impeachment of President Bill Clinton in 1998, when he argued before the House Judiciary Committee that there were degrees of perjury and that President Clinton's did not qualify as "an impeachable high crime." The recipient of several honorary degrees, Higginbotham also received the Raoul Wallenberg Humanitarian Award (1994), the Presidential Medal of Freedom (1995), and the NAACP's Spingarn Medal (1996). After he and his first wife divorced in 1988, Higginbotham married Evelyn Brooks (SEE EVELYN BROOKS HIGGINBOTHAM), a professor at Harvard, and adopted her daughter. He died in a Boston hospital after suffering a series of strokes.

Although he never served on the Supreme Court, Higginbotham's impact on the legal community seems certain to continue. A pioneer among African American jurists, he also made solid contributions in the areas of legal scholarship, training, and civil rights.

FURTHER READING

Higginbotham's papers are held at the John F. Kennedy Presidential Library in Boston, Massachusetts. The Harvard University School of Law in Cambridge, Massachusetts, also maintains a file on Higginbotham. His career on the bench can be traced in issues 223 through 429 of the *Federal Supplement* (for his decisions on the District Court) and in issues 560 through 983 of the *Federal Reporter*.

Higginbotham, A. Leon. "An Open Letter to Justice Clarence Thomas from a Federal Judicial Colleague," *University of Pennsylvania Law Review* 140, no. 1005 (1992).

Bell, Derrick. "Judge A. Leon Higginbotham Jr.'s Legacy," *Rutgers Law Review* 53 (Spring, 2001): 627–640.

Ogletree, Charles, Jr., et al. "In Memoriam: A. Leon Higginbotham Jr.," *Harvard Law Review* 112, no. 8 (June 1999): 1801–1833.

Obituaries: *New York Times, Philadelphia Inquirer,* and *Boston Globe,* 15 Dec. 1998.

This entry is taken from the *American National Biography* and is published here with the permission of the American Council of Learned Societies.

EDWARD L. LACH JR.

Higginbotham, Evelyn Brooks (4 June 1945–), historian, was born Evelyn Titania Brooks in Washington, D.C., the younger of two daughters of Dr. Albert Neal Dow Brooks, a high school principal and historian, and Alma Elaine Campbell, a high school history teacher who later served as the supervisor for history in the Washington, D.C., public school system. The teaching and writing of history played a central role in the Brooks household. Albert N. D. Brooks served as the secretary-treasurer of the Association for the Study of Afro-American Life and History and as the editor of that organization's *Negro History Bulletin.* Albert Brooks was the youngest of ten children of the Reverend WALTER HENDERSON BROOKS, born a slave in Virginia in the 1850s and still alive at his granddaughter Evelyn's birth. A prominent Baptist minister and poet, Walter H. Brooks published an article in one of the earliest volumes of CARTER GODWIN WOODSON's *Journal of Negro History* in the early 1920s.

Given her family background, Higginbotham was exposed at an early age to some of the leading African American historians of the twentieth century, including JOHN HOPE FRANKLIN, BENJAMIN ARTHUR QUARLES, RAYFORD WHITTINGHAM LOGAN, and CHARLES HARRIS WESLEY. But it was her father, with whom she traveled as he gave speeches during Negro History Week, and who worked tirelessly to bring professional respect to the study of black history, who instilled in her a desire to become a historian. Even in elementary school, Higginbotham realized that American history, as taught in the 1950s, did not adequately reflect the contributions of African Americans and others.

After graduating from the Theodore Roosevelt High School in Washington, D.C., in 1963 Higginbotham began her collegiate training in the fall of that year at Howard University. However, in 1965, having married Larry G. Barnett, she left Howard and the Washington area for the Midwest and matriculated at the University of Wisconsin at Milwaukee. As a student, she was active in efforts to develop African American studies programs in Milwaukee's schools and colleges and also supported efforts to integrate black history into the traditional curriculum. Upon graduation with a B.A. in History in June 1969, Higginbotham began to put her activism into practice, by teaching American history and serving as a counselor to eighth-graders at the Francis Parkman Jr. High School in Milwaukee until 1971. Her daughter Nia was born in that year. In 1972 her marriage ended, and she returned to Washington, D.C., where she taught at the city's Woodrow Wilson High School until 1974, the year she earned her M.A. in History from Howard University. At Howard, she worked closely with Rayford W. Logan, author of the classic work on American race relations in the late nineteenth and early twentieth centuries, *The Betrayal of the Negro: From Rutherford B. Hayes to Woodrow Wilson.* That period, from 1880 to 1920, labeled by Logan as the "nadir," was marked by an upsurge in racial violence by whites against blacks and a retreat from the gains of Reconstruction. Higginbotham's own doctoral research would focus on the same era.

Higginbotham worked as a manuscript research associate at Howard's Moorland-Spingarn Research Center in 1974–1975, and learned the methods of historical research from the Center's director, DOROTHY BURNETT PORTER WESLEY. After earning a Certification in Archival Administration and Records Management at the National Archives in Washington, D.C., in 1975, Higginbotham earned a Certificate in Quantitative Methodology in Social Science at the Newberry Library in Chicago two years later. By then she had already begun a doctoral dissertation in history at the University of Rochester, working with the eminent scholar of slavery Eugene D. Genovese as her advisor. Higginbotham's interest in historical theory and gender analysis was influenced during her time at Rochester by a vibrant interdisciplinary faculty which included, among others, the women's historian Elizabeth Fox-Genovese, the cultural historian Christopher Lasch, and the economic historian Stanley F. Engerman.

At the time Higginbotham began her dissertation research in the late 1970s, only a handful of scholars were working on topics in African American women's history. In 1978, however, she was one of the contributors to *Afro-American Woman: Struggles and Images* (1978); edited by Rosalyn Terborg-Penn and Sharon Harley it was the first published anthology examining the experience of African American women from an historical

perspective. Higginbotham's doctoral dissertation examined the struggle for race and gender equality in the black Baptist Church in the late nineteenth and early twentieth century. She argued that black women, who formed three-fifths of church membership, raised much of the money for local churches, and played a leading role in educational and self-help efforts, most notably the National Training School in Washington, D.C., which was dedicated to professionalizing domestic service and was led by NANNIE BURROUGHS, an outspoken leader of the Women's Convention of the National Baptist Convention in the first half of the twentieth century. (Burroughs, a hero in the Brooks household, was a member of Walter H. Brooks's congregation.) Leaders of the Women's Convention worked with white northern female reformers and male African American Baptist leaders to expand work and educational opportunities, and came to develop a distinct "feminist theology."

While completing her dissertation, Higginbotham taught history at Simmons College in Boston during the 1979–1980 academic year; taught at the Harvard Divinity School in the fall of 1980; and was an instructor in the history department at Dartmouth University (her father's *alma mater*) in Hanover, New Hampshire, from 1980 to 1982. She was appointed an assistant professor in the Afro-American Studies Program at the University of Maryland at College Park in 1982, and taught there until 1986, when she secured an appointment in the history department at the University of Pennsylvania in Philadelphia. In 1988, she married A. LEON HIGGINBOTHAM JR., the distinguished federal court judge and legal scholar who also taught at the University of Pennsylvania.

Evelyn Brooks Higginbotham's dissertation primarily employed the traditional historical method of archival research, but in the late 1980s and early 1990s, she began to look more broadly at the role of gender and class in African American history. In "Beyond the Sound of Silence: Black Women in History," published in the inaugural issue of the journal *Gender & History* (1989) she noted that while the black woman's voice "goes largely unheard" (50) in mainstream historical scholarship, recent work on black women had begun to weave "a more intricate, yet more honest narrative" (62) of women, African Americans, and the United States in general. Further studies of African American women, she concluded, would not only reveal a story of gender and racial oppression, but also provide a new narrative of black women's "cultural autonomy … supportive bonding, and survival strategies"(63). In "African-American Women's History and the Metalanguage of Race," published in the feminist journal *Signs* (Winter 1992), Higginbotham's scholarship took a decidedly more theoretical turn. According to one scholar, the essay marked a paradigm shift in black women's history, offering a "new calculus in place of [its] old geometry" (Wilson, 355). Drawing on the work of African American literary and cultural theorists, including HENRY LOUIS GATES JR., as well as the white European scholars Michel Foucault, M. M. Bakhtin, and Jurgen Habermas, Higginbotham examined the racial constructions of gender, class, and sexuality. Following Bakhtin, she posited "race" as a "double-voiced discourse" which served as the voice of black liberation as well as the voice of black oppression. In 1993 the Berkshire Conference of Women Historians awarded the essay its prize for best article published that year.

In 1993 Harvard University Press published Higginbotham's *Righteous Discontent: The Women's Movement in the Black Baptist Church: 1880–1920*. The book, which was adapted from her dissertation, but updated to include the theoretical insights of her *Signs* and *Gender & History* articles, won awards from the American Historical Association, the American Academy of Religion, the Association of Black Women Historians, and the Association for Research on Non-Profit and Voluntary Organizations. It was also a *New York Times* Notable Book in 1993 and 1994. In the latter year the University of Rochester awarded Higginbotham its Distinguished Scholars Medal.

After receiving tenure at the University of Pennsylvania in 1993, Higginbotham moved to Harvard University, where she was appointed a professor of Afro-American Studies in the Faculty of Arts and Sciences and professor of African American Religious History in the Divinity School. In 1998 she became the first African American appointed a full professor within Harvard's History Department and in the 2006–2007 academic year was appointed chair of Harvard's Department of African and African American Studies. She published and presented papers during the later 1990s and early 2000s on topics including black women in politics in the 1920s; African American religion and race records in the 1920s and 1930s; and the racial construction of citizenship. In 2001 she was the editor in chief of a major reference work, *The Harvard Guide to African-American History*, and was the editor in chief with Henry Louis Gates Jr. of the *African American National Biography* (2008), the largest biographical dictionary of African Americans yet to be published. Other projects have included a study for the Lilly Endowment on the history of its grant-making to African American religious institutions and programs. Following the death of her husband in 1998 Evelyn Higginbotham established the A. Leon Higginbotham Papers Project within Harvard's W. E. B. DuBois Institute.

Active in community affairs, Higginbotham was inducted into the Academy of Women Achievers of the Boston YWCA in 2000. The award "recognizes women who have demonstrated leadership and reached exemplary levels of achievement in their professions and communities" (*Harvard Gazette*). From the 1970s on, Evelyn Brooks Higginbotham's scholarship similarly honored and brought into the historical mainstream millions of African American women whose own leadership and exemplary achievements were silenced for far too long.

Higginbotham received several honors after 2007. Among these were the 2008 Carter G. Woodson Scholar Medallion from the Association for the Study of African American Life and History (ASALH), election to American Philosophical Society (2009) and the 2010 Sigma Pi Phi Boule Award. In 2011 Howard University awarded her an honorary Doctorate in Humane Letters in recognition of her contribution to African American history. Professor Higginbotham was also profiled in a cover story for *Howard Magazine* in 2010 that examined her links to Howard University, and her role in thoroughly revising the classic African American history textbook, *From Slavery to Freedom*. The textbook's original author, JOHN HOPE FRANKLIN selected Higginbotham to update the work for a 21st century audience. In addition to updating the story of African American history to include Hurricane Katrina and the election of BARACK OBAMA as president, Higginbotham updated 80 percent of the book's scholarship to reflect new trends in African and African American historiography. The ninth edition of the book was published by McGraw Hill in 2010 to critical and popular acclaim, and also included new digital resources and tools. In 2010-11 Evelyn Brooks Higginbotham was the Inaugural John Hope Franklin Professor of American Legal History at Duke University Law School, Durham, North Carolina.

FURTHER READING

Harris, Paisley. "Gatekeeping and Remaking: The Politics of Respectability in African American Women's History and Black Feminism," *Journal of Women's History*, 15 (Spring 2003): 212–220.

Mitchell, Michele. "Silences Broken, Silences Kept: Gender and Sexuality in African-American History," *Gender & History* 11 (1999): 433–444.

Wilson, Francille Rusan, "'This Past Was Waiting for Me when I Came': The Contextualization of Black Women's History." *Feminist Studies* 22 (Summer 1996): 345–362.

"YWCA to honor Evelyn Brooks Higginbotham as Woman Achiever," *Harvard Gazette*, 11 May 2000.

STEVEN J. NIVEN

Higginbotham, J. C. (11 May 1906–26 May 1973), jazz trombonist, was born Jay C. Higginbotham in Social Circle, Georgia. The names and occupations of his parents are unknown, and little is known about his early family life other than that he was the thirteenth of fourteen children, all of whom were raised in a musical environment. A sister and one brother played trombone, another brother played trumpet, and his niece was a composer.

Higginbotham attended school in Cincinnati, Ohio, where he apprenticed as a tailor at the Cincy Colored Training School and worked at the General Motors factory before joining Wesley Helvey's band as a professional musician in 1924. After two years with Helvey, he left for Buffalo, New York, to work with Eugene Primos and the trombonist Jimmy Harrison. In 1928 he settled in New York, where, while sitting in with the CHICK WEBB Orchestra at the Savoy Ballroom, he was hired by the bandleader LUIS RUSSELL; he remained with Russell until 1931. Higginbotham developed into an especially strong soloist during this period, and he was frequently featured in Russell's band, soloing after LOUIS ARMSTRONG on such recordings as "Mahogany Hall Stomp" and "Dallas Blues" (both 1929). During the next few years Higginbotham migrated through many of the prominent black swing bands of the 1930s, including those led by Webb, FLETCHER HENDERSON, LUCKY MILLINDER, and Benny Carter, before rejoining Russell in 1937 for three years in which Russell's orchestra again provided the backing for Armstrong.

Higginbotham's reputation during the swing years (1930s and early 1940s) continued to grow, culminating in his selection as the winner of the *Down Beat* poll (1941–1944), the *Metronome* poll (1943–1945), and the *Esquire* Gold Award in 1945.

But the arrival of bebop and the rise of younger trombonists (J. J. JOHNSON, Bennie Green, Kai Winding) began to detract from Higginbotham's stature in the late 1940s and early 1950s. With the demand for his skills as a sideman considerably lessened, he began working a succession of modest engagements in Cleveland, Boston, and New York. A recording that he made with the trumpeter BUCK CLAYTON in March 1956 was his first in ten years.

Higginbotham's early recordings of his own original compositions include "Higginbotham Blues" and "Give Me Your Telephone Number," both in 1930, but during the 1930s and 1940s he also recorded with many well-known jazz artists, including LIL ARMSTRONG, Mezz Mezzrow, COLEMAN HAWKINS, Fletcher Henderson, RED ALLEN, Louis Armstrong, LIONEL HAMPTON, COOTIE WILLIAMS, REX STEWART, and TINY GRIMES.

Throughout much of his career Higginbotham was closely associated with the trumpeter Red Allen. Few partnerships in jazz have been so successful, for the two began working together in 1929 while in the Russell orchestra and continued to play together intermittently for more than thirty years in such groups as the Blue Rhythm Band in 1934, and the Russell orchestra, backing Armstrong, from 1937 to 1940. He also played at such places as the Garrick Stage Bar in Chicago in 1942 and the Onyx Club, the Apollo Theater, and Kelly's Stables in New York City in the 1940s. In late 1956 Higginbotham was back with Allen for a stay at the Metropole Café in New York and remained there intermittently until the summer of 1959. During the 1960s Higginbotham fronted a succession of small groups, most of them with a New Orleans revival tinge, but although he continued to play until the early 1970s, these were difficult years for him. The writer Paul Hemphill in 1966 related how the trombonist had fallen on hard times and even had to borrow cab fare in order to participate in a jam session at Eddie Condon's New York club during the mid-1960s.

Higginbotham remained active as a performer almost until his death in New York City, but his contributions as a pioneering jazz trombonist were made early in his career. His powerful tone, surefooted technique, and legato style—a style introduced by Jimmy Harrison but refined by Higginbotham during the 1930s—placed him in the vanguard of jazz trombonists who gradually overcame the problems of technical agility that afflicted the first generation of players. He transformed the trombone into a modern instrument, closer in dexterity to that of other horns, and his consistent ability as an improviser made him the dominant model for an emerging group of younger trombonists that included TRUMMY YOUNG, Bill Harris, and Eddie Bert.

FURTHER READING

Hemphill, Paul. "Repaying Higgy," *Atlanta Journal and Constitution*, 24 Nov. 1966.

Jones, Cliff. *J. C. Higginbotham* (1944).

Schuller, Gunther. *The Swing Era: The Development of Jazz, 1930–1945* (1989).

Obituary: *New York Times*, 28 May 1973.

This entry is taken from the *American National Biography* and is published here with the permission of the American Council of Learned Societies.

CHARLES BLANCQ

Higginbotham, Mitchell (2 Mar. 1921–), Tuskegee Airman, was born in Amherst, Virginia, where he lived with his paternal grandfather until the age of five. The federal judge A. LEON HIGGINBOTHAM was his distant cousin. In Amherst, Mitchell Higginbotham went to school with his older aunts and uncles and learned the alphabet, multiplication, and division before he entered kindergarten. At the age of five, he was taken to live with his parents in Sewickley, Pennsylvania. His parents worked in the steel mills, but during the Great Depression, the mills closed and they entered domestic service. Schools in Sewickley were integrated, but the YMCA, the theaters, and many of the sports programs were closed to African Americans. When Higginbotham enrolled in school in Sewickley, he was so advanced that he skipped first grade. There were six African Americans out of the 106 students in Higginbotham's high school graduating class. He motivated his fellow African American students to integrate the junior/senior prom—this would be the first time that African Americans had even participated. Their appearance at the dance in formal attire caused a furor, but they were admitted and danced with each other. The following year, the prom once again was all white.

Higginbotham graduated from Sewickley High School in 1938 and attended Virginia State College for Negroes (renamed Virginia State College in 1946 and Virginia State University in 1979) in Petersburg, Virginia. Though he thought the "for Negroes" part of the school's name was demeaning and insulting, he attended the college because it was affordable. He majored in physics and chemistry. At the start of his junior year, he was a day late in returning to school, and his room in the newly built dormitory was given to someone else. This angered Higginbotham so much that he got his money back and boarded a train for Tennessee State University in Nashville, where a friend of his was a star athlete. Based on his friend's recommendation, he was accepted to Tennessee State and got a job in the cafeteria. He completed one year there. While in Nashville, he removed a "Whites Only" sign from a trolley car while a friend removed the "Negroes Only" sign. The following year, he worked for the Standard Spring Steel Company in Coraopolis, Pennsylvania, near Sewickley, to save money before returning to school.

In 1940, the draft was instituted. Both Higginbotham and his father (seventeen years his senior) were drafted. His father received a deferment because he worked as a riveter in the shipyards.

Mitchell Higginbotham had developed an interest in aviation in high school, when he participated in the Junior Birdmen of America, an organization of students interested in building model airplanes, and he saw this as an opportunity to fly with the Air Force. He was advised by a white veteran that in order to get into aviation, he should volunteer instead of waiting to be drafted. He learned about the aviation opportunities at Tuskegee through *The Pittsburgh Courier* and from its editor and publisher, ROBERT L. VANN, who was a friend of Higginbotham's father. In 1942, while waiting and hoping to be called by the U.S. Army Air Corps, he moved to Washington, D.C., and secured employment at the U.S. Department of Justice. There he was among the first group of African Americans to integrate the cafeteria. Later that year, he was accepted to the instructor-training program at Tuskegee. In the secondary phase of flying, he and his primary instructor, Philip Lee, had an understanding that Lee would teach him flying and Higginbotham would teach him the intricacies of playing contract bridge. The standard time to solo after flight training is ten hours—Higginbotham soloed in two and a half. Higginbotham completed his instructor training, but the program was discontinued throughout the country because the Army Air Corps had trained enough instructors. Higginbotham and fourteen others were accepted into Class 44K of cadet training. He chose to train as a bomber instead of a fighter pilot since this would later increase his chance of becoming a commercial airline pilot.

In March of 1945, Higginbotham and the 477th Medium Bombardment Group were sent to Freeman Field, an Air Force base in Seymour, Indiana. Freeman Field had two officers clubs—one for white officers and one for African American officers. The club for white officers was outfitted with games, a guesthouse, and other amenities, while the club for African Americans was clearly inferior. Higginbotham was among the African American officers who formed groups of two or three and sought entrance to the white officers' club, which was refused. Later the African American officers were asked to sign a document stating they understood Base Regulation 85-2, which effectively segregated the clubs—clearly in violation of Army Regulation 210-10 (March 1943), which forbade racial segregation on military posts. Higginbotham was one of the 104 officers who refused to sign the order; he was arrested and held in quarters. While 101 of the officers were acquitted, three were court-martialed, and Higginbotham's roommate, ROGER TERRY, was convicted.

Higginbotham was discharged from the U.S. Army Air Corps in October of 1946. He returned to Virginia State and completed his college degree, and he later completed his master's degree at the University of Colorado. The title of his master's thesis was "Labor Relations and Organizations in the Union of South Africa." He served as assistant director of industrial relations of the Pittsburgh Urban League and, in 1956, moved to Southern California where he worked with the juvenile court system.

In 1995, the Tuskegee Airmen National Convention was held in Atlanta, Georgia. Rodney Coleman, who was then secretary of the army, presented a pardon to each of the men arrested at Freeman Field.

FURTHER READING

Warren, James C. *The Tuskegee Airmen Mutiny at Freeman Field* (2001).

LISA M. BRATTON

Higgins, Bertha Grant DeLard (18 Nov. 1872?–30 Dec. 1944), suffragist and political activist, was born in Danville, Virginia, in 1872 (some sources, notably U.S. Census records, say 1874) to Alfred and Barbara Dillard. Little is known of her early life, but she received training as a dressmaker and clothing designer, studying in London and Paris as well as in the United States.

On 28 September 1898 she married William Harvey Higgins, who had recently graduated from medical school in North Carolina. They lived in New York City while he completed some additional training at Long Island Medical College, and during that period Bertha operated her own dressmaking shop. By 1903 William Higgins had opened a medical practice in Providence, Rhode Island, where he was one of the city's few black physicians. As was customary in those days, Higgins gave up her profession after the birth of the couple's first child, Prudence, in 1913. However, she had already developed an interest in politics and had begun working on issues that would benefit the black community. Higgins became active in the club-women's movement, in which middle-class women volunteered their time trying to bring about social change (Hine, 205). By 1914 she was active in the Providence Women's Suffrage Party, campaigning to get women the right to vote in Rhode Island, a right given to the state's men as early as 1870 (Terborg-Penn, 103).

In the Progressive era it was the Republican Party, the "Party of Lincoln," to which most African Americans gravitated, and Higgins was no exception. She became involved with the Julia Ward Howe State Republican Club, an organization she helped to found. She later became an incorporator of the Rhode Island League of Women Voters. She was a passionate public speaker, going out to churches and civic functions to get other black women involved and register them to vote. As society changed, Higgins was there to witness it. When Rhode Island passed a state law giving women the right to vote in presidential elections in 1917, she wrote about how proud she was that one of the first women in Providence to register was a black woman (Terborg-Penn, 143).

Once national women's suffrage had been attained with the ratification of the Nineteenth Amendment in 1920, Higgins continued her efforts to improve the quality of life for African Americans. While she and her husband were both active in the African Methodist Episcopal (AME) Church, it was political activism that remained a focal point for her. As a member of the Women's Political Study Club, she was often in contact with other prominent black women, and made sure she was informed about the causes in which they were involved. Higgins also stayed in constant touch with white politicians, whether incumbent or running for office, reminding them of the importance of policies that would help bring more jobs and show a commitment to equal opportunity. She was a confident woman with a forceful personality, and she refused to be ignored. Politicians found they would be wise to respond whenever she advocated for one of their constituents, because she would continue to write letters until her request was granted (Liberman, 6H).

Higgins became well known for her ability to turn out black female voters for Republican causes, and she regularly used this as leverage to get white politicians to take her ideas more seriously. So, given her roots in Republican politics, it was probably a shock when in 1932, the longtime party loyalist decided to make a dramatic change: she became a Democrat. It was not an easy decision. She had become increasingly disillusioned with the Republican Party as she saw fewer and fewer black women being appointed to leadership roles on state and national committees, and promises that had been made to keep black Republican women involved went unfulfilled. After so many years of faithful support and hard work, she came to feel that the Republicans were taking black voters for granted. With the same energy that she had devoted to Republican political activism, Higgins now devoted her time to Democratic causes. By 1934 she was the director of Rhode Island's Colored Democratic Women's Organization. The election year 1936 found Higgins seriously ill for several weeks during late August, but being in the hospital failed to slow her activism; she continued to help the party with her usual enthusiasm. Later that year, she served as a member of the committee that greeted President Franklin Delano Roosevelt when he visited Providence. Higgins also spoke at Democratic political rallies, explaining why she had left the Republican Party. Her talks were both eloquent and persuasive, and there is some evidence that black women who respected her joined the Democratic Party, although how many is not known. Newspaper reports say her speeches were often greeted with "a great ovation." In addition to her political work, Higgins devoted time to establishing a chapter of the Urban League to Providence, as part of her long-standing commitment to equal employment opportunities.

The remainder of the 1930s brought both joy and sorrow to Higgins. The joy was that her daughter Prudence not only graduated from college in 1936 but also became the first black social worker in Rhode Island's Department of Public Welfare. Given that Higgins had advocated for the hiring of black teachers many years earlier, such a milestone must certainly have been gratifying. But in May

1938 her husband, William, despondent and in poor health, fell to his death, a probable suicide.

Higgins remained politically active until just before her death in 1944. She was reelected head of the Colored Democratic Women several more times. Always an independent and outspoken person, she continued to challenge politicians, especially those whom she felt were not doing their part to stand up for African Americans. With such a significant heritage of activism, it is puzzling that pioneer black activists like Higgins are not as well remembered as their white counterparts. Given her tireless work in getting black women the vote, and her ongoing advocacy for black causes, perhaps one day the name of Bertha G. Higgins will be more widely known and appreciated.

FURTHER READING

Hine, Darlene Clark, ed. *Black Women in America*, 2d ed. (2005).

Liberman, Ellen. "Black Women Then and Now. Bertha Higgins: Marshaling the Black Vote," *Providence (RI) Journal-Bulletin*, 6 Mar. 1997.

"Mrs. Bertha G. Higgins: Private Funeral Held for Well-Known Negro Leader," *Providence Journal*, 3 Jan. 1946.

"Rhode Island Gets Race Social Worker," *Chicago Defender*, 1 May 1937.

Terborg-Penn, Rosalyn. *African American Women in the Struggle for the Vote, 1850–1920* (1998).

DONNA HALPER

Higgins, Billy (11 Oct. 1936–3 May 2001), jazz drummer, teacher, and community activist, was born William Higgins in Los Angeles, California, to Ann Higgins and a father whose name is not known. He began playing the drums as a child when Johnny Kirkwood, a drummer who worked with LOUIS JORDAN and DINAH WASHINGTON and who lived near Higgins, took him around to hear all the bands. Higgins later recalled, "There's always got to be somebody to show you the way, to encourage you. And he also encouraged me in how to live life. I grew up without a father, so he was kind of like a father figure" (Bennett). Higgins attended Foshay Junior High School and Jacob Riis High School, both in Los Angeles.

In 1953 Higgins joined with his schoolmate, the trumpeter DON CHERRY, to form the Jazz Messiahs, which included George Newman on piano and alto saxophone and PeeWee Williams on bass. Traveling up and down the West Coast he met the Texas-born saxophonist James Clay, who introduced him to a fellow Texan, ORNETTE COLEMAN. Higgins and Coleman began working together on a controversial approach to music, one that used a concept of melodic development known as harmolodics. They spent about three years simply rehearsing before anyone gave them a job. The performance in November 1959 of Ornette Coleman's group with Billy Higgins, Don Cherry, and Charlie Haden on bass at the Five Spot Café in New York City became a legendary jazz event, with jazz fans and critics lining up to praise or decry this new approach. The group's initial engagement of two weeks was extended to six weeks. Higgins made such an immediate impression upon his arrival in New York that he began to be in demand for recordings and performances.

Higgins worked with THELONIOUS MONK for about five months in New York, and then he returned to California until JOHN COLTRANE came to Los Angeles and offered him a job. He returned to New York in the early 1960s and worked with Coltrane, SONNY ROLLINS, and LEE MORGAN. It was during that period that Higgins became the house drummer for many of the legendary albums on Blue Note Records. He is featured on recordings by DEXTER GORDON, JACKIE MCLEAN, HANK MOBLEY, HERBIE HANCOCK, Freddie Hubbard, Donald Byrd, Bobby Hutcherson, and many others.

In the 1970s Higgins performed and recorded with Mal Waldron, CLIFFORD JORDAN, and George Coleman, and he was a leader with Bill Lee and BILL HARDMAN of the Brass Company. From 1975 until his death in 2001 Higgins toured and recorded with the Cedar Walton Trio and Quartet, led his own group, and made recordings with MILT JACKSON, Art Pepper, and J. J. JOHNSON.

In 1977 Higgins embraced Islam and took the name Hassan Ahmed Abdul Kareem. He was quoted as saying, "I needed something very strong to get out of the situation I was in." In 1989 he made the pilgrimage to Mecca, which he said was "one of the most fulfilling things that can happen to the human spirit" (Bennett).

In the 1980s Higgins continued to work with Cedar Walton, as well as recording and touring with JOE HENDERSON, Pat Metheny, David Murray, and SLIDE HAMPTON. He also performed and recorded with the Timeless All-Stars and occasionally with Ornette Coleman. In 1986 he had an acting and musical role in the Bertrand Tavernier film *Round Midnight*, starring Dexter Gordon. Higgins co-wrote the tune "Call Sheet Blues" for the soundtrack of the film and won a Grammy for the composition.

In 1989 Higgins and Kamau Daáood, a poet and a community arts activist, founded The World Stage in Leimert Park Village, the heart of Los Angeles's African American cultural community, as an educational and performance arts gallery. Initially it was formed as a loose collective of artists and arts supporters, but it grew into an organization with a schedule of public workshops and programs in music and literature, concerts, jam sessions, master classes, readings, and rehearsals. When not on the road performing, Higgins gave Monday-night drum workshops designed for young people. Many of his students went on to perform and record with the top jazz groups.

In 1996 Higgins had his first liver transplant and needed another one within twenty-four hours when the first one failed. Many jazz fans were surprised when he returned to touring and recording the following year with Ornette Coleman, Charles Lloyd, and Harold Land. In 1997 he was awarded the American Jazz Masters Fellowship from the National Endowment for the Arts and the PHINEAS NEWBORN JR. Award. Higgins was a faculty member of the UCLA Jazz Studies Program and the founder of the Annual Day of the Drum Festival, a Los Angeles event that brought together percussionists from around the world.

In 1999 the First Annual Billy Higgins Fresno State Jazz Festival was presented in Fresno, California. Four months before his death in May 2001 Higgins made his final recordings with his longtime friend and musical associate Charles Lloyd. *Which Way Is East* features duets with Lloyd and has Higgins playing central African *linga* (wooden slit-drum), North African *guimbri* (bass lute), and guitar and singing in English, Spanish, and Arabic. His final performance was in January 2001 at a benefit in Los Angeles to support his fight against liver disease. He died in Daniel Freeman Hospital in Inglewood, California, at the age of sixty-four.

Billy Higgins had four sons—Ronald, William Jr., David, and Benjamin—and two daughters, Ricky and Heidi. Details of his romantic relationships or marriages remain unknown. Charles Lloyd said of Higgins, "Billy made the world a better place. How could he smile like that with all the injustice everywhere? He was somehow able to rise above all that." One of the most recorded drummers in jazz history and known among musicians and fans as "Smiling Billy," Higgins's joy of playing music was obvious to the audience, and his drum style was noted for its understated grace and skill.

FURTHER READING
Bennett, Karen. "Billy Higgins: Time on His Hands," *The Wire* (London) 72 (Feb. 1990).

Chapman, Dale, and Andrew Berish. "Enlightening the Spirit: Billy Higgins, the World Stage, and Transforming Society through Jazz," *Echo* 2.1 (Spring 2000).

Monson, Ingrid. *Saying Something: Jazz Improvisation and Interaction* (1997).

Obituaries: *New York Times* and *Los Angeles Times*, 4 May 2001.

MAXINE GORDON

Hill, "Rabbi" David (20 Nov. 1926?–Dec. 2005), religious leader, fugitive, and political activist, was born David Hill in Nashville, Arkansas. Details of his early years are sketchy, although in interviews he claimed to have served in the navy during World War II and said that he spent many years as a civil rights activist and was persecuted by the government for it.

The government told a different version of Hill's story: it sought him because he was a con man with an arrest record dating back to the 1940s who had jumped bail after being arrested for defrauding people in several states. In 1957, for example, under the name "Reverend Frank Williams," Hill had a small church in Chicago where he claimed to be either a bishop or a minister. In reality he had never been ordained. He also won the trust of a number of Chicago residents, including at least one pastor, and then borrowed about $2,500 from them, ostensibly to invest it in a land deal. But the deal never occurred, and he never repaid the money. It was a pattern that would repeat itself at other times during Hill's life. He lived surrounded by controversy and mystery. He used multiple aliases over the years and was thought by some to be a holy man, while others regarded him as a common criminal.

Whether he had ever really been a civil rights activist before 1969, that summer Hill was thrust into the spotlight of a high-profile civil rights controversy in Cleveland, Ohio. There Ernest Hilliard, a local black minister, challenged the McDonald's hamburger chain because the company seemed unwilling to permit African Americans to become franchise owners. The Reverend Hilliard sought to purchase a franchise and enlisted the help of several men who were known as community organizers, including James A. Raplin and David Hill, who by that time was calling himself "Rabbi" and operating a small storefront church called the House of Israel. The negotiations between Hilliard and McDonald's did not go well, and to complicate matters, Hilliard was then found murdered.

Meanwhile, Hill and Raplin had become involved in Operation Black Unity, a coalition of eighteen civil rights groups, some of which had a reputation for militancy and black nationalism, while others were more moderate and diplomatic. Led by Raplin and Hill, they united to fight for economic justice in Cleveland. They organized boycotts and held pickets at various McDonald's locations. The boycotts were effective and ultimately led McDonald's to change its policies. But in September 1969 Hill and Raplin were suddenly indicted and charged with blackmail for allegedly forcing white franchise owners to sell to blacks. Both Hill and Raplin were portrayed in the conservative white press as radicals and extortionists. An all-white jury convicted both men, although witnesses testified that no intimidation had occurred. Even executives from McDonald's, while saying the boycott had hurt their business, admitted that no laws had been broken. Raplin was sent to prison, where he served twenty-seven months. He was pardoned in 1992. While awaiting an appeal in November 1971, Hill jumped bail and fled. He traveled to several countries before finally settling in Guyana, a country that had no extradition treaty with the United States.

The small nation that would become associated with another controversial religious leader, Jim Jones, now became the home of Hill's House of Israel. Hill began going by the name Rabbi Edward Emmanuel Washington and adopted a new theology similar to that of the Black Hebrew Israelites. The group's belief were based on the premise that Jesus was really a black man, as were all the original Hebrews; that white theology had tried to destroy blacks and so it must be replaced with Afrocentric theology; and that he, the rabbi, had been chosen to lead his followers during what might soon be the end times. He established a commune and expected both obedience and worship from his followers, who called him "master" and "king." They tithed to him a portion of their income, which was derived largely from the salted peanuts and banana chips the commune produced and sold. The tithes enabled "Rabbi Washington" and his wife "Queen Oba," a Guyanese woman, to live in a stately mansion. At its height, he claimed the group had 8,000 followers, although skeptics said the figure was closer to 400. To his detractors, the rabbi was just another cult leader, and a dangerous one: he had the support of Guyana's authoritarian president, Forbes Burnham, who let Hill preach his beliefs on the government's radio station. In return, Hill and his followers provided protection and support to Burnham, including suppressing dissent and clamping down on parties that opposed the government. Some of his critics even accused him of having murdered at least one of Burnham's political opponents.

For a while, Hill lived the good life in Guyana, but when Burnham died in 1985, the new government was not so charitable toward "Rabbi Washington" and his followers. Ultimately four members of the House of Israel, including Hill, were charged with manslaughter for the beating death of a former member of their church. Hill ended up serving six years in a Guyanese prison, and upon his release in 1992 he returned to the United States, accompanied by FBI agents. For reasons that remain unclear, he never served jail time in the United States and ultimately returned one more time to Guyana, where he claimed to be doing research for a book. He was never able to reestablish his former influence in Guyana, and he returned to the United States in 1997 and this time remained there. He died in Newark, New Jersey. He was reported to be seventy-seven years old.

FURTHER READING

Barbash, Fred. "Black Rabbi Symbolizes Guyana's Cult Policy," *Washington Post*, 30 Nov. 1978.
"Call Minister Confidence Man," *Chicago Defender*, 14 Feb. 1957.
Turner, Kernan. "A Black Supremacy Cult in Land Haunted by Jim Jones," *Syracuse (NY) Post-Standard*, 1 Feb. 1984.
Williams, Juan. "Ohio Fugitive Bolsters Guyana's Leader," *Washington Post*, 18 Nov. 1983.
Obituary: *Caribbean Impact*, 22 Dec. 2005.

DONNA HALPER

Hill, Abram (20 Jan. 1910–6 Oct. 1986), theatrical director and playwright, was born in Atlanta, Georgia, the son of John Hill and Minnie (maiden name unknown). His father, a fireman on the Seaboard Air Line Railroad, participated in salary protests that forced him to leave the railroad after World War I; he then became a housepainter.

Abram appeared at the Morehouse College Chapel at the age of seven but did not pursue an interest in the stage. At the age of fourteen he fell ill with a severe case of pneumonia and spent two months in a hospital. The experience inspired him to become a surgeon, and in 1925 the Hill family moved to New York City to provide Abram with more educational opportunities. He attended Theodore Roosevelt High School and graduated from DeWitt Clinton High School in 1929. Hill then spent three years working at Macy's department store as an elevator operator while taking pre-medical courses at the College of the City of New York. According to the *New York Post*, Hill also supported himself as a photographer's assistant, hotel clerk, sandhog in the Westchester water tunnel, factory worker, and delivery boy. During this time Hill began writing short stories and even a novel titled "The Crystal Casket," but these were never published. In 1932 Hill became the drama coach at both St. Philip's Protestant Church and the Abyssinian Baptist Church.

Still interested in the medical profession, Hill went to Lincoln University in Pennsylvania in 1932 to continue his education, but a drama professor, J. Newton Hill, recognized Hill's talents and allowed him to run the school's Little Theatre, for which Hill wrote and directed plays. In 1937 he received his BA, was awarded the Charles W. Conway Prize in English, and stayed on a semester as a faculty assistant in drama. During summer vacations from Lincoln, he worked as drama director for a Temporary Emergency Relief Association (TERA) at Camp Upton, Long Island, adapting plays to reflect a black worldview, and during the summers of 1935 and 1936 he acted as assistant state supervisor of the TERA camps.

After graduating from Lincoln, Hill joined the Federal Theatre Project (FTP). Assigned to work with the national director, Hallie Flanagan, in writing a Living Newspaper-style play depicting the black experience, Hill also became a censor of sorts, reviewing all plays with black characters considered for production by the FTP. Hill kept a number of plays from production that he felt presented a distorted view of black life, and his own play, *Liberty Deferred*, did not reach the stage due to the withdrawal of government funds for the project.

Despite the FTP's demise, Hill continued to write plays. In 1937 his *Hell's Half Acre* was produced both by the Unity Players in the Bronx and by Joseph Ornato. Intent on studying playwriting, Hill took courses at the New School of Social Research and did summer work in theater at Columbia and Atlanta Universities. His gifts brought him to the attention of Theresa Helburn of the Theatre Guild, who awarded Hill a scholarship to the school. At the school he and another promising playwright, Tennessee Williams, studied under John Gassner. With the end of the FTP in 1939, venues for young playwrights were scarce, so Hill tried to sell his plays in the commercial arena. While producers agreed on his talent and promise, few were willing to risk money on an unknown. Erwin Piscator, a German director, wanted to produce one of Hill's plays, but the lack of black actors made casting difficult, and the project was dropped.

Desperately trying to make a living in the theater, Hill approached the NAACP's Public Relations Council, which advised him to organize the black playwrights into a production company the civil rights organization could sponsor. Hill did so, and along with two other prominent black playwrights, THEODORE WARD and LANGSTON HUGHES, founded the Negro Playwrights' Company. Hill stayed with the venture only two months, leaving "quite brokenhearted over the Negro Playwrights' Company's lack of vision and practical planning." Hill thought the group too willing to sacrifice artistic quality for propaganda. While the group was one of the first to challenge stereotypical black representation on the stage, it disbanded after one production. That same year Hill's satire On Strivers' Row was produced by the ROSE McCLENDON Players and ran for sixteen performances.

Encouraged by this success, Hill applied to and was accepted at the Yale School of Drama, but he was unable to afford the tuition. Disappointed, he considered founding his own theater group in New York. Establishing a black theater group had been tried before, but a determined Hill studied these groups and their failures so as not to repeat them. In the spring of 1940 he gathered together other interested parties to form the American Negro Theatre (ANT). According to Hill the ANT "had no money—only enthusiasm." Hill acted as director, and FREDERICK O'NEAL, who had founded the Aldridge Players in St. Louis, became the manager. Its membership comprised both professionals and amateurs, including RUBY DEE. The ANT made its home at the 135th Street Library Theatre in the basement of the Harlem branch library with a threefold purpose: to develop art, to develop a vital black theater, and to develop pride and honor among the black community.

The first major production of the new company was Hill's On Strivers' Row, and although not a critical success, the play ran for 101 performances and came to be considered Harlem's favorite play.

The story of the racial and social issues faced by a young prizefighter trying to make it out of Harlem struck a familiar chord with Harlem audiences. The ANT produced eighteen plays over the next decade, including Henry Ephron and Phoebe Ephron's Three's a Family (1943), a show imported from Broadway that had the distinction of being the only play to run in New York simultaneously with a white and a black cast. The lack of black scripts became a problem for the new company, so Hill began to adapt established and new plays to the ANT's needs. The most important of these adaptations was Philip Yordan's Anna Lucasta, originally about Polish Americans. The play had been rejected by forty-four Broadway producers before Hill secured permission to adapt it for the ANT. It opened in June 1944 under director Harry Wagstaff Gribble and starred HILDA SIMMS, CANADA LEE, ALVIN CHILDRESS, and Earle Hyman. Billboard called the cast "excellent without exception" (June 1944).

The success of Anna Lucasta became both the apogee and the perigee in the life of the ANT. It led to a grant of $9,500 from the Rockefeller Foundation General Education Board in 1944 and another twelve thousand dollars in 1945. It also brought the ANT to the attention of the general theatergoing public. Critics praised the play, particularly for its nontraditional portrayal of the black characters. Burton Rascoe of the New York World-Telegram wrote that Anna Lucasta was important not only for the quality of the production but also because "it is not the usual white theatrical exploitation of the Negro as a ... 'colorful,' 'quaint,' or 'charming' character, but is a serious story of average human beings ... who happen to have pigmented skins." The play's success led to its transplantation to Broadway with its cast, which included Frederick O'Neal. It was equally acclaimed on Forty-seventh Street, but the ANT would not long survive the loss of O'Neal and the others.

The ANT had been founded on the principle that it was a company with no stars, but when part of the Anna Lucasta cast went to Broadway while the others stayed behind in Harlem, the company began to fall apart. The ANT, which had become known for its experimentation, now became a tryout theater for those aspiring to Broadway. In 1947 the Rockefeller grant expired, and financial difficulties settled in for the company. Hill resigned the following year. By 1950 the ANT had stopped producing plays except for the occasional variety show.

From 1951 to 1955 Hill served as director of dramatics at Lincoln University. The remainder of his life was spent teaching and writing plays. He worked as a professor of English at the New York City schools from 1957 to 1980. The best of Hill's later plays include *Power of Darkness* (1948), *Miss Mabel* (1951), and *Split Down the Middle* (1970). Hill died in New York City.

FURTHER READING

Abramson, Doris. *Negro Playwrights in the American Theatre, 1925–1959* (1959).

Bigsby, C. W. E. *A Critical Introduction to Twentieth Century American Drama*, vol. 1 (1982).

Hill, Errol, ed. *The Theatre of Black Americans* (1987).

Isaacs, Edith J. R. *The Negro in the American Theatre* (1947).

Obituary: *New York Times*, 11 Oct. 1986.

This entry is taken from the *American National Biography* and is published here with the permission of the American Council of Learned Societies.

MELISSA VICKERY-BAREFORD

Hill, Andrew (30 June 1937–20 Apr. 2007), pianist and composer, was born in Chicago. As a child he played accordion, danced, and sang on street corners. His talent was first rewarded when he won two Thanksgiving turkeys in a talent show sponsored by the *Chicago Defender*, a black newspaper that he delivered to homes in his neighborhood, including that of the pianist EARL "FATHA" HINES. As a child Hill attended the University of Chicago's experimental Laboratory School, and he began to play the piano seriously around 1950, learning blues changes from the baritone sax player Pat Patrick; within a couple of years Hill was playing in local rhythm and blues groups. He later noted that jazz was everywhere in his Chicago childhood: it was "the spiritual element that kept the community together" (Osby).

Hill made his recording debut on a 1954 Vee-Jay session with a quintet led by the bassist Dave Shipp. At this point he became interested in composition, and his playing was influenced by the pianists ART TATUM, BUD POWELL, and to a great extent THELONIOUS MONK. Hill took lessons from the Chicago bandleader William Russo and sent a composition to the classical composer Paul Hindemith at Yale University; Hindemith worked with the young Hill when he came to Chicago and on several occasions thereafter. Still short of his twentieth birthday, Hill met and often accompanied musicians like saxophonists GENE AMMONS,

Johnny Griffin, BEN WEBSTER, and CHARLIE PARKER, as well as the trumpeters ROY ELDRIDGE and MILES DAVIS. The pianist Barry Harris was a particularly important mentor who helped Hill unravel the complexities of Powell's music. By 1957 Hill was leading his own trio at Roberts' Show Lounge, and he recorded a pair of 45s for Ping Records—two trios and two quintets—with VON FREEMAN on tenor and Patrick on baritone. Hill formed another trio in 1959, recording *So in Love with the Sound of Andrew Hill* for Warwick Records with James Slaughter on drums and Malachi Favors on bass.

In 1961 Hill toured with DINAH WASHINGTON and accompanied JOHNNY HARTMAN on an album titled *Johnny Hartman and the Andrew Hill Trio*. Hill settled in New York City the same year, regularly backing the singers Hartman and Al Hibbler and working with the Johnny Griffin–Eddie Davis group. He also played with the saxophonists JACKIE McLEAN and RAHSAAN ROLAND KIRK, as well as with the trumpeter Kenny Dorham, appearing on albums by Kirk and the vibraphonist Walt Dickerson. Hill then moved to Los Angeles for six months, playing with the Lighthouse All Stars and appearing on Jimmy Woods's 1963 recording *Conflict*. It was during this time that he met and later married the organist Laverne Gillette; the two then moved back to New York City.

As his popularity grew Hill received invitations to appear on JOE HENDERSON's album *Our Thing* and on HANK MOBLEY's *No Room for Squares* (both on Blue Note, 1963). Alfred Lion produced both of these sessions and was so impressed that he signed Hill to a contract with Blue Note. Lion later commented that he had not heard such originality since first listening to Monk and HERBIE NICHOLS. Though he appeared as a sideman on recordings by Bobby Hutcherson and LEE MORGAN, Hill now embarked on a career as a leader in his own right. From 1963 to 1971 he made approximately nineteen recordings for Blue Note with varying personnel. The music revealed qualities that were to remain consistent in Hill's playing: beautiful, asymmetrical melodies and intricate harmonies set against a polyrhythmic backdrop, and angular compositions built from somber, brooding, dissonant fragments that moved beyond postbop yet stopped short of free jazz.

On *Black Fire* (1963), for instance, Henderson, the drummer ROY HAYNES, and the bassist Richard Davis were noted for their willingness to push the mainstream to its limits. *Smokestack* retained Davis and Haynes and has some of Hill's most complex compositions, like the dramatic "Wailing Wall" and "Verne," dedicated to his wife. *Judgement* (1964) substitutes Elvin Jones on drums and adds Hutcherson on vibes; the combination of piano and vibes is most beautiful in pieces like "*Siete Ocho.*" *Point of Departure* (1964) is one of Hill's harmonically and rhythmically freest albums, reflecting the addition of the young TONY WILLIAMS on drums, along with Davis, Henderson, Dorham, and the adventurous saxophonist ERIC DOLPHY. Other notable sessions include *Compulsion* (1965), a quintet that adds two African percussionists; *Grass Roots* and *Dance with Death* (both 1968); and *Lift Every Voice* (1969), a quintet with voices. Several sessions were not released at all until the 1970s or later; perhaps the best of these (from 1965 and 1970) were issued on a two-LP Blue Note album in 1975 and on *Passing Ships*, a 1969 nonet released in 2003.

Hill did not record from 1970 until late 1974, when he reemerged with a flurry of activity. He recorded trio (1974) and quartet (1975) sessions for Steeplechase Records, a trio for Inner City (1976), and a solo recital in 1979 for Artist House. In 1975 he waxed a particularly lyrical and harmonically adventurous album, *Spiral*, for Arista/Freedom that included three quintets and a duet with the altoist Lee Konitz. Hill was awarded a Smithsonian Fellowship in 1975 and toured the country as part of the Smithsonian Heritage Program.

In 1977 Hill and his wife moved to Pittsburg, California, where he continued to tour, sponsored in part by the California Arts Council. He also performed in prisons and taught in California public schools, working with emotionally troubled children. In 1980 he released two recordings for Soul Note: *Strange Serenade*, a harmonically daring trio album, and *Faces of Hope*, a solo effort. He did not record again until 1986, when he released *Shades*, a trio and quartet effort for Soul Note. Clifford Jordan on tenor sax was an ideal partner, while Rufus Reid (bass) and Ben Riley (drums) provided the supple, flexible rhythmic foundation essential to Hill's music. Hill recorded a solo album, *Verona Rag*, shortly thereafter, and it, too, shows a master at the peak of his powers. *Eternal Spirits* (Blue Note, 1989), with Hutcherson, Reid, and Riley, also included the young saxophonist Greg Osby, whose off-center alto playing proved a perfect match for the pianist's angular lines and irregular phrasing. Osby also appeared on 1990's *But Not Farewell*, a romantic, melancholy album that included a younger generation of musicians—Robin Eubanks

on trombone, Lonnie Plaxico on bass, and Cecil Brooks on drums.

Laverne died of breast cancer in 1989, and Hill retreated a bit from performance and recording. He toured England in the early 1990s and married Joanne Robinson, a dancer and dance teacher; they resettled in Portland, Oregon, where Hill taught at Portland State University. He moved to northern New Jersey in 1996, and in 1998 he formed a new sextet for a performance at the Texaco Jazz Festival. Known as the Point of Departure Band, the group reconstructed the original instrumentation of one of Hill's most famed Blue Note recordings, with Ron Horton on trumpet, Greg Tardy on reeds, Marty Ehrlich on alto sax, Scott Colley on bass, and Billy Drummond on drums. The group recorded *Dusk* for Palmetto Records the next year, an album of beautiful melodies and phrasing and shifting meters and tempos. The title piece "Dusk" is inspired by JEAN TOOMER's novel *Cane*, where dusk itself is a recurring motif.

Over the next two years Hill's performance schedule picked up; he performed a series of duets with Hutcherson, the drummer Andrew Cyrille, and the saxophonists David Murray and ARCHIE VERNON SHEPP. He played at the Chicago Jazz Festival and spent part of the summer of 1999 at an Italian artists' colony; he also recorded a life solo performance at a club in Metz, France (*Les Trinitaires*, 1998). *A Beautiful Day* (Palmetto, 2002) is a big band album recorded live at Birdland. Hill finally received long-overdue recognition when he was awarded the Jazzpar Prize in 2003. The resulting album, *The Day the World Stood Still* (2004), is an octet performance with his trio (with Colley and Waits) at the core. He released a final album for Blue Note, *Time Lines*, in 2006, an album of new compositions for quintet, and died of lung cancer on 20 April 2007 at his home in Jersey City. The Berklee College of Music awarded him a posthumous honorary doctorate on 12 May 2007.

Hill defies categorization. His music is filled with beautiful, angular melodies, shifting polyrhythms, irregular phrasing, and structured ensembles that speak to the strengths of his band members. He brings an intellectual perspective to the music that recalls the careers of MUHAL RICHARD ABRAMS, ANTHONY BRAXTON, and CECIL TAYLOR. He was well read, led university symposiums, and wrote unrecorded string quartets, brass quartets, and even an opera. His commitment to the music was illustrated by a story from the Mount Fuji–Blue Note Jazz Festival, where Hill played in August 1986. He arrived at the festival with a suitcase of new music, and two of his band members, Joe Henderson and WOODY SHAW, came to Michael Cuscuna in the wings during the performance, complaining: "This music is hard enough to play. Can you get him to stop rewriting it while we're playing it?"

FURTHER READING

Friis, Soren. "Liner Notes," trans. Paul Banks, for The Andrew Hill Jazzpar Octet +1, *The Day the World Stood Still* (2004).

Osby, Greg. "Reality Lessons," *Down Beat* 70 (Jan. 2003).

Panken, Ted. "Normally Unorthodox," *Down Beat* 68 (Jan. 2001).

Rosenthal, David H. *Hard Bop: Jazz and Black Music, 1955–1965* (1992).

Rusch, Bob. "Andrew Hill: Interview," *Cadence* 1 (Oct. 1976).

Shoemaker, Bill. "Andrew Hill: Point of Return," *Jazz Times* 30 (Aug. 2000).

RONALD P. DUFOUR

Hill, Anita Faye (30 Jul. 1956–), lawyer and educator, was born in rural Lone Tree, Okmulgee County, eastern Oklahoma, near Tulsa. Known as Faye to family and friends, she was the great-granddaughter of slaves and the youngest of thirteen children born to farmers Albert and Erma Hill. Faye grew up in the Baptist Church and remained within that congregation. An excellent student and avid reader, she attended Eram Grade School and in 1973 became the fourth child from her family to be selected as valedictorian at the local Morris High School.

In 1977 Hill earned her B.S. in psychology with honors from Oklahoma State University in Stillwater. On a National Association for the Advancement of Colored People (NAACP) scholarship, she left Oklahoma for the vastly different environment of Yale University Law School, where many classmates had enjoyed considerable financial and social advantages from birth. Graduating with her J.D. in 1980, Hill felt no shame or need to apologize about the boost that her educational ambitions received "in ways small and large, from school lunch programs to grants and loans [to] ... affirmative action .... Such programs provided me ... the opportunity to prove myself, no more, no less" (Hill 1998, p.46).

From 1980 to 1981, Hill worked for the Washington, D.C., law firm of Wald, Harkrader, & Ross. She then contemplated government service. A friend introduced her to another black Yale law graduate, CLARENCE THOMAS, then legal aide to Senator Jack Danforth (R-Missouri). President Ronald Reagan named Thomas assistant secretary, U.S. Department of Education. Although a Democrat, Hill accepted a job as his attorney-advisor because the work interested her. Appointed head of the Equal Employment Opportunity Commission (EEOC) nine months later, Thomas hired Hill as his special assistant.

According to Hill, Thomas started pressuring her for dates and initiating graphic sexual discussions she did not want three months after she started work as his aide. Because his overtures stopped and the work was meaningful to her, Hill followed Thomas to the EEOC, where he resumed the inappropriate conduct. Hill said she confided in only a few close friends about these traumatically humiliating incidents. After hospitalization for stress-related stomach pain in January 1983, she looked for another job.

Anita Hill returned to Oklahoma to be near her family. From 1983 to 1986, she taught law at Oral Roberts University in Tulsa. In 1986, she began to teach commercial and international law at the University of Oklahoma (OU) in Norman, achieving full professor in 1988 and tenure in 1990. During the summer of 1991, Hill was facing difficult treatment decisions about her benign but highly painful uterine tumors when THURGOOD MARSHALL retired from the U.S. Supreme Court and Clarence Thomas was nominated to replace him. The Senate Judiciary Committee contacted Hill after a tip about her sexual harassment allegations. Believing her word was confidential, Hill prepared a statement for them. However, her name and charges were leaked to the press. With her aging parents and many other family members around her, Hill testified publicly in October 1991 before the Committee about her allegations concerning Thomas. Vehemently denying her account, Thomas said he was being subjected to a "high-tech lynching." He was ultimately confirmed and as of 2009, remains on the Court. The Hill–Thomas hearings were carried live on radio and four television networks. They captured the nation's attention, stirring up intense considerations of race and gender. Whites often focused on who was more credible, Hill or Thomas. The hearings raised more complex issues for African Americans. Some disparaged Hill for publicly airing blacks' "dirty laundry" and undermining instead of supporting a black man's rise to power. Many questioned why white feminists so quickly donned "I Believe Anita Hill" buttons,

Anita Hill, University of Oklahoma law professor, testifying before the Senate Judiciary Committee that she was sexually harassed by Clarence Thomas (1991). (AP Images.)

suggesting this was because of sexual-predator stereotypes about black men. There were arguments over whether Hill or Thomas was a traitor to the African American community.

Black feminists and womanists mobilized the group African American Women in Defense of Ourselves. Womanism, a form of women's rights advocacy that acknowledges the concerns and contributions of black women and addresses the racial oppression of both women and men, is a term coined by black women thinkers who believed that "feminism" was a Eurocentric theory that did not consider race and gender equally. In seven black newspapers and the *New York Times*, the group defended Hill, tying attacks against her to a distinct historical context. "Black women have been sexually stereotyped as immoral, insatiable, perverse, the initiators of all sexual contacts—abusive or otherwise" (qtd. in Smitherman 1995, p.47). According to Hill, many critics felt entitled to attack her character and credibility because of sexist beliefs about single women. "[B]eing single does not exile me from my family and its values, or from African American culture. Nor … [does it] equate with the rejection of values" (qtd. in Hill and Jordan 1995, p.284).

After the hearings, Hill turned down interview requests and returned to the University of Oklahoma. Her tumors were surgically removed. She lectured widely on sexual harassment, in general rather than personal terms, and began to write on the subject. In 1993, she went to California for a sabbatical and then a year-long leave of absence. The same year, conservative pundit David Brock published *The Real Anita Hill*, galvanizing further hostility toward her. Despite her many supporters on campus, stiff opposition ended efforts to honor Hill with a professor's chair at OU. Tensions escalated after David Boren became OU president in 1994. As a U.S. Senator, Boren had voted to confirm Clarence Thomas. Hill resigned in October 1996 and spent some months at the University of California at Berkeley. She then taught law, social policy, and women's studies at Brandeis University in Waltham, Massachusetts. She stood by her allegations against Thomas in her 1998 memoir *Speaking Truth to Power*.

In 2001, David Brock recanted his attacks on Anita Hill. In his 2007 memoir *My Grandfather's Son*, Thomas continued to deny Hill's sexual harassment charges. He criticized Hill's job performance and personality and accused her of complicity with "powerful interest groups" who wielded "the age-old blunt instrument of accusing a black man of sexual misconduct" (Associated Press, 28 Sept. 2007). Hill responded, "I will not stand by silently and allow [Thomas], in his anger, to reinvent me" (Associated Press, 2 Oct. 2007). This exchange expressed persistent divisions over race and gender within the black community and among Americans in general. Yet Anita Hill, more than any other one individual, brought the often denied, cross-racial human rights issue of sexual harassment into the national consciousness.

In 2011, Hill published *Reimagining Equality: Stories of Gender, Race, and Finding Home*. The book examines the impact of the subprime-lending crisis that resulted in the loss of homes throughout the United States, but that was particularly damaging to African American and Hispanic households. Hill notes in her book evidence that subprime lenders charged black women and Latinas higher rates and fees than black or Hispanic men or whites, regardless of income.

FURTHER READING

Hill, Anita. *Speaking Truth to Power* (1998).

Hill, Anita, and Emma Coleman Jordan, eds. *Race, Gender, and Power in America: The Legacy of the Hill-Thomas Hearings* (1995).

Associated Press, "16 Years Later, Thomas Fires Back at Hill" [wire release], 28 Sept. 2008.

Associated Press, "Anita Hill: Thomas Harassment Charge True" [wire release], 2 Oct. 2007.

Kuczynski, Alex, and William Glaberson. "Thomas Book Author Says He Lied in His Attacks on Anita Hill," *New York Times*, 27 June 2001.

Morrison, Toni, ed. *Race-ing Justice, En-Gendering Power: Essays on Anita Hill, Clarence Thomas, and the Construction of Social Reality* (1992).

Smitherman, Geneva, ed. *African American Women Speak Out on Anita Hill-Clarence Thomas* (1995).

Thomas, Jo. "Anita Hill Plans to Leave Teaching Post in Oklahoma," *New York Times*, 13 Nov. 1998.

MARY KRANE DERR

Hill, Arzell "Z. Z." (30 Sept. 1935–27 April 1984), blues and soul singer, was born near Naples, Texas. He had three brothers and one sister, but nothing is known of his parents. His date of birth is often given as 1940 or 1941, as he sometimes stated those dates in interviews. He adopted "Z. Z." while performing in the Dallas area because it sounded like the first two initials of B. B. KING's name, a bluesman he admired

and wanted to emulate early in his career. His repertoire and recordings include soul and R&B, but he was most successful as a blues artist.

Hill first sang publicly in the Gethsemane Baptist Church choir and later joined a gospel quintet called the Spiritual Five, a group that performed at local churches. He graduated from high school in 1953 and subsequently moved to Dallas to live with an uncle. Continuing to sing in church, Hill began sitting in with local club musicians, including Big Bo Thomas and Frank Shelton. Performing songs popularized by B. B. King, Bobby "Blue" Bland, and LITTLE RICHARD, and occasionally the soul singers JACKIE WILSON and SAM COOKE, Hill honed his style and technique as a blues, R&B, and soul singer, showing particular skill at blues balladry.

In the early 1960s Hill's older brother Matt was an emerging record producer who owned the label M. H. Matt invited him to move to San Diego, California. While he pursued his singing career, Hill found a varied array of day jobs to support his family. His wife, Offria Lee Watson, gave birth to a daughter, Lisa, in 1960, a second daughter, Bridgette, in 1961, and a son, Arzell Jr. in 1965. He worked in the groceries and produce department at a warehouse, was a truck driver, and loaded and unloaded sugar. Encouraged by OTIS REDDING, Hill continued to sing in local clubs as well as clubs in Los Angeles. Hill made his first recordings in 1963 for his brother's San Diego–based Hill label. His debut single, "You Were Wrong," was produced by his brother (who would serve as Hill's producer for most of his career) and proved successful. The song spent a week on the pop chart and led to a contract with Kent Records in 1964. For the next four years Hill recorded several singles for Kent (most were not blues-oriented but were soul and R&B) that were poorly promoted. Working sporadically in Los Angeles clubs, Hill found success with the top thirty R&B hit "I Need Someone (To Love Me)." These early Kent singles included the adult-themed "Five Will Get You Ten" (1964), "The Right to Love" (1964), "Hey Little Girl" (1965), and "I Found Love" (1966), none of which was successful on the R&B charts. Unhappy with his treatment by Kent and his less-than-successful Kent releases, Hill left Kent in 1968, though the label continued to release his material into the early 1970s.

Hill continued to model his performance style on soul singers, but his most successful recordings were adult-oriented blues, particularly those influenced by Bobby "Blue" Bland, addressing marital infidelity. In the early 1970s Hill was poised for greater success, recording for several record labels. After Kent, Hill recorded briefly for Mankind Records, releasing *The Brand New Z. Z. Hill* in 1971. He then had a brief stint with Atlantic Records. He recorded in Muscle Shoals, where the Fame Studios were located (the studios used by a number of Stax/Volt artists as well as by ARETHA FRANKLIN for her debut recording on the Atlantic label). There he worked with Jerry "Swamp Dogg" Williams on his album *The Second Chance*. His work with Williams led to measured success. Hill also recorded for the Audrey label.

Hill continued to tour and perform live during the 1970s as he struggled to build his recording career. In 1971 he returned to his brother's Hill label and recorded the highest-charting single of his career, the blues ballad "Don't Make Me Pay for His Mistakes." (The song went to number seventeen on the R&B chart.) In 1972 Hill secured a favorable deal with United Artists and released three albums: *The Best Thing That's Happened to Me* (1972), *Keep on Loving You* (1975), and *Pure Soul*. Given better material to record from songwriters such as LAMONT DOZIER, six singles reached the R&B charts. Following two years with United Artists, Hill then signed with Columbia and recorded the albums *Let's Make a Deal* (1978) and *The Mark of Z. Z. Hill* (1979). In 1977 he achieved his greatest commercial success with the single, "Love Is So Good When You're Stealing It."

Hill continued to tour during the late 1970s to support his recording career. His major break came in 1980 when he signed with Malaco Records, a Jackson, Mississippi–based label specializing in southern soul and blues. The label keenly promoted his records and became especially successful at getting them played on black radio—during a time when blues was infrequently programmed. His singles, "Down Home Blues," "Bump and Grind," and "Blue Monday" proved especially popular. He recorded his most successful albums with Malaco: *Down Home Blues, The Rhythm and the Blues,* and *I'm a Blues Man.* Two singles from the first album, "Down Home Blues" and "Somebody Else Is Steppin' In," became blues standards. During the early 1980s Hill worked to preserve the blues tradition by choosing younger blues musicians for his band. In 1983 he won the Blues Foundation's W. C. HANDY Award for Blues Vocalist of the Year. The following year he won another Handy Award for Blues Vocalist. Sadly, just as Hill's career promised even greater success, he died in Dallas on 27 April 1984 of a blood clot resulting from injuries suffered in an automobile accident in February of that year.

FURTHER READING
Cochrane, William A. "Z. Z. Hill," *Living Blues* (Summer/Fall, 1984).
Cochrane, William A. "Z. Z. Hill in Upper Mississippi," *Living Blues* (Spring, 1984).
Miller, Debby. "I'm a Blues Man," *Rolling Stone* (29 Mar. 1984).
O'Neal, Jim. "Living Blues Interview: Z. Z. Hill," *Living Blues* (Summer/Autumn, 1982).
Obituary: *Living Blues* (Summer/Fall, 1984).

GAYLE MURCHISON

Hill, Barney (20 July 1922–25 Feb. 1969), a post office worker who gained notoriety by claiming to have been abducted by extraterrestrial aliens, was born in Newport News, Virginia, the fourth and youngest son of a shipyard worker. Family lore had it that Hill's maternal great-great grandfather was a white plantation owner. Hill's maternal great-grandmother's fair skin allowed her to live inside her father's home, where she was brought up by her aunts, even though technically she was still a slave. When she was married, her father gave her 250 acres of land, and it was on this land near Newport News that Barney Hill grew up along with his parents and an aunt and uncle, who then owned the farm.

Hill was unhappy when his family moved from Virginia to Philadelphia, Pennsylvania, where he attended high school for two years and spent a freshman year at Temple University. He found life in Philadelphia tough and a complete contrast to his previous rural life. At school Hill always fought to protect the underdog, an attitude he maintained throughout his life.

On 10 May 1941 he enlisted in the U.S. Army and served for three years. During this time he married Ruby Horn and had two children, Barney and Darrel. After the couple divorced he married Betty (Eunice Elizabeth Barrett) in 1960 and settled in her hometown, Portsmouth, New Hampshire.

Working nights at South Station post office in Boston, Massachusetts, as an assistant dispatcher meant that Barney had to commute a distance of 120 miles. He nonetheless found time to be active in civil rights issues connected with the police, housing, and the local shipyard. Active in the local branch of the National Association for the Advancement of Colored People, Hill also organized the Rockingham County Community Action Program and became its director for three years.

On 28 August 1963 he attended the March on Washington and heard MARTIN LUTHER KING JR. give his famous "I Have a Dream" speech. Hill and his wife were also active members of their local Unitarian Universalist Church in Portsmouth. On its behalf they acted as envoys to the United Nations. They also supported Lyndon Johnson's 1964 presidential campaign and were invited to his inauguration. As Betty put it, "Everybody knew Barney."

Hill claimed that his abduction experience began on the night of 19 September 1961 when he and Betty were driving back from a brief vacation in Canada. As they drove along U.S. Highway 3, he recalled, a UFO began following them. Stopping his car in the middle of the road at a place called Indian Head, Hill ran into a nearby field to get a better view of the UFO. Using binoculars, he claimed to have seen six uniformed beings working at a large control panel inside the UFO.

Fearing the occupants of the craft were going to capture him, he quickly ran back to his car. As he drove away he and his wife heard a beeping sound. They then turned onto a dirt road and drove a mile, when they experienced drowsiness and a tingling sensation. Some "men" in the road stopped them and after that they had little perception of their journey. On hearing the beeping sound again, they found themselves at Ashland, thirty-five miles south of Indian Head.

Back home in Portsmouth, New Hampshire, they reported their UFO sighting to the nearby Pease Air Force Base. After speaking to Betty and Barney, Major Paul W. Henderson submitted report No. 100-1-61 to Project Blue Book (the U.S. Air Force's UFO investigation project that ran from 1953 to 1969). In a final report dated 27 September 1963, the Project stated they probably saw the planet Jupiter.

When UFO investigators interviewed them, it became apparent that their journey took two hours longer than expected. Anxious about the reality of their experience, they made several trips to find the location of their encounter with the "men." Following the alleged encounter, Hill complained of suffering from neck pain, high blood pressure, ulcers, a ring of warts around his groin, and extreme headaches. He had also become increasingly depressed.

Betty and Barney Hill were also under several forms of stress caused by their own personal situation and problems. The most obvious factor was that they were an interracial couple who felt vulnerable to criticism for this reason alone. Hill was particularly concerned about keeping in contact with his two sons from his previous marriage and the family also had money worries.

During his trip to Canada Hill had experienced many anxious moments. He worried about being rejected by a motel because he was black. He disliked Montreal, which he found busy and confusing. The couple had little cash for motel bills and worried about the roads being blocked by an impending hurricane. "Hoodlums" stared at them in a restaurant but they turned out to be friendly. Immediately before seeing the UFO, he worried about bears coming out of the woods.

Hill attended therapy sessions for his continuing health problems. Here his amnesia regarding the missing two hours was eventually regarded as significant, and he was referred to psychiatrist and neurologist Dr. Benjamin Simon. Dr. Simon conducted hypnotic regression sessions with Betty and Barney Hill from 4 January to 27 June 1964, in which they elaborated on the details of their abduction.

Barney recalled being taken inside the UFO, where he had a physical examination inside an operating room. Semen was allegedly taken from him but this was not publicized because of embarrassment. Betty's recollection of the abduction was more detailed; unlike Barney she recalled that she had conversed with the occupants and was shown a "star map" and an alien book.

At the end of 1965 their story was leaked to newspapers and led to the publication of John Fuller's best-selling book *The Interrupted Journey* the following year. Through the encouragement of film star JAMES EARL JONES, it was made into a TV movie in 1975. *The UFO Incident* was faithful to Hill's recollections and was well received. After it was screened on TV, the movie established the image of alien abductions in popular culture that continues to this day.

Despite (and perhaps because of) numerous interviews, speculation, explanations, and a newly found celebrity status, Barney Hill never really came to terms with what he believed had been his encounter with extraterrestrial lifeforms. Eight years after the incident he died of a cerebral hemorrhage in a Portsmouth hospital.

FURTHER READING

Fuller, John G. *The Interrupted Journey: Two Lost Hours Aboard a Flying Saucer* (1966).

NIGEL WATSON

Hill, Charles Andrew (28 Apr. 1893–8 Feb. 1970), pastor and civil rights activist, was born in Detroit, Michigan, the son of Edward Hill and Mary Lance. He attended local public schools before graduating in 1914 from Cleary Business College in Yipsilanti. He also attended Moody Bible Institute in Chicago and in 1918 entered the ministry. The following year he graduated from Lincoln University near Philadelphia. Hill assisted at the Second Baptist Church and within two years he became pastor of Hartford Avenue Baptist Church, expanding it from thirty-five to several hundred congregates nearly fifty years later. He married Georgia Roberta Underwood in 1919 and began a family of eight children.

A social gospel advocate, Hill combined religious beliefs and community action during the late 1930s. He helped SNOW F. GRIGSBY pressure the Detroit Edison Company into hiring more black utility workers, and before most other ministers he helped the United Automobile Workers (UAW) organize black workers in the industry. During the early 1940s he recruited blacks for the Civil Rights Federation, served on the mayoral Inter-Racial Committee, and presided over the state conference of the National Negro Congress (NNC).

Hill came to the forefront during World War II. An advocate of Double Victory (saving democracy abroad while extending it at home), he chaired committees seeking specific redress. None proved more important than the Sojourner Truth Citizens Committee of 1942, which successfully fought for black occupancy of the federally funded defense project named after the famed abolitionist and feminist. Overseeing this biracial coalition of church, civic, and labor groups, Hill coordinated its inner circle and linked it with community leaders and rank-and-file supporters through luncheons at the Lucy Thurman YWCA and meetings among the black churches. He also contributed to the committee's newspaper, headed rallies, and led delegations to municipal, federal, and congressional offices. He advanced many of the techniques that would be used by civil rights activists in the postwar era.

Hill became popular among militants and leftists. In late 1942 he transformed the housing group into the Citizens Committee for Jobs in War Industries and, encouraged by members of Ford Local 600 and the local NNC, sought to unseat Dr. JAMES J. McCLENDON as president of the local National Association for the Advancement of Colored People (NAACP). He failed, and paid the price of losing association funding and office space

for his committee. Undaunted, he led an unsuccessful effort to bring the Fair Employment Practices Committee into Detroit for public hearings on racial discrimination in war industries in 1943. The combined pressure of his committee, labor leaders, and federal officials fostered improvements in employment. However, following the worst riot of the war, which claimed thirty-four lives and destroyed $2 million worth of property in late June, his organization, along with others, adopted less volatile strategies.

Even as the riot raged Hill sponsored a community-wide meeting with Mayor Edward J. Jeffries Jr. to criticize the police while suggesting ways to end the bloodshed. Thereafter he and others clashed with local, county, and state officials who blamed the violence on black leaders and organizations, especially the NAACP and the *Michigan Chronicle*. When the report of the Governor's Fact-Finding Committee became available, he labeled it a "white wash" of the Detroit Police Department, and he held the mayor and police commissioner responsible for having done nothing to avert the disorder. He initiated a petition for a federal grand jury probe of the outburst, unsuccessfully insisting upon it as a member of the Mayor's Peace Committee. Hill also aligned his jobs committee with other organizations in the Vote Mobilization Committee. That fall, under state senator Charles C. Diggs, it failed to spoil the re-election of Mayor Jeffries or elect a black candidate to common council.

In 1944 Hill mobilized black voters and joined unionists to deny William E. Dowling, former chair of the governor's committee, renomination as the Democratic candidate for Wayne County Prosecutor. During the following year he participated in a similar coalition that failed to elect both a former UAW official for mayor over Jeffries and new councilmen (including himself). Believing that better conditions would come "only to those who use the ballot," he ran for council and lost again in 1947, 1949, and 1951. He also fell short in special primaries for council and congressional vacancies, respectively in 1948 and 1955.

Upon the retirement of McClendon, Hill became president of the Detroit NAACP in 1946. He soon gained the reputation of being not just a poor administrator but, more troubling to executive board members in the growing reactionary climate, an advocate of communist organizations and causes. As a result he lost his election for a second term and moved even more to the left, participating in efforts to free Earl Browder, former president of the U.S. Communist Party.

By the end of the decade Hill was a target of anticommunism. In 1949 his eldest son and namesake, a decorated pilot in World War II and reserve officer, faced charges of disloyalty by the U.S. air force for having read the *Daily Worker* and assisted in the 1945 council campaign. Clearly, Hill's son was being punished for his father's politics—"guilt by relationship"—although his own appeal of the flimsy accusations did force an official apology. Still, he never flew missions again, and in 1951 his father was subpoenaed by the House Un-American Activities Committee (HUAC) to answer, among other charges, for having criticized the Korean War.

No charges were brought against the Reverend Hill, who denied ever having been a communist and continued his activism until retiring in 1968. He died shortly thereafter in Detroit, a native son who combined protest tactics, religious faith, and independent thought. A fearless coalition-builder who inspired others to act, he believed that the struggle for equality required sacrifice and assistance from everyone; like the flight of a bird, to use his own metaphor, it needed a right wing and a left wing. Indeed, his was a lifelong commitment to activism that created opportunities for more radical members of the black and white communities and promoted the ideal of a colorblind society.

FURTHER READING

Wayne State University, Michigan, has information about Hill in its collections on Labor and Urban Affairs, Civil Rights Congress of Michigan, Unionization of the Auto Industry, and its oral history collection on Blacks in the Labor Movement.

Capeci, Dominic J., Jr. *Race Relations in Wartime Detroit: The Sojourner Truth Housing Controversy of 1942* (1984).

Meier, August, and Elliott Rudwick. *Black Detroit and the Rise of the UAW* (1979).

Thomas, Richard W. *Life for Us Is What We Make It: Building Black Community in Detroit, 1915–1945* (1992).

Obituaries: *Detroit Free Press*, 10 Feb. 1970; the *Michigan Chronicle* and the *Detroit Tribune*, both 14 Feb. 1970.

This entry is taken from the *American National Biography* and is published here with the permission of the American Council of Learned Societies.

DOMINIC J. CAPECI

Hill, Chippie (15 Mar. 1905–7 May 1950), dancer and singer, was born Bertha Hill in Charleston, South Carolina, the daughter of John Hill and Ida Jones. From the age of nine she sang in church. The family moved to New York City sometime around 1918, and the following year Hill danced at Leroy's Club in Harlem in a show led by ETHEL WATERS. The owner of Leroy's nicknamed Hill "Chippie" because of her youth.

Hill toured as a singer and a dancer with the Rabbit Foot Minstrels in the early 1920s and as a featured blues singer on the Theater Owners' Booking Association circuit. In St. Louis her "wardrobe was stolen, and several nights later Chippie spotted the thief sitting in the front row. 'I knew her,' says Chippie, 'because she was wearing my best dress.' There was nothing for Chippie to do but leap off the stage in the middle of the show and attack the culprit. 'I tore that rag right off that bitch's back'" (Aurthur, 3).

Hill settled in Chicago in the mid-1920s. She participated in recording sessions with the cornetist LOUIS ARMSTRONG in November 1925 and February 1926, recording "Low Land Blues," "Trouble in Mind," and "Georgia Man." She performed at the Race Records Ball at the Chicago Coliseum in February 1926, and she also won a talent and recording contest at the coliseum. Hill commenced regular performances at the Plantation Café, where she worked with the cornetist KING OLIVER's band in August 1926, and at the Dreamland Café. In November 1926 Hill recorded "Pleadin' for the Blues," "Pratts [*sic*] City Blues," and "Lonesome Weary Blues" (again with Armstrong). Two years later she recorded "Weary Money Blues" and "Christmas Man Blues" with the pianist THOMAS ANDREW DORSEY and the guitarist TAMPA RED as well as a new version of "Trouble in Mind." In 1929 she recorded "I Ain't Gonna Do It No More" and sang at Chicago's Elite No. 2 Club before touring with the pianist LOVIE AUSTIN. That year she married John Offett; they had seven children. Hill continued to work part-time at clubs around Chicago, including engagements at the Annex Café from 1934 to 1937, the Cabin Inn with the clarinetist Jimmie Noone in 1937, and the Club DeLisa from 1939 to 1940.

During the 1940s Hill left music to devote herself to her family, but early in 1946 the writer and promoter Rudi Blesh found her in Chicago and immediately recorded nine tracks, including versions of "Trouble in Mind," "Careless Love," "How Long Blues," and "Around the Clock Blues," all with

Austin's band. Hill resumed working at the Club DeLisa from 1946 to 1947, and she participated in a jazz concert in Chicago before moving to New York, where she starred in Blesh's This Is Jazz concert at the Ziegfeld Theatre in June 1947 and on his weekly radio series This Is Jazz in July and August of that year. In late 1947 and early 1948 Hill appeared at the Village Vanguard in Greenwich Village, and she also sang at Jimmy Ryan's club in midtown.

In the spring of 1948 Hill worked with the trombonist KID ORY in a concert at Carnegie Hall, and she performed in Paris. She held engagements at New York's Central Plaza Club in 1949 and Riviera Club in 1949–1950, and she performed with the pianist Art Hodes's quintet at the Blue Note in Chicago in 1950, and again in New York at the Stuyvesant Casino in 1950. Hill's strong personality remained intact during these final years: "When she arrived in New York she slyly informed the press that she was forty-two. This year [1949] she is forty-one." Although already a grandmother, she could "outcurse and outdrink any truck driver you can dig up, and if you ever get up the nerve to ask her to dance, she'll jitterbug you into exhaustion" (Aurthur, 4). Hill died in a hit-and-run traffic accident in New York.

Like the better-known singers MA RAINEY and BESSIE SMITH, Hill emphasized a southern, African American, "down home" blues vocal style more than the mainstream mannerisms of vaudeville singing—although the latter may be heard in a song such as "Lonesome, All Alone and Blue," which she recorded with Armstrong in February 1926. Sliding blue notes abound in her work. She often moved out of her mid-range voice into a strained, piercing shout-singing; and she sometimes muffled lyrics, as in her first recording, "Low Land Blues." Of the discs from her second career in the 1940s, Blesh writes that "in these she reveals … a rhythmic shouting more forceful than will be found on any of the known records of Ma and Bessie, and a clipped, hot phrasing that barely appears in her earlier work."

FURTHER READING

Aurthur, Bob. "Let the Good Times Roll: An Impression of Chippie Hill," Playback 3 (Feb. 1950).
Blesh, Rudi. Shining Trumpets: A History of Jazz, 2d ed. (1958).
Obituary: Melody Maker, 24 June 1950.
This entry is taken from the American National Biography and is published here with the permission of the American Council of Learned Societies.

BARRY KERNFELD

Hill, Edwin Shelton (1903–19 Feb. 1993), educator and civil rights activist, was born and raised on a cattle ranch on a Choctaw reservation in Oklahoma. His father, a cowboy, and mother, a schoolteacher (whose names are not known) expected their children to work hard and pursue education as a means to a better future. The youngest of three boys, Shelly (as he preferred to be called) developed a strong work ethic on the ranch and held several campus jobs while attending college at Western University in Quindare, Kansas. During the summer, Hill worked as a Pullman porter. Hill had hopes of becoming a doctor, but medical school was too expensive, so he turned to teaching. Black teachers could only expect to find employment in the segregated South, and Hill recalled few positive memories of his early teaching experience. He became assistant principal at an all-black high school in Texas and later, in Oklahoma, principal of a junior high school.

The salary for black educators was so low that Hill was forced to supplement his income by continuing his work as a Pullman porter during school vacations. In the summer of 1925 railroad work brought Hill to Portland, Oregon, for the first time. When he became a labor recruiter for Union Pacific Railroad, he found himself returning regularly to Portland, and in 1941 decided to move there permanently with Helloise, his wife. Hill arrived in Portland as part of a major migration of black war industry workers into West Coast cities. For many Americans, World War II was a pivotal time, testing the adaptability of institutions and challenging old ideas and customs. So it was for Portland, Oregon, where the need for nontraditional sources of labor opened doors previously closed to African Americans. Black newcomers to Portland encountered prejudice and discrimination, but eventually they also significantly altered the city's employment and housing patterns.

City officials and union leaders were comfortable with a homogenous racial policy that had excluded the nonwhite population of Oregon from social and economic equality since the adoption in 1857 of the state constitution. Racial tension became more acute when, because of World War II, the city's black population grew from fewer than 2,000 to approximately 25,000, before settling permanently at just over 10,000. True to his work ethic, Hill became a leader in the fight to promote economic and social equality throughout the city.

Too old for the draft, Hill instead received a War Department appointment as an army education and recreation director assigned to the Fourth Air Force unit at Portland Air Base. "I considered myself a militant Negro," said Hill in a later interview (*Oregonian*, 10 Sept. 1963). Whenever possible, he sought out and challenged discriminatory policies and as employee relations officer became an advocate and a spokesman for minority enlistees.

The war became a catalyst for a change in race relations in Portland as African Americans flocked to the city in support of the national war effort. This influx was a great benefit to Portland's small black community. A larger, more militant population rallied behind Executive Order 8802 which, in 1941, prohibited "discrimination in the employment of workers in defense industries."

Prior to Executive Order 8802, Portland-area employment services had routinely classified all black workers as general laborers, regardless of their individual skill or training. In 1941 skilled shipyard laborers were among the highest-paid wage earners in the country. To protect these high-paying jobs, craft unions continued to discriminate against African Americans. Prior to the 1940s no black person had worked in the Portland shipyards. Pointing out that African Americans were fighting both Hitler and Jim Crow, a more confrontational black community slowly broke down some of the traditional hiring practices.

When efforts to limit black wartime employment were not entirely successful, Portland politicians and businessmen manipulated the housing market to ensure racial segregation. Black newcomers were restricted to a twenty-five-block run-down area in northeast Portland—or, when hastily built federal public housing opened, blacks were assigned to Vanport and Guilds Lake, the two designated projects that accepted black residents and were located outside the city limits.

Race relations became especially sensitive when public officials worked harder to encourage African Americans to leave the area rather than seek means of accommodation. Still, the growth of the Portland black community invigorated the local NAACP and led to the establishment of a local chapter of the Urban League. And black and white activists began to question the traditions and practices that had inhibited good race relations in Portland for many years.

On one hand, Vanport was viewed as the "Negro Project," although the percentage of black families never exceeded 25 percent. However, due to constant pressure from civil rights activists, Vanport hired the first black public school teachers and police deputies in state history. Helloise Hill taught elementary school in Vanport and eventually transferred into the public school system of Portland.

Shelly Hill helped organize the Negro Citizens Tax League of Portland (NCTLP), an organization that attacked discriminatory policies in public accommodations. In 1946 Hill was elected president of the NCTLP and launched a project to register all eligible black voters. African Americans regularly drafted civil rights bills to present at each session of the state legislature. They studied legislation already passed in states such as Washington, Minnesota, and Nebraska. The State of Oregon finally passed a comprehensive civil rights bill in 1953.

Following World War II, as the new industrial relations director for the Portland Urban League, Hill negotiated with employers for jobs previously reserved for whites. In 1946 the unemployment rate for whites was 8 percent while approximately 50 percent of blacks remaining in Portland were unemployed. And, while white war workers were retrained for clerical or sales positions, black men and women were not afforded these same opportunities.

In 1959 Hill was elected as executive director of the local Urban League chapter, a position he held until retiring in 1973. He oversaw important improvements in race relations and provided much-needed charismatic leadership in the black community. He joined the Shriners, the Elks, the City Club, and continued to work hard and fight for the rights of everyone. The governor of Oregon appointed Hill to a committee on the handicapped and he was a long-standing member of Oregon's Civil Rights Advisory Committee.

FURTHER READING
The Oregonian, 10 Sept. 1963.
The Oregonian, 14 Dec. 1973.
Pearson, Rudy. "African Americans in Portland, Oregon, 1940–1950: Work and Living Conditions—A Social History," Ph.D. diss., Washington State University (1996).

RUDY PEARSON

Hill, Elias (1819–28 Mar. 1872), minister, schoolteacher, Union League organizer, and Liberian emigrant, was born into slavery near Yorkville (later York), South Carolina, probably the son of a light-skinned house slave named Dorcas Hill and a man brought as a slave from Africa to South Carolina. At the age of seven, Hill contracted a crippling disease that he called "rheumatism," but that was probably polio. His owner's five-year-old son, Daniel Harvey Hill (the man who would later famously lose a copy of Robert E. Lee's battle plans while serving as a Confederate general at Antietam), seems to have come down with a mild case of the same disease at almost the same time. But Hill got the worst of it. He was never again able to walk. His legs shrunk to the diameter of an average man's wrist. His arms were like those of a small child. His fingers were so contracted that he could barely hold a pen. Hill's severe disabilities made him of little use as a slave. Around 1840 his father (who had bought his own freedom for $150) purchased the freedom of Hill and his mother, Dorcas, from the white Hill family.

Little is known of Hill's life before 1860, when he was listed on the census as a "deformed" freeman in a household with his mother, who was then working as a free domestic servant. After the Civil War, Hill became a leader in each of the three great fields of postwar black activism: religion, education, and politics. He had preached as a Baptist minister since at least 1861, traveling to congregations across the Piedmont with the assistance of several young nephews. Beginning with the end of the war, he taught school in a one-room schoolhouse near Yorkville. And by 1870 Hill was working as a community organizer for the York County Union League chapter. In each of these areas, Hill became known for his unusually powerful voice. It carried long distances, and observers called it "clear and sonorous," a "voice of unusual power and sweetness" (Witt, 113).

Hill's voice also helped draw the attention of the local Ku Klux Klan. The York County Klan was among the most violent in the South. In 1870 and 1871 its leader, Rufus Bratton (who served as a model for Thomas Dixon's white supremacist novel, *The Clansman*), organized a campaign of violent and deadly attacks on upcountry blacks and Republicans. Early in the morning of 6 May 1871 Bratton's Klan arrived at Hill's door. Other black men were sleeping in the woods to avoid the Klan, but Hill's disability made that impossible. The Klansmen pulled Hill out of his home and beat him, attacking him with a horsewhip and demanding that he renounce his affiliations with the Union League and the Republican Party. Thanks to men like Hill and to the efforts of the federal government, however, the Klan seemed to be in retreat by the summer and fall of 1871. In July, while still recovering from his wounds, Hill testified at a congressional hearing on the Klan, describing its campaign and

naming his attackers. That fall, President Ulysses S. Grant suspended the writ of habeas corpus across the South Carolina upcountry and sent in federal troops to restore order. Grant's attorney general, Amos Akerman, initiated a battery of arrests and prosecutions of Klansmen under new civil rights legislation enacted pursuant to the Reconstruction amendments to the U.S. Constitution. Hundreds of Klansmen were indicted by the federal authorities, and dozens were convicted. Facing what seemed like almost certain convictions, Bratton and many of his fellow Klansmen fled to Canada.

Yet in the very same months, Hill chose to leave the country, too. Beginning in April 1871 he had been corresponding with the American Colonization Society, a white Christian organization that had promoted and sometimes financed the emigration of American blacks to Liberia since its founding in 1816. It no longer seemed possible, Hill wrote to the Colonization Society, "for our people to live in this country peaceably" (Witt, 130). In Liberia, by contrast, the Colonization Society seemed to promise an independent constitutional republic (founded in 1847 by former African Americans, some of whom were former slaves) as well as twenty-five acres of land and six months of supplies to each emigrant. In November 1871 Hill and almost 200 of his fellow York County freed people departed by railroad for Virginia and from Virginia by ship to Monrovia on the Liberian coast. From there, Hill and most of the emigrants moved up the St. Paul's River to the fledgling town of Arthington, where they began to build a school and a church.

Hill's emigration began with great hope but ended in tragedy. When Hill and his fellow emigrants arrived in Liberia in December 1871, they found a republic in crisis. A violent coup in October (and the subsequent assassination of the deposed president) touched off a period of political turmoil in Liberia that lasted into the twenty-first century. Social and economic conditions in Liberia were far worse than the Colonization Society had led Hill and his fellow South Carolinians to believe. Already in chronically poor health, Hill fell ill with malaria in January 1872 and died two months later. By May, one-third of the emigrant group had died of malaria and similar ailments. By November 1872 some of the York County emigrants began to trickle back into South Carolina. Among those from Hill's company who stayed in Liberia, however, a still stranger fate awaited. In the 1870s and 1880s American Liberians were turning to a new cash crop: coffee. Two of Hill's nephews, in particular, successfully re-created many of the conditions of their native South Carolina, replete with plantation-style homes and forced labor agriculture, this time from the local indigenous people of the West Africa coast.

FURTHER READING

Elias Hill's extensive correspondence with the American Colonization Society is available in the Library of Congress's microfilm edition of the Records of the American Colonization Society, published in 1971.

Witt, John Fabian. "Elias Hill's Exodus," in *Patriots and Cosmopolitans: Hidden Histories of American Law* (2007).

JOHN FABIAN WITT

Hill, Errol (5 Aug. 1921–15 Sept. 2003), scholar, theater historian, editor, playwright, and director, was born Errol Gaston Hill in Port of Spain, Trinidad, the son of Thomas David and Lydia (Gibson) Hill. Hill's father lived away from the family throughout the boy's childhood, but his mother, a singer and actress in the local Methodist Church, strongly influenced him to pursue a theatrical career. Hill's involvement with drama took a major step forward in the mid-1940s when he co-founded, with the international actor Errol John and others, a local amateur theater group called the Whitehall Players. While writing, acting, and directing in that group, Hill developed an interest in Trinidadian carnival and steel band music. By the early 1950s, with the assistance and support of the Trinidad and Tobago Youth Council, Hill was among the first Trinidadians to air steel band music on the radio. Given the worldwide popularity of the form in ensuing decades, it is safe to say that Hill's efforts contributed significantly to the flowering of this native West Indian musical art form.

Hill took advantage of every opportunity to build upon previous knowledge and experience. Thus one of his earliest plays, *Ping Pong* (1950), is reputedly the first play ever written about a steel band (Funk, 2). Hill dedicates the play to "all those early pan-beaters who, out of adversity and in the face of opposition, created a new type of music" (Funk, 2). Given the socioeconomic hardships facing these musicians at that time, Hill's play seemed to represent, on one level, the struggle of a musical art form to survive. Hill would go on to write ten more plays during his long career, the most acclaimed of which is *Man Better Man* (1964). Most critics agree that this latter drama epitomizes Hill's effort to create a unique, authentic, Caribbean

theater, one firmly rooted in indigenous cultural mores and art. In *Man Better Man*, Hill blended West Indian vernacular, calypso music, stick fighting, and folk magic to tell a compelling story of love, heroism, artistic virtuosity, and community spirit. As Hill himself summed up later: "I can see … in the search for identity which was coming throughout the Caribbean, all the various forms, the speech and the kind of music, the sort of rhythm, the kind of movement in dance. All the things that would give us identity could be found … in the folk forms. And I went up to Jamaica … in 1953—and immediately started to investigate all the folk traditions in Jamaica and immediately started to put out Caribbean plays using Creole and English Creole and French Creole" (Hall et al., 2).

Hill's avid interest in drama and the theater was not limited to playwriting or acting. His larger mission was to identify, authenticate, and promote native art forms. By necessity his efforts in this regard became increasingly academic. In 1949 he received a two-year British Council scholarship to attend the Royal Academy of Dramatic Art in London. He was the only black student in attendance and was "required to be made up white before performances on stage with his white peers" (Funk, 2). Despite many such racial humiliations, Hill made the most of his time at the academy. He saw hundreds of productions, studied classical and Shakespearean theater, and examined the techniques of great British actors like Laurence Olivier and Richard Burton. But on his own, he also staged ethnically diverse productions, using students from the local West Indian communities as actors. After receiving his diploma in 1951 Hill worked for the BBC as a director and an actor. He was also the announcer for the arts-oriented radio program *Calling the Caribbean*, which reached audiences in the West Indies. Later he spent a short time as the stage director for an Arts Council tour of Wales and the North of England. Upon returning home in 1953 he secured a position as tutor in drama and radio at the newly established University of the West Indies, Jamaica, where he taught until 1958. During this time, on 12 August 1956, he married Grace Lucille Eunice Hope of Barbados, a teacher of dance and movement. The couple was married for forty-seven years, until the time of Hill's death. They had four children.

After winning fellowships from the Rockefeller Foundation and the Theater Guild of America (1958, 1960), Hill took a sabbatical from the University of the West Indies to study at the Yale University School of Drama. In four years at Yale he achieved both his B.A. (summa cum laude) and his MFA in theater history and playwriting. He returned to the University of the West Indies, Trinidad, in 1962, then later accepted a teaching fellowship at the University of Ibadan School of Drama in Nigeria (1965–1967). There Hill gained cultural and historical knowledge and insight that would assist him in later book publications, not the least of which was *The Cambridge Guide to African and Caribbean Theater* (1994), co-authored with Martin Banham and George Woodyard. In 1966 Hill received his DFA from Yale.

Hill returned to Trinidad in 1967 but quickly relocated to New York City, probably because the University of the West Indies drama program was small and Hill was ready for more. After one year of teaching at the City University of New York, Hill, with the help of a recommendation from one of his Yale professors and a strong curriculum vitae, secured a position as associate professor of drama at Dartmouth College in New Hampshire. Dartmouth would remain his home academic institution from 1968 until his death in 2003, a total of thirty-five years. He was promoted to full professor in 1969 and retired as emeritus professor in 1989. He was the first African American professor to receive tenure at Dartmouth, served two terms as chair of the drama department, and was the college's affirmative action officer in the early years of that program. In 1976, in recognition of his contributions to teaching, scholarship, and service, Hill was named Dartmouth's John D. Willard Professor of Drama and Oratory. The crowning accolade of his Dartmouth years came in 1991 when he received the college's Presidential Medal for Outstanding Leadership and Achievement. In a press release put out at the time of Hill's death, Dartmouth President James Wright spoke of Hill as "a leader in his academic field and a leader here at Dartmouth.... His accomplishments both in the theater and as a teacher and administrator will resonate for years to come" (*Dartmouth News*, 1).

It was during his time at Dartmouth that Hill's multifaceted talents blossomed fully. By the end of his long career he had taught more than thirteen different courses, acted in more than forty plays, directed a Summer Repertory Program for six seasons, and produced and directed over 120 classical, modern, and contemporary plays (Meryl Streep and Moses Gunn were among those whom he mentored). He was a Fulbright scholar, and he received fellowships from the Rockefeller and Guggenheim foundations and from the National Endowment for the Humanities. He authored or edited fifteen major scholarly books and periodicals, wrote twenty-five major articles on theater history or drama, wrote eleven plays, and received several major awards from professional associations for his creative and scholarly work.

Opinions vary as to which of Errol Hill's many academic publications represents his best work. Some cite his last book, *A History of African American Theatre* (winner of the 2003 Theatre Library Association's George Freedley Memorial Award), as his most important text because, in the words of the reviewer Henry Miller, it is the "first historical source book of this magnitude to be published in this field" (335). Others speak of both *The Trinidad Carnival: Mandate for a National Theatre* (1972, rev. 1997) and *The Jamaican Stage 1655–1900* (1992) as important groundbreaking studies of Caribbean theater in relation to indigenous cultural origins. Then there is the critically acclaimed and award-winning *Shakespeare in Sable: A History of Black Shakespearean Actors* (1984), a text that epitomizes the breadth of Hill's interest in theater and his commitment to documenting all types of African diaspora contributions to drama. Lastly, a number of educators and parents find Hill's 1989 compilation *Black Heroes: Seven Plays* to be his most valuable contribution. This text features plays about seven black historical figures (including HARRIET TUBMAN, PAUL ROBESON, and MARCUS GARVEY) and their heroic struggles for freedom and equality. In the introduction to the anthology Hill articulates what might be seen as the mantra for his life's work as an African American and Caribbean historian: "to identif[y] black heroes and ensur[e] that they are appropriately memorialized for present and future generations" (vii).

Opinions may differ as to which of Hill's publications is his best, but his contribution to his chosen field is clear: he was the foremost historian of African American and Caribbean theater in the latter half of the twentieth century. More broadly, his innovations in Caribbean playwriting, his research of African American and West Indian theater traditions, his research on black actors in Shakespeare, and even his distinction as the first tenured black professor at Dartmouth help to identify Hill as a trailblazer for equality and excellence in every facet of his personal and professional life.

FURTHER READING

Errol Hill's Manuscript Collection is housed at the Berry/Baker Library, Rauner Special Collections, Dartmouth College, Hanover, New Hampshire.

Funk, Ray. "Errol Hill 1921–2003," *Kaiso Newsletter* 42 (2003).

Hall, Tony, Christopher Laird, and Bruce Paddington, interviewers. "Transcript of an Interview with Errol Hill," in *Banyan* (1989). Available at http://www.pancaribbean.com/banyan/errol.htm.

Miller, Henry. "Review of *A History of African American Theater*," *African American Review* 38 (2004).

Obituaries: *Dartmouth News: News Releases*, 16 Sept. 2003; *Yale University Alumni Notes*, Nov.–Dec. 2003.

EDWARD T. WASHINGTON

Hill, Henry Aaron (30 May 1915–17 Mar. 1979), chemist and businessman, was born in St. Joseph, Missouri, the son of William Anthony Hill II, the headwaiter at a local hotel, and Kate Anna Evans. Hill attended public elementary and secondary schools in St. Joseph and graduated from Bartlett High School in 1931. After completing his first year of college at Lewis Institute in Chicago (later a part of the Illinois Institute of Technology), he attended Johnson C. Smith University, an all-black institution in Charlotte, North Carolina. He graduated in 1936 with a B.S. cum laude in Mathematics and Chemistry.

Hill spent the 1937–1938 academic year as a special student at the Massachusetts Institute of Technology. The following year he studied at the University of Chicago, where he was one of two African American graduate students in the chemistry department. While the other black student, WARREN HENRY, went on to earn a Ph.D. at Chicago (1941), Hill returned in 1939 to MIT to complete his doctoral work. The reason for this move is uncertain; it has been suggested that both Hill and Henry were in need of "work-study" assistance to carry them through the program and that the Chicago chemistry department was unwilling to support more than one African American student in this way.

Hill received a Ph.D. in Chemistry from MIT in 1942. His work was supported by fellowships from the Julius Rosenwald Fund, a private foundation with a special interest in educational and other needs of African Americans. One of his mentors at MIT was the chemist James Flack Norris, whom Hill admired for his refusal to make an issue of race. According to Hill, Norris was "the first big man whom I met who was more interested in my ability to learn chemistry than in the identity of my grandparents."

Race proved to be a barrier, however, in the search for employment. Hill's job applications were declined by forty-five companies before North Atlantic Research Corporation in Newtonville, Massachusetts, hired him onto their staff in 1942 as a research chemist in charge of organic research. This job offer coincided with offers from several other firms, all of which occurred after the United States entered World War II. "The impenetrable barrier of race prejudice," Hill wrote to the Rosenwald Fund in 1942, "has been lowered under the pressure of the war effort, and some employers are accepting Negroes in the industries as laborers and even in the so-called professional positions." At North Atlantic he helped develop water-based paints, protein fibers, rubber adhesives, surface coatings, fire-fighting foams, and several types of synthetic rubber. He became director of research in 1943 and company vice president in 1944 and held both positions until his departure in 1946 to join Dewey & Almy Chemical Company in Cambridge, Massachusetts, as a group leader in polymer research. During the war he worked for a brief period as a civilian chemist attached to the Office of Scientific Research and Development. He married the historian ADELAIDE McGUINN CROMWELL (later Gulliver) in 1943; they had one child.

In 1952 Hill cofounded National Polychemicals, Inc., a manufacturer of chemical intermediates used in elastomer and polymer production. He served as the company's assistant manager from 1952 to 1956 and vice president from 1956 to 1961, and was in charge of the company's technical operations in chemistry, engineering, research, and production. He resigned in 1961 to establish his own company, Riverside Research Laboratory, Inc., in Watertown, Massachusetts (later moved to Haverhill, Massachusetts), and was its president until his death. This enterprise provided research, development, and consulting services in the field of organic chemistry, particularly resins, rubbers, textiles, and plastics. Hill was the author of a number of related patents, including "manufacture of azodicarbonide" (1961), "barium azocarbonate as a blowing agent for high melting plastomers" (1963), and "urea-formaldehyde condensates" (1967).

A noted authority on polymer chemistry and fabric flammability, Hill was appointed in 1968 by President Lyndon B. Johnson to the National

Commission on Product Safety, on which Hill served for two years. Thereafter, the focus of his work was on product liability and product safety. He devised and conducted tests for compliance with federal, state, and local safety standards. He was a consultant on product safety to various firms and testified in court as an expert witness in product liability cases—usually on behalf of plaintiffs injured by substandard products. Hill also served in 1969 as a member of the advisory council to the Subcommittee on Consumer Affairs of the U.S. Senate Committee on Commerce. He was a member of the National Motor Vehicle Safety Advisory Council (1970–1973, 1977) and chairman of its compliance committee, as well as a member of an evaluation panel of the National Bureau of Standards (1972–1976). In this latter stage of his career, he played an integral role in the modern consumer-rights movement.

Hill was active in the American Chemical Society. First elected to office in 1958, as chairman of the membership committee of ACS's Northeastern Section, he went on to play a prominent role in regional ACS affairs and served on the national council (beginning in 1964) and board of directors (1971–1978). In line with his evolving interest in community and consumer affairs, he became involved in labor, educational, and other issues of special concern to chemists and chemical engineers. He served, for example, as chairman of ACS's Committee on Professional Relations in 1968 and established an Economic Status Subcommittee and a Division of Professional Relations within ACS. Through these programs, he helped formulate guidelines that became a widely accepted protocol of employment and termination conditions for chemists and chemical engineers; in addition, he investigated periodic mass layoffs in the chemical industry and assisted in the resolution of employment problems faced by individual ACS members. Elected president of ACS in 1976, Hill was the first African American to hold this post.

Hill became a fellow of the American Association for the Advancement of Science in 1964. Other professional affiliations included memberships in the American Association of Textile Chemists and Colorists, New York Academy of Sciences, and American Institute of Chemists. He died in Haverhill, Massachusetts.

FURTHER READING
A file on Hill's work as a graduate student, along with related career information, is in the Julius

Rosenwald Fund Archives, Special Collections Department, Fisk University, Nashville, Tennessee.
Manning, Kenneth R. "Henry C. McBay: Reflections of a Chemist," in *Henry C. McBay: A Chemical Festschrift: Proceedings of a Symposium in Honor of the First Martin Luther King, Jr., Scholar at the Massachusetts Institute of Technology*, eds. William M. Jackson and Billy Joe Evans (1994): 20.
Massie, Samuel P. "Henry A. Hill: The Second Mile," *Chemistry* 44 (Jan. 1971): 11.
Obituary: *Chemical and Engineering News* 57 (26 Mar. 1979): 6–7.

This entry is taken from the *American National Biography* and is published here with the permission of the American Council of Learned Societies.

KENNETH R. MANNING

Hill, Lethia (dates unknown), singer, is a person about whom little personal information is known. Her first name sometimes also appears as "Leitha" and "Aletha." When the Chicago Dreamland Café waiters staged a "Carnival of Joy" on 11 April 1921, the entertainers included Lethia Hill (along with the Wickliffe Ginger band, Georgia White, Elvira Johnson, Lola Jones, and Julia Rector, among others), indicating that she was a professional entertainer before that time. She opened the Chicago Paradise Gardens on 2 March 1923, but by December of that year, she and Mary Bradford were vocalists with Dago Davis's Harmony Seven at the New Entertainers Café, Kansas City. In August 1924 she recorded one single title, the "Old North State Blues," in New York for the Vocalion label, accompanied by BUBBER MILEY (cornet) and Arthur Ray (piano). In February 1925 she was in the cast of *Sunset Rays* at the Chicago Sunset (also featuring Austin & Delaney, BLANCHE DOROTHEA JONES CALLOWAY, Walter Richardson, Johnny Vigal, the "Georgia Peach Chorus," and Sammy Stewart's Famous Orchestra). She is believed to have worked at the Sunset Café until autumn 1925. In December 1925 she was a feature at the *Chicago Defender*'s Christmas Benefit Show as "Lethia Hill (Blues)." She then went on tour with Wen Talbert and His Orchestra (for a Charleston-featuring show on the Pantages circuit).

Hill returned to the Vocalion studios in October 1926 (still with the Wen Talbert Orchestra) and again in January 1927 (with the pianist Porter Grainger), but all three titles remained unissued, as well as her "Cheatin' Daddy," recorded for Okeh in February 1927 (with Porter Grainger's Four). In

November 1926 Talbert's orchestra went into a New York cabaret, after finishing the tour, and Hill soon after began an engagement at the New York Cotton Club. Her specialty there was double-entendre blues. She appeared in many Cotton Club revues over the next eight years, but also had engagements at other New York clubs, such as Connie's Inn, and at theaters such as the Lafayette. Early in 1934 she was a vocalist with the CAB CALLOWAY Orchestra and the following year with LUCKY MILLINDER's Mills Blue Rhythm Band. In August 1935 she briefly returned to Chicago, but rejoined Cab Calloway in October of that year and both appeared in the film *The Singing Kid*. After 1937 Hill worked mainly in Chicago clubs and theaters.

Hill is best remembered for her long association with the Cotton Club, alongside DUKE ELLINGTON and his orchestra. In May 1927 she had a guest appearance with the entire Cotton Club revue at the Lafayette, sharing vocal credits with Aida Ward. In *The Hot Chocolate* revue, which opened on 7 October 1928, she performed the double-entendre song "Handy Man." The *Springbirds* revue, which opened on 31 March 1929, featured her as the "Queen of the blues" (the other singers were Josephine Hall and Maud Russell). She also was in the *Blackberries* revue, which opened on 29 September 1929; and in *Blackberries of 1930*, which opened on 2 March 1930. The *Blackberries Crop of 1931*, better known as *Brown Sugar—Sweet, but Unrefined*, which opened on 28 September 1930, featured her first with the dance team of Swan & Lee in a turn titled "Scat," featuring her song "The Pussy Cat." She then performed a "Specialty Blues" and finally returned to the stage as "fallen woman," performing "Heap O'Misery," accompanied by the entire cast. In April 1931 she was recorded on stage by a German radio reporter, delivering "(Please Give Me) Something to Remember You By," accompanied by Cab Calloway's Cotton Club Band. This cut demonstrated her ability to transform a torch song normally associated with white singers into a blues-inspired, "sandpaper" black version.

FURTHER READING

Bergmeier, Horst, and Rainer E. Lotz. *Live from the Cotton Club* (with audio CD, 2003).

RAINER E. LOTZ

Hill, Mary Elliott (5 Jan. 1907–12 Feb. 1969), organic and analytical chemist, was born in South Mills, North Carolina, the daughter of Robert Elliott and Frances Bass. Little is known about the early part of her life, except that she lived with her parents and two brothers in modest circumstances. After completing elementary and secondary education, she enrolled in Virginia State College in Petersburg, where during her sophomore year, she married Carl McClellan Hill, who in addition to being an honor student at Hampton Institute was also class president and an All-America guard on the school football team. Over the course of their forty-one-year marriage the couple had three children.

In 1929 Hill received a B.S. degree from Virginia State College Laboratory School, where from 1930 to 1937 she was instructor and critic teacher in high school sciences. As critic teacher, Hill advised other staff members, mediated conflicts or disagreements related to the attainment of teaching goals, familiarized herself with the most current books and teaching ideas, and suggested in-house changes, improvements, and course additions when appropriate. At various times between 1932 and 1936, while also teaching at the laboratory school, she taught chemistry at Hampton Institute, where from 1937 to 1940 she was a full-time faculty member and associate professor of chemistry.

Recognizing the practical benefits of advanced study, Hill enrolled in the Graduate School of Arts and Sciences at the University of Pennsylvania, where in 1941 she was awarded a master of science degree in Analytical Chemistry. For the next six years she was an instructor in chemistry at Dudley High School in Greensboro, North Carolina. Until about 1950 intractable racial barriers kept blacks from finding technical employment in the chemical industry or in academia outside of black colleges and universities. In the South during Hill's day, gifted black science students who did not aspire to medicine, dentistry, or agriculture were not encouraged to seek professional careers in science. The conventional wisdom was that unless a student's ambition was to teach in an all-black school, there was no work in science. This belief derived from the well-known and widely publicized experiences of several world-class black scientists, such as the chemist PERCY LAVON JULIAN, the cell biologist ERNEST EVERETT JUST, and the chemistry textbook writer LLOYD FERGUSON. In the South, white college graduates with a doctoral degree in chemistry could choose to work in the chemical industry or to teach at either the high school or college level. For black graduate students with a similar degree, there were no such opportunities in the chemical industry, and teaching opportunities existed only in all-black high schools or colleges. If there were no vacancies in a college, the only options for the black Ph.D. were to teach high school or switch fields.

In 1944, after serving one year as an assistant professor at Bennett College in Greensboro, Hill accepted a teaching position at Tennessee A & I College, a historically black college in Nashville now known as Tennessee State University, where for the next eighteen years she was an associate professor of chemistry; in 1951 she became acting head of the chemistry department. In 1962 her husband, who was dean of Tennessee A & I's School of Arts and Sciences, accepted the position of president of Kentucky State College in Frankfort, a historically black college. Relocating with him, Hill accepted a position as professor of chemistry. With her husband, she collaborated in the writing of *General College Chemistry* (1944), a textbook which Carl Hill coauthored with Myron B. Towns, and *Experiments in Organic Chemistry* (1954), a laboratory manual; the latter volume went through four editions. As an analytical chemist on her husband's research team, she was one of the coauthors of their forty-plus published papers.

Both a skilled classroom teacher and analytical laboratory chemist, Hill preferred the classroom because she enjoyed interacting with students, from whom she always demanded excellence. On the college campuses where she taught, Hill established and supervised student-affiliate chapters of the American Chemical Society, which influenced many African American students to consider careers in science and teaching. A conservative estimate is that at least twenty of her students became college professors. Her powerful influence on students is reflected in her having been designated as one of the top six chemistry teachers in the United States and Canada by the Manufacturing Chemists Association.

Until the early 1950s, Europe, and in particular Germany, was recognized as being the center of work in theoretical and experimental organic chemistry, the thrust of which is to create entirely new substances—preferably with commercial applications—out of existing raw materials. The break in scientific communication between German and U.S. chemists during World War II caused the American chemical industry to grow, and this led in the 1950s and 1960s to the ascendance of brilliant, creative, innovative chemists. Both Mary Hill and Carl Hill were in that category. Among other innovations the Hills used ketenes, which are highly reactive chemical substances with great potential as starting materials for creating new

types of ethers, and for helping a chemist to better understand complex chemical reactions. In much of their work they used the then relatively new chemicals known as Grignard Reagents (named after the inventor, Nobel laureate Victor Grignard), which in controlled chemical reactions promote rearrangements of atoms to positions desired by the synthesis chemist and confirmed by an analytical chemist.

In her role as analytical chemist for her husband's research team, Hill pioneered efforts to create new methods, as well as to modify existing methods, of organic chemical analysis using such instruments as the ultraviolet spectrophotometer. She also established procedures for monitoring the progress of chemical reactions by determining the degree of solubility of reaction species in non-waterbased (nonaqueous) reaction systems. This ability to isolate, identify, and quantify such reaction products enabled synthesis chemists on her team, aided by the Grignard Reagents, to design new materials, including plastics.

The Hills were longtime, active members of St. Andrews Presbyterian Church in Nashville; Mary Elliott Hill was a member of the Women of St. Andrews, a church auxiliary, and also served for a time as church historian. She belonged to several professional and civic organizations, including Alpha Kappa Alpha National Honor Society, the American Chemical Society, the Tennessee Academy of Science, the National Institute of Science, and Beta Kappa Chi Sorority; she was also the assistant editor of the *Bulletin*, the Beta Kappa Chi newspaper. After moving to Frankfort, she became an active member of the Women's Circle of the South Frankfort Presbyterian Church. She died in Frankfort and was interred at Norfolk, Virginia.

FURTHER READING

Davis, Marianna, ed. *Contributions of Black Women to America* (1982).

"Many Components Equal Mary Hill," Louisville *Courier-Journal*, 11 Oct. 1963.

Sammons, Vivian Ovelton. *Blacks in Science and Medicine* (1990).

Taylor, Jacques. *The Negro in Science* (1955).

Obituaries: (Frankfort) *Kentucky State Journal*, 12 Feb. 1969; *Norfolk Virginian-Pilot*, 13 Feb. 1969.

This entry is taken from the *American National Biography* and is published here with the permission of the American Council of Learned Societies.

BILLY SCOTT

Hill, Oliver White (1 May 1907–5 Aug. 2007), NAACP attorney, politician, and civil rights activist, was born Oliver White in Richmond, Virginia, the son of William Henry White Jr. and Olivia Lewis White, both resort employees. His parents divorced in 1911, and when his mother married Joseph C. Hill, Oliver took his stepfather's last name.

Oliver Hill spent much of his youth and adolescent years in Roanoke, Virginia. For most of these years he lived with friends of his family—the Pentecosts—while his mother and stepfather lived and worked in Hot Springs, Virginia, and then in Washington, D.C. Hill went to school in Roanoke until the eighth grade, when he moved to Washington, D.C., to join his mother and stepfather. He then went to Dunbar High School there, which enjoyed a reputation for academic excellence.

Hill obtained his bachelor's and law degrees from Howard University, completing his studies in 1933. He was a close friend and classmate of THURGOOD MARSHALL, who ranked first in the class of 1933. Hill ranked second in the same class. Both Hill and Marshall studied under CHARLES HAMILTON HOUSTON, who oversaw the revitalization of Howard's law school at this time. Under Houston's guidance, the two developed a strong interest in civil rights law and grew committed to utilizing their knowledge to improve the status of African Americans. Hill also met and courted his future wife, Beresenia Walker, while in Washington. Married in 1934, the couple had one son, Oliver White Hill Jr., born in 1949. The marriage lasted until Beresenia Hill passed away in 1993.

In 1934 Hill moved back to Roanoke and began practicing law. Increasingly active in civil rights issues, he helped found the Virginia State Conference of the NAACP in 1935, the first state office of the NAACP in the nation. His private practice struggled, however, and in 1936 Hill returned to Washington to be with his wife, who was teaching in the public schools. In 1939 Hill left Washington and moved to Richmond to practice law. Almost immediately he became involved in the NAACP's equalization campaign, which sought to improve black schools in the South by forcing the southern states to make "separate but equal" a reality. Hill worked as a liaison between the NAACP and the Virginia Teachers Association, which represented the state's black educators. Coordinating his work with that of Thurgood Marshall—who had become the head of the newly created NAACP Legal Defense and Educational Fund (the "Inc. Fund") in 1939, Hill filed lawsuits around the state on behalf of teachers seeking pay equal to that of their white peers. In 1940 he became the head of the Virginia state NAACP legal staff, which made him responsible for overseeing the work of local NAACP attorneys around Virginia. Working closely with these attorneys, he expanded the NAACP's equalization campaign over the course of the decade. From teacher salaries the campaign expanded to include school facilities, transportation, and other aspects of separate but unequal educational opportunities in Virginia. The struggle also expanded geographically, throughout Virginia, and the Virginia NAACP became recognized as the national leader of the equalization campaign. The *Washington Post* once estimated that the Virginia NAACP's equalization lawsuits had forced the state of Virginia to pay nearly $50 million to correct gaps in the state's education system.

Hill served in the military toward the end of World War II and then returned to Richmond to practice law. In the meantime, his close friend SPOTTSWOOD W. ROBINSON III had established a practice with attorney Martin A. Martin. The firm, named Hill, Martin, and Robinson, would handle much of the Virginia NAACP's civil rights litigation for the next decade. In Richmond, Hill also entered into politics, running unsuccessfully for a seat in the state legislature in 1947 and winning election to the Richmond City Council in 1948, the first black to do so since 1898. He also campaigned for President Harry S. Truman in 1948 and was rewarded with an appointment to the President's Committee on Government Contracts Compliance, a predecessor of the Equal Employment Opportunity Commission. By the late 1940s Hill was also personally committed to challenging segregation in his day-to-day actions. He refused to sit in the section set aside for blacks when riding public transportation, attempted to gain service at a variety of restaurants unless he knew they did not serve blacks, and refused to join segregated organizations. These actions, of course, occasionally placed him in unsettling situations.

Following a series of important victories before the United States Supreme Court—including *McLaurin v. Oklahoma State Regents* and *Sweatt v. Painter*—in 1950 the NAACP chose to abandon its equalization campaign in favor of lawsuits directly challenging the constitutionality of segregation. In 1951, after a student strike at the black high school in Farmville, Virginia, Hill and the state NAACP filed *Davis v. County School Board of Prince Edward County, Virginia*, on behalf of local plaintiffs, arguing that segregation was unconstitutional. Hill and his law partner Spottswood Robinson prepared and argued the case in conjunction with Thurgood Marshall and the Inc. Fund. The case eventually became one of the five cases that made up the *Brown v. Board of Education* decision.

Subsequent to the historic *Brown* decision, Hill helped to develop the NAACP's implementation plans, serving as a delegate from Virginia at the May 1954 Atlanta Conference. Afterward he spoke regularly in favor of southern compliance, placing himself squarely at odds with the growing opposition movement in the region. Throughout the later 1950s, during "massive resistance," Hill and the Virginia NAACP doggedly sought to bring about school desegregation in the state. Hill delivered speeches on compliance before the state legislature and at public hearings. To help redirect Virginia's government, he again ran, unsuccessfully, for the state legislature. He also oversaw the development of new legal action, aimed at implementing the *Brown* decision in Virginia, starting in 1956. For their actions, Hill and several members of the Virginia NAACP faced regular threats and harassment from white segregationists. Shortly after the sit-ins began in February 1960, copycat protests began in Richmond. Hill served as the legal representative for participants who were arrested in Richmond, and he and his wife picketed downtown businesses.

Also in 1960 Hill campaigned for the election of John F. Kennedy and, when Kennedy assumed office, was appointed the assistant to the commissioner of the Federal Housing Administration for Intergroup Relations. Returning to Washington, he was charged with the task of helping to develop Kennedy's executive order on fair housing practices. He would remain in Washington until 1966. In that year Hill returned permanently to Richmond and reentered private practice. He retired from practicing law in 1998 but continued to read the law and advise practicing attorneys.

For his work in the realm of civil rights, Hill received a number of honors and awards. In 2000 he received the American Bar Association Medal. He had previously won the Lawyer of the Year Award from the National Bar Association in 1959 and the Simple Justice Award from the NAACP Legal Defense and Educational Fund in 1986. In 1999 he received the Presidential Medal of Freedom, the nation's highest civilian honor. In August 2007, Hill died of a heart ailment at his Richmond home.

FURTHER READING

Hill, Oliver W., Sr., with Jonathan K. Stubbs, eds. *The Big Bang: "Brown v. Board of Education" and Beyond: The Autobiography of Oliver W. Hill, Sr.* (2000).

Kluger, Richard. *Simple Justice: The History of "Brown v. Board of Education" and Black America's Struggle for Equality* (2004).

Obituary: *Washington Post*, 6 Aug. 2007.

BRIAN J. DAUGHERITY

Hill, Pete (12 Oct. 1880–Dec. 1951), baseball player, was born Preston Hill in Pittsburgh, Pennsylvania. His parents' names and details about his early years are unknown, though he reportedly was part Native American. Hill started his career with the Pittsburgh Keystones in 1899, but no statistical records are extant. He left in 1903 to join the Cuban X-Giants, a team of African American players that starred the pitcher RUBE FOSTER, the so-called father of black baseball. The club also featured second baseman Charlie Grant, who had just failed to pass with the Baltimore Orioles as an "Indian," Chief Tokahoma. That autumn the Giants won the informal black championship over the Philadelphia Giants.

The next year Hill and most of his teammates jumped to the Philadelphia Giants, winners of the unofficial 1904 championship. The Giants played mostly against white semipro outfits, occasionally facing other black teams. In two games against the Philadelphia Athletics in 1904, Hill got three hits against the future Hall of Fame pitchers Rube Waddell and Eddie Plank. For the years 1903 to 1906 only fourteen box scores have been found for games against other top black teams; in these games Hill batted .414.

In 1906 Hill and Foster moved to the Chicago Leland Giants, which played at Seventy-ninth and Wentworth. As in Philadelphia, most of their competition came from local semipro teams that often starred former and future major leaguers. In 1907 the Leland Giants reportedly won 110 games (48 in a row) and lost just 10. Hill was the star batter and center fielder, and the Giants was the best black team of its era.

The veteran catcher Frank Duncan (later JACKIE ROBINSON's first manager) recalled Hill as "a great hitter, a lot like Yogi Berra. He was built like Berra. Yogi wasn't as tall, and Pete was kind of bow-legged. Like Berra, he'd spray the ball to all fields." Added the veteran black pitcher Arthur Hardy, "He wasn't a long-ball hitter, but he was a clever base-runner.

He moved so easily that it didn't look like he was putting much effort into it. He had perfect muscular control."

In the spring of 1908 the Lelands were prosperous enough to become the first black team to hire its own private Pullman car to travel to spring training. In the winter of 1909–1910 the players sailed to Cuba, where they met the American League champion Detroit Tigers, who arrived without their star, Ty Cobb. Hill got eight hits in twenty-five at bats as his team won four of the six games. The Tigers were followed by an all-star team that included the pitchers Mordecai Brown of the Chicago Cubs and Howie Camnitz of the Pittsburgh Pirates, and the black team beat them two out of three.

Rube Foster broke with owner Frank Leland in 1910 and formed the American Giants, bringing along Hill, John Henry Lloyd, the pitcher Frank Wickware, the catcher Bruce Petway, and others. The Giants dominated black teams in the Midwest. The heavyweight boxing champion JACK JOHNSON occasionally played first base. Hill batted .522 against other Negro League teams in the few games for which there are box scores, and the American Giants claimed an overall won-lost record of 123–6.

That winter Hill and Lloyd were back in Cuba for another series of games with the Tigers; this time Cobb came along. Although the Tigers won the series, Cobb vowed never to play against blacks again and never did. The Cubans, with Hill and Lloyd in the lineup, then beat the world champion Philadelphia Athletics in three straight games. In all Hill had eight hits in twenty-seven at bats against the big leaguers; his lifetime average against major league opponents was .303.

In 1913 the Giants journeyed to the West Coast and beat the recently retired Cy Young. Based on sketchy records, Hill batted .361 that year. On another jaunt in 1914 the American Giants beat a club that included shortstop Honus Wagner. However, Hill's average for the full year fell to .231. Three more subpar years followed, his batting average falling to as low as .207 in 1917.

In 1919 Hill managed the Detroit Stars, which joined Foster's new Negro National League the following year. Hill's average shot up to .310 that year and to .391 the following year. After a year of managing the Milwaukee Bears in 1923, when he batted .326, Hill moved to Baltimore in 1924 to take over the Baltimore Black Sox in the Eastern Colored League.

Hill dropped out of big-time black baseball after the 1924 season. Details of his later life are cloudy, but he reportedly worked for the Ford Motor Company in Detroit and managed the semipro Buffalo, New York, Red Caps. He died in Buffalo.

FURTHER READING
Lester, Larry. *The Ballplayers* (1990).
This entry is taken from the *American National Biography* and is published here with the permission of the American Council of Learned Societies.

JOHN B. HOLWAY

Hill, Stephen Spencer (fl. 1849–1854), gold miner and rancher who was legally stripped of his property and liberty, was born into slavery, most likely in the early nineteenth century. Nothing is known about him, including the place of his birth or his parents' names, until 1849 when he accompanied his owner Tucker Wood from Arkansas to California.

When Wood returned to Arkansas four years later, Hill stayed in California. A document filed in the county court of Tuolumne County states that Hill bought his freedom from Wood on 1 April 1853. Almost seven months later, on 27 October 1853, Hill filed a claim to 160 acres of land at the top of a canyon on the Stanislaus River in central California, less than five miles from Sonora. The claim was recorded, and Hill began to work his land, clearing and sowing forty acres with wheat and barley. He also built a cabin to live in and planted a vegetable garden. At the same time he continued to mine for gold at Gold Spring. Mining had proved lucrative, paying for Hill's freedom and acreage, stock, and equipment for his farm, as well as ensuring later payment on more land and a cabin purchased from one James Bradley. The *Columbia Gazette* reported on 1 April 1854—one year after Hill's manumission—that "on Steve's claim … a beautiful specimen was taken out, weighing 9 ounces, pure gold."

A few days before the newspaper reported on Hill's nine-ounce nugget, Owen R. Rozier, an acquaintance of Tucker Wood, Hill's former owner, moved to the area, settling on Hill's property. After consulting with an attorney in Sonora, Rozier wrote to Wood, asking if he had freed Hill, who now prospered. If Wood had not, Rozier wrote, then Hill's property legally belonged to Wood, and Rozier asked to be appointed Wood's agent in California, with rights to reclaim Wood's property, including the land, the gold, and the person of Stephen Spencer Hill.

In 1852 California had passed the California Fugitive Slave Law, two years after the passage of the national Fugitive Slave Law of 1850. Under the California law (which was later renewed twice and eventually expired in April 1855), a slave owner was protected in his ownership of a slave for one year. The alleged slave could be seized and presented at trial but could not testify. Anyone aiding the slave, directly or indirectly, was subject to a fine of $500 and imprisonment and could be sued for civil damages by the owner.

Rozier made no secret of the letter that he had written to Wood, and Hill knew that his freedom stood in peril. On 22 July 1854 he advertised the sale of his ranch, crops, and furnishings, in his own name. The next edition of the newspaper reran the ad, but with Rozier's name as "Agent" over Hill's name.

Hill was widely respected and liked by his neighbors, who referred to him as Steve or Black Steve. In spite of the provisions of the law, Hill was advised and helped by friends. Hill fled his ranch after he was warned in advance that Rozier had received the necessary legal agency from Wood, who claimed to be Hill's owner. Hill was soon caught and imprisoned, however. Hill's certificate of manumission would have been vital evidence at Hill's hearing, but it was not found in his home.

Hills friends, including the Englishman John Jolly—who kept a diary of the events—raised the funds necessary to hire the attorney Oliver Wolcott to defend Hill. They also harvested Hill's crops and attempted to remove the stock, equipment, and furniture from his property so that Rozier could not claim or sell it. Rozier came upon Hill's ranch in the middle of this transference and identified two of the men involved: Jeremiah Connelly and William Fullam. Rozier asked for an injunction to stop any other property from being removed from the ranch until a decision was rendered about Hill's status. By the time Rozier returned with the injunction, Hill's neighbors had successfully removed Hill's belongings from his home. All that remained were two empty cabins.

Hill's supporters, all of whom were white and who called themselves the "Gold Spring boys," harassed and taunted Rozier. Samuel Van Nest goaded him to the point that Rozier struck him in the head with a revolver, which resulted in Rozier's arrest for assault and battery. When Rozier could not pay the $100 fine, he found himself incarcerated alongside Hill at the county jail. Van Nest brought a civil suit asking $1,500 damages from Rozier.

Meanwhile in late August 1854 Hill's hearing took place in the county court of Tuolumne County, in Sonora, with the county judge Leander Quint presiding. Although the exact arguments remain unknown, at the conclusion of the trial Hill was declared to be a slave. As for Rozier, he was freed after his attorney filed a confession of judgment for $200 and applied for a writ of habeas corpus.

Rozier now had the right to take Hill back to Arkansas as a slave. The legal outcome was not unexpected, so Hill's friends planned to restore to him as much of his earnings as they could and help him escape.

James Bradley, who had sold Hill land, now claimed that Hill still owed money for the property. He was awarded the land in court, but Rozier, not knowing this, sold the same land to Levi Womack. When Bradley arrived at the cabin, Womack was already there and pistol-whipped Bradley. Another charge of assault and battery resulted, and Womack was arrested. He posted bond, and the charge was at some point dropped from the court calendar. Bradley and Connelly (one of the men whom Rozier identified as removing Hill's property) purchased the land and cabins from the constable two weeks later. Rozier, once he returned Womack's payment, was unable to outbid them, possibly because of the money he already owed to Van Nest for his assault.

Rozier now had the right to take Hill back to Arkansas as a slave, and so he arranged to have Hill transported to Stockton and installed as a prisoner on the steamer *Urilda*, before he himself traveled on to San Francisco. An article in the 25 September 1854 edition of the *San Joaquin Republican* reported that Hill escaped from the steamer while it was still in Stockton. Rozier told the newspaper that Hill had escaped with $13 in cash, Rozier's gold watch, and a draft for $500. Hill was thought to be heading back to Sonora in Tuolumne County.

Where Hill ended up, and what name he lived under after escaping, is unknown. The events of 1854 can only be pieced together from scattered newspaper accounts, which may or may not be accurate, the sparse records of the Tuolumne County courts, the diary of Hill's friend John Jolly, and the family history handed down by the descendants of Owen Rozier.

Hill's was one of several court cases that tested the legal status of all blacks in the state of California, including the 1851 case of Frank in which the judge ruled that the national Fugitive Slave Law of 1850 did not apply, the 1852 case of Robert Perkins who was returned to his master, the 1855 case of Mitchell who was not to be returned to his owner, and the 1858 case of ARCHY LEE who was finally deemed free after several unsuccessful trials.

FURTHER READING
Jolly, John. *Gold Spring Diary: The Journal of John Jolly*, ed. Carlo M. De Ferrari (1966).

VICKEY KALAMBAKAL

Hill, Thomas Arnold (27 Aug. 1888–1 Aug. 1947), National Urban League executive and civil rights leader, was born in Richmond, Virginia, the son of Ruben Hill, a businessman, and Irene Hill. He attended Wayland Academy in Richmond and graduated from Virginia Union University with an AB degree in 1911. He studied economics and sociology at New York University for one year, and in 1914 he was hired as an assistant to EUGENE KINCKLE JONES of the National Urban League (NUL) in New York. In 1916 he was appointed executive secretary of the Chicago Urban League. He was an official in the National Urban League for twenty-four years. He married Sara O. Henderson and they reared two sons.

A man of immense personal and administrative skills, Hill was credited with organizing the Chicago chapter of the Urban League. He was an effective fund-raiser, impressing white philanthropists such as Julius Rosenwald, who supplied much of the Chicago chapter's funding, as a "very conservative, vigorous, educated Negro" (Spear, 170). Hill arrived in Chicago at a time of great turmoil. As one of the main destinations for African Americans migrating north, Chicago was rife with racial tensions, exploding in violent race riots in 1919. Hill worked closely with the University of Chicago sociologist Robert Park, the first president of the Chicago Urban League, to efficiently deliver social and educational services to black migrants. He also became deeply involved in the struggle between black and white workers over union membership and access to industrial jobs. Throughout his career Hill sought to upgrade the status of black workers and challenge the idea that they were fit only for menial tasks.

T. Arnold Hill was widely recognized as pro-labor, a man whose "protestations of amity toward the labor movement were genuine, rather than merely gestures to maintain good relations" (Grossman, 237). Hill was convinced that only unionization would provide black workers with economic security, a stand that was out of step at the time with many Urban League officials who put their faith in employers. At the same time, Hill remained skeptical of the intentions of labor leaders, telling a labor rally in the Chicago stockyards that "if he and his colleagues were expected to advise the colored workers to join the union, they expected the union men themselves to be fair toward [black] workers" (Grossman, 208–209).

Hill was appointed director of industrial relations in the National Urban League's New York office in 1925. During these years he worked closely with A. PHILIP RANDOLPH and JAMES WELDON JOHNSON, among others, trying to convince William Green, president of the American Federation of Labor (AFL) and the executive committee to open its doors to black workers. Hill and the Urban League never succeeded, and he finally soured on the AFL in the early 1930s when Green refused to accept the NUL's help in organizing black workers. But Hill did not abandon his effort to open up unions to black workers.

In 1933 Hill was appointed acting executive secretary of the NUL, replacing Jones, who had been appointed to a position in the Department of Commerce. He held this position until 1936 when Jones returned. Hill was a severe critic of the New Deal, writing in 1936 that "the Negro remains the most forgotten man in a program planned to deal new cards to millions of workers neglected and exploited in the shuffle between labor and capital" (Hill, "The Plight," 40). Because of the exclusion of blacks from the New Deal and the desperate circumstances of black workers in the 1930s, Hill took a militant turn and lobbied for changes in New Deal policies while putting the NUL behind the drive to unionize workers.

Hill was an ever-present figure in New Deal offices and on Capitol Hill during the 1930s. In order to fight discrimination in New Deal programs, he believed that African Americans should seek positions inside the Roosevelt administration or get on key planning committees. Although he did not have a position in the administration until the late 1930s, when he was appointed to the National Youth Administration, Hill was well connected with key administrators and Eleanor Roosevelt. He was one of the more astute observers of the combined effects of the Depression and white racism on black workers, and he used his access to try to convince New Deal administrators of the need for antidiscrimination policies and to help black workers and sharecroppers find work. In 1934 Hill testified before Congress, telling the Senate Committee on Education and Labor that as written the bill would allow unions to discriminate and exclude black workers from the benefits of unionization. He also fought hard to open up Works Progress Administration (WPA) jobs to black workers.

Hill became convinced that administrators and politicians would listen only if black workers were mobilized. To this end he launched Workers Councils in 1934, a nationwide grassroots effort by the NUL to persuade skeptical black workers to join unions. The Workers Councils were based on the idea of "self-determination," reflecting Hill's belief that it would be hard to ignore the voices of 5 million organized workers. Hill appointed Lester Granger to set up the Workers Councils, but it remains unclear how effective the councils were in convincing black workers to join unions. These actions put the NUL squarely on the side of organized labor in the 1930s. In addition to trying to convince black workers of the benefits of an alliance with white workers, Hill reached out to the Congress of Industrial Organizations (CIO), which was far more receptive to organizing blacks than the AFL.

Hill resigned from the NUL in 1940 after an acrimonious split with his mentor, Eugene Jones. The two men had a falling-out over strategy—Hill saw the future of the NUL in mobilizing African Americans while Jones remained committed to building relations with white elites—and a struggle for control of the NUL. From 1940 to 1942 Hill served as the assistant director of the National Youth Administration, but he continued to press for antidiscrimination policies.

T. Arnold Hill was an indefatigable advocate for black workers. He was part of a group of black leaders who believed that the future for African Americans lay with the labor movement, and he dedicated his life to improving the economic status of black workers. He was legitimately described as a "champion of equal rights for Negro in industry" in his obituary. But he was also a skilled administrator and an articulate observer of the condition of black workers in the 1930s. His writings on black labor during the New Deal continue to be worth reading.

FURTHER READING

Brooks, Lester, and Parris Guichard. *Blacks in the City* (1971).
Grossman, James R. *Land of Hope: Chicago, Black Southerners, and the Great Migration* (1991).
Hill, T. Arnold. *The Negro and Economic Reconstruction* (1937).
Hill, T. Arnold. "The Plight of the Negro Industrial Worker," *Journal of Negro Education* 5 (1936): 40–47.
Spear, Allan H. *Black Chicago: The Making of a Negro Ghetto* (1967).
Obituary: *New York Times*, 4 Aug. 1947.

MICHAEL K. BROWN

Hilliard, David (15 May 1942–), political activist, chief of staff of the Black Panther Party, and cofounder of the HUEY P. NEWTON Foundation, was born in Rockville, Alabama, the twelfth and last child of Lela Williams, a farmer from a respected family in Rockville, and Lee Hilliard, a hardworking manual laborer. Growing up in the rural South, Hilliard received his formal education in a one-room schoolhouse and a more practical guide to life from his siblings. The Hilliards worked tirelessly to shield their children from hunger, poverty, and the manifestations of Jim Crow, teaching them the communal ideas and values that would prove integral to David's later work as an activist. David struggled to find his niche while growing up. His family relocated to California while he was still young as part of the wave of Gulf Coast migrants searching for better opportunities. In Oakland, the fusion of multiracialism, militant trade unionism, and Western American culture offered new experiences as it shaped his outlook and perception of the world.

The poverty, unemployment, and economic instability of his youth left Hilliard disillusioned with his surroundings. He repeatedly changed jobs throughout his early twenties as he rejected racism from employers and asserted his dignity. During his quest for self-discovery, he fell in love with and married his girlfriend, Patricia Parks, in 1959. Together they reared three children. Hilliard's life changed during the mid-1960s when he read the autobiography of the former Nation of Islam leader MALCOLM X. Hilliard gained a better understanding of his feelings of purposelessness, isolation, and rage concerning the wretched social realities facing African Americans. The autobiography gave him insights to urban America and the raging protests that burned U.S. cities throughout the decade. He was intrigued when his friend Huey Newton shared plans to create an organization—the Black Panther Party—that would promote education, politics, and social reform supported by a philosophy of self-defense.

Hilliard joined the Black Panther Party as a full-time member shortly after its founding in 1966.

Although he initially hesitated to join because of the high risks involved in activities like community police patrols, Hilliard soon recognized their value and the security they offered in the community. He became captain of National Headquarters and later chief of staff with responsibilities over administrative duties, political education classes, programs such as the party's newspaper, *The Black Panther*, and new chapters. He also served as the party's national and international spokesperson. His wife worked as the party's financial secretary, their children actively participated in Panther activities, and party business became an integral part of their household.

Hilliard encountered serious trouble in the days following the 1968 assassination of Dr. MARTIN LUTHER KING JR. He and other members of the leadership debated how the party should respond to this event. While Hilliard favored a peaceful response, the majority wanted to make a statement by ambushing the police. The plan failed and both sides suffered fatalities. This shootout was only one of numerous hostile encounters between Panthers and law enforcement agencies. Police profiled and arrested Hilliard on dubious charges, including allegations that he had threatened to kill President Nixon in 1969 when he criticized him in a speech. Though the courts dropped most of the charges, he served four years between San Quentin and Folsom State prisons for his involvement in the 1968 shootout. Hilliard's misfortune multiplied during his incarceration. Though he strived to be a model prisoner, the staff consistently denied him proper medical treatment before transferring him to the Vacaville medical facility. Furthermore, the FBI and police incessantly harassed him. At the beginning, he received tremendous support as Panthers attended court and sponsored a David Hilliard Free Shoes program to publicize his case. Party support wavered after his sentencing, however, and communication with the leadership and general body deteriorated as the Panthers fragmented under the chaos created by the FBI's counterintelligence program (Cointelpro). While Hilliard was imprisoned for his activities as a Panther, Newton expelled him from the Party.

After his release in 1974, Hilliard had difficulty adjusting to life without the Panthers. He longed to return to the party he used to know and sought out many former Panthers, including Newton. Their rejection forced him to search for other outlets that would allow him to use the skills he developed as an activist. None of his jobs as a Union Field Representative for Service Employees, a dockworker, or an unskilled laborer offered him the fulfillment of party work. Unable to cope with financial constraints, poor employment opportunities, and the void the party left in his life, he resorted to self-destructive patterns of drug and alcohol abuse that left a long trail of burned bridges. After years of addiction and misery, he struggled to rehabilitate and reconstruct his life. Following his second and final recovery in the mid-eighties, Hilliard's commitment to the Panthers and its principles regained significance in his life. Though his membership in the Panthers occupied a relatively short space of time in his life, it remained a central influence in his activism and scholarship. In 1993, he published his autobiography *This Side of Glory*. He continued working on projects dedicated to the legacy of the Panthers throughout the 1990s and into the twenty-first century including biographical and edited works of the party and its leadership, Black Panther tours, and founding and directing the Dr. Huey P. Newton Foundation, a non-profit organization for social change. He also spent time teaching and lecturing throughout the United States in an effort to preserve the memory and legacy of the Black Panther Party.

FURTHER READING

The Dr. Huey P. Newton Foundation, Inc., Collection is housed in the Department of Special Collections in the Cecil H. Green Library at Stanford University in Palo Alto, California.

Hilliard, David, and Lewis Cole. *This Side of Glory: The Autobiography of David Hilliard and the Story of the Black Panther Party* (1993).

S. SHERRIE TARTT

Hilton, Alfred B. (?–21 Oct. 1864), Civil War soldier and Medal of Honor recipient, was born in Harford County, Maryland. The personal details of his life are unknown, but he was likely a slave before the Civil War began. By 1863 thousands of slaves had fled to the Union army lines seeking their freedom from Southern masters. Their situation in legal limbo, they gained the name "contrabands," as opposed to freemen and -women, as soon as they began appearing in Union lines and were settled in hundreds of regional camps. Many of them, men and women, were employed by the Union Army, not as soldiers, but as laborers building fortifications, stevedores, wagoneers, spies, scouts, guides, cooks, and laundresses. A number of men, such as ROBERT SMALLS, knew well the waters of their native areas and were employed as pilots. The use of blacks as soldiers would not come until midway through the war. While the use of black troops was authorized by the Emancipation Proclamation, the process worked slowly, and not until after the July 1863 battle at Fort Wagner, South Carolina, did the War Department become fully convinced of the efficacy of black troops. Several black regiments had been formed much earlier with tentative War Department approval. These included the First and Second Kansas Colored Volunteers, the former bloodied in battle on the Osage River in Missouri in October 1862; the First Regiment Louisiana Native Guards, also known as the Chasseurs d'Afrique, formed in September 1862 and employed in guarding forts, bridges, and railroads along the Mississippi River; and the First South Carolina Volunteers, which began to form in the summer of 1862 without War Department or congressional approval. Despite the fact that these units performed admirably, the Union refused to muster them as part of the regular army. It was not until the example of the 54th Massachusetts Regiment—authorized in February 1863 under Governor John A. Andrew—that the rest of the North would follow suit.

Given his likely background, Hilton surely knew the lines from an old Negro spiritual that declared "They say the people shall be free, there's a better day a-coming, Oh, sound the Jubilee" (Quarles, 163). Soon enough he would not only become free but would also begin to fight for the freedom of others. How Hilton came to join the Fourth U.S. Colored Troop (USCT) Regiment, organized in Baltimore beginning in July 1863, is uncertain. Perhaps he was a contraband in a Union camp awaiting just such an opportunity, or maybe he was recruited by one of the many agents that scoured the border states encouraging blacks to join the army. Either way, he would be one of the nearly 9,000 blacks from Maryland who would serve in the Union army during the war.

Likely enlisting as a private in the summer of 1863, Hilton was later promoted to the rank of color sergeant in Company H, in charge of carrying the American flag when his regiment went into battle. This is a sure sign of both his soldierly skills as well as his devotion to duty, and he likely was the color sergeant when the 4th USCT fought at Petersburg Heights in its first real battlefield test in June 1864. By late September 1864 Hilton and the men of the 4th USCT, including his fellow sergeant CHRISTIAN ABRAHAM FLEETWOOD and Private CHARLES VEALE, were stationed opposite the Confederate line of fortifications, just south of Richmond at New Market Heights as part of General Benjamin F. Butler's Army of the James. On 29 September the regiment and several other USCT units were assigned the task of capturing Fort Harrison, a key point in the Confederate line. The capture of three other forts was also the objective of the Union army, and the subsequent Battle of New Market Heights would last for two days and cost the Union 5,000 casualties. However, while the battle turned out to be indecisive, with only one fort captured in the heavy fighting, the bulk of the glory in this battle was achieved by the men of the USCT regiments; their capture of Fort Harrison at heavy cost would prove once and for all the capability and courage of black troops in battle.

In the fighting at New Market Heights, at least fifteen black soldiers were credited for gallantry in battle by their commanding officers in four different USCT regiments, including Hilton, Fleetwood, and Veale of the 4th USCT, and fourteen of these men would receive the Medal of Honor, including Hilton. In a letter to his men of the Army of the James dated 11 October 1864, General Butler cited the deeds of many of his black soldiers who fought with valor at New Market Heights. Of Alfred Hilton, he stated that "the bearer of the national colors, when the color sergeant with the regimental standard fell beside him, seized the standard, and struggled forward with both colors, until disabled by a severe wound at the enemy's inner line of abatis, and when on the ground he showed that his thoughts were for the colors and not for himself" (*Official Records*, 169). Severely wounded in battle, Hilton did not long survive, succumbing to his wounds on 21 October 1864 at a Union hospital. He was subsequently buried at the Hampton National Cemetery in Hampton, Virginia. Butler had previously recognized Hilton for his valor, honoring him with "a special medal for gallantry," as well as promoting him to first sergeant (*Official Records*, 169). The "special medal" that Hilton first received was the Colored Troop Medal, later known as the Butler Medal, a silver medal authorized by Benjamin Butler and inspired specifically by the Battle of New Market Heights. However, even after his death, Hilton was not forgotten; nearly six months later, on 6 April 1865, he was honored posthumously with the Medal of Honor.

FURTHER READING

Civil War Medal of Honor Recipients. "Medal of Honor Citations," available online at http://www.army.mil/cmh/mohciv.htm.

Quarles, Benjamin Arthur. *The Negro in the Civil War* (1989).

United States Government Printing Office. *The War of the Rebellion: Official Records of the Union and Confederate Armies* (1893).

GLENN ALLEN KNOBLOCK

Hilton, John Telemachus (Apr. 1801–5 Mar. 1864), abolitionist, civil rights activist, and community leader, was born in Pennsylvania. Almost nothing is known of his parents and early life. He relocated to Boston by the mid-1820s and established himself as a hairdresser, a trade that he would pursue most of his life. In 1825 he married the Bostonian Lavinia F. Ames. The couple had six children over the next dozen years: an unnamed daughter who died in 1826, Lucretia (b. 1828), Louisa (b. 1829), John W. (b. 1831), Henry (b. 1834), and Thomas (b. 1837).

In addition to plying his trade and raising a family, Hilton established himself as a leader in Boston's black community by the late 1820s. He joined the African Baptist Church and became a protégé of the Reverend THOMAS PAUL, the congregation's pastor. With Paul's guidance, he served as a lay leader and often represented the congregation at meetings of the Boston Baptist Association. He also joined the local African Freemasonic Lodge 459, becoming its grand master in 1827. Under his aggressive leadership, Lodge 459 soon declared its independence from white Masonic lodges and established itself as the Grand Lodge for PRINCE HALL Freemasonry in North America. In 1826 he joined other local activists in founding the Massachusetts General Colored Association, the first organization created by African Americans in the North to openly fight for emancipation and equal rights. Later, in the 1830s, he embraced community efforts at moral reform and intellectual improvement, serving as the first president (1838) of the Adelphic Union Library Association and as secretary of the Infant School Association. He was also a prominent figure in the New England Colored Temperance Society.

When William Lloyd Garrison launched the weekly journal known as the *Liberator* in 1831—signaling the start of a new, more militant antislavery movement—Hilton became one of the first African Americans to rally to his side. This began a long working relationship between the two men. Hilton often spoke at local and regional antislavery meetings and served as president of the Colored Liberator Aiding Association, which generated the crucial funds necessary to support the journal in its early years. Like Garrison, he vehemently opposed the American Colonization Society's efforts to relocate African Americans to Liberia on the African continent and led meetings to generate local black opposition to the organization's policies. He organized and presided over receptions for well-known antislavery figures, First of August celebrations to commemorate the end of slavery in the British Empire, and black conventions called to fight for civil rights. For many years Hilton served as the only black member of the board of managers of the Massachusetts Anti-Slavery Society.

Frustrated by the lack of progress in attaining civil rights for black people, Hilton briefly joined an effort to settle free blacks in British Guiana in 1840. He acted as a recruiting agent for the colonial government, trying to persuade other African Americans to become migrants. After abandoning that venture, he focused his energies on pushing for racial integration in local public institutions. He publicly protested segregation and other discrimination found in the churches of Boston and Cambridge. Hilton remained loyal to Garrison and his militant, interracial brand of abolitionism, even after a schism over political involvement, women's rights, and other issues. In 1844 he joined WILLIAM COOPER NELL and Jonas Clark, two other local black activists, to organize a campaign to integrate public education in Boston. The lengthy campaign employed boycotts, petition campaigns, and legal challenges—finally achieving success in 1855 when the Massachusetts legislature prohibited racially segregated schools. Hilton even moved to Cambridge for a few years during the campaign in order to enroll his children in the town's integrated schools. When an attempt was made to establish a racially separate antislavery organization in Boston in 1848, he successfully fought it. He continued to participate in antislavery meetings, helped to operate an employment service for working-class blacks out of the *Liberator* office, and defended Garrison and the *Liberator* against critics inside and outside of the antislavery movement. On occasion, he contributed antislavery essays to the *Liberty Bell*, an annual giftbook published by Massachusetts abolitionists. His wife, Lavinia, often joined in his antislavery work.

Hilton continued to play a prominent role in the community affairs of black Boston in the 1850s. He was one of the few African American members of the Boston Vigilance Committee, which was organized to aid and protect runaway slaves against enforcement of the Fugitive Slave Act of 1850. He frequently chaired community meetings and represented local blacks on the Massachusetts State Council of the Colored People (1854) and at the New England Colored Citizens' Convention (1859)—both were organizations committed to the struggle for equal rights. He remained a respected public figure into his final years.

Hilton died of hepatitis on 5 March 1864 in Brighton, Massachusetts, but he lived long enough to see slavery's death in the South. Upon his death, the *Liberator* noted on 18 March 1864 that "his mental and moral excellencies won for him a prominence among those identified with him by complexion and condition.... He was one of the first colored Americans to greet the Anti-Slavery movement, which received, to his last day, the most devoted, unwavering affection and support.... Whether in promotion of Equal School Rights or other branches of the Anti-Slavery reform, he was unsparing of those who deserved rebuke."

FURTHER READING

Dorman, Franklin A. *Twenty Families of Color in Massachusetts, 1742–1998* (1998).

Hinks, Peter P. *To Awaken My Afflicted Brethren: David Walker and the Problem of Antebellum Slave Resistance* (1997).

Horton, James Oliver, and Lois E. Horton. *Black Bostonians: Family Life and Community Struggle in the Antebellum North* (1979).

Ripley, C. Peter et al., eds. *The Black Abolitionist Papers, 1830–1865*, 5 vols. (1985–1992).

ROY E. FINKENBINE

Hilton, Lavinia F. (18 Apr. 1803–1 Nov. 1882), abolitionist and singer, was born Lavinia (sometimes Lavina) F. Ames in Andover, Massachusetts, to Prince and Eunice (Russ) Ames. Nothing else is known about her early life except that the U.S. census listed her as a mulatto. She married the abolitionist leader John T. Hilton on 31 October 1825. The couple had six children—one died an infant in 1826—Lucretia, Louisa, John W., Henry, and Thomas B. She was active in Boston's African Baptist Church and in April 1833 performed a vocal solo in a concert held in the church by the Baptist Singing Society. While her husband achieved fame as an abolitionist leader and grand master of the Prince Hall Freemason lodge number 459 in Boston, Lavinia pursued her own antislavery work—a contribution that has been largely overlooked by historians.

In April 1833, while her husband helped form a gentleman's temperance society, Lavinia Hilton worked with Susan Paul and others to organize an equivalent ladies' organization, of which she became the treasurer. Throughout the nineteenth century, temperance played a central role in black communities. While at first serving as a badge of respectability, intended to prove black worth to skeptical whites, temperance, by the 1840s, became a vital component of the black abolitionist movement. Rather than a symbolic means to gain white approval and counter racist stereotypes of African Americans, temperance became crucial to blacks for what it did to improve black community life and assert black independence. As the Philadelphia black abolitionist Jacob C. White Jr. asserted, temperance would help secure "our liberties, and our rights" which depended upon black leaders to "fight their battles and contend with our enemies for our rights" (Yacovone, p. 297). As a member of the Boston Female Anti-Slavery Society, Hilton helped organize many antislavery fairs. But her reform work in March 1839 catapulted her into the forefront of radical abolitionism in Boston. She joined with over seventy other Boston women to denounce the commonwealth's antimiscegenation laws. With elite white women like Ann Phillips, Helen E. Garrison, Maria Weston Chapman, and Louisa M. Sewall, Hilton repudiated the state's laws that barred intermarriage as an insult to "all who profess to reverence the law of God, or to regard the rights and dignity of human nature." Hilton signed the petition to the state legislature which regarded the state's laws "relating to marriage and divorce, as unconstitutional, and a violation of the higher law which is above the enactments of all human codes. On the ground of principle, and because they believe such provisions are calculated to bring odium upon a portion of the human family on account of their complexion, they ask that they may be immediately repealed" (*Liberator*, 22 Mar. 1839). One can hardly overestimate the significance of black and white women *together* asking for repeal of laws banning racial intermarriage in 1839.

The next year, Lavinia Hilton proved, if there was any doubt, that she did not stand in the shadow of her activist husband. As the American Anti-Slavery began to fracture over the radicalism of William Lloyd Garrison and his associates, especially over his desire to accord women full standing in the body, the Boston Female Anti-Slavery

Society chose Hilton, Susan Paul, and twelve white women to serve as official delegates to the annual meeting of the Anti-Slavery Society and to oppose the efforts of the society's men who would "throw obstacles in our way, and prevent the exercise of our power in behalf of the cause" as "anti-slavery women." (*Liberator*, 24 Apr. 1840).

In 1882, she died of Bright's Disease in Cambridge. Although Hilton seemed only to briefly grace the historical record, few people of any race or either gender took a more daring stand for human rights in antebellum America.

FURTHER READING

Dorman, Franklin A. *Twenty Families of Color in Massachusetts, 1742–1998* (1998).

Horton, James Oliver, and Lois E. Horton. *Black Bostonians: Family Life and Community Struggle in the Antebellum North* (1999).

Salerno, Beth A. *Sister Societies: Women's Antislavery Organizations in Antebellum America* (2005).

Yacovone, Donald. "The Transformation of Black Temperance, 1827–1854: An Interpretation," *Journal of the Early Republic* 8 (Fall 1988): 281–297.

Yee, Shirley. *Black Women Abolitionists: A Study in Activism, 1828–1860* (1992).

DONALD YACOVONE

Hilyer, Amanda Victoria Gray (24 Mar. 1870–29 June 1957), business owner, civic activist, and clubwoman, was born in Atchison, Kansas. Little is known of her family or early life in Kansas. After high school, she taught school for three years in Kansas. She married Arthur Smith Gray in 1893. He graduated from Howard University in Washington, D.C., the same year. Like many educated blacks in the late nineteenth century seeking to escape Jim Crow conditions in the South, the couple moved to Washington, D.C. Gray taught kindergarten briefly, and Arthur Gray worked as a private secretary to the chief of the Bureau of Statistics. Later in his civil service career, he worked as a statistician in the Bureau of Foreign and Domestic Commerce; he worked as a stenographer and private secretary to the chief of the Bureau of Statistics from 1898 to 1905 and later as a statistician for a government agency until his death in 1917. The Grays had no children.

The Grays, firmly ensconced in respectable middle-class black society, became part of the dynamic cultural and political life of black Washington. They were members of the Berean Baptist Church. An accomplished singer, Gray helped found in 1901 the Coleridge-Taylor Choral Society, which sponsored the British composer Samuel Coleridge-Taylor's first visit to the United States three years later. For sixty years she was a member of the Treble Clef Club founded by Mamie Hilyer, the wife of Andrew F. Hilyer. In 1905 she and several church members and-clubwomen, including ANNA JULIA HAYWARD COOPER, founded the Colored Women's Christian Association (CWCA), the first black YWCA in the city and the first independent black YWCA in the United States. The CWAC received little support from its white sister organization, but it provided housing, training, and social activities for thousands of young black men and women in the city. The organization moved to Rhode Island Avenue and changed its name to the D.C. PHILLIS WHEATLEY YWCA in the 1920s.

Gray became more politically active after 1910. She was probably influenced through her frequent attendance at the Sunday evening socials held at the home of the clubwoman and antilynching activist CARRIE WILLIAMS CLIFFORD. She also continued her participation and leadership in local lyceum clubs like the Booklovers Club, founded by JOSEPHINE BRUCE. Through Clifford's Sunday socials and her club activities, Gray encountered a dynamic mix of cultural and crusading black Washington elite, such as the activist MARY CHURCH TERRELL and the composer HENRY THACKER BURLEIGH. She protested the lynching of Mattie Lomax in 1911 and sought municipal regulation of theaters on Sundays and black youth at public beaches.

An ambitious woman, Gray was tired of teaching. She applied to the pharmacy program at Howard University and graduated with the Pharm.G. degree in 1903. She clearly understood that because of racism and sexism in U.S. society, black families often required the financial support of the women. Black men and women struggled to find positions outside of unskilled labor and domestic service. Those fortunate enough to gain higher education also had difficulty securing positions and salaries commensurate with their education and ambition or that offered possibilities for management positions. But she also realized that black women themselves had few job opportunities, and that well-educated women were often limited to jobs in nursing or teaching. Following in the footsteps of pioneering women pharmacists like Dr. Julia P. H. Coleman, the owner of Columbia Pharmacy in Newport News, Virginia, and Clara Smyth, the owner of the Johnson Pharmacy in Charleston, she and her husband, Arthur, founded the Fountain Pharmacy in 1903.

The Fountain was one of more than a dozen black-owned or-operated pharmacies in Washington in the early 1900s, but it quickly set itself apart from its competition. It was located in True Reformers Hall in the Shaw and U Street District. The fraternal order built the hall in 1903, and it became a symbol of great pride for black Washingtonians who believed it represented the race's progress and its capacity for commercial success. Gray drew a clear distinction between traditional roots and herbal remedies offered at "root shops" and the Fountain's modern chemical preparations, decor, and stock. The store's extensive marketing included publishing a free colored medical directory for patrons and printing circulars in the local newspapers that emphasized the store's unique features.

As co-owner of the Fountain, Gray essentially ran the business; her husband was primarily responsible for record keeping and marketing. At the 1908 National Negro Business League convention in Baltimore, she described how black women could earn a secure living in pharmacy, and she stressed the profession's benefits to black women. As proprietor of her own store, she told delegates, the black woman avoided the kind of environment in white offices or on the factory floor that insulted respectable femininity, such as coarse language and sexual advances. Despite unequivocal statements that women were essential to the world of commerce and business, she carefully framed her business success in normative terms that stressed businesswomen's roles as "helpmeets" and "helpers" rather than "usurpers" in conflict and competition with black men. Also, like many businesswomen in the league, she stressed black women's attraction to business not as a desire for self-interest or greater autonomy within the black family but as a way to help them fulfill traditional roles in unconventional ways.

After the death of her husband in 1917, she sold the pharmacy business to the doctors R. E. Banks and A. C. Burwell, moved to St. Louis, and became active in the war movement. She was among the thousands of black women who supported black participation in the war effort by raising millions for Liberty Bonds, participating in food conservation clubs, and providing services to black troops. They hoped that their patriotism and service during the country's battle for freedom and democracy abroad would translate into greater freedom and democracy at home. However, they met discrimination from organizations such as Red Cross and the YWCA.

The local white YWCAs upheld the color line and refused to work with or provide funding for black YWCAs, including the Colored Women's Christian Association in Washington, D.C. However, in 1918 the War Work Council of the National YWCA set aside more than $400,000 for black women. The black YWCAs used the money to appoint a colored national secretary, fund a national network of field supervisors, and help local organizations set up fifteen black government-sponsored hostess houses in cities near military bases. These hostess houses served as clearinghouses for information about the war, wounded soldiers, and local resources, and they provided social activities for black soldiers and their families or women visitors. They also provided traditional YWCA services, such as training and employment services. Gray worked with the hostess houses at the camps Upton, Dix, and Taylor in the New York area. After the war she settled back into St. Louis and was appointed the executive secretary of the St. Louis Phillis Wheatley YWCA.

In 1923 Gray married Andrew F. Hilyer and moved back to Washington. She and her late husband, Arthur, had been involved with Andrew and his late wife, Mamie, in many Washington civic and cultural clubs. Although Arthur had died two years later, Gray continued to use his name in her professional life. As Amanda Gray Hilyer, she continued her community service and club work. She served as president of Howard University's Women's Club, on the board of Berean Baptist Church, and president and board member of the IONIA WHIPPER Home for Unwed Mothers. Contemporaries described Hilyer as zealous, noble, and stubborn but selflessly devoted to the arts and community service. Hilyer died unexpectedly of a stroke in 1957.

FURTHER READING

Gray, Amanda V. "The Possibilities of Woman in Pharmacy," in *Report of the Ninth Annual Convention of the National Negro Business League, Held in Baltimore, Maryland, August 19–21, 1908* (1908): 103–109.

McGuire, Robert, III. "Hilyer, Amanda V[ictoria] Gray," in *Dictionary of American Negro Biography*, eds. Rayford Whittingham Logan and Michael R. Winston (1982): 313–314.

Obituary: *Journal of Negro History* 43.1 (Jan. 1958): 82–84.

SHENNETTE GARRETT

Himes, Chester Bomar (29 July 1909–12 Nov. 1984), writer, was born in Jefferson City, Missouri, the youngest of three sons to professors Joseph Sandy Himes and Estelle Bomar. Himes believed that his surname derived from paternal ancestors who were skilled artisans owned by a Jewish slaveholding family named Heinz. The Bomar family claimed descent from an American Indian woman or African princess and an Irish overseer. His father Joseph Himes was sent to Claflin College in Orangeburg, South Carolina, where he studied blacksmithing. Himes's mother studied music at Scotia Seminary in Concord, North Carolina. After his parents married in 1901, they held a joint appointment at Georgia State College and then taught at a number of other colleges in the South, including Tuskegee Institute in Alabama. Himes sensed that the tension in his parents' marriage was a reflection of the struggle between white and black manifested in his mother's light complexion and his father's dark one. These perceptions, which were not shared by Himes's siblings, provide the backdrop for his novel *The Third Generation* (1954), and the themes of race, sex, and power recur throughout both his life and work. When Himes was twelve years old, his brother Joseph nearly blinded himself in a chemistry experiment gone awry and was refused medical treatment at the local white hospital. After graduating from Glenville High School in 1926, Himes was working at a Cleveland hotel to earn money for college when he accidentally fell down an open elevator shaft, fracturing three vertebrae. He, too, was denied entry to a white hospital. Thus, when he entered Ohio State University in the fall, still wearing a back brace, he was scarred physically and emotionally. He had gained admission to the university in part because a grade of fifty-six he had received in one course was mistakenly recorded on his transcript as eighty-six; nevertheless, it was later found that he had the fourth-highest IQ of any student entering that year. However, Himes was more interested in the illicit activities he found in the black underworld and in the superficial aspects of campus life than he was in his studies. At the end of his first semester, the highest grade he could muster was a C in English. The shady individuals he associated with later appeared as characters in his crime novels, but in 1927 keeping such company merely helped to get him expelled.

Back on the streets of Cleveland, Himes's delinquent behavior came to include soliciting prostitutes, gambling, and forging checks. His parents, who were going through a divorce, could not stop his

Chester Bomar Himes. His detective novels helped to pioneer a new genre of mystery writing. (Library of Congress.)

downward spiral—though his nearly blind brother was on his way to graduating magna cum laude from Oberlin College and earning a Ph.D. After two prior arrests in 1928 Himes was sentenced to twenty to twenty-five years in the Ohio State Penitentiary for an armed robbery he committed against a white couple. In 1930 the prison was engulfed in a fire that killed more than three hundred inmates. Himes wrote a story about this tragedy called "To What Red Hell," which was published in *Esquire* in 1934. From then on Himes considered himself a writer. His novel *Cast the First Stone* (1954) draws heavily on his prison experience, exploring the problems of crime and punishment and exposing the realities of prison life. *Run Man Run* (1966) presents the absurdity of the "Negro" condition as he saw it—a state of being imprisoned and paralyzed within a racist society.

A year after his release from prison in 1936, Himes married Jean Lucinda Johnson. During the Depression he found work as a laborer with the Works Progress Administration, but was soon assigned to the Ohio Writers' Project, where he worked on a history of Cleveland and wrote an unsigned column for the *Cleveland Daily News*. During this period he met and befriended LANGSTON HUGHES, who assisted his writing career. In 1940 Himes and his wife moved to Los Angeles to work as butler and maid for the novelist Louis Bromfield, whom they hoped would help further Himes's career. When this did not happen, Himes found work in the shipyards and in war industry plants, while Jean found a position with slightly higher wages and status. His frustration with bigotry, liberals, union organizers, communists, and the blacks he encountered at the NAACP, as well as his low opinion of women, found fictional representation in his most ambitious novels, *If He Hollers Let Him Go* (1945) and *Lonely Crusade* (1947).

A Rosenwald Fellowship allowed Himes to move to New York City in 1944 to write full-time. His work received mixed reviews and sold so poorly that when the money ran out, Himes sometimes worked as a caretaker or bellhop to survive. He separated from Jean in 1952 and began a series of relationships with white women—including a violent one with Vandi Haygood that became the basis for *A Case of Rape* (1984), first published in French in 1963. Himes wrote that "the very essence of any relationship between a black man and a white woman in the United States is sex" (Muller, 65). This sentiment gave both *The End of a Primitive* (1955), which Himes considered to be his best work, and the satirical *Pinktoes* (1961) a racial edge that was too unsettling for most Americans.

By the early 1950s Himes had become so disappointed with the United States that he went to Europe and became one of the many American expatriate writers living in Paris. RICHARD WRIGHT helped Himes make his European transition, assisting him professionally and introducing him to JAMES BALDWIN, though Himes considered Wright a rival as much as a friend and preferred to invite comparisons of his own work to William Faulkner's. He lived a peripatetic existence in Europe, taking up with several women before meeting an English columnist, Lesley Packard, in 1958; the two were married in 1965. His writing career entered a new and unexpected phase when the French editor and translator Marcel Duhamel suggested that Himes write commercial detective novels. In 1958 his first attempt, *For Love of Imabelle*, won the French Grand Prix for the year's best detective novel.

At first Himes considered his detective novels to be lucrative projects that he could churn out quickly in order to support his "serious" writing. He did not expect that *The Real Cool Killers* (1959), *The Crazy Kill* (1959), *The Big Gold Dream* (1960), *All Shot Up* (1960), and *Blind Man with a Pistol* (1969) would become as popular as they did. *Cotton Comes to Harlem* (1965) was made into a film directed by OSSIE DAVIS in 1970, and *The Heat's On* (1965) became the film *Come Back, Charleston Blue* in 1974. In Grave Digger Jones and his partner Coffin Ed Johnson, Himes created compelling characters who dispense their own brand of black justice and who have been compared to Dashiell Hammett's Sam Spade. With these books Himes helped to pioneer a new genre of African American mystery writing that continues with such writers as WALTER MOSLEY and Nora DeLoach.

Himes lived the last sixteen years of his life in Spain, where he struggled with a variety of geriatric illnesses. He rarely visited the United States, but he never stayed anyplace in Europe long enough, or learned to speak any of the languages well enough, to consider Europe his home. In his final years, often writing in great arthritic pain, he finished two autobiographies, *The Quality of Hurt* (1972) and *My Life of Absurdity* (1976).

FURTHER READING
Some letters from Himes are located at the Beinecke
　　Rare Book and Manuscript Library, Yale University.
Himes, Chester. *My Life of Absurdity* (1976).
Himes, Chester. *The Quality of Hurt* (1972).
Margolies, Edward, and Michel Fabre. *The Several Lives
　　of Chester Himes* (1997).
Muller, Gilbert H. *Chester Himes* (1976).
Obituary: *New York Times*, 14 Nov. 1984.

SHOLOMO B. LEVY

Hinard, Eufrosina (1777–2 Jan. 1866?), slave owner, was born in New Orleans, Louisiana, to a freed slave and a white man (their names are unknown). Hinard never experienced slavery herself, and her life as a slave-owning black female was far removed from the common experience of most blacks in North America. This anomaly can be explained in part by the political and social turbulence of early New Orleans. By the time Hinard was forty-two, she had lived under French, Spanish, and American rule. In 1791 at the age of fourteen, Hinard was *placéed* (committed) to the white Spaniard Don Nicolás Vidal, the *auditor de guerra*, the Spanish colonial governor. In this lofty position, Vidal provided military and legal counsel for both Louisiana and West Florida. Both the Spanish and the French legislated against racial intermarriage as a way of maintaining pure white blood, but this legislation did not stop white men from cohabitating with black women. Many French and Spanish military officials sent to help govern the territory would take mixed-blood mistresses during their time in Louisiana. Because these unions continued to occur in opposition to the law, an extralegal institution called *placage* developed to provide some formality, as well as some economic and social advantages for the black women.

The *placage* system that brought Vidal and Hinard together developed out of slavery. Many white men freed female slaves after having sexual relations with them, especially if children had resulted. Some of these women encouraged their daughters to also cohabitate with white men. As the system became established, *placage* relationships usually occurred between rich whites and free blacks, who emerged as an "upper class" within their communities. Free black women usually referred white men wishing to enter into this type of relationship to one of the girl's parents (usually the mother) who asked for certain concessions. Once both parties came to an agreement, a ceremony often took place, and then the formal relationship commenced.

While this system developed out of oppression, Hinard and other free black women did benefit from it in certain ways. In New Orleans's racially stratified society, increased whiteness brought more social status and relative financial security for oneself and one's children. While it is certain that many women were forced into these relationships, some most certainly chose *placage* (and its possible benefits) over marriage to a free black man. However, any benefits were tenuous because the *placage* system was never legally binding. Whether coerced or voluntary in the beginning, it seems quite possible that Vidal and Hinard had a genuinely affectionate relationship. The couple had at least two children who grew to adulthood during their fifteen years together: Mercedes (Merced) Vidal and Caroline Maria Vidal.

In 1800 Spain secretly transferred Louisiana back to the French. Within three years Napoleon decided to sell Louisiana to the United States. This decision affected Vidal and Hinard greatly. Vidal and Hinard decided to move to Spanish Florida rather than remain in Louisiana under American rule. Florida would not become American territory until 1819.

When Vidal died in 1806, although he had previously sired another child while stationed in South America (through another *placage* relationship), he left his entire estate to Hinard and their daughters. This was an extremely unusual act and one that would have been illegal had they stayed in New Orleans. Their daughter Merced later caused an international stir by petitioning President Andrew Jackson to help her recover her deceased father's documents. Jackson requested these documents from the Spanish Floridian government, and when he did not receive a satisfactory reply to his inquiry he had the Spanish governor jailed. Merced eventually received the documents.

After Vidal's death, Hinard exhibited considerable business acumen by buying a brick-making business and acquiring a number of slaves. (She owned thirteen by 1840.) While we have no written record of Hinard's thoughts about slavery, she probably maintained views more akin to Spanish sentiments than those associated with English North Americans, allowing her slaves to buy their freedom at a fair market price. Even after the Florida colonial government had outlawed the practice of self-purchase, she continued to buy slaves and hire them out until they could turn a profit for her; free them, and subsequently buy more slaves. In Hinard's case, slavery seems to have remained primarily a source of labor. Historian Virginia Gould has demonstrated that free black women in Gulf Coast cities distinguished themselves from both white women and slave women, and they felt little race-based empathy toward slaves. Black slave owners on the Gulf Coast such as Hinard emancipated their slaves at a rate similar to their white Spanish counterparts. Hinard's actions directly opposed the increasingly prevalent idea in the American South that slaves had no right to freedom; but Hinard's behavior also contradicts gender and racial solidarity theories of some contemporary historians. Hinard's life clearly demonstrates the complexity of slavery and freedom in and around the Gulf Coast at the turn of the dawn of the nineteenth century.

FURTHER READING

Gould, Virginia. "In Full Enjoyment of their Liberty: The Free Women of Color of the Gulf Ports of New Orleans, Mobile, and Pensacola, 1769–1860." Diss., Emory University (1991).

Haas, Edward F. *Louisiana's Legal Heritage* (1983).

DONOVAN S. WEIGHT

Hinderas, Natalie (15 June 1927–22 July 1987), concert pianist, educator, and champion of black classical composers, was born Natalie Leota Henderson in Oberlin, Ohio, the daughter of Abram L.

Henderson, a touring jazz pianist, and Leota Palmer, a classical pianist who later taught at Fisk University, the Cleveland Institute of Music, and Philadelphia's Settlement Music School. Hinderas's great-grandfather was also a musician—a teacher and bandmaster in Due West, South Carolina, and her ethnic heritage included African, Native American, Italian, and possibly even Spanish origins. Hinderas first appeared on stage as a singer and dancer when she was three years old. At age six she began formal lessons on both piano and violin. Two years later, in Cleveland, she offered her first full-length recital and that same year was accepted as a special student at the music conservatory of Oberlin College, where both her parents had studied.

In 1939, at age twelve, Hinderas performed Edvard Grieg's Piano Concerto with the Cleveland Women's Symphony Orchestra. She graduated from Oberlin High School in 1943 and three years later left Oberlin Conservatory with a bachelor of science in Music at just eighteen years of age—the school's youngest graduate to date. She moved to Philadelphia that fall, commuting to study at Juilliard with Olga Samaroff, who (having been born Olga Hickenlooper) encouraged her pupil to assume the more European and exotic name of Hinderas. (The Hispanic sheen of "Hinderas" may have mitigated some of the racism that limited her professional opportunities.) After Samaroff's death in 1948, Hinderas studied with Edward Steuermann for five years at the Philadelphia Conservatory. Several awards and fellowships helped finance her education.

Hinderas played her New York solo recital debut at Town Hall on 13 November 1954 as a benefit for the Urban League, performing works by Mozart, Chopin, Ravel, Hindemith, and Berg. Praising her developing talents, a *New York Times* reviewer noted the "honest musical instincts" with which she "shaped a phrase with real authority, leaving no doubt that a strong controlling force was engaged" (Schonberg, 1954). This performance led to representation by Columbia Artists Management on its Community Concerts roster, an American recital tour, performances with the National Symphony, and a contract with NBC to play recitals, concertos, and variety shows on its owned and operated radio and TV stations. Hinderas embraced broadcast media enthusiastically for they reached a large audience, expanding the appeal of classical music. She married the TV producer Lionel J. Monagas on 12 June 1955 and created radio and public television programs about music, including *Contrasts* and *Footnotes on Gershwin*, beginning in 1959. The couple had one daughter, Michele Lisa, born in 1963.

Under a 1959 Leventritt Foundation award, Hinderas performed concertos with smaller orchestras. Early in 1960 she undertook a four-month U.S. State Department tour, presenting lecture recitals on American music in Sweden, Yugoslavia, Iran, Jordan, Taiwan, and the Philippines. The following year she was invited by the American Society for African Culture to appear at the opening of its cultural center in Lagos, Nigeria. A second State Department tour in 1964 took her to Sweden, Poland, Yugoslavia, and England. Afterward, Hinderas limited her international touring to be with her child. In 1968 Hinderas joined the artists roster of Joanne Rile Management.

Hinderas had studied composition with Vincent Persichetti and sympathized with the challenges faced by all contemporary American classical composers. Further inspired by the civil rights movement, she researched black classical music and in 1968 began offering residencies at black colleges with lively commentary on music by composers including R. NATHANIEL DETT, WILLIAM GRANT STILL, HALE SMITH, GEORGE THEOPHILUS WALKER, Arthur Cunningham, Stephen Chambers (later Talib Rasul Hakim), and OLLY WOODROW WILSON. Hinderas was deeply frustrated by the racist limitations placed on black composers in her time and that black creativity could be recognized or nurtured only in blues-based idioms such as jazz and soul. She worked to convince black audiences that classical music was not just for whites and to convince white listeners that black composers were legitimate artists.

Her acclaimed first commercial recording, *Natalie Hinderas Plays Music by Black Composers* (1971 Desto, rereleased 1993 CRI), ranges widely from blues-based neo-Romantic idioms to serialist, third stream, and works for piano and electronics. Drawing upon her years of live recital performances of these works, the two-LP set offered a powerful and mature artistic realization of black experience. The passion and intensity Hinderas brought to Walker's Sonata No. 1 and Hakim's "Sound-Gone" revealed a commanding artist able to shift suddenly from power to subtlety, a courageous technique fully at the service of expression, pervasive singing melodic lines, and a glorious sensitivity to tone color. This recording won an award from the influential *Saturday Review* and had a catalytic effect on the appreciation and research of black classical music.

In 1971 Hinderas finally got her big professional break. The conductor Eugene Ormandy asked her to perform with the Philadelphia Orchestra for four concerts on its subscription series that November—making her the first black woman instrumentalist to appear with a major American orchestra on its premier series. Hinderas suggested performing the Argentinean composer Alberto Ginastera's Piano Concerto No. 1 (1961), a dramatic work blending modernism, rhythm, and melodic poetry, perfectly suited to her artistic personality. The performance was sensational, and Hinderas was soon invited to perform with the Los Angeles Philharmonic (1972), Boston Pops at the Hollywood Bowl (Gershwin, Concerto in F, 1972), New York Philharmonic (Ginastera, 1 November 1972), Atlanta Symphony (1973), Cleveland Orchestra (Schumann, 1973), and Chicago Symphony (Ravel, Concerto in G, 1974). She also appeared with orchestras in Baltimore, Pittsburgh, Dallas, San Francisco, Washington, D.C., and Toronto, as well as at the Ambler, Blossom, Chautauqua, Grant Park, and Interlochen music festivals. Hinderas helped commission George Walker's Piano Concerto, playing the world premiere in Minneapolis in 1975 and recording it three years later with the Detroit Symphony for CBS Records' Black Composers Series. In 1977 she recorded more traditional repertoire for the Orion label.

A dedicated teacher and savvy professional mentor, she took on her first pupils at age ten, while her first faculty positions were at Philadelphia's Conservatory of Music, Music Academy, and Settlement Music School. In 1966 she joined Temple University's Esther Boyer College of Music as an instructor and was quickly promoted to assistant (1969), associate (1971), and finally full professor (1973), receiving the University's Creative Achievement Award in 1985 and teaching at Temple until her death. Among her students was the classical pianist Leon Bates, a black concert soloist of international renown who, like Hinderas, performs music by canonic European as well as black composers. Hinderas served as a judge for national and international competitions including the Chopin Piano Competition and the International American Music Competition of Carnegie Hall. In 1976 she was awarded an honorary doctorate from Swarthmore College and a year later received a Distinction in Music Award from the National Association of Negro Musicians.

Hinderas's commitment to her community led to her election as the first president of the Union League Guild in Philadelphia in 1958, while from 1974 to 1979 she was a trustee of Oberlin College. She was a deeply spiritual and religious person, often presenting "musical sermons" as part of the worship services at First United Methodist Church of Germantown, Pennsylvania. Hinderas died from cancer at her home in Elkins Park, Pennsylvania, after a brief illness.

FURTHER READING
Archival materials related to Hinderas are held by Joanne Rile Management and Temple University.
Burden, Nancy. "Natalie Hinderas—Musical Militant," *Sunday Bulletin* (Philadelphia), 26 Jan. 1969.
Ericson, Raymond. "A Colored Girl Like You Can't Play Hollywood Bowl," *New York Times*, 19 Nov. 1972.
Fleming, Shirley. "Natalie Hinderas, Musican of the Month," *High Fidelity and Musical America* (Oct. 1973).
Polak, Maralyn Lois. "Program Notes on an Ex-Prodigy," *Today* in the *Philadelphia Inquirer*, 19 Mar. 1978.
Schonberg, Harold C. "Miss Hinderas Plays Debut Piano Recital," *New York Times*, 14 Nov. 1954.
Obituaries: *New York Times* and *Philadelphia Inquirer*, 23 July 1987.

MARK CLAGUE

Hines, Earl "Fatha" (28 Dec. 1905–22 Apr. 1983), jazz pianist and bandleader, was born Earl Kenneth Hines in Duquesne (later absorbed into Pittsburgh), Pennsylvania, the son of Joseph Hines, a foreman on the coal docks. His mother, whose name is unknown, died when he was an infant. From the age of three he was raised by his stepmother, Mary (maiden name unknown), an organist. His father played cornet and led the local Eureka Brass Band, an uncle was an accomplished brass player, and an aunt sang light opera. Thus immersed in musical influences, Hines commenced classical piano studies in 1914. He possessed an immense natural talent. While making rapid progress through the classics he also began playing organ in the Baptist church and covertly entertaining at parties, this last activity a consequence of his ability to learn popular songs by ear. His life, like his music, moved fluidly between middle-class proprieties and more popular pleasures.

Hines lived with his aunt Sadie Phillips from the age of twelve and attended Schenley High School.

Earl Hines, jazz pianist and bandleader, New York City, c. March 1947. (© William P. Gottlieb; www.jazzphotos.com.)

Continuing to perform brilliantly, he nevertheless also learned to be a barber and attempted other trades, none holding his lasting interest. During summer vacation from high school in 1922, he played at the Leader House in a trio under the direction of the singer and saxophonist Lois (also known as Louis) Deppe. Hines was with Deppe's group that in 1923 became a big band and toured the region and recorded for the Gennett label. During this period the rambunctious Hines tried his hand at being a pool shark and a pimp, and he fell into a disastrous and brief marriage to the singer Laura Badge, who used his already considerable reputation to advance her career. The banjoist Harold Birchett taught Hines always to keep a steady tempo, a requirement of the dance-band world that was at odds with his training in the rhythmic freedoms of the European romantic piano tradition. Hines learned the lesson well but retained in his soloing a penchant for rhythmic flights of fancy. Advised that his skills were too great for the Pittsburgh area, in 1924 he left his hometown for an engagement in Chicago, a cradle of jazz in the 1920s.

While working at an after-hours club around 1925, Hines concurrently played with CARROLL DICKERSON's orchestra at the Entertainer's Club.

When the club was padlocked by police—a routine occurrence in Chicago of the 1920s—Dickerson secured a forty-two-week tour on the Pantages theater circuit, taking the band to the West Coast and Canada. On their return to Chicago in 1926, Dickerson's band began an engagement at the Sunset Cafe, where LOUIS ARMSTRONG joined. Earlier each evening Hines and Armstrong also played in Erskine Tate's Vendome Theater Symphony Orchestra. When Dickerson was fired from the Sunset in February 1927, Armstrong was made nominal leader and Hines music director. Also around this time Hines worked as an accompanist for the singer ETHEL WATERS.

In late 1927 in Chicago Hines joined clarinetist Jimmie Noone's Apex Club Orchestra, one of the most important bands in early jazz. He eventually left the group after a dispute with Noone. Meanwhile, in May 1928, Hines began recording a succession of discs that collectively document his stature in early jazz. A good number of these titles were made under Noone's leadership, even as their personal relationship was disintegrating. Perhaps the finest, from the perspective of Hines's contribution, are "Sweet Sue (Just You)," "Four or Five Times," "Every Evening," "Monday Date," "Oh! Sister, Ain't That Hot!," "King Joe," and "Sweet Lorraine" with Noone; "Skip the Gutter" and "A Monday Date" as a member of Armstrong's Hot Five; "Savoyagers' Stomp" alongside Armstrong in Dickerson's orchestra; the duo "Weather Bird" with Armstrong; and the pianist's unaccompanied solos on the popular song "I Ain't Got Nobody" and on his own compositions "Caution Blues" (also known as "Blues in Thirds"), "A Monday Date," and "Fifty-seven Varieties" (a punning reference to his surname and his home, from the advertising slogan of the Pittsburgh food corporation Heinz). These last sides were recorded in December 1928, just after a trip to Long Island City, New York, where he punched eight piano rolls for the QRS company.

Also by 1928 Hines had entered into a relationship with entertainer and violinist Kathryn Perry, who became his second wife by common-law marriage. On his birthday he brought a new big band into the Grand Terrace, where, apart from numerous regional tours, he held an engagement through the end of 1939. Stories abound—humorous, nostalgic, and ugly—from these eleven years. Ballroom owner Ed Fox offered Hines considerable musical opportunities and an unusually stable job in the world of entertainment, while simultaneously taking great advantage of him. Hines seemed unconcerned with developing expertise in the business aspects of music. Gangsters (notably Al Capone) frequented the club and around 1931 took it over, demanding a 20 percent share for "protection" and for preventing Hines's sidemen from leaving for other bands. Some musicians expressed their pleasure at belonging to a band that felt like a happy family (in contrast to the cutthroat divisiveness of many swing-era big bands), owing in no small part to Hines's joyful leadership.

Hines's explanation of how he got his nickname is indicative of how he was viewed by his band members and others who worked with him. One night after he had written the band's theme song, "Deep Forest," in collaboration with the English jazz composer Reginald Foresythe, Hines gave a fatherly scolding to the master of ceremonies for drinking too much. The in-house broadcast on NBC then opened: "Here comes Fatha Hines through the deep forest with his little children." Hence he was thereafter known as "Fatha."

Prominent among artistic highlights at the Grand Terrace, apart from Hines's ever-present piano playing, were the performances of the dancer, singer, and trumpeter VALAIDA SNOW from 1933 to 1934. When Snow left for Europe in 1935, she was replaced by Hines's wife, Perry. During these years his band featured the trumpeters Walter Fuller and George Dixon, the trombonist TRUMMY YOUNG, the alto saxophonists and clarinetists OMER SIMEON and Darnell Howard (who doubled on violin as well), and the tenor saxophonists and arrangers JIMMY MUNDY and Cecil Irwin. The rhythm section provided a wonderful push, with Hines working in conjunction with the guitarist Lawrence Dixon, the bassist Quinn Wilson, and the drummer Wallace Bishop. Their recordings, never especially innovative, were nonetheless characteristically sparky, clean, and swinging, except for the somewhat pretentious mood piece "Harlem Lament" from 1933, which afforded Hines his greatest opportunity as a soloist with the orchestra.

The band's overall level of performance evidently dipped after Irwin died in May 1935. He was immediately replaced by the tenor saxophonist and arranger BUDD JOHNSON, who helped bring the band to another peak a few years later with such prominent new members as the drummer Alvin Burroughs, the singer BILLY ECKSTINE (both joining in 1939), and the alto saxophonist Scoops Carry (1940). A second spate of high-quality recordings included "Grand Terrace Shuffle" and "G. T. Stomp," made before a financial dispute with

Fox led to Hines's final departure from the ballroom at the end of 1939; the hit songs "Jelly, Jelly" (1940) and "Stormy Monday Blues" (1942); and "Skylark" (also 1942), which represented the first time an African American singer (Eckstine) was allowed to debut a romantic ballad. Less inspiring musically but highly profitable was "Boogie Woogie on St. Louis Blues" (1940). Independent of the big band, Hines recorded unaccompanied improvisations in 1939 and 1940, including "The Father's Getaway" and "Reminiscing at Blue Note."

Hines was divorced from his second wife by June 1940. The big band, having lost its home base, toured continuously from that year onward. New members included the drummer SHADOW WILSON (who joined in 1942), the two future giants of bop CHARLIE PARKER (playing tenor rather than alto saxophone) and the trumpeter DIZZY GILLESPIE (both from late 1942 into 1943), and the singer SARAH VAUGHAN (from April 1943). Because of a recording ban, no documentation of their contribution survives. They had all left Hines by the fall of that year and soon would form a big band under Eckstine's leadership. Shifting directions considerably, Hines formed a short-lived, twenty-four-piece orchestra in October 1943, imitating another popular trend by adding a string section (in this instance, all women) and a vocal group (also women) to the standard big-band instrumentation. In March 1944 he briefly led the DUKE ELLINGTON Orchestra while Ellington was suffering from tonsilitis.

In 1946 Hines was in a serious automobile accident that left his right eye permanently damaged. The following year he disbanded the big band and married Janie Moses, who had sung with the group for two years. They had two daughters. After a losing venture running a nightclub from April to August 1947, he joined Jack Teagarden and SID CATLETT in Louis Armstrong's newly formed All Stars in January 1948. The group toured Europe in 1948, giving an acclaimed appearance at the Nice Jazz Festival, and again in 1949. Apart from Armstrong he recorded a fine trio session with the bassist Al McKibbon and the drummer J. C. HEARD in 1950. Hines remained with Armstrong until the fall of 1951, when he quit in a controversy over publicity. Also in 1951 Hines had a small role in a feature film, *The Strip*. During the 1950s and later he appeared occasionally on television as well.

From 1952 to 1954 Hines led small swing groups that included at various times the trumpeter Jonah Jones, the drummer ART BLAKEY, and the trombonist DICKY WELLS. Having interrupted these affiliations to play with a sparky Dixieland band at the Hangover in San Francisco (June 1952 and February 1954), he began a long engagement there in September 1955. He took his family to San Francisco the following year and settled across the bay in Oakland in 1960. Among his sidemen were the trumpeter Muggsy Spanier, the clarinetist Darnell Howard, the trombonist JIMMY ARCHEY, and the bassist POPS FOSTER. During this period Hines also toured England as coleader of a group with Teagarden (September 1957) and led a swing group at the Embers in New York City (1959).

The Dixieland group moved into the Black Sheep in San Francisco in 1961–1962 and then disbanded. In 1964 the writer Stanley Dance convinced a reluctant Hines—who thought of himself as an entertainer rather than a concert-giver—to present three concerts at the Little Theatre in New York. Performing alone and in a trio with bass and drums, he surprised the audience with the quality of his playing and thereby launched the final portion of his career, during which he toured internationally from 1965 into the early 1980s. In these last two decades his working group was usually a quartet in which, initially, he was reunited with Budd Johnson and to which he often added a singer, such as ALBERTA HUNTER. Two LPs in the boxed set *The Father of Modern Piano*, recorded at a later reunion in 1977, capture well the quartet of the mid-1960s to the end of the decade, with the bassist Bill Pemberton and the drummer Oliver Jackson joining Hines and Johnson. Hines divorced Janie Hines in 1980; their daughters had died. He died in Oakland.

It was in his unaccompanied performances that Hines made his greatest contribution, offering profound and original interpretations of American popular songs. The essential qualities of his playing since the 1920s were an extraordinary speed and independence of hands; the ability to reharmonize and to ornament melodies in infinitely varied ways; a hammerlike tone, enhanced further by the presentation of melodies in octaves; and the use of left-hand techniques of ragtime and stride piano playing but in quicksilver, unpredictable sequences. Hines's irrepressible swing rhythms might suddenly give way to impossibly difficult and seemingly irrational rhythmic figures and then, just as suddenly, resume; he could command showy tremolos in either hand and stark and pointed registral contrasts. During the first four decades of his career, Hines often used his talents in a flighty and superficial manner (especially during the big-band decades), as if he were bursting with so many brilliant ideas that he could not control and shape the music. In his later years, however, he was more disciplined and managed to attain high levels of artistic achievement along with commercial success. On his solo work of the 1960s and 1970s Hines was, arguably, the finest jazz pianist ever.

FURTHER READING

Dance, Stanley. *The World of Earl Hines* (1977; rpt. 1983).

Moxhet, Lionel. *A Discography of Earl Hines, 1923–1977: Records, Festivals and Concerts* (1978).

Obituary: *San Francisco Chronicle*, 23 Apr. 1983.

This entry is taken from the *American National Biography* and is published here with the permission of the American Council of Learned Societies.

BARRY KERNFELD

Hines, Gregory (14 Feb. 1946–9 Aug. 2003), tap dancer, actor, recording artist, and choreographer, was born Gregory Oliver Hines in the Sugar Hill section of Harlem, New York, the youngest of two sons of Maurice "Chink" Hines, a drummer and nightclub bouncer, and Alma Lawless, daughter of West Indian immigrants. Before he was three Gregory and his brother Maurice Jr., who was two years older, began studying with the master tapographer HENRY LETANG. In 1954 the siblings debuted at Harlem's Apollo Theater. Also that year the Hines Kids, as they became known professionally, appeared in the Broadway musical *The Girl in Pink Tights*. The following year they began performing at previously all-white Playboy Clubs in Chicago, Kansas City, and New Orleans, and they soon became regular opening act attractions on the liberal Borscht Belt circuit in the Catskill Mountains. Gregory Hines proved to be more than just a gifted tap prodigy. His ability to sing, act, and tell jokes, using his brother as straight man, engendered both cheers and fears from some of the headliners with whom they worked. Opening for the comic Don Rickles at the Westbury Theatre in Long Island got the Hines Kids fired off his tour for being, as the story goes, "a hard act to follow."

Outgoing and aggressive, Gregory overshadowed his shy brother. The ill-matched partnership created a recurring lifelong friction. Impeccably groomed and sophisticated beyond their years, the Hines Brothers (as they were then billed) made their Las Vegas debut in 1955 at the Moulin Rouge, the city's first integrated hotel and casino. Following

Gregory Hines, in January 2001, discussed his role as tap legend Bill "Bojangles" Robinson in the film *Bojangles*. (AP Images.)

that six-month engagement, they returned to a New York whose entertainment scene had changed. Their act, dapper and sophisticated, seemed prissy and anachronistic against the gritty cool of New York's new beat persona. Realizing the need to retool and regroup, the brothers briefly teamed with the actor-singer-dancer Johnny Brown and performed as Hines, Hines and Brown. (Brown went on to star on TV's *Laugh-In* and be featured as the comic building superintendent, Bookman, on the classic 1970s TV series *Good Times*.)

After scattered engagements on the East Coast, Gregory and his brother bid farewell to Brown and returned to Vegas, this time as Hines, Hines and Dad, with their father playing drums in the background. During the next few years the act earned small fees and toured the continent under conditions that were sometimes horrific. Lodgings and eateries that served and/or housed blacks were difficult to find, so they often ate and slept in their

car. Through much of the early and mid-1960s the family lived in Brooklyn when not on the road. Like his father, Gregory was an outstanding athlete who could have been a pro baseball player. An errant and impatient teenager who would rather roughhouse than rehearse, he sustained permanent damage to his right eye after tumbling from a tree and landing face first on a stump, tearing his cornea.

When their act appeared on the popular *Ed Sullivan Show*, it attracted the attention of the manager Stanley Kay, who showcased the act in an intricate and classy medley of songs from Broadway's newest hit, *Fiddler on the Roof*, at Grossinger's in the Catskills, one of the most important hotel showplaces on the Borscht circuit, to great success. The French variety star Charles Aznavour, alerted by the buzz, brought them to Paris for a twelve-week engagement at the Olympic Theatre. The triumph of that engagement netted a recording contract with Columbia Records.

But internal tension was mounting. It was 1966. Rock and roll was the international craze, and the twenty-year-old Hines, a self-taught drummer and rock and roll aficionado, was frustrated. He considered the family act old-fashioned and out of touch, and he complained about his lack of individual identity.

Shortly after their return from Europe, Columbia Records showcased the act at New York's Plaza Hotel, earning bookings on the *Mike Douglas Show*, the *David Frost Show*, and the *Tonight Show*, starring Johnny Carson. On the *Tonight Show* they made an unprecedented thirty-seven appearances. In 1968 Hines married Patricia Panella, a white dance therapist. Their only child, a daughter named Daria, was born in 1970.

Hines's discontent grew. Not even plum engagements with ELLA FITZGERALD and Judy Garland could soothe his restlessness. When Stanley Kay presented the brothers with a medley of songs from the early 1960s Broadway and motion picture classic *My Fair Lady*, Gregory flatly rejected it. In 1971 he quit the act. He also divorced his wife.

Hines then moved to Venice, California, grew his hair long, formed a jazz-rock band aptly named Severance, and worked at various times as a busboy, waiter, and karate instructor. He considered himself liberated. But the band never took off, and by 1976 his circumstances and the shift in social fashion gave him pause. Traditional entertainment was making a stylish comeback, and he knew that he had to do the same. That year he returned to Manhattan and almost immediately landed a key role in a new musical, *The Last Minstrel Show*. The show closed during its Philadelphia pre-Broadway tryout, but it did relaunch Hines's career.

Hines landed a spot in the new Broadway review *Eubie!* So did his estranged brother. When the brothers discovered that they had been cast, their professional reunion was fraught with personal tension that both tried to mask in the name of professional decorum. *Eubie!* opened on 20 September 1978 at the Ambassador Theatre to glowing reviews, and the notices for Gregory were exceptional. He was nominated for the first of four Tony Awards. Although he lost the Tony, he did win the Outer Circle Critics' Award.

Following *Eubie!* Hines starred as a dancing-singing Scrooge in a new musical comedy version of *A Christmas Carol* set in Harlem. This project provided him with his first real acting opportunity and his second Tony Award nomination. When he lost again he pretended not to care, but friends confided that the elusiveness of the award bothered him greatly. For Hines real stardom needed tangible validation.

When illness forced the comic RICHARD PRYOR to drop out of the director Mel Brooks's upcoming film *The History of the World Part 1*, Brooks hired Hines on the recommendation of the actress Madeline Kahn. Standout reviews for Hines in an otherwise tepid film made Hollywood take notice. Other film assignments followed, including a starring role opposite Oscar-winner Albert Finney in *Wolfen*.

Hines met and married Pamela Koslow in 1981, and she brought to the union a daughter, Jessica, from a previous marriage. Hines then returned to New York to star in the Broadway-bound *Sophisticated Ladies*, a high-profile salute to DUKE ELLINGTON. Despite several pluses—a company that featured JUDITH JAMISON, the jazz-pop vocalist Phyllis Hyman, the dancers Hinton Battle and Greg Burge, and the twenty-one-piece Duke Ellington orchestra—the show was in trouble. Hines and the director/choreographer Donald McKayle clashed continuously, resulting in Hines's firing.

Opening-night tryouts in Washington, D.C., were disastrous. The producers, desperate to fix their multimillion-dollar fiasco, fired McKayle and hired the ballet choreographer Michael Smuin to retool the show. Smuin in turn rehired Hines. *Sophisticated Ladies* became one of the biggest hits of the 1980–1981 Broadway season. Hines's performance was one of the highlights of the show, earning him his third Tony Award nomination—and his third loss.

In 1983 a son, Zachary Evan, was born to Gregory and Pamela Koslow Hines. That same year Francis Ford Coppola, the five-time Academy Award–winning director of *The Godfather* and *Apocalypse Now*, was preparing a new film project, *The Cotton Club*. Set during the club's infamous gangster-run infancy, *The Cotton Club* contained a secondary storyline revolving around a black hoofer, Sandman Williams, inspired by the real-life hoofer HOWARD SANDMAN SIMS and his brother Clay, who perform at the club before all-white audiences.

Hines vigorously lobbied for the role of Sandman—his paternal grandmother, Ora Hines, was one of the original Cotton Club dancers—even turning down the lead in the film *48 Hrs.*, which subsequently went to the newcomer EDDIE MURPHY. But little did Hines know that Coppola had fashioned the script with the Hines brothers in mind, borrowing many elements from their lives, including their fiercely guarded private discord. Hines proved to be particularly impressive in the otherwise uneven film, augmenting the choreography with his own step designs. His a capella improvography during his final act staircase-dance solo is considered a cinematic standout.

Following *The Cotton Club*, Hines starred in a string of hit films, including *The Muppets Take Manhattan* (1984), *White Nights* (1985), opposite the ballet dancer Mikhail Baryshnikov, and *Running Scared* (1986), opposite the comic Billy Crystal. In 1987 Hines recorded a self-titled LP for Epic Records, produced by his close friend LUTHER VANDROSS. The previous year he had recorded a duet with Vandross.

But tap was never far from Hines's consciousness. In 1988 he lobbied successfully for the creation of a National Tap Dance Day, won an Emmy Award for his PBS special *Gregory Hines: Tap Dance in America*, and produced and starred in Hollywood's first tap film in more than forty years, *Tap* (1989), which innovatively merged traditional tap with contemporary rock, soul, and funk and brought together the personification of three generations of tap excellence. The film featured the septuagenarian hoof legends Arthur Duncan, Sandman Sims, BUNNY BRIGGS, JIMMY SLYDE, Steve Condos, and HAROLD NICHOLAS and brought them together onscreen for the first and last time. In addition Hines hired his sixteen-year-old protégé SAVION GLOVER, the tap-dancing sensation whom he first noticed in the Paris production of the Broadway-bound musical revue *Black and Blue*. *Tap* is also significant in that it contains the final film performance of Hines's mentor, the showbiz legend SAMMY DAVIS JR.

In 1992 Hines returned to Broadway in his wife's production of *Jelly's Last Jam*, written and directed by the playwright GEORGE C. WOLFE. Portraying the brilliant self-loathing Creole composer and musician JELLY ROLL MORTON proved to be Hines's most challenging role, for which he finally won a Tony Award for the best actor in a musical.

Hines starred in the short-lived CBS sitcom *The Gregory Hines Show* (1994) and made film appearances in *Waiting to Exhale* (1995) and *The Preacher's Wife* (1996). One of his final performances was as the legendary dancer BILL ("Bojangles") ROBINSON in the Showtime cable biographical drama *Bojangles* (2001), for which he received Screen Actors Guild, Emmy, and NAACP Image award nominations. The star of nearly forty films and considered the greatest tap dancer of his generation, dignified by a stylish and effortless technique, Gregory Hines died of liver cancer in Los Angeles.

FURTHER READING

Jowitt, Deborah. "Tapping into History," *Village Voice* (Aug. 2003).

Obituaries: *New York Times* and *Miami Herald*, 11 Aug. 2003.

STANLEY BENNETT CLAY

Hinson, Eugene Theodore (20 Nov. 1873–7 June 1960), physician, was born in Philadelphia, Pennsylvania, the son of Theodore C. Hinson and Mary E. Cooper. He grew up in Philadelphia, where he attended the O. V. CATTO public schools. After his family moved to Camden, New Jersey, across the Delaware River from Philadelphia and where his father was employed at an iron foundry, he was influenced by his principal at the Mount Vernon School, WILLIAM FRANK POWELL, later a U.S. minister to Haiti.

Returning to Philadelphia, Hinson studied at the Quaker Philadelphia Institute for Colored Youth, where the noted educator FANNY JACKSON COPPIN was principal. He graduated in 1892 and taught in Hartford County, Maryland, and then Philadelphia. By 1894 he had decided to pursue a career as a physician and enrolled in the medical school at the University of Pennsylvania. Specializing in gynecology he received his medical degree in 1898 with honors and ranked twelfth in his class.

Because he was black Hinson was unable to secure an internship at the University of Pennsylvania Hospital even though the top fifteen graduates usually were accepted. He also was refused employment at the Philadelphia General and Presbyterian Hospitals. Hinson was welcomed to join the staff at the Frederick Douglass Memorial Hospital, an African American facility established in 1895 by Dr. NATHAN F. MOSSELL, a University of Pennsylvania Medical School alumnus.

Hinson was invited to be on the hospital's board of directors, and he served through 1905. Friction between black physicians and "difficulties of existence" in Philadelphia resulted in the decision to establish another black hospital. Health care for blacks was limited and generally inferior to that for whites, and African American medical professionals sought to improve services.

Hinson led a group of doctors to create Mercy Hospital on 12 February 1907. He was the first member appointed to the new hospital's board of directors and was named chief of gynecological service. He also had a private practice until 1955, when he retired as a result of failing health.

A 1948 merger with the Douglass Hospital resulted in the Mercy-Douglass Hospital, considered the city's second-oldest black hospital. At a June 1948 banquet, the Mercy-Douglass staff recognized Hinson's role in establishing the health care facility and his dedication to bettering health care for the black community. Four years later a testimonial banquet was held in his honor at which he was toasted as "one of Philadelphia's most distinguished and beloved practitioners."

A gifted surgeon as well as a medical pioneer Hinson belonged to a variety of local, state, and national professional organizations. He was a member of the Philadelphia Academy of Medicine, the Philadelphia County Medical Society, the Pennsylvania State Medical Society, the National Medical Association, and the Academy of Medicine. He was pictured on the cover of the May 1956 *Journal of the National Medical Association*.

Hinson married Marie E. Hopewell in November 1902; they had no children. A civic leader and reformer Hinson participated in a variety of activities to enrich his community. He was a lifelong member of the Lombard Central Presbyterian Church and chairman of the Philadelphia National Association for the Advancement of Colored People's Committee on Public Schools. A dedicated educator Hinson donated part of his family's farm at Oxford, Pennsylvania, to Lincoln University, which built its campus on the site. Interested in athletics and student life he was a member of the fraternity Alpha Phi Alpha and co-founder of Sigma Pi Phi, the first black American Greek fraternity.

Hinson died in 1960 in the hospital that he founded. The *Journal of the National Medical Association* lauded his contributions to the African American medical community: "He is one of the early pioneers to whose vision and benefactions the present Mercy-Douglass Hospital stands as a monument."

FURTHER READING

"Eugene Theodore Hinson, M.D., 1873–," *Journal of the National Medical Association* 48 (May 1956).

Morais, Herbert M. *The History of the Afro-American in Medicine* (1976).

Obituary: *Journal of the National Medical Association* 52 (Nov. 1960).

This entry is taken from the *American National Biography* and is published here with the permission of the American Council of Learned Societies.

ELIZABETH D. SCHAFER

Hinton, Chuck (3 May 1934–), baseball player, was born Charlie Edward Hinton Jr. in Rocky Mount, North Carolina, to Charlie Hinton, a cabdriver, and Ada Hinton, a homemaker. The second son of seven children, Hinton became the oldest male child after his older brother Charlie Leonard died of double pneumonia, aged three months.

Hinton starred on the football and basketball teams at Booker T. Washington High School in Rocky Mount, while also playing semipro baseball with older men and his younger brother, James "Checho" Hinton. Following high school, which he graduated in either 1952 or 1953, Hinton briefly played semipro ball in the Washington, D.C., environs, but his brother convinced him to attend Shaw University in Raleigh on a baseball scholarship. Both excelled athletically in college; Checho would later sign with football's New York Titans. Chuck attended Shaw from 1955 to 1956, leaving in the summer of his sophomore year following a major-league tryout.

On a summer off from college, Hinton hitchhiked to Washington to attend a New York Giants baseball tryout in Fredericksburg, Maryland. Though he missed it, Washington's Griffith Stadium held an open tryout the following week. Hinton impressed many scouts, including one for the Orioles, who invited him to his office the following day. He once again hitchhiked to the meeting and left with a $200 a month contract, plus a $500 signing bonus.

In 1956, Hinton was assigned to the Arizona-Mexican league, where he played for the Orioles' affiliate, the Phoenix Suns. Following the season, Hinton proposed to his girlfriend, Irma "Bunny" Macklin, whom he began dating in college, and the two eloped and wed in Greensboro, North Carolina, in October 1956. They lived with Hinton's sister and brother-in-law during the off-season, and Hinton worked at a mill with his brother-in-law. Shortly afterward, he was drafted into the army, where he received a "special forces" assignment that entailed playing football and baseball.

After two years in the army, Hinton reported to spring training for the Orioles in 1959. The club moved him from catcher to third base to outfield, his first taste of becoming a utility player. Hinton was assigned to Aberdeen, South Dakota, in the Northern League, where his blackness was an anomaly. In Hinton's words, when he went to bat, "(k)ids … would rub my hair or touch my skin … to see whether the color came off." Hinton was the batting champion and MVP of the league that season and was sent to the instructional league in Clearwater, Florida, that winter. The following season, Hinton played outfield, first, and third base for Stockton in the California League and once again was the league batting champ and MVP.

Just as he was gaining traction with the Orioles, Hinton was selected that December by the Washington Senators in the expansion draft. In February 1961, Hinton attended spring training camp in Pompano Beach, Florida; because of segregation, he and three black teammates were forced to stay in a house in a different part of town from the rest of the Senators.

Sent down to the minors to start the 1961 season, Hinton soon became a regular for the big-league team. In 1962, he posted his best season, finishing with the fourth-highest batting average in the American League, while playing five different positions for the Senators. Off the field, Hinton had become a successful businessman in Washington, starting an insurance agency his rookie year and opening three new locations the following year. He also began hosting a sports radio show, giving civic speeches, and becoming involved with charitable projects in the city.

Though Hinton was named to the All-Star team in 1964, Washington traded him in the off-season to the Cleveland Indians. He posted average numbers with the Indians for three years before enduring his worst season in 1968 with the California Angels. Hinton returned to the Indians that off-season, retiring after 1971. Known for his versatility in the field—over the course of his career, he would play every position but pitcher—Hinton also batted over .300 twice and finished in the top ten in stolen bases in the American league five times.

Following his playing days, Hinton's popularity remained high in Washington, where he and his wife, Irma, settled with their four children, Charles, Jonquil, Kimberly, and Tiffany. Along with working for the city's Department of Recreation, Hinton was hired in 1972 to helm Howard University's baseball team, where he promptly won the Mid-Eastern Athletic Conference title his first year. He was elected to the Howard University Athletics Hall of Fame in 1998, one year before retiring from the post after twenty-eight seasons coaching.

Ever the sport's ambassador, Hinton cofounded the Major League Baseball Players Alumni Association in 1982, an organization dedicated to promoting the game and raising funds for various charities.

FURTHER READING

Hinton, Chuck, and Sam Lacy. *My Time at Bat: A Story of Perseverance* (2002).

Stann, Francis. "Chuck Hinton: Next AL Bat King?" *Baseball Digest* (1963).

ADAM W. GREEN

Hinton, William Augustus (15 Dec. 1883–8 Aug. 1959), physician and clinical pathologist, was born in Chicago, Illinois, the son of Augustus Hinton, a railroad porter, and Marie Clark; both parents were former slaves. His formal education was completed in Kansas City, Kansas, where his parents moved before his first birthday. After attending the University of Kansas from 1900 to 1902, he transferred to Harvard College, where he received a B.S. in 1905. Postponing a medical school education because of lack of funds, Hinton taught the basic sciences at colleges in Tennessee and Oklahoma and embryology at Meharry Medical College between 1905 and 1909. While teaching at the Agricultural and Mechanical College in Langston, Oklahoma, he met a schoolteacher, Ada Hawes, whom he married in 1909; they had two daughters. During the summers Hinton continued his studies in bacteriology and physiology at the University of Chicago.

Hinton entered Harvard Medical School in 1909 and was awarded an MD in 1912. Scholarships and part-time work in the Harvard laboratories of

William Augustus Hinton in June 1949. He was appointed Clinical Professor of Bacteriology and Immunology in the Harvard Medical School, becoming the first African American to hold a professorship at Harvard University. (AP Images.)

Richard C. Cabot and Elmer E. Southard allowed him to attend medical school and support his family.

Because of racial discrimination, Hinton was prevented from gaining an internship in a Boston hospital. Unable to acquire the specialty training in surgery that he desired, he turned to the laboratory aspect of medicine. In 1912 he began working part-time as a volunteer assistant in the department of pathology of the Massachusetts General Hospital. During the three years he spent at Massachusetts General after medical school graduation, he was asked to perform autopsies on all persons known or suspected to have syphilis. He also acquired a paid position as an assistant in the Wassermann Laboratory (the Massachusetts state laboratory for communicable diseases), based at the Harvard Medical School complex. (This laboratory had been named for August von Wassermann, who devised the first blood serum test for the detection of syphilis in 1906.) Southard was so impressed by Hinton's knowledge of syphilis that he arranged for him to teach its laboratory diagnostic techniques to Harvard medical students. Within two years of his medical school graduation, Hinton had published his first scientific paper on the serology of syphilis in Milton Joseph Rosenau's *Textbook of Preventive Medicine*.

In 1915, when the Wassermann Laboratory was transferred from Harvard to the Massachusetts Department of Public Health, Hinton was appointed assistant director of the Division of Biologic Laboratories and chief of the Wassermann Laboratory. He served as the head of the Wassermann Laboratory for thirty-eight years. At the Peter Bent Brigham Hospital (later called Brigham and Women's Hospital) he observed both inpatients and outpatients, correlating serologic tests with the clinical manifestations and treatment of patients with syphilis. For twelve years, from 1915 to 1927, he immersed himself in the search for a more effective test for syphilis; the Wassermann test and others for syphilis yielded a high percentage of false-positive results, and many doctors had lost confidence in the Wassermann test. Because the treatment of syphilis was long, painful, and dangerous, and it was a seriously debilitating disease, a more accurate test was badly needed.

In 1918 Hinton was appointed instructor of preventive medicine and hygiene at the Harvard Medical School, the beginning of a thirty-four-year teaching career at Harvard. In 1921 his instructional responsibilities were expanded to include bacteriology and immunology.

During the 1920s Hinton carried on intensive research on the pathology of venereal diseases. He was responsible for all syphilis testing in Massachusetts and had responsibility for the diagnosis of rabies for the State Division of Animal Husbandry. When Massachusetts established blood tests for syphilis as a requirement for marriage licenses and for mothers before birth, Hinton supervised the expansion of state laboratories from 10 to 117. His laboratories also conducted research on tuberculosis and influenza for the state.

Hinton's signal, most important contribution to medical science came in 1927, when he perfected what was judged to be the most accurate and sensitive blood serum test for syphilis. His test drastically reduced the percentage of false positives. It also met the requirements of mass screening, quick results, simplicity, replicability, and unambiguity. For the next quarter of a century the Hinton test was universally used, replacing the Wassermann test. Even though the Hinton test was 98 percent accurate, Hinton was not completely satisfied, and he collaborated with John Davies in perfecting his test. By 1931 he had developed an improved version that could be done with smaller amounts of the patient's blood. The Davies-Hinton test was adopted as the official test of the disease by the Massachusetts Department of Public Health. In 1934 the U.S. Public Health Service reported that its evaluation showed the Hinton test to be the best available, using sensitivity and specificity as evaluative standards.

In 1934 Hinton began writing his classic textbook, *Syphilis and Its Treatment* (1936). In this book, praised in both Europe and the United States, Hinton sought to provide "a clear, simple, relatively complete account of syphilis and its treatment for physicians, public health workers and medical students." The book became a standard reference in medical schools and hospitals. Documenting Hinton's years of research and "his experience in clinics with patients and the disease from their point of view," it is believed to be the first medical textbook written by an African American doctor.

Recognition came slowly and late to Hinton. In 1946 he was promoted to the rank of lecturer in bacteriology and immunology at the Harvard Medical School. Three years later, a year before he retired and twenty-two years after he had developed his first test for syphilis, he was elevated to the position of clinical professor—the first African American to attain the title of professor at Harvard.

Hinton was a member of the American Society of Clinical Pathologists, the Society of American Bacteriologists, the American Medical Association, and the American Association for the Advancement of Science, and a fellow of the Massachusetts Medical Society. In 1948 he was elected a life member of the American Social Science Association. He lectured frequently to the medical specialty groups of the National Medical Association. He contributed twenty-one medical-scientific articles to professional journals. He also served as a special consultant to the U.S. Public Health Service.

Hinton died in his home in Canton, Massachusetts. His legacy to American medicine was not forgotten. In 1974, fifteen years after his death, when the new State Laboratory Institute Building of the Massachusetts Department of Public Health in Boston was dedicated, it was named the William A. Hinton Serology Laboratory.

FURTHER READING

Cobb, W. Montague. "William Augustus Hinton, MD, 1883–," *Journal of the National Medical Association* 49 (Nov. 1957): 427–428.

Hayden, Robert C. "William A. Hinton: Pioneer against Syphilis," in *Eleven African American Doctors* (1992).

This entry is taken from the *American National Biography* and is published here with the permission of the American Council of Learned Societies.

ROBERT C. HAYDEN

Hite, Les (13 Feb. 1903–6 Feb. 1962), jazz alto saxophonist and bandleader, was born in Du Quoin, Illinois, to parents whose names are unknown. While attending school in Urbana, Illinois, he played alongside his parents and siblings in a family band. He studied at the University of Illinois, Urbana. The details of his education are unknown.

After local work with the obscure Detroit Shannon band, he toured with a little-known singer named Helen Dewey in a revue that failed in Los Angeles late in 1924. Hite, the trumpeter George Orendorff, and the saxophonist Jimmy Strong decided to stay there. Hite worked with the bands of Reb Spikes, MUTT CAREY, Paul Howard, Curtis Mosby, and Sonny Clay, these last two concurrently in 1928. By early 1929 he was working with Henry "Tin Can" Allen, and when he died Hite took his place as bandleader.

The pool of excellent big-band musicians in the Los Angeles area at this time was not large, and one would expect much interchange among them. By one account the band that Hite was hired to form at the Cotton Club late in 1929 was a continuation of Paul Howard's Quality Serenaders. It may be the case, however, that the band that Hite brought into a second Cotton Club the following year was Howard's old band. Some sources say Howard played in 1930 at this new location with Orendorff and the drummer (and soon to be vibraphonist) LIONEL HAMPTON, both of whom then joined Hite.

Hite's California Syncopators began their stand at the new Cotton Club in an auspicious way by accompanying LOUIS ARMSTRONG, with whom they also made recordings, including "Body and Soul," "Shine," and "Sweethearts on Parade." New bandsmen in 1931 included the trombonist LAWRENCE BROWN, who also had worked with Howard, and the alto saxophonist Marshall Royal, who took over leadership of the saxophone section. Probably by this point Hite had suffered the auto accident in which he severely injured his lower lip. He rarely played thereafter.

In a profession in which changes in personnel are commonplace, Hite's was one of the most stable big bands of the 1930s. The trumpeter DIZZY GILLESPIE explained that Hite had a sponsor, an affluent white woman who kept the band on a modest salary even when there was no work. Through the decade Hite held residencies at Los Angeles's Cotton Club, including a show with FATS WALLER in the summer of 1935. The band also contributed to sixty-five films while in Hollywood, including *Taxi* (1932) starring James Cagney, *Sing, Sinner, Sing* (1933), *The Music Goes Round* (1936), *Gangsters on the Loose (Bargain with Bullets)* (1937), *Fools for Scandal* (1938), and three sound films for video jukeboxes of the 1940s.

In September 1939 Hite disbanded in order to take over the alto saxophonist Floyd Turnham's band, with Turnham remaining as Hite's sideman. At the band's first engagement in Dallas late that month Hite hired T-BONE WALKER, whose singing was admired during performances at New York's Golden Gate Ballroom and Apollo Theater in January 1940. Recordings made in New York around June 1940 and in March 1941 included versions of "That's the Lick" and "T-Bone Blues," which are pioneering discs in the contribution of Los Angeles-based musicians to the development of rhythm and blues. Despite Walker's forthcoming role as one of the most important early electric blues guitarists, he is strictly the singer on "T-Bone Blues"; the guitarist is Frank Pasley.

Hite reorganized his band in New York City in March 1942, when Gillespie and the pianist Gerald Wiggins joined, and again in July of that year, now with the trumpeter GERALD WILSON, the saxophonist Buddy Collette, the trombonist John Ewing, and Wiggins as the notable sidemen. The trumpeter Snooky Young joined in October, remaining into 1943. In 1945 Hite left music, and from 1957 he was a partner in a booking agency. He died in Santa Monica, California.

FURTHER READING

Burke, Tony, and Dave Penny. "Les Hite's Orchestra 'T. Bone Blues,' 1935–42," *Blues and Rhythm: The Gospel Truth* no. 9 (May 1985).

Gillespie, Dizzy, and Al Fraser. *To Be, or Not … to Bop: Memoirs* (1979, 1985).

McCarthy, Albert. *Big Band Jazz* (1974).

This entry is taken from the *American National Biography* and is published here with the permission of the American Council of Learned Societies.

BARRY KERNFELD